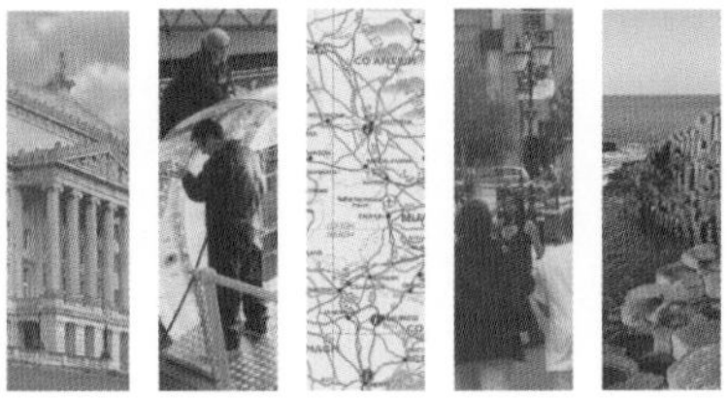

# NORTHERN IRELAND
# **YEARBOOK 2005**

A Comprehensive Reference Guide to the
Political, Economic and Social Life of Northern Ireland

Content written and produced by Lagan Consulting Tel: 028 9262 8777
Editor: Michael McKernan
Public Affairs Editor: Owen McQuade
Research Manager: Sandra Dane
Design: Gareth Duffy



Published by bmf Publishing
TSL House
38 Bachelors Walk
Lisburn, BT28 1XN
Tel: 028 9262 8787
Fax: 028 9262 8789

Distribution and Marketing by tSO Ireland
16 Arthur Street
Belfast, BT1 4GD
Tel: 028 9023 8451

Printed by GPS Colour Graphics, Belfast

ISBN: 095462842X

# A Comprehensive Guide to Northern Ireland

## Foreword

Welcome to the fourth edition of the Northern Ireland Yearbook - a comprehensive guide to the social, economic and political life of Northern Ireland. It remains the only substantial book published that draws together all strands of public life in Northern Ireland and presents detailed information in a useful and insightful format.

We feel we are getting closer to our goal of ensuring that the book features in the offices of most organisations in Northern Ireland, public, private and voluntary sectors and specifically on the desks of all of Northern Ireland's top decision makers. We are also making the Yearbook available in all libraries, schools and institutions as well as in high street bookshops.

This year most chapters have been expanded in scope and detail and we have added a new chapter on the Irish Republic. There is also a uniquely colourful and, we hope, interesting guide to recent elections. In production terms we have adopted a new easier-to-follow format resulting in more information contained in a more user-friendly volume.

It is entirely right that Northern Ireland should have its own substantial Yearbook covering the full political, economic and social spectrum, and we are determined to make this publication a model of its kind. I hope you find this a useful and satisfying addition to your library, home or office.

Michael McKernan
Editor

## Acknowledgments

The authors and publishers owe a debt of gratitude to many people who have contributed their advice and efforts to this substantial publication. Firstly we are indebted to the suppliers of copyright material incorporated into parts of the Yearbook, in particular the Ordnance Survey (OSNI), the Northern Ireland Statistics and Research Agency (NISRA), Ulster Business (including Dun and Bradstreet) and the Northern Ireland Tourist Board (NITB). We have made every effort to ensure that permission has been obtained for all copyrighted material used, and to attribute the source. If there is any lapse in this respect it is entirely accidental.

We are also very appreciative of those whose photographs adorn the Yearbook, particularly the Northern Ireland Tourist Board and Belfast Visitor and Convention Bureau and the political parties and a multitude of organisations and individuals who supplied their own material. (All photographic sources are acknowledged specifically below).

Thanks are due also to the many individuals who helped with the compilation of Chapter 3 including the listings of Civil Servants and other officials and appointees. The result, while by no means exhaustive, remains the most comprehensive presentation of Northern Ireland's senior Civil Service ever produced.

We would like to acknowledge also the many expert individuals who contributed their advice and wisdom to the publication including politicians, leading economists, journalists, educationalists and health professionals. Hopefully the book does them justice.

Finally thanks are due to all the 'hands-on' people who worked so hard to actually produce the 2005 Yearbook. It is a major undertaking. The team at Lagan Consulting; Owen, for all the government insight; Sandra, Sharon and Lynda for research and production; Gareth for all the long hours of design work; designers Gerry and Paddy also; Dan for managing the advertising. The large group of checkers and proof readers. Thanks also to Dan, Michael and Nicola at TSO; Russell at Ulster Business and all other contributors and advertisers.

### Photographs

Northern Ireland Yearbook 2005 Photographic Sources*:

| | (page numbers) |
|---|---|
| Andersonstown News Group | 352 |
| Belfast City Centre Management | 305 |
| Belfast City Hospital HSS Trust | 220, 233, 238 |
| Belfast Visitor & Convention Bureau | 318, 320, 447, 449, 451, 454, 456, 463, 464 |
| Bombardier Aerospace | cover |
| Dungannon & South Tyrone Borough Council | 26 |
| European Commission | 422 |
| FG Wilson | 278 |
| Grand Orange Lodge of Ireland | 14 |
| Hilda Winter | 11 |
| House of Commons | 34, 36, 37 |
| Junction One | 465 |
| Lisburn City Centre Management | cover, 8, 25 |
| Lisburn City Council | 404, 462 |
| Northern Ireland Fire Brigade | 229 |
| Northern Ireland Tourist Board | cover, 23, 445, 446, 456, 466, 477 |
| St Mary's University College | 261 |
| The Queen's University of Belfast | 252 |
| Translink | 471, 472, 473 |

*excludes bmf Business Services private portfolio

### Mapping

Mapping in the Northern Ireland Yearbook is reproduced
with the permission of the Ordnance Survey of Northern Ireland
Permit ID 40399

# Contents

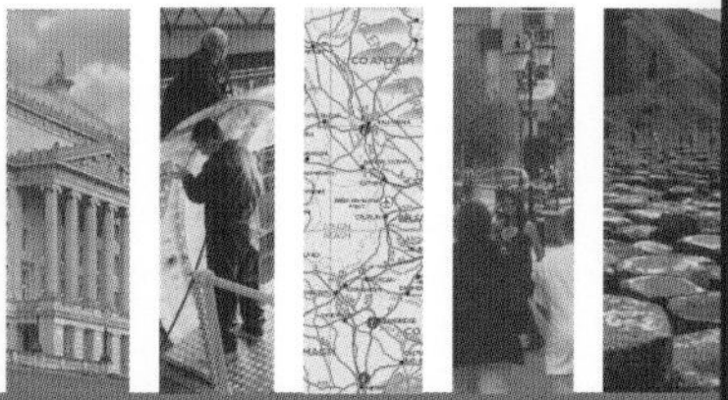

Northern Ireland Yearbook 2005

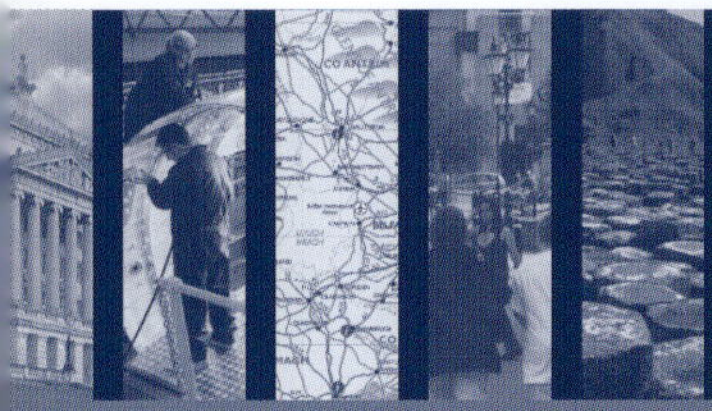

*Market Square, Lisburn*

# Chapter 1

## The Place and Its People

# Northern Ireland: A Brief History

Northern Ireland is a relatively young political entity, having been created in 1920 by the Government of Ireland Act, which partitioned Ireland into two separate jurisdictions. Each was awarded their own executive and Home Rule parliament; a 26 county Southern Ireland was given relative independence but the remaining six counties of Armagh, Antrim, Down, Fermanagh, Londonderry and Tyrone were retained within the United Kingdom, establishing their own devolved administration. Despite its relative brevity, Northern Ireland's history has been coloured with conflict and controversy, characterised by deep and festering divisions between its people, based largely on issues of religion and nationality. In very general terms the division is thus: the Protestant or unionist community look to Britain for political parentage, whilst the Catholic or nationalist community believe ultimately in a unified Irish Republic independent from Britian.

The debate over the terminology used to refer to Northern Ireland is itself indicative of the difficulties inherent in providing an objective commentary on its past. Because Northern Ireland is composed of only six of the nine counties of the ancient Irish province of Ulster, use of the terms 'Ulster', or the 'Province' is perceived as inaccurate by nationalists. They tend to prefer 'Six Counties' or 'the north of Ireland' which in turn often irritates unionists. This example highlights how events, which to an outside observer seem clear-cut and straightforward can be interpreted by different people in different ways. It is generally accepted that no presentation of facts can be considered universally objective. The representation of Northern Ireland's history which follows here may therefore be perceived as too 'orange' or too 'green', depending on the sensitivities of the reader; it has however been intended as neither.

### Pre-Christian Era

The early history of Ireland as a whole is shrouded in semi-myth and legend; indeed anything before around 500AD is extremely difficult to prove. Historians estimate that the Celts came to Ireland from the Rhine and Danube areas in Europe, around 400 BC. They introduced the Gaelic language, along with their own culture and beliefs. Only culture and language unified Celtic Ireland at this stage: the country was divided into about 150 small communities (tuatha). A king ruled each tuath, and an overking ruled a group of tuatha. Similarly, a group of overkings would hold allegiance to a provincial king. Ireland was roughly divided into five provinces: Ulster, Munster, Leinster, Connacht and Mide, although the number and precise boundaries of provinces were in a constant state of flux. The rulers of Ireland fought each other frequently, and while individual leaders variously assumed the title of 'High King' of Ireland, no one person ruled all of Ireland at this time. According to legend, in 300 BC High King Fiachadh founded the Fianna. This was the military elite of Ireland, charged with guarding the High King, although at first it is said to have been a somewhat undisciplined and incoherent group. This changed with the arrival of Fionn mac Cumhail, more commonly known as Finn MacCool who is celebrated as the Fianna's greatest ever leader. Finn challenged the Fianna to become champions of the people, and implemented a code of honour, chivalry and justice.

There are many legends surrounding Finn MacCool and the Fianna; one of the most famous gives an account of the creation of the 'Giant's Causeway', a hexagonal-shaped volcanic rock formation on the north coast of Ireland, which has become Northern Ireland's most popular visitor attraction. A Scottish giant angered Finn by questioning his fighting ability, but was unable to accept the resulting challenge because he could not swim to Ireland. The story says that Finn tore great strips of rock from the coast, and made them into pillars to stretch from Ireland to Scotland. The giant was forced to cross over to Ireland, and Finn chased him back to Scotland, flinging huge chunks of earth at him. The biggest crater caused by this flooded with water and became Lough Neagh, the largest lake in Ireland or Britain, whilst a huge lump of earth fell into the Irish Sea and became the Isle of Man. A similar myth tells how Ulster got its symbol, the Red Hand. Two chiefs, one of whom was of the ancient House of O'Neill, disputed ownership of a piece of land (often claimed to be Ulster). The dispute was to be settled by a race: the chiefs would sail to the shore, and whoever touched it first with his right hand would win the land. O'Neill saw his opponent leading and about to step out of his boat, and so he cut off his right hand with his sword and threw it onto the shore, thus winning the contest.

Perhaps the most famous Ulster hero from the early period is Cu Chulainn, said to have been born around 500 BC. His name was originally Setanta, but as a young man he accidentally killed the guard dog of Culainn, a local warrior, who was distraught at its loss. Setanta took the dog's place to guard Culainn, and was thereafter known as Cu Chulainn, the Hound of Culainn. Cu Chulainn led the so-called 'Red Branch' of Ulster warriors, mainly against forces led by Queen Maeve of Connacht.

### Early Christian Era

The Celts followed a religion based on natural phenomena and related spiritual beliefs until the introduction of Christianity to Ireland, during the 5th century AD. The establishment of Christianity in Ireland is accredited to St. Patrick, although he was by no means the first Christian in Ireland. St Patrick is believed to have been born in western Britain, possibly Wales; a Romanised Celt who was kidnapped and sold into slavery in Ireland. Patrick eventually escaped to the Continent, where he studied for the priesthood until he decided to return to Ireland, traditionally dated 432 AD.

Armagh, once a site associated with pagan rituals, became the centre of Christianity in Ireland after St Patrick supposedly received a cauldron from a powerful Druid (Celtic priest), but angered the druid by saying just a small word of thanks. When the druid demanded the cauldron back, Patrick said the same word of thanks, which induced the druid to repent, giving Patrick not only the cauldron back, but also a piece of land on which to build a church. Armagh still remains the ecclesiastical capital of Ireland, with both Catholic and Church of Ireland cathedrals built on two hilltops overlooking the city. Ireland, north and south, has a plethora of churches named after the island's patron saint. Probably one of the best-known legends about St Patrick is his supposed banishment of all snakes from Ireland. This is probably a metaphor for Patrick's having banished the 'demons of paganism', as it had arguably been documented two centuries earlier that Ireland had no indigenous snakes. 1500 years later, St Patrick has become a symbol of both inspiration and division within Northern Ireland today. He is Ireland's patron saint, celebrated on his feast day, 17th March, by Irish people across the globe. However, in Northern Ireland St Patrick is viewed in different ways. To the majority of Catholics and nationalists, he is a Catholic saint on account of his presence in Ireland long before the Protestant Reformation. The Protestant and unionist majority in Northern Ireland, however, tend to waver between rejecting the saint, and embracing him as a British preacher who civilised the native Irish. Both communities lay claim to St Patrick's final resting place: either at Saul, near Downpatrick (the Catholic view), or in the grounds of Downpatrick Church of Ireland Cathedral (the Protestant belief).

A distinctive feature of the development of early Christianity was the role of monasticism. During the Dark Ages (500-800 AD) religion and scholarship almost disappeared in other European countries, largely as a result of barbarian invasions that did not reach Ireland. Irish monks established communities all over Europe, such as those at St Fursey at Peronne in France and St Columbanus at Bobbio in Italy. In the early centuries AD, missionary success was complemented by Ireland's cultural achievements. Ornate chalices and jewellery were created, while scribes produced magnificently illuminated manuscripts. The Book of Kells is the most famous example, begun around 800 AD. Its name derives from the Abbey of Kells, Co Meath, its home until 1541, although it was probably begun on the island of Iona, between Ireland and Scotland. The Book of Kells marks what many have called the Golden Age of Irish history, the period when Ireland was the 'land of saints and scholars'. The Book of Kells is now permanently on display at Trinity College, Dublin, where a page is turned every day.

From around 800 AD Ireland was initially attacked and then settled by Vikings, raiders and traders from Northern Europe, who founded Dublin, Limerick, Cork and Waterford. Ireland's disunity made the country vulnerable to attacks, and the southern half was conquered easily, while the relative strength of the O'Neill dynasty of kings enabled the northern half to withstand assault. Towards the end of the 10th century Brian Boru became king of Munster, and engaged the Vikings in a battle, which they were ultimately to lose. At the turn of the century Boru gained control of the whole country and was crowned High King of all Ireland. For the first time the country was united under his leadership. After Brian Boru's death in 1014 other Irish kings sought to follow his example; the trend was towards the development of a strong, centralised monarchy, as seen elsewhere in Europe, until the arrival of Norman forces in 1167-9. Brian Boru's grave may still be visited in Armagh City to this day.

The first Normans in Ireland were effectively mercenaries, invited to assist the King of Leinster in his claim to the High Kingship in 1169. Their leader, Richard de Clare, nicknamed Strongbow, succeeded the Leinster throne, and in 1171 the Normans' overlord, Henry II of England, declared himself overlord of the whole of Ireland. Led by John de Courcy, Normans settled in many parts of Ireland, establishing similar systems of law, parliament and administration as they had in England. Norman influence in Ireland was never as strong as it had been in England following the battle of Hastings in 1066; the Normans tended to assimilate themselves into Irish culture, rather than the other way round. French names gradually evolved into Irish forms, for example de Burgh became Burke, and the prefix Fils became Fitz, as in FitzGerald and FitzWilliam.

Meanwhile, the native Gaelic population remained numerically strong and the people intermarried with the Normans. By 1500 English control (previously Norman) had receded to a small area around Dublin called 'the Pale', as Normans in Ireland became increasingly integrated. The modern expression 'beyond the pale' refers to this time, when everything outside the Pale area was considered dangerous and uncivilised. It is interesting that, despite colonising Ireland, the Normans eventually came to be described as 'more Irish than the Irish'.

**The Plantation of Ulster**

From the 16th century English Tudor monarchs began a further conquest of Ireland. Henry VIII became the first English ruler to declare himself king of Ireland in 1541 but the most significant event in the development of the modern Northern Ireland could be said to be the Plantation of Ulster. This involved the systematic introduction of large numbers of English and Scottish settlers, designed to establish English rule and control the native Irish. Mary I was the first English monarch to attempt plantation, mainly in Ulster, from 1556, but it was left to her successor, Elizabeth I, to secure Ireland. Land was taken from the native population and redistributed to settlers, often as a reward for services rendered in Britain. This process was not transacted without resistance: by 1594 Hugh O'Neill, Earl of Ulster, had united the ruling families of the north of Ireland, and begun a rebellion against the English crown that was to last nine years. O'Neill was strengthened by some assistance from Spain, traditional enemies of England, but the battle of Kinsale in 1601 was decisive in quashing the uprising. This was the first time that England had ever established control over the whole of Ireland, and in 1603 O'Neill and other rebellious Gaelic nobles fled to France (an event known as the 'Flight of the Earls').

Having united the English and Scottish thrones, King James I continued with the plantation of Armagh, Derry, Cavan, Donegal, Tyrone and Fermanagh, later adding Down and Antrim. In 1613 James I formed the new county of 'Londonderry', renaming the ancient city by royal charter. The Honourable The Irish Society in London paid for defensive walls to be erected around the city, which was to serve as headquarters for many of the society's commercial projects.

The British government invited their people to settle throughout Ulster, and many skilled and industrious people did just that.

The skill and motivation of many English and French Huguenots formed the basis of a linen industry that was eventually to become the biggest in the world. From being the poorest province of Ireland, Ulster gradually became the most prosperous. Its place as the most industrialised region of Ireland continued until relatively recent times and it was accepted by many as being largely attributable to the British influence on this part of the country.

The influx into the province of Protestant colonists, primarily Presbyterians from Scotland, meant that Ulster became the only part of Ireland where the Protestant religion was established with any real success. As with the Normans some centuries earlier, the Ulster-Scots settlers brought their own culture, the difference being that, unlike the Normans, Ulster-Scots tended to retain their distinct identity rather than integrate themselves into the native culture. In fact the settlers were emphatic in celebrating their religious freedoms which in the case of Presbyterians and non-conformists had been a right denied to them by the king who was head of the establishment Church of England.

Two separate cultural, political and religious identities began to emerge in the north of Ireland: the vast majority of native Irish people were Catholic, and held their allegiance to their native Ireland, whilst Protestant settlers, including Anglican, Methodist and other denominations, considered themselves loyal to Britain. It is argued by many that the Plantation was the event in which much of today's conflict has its roots.

**Seventeenth Century Conflict**

The 17th century English civil war between Charles I and Parliament also had far-reaching consequences in Ireland. Oliver Cromwell, leader of the victorious parliamentary forces, maintained the English presence in Ireland and consolidated his success in Britain by quashing ensuing Irish rebellions. Following Cromwell's military success, the 1653 Act of Settlement involved large-scale confiscation of land. Further colonisation ensured that property and political power passed to loyal Protestants: before 1641, Catholics owned about three-fifths of the land; by the 1680s, they owned one-fifth of it. However, many Catholics did not and had never owned land, and were tenants or serfs already. For them, the change was in landlord and in attitude towards them, but they perceived themselves and their people as dispossessed.

*King Billy*

The accession of the Catholic James II to the British throne in 1685 sparked a new wave of discord in Ireland. The Protestant aristocracy in Britain vehemently opposed the Catholic king who sought to expand his power at their expense. On being deposed, James fled to Ireland, where he found support everywhere apart from the Protestant community in the north. In what have become famous historical events, the predominantly Protestant towns of Derry and Enniskillen closed their gates against James and defied his authority. In the face of a strong military force the governor of Derry, Robert Lundy, was initially prepared to negotiate with James, but Lundy was overthrown and the gates remained closed. In modern-day loyalist circles the name Lundy has become synonymous with 'traitor', and every year his effigy is ritually burned on loyalist bonfires across Northern Ireland in a celebration of the famous siege. James besieged Derry for three months but failed to breach the city's fortified walls. On account of this, Derry became known as 'the Maiden City'.

The British throne, meanwhile, had been offered to a Protestant Dutch prince, William of Orange, as part of a pan-European coalition (supported by the Pope) against the dominant, Catholic French king Louis XIV. William followed James to Ireland as part of a Europe-wide conflict, and fought a number of battles, most notably the militarily decisive Battle of Aughrim and the less significant but more famous Battle of the Boyne in 1690. The Catholic population supported James, who had been sympathetic to their situation, while Protestant settlers (some of whose families had lived in Ireland for several generations) sided with William. The war ended in victory for William and subsequently brought the longest peace that Ulster had ever known. Today 'Protestant King Billy' is a loyalist hero, and is depicted on many Orange banners and also in street murals across the province. Like the Siege of Derry, the Battle of the Boyne has been celebrated enthusiastically by many within the Ulster Protestant community as part of Orange Order demonstrations. The anthem of Ulster loyalism, 'The Sash', refers to an Orange sash (still a symbol of the Orange Order) being worn in 'Derry, Aughrim, Enniskillen and the Boyne', although the Orange Order itself was not actually founded until a century later.

Throughout the 18th century Catholics throughout the British Isles were perceived as a potential threat to the Protestant monarchy, and Ireland in particular was considered a platform for the creation of instability in Britain. Despite the Plantation the Protestant establishment remained a minority in Ireland, although Scots Presbyterians in Ulster had risen in strength alongside the established Church of Ireland (Anglican) ascendancy. A series of Penal Laws were passed which kept the bulk of the Catholic population in a state of relative poverty and without many of the most basic civil rights. As the Penal Laws applied to all non-Anglicans, Presbyterians in Ulster were also denied full civil rights, though to a somewhat lesser extent. This meant that members of the Established Church were the chief beneficiaries of Ulster's newfound prosperity.

By 1782, British rule in Ireland was stable enough to allow the Westminster government to grant full legislative independence to the Irish Parliament (Grattan's Parliament), effectively making

Ireland a separate kingdom sharing the British monarch as head of state (although the Dublin administration would be directly appointed by the British king).

Towards the end of the eighteenth century the British government also began to relax the Penal Laws and proposed Catholic Emancipation (repeal of some of the anti-Catholic legislation) in 1795.

Late 18th century Co Armagh land skirmishes between Protestant Peep o' Day Boys and Catholic Defenders, which culminated in the Battle of the Diamond in September 1795, led to the formation of the Orange Order in Dan Winter's Cottage in Loughgall. The Order was created primarily as a Protestant defence association in support of the British King and the wider Protestant Ascendancy. It had the aim of galvanising the minority Protestant population against rising Catholic power and confidence. The Order, taking its name from William of Orange two or three generations earlier, was oathbound, making use of passwords and signs and was comprised mainly of Protestant weaver-farmers, with initially very few members from the landed gentry. Apart from economic and other considerations the members of the Orange Order feared the historical authoritarianism of Catholicism, and saw the Order as a vehicle for preserving Protestant liberties. Orangemen formed associations know as lodges throughout Ireland (although it was predominant in the North) and organised marches to commemorate the Battle of the Boyne and other events; these marches often led to rioting between Catholics and Protestants. By 1836 the British government had banned Orange marches on account of the rioting that followed, but this ban was defied from 1849 onwards. Over the years the Orange Order founded lodges all over the world with the 'Twelfth of July', the historical date of the Battle of the Boyne, becoming the focal point for Orange parades.

**Act of Union to the Land War**

The United Irishmen, formed in 1791, was a revolutionary group of idealists, inspired by the thinking behind the French Revolution, who aimed to unite Catholic, Protestant and Dissenter against British rule. Inspired as much by radical Protestant liberals as by Catholics, and led by Theobald Wolfe Tone and Lord Edward Fitzgerald the United Irishmen attempted a rebellion against Britain in 1798. Despite French assistance the rebellion, which was accompanied by a smaller uprising in Ulster, was easily suppressed. One result of which was to strengthen the case (which had been growing in the minds of British politicians since the early 1770s) for a legislative union between Britain and Ireland, on the grounds that Ireland represented a security threat to Britain. The idea was opposed by many and varied groups throughout the country (including representatives from Dublin commerce, the law, country gentlemen and the Orange Order) however due to the unrepresentative nature of the Irish parliament and the strength of the Unionist position at Westminster, their arguments had little impact. It took just over a year (and the distribution of much political patronage) to persuade the Irish parliament to vote itself out of existence and the Act of Union took effect from 1 January 1801.

Under the terms of the Act of Union, all Irish parliamentary business was conducted at Westminster with Ireland represented in the new united parliament by 100 MPs who were actually more representative of the Irish population than their predecessors in the Irish parliament had been. The Catholic community, however, remained largely excluded from politics, both in terms of the right to vote and the right to stand for parliament. Various Catholic relief bills were rejected by both the House of Commons and the House of Lords in the early 19th century and proponents of the issue remained largely divided until the 1820s and the formation of the Catholic Association under lawyer Daniel O'Connell.

O'Connell made membership of the Association accessible to everyone with associate membership costing just a penny a month. By mobilising those few Catholics who did have the right to vote, along with liberal Protestant sympathisers, O'Connell was successful in getting first his supporters, and then himself, elected to parliament. The government was faced with the fact that O'Connell had been elected, but due to the nature of the constitution was unable to take his seat, a situation they realised could quickly lead to an uprising in Ireland. In response, parliament passed an emancipation bill in 1829, opening the way to Catholic participation in parliament and to public office.

In the late 1840s Ireland suffered enormous hardship due to the 'Great Famine', precipitated by successive failures of the potato crop, upon which Ireland's labouring poor were dependent as their staple foodstuff. The Famine devastated many parts of Ireland, causing many of its survivors to emigrate, and the population of the island fell from almost 8 million to around 4 million, a combination of death by starvation and disease, and emigration. The industrialised northeast was less affected by this struggle than the rest of Ireland because tenant farming was not the sole local economy, although the Famine and the failure of government to bring adequate relief was an issue of grievance throughout the island.

The Famine had a profound impact on not just the Irish population but the entire way of life. Death, migration and eviction of the very poorest cottiers and labourers, combined with the financial difficulties experienced by the gentry led to the dominance of the farmer class in Irish agricultural society. This trend was accompanied by a change in farming methods with a move away from tillage towards animal husbandry and pastoral farming. Living standards for those who remained also rose with real wages increasing and housing stock and literacy levels improving. In political terms, the most enduring legacy of the Famine was the way in which it highlighted the problems with the Irish land system and popularised the struggle which became associated with these. It was via the land issue that the issue of Irish nationalism came again to the fore towards the end of the 19th century.

**Home Rule**

It was out of the struggle for land reform in the 1870s and 1880s that the movement for 'home government', in the form of restoration of an Irish parliament, gained support, firstly under the leadership of Isaac Butt and then Charles Stuart Parnell. Parnell was successful in creating a modern, highly disciplined political party, the Irish Parliamentary Party, which had Home Rule as its first objective. By 1886, the IPP had won enough seats at Westminster to hold the 'balance of power' thereby forcing Gladstone to introduce a Home Rule Bill in order to restore the Liberal party to power.

Although Parnell had won 85 Westminster seats in Ireland, including a majority of those in Ulster, Home Rule enjoyed far from universal support, both within parliamentary circles and outside. A huge number of Gladstone's own party voted with the opposition to defeat the Bill, a move which was applauded loudly in Ulster and which actually led to the worst riots of the 19th century in Belfast, as Protestants asserted their victory over their Catholic neighbours and colleagues.

By the late nineteenth century Belfast had become a prosperous and growing city, and in 1891 bypassed Dublin to become the largest city in Ireland. In terms of industry Belfast had become renowned worldwide for its linen, engineering, aerated waterworks, tobacco works, distilleries and shipyards. In fact Belfast's shipbuilding and engineering prowess captured the imagination of the world in the form of the most famous ship in history, Titanic, which was built at the Belfast shipyard, Harland and Wolff. Although her maiden voyage ended in disaster, Titanic still brings recognition to Belfast, and to a yard that at its peak employed over 30,000 men on site.

Belfast's industrial and commercial success and the prosperity of the north east of Ulster in general, was largely attributable to its strong links with Britain. Coal and raw materials for Belfast's industries came from mainland Britain, and it was Britain and the Empire which were the destination for many of the province's manufactured goods. Increasingly, this prosperous region was unwilling to be subsumed into a larger but poorer, nationalist Ireland. It was widely felt that a Dublin parliament, dominated by the landed interest, would impose heavy taxes on northern industry and introduce protective tariffs to promote southern self-sufficiency. Economic fears and religious and cultural differences combined to ensure that the suggestion of Home Rule for Ireland, or indeed any degree of self-rule by the Irish, was, met with what ranged from vociferous opposition to, at times, civil unrest in Ulster.

It was in opposition to Home Rule that Conservatives in Ireland organised themselves into a coherent Unionist grouping, under the leadership of Ulster landowner Sir Edward Saunderson. This group enjoyed the support of prominent British Conservatives and was successful in seeing Gladstone's Second Home Rule Bill defeated in 1893.

The Home Rule issue, although in hibernation for almost twenty years re-emerged on the political agenda in 1910, when the Irish Parliamentary Party, under the leadership of John Redmond, was again able to force the Liberals to support Home Rule. The 1911 Parliament Bill reduced the power of the House of Lords to delaying legislation for two years so that when Asquith introduced the Third Home Rule Bill in April 1912 it seemed certain to become law by 1914. Sure in the knowledge that the permanent Conservative majority in the Lords would never accept Home Rule, Unionists had, in 1886 and 1893 been content to confine their objections to Irish self-government to parliamentary means. By 1912, it had become clear that they could only depend on themselves to defend against any Home Rule measure and began to make provisions for less constitutional means of opposition.

Under the leadership of Dublin lawyer Sir Edward Carson and Ulster whiskey millionaire James Craig, Unionist resistance to Home Rule was organised. Preparations were made for a Unionist Provisional Government to come into effect with the passage of any measure of Home Rule; mass demonstrations were organised in Ulster and in Britain; the Solemn League and Covenant was signed, by some in their own blood; the Ulster Volunter Force (UVF) formed and drilling began; guns were brought into Ulster by night. Unionists were showing themselves to be serious in their opposition to Home Rule.

Nationalists were, at the same time, showing themselves to be just as serious in their pursuit of their long-time political objective. An Irish Volunteer Force was formed in opposition to 'Carson's Army' and guns were brought by night into Howth, just as they had been into Larne several months earlier.

*Signing of the Solemn League and Covenant 1912*

Despite all this sabre-rattling, negotiations were ongoing in the period 1912-14 to try and find a peaceful resolution to the Home Rule crisis. Despite Carson's reluctance as a Southern Unionist, as time went on it became increasingly obvious that Unionists could only, realistically, hope to 'save' Ulster from the fate of Home Rule. Their minority was too small to have any hope of preventing the measure taking effect for the rest of Ireland and they preferred to retain an area that they could easily control. By the spring of 1914 the idea of partition seemed to have been accepted in principle by many of the parties concerned. Divisions did however still exist on the precise nature of any agreement which excluded some Ulster counties from Home Rule and focused on whether exclusion should be permanent and to how many counties it should apply.

**Partition**

Thus was the situation with the outbreak of World War I in August 1914. Redmond gave his support to the war effort in return for a promise of Home Rule at the end of the war. Although passed on 18 September 1914, Home Rule was suspended for the duration of the war when amending legislation would make special provision for Ulster. Attempts by Lloyd-George to reach a solution during the war came to nothing and when the issue was re-visited at the end of the international conflict the result was the 1920 Government of Ireland Act, which effectively combined the principles of Home Rule with those of Unionism, creating a six-county Northern Ireland and a 26-county Southern Ireland, each with their own executive and parliament. The powers of the two new jurisdictions were initially limited and provision was made, in the shape of the Council of Ireland, for their amalgamation. This body was never to meet, however and Northern Ireland was there to stay. The Irish 'War of Independence' was fought in the south in the period 1919-21 and led to the signing of the Anglo-Irish Treaty in December 1921, whereby the remaining 26 counties were given the name Irish Free State and dominion status within the British Empire.

The 1920 Government of Ireland Act led to the formation of Northern Ireland as a new political entity. The new jurisdiction was made up of the six north-eastern counties of Antrim, Armagh, Down, Fermanagh, Londonderry and Tyrone. Following elections in May 1921, the first parliament of Northern Ireland was opened on 7 June 1921 by King George V in the Council Chamber of Belfast City Hall, where a Unionist Party government, headed by James Craig was sworn in.

The new government (which became known as the Stormont government, after the splendid new building in which it sat after 1932) was from the outset dominated by the Ulster Unionist Party. Its executive comprised seven departments, headed by the Department of the Prime Minister, which maintained a central co-ordinating role with Westminster and across the six other local ministries of Finance, Home Affairs, Labour, Education, Agriculture and Commerce.

The new Northern Ireland Parliament consisted of two chambers. The first, a 52 member House of Commons, the second, a Senate, consisting of 26 members all elected by the lower chamber except for the two ex-officio seats held by the Lord Mayor of Belfast and the Mayor of Londonderry. Although Northern Ireland was given its own devolved government, Section 75 of the Government of Ireland Act 1920 specified that the supreme authority of the UK parliament would continue. In addition, to continue the formal presence of the monarch in the most peripheral region of the United Kingdom, the office of Governor of Northern Ireland was created under the Act.

From the outset the powers of the new government were clearly defined. All powers relating to defence, armed forces and foreign policy were retained by Westminster and the powers of the northern Government were limited in relation to taxation, with Westminster reserving the power to raise income tax and customs and excise duties.

The continuation of political conflict for several years following the 1921 Treaty of Independence in the South (the Irish Civil War) meant that the anticipated reunification of the two administrations, North and South, did not occur. The Institutions established under the first Craig Government continued relatively uninterrupted until the Second World War with Craig's Ulster Unionist party permanently in government.

## The First Northern Ireland Government

The new Northern Ireland government had a less than auspicious start, facing threats and difficulties from every direction. Internally, it had to cope with sectarian rioting which in the period 1920-22 killed 455 and wounded 1766 people in Belfast alone. By the end of 1920 7,400 people had been driven from their jobs and nearly 23,000 from their homes. This was a situation the new administration found difficult to contain since although having responsibility, it was largely devoid of power to act.

Craig also felt his new state faced an external threat from the Free State Army, a fear which was in part confirmed in May 1922 when Irish troops occupied a triangle of land at Belleek on the Co Fermanagh border and defeated the local Ulster Special Constabulary garrison.

From the outset, the Stormont government was also beset with financial difficulties. Its allocation of funds from Westminster were based on the boom years of 1920-21 which showed that the Northern Ireland government would have a surplus of £2.5 million but in reality the situation was the opposite and the Finance Minister experienced an almost permanent shortfall. Most of the money allocated to Northern Ireland was actually collected by the London Treasury, and only 'handed over' after the imperial contribution and other levies for legal and customs services were deducted. The result in Northern Ireland was uncertainty as to how much money the government would get each year which made budgeting difficult. This was all at a time when Northern Ireland's unemployment rate averaged 19% as a result of the decline of traditional industries in Belfast.

Despite all this the most immediate threat that the new political entity faced in its first few years came in the shape of the Boundary Commission. In the course of negotiations over the Anglo-Irish Treaty in 1921, which had created the Boundary Commission, Lloyd-George had assured Craig that only minor territorial changes would take place whilst leading the Free State side to believe that huge areas would change hands. It wasn't until 1925 that it was decided that no changes would be made and Northern Ireland would be left as it was.

The situation in Northern Ireland was not made any easier by the lack of experience of government ministers. Only Craig had had previous government experience, most of the rest of the posts were allocated as a reward for political service and not necessarily on any basis of suitability or fitness to perform their job. This was compounded by the fact that there had been no pre-planning for a Home Rule parliament in Northern Ireland.

Sometimes criticism of individual ministers for their uninspired style of government can be harsh, considering the atmosphere in which they tried to function when every policy or initiative was subject to accusations of partisanship or sectarianism. One such example was Lord Londonderry's 1923 Education Act which made provision for the establishment of a non-sectarian, secular system of education. Ironically this came under attack from both the Catholic Church (as it took the education of Catholic children out of exclusively Catholic hands) and the Protestant community because it didn't make compulsory the teaching of a programme of Protestant Bible instruction by teachers. The largely 'segregated' system of primary and secondary education that exists today evolved from Church actions rather than by any design of the state.

**Signs of Discontent...**

With the Ulster Unionist party in permanent government and firmly in control of all state institutions, nationalists and Catholics took little part in the new Northern Ireland state. Nationalist leaders initially boycotted the new parliament, but did take their seats from 1925 in an attempt to provide the Catholic minority with some representation at Stormont. Their level of representation was, however, significantly reduced by the abolition of proportional representation for parliamentary elections in 1927. Electoral discrimination was to be one of the biggest grievances of the nationalist community under the Stormont government.

Other, more day-to-day grievances were felt in the areas of housing, policing and employment - in both the public and private sectors. In all these areas Catholics felt that they were deliberately discriminated against by Protestants who, from their positions of power, tended to control decision-making in particular the allocation of housing and jobs.

All this contributed to the mentality that Northern Ireland was a 'Protestant state for a Protestant people'. Whilst at the time of partition in 1920, it had been envisaged by some that Northern Ireland and its southern neighbour might, at some time in the future, come together again, in actual fact the two jurisdictions and their people grew further apart. Partition became entrenched in the inter-war years, and was reinforced by the Southern Ireland's constitutional change in 1948, when it became a Republic. Essentially Northern Ireland over time developed and established a unique political identity, and the Republic of Ireland's leaders in practice made little effort to understand or engage it.

**Parity**

Growing acceptance of the 'principle of parity' in terms of the requirement to treat Northern Ireland citizens on the same basis as the Westminster government would treat citizens of Great Britain had developed throughout this period. However, despite the 'principle of parity' successive governments held relative freedom in their management of the internal administration of the North and were able, amongst other initiatives, to introduce reforms, effectively reinforcing the government's political control at the expense of nationalists.

The establishment of the post-war Labour government at Westminster under the leadership of Clement Atlee had an agenda for social and economic reform, which unsettled the right-of-centre Unionist administration in Northern Ireland from the outset and brought the principle of parity into sharper focus.

In the post war period the financial relationship underpinning parity was extensively developed between London and Belfast. The establishment of parity in public services and taxation in 1946 consequently meant that the Northern Ireland budget had to be 'cleared' in advance by the Treasury in London. Comprehensive National Insurance legislation passed in 1948 consolidated previously separated funds into a single fund for the United Kingdom guaranteeing equal benefits throughout the jurisdiction. This was followed in 1949 by further developments which saw national assistance, family allowances, pensions and health service provisions being put onto an equal footing with the rest of the UK coupled with the guarantee that where the cost of providing these services should be higher in Northern Ireland than in Britain the UK government would fund 80% of the surplus costs. To some extent this was the ancestry of the current system of financial management for Northern Ireland, now administered under the terms of the Barnett Formula.

The passing of the Public Health and Local Government Act of 1946 led to the creation of a new Ministry of Health and Local Government at Stormont with responsibility for rolling out the provisions for the Welfare state as envisaged by the Beveridge Report and originating from Westminster. Greater emphasis was placed on improving the housing stock and social housing was built largely at the expense of the Treasury to be administered by Northern Ireland's local authorities.

Throughout this period inter-communal relations in Northern Ireland were poor and the arrival of 'liberal' Unionist leader Terence O'Neill as Prime Minister in 1963 was to bring matters to a head. On taking office, O'Neill stated that he planned to raise living standards, not just for Catholics, but across the working classes. O'Neill's view was that Catholic discontent could be addressed through a series of relatively modest reforms which, by giving Catholics more of a 'stake' in Northern Ireland affairs, would make them 'normal' citizens. This attracted fierce opposition; both from within O'Neill's own party, and from other unionists, in particular, Ian Paisley. Paisley's main aim was to keep Northern Ireland Protestant at all costs and he opposed O'Neill's reforms vociferously, particularly those granting equality to Catholics and co-operation with the Republic of Ireland.

Paisley commanded substantial support among working-class Protestants. His uncompromising politics provided a strong contrast to those of the upper-class patrician O'Neill. O'Neill's promised reforms were acknowledged by the minority community in terms of the resumption of their Stormont seats by the Nationalist Party, who had previously boycotted the Parliament, but many felt that the reforms did not go far enough. Major government decisions continued to be seen as unfair, in particular the siting of a new 'city' (Craigavon, named after James Craig) and a new university (at Coleraine, as opposed to Derry) in predominantly Protestant areas.

**Civil Rights to Hunger Strikes**
Organisations such as the Campaign for Social Justice and the Northern Ireland Civil Rights Association (NICRA) were formed to demand equal rights for Catholics in housing, employment and voting. A student march, associated with NICRA, from Belfast to Derry in January 1969 broke out into fierce rioting after it passed through predominantly loyalist areas and was attacked by a crowd of loyalists. In the aftermath of the march, widespread rioting broke out across Northern Ireland and the issue started to move away from that of civil rights towards that of religious and national identity.

By the time of O'Neill's resignation in April 1969 (he was succeeded by Major Chichester-Clark), limited reforms had been undertaken, but following the unrest, the RUC (Royal Ulster Constabulary) had banned all similar marches. Continued street violence led to the deployment of British troops in Derry and Belfast in August that year, initially to protect Catholic communities from sectarian attacks.

In 1971, amid further escalations of violence, internment (imprisonment without trial) was reintroduced to Northern Ireland by Unionist Prime Minister Brian Faulkner (who had succeeded Chichester-Clark), albeit with little if any success. Though banned, civil rights marches continued, and on 30th January 1972, a civil rights march ended with the British army shooting dead 13 men in controversial circumstances during a march in Derry. The day has become universally known as 'Bloody Sunday' and is currently the subject of a major long-running public enquiry. Nationalist political passions reached a new pitch not only in Northern Ireland but in the South as well; the British Embassy in Dublin was burned down in protest at the killings. The security situation continued to deteriorate rapidly beyond the control of the Northern Ireland government to the extent that the Conservative government at Westminster led by Prime Minister Ted Heath was forced to suspend the Stormont parliament to allow political negotiations on institutional reform to proceed. The consequent introduction of Direct Rule, meant that Northern Ireland, for the first time since 1921, was to be governed politically from Westminster.

YOU
ARE NOW
ENTERING
FREE DERRY
*Free Derry Corner, Derry*

The 1970s saw an unprecedented resurgence of paramilitary violence, from both republican and loyalist quarters. The chief protagonists were the Provisional IRA, who took their name, following an ideological split, from the old 'official' Irish Republican Army of the Irish Civil War. The IRA saw its support rise dramatically through the 1970s, especially after the British government's re-introduction of internment, and it began a campaign of violence aimed at making the administration of Northern Ireland unprofitable and unmanageable for the British government. They waged war on the economic life of Northern Ireland by bombing numerous commercial and administrative targets, and on the police and army security establishment through direct attacks on personnel.

On the loyalist side, the UVF (the name taken from Carson's 1914 volunteer army, the Ulster Volunteer Force) had become an active armed group intent on defending Ulster from the rising power of Irish nationalism. Following a number of murders and activities the group, led by Gusty Spence was proscribed in 1966. Nonetheless, by the 1970s its membership had risen, along with that of the much larger Ulster Defence Association (UDA). Loyalist paramilitary violence was spontaneous and random, mainly taking the form of indiscriminate shooting of Catholics in retaliation for IRA attacks on police officers, British Army troops and Protestant civilians.

The stakes were raised in 1979 when, amongst many other violent atrocities Lord Mountbatten, a prominent member of the British royal family, and later eighteen British soldiers were murdered in two republican attacks. The subsequent security clampdown brought about the loss of special category (PoW) status in local prisons, which led republican prisoners to go on hunger strike. 10 IRA men starved themselves to death, including the leader of the hunger-strikers, Bobby Sands, who was elected to the Fermanagh/South Tyrone Westminster seat whilst on hunger strike. Their deaths led to further rioting in Northern Ireland and Dublin, symptomatic of continuing polarisation. The long-term significance of the hunger strikes was the stimulus they gave to the development of Sinn Féin and republicanism as a serious mainstream political force. Violence and general civil unrest in Northern Ireland continued throughout the 1970s and 1980s, with devastating impact, until the ceasefires in the early 1990s. Throughout this period many attempts at reaching political agreement were made and these are outlined overleaf.

## Direct Rule and Political Initiatives 1972 - 2003

**Sunningdale**
The British government attempted to introduce various initiatives aimed at establishing a devolved administration for Northern Ireland after the prorogation of the Stormont administration. The first of these was the Sunningdale Agreement of 1973, which emerged following historic British and Irish Government negotiations alongside discussions involving the local political parties. A 78-seat assembly to be elected under proportional representation was proposed. This would establish a power-sharing executive, composed of unionist and nationalist parties. Of the many political parties in Northern Ireland, only three accepted: the Ulster Unionist Party (UUP), the Social Democratic and Labour Party (SDLP) and Alliance. Political opposition to 'Sunningdale' was intense and the agreement ultimately failed to capture the support of a majority of Unionists. The Executive was faced with severe pressure from loyalists who opposed power sharing. A general strike, organised by loyalists and supported by most unionists, brought Northern Ireland to a standstill and the Executive collapsed, replaced again by Direct Rule on 30 May 1974. Despite its failure, the Sunningdale Agreement had established the principle of power sharing in Northern Ireland, which would become an important development in the context of future political initiatives.

Despite numerous and varied political initiatives including attempts to create a gradual re-introduction of a local administration (rolling devolution) Direct Rule was to continue unabated for the next 25 years. This however did not stop the process of ongoing institutional reform.

From 1972 onwards Northern Ireland was governed by a Secretary of State, a full member of the British Cabinet who was assisted by several junior ministers, generally MPs from Britain. The Northern Ireland Office took over responsibility for the law and order functions of the Ministry of Home Affairs and reported to the Secretary of State on broad political matters.

In 1976 the Department of the Civil Service was separated out of the Department of Finance but re-attached in the form of the new Department of Finance and Personnel in 1982. Government departments were again re-formed to comprise six new departments. These were:

- Department of Economic Development;
- Department of the Environment;
- Department of Education;
- Department of Social Services;
- Department of Health;
- Department of Agriculture.

In addition there was a radical reform of local government under the Local Government (Northern Ireland) Act of 1972 providing for the replacement of all previous local authorities with 26 new district councils. This reform coincided with the demise of Stormont and the introduction of Direct Rule and councils were given fewer powers than had previously been envisaged. District councils' responsibilities were confined to the relatively minor functions of street cleaning, refuse collection, cemeteries and leisure facilities. The main functions of health and education were operated by area Boards largely comprised of central government appointees. A new centralised housing authority, the Northern Ireland Housing Executive, assumed all previous local authority housing duties.

**Rolling Devolution**

In the early 1980s, Secretary of State James Prior proposed what became known as 'rolling devolution', the idea being that a Northern Ireland assembly would initially be given limited, consultative powers. These new powers could increase significantly as circumstances permitted, i.e. as a culture of power-sharing and cross-community co-operation evolved. 59 members were elected to a new assembly in October 1982, although the SDLP and Sinn Féin refused to participate in the new institution. The Ulster Unionists boycotted the assembly over security policy, so that the only full participants were the DUP and Alliance. The 'Prior' Assembly offered a limited degree of power-sharing via Committee chairmanships but was doomed to failure when so many of the major parties refused to take part in its precedings.

**The Anglo-Irish Agreement**

The next major political development was the Anglo-Irish Agreement signed on 15 November 1985 by the British and Irish governments, which in an all-round constitutional package gave the Irish Republic, for the first time, a formal albeit consultative, role in the government of Northern Ireland.

The establishment of an Irish Governmental physical presence in Belfast and the involvement of Dublin ministers in a consultative role across a range of policy areas in Northern Ireland created fierce resentment in the Unionist community. The signing of this Agreement in 1985 proved highly unacceptable to unionists, who resigned their Westminster seats in protest, boycotted district councils and generally made it clear that they would not allow the Republic of Ireland any role as of right in Northern Ireland. Unionist politicians were united in opposition to an Agreement, which they felt had, unjustly, been formulated without their input and imposed without their consent, and employed protests, resignations and other tactics in a major campaign to thwart it. Their use of the ongoing Assembly to criticise the Anglo-Irish Agreement eventually led to its dissolution by the British government.

The Anglo-Irish Agreement established a permanent secretariat at Maryfield, on the eastern outskirts of Belfast. In effect the British government, led by Prime Minister Margaret Thatcher, had acknowledged the right of the Republic of Ireland to consultation over the future of Northern Ireland. The British government also asserted that it had no selfish or strategic interest in Northern Ireland and reaffirmed that Northern Ireland could only rejoin the Republic of Ireland if a majority of its people consented, thus establishing what has become known as the 'principle of consent'. Up untill this time the republican movement had refused to accept that 'consent' was necessary in order to achieve a united Ireland.

Despite much pessimism in the early years following the signing of the Anglo-Irish Agreement, the Northern Ireland parties continued in talks to break the political deadlock. Unionists were motivated by a desire to reach an outcome that would create a locally devolved government and shift the trend away from Anglo-Irish joint administration. Unionist leaders increasingly recognised the need to cut a deal with Northern Ireland nationalists to achieve this. Nationalists, buoyed by the backing of the Dublin government, were also looking for a locally based government providing it offered the prospect of power sharing.

## The Peace Process

Towards the end of the 1980s, SDLP leader John Hume had engaged in exploratory talks with Sinn Féin President Gerry Adams, aimed at identifying the political circumstances in which the IRA could move from their military focused stance into the mainstream political arena. By 1993 the Hume-Adams talks had produced a series of documents and statements which were fed into continuing inter governmental discussions. Hume argued that if London stated it had no selfish desire to hold onto Northern Ireland then the IRA would have no reason to continue to fight its 'war'. The Hume-Adams dialogue was taken forward by Taoiseach Albert Reynolds and the Irish government into discussions with London.

### Downing Street Declaration

The ongoing talks between the British and Irish governments were to culminate in the Downing Street Declaration of December 1993, in which the British government acknowledged and accepted the principle of self-determination of the people in both parts of the island of Ireland, together with the principle of consent for any change being made. The Declaration reaffirmed that Britain had no selfish or strategic interest in Northern Ireland and it was hoped that this affirmation would facilitate an IRA ceasefire. Ceasefires were to follow, the IRA in August 1994, with the UVF and the UDA under the banner of the Combined Loyalist Military Command (CLMC) following in October that year. Although the ceasefires did not do a lot to improve trust between Northern Ireland's warring groups, they improved the climate for political talks and these got underway under the auspices of Prime Minister John Major and Taoiseach Albert Reynolds.

### Fresh Talks

The UK general election of 1997 saw the return of a Labour government with a solid parliamentary majority, which enabled the new Prime Minster, Tony Blair, to inject fresh momentum into the peace process. Multi-party talks opened in September, following a three-strand formula. Strand one dealt with the internal administration of Northern Ireland; strand two considered the relationship between North and South, and strand three relations between London and Dublin: the East-West Dimension.

## The Belfast (Good Friday) Agreement

Following considerable personal involvement by Prime Minister Tony Blair, Irish Taoiseach Bertie Ahern, American President Bill Clinton, and intensive discussions between the local political parties, the Belfast Agreement (the 'Good Friday Agreement') was signed on Good Friday, 10th April 1998. The majority of political parties supported the Agreement, notable exceptions being Ian Paisley's DUP and the smaller UKUP, both of whom refused to participate in the talks.

Essentially the Agreement was a balanced constitutional deal which recognised the need to establish institutions which would give expression to three sets of relationships: the two traditions in Northern Ireland; the two traditions in Ireland (North and South); and the two nations Britain and Ireland (East and West). Alongside the Belfast-based institutions there was to be a series of cross-border development bodies with representation from both sides reporting into a North/South Ministerial Council. In addition, there would be a British/Irish Council addressing issues on an East/West basis and a consultative Civic Forum reflective of sectoral and community interests outside of the party political system.

The proposed arrangements, which were voted through the London and Dublin parliaments and put to separate referenda in Northern Ireland and the Republic, created an elected Assembly in Northern Ireland with a power-sharing Executive. The number of Northern Ireland government departments was increased to 10 along with a new unique joint central Office of the First and Deputy First Minister (OFMDFM).

### Belfast Agreement Referenda Results

**Northern Ireland**
Electorate: 1,175,403 Turnout: 80.98%

| | VOTES | PERCENTAGE |
|---|---|---|
| YES | 676,966 | 71.12% |
| NO | 274,879 | 28.88% |

**Republic of Ireland**
Electorate: 2,753,127 Turnout: 56.1%

| | VOTES | PERCENTAGE |
|---|---|---|
| YES | 1,442,583 | 94.4% |
| NO | 85,748 | 5.6% |

Following approval by Westminster, parliament passed the Northern Ireland (Elections) Act 1998, which provided for the holding of Assembly elections on 25 June 1998. The Act also provided for the Assembly to meet in 'shadow' mode, pending the coming into effect of the substantive powers of the new institutions provided for in the Northern Ireland Act 1998.

Elections held on 25 June 1998 returned 108 MLAs to the new Assembly. The Assembly met for the first time on 1 July 1998. David Trimble MP, Leader of the Ulster Unionist Party was elected as First Minister Designate and Séamus Mallon MP, Deputy Leader of the SDLP as Deputy First Minister Designate.

### Assembly Results by Party June 1998

| Party | % total vote | Seats |
|---|---|---|
| SDLP | 22.0 | 24 |
| UUP | 21.3 | 28 |
| DUP | 18.1 | 20 |
| Sinn Fein | 17.6 | 18 |
| Alliance | 6.5 | 6 |
| UKUP | 4.5 | 5 |
| Ind Unionist | 2.9 | 3 |
| PUP | 2.6 | 2 |
| NIWC | 1.6 | 2 |
| Others | 2.9 | 0 |
| **Total** | **100** | **108** |

### Review of the Agreement

However, despite the election of an Assembly there remained some significant political obstacles to the formation of a devolved government, most notably surrounding the decommissioning of paramilitary weapons. The Secretary of State Mo Mowlam announced a review of the implementation of the Agreement, facilitated by US Senator George Mitchell, and focused on how to carry forward matters relating to inclusive devolution and decommissioning. Eventually the Review produced consensus on the issues of the formation of an inclusive Executive and the decommissioning of weapons, enabling the necessary actions to take place in order to trigger devolution.

**Devolution**
Power was finally devolved to the Assembly and its Executive Committee on 2 December 1999. The Assembly succeeded in electing a cross community 12 strong Executive Committee using the d'Hondt system and assigning Ministers to their new Departments.

Despite the devolution of most of the day to day activities and powers of government to the new power-sharing Assembly, and the establishment of North/South bodies, Northern Ireland continued to operate unambiguously as part of the United Kingdom. Northern Ireland would continue to have representation at Westminster and significant governmental powers (excepted matters) would remain with Westminster for the foreseeable future.

However, once established, the Assembly and Executive were dogged by ongoing political difficulties. The continuing delay in paramilitary decommissioning eroded trust and confidence and meant that Ulster Unionists spent much of their time fending off internal critics. While the DUP occupied its two ministerial offices, it refused to participate in the round table Executive Committee which included Sinn Féin. Sinn Féin refused to take up its positions on the Northern Ireland Policing Board and the Ulster Unionist Party on occasions withdrew co-operation from the all-island bodies created under the Agreement.

At the 'backbencher' level, there was unease at what was perceived to be a relatively 'light' legislative programme in the unusual circumstance where all four main parties were effectively in a coalition and there was no effective opposition.

The continuing tensions led to several suspensions of the operation of the Assembly – the first time between February and May 2000. The lack of agreement on decommissioning forced further suspensions in August and September 2001. Finally, following a series of security-related 'breaches' attributed by Unionists to Sinn Féin, the Assembly and its institutions were suspended once again in October 2002. Despite ongoing negotiations the natural life of the Assembly expired in May 2003 before any agreement on restoration could be reached. The lack of agreement on the circumstances under which devolution could be restored, led the British government to postpone the Assembly elections which had been due to be held in May 2003.

**Devolved Government in Operation**
Despite the general disappointment at the failure to reach agreement – except of course for the minority totally opposed to the Agreement in the first place – the experience of devolution in practice was generally regarded as positive. Some of the local politicians were seen to have risen to the challenge of ministerial office and for the first time in many years Northern Ireland had leaders capable of effecting change.

The new administration had some notable successes – the rapid introduction, as promised, of free transport for citizens of pensionable age; the decisive management of the Foot and Mouth Disease crisis which had bedevilled the UK mainland and the tireless efforts to promote Northern Ireland abroad as an investment location. New methods were sought for funding public infrastructure which included the major Reinvestment and Reform Initiative (RRI). The Initiative established a new body, the Strategic Investment Board (SIB) to oversee a major new investment programme.

The Assembly Committees worked effectively scrutinising ministerial proposals and evolving into an 'opposition' role. At the operational level, Committee members comprising, in many cases, totally opposing parties, went about their business calmly and effectively. At the level of the citizen, Northern Ireland individuals and groups enjoyed comparatively easy access to ministerial decision-makers and the opportunity to have real influence over government decisions and policies.

**Future Devolution**
Efforts to 'do a deal' during the summer of 2003, despite further weapons decommissioning in October, came to nothing and the government finally called the Assembly election for 26 November 2003, in the absence of any agreement on how the institutions could be restored.

The election resulted in a hardening of attitudes in both communities with the anti-Agreement DUP getting the largest single share of the vote and 30 seats. The Ulster Unionist Party held on to 27 seats. The DUP representation was increased when, shortly after the election 3 Ulster Unionist MLAs left the party to join the DUP. On the nationalist side Sinn Féin emerged as the larger party winning 24 seats against the SDLP's 18. Apart from the Alliance Party, which retained its 6 seats, the smaller parties were, for the most part, squeezed out.

The period since the election has seen the DUP and Sinn Féin inch towards each other in the recognition that they, the two leading parties, now for the first time carry the greatest onus of responsibility for finding a way forward. Intensive all-party talks were held at Leeds Castle, Kent in September 2004 where many of the protagonists claimed that the parties were close to a 'deal'. However, fundamental issues including decommissioning, demilitarisation and, more recently, accountability continue to delay any prospect of a rapid return to devolved government.

## Looking Forward...
Although inter-communal strife is still going on in many parts of Northern Ireland, for the most part, generally, Northern Ireland has prospered during peacetime. New buildings, shops, restaurants and other entertainment venues are appearing all over the province and the numbers of visitors is increasing.

It is clear however that there is still a long way to go towards a 'normalisation' of the political and security situation here, but it is accepted by many that the crucial constitutional issues relating to the status of Northern Ireland itself have been decided, for the short term at least. Nonetheless divisions nurtured over centuries remain deep-rooted and will not disappear easily. The future, however, is not without hope. Most people recognise that Northern Ireland is now a better place, in which to live, visit or do business, than it was before the ceasefires. The long term signs indicate a trend towards a more peaceful future.

# Northern Ireland: The Place

## Geographical Overview

Northern Ireland occupies 5461 square miles in the northeast of the island of Ireland, which itself lies on the extreme northwest of the European continent. Its area takes up around one sixth of the island, approximately the size of Connecticut or Yorkshire. On the east it is separated from Scotland by the North Channel and from England by the Irish Sea; to the west and south it borders the Republic of Ireland. Its greatest distance north-south measures 85 miles, east-west 111 miles.

Northern Ireland's landscape consists mainly of low hill country, although there are two significant mountain ranges: the Mournes, which extend from South Down to Strangford Lough in the east, and the Sperrins, reaching through the northwest boundaries of Northern Ireland. The highest point in Northern Ireland is one of the twelve peaks of the Mournes: Slieve Donard in Co Down, some 2796 ft above sea level. From the top of Slieve Donard the Isle of Man is visible and in favourable conditions, the Scottish coast, Mount Snowdon in Wales and even the Cumbrian Hills of England may be seen. There is also a substantial tract of high land in Co Antrim known as the Antrim Plateau, or more commonly the 'Glens of Antrim'. In contrast, the lowest lying point in Northern Ireland is The Marsh, near Downpatrick, actually 1.3 ft below sea level.

There are also over 60 forests, including 9 forest parks, and a number of wooded areas. The southwest is mainly forested, with a number of small lakes and rivers which drain into Lough Erne. The lake, split into Upper and Lower Lough Erne, is a 50-mile waterway favoured by many for fishing and pleasure boating, particularly following the recent development of the Shannon-Erne waterway.

A basalt plateau extends throughout Northern Ireland, leading to brown earth soil that varies as a result of glacially transported material. This can appear as drumlins, smooth mounds that occur principally in parts of South Down and Armagh. Glaciation also created the area's principal valleys: the River Bann in the north, the Blackwater in the southwest and the Lagan in the east. These valleys have always been vital in providing routes through the heart of the North, and the waterways are still used commercially and for pleasure. Land between the estuary of the River Roe and the city of Derry was reclaimed from the sea in the nineteenth century for flax growing. As the land is below sea level, it is drained artificially and the estuary itself is now a nature reserve.

Lough Neagh is the largest freshwater lake on the whole island; the largest in the British Isles and one of the largest in Europe. It covers an area of 153 square miles out of Northern Ireland's total of 246 square miles of inland water and tideways. As well as providing all kinds of freshwater fish, the Lough is also the centre of a centuries-old eel fishery, which exports hundreds of tonnes of Ulster eels every year. The best view of Lough Neagh is generally available from a plane flying into Belfast International Airport: the surrounding land is very flat, making the Lough, despite its size, a somewhat hidden feature of Northern Ireland.

Farming land in Northern Ireland varies from the fertile arable expanses of North Down and South Antrim to the boggy low lying lands of the Fermanagh lakelands and the stony upland of mid Ulster and the Sperrins.

### Northern Ireland: Main Geographical Features

**Area of Counties**

| | |
|---|---|
| Antrim | 1176 sq miles |
| Armagh | 513 sq miles |
| Down | 982 sq miles |
| Fermanagh | 715 sq miles |
| Londonderry | 814 sq miles |
| Tyrone | 1261 sq miles |
| Total | 5461 sq miles |

**Mountains**

| | |
|---|---|
| Slieve Donard Co Down | 2796 ft |
| Sawel Co Tyrone / Co Londonderry border | 2240 ft |
| Cuilcagh Co Fermanagh | 2188 ft |
| Slieve Gullion Co Armagh | 1894 ft |
| Trostan Co Antrim | 1817 ft |

**Lakes**

| | |
|---|---|
| Lough Neagh | 153 sq miles |
| Lower Lough Erne | 42 sq miles |
| Upper Lough Erne | 13 sq miles |

**Rivers**

Upper Bann: 47 miles from Mourne Mountains to Lough Neagh

Lower Bann: 38 miles from Lough Neagh to the Atlantic Ocean

Lagan: 32 miles from the Mournes to Belfast Lough

Nonetheless there is sufficient quality land to support a major agricultural industry with the abundance of pasture giving dairy and livestock industries a competitive advantage. Peat soils, historically the main source of fuel for peasant farmers, are a feature of the island and quite common in the North. Peat and turf are still cut extensively for fuel, although mainly for private domestic use as commercially they are not particularly significant. Few mineral resources are naturally present in Northern Ireland although gravel, clays, chalk and limestone provide the basis for the manufacture of lime, bricks and cement. Most other raw materials, such as oil and coal, are not rich in Northern Ireland and need to be imported. In fact Northern Ireland is at something of a competitive disadvantage in that it is entirely dependent on imported fuels to meet its energy requirements. The town of Coalisland is named after a vein of coal that, although present, has never been successfully mined. There is also a significant deposit of lignite on the western shores of Lough Neagh but this has yet to be proven commercially viable.

Northern Ireland's climate is temperate, although much affected by its maritime location. High winds are common, especially in the north and on the east coast, and south westerly winds tend to drive away clouds from the Atlantic. As a result, the weather in Northern Ireland can be fairly changeable, going from overcast to a blue sky in a short space of time. Rainfall varies from as little as 32.5 inches to 80 inches per year, generally increasing towards eastern areas. Spring is relatively dry; summer and winter are disproportionately wet. Winters are generally long because of Northern Ireland's location north and west, which also leads to shorter days in the winter months. Snow is not uncommon, but rarely settles and is seldom severe. However, summer days are also proportionately longer than average. Average temperatures range from 3.3 degrees centigrade in winter to 18 degrees in the summer, indicating few extremes of hot and cold. The mildness and humidity of Northern Ireland's climate, together with slow natural drainage, has given the area a reputation for lush green fields and constant rain, although conditions are generally quite pleasant. Northern Ireland is also widely noted for its breathtaking scenery, including some 330 miles of coastal road. In fact, over 20% of the land has been designated as Areas of Outstanding Natural Beauty. This has been helped by low population density in many areas, leaving the countryside largely unspoilt.

The generous natural landscape has also led to the growth of all kinds of outdoor pursuits. There are several championship standard golf courses, as well as opportunities for coarse fishing, as salmon and trout are plentiful in rivers. Watersports such as sailing and windsurfing are also popular, as are climbing, hiking and horse riding.

*Northern Ireland: Towns and Roads*

## The Six Counties...

Northern Ireland is comprised of six of Ireland's 32 counties. Although often thought of as having some ancient tribal or cultural significance, the county divisions were entirely a British administrative creation in the 19th Century. The six counties of Northern Ireland each have their own unique image and characteristics and are described briefly below.

*Giants Causeway, Co Antrim*

### Antrim

Antrim occupies the north-east corner of Northern Ireland, stretching from Belfast in the south to the north coast. To the east is the Irish Sea, and Antrim's western boundary for the most part is Lough Neagh and the River Bann. It is Northern Ireland's second largest county by size. County Antrim is a mixture of urban centres including most of north and west Belfast, the towns of Ballymena, Larne, Carrickfergus, Ballymoney and Antrim town itself, and large rural stretches. Antrim is possibly best known for its picturesque 'Glens', home to traditional rural lifestyles and splendid mountain scenery, and its rugged north coast where Northern Ireland's premier visitor attraction, the Giant's Causeway, is located.

### Armagh

Armagh is Northern Ireland's smallest county, characterised by the large towns of Lurgan and Portadown (Craigavon) to the north, the ecclesiastical city of Armagh itself mid-county and drumlin country in the south. Known in Ireland and worldwide as the 'Orchard County', Armagh has a major apple production and processing industry, famous for the local 'Bramley' cooking apple. The cathedral city itself, with its religious significance, is described below under 'cities'. The border areas have witnessed much of the anti-British violence carried out during the Troubles and the area of South Armagh, near the Irish border, earned the unfavourable tag of 'bandit country' during the 1970s and 1980s. However South Armagh offers fine scenery around Slieve Gullion and many interesting attractions.

### Londonderry

County Londonderry – the 'Oak Leaf' county - lies to the north west of Northern Ireland, and combines the major population centres of Derry city and Coleraine with numerous small towns and villages becoming ever more rural toward the south of the county. Northern Ireland's second largest mountain range, the Sperrins, runs through the heart of the county and 'Crossing the Sperrins', through the steep 'Glenshane Pass', is a well known feature of any journey between Derry and Belfast. The county is defined geographically by four main river valleys: the Bann, the Roe, the Faughan and the Foyle.

### Down

Like Antrim, County Down incorporates a major slice of Belfast – most of the south and east of the city. The other substantial towns in the county are Bangor and Newtownards in the north-east, Lisburn in the north-west, Banbridge and Ballynahinch in mid-county and Newcastle, Downpatrick and Newry in the south. Down is home to the Mountains of Mourne, Northern Ireland's highest mountain range and source of the River Bann. It also encloses Northern Ireland's second largest inland waterway, Strangford Lough, which opens up to the Irish sea.
Down incorporates the industrial with the rural and with numerous attractive small towns such as Moira, Hillsborough and Castlewellan. It has a significant tourism industry centred around the popular tourist resorts of Newcastle and Bangor.

### Fermanagh

Fermanagh is a predominantly rural county located to the south-west of Northern Ireland. It has by far the smallest population of any of the six counties and its main industries are agriculture and tourism. The tourism industry is largely based around Fermanagh's two major internal waterways: Lower and Upper Lough Erne. These lakes are a major attraction to anglers and a centre for boating holidays. Fermanagh's main centre is the picturesque town of Enniskillen, the regional administrative centre which is built around a series of islands at the mouth of Lower Lough Erne. Other significant towns, providing employment and centres of population are Lisnaskea, in the south of the county and Irvinestown in the north.

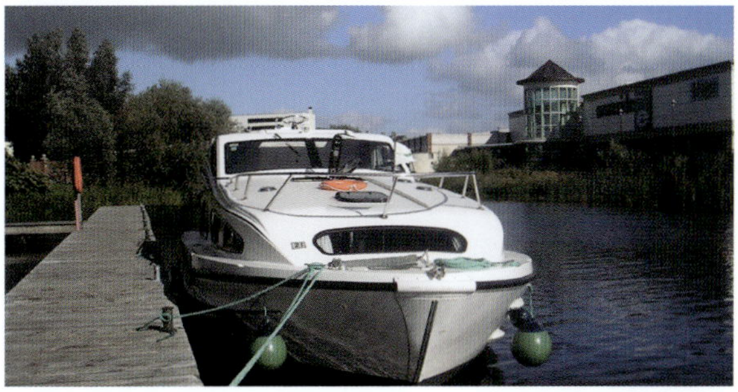

*Lough Erne, Enniskillen*

### Tyrone

Tyrone is Northern Ireland's largest county by size and stretches from Lough Neagh in the East to the border with Donegal in the West. There is no dominant town in the county, the four main ones being Strabane to the north west, Cookstown to the east, Omagh in the centre and Dungannon to the south. The main industry is agriculture although there is a spread of industry throughout the main towns. Tyrone, meaning Eoin's Land, is the ancient home of the O'Neill clan, once the dominant rulers of Ulster. The 'Red Hand' of Ulster remains the symbol of the county to this day. Tyrone's main rivers include the Ballinderry, the Owenreagh and Strule and are known to anglers for the quality of their fishing.

*Albert Clock, Belfast*

## Cities in Northern Ireland

Northern Ireland now has five cities: Belfast, Derry/ Londonderry, Armagh, Lisburn and Newry although these are quite different from each other in size and all are very small by global standards. Lisburn and Newry were awarded city status during the 2002 Golden Jubilee celebrations.

### Belfast

The capital city of Northern Ireland, Belfast is also its administrative, industrial and commercial centre. It has a population of around 350,000 and enjoys an enviable setting, facing out to sea and cradled on all sides by ranges of hills and mountains. The name Belfast itself is derived from the Irish béal feirste. This literally means 'mouth of the river' and came from Belfast's position at the head of the River Lagan, which becomes Belfast Lough as it joins the Irish Sea. Originally a small town, Belfast saw its population increase significantly with the Industrial Revolution. In 1800 its population was around 20,000 but the enormous growth of the linen industry caused Belfast to expand rapidly. Rows of small terraced housing serve as a reminder of the thousands of mill and factory workers who moved from the countryside and settled in the city. In 1888, Belfast became a city by royal charter and by the end of the 19th century had overtaken Dublin in terms of population. By the beginning of the Second World War, during which Belfast experienced bombing at the hands of German planes targeting its shipyards and engineering works, its population had exceeded 400,000.

The city also suffered heavily in economic and social terms during the 'Troubles', when it became a frequent target of paramilitary bombs. In recent years however it has enjoyed a major revival of cultural activities and a more positive atmosphere, with new hotels, restaurants and entertainment venues springing up all over the city. Belfast is also a district, in local government terms, covering some 44 square miles (115 square km), taking in several smaller towns and villages around its limits. The most recent figures (2003 mid-year estimate) put the population of Belfast's local government district at 271,596, over 15% of the total population of Northern Ireland.

### Derry (Londonderry)

Derry, the 'Maiden City', is located on the river Foyle in the north west of Northern Ireland, and has a population of around 100,000. It is one of the oldest settlements on the island of Ireland, having traditionally been founded in 546 AD by St Columba. The name Derry comes from the Irish word Doire or Daire, meaning oak grove, in particular one surrounded by water or a peat bog. This was the case in Derry, the grove being on an island in the River Foyle. The water beside the island gradually dried out, leaving a boggy area that became known as the 'Bogside'. In the early seventeenth century, King James I gave the City of London responsibility for settling this area of Ireland. Derry was fortified in 1613 and renamed Londonderry by royal charter as part of the Plantation of Ulster. The debate over what the city should be called is a long-standing one with some people now adopting the phrase 'Stroke City' as a humourous and inoffensive option.

Although much smaller than Belfast and no bigger than a typical English town the inhabitants of Derry are very proud of their City status and their rich heritage. The defined area of Derry city itself is relatively small, only 3.4 square miles. Unemployment in Derry has historically tended to be above the Northern Ireland average. Traditionally it has had a particular problem with male unemployment as its well-established shirtmaking industry has tended to provide more jobs taken up by women. Poverty remains a problem in the city. In recent years, although the shirt factories have been closing there has been an influx of new engineering and high-tech investments in the city, and Derry has developed a new economic self-confidence.

It is expected that initiatives such as re-locating public sector jobs to the city will help go some way towards further alleviating unemployment.

Despite its image as a divided city Derry is developing a vibrant cultural life with its new Millennium Forum hosting many famous musicians and theatrical productions. Each October the entire city comes alive for the annual Halloween festival, when houses are decorated and people dress up to enjoy the festivities. Architecturally the city boasts the famous City Walls and the Guildhall, which are both must-see sights for any visitor. The emergence of new hotels, bars and restaurants have meant that Derry city has become more appealing as a place for people to visit as well as to live and work.

### Armagh

Armagh is similarly an historical city, first founded on the hill fort of Ard Mhacha in the 4th century AD. It has a population of less than 20,000 and barely merits inclusion in the top 10 of Northern Ireland's towns (by population). Important in terms of Ulster and Ireland as a whole, it is the ancient city of St Patrick. Both Church of Ireland and Catholic cathedrals in the city are named after the patron saint of Ireland and both churches' archbishops are based in the ecclesiastical city.

Armagh city also boasts an observatory (founded in 1765) and planetarium. Of particular note is the fine Regency and Georgian architecture that is prominent around the City Centre in the area of the Mall. The wider Armagh local Government district covers an area of 261 square miles, and, according to the 2001 Census figures has a population of 54,263 indicating low population density in what is a heavily rural area. The county of Armagh is known as the Orchard County; famous for fruit growing, in particular apples, although there are a number of light industrial centres as well.

**Lisburn**

*Market Square, Lisburn*

Lisburn, some 8 miles southwest of Belfast and increasingly merging with the south western outskirts of the city, was a small village until plantation. The English government invited French Huguenots to settle there, who nurtured the growing linen industry by the introduction of new Dutch looms. Lisburn quickly became a major linen producer, although today this focus has progressed to synthetic fabrics. The River Lagan, runs through the centre of Lisburn and although the linen industry based around the river has declined, Lisburn remains an important centre for commerce and industry in Northern Ireland and is also a popular residential location, acting as a 'commuter town' for Belfast.

**Newry**

Newry is notable for having the first inland waterway in the British Isles, which contributed greatly to the town's prosperity in the nineteenth century. The canal had 14 locks and provided a means to export mainly linen and stone. By 1840 its importance had declined, however. The name Newry is derived from the Gaelic for a yew tree, which was according to legend planted by St Patrick in the area. Newry has experienced rapid growth in population and economic activity in recent years and today is a busy city benefiting from its close proximity to the border with the Republic of Ireland. The city itself is strategically located some forty miles south of Belfast and only sixty miles north of Dublin.

## Major Towns in Northern Ireland

Many of Northern Ireland's towns date from the seventeenth century, when London companies formed the Honourable The Irish Society. They planned and built towns around a central meeting place, known as a diamond. Two streets would intersect the diamond and the town itself would be built on a grid pattern. These towns would usually include fortifications around the town's boundary, a market house and a planter's residence. Limavady and Coleraine in County Londonderry are good examples of 'plantation towns'.

Later, in the nineteenth century, smaller 'mill villages' such as Bessbrook in County Armagh, were planned around greens which may have been used as 'bleach greens' for bleaching linen. These villages and small towns were characterised by terraces of small, neat mill-workers houses, many of which have been modernised but are preserved in their original architectural form.

Other larger market towns tend to have a long, wide main street. For example, Cookstown in County Tyrone is known for its main street, 1.25 miles long and 130 ft wide. Lurgan in County Armagh is another example. Given the rural environment, there are many small market towns throughout the area. Northern Ireland also has an abundance of tiny villages and hamlets, especially in more remote areas. The smallest Irish description of a rural district is a 'townland' which could be as little as 300 acres. In 1846 Ordnance Survey recorded more than 60,000 of these townlands across the island of Ireland. In some parts of Northern Ireland, people are very proud of their townlands and actively try to preserve them by using them in preference to their official road or street name as part of their postal address.

During the seventeenth century plantation, the majority of place names all over Ireland were 'anglicised', from their original Gaelic Irish. Translation meant that many place names are remarkably similar, especially in terms of prefix; the basic difference being a spelling closer to the English phonetics of the original Gaelic name. Common examples include Bally-, from Baile, meaning town; and Drum- or Drom-, from droim, meaning ridge. Knock comes from the Irish word cnoc meaning hill, and Carrick from the Irish carraig, meaning rock.

The Bann river is often seen as a political and economic dividing line in Northern Ireland: the more prosperous east and the less prosperous, less populated west. Derry is unquestionably the major population centre of the West and local businesses often complain that Northern Ireland stops 'left of the Bann'. Most people live east of the Bann and few of the towns to the west have more than 10,000 inhabitants. Northern Ireland's main towns are described briefly below:

**Bangor**

Third in terms of population after Belfast and Derry, Bangor is a large town located on the affluent North Down coastline, some 16 miles east of Belfast. The town centre is very close to the sea front at the mouth of Belfast Lough. Although it is a commercial and administrative centre in its own right Bangor is also a residential location for many people whose employment is in Belfast. Bangor is a popular seaside tourist resort attracting many visitors, particularly to its splendid marina, during the summer months.

**Ballymena**

Ballymena is also one of Northern Ireland's largest and busiest towns, and is the main administrative centre for the north east region of Northern Ireland. The town is home to some major manufacturing industries and also services a large and prosperous rural population, enjoying one of the lowest rates of unemployment in the North. Ballymena is highly regarded in terms of the quality of its shops and its people maintain a reputation for friendliness and warmth.

*Lurgan, Co Armagh*

**Craigavon,** including **Lurgan** and **Portadown**

Craigavon, Portadown and Lurgan are all part of a south west extension of the Lagan Valley and Belfast's industrial area. The central Craigavon area was originally designated a 'new town' in the late 1960s, hoping to create a new lifestyle in a modern environment with a fully integrated approach to planning. The town, named after unionist Prime Minister James Craig, later Lord Craigavon, was designed to join together the established towns of Lurgan and Portadown (just 5 miles apart) and provide relief for the overcrowding experienced in Belfast at that time.

However, people did not move to Craigavon in the numbers anticipated and, particularly in the 1970s, there was insufficient employment available for those who did. The result was surplus, unwanted public housing alongside economic deprivation. Its popularity did not reach expectations at the time of its creation, although more recently Craigavon is becoming a favoured location for Belfast-bound commuters.

The Craigavon area with its proximity to Lough Neagh and good communications infrastructure is increasingly developing a very positive lifestyle image built around recreation and leisure.

**Coleraine**

Coleraine is in County Londonderry, although it is the main town on the north east coast of Northern Ireland, which mainly falls under County Antrim. The town is centred where Northern Ireland's biggest river, the Bann, joins the Sea. It is a busy industrial centre and market town, as well as being a University town with a major campus located on its northern outskirts. Coleraine is a popular base for touring the north Antrim coast, and is close to two of Northern Ireland's most popular holiday resorts, Portrush and Portstewart.

**Larne**

Larne is home to Northern Ireland's second most important port (only Belfast ranks above it), as well as a busy commercial centre. Situated about 20 miles north east of Belfast and sheltered by the Islandmagee headland, Larne is a busy ferryport, taking heavy volumes of passengers and cargo to the Scottish ports of Stranraer and Cairnryan. It is also home to some of Northern Ireland's busiest industries, with a narrow stretch of water separating it from the North's biggest power station, Ballylumford.

**Omagh**

Omagh has seen significant growth as a result of increased administration in the western regions of Northern Ireland. In more recent times it experienced the worst single atrocity of the Northern Ireland troubles – a bomb in the town centre in August 1998 which killed 29 people. Omagh is a busy market town and its location in the rural centre of Northern Ireland means that it serves a substantial rural hinterland. Its people have earned extensive recognition for the dignified manner in which the community has rebuilt itself following the 1998 atrocity.

**Strabane**

Strabane is situated on the border, some 20 miles south of Derry, and sits to the east of the River Foyle. It is the gateway to North Donegal. Strabane has historically experienced some of the highest levels of unemployment in any of Northern Ireland's large towns. However, its heritage is rich, as Strabane was an important printing and publishing centre in the eighteenth century and the American Declaration of Independence was printed there.

**Enniskillen**

Enniskillen is the unofficial capital of the Fermanagh lakelands, as well as being the administrative and commercial centre for the county. It is possibly Northern Ireland's most picturesque large town. With its island location and accompanying attractions Enniskillen is a popular tourist centre, particularly for boating and angling enthusiasts.

*Dungannon, Co Tyrone*

**Dungannon**

Dungannon town is situated in the south of County Tyrone in the centre of Northern Ireland. Its Irish name is Dún Geanainn, meaning Gannon's fort. Today Dungannon is a market town, also hosting light industries including food processing, crystal and fabrics. Dungannon is the main commercial centre for the largely rural area of South Tyrone. It is well located as the gateway to the West of Northern Ireland, adjacent to the M1 Motorway.

## Northern Ireland: The People

Northern Ireland's 'Troubles' are rooted in social and cultural differences that go back many hundreds of years and it is impossible to describe the people without reference to history and religion. The area has always had strong links with the western areas of Scotland as a consequence of its close proximity. English and Scottish settlers during the Plantation found that apart from their nationality, their Protestant faith marked them as separate from the native Irish. Unlike the Norman invaders of 1170, the English and Scottish planters of the 16th and 17th centuries resisted any integration of their culture into that of the native population. Over time they came to form the majority of the population in County Antrim, North Down and the Lagan Valley.

The Protestant planters of Ulster contributed greatly to the government's anglicisation of Ireland. They did this by translating place names from Irish, and establishing English over Gaelic as the official language. Scottish influence is especially striking in the regional accents and dialects of Northern Ireland. Areas with stronger Scottish links, such as the county of Antrim and parts of county Down, have discernible Scottish accents; indeed inhabitants of towns like Ballymena are often mistaken for Scots by visitors. Similarly, areas close to the border with the Republic of Ireland show southern characteristics in language, for example people from Derry and Donegal sound quite similar.

There is an uneven distribution of Protestant and Catholic communities throughout Northern Ireland. Protestants are concentrated in large numbers in the east of Northern Ireland, and particularly so in the areas immediately surrounding Belfast. Meanwhile areas such as Newry and Mourne and Derry, in the South and West respectively have overwhelmingly Catholic populations. The broad overall picture is that Northern Ireland tends to be more Catholic overall west of the Bann and more Protestant to the east of the river.

## Population

### Size and Composition

The population of Northern Ireland on 30 June 2003 (estimated) was 1,702,628; a 10% increase on the 1981 figure. Over the period 1981-2003 all local government districts experienced population growth, except Belfast, where the population has fallen by around 15%. Correspondingly, the biggest increases in population were in the areas around Belfast – notably Carrickfergus, Lisburn and Ards (a significant increase in population occurred in the Banbridge area, but this can partly be attributed to the transfer of part of the area of Newry and Mourne to the Banbridge district in the early 1990s).

The three key determinants of population size are the birth rate, death rate and net inward or outward migration. Although Northern Ireland's birth rate has always outpaced the death rate, the natural growth in population has tended to be checked by a high degree of net outward migration. Birth rates are generally higher in the West and South of Northern Ireland than in the East and North. These factors impacting population growth are discussed in greater detail later. The latest figures (estimated) for the population of Northern Ireland are set out in Table 1.1.

**Table 1.1 Northern Ireland Population (June 2003)**

| | 0-15 | 16-59/64 | 60+/65+ | Total |
|---|---|---|---|---|
| 1961 | 438,404 | 808,338 | 180,649 | 1,427,391 |
| 1971 | 482,744 | 852,738 | 204,931 | 1,540,413 |
| 1981 | 444,058 | 874,440 | 224,466 | 1,542,964 |
| 1991 | 416,539 | 944,645 | 246,111 | 1,607,295 |
| 2001 | 397,150 | 1,029,958 | 262,211 | 1,689,319 |
| 2003 | 388,143 | 1,043,893 | 270,592 | 1,702,628 |

Source: NISRA

### Population Density

The overall population density of Northern Ireland in 2003 was estimated at 125 persons per square kilometre. Population density varies considerably across Northern Ireland tending to be at its lowest in the west (Local Government Districts Fermanagh, Omagh and Strabane) and in the very north of the province (Moyle, which includes the low population on Rathlin Island) and higher in the east and in the hinterlands of the larger towns and cities.

**Table 1.2 Population by Local Government District 1981-2003 and Population Density 2003**

| | Population Estimates | | | Population Density |
|---|---|---|---|---|
| | 1981 | 2001 | 2003 | 2003 |
| NI | 1,542,964 | 1,689,319 | 1,702,628 | 125.4 |
| Antrim | 46,066 | 48,761 | 49260 | 116.9 |
| Ards | 57,996 | 73,435 | 74369 | 195.5 |
| Armagh | 49,337 | 54,462 | 55449 | 82.6 |
| Ballymena | 54,999 | 58,801 | 59516 | 94.5 |
| Ballymoney | 22,983 | 27,007 | 27809 | 66.8 |
| Banbridge | 30,084 | 41,549 | 43083 | 95.4 |
| Belfast | 316,358 | 277,170 | 271596 | 2477.6 |
| Carrickfergus | 28,704 | 37,730 | 38466 | 475.9 |
| Castlereagh | 60,906 | 66,533 | 66076 | 777.4 |
| Coleraine | 46,869 | 56,408 | 56024 | 115.4 |
| Cookstown | 28,403 | 32,712 | 33387 | 65.0 |
| Craigavon | 73,504 | 80,931 | 82155 | 291.8 |
| Derry | 90,157 | 105,335 | 106456 | 279.7 |
| Down | 53,782 | 64,147 | 65195 | 100.5 |
| Dungannon | 43,922 | 47,849 | 48695 | 63.0 |
| Fermanagh | 52,108 | 57,687 | 58705 | 34.5 |
| Larne | 29,105 | 30,811 | 30948 | 92.0 |
| Limavady | 27,309 | 32,639 | 33571 | 57.3 |
| Lisburn | 85,188 | 108,997 | 109565 | 245.3 |
| Magherafelt | 32,718 | 39,891 | 40837 | 72.4 |
| Moyle | 14,452 | 15,961 | 16302 | 33.0 |
| Newry & Mourne | 77,515 | 87,399 | 89644 | 99.8 |
| Newtownabbey | 72,450 | 80,144 | 80285 | 532.8 |
| North Down | 66,926 | 76,578 | 77110 | 953.4 |
| Omagh | 44,778 | 48,109 | 49560 | 43.9 |
| Strabane | 36,345 | 38,273 | 38565 | 44.8 |

Source: NISRA

Moyle has the lowest population density in Northern Ireland at just 33 persons per square kilometre, in comparison to the 2,477 in Belfast. High population densities are also recorded in North Down, Newtownabbey and Castlereagh.

Another unusual dimension to the population distribution of Northern Ireland is that it is not overwhelmingly concentrated in cities and towns. Although the Greater Belfast area accounts for almost one third of the total population in Northern Ireland, most of the remaining inhabitants are to be found in numerous small towns, villages, hamlets and relatively remote rural locations. Two thirds of Northern Ireland's land mass is west of the River Bann, and there are virtually no towns of population greater than 15,000 people (excluding the city of Derry).

**Life Expectancy and Population Growth**

Birth rates in Northern Ireland are generally high by UK standards although the overall birth rate for the region has slowed down significantly in recent years. In 1971 there were 20.6 births per 1,000 of population in Northern Ireland, falling to 17.6 in 1981, 16.2 in 1991 and down to 13.0 in 2001. This figure has fallen again in 2003 to 12.7. Birth rates are generally higher in the West and South of Northern Ireland than in the East and North.

Death rates have also been falling over the same period, albeit more slowly (see Table 1.3), reflecting the general tendency for people to live longer. Indeed life expectancy for children born in the period 2000-2002 is calculated to be 80 (women) and 75 (men); the highest ever. At the turn of the 20th century (1900-02) life expectancy for men and women was just 47. Table 1.4 illustrates trends in life expectancy in Northern Ireland since 1970.

**Table 1.3 Rates of Births, Marriages and Deaths in Northern Ireland 1971-2003***

| Year | Births | Marriages | Deaths |
|---|---|---|---|
| 1971 | 20.6 | 7.9 | 10.5 |
| 1981 | 17.6 | 6.2 | 10.5 |
| 1991 | 16.2 | 5.7 | 9.4 |
| 2001 | 13.0 | 4.3 | 8.6 |
| 2003 | 12.7 | 4.6 | 8.5 |

* per 1000 population

Source: NISRA

Marriage rates in Northern Ireland have been falling steadily over the past 30 years. Whilst in 1971 there were 7.9 marriages per 1000 of population, the figure for 2003 has fallen to just 4.6. This is indicative of changing trends in society, whereby it has become increasingly common for people to live together without getting married.

**Table 1.4 Life Expectancy (from birth) 1970 - 2002****

| | Male | Female |
|---|---|---|
| 1970-72 | 67.6 | 73.7 |
| 1980-82 | 69.2 | 75.6 |
| 1990-92 | 72.6 | 78.4 |
| 1991-93 | 72.8 | 78.7 |
| 1998-00 | 74.5 | 79.6 |
| 1999-01 | 74.8 | 79.8 |
| 2000-02 | 75.2 | 80.1 |

**years

Source: NISRA

With increasing life expectancy, and death rates which are falling more dramatically than birth rates, it would be expected that the population of Northern Ireland would be increasing rapidly. As it happens, the population is increasing, but at a fairly slow rate (2001 census figures show an increase of around 82,000 people on the 1991 figures). This may be partly explained by the level of outward migration from Northern Ireland, which has traditionally been high, with many young people (especially) leaving to seek education and employment in Great Britain and beyond. It would appear that with the advent of more peaceful times, this trend has slowed, but the overall effect will not be seen for some time.

**Table 1.5 Northern Ireland Population Projection to 2043 (thousands)**

| | 2003 | 2008 | 2013 | 2018 | 2023 |
|---|---|---|---|---|---|
| Total | 1,703 | 1,735 | 1,765 | 1,795 | 1,821 |
| | **2028** | **2031** | **2036** | **2041** | **2043** |
| Total | 1,837 | 1,840 | 1,839 | 1,829 | 1,823 |

Source: NISRA

Future projections of population (see table 1.5 above) indicate a steady population increase until 2031 then a slow reduction thereafter. The NISRA long-term forecast shows Northern Ireland's population being only 7.0% higher in 2043 than it was in 2003.

**Population and Religion**
One of the key insights into Northern Ireland – from a political perspective – is the changing religious composition of the population. Given that political affiliations correlate significantly with religious divisions, any changes in the relative numbers of the two communities are assumed to have political implications. In most other parts of the western world the religious breakdown of the population would only be of academic interest but in Northern Ireland it attracts much more attention for this reason.

Of considerable political significance is the perception that the birth rate in the Catholic community is traditionally much higher than in the Protestant community, adding weight to the majority community's fear that political power would shift from the declining Protestant majority to the growing Catholic minority. Over recent years both birth rates have slowed down and the gap has narrowed significantly.

## Religious Affiliation

Northern Ireland is home to people from a variety of ethnic and religious backgrounds. However, most people in the region describe themselves in terms of the principal Christian denominations found throughout the English-speaking world: the Roman Catholic Church; the Church of Ireland (Anglican); the Presbyterian Church; or other, smaller Protestant denominations. In the 2001 Northern Ireland Census of population, 40% of the population stated directly that they were Roman Catholic, with 46% stating they belonged to other Christian religions, the vast majority of which were Protestant.

Other religions and philosophies were stated by only 0.3% of those responding. In the 2001 census 14% responded as having no religion or not stating it, which represented a significant increase on 4% recorded in 1991. Examining the census results at a Local Government District level it is apparent that there is a much higher incidence of people in urban areas recording no religion (or not stating it). Highest percentages are to be found in North Down (25%), Carrickfergus (23%) and Ards (21%) while the lowest figures are in Strabane and Magherafelt (both 6%) and Cookstown (7%).

*Church of Ireland Cathedral, Armagh*

The second largest denomination in Northern Ireland after Roman Catholic is the Presbyterian Church followed by the Church of Ireland (Anglican) with Methodists a distant fourth. In addition there are numerous other smaller Protestant denominations, some characterised by a more evangelical and fundamentalist outlook. Unlike many Western countries where the Catholic Church would tend to find itself on the right wing of social policy, in Northern Ireland some of the smaller churches also exert a conservative influence on social policy; being opposed for example to abortion and euthanasia (like Roman Catholics) but also to homosexuality and failure to observe the Sabbath Day. As a result some parts of Northern Ireland observe a regime on Sundays where working or participation in organised leisure activities is not encouraged. For the majority however secularism has strengthened in line with overall trends in Britain and Ireland.

*Gospel Hall, Co Down*

These results are interesting when compared with the figures for community background which includes religion or religion brought up in: just 3% of the population responded as having been brought up with no religious or community background. This suggests that around 10% of the population have chosen not to adhere to the traditional religious beliefs in which they were brought up. Again, there is a much higher than average incidence of people having been brought up with no religious or community background in urban areas – figures are highest in North Down, Carrickfergus and Ards and are lowest (under 1%) in Strabane, Newry and Mourne and Dungannon. This all implies that people are more likely to continue to adhere to the beliefs in which they were brought up in rural areas, where there is a higher percentage of the population who are brought up within a religious or community background.

Northern Ireland has higher rates of church attendance than elsewhere in the United Kingdom and religion is, in its own right, important to the life of the area. Even people who have little formal religious commitment often have a social background which is linked to one or other of the two main religious communities. Frequently it is on this basis that they are perceived by others to belong to either the Protestant or Catholic community.

The community to which a person belongs often influences many other aspects of their life: their national identity, language, the area in which they live, the school they or their children attend, the political party they support and even their name. Religious community background (rather than theological belief) as the principal source of social identity in Northern Ireland has been the subject of considerable academic attention.

**Religious Segregation**

Overall the 2001 census figures show that 44% of respondents were brought up in the Catholic religion/background and 53% were brought up with Protestant and other Christian backgrounds. These are the figures for Northern Ireland as a whole and suggest an increasingly even Catholic/Protestant split. The situation is somewhat different when examined in greater detail.

In the Local Government Districts of Carrickfergus, Ards, North Down, Castlereagh and Newtownabbey over 75% responded as being brought up within the Protestant community. In Newry and Mourne and Derry over 75% responded as being brought up within the Catholic community. This all points to the fact that while, overall Northern Ireland appears a fairly mixed community, when examined in greater detail, many areas remain dominated by one or other of the main religions.

*St. Patrick's Roman Catholic Cathedral, Armagh*

**Language and Identity**

The Northern Ireland Social Attitudes Survey was first conducted in 1989. Focusing on a range of social and political issues, it collected the opinions of a representative sample of persons aged 18 or over who live in private households. In the 1995 survey, 63% of Catholic respondents described themselves as 'Irish' compared with 5% of Protestants. In contrast, 64% of Protestant respondents described themselves as 'British' compared with 11% of Catholics.

The 2001 Census also contained a question on knowledge of the Irish language, which was to be answered in respect of the population aged three or over. Just over one in ten people (10.35%) had some knowledge of Irish (ie could speak, read or write the language). In 1995-96, 1038 pupils in Northern Ireland, equating to 0.3% of all school enrolments, were taught through the medium of Irish.

## Northern Ireland Households

**Household size and Type**

Households in Northern Ireland tend to be larger than the average for the United Kingdom as a whole. The average Northern Ireland household comprised 3 persons in 2003-04, with people living alone representing over a quarter of the region's households.

In 2003-04 30% of Northern Ireland households comprised 4 or more people. Traditionally Northern Ireland's households have been larger than the UK average, partly because of the tendency for Northern Ireland families to have more children, and also the fact that the traditional extended family (including grandparents) has survived to a greater extent in Northern Ireland.

Although family sizes remain higher in Northern Ireland than the rest of the UK, they have been coming down steadily in absolute terms. Higher expectations about living standards and changes to the structure of living costs has meant that many families on average incomes would now struggle to maintain their desired standard of living for larger household sizes, i.e. with more than 2 or 3 children. Economic forces therefore, combined with social and attitudinal change in relation to family planning have put downward pressure on family size. This trend has been apparent in both religious communities.

**Table 1.6 Number of Persons in Household 1983 to 2003-04**

| No of persons | Northern Ireland | | | | |
|---|---|---|---|---|---|
| | 1983 | 91-92 | 01-02 | 02-03 | 03-04 |
| 1 | 20 | 22 | 26 | 28 | 26 |
| 2 | 26 | 28 | 29 | 29 | 31 |
| 3 | 16 | 16 | 18 | 16 | 14 |
| 4 | 17 | 17 | 15 | 15 | 17 |
| 5 | 10 | 10 | 7 | 8 | 7 |
| >6 | 11 | 7 | 5 | 4 | 4 |
| Average Household size | 3.14 | 2.91 | 2.67 | 2.58 | 2.61 |

Source: NISRA

There is a predominant tendency for lone parents to be mothers rather than fathers. Of all families with dependent children, 25% are lone mothers and just 2% are lone fathers. Of the 25% who are lone mothers, 13% of these are single (as opposed to being widowed, divorced or separated), a figure which has risen significantly from the 8% recorded in 1996-97.

**Table 1.7 Type of Household 1983 to 2003-04**

| | 1983 | 91-92 | 01-02 | 02-03 | 03-04 |
|---|---|---|---|---|---|
| 1 person only | 20 | 22 | 26 | 28 | 26 |
| 2 or more adults | 4 | 3 | 3 | 3 | 3 |
| Married/Cohabiting couple: | | | | | |
| with dependent children | 38 | 34 | 27 | 27 | 27 |
| with non-dependent children only | 8 | 8 | 8 | 7 | 7 |
| no children | 19 | 21 | 22 | 23 | 23 |
| Lone parent: | | | | | |
| with dependent children | 4 | 7 | 10 | 8 | 9 |
| with non-dependent children only | 6 | 4 | 4 | 4 | 4 |
| Two or more families | 1 | 1 | 1 | 1 | 1 |

Source: NISRA; General Household Survey

The number of lone parent households with dependent children rose sharply from 4% of all households in 1983 to 10% in 2001-02 (see Table 1.7 above). This has eased back to 9% in 2003/04.

**Household Income**

From Table 1.8, it is apparent that gross household income in Northern Ireland is significantly below the UK average, although it is very close to the average income level in Wales. It is worth noting, however, that disposable income, as a percentage of total income in Northern Ireland is 84%, just slightly higher than the UK average of 82%. Traditionally, disposable income in Northern Ireland, as a percentage of total income has been higher than for the rest of the UK mainly because of lower housing costs. The fact that the figures have now converged can largely be attributed to the rising cost of housing in Northern Ireland, following six years of rapid house price inflation.

**Table 1.8 Weekly Household Income Across UK Countries (£) 2001/02 - 2002/03**

| | Gross | Disposable |
|---|---|---|
| Northern Ireland | 448 | 380 |
| United Kingdom | 546 | 448 |
| England | 561 | 459 |
| Wales | 451 | 381 |
| Scotland | 490 | 404 |

Source: Office for National Statistics

Table 1.9 shows the percentage of households with durable goods across the UK countries. Northern Ireland is below the UK average (but above Scotland) in terms of car ownership and above all the other UK countries in ownership of dishwashers! The figures show that in terms of information technology, Northern Ireland is below the UK average for both ownership of a home computer and internet connections.

**Table 1.9 % of Households with Durable Goods Across UK Countries 2001/02-2002/03**

| | Car/ Van | Dish-washer | Home PC | Internet Connection |
|---|---|---|---|---|
| Northern Ireland | 71 | 33 | 41 | 33 |
| England | 75 | 29 | 53 | 43 |
| Wales | 74 | 22 | 46 | 34 |
| Scotland | 66 | 24 | 47 | 39 |
| United Kingdom | 74 | 28 | 52 | 42 |

Source: Office for National Statistics

*(Further related socio-economic information is set out in Chapter 7 'The Northern Ireland Economy' with more about household tenure covered in Chapter 5 'Health and Housing in Northern Ireland').*

*Parliament Buildings, Stormont*

The Government and Politics of Northern Ireland

# Chapter 2

# The Governance of Northern Ireland

## The Role of Westminster

As part of the United Kingdom, Northern Ireland is subject to the authority of the Westminster Parliament. There has generally been a consensus both in London and Belfast however, that Northern Ireland should ideally govern itself according to local policy priorities. There is a general view that a devolved administration offers greater policy sensitivity for Northern Ireland as well as greater accessibility to government in terms of influencing the formulation and execution of policy and the final allocation of resources.

Despite the creation of the new state in 1920, and the devolution of powers to the first Northern Ireland administration, Westminster has always retained ultimate sovereignty over Northern Ireland. Northern Ireland has always continued to send its quota of MPs to the Westminster parliament. Exactly how Westminster has impacted upon Northern Ireland, and what powers it has had, has varied considerably, depending on whether or not Northern Ireland has had its own devolved government at any given time.

During the period 1921-1972, Northern Ireland had its own administration, based at Stormont (from 1932) and legislation for Northern Ireland was made in the form of Acts of Parliament debated and passed through the Northern Ireland parliament, which comprised a 52 member elected House of Commons and a 26 member nominated House of Lords.

From 1972, following the suspension of the Northern Ireland parliament, Northern Ireland was governed directly from Westminster. The government was represented in Northern Ireland by a Secretary of State and the vast bulk of Northern Ireland's primary legislation was carried into effect by means of Orders in Council. From the late seventies certain Acts relating to Great Britain contained clauses known as 'parity orders', enabling the same legislation to be issued for Northern Ireland.

*Palace of Westminster*

Since 1972 there have been three devolved assemblies, 1974, 1982-86 and the most recent assembly established under the terms of the Northern Ireland Act 1998. The Assembly of 1974 and the 1998 Assembly were given legislative powers, transferred from Westminster; the Assembly of 1982-86 had no legislative powers. (The current assembly elected in late 2003 has yet to convene).

## The Belfast Agreement 1998

The Belfast Agreement saw the reestablishment of a Northern Ireland Assembly implemented by the Northern Ireland Act 1998. In elections using proportional representation in the existing eighteen Westminster constituencies one hundred and eight members were elected to the new Assembly. When the Assembly first met on 1 July 1998 it held no legislative powers until devolution on 2 December 1999, when a range of legislative powers were transferred from Westminster to the Assembly and executive power to the power-sharing Executive.

The terms of the Northern Ireland Act 1998 provide for the establishment of a legislative assembly and the creation of an Executive with a First Minister, Deputy First Minister and ten ministers appointed under the d'Hondt voting procedure. The establishment of new institutions such as the North/South Ministerial Council were also provided for under the Act. Areas which were devolved to the Assembly and Executive include education, social services, the arts and agriculture, broadly corresponding with those areas devolved to the Welsh Assembly and Scottish Parliament. Full details of exactly which areas of responsibility were devolved and which remain under the control of Westminster are set out below.

## Excepted and Reserved Matters

Even under devolution the Secretary of State retains certain clearly defined powers. These include constitutional and security matters relating to Northern Ireland and policing and relationships with the European Union which are not devolved matters under the terms of the Northern Ireland Act 1998. Under the terms of the Northern Ireland Act 1998 Westminster continues to legislate in non-devolved or excepted matters in the form of Orders in Council, Acts and Statutory Instruments. Some reserved matters including criminal law and civil defence may eventually be transferred to the Northern Ireland legislature. However, excepted matters will remain permanently under the control of Westminster.

The main areas of government which remain 'reserved' or 'excepted' are set out below.

| Reserved | Excepted | Transferred |
|---|---|---|
| • Policing<br>• Security<br>• Prisons<br>• Criminal Justice<br>• Income Tax<br>• National Insurance<br>• Regulation of Telecommunications and Broadcasting | • Elections<br>• Europe<br>• Peace and Reconciliation<br>• Foreign Policy | • All matters not excepted or reserved |

## The United Kingdom Government

### Parliament

Parliament is the institution responsible for making and repealing UK law and is the highest legislative authority in the United Kingdom. It consists of three constituent parts:

- House of Commons
- House of Lords
- Crown.

The principal functions of parliament are to:

- make laws
- examine the work of government
- control finance
- protect the individual
- examine European proposals
- debate current affairs.

### House of Lords

The unelected House of Lords is the second chamber of the UK Houses of Parliament. Members of the House of Lords (peers) consist of Lords Spiritual (senior bishops) and Lords Temporal (lay peers). Law Lords (senior judges) also sit as Lords Temporal. Originally, they were drawn from the nobility, but now only 92 peers sit by virtue of hereditary peerage, with the majority of members now being life peers. There were 666 peers in total on 1st March 2004.

Around two thirds of Lords align themselves with a political party, with one third of cross bench peers not affiliated to any party group. Some members of the Lords are former MPs, who have been elevated to the Lords in recognition of their contribution to politics or other aspects of public life.

### Role of the House of Lords

In general, the functions of the House of Lords are similar to those of the House of Commons in legislating, debating and questioning the executive. However, members of the Lords are not involved in matters of taxation and finance. All bills go through both Houses before becoming Acts, and may start in either House. Normally, the consent of the Lords is required before Acts of Parliament can be passed, and the Lords can amend all legislation, with the exception of bills to raise taxation.

The House of Lords is also the final court of appeal for civil cases in the United Kingdom and for criminal cases in England, Wales and Northern Ireland. Only the Lords of Appeal (Law Lords) - of whom there are 12 employed full-time - take part in judicial proceedings.

### House of Commons

The House of Commons is currently made up of 659 Members of Parliament (MPs), each elected to represent an individual constituency. Of the 659 seats, 529 are for England, 40 for Wales, 72 for Scotland and 18 for Northern Ireland.

A government can only remain in office for as long as it has the support of a majority in the House of Commons. As with the House of Lords, the House of Commons debates new primary legislation as part of the process of making an Act of Parliament, but the Commons has primacy over the non-elected House of Lords. 'Money bills', concerned solely with taxation and public expenditure, are always introduced in the Commons and must be passed by the Lords promptly and without amendment. The House of Commons also scrutinises the work of the government - it does that by various means, including questioning ministers in the Chamber and through the Select Committee system.

### Parliamentary Legislative Process at Westminster

At the beginning of each Session of Parliament, the government announces its legislative plan for the coming session in the Queen's speech. The following is the process followed when enacting legislation in the Westminster parliament.

#### Preparatory Stages

The bill is drafted by lawyers in the Parliamentary Counsel Office, part of the Cabinet Office, on instruction of the relevant government department. Before introduction of the bill a Green (ie consultative) or White (ie statement of policy) Paper may have been issued or the bill may simply be presented without any prior announcement. Bills consist of clauses, becoming sections and schedules in the resulting act. Draft bills provide the opportunity for pre-legislative scrutiny.

#### First Reading

The Order Paper contains a Notice of Presentation of the bill. The title of the bill is read to the House by a Clerk, the Minister concerned or government Whip names the date for the Second Reading. The First Reading stage forms the House's order to print the bill. The Public Bill Office of the House of Commons exercises a supervisory role during the passage of the bill through the House. There is no debate at first reading.

#### Second Reading

The first substantive stage of a bill is at second reading. The date of the debate on the bill is announced by the Leader of the House in a Business Statement. The Opposition may table a 'reasoned amendment', technically an amendment to the question before the House at Second Reading, giving the reasons for objecting to the bill. The Second Reading is a debate on the principles behind the bill.

#### Second Reading Committee

Some non-controversial bills are dealt with in a Second Reading Committee. A Second Reading Committee does not have the power to give a bill a Second Reading, it may only recommend that the bill be read a second time. Such bills are given a second reading in the House soon afterwards, without debate. Following a second reading and before consideration by Committee, provisions requiring Money or Ways and Means Resolutions must be dealt with.

#### Committee Stage

In the Committee Stage, usually by Standing Committee, the contents of a bill, its clauses and schedules are examined in detail and amendments can be made by agreement or by a majority vote. It is usually an opportunity for a small number of

MPs in the House of Commons to look in depth at a bill to make sure that every part of the proposed law has been considered. Committee stage allows interested parties to press parliamentarians to make amendments.

**Standing Committee Stage**
A Standing Committee generally has about 18 members and its membership reflects the composition of the House. At least one Minister from the government department in charge of the bill will be on the committee, as well as a front-bench spokesman from each of the opposition parties represented. A Standing Committee may dispose of a short bill in a single sitting, but a long or controversial bill might take many weeks. A new Standing Committee is appointed for each bill.

**Special Standing Committees**
Very occasionally, a bill may be committed to a Special Standing Committee, which spends a limited time investigating the issues involved before going through the bill in the usual way as a normal Standing Committee.

**Committee of the whole House**
The whole House may consider certain bills at committee stage, generally bills of constitutional importance, such as the House of Lords Bill 1998/99, those requiring a very rapid passage, and certain financial measures, including at least part of each year's Finance Bill. If a Committee amends a bill it is reprinted and given a new bill number. This version of the bill carries a rubric on the front page, 'As Amended in Standing Committee A' or 'As Amended in Committee', if it is considered in Committee of the Whole House.

**Report Stage (or Consideration Stage)**
The House may make further amendments to the bill but does not consider those clauses and schedules to which no amendments have been tabled. The Consideration Stage provides an opportunity for MPs not on the Standing Committee to move amendments to the bill. The House may reverse or amend changes made by Standing Committee. If a bill has been dealt with by a Committee of the whole House, and not amended, it progresses to Third Reading without Consideration Stage.

**Third Reading**
The final Commons stage of the bill is the Third Reading. This enables the House to take an overview of the bill, as amended in Committee or on Consideration. No amendments may be made at this stage. Debates on Third Reading are usually very short. After Third Reading in the Chamber in which the bill was introduced the bill moves to first reading in the Second chamber, the House of Lords.

**Lords Stages and Amendments**
Having passed Third Reading in the Commons, the bill is sent to the Lords, usually but not necessarily on the next sitting day. The legislative process in the House of Lords is broadly similar to that in the House of Commons. The Lords and Commons must finally agree a text of each bill. A bill may travel backwards and forwards between the two chambers several times before agreement on all amendments is reached. The House of Lords may delay a piece of legislation which emanates from the Commons, but under the Parliament Act 1911, may not block it indefinitely or insist on amendments.

**Royal Assent**
When a text has been agreed between the Houses, the bill is submitted for Royal Assent. The Royal Assent is the Monarch's agreement to make a bill into an act of parliament. The Monarch, as the third element in parliament's composition, actually has the right to refuse Royal Assent, something which has not happened since 1707. After signification of Royal Assent, the bill becomes an act, and is printed both individually and in the annual series of Public and General Acts.

**The current state of the parties in the House of Commons is as follows:**

| | |
|---|---|
| Labour | 407 |
| Conservative | 163 |
| Liberal Democrat | 55 |
| Scottish National Party | 5 |
| Plaid Cymru | 4 |
| Democratic Unionist Party | 6 |
| Ulster Unionist Party | 5 |
| *Sinn Féin | 4 |
| SDLP | 3 |
| Independent | 1 |
| Independent Conservative | 1 |
| Independent Labour | 1 |
| **Speaker & 3 Deputies | 4 |
| Total | 659 |
| Government Majority | 159 |

*(Sinn Féin members do not take their seats)
**(do not normally vote)

*Details of Northern Ireland MPs elected to Westminster are set out in Chapter 2 on page 40.*

## The Government
According to the constitution, following a general election, the monarch invites the leader of the party which has won the most seats to form the government. The party leader then becomes Prime Minister and appoints a Cabinet of around 20 senior ministers, who take responsibility for a major department of state. Cabinet ministers are supported by a number of junior (non-cabinet) ministers who work within their departments.

The government is made up from the party which wins the most seats in the House of Commons in a general election. The last general election took place on 7 June 2001, and returned a Labour government to office, with Tony Blair continuing as Prime Minister. Full details of the UK government are set out below.

## The Cabinet

**Prime Minister, First Lord of the Treasury and Minister for the Civil Service**
The Rt Hon Tony Blair MP

**Deputy Prime Minister**
The Rt Hon John Prescott MP

**Chancellor of the Exchequer**
The Rt Hon Gordon Brown MP

**Secretary of State for Foreign and Commonwealth Affairs**
The Rt Hon Jack Straw MP

**Secretary of State for the Home Department**
The Rt Hon David Blunkett MP

**Secretary of State for Environment, Food and Rural Affairs**
The Rt Hon Margaret Beckett MP

**Secretary of State for Transport and Secretary of State for Scotland**
The Rt Hon Alistair Darling MP

**Secretary of State for Health**
The Rt Hon Dr John Reid MP

**Chancellor of the Duchy of Lancaster**
The RT Hon Alan Milburn MP

**Secretary of State for Northern Ireland**
The Rt Hon Paul Murphy MP

**Secretary of State for Defence:**
The Rt Hon Geoff Hoon MP

**Secretary of State for Trade and Industry and Minister for Women**
The Rt Hon Patricia Hewitt MP

**Secretary of State for Culture, Media and Sport**
The Rt Hon Tessa Jowell MP

**Parliamentary Secretary to the Treasury and Chief Whip**
The Rt Hon Hilary Armstrong MP

**Secretary of State for Education and Skills**
The Rt Hon Charles Clarke MP

**Chief Secretary to the Treasury**
The Rt Hon Paul Boateng MP

**Leader of the House of Commons, Lord Privy Seal and Secretary of State for Wales**
The Rt Hon Peter Hain MP

**Minister without Portfolio**
The Rt Hon Ian McCartney MP

**Leader of the House of Lords & Lord President of the Council**
The Rt Hon Baroness Amos

**Secretary of State for Constitutional Affairs and Lord Chancellor for the transitional period**
The Rt Hon Lord Falconer of Thoroton QC

**Secretary of State for International Development**
The Rt Hon Hilary Benn MP

**Secretary of State for Work and Pensions**
The Rt Hon Alan Johnson MP

*House of Commons*

### Also attending cabinet:

**Lords Chief Whip and Captain of the Gentlemen at Arms**
The Rt Hon The Lord Grocott

### Law Officers

**Attorney General**
The Rt Hon Lord Goldsmith QC

**Solicitor General**
The Rt Hon Harriet Harman QC MP

**Advocate General for Scotland**
Dr Lynda Clark QC MP

### Office of the Deputy Prime Minister

**Ministers of State**
The Rt Hon Nick Raynsford MP
The Rt Hon Lord Rooker
The Rt Hon Keith Hill MP

**Parliamentary Under-Secretaries**
Yvette Cooper MP
Phil Hope MP (unpaid)

### Cabinet Office

**Minister for the Cabinet Office**
Ruth Kelly MP

### HM Treasury

**Paymaster General**
The RT Hon Dawn Primarolo MP

**Financial Secretary**
Stephen Timms MP

**Economic Secretary**
John Healey MP

### Leader of the House of Commons
**Parliamentary Under-Secretary**
Philip Woolas MP

### Department for Constitutional Affairs
**Parliamentary Under-Secretaries**
Christopher Leslie MP
David Lammy MP
Baroness Ashton of Upholland

**Parliamentary Under-Secretary for Scotland Office (reporting to the Secretary of State for Scotland)**
Anne McGuire MP

**Parliamentary Under-Secretary for Wales Office (reporting to the Secretary of State for Wales)**
Don Touhig MP

### Foreign and Commonwealth Office
**Minister of State (Trade)**
Douglas Alexander (also Minister of State in the Department of Trade and Industry)

**Minister of State (Europe)**
Dr Denis MacShane MP

**Minister of State (Middle East)**
The Rt Hon Baroness Symons of Vernham Dean

**Parliamentary Under-Secretaries**
Bill Rammell MP
Chris Mullin MP

### Home Office
**Ministers of State**
Hazel Blears MP
The Rt Hon Baroness Scotland of Asthal QC
Desmond Browne MP

**Parliamentary Under-Secretaries**
Caroline Flint MP
Fiona Mactaggart MP
Paul Goggins MP

### Department for Environment, Food and Rural Affairs
**Minister of State (Environment)**
Elliot Morley MP

**Minister of State (Rural Affairs)**
The Rt Hon Alun Michael MP

**Parliamentary Under-Secretaries**
The Lord Whitty
Ben Bradshaw MP

### Department for International Delevopment
**Parliamentary Under-Secretary**
Gareth Thomas MP (Harrow West)

### Department for Work and Penisons
**Minister for Pensions**
Malcolm Wicks MP

**Minister for Work**
Jane Kennedy MP

**Parliamentary Under-Secretaries**
The Rt Hon Baroness Hollis of Heigham DL
Maria Eagle MP
Chris Pond MP

### Department for Transport
**Minister of State**
Tony McNulty MP

**Parliamentary Under-Secretaries**
David Jamieson MP
Charlotte Atkins MP *

### Department for Health
**Ministers of State**
The Rt Hon John Hutton MP
Rosie Winterton MP

**Parliamentary Under-Secretaries**
Melanie Johnson MP (Minister for Public Health)
The Lord Warner
Dr Stephen Ladyman MP

* Charlotte Atkins MP will be taking on this role on a temporary basis in addition to her position as a Government Whip.

### Northern Ireland Office
**Ministers of State**
The Rt Hon John Spellar MP

**Parliamentary Under-Secretaries**
Ian Pearson MP
Angela Smith MP
Barry Gardiner MP

### Ministry of Defence
**Minister of State**
The Rt Hon Adam Ingram MP

**Parliamentary Under-Secretaries**
The Lord Bach
Ivor Caplin MP

### Department of Trade and Industry
**Minister of State**
Mike O'Brien MP

**Minister of State (Trade)**
Douglas Alexander MP

**Minister of State and Deputy Minister for Women**
Jacqui Smith MP

**Parliamentary Under-Secretaries**
Nigel Griffiths MP
Gerry Sutcliffe MP
Lord Sainsbury of Turville (unpaid)

### Department for Education and Skills
**Minister of State (Children)**
The Rt Hon Margaret Hodge MBE MP

**Minister of State (Schools)**
David Miliband MP

**Minister of State (Universities)**
Dr Kim Howells MP

**Parliamentary Under-Secretaries**
The Lord Filkin CBE
Ivan Lewis MP
Stephen Twigg MP

### Department for Culture, Media and Sport
**Minister of State (Sport)**
The Rt Hon Richard Caborn MP

**Minister of State (Arts)**
The Rt Hon Estelle Morris MP

**Parliamentary Under-Secretary**
The Rt Hon Lord McIntosh of Haringey

## House of Lords

**Captain of the Yeoman (Deputy Chief Whip)**
The Lord Davies of Oldham

**Lords in Waiting**
The Lord Bassam of Brighton
The Lord Evans of Temple Guiting CBE
The Lord Triesman

**Baronesses in Waiting**
Baroness Farrington of Ribbleton
Baroness Andrews OBE
Baroness Crawley

## House of Commons

**Deputy Chief Whip and Treasurer of HM Household**
Bob Ainsworth MP

**Comptroller of HM Household**
The Rt Hon Thomas McAvoy MP

**Vice Chamberlain of HM Household**
Jim Fitzpatrick MP

**Lord Commissioners**
Jim Murphy MP
John Heppell MP
Joan Ryan MP
Nick Ainger MP
Derek Twigg MP

**Assistant Government Whips**
Fraser Kemp MO
Gillian Merron MP
Paul Clark MP
Vernon Coaker MP
Margaret Moran MP
Bridget Prentice MP
Tom Watson MP (unpaid)

**Parliamentary Private Secretary to the Prime Minister**
David Hanson MP

## Members of the Shadow Cabinet

**Leader of Her Majesty's Official Opposition & Leader of the Conservative Party**
Rt Hon Michael Howard QC MP

**Shadow Secretary of State for International Development, Shadow Foreign Secretary & Deputy Leader of Her Majesty's Official Opposition**
Rt Hon Michael Ancram QC MP

**Leader of Her Majesty's Official Opposition in the House of Lords**
Rt Hon Lord Strathclyde

**Shadow Secretary of State for Economic Affairs & Shadow Chancellor of the Exchequer**
Rt Hon Oliver Letwin MP

**Shadow Secretary of State for Defence**
Hon Nicholas Soames MP

**Shadow Secretary of State for Deregulation**
Rt Hon John Redwood MP

**Shadow Secretary of State for Education**
Tim Collins MP

**Shadow Secretary of State for Health**
Andrew Lansley CBE MP

**Shadow Secretary of State for Home Affairs & Shadow Home Secretary**
Rt Hon David Davis MP

**Shadow Secretary of State for Environment & Transport**
Tim Yeo MP

**Shadow Secretary of State for the Family**
Rt Hon Theresa May MP

**Shadow Secretary of State for Local and Devolved Government Affairs**
Mrs Caroline Spelman MP

**Shadow Secretary of State for Work and Pensions & Welfare Reform**
David Willetts MP

**Co-Chairman of the Conservative Party**
Dr Liam Fox MP, Lord Saatchi

**Opposition Chief Whip (Commons)**
Rt Hon David Maclean MP

**Head of Policy Co-ordination**
David Cameron MP

**Shadow Secretary of State for Northern Ireland**
David Lidington MP (not a member of the Shadow Cabinet)

## Northern Ireland Elected Representation at Westminster

Northern Ireland currently returns 18 MPs to Westminster, but in the past it had a disproportionately lower representation. From the enactment of the Government of Ireland Act 1920 until 1983 it had a representation of 12 MPs. However, the Boundary Commission in 1983 revised the level of representation and five extra seats were created. These were contested for the first time in the June 1983 general election. In 1995, the Boundary Commission examined the situation again and created a further seat bringing the total to eighteen for the May 1997 election.

Provisional Recommendations from the present review of Northern Ireland's parliamentary constituencies, published in May 2004, suggest retaining 18 constituencies, but propose changes to some of the constituency boundaries, particularly for the Belfast and surrounding constituencies. The recommendations suggest extending the four Belfast constituencies 'outwards', and that the constituency of East Antrim should be redrawn to take in the Glens of Antrim and Ballycastle. This constituency would then be renamed as Antrim Coast and Glens. Minor changes are suggested to some of the other constituencies, with Fermanagh and South Tyrone, Mid Ulster, North Down and West Tyrone preserved in tact. The Commission will make Final Recommendations in 2005.

In addition to its MPs, Northern Ireland also has significant representation in the House of Lords. Details of Ulster Unionist Party members of the House of Lords are set out on page 66.

**Current Westminster MPs (elected in 2001)**

| Constituency | Name | Party |
|---|---|---|
| Belfast East | Peter Robinson | DUP |
| Belfast North | Nigel Dodds | DUP |
| Belfast South | Rev Martin Smyth | UUP |
| Belfast West | Gerry Adams | SF |
| East Antrim | Roy Beggs | UUP |
| East Londonderry | Gregory Campbell | DUP |
| Fermanagh & South Tyrone | Michelle Gildernew | SF |
| Foyle | John Hume | SDLP |
| Lagan Valley | Jeffrey Donaldson | DUP* |
| Mid Ulster | Martin McGuinness | SF |
| Newry and Armagh | Séamus Mallon | SDLP |
| North Antrim | Rev Ian Paisley | DUP |
| North Down | Sylvia Hermon | UUP |
| South Antrim | David Burnside | UUP |
| South Down | Eddie McGrady | SDLP |
| Strangford | Iris Robinson | DUP |
| West Tyrone | Pat Doherty | SF |
| Upper Bann | David Trimble | UUP |

**Seats By Party**

| | | | |
|---|---|---|---|
| DUP | 6 | SF | 4 |
| UUP | 5 | SDLP | 3 |
| Total | 18 | | |

## Contact Details for Northern Ireland Westminster MPs

**Gerry Adams**
Constituency: Belfast West
Party: **Sinn Féin**
51-55 Falls Road
Belfast, BT12 4PD
Tel: 028 9022 3000 / Fax: 028 9022 5553

**Roy Beggs**
Constituency: East Antrim
Party: **Ulster Unionist Party**
41 Station Road, Larne, BT40 3AA
Tel: 028 2827 3258 / Fax: 028 2828 3007
Westminster: Tel: 020 7219 6305 / Fax: 020 7219 3889

**David Burnside**
Constituency: South Antrim
Party: **Ulster Unionist Party**
24 Fountain Street, Antrim, BT41 4BB
Tel: 028 9446 1211
Westminster: Tel: 020 7219 8493

**Gregory Campbell**
Constituency: East Londonderry
Party: **DUP**
25 Bushmills Road, Coleraine, BT52 2BP
Tel: 028 7032 7327
Fax: 028 7032 7328

**Nigel Dodds**
Constituency: Belfast North
Party: **DUP**
210 Shore Road, Belfast, BT15 3QB
Tel: 028 9077 4774
Fax: 028 9077 7685

**Jeffrey Donaldson***
Constituency: Lagan Valley
Party: **DUP**
The Old Town Hall
Castle Street, Lisburn, BT27 4XD
Tel: 028 9266 8001
Fax: 028 9267 1845
Westminster:Tel: 020 7219 3407 / Fax: 020 7219 0696

* Jeffrey Donaldson was elected for the UUP but has subsequently joined the DUP

**Pat Doherty**
Constituency: West Tyrone
Party: **Sinn Féin**
1 Melvin Road, Strabane, BT82 9AE
Tel: 028 7188 6464
Fax: 028 7188 6466

**Michelle Gildernew**
Constituency: Fermanagh/South Tyrone
Party: **Sinn Féin**
60 Irish Street, Dungannon, BT70 1DQ
Tel: 028 8772 2776
Fax: 028 8772 2776

**Sylvia Hermon**
Constituency: North Down
Party: **Ulster Unionist Party**
77a High Street, Bangor, BT20 5BD
Tel: 028 9147 0300 / Fax: 028 9147 0301
Westminster: Tel: 020 7219 8491

**John Hume**
Constituency: Foyle
Party: **SDLP**
5 Bayview Terrace, Derry, BT48 7EE
Tel: 028 7126 5340 / Fax: 028 7136 3423

**Seamus Mallon**
Constituency: Newry and Armagh
Party: **SDLP**
2 Bridge Street, Newry, BT35 8AE
Tel: 028 3026 7933 / Fax: 028 3026 7828

**Eddie McGrady**
Constituency: South Down
Party: **SDLP**
32 Saul Street, Downpatrick, BT30 6NQ
Tel: 028 4461 2882 / Fax: 028 4461 9574

**Martin McGuinness**
Constituency: Mid Ulster
Party: **Sinn Féin**
32 Burn Road, Cookstown, BT80 8DN
Tel: 028 8676 5850 / Fax: 028 8676 6734

**Ian Paisley**
Constituency: North Antrim
Party: **DUP**
256 Ravenhill Road, Belfast, BT6 8GJ
Tel: 028 9045 8900 / Fax: 028 9045 7783

**Iris Robinson**
Constituency: Strangford
Party: **DUP**
2b James Street, Newtownards, BT23 4DY
Tel: 028 9182 7701 / Fax: 028 9182 7703

**Peter Robinson**
Constituency: Belfast East
Party: **DUP**
Strandtown Hall
96 Belmont Avenue, Belfast, BT4 3DE
Tel: 028 9047 3111 / Fax: 028 9047 1797

**Martin Smyth**
Constituency: South Belfast
Party: **Ulster Unionist Party**
117 Cregagh Road, Belfast, BT6 0LA
Tel: 028 9045 7009 / Fax: 028 9045 0837
Westminster: Tel: 020 7219 4098 / Fax: 020 7219 2347

**David Trimble**
Constituency: Upper Bann
Party: **Ulster Unionist Party**
2 Queen Street, Lurgan, BT66 8BQ
Tel: 028 3832 8088 / Fax: 028 3832 2343
Westminster: Tel: 020 7219 6987 / Fax: 020 7219 2489

## Northern Ireland Business at Westminster

The right to debate matters pertaining to Northern Ireland and legislate in those areas not devolved to the Northern Ireland Assembly is retained by Westminster.

Northern Ireland business in the Commons is conducted in a number of ways:

- For Primary legislation, through the full Westminster legislative process;
- Through the Northern Ireland Grand Committee;
- Through the Northern Ireland Affairs Select Committee;
- Through questions addressed to the Secretary of State for Northern Ireland.

### The Committee's Remit

The Northern Ireland Affairs Committee is appointed by the House of Commons to examine the expenditure, administration and policy of the Northern Ireland Office; administration and expenditure of the Crown Solicitor's Office (but excluding individual cases and advice given by the Crown Solicitor); and other matters within the responsibilities of the Secretary of State for Northern Ireland (but excluding the expenditure, administration and policy of the Office of the Director of Public Prosecutions, Northern Ireland and the drafting of legislation by the Office of the Legislative Counsel).

### Membership of the Committee

The Committee consists of 13 Members of Parliament, of whom a quorum of 4 is required for the Committee to conduct formal business. The Committee is nominated by the House at the beginning of each Parliament for the duration of the Parliament, although individual Members may be discharged or added during the course of the Parliament. The membership reflects the party strengths in the House as a whole. Thus, in the present Parliament, there are 7 Labour Members, 2 Conservative Members, 2 Ulster Unionist Members, 1 Democratic Unionist Member and 1 Social Democratic and Labour Member. The Committee appoints one of its number as Chairman.

### The Committee's Work

Select Committees operate normally by conducting inquiries into subjects within its area of responsibility. Once a subject has been chosen, and the terms of reference of the inquiry have been agreed, the Committee requests written memoranda from interested organisations. Formal evidence sessions are then arranged with the individuals and bodies principally concerned. Informal briefing sessions may be held and/or visits conducted. On the basis of the evidence, a report is drafted under the direction of the Chairman, which the Committee considers, may amend, and finally agree to. A report is then published. The Government is obliged to respond to the Committee's recommendations within 2 months.

Issues which have recently been under inquiry by the Northern Ireland Affairs Committee have included:

- Electoral registration;
- The Parades Commission and Public Processions (Northern Ireland) Act 1998;
- The functions of the Office of the Police Ombudsman
- Hate crime in Northern Ireland;
- The functions of the Northern Ireland Policing Board.

The Northern Ireland Affairs Committee also has a sub-committee which was set up to undertake more scrutiny of previously devolved issues. This sub-committee undertakes inquiries into matters that previously fell within the remit of the Northern Ireland Assembly. The sub-committee will be chaired by Tony Clarke, MP with all members of the existing Northern Ireland Affairs Committee eligible to participate in inquiries. Issues recently under inquiry include:

- Social housing provision in Northern Ireland;
- Waste management in Northern Ireland;
- Air transport services in Northern Ireland.

**Contact Details:**
Northern Ireland Affairs Committee
House of Commons, 7 Millbank
Westminster, London, SW1P 3JA
Tel: 020 7219 2172 / Fax: 020 7219 0300
Web: www.parliament.uk
Email: northircom@parliament.uk
Committee Clerk: Dr John Patterson Tel: 020 7219 2171
Sub-committee Clerk: Hugh Farren Tel: 028 9052 1360
Committee Specialist: Dr Aileen O'Neill Tel: 020 7219 8899
Committee Assistant: Tony Catinella Tel: 020 7219 2173

**Membership of the Northern Ireland Affairs Select Committee**

| Member | Party | Constituency |
|---|---|---|
| Adrian Bailey | Lab | West Bromwich West |
| Harry Barnes | Lab | North East Derbyshire |
| Roy Beggs | UUP | East Antrim |
| Gregory Campbell | DUP | East Londonderry |
| Tony Clarke | Lab | Northampton South |
| Stephen Hepburn | Lab | Jarrow |
| Iain Luke | Lab | Dundee East |
| Eddie McGrady | SDLP | South Down |
| Stephen Pound | Lab | Ealing North |
| Martin Smyth | UUP | Belfast South |
| Hugo Swire | Cons | East Devon |
| Mark Tami | Lab | Alyn & Deeside |
| Bill Tynan | Lab | Hamilton South |
| Michael Mates(Chair) | Cons | East Hampshire |

## Secretary of State for Northern Ireland: Questions

The Secretary of State and the Northern Ireland Ministers take questions approximately every Fourth Wednesday. MPs from any part of the UK may raise questions relating to Northern Ireland affairs. However, during the existence of the Assembly in Northern Ireland, MPs were not allowed to raise matters falling under the remit of the Stormont government in Westminster, a convention strongly criticised by many.

## The Northern Ireland Grand Committee

The Northern Ireland Grand Committee provides a further vehicle for the discussion of Northern Ireland affairs. The Committee consists of all 18 members representing constituencies in Northern Ireland and not more than 25 other members nominated by the Committee of Selection. The quorum is 10.

The Committee may take oral questions for answer by the Secretary of State or other government minister in addition to those taken in the House. All questions tabled must specify that they are for answer in Grand Committee.

The Northern Ireland Committee Order book in the Vote Office contains details of the times, locations, dates of sittings and the agenda of the Grand Committee.

**Membership of the Northern Ireland Grand Committee**

Chair: Roger Gal
Members:

| | | | |
|---|---|---|---|
| Harry Barnes | Lab | David Lidington | Cons |
| Roy Beggs | UUP | Iain Luke | Lab |
| Kevin Brennan | Lab | Stephen McCabe | Lab |
| David Burnside | UUP | Eddie McGrady | SDLP |
| Gregory Campbell | DUP | Andrew Mackay | Cons |
| Alistair Carmichael | Lib Dem | Kevin McNamara | Lab |
| Geoffrey Clifton-Brown | Cons | Tony McWalter | Lab |
| Vernon Coaker | Lab | Seamus Mallon | SDLP |
| Nigel Dodds | DUP | Michael Mates | Cons |
| Jeffrey Donaldson | DUP | Bill O'Brien | Lab |
| Louise Ellman | Lab | Lembit Opik | Lib Dem |
| Mark Field | Cons | Ian Paisley | DUP |
| Tom Harris | Lab | Stephen Pound | Lab |
| Sylvia Hermon | UUP | Iris Robinson | DUP |
| John Hume | SDLP | Peter Robinson | DUP |
| Andrew Hunter | Ind Cons | Martin Smyth | UUP |
| Huw Irranca-Davies | Lab | Gareth Thomas | Lab |
| Helen Jackson | Lab | David Trimble | UUP |
| Eric Joyce | Lab | | |

# The Northern Ireland Assembly

The Northern Ireland Assembly
Parliament Buildings, Belfast, BT4 3XX
Tel: 028 9052 1862 / Fax: 028 9052 1959
Web: www.ni-assembly.gov.uk

## Northern Ireland Assembly 1998-2003

The Northern Ireland Assembly was established as a result of the Belfast Agreement of 10 April 1998. The Agreement was endorsed by referenda north and south (results of referenda set out in Chapter 1 on page 19) held on 22 May 1998. The Assembly was established as one of a series of inter-related bodies with full legislative and executive authority for all matters which are the responsibility of the Northern Ireland government department, known as transferred matters. (A full list of all transferred, reserved and excepted matters is set out earlier in this chapter, on page 34). Other institutions of the Belfast Agreement include a North/South Ministerial Council, a British-Irish Intergovernmental Conference and a Civic Forum – see diagram below.

The members of the first Northern Ireland Assembly were elected on 25 June 1998, using proportional representation within the existing 18 Westminster constituencies with 6 members elected for each constituency. The Assembly met for the first time on 1 July 1998 when Lord Alderdice was appointed as Presiding Officer (Speaker). David Trimble and Seamus Mallon were also elected as First Minister (Designate) and Deputy First Minister (Designate) respectively.

In early 1999 agreement was reached on the structure and titles of the new government departments, which remain in place although devolution has been suspended. Nominations to ministerial positions were made by the parties (three each from the UUP and SDLP and two each from the DUP and Sinn Fein) at the end of November 1999 and power was devolved to the new Assembly on 2 December 1999, with Lord Alderdice confirmed as Speaker. Chairpersons and Deputy Chairpersons for the ten standing committees were also nominated, with Committee membership subsequently allocated according to the d'Hondt system with individual nominees agreed among the Party Whips. Two Junior Ministers were later appointed, one each from the UUP and SDLP.

Throughout its life the 1998 Assembly was dogged by instability. Due to unresolved difficulties surrounding the issue of decommissioning the Assembly was in suspension during the period of February to May 2000. Further 24 hour suspensions took place in August and September 2001 during the time when David Trimble had resigned as First Minister. November 2001 saw David Trimble's re-election to the position of First Minister, along with Mark Durkan, who had replaced Seamus Mallon in the position of Deputy First Minister.

During the period November 2001 – October 2002 the Executive, Assembly and its Committees met regularly and transacted a significant amount of business including the publication of many reports; the passage of 31 Acts; and the debating of issues such as the future of education, public accounts and telecommunications.

Following further political difficulties between the parties, the Assembly was finally suspended by the Secretary of State at midnight on 14 October 2002. Following suspension, legislation being considered by the Assembly was processed instead through Westminster in the form of Orders in Council. The Assembly was formally dissolved on 28 April 2003 in anticipation of an election in May 2003. The election was postponed and took place on 26 November 2003. Since January 2004, political parties have been engaged in a review of the Belfast Agreement, aimed at restoring the devolved institutions.

**Assembly Staff**

During the current state of suspension, some Assembly secretariat staff have been retained to carry out essential duties.

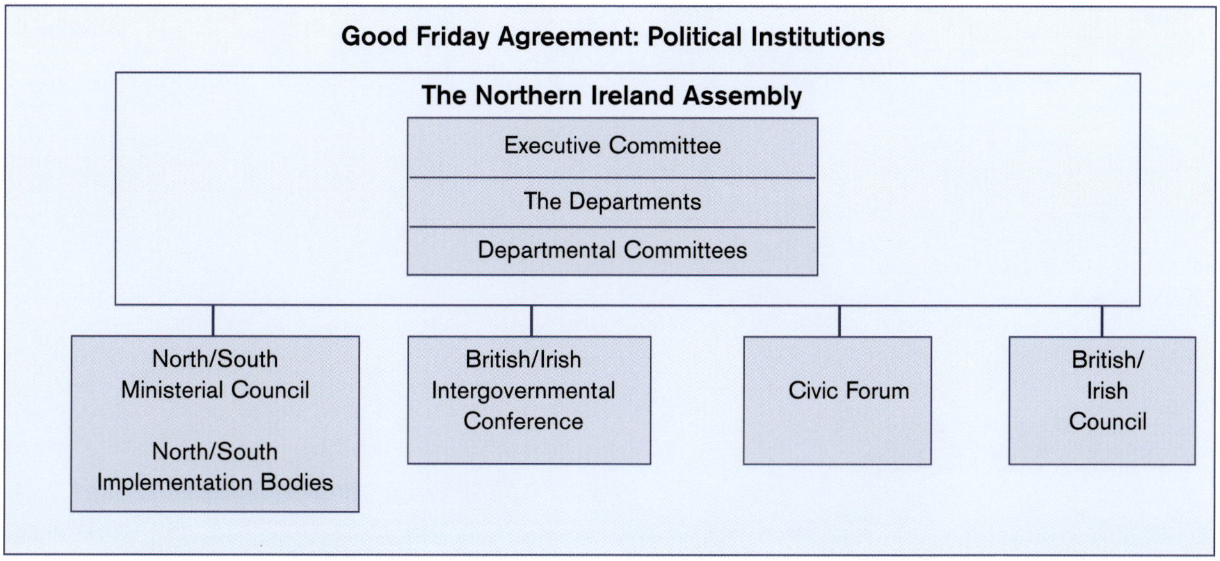

### The Speaker
The Office of the Presiding Officer of the Assembly, known as the Speaker, was held by Lord Alderdice until his retirement on 29 February 2004. The role of the Speaker is to preside over the proceedings of the Assembly, selecting amendments to Bills and Motions for debate and selecting questions for oral answer. The ruling of the Speaker is final on all questions of matter and procedure in the Assembly. The Speaker also chairs the Business Committee and the Assembly Commission.

### Office of the Clerk and Records of the Assembly
The Clerk notes all proceedings of the Assembly and the minutes of proceedings, having been perused and signed by the Speaker, are printed and constitute the Journal of the Proceedings of the Assembly. The Clerk is the custodian of all Journals of Proceedings, records and other documents belonging to the Assembly.

### The Assembly Commission
The Assembly Commission is the corporate body of the Assembly and is responsible for providing the Assembly with the property, staff and services it requires to function. Its task is to represent the interests of the Assembly and its 108 elected Members. The Assembly Commission has five members and is chaired by the Speaker.

### The Office of the Clerk to the Northern Ireland Assembly
The function of the Office of the Clerk to the Northern Ireland Assembly is to provide a central policy and management function and to offer a range of corporate services to the Assembly.

### Clerk Assistant's Directorate
The function of the Clerk Assistant's Directorate is to meet the needs of Members and Committees when carrying out Assembly business, to establish a team of trained staff and maintain a programme of continuous staff training and development and to maximise resources within its budget.

### Office of the Official Report (Hansard)
The Function of the Office of the Official Report is to produce the Official Report of all sittings of the Assembly including details of debates, resolutions, questions, votes and appropriate Committee sessions. The Hansard report, which is available to the public, lists the names of all the Members, reports what they say and records all the Assembly's decisions.

### Keeper of the House Directorate
The function of the Keeper of the House Directorate is to deliver the best possible service to Members, the public and all those who work in or visit Parliament Buildings. Key areas of work include events, support services, works, health and safety and security.

### Research and Information Directorate
The function of the Research and Information Directorate is to source, process, transform and communicate information for and within the Assembly and to ensure that its business is open to public interest and scrutiny.

### Finance and Personnel Directorate
The function of the Finance and Personnel Directorate is to provide support for Members and the Secretariat ranging from recruitment to pensions.

## Elected Members of the Assembly (2003)

The table below summarises the outcome of the 2003 Northern Ireland Assembly elections in terms of party strength.

**Overall Assembly Election Results by Party November 2003**

| Party | % 1st pref Votes | Seats |
|---|---|---|
| DUP | 25.7 | 30 |
| UUP | 22.7 | 27 |
| Sinn Féin | 23.5 | 24 |
| SDLP | 17.0 | 18 |
| Alliance | 3.7 | 6 |
| UKUP | 0.8 | 1 |
| PUP | 1.2 | 1 |
| Others | 5.4 | 1 |
| **Total** | **100** | **108** |

What follows is a detailed listing of the elected members firstly by party affiliation, then by constituency and then A-Z with contact details.

## Assembly Members by Party Affiliation (as elected in Nov 2003)

### Democratic Unionist Party (30)

| | |
|---|---|
| Paul Berry | Newry and Armagh |
| Thomas Buchanan | West Tyrone |
| Gregory Campbell | East Londonderry |
| Wilson Clyde | South Antrim |
| George Dawson | East Antrim |
| Dianne Dodds | Belfast West |
| Nigel Dodds | Belfast North |
| Alex Easton | North Down |
| George Ennis | Strangford |
| Paul Girvan | South Antrim |
| William Hay | Foyle |
| David Hilditch | East Antrim |
| Nelson McCausland | Belfast North |
| Rev William McCrea | Mid Ulster |
| Maurice Morrow | Fermanagh and South Tyrone |
| Stephen Moutray | Upper Bann |
| Robin Newton | Belfast East |
| Rev Ian Paisley | North Antrim |
| Ian Paisley Jr | North Antrim |
| Edwin Poots | Lagan Valley |
| George Robinson | East Londonderry |
| Iris Robinson | Strangford |
| Mark Robinson | Belfast South |
| Peter Robinson | Belfast East |
| Jim Shannon | Strangford |
| David Simpson | Upper Bann |
| Mervyn Storey | North Antrim |
| Peter Weir | North Down |
| Jim Wells | South Down |
| Sammy Wilson | Belfast East |

### Ulster Unionist Party (27)

| | |
|---|---|
| Billy Armstrong | Mid Ulster |
| Norah Beare* | Lagan Valley |
| Roy Beggs | East Antrim |
| Billy Bell | Lagan Valley |
| Dr Esmond Birnie | Belfast South |
| David Burnside | South Antrim |
| Fred Cobain | Belfast North |
| Michael Copeland | Belfast East |
| Rev Robert Coulter | North Antrim |
| Leslie Cree | North Down |
| Jeffrey Donaldson* | Lagan Valley |
| Tom Elliott | Fermanagh/South Tyrone |
| Sir Reg Empey | Belfast East |
| Arlene Foster* | Fermanagh/South Tyrone |
| Samuel Gardiner | Upper Bann |
| Norman Hillis | East Londonderry |
| Derek Hussey | West Tyrone |
| Danny Kennedy | Newry and Armagh |
| David McClarty | East Londonderry |
| Alan McFarland | North Down |
| Michael McGimpsey | Belfast South |
| David McNarry | Strangford |
| Dermot Nesbitt | South Down |
| Ken Robinson | East Antrim |
| John Taylor | Strangford |
| David Trimble | Upper Bann |
| Jim Wilson | South Antrim |

* Jeffrey Donaldson, Arlene Foster and Norah Beare subsequently joined the DUP raising DUP representation to 33 seats and reducing UUP representation to 24.

### Sinn Féin (24)

| | |
|---|---|
| Gerry Adams | Belfast West |
| Bairbre de Brún* | Belfast West |
| Francis Brolly | East Londonderry |
| Willie Clarke | South Down |
| Pat Doherty | West Tyrone |
| Geraldine Dougan | Mid Ulster |
| Michael Ferguson | Belfast West |
| Michelle Gildernew | Fermanagh/South Tyrone |
| Davy Hyland | Newry and Armagh |
| Gerry Kelly | Belfast North |
| Alex Maskey | Belfast South |
| Fra McCann | Belfast West |
| Barry McElduff | West Tyrone |
| Philip McGuigan | North Antrim |
| Martin McGuinness | Mid Ulster |
| Mitchel McLaughlin | Foyle |
| Francie Molloy | Mid Ulster |
| Conor Murphy | Newry and Armagh |
| Mary Nelis** | Foyle |
| John O'Dowd | Upper Bann |
| Pat O'Rawe | Newry and Armagh |
| Thomas O'Reilly | Fermanagh/South Tyrone |
| Caitriona Ruane | South Down |
| Kathy Stanton | Belfast North |

*Bairbre de Brún has resigned from the Assembly, to be replaced by Sue Ramsey **Mary Nelis has resigned from the Assembly and has been replaced by Raymond McCartney

### Social Democratic and Labour Party (18)

| | |
|---|---|
| Alex Attwood | Belfast West |
| Dominic Bradley | Newry and Armagh |
| PJ Bradley | South Down |
| Mary Bradley | Foyle |
| Thomas Burns | South Antrim |
| John Dallat | East Londonderry |
| Mark Durkan | Foyle |
| Dr Sean Farren | North Antrim |
| Tommy Gallagher | Fermanagh and South Tyrone |
| Carmel Hanna | Belfast South |
| Dolores Kelly | Upper Bann |
| Patricia Lewsley | Lagan Valley |
| Alban Maginness | Belfast North |
| Dr Alasdair McDonnell | Belfast South |
| Patsy McGlone | Mid Ulster |
| Eugene McMenamin | West Tyrone |
| Pat Ramsay | Foyle |
| Margaret Ritchie | South Down |

### Alliance Party (6)

| | |
|---|---|
| Eileen Bell | North Down |
| Seamus Close | Lagan Valley |
| David Ford | South Antrim |
| Naomi Long | Belfast East |
| Kieran McCarthy | Strangford |
| Sean Neeson | East Antrim |

### United Kingdom Unionist Party (1)

| | |
|---|---|
| Robert McCartney | North Down |

### Progressive Unionist Party (1)

| | |
|---|---|
| David Ervine | Belfast East |

### Independent (1)

| | |
|---|---|
| Kieran Deeny | West Tyrone |

## Assembly Members by Constituency (as elected in November 2003)

### Belfast East

| | |
|---|---|
| Michael Copeland | UUP |
| Sir Reg Empey | UUP |
| David Ervine | PUP |
| Naomi Long | All |
| Robin Newton | DUP |
| Peter Robinson | DUP |

### Belfast North

| | |
|---|---|
| Fred Cobain | UUP |
| Nigel Dodds | DUP |
| Gerry Kelly | SF |
| Alban Maginness | SDLP |
| Nelson McCausland | DUP |
| Kathy Stanton | SF |

### Belfast South

| | |
|---|---|
| Esmond Birnie | UUP |
| Carmel Hanna | SDLP |
| Alex Maskey | SF |
| Alasdair McDonnell | SDLP |
| Michael McGimpsey | UUP |
| Mark Robinson | DUP |

### Belfast West

| | |
|---|---|
| Gerry Adams | SF |
| Alex Attwood | SDLP |
| Bairbre de Brún* | SF |
| Dianne Dodds | DUP |
| Michael Ferguson | SF |
| Fra McCann | SF |

*Bairbre de Brún has resigned from the Assembly, to be replaced by Sue Ramsey

### East Antrim

| | |
|---|---|
| Roy Beggs Jr | UUP |
| George Dawson | DUP |
| David Hilditch | DUP |
| Sean Neeson | All |
| Ken Robinson | UUP |
| Sammy Wilson | DUP |

### East Londonderry

| | |
|---|---|
| Francis Brolly | SF |
| Gregory Campbell | DUP |
| John Dallat | SDLP |
| Norman Hillis | UUP |
| David McClarty | UUP |
| George Robinson | DUP |

### Fermanagh and South Tyrone

| | |
|---|---|
| Tom Elliott | UUP |
| Arlene Foster* | UUP |
| Tommy Gallagher | SDLP |
| Michelle Gildernew | SF |
| Maurice Morrow | DUP |
| Thomas O'Reilly | SF |

*Arlene Foster subsequently joined the DUP

### Foyle

| | |
|---|---|
| Mary Bradley | SDLP |
| Mark Durkan | SDLP |
| William Hay | DUP |
| Mitchel McLaughlin | SF |
| Mary Nelis* | SF |
| Pat Ramsay | SDLP |

*Mary Nelis has resigned from the Assembly and has been replaced by Raymond McCartney

### Lagan Valley

| | |
|---|---|
| Norah Beare* | UUP |
| Billy Bell | UUP |
| Seamus Close | All |
| Jeffrey Donaldson* | UUP |
| Patricia Lewsley | SDLP |
| Edwin Poots | DUP |

*Norah Beare and Jeffrey Donaldson subsequently joined the DUP

### Mid Ulster

| | |
|---|---|
| Billy Armstrong | UUP |
| Geraldine Dougan | SF |
| Rev William McCrea | DUP |
| Patsy McGlone | SDLP |
| Martin McGuinness | SF |
| Francie Molloy | SF |

### Newry and Armagh

| | |
|---|---|
| Paul Berry | DUP |
| Dominic Bradley | SDLP |
| Davy Hyland | SF |
| Danny Kennedy | UUP |
| Conor Murphy | SF |
| Pat O'Rawe | SF |

### North Antrim

| | |
|---|---|
| Rev Robert Coulter | UUP |
| Sean Farren | SDLP |
| Philip McGuigan | SF |
| Rev Ian Paisley | DUP |
| Ian Paisley Jr | DUP |
| Mervyn Storey | DUP |

### North Down

| | |
|---|---|
| Eileen Bell | All |
| Leslie Cree | UUP |
| Alex Easton | DUP |
| Robert McCartney | UKUP |
| Alan McFarland | UUP |
| Peter Weir | DUP |

### South Antrim

| | |
|---|---|
| Thomas Burns | SDLP |
| David Burnside | UUP |
| Wilson Clyde | DUP |
| David Ford | All |
| Paul Girvan | DUP |
| Jim Wilson | UUP |

### South Down

| | |
|---|---|
| PJ Bradley | SDLP |
| Willie Clarke | SF |
| Dermot Nesbitt | UUP |
| Margaret Ritchie | SDLP |
| Caitriona Ruane | SF |
| Jim Wells | UUP |

### Strangford

| | |
|---|---|
| George Ennis | DUP |
| Kieran McCarthy | All |
| David McNarry | UUP |
| Iris Robinson | DUP |
| Jim Shannon | DUP |
| John Taylor | UUP |

### Upper Bann

| | |
|---|---|
| Samuel Gardiner | UUP |
| Dolores Kelly | SDLP |
| Stephen Moutray | DUP |
| John O'Dowd | SF |
| David Simpson | DUP |
| David Trimble | UUP |

### West Tyrone

| | |
|---|---|
| Thomas Buchanan | DUP |
| Kieran Deeny | Ind |
| Pat Doherty | SF |
| Derek Hussey | UUP |
| Barry McElduff | SF |
| Eugene McMenamin | SDLP |

## A-Z of Assembly Members with Contact Details

Due to the ongoing suspension of the Assembly following the 2003 Assembly elections, each *party* was allocated offices at Stormont, rather than each *individual member* as was previously the case. Contact details for parties at Stormont are as follows:

**Democratic Unionist Party (DUP)**
Room 207, Parliament Buildings
Stormont Estate
Belfast BT4 3XX
Tel: 028 9052 1323

**Ulster Unionist Party (UUP)**
Room 209, Parliament Buildings
Stormont Estate
Belfast BT4 3XX
Tel: 028 9052 1328

**Sinn Féin (SF)**
Room 263
Parliament Buildings
Stormont Estate
Belfast BT4 3XX
Tel: 028 9052 1144

**Social Democratic & Labour Party (SDLP)**
Room 272
Parliament Buildings
Stormont Estate
Belfast BT4 3XX
Tel: 028 9052 1319

**The Alliance Party of Northern Ireland (All)**
Room 220
Parliament Buildings
Stormont Estate
Belfast BT4 3XX
Tel: 028 9052 1315

**United Kingdom Unionist Party (UKUP)**
Room 214
Parliament Buildings
Stormont Estate
Belfast BT4 3XX
Tel: 028 9052 1482

**Progressive Unionist Party (PUP)**
Room 260
Parliament Buildings
Stormont Estate
Belfast BT4 3XX
Tel: 028 9052 1143

## Members

**Adams, Gerry MP,** Sinn Féin
Constituency: Belfast West

Constituency Office:
53 Falls Road
Belfast, BT12 4PD
Tel: 028 9022 3000

**Armstrong, Billy**
Ulster Unionist
Constituency: Mid Ulster

Constituency Office:
Prospect House
Coagh House
Dungannon, BT71 5JH
Tel: 028 8773 8641

**Attwood, Alex**, SDLP
Constituency : Belfast West

Constituency Office:
60 Andersonstown Road,
Belfast
Tel: 028 9080 7808

***Beare, Norah**, DUP
Constituency: Lagan Valley

Constituency Office:
The Old Town Hall
Castle Street
Lisburn, BT27 4XD
Tel: 028 9266 8001

**Beggs, Roy MP**
Ulster Unionist
Constituency: East Antrim

Constituency Office:
41 Station Road
Larne, BT30 3AA
Tel: 028 2827 3258

**Bell, Billy,** Ulster Unionist
Constituency: Lagan Valley

Constituency Office:
2 Sackville Street,
Lisburn, BT27 4AB
Tel: 028 9262 9171

**Bell, Eileen,** Alliance
Constituency: North Down

Constituency Office:
27 Maryville Road
Bangor, BT20 3RH
Tel: 028 9145 2321

*Norah Beare was elected for the UUP but subsequently joined the DUP.

**Berry, Paul,** DUP
Constituency: Newry and Armagh

Constituency Office:
78 Market Street
Tandragee, BT62 2BP
Tel: 028 3884 1668

**Birnie, Dr Esmond**
Ulster Unionist
Constituency: Belfast South

Constituency Office:
117 Cregagh Road
Belfast, BT6 0LA
Tel: 028 9087 3794

**Bradley, Dominic,** SDLP
Constituency:
Newry and Armagh

Constituency Office:
2 Bridge Street
Newry, BT35 8AE
Tel: 028 3026 7933

**Bradley, Mary,** SDLP
Constituency: Foyle

Constituency Office:
7B Messines Terrace
Derry, BT48 7QJ
Tel: 028 7136 0700

**Bradley, PJ**, SDLP
Constituency: South Down

Constituency Office:
2 East Street
Warrenpoint, BT34 3JE
Tel: 028 4177 2228

**Brolly, Francis,** Sinn Féin
Constituency: East Londonderry

Constituency Office:
Contact Party HQ
53 Falls Road
Belfast, BT12 4PD
Tel: 028 9022 3000

**Buchanan, Thomas,** DUP
Constituency: West Tyrone

Constituency Office:
c/o 46 Kirlish Road,
Drumquin
Omagh, BT78 4PY
Tel: 07803 190157

**Burns, Thomas,** SDLP
Constituency: South Antrim

Constituency Office:
25D New Street
Randalstown, BT41 3AF
Tel: 028 9447 8315

**Burnside, David**
Ulster Unionist
Constituency: South Antrim

Constituency Office:
24 Fountain Street
Antrim, BT41 4BB
Tel: 028 9446 1211

**Campbell, Gregory MP,** DUP
Constituency: East
Londonderry

Constituency Office:
25 Bushmills Road
Coleraine, BT52 2BP
Tel: 028 7032 7327

**Clarke, Willie,** Sinn Féin
Constituency: South Down

Constituency Office:
Contact Party HQ
53 Falls Road
Belfast, BT12 4PD
Tel: 028 9022 3000

**Close, Seamus,** Alliance
Constituency: Lagan Valley

Constituency Office:
123 Moira Road
Lisburn, BT28 1RJ
Tel: 028 9267 0639

**Clyde, Wilson,** DUP
Constituency: South Antrim

Constituency Office:
69 Church Street
Antrim, BT41 4BG
Tel: 028 9446 2280

**Cobain, Fred,** Ulster Unionist
Constituency: Belfast North

Constituency Office:
23a York Road
Belfast, BT15 3GU
Tel: 028 9059 4801

**Copeland, Michael**
Ulster Unionist
Constituency: Belfast East

Constituency Office:
4A Belmont Road
Belfast, BT4 2AN
Tel: 028 9065 8217

**Coulter, Rev Robert**
Ulster Unionist
Constituency: North Antrim

Constituency Office:
30A Ballmoney Street
Ballymena, BT43 6AL
Tel: 028 2564 2262

**Cree, Leslie,** Ulster Unionist
Constituency: North Down

Constituency Office:
77A High Street
Bangor, BT20 5BD
Tel: 028 9147 0300

**Dallat, John,** SDLP
Constituency: East
Londonderry

Constituency Office:
11 Bridge Street
Kilrea, BT51 5RR
Tel: 028 2954 1880

**Dawson, George,** DUP
Constituency: East Antrim

Constituency Office:
121 Doagh Road
Newtownabbey, BT36 6AA
Tel: 028 9036 5559

****de Brún, Bairbre,** Sinn Féin
Constituency: Belfast West

Constituency Office:
53 Falls Road
Belfast, BT12 4PD
Tel: 028 9022 3000

**Deeny, Kieran Dr,** Ind
Constituency: West Tyrone

Assembly Office:
Room 223 Parliment
Buildings
Stormont Estate,
Belfast BT4 3XX
Tel: 028 9052 0464

Constituency Office:
c/o Carrickmore Health Centre
4 Termon Road
Carrickmore, BT79 9JR
Tel: 028 8076 1242

**Dodds, Nigel MP,** DUP
Constituency: Belfast North

Constituency Office:
210 Shore Road
Belfast, BT15 3QB
Tel: 028 9077 4774

**Dodds, Dianne,** DUP
Constituency: Belfast West

Constituency Office:
210 Shore Road
Belfast, BT15 3QB
Tel: 028 9077 4774

**Bairbre de Brún has resigned from the Assembly, to be replaced by Sue Ramsey

**Doherty, Pat MP,** Sinn Féin
Constituency: West Tyrone

Constituency Office:
1A Melvin Road
Strabane, BT82 9PP
Tel: 028 7188 1020

***Donaldson, Jeffrey MP**
DUP
Constituency: Lagan Valley

Constituency Office:
The Old Town Hall
Castle Street
Lisburn, BT27 4XD
Tel: 028 9266 8001

**Dougan, Geraldine**
Sinn Féin
Constituency: Mid Ulster

Constituency Office:
32 Burn Road
Cookstown, BT80 8DN
Tel: 028 8676 5850

**Durkan, Mark,** SDLP
Constituency: Foyle

Constituency Office:
7B Messines Terrace,
Racecourse Road
Derry, BT48 7QJ
Tel: 028 7136 0700

**Easton, Alex,** DUP
Constituency: North Down

Constituency Office:
94 Abbey Street
Bangor, BT20 4JB
Tel: 028 9145 4500

**Elliott, Tom,** Ulster Unionist
Constituency:
Fermanagh/South Tyrone

Constituency Office:
1 Regal Pass
Enniskillen, BT74 7NT
Tel: 028 6634 2846

**Empey, Sir Reg**
Ulster Unionist
Constituency: Belfast East

Constituency Office:
4A Belmont Road
Belfast, BT4 2AN
Tel: 028 9065 8217

*Jeffrey Donaldson was elected for the UUP but subsequently joined the DUP.

**Ennis, George**, DUP
Constituency: Strangford

Constituency Office:
34A Frances Street
Newtownards, BT23 7DN
Tel: 028 9182 7990

**Ervine, David,** PUP
Constituency: Belfast East

Constituency Office:
299 Newtownards Road
Belfast, BT4 1AG
Tel: 028 9022 5040

**Farren, Dr Sean**, SDLP
Constituency: North Antrim

Constituency Office:
Bryan House, 16-18 Bryan Street
Ballymena, BT43 6DN
Tel: 028 2563 8765

**Ferguson, Micheal**, Sinn Féin
Constituency: Belfast West

Constituency Office:
53 Falls Road
Belfast, BT12 4PD
Tel: 028 9022 3000

**Ford, David**, Alliance
Constituency: South Antrim

Constituency Office:
9 Carnmoney Road
Newtownabbey, BT36 6HL
Tel: 028 9084 0930

***Foster, Arlene,** DUP
Constituency:
Fermanagh/South Tyrone

Constituency Office:
21 Belmore Street
Enniskillen, BT74 6AA
Tel: 028 6632 0722

**Gallagher, Tommy**, SDLP
Constituency:
Fermanagh/South Tyrone

Constituency Office:
39 Darling Street
Enniskillen, BT74 7DP
Tel: 028 6634 2848

**Gardiner, Samuel,** Ulster Unionist
Constituency: Upper Bann

Constituency Office:
2 Queen Street
Lurgan, BT66 8BQ
Tel: 028 3832 8088

*Arlene Foster was elected for the UUP but subsequently joined the DUP

**Gildernew, Michelle MP,**
Sinn Féin
Constituency:
Fermanagh/South Tyrone

Constituency Office:
60 Irish Street
Dungannon, BT70 1DQ
Tel: 028 8772 2776

**Girvan, Paul,** DUP
Constituency: South Antrim

Constituency Office:
69 Church Street
Antrim, BT41 4BG
Tel: 028 9446 2280

**Hanna, Carmel**, SDLP
Constituency: Belfast South

Constituency Office:
102 Lisburn Road
Belfast, BT9 6BD
Tel: 028 9068 3535

**Hay, William,** DUP
Constituency: Foyle

Constituency Office:
9 Ebrington Terrace
Waterside
Londonderry, BT47 1JS
Tel: 028 7134 6271

**Hilditch, David,** DUP
Constituency: East Antrim

Constituency Office:
22 High Street
Carrickfergus, BT38 7AA
Tel: 028 9332 9980

**Hillis, Norman,**
Ulster Unionist
Constituency: East Londonderry

Constituency Office:
12 Dunmore Street
Coleraine, BT52 1EI
Tel: 028 7032 7294

**Hussey, Derek,** Ulster Unionist
Constituency: West Tyrone

Constituency Office:
48 Main Street
Castlederg, BT81 7BP
Tel: 028 8167 9299

**Davy Hyland,** Sinn Féin
Constituency: Newry and Armagh

Constituency Office:
38 Irish Street
Armagh, BT61 7EP
Tel: 028 3751 1797

**Kelly, Dolores,** SDLP
Constituency: Upper Bann

Constituency Office:
7 William Street Street
Lurgan, BT66 6JA
Tel: 028 3832 2140

**Kelly, Gerry**, Sinn Féin
Constituency: Belfast North

Constituency Office:
291 Antrim Road
Belfast, BT15 2GZ
Tel: 028 9074 0817

**Kennedy, Danny**
Ulster Unionist
Constituency: Newry & Armagh

Constituency Office:
3 Mallview Terrace
Armagh, BT61 9AN
Tel: 028 3751 1655

**Lewsley, Patricia**, SDLP
Constituency: Lagan Valley

Constituency Office:
21B Railway Street
Lisburn, BT28 1XG
Tel: 028 9266 9974

**Long, Naomi,** Alliance
Constituency: Belfast East

Constituency Office:
44A Newtownards Road
Belfast, BT4
Tel: 028 9073 8703

**Maginness, Alban**, SDLP
Constituency: Belfast North

Constituency Office:
228 Antrim Road
Belfast, BT15 2AN
Tel: 028 9022 0520

**Maskey, Alex**, Sinn Féin
Constituency: Belfast South

Constituency Office:
Contact Party HQ
53 Falls Road
Belfast, BT12 4PD
Tel: 028 9022 3000

**McCann, Fra**, Sinn Féin
Constituency: Belfast West

Constituency Office:
53 Falls Road
Belfast, BT12 4PD
Tel: 028 9022 3000

**McCarthy, Kieran**, Alliance
Constituency: Strangford

Constituency Office:
13 Court Street,
Newtownards, BT23 7NX
Tel: 028 9183 2004

**McCartney, Robert**, UKUP
Constituency: North Down

Constituency Office:
10 Central Avenue
Bangor, BT20 3AF
Tel: 028 9147 9860

**McCausland, Nelson**, DUP
Constituency: Belfast North

Constituency Office:
210 Shore Road
Belfast, BT15 3QB
Tel: 028 9077 4774

**McClarty, David**
Ulster Unionist
Constituency: East Londonderry

Constituency Office:
12 Dunmore Street
Coleraine, BT52 1EI
Tel: 028 7032 7294

**McCrea, Rev William**, DUP
Constituency: Mid Ulster

Constituency Office:
10 Highfield Road
Magherafelt, BT45 5JD
Tel: 028 7963 2664

**McDonnell, Dr Alasdair**
SDLP
Constituency: Belfast South

Constituency Office:
143 Ormeau Road
Belfast, BT7 2EB
Tel: 028 9024 2474

**McElduff, Barry**, Sinn Féin
Constituency: West Tyrone

Constituency Office:
21 Main Street
Carrickmore, BT79 9NH
Tel: 028 8076 1744

**McFarland, Alan**
Ulster Unionist
Constituency: North Down

Constituency Office:
77A High Street
Bangor, BT20 5BD
Tel: 028 9147 0300

**McGimpsey, Michael**
Ulster Unionist
Constituency: Belfast South

Constituency Office:
Unit 2, 127-145 Sandy Row
Belfast, BT12 5ET
Tel: 028 9024 5801

**McGlone, Patsy**, SDLP
Constituency: Mid Ulster

Constituency Office:
54A William Street
Cookstown, BT80 8NB
Tel: 028 7964 5424

**McGuigan, Philip**, Sinn Féin
Constituency: North Antrim

Constituency Office:
Contact Party HQ
53 Falls Road
Belfast, BT12 4PD
Tel: 028 9022 3000

**McGuinness, Martin MP**,
Sinn Féin
Constituency: Mid Ulster

Constituency Office:
32 Burn Road
Cookstown, BT80 8DN
Tel: 028 8676 5850

**McLaughlin, Mitchel**
Sinn Féin
Constituency: Foyle

Constituency Office:
15 Cable Street
Derry, BT48 9HF
Tel: 028 7130 9264

**McMenamin, Eugene**, SDLP
Constituency: West Tyrone

Constituency Office:
33A Abercorn Square
Strabane, BT82 9AQ
Tel: 028 7188 6633

**McNarry, David**, Ulster Unionist
Constituency: Strangford

Constituency Office:
6 William Street
Newtownards, BT23 4AE
Tel: 028 9181 4123

**Molloy, Francie**, Sinn Féin
Constituency: Mid Ulster

Constituency Office:
7-9 The Square
Coalisland, BT71 4LN
Tel: 028 8774 8689

**Morrow, Maurice**, DUP
Constituency:
Fermanagh/South Tyrone

Constituency Office:
62B Scotch Street
Dungannon, BT70 1BJ
Tel: 028 8775 2799

**Moutray, Stephen**, DUP
Constituency: Upper Bann

Constituency Office:
10 Windsor Avenue
Lurgan, BT67 9BG
Tel: 028 3834 6111

**Murphy, Conor**, Sinn Féin
Constituency: Newry & Armagh

Constituency Office:
35 Main Street
Camlough, BT35 7JG
Tel: 028 3083 9470

**Neeson, Sean**, Alliance
Constituency: East Antrim

Constituency Office:
North Street
Carrickfergus, BT38 7AQ
Tel: 028 9335 0286

***Nelis, Mary**, Sinn Féin
Constituency: Foyle

Constituency Office:
21A Glenbrook Terrace
Derry, BT48 0DY
Tel: 028 7137 7551

**Nesbitt, Dermot**
Ulster Unionist
Constituency: South Down

Constituency Office:
19 Causeway Road
Newcastle, BT33 0DL
Tel: 028 4372 4400

**Newton, Robin**, DUP
Constituency: Belfast East

Constituency Office:
13 Castlereagh Road
Belfast, BT5 5FB
Tel: 028 9045 9500

*Mary Nelis has resigned from the Assembly and has been replaced by Raymond McCartney

**O'Dowd, John,** Sinn Féin
Constituency: Upper Bann

Constituency Office:
77 North Street
Lurgan, BT67 9AH
Tel: 028 3834 9675

**O'Rawe, Pat**, Sinn Féin
Constituency: Newry & Armagh

Constituency Office:
38 Irish Street
Armagh, BT61 7EP
Tel: 028 3751 1797

**O'Reilly, Thomas,** Sinn Féin
Constituency:
Fermanagh/South Tyrone

Constituency Office:
7 Market Street
Enniskillen, BT74 7DS
Tel: 028 6632 8214

**Paisley, Dr Rev Ian,** DUP
Constituency: North Antrim

Constituency Office:
46 Hill Street
Ballymena, BT43 6BH
Tel: 028 2564 1421

**Paisley, Ian Jnr,** DUP
Constituency: North Antrim

Constituency Office:
46 Hill Street
Ballymena, BT43 6BH
Tel: 028 2564 1421

**Poots, Edwin,** DUP
Constituency: Lagan Valley

Constituency Office:
The Old Town Hall
Castle Street Lisburn, BT27 4XD
Tel: 028 9266 8001

**Ramsay, Pat,** SDLP
Constituency: Foyle

Constituency Office:
7B Messines Terrace,
Racecourse Road
Derry, BT48 7QJ
Tel: 028 7136 0700

**Ritchie, Margaret,** SDLP
Constituency: South Down

Constituency Office:
32 Saul Street
Downpatrick, BT30 6NQ
Tel: 028 4461 2882

**Robinson, George,** DUP
Constituency: East Londonderry

Constituency Office:
25 Bushmills Road
Coleraine, BT52 2BP
Tel: 028 7032 7327

**Robinson, Iris MP,** DUP
Constituency: Strangford

Constituency Office:
2B James Street
Newtownards, BT23 4DY
Tel: 028 9182 7701

**Robinson, Ken**
Ulster Unionist
Constituency: East Antrim

Constituency Office:
32c North Street
Carrickfergus, BT38 7AQ
Tel: 028 9336 2995

**Robinson, Mark,** DUP
Constituency: Belfast South

Constituency Office:
215A Lisburn Road
Belfast, BT9 7EJ
Tel: 028 9022 5969

**Robinson, Peter,** DUP
Constituency: Belfast East

Constituency Office:
Strandtown Hall, 96 Belmont Avenue
Belfast, BT4 3DE
Tel: 028 9047 3111

**Ruane, Caitriona,** Sinn Féin
Constituency: South Down

Constituency Office:
17 Circular Road
Castlewellan, BT31 9ED
Tel: 028 4377 0185

**Shannon, Jim,** DUP
Constituency: Strangford

Constituency Office:
34A Frances Street
Newtownards, BT23 7DN
Tel: 028 9182 7990

**Simpson, David,** DUP
Constituency: Upper Bann

Constituency Office:
10 Windsor Avenue
Lurgan, BT67 9BG
Tel: 028 3834 6111

**Stanton, Kathy,** Sinn Féin
Constituency: Belfast North

Constituency Office:
291 Antrim Road
Belfast, BT15 2GZ
Tel: 028 9074 0817

**Storey, Mervyn,** DUP
Constituency: North Antrim

Constituency Office:
142A Main Street
Bushmills, BT57 8QE
Tel: 028 2073 1303

**Taylor, John**, Ulster Unionist
Constituency: Strangford

Constituency Office:
6 William Street
Newtownards, BT23 4AE
Tel: 028 9181 4123

**Trimble, David MP,** Ulster Unionist
Constituency: Upper Bann

Constituency Office:
2 Queen Street
Lurgan, BT66 8BQ
Tel: 028 3832 8088

**Weir, Peter,** DUP
Constituency: North Down

Constituency Office:
94 Abbey Street
Bangor, BT20 4JB
Tel: 028 9145 4500

**Wells, Jim,** DUP
Constituency: South Down

Constituency Office:
2 Belfast Road
Ballynahinch, BT24 8DZ
Tel: 028 9756 4200

**Wilson, Jim,** Ulster Unionist
Constituency: South Antrim

Constituency Office:
3a Rashee Road
Ballyclare, BT39 9HJ
Tel: 028 9332 4461

**Wilson, Sammy,** DUP
Constituency: East Antrim

Constituency Office:
13 Castlereagh Road
Belfast, BT5 5FB
Tel: 028 9045 9400

*Norah Beare, Jeffrey Donaldson and Arlene Foster were elected for the UUP but subsequently joined the DUP.

## The Executive Committee

Strand 2 of the Good Friday Agreement provided for executive authority to be discharged on behalf of the Assembly by an executive committee comprising a First Minister, Deputy First Minister and up to ten Ministers with Departmental responsibilities. The First and Deputy First Minister are elected on a cross community basis and following their election the posts of Ministers allocated to parties on the basis of the d'Hondt system by reference to the number of seats each party has in the Assembly. The Ministers constitute an Executive Committee convened and presided over jointly by the First and Deputy First Minister.

The Executive Committee (effectively Northern Ireland's Cabinet) provides a forum for the discussion of issues which cut across the responsibilities of two or more Ministers, prioritising executive and legislative proposals and recommending a common position where necessary in dealing with external relationships. Ministers hold full executive authority in their respective areas of responsibility within any broad programme agreed by the Executive Committee and endorsed by the Assembly as a whole.

A party may decline the opportunity to nominate a person to serve as a Minister or subsequently change its nominee. All Northern Ireland Departments are headed by a Minister who liaises with his/her respective statutory Committee. As a condition of appointment Ministers must affirm the pledge of office undertaking to discharge effectively and in good faith all the responsibilities attaching to their office.

Since the suspension of the Assembly and other institutions of the Belfast Agreement in October 2002, the Northern Ireland government departments have been headed up by four Direct Rule Ministers. *(Details of ministerial responsibilities under Direct Rule are set out in Chapter 3)*

The Northern Ireland Executive is a body unique in the multi party membership of its composition in contrast to the one party representation in the British Cabinet. Experience of the first Executive established under the Belfast Agreement indicated that the structure could work quite effectively. However experience of the first Assembly demonstrated that the 'whip' system was not as thoroughgoing as in the Westminster model and there were instances where legislative proposals brought by the Executive Committee to the floor of the Assembly could actually be defeated.

## The First Minister and Deputy First Minister

The First and Deputy First Minister must stand for election as a pair of candidates, one from each of the two political traditions, and must be elected by the Assembly as a pair. The First Minister and Deputy First Minister must be elected within six weeks following the election of the Assembly, otherwise the procedures operational under the Belfast Agreement launch a period of Review. Together they must have the support of an absolute majority of the Assembly, plus a majority of nationalist and a majority of unionist members. If there is an absence of a viable option for the election of First Minister or Deputy First Minister, another Minister may hold the position as acting First or Deputy First Minister for a period of six weeks.

An individual member, committee or Minister may initiate legislation. Voting is by simple majority unless cross-community support is required. A petition of 30 concerned members can trigger such a voting procedure. In these cases, parallel consent or a weighted majority of 60% of those members present and voting, is required.

### Cross Community Decision-Making

Arrangements to ensure decisions are taken on a cross community basis:

(i) Either parallel consent, i.e. a majority of those members present and voting, including a majority of the unionist and nationalist designations present and voting;

(ii) Or a weighted majority (60 per cent) of members present and voting, including at least 40 per cent of each of the nationalist and unionist delegations present and voting.

Key decisions requiring cross-community support will be designated in advance, including election of the Chair of the Assembly, the First Minister and Deputy First Minister, standing orders and budget allocations. In other cases, such decisions could be triggered by a Petition of Concern brought by a minimum of 30 Assembly Members.

The duties defined for the First Minister and the Deputy First Minister include dealing with and co-coordinating the work of the Executive Committee and the response of the Northern Ireland Executive to external business.

### Junior Ministers

In the first Northern Ireland Executive established under the Belfast Agreement there were two junior ministers appointed to OFMDFM, one from each of the two largest parties.

### Programme for Government

It was agreed in the Good Friday Agreement that in order to create effective government for Northern Ireland:

*'The Executive Committee will seek to agree each year, and review as necessary a programme incorporating an agreed budget linked to policies and programmes, subject to approval by the Assembly, after scrutiny in Assembly Committees, on a cross-community basis'.*

The Programme for Government is the administration's core policy document providing a strategic overview of the planned work of the Executive and demonstrating how policies and programmes delivered by different departments and agencies may be combined to achieve agreed priorities. The Programme for Government may be best described as an amalgamation of departmental business plans into the overall corporate plan.

The First Minister and Deputy First Minister hold responsibility for setting the overall priorities for government through the Programme for Government. Ministers are expected to adhere to these priorities.

In the first Assembly 1999-2003, four important areas were identified for greater emphasis within the Programme for Government:

- Investment in infrastructure;
- Improved service delivery;
- Tackling social exclusion, in particular poverty;
- Partnership.

# Assembly Committees

## Introduction

The executive structures under the Good Friday Agreement have the effect of creating a strong inclusive government but weakening the possibility of having a strong formal opposition. The architects of the Agreement therefore saw the need to create a strong committee system where elected members would play a robust formal role in interfacing with the Executive.

The Good Friday Agreement sets out the formal powers of the Committees, which include a 'scrutiny, policy development, and consultation role with respect to the Department with which each is associated'. The Committees also play a role in the 'initiation of legislation', a significant and considerable power to vest in a legislative committee. However, based on the experience of the first Assembly, the main focus of Committee work has tended to be driven by the Executive Programme, although in terms of reporting and the breadth of their inquiries they have shown a readiness to take the initiative.

## Scrutiny Role of Committees

In effect the Committees act as a democratic check and balance on the power of Ministers and the Executive in the absence of an 'opposition' as is traditionally understood within the UK Westminster model.

The ability of Committees to scrutinise effectively and hold the Executive to account is hampered by the inclusive nature of the Executive, and the fact that the majority of seats on each committee are held by the larger parties who also hold the majority of Executive positions.

# Statutory Committees (Departmental Committees)

The Good Friday Agreement created an Assembly which had 10 statutory committees, corresponding to the 10 government departments. The allocation of seats on Statutory Committees (which consist of 11 members) reflects the diversity of political parties represented within the Assembly.

The number of seats allocated to each party should be proportionate to its membership of the Assembly. The Chair and Deputy Chair of the committees are elected using the d'Hondt system which allocates positions on the basis of numerical representation. The Business Committee holds responsibility for the allocation of seats to individual members or the parties subject to approval by the Assembly.

There are no co-opted members on to any of the Committees, whether Statutory, Standing or Ad Hoc. However Statutory Committees do appoint specialist advisors where they deem it appropriate to the conduct of their work.

Statutory Committees have the power 'to consider and advise on departmental budgets and annual plans in the context of the overall budget allocation'. The procedure for processing the budget requires each of the Statutory Committees to examine and scrutinise departmental allocations in line with the current Programme for Government and to submit their views to the Finance and Personnel Committee who interpret and draw together the respective views. These views are then submitted to the Department of Finance and Personnel, enabling the Minister to bring forward a revised budget for consideration.

The quorum for the Statutory Committees is set at five and a member in attendance by video link is deemed to be admissible in meeting the quorum requirement. Simple majority passes votes by a show of hands. The duration of the Committees is the life of the Assembly, although Committee members may resign and be replaced by another member during this time.

# Non-Statutory Committees

Standing Committees and Ad Hoc Committees are the two types of non-statutory committee in the Assembly.

## Standing Committees

Standing Committees are permanent Assembly Committees whose chair and deputy chair are filled utilising the same procedures for Statutory Committees. However the process for nomination of chairs and deputies to Statutory and Non Statutory Committees is different.

With respect to other matters such as quorum and nomination of members the same procedures apply as those for Statutory Committees. The first Assembly established a number of standing committees, to take care of the many aspects of running a legislative forum. These are:

- The Business Committee;
- Committee on Procedures;
- Committee of the Centre;
- Public Accounts Committee;
- Committee on Standards and Privilege;
- Audit Committee.

### Business Committee

The Business Committee which is chaired by the Speaker discusses forthcoming business and makes arrangements for the business of the Assembly. The Committee consists of thirteen members, with two members appointed to act as Chair in the absence of the Speaker.

**Committee on Procedures**
The Committee on Procedures was established to consider and review the Standard Orders and procedures of the Assembly. The Committee has a membership of 11, including a Chairperson and Deputy Chairperson and a quorum of 5.

**Committee of the Centre**
The Committee of the Centre was established to scrutinise the Office of the First Minister and Deputy First Minister, although it is restricted by its remit to only some of the functions of the OFMDFM, including the following:

- Economic Policy Unit;
- Equality Unit;
- Civic Forum;
- European Affairs and International Matters;
- Community Relations;
- Public Appointments Policy;
- Freedom of Information;
- Victims;
- Nolan Standards;
- Public Service Office;
- Emergency Planning;
- Women's Issues;
- Functions of the Planning Appeals Commission and Water Appeals Commission transferred to OFMDFM.

The Committee consists of 17 members and has the power to send for persons and papers as required in conjunction with its role in the legislative process. The Committee of the Centre replaces the Standing Committees on Human Rights and Community Relations, European Affairs and Equality.

**The Public Accounts Committee**
The role of the Public Accounts Committee is 'to consider accounts, and reports on accounts laid before the Assembly'. It is in effect the 'financial watchdog' of the Assembly. The Committee has the power to send for persons, papers and records and neither the Chair nor the Deputy Chairperson of the Committee can be a member of the same political party as the Minister of Finance and Personnel or of any Junior Minister appointed to the Department of Finance and Personnel. The Public Accounts Committee has eleven menbers, including a Chairperson and a Deputy Chairperson.

**Committee on Standards and Privileges**
The role of the Committee on Standards and Privileges is to consider specific matters relating to privileges referred to it by the Assembly. The Committee on Standards and Privileges has 11 members, including a Chairperson and a Deputy Chairperson. The Committee is appointed at the start of every Assembly and oversees all matters relating to the Register of Members' interests and the conduct of Members.

**Audit Committee**
The Audit Committee is governed by procedures set out in Standing Order 53. Under the terms of the order no more than one member of the Committee may simultaneously be a member of the Public Accounts Committee. The Audit Committee has a membership of five and quorum of two.

### Ad Hoc Committees
Ad Hoc Committees are established to deal with specific time-bounded terms of reference that the Assembly may set. Their role is often to consider a piece of draft legislation and produce a written report on it. During the first Assembly, ad-hoc committees were established to look at issues including: flags; financial investigations; criminal injuries compensation; criminal justice reform and firearms.

### Sub Committees
Each Committee has the authority to establish sub Committees. However, unless approved by the Business Committee, no Committee may have more than one sub Committee in operation at any one time. Sub Committees may be appointed to consider specific, time-bounded matters within the terms of reference set by the parent Committee. Once these matters have been resolved the sub committee will report to the Parent Committee and be dissolved.

Each sub Committee should reflect the party strengths in the Assembly as far as possible and the parent committee will determine the quorum for the sub committee.

## Other Institutions of the Belfast Agreement
### Introduction
The Good Friday Agreement radically transformed British and Irish government institutional and constitutional relationships with Northern Ireland. Under the terms of the Agreement both governments made significant constitutional and legislative changes altering their expressions of sovereignty over Northern Ireland. Following the agreement of the Republic of Ireland to amend Articles 2 and 3 of the Irish Constitution, the British Government repealed the Government of Ireland Act 1920. These changes became effective with the enactment of the Northern Ireland Act 1998, which became law on 19 September 1998, thereby implementing the Agreement.

### New Structures
To reflect the changed expressions of British and Irish sovereignty over Northern Ireland, new institutions were created within the three strands of the Agreement – Northern Ireland, North/South and East/West. Within the Northern Ireland strand, the Civic Forum was created as a consultative body, inclusive of all sectors. New North/South institutions created included the North/South Ministerial Council and the six North/South Implementation Bodies. Provisions were also made for a North/South Consultative Forum, although this was not established. Relationships East/West were to be enhanced with the establishment of a British/Irish Council, British/Irish Intergovernmental Conference and Joint Ministerial Committee on Devolution. Details of all these institutions are set out below.

### The Civic Forum
Civic Forum Secretariat
Tel: 028 9052 8841 / Fax: 028 9052 8833
Email: secretariat@civicforum-ni.org
Web: www.civicforum-ni.org

The Civic Forum is a consultative body, with no formal legislative or governmental powers consisting of 60 members plus a Chairperson. Members are representative of the voluntary, business, agriculture, trade union, education, culture, community relations and fisheries sectors. The Civic Forum was suspended, along with the other devolved institutions, in October 2002.

## North/South Bodies

### The North/South Ministerial Council

The North/South Ministerial Council (NSMC) was established on 2 December 1999, under the terms of the Good Friday Agreement and is the lead institution in developing all aspects of North/South co-operation, bringing together Ministers from Northern Ireland and the Irish Government. The role of the Council is to develop consultation, co-operation and action on all-island and cross-border matters of mutual interest. It also provides leadership and direction for the six North/South implementation bodies.

The North/South Ministerial Council, meets in plenary format twice a year with Northern Ireland represented by the First and Deputy First Minister and other relevant ministers and the Irish government by the Taoiseach and relevant ministers. Smaller groups meet on a 'regular and frequent' basis to discuss specific cross-border issues with each side represented by the appropriate minister. The Council may also meet to resolve disagreements and discuss common issues and concerns.

Within the NSMC, government ministers have considerable discretion but they remain accountable to their legislatures, the Assembly and the Oireachtas respectively. The First and Deputy First Minister have a duty to ensure 'cross-community participation' on the Council. The Council is supported by a Joint Secretariat in Armagh staffed by personnel from OFMDFM and the Irish Civil service.

Responsibility for arranging NSMC meetings in sectoral and plenary formats, arranging papers for the meetings and monitoring the work of the bodies rests with the Joint Secretariat.

**NSMC Joint Secretariat**
39 Abbey Street, Armagh, BT61 7EB
Web: www.northsouthministerialcouncil.org
Northern Ireland Joint Secretary: Peter Smyth
Tel: 028 3751 5002
Irish Joint Secretary: Tim O'Connor / Tel: 028 3751 5001

### North/South Implementation Bodies

On 2 December 1999 under the aegis of the North/South Ministerial Council, six North/South Implementation Bodies, established between the British and Irish Governments came into being. These bodies exist to implement policies agreed by Ministers in the North/South Ministerial Council and are expected to develop cross-border co-operation on practical matters of mutual concern.

The bodies operate under the North/South Ministerial Council and are funded from grants made by the relevant government departments, North and South. They are staffed by a combination of civil servants (either transferred or seconded from their parent Departments, North and South) and, increasingly beyond the initial period, directly recruited staff. With the agreement of the Northern Ireland Assembly and the Oireachtas it will be open to the North/South Ministerial Council to set up additional Implementation Bodies in the future. The six North/South Implementation Bodies are: Waterways Ireland; The Food Safety Promotion Board; Inter*Trade*Ireland; The Special EU Programmes Body; The Foyle, Carlingford and Irish Lights Commission; The North/South Language Body (includes twin agencies promoting Irish and Ulster Scots). The work of these bodies is continuing, although devolution has been suspended.

Tha Boord o Ulstér-Scotch/The Ulster-Scots Agency

Tha Boord o Ulstèr-Scotch
Ulster-Scots Agency

| NI Office: | ROI Office: |
| --- | --- |
| Franklin House | Moffat Building |
| 10-12 Brunswick Street, | The Diamond |
| Belfast | Raphoe |
| BT2 7GE | Co. Donegal |
| Tel: 028 90231113 | Tel: 00 353 (7491) 73 876 |
| Email: info@ulsterscotsagency.org.uk | Email: ulsterscotsagency@eircom.net |

**Web: www.ulsterscotsagency.com**

Chief Executive Officer
George Patton

Tha Boord o Ulstér-Scotch/The Uster-Scots Agency is the body responsible for the promotion of the Ulster-Scots language and culture on the island of Ireland. It is part of the North/South Language Implementation Body that was set up under the Belfast Agreement. The Agency is responsible to the North/South Ministerial Council, and in particular to the two sponsoring ministers in Northern Ireland and Dail Eireann, whose remits include language and culture.

**Board Members**
Chairman: Jim Devenney (acting)

| | |
| --- | --- |
| Alistair Simpson | Eddie O'Donnell |
| Dr Linde Lunney | Bob Stoker |
| Dr Ian Adamson | Pat Wall |

**Staff**
Deputy CEO/Director of Culture - George Holmes
Development Officer West - Derek Reaney

## The Food Safety Promotion Board

7 Eastgate Avenue, Eastgate, Little Island, Cork
Tel: 00 353 21 230 4100 / Fax: 00 353 21 230 4111
Web: safefoodonline.com
Bertie Kerr, Fermanagh District Council (Chair)
Chief Executive: Martin Higgins

The Food Safety Promotion Board is principally charged with promoting food safety – through public campaigns, conferences, training and advising professionals and the general public. It is also involved in supporting North/South scientific co-operation, and links between institutions working in the field of food safety. The Food Safety Promotion Board operates under the trade name of safefood

## Foras na Gaeilge

Foras na Gaeilge

7 Cearnóg Mhuirfean
Baile Átha Cliath 2
Teil: (00353 1) 639 8400
1850 325 325
Tuaisceart: 0845 309 8142
Facs: (00353 1) 639 8401
Email: eolas@forasnagaeilge.ie
Web: www.gaeilge.ie

Cathaoirleach
Maighréad Uí Mháirtín

Bunaíodh Foras na Gaeilge ar 2 Nollaig 1999 faoin Acht um Chomhaontú na Breataine - na hÉireann agus is í an príomhaidhm atá ag an bhForas ná an Ghaeilge a chur chun cinn ar fud oileán na hÉireann.

Foras na Gaeilge was established on 2 December 1999 under the terms of the British-Irish Agreement Act, and the main objective of the Foras is to promote the Irish language on the island of Ireland.

The main functions of the Foras are: promotion of the Irish language; facilitating and encouraging its use in speech and writing in public and in private life in the south, and in the context of part III of the European Charter for Regional or Minority Languages, in Northern Ireland where there is appropriate demand; advising both administrations, public bodies and other groups in the private and voluntary sectors; undertaking supportive projects, and grant aiding bodies and groups as considered necessary; undertaking research, promotional campaigns, and public and media relations; developing terminology and dictionaries; supporting Irish medium education and teaching of Irish.

**Board Members**
Chairperson: Maighréad Uí Mháirtín
Anne Craig
Gordon McCoy
Aodán MacPóilín
Liam Corey
Patsy McGlone
Gearoíd MacSiacais
Gearoíd O'hEara
Treasa Ni Ailpin
Brid Uí Néill
Maolsheachlainn O Caollaí
Padraig O Duibhir
Leachlann Ó Catháin
Mairéad Nic Sheaghain
Caitríona Ní Cheallaigh
Diarmuid Ó Murchú

## The Foyle, Carlingford and Irish Lights Commission

At present one Agency has been established (Loughs Agency). A second Agency (Lights Agency) will be established once the appropriate legislation is in place.

## InterTradeIreland

InterTradeIreland
TRADE & BUSINESS DEVELOPMENT BODY

The Old Gasworks Business Park
Kilmorey Street
Newry, BT34 2DE
Tel: 028 3083 4100
Fax: 028 3083 4155
Email: info@intertradeireland.com
Web: www.intertradeireland.com

Chief Executive
Liam Nellis

Inter*Trade*Ireland was established in 1999 as part of the Belfast Agreement between the Government of Ireland and the Government of the United Kingdom of Great Britain and Northern Ireland. Inter*Trade*Ireland's mission is to expand cross-border trade and business on the island of Ireland.

Inter*Trade*Ireland provides a range of funding opportunities and business support initiatives on a cross-border basis. Some of the programmes administered by Inter*Trade*Ireland include:

**Acumen:** Concentrates on stimulating cross-border trade by assisting SMEs North and South by providing tailored consultancy and sales salary support.

**Focus:** An all-island sales and marketing initiative emphasising the promotion of all-island trade - identifying new market opportunities and delivering cross-border sales.

**Go Source** (www.Go-Source.com): An online directory aimed at suppliers interested in tackling the all-island €13bn public procurement market.

**Supplier Education Programme:** Provides guidance to SMEs in Northern Ireland and the Republic in the area of bidding for and servicing public sector contracts.

## Loughs Agency

Foyle Carlingford and Irish Lights
Commission (FCILC)
Loughs Agency Headquarters
22 Victoria Road
Londonderry
BT47 2AB

Email: general@loughs-agency.org
Web: www.loughs-agency.org
Tel: 0044 (0)28 7134 2100
Fax: 0044 (0)28 7134 2720

Carlingford Regional Office
Old Quay Lane
Carlingford, Co Louth
Email: carlingford@loughs-agency.org
Tel/Fax: 00353 (0)42 9383888

Chief Executive
Derick Anderson

Senior Policy Officer: John Pollock
Chief Inspector: Stanley Thorpe
Biologist: Patrick Boylan

**FCILC Board**
Peter Savage (Chair)
Lord Cooke of Islandreagh (Vice Chair)
Jack Allen
Keith Anderson
Dick Blakiston-Houston
Francis Feely
Pat Griffin
Siobhan Logue
Joseph Martin
Tarlach O Crosain
Jacqui McConville
Andrew Ward

**MISSION**
The Loughs Agency aims to provide sustainable social, economic and environmental benefits through the effective conservation, management, promotion and development of the fisheries and marine resources of the Foyle and Carlingford Areas.

## Special European Union Programmes Body (SEUPB)

Headquarters: EU House
6 Cromac Place
Belfast, BT7 2JB
Tel: +44 (0) 28 9026 6660
Fax: +44 (0) 28 9026 6661
Email: info@seupb.org
Web: www.seupb.org

Chief Executive
Pat Colgan

The SEUPB is one of the six cross border Bodies set up under the "Agreement between the Government of Ireland and the Government of the United Kingdom of Great Britain and Northern Ireland establishing implementing bodies".

The SEUPB is the managing authority for the EU Programme for Peace and Reconciliation in Northern Ireland and the Border Region of Ireland and INTERREG IIIA. The Body is also involved in the cross border elements of other Community Initiatives (Leader+, Urban II and Equal) and are responsible for implementing the Common Chapter.

A principal aim of the Special European Union Programmes Body is to promote cross border co-operation through the administration of the cross border element of the Peace II programme and the monitoring and promotion of cross border activities in the context of the National Development Plan 2000-2006 for Ireland and the Structural Funds Plan 2000-2006 for Northern Ireland.

**SEUPB Management Team**
Nuala Kerr, Deputy Chief Executive
Jack O'Connor, Director, Community Initiatives
Shaun Henry, Director, PEACE II
Gina McIntyre, Director, Corporate Services

## The North/South Language Body

(Includes Irish Language and Ulster-Scots Agencies)
The Language Body is a single body reporting to the North/South Ministerial Council, but composed of two separate and largely autonomous agencies: the Irish Language Agency, Foras na Gaeilge, and the Ulster-Scots Agency, Tha Boord o Ulster-Scotch. Each of these agencies has a separate board, which together constitutes the Board of the North/South Language Body.

Tourism Ireland

Tourism Ireland
*Marketing the island of Ireland overseas*

5th Floor, Bishop's Square
Redmond's Hill, Dublin 2
Tel: +353 (0)1 476 3400
Fax: +353 (0)1 476 3666

Beresford House, 2 Beresford Road
Coleraine, BT52 1GE
Tel: 028 7035 9200
Fax: 028 7032 6932

Corporate website: www.tourismireland.com/corporate

Chief Executive Officer
Paul O'Toole

Tourism Ireland was established as one of the 'six areas of co-operation' under the Belfast Agreement and is responsible for marketing the island of Ireland overseas as a tourist destination, with a special remit to support Northern Ireland in realising its tourism potential.

2005 will be the company's fourth year in operation, during which time overseas visitor numbers to the island of Ireland are forecast to have increased by 15.5% over 2002. Within this figure, the increase in the number of overseas visitors to Northern Ireland is forecast to be 30.6% over 2002. Moving forward, Tourism Ireland will continue to work closely with all its tourism industry partners and employ a wide range of marketing tools including an extensive suite of branded literature, available in nine languages, direct marketing, and advertising. The company will also continue to develop its online presence, with local language Tourism Ireland websites

## North South Consultative Forum

Although it was not established during the lifetime of the first Assembly, the Belfast Agreement specifically provided for the possibility of establishing an equivalent of the Civic Forum, structured on an all island basis.

Supporters of the concept, particularly in the voluntary and community sector, see considerable benefits in such an institution although the Republic does not at present have a direct 'mirror' institution to Northern Ireland's Civic Forum from which to draw the southern membership of the new body.

Waterways Ireland

Waterways Ireland
Uiscebhealaí Éireann Watterweys Airlann

Headquarters, 5-7 Belmore Street
Enniskillen, Co Fermanagh, BT74 6AA
Tel: + 44 (0)28 6632 3004
Fax: + 44 (0)28 6634 6237
Website: www.waterwaysireland.org
Email: information@waterwaysireland.org

Chief Executive Officer
John Martin

Directors:
Brian D'Arcy (Operations)
Colin Brownsmith
(Finance and Personnel)
Martin Dennany
(Marketing and Communications)
Nigel Russell (Technical Services)
Acting Director:
Brian McTeggart (Corporate Services)

Waterways Ireland is one of six North-South implementation Bodies established under the British-Irish Agreement in 1999 and has responsibility for the management, maintenance, development and restoration of Ireland's inland navigations, principally for recreational purposes.

Lights Agency

British and Irish legislation, when implemented, will allow transfer of the Commissioner of Irish Lights functions to the Foyle, Carlingford and Irish Lights Commission, and such functions will be exercised through an agency of the FCILC known as the Lights Agency. FCILC will become the General Lighthouse Authority for the island of Ireland.

## Other Areas Identified for North/South Co-operation

In addition to the six Implementation Bodies a further six areas have initially been identified for co-operation between existing government departments and other bodies, North and South. They cover aspects of transport, agriculture, education, health, environment and tourism.

In regard to these areas, common policies and approaches are agreed in the North/South Ministerial Council, but are implemented separately in each jurisdiction. Within each of the six identified Areas for Co-operation, certain specific aspects have been agreed for consideration and these are outlined below.

**Transport**
Strategic planning and development of cross-border co-operation (while co-operation would primarily arise in respect of road and rail planning, it would take account of issues arising in the port and airport sectors and public transport) and road and rail safety;

**Agriculture**
Discussion of Common Agricultural Policy (CAP) issues, animal and plant health policy and research and rural development, between North and South;

**Education**
Education for children with special needs (e.g. autism, dyslexia), educational underachievement, teacher qualifications, and school, youth and teacher exchanges on a cross-border basis;

**Health**
Accident and emergency planning, emergency services, co-operation on high technology equipment, cancer research and health promotion. Joint Working Groups of officials from the two Departments of Health have been set up to bring forward proposals for action in the following areas:

- Cancer research;
- Major emergencies;
- High-technology equipment;
- Health promotion;
- Accident & emergency services.

**Environment**
Research into environmental protection, water quality management and waste management in a cross-border context;

**Tourism**
North/South co-operation on tourism has led to the creation of the all-island tourism organisation Tourism Ireland Limited.

## British Irish Institutions

### The British Irish Council

The British-Irish Council was established to 'promote the harmonies and mutually beneficial development of relationships among the peoples of the United Kingdom and Ireland'. It is made up of representatives of the British and Irish Governments, of the devolved institutions in Northern Ireland, Scotland, Wales, the Isle of Man and the Channel Islands.

The work of the British-Irish Council is centred around the following areas:

- Drugs;
- Environment;
- Health/telemedicine;
- Knowledge economy;
- Minority and lesser-used languages;
- Tourism;
- Transport;
- Social inclusion;

**British-Irish Council Secretariat**
Department of Foreign Affairs
Iveagh House, Dublin 2
Irish Joint Secretary: Úna Ní Dhubhghaill
Tel: 00 353 1 408 2351

**British-Irish Council Secretariat**
Department for Constitutional Affairs
66 Whitehall, London, SW1A 2AU
UK Joint Secretary: Peter Thompson
Tel: 0207 270 6779

### British-Irish Intergovernmental Conference

The British-Irish Intergovernmental Conference was designed to replace the Anglo-Irish Intergovernmental Council and the Intergovernmental Conference established under the 1985 Anglo-Irish Agreement.

The Conference is supported by British and Irish governments including a Joint Secretariat of officials dealing with non-devolved Northern Ireland matters. The Conference brings together both governments to promote bilateral co-operation on all non-devolved matters of mutual interest, including the areas of security, rights, justice, prisons and policing.

### Joint Ministerial Committee on Devolution

A Joint Ministerial Committee on Devolution has been established to enable Ministers from the devolved governments of Scotland, Wales and Northern Ireland to take forward joint action. The role of the Committee is to examine non-devolved matters which may conflict with responsibilities devolved in the regions. Joint Ministerial Committees have been created on the Knowledge Economy, Health and Poverty. Ministers have also engaged in less formal meetings to discuss matters such as Housing, Agriculture and the Environment.

The Prime Minister of the United Kingdom is the Chair of the Joint Ministerial Committee on Devolution. Meetings are attended by the Secretaries of State for Scotland, Wales and Northern Ireland and may be located anywhere in the UK. Whilst the agenda and location are made public the content of these meetings is confidential. A secretariat comprising staff from the UK cabinet office and staff from each of the devolved regions in the UK supports the work of the committee.

# Electoral Systems, Political Parties and Election Results

## Electoral Systems

By UK standards Northern Ireland is something of a 'guinea-pig' when it comes to the application of electoral systems. Northern Ireland maintains a consistency with the rest of the UK in terms of how Westminster elections and European elections are conducted, but is radically different in the approach taken to regional assemblies and local government.

At the heart of Northern Ireland's differentiated treatment is the recognition that in a place that is deeply divided it is all the more important that the election results reflect the wishes of the electorate proportionately. The second most important consideration after proportionality is inclusiveness – and in recent years there has been a considerable effort to ensure that the electoral system does not crowd out the smaller parties.

## First-past-the-post (Simple Plurality)

The first-past-the-post electoral system is used throughout the UK for local (except in Northern Ireland) and general elections. Each constituency returns a single winner, the candidate with the most votes. The winner does not require a majority of votes cast, merely more votes than the closest rival.

First past the post is particularly disproportionate in its translation of votes into seats and this has a number of highly significant ramifications with regard to the composition and operation of parliament and political leadership.

The first-past-the-post system has generally delivered stability in the UK in that the leading party, even though it achieves less than 50 per cent share of vote, can gain a comfortable majority of seats in parliament. In Northern Ireland this less representative system has occasioned considerable 'tactical voting' where people will often vote for a candidate who would not be their first choice in an STV election in order to defeat a candidate to whom they are strongly opposed.

## Proportional Representation

### Single Transferable Vote (STV)

A number of proportional representation alternatives exist to the first past the post electoral model, which seek to ensure a direct, and close correlation between total votes cast for each party and the number of seats won. The first past the post system, properly referred to as simple plurality, is the one that is least connected to the principle of proportional representation.

The single transferable vote system (STV), used for local, European and Northern Ireland Assembly elections under the Northern Ireland Act 1998, is based on multi member constituencies in which voter preferences for candidates are expressed in numerical order. Voters rank candidates in order of preference (1 for their most preferred candidate, 2 for their second choice, etc). A quota is calculated by dividing the number of votes cast plus one by the number of seats available plus one. If a candidate has enough votes to reach the quota, he or she is elected. If the candidate has more votes than the quota, the surplus votes are taken and redistributed proportionately according to the voter's next choice.

The candidate with the least number of votes is eliminated, and their votes redistributed in the same way. The process continues until all available seats have been filled. A candidate can be elected under STV without reaching the quota, in circumstances where further re-distribution of votes would not alter the outcome.

### The d'Hondt Mechanism

Proportional representation has a role in the Northern Ireland Assembly beyond the election of Members to the Assembly. The d'Hondt system of proportional representation is the designated method for the appointment of Ministers in the Assembly and for the assignment of committee chairmanships.

The d'Hondt mechanism has its origins in Belgium where it was first applied in 1889 between the Flemings and Walloons to ensure representation for whichever ethnic group was in a minority. The formulae to allocate seats under the mechanism were also devised by a Belgian, H.R. Droop who produced the procedure for establishing the quota in multi member constituencies. The d'Hondt system takes the number of seats obtained by each party and divides them by one, two, three, four, etc. The ministries are then given to the parties with the twelve largest quotients ranked from the largest to the smallest quotient. Although, the majority party is favoured under d'Hondt the advantage is that minority interests also gain representation, a critical factor for the success of the new Assembly and power sharing in the Northern Ireland Executive. However it does make it unlikely that significantly smaller parties would be able to obtain a ministry under this system.

## The Office of the Chief Electoral Officer

The Chief Electoral Officer position is unique to Northern Ireland. He is an independent officer responsible for the conduct of all elections in Northern Ireland. The Chief Electoral Officer has no direct counterpart in Great Britain, where electoral registration and the conduct of all elections are primarily the responsibility of local authorities.

The Chief Electoral Officer is the registration and returning officer for each parliamentary constituency in Northern Ireland, and the returning officer for European parliamentary elections, Assembly elections and district council elections. He is responsible for the preparation of polling station schemes, the maintenance of election equipment and all other administrative matters relating to elections in Northern Ireland.

The Chief Electoral Officer has a small number of Deputy Electoral Officers and Assistant Electoral Officers to assist him, primarily in the compilation of the electoral register and related duties, but they also act as Deputy Returning Officers, except for local government elections where the Clerk of the particular Council is the ex-officio Returning Officer but acts under the control and supervision of the Chief Electoral Officer. The Chief Electoral Officer is supported by the Electoral Office for Northern Ireland in carrying out his statutory activities.

## The Electoral Office

Headquarters
15 Church Street, Belfast, BT1 1ER
Tel: 028 9024 5353
Web: www.electoralofficeni.gov.uk
Chief Electoral Officer: Denis Stanley
Tel: 028 9033 9955

**Area Electoral Offices**

*Foyle and East Londonderry*
20 Queen Street, Londonderry, BT48 7EQ
Tel: 028 7136 2761

*North Antrim and Mid Ulster*
9A Linenhall Street, Ballymoney, BT53 6DP
Tel: 028 2766 5052

*West Tyrone and Fermanagh and South Tyrone*
21 Kevlin Avenue, Omagh, BT78 1ER
Tel: 028 8224 3600

*Upper Bann, Newry and Armagh, South Down and Lagan Valley*
52 Bridge Street, Banbridge, BT32 3JU
Tel: 028 4066 2857

*East Antrim and South Antrim*
1-3 Portland Avenue, Glengormley, Newtownabbey, BT36 5EY
Tel: 028 9034 2263

*Strangford and North Down*
2B Regent Street, Newtownards, BT23 4LH
Tel: 028 9181 8576

*Belfast East, Belfast North, Belfast South and Belfast West*
6-10 William Street, Belfast, BT1 1PR
Tel: 028 9023 1443

### Electoral Fraud

Increasingly in recent years, there have been many allegations of various kinds of electoral fraud, the most common being 'vote stealing' by impersonation. Although the electoral authorities have failed to find evidence of systematic or wide ranging electoral fraud taking place, Northern Ireland elections now operate under tight regulations governing identification at the polling station. 2003 saw the compilation of a new electoral register, which required individuals to actively register their right to vote. Failure to do so would result in disenfranchisement.

**The Electoral Commission**

Seatem House, 28-32 Alfred Street, Belfast, BT2 8EN
Web: www.electoralcommission.org.uk
Head of The Electoral Commission (Northern Ireland):
Seamus Magee

The Electoral Commission is an independent body set up by the UK Parliament in 2000. Its aim is to gain public confidence and encourage people to take part in the democratic process within the United Kingdom by modernising the electoral process. Any group that wishes to become a registered political party must register with the Electoral Commission. The Electoral Commission also has a role in regulating all expenditure incurred by political parties for electoral purposes.

### Boundary Commission for Northern Ireland

Forestview, Purdy's Lane, Newtownbreda
Belfast, BT8 4AX
Tel: 028 9069 4800 / Fax: 028 9069 4801
Email: bcni@belfast.org.uk
Web: www.boundarycommission.org.uk

Chairman: Rt Hon Michael Martin, MP
Deputy Chairman: Justice Coghlin
Members: Richard Mackenzie, CB, Joan Ruddock, CBE
Secretary to the Commission: John Fisher

The Boundary Commission is an independent body which is required to make periodic reports on the number and design of Northern Ireland's electoral constituencies. These reports must be submitted to the Secretary of State not less than 8 or more than 12 years from the submission of the previous report. The latest recommendations of the Commission are currently out for the consultation and final recommendations will be published during 2005 *(see page 40 for details of provisional recommendations).*

## Political Parties

Northern Ireland has around 40 registered political parties although throughout the last 20 years electoral politics have been dominated by 4 or 5 major parties. The minor parties comprise in the main fringe unionist parties and socialist groups, along with a number of sectional interests.

There are two large unionist parties: the Ulster Unionist Party (UUP) and the Democratic Unionist Party (DUP). Two main parties also represent the nationalist community: the Social Democratic and Labour Party (SDLP) and Sinn Féin. In some sense there is symmetry between these alignments, with the UUP and SDLP appealing increasingly to middle-class and middle-ground unionists and nationalists respectively. The more aggressive and uncompromising DUP and Sinn Féin tend to attract more support among the working classes and young voters. The fifth biggest group, the Alliance Party, straddles the two political communities, although its support base has been severely eroded in recent years. The following is a list of all political parties registered in Northern Ireland with the Electoral Commission.

Alliance – The Alliance Party of Northern Ireland
Children's Party (The)
Community Awareness Party/Protecting Children
Congressional Party (The)
Conservative and Unionist Party (The)
Democratic Party (The)
Democratic Unionist Party – D.U.P.
Europe First
Flauntit.Net Internet Party (The)
Green Party

Labour (Federation of Labour Groups)
Liberal Unionist Party
National Front
New Party (The)
New World Socialist Green Party (The)
Newtownabbey Ratepayers Association
Northern Ireland Unionist Party
Northern Ireland Women's Coalition
Official Monster Raving Loony Party (The)
Party for True Democracy
People's Progressive Party (The)
Progressive Unionist Party of Northern Ireland
Real Democracy Party
Renaissance Independent Party of Europe (The)
SDLP (Social Democratic & Labour Party)
Sinn Féin
Socialist Environmental Alliance
Socialist Party (Northern Ireland)
Support the Ulster Hospital
Ulster Protestant League (The)
Ulster Third Way
Ulster Unionist Party (UUP)
United Kingdom Independence Party
United Kingdom Unionist Party U.K.U.P.
United Unionist Coalition
Vote for Yourself
Workers Party (The)
World
Your Party

## Political Parties Religious/Ethnic Spectrum

As a consequence of historical political divisions it is very difficult to attempt to show Northern Ireland parties on a traditional left-right spectrum. The parties themselves place tremendous emphasis on the constitutional issue of Northern Ireland in their manifestoes, leaving more traditional economic and social issues aside as secondary considerations. Some politicians would contend that their ideologies and policies do exist, but are overshadowed by 'sectarian politics', and that most people in Northern Ireland tend to vote according to religion and nationality, leaving less 'demand' for other policies.

**Catholic/Nationalist:** SDLP; Sinn Féin; Workers Party
**Centre/Other:** Alliance; Northern Ireland Women's Coalition
**Protestant/Unionist**: Ulster Unionist Party; DUP; Progressive Unionist Party; Northern Ireland Unionist Party; UK Unionist Party

## Pro/Anti Agreement Spectrum

The UUP is broadly pro-Agreement, but has a significant anti-Agreement faction, which gained in strength over the lifetime of the first Assembly. All of the nationalist parties represented in the Northern Ireland Assembly are pro-Agreement.

**Pro-Agreement**: Ulster Unionist Party; SDLP; Sinn Féin; Northern Ireland Women's Coalition; Alliance; Progressive Unionist Party
**Anti-Agreement:** DUP; United Kingdom Unionist Party; Northern Ireland Unionist Party

## Main Political Parties in Northern Ireland

### Democratic Unionist Party (DUP)

91 Dundela Avenue, Belfast, BT4 3BU
Tel: 028 9047 1155
Fax: 028 9047 1797
Email: info@dup.org.uk
Web: www.dup.org.uk

Leader: Rev Ian Paisley MP MEP (pictured)
Deputy: Peter Robinson MP
Secretary: Nigel Dodds MP
Chairperson: Maurice Morrow
President: Jim McClure
Chief Executive: Allan Ewart

The DUP is staunchly anti agreement, in contrast to the Ulster Unionists although sharing their core belief that Northern Ireland should remain within the United Kingdom. Founded in 1971 by the Rev Ian Paisley, replacing his Protestant Unionist Party the party is popularised by its uncompromising stance on the constitutional status of Northern Ireland as part of the UK and resistance towards co-operation with the Irish Republic.

The party currently holds six Westminster seats and won 30 Assembly seats in the 2003 Assembly elections to become the largest Unionist party, overtaking the Ulster Unionist Party. Their position was further enhanced by the decisions of Jeffrey Donaldson, Arlene Foster and Norah Beare to resign from the Ulster Unionist Party and join the DUP. The DUP was the only party to secure representation in all 18 constituencies.

Despite its opposition to the Agreement, and public stance of non-cooperation with Sinn Féin, the DUP accepted its Ministerial positions during the first Assembly and participated in the cross party committees.

After many years of leading the opposition to political change in Northern Ireland, the DUP is now for the first time Northern Ireland's largest political party and has acknowledged that it has a responsibility to table new proposals for political progress.

#### DUP Leadership

Ian Paisley is the leader of the DUP, MP for North Antrim since 1970 and was a popular MEP between 1979 and 2004, consistently topping the poll in European elections. Unyielding in his opposition to republicanism, he is vociferously critical of the peace process and the involvement of the Ulster Unionist party. As leader of the Free Presbyterian Church Dr Paisley is a staunch opponent of ecumenism and his attitude to the Roman Catholic faith draws much criticism from his opponents.

## DUP Elected Representation

**European Parliament:** Jim Allister MEP

**Westminster:** 6 MPs *(see pages 40-41 for details)*

**Northern Ireland Assembly:**
A full list of all DUP members elected to the Northern Ireland Assembly in the 2003 elections can be found on page 45.

**Local Government:**
DUP Councillors (A-Z by Council)
Total number of DUP Councillors: 130

*Antrim Borough Council (5)*
Wilson Clyde; Samuel Dunlop; Brian Graham; William Harkness; John Smyth.

*Ards Borough Council (9)*
Margaret Craig; Robin Drysdale; George Ennis; David Gilmore Hamilton Gregory; Hamilton Lawther; William Montgomery Jim Shannon; Terence Williams.

*Armagh City and District Council (4)*
Paul Berry; Heather Black; Freda Donnelly; William Irwin.

*Ballymena Borough Council (11)*
Elizabeth Adger; James Alexander; Martin Clarke; Samuel Gaston; Roy Gillespie; Samuel Hanna; Maurice Mills; Thomas Nicholl; Hubert Nicholl; Robin Stirling; David Tweed

*Ballymoney Borough Council (8)*
Frank Campbell; Cecil Cousley; John Finlay; Robert Halliday Bill Kennedy; Ian Stevenson; Mervyn Storey; Robert Wilson.

*Banbridge District Council (5)*
Norah Beare; David Herron; Stephen Herron; Jim McElroy; Wilfred McFadden.

*Belfast City Council (10)*
Wallace Browne; Ian Crozier; Nigel Dodds; Nelson McCausland; Elaine McMillen; Robin Newton; Ruth Patterson; Eric Smyth; Harry Toan; Sammy Wilson

*Carrickfergus Borough Council (6)*
William Ashe; May Beattie; Terence Clements; David Hilditch James McClurg; Patricia McKinney.

*Castlereagh Borough Council (9)*
John Beattie; Joanne Bunting; Claire Ennis; John Norris; Iris Robinson; Peter Robinson; Mark Robinson; Vivienne Stevenson; Jim White.

*Coleraine Borough Council (7)*
Maurice Bradley; William Creelman; Timothy Deans; Phyllis Fielding; James McClure; Adrian McQuillan; Desmond Stewart.

*Cookstown District Council (2)*
Anne McCrea; Ian McCrea.

*Craigavon Borough Council (6)*
Jonathan Bell; Alan Carson; Stephen Moutray; David Simpson Robert Smith; Woolsey Smith.

*Derry City Council (4)*
Gregory Campbell; Mildred Garfield; William Hay; Joe Miller.

*Down District Council (2)*
William Dick; Jim Wells

*Dungannon and South Tyrone Borough Council (3)*
Roger Burton; Johnston McIlwrath; Maurice Morrow.

*Fermanagh District Council (2)*
Joe Dodds; Bert Johnston

*Larne Borough Council (4)*
Winston Fulton; Bobby McKee; Gregg McKeen; Rachel Rea.

*Limavady Borough Council (2)*
Leslie Cubitt; George Robinson.

*Lisburn City Council (7)*
Cecil Calvert; Jonathan Craig; Joe Lockhart; Lorraine Martin Edwin Poots; Paul Porter; James Tinsley.

*Magherafelt District Council (3)*
Thomas Catherwood; Paul McLean; William McCrea.

*Moyle District Council (3)*
George Hartin; Gardiner Kane; David McAllister.

*Newry and Mourne District Council (1)*
William Burns.

*Newtownabbey Borough Council (8)*
William de Courcy; Paul Girvan; Nigel Hamilton; Pamela Hunter; Victor Robinson; John Mann; Arthur Templeton; Dineen Walker.

*North Down Borough Council (5)*
Ruby Cooling; Gordon Dunne; Alexander Easton; Alan Graham; John Montgomery.

*Omagh District Council (2)*
Thomas Buchanan.

*Strabane District Council (3)*
Allan Bresland; John Donnell; Thomas Kerrigan.

## Sinn Féin (SF)

51/55 Falls Road, Belfast, BT12 4PD
Tel: 028 9022 3000
Fax: 028 9022 3001
Email: sinnfein@iol.ie
Web: www.sinnfein.ie

President: Gerry Adams MP (pictured)
Vice-President: Pat Doherty MP
Chairperson: Mitchel McLaughlin
General Secretary: Robbie Smyth

Representing republicanism within the Northern Ireland political spectrum, Sinn Féin's share of the catholic/nationalist vote has continued to rise, attracting more first preference votes than the SDLP, and overtaking that party in the 2003 Assembly elections. Sinn Féin dates its all-island origins from the independence movement that gathered momentum at the end of World War I in 1918. Linked with the Provisional IRA, Sinn Féin followed a policy of abstentionism in politics until the 1980s, and the party continues to abstain from taking its Westminster seats.

A significant shift in party policy occurred in 1998 when members voted to change the party's constitution and allowed elected party representatives to take their seats in a devolved Northern Ireland Assembly. They have not, however, taken their seats on the Policing Board. Whilst Unionist scepticism remains about the durability of Sinn Féin's commitment to the peace process, recent movement on decommissioning by the IRA has helped demonstrate the party's commitment to constitutional politics.

**Sinn Féin Leadership**
Gerry Adams, President of Sinn Féin since 1990, has been credited with the transformation of Sinn Féin from a political vehicle representing the aims of the IRA to a sophisticated well-organised political party. An MP for West Belfast from 1982 to 1992 and again from 1997, he acknowledged as early as 1980 that Republican aims were unlikely to be satisfied through military means alone.

## Sinn Féin Elected Representation

**European Parliament:** Bairbre de Brun, MEP
**Westminster:** 4 MPs *(see pages 40-41 for details)*
**Dail Eireann:** 5 seats

**Northern Ireland Assembly:**
A full list of all SF members elected to the Northern Ireland Assembly in the 2003 elections can be found on 45

**Local Government:** Sinn Féin Councillors (A-Z by Council)
Total Number of Sinn Féin Councillors: 108

*Antrim Borough Council (2):* Martin McManus; Martin Meehan.

*Armagh City and District Council (5)*
Paul Corrigan; Brian Cunningham; Pat McNamee; Pat O'Rawe Cathy Rafferty.

*Ballymoney Borough Council (1)* Philip McGuigan.

*Belfast City Council (14)* Gerald Brophy; Michael Browne; Máire Cush; Tom Hartley; Danny Lavery; Alex Maskey; Paul Maskey; Chrissie McAuley; Fra McCann; Margaret McClenaghan; Marie Moore; Eoin O'Broin; Joseph O'Donnell; Gerard O'Neill.

*Coleraine Borough Council (1)* Billy Leonard

*Cookstown District Council (6)*
Seamus Campbell; Dessie Grimes; Pearse McAleer; Michael McIvor; John McNamee; Oliver Molloy.

*Craigavon Borough Council (4)*
Maurice Magill; Brian McKeown; Francie Murray; John O'Dowd.

*Derry City Council (10)*
Peter Anderson; Cathal Crumley; Lynn Fleming; Paul Fleming; Tony Hassan; Gerry MacLochlainn; Maeve McLaughlin; Barney O'Hagan; Gearoid O'hEara; William Page.

*Down District Council (4)* Francis Braniff; Willie Clarke; Eamonn McConvey; Francis McDowell.

*Dungannon and South Tyrone Borough Council (8)*
Desmond Donnelly; Seamus Flanagan; Phelim Gildernew; Michael Gillespie; Sean McGuigan; Larry McLarnon; Francie Molloy; Barry Monteith.

*Fermanagh District Council (9)* Joe Cassidy; Pat Cox; Patrick Gilgunn; Stephen Huggett; Ruth Lynch; Robin Martin; Brian McCaffrey; Gerry McHugh, Thomas O'Reilly.

*Limavady Borough Council (4)* Anne Brolly; Brenda Chivers; Marion Donaghy; Martin McGuigan

*Lisburn City Council (4)*
Paul Butler; Micheal Ferguson; Sue Ramsey; Veronica Willis.

*Magherafelt District Council (7)*
Patrick Groogan; Oliver Hughes; Sean McPeake; Sean Kerr; Hugh Mullan; Seamus O'Brien; Seamus O'Neill.

*Moyle District Council (1)* Monica Digney.

*Newry and Mourne District Council (12)* Colman Burns; Charlie Casey; Brendan Curran; Terry Hearty; Breandan Lewis; Elena Martin; Marian Mathers; Jimmy McCreesh; Packie McDonald; Pat McGinn; Mick Murphy; Michael Ruane.

*Newtownabbey Borough Council (1)* Briege Meehan.

*Omagh District Council (8)* Sean Begley; Sean Clarke; Damien Curran; Peter Kelly; Barney McAleer; Michael McAnespie; Barry McElduff; Patrick Watters.

*Strabane District Council (7)*
Ivan Barr; Daniel Breslin; Eamon McGarvey; Claire McGill; Charlie McHugh; Brian McMahon; Jarlath McNulty.

## Ulster Unionist Party (UUP)

UlsterUnionists

Cunningham House,
429 Holywood Road
Belfast, BT4 2LN
Tel: 028 9076 5500
Fax: 028 9076 9419
Email: uup@uup.org
Web: www.uup.org

**Westminster:**
House of Commons, Westminster, London, SW1A 0AA
Tel: 020 7219 0505 / Fax: 020 7219 1575
Email: whiteb@parliament.uk

**Washington, USA:**
Ulster Unionist Party, North American Bureau
1919 Pennsylvania Avenue, NW, Suite 200
Washington, DC 20006, USA
Tel: (202) 828-9866 / Fax: (202) 223-2278
Email: aws.uupna@earthlink.net

Leader: David Trimble MP (pictured)
Deputy: John Taylor
President: Lord Rogan
Vice-President: Lord Maginnis of Drumglass
Vice-President: Sir Reg Empey
Vice-President: Jim Nicholson MEP
Vice-President: Cllr Jim Rodgers
Vice-President: May Steele
Chairman of Executive Committee: James Cooper
Vice-Chairman of Executive Committee: David Campbell
Honorary Secretary: Michael McGimpsey MLA
Honorary Secretary: Danny Kennedy
Honorary Secretary: Dermot Nesbitt
Honorary Secretary: Joan Carson
Honorary Treasurer: Jack Allen OBE
Assistant Honorary Treasurer: Eddie Keown

The Ulster Unionist Party is the oldest political party in Northern Ireland. Its central cause is the maintenance of Northern Ireland's position within the UK and the legitimacy of Northern Ireland as a distinct political, economic and cultural entity. While supportive of the co-operative relationships with the Irish Republic, the UUP prefers cross border matters to be considered within the economic rather than political arena.

## UUP Leadership

David Trimble, MP for the Upper Bann constituency was elected leader of the Ulster Unionist party in 1995. Throughout his career David Trimble has moved along the spectrum of Unionism from being a member of the loyalist Vanguard movement in the 1970s, to a more pragmatic leader supporting the Good Friday Agreement and accepting limited cross border bodies. In 1998 he and John Hume, then leader of the SDLP shared the Noble Peace Prize for their efforts in securing the Agreement. David Trimble has undergone much criticism from Unionists, both within his own party and from outside of it as a result of the number of 'concessions' he has made to political opponents, which it has been argued have weakened the cause of Unionism.

## UUP Elected Representation

**European Parliament:** Jim Nicholson MEP

**Westminster:** 4 MPs *(see pages 40-41 for details)*

**Members of House of Lords**
Lord Cooke of Islandreagh
The Rt Hon The Lord Kilclooney of Armagh
Lord Maginnis of Drumglass
The Rt Hon The Lord Molyneaux of Killead KBE
Lord Laird of Artigarvan
Lord Rogan of Lower Iveagh
Westminster: Tel: 020 7219 5679

**Northern Ireland Assembly:**
A full list of all UUP members elected to the Northern Ireland Assembly in the 2003 elections can be found on page 45.

**Local Government:**
Ulster Unionist Party Councillors (A-Z by Council)
Total number of UUP Councillors: 149

*Antrim Borough Council (8)*
Adrian Cochrane-Watson; Paddy Marks; Paul Michael; Stephen Nicholl; Mervyn Rea; Drew Ritchie; Roy Thompson; Edgar Wallace.

*Ards Borough Council (8)*
Angus Carson; Ronnie Ferguson; Robert Gibson; Tom Hamilton; Jeffrey Magill; John Shields; Philip Smith; David Smyth.

*Armagh City and District Council (7)*
James Clayton; Evelyn Corry; Sylvia McRoberts; Charles Rollston; Eric Speers; Jim Speers; Robert Turner.

*Ballymena Borough Council (7)*
Neil Armstrong; Peter Brown; David Clyde; James Currie; Joseph McKernan; William McNeilly; Lexie Scott.

*Ballymoney Borough Council (5)*
Joe Gaston; William Logan; Tom McKeown; John Ramsay; James Simpson.

*Banbridge District Council (6)*
Joan Baird; Derrick Bell; Ian Burns; John Hanna; John Ingram; William Martin

*Belfast City Council (11)*
Dr Ian Adamson; David Browne; Jim Clarke; Margaret Clarke; Margaret Crooks; Alan Crowe; Sir Reg Empey; Dr Chris McGimpsey; Michael McGimpsey; Jim Rodgers; Robert Stoker.

*Carrickfergus Borough Council (4)*
Roy Beggs; Darin Ferguson; Eric Ferguson; Gwen Wilson.

*Castlereagh Borough Council (5)*
Michael Copeland; David Drysdale; Cecil Hall; Michael Henderson; Barbara McBurney.

*Coleraine Borough Council (9)*
David Barbour; Toye Black; Olive Church
Norman Hillis; Elizabeth Johnston; William A. King;
David McClarty; Robert McPherson; Jim Watt.

*Cookstown District Council (3)*
Sam Glasgow; Walter Greer; Trevor Wilson.

*Craigavon Borough Council (7)*
Sydney Cairns; Fred Crowe; Meta Crozier;
Samuel Gardiner; Arnold Hatch; George Savage;
Kenneth Twyble.

*Derry City Council (2)* Ernest Hamilton; Mary Hamilton.

*Down District Council (6)*
Peter Bowles; Robert Burgess; Albert Colmer;
Gerald Douglas; Jack McIlheron; Edward Rea.

*Dungannon and South Tyrone Borough Council (6)*
Norman Badger; Walter Cuddy; Jim Hamilton; Derek Irwin;
Lord Maginnis of Drumglass; Robert Mulligan.

*Fermanagh District Council (7)*
Harold Andrews; Tom Elliott; Wilson Elliott; Raymond Ferguson;
Robert Irvine; Bertie Kerr; Cecil Noble.

*Larne Borough Council (3)*
Roy Beggs; Dr Brian Dunn; Joan Drummond.

*Limavady Borough Council (3)*
Jackie Dolan; Jack Rankin; Edwin Stevenson.

*Lisburn City Council (12)*
David W Archer; T David Archer; James Baird; Billy Bell;
Ronnie Crawford; Ivan Davis; Jim Dillon; Ned Falloon;
Bill Gardiner-Watson; Sam Johnston; Harry Lewis;
William Ward.

*Magherafelt District Council (2)* John Junkin; George Sheils

*Moyle Borough Council (3)*
William Graham; Helen Harding; Robert McIlroy

*Newry and Mourne District Council (4)*
Isaac Hanna; Danny Kennedy; Andrew Moffett; Henry Reilly.

*Newtownabbey Borough Council (8)* Jim Bingham;
Janet Crilly; Barbara Gilliland; Ivan Hunter; Vera McWilliam;
Ken Robinson; Vi Scott; Edward Turkington.

*North Down Borough Council (8)*
Irene Cree; Leslie Cree; Roy Davies; Roberta Dunlop; Ian Henry;
Ellie McKay; Diana Peacocke; Marion Smith

*Omagh District Council (3)* Reuben McKelvey; Allan Rainey;
Robert Wilson.

*Strabane District Council (2)* James Emery; Derek Hussey.

## Social Democratic and Labour Party (SDLP)

121 Ormeau Road, Belfast, BT7 1SH
Tel: 028 9024 7700
Fax: 028 9023 6699
Email: sdlp@indigo.ie
Web: www.sdlp.ie

Leader: Mark Durkan (pictured)
Deputy: Alasdair McDonnell
General Secretary: Gerry Cosgrove
Chairperson: Patricia Lewsley

For the past 30 years, the SDLP had been recognised as the main nationalist party attracting the majority of the 'Catholic' vote. Recent elections have seen Sinn Féin erode the position of the SDLP, and in the 2003 Assembly elections Sinn Féin comfortably overtook the SDLP as the largest nationalist party.

Founded in 1970 by a group including John Hume and the socialist Gerry Fitt following the civil rights agitation, the SDLP sought to replace the old Nationalist party with a more dynamic version of politics. The SDLP supports the principle of Irish unity advocating the achievement of this through exclusively constitutional political means and the principle of consent of the majority. The SDLP is highly supportive of the Good Friday Agreement.

### SDLP Leadership

Mark Durkan stood unopposed as leader of the SDLP in succession to John Hume and was subsequently elected Deputy First Minister on 6 November 2001.

Previously Mark Durkan was Chairperson of the SDLP from 1990-1995 and a Member of the Forum for Peace and Reconciliation from 1994 until 1996. Durkan was also one of the SDLP's chief negotiators at the inter-party talks leading to the Good Friday Agreement and was widely regarded as being the principal author of the Good Friday Agreement.

### SDLP Elected Representation

**Westminster:** 3 MPs *(see pages 40-41 for details)*

**Northern Ireland Assembly:**
A full list of all SDLP members elected to the Northern Ireland Assembly in the 2003 elections can be found on page 46.

**Local Government:**
SDLP Councillors (A-Z by Council)
Total number of SDLP Councillors: 113

*Antrim Borough Council (4):* Thomas Burns; Oran Keenan;
Bobby Loughran; Donovan McClelland.

*Armagh City and District Council (6)*
Pat Brannigan; Anna Brolly; John Campbell; Tom Canavan;
Tommy Kavanagh; James McKernan.

*Ballymena Borough Council (4)*
Margaret Gribben; Seamus Laverty; PJ McAvoy; Declan O'Loan.

*Ballymoney Borough Council (2)*
Harry Connolly; Malachy McCamphill.

*Banbridge District Council (3)*
Seamus Doyle; Pat McAleenan; Catherine McDermott.

*Belfast City Council (9)* Alex Attwood; Patrick Convery; Carmel Hanna; Alban Maginness; Patrick McCarthy; Catherine Molloy; Martin Morgan; Peter O'Reilly; Margaret Walsh.

*Castlereagh Borough Council (2)* Brian Hanvey; Rosaleen Hughes

*Coleraine Borough Council (3)*
John Dallat; Gerry McLaughlin; Eamon Mullan.

*Cookstown District Council (4)*
Mary Baker; Peter Cassidy; James McGarvey; Patsy McGlone

*Craigavon Borough Council (7)*
Kieran Corr; Ignatius Fox; Dolores Kelly; Patricia Mallon; Mary McAlinden; Nuala McAlinden; Tony Elliott.

*Derry City Council (13)* Mary Bradley; Sean Carr; Jim Clifford; Thomas Conway; Gerard Diver; Shaun Gallagher; John Kerr; Kathleen McCloskey; Jim McKeever; William O'Connell; Helen Quigley; Pat Ramsey; Martin Reilly.

*Down District Council (9)*
Peter Craig; Dermot Curran; John Doris; Peter Fitzpatrick; Anne McAleenan; Carmel O'Boyle; Eamonn O'Neill; Margaret Ritchie; Patrick Toman.

*Dungannon and South Tyrone (4)*
Jim Cavanagh; Vincent Currie; Patsy Daly; Anthony McGonnell.

*Fermanagh District Council (4)*
Frank Britton; Gerry Gallagher; Fergus McQuillan; John O'Kane.

*Larne Borough Council (2)* Daniel O'Connor; Martin Wilson.

*Limavady Borough Council (4)*
Michael Carten; Michael Coyle; Dessie Lowry; Gerard Mullan.

*Lisburn City Council (3)* Patricia Lewsley; William McDonnell; Peter O'Hagan

*Magherafelt District Council (3)* Kathleen Lagan; Joseph McBride; Patrick McErlean.

*Moyle District Council (4)* Madeline Black; Christine Blaney; Catherine McCambridge; Michael Molloy.

*Newry and Mourne District Council (10)*
PJ Bradley; Paul McKibbin; Michael Carr; Michael Cole; John Fee; John Feehan; Frank Feeley; John McArdle; Pat McElroy; Josephine O'Hare.

*Newtownabbey Borough Council (2)*
Noreen McClelland; Tommy McTeague.

*Omagh District Council (6)*
Joe Byrne; Josephine Deehan; Patrick McDonnell; Liam McQuaid; Gerry O'Doherty; Seamus Shields.

*Strabane District Council (4)*
Ann Bell; Tom McBride; Eugene McMenamin; Bernadette McNamee.

## The Alliance Party of Northern Ireland

Alliance — The Alliance Party of Northern Ireland

88 University Street
Belfast, BT7 1HE
Tel: 028 9032 4274
Fax: 028 9033 3147
Email: alliance@allianceparty.org
Web: www.allianceparty.org

Leader: David Ford (pictured)
Deputy: Eileen Bell
General Secretary: Stephen Farry
President: Tom Ekin
Chairperson: Trevor Lunn

The Alliance Party describes itself as a non-sectarian political group, dedicated to co-operation between all the people of Northern Ireland. The party was formed in 1970 to give political expression to those who felt that nationalist and unionist political parties did not reflect their views. Alliance draws its members from all religious and political perspectives.

The 2003 Assembly elections saw Alliance's share of the 1st preference vote decrease significantly to 3.7% from 6.5% in 1998. The party did, however, retain all 6 seats it had held by gaining transfers from other candidates. Despite running candidates in successive Westminster elections, the Alliance Party has never held a Westminster seat.

**Alliance Party Leadership**
The Alliance Party is led by David Ford, a member of Antrim Borough Council since 1993 and elected Assembly Member for South Antrim. He was elected leader of the Alliance party in October 2001, following roles as Party General Secretary from 1990-1998 and Chief Whip.

## Alliance Elected Representation

**Northern Ireland Assembly:**

A full list of all Alliance members elected to the Northern Ireland Assembly in the 2003 elections can be found on page 46.

**Local Government:**

Alliance Party Councillors (A-Z by Council)
Total number of Alliance Party Councillors: 28

*Ards Borough Council (4)*
Linda Cleland; Jim McBriar; Alan McDowell; Kieran McCarthy.

*Banbridge District Council (1)*
Frank McQuaid.

*Belfast City Council (3)*
David Alderdice; Thomas Ekin; Naomi Long.

*Carrickfergus Borough Council (5)*
Robert Cavan; Janet Crampsey; Stewart Dickson; Shireen Bell, Sean Neeson

*Castlereagh Borough Council (4)*
Sara Duncan; Michael Long; Peter Osborne; Geraldine Rice.

*Larne Borough Council (2)*
John Mathews; Geraldine Mulvenna.

*Lisburn City Council (3)*
Elizabeth Campbell; Seamus Close; Trevor Lunn.

*Newtownabbey Borough Council (1)*
Lynn Frazer.

*North Down Borough Council (5)*
Stephen Farry; Marsden Fitzsimons; Tony Hill; Susan O'Brien Anne Wilson.

## United Kingdom Unionist Party (UKUP)

10 Central Avenue
Bangor, BT20 3AF
Tel: 028 9147 9860
Web: www.ukup.org
Email: info@ukup.org

Leader: Robert McCartney (pictured)

Founded by Robert McCartney in 1996 the UKUP campaigned for a No vote in the Referendum, and returned 5 members to the first Assembly in 1998. In January 1999, 4 members left the party, leaving the UKUP with Robert McCartney as its sole representative in the Assembly. He was also the only candidate returned for the party in the 2003 election where overall support for the party fell. The party is staunchly unionist believing the maintenance of the union to be 'in the best interests of all of the people of Northern Ireland'.

## UKUP Elected Representation

**Northern Ireland Assembly:**

Robert McCartney

**Local Government:**

Total number of UKUP Councillors: 2

*North Down Borough Council (2)*
Bill Keery; Valerie Kinghan

## Progressive Unionist Party (PUP)

182 Shankill Road, Belfast, BT13 2BH
Tel: 028 9032 6233 / Fax: 028 9024 9602
Email: central@pup-ni.org.uk
Web: www.pup-ni.org.uk

Leader: David Ervine (pictured)
Secretary: William Mitchell
Chairperson: William Smyth

Formed in 1977, the Progressive Unionist Party seeks to represent loyalist working class voters and is linked to the paramilitary UVF. The party has adopted a pro agreement stance believing that there must be 'sharing of responsibility' between Unionists and Nationalists, whilst maintaining their firm belief in the Union with Great Britain.

## PUP Elected Representation

**Northern Ireland Assembly:**

David Ervine

**Local Government:**

PUP Councillors (A-Z by Council)
Total number of PUP Councillors: 4

*Belfast City Council (3)*
David Ervine; Billy Hutchinson; Hugh Smyth

*Castlereagh Borough Council (1)* Thomas Sandford

## Northern Ireland Women's Coalition (NIWC)

50 University Street, Belfast, BT7 1HB
Tel: 028 9023 3100 / Fax: 028 9024 0021
Email: info@niwc.org
Web: www.niwc.org

Leader: Monica McWilliams (pictured)
Chairperson: Helen Crickard
Contact: Elizabeth Byrne McCullough

The Northern Ireland Women's Coalition, which is strongly pro-Agreement, was established in 1996 with the aim of putting forward an agenda of 'reconciliation through dialogue, accommodation and inclusion' and ensuring that women were represented in the Forum talks on the future of Northern Ireland. Like Alliance the party seeks to draw members from all religious and political persuasions, but with an emphasis on the involvement of women. Leader Monica McWilliams, along with Jane Morrice represented the Women's Coalition in the first Assembly but both were unsuccessful in the 2003 election campaign.

## NIWC Elected Representation

**Local Government:**

Total number of NIWC Councillors: 1

*North Down Borough Council (1)*
Patricia Wallace

## Northern Ireland Unionist Party (NIUP)

c/o 2B Ann Street, Newtownards, BT23 7AB
Tel: 028 9181 0484
Email: info@niup.org
Web: www.niup.org
Leader: Cedric Wilson

Following the resignation of four Assembly members from the UKUP the NIUP was formed on the 5 January 1999. The Northern Ireland Unionist Party is pro union and anti agreement. The party is led by Cedric Wilson. The party which describes its position as 'principled unionism' unsuccessfully contested the 2003 Assembly elections and will not be represented in any new Assembly.

## Green Party

537 Antrim Road, Belfast, BT15 3BU
Tel: 028 9077 6731
Email: vote@greens-in.org
Web: www.greens-in.org
Leader: John Barry

The Green Party has contested Northern Ireland elections since 1990, albeit with very little success. Despite running candidates in most elections, the party remains among the smallest in Northern Ireland, campaigning on ecological and environmental issues. Most recently, Lindsay Whitcroft stood for the party in the 2004 European election, but received less than 1% of the first preference vote.

## The Conservative Party

PO Box 537
Belfast, BT16 1YF
Conservative Party Northern Ireland Chairman:
Julian Robertson

The Conservative Party is the only mainstream political party to contest elections in all four parts of the United Kingdom.

In the 1980s there was pressure within the Conservative Party to stand candidates in Northern Ireland elections. A small number of Conservative Councillors have previously been elected in North Down, but the party was unsuccessful in the 2003 Assembly elections and has currently no elected representation in Northern Ireland.

## Workers' Party

6 Springfield Road, Belfast, BT12 7AG
Tel: 028 9032 8663
Fax: 028 9033 3475
Email: info@workers-party.org
Web: www.workers-party.org

Northern Ireland Secretary: Thomas Owens
President: Sean Garland
General Secretary: John Lowry

The Workers' Party has republican origins and is strongly socialist. Formed after a split within Sinn Féin in the 1970s it proceeded to adopt a Marxist ideology. The party suffered a split in 1992. The Workers Party has seen its share of the vote decrease substantially in recent elections, and currently has no political representation at any level.

# Election Results

Northern Ireland is unique within the United Kingdom in that it conducts all its elections, except those to the Westminster Parliament, by proportional representation.

## Introduction

The legislative and institutional framework of the electoral system for Northern Ireland is also unique in a number of aspects within the UK. All elections and electoral matters, including the franchise and electoral registration are excepted matters, and therefore remain the responsibility of the Government at Westminster regardless of devolution.

Four types of election are held in Northern Ireland:

- Local government;
- Northern Ireland Assembly;
- Westminster parliament;
- European parliament.

Proportional representation, the single transferable vote (STV), is used for all elections except Westminster where, in keeping with the rest of the UK, simple plurality, the 'first past the post' system is applied. Although arguably less democratic than STV, 'first past the post' has continued to be favoured by successive governments as this electoral approach provides a successful UK government with a substantial majority of seats.

## Electoral Results and Analysis

Northern Ireland has had 18 elections during the period 1982-2003, and despite their plentiful nature each has been vigorously contested and generated keen interest in the community. Whilst voting patterns have shown strong adherence to traditional allegiances, the longer-term trend would suggest that nationalist parties are gaining ground on their unionist counterparts and centre parties are finding it difficult to hold their votes against more uncompromising rivals in both communities.

An interesting development within the electoral landscape has been the emerging struggle for dominance not only between, but also within the two religio-political groupings, i.e. between UUP and DUP, SDLP and Sinn Féin. At present, this is a struggle which has resulted in the two more 'extreme' parties coming out strongest - the DUP on the unionist side and Sinn Féin on the nationalist side.

The table below shows each party's electoral results for all major elections since 1982. This includes elections to the various political initiatives such as the Assembly of 1982 and the Forum of 1996. It excludes by-elections, including the multiple by-elections of 1986, as they are not as significant in terms of long-term trends.

**Northern Ireland Elections 1982-2003**
**Parties' share of vote (%)**

| Year | Election to | UUP | DUP | SDLP | SF | All | PUP | NIWC | UKUP | Other |
|---|---|---|---|---|---|---|---|---|---|---|
| **1982** | Assembly | 29.7 | 23.0 | 18.8 | 10.1 | 9.3 | - | - | - | 9.1 |
| **1983** | Westminster | 34.0 | 20.0 | 18.0 | 13.4 | 8.0 | - | - | - | 6.6 |
| **1984** | European | 21.5 | 33.6 | 22.1 | 13.3 | 5.0 | - | - | - | 4.5 |
| **1985** | Local Government | 29.5 | 24.3 | 17.8 | 11.8 | 7.1 | - | - | - | 9.5 |
| **1987** | Westminster | 37.8 | 11.7 | 21.1 | 11.4 | 10.0 | 0.9 | - | - | 7.1 |
| **1989** | Local Government | 31.3 | 17.7 | 21.0 | 11.2 | 6.9 | - | - | - | 11.9 |
| **1989** | European | 22.2 | 30.0 | 25.5 | 9.2 | 5.2 | - | - | - | 7.9 |
| **1992** | Westminster | 34.5 | 13.1 | 23.5 | 10.0 | 8.7 | - | - | - | 10.3 |
| **1993** | Local Government | 29.4 | 17.3 | 22.0 | 12.4 | 7.6 | - | - | - | 11.3 |
| **1994** | European | 23.8 | 29.2 | 28.9 | 9.9 | 4.1 | - | - | - | 4.1 |
| **1996** | NI Forum | 24.2 | 18.8 | 21.4 | 15.5 | 6.5 | 3.5 | 1.0 | 3.6 | 5.5 |
| **1997** | Westminster | 32.7 | 13.6 | 24.1 | 16.1 | 8.0 | 1.4 | 0.4 | 1.6 | 2.1 |
| **1997** | Local Government | 27.9 | 15.6 | 20.6 | 16.9 | 6.6 | 2.2 | 0.5 | 0.5 | 9.2 |
| **1998** | Assembly | 21.3 | 18.1 | 22.0 | 17.6 | 6.5 | 2.6 | 1.6 | 4.5 | 5.8 |
| **1999** | European | 17.6 | 28.4 | 28.1 | 17.3 | 2.1 | 3.3 | - | 3.0 | 0.2 |
| **2001** | Westminster | 26.8 | 22.5 | 21.0 | 21.7 | 3.6 | 0.6 | 0.4 | 1.7 | 1.7 |
| **2001** | Local Government | 22.9 | 21.4 | 19.4 | 20.6 | 5.1 | 1.6 | 0.4 | 0.6 | 8.0 |
| **2003** | Assembly | 22.7 | 25.7 | 17.0 | 23.5 | 3.7 | 1.2 | 0.8 | 0.8 | 4.6 |

## Northern Ireland Westminster Elections

In Northern Ireland the law governing Westminster parliamentary elections is the Representation of the People Act 1983 as amended. The number of Westminster constituencies is determined by the Boundary Commission for Northern Ireland. *(Details on the Boundary Commission can be found on page 62).*

Northern Ireland currently returns 18 MPs to Westminster out of a total for the United Kingdom of 635. MPs are elected under the first-past-the-post electoral system. From its conception under the Government of Ireland Act, 1920, until 1983 it had just 12 MPs. In 1983 the number of MPs was reconsidered by the Boundary Commission and five extra seats were created. These were contested for the first time in the June 1983 general election. In 1995, the Boundary Commission examined the situation again and created a further seat for Northern Ireland, bringing the total to eighteen for the election of May 1997.

Northern Ireland's MPs until recently were somewhat of an anomaly within the British political system. During the existence of the Stormont government, Northern Ireland MPs were not allowed to rise in Westminster matters that came under the remit of the Stormont government, a convention that was strongly criticised by many. Legislation passed in Westminster has tended to exclude Northern Ireland, which has had its own customised version of each Westminster Act. This has resulted in Northern Ireland legislation differing from the rest of the UK, perhaps most notably in recent years, the Provision of Abortion Act, which at present is in effect everywhere in the UK except Northern Ireland.

**Westminster MPs as elected in 2001**

| Constituency | Name | Party |
|---|---|---|
| Belfast East | Peter Robinson | DUP |
| Belfast North | Nigel Dodds | DUP |
| Belfast South | Rev Martin Smyth | UUP |
| Belfast West | Gerry Adams | SF |
| East Antrim | Roy Beggs | UUP |
| East Londonderry | Gregory Campbell | DUP |
| Fermanagh & South Tyrone | Michelle Gildernew | SF |
| Foyle | John Hume | SDLP |
| Lagan Valley | Jeffrey Donaldson* | UUP |
| Mid Ulster | Martin McGuinness | SF |
| Newry and Armagh | Séamus Mallon | SDLP |
| North Antrim | Rev Ian Paisley | DUP |
| North Down | Sylvia Hermon | UUP |
| South Antrim | David Burnside | UUP |
| South Down | Eddie McGrady | SDLP |
| Strangford | Iris Robinson | DUP |
| West Tyrone | Pat Doherty | SF |
| Upper Bann | David Trimble | UUP |

*Jeffrey Donaldson subsequently joined the DUP

*(Contact details for Westminster MPs can be found earlier in this chapter on page 40-41).*

The performance of the principal parties in Northern Ireland in Westminster elections can be seen in the table below. The Ulster Unionists, the SDLP, the DUP, the Alliance Party and Sinn Féin have tended to dominate Westminster elections. However, the Alliance Party is the only one of the five never to have won a Westminster seat, despite capturing up to 12 per cent of the total vote on occasions.

**Northern Ireland Westminster Elections 1979-2001: Parties' % share of vote**

| Party | 1979 | 1983 | 1987 | 1992 | 1997 | 2001 |
|---|---|---|---|---|---|---|
| UUP | 36.6 | 34.0 | 37.8 | 34.5 | 32.7 | 26.8 |
| SDLP | 18.2 | 17.9 | 21.1 | 23.5 | 24.1 | 21.0 |
| DUP | 10.2 | 20.0 | 11.7 | 13.1 | 13.6 | 22.5 |
| SF | - | 13.4 | 11.4 | 10.0 | 16.1 | 21.7 |
| All | 11.9 | 8.0 | 10.0 | 8.7 | 8.0 | 3.6 |
| WP | - | 2.0 | 2.6 | 0.5 | 0.3 | 0.3 |
| PUP | - | - | - | - | 1.4 | 0.6 |
| NIWC | - | - | - | - | 0.4 | 0.4 |
| UKUP | - | - | | - | 1.6 | 1.7 |
| Others | 23.1 | 4.7 | 5.4 | 9.7 | 1.8 | 1.4 |
| Turnout % | 68.4 | 73.3 | 67.4 | 69.7 | 67.1 | 68.0 |

The table of seats gained, shown below, reflects the two-party battle within unionism and the similar contest between the two nationalist parties. In 1992 the Ulster Unionists and SDLP enjoyed the majority of votes from their respective communities, but by 2001 the DUP and Sinn Féin had caught up, Sinn Féin overtaking the SDLP for the first time. Smaller parties usually suffer under the first-past-the-post electoral system in Westminster elections, although the figures have previously shown one or two seats going to independents (nationalist or unionist), and unionist breakaway parties such as James Kilfedder's Ulster Popular Unionist Party from 1983 to 1992, and Robert McCartney's UK Unionist Party in 1997.

**Northern Ireland Westminster Elections 1979-2001: Parties' Share of Seats**

| Party | 1979 | 1983 | 1987 | 1992 | 1997 | 2001 |
|---|---|---|---|---|---|---|
| UUP | 8 | 11 | 9 | 10 | 10 | 6 |
| SDLP | 1 | 1 | 3 | 4 | 3 | 3 |
| DUP | 3 | 3 | 3 | 3 | 2 | 5 |
| SF | - | 1 | 1 | - | 2 | 4 |
| Other Unionists | 2 | 1 | 1 | 1 | 1 | - |
| Others | 1 | - | - | - | - | - |

The influence of 'electoral pacts' between unionist parties is also highly significant. In areas with a large nationalist minority, the UUP and DUP have sometimes agreed that one of their candidates stand down, to allow a straight run for a single unionist candidate and avoid losing the seat to nationalists by splitting the unionist majority. Conversely, the SDLP and Sinn Féin have not entered into such agreements, even where the arithmetic suggested that a single nationalist candidate could comfortably win a seat.

Set out in the table on page 72 is the historical electoral performance of Northern Ireland's political parties in Westminster elections from 1979-2001 in terms of share of popular vote.

Detailed results from the 2001 general election are set out on the following pages.

Northern Ireland Parliamentary Constituencies (1995)

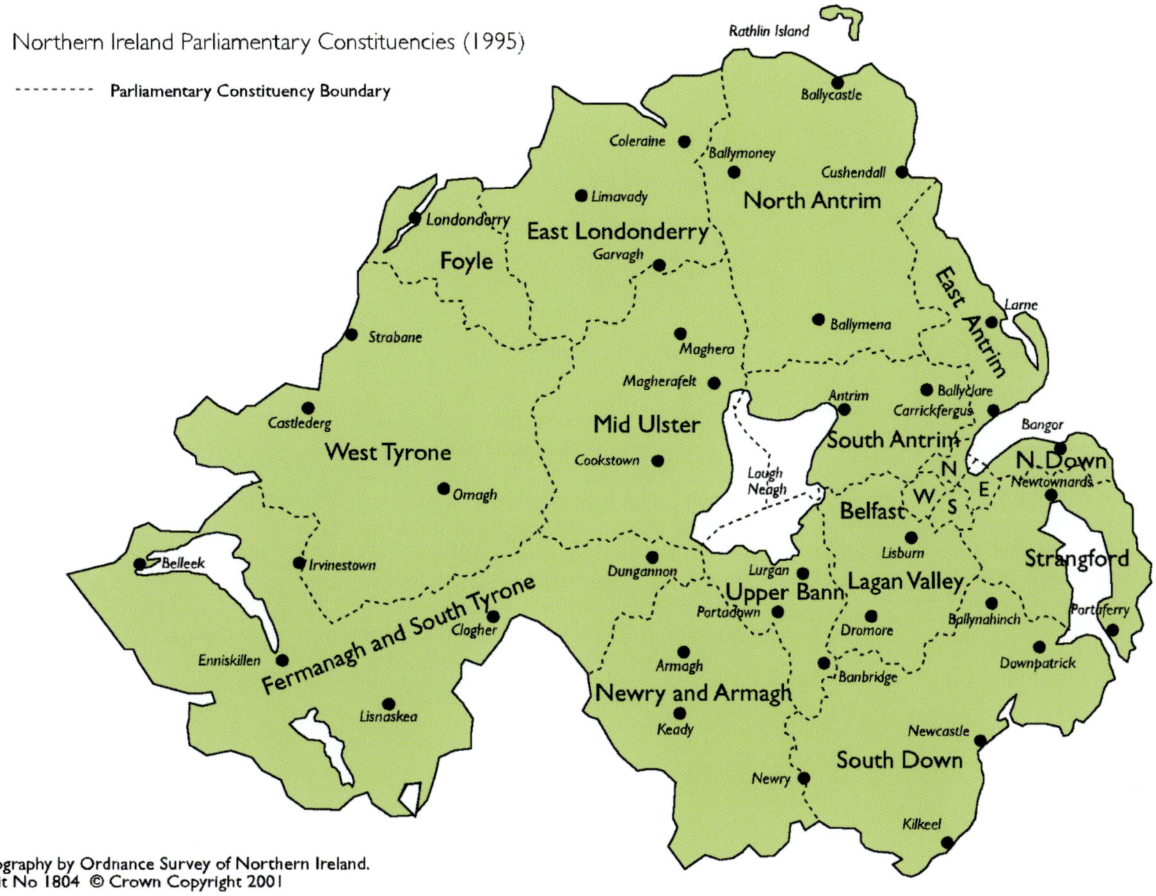


Cartography by Ordnance Survey of Northern Ireland.
Permit No 1804 © Crown Copyright 2001

# The 2001 UK Westminster Government General Election

| | |
|---|---|
| **Electorate** | **1,191,070** |
| **Turnout** | **68.0%** |
| **Total Votes Polled** | **810,381** |
| **Spoiled Votes** | **7,074** |

## Results by Constituency

### Belfast East

| | |
|---|---|
| **Electorate** | **58,455** |
| **Valid Vote** | **36,829** |
| **Turnout** | **63.4%** |
| **DUP Majority** | **7,117** |

| Name | Party | Votes | % vote |
|---|---|---|---|
| **Peter Robinson*** | **DUP** | **15,667** | **42.5** |
| Tim Lemon | UUP | 8,550 | 23.2 |
| David Alderdice | All | 5,832 | 15.8 |
| David Ervine | PUP | 3,669 | 10.0 |
| Joseph O'Donnell | SF | 1,237 | 3.4 |
| Ciara Farren | SDLP | 888 | 2.4 |
| Terry Dick | Cons | 800 | 2.2 |
| Joseph Bell | WP | 123 | 0.3 |
| Rainbow George Weiss | VFY | 71 | 0.2 |

**Sitting MP*

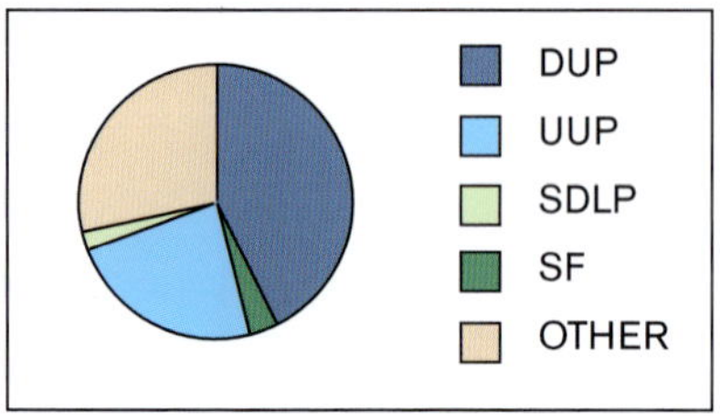


East Belfast held by Peter Robinson of the DUP since 1979 has a substantial unionist majority. Robinson's nearest rivals were the UUP and Alliance, although the DUP majority was well over seven thousand votes.

### Belfast North

| | |
|---|---|
| **Electorate** | **60,941** |
| **Valid Vote** | **40,932** |
| **Turnout** | **67.8%** |
| **DUP Majority** | **6,387** |

| Name | Party | Votes | % vote |
|---|---|---|---|
| **Nigel Dodds** | **DUP** | **16,718** | **40.8** |
| Gerry Kelly | SF | 10,331 | 25.2 |
| Alban Maginness | SDLP | 8,592 | 21.0 |
| Cecil Walker* | UUP | 4,904 | 12.0 |
| Marcella Delaney | WP | 253 | 0.7 |
| Rainbow George Weiss | VFY | 134 | 0.3 |

**Sitting MP*

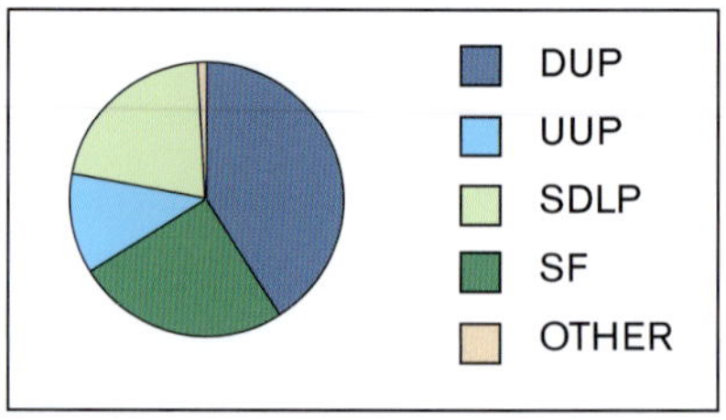


North Belfast is one of the most deeply divided areas in Northern Ireland, and this is reflected in its elections. Cecil Walker held the seat for the Ulster Unionist Party since 1983, unopposed by candidates from the other Unionist parties until the 2001 election when Nigel Dodds of the DUP ran in direct competition. Nigel Dodds won two fifths of the vote, beating Walker into 4th place, behind SDLP and Sinn Féin.

### Belfast South

| | |
|---|---|
| **Electorate** | **59,436** |
| **Valid Vote** | **37,952** |
| **Turnout** | **64.3%** |
| **UUP majority** | **5,399** |

| Name | Party | Votes | % vote |
|---|---|---|---|
| **Martin Smyth*** | **UUP** | **17,008** | **44.8** |
| Alasdair McDonnell | SDLP | 11,609 | 30.6 |
| Monica McWilliams | NIWC | 2,968 | 7.8 |
| Alex Maskey | SF | 2,894 | 7.6 |
| Geraldine Rice | All | 2,042 | 5.4 |
| Dawn Purvis | PUP | 1,112 | 2.9 |
| Patrick Lynch | WP | 204 | 0.6 |
| Rainbow George Weiss | VFY | 115 | 0.3 |

**Sitting MP*

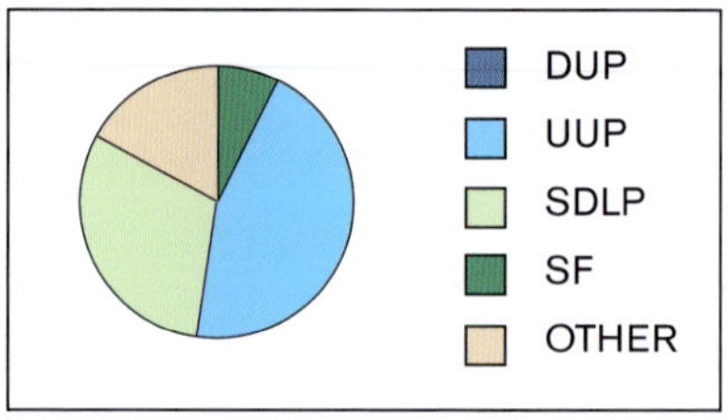


The Ulster Unionist Party candidate Martin Smyth retained South Belfast. Smyth's closest rival was the SDLP's Dr Alasdair McDonnell with Monica McWilliams coming third.

## Belfast West

**Electorate** 59,617
**Valid Vote** 40,982
**Turnout** 69.9%
**SF Majority** 19,342

| Name | Party | Votes | % vote |
|---|---|---|---|
| **Gerry Adams*** | **SF** | **27,096** | **66.1** |
| Alex Attwood | SDLP | 7,754 | 18.9 |
| Eric Smyth | DUP | 2,641 | 6.4 |
| Chris McGimpsey | UUP | 2,541 | 6.2 |
| John Lowry | WP | 736 | 1.8 |
| David Kerr | UTW | 116 | 0.3 |
| George Weiss | VFY | 98 | 0.2 |

*Sitting MP

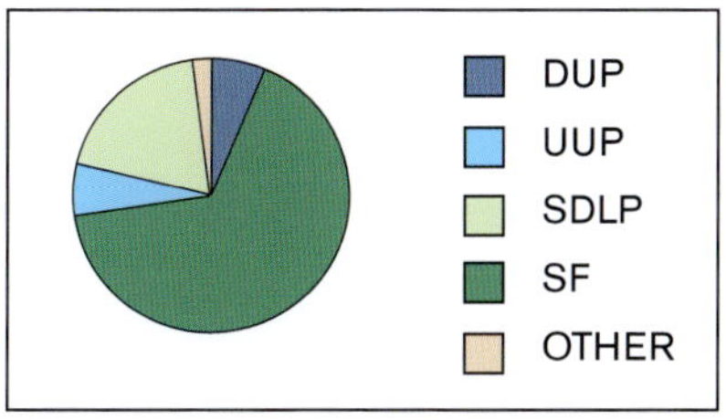


This constituency has a very strong nationalist majority, although it includes much of the loyalist Shankill Road. Gerry Adams of Sinn Féin won the seat first in 1983. Although Dr Joe Hendron of the SDLP won the seat back for the SDLP in 1992, Adams was successful in both 1997 and 2001 recording increased majorities.

## East Antrim

**Electorate** 60,897
**Valid Vote** 36,000
**Turnout** 59.7%
**UUP Majority** 128

| Name | Party | Votes | % vote |
|---|---|---|---|
| **Roy Beggs*** | **UUP** | **13,101** | **36.4** |
| Sammy Wilson | DUP | 12,973 | 36.0 |
| John Matthews | All | 4,483 | 12.5 |
| Danny O'Connor | SDLP | 2,641 | 7.4 |
| Robert Mason | Ind | 1,092 | 3.0 |
| Janette Graffin | SF | 903 | 2.5 |
| Alan Greer | Cons | 807 | 2.2 |

*Sitting MP

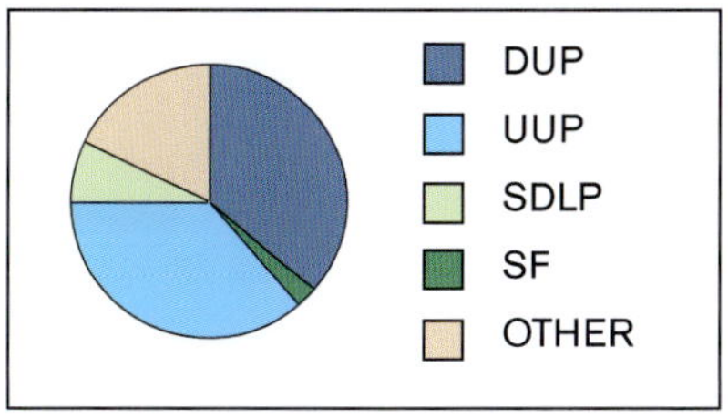


East Antrim is one of the smaller constituencies and has an overwhelming unionist majority. Since its establishment by the Boundary Commission in 1983 Roy Beggs of the UUP has held the seat with increasingly strong opposition coming from the DUP Prominent DUP Assemblyman Sammy Wilson is strongly fancied to win the seat in the 2005 election.

## East Londonderry

**Electorate** 60,215
**Valid Vote** 39,869
**Turnout** 66.9%
**DUP majority** 1,901

| Name | Party | Votes | % vote |
|---|---|---|---|
| **Gregory Campbell** | **DUP** | **12,813** | **32.1** |
| Willie Ross* | UUP | 10,912 | 27.4 |
| John Dallat | SDLP | 8,298 | 20.8 |
| Francie Brolly | SF | 6,221 | 15.6 |
| Yvonne Boyle | All | 1,625 | 4.1 |

*Sitting MP

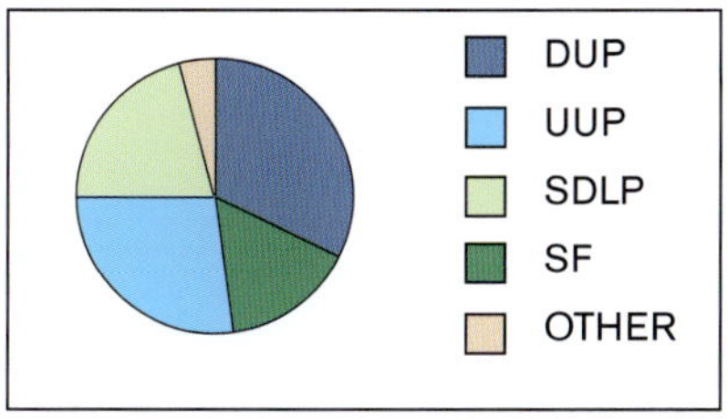


Gregory Campbell of the DUP took the East Londonderry seat from Willie Ross of the UUP who had held it with a majority of 4,000.The loss of this seat for the UUP was unexpected not least because of the hard-line anti-Agreement and anti-Trimble stance of the incumbent MP.

## Fermanagh & South Tyrone

**Electorate** 66,640
**Valid Vote** 51,974
**Turnout** 79.0%
**SF majority** 53

| Name | Party | Votes | % vote |
|---|---|---|---|
| **Michelle Gildernew** | **SF** | **17,739** | **34.1** |
| James Cooper | UUP | 17,686 | 34.0 |
| Tommy Gallagher | SDLP | 9,706 | 18.7 |
| Jim Dixon | Ind | 6,843 | 13.2 |

*Sitting MP

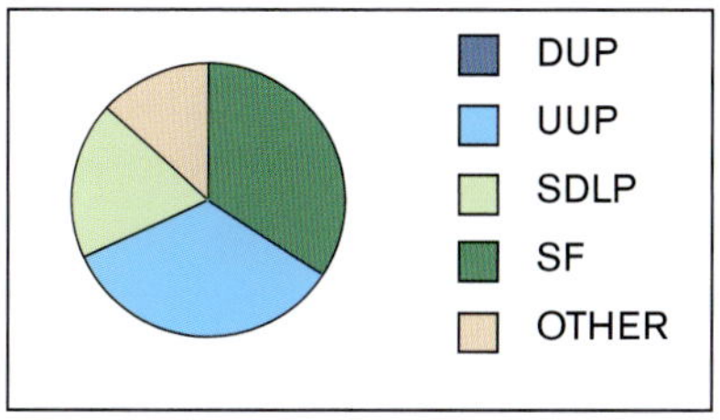


Ken Maginnis had held Fermanagh South Tyrone since 1983 but his decision not to stand for re-election in 2001 and the entry of independent unionist Jim Dixon enabled Michelle Gildernew of Sinn Féin to win the seat.

## Foyle

**Electorate** 70,943
**Valid Vote** 48,879
**Turnout** 69.6%
**SDLP majority** 11,550

| Name | Party | Votes | % vote |
|---|---|---|---|
| **John Hume*** | **SDLP** | **24,538** | **50.2** |
| Mitchel McLaughlin | SF | 12,988 | 26.6 |
| William Hay | DUP | 7,414 | 15.2 |
| Andrew Davidson | UUP | 3,360 | 6.9 |
| Colm Cavanagh | All | 579 | 1.1 |

*Sitting MP

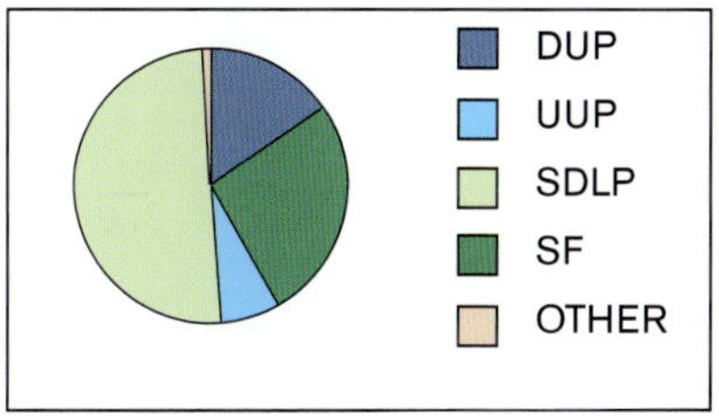


John Hume, has held the constituency since 1983. Despite big swings elsewhere from SDLP to Sinn Féin, the seat was retained by the SDLP with a comfortable majority. Foyle was possibly the only nationalist constituency where Sinn Féin did not gain significant ground on the SDLP.

## Lagan Valley

| | |
|---|---|
| **Electorate** | **72,671** |
| **Valid Vote** | **45,941** |
| **Turnout** | **63.6%** |
| **UUP majority** | **18,342** |

| Name | Party | Votes | % vote |
|---|---|---|---|
| **Jeffrey Donaldson*** | **UUP** | **25,966** | **56.5** |
| Seamus Close | All | 7,624 | 16.6 |
| Edwin Poots | DUP | 6,164 | 13.4 |
| Patricia Lewsley | SDLP | 3,462 | 7.6 |
| Paul Butler | SF | 2,725 | 5.9 |

*Sitting MP*

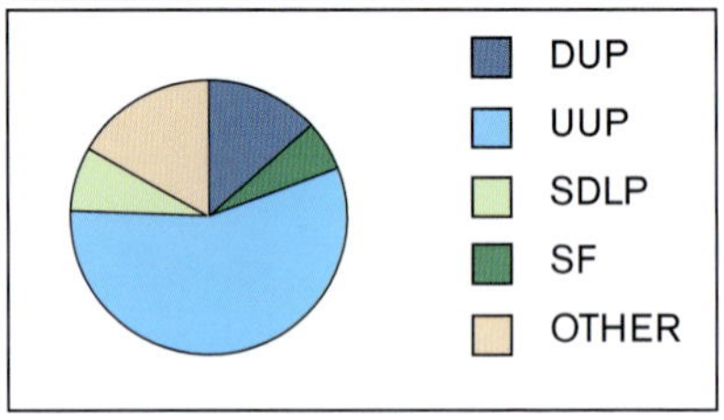


Jeffrey Donaldson has held Lagan Valley since 1997, when he replaced the retiring UUP leader, Jim Molyneaux. Donaldson won over 50 per cent of the vote in 2001, with his nearest rival, Alliance's Seamus Close, 18,000 votes behind. Jeffrey Donaldson has subsequently joined the DUP, taking the Lagan Valley seat out of Ulster Unionist control.

## Mid Ulster

| | |
|---|---|
| **Electorate** | **61,390** |
| **Valid Vote** | **49,936** |
| **Turnout** | **82.1%** |
| **SF majority** | **9,953** |

| Name | Party | Votes | % vote |
|---|---|---|---|
| **Martin McGuinness*** | **SF** | **25,502** | **51.1** |
| Ian McCrea | DUP | 15,549 | 31.1 |
| Eilish Haughey | SDLP | 8,376 | 16.8 |
| Francie Donnelly | WP | 509 | 1.0 |

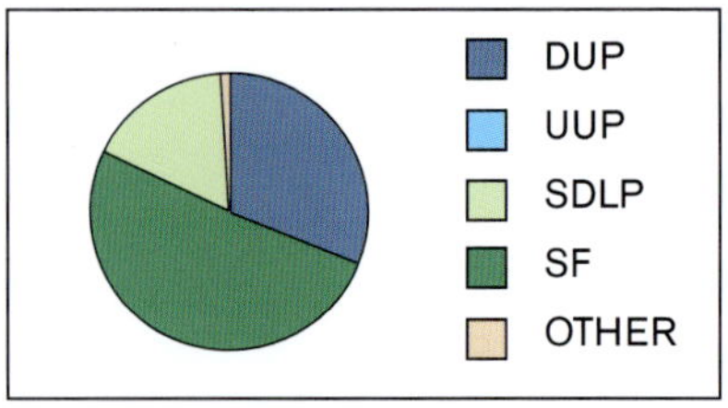


Martin McGuinness retained Mid-Ulster for Sinn Féin, increasing his majority from 1,900 to almost 10,000 votes. The SDLP continued to drop behind the two leading parties in an area with very high turnout.

## Newry and Armagh

| | |
|---|---|
| **Electorate** | **72,466** |
| **Valid Vote** | **55,621** |
| **Turnout** | **77.6%** |
| **SDLP majority** | **3,575** |

| Name | Party | Votes | % vote |
|---|---|---|---|
| **Séamus Mallon*** | **SDLP** | **20,784** | **37.4** |
| Conor Murphy | SF | 17,209 | 30.9 |
| Paul Berry | DUP | 10,795 | 19.4 |
| Sylvia McRoberts | UUP | 6,833 | 12.3 |

*Sitting MP*

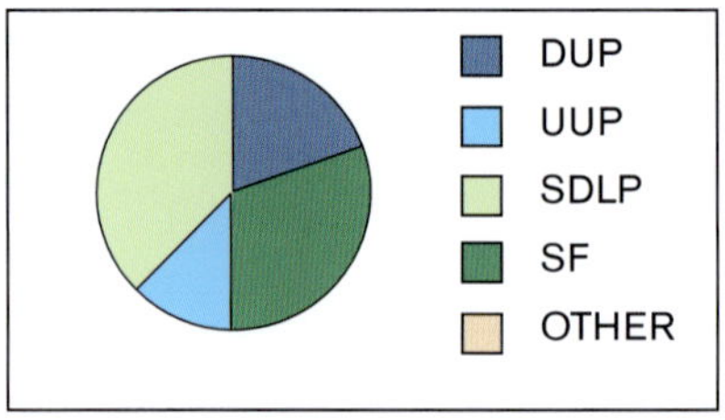


The SDLP Deputy Leader Seamus Mallon retained Newry and Armagh, with a much-reduced majority of 3,500 votes over Sinn Féin's Conor Murphy. The DUP decided to run a candidate, contrary to their previous tactic of allowing the UUP to present a single unionist. Paul Berry, at 10,795 votes, pushed the UUP's Sylvia McRoberts into 4th place.

## North Antrim

| | |
|---|---|
| **Electorate** | **74,451** |
| **Total Valid Vote** | **49,217** |
| **Turnout** | **66.6%** |
| **DUP Majority** | **14,224** |

| Name | Party | Votes | % vote |
|---|---|---|---|
| **Ian Paisley*** | **DUP** | **24,539** | **49.9** |
| Lexie Scott | UUP | 10,315 | 21.0 |
| Sean Farren | SDLP | 8,283 | 16.8 |
| John Kelly | SF | 4,822 | 9.8 |
| Jayne Dunlop | All | 1,258 | 2.5 |

*Sitting MP*

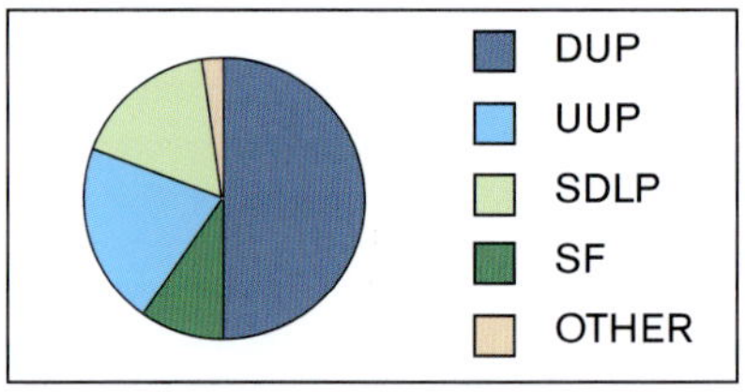


North Antrim is the stronghold of the DUP leader, Ian Paisley since he first won the seat in 1970 with the UUP coming consistently second. The constituency has a substantial unionist majority.

## North Down

| | |
|---|---|
| **Electorate** | **63,212** |
| **Valid Vote** | **37,189** |
| **Turnout** | **59.1%** |
| **UUP Majority** | **7,324** |

| Name | Party | Votes | % vote |
|---|---|---|---|
| **Sylvia Hermon** | **UUP** | **20,833** | **56.0** |
| Robert McCartney* | UKUP | 13,509 | 36.3 |
| Marietta Farrell | SDLP | 1,275 | 3.4 |
| Julian Robertson | Cons | 815 | 2.2 |
| Chris Carter | UIV | 444 | 1.2 |
| Eamon McConvey | SF | 313 | 0.9 |

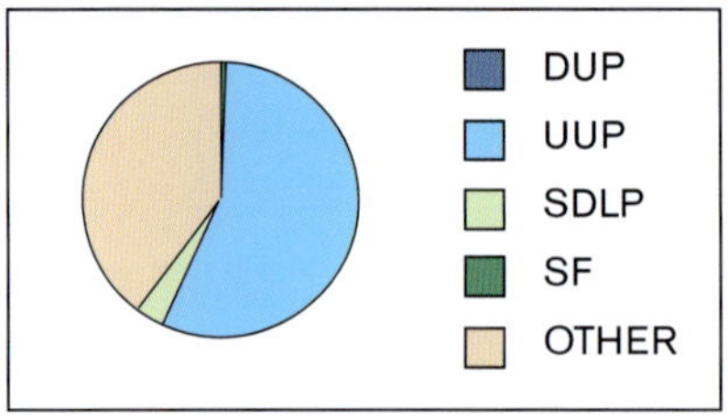


North Down had not been held by any of the main political parties for over 20 years, Independent Unionist James Kilfedder holding the seat throughout the 70's and 80's succeeded by another Independent Unionist, Robert McCartney in 1995.

McCartney had held the North Down seat since the by-election in 1995. In 2001 the Alliance party withdrew in support of the pro-Agreement UUP candidate, Lady Sylvia Hermon. Its support proved crucial to the UUP. Sylvia Hermon took North Down with a majority of 7,324.

## South Antrim

| | |
|---|---|
| **Electorate** | **70,651** |
| **Valid Vote** | **44,158** |
| **Turnout** | **62.5%** |
| **UUP Majority** | **1,011** |

| Name | Party | Votes | % vote |
|---|---|---|---|
| **David Burnside** | **UUP** | **16,366** | **37.1** |
| Willie McCrea* | DUP | 15,355 | 34.8 |
| Sean McKee | SDLP | 5,336 | 12.1 |
| Martin Meehan | SF | 4,160 | 9.4 |
| David Ford | All | 1,969 | 4.4 |
| Norman Boyd | NIUP | 972 | 2.2 |

*Sitting MP*

Clifford Forsythe of the Ulster Unionists held this seat from 1983 until his death in April 2000. Since then it has been very keenly contested between the two main Unionist parties.

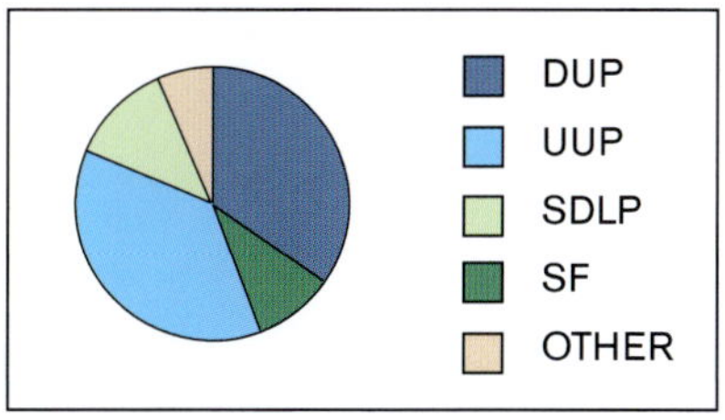


In the 2000 by-election Willie McCrea of the DUP won the seat with a majority of 822 votes. However, the situation was reversed in 2001, when David Burnside won the seat back for the UUP by just over 1,000 votes.

## South Down

| | |
|---|---|
| **Electorate** | **73,519** |
| **Valid Vote** | **52,074** |
| **Turnout** | **71.6%** |
| **SDLP Majority** | **13,858** |

| Name | Party | Votes | % vote |
|---|---|---|---|
| **Eddie McGrady*** | **SDLP** | **24,136** | **46.4** |
| Mick Murphy | SF | 10,278 | 19.7 |
| Dermot Nesbitt | UUP | 9,173 | 17.6 |
| Jim Wells | DUP | 7,802 | 15.0 |
| Betty Campbell | All | 685 | 1.3 |

**Sitting MP*

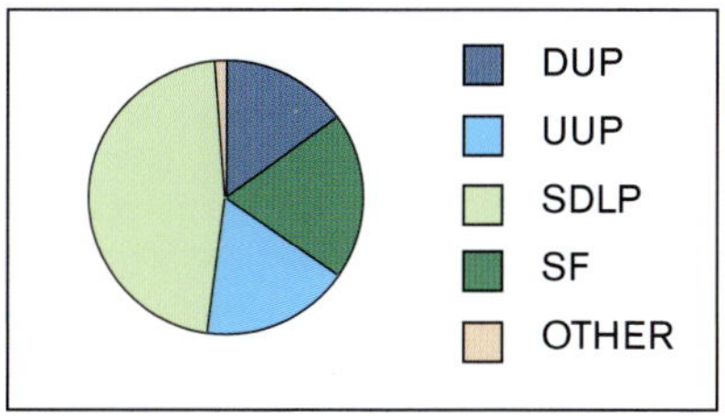


Eddie McGrady of the SDLP has held South Down since 1987, when he displaced Enoch Powell of the UUP by just over 700 votes. Since then, McGrady has increased his majority to almost 14,000 votes in 2001.

## Strangford

| | |
|---|---|
| **Electorate** | **72,192** |
| **Valid Vote** | **43,254** |
| **Turnout** | **60.2%** |
| **DUP majority** | **1,110** |

| Name | Party | Votes | % vote |
|---|---|---|---|
| **Iris Robinson** | **DUP** | **18,532** | **42.8** |
| David McNarry | UUP | 17,422 | 40.3 |
| Kieran McCarthy | All | 2,902 | 6.7 |
| Danny McCarthy | SDLP | 2,646 | 6.1 |
| Liam Johnson | SF | 930 | 2.2 |
| Cedric Wilson | NIUP | 822 | 1.9 |

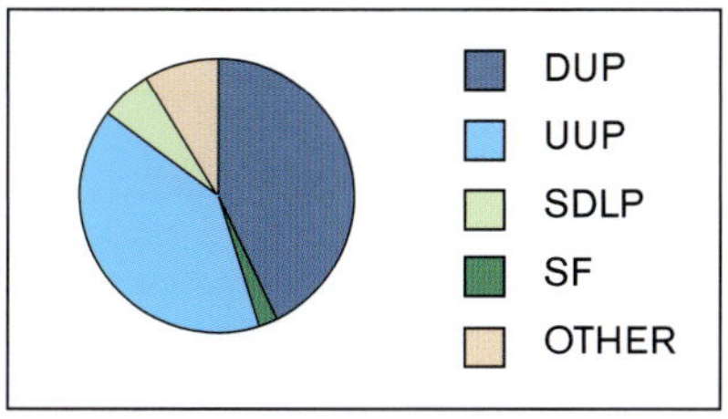


The contest for the Strangford seat, vacated by the UUP's John Taylor was close with David McNarry coming within 1,100 votes of retaining the seat for the UUP. Iris Robinson, DUP, was the eventual winner.

## Upper Bann

| | |
|---|---|
| **Electorate** | **72,574** |
| **Valid Vote** | **51,037** |
| **Turnout** | **70.8%** |
| **UUP majority** | **2,058** |

| Name | Party | Votes | % vote |
|---|---|---|---|
| **David Trimble*** | **UUP** | **17,095** | **33.5** |
| David Simpson | DUP | 15,037 | 29.5 |
| Dara O'Hagan | SF | 10,771 | 21.1 |
| Dolores Kelly | SDLP | 7,607 | 14.9 |
| Tom French | WP | 527 | 1.0 |

**Sitting MP*

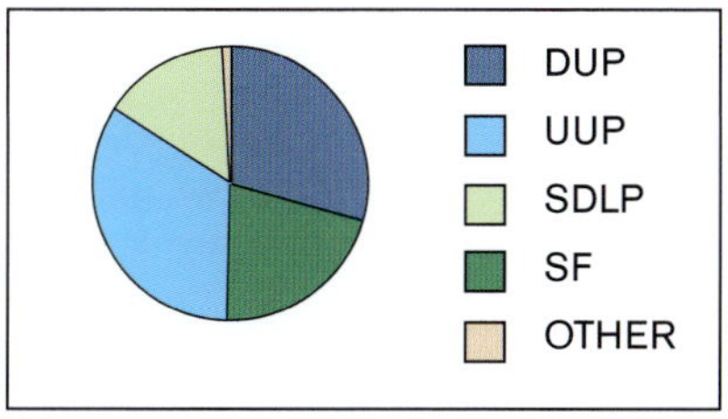


Until 2001 the UUP leader, David Trimble, had comfortably held Upper Bann. In 1997 Trimble enjoyed a majority of over 9,000 votes, with the two nationalist candidates placed between himself and the DUP. In 2001, however, the DUP's David Simpson came within 2,000 votes of winning the seat and causing a major upset.

In the absence of SDLP candidate Bríd Rodgers, the Sinn Féin vote increased significantly, largely at the expense of the SDLP.

## West Tyrone

| | |
|---|---|
| **Electorate** | **60,739** |
| **Total Valid Vote** | **48,530** |
| **Turnout** | **80.6%** |
| **SF majority** | **5,040** |

| Name | Party | Votes | % vote |
|---|---|---|---|
| **Pat Doherty** | **SF** | **19,814** | **40.8** |
| Willie Thompson* | UUP | 14,774 | 30.4 |
| Bríd Rodgers | SDLP | 13,942 | 28.8 |

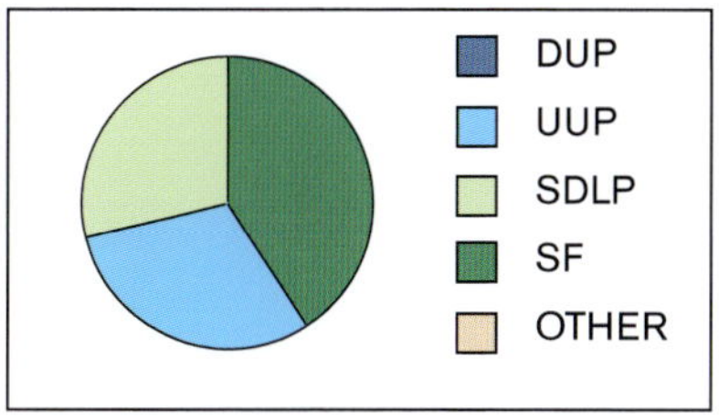


In West Tyrone Pat Doherty of Sinn Féin beat the UUP's Willie Thompson by a majority of over 5,000 votes. The SDLP had hoped to achieve success in this constituency by fielding Bríd Rodgers away from her usual Upper Bann constituency, however this tactic proved unsuccessful.

## Northern Ireland Assembly Elections

Over the years, Northern Ireland has elected a number of different local 'assemblies'. Most of these were associated with various initiatives by UK governments to establish a form of devolved administration in Northern Ireland. Given that these initiatives varied in scope and context the results are not readily comparable with the recently elected legislative assembly.

Elections were contested for the first Northern Ireland Assembly on Thursday 25 June 1998. The 18 Westminster constituencies were used, each to return 6 Assembly members. The electoral system used was a form of proportional representation, the Single Transferable Vote (STV).

The result suggested a 70% pro-Agreement majority, against a 30% anti-Agreement minority spearheaded by the DUP. In reality however the result was possibly somewhat closer. A number of elected members in David Trimble's ostensibly pro-Agreement Ulster Unionist Party were either actually personally against the Agreement, or had not fallen decisively on either side of the argument.

### Valid Votes and Poll

| Constituency | Eligible Electorate | % Poll |
|---|---|---|
| Belfast East | 51,937 | 60.70 |
| Belfast North | 51,353 | 62.31 |
| Belfast South | 50,707 | 62.59 |
| Belfast West | 50,861 | 65.92 |
| East Antrim | 55,473 | 56.50 |
| East Londonderry | 56,203 | 61.75 |
| Fermanagh & S.Tyrone | 64,336 | 72.86 |
| Foyle | 65,303 | 63.45 |
| Lagan Valley | 67,910 | 61.44 |
| Mid Ulster | 60,095 | 74.92 |
| Newry & Armagh | 68,731 | 70.18 |
| North Antrim | 70,489 | 63.32 |
| North Down | 57,422 | 54.54 |
| South Antrim | 63,640 | 59.49 |
| South Down | 70,149 | 65.59 |
| Strangford | 66,308 | 57.06 |
| Upper Bann | 68,814 | 64.15 |
| West Tyrone | 57,795 | 73.24 |
| Total | **1,097,526** | **63.98** |

## 2003 Assembly Election Overview

The 2003 Northern Ireland Assembly election was originally scheduled for May 2003, but was deferred because the previous devolved administration had collapsed and there was no agreement between the pro-agreement parties on how to re-establish the institutions. The Westminster government finally called an election for 26th November 2003 to go ahead whether there was an agreement to take forward and present to the electorate or not.

The election took place in the absence of a 'deal' between the pro-Agreement parties with the DUP standing on a clear anti-Belfast Agreement platform. The two nationalist parties maintained the stance that there would be no renegotiation of the Agreement. The Ulster Unionist Party, while overall maintaining its support for the Agreement, had a significant minority of its officially selected candidates (the most prominent being the Lagan Valley MP Jeffrey Donaldson) running on an anti-Agreement ticket.

A total of 256 candidates contested the 108 seats with a minimum of 11 candidates fielded in Newry and Armagh and a maximum of 19 runners in East Antrim and in North Down.

The campaign was relatively calm and despite attempts to liven up the debate with battle-buses and videos etc and various 'stunts' the media reported that the general public had not been greatly absorbed in the contest.

This observation was reflected in the eventual turnout, which at just under 64% was unusually low for a Northern Ireland election. Some electoral pundits did however attribute the low turnout to the inclement weather as much as to voter indifference. In what is effectively a 4 party system – two main unionist parties and two main nationalist parties – the election could be seen almost in terms of two different electoral tests – one in each community.

As anticipated in the run-up to the election, the overall result reflected a hardening of attitudes in both the unionist and nationalist communities in Northern Ireland with Ian Paisley's Democratic Unionist Party (DUP) and Gerry Adams' Sinn Féin emerging as the biggest winners. While Sinn Féin made its gains largely at the expense of its main opponent the SDLP, the DUP gains were not so much at the expense of the rival Ulster Unionist Party but from a number of smaller unionist parties.

#### Winners and Losers

The election presented few suprises overall. The DUP had been expected to gain seats and Sinn Féin had been expected to open up a gap on the SDLP – although perhaps not by as much as they actually achieved. One surprise in an election that saw the demise of many smaller parties and independents was the election of a single-issue independent 'hospital' candidate in West Tyrone. Other surprises included the DUP capturing a seat in West Belfast where previously there had been no Unionist representation. Dianne Dodds took the seat at the expense of long-serving SDLP MLA and former Westminster MP Dr Joe Hendron.

Although David Trimble's pro Agreement UUP performed robustly – and better than many had expected – a number of the anti-Agreement UUP dissidents scored electoral successes. Anti-Agreement UUP Jeffrey Donaldson recorded the top vote of any candidate in the election and other prominent dissidents Arlene Foster (Fermanagh/South Tyrone) and David Burnside (South Antrim) were comfortably elected.

## Overall Result by Party Share and Seats

| | Votes | % Share of Vote | | Number of Seats | | |
|---|---|---|---|---|---|---|
| | | 2003 | (1998) | 2003 | (1998) | +/- since 1998 |
| DUP | 177,944 | 25.7 | 18.1 | 30 | 20 | +10 |
| SF | 162,758 | 23.5 | 17.6 | 24 | 18 | +6 |
| UUP | 156,931 | 22.7 | 21.5 | 27 | 28 | -1 |
| SDLP | 117,547 | 17.0 | 22.0 | 18 | 24 | -6 |
| Alliance | 25,372 | 3.7 | 6.5 | 6 | 6 | 0 |
| UKUP | 5,700 | 0.8 | 4.5 | 1 | 5 | -4 |
| PUP/UDP | 8,032 | 1.2 | 3.6 | 1 | 2 | -1 |
| NIWC | 5,785 | 0.8 | 1.6 | 0 | 2 | -2 |
| Others | 31,959 | 4.6 | 4.5 | 1 | 3 | -2 |
| Total | 692,028 | 100 | 100 | 108 | 108 | |

However in David Trimble's own constituency where he achieved a high personal vote, the dissident UUP candidate and sitting MLA George Savage, was eclipsed by pro-Agreement Samuel Gardiner.

The decision of anti-Agreement unionists Jeffrey Donaldson, Arlene Foster and Norah Beare to join the DUP left the Ulster Unionist Party with 24 seats to the DUP's 33. This means the DUP is the largest unionist party as well as the largest overall party in Northern Ireland's political system.

For the SDLP the 2003 election overall was a major disappointment. The 1998 result of the SDLP/Sinn Féin contest 24-18 in favour of the SDLP was completely reversed. In a number of constituencies Sinn Féin took over from the SDLP in share of the vote terms for the first time, while in SDLP strongholds the party made significant inroads. The most disastrous result for the SDLP was possibly Newry and Armagh, an SDLP Westminster seat held by Seamus Mallon, where SDLP was reduced to only 1 seat out of the six.

## Parties' Percentage Share of the Vote by Constituency

| Constituency / Party | DUP | SF | UUP | SDLP | Alliance | Other |
|---|---|---|---|---|---|---|
| Belfast East | 39.2 | 3.8 | 33.1 | 3.1 | 9.0 | 11.8 |
| Belfast North | 34.2 | 27.0 | 9.4 | 16.8 | 1.0 | 11.7 |
| Belfast South | 20.8 | 12.6 | 27.0 | 22.9 | 5.9 | 10.8 |
| Belfast West | 7.7 | 65.0 | 3.6 | 19.0 | 0.2 | 4.4 |
| East Antrim | 34.1 | 2.5 | 28.7 | 7.8 | 10.9 | 16.0 |
| East Londonderry | 32.4 | 17.9 | 22.7 | 16.3 | 2.2 | 8.6 |
| Fermanagh & S.Tyrone | 18.7 | 34.4 | 28.7 | 16.3 | 0.1 | 1.4 |
| Foyle | 15.0 | 32.4 | 8.1 | 36.1 | 0.1 | 7.8 |
| Lagan Valley | 20.5 | 7.9 | 46.2 | 7.6 | 10.7 | 7.1 |
| Mid Ulster | 20.8 | 45.5 | 14.4 | 18.3 | 0.1 | 0.5 |
| Newry & Armagh | 18.1 | 39.8 | 15.5 | 24.6 | 0.1 | 1.3 |
| North Antrim | 45.9 | 14.0 | 21.6 | 13.6 | 2.0 | 2.8 |
| North Down | 23.5 | 0.9 | 32.1 | 4.9 | 8.6 | 30.0 |
| South Antrim | 30.6 | 11.5 | 29.8 | 14.4 | 9.1 | 4.6 |
| South Down | 15.0 | 26.5 | 18.2 | 35.1 | 1.1 | 4.2 |
| Strangford | 47.9 | 3.0 | 28.9 | 7.8 | 7.4 | 5.0 |
| Upper Bann | 28.5 | 21.8 | 29.4 | 15.7 | 1.3 | 3.2 |
| West Tyrone | 17.5 | 38.6 | 13.6 | 14.6 | 0.4 | 15.3 |

## Parties' Share of Seats by Constituency

| Constituency / Party | DUP | UUP | SDLP | SF | Alliance | Other |
|---|---|---|---|---|---|---|
| Belfast East | 2 | 2 | 0 | 0 | 1 | 1 |
| Belfast North | 2 | 1 | 1 | 2 | 0 | 0 |
| Belfast South | 1 | 2 | 2 | 1 | 0 | 0 |
| Belfast West | 1 | 0 | 1 | 4 | 0 | 0 |
| East Antrim | 3 | 2 | 0 | 0 | 1 | 0 |
| East Londonderry | 2 | 2 | 1 | 1 | 0 | 0 |
| Fermanagh & South Tyrone | 1 | 2 | 1 | 2 | 0 | 0 |
| Foyle | 1 | 0 | 3 | 2 | 0 | 0 |
| Lagan Valley | 1 | 3 | 1 | 0 | 1 | 0 |
| Mid Ulster | 1 | 1 | 1 | 3 | 0 | 0 |
| Newry & Armagh | 1 | 1 | 1 | 3 | 0 | 0 |
| North Antrim | 3 | 1 | 1 | 1 | 0 | 0 |
| North Down | 2 | 2 | 0 | 0 | 1 | 1 |
| South Antrim | 2 | 2 | 1 | 0 | 1 | 0 |
| South Down | 1 | 1 | 2 | 2 | 0 | 0 |
| Strangford | 3 | 2 | 0 | 0 | 1 | 0 |
| Upper Bann | 2 | 2 | 1 | 1 | 0 | 0 |
| West Tyrone | 1 | 1 | 1 | 2 | 0 | 1 |
| Total | 30 | 27 | 18 | 24 | 6 | 3 |

The election was a major success for the Democratic Unionist Party jumping from 20 seats in 1998 to 30 seats in 2003. The seats were gained primarily from the smaller unionist parties, which, apart from the PUP's leader David Ervine in East Belfast and UKUP leader Robert McCartney in North Down, were effectively obliterated as a force in any new Assembly. The DUP vote share improved in just about every constituency and with better vote management possibly more seats could have been won by the party.

The rise of Sinn Féin continued in the 2003 election with notable gains in North Antrim, South Belfast, North Belfast, South Down, Newry and Armagh and East Londonderry. Taking account of its elected representation in the Irish Republic some party spokespersons prefer the title of 'third largest party in Ireland'.

Perhaps the most outstanding performance in terms of seats for votes and in the context of an overall squeeze on centre parties was that of the Alliance Party. The party experienced a 40% drop in its overall first preference vote, yet retained its six seats. As mentioned above the smaller parties were largely eclipsed in the 2003 Assembly election. The NI Women's Coalition lost its two seats and prominent representatives of minor unionist parties  The table above and those on page 79 show the results in detail.

## 2003 Election: Detailed Results

What follows over the next 36 pages is the detailed results including all the counts from each of the 18 constituencies. Information included for each constituency includes a full list of candidates and their parties and the number of votes they received at each stage of the count, together with the cumulative totals and the number of non-transferable votes. Also shown is a summary table highlighting how the parties performed in terms of share of the vote and seats.

The asterisks indicate those candidates who were members of the 1998 Assembly.  In the detailed count information, the numbers highlighted in bold indicate the 'active' votes being re-distributed at that stage of the counting.

The successful candidates are pictured, and their details are colour-coded by party as per the following key:

| | | | |
|---|---|---|---|
| ■ | DUP | ■ | SF |
| ■ | UUP | ■ | SDLP |
| ■ | Alliance | ■ | Others |

we've got it
covered

# Belfast East

**Total Valid Pole 30965** **Quota 4424** **Turnout 60.7%**

**Party performance**

| Party | Seats | 1st Pref Vote | % | (1998)% |
|---|---|---|---|---|
| DUP | 2 | 12132 | 39.2 | 30.9 |
| SF | - | 1180 | 3.8 | 2.3 |
| UUP | 2 | 10252 | 33.1 | 24.3 |
| SDLP | - | 967 | 3.1 | 2.6 |
| Alliance | 1 | 2774 | 9.0 | 18.0 |
| Others | 1 | 3660 | 11.8 | 21.9 |

**At a glance...**

No surprises in this predominantly unionist constituency with the party share out of the six seats remaining unchanged. Local MP Peter Robinson (DUP) topped the poll as expected followed by Sir Reg Empey (UUP). Despite a significant reduction in first preference votes David Ervine (PUP) and Naomi Long (All), the latter running in place of Lord Alderdice, held on to their party seats. Runner-up overall was UUP former Lord Mayor Jim Rodgers. The total nationalist vote was less than half a quota.

| | | Stage 1<br>1st preference votes 30,965 | Stage 2<br>Transfer of Robinson's surplus |
|---|---|---|---|
| Joseph Bell | WP | 125 | (+3.12)<br>128.12 |
| Thomas Black | Soc | 176 | (+5.2)<br>181.2 |
| *Michael Copeland | UUP | 2291 | (+63.96)<br>2354.96 |
| Terry Dick | Cons | 232 | (+2.08)<br>234.08 |
| *Reg Empey | UUP | 6459 | (n/a)<br>6459 |
| David Ervine | PUP | 2990 | (+221.52)<br>3211.52 |
| Naomi Long | All | 2774 | (+20.28)<br>2794.28 |
| John McBlain | Ind | 72 | (+6.76)<br>78.76 |
| Robin Newton | DUP | 1475 | (+2943.2)<br>4418.2 |
| Joseph O'Donnell | SF | 1180 | (+4.16)<br>1184.16 |
| *Peter Robinson | DUP | 9254 | **(-4830)**<br>4424 |
| Jim Rodgers | UUP | 1502 | (+288.6)<br>1790.6 |
| Harry Toan | DUP | 1403 | (+1230.32)<br>2633.32 |
| Leo Van Es | SDLP | 967 | (2.6)<br>969.6 |
| George Weiss | VFY | 65 | (+1.56)<br>66.56 |
| | Non-transferable | | (36.64)<br>36.64 |

| Candidates Elected | Count |
|---|---|
| Peter Robinson DUP | 1st |
| Reg Empey UUP | 1st |
| Robin Newton DUP | 3rd |
| David Ervine PUP | 6th |
| Naomi Long All | 6th |
| Michael Copeland UUP | 6th |

Peter Robinson

Reg Empey

Robin Newton

David Ervine

Naomi Long

Michael Copeland

| Stage 3 | Stage 4 | Stage 5 | Stage 6 |
|---|---|---|---|
| Transfer of Empey's surplus | Exclusion of Weiss, McBlain, Bell, Black & Dick | Exclusion of Van Es & O'Donnell | Exclusion of Toan |
| (+0.93)<br>129.05 | **(-129.05)**<br>0 | - | - |
| (+2.48)<br>183.68 | **(-183.68)**<br>0 | - | - |
| (+777.79)<br>3132.75 | (+87.76)<br>3220.51 | (+77.41)<br>3297.92 | (+352.57)<br>3650.49 |
| (+16.43)<br>250.51 | **(-250.51)**<br>0 | - | - |
| **(-2035)**<br>4424 | (0)<br>4424 | (0)<br>4424 | (0)<br>4424 |
| (+165.85)<br>3377.37 | (+132.11)<br>3509.48 | (+151.31)<br>3660.79 | (+602.60)<br>4263.39 |
| (+83.08)<br>2877.36 | (+133.31)<br>3010.67 | (1001.34)<br>4012.01 | (+44.53)<br>4056.54 |
| (+2.48)<br>81.24 | **(-81.24)**<br>0 | - | - |
| (+26.04)<br>4444.24 | (0)<br>4424.24 | (0)<br>4424.24 | (0)<br>4424.24 |
| (+1.55)<br>1185.71 | (+20)<br>1205.71 | **(-1205.71)**<br>0 | - |
| (0)<br>4424 | (0)<br>4424 | (0)<br>4424 | (0)<br>4424 |
| (+891.25)<br>2681.85 | (+100.8)<br>2782.65 | (+56.72)<br>2839.37 | (+457.11)<br>3296.48 |
| (+9.92)<br>2643.24 | (+73.42)<br>2716.66 | (+11.12)<br>2727.78 | **(-2727.78)**<br>0 |
| (+16.43)<br>986.03 | (+49.62)<br>1035.65 | **(-986.03)**<br>0 | - |
| (+0.62)<br>67.18 | **(-67.18)**<br>0 | - | - |
| (40.15)<br>76.79 | (114.64)<br>191.43 | (943.46)<br>1134.89 | (1270.97)<br>2405.86 |

# Belfast North

**Total Valid Pole 31532 Quota 4505 Turnout 62.3**

**Party performance**

| Party | Seats | 1st Pref Vote | % | (%1998) |
|---|---|---|---|---|
| DUP | 2 | 10776 | 34.2 | 21.3 |
| SF | 2 | 8514 | 27.0 | 21.3 |
| UUP | 1 | 2961 | 9.4 | 10.9 |
| SDLP | 1 | 5294 | 16.8 | 21.1 |
| Alliance | - | 305 | 1.0 | 3.1 |
| Others | - | 3682 | 11.7 | 22.3 |

**At a glance...**

DUP MP Nigel Dodds topped the poll (with 2 quotas) followed by Sinn Féin's Gerry Kelly. The main change in North Belfast was Kathy Stanton's winning of a second seat for Sinn Féin, ultimately that held previously by the PUP's Billy Hutchinson. The poll witnessed a substantial increase in DUP and Sinn Féin vote share, mainly at the expense of the SDLP and PUP. The UUP vote slipped to under 3,000 for the first time, although candidate Fred Cobain was comfortably elected, as was Alban Maginness for the SDLP. Overall North Belfast reflected the two main features of the election overall - gains by SF and the DUP and a real squeeze of the smaller parties.

| | | Stage 1 | Stage 2 | Stage 3 | Stage 4 | Stage 5 |
|---|---|---|---|---|---|---|
| | | 1st pref votes 31,532 | Transfer of Dodds' surplus | Transfer of Kelly's surplus | Transfer of McCausland's surplus | Exclusion of Gallagher & Delaney |
| *Fraser Agnew | UUC | 802 | (+198.39) 1000.39 | (0) 1000.39 | (+157.05) 1157.44 | (+0.09) 1157.53 |
| Elizabeth Byrne-McCullough | NIWC | 467 | (+11.22) 478.22 | (+4.14) 482.36 | (+3.24) 485.6) | (+12.6) 498.2 |
| *Fred Cobain | UUP | 2961 | (+377.91) 3338.91 | (+0.36) 3339.27 | (+170.19) 3509.46 | (+5.18) 3514.64 |
| Pat Convery | SDLP | 2108 | (+5.61) 2113.61 | (+45.18) 2158.79 | (+1.71) 2160.5 | (+23.18) 2183.68 |
| Marcella Delaney | WP | 90 | (+1.02) 91.02 | (+0.18) 91.2 | (+0.72) 91.92 | **(-91.92)** 0 |
| *Nigel Dodds | DUP | 9276 | **(-4771)** 4505 | (0) 4505 | (0) 4505 | (0) 4505 |
| Peter Emerson | Green | 261 | (+8.16) 269.16 | (+2.34) 271.5 | (+6.39 277.89 | (+21.51) 299.4 |
| John Gallagher | VFY | 17 | (+2.55) 19.55 | (0) 19.55 | (+0.36) 19.91 | **(-19.91)** 0 |
| Margaret Hawkins | All | 305 | (+8.67) 313.67 | (+1.62) 315.29 | (+3.06) 318.35 | (+7.51) 325.86 |
| *Billy Hutchinson | PUP | 1358 | (+329.46) 1687.46 | (+0.9) 1688.36 | (+122.76) 1811.12 | (+7.53) 1818.65 |
| *Gerry Kelly | SF | 5524 | (n/a) 5524 | **(-1019)** 4505 | (0) 4505 | (0) 4505 |
| *Alban Maginness | SDLP | 3186 | (+13.26) 3199.26) | (+111.42) 3310.68 | (+2.25) 3312.93 | (+10) 3322.93 |
| Nelson McCausland | DUP | 1500 | (+3600.6) 5100.6 | (n/a) 5100.6 | **(-595.6)** 4505 | (0) 4505 |
| Raymond McCord | Ind | 218 | (+66.81) 284.81 | (+1.8) 286.61 | (+38.52) 325.13 | (+4.69) 329.82 |
| Frank McCoubrey | Ind | 469 | (+82.62) 551.62 | (+0.36) 551.98 | (+66.6) 618.58 | (+0.18) 618.76 |
| Kathy Stanton | SF | 2990 | (0) 2990 | (+813.78) 3803.87 | (+0.09) 3803.78 | (+9) 3812.87 |
| | Non-transferable | | (64.72) 64.72 | (36.92) 101.64 | (22.66) 124.3 | (10.36) 134.66 |

| Candidates Elected | Count |
|---|---|
| Nigel Dodds DUP | 1st |
| Gerry Kelly SF | 1st |
| Nelson McCausland DUP | 2nd |
| Fred Cobain UUP | 10th |
| Alban Maginness SDLP | 12th |
| Kathy Stanton SF | 12th |

Nigel Dodds

Gerry Kelly

Nelson McCausland

Fred Cobain

Alban Maginness

Kathy Stanton

| Stage 6 | Stage 7 | Stage 8 | Stage 9 | Stage 10 | Stage 11 | Stage 12 |
|---|---|---|---|---|---|---|
| Exclusion of Emerson | Exclusion of McCord | Exclusion of Hawkins | Exclusion of McCoubrey | Exclusion of Byrne-McCullough & Agnew | Transfer of Cobain's surplus | Exclusion of McCoubrey |
| (+10.74)<br>1168.27 | (+49.37)<br>1217.64 | (+16.98)<br>1234.62 | (+100.6)<br>1335.22 | **(-1335.22)**<br>0 | - | - |
| (+74.96)<br>573.16 | (+12.41)<br>585.57 | (+107.98)<br>693.55 | (+8.69)<br>702.24 | **(-702.24)**<br>0 | - | - |
| (+24.34)<br>3538.98 | (+68.79)<br>3607.77 | (+88.52)<br>3696.29 | (+205.21)<br>3901.50 | (654)<br>4555.5 | **(-50.5)**<br>4505 | (0)<br>4505 |
| (+29.54)<br>2213.22 | (+15.18)<br>2228.4 | (+44.36)<br>2272.76 | (+6.6)<br>2279.36 | (+201.1)<br>2480.46 | (+6.51)<br>2486.97 | **(-2486.97)**<br>0 |
| - | - | - | - | - | - | - |
| (0)<br>4505 | (0)<br>4505 | (0)<br>4505 | (0)<br>4505 | (0)<br>4505 | (0)<br>4505 | (0)<br>4505 |
| **(-299.4)**<br>0 | - | - | - | - | - | - |
| - | - | - | - | - | - | - |
| (+44.29)<br>370.15 | (+13.18)<br>383.33 | **(-383.33)**<br>0 | - | - | - | - |
| (+17.79)<br>1836.44 | (+37.84)<br>1874.28 | (+13.29)<br>1887.57 | (+199.85)<br>2087.42 | (+404.53)<br>2491.95 | (34.41)<br>2526.36 | (+78.69)<br>2605.05 |
| (0)<br>4505 | (0)<br>4505 | (0)<br>4505 | (0)<br>4505 | (0)<br>4505 | (0)<br>4505 | (0)<br>4505 |
| (+27)<br>3349.93 | (+15.87)<br>3365.8 | (+70.74)<br>3436.54 | (+7.54)<br>3444.08 | (+223.02)<br>3667.1 | (+8.37)<br>3675.47 | (+1894)<br>5569.47 |
| (0)<br>4505 | (0)<br>4505 | (0)<br>4505 | (0)<br>4505 | (0)<br>4505 | (0)<br>4505 | (0)<br>4505 |
| (10.87)<br>340.69 | **(-340.69)**<br>0 | - | - | - | - | - |
| (+2.09)<br>620.85 | (+55.68)<br>676.53 | (+6)<br>682.53 | **(-682.53)**<br>0 | - | - | - |
| (+20.05)<br>3832.92 | (+5.36)<br>3838.28 | (+3.36)<br>3841.64 | (+0.18)<br>3841.82 | (+53.62)<br>3895.44 | (+0.93)<br>3896.37 | (+222.06)<br>4118.43 |
| (37.73)<br>172.39 | (67.01)<br>239.4 | (32.1)<br>271.5 | (153.86)<br>425.36 | (501.19)<br>926.55 | (0.28)<br>926.83 | (292.22)<br>1219.05 |

# Belfast South

Total Valid Pole 31330 Quota 4476 Turnout 62.6

**Party performance**

| Party | Seats | 1st Pref Vote | % | (%1998) |
|---|---|---|---|---|
| DUP | 1 | 6529 | 20.8 | 13.1 |
| SF | 1 | 3933 | 12.6 | 6.4 |
| UUP | 2 | 8469 | 27.0 | 23.4 |
| SDLP | 2 | 7176 | 22.9 | 21.7 |
| Alliance | - | 1849 | 5.9 | 10.0 |
| Others | - | 3374 | 10.8 | 25.4 |

## At a glance...

The headline news from South Belfast was Sinn Féin's Alex Maskey gaining the party's first ever seat in the constituency – in this case at the expense of outgoing MLA and Northern Ireland Women's Coalition leader Monica McWilliams. Former Arts and Culture Minister Michael McGimpsey topped the poll and was returned with colleague Esmond Birnie. The SDLP, in one of the few constituencies where its vote share actually increased, held on to its two seats. Mark Robinson easily retained the single DUP seat, with the party raising its vote share at the expense of the smaller unionist parties.

| | | Stage 1 | Stage 2 | Stage 3 | Stage 4 | Stage 5 |
|---|---|---|---|---|---|---|
| | | 1st pref Vote 31,330 | Transfer of McGimpsey's surplus | Elimination of Steven | Elimination of Lynn | Elimination of Barbour & Lomas |
| James Barbour | Soc | 167 | (+1.19) 168.19 | (+2) 170.19 | (+11) 181.19 | **(-181.19)** 0 |
| *Esmond Birnie | UUP | 2311 | (+551.99) 2862.99 | (0) 2862.99 | (+3) 2865.99 | (+56.19) 2922.18 |
| Tom Ekin | All | 664 | (+8.5) 672.5 | (+1) 673.5 | (+5) 678.5 | (+19.68) 698.18 |
| *Carmel Hanna | SDLP | 3910 | (+12.92) 3922.92 | (+3) 3925.92 | (+10) 3935.92 | (+17.17) 3953.09 |
| John Hiddleston | UUP | 769 | (+199.75) 968.75 | (+1) 969.75 | (+1.17) 970.92 | (+19.68) 990.6 |
| Roger Lomas | Cons | 116 | (+3.06) 119.06 | (+1) 120.06 | (0) 120.06 | **(-120.06)** 0 |
| Patrick Lynn | WP | 96 | (+0.17) 96.17 | (-1) 97.17 | **(-97.17)** 0 | - |
| *^Alex Maskey | SF | 3933 | (+2.55) 3935.55 | (+2) 3937.55 | (+10) 3947.55) | (+21) 3968.55 |
| *Alasdair McDonnell | SDLP | 3266 | (+17) 3283 | (+4) 3287 | (+20) 3307 | (+10.34) 3317.34 |
| *Michael McGimpsey | UUP | 5389 | **(-913)** 4476 | (0) 4476 | (0) 4476 | (0) 4476 |
| Monica McWilliams | NIWC | 2150 | (+30.43) 2180.43 | (+5) 2185.434 | (+18) 2203.43 | (+45) 2248.43 |
| Thomas Morrow | PUP | 495 | (+14.62) 509.62 | (0) 509.62 | (+2) 511.62 | (+9) 520.62 |
| Ruth Patterson | DUP | 2538 | (+18.7) 2556.7 | (0) 2556.7 | (0) 2556.7 | (+19.34) 2576.04 |
| Geraldine Rice | All | 1185 | (+13.94) 1198.94 | (+3) 1201.94 | (+1) 1202.94 | (+12) 1214.94 |
| *Mark Robinson | DUP | 3991 | (+33.32) 4024.32 | (0) 4024.32 | (+1) 4025.32 | (+14.34) 4039.66 |
| Lindsay Steven | VFY | 42 | (+0.17) 42.17 | **(-42.17)** 0 | - | - |
| John Wright | GP | 308 | (+1.19) 309.19 | (+16.17) 325.36 | (+5) 330.36 | (+37.17) 367.53 |
| ^Alex Maskey was previously MLA for Belfast West | Non- transferable | | (3.5) 3.5 | (3) 6.5 | (10) 16.5 | (20.34) 36.84 |

| Candidates Elected | Count |
|---|---|
| Michael McGimpsey UUP | 1st |
| Mark Robinson DUP | 11th |
| Esmond Birnie UUP | 11th |
| Carmel Hanna SDLP | 12th |
| Alex Maskey SF | 12th |
| Alasdair McDonnell | 12th |

Michael McGimpsey

Mark Robinson

Esmond Birnie

Carmel Hanna

Alex Maskey

Alasdair McDonnell

| Stage 6 | Stage 7 | Stage 8 | Stage 9 | Stage 10 | Stage 11 | Stage 12 |
|---|---|---|---|---|---|---|
| Elimination of Wright | Elimination of Morrow | Elimination of Ekin | Elimination of Hiddleston | Elimination of Rice | Elimination of Patterson | Transfer of Robinson's surplus |
| - | - | - | - | - | - | - |
| (+16.51)<br>2938.69 | (+99.4)<br>3038.09 | (+50.02)<br>3088.11 | (+783.2)<br>3871.31 | (+441.18)<br>4312.49 | (+224)<br>4536.49 | (n/a)<br>4536.49 |
| (+28.17)<br>726.35 | (+13.51)<br>739.86 | **(-739.86)**<br>0 | - | - | - | - |
| (+29.17)<br>3982.26 | (+8.51)<br>3990.77 | (+65.53)<br>4056.3 | (+6.38)<br>4062.68 | (+270.02)<br>4332.7 | (+4.85)<br>4337.55 | (+67)<br>4404.55 |
| (+5)<br>995.6 | (+94.21)<br>1089.81 | (+21.19)<br>1111 | **(-1111)**<br>0 | - | - | - |
| - | - | - | - | - | - | - |
| - | - | - | - | - | - | - |
| (+19)<br>3987.55 | (+2)<br>3989.55 | (+2)<br>3991.55 | (0)<br>3991.55 | (+12)<br>4003.55 | (+8)<br>4011.55 | (+1)<br>4012.55 |
| (+23)<br>3340.34 | (+10.17)<br>3350.51 | (+30.51)<br>3381.02 | (+8.53)<br>3389.55 | (+199.55)<br>3589.1 | (+10.87)<br>3599.97 | (+50)<br>3649.97 |
| (0)<br>4476 | (0)<br>4476 | (0)<br>4476 | (0)<br>4476 | (0)<br>4476 | (0)<br>4476 | (0)<br>4476 |
| (+139.17)<br>2387.6 | (+43.53)<br>2431.13 | (+86.87)<br>2518 | (+24.23)<br>24542.23 | (+626.25)<br>3168.48 | (+40.06)<br>3208.54) | (+314)<br>3522.54 |
| (+8)<br>528.62 | **(-528.62)**<br>0 | - | - | - | - | - |
| (+4)<br>2580.04 | (+100.21)<br>2680.25 | (+3.17)<br>2683.42 | (+135.25)<br>2818.67 | (+20.17)<br>2838.84 | **(-2838.84)**<br>0 | - |
| (+55)<br>1269.94 | (+14.68)<br>1284.62 | (+462.72)<br>1747.34 | (+15.38)<br>1762.72 | **(-1762.72)**<br>0 | - | - |
| (+9.17)<br>4048.83 | (+102.04)<br>4150.87 | (+4.34)<br>4155.21 | (+91.61)<br>4246.82 | (+21.34)<br>4268.16 | (+2393)<br>6661.16 | **(-2185.16)**<br>4476 |
| - | - | - | - | - | - | - |
| **(-367.53)**<br>0 | - | - | - | - | - | - |
| (31.34)<br>68.18 | (40.36)<br>108.54 | (13.51)<br>122.05 | (46.42)<br>168.47 | (172.21)<br>340.68 | (158.06)<br>498.74 | (1753.16)<br>2251.9 |

# Belfast West

**Total Valid Pole 32854 Quota 4694 Turnout 65.9**

**Party performance**

| Party | Seats | 1st Pref Vote | % | (%1998) |
|---|---|---|---|---|
| DUP | 1 | 2544 | 7.7 | 3.2 |
| SF | 4 | 21368 | 65.0 | 59.0 |
| UUP | - | 1170 | 3.6 | 3.9 |
| SDLP | 1 | 6250 | 19.0 | 24.9 |
| Alliance | - | 75 | 0.2 | 0.3 |
| Others | - | 1447 | 4.4 | 8.6 |

**At a glance...**

Sinn Féin confirmed their dominance of nationalist West Belfast, narrowly missing out on taking a fifth seat out of six, despite impressive vote management. Dianne Dodds regained a unionist seat ultimately at the expense of SDLP veteran Dr Joe Hendron. Sinn Féin retained four, although sitting MLA Sue Ramsey lost out to a party colleague. Despite further slippage in SDLP vote share, party policing spokesman Alex Attwood comfortably retained his seat. Sitting MP and Sinn Féin President Gerry Adams topped the poll followed immediately by three Sinn Féin colleagues.

The 65% Sinn Féin share of the vote was the highest recorded by any party in any of the 18 constituencies.

| | | 1st stage | 2nd stage |
|---|---|---|---|
| | | 1st preference votes 32,854 | Transfer of Adams' surplus |
| *Gerry Adams | SF | 6199 | (-1505) 4694 |
| *Alex Attwood | SDLP | 3667 | (+129.6) 3796.6 |
| Mary Ayers | All | 75 | (+3.12) 78.12 |
| ^*Bairbre de Brun | SF | 4069 | (+407.58) 4476.52 |
| Dianne Dodds | DUP | 2544 | (0) 2544 |
| Michael Ferguson | SF | 3849 | (+63.84 3912.84 |
| *Joe Hendron | SDLP | 2583 | (+71.28) 2654.28 |
| David Kerr | UTW | 16 | (0) 16 |
| John Lowry | WP | 407 | (+3.84) 410.84 |
| John MacVicar | Ind | 211 | (+0.24) 211.24 |
| Fra McCann | SF | 4263 | (+74.16) 4337.16 |
| Chris McGimpsey | UUP | 1170 | (+4.56) 1174.56 |
| *Sue Ramsey | SF | 2988 | (+685.2) 3673.2 |
| Hugh Smyth | PUP | 813 | (+1.68) 814.68 |
| | Non-transferable | | (59.96) 59.96 |

^ Bairbre de Brún has resigned from the Assemby to be replaced by Sue Ramsey

| Candidates Elected | Count |
|---|---|
| Gerry Adams SF | 1st |
| Alex Attwood SDLP | 5th |
| Bairbre de Brun SF | 6th |
| Fra McCann SF | 6th |
| Michael Ferguson SF | 8th |
| Dianne Dodds DUP | 8th |

Gerry Adams

Alex Attwood

Bairbre de Brun

Fra McCann

Michael Ferguson

Dianne Dodds

| 3rd stage | 4th stage | 5th stage | 6th stage | 7th stage | 8th stage |
|---|---|---|---|---|---|
| Elimination of Kerr, Ayers, MacVicar & Lowry | Elimination of Smyth & McGimpsey | Elimination of Hendron | Transfer of Attwood's surplus | Transfer of de Brun's surplus | Transfer of McCann's surplus |
| (0) 4694 | (0) 4694 | (0) 4694 | (0) 4694 | (0) 4694 | (0) 4694 |
| (+104.44) 3901.04 | (+55.24) 3956.28 | (+2140) 6096.28 | **(-1402.28)** 4694 | (0) 4694 | (0) 4694 |
| **(-78.12)** 0 | - | - | - | - | - |
| (+18.44) 4494.96 | (+9.24) 4504.2 | (+161.48) 4665.68 | (+564) 5229.68 | **(-535.68)** 4694 | (0) 4694 |
| (+87) 2631 | (+1513.24) 4144.24 | (+112) 4256.24 | (+16) 4272.24 | (+2) 4274.24 | (+2.85) 4277.09 |
| (+8.72) 3921.56 | (+23.56) 3945.12 | (+54.88) 4000 | (+117) 4117 | (+229) 4346 | (+102.6) 4448.6 |
| (+195.44) 2849.72 | (+259) 3108.72 | **(-3108.72)** 0 | - | - | - |
| **(-16)** 0 | - | - | - | - | - |
| **(-410.84)** 0 | - | - | - | - | - |
| **(-211.24)** 0 | - | - | - | - | - |
| (+23.72) 4360.88 | (+2.48) 4363.36 | (+161.64) 4525 | (+380) 4905 | (n/a) 4905 | **(-211)** 4694 |
| (+124) 1298.56 | **(-1298.56)** 0 | - | - | - | - |
| (+26.48) 3699.68 | (+6.24) 3705.92 | (+62.92) 3768.84 | (+155) 3923.84 | (+161) 4084.84 | (+105.45) 4190.26 |
| (+48) 862.68 | **(-862.68)** 0 | - | - | - | - |
| (79.96) 139.92 | (292.24) 432.16 | (415.8) 847.96 | (170.28) 1018.24 | (143.68) 1161.92) | (0.1) 1162.02 |

# East Antrim

**Total Valid Pole 30952 Quota 4422 Turnout 56.5**

**Party performance**

| Party | Seats | 1st Pref Vote | % | (%1998) |
|---|---|---|---|---|
| DUP | 3 | 10563 | 34.1 | 22.2 |
| SF | - | 768 | 2.5 | 2.1 |
| UUP | 2 | 8883 | 28.7 | 29.6 |
| SDLP | - | 2428 | 7.8 | 5.9 |
| Alliance | 1 | 3372 | 10.9 | 20.1 |
| Others | - | 4938 | 16.0 | 20.1 |

### At a glance...

A significant increase in DUP vote share in this predominantly unionist constituency resulted in the party gaining a third seat. The UUP vote share held firm and the party retained its two seats. Despite increasing his share of the vote it was SDLP sitting MLA Danny O'Connor who lost out. The Alliance party former leader Sean Neeson held on to his seat despite the Alliance vote almost halving – further evidence of the overall hardening of attitudes across Northern Ireland. Roy Beggs Junior (UUP) topped the poll, closely followed by DUP education spokesman Sammy Wilson, who ran in this constituency instead of his usual Belfast East.

| | | 1st stage | 2nd stage | 3rd stage | 4th stage | 5th stage | 6th stage |
|---|---|---|---|---|---|---|---|
| | | 1st pref votes 30,952 | Transfer of Beggs' surplus | Transfer of Wilson's surplus | Elimination of Frew | Elimination of Greer | Elimination of Monaghan |
| John Anderson | Ind | 348 | (+5.18) 353.18) | (+0.32) 353.5 | (+10) 363.5 | (+8.02) 371.52) | (+17) 388.52 |
| Roy Beggs | UUP | 5175 | **(-753)** 4422 | (0) 4422 | (0) 4422 | (0) 4422 | (0) 4422 |
| George Dawson | DUP | 3163 | (+34.3) 3197.3 | (+21.48) 3218.78 | (+5.14) 3223.92 | (+14.18) 3238.1 | (+6.04) 3244.14 |
| Stewart Dickson | All | 1192 | (+23.38) 1215.38 | (+0.3) 1215.68 | (+27) 1242.68 | (+24.28) 1266.96 | (+62.14) 1329.1 |
| Andrew Frew | Green | 165 | (+0.7) 165.7 | (+0.04) 165.74 | **(-165.74)** 0 | - | - |
| Alan Greer | Cons | 196 | (+5.74) 201.74 | (+0.14) 201.88 | (+9) 210.88 | **(-210.88)** 0 | - |
| *David Hilditch | DUP | 2856 | (+27.44) 2883.44 | (+56.88) 2940.32 | (+3.02) 2943.34 | (+20.58) 2963.92 | (+11.14) 2975.06 |
| Carolyn Howarth | PUP | 534 | (+5.74) 539.74 | (0) 539.74 | (+3) 542.74 | (+7.42) 550.16 | (+16.14) 566.3 |
| *Roger Hutchinson | Ind | 1011 | (+8.4) 1019.4 | (+0.96) 1020.36 | (+2.14) 1022.5 | (+8.28) 1030.78 | (+5) 1035.78 |
| Robert Mason | Ind | 354 | (+3.78) 367.78 | (+0.54) 368.32 | (+17.14) 385.46 | (+8.14) 393.6 | (+15.14) 408.74 |
| Roy McCune | UUP | 1646 | (+448.28) 2094.28 | (+0.98) 2095.26 | (+8.14) 2103.4 | (+30.24) 2133.64 | (+17.28) 2150.92 |
| Jack McKee | Ind | 1449 | (+17.92) 1466.92 | (+3.96) 1470.88 | (0) 1470.88 | (+2.14) 1473.02 | (+2) 1475.02 |
| Jack McMullan | SF | 768 | (+0.28) 768.28 | (0) 768.28 | (+1) 769.28 | (+1) 770.28 | (+5) 775.28 |
| Anne Monaghan | NIWC | 307 | (+2.38) 309.38 | (+0.12) 309.5 | (+31) 340.5 | (+7) 347.5 | **(-347.5)** 0 |
| *Sean Neeson | All | 2180 | (+28.28) 2208.28 | (+0.98) 2209.26 | (+26.14) 2235.4 | (+22.42) 2257.82 | (+110.46) 2368.28 |
| *Daniel O'Connor | SDLP | 2428 | (+4.62) 2432.62 | (+0.12) 2432.74 | (+8) 2440.74 | (1) 2441.74 | (+39.42) 2481.16 |
| *Ken Robinson | UUP | 2062 | (+94.08) 2156.08 | (+1.68) 2157.76 | (+6) 2163.76) | (+28.7) 2192.46 | (+11.44) 2203.9 |
| Thomas Robinson | UKUP | 564 | (+9.52) 573.52 | (+1.9) 575.42 | (0) 575.42 | (+16.02) 591.44 | (+3.14) 594.58 |
| *^Sammy Wilson | DUP | 4544 | (n/a) 4544 | **(-122)** 4422 | (0) 4422 | (0) 4422 | (0) 4422 |
| ^Sammy Wilson was previously MLA for Belfast East | Non- transferable | | (32.98) (32.98) | (31.6) 64.58 | (9.02) 73.6 | (11.46) 85.06 | (26.16) 111.22 |

| **Candidates Elected** | **Count** |
|---|---|
| Roy Beggs UUP | 1st |
| Sammy Wilson DUP | 1st |
| Ken Robinson UUP | 15th |
| Sean Neeson All | 15th |
| David Hilditch DUP | 15th |
| George Dawson DUP | 15th |

Roy Beggs

Sammy Wilson

Ken Robinson

Sean Neeson

David Hilditch

George Dawson

| 7th stage | 8th stage | 9th stage | 10th stage | 11th stage | 12th stage | 13th stage | 14th stage | 15th stage |
|---|---|---|---|---|---|---|---|---|
| Elimination of Anderson | Elimination of Mason | Elimination of Howarth | Elimination of TD Robinson | Elimination of McMullan | Elimination of Hutchinson | Elimination of Dickson | Elimination of McKee | Elimination of McCune |
| **(-388.52)**<br>0 | - | - | - | - | - | - | - | - |
| (0)<br>4422 | (0)<br>4422 | (0) 4422 | (0)<br>4422 | (0)<br>4422 | (0)<br>4422 | (0)<br>4422 | (0)<br>4422 | (0)<br>4422 |
| (+29.22)<br>3273.36 | (+19.1)<br>3292.46 | (+89.28)<br>3381.74 | (+90.3)<br>3472.04 | (0)<br>3472.04 | (+180.44)<br>3652.48 | (+18.02)<br>3670.5 | (+390.6)<br>4061.1 | (+67.3)<br>4128.4 |
| (+33.84)<br>1362.94 | (+35)<br>1397.94 | (+12.56)<br>1410.5 | (+20.28)<br>1430.78 | (+9)<br>1439.78 | (+20.42)<br>1460.2 | **(-1460.2)**<br>0 | - | - |
| - | - | - | - | - | - | - | - | - |
| - | - | - | - | - | - | - | - | - |
| (+5.26)<br>2980.32 | (+23.14)<br>3003.46 | (+96.14)<br>3099.6 | (+89.26)<br>3188.86 | (0)<br>3188.86 | (+239.92)<br>3428.78 | (+35.78)<br>3464.56 | (+569.74)<br>4034.3 | (+107.82)<br>4142.12 |
| (+7.28)<br>573.58 | (+17.16)<br>590.74 | **(-590.74)**<br>0 | - | - | - | - | - | - |
| (+25.14)<br>1060.92 | (+40.34)<br>1101.26 | (+48.28)<br>1149.54 | (+30)<br>1179.54 | (+2)<br>1181.54 | **(-1181.54)**<br>0 | - | - | - |
| (+106.22)<br>514.96 | **(-514.96)**<br>0 | - | - | - | - | - | - | - |
| (+39.12)<br>2190.04 | (+33)<br>2223.04 | (+91.64<br>2314.68 | (+109.82)<br>2424.5 | (+5)<br>2429.5) | (+62.1)<br>2491.6 | (+61.72)<br>2533.32 | (+166.52)<br>2719.84 | **(-2719.84)**<br>0 |
| (+31.44)<br>1506.46 | (+95.98)<br>1602.44 | (+25)<br>1627.44 | (+117.1)<br>1744.54 | (+3)<br>1747.54 | (+226.08)<br>1973.62 | (+10.84)<br>1984.46 | **(-1984.46)**<br>0 | - |
| (+1)<br>776.28 | (+2)<br>778.28 | (0)<br>778.28 | (+1)<br>779.28 | (-779.28)<br>0 | - | - | - | - |
| - | - | - | - | - | - | - | - | - |
| (+56.42)<br>2424.7 | (+93.42)<br>2518.12 | (+49.56)<br>2567.68 | (+36.16)<br>2603.84 | (+59.14)<br>2662.98 | (+49.74)<br>2712.72 | (+1207.58)<br>3920.3 | (+105.04)<br>4025.34 | (+239.28)<br>4264.62 |
| (+13)<br>2494.16 | (+42.14)<br>2536.3 | (+9.14)<br>2545.44 | (+10.14)<br>2555.58 | (+648)<br>3203.58 | (+11.02)<br>3214.6 | (+37.84)<br>3252.44 | (+46.04)<br>3298.48 | (+33.42)<br>3331.9 |
| (+19.58)<br>2223.48 | (+27.6)<br>2251.08 | (+94.56)<br>2345.64 | (+104.26)<br>2449.9 | (+2.14)<br>2452.04 | (+79.26)<br>2531.3 | (+29)<br>2560.3 | (+226.16)<br>2786.46 | (+2051.56)<br>4838.02 |
| (+8)<br>602.58 | (+29.04)<br>631.62 | (+20)<br>651.62 | **(-651.62)**<br>**0** | - | - | - | - | - |
| (0)<br>4422 | (0)<br>4422 | (0)<br>4422 | (0)<br>4422 | (0)<br>4422 | (0)<br>4422 | (0)<br>4422 | (0)<br>4422 | (0)<br>4422 |
| (13)<br>124.22 | (57.04)<br>181.26 | (54.58)<br>235.84 | (43.3)<br>279.14 | (51)<br>330.14 | (312.56)<br>642.7 | (59.42)<br>702.12 | (480.36)<br>1182.48 | (220.46)<br>1402.94 |

# East Londonderry

**Total Valid Pole 34273** **Quota 4897** **Turnout 61.8**

**Party performance**

| Party | Seats | 1st Pref Vote | % | (%1998) |
|---|---|---|---|---|
| DUP | 2 | 11091 | 32.4 | 23.7 |
| SF | 1 | 6121 | 17.9 | 9.8 |
| UUP | 2 | 7769 | 22.7 | 25.2 |
| SDLP | 1 | 5584 | 16.3 | 23.6 |
| Alliance | - | 762 | 2.2 | 6.1 |
| Others | - | 2946 | 8.6 | 11.7 |

## At a glance...

Overall in terms of seats this constituency retained its 4-2 unionist/nationalist balance although on the unionist side the DUP collected a second seat from former UKUP MLA Boyd Douglas. Sinn Féin won its first seat in this constituency from the SDLP's Michael Coyle. The Ulster Unionist Party retained its two seats on a smaller share of the vote with Norman Hillis replacing disenchanted former MLA Pauline Armitage who ran unsuccessfully as a UKUP candidate. As elsewhere, the DUP and Sinn Féin increased their vote share significantly, with the Alliance vote diminishing.

| | | 1st stage | 2nd stage | 3rd stage | 4th stage | 5th stage |
|---|---|---|---|---|---|---|
| | | **1st pref votes 34,273** | Elimination of Baur & Boyle | Elimination of Armitage | Elimination of Stevenson | Transfer of McClarty's surplus |
| *Pauline Armitage | UKUP | 906 | (+31) 937 | **(-937)** 0 | - | - |
| Marion Baur | Soc Env All | 137 | **(-137)** 0 | - | - | - |
| Yvonne Boyle | All | 762 | **(-762)** 0 | - | - | - |
| Maurice Bradley | DUP | 2836 | (+12) 2848 | (+187) 3035 | (+5) 3040 | (+3.33) 3043.33 |
| Francis Brolly | SF | 4019 | (+32) 4051 | (+5) 4056 | (0) 4056 | (+0.37) 4056.37 |
| *Gregory Campbell | DUP | 4789 | (+14) 4803 | (+220) 5023 | (n/a) 5023 | (n/a) 5023 |
| Michael Coyle | SDLP | 2394 | (+131) 2525 | (+7) 2532 | (+14) 2546 | (+2.59) 2548.59 |
| *John Dallat | SDLP | 3190 | (+240) 3430 | (+25) 3455 | (+13) 3468 | (+4.81) 3472.81 |
| *Boyd Douglas | UUC | 1903 | (+20) 1923 | (+126) 2049 | (+122) 2171) | (+19.61) 2190.61 |
| Norman Hillis | UUP | 2292 | (+85) 2377 | (+150) 2527 | (+432) 2959 | (+240.87) 3199.87 |
| *David McClarty | UUP | 4069 | (+219) 4288 | (+126) 4414 | (+762) 5176 | **(-279)** 4897 |
| Cliona O'Kane | SF | 2102 | (+8) 2110 | (+1) 2111 | (+3) 2114 | (0) 2114 |
| George Robinson | DUP | 3466 | (+8) 3474 | (+40) 3514 | (+99) 3613 | (+4.07) 3617.07 |
| Edwin Stevenson | UUP | 1408 | (+35) 1443 | (+23) 1466 | **(-1466)** 0 | - |
| | **Non-transferable** | | (64) 64 | (27) 91 | (16) 107 | (3.35) 110.35 |

| Candidates Elected | Count |
|---|---|
| Gregory Campbell DUP | 3rd |
| David McClarty UUP | 4th |
| Francis Brolly SF | 7th |
| George Robinson DUP | 10th |
| Norman Hillis UUP | 11th |
| John Dallat SDLP | 12th |

Gregory Campbell

David McClarty

Francis Brolly

George Robinson

Norman Hillis

John Dallat

| 6th stage | 7th stage | 8th stage | 9th stage | 10th stage | 11th stage | 12th stage |
|---|---|---|---|---|---|---|
| Transfer of Campbell's surplus | Elimination of O'Kane | Transfer of Brolly's surplus | Elimination of Douglas | Elimination of Bradley | Transfer of Robinson's surplus | Transfer of Hillis's surplus |
| - | - | - | - | - | - | - |
| - | - | - | - | - | - | - |
| - | - | - | - | - | - | - |
| (+47.74)<br>3091.07 | (+4)<br>3095.07 | (+1.66)<br>3096.73 | (+276.79)<br>3373.52 | **(-3373.52)**<br>0 | - | - |
| (+0.62)<br>4056.99 | (+1839)<br>5895.99 | **(-998.99)**<br>4897 | (0)<br>4897 | (0)<br>4897 | (0)<br>4897 | (0)<br>4897 |
| **(-126)**<br>4897 | (0)<br>4897 | (0)<br>4897 | (0)<br>4897 | (0)<br>4897 | (0)<br>4897 | (0)<br>4897 |
| (0)<br>2548.59 | (+152)<br>2700.59 | (+814.23)<br>3514.82 | (+12)<br>3526.82 | (+7.65)<br>3534.47 | (+11)<br>3545.47 | (+107)<br>3652.47 |
| (+1.24)<br>3474.05 | (+91)<br>3565.05 | (+169.32)<br>3734.37 | (+25.62)<br>3759.99 | (+18.24)<br>3778.23 | (+16)<br>3794.23 | (+76)<br>3870.23 |
| (+29.14)<br>2219.75 | (1)<br>2220.75 | (+0.83)<br>2221.58 | **(-2221.58)**<br>0 | - | - | - |
| (+21.08)<br>3220.95 | (+2)<br>3222.95 | (+0.83)<br>3223.78 | (+660.06)<br>3883.84 | (436.08)<br>4319.92 | (+1027)<br>5346.92 | **(-449.92)**<br>4897 |
| (0)<br>4897 | (0)<br>4897 | (0)<br>4897 | (0)<br>4897 | (0)<br>4897 | (0)<br>4897 | (0)<br>4897 |
| (0)<br>2114 | **(-2114)**<br>0 | - | - | - | - | - |
| (+24.8)<br>3641.87 | (+2)<br>3643.87 | (+0.83)<br>3644.7 | (+1097.29)<br>4741.99 | (+2605)<br>7346.99 | **(-2449.99)**<br>4897 | (0)<br>4897 |
| - | - | - | - | - | - | - |
| (1.38)<br>111.73 | (23)<br>134.73 | (11.29)<br>146.02 | (149.82)<br>295.84 | (306.55)<br>602.39 | (1395.99)<br>1998.38 | (266.92)<br>2265.3 |

# Fermanagh & South Tyrone

**Total Valid Pole 46160 Quota 6595 Turnout 72.9**

**Party performance**

| Party | Seats | 1st Pref Vote | % | (%1998) |
|---|---|---|---|---|
| DUP | 1 | 8630 | 18.7 | 13.9 |
| SF | 2 | 15901 | 34.4 | 26.9 |
| UUP | 2 | 13229 | 28.7 | 24.6 |
| SDLP | 1 | 7507 | 16.3 | 21.6 |
| Alliance | - | 243 | 0.5 | 1.2 |
| Others | - | 650 | 1.4 | 11.9 |

**At a glance...**

No change to party share of seats with an as-you-were result of 2 Sinn Féin, 2 UUP, 1 DUP and 1 SDLP. Sitting MP Michelle Gildernew of Sinn Féin topped the poll followed by Tom Elliott of the UUP. However there were some personnel changes with former UUP Minister Sam Foster (who retired) being replaced by colleague Tom Elliott and Sinn Féin veteran Gerry McHugh surprisingly losing out to newcomer Thomas O'Reilly. SDLP Education spokesman Tommy Gallagher comfortably held his seat, despite an increased vote for Sinn Féin. Turnout at under 73% was relatively low for this traditionally high turnout constituency. Shortly after the election newly-elected MLA Arlene Foster switched allegiance from UUP to DUP.

| | | 1st stage | 2nd stage |
|---|---|---|---|
| | | 1st pref votes 46,160 | Elimination of Cleland & McNulty |
| Frank Britton | SDLP | 2772 | (+206) 2978 |
| Linda Cleland | All | 243 | (-243) 0 |
| Tom Elliott | UUP | 6181 | (+103) 6284 |
| Arlene Foster | UUP | 4938 | (+66) 5004 |
| *Tommy Gallagher | SDLP | 4735 | (+249) 4984 |
| *Michelle Gildernew | SF | 6489 | (+73) 6562 |
| Bert Johnston | DUP | 3094 | (+19) 3113 |
| *Gerry McHugh | SF | 4393 | (+39) 4432 |
| Eithne McNulty | NIWC | 650 | (-650) 0 |
| *Maurice Morrow | DUP | 5536 | (+10) 5546 |
| Robert Mulligan | UUP | 2110 | (+39) 2149 |
| Thomas O'Reilly | SF | 5019 | (+30) 5049 |
| | Non-transferable | | (59) 59 |

## Candidates Elected

| Candidates Elected | Count |
|---|---|
| Tom Elliott UUP | 3rd |
| Thomas Gallagher SDLP | 5th |
| Michelle Gildernew SF | 5th |
| Arlene Foster UUP | 5th |
| Maurice Morrow DUP | 6th |
| Thomas O'Reilly SF | 8th |

Tom Elliott

Thomas Gallagher

Michelle Gildernew

Arlene Foster

Maurice Morrow

Thomas O'Reilly

| 3rd stage | 4th stage | 5th stage | 6th stage | 7th stage | 8th stage |
|---|---|---|---|---|---|
| Elimination of Mulligan | Transfer of Elliott's surplus | Elimination of Britton | Elimination of Johnston | Transfer of Morrow's surplus | Transfer of Gallagher's surplus |
| (+16)<br>2994 | (+17.75)<br>3011.75 | **(-3011.75)**<br>0 | - | - | - |
| - | - | - | - | - | - |
| (+1088)<br>7372 | **(-777)**<br>6595 | (0)<br>6595 | (0)<br>6595 | (0)<br>6595 | (0)<br>6595 |
| (+864)<br>5868 | (+696.51)<br>6564.51 | (+35)<br>6599.51 | (n/a)<br>6599.51 | (n/a)<br>6599.51 | (n/a)<br>6599.51 |
| (+19)<br>5003 | (+31.95)<br>5034.95 | (+2325)<br>7359.95 | (n/a)<br>7359.95 | (n/a)<br>7359.95 | **(-764.95)**<br>6595 |
| (+3)<br>6565 | (0)<br>6565 | (+154)<br>6719 | (n/a)<br>6719 | (n/a)<br>6719 | (n/a)<br>6719 |
| (+20)<br>3133 | (+6.39)<br>3139.39 | (+23.42)<br>3162.81 | **(-3162.81)**<br>0 | - | - |
| (+4)<br>4436 | (0)<br>4436 | (+158)<br>4594 | (+8.71)<br>4602.71 | (+89)<br>4691.71 | (+519.79)<br>5211.5 |
| - | - | - | - | - | - |
| (+124)<br>5670 | (+14.2)<br>5684.2 | (+5.71)<br>5689.91 | (+2980)<br>8669.91 | **(-2074.91)**<br>6595 | (0)<br>6595 |
| **(-2149)**<br>0 | - | - | - | - | - |
| (+2)<br>5051 | (0)<br>5051 | (+92)<br>5143 | (+9)<br>5152 | (+88)<br>5240 | (233.64)<br>5473.64 |
| (9)<br>68 | (10.2)<br>78.2 | (218.62)<br>296.82 | (165.1)<br>461.92 | (1897.91)<br>2359.83 | (11.52)<br>2371.35 |

# Foyle

Total Valid Pole 40806 Quota 5830 Turnout 63.5

## Party performance

| Party | Seats | 1st Pref Vote | % | (%1998) |
|---|---|---|---|---|
| DUP | 1 | 6101 | 15.0 | 12.5 |
| SF | 2 | 13214 | 32.4 | 26.0 |
| UUP | - | 3322 | 8.1 | 9.6 |
| SDLP | 3 | 14746 | 36.1 | 47.8 |
| Alliance | - | 227 | 0.6 | 2.2 |
| Others | - | 3196 | 7.8 | 1.9 |

### At a glance...

This predominantly nationalist constituency registered an as-you-were outcome with SDLP (3), Sinn Féin (2) and DUP (1) retaining their seats. The most striking aspect of the result was how close Sinn Féin came to taking a third seat from the SDLP – a party greatly weakened by the absence from the ticket of former party leader and Westminster MP John Hume. However, current SDLP leader Mark Durkan topped the poll alongside strong performances from Sinn Féin's Mitchel McLaughlin and the DUP's William Hay. Another interesting feature was the impressive vote gathered by veteran socialist journalist Eamon McCann running for the Socialist and Environmental Alliance for the first time.

| | | 1st stage | 2nd stage | 3rd stage |
|---|---|---|---|---|
| | | 1st pref votes 40,806 | Transfer of Durkan's surplus | Transfer of Hay's surplus |
| Mary Bradley | SDLP | 3345 | (+254.24) 3599.24 | (+1.2) 3600.44 |
| Alan Castle | All | 227 | (+4.62) 231.62 | (+1.52) 233.14 |
| *Annie Courtney | Ind | 802 | (+33.18) 835.18 | (+8.08) 843.26 |
| Gerald Diver | SDLP | 1769 | (+209.3) 1978.3 | (+1.64) 1979.94 |
| *Mark Durkan | SDLP | 6806 | (-976) 5830 | (0) 5830 |
| Mary Hamilton | UUP | 3322 | (+10.5) 3332.5 | (+204.32) 3536.82 |
| *William Hay | DUP | 6101 | (n/a) 6101 | (-271) 5830 |
| Danny McBrearty | Ind | 137 | (+3.64) 140.64 | (+0.52) 141.16 |
| Eamon McCann | Soc Env All | 2257 | (+31.64) 2288.64 | (+1.04) 2289.68 |
| Raymond McCartney | SF | 3679 | (+22.12) 3701.12 | (+0.12) 3701.24 |
| *Mitchel McLaughlin | SF | 6036 | (n/a) 6036 | (n/a) 6036 |
| ^*Mary Nelis | SF | 3499 | (+35.7) 3534.7 | (+0.24) 3534.94 |
| Pat Ramsey | SDLP | 2826 | (+340.62) 3166.62 | (+2.4) 3169.02 |
| | Non-transferable | | (30.44) 30.44 | (49.92) 80.36 |

^ Mary Nelis has resigned from the Assemby and has been replaced by Raymond McCartney

| Candidates Elected | Count |
|---|---|
| Mark Durkan SDLP | 1st |
| William Hay DUP | 1st |
| Mitchel McLaughlin SF | 1st |
| Mary Bradley SDLP | 8th |
| Pat Ramsey SDLP | 9th |
| Mary Nelis SF | 9th |

Mark Durkan

William Hay

Mitchel McLaughlin

Mary Bradley

Pat Ramsey

Mary Nelis

| 4th stage | 5th stage | 6th stage | 7th stage | 8th stage | 9th stage |
|---|---|---|---|---|---|
| nsfer of McLaughlin's surplus | Elimination of McBrearty, Castle & Courtney | Elimination of Diver | Elimination of McCann | Elimination of Hamilton | Transfer of Bradley's surplus |
| (+2.88) 3603.32 | (+227.43) 3830.75 | (+928.01) 4758.76 | (+497.87) 5256.63 | (+674) 5930.63 | **(-100.63)** 5830 |
| (+0.12) 233.26 | **(-233.26)** 0 | - | - | - | - |
| (+2.31) 845.57 | **(-845.57)** 0 | - | - | - | - |
| (+2.49) 1982.43 | (+170.12) 2152.55 | **(-2152.55)** 0 | - | - | - |
| (0) 5830 | (0) 5830 | (0) 5830 | (0) 5830 | (0) 5830 | (0) 5830 |
| (+0.12) 3536.94 | (+183.38) 3720.32 | (+29.9) 3750.22 | (+54.79) 3805.01 | **(-3805.01)** 0 | |
| (0) 5830 | (0) 5830 | (0) 5830 | (0) 5830 | (0) 5830 | (0) 5830 |
| (+0.39) 141.55 | **(-141.55)** 0 | - | - | - | - |
| (+4.83) 2294.51 | (+193.58) 2488.09 | (+97.94) 2586.03 | **(-2586.03)** 0 | - | - |
| (+53.01) 3754.25 | (+64.18) 3818.43 | (+64.44) 3882.87 | (+441.53) 4324.4 | (+17) 4341.4 | (+1.4) 4342.8 |
| **(-206)** 5830 | (0) 5830 | (0) 5830 | (0) 5830 | (0) 5830 | (0) 5830 |
| (+107.67) 3642.61 | (+83.66) 3726.27 | (+57.74) 3784.01 | (+554.23) 4338.24 | (+12.75) 4350.99 | (+0.28) 4351.27 |
| (+4.86) 3173.88 | (+160.27) 3334.15 | (+843.93) 4178.08 | (+500.98) 4679.06 | (+1018.5) 5697.56 | (+66.64) 5764.2 |
| (27.32) 107.68 | (137.76 245.44 | (130.59) 376.03 | (536.63) 912.66 | (2082.76) 2995.42 | (32.31) 3027.73 |

# Lagan Valley

**Total Valid Pole 41254** **Quota 5894** **Turnout 61.4**

## Party performance

| Party | Seats | 1st Pref Vote | % | (%1998) |
|---|---|---|---|---|
| DUP | 1 | 8475 | 20.5 | 18.0 |
| SF | - | 3242 | 7.9 | 4.3 |
| UUP | 3 | 19069 | 46.2 | 30.8 |
| SDLP | 1 | 3133 | 7.6 | 8.7 |
| Alliance | 1 | 4408 | 10.7 | 14.6 |
| Others | - | 2927 | 7.1 | 23.6 |

### At a glance...

In a difficult-to-interpret predominantly unionist constituency, the Ulster Unionist Party and to a lesser extent the DUP increased their vote share at the expense of smaller unionist parties. The UUP took three seats, narrowly squeezing out former Tory spokesman turned DUP candidate Andrew Hunter. The departure of Jeffrey Donaldson and newly elected colleague Norah Beare to the DUP shortly after the election makes it impossible to assess the relative strengths of the two main unionist parties in Lagan Valley. Alliance MLA Seamus Close and the SDLP's Patricia Lewsley held their seats although in Lewsley's case only just, following a strong challenge from Sinn Féin's Paul Butler.

| | | 1st stage | 2nd stage | 3rd stage | 4th stage |
|---|---|---|---|---|---|
| | | 1st pref votes 41,254 | Transfer of Donaldson's surplus | Elimination of McCarthy, Park & Johnston | Transfer of Poots' surplus |
| Norah Beare | UUP | 1508 | (+1813.66) 3321.66 | (+116.04) 3437.7 | (+96.96) 3534.66 |
| *Billy Bell | UUP | 2782 | (+1957.5) 4739.5 | (+117.3) 4856.8 | (+105.92) 4962.72 |
| Paul Butler | SF | 3242 | (+9.28) 3251.28 | (+10.58) 3261.86 | (+1.28) 3263.14 |
| *Seamus Close | All | 4408 | (+259.84) 4667.84 | (+179.34) 4847.18 | (+33.6) 4880.78 |
| *Ivan Davis | Ind | 2223 | (+316.1) 2539.1 | (+98.38) 2637.48 | (+24.96) 2662.44 |
| Jeffrey Donaldson | UUP | 14104 | **(-8210)** 5894 | (0) 5894 | (0) 5894 |
| Andrew Hunter | DUP | 3300 | (+785.32) 4085.32 | (+101.84) 4187.16 | (+479.36) 4666.52 |
| Joanne Johnston | Cons | 395 | (+67.86) 462.86 | **(-462.86)** 0 | - |
| Jim Kirkpatrick | UUP | 675 | (+1282.96) 1957.96 | (+65.4) 2023.36 | (+70.72) 2094.08 |
| *Patricia Lewsley | SDLP | 3133 | (+20.88) 3153.88 | (+78.74) 3232.62 | (+3.84) 3236.46 |
| Frances McCarthy | WP | 97 | (+6.38) 103.38 | **(-103.38)** 0 | - |
| Andrew Park | PUP | 212 | (+44.66) 256.66 | **(-256.66)** 0 | - |
| *Edwin Poots | DUP | 5175 | (+1539.32) 6714.32 | (n/a) 6714.32 | **(-820.32)** 5894 |
| | Non-transferable | | (106.24) 106.24 | (55.28) 161.52 | (3.68) 165.2 |

| Candidates Elected | Count |
|---|---|
| Jeffrey Donaldson UUP | 1st |
| Edwin Poots DUP | 2nd |
| Billy Bell UUP | 6th |
| Seamus Close All | 7th |
| Patricia Lewsley SDLP | 9th |
| Norah Beare UUP | 10th |

Jeffrey Donaldson

Edwin Poots

Billy Bell

Seamus Close

Patricia Lewsley

Norah Beare

| 5th stage | 6th stage | 7th stage | 8th stage | 9th stage | 10th stage |
|---|---|---|---|---|---|
| mination of Kirkpatrick | Elimination of Davis | Transfer of Bell's surplus | Transfer of Close's surplus | Elimination of Butler | Transfer of Lewsley's surplus |
| (+840.9) 4375.56 | (+391.8) 4767.36 | (+428) 5195.36 | (+105) 5300.36 | (+28.44) 5328.8 | (+328.64) 5657.44 |
| (+876.76) 5839.48 | (+1094) 6933.48 | **(-1039.48)** 5894 | (0) 5894 | (0) 5894 | (0) 5894 |
| (+3.06) 3266.2 | (+10.06) 3276.26 | (+1) 3277.26 | (+1) 3278.26 | **(-3278.26)** 0 | - |
| (+74.36) 4955.14 | (+870.26) 5825.4 | (+470) 6295.4 | **(-401.4)** 5894 | (0) 5894 | (0) 5894 |
| (+72.56) 2735 | **(-2735)** 0 | - | - | - | - |
| (0) 5894 | (0) 5894 | (0) 5894 | (0) 5894 | (0) 5894 | (0) 5894 |
| (+138.42) 4804.94 | (+124.76) 4929.7 | (+48) 4977.7 | (+23) 5000.7 | (+13.06) 5013.76 | (+30.81) 5044.57 |
| - | - | - | - | - | - |
| **(-2094.08)** 0 | - | - | - | - | - |
| (+14.64) 3251.1 | (+91.64) 3342.74 | (+39) 3381.74 | (+154) 3535.74 | (+2721) 6256.74 | **(-362.74)** 5894 |
| - | - | - | - | - | - |
| - | - | - | - | - | - |
| (0) 5894 | (0) 5894 | (0) 5894 | (0) 5894 | (0) 5894 | (0) 5894 |
| (73.38) 238.58 | (152.48) 391.06 | (53.48) 444.54 | (118.4) 562.94 | (515.76) 1078.7 | (3.29) 1081.99 |

# Mid Ulster

**Total Valid Pole 44362 Quota 6338 Turnout 74.9**

**Party performance**

| Party | Seats | 1st Pref Vote | % | (%1998) |
|---|---|---|---|---|
| DUP | 1 | 9240 | 20.8 | 21.4 |
| SF | 3 | 20194 | 45.5 | 40.8 |
| UUP | 1 | 6394 | 14.4 | 13.9 |
| SDLP | 1 | 8138 | 18.3 | 22.2 |
| Alliance | - | 166 | 0.4 | 1.0 |
| Others | - | 230 | 0.5 | 0.7 |

**At a glance...**

Mid Ulster was the only constituency in the election where the DUP vote went down and the UUP vote increased although the movement was small. The result was as-you-were in terms of seats (Sinn Féin 3, DUP 1, UUP and SDLP 1 each) although there were two new faces - Geraldine Dougan of Sinn Féin replacing John Kelly (who didn't run again) and Patsy McGlone edging out party colleague Denis Haughey. The poll-topper was DUP veteran Rev. William McCrea followed closely by the MP for the area Martin McGuinness of Sinn Féin. At 74.9% Mid Ulster registered the highest turnout of all 18 constituencies.

| | | 1st stage | 2nd stage |
|---|---|---|---|
| | | 1st pref votes 44,362 | Transfer of McCrea's surplus |
| *Billy Armstrong | UUP | 4323 | (+138.6) 4461.6 |
| Francis Donnelly | WP | 230 | (+0.22) 230.22 |
| Geraldine Dougan | SF | 5827 | (+0.22) 5827.22 |
| Cora Groogan | SF | 984 | (0) 984 |
| *Denis Haughey | SDLP | 3843 | (+1.32) 3844.32 |
| James Holmes | All | 166 | (+1.1) 167.1 |
| *William McCrea | DUP | 8211 | (-1873) 6338 |
| Patsy McGlone | SDLP | 4295 | (+5.06) 4300.06 |
| *Martin McGuinness | SF | 8128 | (n/a) 8128 |
| Alan Millar | DUP | 1029 | (+1536.7) 2565.7 |
| *Francis Molloy | SF | 5255 | (+0.44) 5255.44 |
| Trevor Wilson | UUP | 2071 | (+111.54) 2182.54 |
| | Non-transferable | | (77.8) 77.8 |

| Candidates Elected | Count |
|---|---|
| William McCrea DUP | 1st |
| Martim McGuinness SF | 1st |
| Geraldine Dougan SF | 4th |
| Francis Molloy SF | 4th |
| Billy Armstrong UUP | 7th |
| Patsy McGlone SDLP | 8th |

William McCrea

Martin McGuinness

Geraldine Dougan

Francis Molloy

Billy Armstrong

Patsy McGlone

| 3rd stage | 4th stage | 5th stage | 6th stage | 7th stage | 8th stage |
|---|---|---|---|---|---|
| Transfer of McGuinness's surplus | Elimination of Donnelly, Groogan & Holmes | Transfer of Dougan's surplus | Elimination of Wilson | Elimination of Millar | Transfer of Armstrong's surplus |
| (+0.22) 4461.82 | (+47.42) 4509.24 | (+5) 4514.24 | (+1651.08) 6165.32 | (+883) 7048.32 | **(-710.32)** 6338 |
| (+7.26) 237.48 | **(-237.48)** 0 | - | - | - | - |
| (+171.16) 5998.38 | (+918) 6916.38 | **(-578.38)** 6338 | (0) 6338 | (0) 6338 | (0) 6338 |
| (+160.16) 1144.16 | **(-1144.16)** 0 | - | - | - | - |
| (+96.14) 3940.46 | (+170.88) 4111.34 | (+101) 4212.34 | (+38.1) 4250.44 | (+208.24) 4458.68 | (+153) 4611.68 |
| (+1.76) 168.86 | **(-168.86)** 0 | - | - | - | - |
| (0) 6338 | (0) 6338 | (0) 6338 | (0) 6338 | (0) 6338 | (0) 6338 |
| (+205.26) 4505.32 | (+188.32) 4693.64 | (+257) 4950.64 | (+34.2) 4984.84 | (+155.38) 5140.22 | (+106) 5246.22 |
| **(-1790)** 6338 | (0) 6338 | (0) 6338 | (0) 6338 | (0) 6338 | (0) 6338 |
| (+5.94) 2571.64 | (+8.88) 2580.52 | (+1) 2581.52 | (+453.8) 3035.32 | **(-3035.32)** 0 | - |
| (+1121.78) 6377.22 | (n/a) 6377.22 | (n/a) 6377.22 | (n/a) 6377.22 | (n/a) 6377.22 | (n/a) 6377.22 |
| (+1.1) 2183.64 | (+44.88) 2228.52 | (+5) 2233.52 | **(-2233.52)** 0 | - | - |
| (19.22) 97.02 | (172.12) 269.14 | (209.38) 478.52 | (56.34) 534.86 | (1788.7) 2323.56 | (451.32) 2774.88 |

# Newry & Armagh

**Total Valid Pole 47378  Quota 6769  Turnout 70.2**

**Party performance**

| Party | Seats | 1st Pref Vote | % | (%1998) |
|---|---|---|---|---|
| DUP | 1 | 8599 | 18.1 | 13.3 |
| SF | 3 | 18852 | 39.8 | 26.0 |
| UUP | 1 | 7347 | 15.5 | 18.1 |
| SDLP | 1 | 11637 | 24.6 | 35.0 |
| Alliance | - | 311 | 0.7 | 1.4 |
| Others | - | 632 | 1.3 | 6.1 |

**At a glance...**

No change in the balance between nationalists and unionist (which remained 4-2) with the big change being the increase in support for Sinn Féin at the expense of the SDLP. This was also reflected in terms of seats won with Sinn Féin increasing to 3 and the SDLP slipping down to 1. The SDLP had been weakened by the absence of sitting MP and former Deputy Leader Seamus Mallon from the ticket although the result was still possibly the party's worst of the 18 constituencies. The DUP's Paul Berry topped the poll followed by Sinn Féin's Conor Murphy and UUP's Danny Kennedy – all three returning MLAs. SDLP sitting MLA John Fee lost his seat.

| | | 1st Stage | 2nd Stage |
|---|---|---|---|
| | | 1st Pref Votes 47378 | Transfer of Berry's surplus |
| *Paul Berry | DUP | 8125 | (-1356) 6769 |
| Dominic Bradley | SDLP | 4111 | (+8.8) 4119.8 |
| Freda Donnelly | DUP | 474 | (+1164.64) 1638.64 |
| *John Fee | SDLP | 3410 | (+1.28) 3411.28 |
| William Frazer | Ind | 632 | (+111.36) 743.36 |
| Davy Hyland | SF | 5779 | (+0.48) 5779.48 |
| *Danny Kennedy | UUP | 7347 | (n/a) 7347 |
| Jim Lennon | SDLP | 4116 | (+2.88) 4118.88 |
| *Conor Murphy | SF | 7595 | (n/a) 7595 |
| Pat O'Rawe | SF | 5478 | (+0.16) 5478.16 |
| Peter Whitcroft | All | 311 | (+2.72) 313.72 |
| | Non-transferable | | (63.68) 63.68 |

| Candidates Elected | Count |
|---|---|
| Paul Berry DUP | 1st |
| Conor Murphy SF | 1st |
| Danny Kennedy UUP | 1st |
| Dominic Bradley SDLP | 5th |
| Davy Hyland SF | 5th |
| Pat O'Rawe SF | 5th |

Paul Berry

Conor Murphy

Danny Kennedy

Dominic Bradley

Davy Hyland

Pat O'Rawe

| 3rd Stage | 4th Stage | 5th Stage |
|---|---|---|
| Transfer of Murphy's surplus | Elimination of Whitcroft, Frazer & Donnelly | Elimination of Fee |
| (0)<br>6769 | (0)<br>6769 | (0)<br>6769 |
| (+15.2)<br>4135 | (+265.14)<br>4400.14 | (+2383)<br>6783.14 |
| (+0.3)<br>1638.94 | **(-1638.94)**<br>0 | - |
| (+48.1)<br>3459.38 | (+197.58)<br>3656.96 | **(-3656.96)**<br>0 |
| (+0.7)<br>744.06 | **(-744.06)**<br>0 | - |
| (+567.9)<br>6347.38 | (+19.62)<br>6367 | (+266.9)<br>6633.9 |
| (n/a)<br>7347 | (n/a)<br>7347 | (n/a)<br>7347 |
| (+7.1)<br>4125.98 | (+265)<br>4390.98 | (+721.52)<br>5112.5 |
| **(-826)**<br>6769 | (0)<br>6769 | (0)<br>6769 |
| (+112.5)<br>5590.66 | (+12.66)<br>5603.32 | (+108.68)<br>5712 |
| (+1)<br>314.72 | **(-314.72)**<br>0 | - |
| (73.2)<br>136.88 | (1937.72)<br>2074.6 | (176.86)<br>2251.46 |

# North Antrim

**Total Valid Pole 44099** **Quota 6300** **Turnout 63.3**

**Party performance**

| Party | Seats | 1st Pref Vote | % | (%1998) |
|---|---|---|---|---|
| DUP | 3 | 20235 | 45.9 | 37.6 |
| SF | 1 | 6195 | 14.0 | 8.1 |
| UUP | 1 | 9538 | 21.6 | 22.3 |
| SDLP | 1 | 6009 | 13.6 | 16.9 |
| Alliance | - | 867 | 2.0 | 4.6 |
| Others | - | 1255 | 2.8 | 10.5 |

## At a glance...

North Antrim saw a powerful performance by the DUP, which with two Ian Paisleys topping the poll, comfortably held on to its three seats. The big surprise was the election of a Sinn Féin representative Philip McGuigan, eventually taking one of the UUP seats. The remaining UUP seat was held by Robert Coulter while former Finance and Personnel Minister Sean Farren held onto the final seat for the SDLP on a reduced share of the vote. Overall the smaller unionist parties lost ground to the larger two parties.

| | | 1st stage | 2nd stage | 3rd stage |
|---|---|---|---|---|
| | | 1st Pref Votes 44,099 | Transfer of Paisley (Snr) surplus | Transfer of Paisley (Jnr) surplus |
| *Robert Coulter | UUP | 6385 | (n/a) 6385 | (n/a) 6385 |
| James Currie | UUP | 3153 | (+94.08) 3247.08 | (+73.6) 3320.68 |
| Jayne Dunlop | All | 867 | (+6.44) 873.44 | (+10.2) 883.64 |
| *Sean Farren | SDLP | 3648 | (+1.68) 3649.68 | (+2.4) 3652.08 |
| *Gardiner Kane | Ind | 623 | (+54.6) 677.6 | (+25.6) 703.2 |
| William McCaughey | PUP | 230 | (+14.84) 244.84 | (+9.2) 254.04 |
| Philip McGuigan | SF | 6195 | (0) 6195 | (+0.2) 6195.2 |
| Declan O'Loan | SDLP | 2361 | (+1.68) 2362.68 | (+1) 2363.68 |
| *Ian Paisley Jnr | DUP | 7898 | (n/a) 7898 | **(-1598)** 6300 |
| *Rev Ian Paisley | DUP | 8732 | **(-2432)** 6300 | (0) 6300 |
| Nathaniel Small | UKUP | 402 | (+42) 444 | (+61) 505 |
| Mervyn Storey | DUP | 3605 | (+2182.6) 5787.6 | (+1364.6) 7152.2 |
| | Non-transferable | | 34.08 (34.08 | (50.2) 84.28 |

| Candidates Elected | Count |
|---|---|
| Rev Ian Paisley DUP | 1st |
| Ian Paisley (Jnr) DUP | 1st |
| Rev Robert Coulter UUP | 1st |
| Mervyn Storey DUP | 3rd |
| Philip McGuigan SF | 9th |
| Sean Farren SDLP | 9th |

Rev Ian Paisley

Ian Paisley (Jnr)

Robert Coulter

Mervyn Storey

Philip McGuigan

Sean Farren

| 4th stage | 5th stage | 6th stage | 7th stage | 8th stage | 9th stage |
|---|---|---|---|---|---|
| Transfer of Storey's surplus | Elimination of McCaughey | Transfer of Coulter's surplus | Elimination of Kane | Elimination of Dunlop & Small | Elimination of O'Loan |
| (n/a)<br>6385 | (n/a)<br>6385 | **(-85)**<br>6300 | (0)<br>6300 | (0)<br>6300 | (0)<br>6300 |
| (+278)<br>3598.68 | (+77.68)<br>3676.36 | (+59.62)<br>3735.98 | (+305.26)<br>4041.24 | (+933.8)<br>4975.04 | (+74.93)<br>5049.97 |
| (+13)<br>896.64 | (+17.76)<br>914.4 | (+0.8)<br>915.2 | (+37.94)<br>953.14 | **(-953.14)**<br>0 | - |
| (+2.8)<br>3654.88 | (+11.4)<br>3666.28 | (+0.33)<br>3666.61 | (+22.99)<br>3689.6 | (+231.22)<br>3920.82 | (+2059.61)<br>5980.43 |
| (+85)<br>788.2 | (+31.68)<br>819.88 | (+0.86)<br>820.74 | **(-820.74)**<br>0 | - | - |
| (+43.6)<br>297.64 | **(-297.64)**<br>0 | - | - | - | - |
| (0)<br>6195.2 | (+3)<br>6198.2 | (+0.06)<br>6198.26 | (+1.2)<br>6199.46 | (+8.48)<br>6207.94 | (+289)<br>6496.94 |
| (+1.4)<br>2365.08 | (+9.28)<br>2374.36 | (+0.12)<br>2374.48 | (+7.21)<br>2381.69 | (+133.67)<br>2515.36 | **(-2515.36)**<br>0 |
| (0)<br>6300 | (0)<br>6300 | (0)<br>6300 | (0)<br>6300 | (0)<br>6300 | (0)<br>6300 |
| (0)<br>6300 | (0)<br>6300 | (0)<br>6300 | (0)<br>6300 | (0)<br>6300 | (0)<br>6300 |
| (+274.4)<br>779.4 | (+45.56)<br>824.96 | (+0.64)<br>825.6 | (+171.6)<br>997.2 | **(-997.2)**<br>0 | - |
| **(-852.2)**<br>6300 | (0)<br>6300 | (0)<br>6300 | (0)<br>6300 | (0)<br>6300 | (0)<br>6300 |
| (154)<br>238.28 | (101.28)<br>339.56 | (22.57)<br>362.13 | (274.54)<br>636.67 | (643.17)<br>1279.84 | (91.82)<br>1371.66 |

# North Down

**Total Valid Pole 30835 Quota 4406 Turnout 54.5**

**Party performance**

| Party | Seats | 1st Pref Vote | % | (%1998) |
|---|---|---|---|---|
| DUP | 2 | 7245 | 23.5 | 6.9 |
| SF | - | 264 | 0.9 | 0.0 |
| UUP | 2 | 9887 | 32.1 | 32.6 |
| SDLP | - | 1519 | 4.9 | 5.5 |
| Alliance | 1 | 2655 | 8.6 | 14.4 |
| Others | 1 | 9265 | 30.0 | 40.7 |

**At a glance...**

The main change in the predominantly unionist North Down constituency was the capture by the DUP of two seats at the expense of Northern Ireland Women's Coalition and also the Ulster Unionist Party, who were reduced from 3 to 2. This was not surprising given the general trend overall and the departure of former UUP MLA Peter Weir to the DUP mid-term. Although known for its 'independent' streak the squeeze on smaller parties also impacted in North Down, where former MP Robert McCartney held on to his UKUP seat (elected sub-quota) and Northern Ireland Women's Coalition MLA Jane Morrice lost out. Alliance Deputy Leader Eileen Bell retained her seat.

| | | 1st stage | 2nd stage | 3rd stage | 4th stage | 5th stage |
|---|---|---|---|---|---|---|
| | | 1st pref votes 30,835 | Elimination of Carter | Elimination of Sheridan | Elimination of George | Elimination of Rose |
| John Barry | Green | 730 | (+3) 733 | (+1) 734 | (+14) 748 | (+14) 762 |
| *Eileen Bell | All | 1951 | (+6) 1957 | (+5) 1962 | (+8) 1970 | (+13) 1983 |
| Chris Carter | Ind | 109 | (-109) 0 | - | - | - |
| Alan Chambers | Ind | 1077 | (+22) 1099 | (+3) 1102 | (0) 1102 | (+17) 1119 |
| Leslie Cree | UUP | 3900 | (+8) 3908 | (+11) 3919 | (+1) 3920 | (+30) 3950 |
| Alex Easton | DUP | 3570 | (+9) 3579 | (+10) 3589 | (0) 3589 | (+22) 3611 |
| Stephen Farry | All | 704 | (+4) 708 | (+3) 711 | (+11) 722 | (+6) 728 |
| Alan Field | Ind | 428 | (+2) 430 | (+2) 432 | (0) 432 | (+16) 448 |
| Maria George | SF | 264 | (+1) 265 | (0) 265 | (-265) 0 | - |
| William Logan | SDLP | 1519 | (+3) 1522 | (+1) 1523 | (+209) 1732 | (+2) 1734 |
| *Robert McCartney | UKUP | 3374 | (+13) 3387 | (+98) 3485 | (+3) 3488 | (+25) 3513 |
| *Alan McFarland | UUP | 3421 | (+8) 3429 | (+8) 3437 | (+2) 3439 | (+28) 3467 |
| *Jane Morrice | NIWC | 1181 | (+7) 1188 | (+4) 1192 | (+9) 1201 | (+18) 1219 |
| Diana Peacocke | UUP | 2566 | (+2) 2568 | (+19) 2587 | (+2) 2589 | (+34) 2623 |
| Julian Robertson | Cons | 491 | (+1) 492 | (+5) 497 | (0) 497 | (+4) 501 |
| David Rose | PUP | 316 | (+1) 317 | (+10) 327 | (0) 327 | (-327) 0 |
| Thomas Sheridan | UKUP | 209 | (+1) 210 | (-210) 0 | - | - |
| *Peter Weir | DUP | 3675 | (+6) 3681 | (+23) 3704 | (0) 3704 | (+57) 3761 |
| Brian Wilson | Ind | 1350 | (+5) 1355 | (+2) 1357 | (+2) 1359 | (+12) 1371 |
| | Non-transferable | | (7) 7 | (5) 12 | (4) 16 | (29) 45 |

| Candidates Elected | Count |
|---|---|
| Leslie Cree UUP | 12th |
| Eileen Bell All | 13th |
| Alan McFarland UUP | 14th |
| Robert McCartney UKUP | 14th |
| Peter Weir DUP | 14th |
| Alex Easton DUP | 14th |

Leslie Cree

Eileen Bell

Alan McFarland

Robert McCartney

Peter Weir

Alex Easton

| 6th stage | 7th stage | 8th stage | 9th stage | 10th stage | 11th stage | 12th stage | 13th stage | 14th stage |
|---|---|---|---|---|---|---|---|---|
| Elimination of Field | Elimination of Robertson | Elimination of Farry | Elimination of Barry | Elimination of Chambers | Elimination of Morrice | Elimination of Wilson | Elimination of Logan | Transfer of Bell's surplus |
| (+6)<br>768 | (+18)<br>786 | (+14)<br>800 | **(-800)**<br>0 | - | - | - | - | - |
| (+9)<br>1992 | (+16)<br>2008 | (+587)<br>2595 | (+225)<br>2820 | (+126)<br>2946 | (+656)<br>3602 | (+535)<br>4137 | (+1100)<br>5237 | **(-831)**<br>4406 |
| - | - | - | - | - | - | - | - | - |
| (+66)<br>1185 | (+21)<br>1206 | (+8)<br>1214 | (+28)<br>1242 | **(-1242)**<br>0 | - | - | - | - |
| (+39)<br>3989 | (+30)<br>4019 | (+13)<br>4032 | (+41)<br>4073 | (+232)<br>4305 | (+97)<br>4402 | (+80)<br>4482 | (n/a)<br>4482 | (n/a)<br>4482 |
| (+39)<br>3650 | (+13)<br>3663 | (+4)<br>3667 | (+22)<br>3689 | (+81)<br>3770 | (+13)<br>3783 | (+38)<br>3821 | (+6)<br>3827 | (+12)<br>3839 |
| (+12)<br>740 | (+11)<br>751 | **(-751)**<br>0 | - | - | - | - | - | - |
| **(-448)**<br>0 | - | - | - | - | - | - | - | - |
| - | - | - | - | - | - | - | - | - |
| (+4)<br>1738 | (+3)<br>1741 | (+44)<br>1785 | (+66)<br>1851 | (+19)<br>1870 | (+207)<br>2077 | (+81)<br>2158 | **(-2158)**<br>0 | - |
| (+77)<br>3590 | (+49)<br>3639 | (+9)<br>3648 | (+27)<br>3675 | (+172)<br>3847 | (+65)<br>3912 | (+134)<br>4046 | (+26)<br>4072 | (+30)<br>4102 |
| (+47)<br>3514 | (+43)<br>3557 | (+13)<br>3570 | (+36)<br>3606 | (+124)<br>3730 | (+103)<br>3833 | (+250)<br>4083 | (+209)<br>4292 | (+210)<br>4502 |
| (+23)<br>1242 | (+17)<br>1259 | (+28)<br>1287 | (+191)<br>1478 | (+109)<br>1587 | **(-1587)**<br>0 | - | - | - |
| (+13)<br>2636 | (+41)<br>2677 | (+11)<br>2688 | (+41)<br>2729 | (+66)<br>2795 | (+139)<br>2934 | (+131)<br>3065 | (+193)<br>3258 | (+160)<br>3418 |
| (+7)<br>508 | **(-508)**<br>0 | - | - | - | - | - | - | - |
| - | - | - | - | - | - | - | - | - |
| - | - | - | - | - | - | - | - | - |
| (+41)<br>3802 | (+20)<br>3822 | (+4)<br>3826 | (+13)<br>3839 | (+67)<br>3906 | (+16)<br>3922 | (+96)<br>4018 | (+8)<br>4026 | (+5)<br>4031 |
| (+44)<br>1415 | (+14)<br>1429 | (+8)<br>1437 | (+52)<br>1489 | (+109)<br>1598 | (+120)<br>1718 | **(-1718)**<br>0 | - | - |
| (21)<br>66 | (212)<br>278 | (8)<br>286 | (58)<br>344 | (137)<br>481 | (171)<br>652 | (373)<br>1025 | (616)<br>1641 | (414)<br>2055 |

# South Antrim

Total Valid Pole 37421 Quota 5346 Turnout 59.5

**Party performance**

| Party | Seats | 1st Pref Vote | % | (%1998) |
|---|---|---|---|---|
| DUP | 2 | 11452 | 30.6 | 20.1 |
| SF | - | 4295 | 11.5 | 7.3 |
| UUP | 2 | 11154 | 29.8 | 29.9 |
| SDLP | 1 | 5403 | 14.4 | 17.7 |
| Alliance | 1 | 3393 | 9.1 | 8.6 |
| Others | - | 1724 | 4.6 | 16.3 |

**At a glance...**

The main change in South Antrim was the DUP's picking up Northern Ireland Unionist Party candidate Norman Boyd's former UKUP seat. The UUP held its two seats with local MP and prominent anti-Agreement campaigner David Burnside topping the poll. Alliance Party leader David Ford narrowly held on to his seat actually increasing the Alliance share of the vote and eventually edging out Sinn Féin hopeful Martin Meehan. The SDLP retained its single seat although Tommy Burns took the seat from colleague and former MLA Donovan McClelland. In line with the trend right across Northern Ireland, South Antrim saw a major squeeze of the smaller parties.

| | | 1st stage | 2nd stage | 3rd stage | 4th stage |
|---|---|---|---|---|---|
| | | 1st pref votes 37,421 | Transfer of Burnside's surplus | Elimination of Docherty | Elimination of Cosgrove & Wilkinson |
| *Norman Boyd | NIUP | 774 | (+52.56) 826.56 | (+11.96) 838.52 | (+42.48) 881 |
| Thomas Burns | SDLP | 2732 | (+16.56) 2748.56 | (+3) 2751.56 | (+65) 2816.56 |
| David Burnside | UUP | 7066 | **(-1720)** 5346 | (0) 5346 | (0) 5346 |
| *Wilson Clyde | DUP | 5131 | (+124.56) 5255.56 | (+4.24) 5259.8 | (+42.2) 5302 |
| Adrian Cochrane-Watson | UUP | 953 | (+900.72) 1853.72 | (+35.96) 1889.68 | (+75.12) 1964.8 |
| Joan Cosgrove | NIWC | 465 | (+9.36) 474.36 | (+10) 484.36 | **(-484.36)** 0 |
| Jason Docherty | Cons | 174 | (+5.52) 179.52 | **(-179.52)** 0 | - |
| *David Ford | All | 3393 | (+63.6) 3456.6 | (+47.44) 3504.04 | (+250.6) 3754.64 |
| Paul Girvan | DUP | 4820 | (+80.4) 4900.4 | (+13.72) 4914.12 | (+62.2) 4976.32 |
| *Donovan McClelland | SDLP | 2671 | (+6.24) 2677.24 | (+1) 2678.24 | (+45.48) 2723.72 |
| Martin Meehan | SF | 4295 | (+1.2) 4296.2 | (+2) 4298.2 | (+13) 4311.2 |
| John Smyth | DUP | 1501 | (+29.52) 1530.52 | (+2) 1532.52 | (+67.96) 1600.48 |
| Kenneth Wilkinson | PUP | 311 | (+12.24) 323.24 | (+4.24) 327.48 | **(-327.48)** 0 |
| *Jim Wilson | UUP | 3135 | (+384.96) 3519.96 | (+35.48) 3555.44 | (+112.36) 3667.8 |
| | Non-transferable | | (32.56) 32.56 | (8.48) 41.04 | (35.44) 76.48 |

| Candidates Elected | Count |
|---|---|
| David Burnside UUP | 1st |
| Wilson Clyde DUP | 5th |
| Paul Girvan DUP | 6th |
| Jim Wilson UUP | 11th |
| Thomas Burns SDLP | 11th |
| David Ford All | 11th |

David Burnside

Wilson Clyde

Paul Girvan

Jim Wilson

Thomas Burns

David Ford

| 5th stage | 6th stage | 7th stage | 8th stage | 9th stage | 10th stage | 11th stage |
|---|---|---|---|---|---|---|
| Elimination of Boyd | Elimination of Smyth | Transfer of Girvan's surplus | Transfer of Clyde's surplus | Elimination of Cochrane-Watson | Transfer of Wilson's surplus | Elimination of McClelland |
| **(-881)** 0 | - | - | - | - | - | - |
| (+38.92) 2855.48 | (+8.72) 2864.2 | (+11) 2875.2 | (+1) 2876.2 | (+85.16) 2961.36 | (+31) 2992.36 | (+1986.88) 4979.24 |
| (0) 5346 | (0) 5346 | (0) 5346 | (0) 5346 | (0) 5346 | (0) 5346 | (0) 5346 |
| (+231) 5533 | (n/a) 5533 | (n/a) 5533 | **(-187)** 5346 | (0) 5346 | (0) 5346 | (0) 5346 |
| (+154.68) 2119.48 | (+143.68) 2263.16 | (+349) 2612.16 | (+84) 2696.16 | **(-2696.16)** 0 | - | - |
| - | - | - | - | - | - | - |
| - | - | - | - | - | - | - |
| (+66.84) 3821.48 | (+50.88) 3872.36 | (+82) 3954.36 | (+15) 3969.36 | (+519.48) 4488.84 | (+208) 4696.84 | (+269.36) 4966.2 |
| (+199.68) 5176 | (+1238) 6414 | **(-1068)** 5346 | (0) 5346 | (0) 5346 | (0) 5346 | (0) 5346 |
| (+3.24) 2726.96 | (+5.24) 2732.2 | (+6) 2738.2 | (+1) 2739.2 | (+44.2) 2783.4 | (+19) 2802.4 | **(-2802.4)** 0 |
| (+1) 4312.2 | (+1) 4313.2 | (+1) 4314.2 | (0) 4314.2 | (+3.72) 4317.92 | (+1) 4318.92 | (+466.72) 4785.64 |
| (+35.36) 1635.84 | **(-1635.84)** 0 | - | - | - | - | - |
| - | - | - | - | - | - | - |
| (+1048.68) 3772.48 | (+105.84) 3878.32 | (+268) 4146.32 | (+68) 4214.32 | (+1392) 5606.32 | **(-260.32)** 5346 | (0) 5346 |
| (45.6) 122.08 | (82.48) 204.56 | (351) 555.56 | (18) 573.56 | (651.6) 1225.16 | (1.32) 1226.48 | (79.44) 1305.92 |

# South Down

**Total Valid Pole 46012** **Quota 6479** **Turnout 65.6**

**Party performance**

| Party | Seats | 1st Pref Vote | % | (%1998) |
|---|---|---|---|---|
| DUP | 1 | 6789 | 15.0 | 9.4 |
| SF | 2 | 12007 | 26.5 | 15.1 |
| UUP | 1 | 8253 | 18.2 | 14.4 |
| SDLP | 2 | 15922 | 35.1 | 45.3 |
| Alliance | - | 489 | 1.1 | 2.9 |
| Others | - | 1886 | 4.2 | 12.8 |

**At a glance...**

The big change in South Down was the capture of a second seat by Sinn Féin at the expense of the SDLP who had been expected to hold 3. Again like in Foyle and Newry/Armagh the SDLP ticket had been weakened by the absence of sitting Westminster MP, in this case Eddie McGrady. On the Unionist side it remained one seat apiece with Jim Wells (DUP) who topped the poll, and Dermot Nesbitt (UUP) being reelected. In the end there were three new faces, Caitriona Ruane and Willie Clarke of Sinn Féin and Margaret Ritchie of SDLP. As elsewhere the smaller parties were squeezed out of contention by the 'big 4'. SDLP's Eamonn O'Neill was the one to lose out.

| | | 1st stage | 2nd stage | 3rd stage |
|---|---|---|---|---|
| | | 1st pref votes 46,012 | Transfer of Wells's surplus | Elimination of Curran & O'Hagan |
| Raymond Blaney | Green | 799 | (+0.76) 799.76 | (+52) 851.76 |
| *PJ Bradley | SDLP | 5337 | (+0.36) 5337.36 | (+18) 5355.36 |
| Willie Clarke | SF | 4083 | (+0.08) 4083.08 | (+9) 4092.08 |
| Malachi Curran | Ind | 162 | (+0.08) 162.08 | (-162.08) 0 |
| Jim Donaldson | UUP | 2885 | (+99.52) 2984.52 | (+5) 2989.52 |
| Marian Fitzpatrick | SDLP | 2382 | (+0.44) 2382.44 | (+27) 2409.44 |
| Eamonn McConvey | SDLP | 2806 | (+0.12) 2806.12 | (+27) 2833.12 |
| Trudy Miller | NIWC | 565 | (+0.6) 565.6 | (+24) 589.6 |
| *Dermot Nesbitt | UUP | 5368 | (+43) 5411 | (+9) 5420 |
| Desmond O'Hagan | WP | 115 | (+0.08) 115.08 | (-115.08) 0 |
| *Eamonn O'Neill | SDLP | 3942 | (+0.92) 3942.92 | (+21) 3963.92 |
| Neil Powell | All | 489 | (+0.48) 489.48 | (+6) 495.48 |
| Margaret Ritchie | SDLP | 4261 | (+0.76) 4261.76 | (+52) 4313.76 |
| Caitriona Ruane | SF | 5118 | (0) 5118 | (+6) 5124 |
| *Jim Wells | DUP | 6789 | (-310) 6479 | (0) 6479 |
| Jim Wharton | UKUP | 245 | (+115.64) 360.64 | (+2.08) 362.72 |
| | Non-transferable | 666 | (47.16) 713.16 | (19.08) 732.24 |

| **Candidates Elected** | **Count** |
|---|---|
| Jim Wells DUP | 1st |
| PJ Bradley SDLP | 2nd |
| Dermot Nesbitt UUP | 8th |
| Caitriona Ruane SF | 9th |
| Willie Clarke SF | 9th |
| Margaret Ritchie SDLP | 9th |

Jim Wells

PJ Bradley

Dermot Nesbitt

Caitriona Ruane

Willie Clarke

Margaret Ritchie

| 4th stage | 5th stage | 6th stage | 7th stage | 8th stage | 9th stage |
|---|---|---|---|---|---|
| Elimination of Blaney, Powell & Wharton | Elimination of Fitzpatrick | Transfer of Bradley's surplus | Elimination of McConvey | Elimination of Donaldson | Transfer of Nesbitt's surplus |
| **(-851.76)**<br>0 | - | - | - | - | - |
| (+327.6)<br>5682.96 | (+1454)<br>7136.96 | **(-657.96)**<br>6479 | (0)<br>6479 | (0)<br>6479 | (0)<br>6479 |
| (+93.08)<br>4185.16 | (+83.04)<br>4268.2 | (+10.58)<br>4278.78 | (+1641.96)<br>5920.74 | (+5.7)<br>5926.44 | (+8)<br>5934.44 |
| - | - | - | - | - | - |
| (+265.44)<br>3254.96 | (+9.16)<br>3264.12 | (+1.84)<br>3265.96 | (+3.46)<br>3269.42 | **(-3269.42)**<br>0 | - |
| (+146.2)<br>2555.64 | **(-2555.64)**<br>0 | - | - | - | - |
| (+128.04)<br>2961.14 | (+25)<br>2986.16 | (+4.14)<br>2990.3 | **(-2990.3)**<br>0 | - | - |
| (-589.6)<br>0 | - | - | - | - | - |
| (+339.04)<br>5759.04 | (+38.16)<br>5797.2 | (+5.52)<br>5802.72 | (+20)<br>5822.72 | (+2503)<br>8325.72 | **(-1846.72)**<br>6479 |
| - | - | - | - | - | - |
| (+256.32)<br>4220.24 | (+472.08)<br>4692.32 | (+523.02)<br>5215.34 | (+135)<br>5350.34 | (+61.18)<br>5411.52 | (+286)<br>5697.52 |
| **(-495.48)**<br>0 | - | - | - | - | - |
| (+351.56)<br>4665.32 | (+183.04)<br>4848.36 | (+73.14)<br>4921.5 | (+498.46)<br>5419.96 | (+58)<br>5477.96 | (+256)<br>5733.96 |
| (+87.08)<br>5211.08 | (+204)<br>5415.08 | (+34.96)<br>5450.04 | (+574.38)<br>6024.42 | (+2.12)<br>6026.54 | (+9)<br>6035.54 |
| (0)<br>6479 | (0)<br>6479 | (0)<br>6479 | (0)<br>6479 | (0)<br>6479 | (0)<br>6479 |
| **(-362.72)**<br>0 | - | - | - | - | - |
| (305.2)<br>1037.44 | (87.16)<br>1124.6 | (4.76)<br>1129.36 | (117.04)<br>1246.4 | (639.42)<br>1885.82 | (1287.72)<br>3173.54 |

# Strangford

Total Valid Pole 37250 Quota 5322 Turnout 57.1

### Party performance

| Party | Seats | 1st Pref Vote | % | (%1998) |
|---|---|---|---|---|
| DUP | 3 | 17857 | 47.9 | 27.7 |
| SF | - | 1105 | 3.0 | 1.4 |
| UUP | 2 | 10781 | 28.9 | 34.4 |
| SDLP | - | 2906 | 7.8 | 9.0 |
| Alliance | 1 | 2741 | 7.4 | 12.2 |
| Others | - | 1860 | 5.0 | 15.3 |

### At a glance...

Strangford saw another strong performance by the DUP, easily increasing its haul of seats from 2 to 3. The loser in this instance was NIUP leader Cedric Wilson, elected previously for the UKUP. The UUP held its two seats and despite a sizeable fall in vote share the Alliance MLA Kieran McCarthy held on from SDLP challenger Joe Boyle. Sitting Westminster MP Iris Robinson comfortably topped the poll with former UUP Strangford MP Lord Kilclooney (John Taylor) coming second.

| | | 1st stage | 2nd stage | 3rd stage | 4th stage |
|---|---|---|---|---|---|
| | | 1st pref votes 37,250 | Transfer of Robinson's surplus | Transfer of Ennis's surplus | Transfer of Shannon's surplus |
| Joe Boyle | SDLP | 2906 | (+3.33) 2909.33 | (+0.74) 2910.07 | (+5.94) 2916.01 |
| George Ennis | DUP | 4606 | (+1532.54) 6138.54 | **(-816.54)** 5322 | (0) 5322 |
| Dermot Kennedy | SF | 1105 | (+1.11) 1106.11 | (+1.48) 1107.59 | (+3.3) 1110.89) |
| *Lord Kilclooney | UUP | 5658 | (n/a) 5658 | (n/a) 5658 | (n/a) 5658 |
| Robert Little | UUP | 2123 | (+49.21) 2172.21 | (+199.8) 2372.01 | (+222.75) 2594.76 |
| Danny McCarthy | Ind | 319 | (+1.48) 320.48 | (+15.17) 335.65 | (+13.86) 349.51 |
| *Kieran McCarthy | All | 2741 | (+22.57) 2763.57 | (+27.75) 2791.32 | (+44.55) 2835.87 |
| David McNarry | UUP | 3000 | (+55.5) 3055.5 | (+113.96) 3169.46 | (+134.64) 3304.1 |
| Colin Neill | PUP | 540 | (+18.87) 558.87 | (+61.42) 620.29 | (+48.51) 668.8 |
| Philip Orr | Green | 425 | (+12.58) 437.58 | (+24.05) 461.63 | (+21.12) 482.75 |
| *Iris Robinson | DUP | 8548 | **(-3226)** 5322 | (0) 5322 | (0) 5322 |
| *Jim Shannon | DUP | 4703 | (+1402.67) 6105.67 | (n/a) 6105.67 | **(-783.67)** 5322 |
| *Cedric Wilson | NIUP | 576 | (+42.55) 618.55 | (+365.19) 983.74 | (+282.15) 1265.89 |
| | Non-transferable | | (83.59) 83.59 | (6.98) 90.57 | (6.85) 97.42 |

## Candidates Elected

| Candidates Elected | Count |
|---|---|
| Iris Robinson DUP | 1st |
| Lord Kilclooney UUP | 1st |
| George Ennis DUP | 2nd |
| Jim Shannon DUP | 2nd |
| David McNarry UUP | 10th |
| Kieran McCarthy All | 11th |

Iris Robinson

Lord Kilclooney

George Ennis

Jim Shannon

David McNarry

Kieran McCarthy

| 5th stage | 6th stage | 7th stage | 8th stage | 9th stage | 10th stage | 11th stage |
|---|---|---|---|---|---|---|
| Transfer of Kilclooney's surplus | Elimination of D McCarthy | Elimination of Orr | Elimination of Neill | Elimination of Kennedy & Wilson | Elimination of Little | Transfer of McNarry's surplus |
| (+4.68) 2920.69 | (+69.7) 2990.39 | (+56.74) 3047.13 | (+24.97) 3072.1 | (+878.57) 3950.67 | (+143.04) 4093.71 | (+66.34) 4160.05 |
| (0) 5322 | (0) 5322 | (0) 5322 | (0) 5322 | (0) 5322 | (0) 5322 | (0) 5322 |
| (+0.72) 1111.61 | (+61) 1172.61 | (+13.74) 1186.35 | (+2.7) 1189.05 | **(-1189.05)** 0 | - | - |
| **(-336)** 5322 | (0) 5322 | (0) 5322 | (0) 5322 | (0) 5322 | (0) 5322 | (0) 5322 |
| (+218.52) 2813.28 | (+21.1) 2834.38 | (+59.6) 2893.98 | (+169.48) 3063.46 | (+314.37) 3377.83 | **(-3377.83)** 0 | - |
| (+2.1) 351.61 | **(-351.61)** 0 | - | - | - | - | - |
| (+11.16) 2847.03 | (+121.33) 2968.36 | (+178.06) 3146.42 | (+64.61) 3211.03 | (+401.9) 3612.93 | (+619.69) 4232.62 | (+218.86) 4451.48 |
| (+90.24) 3394.34 | (+19.47) 3413.81 | (+35.33) 3449.14 | (+139.87) 3589.01 | (+295.49) 3884.5 | (+1726) 5610.5 | **(-288.5)** 5322 |
| (+3.36) 672.16 | (+3.85) 676.01 | (+21.09) 697.1 | **(-607.1)** 0 | - | - | - |
| (+1.02) 483.77 | (+18.2) 501.97 | **(-501.97)** 0 | - | - | - | - |
| (0) 5322 | (0) 5322 | (0) 5322 | (0) 5322 | (0) 5322 | (0) 5322 | (0) 5322 |
| (0) 5322 | (0) 5322 | (0) 5322 | (0) 5322 | (0) 5322 | (0) 5322 | (0) 5322 |
| (+3.78) 1269.67 | (+7.87) 1277.54 | (+37.28) 1314.82 | (+110.81) 1425.63 | **(-1425.63)** 0 | - | - |
| (0.42) 97.84 | (29.09) 126.93 | (100.13) 227.06 | (184.66) 411.72 | (724.35) 1136.07 | (889.1) 2025.17 | (3.3) 2028.47 |

# Upper Bann

**Total Valid Pole 43482 Quota 6212 Turnout 64.2**

**Party performance**

| Party | Seats | 1st Pref Vote | % | (%1998) |
|---|---|---|---|---|
| DUP | 2 | 12400 | 28.5 | 15.5 |
| SF | 1 | 9494 | 21.8 | 14.3 |
| UUP | 2 | 12786 | 29.4 | 28.9 |
| SDLP | 1 | 6818 | 15.7 | 23.7 |
| Alliance | - | 571 | 1.3 | 3.1 |
| Others | - | 1413 | 3.2 | 14.5 |

## At a glance...

Although the DUP increased its vote-share significantly and gained a seat at the expense of an independent unionist the main story was the robust performance of the UUP and under-fire leader David Trimble. In the event the UUP held on comfortably to its two seats with Trimble registering a strong personal poll-topping vote. In addition UUP voters returned his pro-Agreement running-mate Samuel Gardiner (as opposed to outgoing MLA George Savage) a further sign of local solidarity with Trimble. On the nationalist side Sinn Féin overtook the SDLP as the largest nationalist party although both held their seats fairly comfortably with new candidates Dolores Kelly (SDLP) and John O'Dowd (SF).

| | | 1st stage | 2nd stage | 3rd stage | 4th stage |
|---|---|---|---|---|---|
| | | 1st pref votes 43,482 | Transfer of Trimble's surplus | Elimination of French | Elimination of Anderson |
| Sidney Anderson | Ind | 581 | (+26.24) 607.24 | (+0.64) 607.88 | **(-607.88)** 0 |
| Kieran Corr | SDLP | 3157 | (+38.72) 3195.72 | (+55.92) 3251.64 | (+9) 3260.64 |
| Thomas French | WP | 247 | (+13.12) 260.12 | **(-260.12)** 0 | - |
| Samuel Gardiner | UUP | 2359 | (+1060.48) 3419.48 | (+16.24) 3435.72 | (+44.72) 3480.44 |
| David Jones | Ind | 585 | (+26.56) 611.56 | (+1) 612.56 | (+403.56) 1016.12 |
| Dolores Kelly | SDLP | 3661 | (+50.56) 3711.56 | (+74.52) 3786.08 | (+1) 3787.08 |
| Francis McQuaid | All | 571 | (+62.08) 633.08 | (+37.24) 670.32 | (+0.32) 670.64 |
| Stephen Moutray | DUP | 4697 | (+30.08) 4727.08 | (+7) 4734.08 | (+18.64) 4752.72 |
| John O'Dowd | SF | 5524 | (+6.4) 5530.4 | (+27) 5557.4 | (+2) 5559.4 |
| *Dara O'Hagan | SF | 3970 | (+13.44) 3983.44 | (+21) 4004.44 | (0) 4004.44 |
| *George Savage | UUP | 1269 | (+1423.36) 2692.36 | (+4.92) 2697.28 | (+29.2) 2726.48 |
| David Simpson | DUP | 5933 | (+99.52) 6032.52 | (+1.64) 6034.16 | (+69.12) 6103.32 |
| *David Trimble | UUP | 9158 | **(-2946)** 6212 | (0) 6212 | (0) 6212 |
| *Denis Watson | DUP | 1770 | (+62.08) 1832.08 | (+2) 1834.08 | (+18.64) 1852.72 |
| | Non-transferable | | (33.36) 33.36 | (11) 44.36 | (11.64) 56 |

| Candidates Elected | Count |
|---|---|
| David Trimble UUP | 1st |
| David Simpson DUP | 5th |
| Stephen Moutray DUP | 6th |
| Samuel Gardiner UUP | 9th |
| Dolores Kelly SDLP | 11th |
| John O'Dowd SF | 11th |

David Trimble

David Simpson

Stephen Moutray

Samuel Gardiner

Dolores Kelly

John O'Dowd

| 5th stage | 6th stage | 7th stage | 8th stage | 9th stage | 10th stage | 11th stage |
|---|---|---|---|---|---|---|
| Elimination of McQuaid & Jones | Elimination of Watson | Transfer of Moutray's surplus | Transfer of Simpson's surplus | Elimination of Savage | Transfer of Gardiner's surplus | Elimination of Corr |
| - | - | - | - | - | - | - |
| (+151.32)<br>3411.96 | (+3.32)<br>3415.28 | (+2.61)<br>3417.89 | (+1.64)<br>3419.53 | (+42.66)<br>3462.99 | (206.72)<br>3668.91 | **(-3668.91)**<br>0 |
| - | - | - | - | - | - | - |
| (+250.24)<br>3730.68 | (+158.24)<br>3888.92 | (+101.79)<br>3990.71 | (+41.82)<br>4032.53 | (+2840.06)<br>6872.59 | **(-660.59)**<br>6212 | (0)<br>6212 |
| **(-1016.12)**<br>0 | - | - | - | - | - | - |
| (+186.32)<br>3973.4 | (+2.96)<br>3976.36 | (+2.61)<br>3978.97 | (+2.46)<br>3981.43 | (+77.75)<br>4059.18 | (+271.36)<br>4330.54 | (+2648)<br>6978.54 |
| **(-670.64)**<br>0 | - | - | - | - | - | - |
| (+189.88)<br>4942.6 | (+1516)<br>6458.6 | **(-246.6)**<br>6212 | (0)<br>6212 | (0)<br>6212 | (0)<br>6212 | (0)<br>6212 |
| (+19)<br>5578.4 | (+2.32)<br>5580.72 | (+0.87)<br>5581.59 | (0)<br>5581.59 | (+3.14)<br>5584.73 | (+1.6))<br>5586.33 | (+326.27)<br>5912.6 |
| (+21.64)<br>4026.08 | (+1)<br>4027.08 | (0)<br>4027.08 | (0)<br>4027.08 | (+1.96)<br>4029.04 | (+1.92)<br>4030.96 | (+270.16)<br>4301.12 |
| (+265.12)<br>2991.6 | (+250.24)<br>3241.84 | (+132.24)<br>3374.08 | (+45.1)<br>3419.18 | **(-3419.18)**<br>0 | - | - |
| (+200)<br>6303.32 | (n/a)<br>6303.32 | (n/a)<br>6303.32 | **(-91.32)**<br>6212 | (0)<br>6212 | (0)<br>6212 | (0)<br>6212 |
| (0)<br>6212 | (0)<br>6212 | (0)<br>6212 | (0)<br>6212 | (0)<br>6212 | (0)<br>6212 | (0)<br>6212 |
| (+260.44)<br>2113.16 | **(-2113.16)**<br>0 | - | - | - | - | - |
| (142.8)<br>198.8 | (179.08)<br>377.88 | (6.48)<br>384.36 | (0.3)<br>384.66 | (453.61)<br>838.27 | (178.99)<br>1017.26 | (424.48)<br>1441.74 |

# West Tyrone

**Total Valid Pole 41729** **Quota 5962** **Turnout 73.2**

**Party performance**

| Party | Seats | 1st Pref Vote | % | (%1998) |
|---|---|---|---|---|
| DUP | 1 | 7286 | 17.5 | 17.4 |
| SF | 2 | 16111 | 38.6 | 34.1 |
| UUP | 1 | 5667 | 13.6 | 15.7 |
| SDLP | 1 | 6110 | 14.6 | 25.7 |
| Alliance | - | 164 | 0.4 | 2.2 |
| Others | 1 | 6391 | 15.3 | 4.8 |

**At a glance...**

Perhaps the single most surprising result in the entire election was the election at the top of the poll of Independent 'hospital' candidate Carrickmore GP Dr Kieran Deeny. His election at the expense of SDLP MLA Joe Byrne reflected the anger in West Tyrone at the proposed downgrading of Omagh Hospital. Aside from this upset Sinn Féin held its two seats very easily, and sitting MLAs Derek Hussey (UUP) and Eugene McMenamin (SDLP) held on to theirs. The DUP seat formerly held by veteran Oliver Gibson (who did not run for election) passed on to colleague Thomas Buchanan. Sinn Féin MP for the area Pat Doherty was elected on the first count just behind Dr Deeny.

| | | 1st stage | 2nd stage |
|---|---|---|---|
| | | 1st pref votes 41,729 | Transfer of Deeny's surplus |
| Steven Alexander | All | 164 | (+7.47) 717.47 |
| Thomas Buchanan | DUP | 4739 | (+4.8) 4743.8 |
| *Joe Byrne | SDLP | 2645 | (+73.2) 2718.2 |
| Kieran Deeny | Ind | 6158 | (-196) 5962 |
| *Pat Doherty | SF | 6019 | (n/a) 6019 |
| *Derek Hussey | UUP | 3733 | (+9.66) 3742.66 |
| *Barry McElduff | SF | 5642 | (+47.27) 5689.25 |
| Brian McMahon | SF | 4450 | (+6.99) 4456.99 |
| *Eugene McMenamin | SDLP | 3465 | (+14.07) 3479.07 |
| Derek Reaney | DUP | 2547 | (+2.04) 2549.04 |
| Samuel Reid | PUP | 233 | (+0.57) 233.57 |
| Bert Wilson | UUP | 1934 | (+6.12) 1940.12 |
| | Non-transferable | | (23.83) 23.83 |

| Candidates Elected | Count |
|---|---|
| Kieran Deeny Ind | 1st |
| Pat Doherty SF | 1st |
| Thomas Buchanan DUP | 5th |
| Derek Hussey UUP | 6th |
| Barry McElduff SF | 8th |
| Eugene McMenamin SDLP | 8th |

Kieran Deeny

Pat Doherty

Thomas Buchanan

Derek Hussey

Barry McElduff

Eugene McMenamin

| 3rd stage | 4th stage | 5th stage | 6th stage | 7th stage | 8th stage |
|---|---|---|---|---|---|
| Elimination of Alexander, Reid & Wilson | Transfer of Doherty's surplus | Elimination of Reaney | Transfer of Buchanan's surplus | Transfer of Hussey's surplus | Elimination of Byrne |
| **(-717.47)**<br>0 | - | - | - | - | - |
| (+233.84)<br>4977.64 | (+0.03)<br>4977.67 | (+2245)<br>7222.67 | **(-1260.67)**<br>5962 | (0)<br>5962 | (0)<br>5962 |
| (+56.72)<br>2774.92 | (+2.95)<br>2777.87 | (+13.12)<br>2790.99 | (+11.25)<br>2802.24 | (+189)<br>2991.24 | **(-2991.24)**<br>0 |
| (0)<br>5962 | (0)<br>5962 | (0)<br>5962 | (0)<br>5962 | (0)<br>5962 | (0)<br>5962 |
| (n/a)<br>6019 | **(-57)**<br>5962 | (0)<br>5962 | (0)<br>5962 | (0)<br>5962 | (0)<br>5962 |
| (+1734.67)<br>5477.33 | (+0.14)<br>5477.47 | (+425.47)<br>5902.94 | (+1235.25)<br>7138.19 | **(-1176.99)**<br>5962 | (0)<br>5962 |
| (+4.15)<br>5693.4 | (+29.44)<br>5722.84 | (+3.07)<br>5725.91 | (0)<br>5725.91 | (0)<br>5725.91 | (+372)<br>6097.91 |
| (+7.06)<br>4464.05 | (+19.9)<br>4483.95 | (+1.03)<br>4484.98 | (0)<br>4484.98 | (0)<br>4484.98 | (+73.71)<br>4558.69 |
| (+38.08)<br>3517.15 | (+1)<br>3518.15 | (+15.09)<br>3533.24 | (+12)<br>3545.24 | (+147.75)<br>3692.99 | (+2282.69)<br>5975.68 |
| (+225.48)<br>2774.52 | (+0.03)<br>2774.55 | **(-2774.55)**<br>0 | - | - | - |
| **(-233.57)**<br>0 | - | - | - | - | - |
| **(-1940.12)**<br>0 | - | - | - | - | - |
| (45.16)<br>68.99 | (3.51)<br>72.5 | (71.77)<br>144.27 | (2.17)<br>146.44 | (839.44)<br>985.88 | (262.84)<br>1248.72 |

## Local Government Elections

Elections to the twenty-six district councils of Northern Ireland are also conducted by proportional representation using the STV system. Each local government area is divided into a number of wards, which are then grouped together for the purposes of STV into District Electoral Areas. Each District Electoral Area returns a number of councillors. Belfast has 9 District Electoral Areas, but most other councils have between three and five.

The number and boundaries of each local government area (the area controlled by a district council), and ward boundaries, are determined by the Local Government Boundaries Commissioner. The District Electoral Areas Commissioner determines the grouping of wards. Both these Commissioners are entirely independent and submit recommendations to the Government every 10-15 years.

Local government elections are held every four years in Northern Ireland, the last taking place on 7 June 2001, the same day as the general election.

Details of the election results are set out in Chapter Four, Local Government, but summary results are outlined here. Since Northern Ireland's local government structure was reformed in 1973 there have been 8 local government elections across the 26 Local Government Districts (LGDs). Results for the main parties have tended to correspond with overall performance in other elections although independents have featured more strongly.

Turnout for local elections is generally around 50-60 per cent, which is significantly lower than UK government elections, and also lower than the Assembly elections in 1998 or 2003. This is probably reflective of the fact that the responsibilities of local authorities include areas such as waste disposal, cemeteries and parks, which although vital in everyday life, go largely unnoticed in comparison with mainstream political issues. Nevertheless the parties and candidates fiercely contest the elections, although issues raised at the hustings are matters over which they actually have little authority.

However, turnout for the 2001 local government election, at 66 per cent, was significantly higher than usual. This was largely due to the fact that Westminster elections were held on the same day. *(Further detailed information on Local Councils and their political composition is set out in Chapter 4.)*

## European Parliament Elections
### Members of the European Parliament

The European Parliament is composed of members from each of the 25 member states in broad proportion to their population. The UK has an entitlement of 78 European Parliament seats. Of this, Northern Ireland returns 3 MEPs by an election held every 5 years. Northern Ireland is a single constituency, and the European MPs are elected by proportional representation, (STV). The European Parliament is divided along a traditional left/right spectrum, with members belonging to a number of political groupings reflecting this division.

### Northern Ireland MEPs

The current MEPs, returned in June 2004, are set out below. Full contact details for the three MEPs are set out in Chapter 12.

Name: **Jim Allister, DUP**
European Political Group: Non-attached

Name **Bairbre de Brun, Sinn Fein**
European Political Group Party of European Socialists

Name **Jim Nicholson, UUP**
European Political Group European People's Party and European Democrats

*(There is further detailed information about the European Union in the context of Northern Ireland in Chapter 12 Europe).*

### The 2004 European Parliamentary Election

Traditionally, European Parliament elections in Northern Ireland have been less vigorously contested than Westminster or Assembly elections and are characterised by a lower turnout. The 2004 election turnout was no different with a turnout of 51.7%. The other prime feature of European Parliament elections in Northern Ireland has been the predominance of two Ian Paisley and John Hume, who have been elected comfortably in every contest since 1979.

In the 2004 election: both Ian Paisley and John Hume decided not to seek re-election, but their successors fared very differently. DUP candidate Jim Allister produced a Paisley style poll topping performance, while SDLP candidate Martin Morgan missed out altogether, dropping to fourth place. Sitting Ulster Unionist MEP Jim Nicholson was returned in a comfortable third place well behind the DUP and Sinn Féin candidates. Sinn Féin's Bairbre de Brun became Northern Ireland's first ever female MEP.

**Party % of Total 1st Preference Vote for European Elections**

| Party | 1979 | 1984 | 1989 | 1994 | 2004 |
|---|---|---|---|---|---|
| UUP | 21.9 | 21.5 | 22.2 | 23.8 | 16.6 |
| SDLP | 24.6 | 22.1 | 25.5 | 28.9 | 16 |
| DUP | 29.8 | 33.6 | 29.9 | 29.2 | 32 |
| Sinn Féin | - | 13.3 | 9.1 | 9.9 | 26.3 |
| Alliance | 6.8 | 5.0 | 5.2 | 4.1 | 2.1 |
| Other | 16.9 | 4.5 | 8.1 | 4.1 | - |

*Details of the earlier European Parliamentary Elections are set out overleaf.*

# European Election Results 1979-1999

## 2004 European Election

**Electorate** 1,072,669 **Total Valid Vote** 549,277
**Quota** 137,320 **Turnout** 51.72%

| Name | Party | 1st Pref Votes | Total % Vote | Count Elected |
|---|---|---|---|---|
| Jim Allister | DUP | 175,761 | 32 | 1st |
| Bairbre de Brun | SF | 144,541 | 26 | 1st |
| John Gilliand | Ind | 36,270 | 6 | |
| *Eamon McCann | SEA | 9,172 | 2 | |
| Martin Morgan | SDLP | 87,559 | 16 | |
| Jim Nicholson | UUP | 91,164 | 17 | 3rd |
| Lindsay Whitcroft | UUP | 4,810 | 1 | |

*Socialist/Environmental Alliance

## 1999 European Election

**Electorate** 1,190,160 **Total Valid Vote** 678,809
**Quota** 169,703 **Turnout** 57.7%

| Name | Party | 1st Pref Votes | Total % Vote | Count Elected |
|---|---|---|---|---|
| Rev I Paisley | DUP | 192,762 | 28.4 | 1st |
| J Hume | SDLP | 190,731 | 28.1 | 1st |
| J Nicholson | UUP | 119,507 | 17.6 | 3rd |
| M McLaughlin | SF | 117,643 | 17.3 | |
| D Ervine | PUP | 22,494 | 3.3 | |
| R McCartney | UKUP | 20,283 | 3.0 | |
| S Neeson | All | 14,391 | 2.1 | |
| J Anderson | NLP | 998 | 0.2 | |

## 1994 European Election

**Electorate** 1,162,344 **Total Valid Vote** 559,867
**Quota** 139,967 **Turnout** 49.4%

| Name | Party | 1st Pref Votes | Total % Vote | Count Elected |
|---|---|---|---|---|
| Rev I Paisley | DUP | 163,246 | 29.2 | 1st |
| J Hume | SDLP | 161,992 | 28.9 | 1st |
| J Nicholson | UUP | 133,459 | 23.8 | 2nd |
| M Clark-Glass | All | 23,157 | 4.1 | |
| T Hartley | SF | 21,273 | 3.8 | |
| A McGuinness | SF | 17,195 | 3.1 | |
| F Molloy | SF | 16,747 | 3.0 | |
| Rev H Ross | UIM | 7,858 | 1.4 | |
| Myrtle Boal | Cons | 5,583 | 1.0 | |
| J Lowry | WP | 2,543 | 0.5 | |
| N Cusack | Lab | 2,464 | 0.4 | |
| J Anderson | NLP | 1,418 | 0.2 | |
| J Campion | Peace | 1,088 | 0.2 | |
| D Kerr | Ind Ulst. | 571 | 0.1 | |
| S Thompson | NLP | 454 | 0.1 | |
| M Kennedy | NLP | 419 | 0.1 | |
| R Mooney | Con. Ind | 400 | 0.1 | |

Lab: Labour Party; Peace: Peace Coalition; Ind Ulst: Independent Ulster; Con. Ind: Constitutional Independent

## 1989 European Election

**Electorate** 1,106,852 **Total Valid Vote** 534,811
**Quota** 133,703 **Turnout** 48.3%

| Name | Party | 1st Pref Votes | Total % Vote | Count Elected |
|---|---|---|---|---|
| Rev I Paisley | DUP | 160,110 | 29.9 | 1st |
| J Hume | SDLP | 136,335 | 25.5 | 1st |
| J Nicholson | UUP | 118,785 | 22.2 | 2nd |
| D Morrison | SF | 48,914 | 9.1 | |
| J Alderdice | All | 27,905 | 5.2 | |
| A Kennedy | Cons | 25,789 | 4.8 | |
| M Samuel | GP | 6,569 | 1.2 | |
| S Lynch | WP | 5,590 | 1.0 | |
| M Langhammer | LRG | 3,540 | 0.7 | |
| B Caul | Lab '87 | 1,274 | 0.2 | |

GP: Green Party; LRG: Labour Representation Group; Lab '87: Labour '87

## 1984 European Election

**Electorate** 1,065,363 **Total Valid Vote** 685,317
**Quota** 171,330 **Turnout** 65.4%

| Name | Party | 1st Pref Votes | Total % Vote | Count Elected |
|---|---|---|---|---|
| Rev I Paisley | DUP | 230,251 | 33.6 | 1st |
| J Hume | SDLP | 151,399 | 22.1 | 4th |
| J Taylor | UUP | 147,169 | 21.5 | 2nd |
| D Morrison | SF | 91,476 | 13.3 | |
| D Cook | All | 34,046 | 5.0 | |
| J Kilfedder | UPUP | 20,092 | 2.9 | |
| S Lynch | WP | 8,712 | 1.3 | |
| C McGuigan | Ecology | 2,172 | 0.3 | |

## 1979 European Election

**Electorate** 1,029,490 **Total Valid Vote** 572,239
**Quota** 143,060 **Turnout** 55.6%

| Name | Party | 1st Pref Votes | Total % Vote | Count Elected |
|---|---|---|---|---|
| Rev I Paisley | DUP | 170,688 | 29.8 | 1st |
| J Hume | SDLP | 140,622 | 24.6 | 3rd |
| J Taylor | UUP | 68,185 | 11.9 | 6th |
| H West | UUP | 56,984 | 10.0 | |
| O Napier | All | 39,026 | 6.8 | |
| J Kilfedder | Ulster Unionist | 38,198 | 6.7 | |
| B McAliskey | Ind | 33,969 | 5.9 | |
| D Bleakley | Utd. Community | 9,383 | 1.6 | |
| P Devlin | ULP | 6,122 | 1.1 | |
| E Cummings | UPNI | 3,712 | 0.6 | |
| B Brennan | Rep C | 3,258 | 0.6 | |
| F Donnelly | Rep C | 1,160 | 0.2 | |
| J Murray | U. Lib | 932 | 0.2 | |

ULP: United Labour Party; UPNI: Unionist Party of Northern Ireland; Rep C: Republican Clubs; U. Lib:Ulster Liberal Party

*Castle Buildings, Stormont*

# Chapter 3

# Guide to Government Departments and Agencies

## The Northern Ireland Office

The Northern Ireland Office (NIO) is a government department, headed by the Secretary of State who is a UK Cabinet Minister, The role of the Northern Ireland Office is to support the Secretary of State and to work closely with UK departments and the Northern Ireland Assembly, to advise, offer guidance and ensure effective consultation between the UK and the Northern Ireland devolved administration.

### The Secretary of State

**The Role of the Secretary of State under Direct Rule**

Under Direct Rule, the Secretary of State, assisted by Direct Rule Ministers, assumes responsibility for all matters relating to the governance of Northern Ireland, including all those matters which would usually be devolved to the local administration.

Secretary of State: Paul Murphy (pictured)
Minister of State: John Spellar
Parliamentary Under Secretary: Ian Pearson
Parliamentary Under Secretary: Angela Smith
Parliamentary Under Secretary: Barry Gardiner

*Full details of how ministerial responsibilities are shared between the above Direct Rule Ministers is set out later in this chapter.*

**NIO Belfast Office**
Castle Buildings
Belfast, BT4 3ST
Tel: 028 9052 0700

**NIO London Office**
11 Millbank, London, SW1P 4PN
Tel: 020 7210 3000
Web: www.nio.gov.uk

**Northern Ireland Secretaries of State 1972-2004**

| | | |
|---|---|---|
| Paul Murphy | Labour | 2002 – present |
| Dr John Reid | Labour | 2000 – 2002 |
| Peter Mandelson | Labour | 1999 – 2000 |
| Mo Mowlam | Labour | 1997 – 1999 |
| Patrick Mayhew | Conservative | 1992 – 1997 |
| Peter Brooke | Conservative | 1989 – 1992 |
| Tom King | Conservative | 1985 – 1989 |
| Douglas Hurd | Conservative | 1984 – 1985 |
| James Prior | Conservative | 1981 – 1984 |
| Humphrey Atkins | Conservative | 1979 – 1981 |
| Roy Mason | Labour | 1976 – 1979 |
| Merlyn Rees | Labour | 1974 – 1976 |
| Francis Pym | Conservative | 1973 – 1974 |
| William Whitelaw | Conservative | 1972 – 1973 |

**The Role of the Secretary of State under Devolution**

Under devolution the Secretary of State continues to represent Northern Ireland interests within the Cabinet. Provision for consultation, co-operation and exchanges of information in relation to the interests of the devolved administration in the policies of the UK government are provided for by the Memorandum of Understanding and associated system of concordats between the Northern Ireland Office and the Northern Ireland Executive Committee.

Excepted matters as set out in the Northern Ireland Act 1998 cover areas of national responsibility, which it is envisaged, will always remain the responsibility of the UK parliament. Reserved matters set out in the Act are also matters of national policy, although the Assembly may at some stage make provision for dealing with them, subject to the consent of the Secretary of State and parliamentary control. Reserved matters which currently remain within the responsibility of the Secretary of State include policing, security, prisions and criminal justice. It is envisaged within the terms of the Good Friday Agreement that these matters may, at some future time, be transferred to the administration in Northern Ireland. Transferred matters – which are all matters that are not excepted or reserved fall within the responsibility of the devolved administration, the Northern Ireland Assembly when devolution is in place. (*For a full list of all those matters which are transferred, excepted and reserved, see Chapter 2, page 34.*)

A fundamental government power, the power to levy taxation remains a reserved matter. The Northern Ireland Finance Minister is therefore quite constrained in determining the size of the budget of the Northern Ireland government and more involved in how the public expenditure budget is allocated amongst the various departments.

In addition to representing Northern Ireland interests in all matters in Cabinet, in financial matters the Secretary of State has responsibility for advising the Chancellor, particularly where Northern Ireland bids for additional funding. There are other excepted and reserved matters, which continue to be the responsibility of the Lord Chancellor in Northern Ireland, such as judicial appointments and matters relating to the courts.

The Secretary of State has statutory responsibility for giving consent to Assembly bills where these impact on reserved matters and for forwarding all Assembly bills for Royal Assent. Should the Secretary of State consider a bill to be incompatible with international obligations, defence, national security or public order he may choose not to submit it for Royal Assent.

In relation to reserved or excepted matters, UK departments have certain responsibilities extending to Northern Ireland.

In the conduct of its duties the Northern Ireland Office also operates a number of Executive Agencies across a range of activities. *(More information on these, together with their contact details are included later in this chapter).*

### NIO Public Expenditure

The Northern Ireland Office currently employs approximately 4000 staff, over half of whom are prison warders or auxiliaries. It is one of the highest-spending of Northern Ireland's government departments (after health and education). See table below for NIO budgets up to 2005-06.

**NIO Budgets 2003-04 to 2005-06**

| £ Million | 2003-04 | 2004-05 | 2005-06 |
|---|---|---|---|
| Resource Budget | 1,088 | 1,128 | 1,162 |
| Capital Budget | 64 | 57 | 72 |
| Total Departmental Expenditure Limit | 1,114 | 1,144 | 1,190 |

Source: Northern Ireland Office

It is hoped that NIO security related expenditure would drop markedly as a result of the peace process, and that the peace 'dividend' would be yielded in terms of extra resources being ploughed into areas of need.

## The Administration of Justice in Northern Ireland

## The Criminal Justice System

The administration of the Criminal Justice System remains a 'reserved matter' under the Good Friday Agreement so it is currently under the authority of the Northern Ireland Office, but may, at some time in the future become a devolved matter, to be controlled by a future Northern Ireland Executive. In addition to the Northern Ireland Office, the main agencies and organisations which make up the Northern Ireland Criminal Justice System are:

- The Northern Ireland Court Service;
- The Department of the Director of Public Prosecutions;
- The Northern Ireland Prison Service;
- The Northern Ireland Probation Board;
- The Police Service of Northern Ireland.

### Ministerial Responsibility for the Criminal Justice System

The Secretary of State for Northern Ireland has responsibility for policing and for criminal justice matters generally. He/she is also responsible for a number of agencies and other bodies: the Northern Ireland Prison Service, Forensic Science Northern Ireland and the Probation Board for Northern Ireland and also funds the independent Department of the Director of Public Prosecutions.

The Secretary of State for Constitutional Affairs is responsible for the Northern Ireland Court Service, and has overall responsibility for the effective management of the courts, the appointments of judges and magistrates, policy in respect of legal aid and providing funds to make legal aid payments. The Attorney General superintends the Director of Public Prosecutions for Northern Ireland.

## Review of the Criminal Justice System

The Good Friday Agreement committed the British government to establishing a wide-ranging review of the Northern Ireland criminal justice system. The Agreement indicated that the criminal justice system should be fair and impartial, responsive to the community and encouraging of its involvement, have the confidence of all parts of the community and deliver justice efficiently and effectively.

### Terms of Reference

The Review was tasked with addressing the structure, management and resourcing of publicly funded elements of the criminal justice system and to bring forward proposals for future criminal justice arrangements covering issues such as:

- Appointments to the judiciary and magistracy;
- The organisation and supervision of the prosecution process;
- Improving the responsiveness and accountability of, and any lay participation in the criminal justice system;
- Law reform;
- Co-operation between the criminal justice agencies on both parts of the island;
- How criminal justice functions could be devolved to an Assembly, including the possibility of the establishment of a Department of Justice.

### Members of the Criminal Justice Review

Chairman: Jim Daniell, Director of Criminal Justice at the NIO; Glenn Thompson, Director of the Northern Ireland Court Service; David Seymour, Legal Secretary to the Law Officer; Brian White, Head of Criminal Justice Policy Division at the NIO; Prof Joanna Shapland, Professor of Criminal Justice at Sheffield University and Director of the Institute for the Study of the Legal Profession; Prof John Jackson, Professor of Public Law and Head of the School of Law at Queen's University; Eugene Grant QC, a barrister in criminal practice in Northern Ireland; Dr Bill Lockhart, Director of Extern and Director of the Centre for Independent Research and Analysis of Crime; His Honour John Gower QC, a retired English circuit judge.

### Progress of the Review

June 1998: The Review Group was formally established;

March 2000: publication of Review Group report, containing 294 recommendations. The government conducted a series of consultation processes with interested parties – the recommendations were broadly welcomed by all parts of the community;

November 2001: government publication of preliminary Implementation Plan and draft Justice (Northern Ireland) Bill;

July 2002: Justice (Northern Ireland) Act receives Royal Assent;

June 2003: government publication of updated Implementation Plan providing details of the 294 recommendations – with revised targets and timescales for those which are still in the process of being implemented. The updated Implementation Plan was agreed between the Secretary of State, the Lord Chancellor and the Attorney-General.

May 2004: Justice (Northern Ireland) Act 2004 receives Royal Assent.

**Key recommendations in the Criminal Justice Review**
Among the 294 recommendations in the Review, significant initiatives, and progress made so far include:

- A new Public Prosecution Service: scheduled for completion by December 2006 – work already underway in restructuring and extending the remit of the DPP(NI) including 2 pilots;
- Criminal Justice Inspectorate Northern Ireland established in October 2004 to be responsible for the inspection of all aspects of criminal justice system, other than the courts. Kit Chivers appointed as Chief Inspector;
- Community Safety Strategy: strategy document, 'Creating a Safer Northern Ireland' published in March 2003 with the aim of creating the conditions to promote an inclusive partnership-based approach in developing community safety initiatives;
- Judicial Appointments Commission to be established by spring 2005 with responsibility for making recommendations on judicial appointments up to the level of High Court judge;
- An independent Northern Ireland Law Commission: A body with responsibilities to include review of both civil and criminal law, including practice and procedure, and making recommendations for change to the government;
- Creation of a Youth Justice Agency: created on 1 April 2003, assuming the range of functions and responsibilities which previously fell to the Juvenile Justice Board. Will focus on the prevention of offending and re-offending and will take forward the major changes recommended by the Review for youth justice;
- Youth Conferences: designed to address the needs of victims, to focus on offending behaviour and repairing damaged relationships;
- Victims: The Review recommended that the interests of victims of crime should feature in the codes of practice and plans of all criminal justice organisations that interface with them.

Also in June 2003, the Government appointed The Rt Hon the Lord Clyde as Justice Oversight Commissioner who will provide public assurance about the implementation of the changes in criminal justice arrangements.

Lord Clyde's first and second reports were published in January 2004 and June 2004 respectively.

## The Northern Ireland Court Service

21st Floor, Windsor House, 9-15 Bedford Street, Belfast BT2 7LT
Tel: 028 9032 8594 / Fax: 028 9032 8494
Web: www.courtsni.gov.uk
Director General: David Lavery

*Laganside Court Complex*

The Court Service was established in 1979 by the Judicature (Northern Ireland) Act 1978 as 'a unified and distinct Civil Service of the Crown' and is a separate civil service in its own right. The role of the Court Service is to support the administration of justice in Northern Ireland, within the following strategic aims:

- To facilitate the conduct of the business of the Supreme Court, county courts, magistrates courts and coroners, courts and certain tribunals;
- To give effect to judgments to which the Judgments Enforcement (Northern Ireland) Order 1981 applies;

The Northern Ireland Court Service is part of the Department of Constitutional Affairs and is accountable to Parliament at Westminster through the Secretary of State at the Department of Constitutional Affairs. Lord Falconer was appointed first Secretary of State for Constitutional Affairs in June 2003 as part of a continuing government drive to modernise the constitution and public service. The Court Service employs some 750 staff across 21 venues throughout Northern Ireland and at its headquarters in Belfast.

## Northern Ireland Court Service Contact Details

All offices can be contacted by phone from 9:00am to 5:00pm Monday to Friday, excluding public and bank holidays.

**Information Centre**
Tel: 028 9041 2387 / Fax: 028 9023 6361
Email: informationcentre@courtsni.gov.uk

**Coroner's Office**
Tel: 028 9072 8202 / Fax: 028 9072 4559
Email: coronersoffice@courtsni.gov.uk

**Court Funds Office**
Tel: 028 9072 8888 / Fax: 028 9072 8866
Email: courtfundsoffice@courtsni.gov.uk

**Enforcement of Judgments Office**
Tel: 028 9024 5081 / Fax: 028 9031 3520
Email: ejo@courtsni.gov.uk

**Fixed Penalty Office**
Tel: 028 9072 8233 / Fax: 028 9031 0227
Email: fixedpenaltyoffice@courtsni.gov.uk

**Office of the Social Security Commissioners and Child Support Commissioners**
Tel: 028 9033 2344 / Fax: 028 9031 3510
Email: socialsecuritycommissioners@courtsni.gov.uk

**Royal Courts of Justice**
Tel: 028 9032 8594 / Fax: 028 9031 3508

## Court Offices in Northern Ireland (A-Z)

**Antrim Court Office**
Tel: 028 9446 2661 / Fax: 028 9446 3301
Email: antrimcourthouse@courtsni.gov.uk

**Armagh Court Office**
Tel: 028 3752 2816 / Fax: 028 3752 8194
Email: armaghcourthouse@courtsni.gov.uk

**Ballymena Court Office**
Tel: 028 2564 9416 / Fax: 028 2565 5371
Email: ballymenacourthouse@courtsni.gov.uk

**Banbridge Court Office**
Tel: 028 4062 3622 / Fax: 028 4062 3059
Email: banbridgecourthouse@courtsni.gov.uk

**Bangor Court Office**
Tel: 028 9147 2626 / Fax: 028 9127 2667

Email: bangorcourthouse@courtsni.gov.uk

**Belfast County Court**
Tel: 028 9072 8223 / Fax: 028 9031 3771
Email: belfastcountycourt@courtsni.gov.uk

**Belfast Crown Court Jury Line**
Tel: 028 9024 2099 (available from 5:00pm to 9:00am)

**Belfast Crown Court**
Tel: 028 9072 4758 / Fax: 028 9024 2078
Email: belfastcrowncourt@courtsni.gov.uk

**Belfast Magistrates' Court**
Tel: 028 9072 4550 / Fax: 028 9023 9472
Email: belfastmagistratescourt@courtsni.gov.uk

**Coleraine Court Office**
Tel: 028 7034 3437 / Fax: 028 7032 0156
Email: colerainecourthouse@courtsni.gov.uk

**Craigavon Court Office**
Tel: 028 3834 1324 / Fax: 028 3834 1243
Email: craigavoncourthouse@courtsni.gov.uk

**Downpatrick Court Office**
Tel: 028 4461 4621 / Fax: 028 4461 3969
Email: downpatrickcourthouse@courtsni.gov.uk

**Dungannon Court Office**
Tel: 028 8772 2992 / Fax: 028 8772 8169
Email: dungannoncourthouse@courtsni.gov.uk

**Enniskillen Court Office**
Tel: 028 6632 2356 / Fax: 028 6632 3636
Email: enniskillencourthouse@courtsni.gov.uk

**Laganside Courts (Customer Service)**
Tel: 028 9072 4570 / Fax: 028 9031 0227
Email: csmlaganside@courtsni.gov.uk

**Larne Court Office**
Tel: 028 2827 2927 / Fax: 028 2827 6414
Email: larnecourthouse@courtsni.gov.uk

**Limavady Court Office**
Tel: 028 7772 2688 / Fax: 028 7776 8794
Email: limavadycourthouse@courtsni.gov.uk

**Lisburn Court Office**
Tel: 028 9267 5336 / Fax: 028 9260 4107
Email: lisburncourthouse@courtsni.gov.uk

**Londonderry Court Office**
Tel: 028 7136 3448 / Fax: 028 7137 2059
Email: londonderrycourthouse@courtsni.gov.uk

**Magherafelt Court Office**
Tel: 028 7963 2121 / Fax: 028 7966 8794
Email: magherafeltcourthouse@courtsni.gov.uk

**Newry Court Office**
Tel: 028 3025 2040 / Fax: 028 3026 9830
Email: newrycourthouse@courtsni.gov.uk

**Newtownards Court Office**
Tel: 028 9181 4343 / Fax: 028 9181 8024
Email: newtownardscourthouse@courtsni.gov.uk

**Omagh Court Office**
Tel: 028 8224 2056 / Fax: 028 8225 1198
Email: omaghcourthouse@courtsni.gov.uk

**Royal Courts of Justice**
Tel: 028 9023 5111 / Fax: 028 9031 3508
Email: adminoffice@courtsni.gov.uk

**Strabane Court Office**
Tel: 028 7138 2544 / Fax: 028 7138 8209
Email: strabanecourthouse@courtsni.gov.uk

## The Work of the Different Types of Court

### The Court of Appeal

The Court of Appeal sits at the Royal Courts of Justice in Belfast. The judges of the Court of Appeal are the Lord Chief Justice (who is the President) and three Lords Justices of Appeal. The Court of Appeal hears appeals in criminal matters from the crown court and in civil matters from the High Court. It also hears appeals on points of law from the county courts, magistrates' courts and certain tribunals. A Court of Appeal case will usually be heard by three judges and sometimes by two. Incidental matters may be heard by a single judge.

### The High Court

In Northern Ireland civil justice is administered mainly by the county courts and the High Court. County courts deal with cases of lesser value while the High Court handles cases of greater value or certain complex cases or applications (such as judicial review). Where cases suitable for trial in the county courts are commenced in the High Court, the High Court may remit a case to a county court. Similarly, appropriate cases may be removed from the county court to the High Court.

The High Court normally sits at the Royal Courts of Justice in Belfast. It consists of the Lord Chief Justice (who is the President) and other judges (puisne judges) of whom there were nine at 31 March 2004.

The High Court has three Divisions, handling different types of work: the Chancery Division, Queen's Bench Division and Family Division.

#### Chancery Division

The principal business assigned to the Chancery Division is:

- land and property matters;
- the execution or declaration of trusts;
- bankruptcy and winding up proceedings;
- the dissolution of partnerships.
- contentious probate matters

#### Queen's Bench Division

The Queen's Bench Division deals principally with:

- actions in contract;
- actions in tort (typically personal injury actions arising from road traffic accidents, industrial accidents, false imprisonment and medical negligence);
- public law cases (for example, applications for judicial review of the decisions of the inferior courts, tribunals, public bodies or Government Ministers);
- defamation (libel and slander); and
- Admiralty.

#### Family Division

The principal business assigned to the Family Division is:

- matrimonial causes (such as divorce, judicial separation and ancillary matters involving custody of, and access to, children of the marriage and financial provision orders);
- adoption;
- wardship of children;
- applications under the Children (Northern Ireland) Order 1995;
- patients' affairs (dealing with persons who, by reason of mental incapacity, require the protection of the court);
- the granting or revocation of probate or letters of administration.

### The Crown Court

The Crown Court has exclusive jurisdiction to try offences charged on indictment. Offences tried on indictment are the more serious offences. Some offences will always be tried summarily (ie by the magistrates' courts) and others may be tried either summarily or on indictment. The Lord Chief Justice is President of the Crown Court and the Lords Justices of Appeal, High Court judges and county court judges all sit in the Crown Court from time to time, although directions of the Lord Chancellor restrict the hearing of the most serious offences to the more senior judges. The Crown Court normally sits at nine venues in Northern Ireland.

### County Courts

In Northern Ireland there are seven county court divisions although the court may sit in more than one location within the division. There is a present complement of fifteen county court judges and four district judges. The county court judges may also sit in the Crown Court to hear criminal cases but district judges deal exclusively with civil business. A number of deputy county court judges and deputy district judges have been also appointed.

#### Civil Business

Ordinary civil cases (eg contract or tort actions) are commenced in the County Court if the value of the case is less than £15,000 or less than £45,000 in equity matters (eg matters concerning wills). The County Court has jurisdiction in disputes relating to land where the net annual value of the land in question does not exceed £500 (or £3,200 in respect of 'commercial' property). If the value of the case or land is above these limits the case will be commenced in the High Court. The County Court may also hear claims for libel or slander (value up to £3,000).

A county court judge will normally determine contested civil cases above £3,000. District judges hear uncontested matters up to £15,000 and contested cases up to a value of £5,000.

Many cases in which the sum involved does not exceed £2,000 will be dealt with by the district judge by way of arbitration, often called the small claims procedure, which is primarily designed to resolve simple consumer disputes. Arbitrations are informal and do not adhere strictly to the rules of evidence and county court procedure. Parties are encouraged to handle small claims by themselves rather than being legally represented, and legal aid is not available for representation in such cases.

County courts also have jurisdiction to hear applications for adoptions and undefended divorces. The county courts have jurisdiction to determine appeals against decisions made by the Secretary of State for Northern Ireland by claimants for compensation under the criminal injuries and criminal damage legislation. Applications for the grant of intoxicating liquor licences and certificates of registration for clubs are also made to the county courts. In addition to its original civil jurisdiction the county court hears appeals under a number of statutory provisions from the magistrates' courts or from other tribunals. All these matters will be dealt with by the county court judge.

Three county courts have been designated as family care centres to deal with certain applications or appeals relating to the care or welfare of a child or young person under the Children (Northern Ireland) Order 1995. When dealing with civil matters in relation to children under 17 under the Children (Northern Ireland) Order 1995 it is known as a Family Proceedings Court.

**Criminal Business**
The County Courts' criminal jurisdiction is limited to hearing appeals from the magistrates' courts against conviction or sentence.

## Magistrates' Courts

There are twenty-one petty sessions districts in Northern Ireland which are spread throughout the seven county court divisions. A magistrates' court sitting in petty sessions (other than a youth court or family proceedings court) is presided over by a resident magistrate sitting alone. The present complement of resident magistrates is 19. There are also a number of deputy resident magistrates.

**Criminal Business**
Magistrates' courts exercise two basic functions in respect of criminal proceedings:

- the summary trial of relatively minor offences or of indictable offences which may be tried summarily. The vast majority of criminal cases in Northern Ireland are dealt with by the magistrates' courts. Summary trial is quicker and less expensive than a crown court trial on indictment.

- An examination of the case against an accused who is to be tried on indictment in the Crown Court. The initial examination can take the form of a preliminary inquiry (where the witnesses' statements are handed into court) or a preliminary investigation (where witnesses appear to give their evidence orally and on oath). These hearings are referred to as committal proceedings as the purpose is to determine whether there is sufficient evidence against the accused to warrant committing him for trial at the Crown Court.

Youth Courts are specially constituted courts of summary jurisdiction composed of a resident magistrate and two lay members (of whom at least one must be a woman) which deal with criminal matters in relation to children under 17.

**Civil Business**
The main types of civil business transacted by the magistrates' courts are domestic proceedings, small debts, and applications for certain licences.

## Coroners Courts

The jurisdiction of the Coroner in Northern Ireland is defined principally by the Coroners Act (Northern Ireland) 1959 as supplemented by the Coroners (Practice and Procedure) Rules (Northern Ireland) 1963 [SR 1963 No 199], as amended.

There is one full-time Coroner in Northern Ireland and six part-time Coroners. There are also six Deputy Coroners. Each Coroner is responsible for the investigation of deaths which occur in his particular district. There are presently seven Coroners districts in Northern Ireland.

Where a Coroner considers it is necessary to hold an inquest into a particular death, he may direct a post-mortem examination. This may be followed by the holding of a formal inquest, which may either be presided over by the Coroner only or by a Coroner with the assistance of a jury. The purpose of an inquest is to establish how, when and where the death of the deceased occurred. An inquest does not determine questions of criminal or civil liability.

## Social Security Commissioners and Child Support Commissioners

Social Security Commissioners are appointed under the Social Security Administration (Northern Ireland) Act 1992. They hear appeals from Appeal Tribunals in relation to matters arising under the social security system. Child Support Commissioners are appointed under the Child Support Act 1991 and they hear appeals from Child Support Appeal Tribunals.

Commissioners are barristers or solicitors of at least ten years standing. Apart from the Chief Commissioner there is one other full-time Commissioner.

An appeal against the decision of a Commissioner can be made on a point of law to the Court of Appeal if leave to do so is given by the Commissioner or the Court. Detailed rules regulating the conduct of proceedings before Commissioners are set out in The Social Security Commissioners (Procedure) Regulations (Northern Ireland) 1999 [SR 1999 No.225] and in The Child Support Commissioners (Procedure) Regulations (Northern Ireland) 1999 [SR 1999 No.226].

## The Court Structure in Northern Ireland (and the UK)

**The House of Lords**

Final Court of Appeal in the UK

Hears appeals on points of law in cases of major importance

**The Court of Appeal**

Hears appeals on points of law in criminal and civil cases from all courts

**The High Court**

Hears complex or important civil cases in three divisions and also appeals from county courts

- **Queen's Bench Division**
- **Chancery Division**
- **Family Division**

**County Courts including Family Care Centres (7 Divisions)**

Hear a wide range of civil actions from magistrates' courts

**Small Claims Courts**

Hear consumer claims and minor civil cases

**The Crown Court**

Hears all serious criminal cases

**Magistrates' Courts (including Juvenvile Courts and Family Proceedings Courts)**
(21 Petty Sessions Districts)

Conduct preliminary hearings in more serious criminal cases, cases involving juveniles and some civil and domestic cases, including family proceedings

**Coroners' Courts**

Investigates the circumstances of sudden, violent or unnatural deaths

**The Enforcement of Judgments Office**

Enforces money and other judgments

## The Enforcement of Judgments Office

The Enforcement of Judgments Office (EJO) mainly deals with enforcing money judgments but it also enforces other types of civil judgments such as those that are connected with the possession of land and property. It is not a debt-collecting agency. It deals with an ever-present social problem and when necessary it works with the welfare departments that are involved in the case.

## The House of Lords

The House of Lords deals mainly with appeals from the Court of Appeal, or direct from the High Court, where the case involves a point of law or general public importance. Appeals are mostly about civil cases although the Lords do deal with some criminal appeals.

## The Court of First Instance

The Court of First Instance is based in Luxembourg. A case can be taken to this court if European Community law has not been implemented properly by a national government or if there is confusion over its interpretation or if it has been ignored. A case which is lost at the Court of First Instance may be able to be appealed against at the European Court of Justice.

## The European Court of Justice

The European Court of Justice advises on interpretation of European Community law and takes action against infringements. It examines the validity of acts of the European Community institutions and clarifies European Community law by making preliminary rulings. It also hears appeals against decisions made by the Court of First Instance.

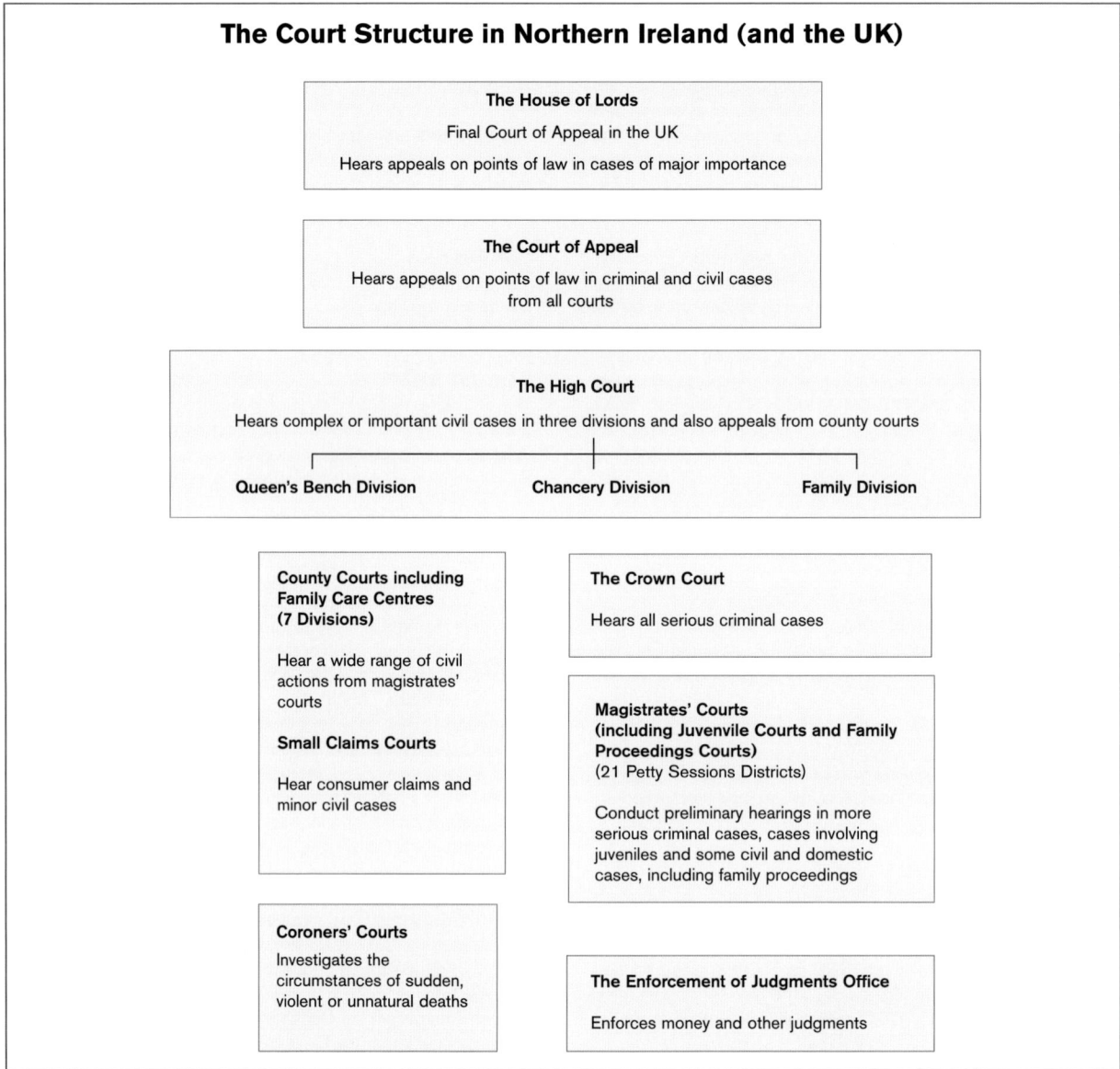

## The European Court of Human Rights

The European Court of Human Rights deals with cases in which a person thinks their human rights have been contravened and there is no legal remedy within the national legal system.

The Lord Chancellor holds responsibility for a wide range of functions affecting the administration of justice in Northern Ireland and has the leading role in appointments to judicial, quasi-judicial offices and Queen's Counsel. He holds ministerial responsibility for legal aid, matters affecting the provision of legal services to the public, and determining the statutory framework for the structure, jurisdiction and operation of the courts in Northern Ireland. The role of the Court Service is to support the Lord Chancellor in the discharge of these responsibilities.

## Work of the Northern Ireland Court Service

The work of the Court Service is to:

- Provide administrative support for the Supreme Court, county courts, magistrates' courts, coroners' courts and certain tribunals;
- Give effect to judgments to which the Judgments Enforcement (Northern Ireland) Order 1981 applies;
- Support the Lord Chancellor and Secretary of State for Constitutional Affairs in discharging his ministerial responsibilities in Northern Ireland.

### Structure

The Court Service is accountable to Parliament at Westminster through the Lord Chancellor and Secretary of State for Constitutional Affairs, Lord Falconer.

The Director of the Court Service, Mr David A Lavery, is the Head of Department, Principal Accounting Officer and Accountant General of the Supreme Court of Judicature of Northern Ireland.

In running the department the Director is supported by a Management Board comprising five Divisional Heads and two Non-Executive Members.

The Head of Operations Division, George Keatley, is responsible for:

- The administration of court business;
- The Enforcement of Judgments Office;
- Administrative support to the Social Security and Child Support Commissioners, the Pension Appeals Tribunal and the Tribunal established under section 91 of the Northern Ireland Act 1988;
- The Fixed Penalty Office;
- Meeting the standards laid down in the Courts Charter for Northern Ireland.

The Head of Policy and Legislation Division, Laurene McAlpine, is responsible for:

- Providing advice to the Lord Chancellor on the policy and legislative framework within which Northern Ireland courts operate;
- Providing legal services for the Court Service;
- Handling legislation for which the Lord Chancellor is responsible for in Northern Ireland;
- Carrying out the functions of the Central Authority under the European and Hague Conventions on Child Abduction;
- Providing the Secretariat to Court Rules Committees.

The Head of Corporate Services and Modernisation Division, Anthony Carleton, has responsibility for:

- Providing a range of services in support of other divisions and the judiciary including personnel and training, resource management, procurement, including capital projects, information services and information technology;
- Providing an internal audit function;
- Managing funds lodged in court on behalf of adults and minors.

The Head of Public Legal Services Division, Linda Devlin, has responsibility for:

- Reform of public funded legal services;
- Oversight of the Legal Services Commission's administration of publicly funded legal services;
- Formulating and implementing legal aid policy and initiatives.

The Head of Judicial Services Division, Alan Hunter, has responsibility for;

- Supporting the Lord Chancellor on the administration of judicial appointments in Northern Ireland including advising on appointments policy.
- Working closely with the Commissioner for Judicial Appointments for Northern Ireland who oversees the judicial appointments processes.
- The establishment of, and the appointment of individuals to the new judicial office of Lay Magistrate.

### Court Service Organisational Structure

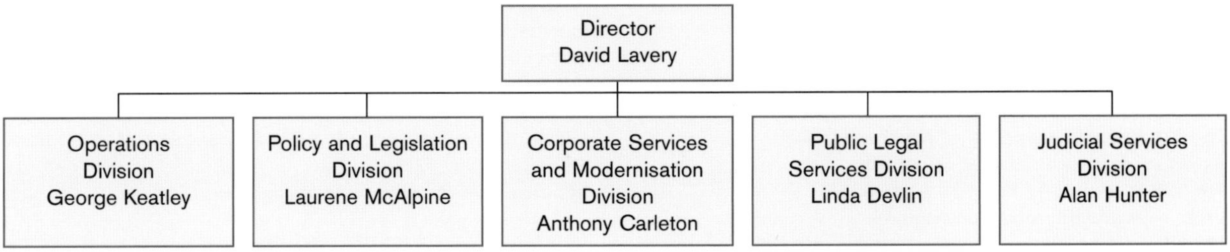

**Policy and Legislative Programme**
The Court Service aims to provide policy advice and deliver an agreed programme of legislation including court rules involving the formulation of non executive policy, including civil and criminal policy, advice on such policy to ministers and on the general administration of justice. The Court Service also advises the Chancellor on judicial and public appointments and the operation of recruitment procedures.

## The Department of the Director of Public Prosecutions
The aim of the Department is to provide the people of Northern Ireland with an independent, fair and effective prosecution service. The Department of the Director of Public Prosecutions in Northern Ireland was established by the Prosecution of Offences (Northern Ireland) Order 1972. The current Director of Public Prosecutions in Northern Ireland is Sir Alasdair Fraser CB QC.

**Functions of the DPP**
The main function of the Director is to consider facts or information contained in police investigation files and reach decisions as to a prosecution or no prosecution. Where the decision is for prosecution:

- Prosecute in the Crown Court – this generally occurs for the most serious offences (eg murder, serious assaults); or
- Prosecute certain offences in the Magistrates' Courts – generally these prosecutions are for the more serious offences (eg criminal damage, minor sexual assaults) which can be heard in the Magistrates' Courts including where the prosecution is of a police officer or a member of the security forces.

The Director also considers, with a view to prosecution, investigation files from government departments. Other duties include making representations in bail applications and in cases which go on appeal to the County Court, the Court of Criminal Appeal and the House of Lords.

**Relationship with the Attorney General and Others**
The Director and Deputy Director of Public Prosecutions are appointed by the Attorney General for Northern Ireland, currently The Right Honourable The Lord Goldsmith QC. The Director and his staff are wholly independent of government and the police.

**Attorney General's Office**
Legal Secretariat to Law Officers
Attorney General's Chambers
9 Buckingham Gate, London, SWI1 6JP
Tel: 0207 271 2412
Web: www.lslo.gov.uk

**The Youth Justice Agency of Northern Ireland**
41-43 Waring Street, Belfast, BT1 2DY
Tel: 028 9031 6400 / Fax: 028 9031 6402
Web: www.youthjusticeagencyni.gov.uk
Chief Executive: Bill Lockhart

The creation of the Youth Justice Agency came about as a result of recommendations from the Criminal Justice Board. The main aim of the youth justice system is to prevent offending by children, and the Youth Justice Agency works to divert children from crime and assist their integration into the community.

## The Northern Ireland Judiciary
The role of the Court Service is to ensure the efficient and effective disposal of court business and support the Judiciary. The relationship between the Judiciary and the Courts Service is crucial in the administration of the courts and tribunals. However, whilst close co-operation is required it is imperative that the independence of the judiciary is maintained.

**Full and Part Time Judiciary (March 2004)**

| | |
|---|---|
| **Supreme Court** | |
| Lord Chief Justice | 1 |
| Lord Justices of Appeal | 3 |
| High Court Judges | 9 |
| Masters of the Supreme Court | 7 |
| Principal Private Secretary to the Lord Chief Justice | 1 |
| **County Courts** | |
| County Court Judges | 15 |
| District Judges | 4 |
| **Magistrate's Courts** | |
| Resident Magistrates | 19 |
| Chief Social Security & Child Support Commissioner | 1 |
| Social Security and Child Support Commissioner | 1 |
| Coroner | 1 |
| Total | 62 |

**Lord Chief Justice for Northern Ireland**
Royal Courts of Justice
Chichester Street, Belfast, BT1 3JF
Tel: 028 9023 5111
Web: www.courtsni.gov.uk

The Lord Chief Justice for Northern Ireland is currently The Honourable Sir Brian Kerr. Sir Brian took up his position in January 2004 following the elevation of his predecessor Sir Robert Carswell to the House of Lords as a Law Lord.

## Appointments to the Judiciary
Recommendations to the Lord Chancellor are made by Advisory Committees on the appointment of Justices of the Peace, Lay Panel Members and General Commissioners of Income Tax. The manager of the Judicial Appointments Branch performs the role of Assistant Secretary of Commissions (Northern Ireland) to each Committee. This system is currently being revised under the Review of the Criminal Justice System, which has recommended the establishment of a Judicial Appointments Commission to recommend on judicial appointments up to the level of High Court Judge.

## The Legal Profession in Northern Ireland

The legal profession in Northern Ireland is composed of two separate and complementary branches:

- Barristers;
- Solicitors.

Differences in the services each provide are reflected by the differences in their training and organisation. Solicitors provide the first point of contact for those seeking legal advice and in many cases such as conveyancing, making wills or matrimonial matters may be the only contact necessary. However a barrister may be required to advise or represent a client in court. Contact in the first instance is usually through the client's solicitor rather than directly with the client, this is thought to aid the maintenance of impartiality.

Should a case proceed, the solicitor may undertake the preparatory work although barristers with their experience of litigation and knowledge of the procedures of the court and judiciary will focus on the presentation of the matter. The client and solicitor meet as and if required by the nature of the case, which is determined by the likelihood of the case succeeding.

In April 2003 there were 555 barristers in independent practice in Northern Ireland. There are 66 Queen's Counsel, barristers who have earned a high reputation and are appointed by the Queen on the recommendation of the Lord Chancellor as senior advocates and advisers. The title does not imply an association with the State. Barristers who are not Queen's Counsel are called Junior Counsel. This term is misleading since many members of the Junior Bar are experienced barristers with considerable expertise.

**The Executive Council and the Bar Council**
The General Council of the Bar of Northern Ireland
PO Box 414
Royal Courts of Justice
Chichester Street, Belfast, BT1 3JP
Tel: 028 9056 2349 / Fax: 028 9056 2350
Web: www.barlibrary.com

The Executive Council is involved with Barrister education; fees of students; calling counsel to the Bar (although the call to the Bar is performed by the Lord Chief Justice on the invitation of the Benchers); administration of the Bar Library, (to which all practising members of the Bar belong) and liaising with corresponding bodies in other countries.

The Bar Council is responsible for the maintenance of the standards, honour and independence of the Bar and, through its Professional Conduct Committee, receives and investigates complaints against members of the Bar as professionals.

The Bar Library is the base of all practising barristers in Northern Ireland, providing office and other support and facilities as well as library and information services. The new Bar Library building opened in April 2003.

***The Bar Library***
91 Chichester Street, Belfast, BT1 3JQ

**The Law Society of Northern Ireland**
Law Society House
98 Victoria Street
Belfast, BT1 3JZ
Tel: 028 9023 1614 / Fax: 028 9023 2606
Web: www.lawsoc-ni.org
Chief Executive: John Bailie

The Law Society is set up by Royal charter, and its powers and duties are to regulate the solicitor's profession in Northern Ireland. It operates through a Council of thirty members, all practicing solicitors who serve on a voluntary basis. Any solicitor whose name is on the Roll of Solicitors in Northern Ireland and who has not been suspended from practising as a solicitor may become a member of the Society on payment of the annual subscription. There are approximately 1850 solicitors currently practising in Northern Ireland.

**Legal Aid Administration**
The Law Society of Northern Ireland holds statutory responsibility for the civil legal aid scheme and administers criminal legal aid on behalf of the Lord Chancellor. The Legal Aid department is managed by the Legal Aid Committee of the Law Society composed of solicitors and barristers, one of whom is appointed by the Lord Chancellor. Financial memoranda and management statements govern relationships between the Law Society, its Legal Aid committee and department and the Court Service. The Court Service facilitates the administration of legal aid by the Legal Aid department.

## The Compensation Agency

Royston House, 34 Upper Queen Street
Belfast, BT1 6FD
Tel: 028 9024 9944
Web: www.compensationni.gov.uk
Chief Executive: Anne McCleary

The Compensation Agency was established in April 1992 to support the victims of violent crime by providing compensation to those who sustain loss as a result of actions taken under emergency provisions legislation. This work is carried out on behalf of the Secretary of State for Northern Ireland.

## Elections Administration

The Secretary of State for Northern Ireland also retains overall responsibility for elections in Northern Ireland although day to day executive responsibility rests with the Electoral Office headed up by the Chief Electoral Officer. The Secretary of State appoints the Chief Electoral Officer.

**The Electoral Office Headquarters**
15 Church Street
Belfast, BT1 1ER
Tel: 028 9023 9431
Chief Electoral Officer: Denis Stanley

*(More detailed information on elections including recent results is included in Chapter 2).*

## Security in Northern Ireland

The government's security policy is designed to secure lasting peace in Northern Ireland based on the Good Friday Agreement. The government has expressed its desire to achieve a return to normal security and policing arrangements, with the army assuming a peacetime role within Northern Ireland, the removal of military bases and barriers, a reduction in troop levels and a cessation of emergency legislation.

It remains a priority for the government to maintain security policies for Northern Ireland, supported by a sufficient capability for counter-terrorism. Although progress towards 'normalisation' has been made, the estimated threat of further terrorist attack and concern for public safety determine the rate at which long-term objectives can be achieved.

*Watchtower at HMP Maze*

Since the reinstatement of the IRA ceasefire in 1997, a wide range of security measures have been implemented:

- Currently just over 11,000 troops in Northern Ireland, the lowest level since 1970. Troop levels have decreased year on year since 1992, when there were approximately 18,200;
- Closure, demolition or vacation by the Army of 64 of the 105 military bases and installations occupied in 1997;
- Demolition of almost half of the surveillance sites which were in existence at the time of the ceasefire;
- Castlereagh, Strand Road and Gough Holding Centres now closed;
- 102 cross-border roads re-opened;

The current role of the army in Northern Ireland is to support the PSNI in countering the threat of terrorism and assist in the government's objective of restoring normality to the province.

Northern Ireland's politicians are deeply divided on security with most unionists concerned at the relaxation of security and the reduction in capability, while nationalists want to see a much faster rate of 'normalisation' particularly in border areas.

## Prisons Administration in Northern Ireland

**Northern Ireland Prison Service**
Dundonald House
Upper Newtownards Road
Belfast, BT4 3SU
Tel: 028 9052 2922 / Fax: 028 9052 5160
Email: info@niprisonservice.gov.uk
Web: www.niprisonservice.gov.uk
Director General: Peter Russell

The Northern Ireland Prison Service is an executive agency of the Northern Ireland Office. It is responsible for providing prison services in Northern Ireland and is a major component of the wider criminal justice system. The Secretary of State is the minister responsible for the Prison Service and is accountable to parliament.

The Prison Service currently has three operational establishments and a staff training facility, the Prison Service College.

**Hydebank Wood**
**Young Offenders Centre**
Hospital Road
Belfast, BT8 8NA
Tel: 028 9025 3666

**Maghaberry Prison**
Old Road
Ballinderry Upper
Lisburn, BT28 2PT
Tel: 028 9261 1888

**Magilligan Prison**
Point Road
Limavady, BT49 0LR
Tel: 028 7776 3311

**Prison Service College**
Woburn House
Millisle, BT22 2HS
Tel: 028 9186 3000

**The Prison Population (October 2004)**

| | Sentenced | Remand | Total |
|---|---|---|---|
| Maghaberry | 367 | 356 | 723 |
| Magilligan | 348 | 0 | 348 |
| Hydebank Wood YOC | 120 | 143 | 263 |
| Total | 835 | 499 | 1334 |

The Hydebank Wood total includes 32 female prisoners (13 sentenced and 19 remand). The bulk of the prison population in Northern Ireland is now made up of people convicted of non-terrorist related offences.

### Life Sentence Prisoners

As of 10 August 2004 there were 123 life sentence prisoners including 3 prisoners detained at the Secretary of State's pleasure. Since 1981 special arrangements have been in place for the release on licence of life sentence prisoners and under these arrangements 468 prisoners have been released to date.

The power to release a life sentence prisoner rests with the Secretary of State, after consultation with the Lord Chief Justice of Northern Ireland and the trial judge.

The non-statutory Life Sentence Review Board formally advises the Secretary of State on the release of such prisoners. The average sentence served by a life sentence prisoner is 15 years.

**Accelerated Release Prisoners**
Under the terms of the Good Friday Agreement, the Northern Ireland (Sentences) Act was introduced in July 1998. Prisoners convicted of such offences and attracting a sentence of five years or more became eligible to apply for early release from the Independent Sentence Review Commission.

**Staffing Statistics (July 2004)**
The Northern Ireland Prison Service employs around 2,000 staff. The Prisoner Escort Group – responsible for producing people to and returning them from courts – has staff based at courtrooms throughout Northern Ireland.

**Prison Service Staff by Location and Category (July 2004)**

| Location | Civilian Staff | Prison Staff-Uniformed | Prison Staff Civilian | Total |
|---|---|---|---|---|
| PSHQ* | 201 | 44 | 8 | 254 |
| Maghaberry | 69 | 839 | 30 | 939 |
| Magilligan | 41 | 341 | 22 | 404 |
| Hydebank Wood YOC | 32 | 277 | 9 | 318 |
| Prisoner Escort Group | 3 | 77 | 1 | 81 |
| Total | 347 | 1579 | 70 | 1996 |

*total for PSHQ includes those employed at the Prison Service College

Civilian staff includes administrative officers as well as psychologists, teachers, special advisors and a health and safety officer.

Prison staff (uniform) includes all governor, principal officer, senior officer, officer and auxiliary officer grades including specialists eg dog handlers, hospital officers and physical education instructors. Prison staff (civilian) includes searchers, cooks, drivers, cleaners.

## The Probation Board for Northern Ireland

80-90 North Street, Belfast, BT1 1LD
Tel: 028 9026 2400 / Fax: 028 9026 2470
Web: www.pbni.org.uk / Email: info@pbni.org.uk
Chairman: Ronnie Spence
Chief Executive: Noel Rooney

The Probation Board is a non-departmental body with the aim of reducing crime and the harm it does. Its mission is to integrate offenders successfully into the community by reducing re-offending.

The Probation Board has a number of functions:

- To carry out assessments and provide reports to courts to make a contribution to the decisions which Judges make in relation to sentencing;
- To have staff who work in prisons providing a range of social welfare services.

The Probation Board may fund organisations that provide hostels for offenders and run projects in the community, which address the offending behaviour of offenders who are under Probation Board supervision. The Secretary of State for Northern Ireland has responsibility for appointments to the Board.

## Victims

The Belfast Agreement makes a commitment towards addressing the needs of the victims and survivors of the Troubles. The government has appointed a Victims Minister (currently Angela Smith) with administrative support units within both OFMDFM and the Northern Ireland Office. More than £20m has been invested in victims' initiatives since 1998, which has financed the implementation of the Bloomfield Report 'We Will Remember Them'. Projects completed to date have provided for:

- Financial support for victims' groups;
- The establishment of a memorial fund;
- The establishment of two trauma centres;
- The analysis of the needs of victims and survivors who live in GB;
- The development and rolling out of a strategy for the NI departments to deliver practical help and services to victims and survivors.

**Contact:**
Victims Unit, OFMDFM, Castle Buildings, Stormont
Belfast BT3 3SR
Tel: 028 9052 3445
Fax: 028 9052 8354
Web: www.victimsni.gov.uk
Email: info@victimsni.gov.uk

Victims Unit, NIO, Room 123, Stormont House Annex
Belfast, BT4 3SH
Tel: 028 9052 7902
Web: www.nio.gov.uk
Email: victims.liaison.nio@nics.gov.uk

## Policing in Northern Ireland

Policing and security have been a source of great political and social division in Northern Ireland. With over 3,000 civilians, including hundreds of security force personnel as well as members of government killed throughout the thirty years of the 'Troubles', policing and the role of the Police Service in Northern Ireland remains an emotive issue within all sections of the community. Recent reforms under Patten, the launch of the PSNI and controversial unresolved matters such as alleged security force collusion in paramilitary crimes have continued to maintain the high priority of policing on the general political agenda.

## The Review of Policing in Northern Ireland

The Good Friday Agreement proposed the establishment of an Independent Commission on Policing for Northern Ireland. The Rt Hon Chris Patten was appointed to chair this Commission and it published its plans for the future of policing (known as the 'Patten Report') in September 1999. The process of implementation of the Patten recommendations is already well underway with progress to date including:

- *31 May 2000:* Oversight Commissioner, Tom Constantine appointed to oversee the change process;
- *6 November 2000:* Police (Northern Ireland) Act 2000;
- *1 April 2001:* establishment of police district command units based on council areas;
- *17 August 2001:* revised Implementation Plan published;
- *29 September 2001* – appointment of a new Policing Board (to replace the Police Authority);
- *4 November 2001:* first new recruits enter training;
- *4 November 2001:* Policing Board assumes its powers;
- *4 November 2001:* RUC changes name to Police Service of Northern Ireland (PSNI);
- *14 November 2001:* names of trustees on RUC George Cross Foundation and Northern Ireland Police Fund announced;
- *5 April 2002:* new uniform and emblem comes into service; first recruits under 50:50 graduate; new flag-flying rules introduced;
- *29 April 2002:* intergovernmental agreement signed between the UK and Republic of Ireland on police co-operation;
- *4 March 2003:* public appointments to DPPs;
- *8 April 2003:* Police (Northern Ireland) Act 2003;
- *December 2003:* The new oversight commissioner Al Hutchison succeeds Tom Constantine

## Oversight Commissioner

Tom Constantine was appointed as Oversight Commissioner on 31 May 2000 and was succeeded by Al Hutchinson in December 2003. He is responsible under the 2000 Act for overseeing the implementation of the changes in policing arrangements and structures recommended in the context of the Patten Report. In carrying out the evaluation process, the Oversight Commissioner is supported by a team of experienced policing professionals, including Chief of Staff, Mark Reber.

### Tripartite Policing Responsibilities

Policing in Northern Ireland is governed by the 'tripartite structure' involving the Secretary of State for Northern Ireland, the Policing Board and the Chief Constable. The detailed provisions for this arrangement are set out in the Police (NI) Act 2000, as amended by the Police (Northern Ireland) Act 2003, which implements the Patten recommendations.

## The Role of the Secretary of State

The Secretary of State sets the statutory framework for policing, (which remains a reserved matter) and is empowered to set long term policing objectives. In addition the Secretary of State obtains and provides the annual police grant and approves the appointment of senior police officers. He makes regulations which set out the terms and conditions of service of police officers and may regulate on the emblems and flags of the police service.

He appoints the independent members of the Policing Board as well as the Oversight Commissioner and is involved in the process of appointing the Police Ombudsman. The Secretary of State may issue codes of practice to the Policing Board and a code on the appointment of independent members to District Policing Partnerships (DPPs). He may also issue guidance on the use of public order equipment. He appoints inspectors of constabulary to inspect the police service and has responsibility for issues concerning national security.

## The Chief Constable

The Police Service of Northern Ireland is led by the Chief Constable, currently Hugh Orde, who took up his post on 2 September 2002. The Chief Constable is responsible for the operational direction and control of the police service with managerial responsibility for the police and other staff of the service and the use of resources.

Under the terms of the Police (NI) Act 2000, as amended by the Police (Northern Ireland) Act 2003, the Chief Constable is required to:

- Produce a draft of the policing plan detailing how he will police Northern Ireland in line with priorities set by the Secretary of State and the Policing Board. The Policing Board approves and publishes this plan before the commencement of each financial year;
- District Commanders are required to produce local policing plans, consistent with the annual plan after consultation with the local District Policing Partnership;
- Bring to the attention of all officers the terms of the new declaration (or oath);
- Draft an action plan for increasing the number of women in the Police Service should the Board require;
- Provide guidance to officers on the registration of notifiable memberships (memberships of an organisation which might be regarded as affecting the ability of an officer to discharge his duties effectively and impartially);
- Ensure officers read and understand the code of ethics;
- Report on any matter connected with policing to the Board. The Chief Constable may 'appeal' against such a request to the Secretary of State in specific grounds as set out in the Act;
- Produce and publish an annual report.

www.psni.police.uk
PSNI Headquarters
65 Knock Road
Belfast BT5 6LE
Our Purpose
Making Northern Ireland safer for everyone through professional, progressive policing
Vision
A service everyone can be proud of because it provides policing at its best
Values
Honesty and openness, fairness and courtesy, partnerships, performance and professionalism, respect for the rights of all

## The Police Service of Northern Ireland

PSNI Headquarters
65 Knock Road, Belfast, BT5 6LE
Tel: 028 9065 0222
Web: www.psni.police.uk

The Police Service of Northern Ireland (PSNI) came into being on 4 November 2001. The Service is divided into 2 geographical areas – Urban and Rural Regions. Each region is commanded by an Assistant Chief Constable.

The two regions are made up of 29 smaller District Command Units (DCUs). Twenty-five of these match the boundaries of District Council areas outside Belfast. For administrative and logistical reasons Belfast City Council area has been split into four DCUs – North, South, East and West.

The Urban Region covers 12 District Command Units and the Rural Region covers 17 District Command Units.

The development of DCUs is in line with the RUC's own 'Fundamental Review of Policing' published in 1996 and with one of the central recommendations in the Patten Report that policing should be delivered with and for the community. The new structure devolves decision making about resources, personnel, services and budgets to local District Commanders.

The Police Service is accountable to the Northern Ireland Policing Board, which in addition to independent members drawn from the broader Northern Ireland community, has representatives from almost all the main political parties.

**Aims of the PSNI:**

- To promote safety and reduce disorder;
- To reduce crime and the fear of crime;
- To contribute to delivering justice in a way which secures and maintains public confidence in the rule of law;
- To implement the programme of change.

**Policing Resources**

The Secretary of State has established a grant for policing for the 2004/05 financial year of £705.4 million. Of this some £484 million is required for staff costs.

The Northern Ireland Policing Board has overall financial responsibility for police resources but it delegates the day to day management and control of these (except acquisition of land) to the Chief Constable who is responsible for delivering the policing service.

The following table shows the strength of the police service on 31 August 2003.

**PSNI Personnel by Gender (August 2003)**

| Category | Male | Female | Total |
|---|---|---|---|
| Regulars | 5967 | 1056 | 7023 |
| Reserve (Full Time) | 1565 | 158 | 1723 |
| Reserve (Part Time) | 569 | 323 | 892 |
| Support Staff | 1123 | 2306 | 3429 |
| **Overall total** | **9224** | **3843** | **13067** |

| DPP/DCU Commander | Telephone | Extension |
|---|---|---|
| **Antrim** | | |
| Chief Supt Bill Woodside | 028 9065 0222 | extn 36198 |
| **Ards** | | |
| Temp Supt David Greene | 028 9181 8080 | Ext 40002 |
| **Armagh** | | |
| Supt Bob Moore | 028 3752 3311 | |
| **Ballymena** | | |
| Supt Terence Shevlin | 028 9065 0222 | extn 41000 |
| **Ballymoney** | | |
| Supt P Corrigan | 028 2766 2222 | ext 40950 |
| **Banbridge** | | |
| Supt Mervyn Waddell | 028 4066 2222 | |
| **Belfast** | | |
| **East Belfast** | | |
| Chief Supt Henry Irvine | 028 9065 0222 | |
| **North Belfast** | | |
| Chief Supt Julie Lindsay-White | 028 9065 0222 | extn 30406 |
| **South Belfast** | | |
| Chief Supt Stephen Grange | 028 9065 0222 | |
| **West Belfast** | | |
| Chief Supt Cecil Craig | 028 9065 0222 | extn 26705 |
| **Carrickfergus** | | |
| Temp Supt Bill Robinson | 028 9065 0222 | extn 30630 |
| **Castlereagh** | | |
| Supt Gordon Reid | 028 9065 0222 | extn 21202 |
| **Coleraine** | | |
| Supt Dawson Cotton | 028 7034 4122 | extn 63900 |
| **Cookstown** | | |
| Supt Ivan Johnston | 028 8676 6000 | extn 40400 |
| **Craigavon** | | |
| Acting Chief Supt Henery McMullen | 028 3832 5144 | extn 40304 |
| **Derry (Foyle DCU)** | | |
| Chief Supt Richard Russell | 028 7136 7337 | |
| **Down** | | |
| Chief Supt Robert Robinson | 028 4461 5011 | |
| **Dungannon & South Tyrone** | | |
| Supt Ken Henning | 028 8775 2525 | extn 40512 |
| **Fermanagh** | | |
| Chief Supt Gerry O'Callaghan | 028 6632 2828 | extn 40567 |
| **Larne** | | |
| Supt Tom Haylett | 028 2827 2266 | extn 88053 |
| **Limavady** | | |
| Acting Supt David Hamilton | 028 7776 6797 | |
| **Lisburn** | | |
| Chief Supt Brendan Mcguigan | 028 9266 5212 | extn 36972 |
| **Magherafelt** | | |
| Temp Supt John Lindsay | 028 7963 3701 | extn 40450 |
| **Moyle** | | |
| Chief Insp David Wallace | 028 2076 2312 | extn 40946 |
| **Newry & Mourne** | | |
| Chief Supt Alan Caldwell | 028 3026 5500 | extn 42265 |
| **Newtownabbey** | | |
| Supt Murray Sterritt | 028 9065 0222 | extn 30302 |
| **North Down** | | |
| Supt Graham Shields | 028 9065 0222 | extn 37950 |
| **Omagh** | | |
| Supt Michael Skuce | 028 8225 6177 | extn 40650 |
| **Strabane** | | |
| Supt Clifford Best | 028 7137 9814 | |

## Police Service of Northern Ireland Organisational Chart

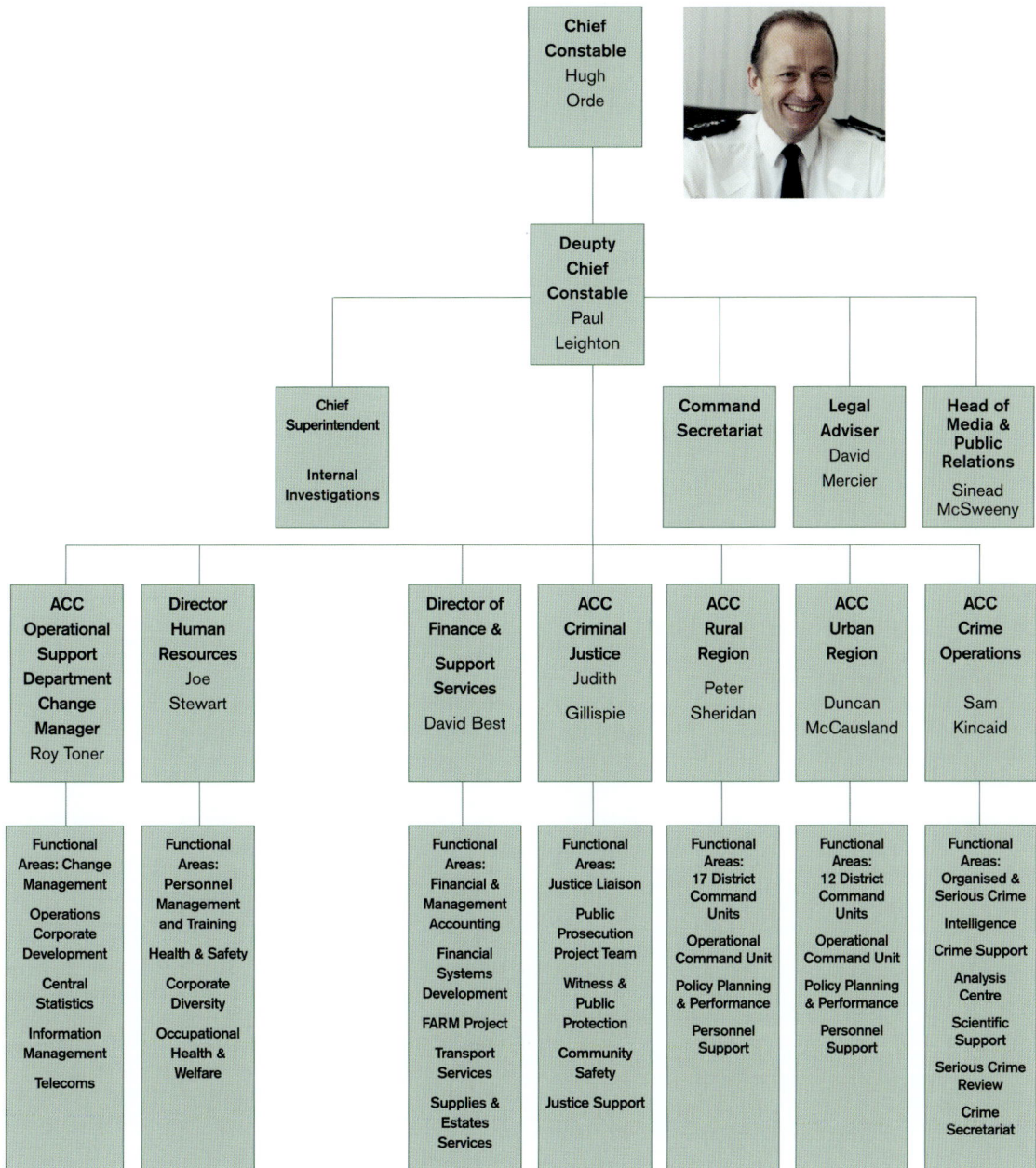

- **Chief Constable** Hugh Orde

- **Deupty Chief Constable** Paul Leighton
  - Chief Superintendent – Internal Investigations
  - **Command Secretariat**
  - **Legal Adviser** David Mercier
  - **Head of Media & Public Relations** Sinead McSweeny
  - **ACC Operational Support Department Change Manager** Roy Toner
    - Functional Areas: Change Management
    - Operations Corporate Development
    - Central Statistics
    - Information Management
    - Telecoms
  - **Director Human Resources** Joe Stewart
    - Functional Areas: Personnel Management and Training
    - Health & Safety
    - Corporate Diversity
    - Occupational Health & Welfare
  - **Director of Finance & Support Services** David Best
    - Functional Areas: Financial & Management Accounting
    - Financial Systems Development
    - FARM Project
    - Transport Services
    - Supplies & Estates Services
  - **ACC Criminal Justice** Judith Gillispie
    - Functional Areas: Justice Liaison
    - Public Prosecution Project Team
    - Witness & Public Protection
    - Community Safety
    - Justice Support
  - **ACC Rural Region** Peter Sheridan
    - Functional Areas: 17 District Command Units
    - Operational Command Unit
    - Policy Planning & Performance
    - Personnel Support
  - **ACC Urban Region** Duncan McCausland
    - Functional Areas: 12 District Command Units
    - Operational Command Unit
    - Policy Planning & Performance
    - Personnel Support
  - **ACC Crime Operations** Sam Kincaid
    - Functional Areas: Organised & Serious Crime
    - Intelligence
    - Crime Support
    - Analysis Centre
    - Scientific Support
    - Serious Crime Review
    - Crime Secretariat

### Organised Crime Task Force

The Organised Crime Task Force (OCTF) was created as part of a multi-agency approach to tackling organised crime. The OCTF aims to tackle, amongst other things: extortion, the drugs trade, the smuggling of fuel, tobacco and alcohol, money laundering, counterfeit goods and armed robbery. The OCTF brings together government, law enforcement and a wide range of other agencies.

### Assets Recovery Agency

The Assets Recovery Agency (ARA) is an independent government department, which became operational in February 2003 with the aim of reducing crime and recovering the assets of crime by criminal confiscation, civil recovery or taxation. The Assets Recovery Agency's Belfast operation is headed by Alan McQuillan who consults with the Secretary of State with regard to the organisation's strategy for Northern Ireland.

### Forensic Science Northern Ireland

151 Belfast Road, Carrickfergus, BT38 8PL
Tel: 028 9036 1888 / Fax: 028 9036 1900
Web: www.fsni.gov.uk Email: forensic.science@fsni.gov.uk
Chief Executive: Brett Hannon

Forensic Science Northern Ireland is an Executive Agency within the Northern Ireland Office. It provides: scientific support for the investigation of crime, court proceedings and investigations

## Northern Ireland Policing Board

Northern Ireland Policing Board
Waterside Tower, 31 Clarendon Road
Clarendon Dock, Belfast, BT1 3BG
Tel: 028 9040 8541 / Fax: 028 9040 8500
Web: www.nipolicingboard.org.uk
Email: information@nipolicingboard.org.uk
Chairman: Professor Desmond Rea
Chief Executive: Trevor Reaney (Pictured)

A key element of the 2000 Act and a central aspect of police reform is the creation of a new Policing Board. It replaced the Police Authority on 4 November 2001 and is made up of 10 democratically elected Assembly members chosen by parties and 9 independents, appointed by the Secretary of State on the basis of their skills and experience.

The Policing Board has responsibility for the accountability of the police and monitoring and evaluating the service provided. The powers of the Board include:

- Ensuring the efficiency & effectiveness of the service;
- Setting objectives and performance targets for the annual Policing Plan published by the Board;
- Monitoring the performance against the plan;
- Monitoring human rights performance of the service;
- Maintaining the knowledge of the Board in relation to patterns of recruitment and assessment of the effectiveness of recruitment procedures;
- Assessing the effectiveness of the new police code of ethics;
- Assessing public satisfaction with police and district policing partnerships;
- Requiring the Chief Constable to report on any matter connected with policing and the option to establish an inquiry;
- Determining the policing budget;
- Appointing senior officers subject to approval of the Secretary of State;
- Making arrangements to secure the economy, efficiency and effectiveness of the Board and police service;
- Production of an annual report.

The Board in fulfilling its function is required to give consideration to the principle that policing should be impartial and to the overall policing plan.

**Members of the Policing Board**

**Chairman: Professor Desmond Rea**

| **Denis Bradley** | **Vice-Chairman** |
|---|---|
| Alex Attwood | SDLP |
| Viscount Brookeborough | UUP |
| Joe Byrne | SDLP |
| Fred Cobain | UUP |
| Brian Dougherty | Non-Party |
| Barry Gilligan | Non-Party |
| William Hay | DUP |
| Tom Kelly | Non-Party |
| Lord Kilclooney | UUP |
| Sam Foster | UUP |
| Pauline McCabe | Non-Party |
| Alan McFarland | UUP |
| Eddie McGrady | SDLP |
| Rosaleen Moore | Non-Party |
| Ian Paisley (Junior) | DUP |
| Suneil Sharma | Non-Party |
| Sammy Wilson | DUP |

Following the Secretary of State's decision to suspend devolved government the work of the Board continued without interruption. District Policing Partnerships have now been established in all Local Government Districts. For the most part the DPPs have gone about their public business with very little rancour or controversy. There have however been a few instances of intimidation of DPP members at local level.

**Devolution of Policing**

Once the devolved institutions are working effectively, the Westminster government intends to devolve responsibility for policing and justice functions, as set out in the Belfast Agreement. Before it can do this, it needs to take some major steps to implement the Criminal Justice Review and to make some more progress on detailed implementation of the Patten Report. A final decision to devolve these functions will only be taken in the context of security political progess and other relevant considerations.

## Police Ombudsman For Northern Ireland

New Cathedral Buildings, St Anne's Square
11 Church Street, Belfast, BT1 1PG
Tel: 028 9082 8600 / 0845 601 2931
Fax: 028 9082 8659
Email: info@policeombudsman.org
Web: www.policeombudsman.org
Police Ombudsman: Mrs Nuala O'Loan (pictured)
Chief Executive: Mr Sam Pollock
Executive Director: Mr David Wood

The Office of the Police Ombudsman for Northern Ireland is an independent system for dealing with complaints against police officers in Northern Ireland. The system is independent of the police. All complaints against the police in Northern Ireland, including the Harbour, Airport and Ministry of Defence police, are dealt with by the Police Ombudsman's Office. The process is free and members of the public do not need to make an appointment. The Police Ombudsman's role is to:

- Receive complaints about how police officers do their jobs. Such complaints may involve allegations that a police officer may have been involved in criminal behaviour or has broken their Code of Ethics.
- Deal with complaints. This may involve seeking to resolve appropriate complaints informally while investigating more serious allegations.
- Decide the outcome of complaints. On the completion of an investigation the Police Ombudsman may send a file to the DPP and/or recommend that an officer be subject to disciplinary proceedings.
- Monitor trends in complaints against the police.
- Make recommendations for improvements in police policy and practice

The primary role of the Police Ombudsman's Office is to deal with complaints from members of the public about the conduct of police officers in Northern Ireland. Normally the incident complained about must have happened within the previous 12 months. However we can investigate complaints about things that happened more than a year before they are reported to us. These will be cases where:

- There was no previous investigation and the Police Ombudsman considers that your complaint is grave or exceptional or
- There was a previous investigation but there is now new evidence, and the Ombudsman believes the complaint is grave or exceptional.

The Office can investigate matters if asked to by the PSNI Chief Constable, the Policing Board or the Secretary of State for Northern Ireland. The Police Ombudsman may also investigate a matter, even if she has not received a complaint about it, if she believes it in the public interest to do so. The Office has a budget of £7 million and has 128 staff.

# Northern Ireland's Government Departments

## Introduction

Although Northern Ireland had its own devolved government from the foundation of the state in 1920 until 1972, for most of the last 30 years the province has been governed directly from Westminster. Following the signing of the Belfast Agreement in 1998, power was devolved to the new Assembly in December 1999. Northern Ireland was governed by a power sharing Executive and eleven new government departments.

Up until the suspension of the first Assembly in October 2002, local politicians headed the ten government departments (as listed below). An eleventh, joint department, the Office of the First Minister and Deputy First Minister was established to oversee the work of the other departments and, before suspension, was headed by First Minister David Trimble and Deputy First Minister Mark Durkan.

The eleven government departments during the Assembly were as follows:

Office of the First Minister and Deputy First Minister
Department of Agriculture and Rural Development
Department of Culture, Arts and Leisure
Department of Education
Department for Employment and Learning
Department of Enterprise, Trade and Investment
Department of the Environment
Department of Finance and Personnel
Department of Health, Social Services and Public Safety
Department for Regional Development
Department for Social Development

Following the suspension of the Northern Ireland Assembly ministers from Westminster, who operate under the Northern Ireland Office, replaced local ministers representing the eleven departments on the Northern Ireland Executive.

**Northern Ireland Office Team**

| | |
|---|---|
| Secretary of State | Paul Murphy MP |
| Minister of State | John Spellar MP |
| Parliamentary Under Secretary | Ian Pearson MP |
| Parliamentary Under Secretary | Angela Smith MP |
| Parliamentary Under Secretary | Barry Gardiner MP |

**Secretary of State Paul Murphy**
Following the introduction of direct rule, the ministerial portfolios were allocated as follows:

Four ministers support the Northern Ireland Office headed by the Secretary of State Paul Murphy and together they are responsible for the governance of Northern Ireland and the management of the ten departments whilst direct rule is in place.

**Minister of State John Spellar MP** has responsibility for political development, criminal justice, human rights and equality. He is also Minister at the Department for Social Development and the Department for Regional Development, as well as part of OFMDFM.

**Parliamentary Under Secretary of State Ian Pearson MP** has responsibility for security and policing, prisons, the Assets Recovery Agency and Organised Task Force and Europe (European Preparations Committee). He is also Minister at the Department of Finance and Personnel, the Department of Agriculture and Rural Development and has responsibility for part of OFMDFM.

**Parliamentary Under Secretary of State Angela Smith MP** has responsibility for victims and reconciliation as well as the Department of the Environment, Department of Health, Social Services and Public Safety and the Department of Culture, Arts and Leisure.

**Parliamentary Under Secretary of State Barry Gardiner MP** has responsibility for the Department of Enterprise, Trade and Investment, the Department for Employment and Learning and the Department of Education.

Details of the Northern Ireland government departments and their senior personnel are set out as follows.

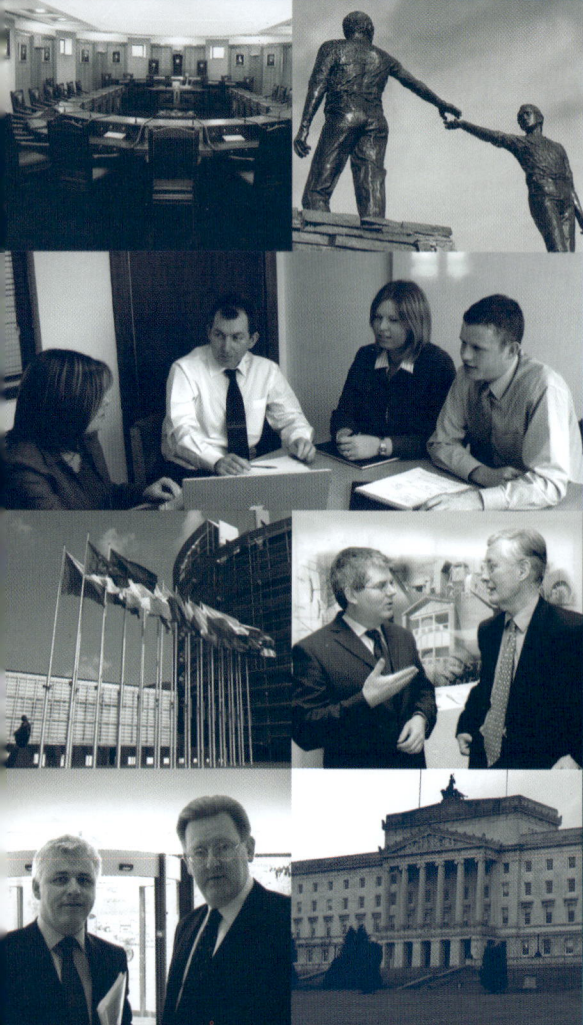

## Office of the First Minister and Deputy First Minister (OFMDFM)

Castle Buildings
Stormont, Belfast, BT4 3SR
Tel: 028 9052 8400
Fax: 028 9052 2933
Web: www.ofmdfmni.gov.uk

**Head of the Civil Service:**
Nigel Hamilton
Tel: 9037 8133

**Private Office:**
Private Secretary: Debbie Sweeney
Tel: 028 9037 8132

The Office of the First Minister and Deputy First Minister was established as a department on 1 December 1999 following the devolution of power to Northern Ireland.

The work of the department revolves around three interrelated roles:

- To support the work of the Executive (during devolution);
- To undertake a wide range of departmental functions allocated to the First Minister and Deputy First Minister;
- To provide a service to other government departments.

**Functions**

- Brussels Office;
- Central Emergency Planning Unit;
- Children and Young Peoples Unit;
- Civic Forum Secretariat;
- Community Relations Unit;
- Economic Policy Unit;
- Equality Unit;
- Executive Information Service;
- Executive Secretariat;
- Honours;
- Human Rights;
- Machinery of Government;
- North/South Ministerial Council;
- Northern Ireland Bureau in Washington;
- Northern Ireland eGovernment Unit;
- Public Appointments;
- Public Service Reform Unit;
- Review of Public Administration;
- Secretariat for Commissioner for Public Appointments;
- Victims Unit.

### Legal Services Directorate

Director: Denis McCartney
Tel: 028 9037 8125
Fax: 028 9037 8037
Email: irena.elliott@ofmdfmni.gov.uk
Contact: Caroline Webb
Tel: 028 9037 8126
Fax: 028 9037 8037
Email: caroline.webb@ofmdfmni.gov.uk

### Executive Information Service

Director: Stephen Grimason
Tel: 028 9037 8101
Fax: 028 9037 8013
Email: stephen.grimason@ofmdfmni.gov.uk
Deputy Director: Colm Shannon
Tel: 028 9037 8103
Fax: 028 9037 8013
Email: colm.shannon@ofmdfmni.gov.uk

The Executive Information Service (EIS), provides the full range of news and public relations services to ministers and their departments. It seeks to present policy and activity of the Northern Ireland Administration. The central unit of EIS is based in Castle Buildings with staff out posted to provide an information service in each department.

**Public Relations Unit**
Contact: Lorna Armstrong
Tel: 028 9037 8018
Fax: 028 9037 8112
Email: lorna.armstrong@ofmdfmni.gov.uk

**Press Office**
Contact: Don McAleer
Tel: 028 9037 8105
Fax: 028 9037 8016
Email: don.mcaleer@ofmdfmni.gov.uk

Contact: Paul Pringle
Tel: 028 9037 8106
Fax: 028 9037 8016
Email: paul.pringle@ofmdfmni.gov.uk

**Co-ordination and Planning**
The Co-ordination and Planning unit co-operates with departments to provide a mechanism to maximise the impact of announcements and reduce the possibility of clashes of events.

Contact: Don McAleer
Tel: 028 9037 8105
Fax: 028 9037 8016
Email: don.mcaleer@ofmdfmni.gov.uk

Press officers assigned to other Ministers can be contacted at Department headquarters as follows:

**Department of Agriculture and Rural Development**
Contact: Bernie McCusker
Tel: 028 9052 4619
Fax: 028 9052 5003
Email:
bernadette.mccusker@dardni.gov.uk

**Department of Culture, Arts and Leisure**
Contact: Jill Heron
Tel: 028 9025 8900
Fax: 028 9025 8906
Email: jill.heron@dcalni.gov.uk

**Department of Education**
Contact: Jill Garrett
Tel: 028 9127 9356
Fax: 028 9127 9271
Email: jill.garrett@deni.gov.uk

**Department of Enterprise, Trade and Investment**
Contact: Anne Martin
Tel: 028 9052 9353
Fax: 028 9052 9546
Email: anne.martin@detini.gov.uk

**Department of the Environment**
Contact: Brian Kirk
Tel: 028 9054 0013
Fax: 028 9054 1129
Email: brian.kirk@doeni.gov.uk

**Department of Finance and Personnel**
Contact: Colin Ross
Tel: 028 9052 7375
Fax: 028 9052 7149
Email: colin.ross@dfpni.gov.uk

**Department of Health, Social Services and Public Safety**
Contact: Philip Maguire
Tel: 028 9052 0636
Fax: 028 9052 0572
Email: philip.maguire@dhsspsni.gov.uk

**Department for Employment and Learning**
Contact: Gwyn Treharne
Tel: 028 9025 7790
Fax: 028 9025 7795
Email: gwyn.treharne@dhfeteni.gov.uk

**Department for Regional Development**
Contact: Paddy Cullen
Tel: 028 9054 0817
Fax: 028 9054 0029
Email: paddy.cullen@drdni.gov.uk

## OFMDFM Organisation Chart

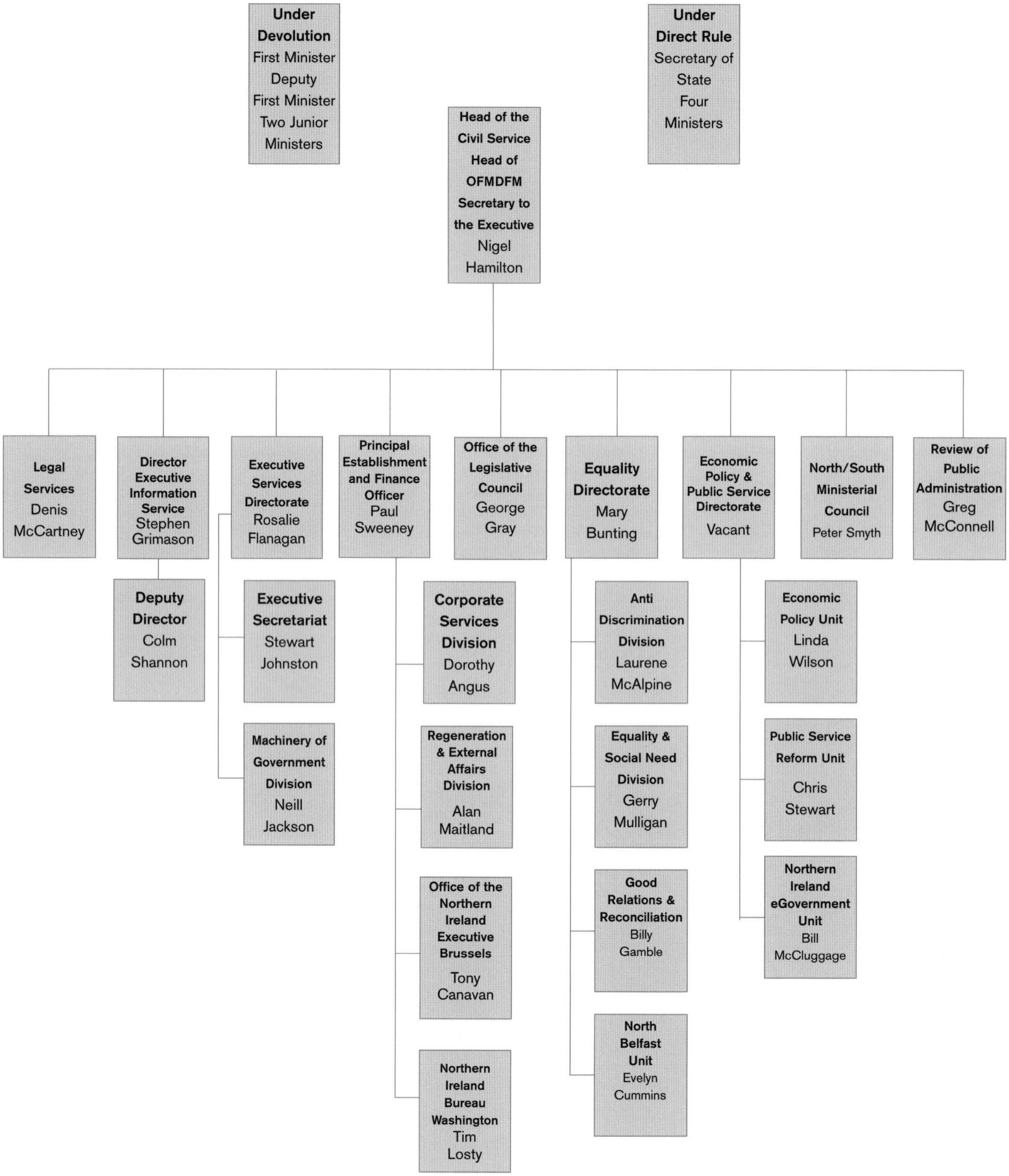
Under Devolution
First Minister
Deputy First Minister
Two Junior Ministers
Under Direct Rule
Secretary of State
Four Ministers
Head of the Civil Service
Head of OFMDFM
Secretary to the Executive
Nigel Hamilton
Legal Services
Denis McCartney
Director Executive Information Service
Stephen Grimason
Deputy Director
Colm Shannon
Executive Services Directorate
Rosalie Flanagan
Executive Secretariat
Stewart Johnston
Machinery of Government Division
Neill Jackson
Principal Establishment and Finance Officer
Paul Sweeney
Corporate Services Division
Dorothy Angus
Regeneration & External Affairs Division
Alan Maitland
Office of the Northern Ireland Executive Brussels
Tony Canavan
Northern Ireland Bureau Washington
Tim Losty
Office of the Legislative Council
George Gray
Equality Directorate
Mary Bunting
Anti Discrimination Division
Laurene McAlpine
Equality & Social Need Division
Gerry Mulligan
Good Relations & Reconciliation
Billy Gamble
North Belfast Unit
Evelyn Cummins
Economic Policy & Public Service Directorate
Vacant
Economic Policy Unit
Linda Wilson
Public Service Reform Unit
Chris Stewart
Northern Ireland eGovernment Unit
Bill McCluggage
North/South Ministerial Council
Peter Smyth
Review of Public Administration
Greg McConnell

**Department for Social Development**
Contact: Jim Hamilton
Tel: 028 9056 9211
Fax: 028 9056 9269
Email: jim.hamilton@dsdni.gov.uk

## Executive Services Directorate

Director: Rosalie Flanagan
Tel: 028 9037 8123
Fax: 028 9037 8035
Email: rosalie.flanagan@ofmdfmni.gov.uk

## Executive Secretariat (including North/South Ministerial Council, British Irish Council)

Head of Division: Stewart Johnston
Tel: 028 9037 8149
Fax: 028 9037 8035
Email: stewart.johnston@ofmdfmni.gov.uk

Contact: Tom Watson
Tel: 028 9052 3173
Fax: 028 9052 8697
Email: tom.watson@ofmdfmni.gov.uk

**NSMC, BIC and Civic Forum Liaison**
Contact: Gail McKibbin
Tel: 028 9052 3191
Fax: 028 9052 8697
Email: gail.mckibbin@ofmdfmni.gov.uk

## Machinery of Government Division

Head of Division: Neill Jackson
Tel: 028 9052 2619
Fax: 028 9076 5720
Email: neill.jackson@ofmdfmni.gov.uk

Machinery of Government Division performs an internal support and advisory function within the Northern Ireland administration. It operates at the interface of OFMDFM and other government departments and the Northern Ireland Assembly, co-ordinating and monitoring of information and providing guidance on a range of issues.

**Machinery of Government**
Contact: Dr Deirdre Griffith
Tel: 028 9076 5701
Fax: 028 9076 5720
Email: deirdre.griffith@ofmdfmni.gov.uk

**Assembly Section**
Contact: Alan Rogers
Tel: 028 9076 5702
Fax: 028 9076 5720
Email: alan.rogers@ofmdfmni.gov.uk

**Legislation Progress Unit**
Contact: Jim Hamilton
Tel: 028 9052 2440
Fax: 028 9052 2928
Email: jim.hamilton@ofmdfmni.gov.uk

## The North/South Ministerial Council Joint Secretariat

Joint Secretary: North: Dr Peter Smyth
Tel: 028 3751 5002
Fax: 028 3751 5032
Email: peter.smyth@ofmdfmni.gov.uk

Contact: Pat Donaghy
Tel: 028 3751 5008
Fax: 028 3751 1874
Email: pat.donaghy@ofmdfmni.gov.uk

Contact: Grainne Killen
Tel: 028 3751 5042
Fax: 028 3751 1874
Email: grainne.killen@ofmdfmni.gov.uk

North/South Ministerial Council
Joint Secretariat
39 Abbey Street, Armagh, BT61 7EB

## Equality Directorate

Director: Mary Bunting
Tel: 028 9052 2857
Fax: 028 9052 0761
Email: mary.bunting@ofmdfmni.gov.uk

## Anti-Discrimination Division

Head of Division: Laurene McAlpine
Tel: 028 9052 3156
Fax: 028 9052 8300
Email: laurene.mcalpine@ofmdfmni.gov.uk

**Single Equality Bill**
Contact: Ivan Millen
Tel: 028 9052 3365
Fax: 028 9052 3272
Email: ivan.millen@ofmdfmni.gov.uk

**Race, Fair Employment and Treatment and Disability Discrimination Legislation**
Contact: Ken Walker
Tel: 028 9052 3158
Fax: 028 9052 3272
Email: ken.walker@ofmdfmni.gov.uk

**Disability Bill**
Contact: Beverley Cowan
Tel: 028 9052 3124
Fax: 028 9052 3272
Email: beverley.cowan@ofmdfmni.gov.uk

**Sex, Age and Sexual Orientation Discrimination and Equal Pay**
Director: Drew Haire
Tel: 028 9052 0088
Fax: 028 9052 3272
Email: drew.haire@ofmdfmni.gov.uk

**Oversight of Equality Commission**
Director: Drew Haire
Tel: 028 9052 0088
Fax: 028 9052 3272
Email: drew.haire@ofmdfmni.gov.uk

## Equality and Social Need Division

Head of Division: Gerry Mulligan
Tel: 028 9052 3148
Fax: 028 9052 8300
Email: gerry.mulligan@ofmdfmni.gov.uk

**Anti-Poverty Unit**
Contact: Pauline Millar
Tel: 028 9052 2048
Fax: 028 9052 3323
Email: pauline.millar@ofmdfmni.gov.uk

**Statutory Duty and Human Rights Unit**
Contact: Claire Archbold
Tel: 028 9052 3140
Fax: 028 9052 3272
Email: claire.archbold@ofmdfmni.gov.uk

**Equality Unit**
Contact: Hilary Harbinson
Tel: 028 9052 8194
Fax: 028 9052 3323
Email: hilary.harbinson@ofmdfmni.gov.uk

**Research Branch**
Contact: Dr Stephen Donnelly
Tel: 028 9052 8273
Fax: 028 9052 8273
Email: stephen.donnelly@ofmdfmni.gov.uk

## Good Relations and Reconciliation Division

Head of Division: Billy Gamble
Tel: 028 9052 8351
Fax: 028 9052 8474
Email: billy.gamble@ofmdfmni.gov.uk

**Community Relations Unit**
Contact: Denis Ritchie
Tel: 028 9052 3460
Fax: 028 9052 8426
Email: denis.ritchie@ofmdfmni.gov.uk

**Race Equality Unit**
Contact: Ken Fraser
Tel: 028 9052 2615
Fax: 028 9052 8354
Email: ken.fraser@ofmdfmni.gov.uk

**Victims Unit**
Contact: John Clarke
Tel: 028 9052 3167
Fax: 028 9052 8354
Email: johnv.clarke@ofmdfmni.gov.uk

**Children and Young People's Unit**
Contact: Vacant
Tel: 028 9052 3118
Fax: 028 9052 8426

## North Belfast Community Action Unit

Head of Unit: Evelyn Cummins
Tel: 028 9072 6014
Fax: 028 9072 6102
Email: evelyn.cummins@ofmdfmni.gov.uk

The North Belfast Community Action Unit is part of OFMDFM but also reports to the Department for Social Development. The Unit is guided by a steering group of officials from both these departments and has responsibility for developing a long term strategic action plan; encouraging partnerships; building community capacity; and addressing interface issues in North Belfast. The Unit is also responsible for the development and regeneration of the Crumlin Road Gaol.

**Principal Establishment and Finance Officer**
Contact: Paul Sweeney
Tel: 028 9052 8615
Fax: 028 9052 2262
Email: paul.sweeney@ofmdfmni.gov.uk

## Corporate Services Division

Head of Division: Dorothy Angus
Tel: 028 9052 8153
Fax: 028 9052 0748
Email: dorothy.angus@ofmdfmni.gov.uk

**Finance**
Contact: Aubrey Playfair
Tel: 028 9052 3440
Fax: 028 9052 8135
Email: aubrey.playfair@ofmdfmni.gov.uk

**Personnel and Office Services**
Contact: Liz Elliott
Tel: 028 9052 2119
Fax: 028 9052 2339
Email: liz.elliott@ofmdfmni.gov.uk

**Information Technology**
Contact: Robert Fee
Tel: 028 9052 2670
Fax: 028 9052 3452
Email: robert.fee@ofmdfmni.gov.uk

**Knowledge Network Team**
Contact: Robert Fee
Tel: 028 9052 2670
Fax: 028 9052 3452
Email: robert.fee@ofmdfmni.gov.uk

**Central Management Branch**
Contact: Geoffrey Simpson
Tel: 028 9052 3245
Fax: 028 9052 2933
Email: geoffrey.simpson@ofmdfmni.gov.uk

**Central Appointments Unit (CAU)**
Contact: Geoffrey Simpson
Tel: 028 9052 3245
Fax: 028 9052 8125
Email:geoffrey.simpson@ofmdfmni.gov.uk

**Honours**
Contact: Gary Smyth
Tel: 028 9052 8162
Fax: 028 9052 8200
Email: gary.smyth@ofmdfmni.gov.uk

**Central Emergency Planning Unit (CEPU)**
Contact: John Hinds
Tel: 028 9052 8860
Fax: 028 9052 8875
Email: john.hinds@ofmdfmni.gov.uk

## Regeneration and External Affairs Division

Head of Division: Alan Maitland
Tel: 028 9052 8389
Fax: 028 9052 2262
Email: alan.maitland@ofmdfmni.gov.uk

This Division comprises the European Policy and Co-ordination Unit and Reform Initiatives Sites Team.

**European Policy & Co-ordination Unit European Policy Issues**
Contact: Alison Coey
Tel: 028 9052 3105
Fax: 028 9052 2552
Email: alison.coey@ofmdfmni.gov.uk

**Measure 4.1 and Interface with NI EU Interests**
Contact: Paul Geddis
Tel: 028 9052 8445
Fax: 028 9052 2552
Email: paul.geddis@ofmdfmni.gov.uk

**Reinvestment and Reform Initiative**
Contact: Alan Maitland
Tel: 028 9052 8389
Fax: 028 9052 2552
Email: alan.maitland@ofmdfmni.gov.uk

## Economic Policy Unit and Public Service Directorate

Director: Vacant
Tel: 028 9052 8505
Fax: 028 9052 2262

**Economic Policy Unit**
Head of Division: Linda Wilson
Tel: 028 9052 3198
Fax: 028 9052 2262
Email: linda.wilson@ofmdfmni.gov.uk

**Economic Policy and Effectiveness**
Contact: Bobby Clulow
Tel: 028 9052 8472
Fax: 028 9052 2552
Email: robert.clulow@ofmdfmni.gov.uk

**Programme for Government and Financial Resources Programme for Government and PSAs**
Contact: Robbie Saulters
Tel: 028 9052 2516
Fax: 028 9052 2552
Email: robbie.saulters@ofmdfmni.gov.uk

**Finance Issues**
Contact: John McKenna
Tel: 028 9052 2742
Fax: 028 9052 2552
Email: john.mckenna@ofmdfmni.gov.uk

**Public Private Investment Unit**
Contact: James McAleer
Tel: 028 9052 2752
Fax: 028 9052 2552
Email: james.mcaleer@ofmdfmni.gov.uk

**Policy Innovation Unit**
Contact: Tom Reid
Tel: 028 9052 8439
Fax: 028 9252 2552
Email: tom.reid@ofmdfmni.gov.uk

## Public Service Reform Unit

Head of Division: Chris Stewart
Tel: 028 9076 5308
Fax: 028 9052 4916
Email: chris.stewart@ofmdfmni.gov.uk

**Public Service Delivery Improvement Team**
Contact: Gerry O'Neill
Tel: 028 9076 5520
Fax: 028 9076 5834
Email: gerry.oneill@ofmdfmni.gov.uk

**Investors in People (IIP) Standard/Chartermark/EDRM**
Contact: Gerry O'Neill
Tel: 028 9076 5820
Fax: 028 9076 5834
Email: gerry.oneill@ofmdfmni.gov.uk

**Reform Strategy Team**
Contact: Geoff Beattie
Tel: 028 9076 5824
Fax: 028 9076 5834
Email: geoff.beattie@ofmdfmni.gov.uk

**Central Freedom of Information Team**
Contact: David Lammey
Tel: 028 9076 5523
Fax: 028 9076 5834
Email: david.lammey@ofmdfmni.gov.uk

**Electronic Document Record Management Systems**
Contact: Mike Beare
Tel: 028 9076 5829
Fax: 028 9076 5834
Email: mike.beare@ofmdfmni.gov.uk

## Northern Ireland eGovernment Unit

Head of Division: Bill McCluggage
Tel: 028 9052 4700
Fax: 028 9052 4916
Email: bill.mccluggage@ofmdfmni.gov.uk

**eGovernment Strategy and Policy**
Contact: Ray Wright
Tel: 028 9052 4368
Fax: 028 9052 4916
Email: ray.wright@ofmdfmni.gov.uk

**eGovernment Technology Standards and Architecture**
Contact: John McKernan
Tel: 028 9052 4359
Fax: 028 9052 4916
Email: john.mckernan@ofmdfmni.gov.uk

**Citizen Facing Solutions, eDelivery Team and Digital Inclusion**
Contact: John Price
Tel: 028 9052 4980
Fax: 028 9052 4916
Email: john.price@ofmdfmni.gov.uk

## Office of the Northern Ireland Executive Brussels

Head of Division: Tony Canavan
Tel: 00 322 290 1335
Fax: 00 322 290 1332
Email: tony.canavan@ofmdfmni.gov.uk

Deputy Director: William Dukelow
Tel: 00 322 290 1334
Fax: 00 322 290 1332
Email: william.dukelow@ofmdfmni.gov.uk

Agriculture Policy Advisor: Eileen Kelly
Tel: 00 322 290 1342
Fax: 00 322 290 1332
Email: eileen.kelly@ofmdfmni.gov.uk

## Northern Ireland Bureau Washington

Contact: Tim Losty, Director/Counsellor
Tel: 001 202 367 0461
Fax: 001 202 367 0468
Email: tlosty@nibureau.com

Deputy Director/First Secretary:
Michael Gould
Tel: 001 202 367 0462
Fax: 001 202 367 0468
Email: mgould@nibureau.com
Web: www.nibureau.com

**Review of Public Administration**
Chief Operating Officer: Greg McConnell
Tel: 028 9027 7688
Fax: 028 9027 7610
Email: greg.mcconnell@rpani.gov.uk

Deputy Chief Operating Officer:
David Finegan Tel: 028 9027 7687
Email: david.finegan@rpani.go.uk

**Project Officers**
Joan Cassells Tel: 028 9027 7601
Email: joan.cassells@rpani.gov.uk

Debbie Donnelly: Tel: 028 9027 7602
Email: debbie.donnelly@rpani.gov.uk

## Office of the Legislative Counsel

Head of Directorate: George Gray
Tel: 028 9052 1307
Fax: 028 9052 1306
Email: george.gray@ofmdfmni.gov.uk

## Agencies, Non Departmental Public Bodies and other organisations within OFMDFM

**Advisory Council on Infrastructure Investment**
E5.20 Castle Buildings, Stormont Estate
Upper Newtownards Road
Belfast, BT4 3SR
Tel: 028 9052 2428
Fax: 028 9052 2552
Email: kathryn.menary@ofmdfmni.gov.uk
Chiar: John Keanie MBA

**Community Relations Council**
6 Murray Street, Belfast, BT1 6DN
Tel: 028 9022 7500
Fax: 028 9022 7551
Chief Executive: Dr Duncan Morrow

**Economic Research Institute of Northern Ireland**
Pearl Assurance House
1-3 Donegall Square East
Belfast, BT1 5HB
Tel: 028 9023 2125
Fax: 028 9033 1250
Web: www.niec.org.uk
Director: Victor Hewitt

**Equality Commission for Northern Ireland**
Equality House, 7-9 Shaftesbury Square
Belfast, BT2 7DP
Tel: 028 9050 0600
Fax: 028 9033 1544
Web: www.equalityni.org
Email: information@equalityni.org
Chief Executive: Evelyn Collins
Chief Commissioner: Dame Joan Harbison

**Office of the Commissioner for Public Appointments (Northern Ireland)**
A5.34, Castle Buildings
Stormont Estate, Upper Newtownards Road, Belfast, BT4 3SR
Tel: 028 9052 8187
Fax: 028 9052 8237
Web: www.ocpani.gov.uk
Commissioner: Dame Rennie Fritchie

**Planning Appeals Commission**
Park House, 87-91 Great Victoria Street
Belfast, BT2 7AG
Tel: 028 9024 4710
Fax: 028 9031 2536
Web: www.pacni.gov.uk
Email: info@pacni.gov.uk
Chief Commissioner: John Warke

**Strategic Investment Board**
Level 5, Block A
Castle Buildings, Stormont Estate
Upper Newtownards Road
Belfast, BT4 3SR
Tel: 028 9052 8666
Fax: 028 9052 2432
Web: www.sibni.org
Email: contact.sib@sibni.org
Chief Executive: David Gavaghan

**Water Appeals Commission**
Park House, 87-91 Great Victoria Street
Belfast, BT2 7AG
Tel: 028 9024 4710
Fax: 028 9031 2536
Web: www.pacni.gov.uk
Email: info@pacni.gov.uk

## Department of Agriculture and Rural Development

Dundonald House
Upper Newtownards Road
Belfast, BT4 3SB
Tel: 028 9052 4999
Fax: 028 9052 5003
Web: www.dardni.gov.uk

**Direct Rule Minister:** Ian Pearson

**Permanent Secretary:** Pat Toal
Tel: 028 90 52 4608
Fax: 028 90 52 4813
Email: Pat.Toal@dardni.gov.uk

**Press Office**
Principal Information Officer:
Bernie McCusker
Tel: 028 90 52 4619
Fax: 028 90 52 5003
Email: Bernie.McCusker@dardni.gov.uk

The Department of Agriculture and Rural Development (DARD) aims to promote sustainable economic growth and the development of the countryside in Northern Ireland. The department assists the competitive development of the agri-food, fishing and forestry sectors of the Northern Ireland economy having regard for the need of the consumers, the welfare of animals and the conservation and enhancement of the environment.

DARD has responsibility for food, farming and environmental policy, as well as development of the agricultural, forestry and fishing industries in Northern Ireland. It provides a business development service for farmers, and a veterinary service with administration of animal health and welfare. It is responsible to the Department of the Environment, Food and Rural Affairs (Defra) in Great Britain, for the administration in Northern Ireland of schemes affecting the whole of the United Kingdom. The department also oversees the application of European Union agricultural policy to Northern Ireland.

### Central Policy Group

Deputy Secretary: Tony McCusker
Tel: 028 9052 4628
Fax: 028 9052 4077
Email: Tony.McCusker@dardni.gov.uk

### Animal Health and Welfare Policy Division

Director: Liam McKibben
Tel: 028 9052 4193
Fax: 028 9052 4077
Email: Liam.McKibben@dardni.gov.uk

**Animal Welfare & Trade Branch**
Contact: Colette Connor
Tel: 028 9052 4290
Fax: 028 9052 5281
Email: Colette.Connor@dardni.gov.uk

**Animal Disease Control Branch**
Contact: Colette McMaster
Tel: 028 9052 4660
Fax: 028 9052 4982
Email: Colette.McMaster@dardni.gov.uk

**TSE Branch**
Contact: Kate Davey
Tel: 028 90 52 4408
Fax: 028 9052 4982
Email: Kate.Davey@dardni.gov.uk

### Farm, Food and Environmental Policy Division

Director: David Small
Tel: 028 9052 4479
Fax: 028 9052 4077
Email: David.Small@dardni.gov.uk

**Environmental Policy Branch:**
Contact: Ian McKee
Tel: 028 9052 4773
Fax: 028 9052 4059
Email: Ian.McKee@dardni.gov.uk

**Food Policy Branch:**
Contact: Peter Scott
Tel: 028 9052 4496
Fax 028 9052 4574
Email: Peter.Scott@dardni.gov.uk

**Farm Policy Branch:**
Contact: Joe Cassells
Tel: 028 9052 4493
Fax: 028 9052 4266
Email: Joe.Cassells@dardni.gov.uk

### Policy and Economics Division

Director: Tom Stainer
Tel: 028 9052 4655
Fax: 028 9052 4804
Email: Tom.Stainer@dardni.gov.uk

**Economics and Statistics Unit**
Contact: Stanley McBurney
Tel: 028 9052 4300
Fax: 028 9052 4676
Email: Stanley.McBurney@dardni.gov.uk

**Co-ordination & Central Support Branch**
Contact: Damien Kerr
Tel: 028 9052 4192
Fax: 028 9052 4676
Email: Damien.Kerr@dardni.gov.uk

**Research & Education Policy Branch**
Contact: Elaine McCrory
Tel: 028 9052 4372
Fax 028 9052 4676
Email: Elaine.McCrory@dardni.gov.uk

**Policy Development Branch:** Vacant

**Agricultural Economy Branch**
Contact: Dr Seamus McErlean
Tel: 028 9052 4675
Fax: 028 9052 4676
Email: Seamus.McErlean@dardni.gov.uk

**Farm Accounts Branch**
Contact: Andrew Crawford
Tel: 028 9052 4682
Fax: 028 9052 4676
Email: Andrew.Crawford@dardni.gov.uk

**Farm Census Branch**
Contact: Dr Paul Caskie
Tel: 028 9052 4427
Fax: 028 9052 4676
Email: Paul.Caskie@dardni.gov.uk

**CAP Reform Branch**
Contact: Norman Fulton
Tel: 028 9052 4419
Fax: 028 9052 4676
Email: Norman.Fulton@dardni.gov.uk

### Fisheries Division

Director: Noel Cornick
Tel: 028 9052 4387
Fax: 028 9052 4804
Email: Noel.Cornick@dardni.gov.uk

**Aquaculture and Fish Health Branch:**
Contact: Anne Dorbie
Tel: 028 9052 2648
Fax: 028 9052 3121
Email: Anne.Dorbie@dardni.gov.uk

**Sea Fisheries Policy and Grants Branch:**
Contact: Eileen Sung
Tel: 028 9052 2385
Fax: 028 9052 3121
Email: Eileen.Sung@dardni.gov.uk

**Fisheries Inspectorate Branch**
Contact: Mark McCaughan
Tel: 028 9052 2217
Fax: 028 9052 3121
Email: Mark.McCaughan@dardni.gov.uk

## Department of Agriculture and Rural Development Organisation Chart

**Minister**
Ian Pearson

**Permanent Secretary**
Pat Toal

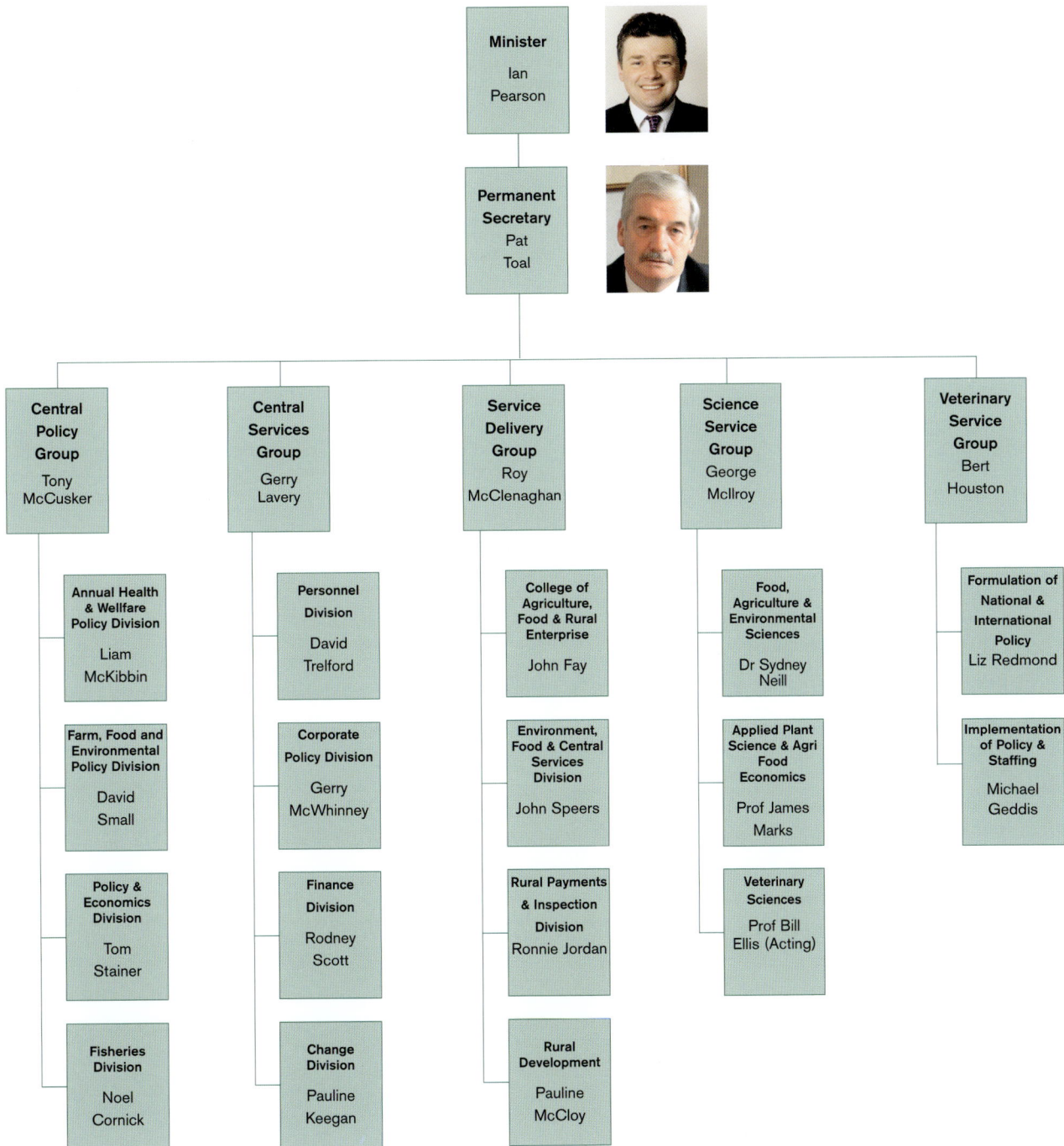

- **Central Policy Group** – Tony McCusker
  - Annual Health & Wellfare Policy Division – Liam McKibbin
  - Farm, Food and Environmental Policy Division – David Small
  - Policy & Economics Division – Tom Stainer
  - Fisheries Division – Noel Cornick
- **Central Services Group** – Gerry Lavery
  - Personnel Division – David Trelford
  - Corporate Policy Division – Gerry McWhinney
  - Finance Division – Rodney Scott
  - Change Division – Pauline Keegan
- **Service Delivery Group** – Roy McClenaghan
  - College of Agriculture, Food & Rural Enterprise – John Fay
  - Environment, Food & Central Services Division – John Speers
  - Rural Payments & Inspection Division – Ronnie Jordan
  - Rural Development – Pauline McCloy
- **Science Service Group** – George McIlroy
  - Food, Agriculture & Environmental Sciences – Dr Sydney Neill
  - Applied Plant Science & Agri Food Economics – Prof James Marks
  - Veterinary Sciences – Prof Bill Ellis (Acting)
- **Veterinary Service Group** – Bert Houston
  - Formulation of National & International Policy – Liz Redmond
  - Implementation of Policy & Staffing – Michael Geddis

## Central Services Group
Deputy Secretary: Gerry Lavery
Tel: 028 9052 4638
Fax: 028 9052 4813
Email: Gerry.Lavery@dardni.gov.uk

## Personnel Division
Assistant Secretary: David Trelford
Tel: 028 9052 4287
Fax: 028 9052 4148
Email: David.Trelford@dardni.gov.uk

**Personnel Management Branch:**
Principal: Robert Campton
Tel: 028 9052 4766
Fax: 028 9052 5544
Email: Robert.Campton@dardni.gov.uk

**Personnel Services Branch**
Principal: Eamonn Dickson
Tel: 028 9052 4301
Fax: 028 9052 5544
Email: Eamonn.Dickson@dardni.gov.uk

**Business Development Branch:**
Principal: Moya Cushley
Tel: 028 9052 5513
Fax: 028 9052 4018
Email: Moya.Cushley@dardni.gov.uk

## Corporate Policy Division
Assistant Secretary: Gerry McWhinney
Tel: 028 9052 4272
Fax: 028 9052 4148
Email: Gerry.McWhinney@dardni.gov.uk

**Media Services Branch**
Principal: Bernie McCusker
Tel: 028 9052 4619
Fax: 028 9052 5003
Email: Bernie.McCusker@dardni.gov.uk

**Central Management Branch**
Principal: Edwin Gallagher
Tel: 028 9052 4331
Fax: 028 9052 4884
Email: Edwin.Gallagher@dardni.gov.uk

**Equality and Rural Proofing Branch**
Principal: Lindsay Hodges
Tel: 028 9052 5057
Fax: 028 9052 4884
Email: Lindsay.Hodges@dardni.gov.uk

## Finance Division
Assistant Secretary: Rodney Scott
Tel: 028 9052 4678
Fax: 028 9052 4148
Email: Rodney.Scott@dardni.gov.uk

**Financial Systems Branch:**
Principal: Vacant

**Resource Control Branch:**
Principal: T Rodgers
Tel: 028 9052 4544
Fax: 028 9052 4906
Email: Tom.Rodgers@dardni.gov.uk

**Internal Audit Branch:**
Principal: Sean McGuinness
Tel: 028 9052 4046
Fax: 028 9052 4071
Email: Sean.McGuinness@dardni.gov.uk

**Financial Reporting Branch:**
Principal: Dennis Foy
Tel: 028 9052 5035
Fax: 028 9052 0903
Email: Dennis.Foy@dardni.gov.uk

**Financial Policy and Investigations Branch:**
Principal: Jim Ditchfield
Tel: 028 9052 4551
Fax: 028 9052 5092
Email: Jim.Ditchfield@dardni.gov.uk

## Change Division
Assistant Secretary: Pauline Keegan
Tel: 028 9052 4557
Fax 028 9052 4148
Email: Pauline.Keegan@dardni.gov.uk

**Modernisation Unit**
This Unit takes a lead role in the DARD modernisation programme, which is geared to improving the efficiency of operations and the delivery of services to the public.

Principal: Michael Thompson
Tel: 028 9052 4736
Email: Michael.Thompson@dardni.gov.uk

Principal: Hilda Hagan
Tel: 028 9052 5457
Email: Hilda.Hagan@dardni.gov.uk

**Information Management Branch**
Principal: Charlie Bennett
Tel: 028 9052 4211
Fax: 028 9052 4196
Email: Charlie.Bennett@dardni.gov.uk

Principal: Fiona Coulter
Tel: 028 9052 4231
Fax 028 9052 4196
Email: Fiona.Coulter@dardni.gov.uk

**Information Services (ISB) and Estate Management (OSEM)**
Senior Principal: Earl Long
Tel: 028 9052 4714
Fax: 028 9052 0876
Email: Earl.Long@dardni.gov.uk

Principal: Geoff Cromey
Tel: 028 9052 4774
Fax: 028 9052 0876
Email: Geoff.Cromey@dardni.gov.uk

ISB provides an in-house ICT service to the Department. OSEM is responsible for the co-ordination and provision of a wide range of Estate, Accommodation, Construction, Office and office-related services to DARD.

## Service Delivery Group
Deputy Secretary: Roy McClenaghan
Tel: 028 9052 4589
Fax: 028 9052 4060
Email: Roy.McClenaghan@dardni.gov.uk

## College of Agriculture/Food and Rural Enterprise
Director: John Fay
Tel: 028 9442 6600
Email: John.Fay@dardni.gov.uk

**Development Service**
Deputy Director: Paul McGurnaghan
Tel: 028 9442 6620
Fax: 028 9442 6606
Email: Paul.McGurnaghan@dardni.gov.uk

**Beef and Sheep Development Branch**
Head of Branch: John Herron
Tel: 028 9442 6740
Fax: 028 9442 6777
Email: John.Herron@dardni.gov.uk

**Dairy and Pigs Development Branch**
Head of Branch: Ian McCluggage
Tel: 028 9442 6760
Fax: 028 9442 6777
Email: Ian.McCluggage@dardni.gov.uk

**Crops and Horticulture Development Branch:** Vacant

**Food Technology Development Branch**
Head of Branch: Denis Legge
Tel: 028 8676 8134
Fax: 028 8676 1043
Email: Denis.Legge@dardni.gov.uk

**Educational Development Branch**
Head of Branch: James O'Boyle
Tel: 028 9442 6608
Fax: 028 9442 6777
Email: James.O'Boyle@dardni.gov.uk

**Education Service**
Deputy Director: Ian Titterington
Tel: 028 9442 6610
Fax: 028 9442 6606
Email: Ian.Titterington@dardni.gov.uk

**Higher Education Branch:**
Head of Branch: Sam Kennedy
Tel: 028 9442 6660
Email: Sam.Kennedy@dardni.gov.uk

**Further Education Branch:**
Head of Branch: Herbi Jones
Tel: 028 9442 6792
Email: Herbi.Jones@dardni.gov.uk

**Supply and Packaging Branch**
Head of Branch: Derek McDowell
Tel: 028 8676 8150
Email: Derek.McDowell@dardni.gov.uk

**Food Technology Education Branch**
Head of Branch: John Crawford
Tel: 028 8676 8138
Email: John.Crawford@dardni.gov.uk

**Equine and Rural Enterprise Branch**
Head of Branch: Seamus McAlinney
Tel: 028 6634 4855
Email: Semus.McAlinney@dardni.gov.uk

## Environment, Food and Central Services Division

This Division is responsible for organisational improvement; provision of technical support; education and financial management; the Rural Connect service; and the delivery of food and environmental polices through Countryside Management and Supply Chain Development.

Director: John Speers
Tel: 028 9052 4324
Email: John.Speers@dardni.gov.uk

**Countryside Management Branch**
Head of Branch: Harry Gracey
Tel: 028 9052 4713
Email: Harry.Gracey@dardni.gov.uk

**Supply Chain Development Branch**
Head of Branch: Steven Millar
Tel: 028 9442 6789
Email: Steven.Millar@dardni.gov.uk

**Organisational Improvement Branch**
Head of Branch: Eric Long
Tel: 028 9052 4788
Email: Eric.Long@dardni.gov.uk

**Technical Promotions Branch**
Head of Branch: Barry Niblock
Tel: 028 9052 4576
Fax: 028 9052 4788
Email: Barry.Niblock@dardni.gov.uk

**Education and Finance Branch**
Head of Branch: Pauline Rooney
Tel: 028 9052 4413
Email: Pauline.Rooney@dardni.gov.uk

**Rural Connect Branch**
Head of Branch: Jim Torney
Tel: 028 9052 4529
Fax: 028 9052 0815
Email: Jim.Torney@dardni.gov.uk

## Rural Payments and Inspection Division

The Division deals with Policy, Payments and Inspection for various schemes and quotas administered by DARD. The Division is leading on the implementation of the new Single Farm Payment, due to be introduced in 2005 under the CAP Reform agreement. The Division is also responsible for the implementation of agri-food legislation pertaining to food safety, plant health, product certification, marketing standards and industry support.

Head of Division: Ronnie Jordan
Tel: 028 9052 4555
Email: Ronnie.Jordan@dardni.gov.uk

**Grants and Subsidies Policy Branch**
Head of Branch: Valerie Bell
Tel: 028 9052 4595
Email: Valerie.Bell@dardni.gov.uk

**Grants and Subsidies Payments Branch**
Head of Branch: Seamus Doran
Tel: 028 7131 9899
Email: Seamus.Doran@dardni.gov.uk

**Implementation of the Single Farm Payment**
Project Manager: Bregeen Glendinning
Tel: 028 7131 9860

**Grants and Subsidies Inspection Branch**
Head of Branch: Willis McWhirter
Tel: 028 2566 2829
Email: Willis.Mcwhirter@dardni.gov.uk

**Quality Assurance Branch**
Head of Branch: Wilf Weatherup
Tel: 028 9052 4685
Email: Wilf.Weatherup@dardni.gov.uk

## Rural Development

This Division is responsible for the administration of the Rural Development Programme which aims to contribute to the economic, environmental, social and cultural well being of the rural community for the benefit of the whole community of Northern Ireland.

Assistant Secretary: Pauline McCloy
Tel: 028 9052 4586
Email: Pauline.McCloy@dardni.gov.uk

General enquires concerning the RDP should be directed to:

**Rural Development Division - Central**
Head of Branch: Michael McLernon
Tel: 028 9052 4578
Email: Michael.McLernon@dardni.gov.uk

Key Programme Contacts:

**Rural Development Division – North**
LEADER+, National Resource Rural Tourism Initiative (NRRTi)
Head of Branch: Gareth Evans
Tel: 028 2563 2199
Email: Gareth.Evans@dardni.gov.uk

**Rural Development Division – West**
Interreg IIIA
Head of Branch: Sean Nugent
Tel: 028 8225 5701
Email: Sean.Nugent@dardni.gov.uk

**Rural Development Division – South**
Programme for Building Sustainable Prosperity (PBSP)
Head of Branch: Vince McKevitt
Tel: 028 3025 3259
Email: Vince.McKevitt@dardni.gov.uk

**Rural Development Division - Peace Branch**
PEACE II Programme
Head of Branch: Brian Morrison
Tel: 028 9054 7188
Email: Brian.Morrison@dardni.gov.uk

Head of Peace Projects: Michael Mullan
Tel: 028 8676 8126
Email: Michael.Mullan@dardni.gov.uk

## Science Service Group

Chief Scientific Officer:
Dr George McIlroy
Tel: 028 9052 4635
Email: George.McIlroy@dardni.gov.uk
Web: www.afsni.ac.uk

## Agricultural, Food & Environmental Sciences

Deputy Chief Scientific Officer:
Dr Sydney Neill
Tel: 028 9052 5349
Email: Sydney.Neill@dardni.gov.uk

## Applied Plant Science and Agri-food Economics

Deputy Chief Scientific Officer:
Dr M Camlin (Acting)
Tel: 028 9025 5281
Email: Michael.Camlin@dardni.gov.uk

### Veterinary Sciences
Deputy Chief Scientific Officer: Prof William Ellis (Acting)
Tel: 028 9052 5062
Email: Bill.Ellis@dardni.gov.uk
Deputy Chief Veterinary Research Officers: Dr D Bryson, Dr S Kennedy

### Veterinary Service Group
Chief Veterinary Officer: Bert Houston
Tel: 028 9052 4669
Email: Robert.Houston@dardni.gov.uk

### Formulation of National and International Policy
Deputy Chief Veterinary Officer: Liz Redmond
Tel: 028 9052 4670
Email: Liz.Redmond@dardni.gov.uk

### Implementation of Policy and Staffing
Deputy Chief Veterinary Officer: Michael Geddis
Tel: 028 9052 4643
Email: Michael.Geddis@dardni.gov.uk

## Agencies, Non Departmental Public Bodies and other organisations within the Department of Agriculture and Rural Development

### Agricultural Research Institute of Northern Ireland
Large Park, Hillsborough, BT26 6DR
Tel: 028 9268 2484
Fax: 028 9268 9594
Web: www.arani.ac.uk
Director: Dr Sinclair Mayne

### Agricultural Wages Board
Agricultural Wages Secretariat
Room 910, Dundonald House
Upper Newtownards Road
Belfast, BT4 3SB
Tel: 028 9052 0813
Fax: 028 9052 4266

### Drainage Council
c/o Alan Morton, The Secretary
Rivers Agency, Hydebank
4 Hospital Road, Belfast, BT8 8JP
Tel: 028 9025 3357
Chairman: Dr Robert Myers

### Forest Service
Dundonald House
Upper Newtownards Road
Belfast, BT4 3SB
Tel: 028 9052 4480
Fax: 028 9052 4570
Web: www.forestserviceni.gov.uk
Chief Executive: Malcolm Beatty
Tel: 028 9052 4463
Fax: 028 9052 4570
Email: Malcolm.Beatty@dardni.gov.uk

#### Corporate Services
Director: Crawford McCully
Tel: 028 9052 4458
Fax: 028 9052 4570
Email: Crawford.McCully@dardni.gov.uk

#### Operations
Director: John Joe O'Boyle
Tel: 028 9052 4464
Fax: 028 9052 4570
Email: John.O'Boyle@dardni.gov.uk

#### Policy and Standards
Director: Pat Hunter Blair
Tel: 028 9052 4465
Fax: 028 9052 4570
Email: pat.hunter-blair@dardni.gov.uk

### Foyle, Carlingford and Irish Lights Commission
The Loughs Agency
22 Victoria Road, Waterside
Londonderry, BT47 2AB
Tel: 028 7134 2100
Fax: 028 7134 2720
Web: www.loughs-agency.org
Email: general@loughs-agency.org

### Livestock and Meat Commission for Northern Ireland
Lissue House, 31 Ballinderry Road
Lisburn, BT28 2SL
Tel: 028 9263 3000
Fax: 028 9263 3001
Web: www.lmcni.com
Email: info@lmcni.com
Chief Executive: David Rutledge

### Northern Ireland Fishery Harbour Authority
3 St Patrick's Avenue
Downpatrick, BT30 6DW
Tel: 028 4461 3844
Fax: 028 4461 7128
Web: www.nifha.fsnet.co.uk
Email: info@nifha.fsnet.co.uk
Chief Executive: Chris Warnock

### Pig Production Development Committee
c/o Farm Policy Division
Room 910, Dundonald House
Upper Newtownards Road
Belfast, BT4 3SB
Tel: 028 9052 4873
Fax: 028 9052 4266
Email: joyce.miskimmons@dardni.gov.uk

### Rivers Agency
Hydebank
4 Hospital Road, Belfast, BT8 8JP
Tel: 028 9025 3355
Fax: 028 9025 3455

The Agency is responsible for the maintenance of designated watercourses and sea defences; execution of drainage/flood defence schemes and management of Lough Neagh/Erne levels within statutory limits

Chief Executive: John Hagan
Tel: 028 9025 3440
Email: John.Hagan@dardni.gov.uk

#### Corporate Services
Director of Corporate Services: Alan Morton
Tel: 028 9052 3357
Email: Alan.Morton@dardni.gov.uk

#### Operations
Director of Operations: Melvyn Hamilton
Tel: 028 9025 3358
Email: Melvyn.Hamilton@dardni.gov.uk
Principal Engineers: P Aldridge, A Kirkwood, P McCrudden

#### Development
Director of Development: Ronald White
Tel: 028 9025 3424
Email: Ronald.White@dardni.gov.uk
Principal Engineers: J Clarke, S Dawson, P Mehaffey, J Nicholson

### Rural Development Council
17 Loy Street
Cookstown, BT80 8PZ
Tel: 028 8676 6980
Fax: 028 8676 6922
Web: www.rdc.org.uk
Email: info@rdc.org.uk
Chief Executive: Martin McDonald

## Department of Culture, Arts and Leisure

Interpoint
20-24 York Street
Belfast, BT15 1AQ
Tel: 028 9025 8825
Fax: 028 9025 8906
Web: www.dcalni.gov.uk

**Direct Rule Minister**: Angela Smith MP
Permanent Secretary:
Dr Aideen McGinley OBE
Tel: 028 9025 8814
Deputy Secretary: Edgar Jardine
Tel: 028 9025 8848
Fax: 028 9025 8951

**Private Office**
Private Secretary: Julie Childs
Tel: 028 9025 8807

**Press Office**
Principal Information Officer: Jill Heron
Tel: 028 9025 8900
Fax: 028 9025 8951

The Department of Culture, Arts and Leisure (DCAL) is responsible for developing policy, service delivery, administration and monitoring of: arts and creativity; museums; libraries; sport and leisure; visitor amenities; inland waterways and inland fisheries; Ordnance Survey; the Public Record Office; language policy; and for advising on matters relating to National Lottery distribution.

The core department is structured into three Divisions – Culture: Sport, Museums and Recreation; and Corporate Services – and two Executive Agencies – Ordnance Survey of Northern Ireland and the Public Record Office of Northern Ireland. The Department also draws on the expertise of the Education and Training Inspectorate.

DCAL works with a wide range of statutory bodies including the Armagh Planetarium and Observatory, the Arts Council of Northern Ireland, the Education and Library Boards, the Fisheries Conservancy Board, the Museums and Galleries of Northern Ireland, the Northern Ireland Events Company, the Northern Ireland Museums Council, the Northern Ireland Water Council and the Sports Council for Northern Ireland. DCAL also works with the two North/South Implementation Bodies, Waterways Ireland and the Language Body, comprising the Ulster Scots Agency and Foras na Gaeilge, as well as with all government departments and 'sister' departments in Great Britain and the Republic of Ireland.

Further working relationships have been forged over the past 4 years, through the Cultural Forum. The Forum acts in an advisory capacity to the Department on a range of issues, with representatives from across the Museums, Libraries, Heritage, Arts and Sports sectors, as well as Lottery Distributors, Local Government, the Education and Library Boards, other departments and interested parties such as the British Council and the Community Relations Council.

The Department also seeks to raise the profile of Northern Ireland culture internationally and to this end funds the post of Cultural Affairs Officer of the Northern Ireland Bureau in Washington DC.

### Corporate Services

Head of Division: Damian Prince
Tel: 028 9025 8821
Fax: 028 9025 8987
Email: damian.prince@dcalni.gov.uk

**Press Office:**
Contact: Jill Heron
Tel: 028 9025 8900
Fax: 028 9025 8906
Email: jill.heron@dcalni.gov.uk

**Policy Evaluation & Review Unit:**
Contact: Denis McCoy
Tel: 028 9025 8917
Fax: 028 9025 8942
Email: denis.mccoy@dcalni.gov.uk

**Research & Statistics:**
Contact: Michael Willis
Tel: 028 902
Email: michael.willis@dcalni.gov.uk

**MPSO/Central Management Branch:**
Contact: David Craig
Tel: 028 9025 8867
Email: david.craig@dcalni.gov.uk

**Economics:**
Contact: Tom Flynn
Tel: 028 9025 8963
Email: tom.flynn@dcalni.gov.uk

**Financial Planning:**
Contact: Michelle Estler
Tel: 028 9025 8910
Fax: 028 9025 8883
Email: michelle.estler@dcalni.gov.uk

**Accounts and Accountability:**
Contact: Eddie Magowan
Tel: 028 9025 8859
Fax 028 9025 8987
Email: eddie.magowan@dcalni.gov.uk

**Human Resources:**
Contact: Sharon Irwin
Tel: 028 9025 8937
Fax: 028 9025 8934
Email: sharon.Irwin@dcalni.gov.uk

**Freedom of Information:**
Contact: Paul McAllister
Tel: 028 9025 4256

### Culture

Head of Division: Colin Jack
Tel: 028 9025 8843
Fax: 028 9025 8987
Email: colin.jack@dcalni.gov.uk

**Arts:**
Contact: Mark Mawhinney
Tel: 028 9025 8824
Fax: 028 9025 8879
Email: arci@dcalni.gov.uk

**Libraries:**
Contact: Phillips Wilson
Tel: 028 9025 8927
028 9025 8876
Email: phillips.wilson@dcalni.gov.uk

**Linguistic Operations:**
Contact: Ian Sloan
Tel: 028 9025 4216
Email: ian.sloan@dcalni.gov.uk

**Cultural & Language Diversity Policy Branch:**
Contact: Victor Douglas
Tel: 028 9025 4239
Email: victor.douglas@dcalni.gov.uk

**Sports, Museums & Recreation:**
Head of Division: Nigel Carson
Tel: 028 9025 8801
Fax: 028 9025 8951
Email: nigel.carson@dcalni.gov.uk

**Sports:**
Contact: Jack Palmer
Tel: 028 9025 8935
Email: jack.palmer@dcalni.gov.uk

## Department of Culture, Arts and Leisure Organisation Chart

- **Minister** Angela Smith

- **Permanent Secretary** Dr Aideen McGinley

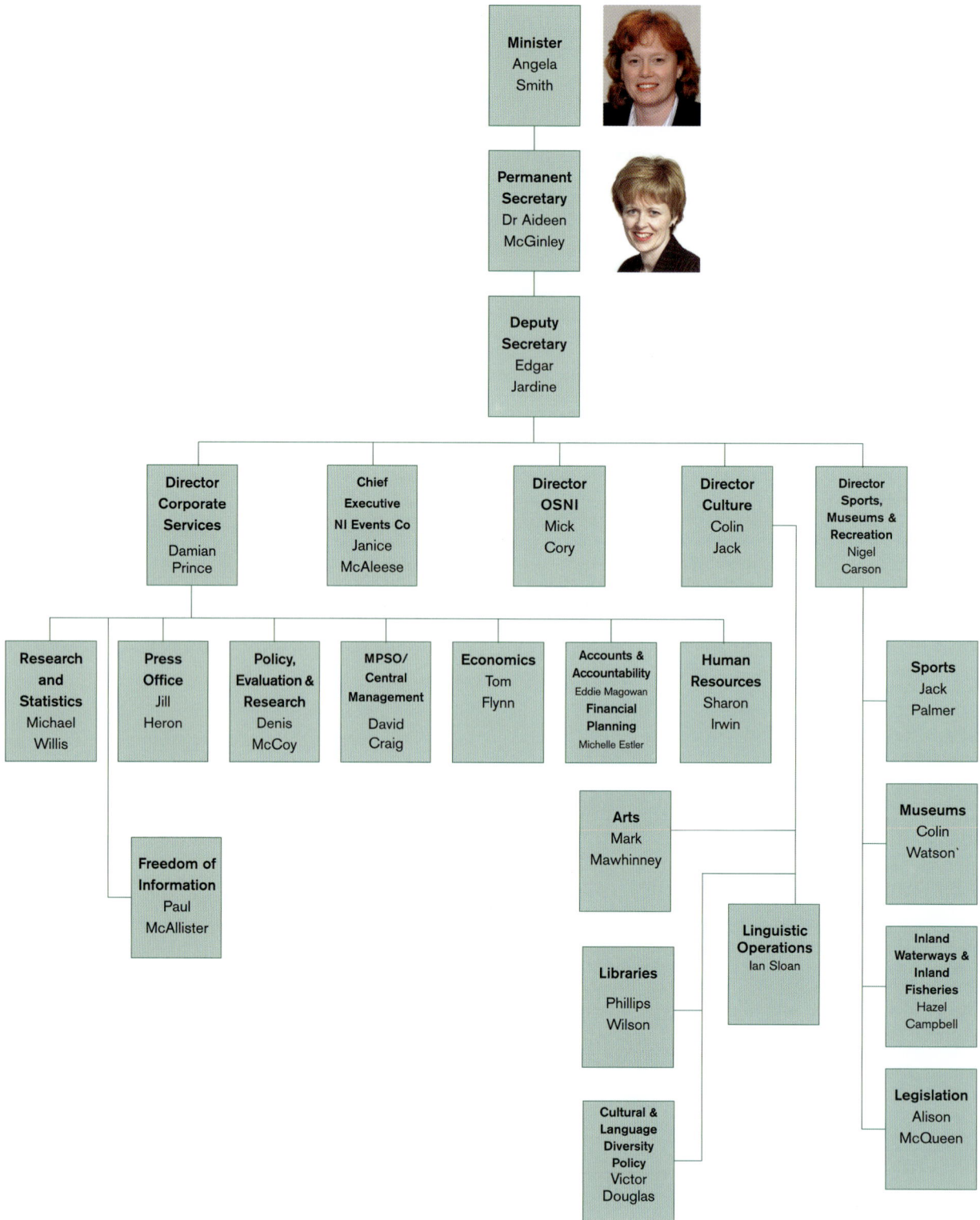

- **Deputy Secretary** Edgar Jardine
  - **Director Corporate Services** Damian Prince
    - **Research and Statistics** Michael Willis
    - **Freedom of Information** Paul McAllister
    - **Press Office** Jill Heron
    - **Policy, Evaluation & Research** Denis McCoy
    - **MPSO/ Central Management** David Craig
    - **Economics** Tom Flynn
    - **Accounts & Accountability** Eddie Magowan; **Financial Planning** Michelle Estler
    - **Human Resources** Sharon Irwin
  - **Chief Executive NI Events Co** Janice McAleese
  - **Director OSNI** Mick Cory
  - **Director Culture** Colin Jack
    - **Arts** Mark Mawhinney
    - **Linguistic Operations** Ian Sloan
    - **Libraries** Phillips Wilson
    - **Cultural & Language Diversity Policy** Victor Douglas
  - **Director Sports, Museums & Recreation** Nigel Carson
    - **Sports** Jack Palmer
    - **Museums** Colin Watson`
    - **Inland Waterways & Inland Fisheries** Hazel Campbell
    - **Legislation** Alison McQueen

**Museums:**
Contact: Colin Watson
Tel: 028 9025 8862
Fax: 028 9025 8942
Email: colin.watson@dcalni.gov.uk

**Inland Waterways & Inland Fisheries:**
Contact: Hazel Campbell
Tel: 028 9025 8862
Fax: 028 9025 8898
Email: hazel.campbell@dcalni.gov.uk

**Legislation:**
Contact: Alison McQueen
Tel: 028 9025 4228
Email: alison.mcqueen@dcalni.gov.uk

## Agencies, Non Departmental Public Bodies and other organisations within Department of Culture, Arts and Leisure

### Armagh Observatory
College Hill, Armagh, BT61 9DG
Tel: 028 3752 2928
Fax: 028 3752 7174
Web: www.arm.ac.uk

Director: Prof Mark Bailey
Tel: 028 3751 2957
Fax: 028 3752 7174
Email: meb@star.arm.ac.uk

### Armagh Planetarium
College Hill, Armagh, BT61 9DG
Tel: 028 3752 4725
Fax: 028 3752 6187
Web: www.armaghplanet.com
Director: Dr Tom Mason
Email: tom@armaghplanet.com

### Arts Council of Northern Ireland
MacNeice House, 77 Malone Road
Belfast, BT9 6AQ
Tel: 028 9038 5200
Fax: 028 9066 1715
Web: www.artscouncil-ni.org
Email: info@artscouncil-ni.org
Chief Executive: Roisin McDonough

### Fisheries Conservancy Board
1 Mahon Road
Portadown, BT62 3EE
Tel: 028 3833 4666
Fax: 028 3833 8912
Web: www.fcbni.com
Chief Executive: Karen Simpson

### Museums & Galleries of Northern Ireland (MAGNI)
Ulster Museum
Botanic Gardens
Belfast, BT9 5AB
Tel: 028 9038 3000
Fax: 028 3083 3003
Web: www.magni.org.uk

Chief Executive: Tim Cooke
Tel: 028 9038 3095
Fax: 028 9038 3006
Email: director.um@nics.gov.uk

### Ordnance Survey of Northern Ireland
Colby House, Stranmillis Court
Malone Lower, Belfast, BT9 5BJ
Tel: 028 9025 5755
Fax: 028 9025 5700
Web: www.osni.gov.uk
Chief Executive: Mick G Cory

### Northern Ireland Museums Council
6 Crescent Gardens
Belfast, BT7 1NS
Tel: 028 9055 0215
Fax: 028 9055 0216
Web: www.nimc.co.uk
Email: info@nimc.co.uk
Director: Chris Bailey
Email: dir@nimc.co.uk

### Northern Ireland Events Company
Redwood House
66 Newforge Lane
Belfast, BT9 5NT
Tel: 028 9066 6661
Fax: 028 9066 8040
Web: www.nievents.co.uk
Email: info@nievents.co.uk
Chief Executive: Janice McAleese

### North/South Language Body
The North/South Language Body is a single body composed of two separate and largely autonomous agencies:

**Ulster Scots Agency**
Franklin House, 10-12 Brunswick Street
Belfast, BT2 7GE
Tel: 028 9023 1113
Fax: 028 9023 1898
Web: www.ulsterscotsagency.com
Email: info@ulsterscotsagency.org.uk
Chief Executive: George Patten
Acting Chair: Jim Devenney

**Foras na Gaeilge**
7 Merrion Square, Dublin
Tel: 00 353 1 639 8400
Fax: 00 353 1 639 8401
Web: www.forasnagaeilge.ie
Email: eolas@forasnagaeilge.ie
Chief Executive: Seosamh MacDonncha
Chairperson: Maighread Ní Mhairtin

### Public Record Office of Northern Ireland
66 Balmoral Avenue, Belfast, BT9 6NY
Tel: 028 9025 1318
Fax: 028 9025 5999
Web: www.proni. gov.uk
Email: proni@dcalni.gov.uk
Chief Executive: Dr Gerry Slater

Head of Access: Aileen McClintock
Head of Records Management and Administration and of Preservation: Patricia Kernaghan
Head of Corporate Services: Tom Robinson
Head of Education, Learning and Outreach: Valerie Adams
Head of Public Service (Readers): Cecilia McCormick
Head of Information Systems: Hugh Campbell
New Archive Legislation Officer: Roger Strong
New Accommodation Project Manager: Marie Garvey

### Sports Council for Northern Ireland
House of Sport, Upper Malone Road
Belfast, BT9 5LA
Tel: 028 9038 1222
Fax: 028 9068 2757
Minicom: 028 9068 2593
Web: www.sportni.net
Chief Executive Officer: Eamonn G McCartan

### Waterways Ireland
20 Darling Street
Enniskillen, BT74 7EW
Web: www.waterwaysireland.org
Email: info@waterwaysireland.org
Chief Executive: John Martin

*Note: DCAL is also the sponsoring department of the 5 Education and Library Boards in respect of library services. Contact details for the Boards may be found on pages 272-273.*

## Department of Education

Rathgael House
Balloo Road
Bangor, BT19 7PR
Tel: 028 9127 9279
Fax: 028 9127 9100
Web: www.deni.gov.uk

**Direct Rule Minister**: Barry Gardiner

**Permanent Secretary**: Gerry McGinn
Tel: 028 9127 9309

**Deputy Secretary**: Eddie Rooney
Tel: 028 9127 9313

**Private Office**
Private Secretary: Patricia McBride
Tel: 028 9127 9307
Email: patricia.mcbride@deni.gov.uk

**Press Office**
Principal Information Officer: Jill Garrett
Tel: 028 9127 9356
Email: jill.garrett@deni.gov.uk

The Department of Education has responsibility for aspects of education relating to schools and the Youth Service. This includes policy, legislation and resource issues for both areas.

As regards the Education Service, the Department of Education has responsibility for strategic planning and accounting for public expenditure. The Department manages the funding and administration of schools. It monitors schools' effectiveness, and oversees school planning and provision. The Department also has an inspectorate, and makes appointments to the five Education and Library Boards.

The Department develops policy regarding schools curriculum, and the assessment of pupils, including examinations. It oversees transfer procedures and school enrolment, and provides special education services and pupil support.

The Department of Education also has responsibility for community relations among young people, which is part of its overall youth services remit. The Department provides a comprehensive youth service, and supports many associated organisations.

### School Improvement & Teacher Development

Head of Division: Christine Jendoubi
Tel: 028 9127 9383

**Teachers Negotiating Committee Branch**
Principal: Alastair Bradley
Tel: 028 9127 9258

Functions: Policy on Teachers' Salaries and Conditions of Service, including Teachers' Health and Wellbeing.

**School Improvement Branch**
Principal: Peter Lowry
Tel: 028 9127 9562
Functions: School Improvement and Support Programmes; Reading Recovery; Literacy/Numeracy Strategy; Out of School Hours Learning Activities; Reducing the Bureaucratic Burden; Dissemination of Good Practice; School Library Service; Education Action Zones.

**Teacher Education Branch**
Principal: Ron Armstrong
Tel: 028 9127 9288
Functions: Teacher Education – Initial, Induction and Early Professional Development; Continuing Professional Development; CASS; Professional Qualification for Headship; GTC.

**Teachers Pay, Pensions & Administration Branch**
(Waterside House)
Principal: Mervyn Gregg
Tel: 028 9127 9166
Functions: Teachers Pay & Pension Project; Teachers' Pay & Administration; Teachers' Pensions.

### Schools and Pupil Services

Head of Division: June Ingram
Tel: 028 9127 9322

**Equality, Rights & Social Inclusion Unit**
Principal: Sharon Lawlor
Tel: 028 9127 9342
Functions: Equality issues; Anti-Poverty Strategy Action Plan; Human Rights; Racial; Education of Travellers & other Ethnic Minorities; Disability Rights.

**Pupil Support Branch**
Principal: Mary Potter
Tel: 028 9127 9386
Functions: Policy for Pupils 'at risk', including looked after children, school age mothers, young offenders & victims of violence; academically gifted children; school discipline (bullying, suspensions, expulsions); child protection in schools; Education Otherwise Than At School (EOTAS).

**Open Enrolment & Transfer Procedure Branch**
Principal: John Leonard
Tel: 028 9127 9693
Functions: Open Enrolment Policy; Legislation and Administration; Transfer/Procedure Policy; Class sizes (KS1) Policy and Legislation, Implementation; Pupil Placement issues.

**Special Education Branch**
Principal: Irene Murphy
Tel: 028 9127 9419
Functions: Special Educational Needs Policy; Legislation; Code of Practice. All aspects of special educational needs 0-19, but especially: autism & dyslexia; NorthSouth Links: NS Ministerial Council, St Joseph's Middletown; Children in Care – Lakewood Special School; Integration/Inclusion; Statementing inc. servicing SEN Tribunal; Medical Needs, Nursing; Education Psychology Service; Code of Practice and Special Schools Funding; Liaison with DEL/DHSSPS; Liaison with relevant voluntary organisations.

### Resource Allocation Division

Head of Division: Katrina Godfrey
Tel: 028 9127 9524

**School Finance Branch**
Principal: Rose Morrow
Tel: 028 9127 9967
Functions: School Finance (bids and monitoring); Funding of Making a Good Start Initiative. Common LMS Scheme and formula. Recurrent funding of voluntary grammar & grant maintained integrated schools.

**School Administration Branch**
Principal: Brian Hill
Tel: 028 9127 9630
Functions: Home to School Transport; School Meals Service; Boarding & Clothing Allowances; Educational Maintenance Allowance; Funding and Administration of CCMS; Primary & Secondary Standing Conferences; Children (Public Performances) Regulations. General administration and

## Department of Education Organisation Chart

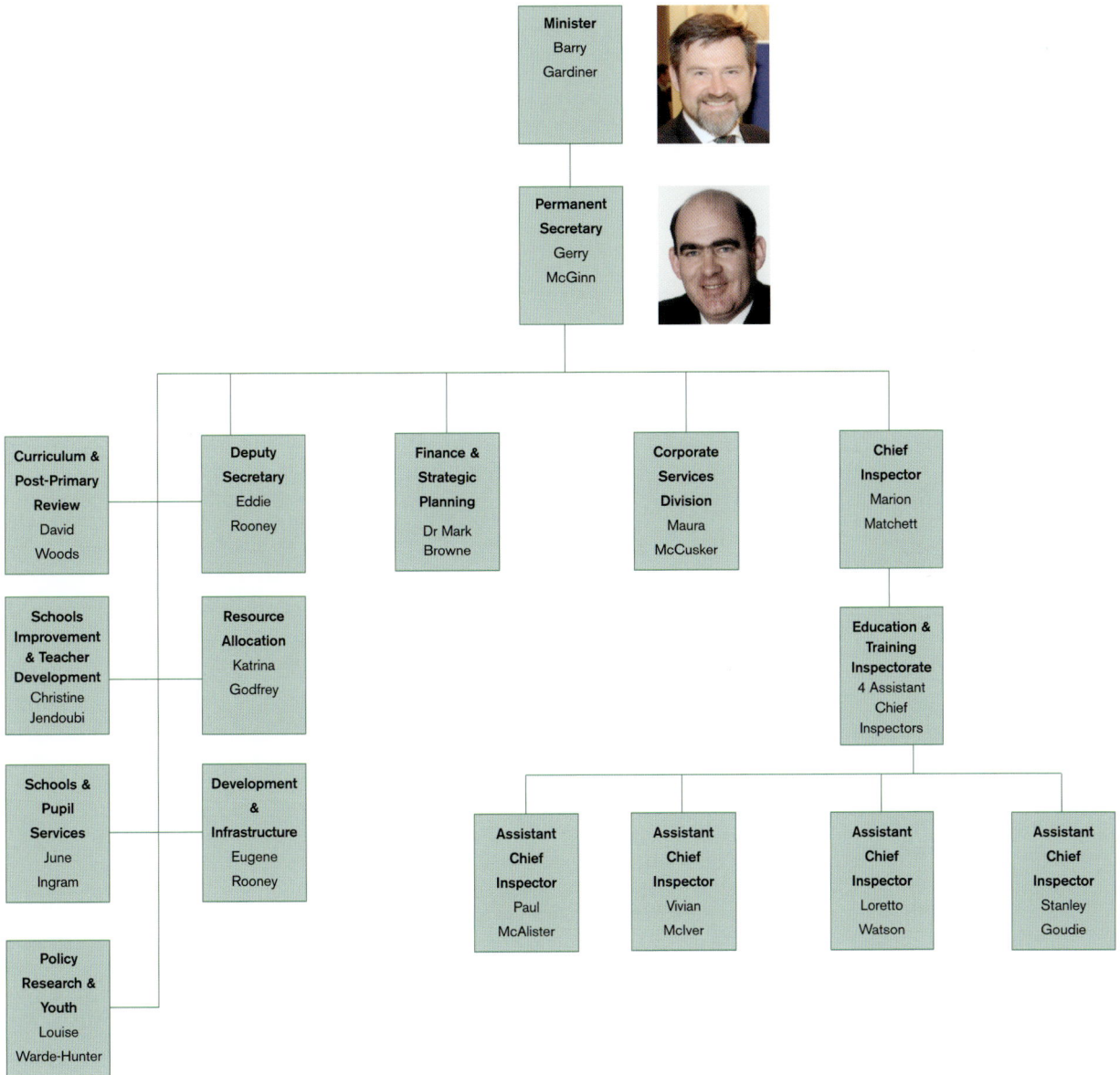

- **Minister** Barry Gardiner

  - **Permanent Secretary** Gerry McGinn

    - **Deputy Secretary** Eddie Rooney
      - **Curriculum & Post-Primary Review** David Woods
      - **Schools Improvement & Teacher Development** Christine Jendoubi
      - **Schools & Pupil Services** June Ingram
      - **Policy Research & Youth** Louise Warde-Hunter
      - **Resource Allocation** Katrina Godfrey
      - **Development & Infrastructure** Eugene Rooney
    - **Finance & Strategic Planning** Dr Mark Browne
    - **Corporate Services Division** Maura McCusker
    - **Chief Inspector** Marion Matchett
      - **Education & Training Inspectorate** 4 Assistant Chief Inspectors
        - **Assistant Chief Inspector** Paul McAlister
        - **Assistant Chief Inspector** Vivian McIver
        - **Assistant Chief Inspector** Loretto Watson
        - **Assistant Chief Inspector** Stanley Goudie

school management issues; Schemes of Management, Appointments to Boards of Governors, and School Security; Registration of Independent Schools; North Belfast Initiative Coordination; Review of School Governance.

**Area Board Resource Allocation & Monitoring Branch (ABRAM)**
Principal: Chris Bradley
Tel: 028 9127 9315
Functions: Resource Distribution to ELBs; Budgeting Control & Monitoring, ELB Personnel & Accountability Issues; Staff Commission; Best Value.

## Development and Infrastructure Division
Head of Division: Eugene Rooney
Tel: 028 9127 9334

**Building Branch**
Principal: Sean Johnston
Tel: 028 9127 9467
Functions: Finance and Energy Efficiency Section. School major & minor works programme (including Education Reform); Building Handbook Review.

**Development Branch**
Principal: Russell Welsh
Tel: 028 9127 9628
Functions: Economic Appraisals; Development Proposals & Capital Priorities in respect of Primary, Special, Nursery; Pre-school Expansion Programme; SELB/NEELB. Estates Management Project. Economic Appraisals, Development Proposals & Capital Priorities in respect of Secondary, Grammar Schools, Pre-School Expansion Programme SEELB/BELB/WELB.

**Public Private Partnership & Strategy Unit**
Principal: Patrick McNally
Tel: 028 9127 9291
Functions: Policy & Development of Public Private Partnerships (PPP) in Education; General PPP Guidance; Standardisation of PPP Documentation. Strategy Unit; ICT in Schools (C2K).

## Policy Research and Youth
Head of Division: Louise Warde-Hunter
Tel: 028 9127 9263

**Youth Services Branch**
Principal: Tom McCready
Tel: 028 9127 9541
Functions: Development & Implementation of Policy in respect of the NI Youth Service; Youth Council for Northern Ireland; Capital Grants to recognised Voluntary Youth Organisations; Grants for Training of Youth Workers; North South Youth Exchanges.

**Community Relations Branch**
Principal: Tom McCready
Tel: 028 9127 9541
Functions: The Promotion of Community Relations between Young People; Schools Community Relations Programme; Youth Service Community Relations Support Scheme; Community Relations Core Funding Scheme; Cultural Traditions Programme.

**Statistics & Research Branch**
Principal: Dr Ivor Johnston
Tel: 028 9127 9677
Functions: Research; Statistical Series; Analysis.

School Policy Branch
Principal: Stephen Sandford
Tel: 028 9127 9670
Functions: Pre-school Education Programme and Policy. Policy on Provision of Integrated Education; Irish Medium Education; Funding of NICIE & Comhairle na Gaelscolaíochta.

**Economic Advisory Unit**
Principal: Mike Archer
Tel: 028 9127 9601
Functions: Economic advice on Policy issues; advice on value for money of projects and in relation to specific issues.

**Policy Support Unit**
Principal: John Caldwell
Tel: 028 9127 9593
Functions: To take forward policy reviews as determined by senior management team.

## Curriculum and Post Primary Review
Head of Division: David Woods
Tel: 028 9127 9427

**Curriculum and Qualifications**
Principal: Richard Cushnie
Tel: 028 9127 9540
Functions: CCEA; Curriculum 0-14; Assessment 4-14; Religious Education; Creativity/Culture; Qualifications and Key Skills.

**Post Primary Support Team**
Principal: Leslie Ashe
Tel: 028 9127 9700
Functions: Development of policy on new arrangements for Post-Primary Education.

Contact: Jacqui McLaughlin
Tel: 028 9127 9734
Functions: Contributing to policy development on new arrangements for post-primary education. Management of the 'development package'. Liaison with DEL on 14-19 issues.

## Finance and Strategic Planning
Head of Division: Dr Mark Browne
Tel: 028 9127 9338

**Financial Planning Branch**
Principal: Brian Morrow
Tel: 028 91279378
Functions: Public Expenditure Planning, Budgeting & Monitoring; Resource Budgeting; Main & Supplementary Estimates.

**Accounts Branch**
Principal: Ronnie McQuitty
Tel: 028 9127 9696
Functions: Payment Processing; Appropriation Accounts; Resource Accounts; Accountability Issues.

**Strategy Management Unit**
Principal: Dr Chris Hughes
Tel: 028 9127 9216
Functions: Strategic, Corporate & Business Planning; NDPB accountability Reviews; Strategic Education Partnership; Programme for Government.

**Internal Audit Branch**
Principal: Michelle Anderson
Tel: 028 9127 9669
Functions: Internal Audit; corporate governance & risk management issues & monitoring of systems of internal control.

**Special Funding Initiatives Unit**
Principal: Alison Clydesdale
Tel: 028 9127 9595
Functions: EU Structural Funds Monitoring; Belfast Regeneration, Londonderry Regeneration.

## Corporate Services Division
Head of Division: Maura McCusker
Tel: 028 9127 9300

**Central Policy and Management Branch**
Contact: Trevor Brant
Tel: 028 9127 9580

(Acting) Deputy Principal: Catherine Bell
Tel: 028 9127 9558
Functions: Co-ordination of business & development of relations with Westminster; Legislation; Emergency Planning; The British Council; International Relations.

**Minister's Private Office**
Contact: Liam Barr (Grade 7)
Tel: 028 9127 9978
Private Secretary: Patricia McBride
Tel: 028 9127 9307

**Personnel & Development Services**
Principal: Paul Cartwright
Tel: 028 9127 9460
Functions: Records Management; Security; Equal Opportunities. Personnel DRC; Promotion; Pay, Transfers; Travel & Subsistence; Appraisal; Sick Absence, HRMS; Staff Welfare Service; Staff Development; IIP;

**Business Services**
Principal: Mary Cromey
Tel: 028 9127 9456
Functions: Modernising Government; Information Systems Strategy; Information Systems Development & Support; Web Development; Teachers System Support; Technical Infrastructure; IT Security.

**Information Management and Services Branch**
Principal: Veronica Bintley
Tel: 028 9127 9983
Functions: Accommodation, Office & Support Services, Health & Safety, Freedom of Information, Data Protection, Records Management, Accommodation, Security, Knowledge Network, EDRMS.

**Press Office**
Press Officer: Jill Garrett
Tel: 028 9127 9356
Functions: Media Queries; Daily News Digests; Media Monitoring and Advice; Press Releases; Press Conferences and Staff Magazine.

## Education and Training Inspectorate
Chief Inspector: Marion Matchett
Tel: 028 9127 9359

Assistant Chief Inspector:
Stanley Goudie
Tel: 028 9127 9555
Functions: policy, planning and improvement

Assistant Chief Inspector: Paul McAlister
Tel: 028 9127 9697
Functions: youth and community; alternative education provision; culture, arts and leisure

Assistant Chief Inspector: Vivian McIver
Tel: 028 9127 9532
Functions: Post-16 education including schools, further educations, training, higher education and teacher education

Assistant Chief Inspector: Loretto Wilson
Tel: 028 9127 9364
Functions: Pre-16 education, including pre-school, primary and post-primary

**Inspection Services Branch (ISB)**
Contact: Jenny McIlwain
Tel: 028 9127 9596
Functions: ISB administers the inspection schedule and publishes inspection reports within agreed targets. It also provides an alternative administrative and professional support service to facilitate the delivery of advice to relevant organisations and individuals.

## Other Agencies
**Comhairle na Gaelscolaíochta**
Teach an Gheata Thiar
4 Stráid na Banríona
Béal Feirste, BT1 6ED
Guthán: 028 9032 1475
Príomhfheidhmeannach: Seán Ó Coinn

**Council for Catholic Maintained Schools**
160 High Street
Holywood, BT18 9HT
Tel: 028 9042 6972
Fax: 028 9042 4255
Chief Executive: Donal Flanagan

**General Teaching Council for Northern Ireland**
4th Floor, Albany House
73-75 Great Victoria Street
Belfast, BT2 7AF
Tel: 028 9033 3390

**Integrated Education Fund**
41 University Street
Belfast, BT7 1FY
Tel: 028 9033 0031
Director: Tina Merron

**Iontaobhas na Gaelscolaiochta**
199 Bothár na bhFal
Béal Feirste, BT12 6FB
Guthán: 028 9024 1510
Príomhfheidhmeannach: Pilib Ó Runaidh

**Northern Ireland Council for Curriculum, Examinations and Assessment**
29 Clarendon Road
Clarendon Dock, Belfast, BT1 3BG
Tel: 028 9026 1200
Chief Executive: Gavin Boyd

**Northern Ireland Council for Integrated Education**
Aldershot House, 13-19 University Road
Belfast, BT7 1NA
Tel: 028 9023 6200
CEO: Michael Wardlow

**Staff Commission for Education and Library Boards**
Purdy's Lane, Belfast, BT8 4TA
Tel: 028 9049 1461
Chairman: Bernard Cullen

**Youth Council for Northern Ireland**
Purdy's Lane, Belfast, BT8 7AR
Tel: 028 9064 3882
Chief Executive: David Guilfoyle

## Department for Employment and Learning (DEL)

Adelaide House
39-49 Adelaide Street, Belfast, BT2 8FD
Tel: 028 9025 7777
Web: www.delni.gov.uk
Email: del@nics.gov.uk

**NIO Minister:** Barry Gardiner MP
**Permanent Secretary:** Will Haire
Tel: 028 9025 7834
Fax: 028 9025 7878
**Private Office**
Private Secretary: Jill Patton
Tel: 028 9025 7791
Fax: 028 9025 7919
Email: jill.patton@delni.gov.uk
**Press Office**
Principal Information Officer:
Gwyn Treharne
Tel: 028 9025 7790
Fax: 028 9025 7592
Email: gwyn.treharne@delni.gov.uk

The Department for Employment and Learning (DEL) manages a range of training and employment measures and programmes and provides funding for institutions in the Further and Higher Education sectors.

It operates within a number of policy frameworks and guidelines set at national, regional and European level.

At national level these include Welfare Reform and Modernisation, New Deal, widening access to further education and lifelong learning. Within Northern Ireland, issues such as quality and standards in Higher and Further Education, essential skills of literacy and numeracy, equality and employability figure prominently. North-South and East West collaboration is also an important factor. All or these are consistent with key European themes on employability, entrepreneurship, adaptability and equal opportunities.

One common vein is evident throughout all the work the Department undertakes – the need to keep a clear economic imperative to the fore. This in turn will help to create an environment in which business is supported and allowed to thrive, where entrepreneurs are encouraged and where people have the chance to learn and earn.

### Head of Policy for Employment Services & Employment Rights

Deputy Secretary: Dr Robson Davison
Tel: 028 9025 7876
Email: robson.davison@delni.gov.uk

### Preparation for Work Division

Head of Division: Patricia McAuley
Tel: 028 9025 7806
Email: patricia.mcauley@delni.gov.uk

The main areas of work through which the division delivers its service are:

- Welfare Reform and Modernisation
- Employment Service
- Targeted Initiatives
- Focus for work
- New Deal
- Disablement Advisory Programme

**Regional Operations (Grade 6)**
Contact: Daragh Shields
Tel: 028 9025 7865
Email: daragh.shields@delni.gov.uk

Regional Manager, Northern Region
Contact: Ann Williams
Tel: 028 9442 6574
Email: ann.williams@delni.gov.uk

Regional Manager, Southern Region
Contact: Peter Poland
Tel: 028 3026 5197
Email: peter.poland@delni.gov.uk

Regional Manager, Belfast
Contact: Harriet Ferguson
Tel: 028 9025 2289
Email: harriet.ferguson@delni.gov.uk

**Employment Service Policy**
Contact: Tom Hunter
Tel: 028 9072 6794
Email: tom.hunter@delni.gov.uk

**Disablement Advisory Service**
Contact: John Campbell
Tel: 028 9025 2261
Email: john.campbell@delni.gov.uk

**Partnerships**
Contact: Sheena Mairs
Tel: 028 9072 6709
Email: sheena.mairs@delni.gov.uk

**Service Delivery Development and Support**
Contact: Kieran Brazier
Tel: 028 9072 6796
Email: kieran.brazier@delni.gov.uk

**Programme and Product Management and Development**
Contact: Liz Young
Tel: 028 9025 7887
Email: liz.young@delni.gov.uk

### Corporate Services Division

Head of Division: Daryl Young (Acting)
Tel: 028 9052 7769
Fax: 028 9025 7817
Email: daryl.young@delni.gov.uk

The role of Corporate Services Division is to provide a range of support services to the rest of the Department. It also has responsibility for ensuring effective communication with both internal and external customers and the press.

**Personnel**
Contact: Mervyn Langtry
Tel: 028 9025 7883
Email: mervyn.langtry@delni.gov.uk

**CIS**
Contact: Geoff Harrison
Tel: 028 9025 7608
Email: geoff.harrison@delni.gov.uk

**Planning and Equality**
Contact: Briege Rainey (Acting)
Tel: 028 9025 7627
Email: briege.rainey@delni.gov.uk

**Media and Marketing Unit**
Contact: Gwyn Treharne
Tel: 028 9025 7790
Email: gwyn.treharne@delni.gov.uk

**Information Management**
Contact: Martin Caher
Tel: 028 9025 7431
Email: martin.caher@delni.gov.uk

### Finance & European Division

Head of Division: George O'Doherty
Tel: 028 9025 7810
Email: george.odoherty@delni.gov.uk

The Division is responsible for budget management, expenditure reporting, audit and accountability and accounting arrangements in the department. A European Unit administers European Social Funding under the two main European Programmes and the EQUAL programme for Northern Ireland.

**Finance (1)**
Contact: Graeme Wilkinson
Tel: 028 9025 7702
Fax: 028 9025 7611
Email: graeme.wilkinson@delni.gov.uk

## Department for Employment and Learning Organisation Chart

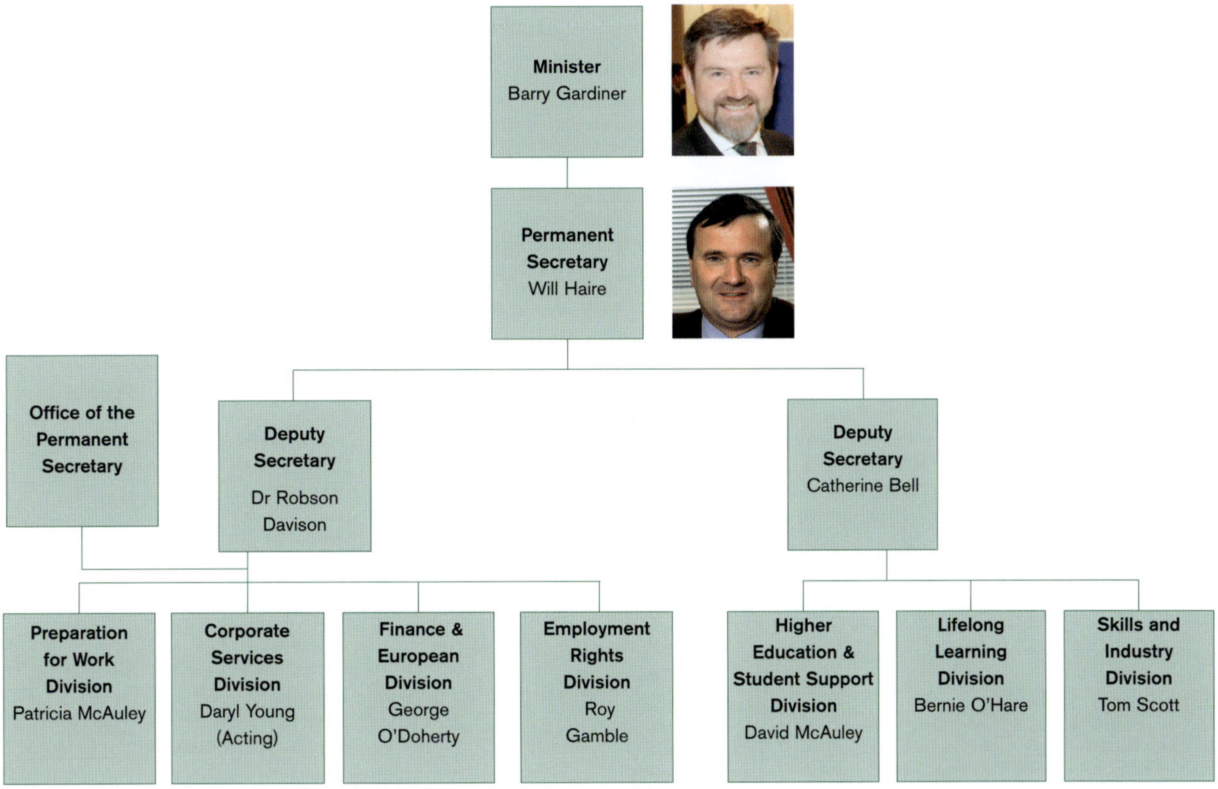


**Finance (2)**
Contact: Jim Russell
Tel: 028 9025 7651
Email: jim.russell@delni.gov.uk

**European Policy Unit**
Contact: Raymond Little
Tel: 028 9025 7988
Email: raymond.little@delni.gov.uk

**European Unit**
Contact: John Neill
Tel: 028 9025 7874
Email: john.neill@delni.gov.uk

### Employment Rights Division
Head of Division: Roy Gamble
Tel: 028 9025 7806
Email: roy.gamble@delni.gov.uk
Contact: Monica O'Kane
Tel: 028 9025 7948
Email: monica.okane.delni.gov.uk

Employment legislation covers individual and collective employment rights and means of redress when these are infringed, together with legislation relating to trade unions and the regulation of their affairs. Employment Rights Division has a programme of primary and subordinate legislation at various stages of completion. The Division administers the Redundancy Payments Service and has responsibility for supporting the Office of the Industrial Tribunals and the Fair Employment Tribunal (OITFET), the Industrial Court, the Labour Relations Agency (LRA), and the Certification Officer.

**Employment Rights (1)**
Contact: Tim Devine
Tel: 028 9025 7520
Email: tim.devine@delni.gov.uk

**Employment Rights (2)**
Contact: Valerie Reilly
Tel: 028 9025 7560
Email: valerie.reilly@delni.gov.uk

**Bill Team**
Contact: Lynne Taylor (acting)
Tel: 028 9025 7677
Email: lynne.taylor@delni.gov.uk

**Office of Industrial Tribunals and Fair Employment Tribunals**
Contact: Jim Walker
Tel: 028 9034 7454
Email: jim.walker@delni.gov.uk

### Head of Further & Higher Education, Skills and Industry Policy
Deputy Secretary: Catherine Bell
Tel: 028 9025 7805
Email: catherine.bell@delni.gov.uk

### Higher Education and Analytical Services Division
Head of Division: David McAuley
Tel: 028 9025 7811
Email: david.mcauley@delni.gov.uk
Contact: Christine McFarland
Tel: 028 9025 7886
Email: christine.mcfarland@delni.gov.uk

The Division is responsible for a broad range of policy initiatives aimed at sustaining an internationally competitive higher education sector in Northern Ireland. The Division operates under advice from the Northern Ireland Higher Education Council (NIHEC) and its remit includes: learning and teaching quality; university research and knowledge transfer; widening access and student finance. The Division also provides an economic and statistical research and evaluation service for the whole of the Department.

**Student Finance Branch**
Head of Unit: Sean McGarry
Tel: 028 9025 7712
Email: sean.mcgarry@delni.gov.uk

**Higher Education Finance Branch**
Head of Unit: Vacant
Contact: Bernard McClure
Tel: 028 9025 7718
Email: bernard.mcclure@delni.gov.uk

**Higher Education Research Policy Branch**
Head of Unit: Dr Linda Bradley
Tel: 028 9025 7607
Email: linda.bradley@delni.gov.uk

**Higher Education Policy Branch**
Head of Unit: Siobhan Logue
Tel: 028 9025 7573
Email: siobhan.logue@delni.gov.uk

**Tertiary Education Analytical Services Branch**
Head of Unit: Victor Dukelow
Tel: 028 9025 7610
Email: victor.dukelow@delni.gov.uk

**Research and Evaluation Branch**
Head of Unit: Dave Rogers
Tel: 028 9025 7510
Email: dave.rogers@delni.gov.uk

## Skills and Industry Division

Head of Division: Tom Scott
Tel 028 9025 7807
Email: tom.scott@delni.gov.uk

The Division is responsible for policy and programmes in relation to: Skills Strategy, including Sector Skills and Management Development; Careers and Guidance Services, Youth training including Jobskills and Modern Apprenticeships; Bridge to Employment initiative and a Supplier Services Branch which covers relationships with training providers.

**Management Development**
Contact: Paul Bryans (Acting)
Tel: 028 9044 1773
Email: paul.bryans@delni.gov.uk

**Sectoral Development**
Contact: Jim Hanna
Tel: 028 9044 1803
Email: jim.hanna@delni.gov.uk

**Supplier Services**
Contact: Ann Loney
Tel: 028 9044 1746
Email: ann.loney@delni.gov.uk

**Training Programmes/IFI**
Contact: Tommy McVeigh
Tel: 028 9044 1841
Email: tommy.mcveigh@delni.gov.uk

**Careers & Adult Guidance**
Contact: John McKeown
Tel: 028 9044 1840
Email: john.mckeown@delni.gov.uk

**Training Services**
Contact: Francis Creagh (Acting)
Tel: 028 9044 1834
Email: francis.creagh@delni.gov.uk

**Skills Unit**
Contact: Terry Morahan
Tel: 028 9044 1838
Email: terry.morahan@delni.gov.uk

## Lifelong Learning Division

Head of Division: Bernie O'Hare
Tel: 028 9025 7856
Email: bernie.ohare@delni.gov.uk

**Further Education Corporate Governance & Accountability**
Contact: Denis Lowry
Tel: 028 9025 7620
Fax: 028 9025 7529
Email: denis.lowry@delni.gov.uk

**Further Education Finance**
Contact: John McGuigan
Tel: 028 9025 7513
Email: john.mcguigan@delni.gov.uk

**Further Education Capital Development**
Contact: Tom Redmond
Tel: 028 9025 7546
Email: tom.redmond@delni.gov.uk

**Further Education Policy and Strategic Development**
Contact: Richard Kenny
Tel: 028 9025 7690
Email: richard.kenny@delni.gov.uk

**Essential Skills Branch**
Contact: Deirdre McGill
Tel: 028 9025 7785
Email: deirdre.mcgill@delni.gov.uk

**Learning and Curriculum Policy**
Contact: Marian Cree
Tel: 028 9025 7824
Email: marian.cree@delni.gov.uk

## Agencies, Non Departmental Public Bodies and other organisations within the Department for Employment and Learning

**Construction Industry Training Board**
Nutts Corner Training Centre
17 Dundrod Road, Crumlin, BT29 4SR
Tel: 028 9082 5466
Web: www.citbni.org.uk
Email: info@citbni.org.uk
Chief Executive: Allan McMullen

**Enterprise Ulster**
The Close, Ravenhill Reach
Belfast, BT6 8RB
Tel: 028 9073 6400
Web: www.enterpriseulster.co.uk
Email: hq@eulster.globalnet.co.uk
Chief Executive: Joe Eagleson

**Labour Relations Agency**
Head Office, 2-8 Gordon Street
Belfast, BT1 2LG
Tel: 028 9032 1442
Web: www.lra.org.uk
Email: info@lra.org.uk
Chief Executive: William Patterson

**Northern Ireland Higher Education Council**
39-49 Adelaide Street, Belfast, BT2 8FD
Tel: 028 9025 7886
Chairman: Tony Hopkins CBE
Contact: Christine McFarland
Tel: 028 9025 7886
Email: christine.mcfarland@delni.gov.uk

**Northern Ireland Industrial Court**
Room 204, Adelaide House
39-49 Adelaide Street
Belfast, BT2 8FD
Tel: 028 9025 7601
Web: www.delni.gov.uk/er
Senior Case Manager: Joanna Calixto

**Ulster Supported Employment Limited**
182-188 Cambrai Street
Belfast, BT13 3JH
Tel: 028 9035 6600
Web: www.usel.co.uk
Email: info@usel.co.uk
Chief Executive: Mitchell Wylie

## Department of Enterprise, Trade and Investment

Netherleigh House, Massey Avenue
Belfast, BT4 2JP
Tel: 028 9052 9900
Fax: 028 9052 9550
Web: www.detini.gov.uk

**Direct Rule Minister**: Barry Gardiner
Permanent Secretary: Bruce Robinson
Tel: 028 9052 9441
**Private Office**
Private Secretary: William Donaghy
Tel: 028 9052 9208
**Press Office**
Acting Press Officer: Anne Marting
Tel: 028 9052 9201

DETI is responsible for economic development policy, energy, telecommunications, tourism, mineral development, health and safety at work, Companies Registry, Insolvency Service, consumer affairs, social economy, professional economic advice and research and labour market and economic statistics services. Financial and personnel management services are provided centrally within the department.

DETI has four agencies to assist in strategy implementation.

- Invest Northern Ireland (Invest NI), which supports business growth and inward investment, promotes innovation, research and development and in-company training, encourages exports and supports local economic development and company start up:
- The Northern Ireland Tourist Board (NITB), which is responsible for the development, promotion and marketing of Northern Ireland as a tourist destination:
- The Health and Safety Executive for Northern Ireland (HSENI), which is responsible for health, safety and welfare at work: and
- The General Consumer Council for Northern Ireland (GCCNI), which is responsible for promoting and safeguarding the interests of consumers and campaigning for the best possible standards of service and protection.

### Policy Group
Director: Wilfie Hamilton
Tel: 028 9052 9203
Email: wilfie.hamilton@detini.gov.uk

### Strategic Policy:
Head of Division: Malcolm Briant
Tel: 028 9052 9202
Fax: 028 9052 9543
Email: malcolm.briant@detini.gov.uk

**Strategy Unit**
Principal: Rosemary Crawford
Tel: 028 9052 9416
Fax: 028 9052 9533
Email: rosemary.crawford@detini.gov.uk

**Policy Innovation Unit**
Principal: Mark Pinkerton
Tel: 028 9052 9267
Fax: 028 9052 9533
Email: mark.pinkerton@detini.gov.uk

**Planning Unit**
Principal: Paul Dolaghan (Acting)
Tel: 028 9052 9254
Fax: 028 9052 9533
Email: paul.dolaghan@detini.gov.uk

**Telecomms**
Principal: Anne Conaty
Tel: 028 9052 9448
Email: anne.conaty@detini.gov.uk

### Tourism, Agency Liaison & Equality
Head of Division: Robin McMinnis

**Tourism Policy**
Principal: Norman Houston
Tel: 028 9052 9404
Fax: 028 9052 9321
Email: norman.houston@detini.gov.uk

**Equality/New Human Rights/West Belfast & Greater Shankill Taskforces:**
Mike Maxwell
Tel: 028 9052 9226
Fax: 028 9052 9542
Email: mike.maxwell@detini.gov.uk

**Policy Services Unit/IFI BEP/ State Aids**
Principal: Ashley Ray
Tel: 028 9052 9634
Fax: 028 9052 9542
Email: ashley.ray@detini.gov.uk

**Minerals**
Principal: Jim King
Tel: 028 9052 9367
Fax: 028 9052 9549
Email: jim.king@detini.gov.uk

**Invest NI/InterTradeIreland Unit**
Principal: Gerry McGeown
Tel: 028 9052 9247
Fax: 028 9052 9550
Email: gerry.mcgeown@detini.gov.uk

**Tourism Special Projects**
Principal: Ciaran McGarrity
Tel: 028 9052 9566
Fax: 028 9052 9550

### Energy
Head of Division: Jenny Pyper
Tel: 028 9052 9577
Fax: 028 9052 9549
Email: jenny.pyper@detini.gov.uk

**Gas Regulation**
Principal: Tony Doherty
Tel: 028 9052 9272
Fax: 028 9052 9549
Email: tony.doherty@detini.gov.uk

**Electricity Regulation**
Acting Principal: George McNally
Tel: 028 9052 9281
Fax: 028 9052 9549
Email: george.mcnally@detini.gov.uk

**Sustainable Energy**
Principal: David Stanley
Tel: 028 9052 9240
Fax: 028 9052 9549
Email: david.stanley@detini.gov.uk

**All Island Energy**
Principal: Peter Hughes
Tel: 028 9052 9405
Fax: 028 9052 9549
Email: peter.hughes@detini.gov.uk

### Economics and Statistics Division
Head of Division: Fiona Hepper
Tel: 028 9052 9215
Fax: 028 9052 9550
Email: fiona.hepper@detini.gov.uk

**Economics**
Principal Economist: Philip Rodgers
Tel: 028 9052 9371
Fax: 028 9052 9542
Email: philip.rodgers@detini.gov.uk

**Statistics Research**
Senior Principal Statistician:
James Gillan
Tel: 028 9052 9573
Email: james.gillan@detini.gov.uk

Principal Statistician:
Joanne McCutcheon
Tel: 028 9052 9425
Email: joanne.mccutcheon@detini.gov.uk

## Department of Enterprise, Trade and Investment Organisation Chart

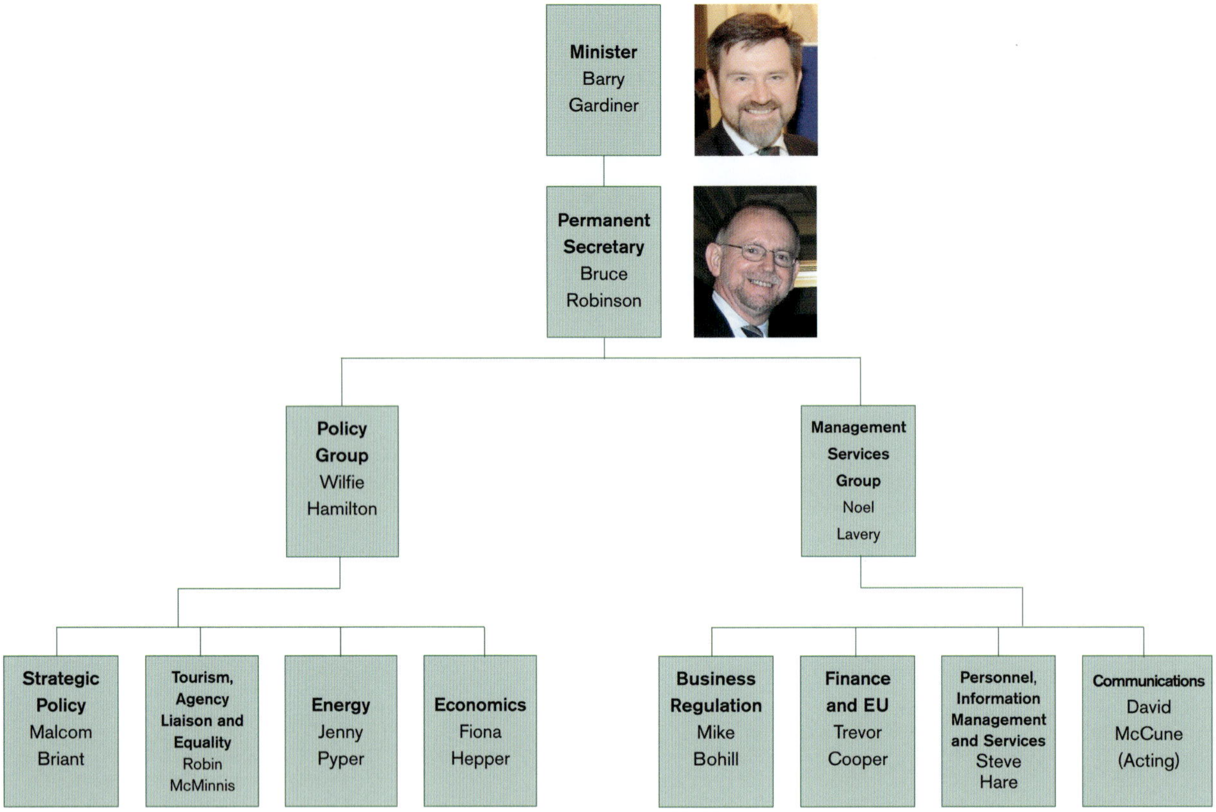


### Management Services Group
Director: Noel Lavery
Tel: 028 9052 9226
Email: noel.lavery@detini.gov.uk

### Business Regulation
Head of Division: Mike Bohill
Email: mike.bohill@detini.gov.uk

**Insolvency**
Director: Reg Nesbitt
Email: reg.nesbitt@detini.gov.uk
Principals: Joe Hasson, Leslie Gawley

**Consumer Affairs**
Principal: David Livingstone

**Companies Registry**
Principal: Rosaleen McMullan

**Social Economy**
Principal: Anne-Marie Davison

**Company Law**
Contact: Juliet Whitford
Tel: 028 9025 2548
Fax: 028 9025 2481
Email: juliet.whitford@detini.gov.uk

### Finance and EU
Head of Division: Trevor Cooper

**Finance Branch and Accounts Branch**
Principal: Rodney Brown

**Resource Accounting**
Principal: Rodney Brown

**Invest Northern Ireland Accounts Project**
Principal: Erroll Crooks

**Internal Audit**
Principal: Alan Magee

**European Programmes**
Principal: Howard Keery

**Accountability and Invest NI Casework**
Principal: Alberta Pauley

**Finance**
Principal: Bernie Brankin

### Personnel, Information Management and Services
Head of Division: Steve Hare
Tel: 028 9052 9402
Email: steve.hare@detini.gov.uk

**Personnel**
Principal: Alan Lamont
Tel: 028 9052 9339

**Development and Training**
Principal: Paula McCreary
Tel: 028 9090 5297
Email: paula.mccreary@detinig.vo.uk

**Corporate Services**
Principal: Terry Long
Tel: 028 9052 9337

**Information Management**
Principal: Joe O'Hare
Tel: 028 9052 9596
Email: joe.o'hare@detini.gov.uk

**Information Technology**
Principal: Pat Cunningham
Tel: 028 9052 9253
Email: pat.cunningham@detini.gov.uk

### Communications
Head of Division (Acting):
David McCune
Tel: 028 9052 9422
Fax: 028 9052 9894
Email: david.mccune@detini.gov.uk

**Press Office**
Acting Information Officer: Anne Martin
Tel: 028 9052 9263
Fax: 028 9052 9546
Email: anne.martin@detini.gov.uk

**Private Office/Central Management & Public Appointments/Parliamentary Support & Legislative Monitoring**
Principal (Acting): John Simms
Tel: 028 9052 9401
Fax: 028 9052 9550
Email: john.simms@detini.gov.uk

**Marketing and Communication**
Deputy Principal: Angela Jackson
Tel: 028 9052 9536
Fax: 028 9052 9550
Email: angela.jackson@detini.gov.uk

### Agencies, Non Departmental Public Bodies and other organisations within the Department of Enterprise, Trade and Investment

**General Consumer Council for Northern Ireland**
116 Holywood Road, Belfast, BT4 1NY
Tel: 028 9067 2488
Fax: 028 9065 7701
Web: www.gccni.org.uk
Chief Executive: Eleanor Gill

**Health and Safety Executive for Northern Ireland**
83 Ladas Drive, Belfast, BT6 9FR
Tel: 028 9024 3249
Fax: 028 9023 5383
Web: www.hseni.gov.uk
Email: hseni@detini.gov.uk
Chief Executive: Jim Keyes

**Inter*Trade*Ireland**
Old Gasworks Business Park
Kilmorey Street, Newry, BT34 2DE
Tel: 028 3083 4100
Fax: 028 3083 4155
Web: www.intertradeireland.com
Email: info@intertradeireland.com
Chief Executive: Liam Nellis

**Invest Northern Ireland**
Goodwood House, 44-58 May Street
Belfast, BT1 4NN
Tel: 028 9023 9090
Fax: 028 9049 0490
Web: www.investni.com
Chief Executive: Leslie Morrison
Managing Directors: Colin Lewis, Tracy Meharg, Leslie Ross, Terri Scott

**Northern Ireland Tourist Board**
St Anne's Court, 59 North Street
Belfast, BT1 1NB
Tel: 028 9023 1221
Fax: 028 9024 0960
Web: www.nitb.com
Chief Executive: Alan Clarke

**Tourism Ireland Limited**
Beresford House, 2 Beresford Road
Coleraine, BT52 1GE
Tel: 028 7035 9200
Fax: 028 7032 6932
Chief Executive: Paul O'Toole

# Department of the Environment (DOE)

Clarence Court
10-18 Adelaide Street
Belfast, BT2 8GB
Tel: 028 9054 0540
Fax: 028 9054 0024
Web: www.doeni.gov.uk
Email: cmb@doeni.gov.uk

**Minister:** Angela Smith
**Permanent Secretary:** Stephen Peover
Tel: 028 9054 0002
Fax: 028 9054 0082
Email: stephen.peover@doeni.gov.uk

**Private Office**
Private Secretary: Stuart McDougall
Tel: 028 9054 1166
Email: stuart.mcdougall@doeni.gov.uk

**Press Office**
Contact: Brian Kirk
Tel: 028 9054 0013
Fax: 028 9054 1199
Email: brian.kirk@doeni.gov.uk

Contact: Paddy Murphy
Tel: 028 9054 0014
Fax: 028 9054 1199
Email: paddy.murphy@doeni.gov.uk

The Department's aim is to improve the quality of life in Northern Ireland, now and for the future, by promoting a better and safer environment and supporting effective and efficient local government.

The work of the Department revolves around four main objectives: -

- to protect, conserve and enhance the natural environment and built heritage;
- to improve the quality of life of the people of Northern Ireland by planning and managing development in ways which are sustainable and which contribute to creating a better environment;
- to reduce road casualties;
- to support a system of Local Government which meets the needs of residents and ratepayers.

**Functions**
Environmental Policy Group; Local Government Division; Driver & Vehicle Testing Agency; Driver and Vehicle Licensing Northern Ireland; Planning Service; Road Safety and Vehicle Standards Division.

## Corporate Services

Director: Dr Murray Power
Tel: 028 9054 0820
Fax: 028 9027 9430
Email: murray.power@doeni.gov.uk

## Environmental Policy Group

Deputy Secretary: Felix Dillon
Tel: 028 9054 0649
Email: felix.dillon@doeni.gov.uk

Director of Environmental Policy:
Ian Maye
Tel: 028 9054 4525
Fax: 028 9054 4564
Email: ian.maye@doeni.gov.uk

Director of Sustainable Development:
Judena Goldring
Tel: 028 9025 7360
Fax: 028 9025 7390
Email: judena.goldring@doeni.gov.uk

Environmental Policy Group is tasked with developing policy and drafting legislation on a broad range of environmental issues. It also has lead responsibility for promoting sustainable development and the development of and oversight of Northern Ireland's Sustainable Development Strategy.

Environmental Policy Division deals with policy on waste management, air quality, noise, litter, dangerous wild animals and environmental information issues. Sustainable Development Division, in addition to its sustainable development responsibilities, including climate change and greening government, is responsible for policy on water quality, natural and built heritage and biotechnology. Much of the work centres on contributing to the development of UK and European sustainable development and environmental policy and on transposing the requirements of EU Environmental Directives into Northern Ireland law.

## Local Government and Safety Group

Deputy Secretary: Cynthia Smith
Tel: 028 90540001
Fax: 028 9054 1153
Email: cynthia.smith@doeni.gov.uk

## Local Government Division

Director of Local Government:
John Ritchie
Tel: 028 9054 0844
Email: john.ritchie@doeni.gov.uk
Web: www.doeni.gov.uk/lgd

Local Government Division aims to support a system of local government which meets the needs of residents, ratepayers and users of district council services and facilities.

## Road Safety and Vehicle Standards Division (RSVSD)

Director: Wesley Shannon
Tel: 028 9054 0843
Fax: 028 9054 0775
Email: wesley.shannon@doeni.gov.uk
Web: www.doeni.gov.uk/roadsafety

Road Safety and Vehicle Standards Division has responsibility for promotion of road safety and for delivery through education, training and publicity, improvements in road user attitudes and behaviour, to contribute to a reduction in road casualties.

The Division is also tasked with developing policy and legislation to ensure the proper regulation of drivers, vehicles and transport operators.

## Department of the Environment Organisation Chart

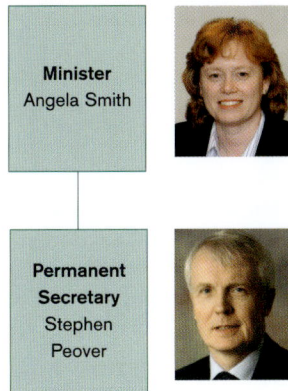

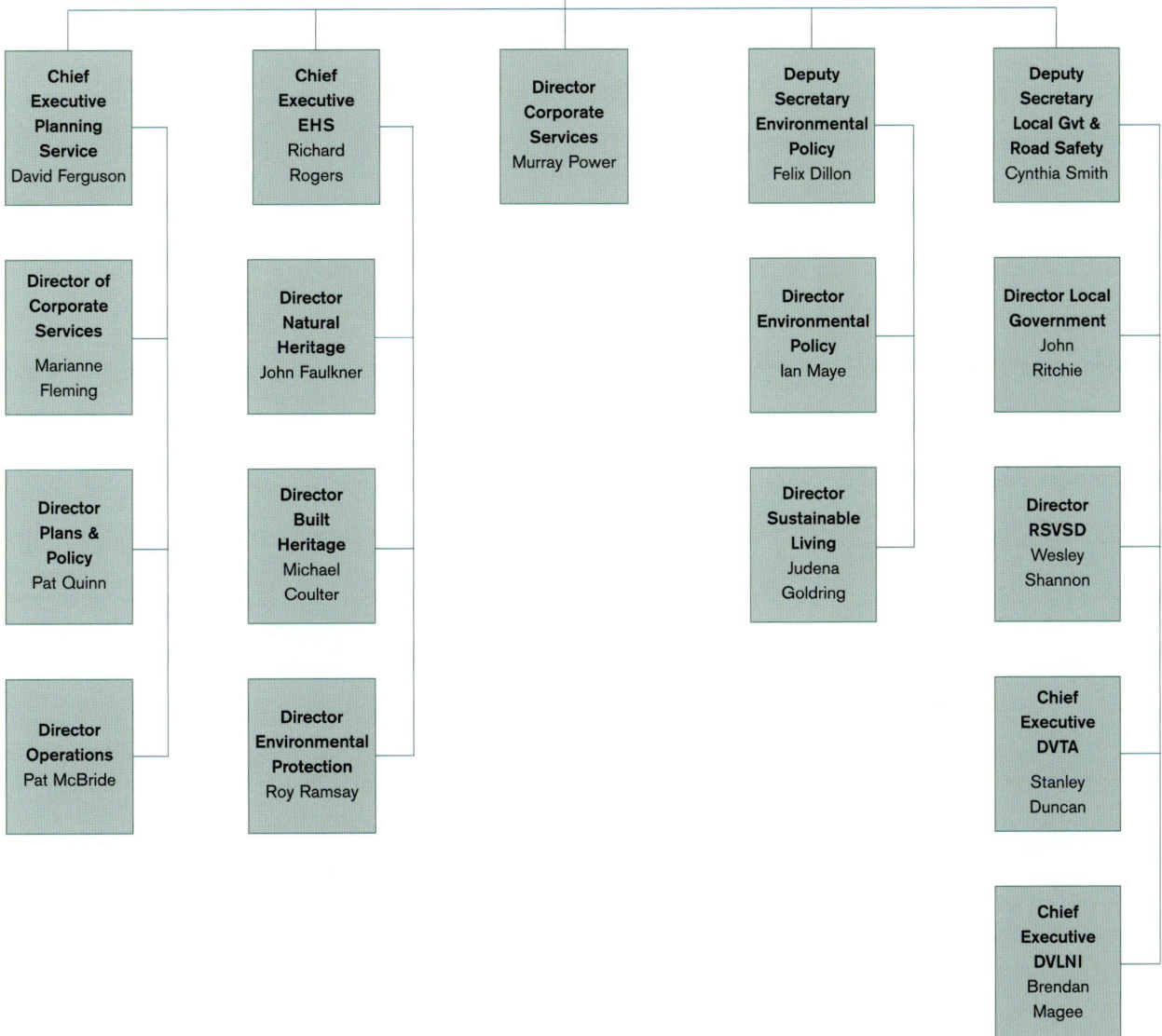

- **Minister** Angela Smith

  - **Permanent Secretary** Stephen Peover

    - **Chief Executive Planning Service** David Ferguson
      - **Director of Corporate Services** Marianne Fleming
      - **Director Plans & Policy** Pat Quinn
      - **Director Operations** Pat McBride
    - **Chief Executive EHS** Richard Rogers
      - **Director Natural Heritage** John Faulkner
      - **Director Built Heritage** Michael Coulter
      - **Director Environmental Protection** Roy Ramsay
    - **Director Corporate Services** Murray Power
    - **Deputy Secretary Environmental Policy** Felix Dillon
      - **Director Environmental Policy** Ian Maye
      - **Director Sustainable Living** Judena Goldring
    - **Deputy Secretary Local Gvt & Road Safety** Cynthia Smith
      - **Director Local Government** John Ritchie
      - **Director RSVSD** Wesley Shannon
      - **Chief Executive DVTA** Stanley Duncan
      - **Chief Executive DVLNI** Brendan Magee

## Executive Agencies

### Driver and Vehicle Licensing Northern Ireland (DVLNI)

County Hall, Castlerock Road
Coleraine, BT51 3TA
Web: www.doeni.gov.uk/dvlni
Email: dvlni@doeni.gov.uk
Chief Executive: Brendan Magee
Tel: 028 703 41249
Fax: 028 703 41424
Email: brendan.magee@doeni.gov.uk

Director of Development: Trevor Evans
Tel: 028 703 41248
Fax: 028 703 41424
Email: trevor.evans@doeni.gov.uk

Director of Drivers and Road Transport Licensing: Colin Campbell
Tel: 028 703 41448
Fax: 028 703 41424
Email: colin.campbell@doeni.gov.uk

Director of Programmes:
Bernie Cosgrove
Tel: 028 703 41242
Fax: 028 703 41424
Email: bernie.cosgrove@doeni.gov.uk

Director of Vehicle Licensing:
Ann McCabe
Tel: 028 703 41206
Fax: 028 703 41424
Email: ann.mccabe@doeni.gov.uk

Director of Corporate Services:
Seamus McClean
Tel: 028 703 41368
Fax: 028 703 41424
Email: seamus.mcclean@doeni.gov.uk

Director of Finance: Lucia O'Connor
Tel: 028 703 41352
Fax: 028 703 41424
Email: lucia.o'connor@doeni.gov.uk

Driver Licensing Division
Tel: 028 7034 1469
Fax: 028 7034 1398
Email: dvlni@doeni.gov.uk

**Vehicle Licensing Division**
Tel: 028 7034 1461
Fax: 028 7034 1422
Email: dvlni@doeni.gov.uk

**Vehicle Licensing Central Office**
Telephone Re-Licensing Section
Tel: 028 7034 1514
Email: dvlni@doeni.gov.uk

**Sale of Mark Section**
Tel: 028 7034 1244
Fax: 028 703 41441
Email: dvlni@doeni.gov.uk

**Commercial Operator Licensing**
148-158 Corporation Street
Belfast, BT1 3DH
Tel: 028 9025 4100
Fax: 028 9025 4086
Email: dvlni@doeni.gov.uk

**Local DVLNI Offices**
Opening hours for all local offices:
9.15am – 4.00pm

*Armagh*
Dobbin Centre
Dobbin Lane, Armagh, BT61 7QP
Tel: 028 3752 7305
Fax: 028 3752 8721
Contact: Jill Kane
Email: jill.kane@doeni.gov.uk

*Ballymena*
County Hall, Galgorm Road
Ballymena, BT42 1HN
Tel: 028 2565 3333
Fax: 028 2566 2067
Contact: Ronnie Rowe
Email: ronnie.rowe@doeni.gov.uk

*Belfast*
Royston House, Upper Queen Street,
Belfast, BT1 6FA
Tel: 028 9054 2042
Fax: 028 9054 7379
Contact: Christine Clark
Email: christine.clark@doeni.gov.uk

*Coleraine*
County Hall, Castlerock Road, Coleraine
Tel: 028 7034 1417
Fax: 028 7034 1418
Contact: Clare Wilson
Email: clare.wilson@doeni.gov.uk

*Downpatrick*
Rathkeltair House, Market Street,
Downpatrick, BT30 6AJ
Tel: 028 4461 2211
Fax: 028 4461 8089
Contact: Mary Keenan
Email: mary.keenan@doeni.gov.uk

*Enniskillen*
County Buildings
East Bridge Street
Enniskillen, BT74 7BW
Tel: 028 6634 6555
Tel: 028 6632 2750
Contact: Kate Charity
Email: kate.charity@doeni.gov.uk

*Londonderry*
Orchard House, 40 Foyle Street,
Londonderry, BT48 6AT
Tel: 028 7131 9900
Fax: 028 71319819
Contact: Terence Healey
Email: terence.healey@doeni.gov.uk

Omagh
Boaz House, 15 Scarffes Entry
Omagh, BT78 1JE
Tel: 028 8225 4700
Fax: 028 8225 4711
Contact: Annie Alexander
Email: annie.alexander@doeni.gov.uk

### Driver and Vehicle Testing Agency (DVTA)

Balmoral Road, Belfast, BT12 6QL
Tel: 028 9068 1831
Fax: 028 9066 5520
Web: www.doeni.gov.uk/dvta
Chief Executive: Stanley Duncan
Tel: 028 9054 7943
Fax: 028 9027 9464
Email: stanley.duncan@doeni.gov.uk

Director of Finance: Colin Berry
Tel: 028 9054 7934
Fax: 028 9066 5520
Email: colin.berry@doeni.gov.uk

Director of Personnel & Customer Services: John Crosby
Tel: 028 9054 7987
Fax: 028 9054 7950
Email: john.crosby@doeni.gov.uk

Director of Corporate Services:
Trevor Hassin
Fax: 028 9066 5520
Email: trevor.hassin@doeni.gov.uk

Director of Operations: Martin Woods (Acting)
Tel: 028 9054 7982
Fax: 028 9066 5520
Email: martin.woods@doeni.gov.uk

Director of Technical Policy and Legislation: Alastair Peoples
Tel: 028 9054 7942
Fax: 028 9054 7964
Email: alastair.peoples@doeni.gov.uk
Director of Compliance & Planning:
David Wilson
Tel: 028 9054 1827
Fax: 028 9066 5520
Email: david.wilson@doeni.gov.uk

**Local DVTA Offices**

*Armagh*
47 Hamiltonsbawn Road
Armagh, BT60 1HW
Tel: 028 3752 2699
Fax: 028 9025 4086
Email: armaghde.dvta@doeni.gov.uk

*Ballymena*
Pennybridge Industrial Estate
Larne Road, Ballymena, BT42 3ER
Tel: 028 2565 6801
Fax: 028 9025 4086
Email: ballymenade.dvta@doeni.gov.uk

*Belfast*
Balmoral Road, Belfast, BT12 6QL
Tel: 028 9068 1831
Fax: 028 9025 4086
Email: belfastde.dvta@doeni.gov.uk

*Coleraine*
2 Loughan Hill Industrial Estate
Gateside Road, Coleraine, BT52 2NJ
Tel: 028 7034 3819
Fax: 028 9025 4086
Email: colerainede.dvta@doeni.gov.uk

*Cookstown*
Sandholes Road, Cookstown, BT80 9AR
Tel: 028 8676 4809
Fax: 028 9025 4086
Email: cookstownde.dvta@doeni.gov.uk

*Craigavon*
3 Diviny Drive
Carn Industrial Estate
Craigavon, BT63 5RY
Tel: 028 3833 6188
Fax: 028 9025 4086
Email: craigavonde.dvta@doeni.gov.uk

*Downpatrick*
Cloonagh Road, Flying Horse Road
Downpatrick, BT30 6DU
Tel: 028 4461 4565
Fax: 028 9025 4086
Email: downpatrickde.dvta@doeni.gov.uk

*Enniskillen*
Chanterhill, Enniskillen, BT74 6DE
Tel: 028 6632 2871
Fax: 028 9025 4086
Email: enniskillende.dvta@doeni.gov.uk

*Larne*
Ballyboley Road, Ballyloran
Larne, BT40 2SY
Tel: 028 2827 8808
Fax: 028 9025 4086
Email: larnede.dvta@doeni.gov.uk

*Lisburn*
Ballinderry Industrial Estate
Ballinderry Road, Lisburn, BT28 2SA
Tel: 028 9266 3151
Fax: 028 9025 4086
Email: lisburnde.dvta@doeni.govuk

*Londonderry*
New Buildings Industrial Estate
Victoria Road, Londonderry
Tel: 028 7134 3674
Fax: 028 9025 4086
Email: londonderryde.dvta@doeni.gov.uk

*Mallusk*
Commercial Way
Hydepark Industrial Estate
Newtownabbey, BT36 8YY
Tel: 028 9084 2111
Fax: 028 9025 4086
Email: malluskde.dvta@doeni.gov.uk

*Newry*
51 Rathfriland Road, Newry, BT34 1LD
Tel: 028 3026 2853
Fax: 028 9025 4086
Email: newryde.dvta@doeni.gov.uk

*Newtownards*
Jubilee Road, Newtownards, BT23 4XP
Tel: 028 9181 3064
Fax: 028 9025 4086
Email: newtownardsde.dvta@doeni.gov.uk

*Omagh*
Gortrush Industrial Estate, Derry Road
Omagh, BT78 5EJ
Tel: 028 8224 2540
Fax: 028 9025 4086
Email: omaghde.dvta@doeni.gov.uk

## Environment and Heritage Service

Chief Executive: Richard Rogers
Tel: 028 9054 6570
Fax: 028 9054 6513
Email: richard.rogers@doeni.gov.uk

Director of Built Heritage:
Michael Coulter
Tel: 028 9054 3029
Fax: 028 9054 3135
Email: michael.coulter@doeni.gov.uk

Director of Corporate Services:
Damian Campbell
Tel: 028 9054 6679
Fax: 028 9054 6512
Email: damian.campbell@doeni.gov.uk

Director of Environmental Protection:
Dr Roy Ramsay
Fax: 028 9054 6512
Email: roy.ramsay@doeni.gov.uk

Director of Natural Heritage:
Dr John Faulkner
Tel: 028 9054 6571
Fax: 028 9054 6512
Email: john.faulkner@doeni.gov.uk

**Finance, Industrial Pollution and Radiochemical Inspectorate and, Water Management**
Calvert House, 23 Castle Place
Belfast, BT1 1FY
Tel: 028 9025 4754
Fax: 028 9025 4793 / 4865 / 4700

**Air and Environmental Quality, Biodiversity, Conservation Designations and Protection, Conservation Science, Co-ordination Unit, Corporate Communications, Countryside and Coast, Drinking Water Inspectorate, Regional Operations, Waste Management**
Commonwealth House, 35 Castle Street
Belfast, BT1 1GU
Tel: 028 9025 1477
Fax: 028 9054 6660

**Historic Monuments and Buildings**
Waterman House, 5-33 Hill Street,
Belfast, BT1 2LA
Tel: 028 9054 3076
Fax: 028 9054 3102
3080

**Personnel and Development Service**
6th Floor, Royston House, Upper Queen Street, Belfast, BT1 6FD
Tel: 028 9025 1477
Fax: 028 9054 2086

**Water Management (Lisburn)**
17 Antrim Road, Lisburn, BT28 3AB
Tel: 028 9262 3100
Fax: 028 9262 3225

Environment and Heritage Service (EHS) takes the lead in advising on, and in implementing, the Government's environmental policy and strategy in Northern Ireland.

The Agency carries out a range of activities, which promote the Government's key themes of sustainable development, biodiversity and climate change. Our overall aims are to protect and conserve Northern Ireland's natural heritage and built environment, to control and regulate pollution and to promote the wider appreciation of the environment and best environmental practices.

## Planning Service

Millennium House
17-25 Great Victoria Street
Belfast, BT2 7BN
Tel: 028 9041 6700
Fax: 028 9041 6983
Web: www.planningni.gov.uk
Chief Executive: David Ferguson
Tel: 028 9041 6993
Email: david.ferguson@doeni.gov.uk

Planning Service is responsible for developing, and implementing, Government planning policies and development plans in Northern Ireland. Our aim is to plan and manage development in ways which will contribute to a quality environment and seek to meet the economic and social aspirations of present and future generations.

Director Corporate Services:
Marianne Fleming
Tel: 028 9041 6994
Fax: 028 9041 6983
Email: marianne.fleming@doeni.gov.uk

Director Planning Policy: Pat Quinn
Tel: 028 9041 6528
Fax: 028 9041 6983
Email: pat.quinn@doeni.gov.uk

Director Operations: Pat McBride
Tel: 028 9041 6526
Fax: 028 9041 6983
Email: pat.mcbride@doeni.gov.uk

Professional Services Manager:
Anne Garvey
Tel: 028 9041 6995
Fax: 028 9041 6983
Email: anne.garvey@doeni.gov.uk

**Divisional Planning Offices**

*Ballymena*
County Hall, 182 Galgorm Hall,
Ballymena, BT42 1QF
Tel: 028 2565 3333
Fax: 028 2566 2127
Divisional Planning Manager:
Helena O'Toole

*Belfast*
Bedford House, 16-22 Bedford Street,
Belfast, BT2 7FD
Tel: 028 9025 2800
Fax: 028 9025 2828
Divisional Planning Manager: Vacant

*Craigavon*
Marlborough House, Central Way
Craigavon, BT64 1AD
Tel: 028 3834 1144
Fax: 028 3834 1065
Divisional Planning Manager:
Hilary Heslip

*Downpatrick*
Rathkeltair House, Market Street,
Downpatrick, BT30 6EJ
Tel: 028 4461 2211
Fax: 028 4461 8196
Divisional Planning Manager:
Clifford McIlwaine

*Londonderry*
Orchard House, 40 Foyle Street
Londonderry, BT48 6AT
Tel: 028 7131 9900
Fax: 028 7131 9777
Divisional Planning Manager:
Mary McIntyre

*Omagh*
County Hall, Drumragh Avenue
Omagh, BT79 7AE
Tel: 028 8225 4000
Fax: 028 8225 4009
Divisional Planning Manager:
Brian Hughes

**Sub-Divisional Planning Offices**

*Coleraine*
County Hall, Castlerock Road
Coleraine, BT51 3HS
Tel: 028 7034 1300
Fax: 028 7034 1434
Divisional Planning Manager:
Mary McIntyre

*Enniskillen*
County Buildings, 15 East Bridge Street
Enniskillen, BT74 7BW
Tel: 028 6634 6555
Fax: 028 6634 6550
Divisional Planning Manager:
Brian Hughes

## Non-Departmental Public Bodies

### Council for Nature Conservation and the Countryside (CNCC)

Waterman House, 5-33 Hill Street
Belfast, BT1 2LA
Tel: 028 9054 3076
Fax: 028 9054 3047
Email: secretariat-hillst@doeni.gov.uk
Chairman: Dr Lucinda Blakiston Houston

### Historic Buildings Council

Secretariat, Waterman House
5-33 Hill Street, BT1 2LA
Tel: 028 9054 3076
Fax: 028 9054 3047
Email: secretariat-hillst@doeni.gov.uk
Chairman: Ian McQuiston

### Historic Monuments Council

Secretariat, Waterman House
5-33 Hill Street, BT1 2LA
Tel: 028 9054 3076
Fax: 028 9054 3047
Email: secretariat-hillst@doeni.gov.uk
Chairman: Richard Black

### Local Government Staff Commission

Commission House
18-22 Gordon Street, Belfast, BT1 2LG
Tel: 028 9031 3200
Fax: 028 9031 3151
Web: www.lgsc.org.uk
Email: info@lgsc.org.uk
Chief Executive: Adrian Kerr

### Northern Ireland Local Government Officers Superannuation Committee

Templeton House, 411 Holywood Road,
Belfast, BT4 2LP
Tel: 028 9076 8025
Fax: 028 9076 8790
Web: www.nilgosc.org.uk
Email: info@nilgosc.org.uk
Chairman: John Galbraith

### Waste Management Advisory Board for Northern Ireland

Waterman House, 5-33 Hill Street,
Belfast, BT1 2LA
Tel: 028 9054 3086
Fax: 028 9054 3106
Email: wmabni@doeni.gov.uk
Chairman: Professor Deborah Boyd

## Department of Finance and Personnel

Rathgael House
Balloo Road, Bangor, BT19 7NA
Tel: 028 9127 9279
Fax: 028 9185 8104
Web: www.dfpni.gov.uk

**Direct Rule Minister:** Ian Pearson MP
**Private Office:**
Private Secretary: David McCreedy
Tel: 028 9052 9140
Email: private.office@dfpni.gov.uk

**Permanent Secretary**: John Hunter
Tel 028 9185 8166
Email: perm.sec@dfpni.gov.uk
**Second Permanent Secretary:**
Dr Andrew McCormick
Tel 028 9052 7437
Email: andrew.mccormick@dfpni.gov.uk

The Department of Finance and Personnel, or DFP, has a wide range of functions, many of which are carried out centrally either by the department directly or through an agency on behalf of the Civil Service in Northern Ireland.

DFP is responsible for public expenditure, including the formulation of an annual Budget. It seeks to secure appropriate funding from various sources, including the European Union. It is also responsible for personnel, which translates as the general management of the Civil Service (including the areas of policy, pay, recruitment and security). The Department is also responsible for law reform and the provision of legal services to other Northern Ireland departments.

The Department provides procurement services for goods, services and works to the Northern Ireland government departments and their associated public bodies. It is also responsible for the development of procurement policy for the Civil Service in Northern Ireland and the dissemination of best practice and provides a single point of contact for advice on procurement matters.

It provides a valuation service to the public sector, and through the Rate Collection Agency (RCA), collects rates in Northern Ireland. The Department is also responsible for the Land Registers of Northern Ireland, and also provides a range of design, maintenance and advisory services on construction matters to the Northern Ireland public sector.

DFP oversees the work of NISRA, the Northern Ireland Statistics and Research Agency, which provides a service to support the development, monitoring and evaluation of social and economic policy, as well as providing information to the general public, and organising the Census of Population.

### Central Finance Group

Budget Director: Leo O'Reilly
Tel: 028 9127 7601
Fax: 028 9127 7672
Email: leo.o'reilly@dpni.gov.uk

**Central Expenditure Division**
Head of Division: Richard Pengelly
Tel: 028 9185 8240
Fax: 028 9185 8262
Email: richard.pengelly@dfpni.gov.uk

**European Union Division**
Head of Division: Bill Pauley
Tel: 028 9052 3707
Fax: 028 9052 3949
Email; bill.pauley@dfpni.gov.uk

**Rating Policy Division**
Head of Division: Brian McClure
Tel: 028 9127 7668
Fax: 028 9185 8008
Email: brian.mcclure@dpni.gov.uk

**Strategic Policy Division**
Head of Division: Michael Brennan
Tel: 028 9185 8151
Fax: 028 9185 8098
Email: michael.brennan@dfpni.gov.uk

### Treasury Officer of Accounts:

David Thomson
Tel: 028 9185 8150
Fax: 028 9185 8261
Email: david.thomson@dfpni.gov.uk

**Supply 1** (responsible for DCAL, DETI, DARD, OFMDFM and Minor Departments)
Head of Division: Jack Layberry
Tel: 028 9185 8212
Fax: 028 9185 8262
Email: jack.layberry@dfpni.gov.uk

**Supply 2** (responsible for DRD, DoE and DHSSPS)
Head of Division: Mary McIvor
Tel: 028 9185 8205
Fax: 028 9185 8262
Email: mary.mcivor@dfpni.gov.uk

**Supply 3** (responsible for DE, DEL, DFP and DSD)
Head of Division: Ciaran Doran
Tel: 028 9127 7653
Fax: 028 9185 8262
Email: ciaran.doran@dfpni.gov.uk

**Accountability and Accountancy Services Division**
Head of Division: Derek Lynn
Tel: 028 9185 8203
Fax: 028 9127 7690
Email: derek.lynn@dfpni.gov.uk

### Central Personnel Group

Director: Linda Brown
Tel: 028 9052 6166
Fax: 028 9052 6466
Email: linda.brown@dfpni.gov.uk

**Equal Opportunities and Appointments Division**
Head of Division: John McKervill
Tel: 028 9052 6161
Fax: 028 9052 6466
Email: john.mckervill@dfpni.gov.uk

**Employment Conditions and Pensions Division**
Head of Division: Michael Daly
Tel: 028 9052 6168
Fax: 028 9052 6407
Email: michael.daly@dfpni.gov.uk

**Pay and Development Division**
Head of Division: Gareth Johnston
Tel: 028 9052 6169
Fax: 028 9052 6407
Email: gareth.johnston@dfpni.gov.uk

**Information Management Services Division**
Head of Division: Robin Foote
Tel: 028 9052 6696
Fax: 028 9052 6833
Email: robin.foote@dfpni.gov.uk

### Central Procurement Directorate

Director: John McMillen
Tel: 9082 3151
Fax: 028 9082 3199
Email: john.mcmillen@dfpni.gov.uk

Supplies and Services Division
Deputy Director: Roy Bell
Tel: 028 9052 6622
Fax: 028 9052 6440
Email: roy.bell@dfpni.gov.uk

## Department of Finance and Personnel Organisation Chart

- **Minister** Ian Pearson 
  - **Permanent Secretary** John Hunter 
    - **2nd Permanent Secretary** Andrew McCormick
      - **Central Finance Group**
        - **Budget Director** Leo O'Reilly
          - **Central Expenditure Division** Richard Pengelly
          - **Strategic Policy Division** Michael Brennan
          - **European Division** Bill Pauley
          - **Rating Policy Division** Brian McClure
        - **Supply Director** David Thomson
          - **Supply 1** Jack Layberry
          - **Supply 2** Mary McIvor
          - **Supply 3** Ciaran Doran
          - **Head of Accountability & Accountancy Division** Name
      - **Central Procurement Directorate** John McMillen
        - **Supplies & Services Division** Roy Bell
        - **Professional Services Division** Sid Fairfield
        - **Construction & Advisory Division** Des Armstrong
        - **Policy and Support Division** Fergus Devit
    - **DFP Agencies**
    - **Office and Law Reform Director** Ethne Harkness
      - **Senior Legal Assistant** Laura McPolin
      - **Senior Legal Assistant** Michael Foster
      - **Senior Legal Assistant** Orla Ward
    - **Central Personnel Group** Linda Brown
      - **Equal Opportunities & Appointments Division** John McKervill
      - **Employment Conditions & Pensions Division** Michael Daly
      - **Pay & Development Division** Gareth Johnston
      - **Information Management Services Division** Robin Foote
    - **Departmental Solicitors Office** Robin Cole
      - **Deputy Head of Legal Services** Brian Doherty
    - **Corporate Services Group** Chris Thompson
      - **Central Support Division** Norman Taylor
      - **Finance & Information Services Division** Jim O'Hagan
      - **Office Estates & Building Standards Division** Bernie Stuart
      - **Department Personnel Division** Gerry Cosgrave

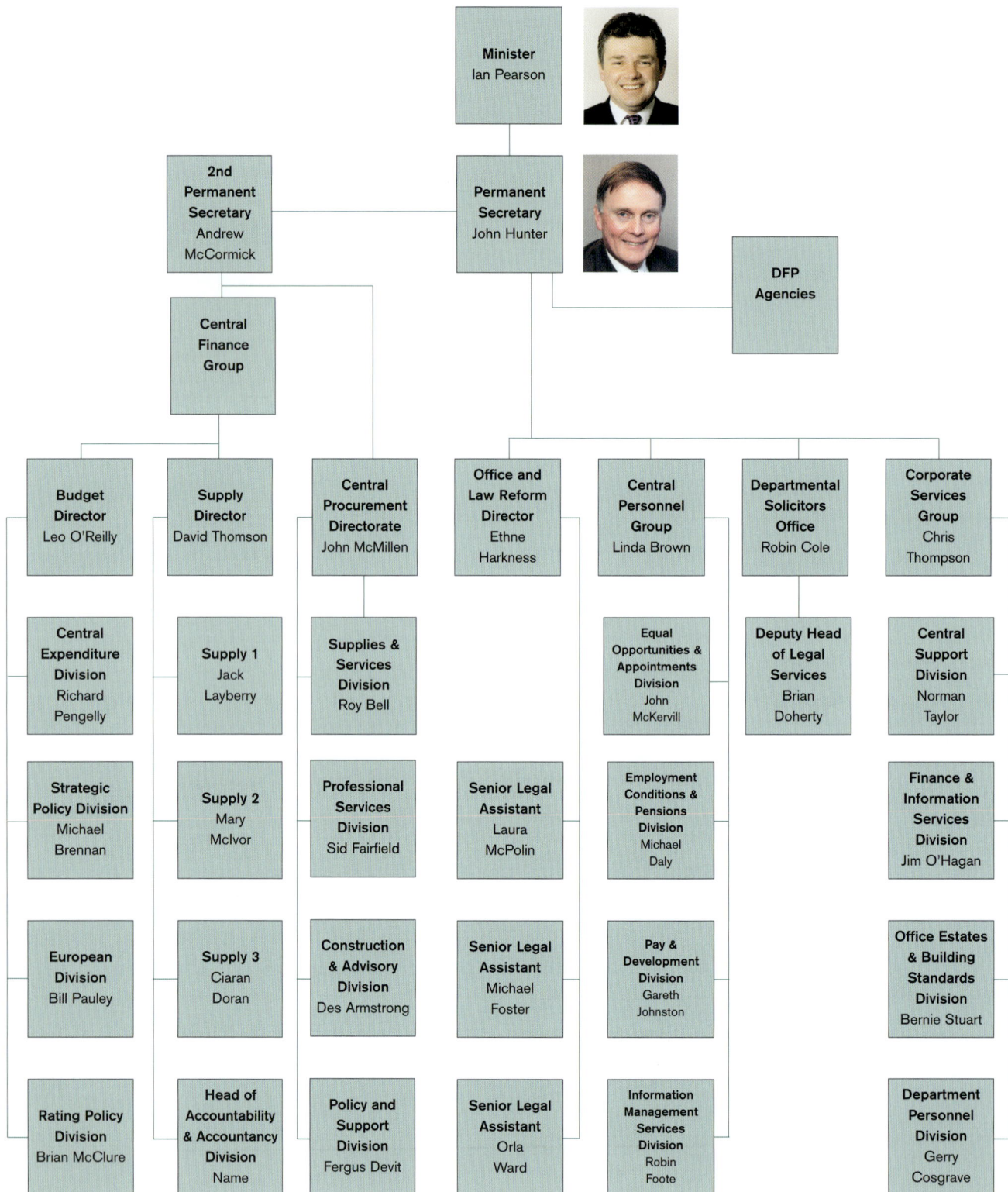

**Professional Services Division**
Deputy Director: Sid Fairfield
Tel: 028 9082 3302
Fax: 028 9082 3241
Email: sid.fairfield@dfpni.gov.uk

**Construction and Advisory Division**
Deputy Director: Des Armstrong
Tel: 028 9082 3201
Fax: 028 9082 3241
Email: des.armstrong@dfpni.gov.uk

**Policy and Support Division**
Deputy Director: Fergus Devitt
Tel: 028 9082 3152
Fax: 028 9082 3199
Email: fergus.devitt@dfpni.gov.uk

## Corporate Services Group

Director: Chris Thompson
Tel: 028 9185 8044
Fax: 028 9185 8048
Email: chris.thompson@dfpni.gov.uk

**Central Support Division**
Head of Division: Norman Taylor
Tel: 028 9185 8128
Fax: 028 9185 8048
Email: normant.taylor@dfpni.gov.uk

**Departmental Personnel Division**
Head of Division: Gerry Cosgrave
Tel: 028 9185 8265
Fax: 028 9185 8067
Email: gerry.cosgrave@dfpni.gov.uk

**Finance and Information Services Division**
Head of Division; Jim O'Hagan
Tel: 028 9185 8278
Fax: 028 9127 7602
Email: jim.o'hagan@dfpni.gov.uk

**Office Estates and Building Standards Division**
Head of Division: Dr Bernie Stuart
Tel: 028 9051 8322
Fax: 028 9051 8344
Email: bernie.stuart@dfpni.gov.uk

## Departmental Solicitors Office

Head of Legal Services: Robin Cole
Tel: 028 9025 1222
Fax: 028 9025 1235
Email: robin.cole@dfpni.gov.uk

Deputy Head of Legal Services:
Brian Doherty
Tel: 028 9025 1223
Fax: 028 9025 1235
Email: brian.doherty@dfpni.gov.uk

Assistant Solicitor: Noel Kelly
Tel: 028 9025 1241
Email: noel.kelly@dfpni.gov.uk

Assistant Solicitor: Philip Gunn
Tel: 028 9025 1241
Email: philip.gunn@dfpni.gov.uk

Assistant Solicitor: Paul McGinn
Tel: 028 9025 1242
Email: paul.mcginn@dfpni.gov.uk

Assistant Solicitor: Jeanette Diamond
Tel: 028 9055 6614
Email: jeanette.diamond@dfpni.gov.uk

Assistant Solicitor: Edmund Quiery
Tel: 028 9054 2320
Email: edmund.quiery@dfpni.gov.uk

## Office of Law Reform

Director: Ethne Harkness
Tel: 028 9054 2901
Fax: 028 9054 2909
Email: ethne.harkness@dfpni.gov.uk

Assistant Director: Laura McPolin
Tel: 028 9054 2902
Fax: 028 9054 2909
Email: laura.mcpolin@dfpni.gov.uk

Assistant Director: Michael Foster
Tel: 028 9054 2903
Email: michael.foster@dfpni.gov.uk

Assistant Director: Orla Ward
Tel: 028 9054 2908
Email: orla.ward@dfpni.gov.uk

## Agencies, Non Departmental Public Bodies and other organisations within DFP

**Business Development Service**
Craigantlet Buildings, Stoney Road
Belfast, BT4 3SX
Tel: 028 9052 0444
Fax: 028 9052 7447
Web: www.bdsni.gov.uk
Chief Executive: Ray Long
Tel: 028 9052 7406
Email: ray.long@dfpni.gov.uk

**Land Registers of Northern Ireland**
Lincoln Building
27-45 Great Victoria Street
Belfast, BT2 7SL
Tel: 028 9025 1515
Fax: 028 9025 1550
Web: www.lrni.gov.uk
Chief Executive: Patricia Montgomery
Tel: 028 9025 1663
Email: patricia.montgomery@dfpni.gov.uk

**Law Reform Advisory Committee for Northern Ireland**
Lancashire House, 5 Linenhall Street
Belfast, BT2 8AA
Tel: 028 9054 2900
Fax: 028 9054 2909
Web; www.olrni.gov.uk
Secretary: Clare Irvine
Email: claire.irvine@dfpni.gov.uk

**Northern Ireland Building Regulations Advisory Committee**
Building Regulations Unit
Office Estates & Building Standards Division
3rd Floor, Lancashire House
3 Linenhall Street, Belfast, BT2 8AA
Tel: 028 9054 2923
Fax: 028 9054 7866
Secretary: Hugh Murray

**Northern Ireland Statistics and Research Agency**
McAuley House, 2-14 Castle Street
Belfast, BT1 1SA
Tel: 028 9034 8100
Fax: 028 9034 8106
Web: www.nisra.gov.uk
Chief Executive: Norman Caven
Tel: 028 9034 8102
Email: norman.caven@dfpni.gov.uk

**Rate Collection Agency**
Oxford House, 49-55 Chichester Street
Belfast, BT1 4HH
Tel: 028 9052 2252
Fax: 028 9052 2113
Web: www.ratecollectionagencyni.gov.uk
Chief Executive: Arthur Scott
Tel: 028 9025 2110
Fax: 028 9025 2046
Email: arthur.scott@dfpni.gov.uk

**Valuation and Lands Agency**
Queen's Court
56-66 Upper Queen Street
Belfast, BT1 6FD
Tel: 028 9025 0700
Fax: 028 9054 3750
Chief Executive: Nigel Woods
Web: www.vla.nics.gov.uk
Tel: 028 9054 3923
Fax: 028 9054 3800
Email: nigel.woods@dfpni.gov.uk

# Department of Health, Social Services and Public Safety

Castle Buildings, Stormont Estate
Upper Newtownards Road
Belfast, BT4 3SQ
Tel: 028 9052 0500
Fax: 028 9025 0572
Web: www.dhsspsni.gov.uk

**Direct Rule Minister**: Angela Smith
Permanent Secretary: Clive Gowdy
Tel: 028 9052 0559
Fax: 028 9052 0573

**Private Office**
Private Secretary: Sharon Lindsay
Tel: 028 9052 0642
Fax: 028 9052 0557

**Information Office**
Press Officer: Philip Maguire
Tel: 028 9052 0636
Fax: 028 9052 0572

The Department of Health, Social Services and Public Safety (DHSSPS) has three main business responsibilities:

- **Health and Personal Social Services**, which includes policy and legislation for hospitals, family practitioner services and community health and personal social services;
- **Public Health**, which covers policy, legislation and administrative action to promote and protect the health and well-being of the population and emergency planning;
- **Public Safety**, which includes responsibility for the policy and legislation for public safety policies, including Ambulance Services, and Fire Services.

The Department's mission is to improve everyone's health and social well-being. It does so by ensuring the provision of appropriate health and social care services, both in clinical settings, such as hospitals and GPs' surgeries, and in the community, through nursing, social work and other professional services. It also supports programmes of health promotion and education to encourage the community to adopt activities, behaviours and attitudes that will lead to better health and well-being.

**Primary, Secondary and Community Care Group**
Deputy Secretary: Andrew Hamilton
Tel: 028 9052 3263

This Group deals with the operational issues relating to the commissioning and delivery of services in the Health and Personal Social Services. It maintains a close relationship with the various bodies making up the HPSS and works with them to ensure that they operate within the policy framework set by Ministers.

## Primary Care Directorate

Director: Dr Jim Livingstone
Tel: 028 9052 2788

**Secondary Care Directorate**
Director: Dean Sullivan
Tel: 028 9052 2101

**Community Care Directorate**
Director: Leslie Frew
Tel: 028 9052 2786

## Resources and Performance Management Group

Deputy Secretary: Don Hill
Tel: 028 9052 0560

This Group negotiates and has management of financial resources for the DHSSPS, departmental staffing policy and resources and internal audit arrangements for the Department. It also deals with the collection and provision of information and analysis on HPSS matters and is responsible for monitoring and management of the performance of the HPSS.

**Personnel & Corporate Services Directorate**
Director: Paul Conliffe
Tel: 028 9052 2825

**Finance Directorate**
Director: Julie Thompson
Tel: 028 9052 2446

**Information & Analysis Directorate**
Director: Dr Liz McWhirter
Tel: 028 9052 2522

**Planning & Performance Management Directorate**
Director: Noel McCann
Tel: 028 9052 2795

## Strategic Planning and Modernisation Group

Deputy Secretary: Paul Simpson
Tel: 028 9052 2667

This Group has responsibility for strategic management, planning, IT and public safety issues for the DHSSPS. It manages the capital development programme and provides strategic direction on human resources services for the HPSS. It has responsibility for ambulance services, fire services, regional transport services, IT services for the department and the HPSS, the regional strategy for health and social well-being, and overall co-ordination of the New TSN, Equality and Human Rights.

Support Services Unit
Head: Patricia Blacker
Tel: 028 9052 3184

Directorate of Information Systems/ITG
Director: Garry Williams
Tel: 028 9054 2201

Human Resources Directorate
Director: David Bingham
Tel: 028 9052 0781

Strategy Inclusion and Public Safety Directorate
Director: Andrew Elliott

## Public Health, Medical and Allied Group

**Chief Medical Officer**
Dr Henrietta Campbell
Tel: 028 9052 0563
The Public Health, Medical and Allied Group, led by the Chief Medical Officer, provides advice and specific medical services for the Department, the wider Northern Ireland Civil Service, and the Prison Service. This Group is also responsible for the public health business area, comprising the Investing for Health initiative; health protection; health promotion; emergency planning and strategies on smoking, drugs and alcohol.

## Department of Health, Social Services and Public Safety Organisation Chart

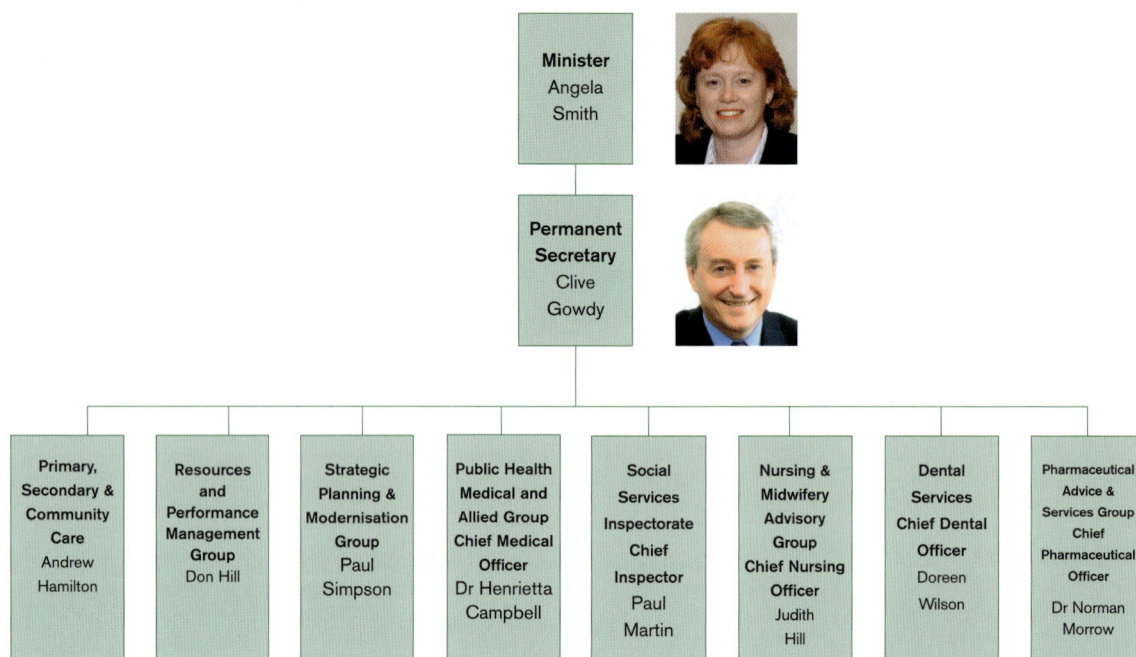

**Minister**
Angela Smith

**Permanent Secretary**
Clive Gowdy

- **Primary, Secondary & Community Care** Andrew Hamilton
- **Resources and Performance Management Group** Don Hill
- **Strategic Planning & Modernisation Group** Paul Simpson
- **Public Health Medical and Allied Group Chief Medical Officer** Dr Henrietta Campbell
- **Social Services Inspectorate Chief Inspector** Paul Martin
- **Nursing & Midwifery Advisory Group Chief Nursing Officer** Judith Hill
- **Dental Services Chief Dental Officer** Doreen Wilson
- **Pharmaceutical Advice & Services Group Chief Pharmaceutical Officer** Dr Norman Morrow

### Social Services Inspectorate
Chief Inspector: Paul Martin
Tel: 028 9052 0561

The Social Services Inspectorate, under the leadership of the Chief Inspector, provides advice and support to Ministers, the Department, other Government Departments and agencies in the field of Social Care. An Annual Inspection Programme across a range of services and providers is carried out for the Department and the Northern Ireland Office. The Inspectorate also carries responsibility for policy on social work and social care training and education including the disbursement of postgraduate social work bursaries and other training support funding linked to the PSS Training Strategy.

### Nursing and Midwifery Advisory Group
Chief Nursing Officer: Judith Hill
Tel: 028 9052 0562

The Nursing & Midwifery Advisory Group, led by the Chief Nursing Officer, is responsible for advising the Department, the wider Northern Ireland Civil Service and the Prison Service on all aspects of policy which affect nursing, midwifery and health visiting, education and services.

### Dental Services Group
Chief Dental Officer: Doreen Wilson
Tel: 028 9052 2940

Dental Services Group, led by the Chief Dental Officer, provides advice on oral health to the Department, the wider Northern Ireland Civil Service and other bodies and agencies. Monitoring of dental treatment provided by general dental practitioners is carried out by the Referral Dental Service. It also delivers direct dental services to the Prisons and Young Offenders Centre.

### Pharmaceutical Advice and Services Group
Chief Pharmaceutical Officer:
Dr Norman Morrow
Tel: 028 9052 3219

The Pharmaceutical Advice and Services Group, led by the Chief Pharmaceutical Officer, is responsible for the provision of specialist advice in respect of medicines and pharmaceutical services. It also has responsibility for medicines legislation, including inspection and enforcement under that legislation pertaining to both human and veterinary medicines.

### Health Estates
Health Estates determines policy on estate issues in relation to the delivery of health and social care. The Agency's task is to provide professional and technical advice, guidance and support on estate matters, at both strategic and operational levels, to the various bodies charged with responsibility for the Health and Social Services estate.

**Health Estates**
Stoney Road, Dundonald
Belfast, BT16 1US
Tel: 028 9052 0025
Fax: 028 9052 3900
Web: www.dhsspsni.gov.uk/hea

Chief Executive: John Cole
Tel: 028 905 23823
Estates Development

Director: Eddie Brett
Tel: 028 905 23702
Estates Policy / Director: Stan Blayney
Tel: 028 905 23763

## Agencies, Non Departmental Public Bodies and other organisations within DHSSPS

**Altnagelvin Hospitals HSST**
Glenshane Road
Londonderry, BT47 6SB
Tel: 028 7134 5171
Fax: 028 7161 1219
Chairman: Denis Desmond CBE
Chief Executive: Stella Burnside

**Armagh and Dungannon HSST**
St Luke's Hospital
Armagh, BT61 7NQ
Tel: 028 3752 2381
Fax: 028 3741 2521
Chairman: Deirdre Dorman
Chief Executive: Pauline Stanley

**Belfast City Hospital HSST**
51 Lisburn Road, Belfast, BT9 7AB
Tel: 028 9026 3564
Fax: 028 9032 6614
Chairman: Joan Ruddock OBE
Chief Executive: Quentin Coey

**Central Services Agency**
25-27 Adelaide Street, Belfast, BT2 8FH
Tel: 028 9032 4431
Fax: 028 9023 2304
Web: www.centralservicesagency.com
Email: chiefexec@csa.n-i.nhs.uk
Chairperson:
Professor John Frances Fulton
Chief Executive: Stephen Hodkinson

**Causeway HSST**
80 Coleraine Road
Ballymoney, BT53 6BP
Tel: 028 2766 6600
Fax: 028 7166 1200
Chairman: Jean Jefferson
Chief Executive (Acting): Alan Braiden

**Craigavon and Banbridge Community HSST**
Bannvale House, 10 Moyallen Road
Gilford, BT63 5JX
Tel: 028 3883 1983
Fax: 028 3883 1993
Chairman: Joseph Graham Martin
Chief Executive: Glenn Houston

**Craigavon Area Hospital HSST**
68 Lurgan Road
Craigavon, BT63 5QQ
Tel: 028 3861 2550
Fax: 028 3839 4955
Chairman: E McClurg
Chief Executive: John Templeton

**Distinction and Meritorious Service Awards Committee**
Room D.13, Castle Buildings, Stormont
Belfast, BT4 3SJ
Tel: 028 9052 2817
Fax: 028 9052 2912
Secretary: John Nesbitt

**Down Lisburn HSST**
Lisburn Health Centre
25 Linenhall Street
Lisburn, BT28 1LU
Tel: 028 9250 1309
Fax: 028 9250 1210
Chairman: Denise Fitzsimnons
Chief Executive: John Compton

**Eastern Health and Social Services Board**
Champion House
12-22 Linenhall Street
Belfast, BT2 8BS
Tel: 028 9032 1313
Fax: 028 9055 3681
Chairman: David Russell
Chief Executive: Paula Kilbane

**Eastern Health and Social Services Council**
1st Floor McKelvey House
24-27 Wellington Place
Belfast, BT1 6GQ
Tel: 028 9032 1230
Fax: 028 9032 1750
Chairman: Patricia McMillan
Chief Officer: Jane Graham

**Fire Authority for Northern Ireland**
Brigade Headquarters
1 Seymour Street, Lisburn, BT27 4SX
Tel: 028 9266 4221
Fax: 028 9267 7402
Web: www.nifb.org.uk
Chairman: William Gillespie
Chief Fire Officer: Colin Lammey

**Food Safety Promotion Board**
7 Eastgate Avenue
Eastgate, Little Island, Cork
Tel: 00 353 21 230 4100
Fax: 00 353 21 230 4111
Web: www.safefoodonline.com
Chief Executive: Martin Higgins

**Foyle HSST**
Riverview House, Abercorn Road
Londonderry, BT48 6FB
Tel: 028 7126 6111
Fax: 028 7126 0806
Chairman: Anthony Jackson
Chief Executive: Elaine Way

**Green Park Healthcare HSST**
20 Stockman's Lane
Belfast, BT9 7JB
Tel: 028 9066 9501
Fax: 028 9038 2008
Chairman: Ian Doherty
Chief Executive: Hilary Boyd

**Health Estates Agency**
Stoney Road, Dundonald
Belfast, BT16 1US
Tel: 028 9052 0025
Fax: 028 9052 3900
Web: www.dhsspsni.gov.uk/hea
Chief Executive: John Cole

Estates Development
Director: Eddie Brett
Tel: 028 9052 3702

Estates Policy
Director: Stan Blayney
Tel: 028 9052 3763

**Health Promotion Agency for Northern Ireland**
18 Ormeau Avenue, Belfast, BT2 8HS
Tel: 028 9031 1611
Fax: 028 9031 1711
Email: info@hpani.org.uk
Chairman: Alice Quinn
Chief Executive: Dr Brian Gaffney

**Homefirst HSST**
The Cottage, 5 Greenmount Avenue
Ballymena, BT43 6DA
Tel: 028 2563 3700
Fax: 028 2563 3733
Chairman: Robert Ferguson
Chief Executive: Norman Evans

**Mater Infirmorum HSST**
45-51 Crumlin Road
Belfast, BT14 6AB
Tel: 028 9074 1211
Fax: 028 9074 9784
Chairman: Lady McCollum
Chief Executive: Sean Donaghy

**Mental Health Commission**
Elizabeth House
118 Holywood Road, Belfast, BT4 1NY
Tel: 028 9065 1157
Email: mhc@dhsspsni.gov.uk
Chairperson: Marian O'Neill
Acting Chief Executive: Stephen Jackson

**Mental Health Review Tribunal**
Room 11 Annex 6
Castle Buildings, Stormont
Belfast, BT4 3SQ
Tel: 028 9052 3388
Chairman: Fraser Elliott QC
Secretary: Esther Clarke/Alison Bray

**Newry and Mourne HSST**
5 Downshire Place
Downshire Road, Newry, BT34 1DZ
Tel: 028 3026 0505
Fax: 028 3026 9064
Chairman: Sean Hogan
Chief Executive: Eric Bowyer

**North and West Belfast HSST**
Glendinning House
6 Murray Street, Belfast, BT1 6DP
Tel: 028 9082 1209
Fax: 028 9082 1284
Chairman: Patrick McCarten
Chief Executive: Richard Black

**Northern Health and Social Services Board**
County Hall, 182 Galgorm Road
Ballymena, BT42 1HN
Tel: 028 2566 2311
Fax: 028 2565 5112
Chairman: Michael Wood
Chief Executive: Stuart Macdonnell

**Northern Health and Social Services Council**
8 Broadway Avenue
Ballymena, BT43 7AA
Tel: 028 2565 5777
Fax: 028 2565 5112
Chairman (Acting): Thomas Creighton
Chief Executive: Noel Graham

**Northern Ireland Ambulance Services HSST**
Knockbraken Healthcare Park
Saintfield Road, Belfast, BT8 8SG
Tel: 028 9040 0999
Fax: 028 9040 0900
Chairman: Doug Smyth
Chief Executive: Paul McCormick

**Northern Ireland Blood Transfusion Service Agency**
Belfast City Hospital Complex
51 Lisburn Road, Belfast, BT9 7TS
Tel: 028 9053 4662
Fax: 028 9043 9017
Web: www.nibts.org
Email: chiefexec@nibts.n-i.nhs.uk
Chairperson: Stephen Costello
Chief Executive: Morris McClelland

**Northern Ireland Council for Medical and Dental Education**
5 Annadale Avenue, Belfast, BT7 3JH
Tel: 028 9049 2731
Fax: 028 9064 2279
Web: www.nicpmde.com
Email: nicpmde@nicpmde.gov.uk
Chairperson: Dr Don Keegan
Chief Executive: Dr JR McCluggage

**Northern Ireland Guardian Ad Litem Agency**
Centre House
79 Chichester Street, Belfast, BT1 4JE
Tel: 028 9031 6550
Fax: 028 9031 9811
Web: www.nigala.n-i.nhs.uk
Email: admin@nigala.n-i.nhs.uk
Chairperson: Jim Currie
Chief Executive: Ronnie Williamson

**Northern Ireland Practice and Education Council for Nursing and Midwifery**
Centre House, 79 Chichester Street
Belfast, BT1 4JE
Tel: 028 9023 8152
Fax: 028 9033 3298
Web: www.nipec.n-i.nhs.uk
Email: enquiries@ nipec.n-i.nhs.uk
Chairperson: Maureen Griffith
Chief Executive: Ms Paddy Blaney

**Northern Ireland Regional Medical Physics Agency**
Musgrave and Clarke House
Royal Hospitals Site
Grosvenor Road, BT12 6BA
Tel: 028 9034 6488
Fax: 028 9031 3040
Web: www.medicalphysics.n-i.nhs.uk
Chairperson: Professor David Walmsley
Chief Executive: Professor Peter Jaritt

**Northern Ireland Social Care Council**
7th Floor Millennium House
19-25 Great Victoria Street
Belfast, BT2 7AQ
Tel: 028 9041 7600
Fax: 028 9041 7601
Web: www.niscc.info
Chief Executive: Brendan Johnston
Chairman: Jeremy Harbison

**Royal Group of Hospitals and Dental Hospital HSST**
Grosvenor Road, Belfast, BT12 6BA
Tel: 028 9024 0503
Fax: 028 90 24 0899
Chairman: Paul McWilliams
Chief Executive: William McKee

**South and East Belfast HSST**
Knockbracken Healthcare Park
Saintfield Road, Belfast, BT8 8BH
Tel: 028 9056 5656
Fax: 028 9056 5813
Chairman: Robin Harris
Chief Executive: Patricia Gordon

**Southern Health and Social Services Board**
Tower Hill, Armagh, BT61 9DR
Tel: 028 3741 0041
Fax: 028 3741 4550
Chairman: Fionnuala Cook OBE
Chief Executive: Colm Donaghy

**Southern Health and Social Services Council**
Quaker Buildings, High Street
Lurgan, BT66 8BB
Tel: 028 3834 9900
Fax: 028 3834 9858
Chairman: Roisin Foster
Chief Executive: Stella Cunningham

**Sperrin Lakeland HSST**
Strathdene House
Tyrone and Fermanagh Hospital
Omagh, BT79 0NS
Tel: 028 8283 5285
Fax: 028 8283 5286
Chairman: Richard Scott
Chief Executive: Hugh Mills

**Ulster Community and Hospitals HSST**
39 Regent Street
Newtownards, BT23 4AD
Tel: 028 9151 2201
Fax: 028 9182 0140
Chairman: Siubhan Grant
Chief Executive: Jim McCall

**United Hospital HSST**
Bush House, 45 Bush Road
Antrim, BT41 2QB
Tel: 028 9442 4673
Fax: 028 9442 4654
Chairman: Raymond Milnes
Chief Executive: Bernard Mitchell

**Western Health and Social Services Board**
15 Gransha Park, Clooney Road
Londonderry, BT47 6FN
Tel: 028 7186 0086
Fax: 028 7186 0311
Chairman: J Bradley
Chief Executive: S Lindsay

**Western Health and Social Services Council**
Hilltop, Tyrone and Fermanagh Hospital
Omagh, BT79 0NS
Tel: 028 8225 2555
Fax: 028 8225 2544
Chairman: Patrick McGowan
Chief Executive: Maggie Reilly

## Department for Regional Development

Clarence Court, 10-18 Adelaide Street
Belfast, BT2 8GB
Tel: 028 9054 0540
Fax: 028 9054 0024
Web: www.drdni.gov.uk

**Direct Rule Minister:** John Spellar
**Permanent Secretary:** Stephen Quinn
Tel: 028 9054 1175
**Private Office**
Private Secretary: Paul Gill
Tel: 028 9054 0105
Principal Information Officer:
Paddy Cullen
Tel: 028 9054 0817

The Department for Regional Development (DRD) is charged with strategic and transport planning in Northern Ireland. It is responsible for the provision and maintenance of roads, water and sewage services. The Department also develops policy relating to public transport, including rail, bus, ports and airports. Much of DRD's operational work is carried out by its two executive agencies: the Roads Service and the Water Service. The department has recently published a ten-year development strategy, which has created considerable interest in future infrastructural development priorities.

### Regional Planning and Transportation

Deputy Secretary: Doreen Brown
Tel: 028 9084 0100

Director of Public
Transport Division: Brian White
Tel: 028 9054 0651
Fax: 028 9054 0593

Director of Regional Planning and
Transportation Division: Mike Thompson

Director of Public Transport Performance
Division: Jack McGibbon
Tel: 028 9054 0650
Fax: 028 9054 0662

### Resources and Management Services

Deputy Secretary:
Principal Establishment and Finance
Officer: David Sterling
Tel: 028 9054 1180

Director of Personnel: Wendy Johnston
Tel: 028 9054 1070

Director of CPMU: Alan McArthur
Tel: 028 9054 1195

Director of Finance: Donald Henry
Tel: 028 9054 0848
Fax: 028 9054 0851
Email: donald.henry@drdni.gov.uk

Director of Infrastructure Funding:
Nigel McCormick
Tel: 028 9054 2990
Fax: 028 9054 7875
Email: Nigel.mccormick@drdni.gov.uk

Internal Audit: Ronnie Balfour

CCU: Stephen Murphy

### Roads Service

Chief Executive: Malcolm McKibbin
Tel: 028 9054 0531
Email: Malcolm.mckibbin@drdni.gov.uk

Director of Corporate Services:
Jim Carlisle
Tel: 028 9054 0906
Email: jim.Carlisle@drdni.gov.uk

Director of Network Services: David Orr
Tel: 028 9054 0462
Email: david.orr@drdni.gov.uk

Director of Engineering: Geoff Allister
Tel: 028 9054 0471
Email: geoff.allister@drdni.gov.uk

Director of Finance: John McNeill
Tel: 028 9054 0469
Email: john.mcneill@drdni.gov.uk

### Water Service

Chief Executive: Katharine Bryan
Tel: 028 9034 5800
Fax: 028 9035 4685
Email: Katharine.Bryan@waterni.gov.uk

**Executives Directors**
Director of Operations: John Kelly
Tel: 028 9035 4744
Fax: 028 9035 4798
Email: John.Kelly@waterni.gov.uk

Director of Corporate Services:
Robin Mussen
Tel: 028 9035 4794
Fax: 028 9035 4798
Email: Robin.Mussen@waterni.gov.uk

Director of Customer Services:
William Duddy
Tel: 028 9035 7636
Fax: 028 9035 4888
Email: William.Duddy@waterni.gov.uk

Director of Development: Trevor Haslett
Tel: 028 9035 4772
Fax: 028 9035 4798
Email: Trevor.Haslett@waterni.gov.uk

Business Transformation Director:
Peter May
Tel: 028 9035 4746
Fax: 028 9035 4888
Email: Peter.May@waterni.gov.uk

Interim Director of Standards &
Regulation: Jim Graham
Tel: 028 9035 7689
Fax: 028 9035 4888
Email: Jim.Graham@waterni.gov.uk

Director of Finance: David Carson
Tel: 028 9035 4753
Fax: 028 9035 7601
Email: David.Carson@waterni.gov.uk

PPP Director: Sue Holmes
Tel: 028 9035 7588
Fax: 028 9035 4993
Email: Sue.Holmes@waterni.gov.uk

**Networks South East Region**
Manager: Bill Gowdy
34 College Street
Belfast BT1 6DP
Tel: 028 9032 8161
Fax: 028 9035 4828
Email: Bill.Gowdy@waterni.gov.uk

**Wastewater Services**
Manager: Alec McQuillan
Academy House
121A Broughshane Street
Ballymena BT43 6BA
Tel: 028 2565 3655
Fax: 028 2566 3131
Email: Alec.McQuillan@waterni.gov.uk

**Water Supply**
Manager: Sidney McKee
Marlborough House, Central Way
Craigavon, BT64 1AD
Tel: 028 3834 1100
Fax: 028 3832 0555
Email: Sidney.McKee@waterni.gov.uk

**Networks North West Region**
Manager: Joe Millar
1A Belt Road, Altnagelvin
Londonderry BT47 2LL
Tel: 028 7131 2221
Fax: 028 7131 0330
Email: Joe.Millar@waterni.gov.uk

**Customer Services**
Waterline: 0845 744 0088
Leakline: 0800 028 2011

## Department for Regional Development Organisation Chart

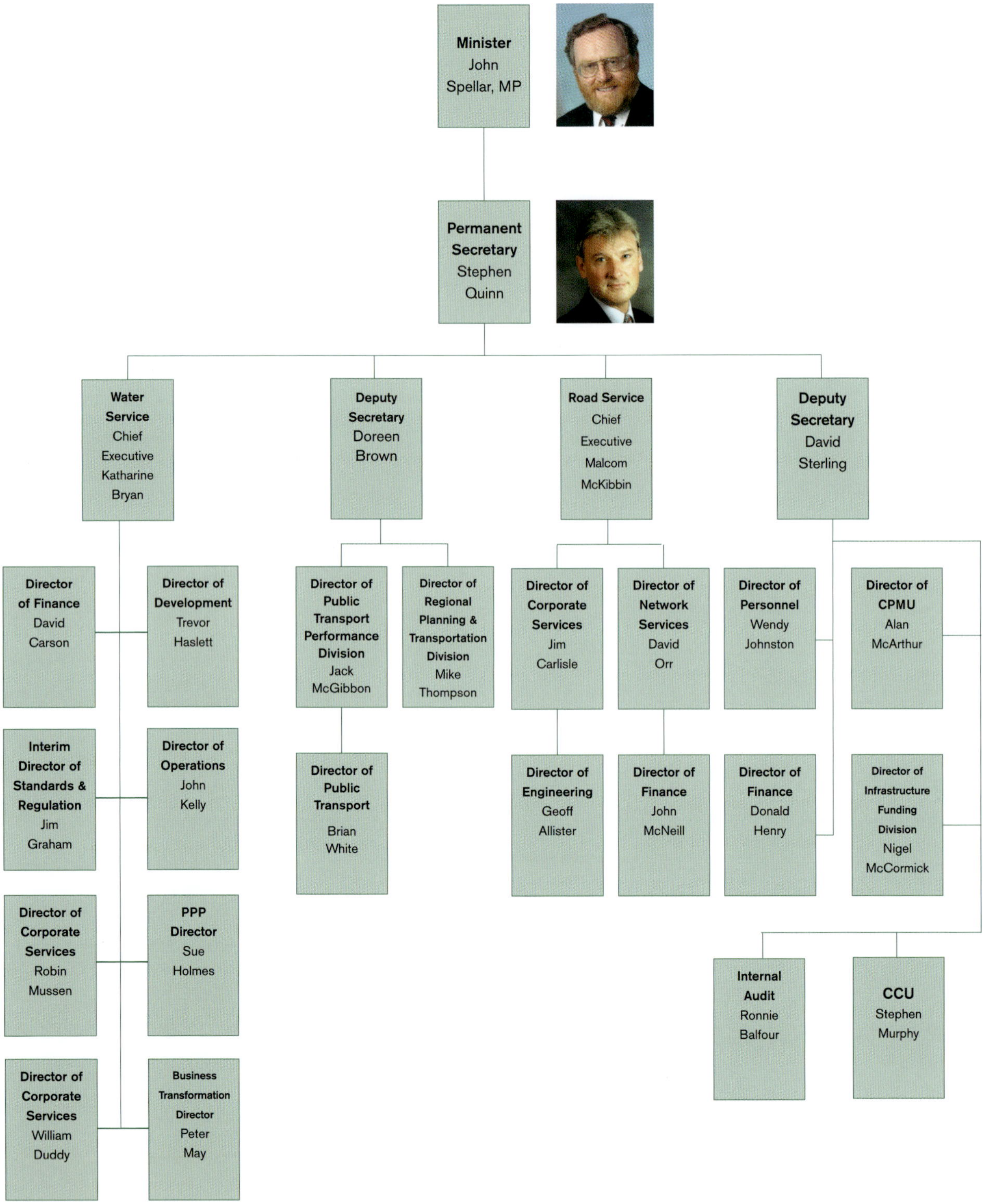
Minister John Spellar, MP
Permanent Secretary Stephen Quinn
Water Service Chief Executive Katharine Bryan
Deputy Secretary Doreen Brown
Road Service Chief Executive Malcom McKibbin
Deputy Secretary David Sterling
Director of Finance David Carson
Director of Development Trevor Haslett
Interim Director of Standards & Regulation Jim Graham
Director of Operations John Kelly
Director of Corporate Services Robin Mussen
PPP Director Sue Holmes
Director of Corporate Services William Duddy
Business Transformation Director Peter May
Director of Public Transport Performance Division Jack McGibbon
Director of Regional Planning & Transportation Division Mike Thompson
Director of Public Transport Brian White
Director of Corporate Services Jim Carlisle
Director of Network Services David Orr
Director of Engineering Geoff Allister
Director of Finance John McNeill
Director of Personnel Wendy Johnston
Director of CPMU Alan McArthur
Director of Finance Donald Henry
Director of Infrastructure Funding Division Nigel McCormick
Internal Audit Ronnie Balfour
CCU Stephen Murphy

## Agencies, Non Departmental Public Bodies and other organisations within DRD

### Coleraine Harbour
Harbour Office, 4 Riversdale Road,
Coleraine, BT52 1RY
Tel: 028 7034 2012
Fax: 028 7035 2000
Web: www.coleraineharbour.f9.co.uk
Email: info@ coleraineharbour.f9.co.uk

### Londonderry Port and Harbour
Harbour Office, Port Road, Lisahally
Londonderry, BT47 6FL
Tel: 028 7186 0555
Fax: 028 7186 1168
Web: www.londonderryport.com
Email: info@londonderry-port.co.uk
Chief Executive: Brian McGrath

### Northern Ireland Transport Holding Company
Chamber of Commerce House
22 Great Victoria Street
Belfast, BT2 7LX
Tel: 028 9024 3456
Fax: 028 9043 8717
Web: www.translink.co.uk/nithco
Email: nithc@dialstart.net
Chairperson: Dr Joan Smyth
Corporate Director: Jim Aiken

### Port of Belfast
Belfast Harbour Commissioners
Belfast, BT1 3AL
Tel: 028 9055 4422
Fax: 028 9055 4411
Web: www.belfast-harbour.co.uk
Email: info@belfast-harbour.co.uk
Chief Executive: John Doran

### Roads Service
Clarence Court
10-18 Adelaide Street,
Belfast, BT2 8GB
Tel: 028 9054 0540
Fax: 028 9054 0024
Web: www.roadsni.gov.uk
Email: roads@drdni.gov.uk
Chief Executive: Dr Malcolm McKibben

**Regional Offices**

*Eastern Division*
Hydebank, 4 Hospital Road
Belfast, BT8 8JL
Tel: 028 9025 3000
Fax: 028 9025 3220
Email: roads.eastern@drdni.gov.uk
Divisional Manager: Joe Drew

*Northern Division*
County Hall
Castlerock Road, Coleraine, BT51 3HS
Tel: 028 7034 1300
Fax: 028 7034 1430
Email: roads.northern@drdni.gov.uk
Divisional Manager: Dr Andrew Murray

*Southern Division*
Marlborough House
Central Way, Craigavon, BT64 1AD
Tel: 028 3834 1144
Fax: 028 3834 1867
Email: roads.southern@drdni.gov.uk
Divisional Manager: John White

*Western Division*
County Hall
Drumragh Avenue, Omagh, BT79 7AF
Tel: 028 8225 4111
Fax: 028 8225 4010
Email: roads.western@drdni.gov.uk
Divisional Manager: Pat Doherty

*Roads Service Consultancy*
Rathkeltair House, Market Street
Downpatrick, BT30 6AJ
Tel: 028 4461 2211
Fax: 028 4461 8188
Email: roads.consultancy@drdni.gov.uk
Head of Roads Service Consultancy:
Mr R J M Cairns

### Warrenpoint Harbour
Warrenpoint Harbour Authority
Warrenpoint, BT34 3JR
Tel: 028 4177 3381
Fax: 028 4175 2875
Web: www.warrenpointharbour.co.uk
Email: info@warrenpointharbour.co.uk
Chief Executive: Quintin Goldie

### Water Council
Water Service Strategic Policy Branch
Room 1.08, 34 College Street
Belfast, BT1 6DR
Tel: 028 9054 1158
Fax: 028 9054 1156
Web: www.watercouncilni.gov.uk
Email: secretary@watercouncilni.gov.uk

### Water Service
Northland House
3 Frederick Street, Belfast, BT1 2NR
Tel: 028 9024 4711
Fax: 028 9032 4888
Web: www.waterni.gov.uk
Email: waterline@waterni.gov.uk
Chief Executive: Katharine Bryan
Tel: 028 9034 5800
Fax: 028 9035 4798

**Regional Offices**

*Eastern Division*
34 College Street
Belfast, BT1 6DR
Tel: 028 9032 8161
Fax: 028 9035 4828

*Northern Division*
Academy House
121A Broughshane Street
Ballymena, BT43 6BA
Tel: 028 2565 3655
Fax: 028 2566 3131

*Southern Division*
Marlborough House
Central Way
Craigavon, BT64 1AD
Tel: 028 3834 1100
Fax: 028 3832 0555

*Western Division*
Belt Road
Altnagelvin
Londonderry, BT47 2LL
Tel: 028 7131 2221
Fax: 028 7131 0330

## Department for Social Development

Lighthouse Building
1 Cromac Place
Gasworks Business Park
Ormeau Road, Belfast BT7 2JB
Tel: 028 9082 9000
Fax: 028 9082 9548

**Direct Rule Minister:** John Spellar
**Permanent Secretary:** Alan Shannon
Tel: 028 9082 9044
**Private Secretary** Tel: 028 9082 9034
**Principal Information Officer:**
Jim Hamilton Tel: 028 9082 9490

The Department for Social Development (DSD) brings together areas of work from both the former Department of Health and Social Services and the Department of the Environment. DSD is responsible for housing policy, urban regeneration and community development, along with social and charities legislation and the voluntary and community unit. It administers the social security, child support and pension schemes and associated appeals services.

The department sponsors a number of non-departmental public bodies. These include the Northern Ireland Housing Executive (NIHE), Laganside Corporation and several advisory and tribunal bodies.

The Department's mission is to promote individual and community wellbeing through integrated social and economic action. Many of its policies impact on health, particularly housing. It interacts with many of the poorest in society, and has responsibility for improving housing, delivering social security benefits, providing child support services and developing community infrastructure. Key elements of current DSD strategies include providing, through the Northern Ireland Housing Executive and Housing Associations, high quality affordable social housing for those on low incomes and in greatest need.

### Central Policy and Co-ordination Unit

Director: Philip Angus
Tel: 028 9082 9015
Fax: 028 9082 9557
Email: philip.angus@dsdni.gov.uk

**Office of the Permanent Secretary**
Principal: Vacant

**Information Office**
Principal: Jim Hamilton
Tel: 028 9082 9490
Fax: 028 9082 9536
Email: jim.hamilton@dsdni.gov.uk

**Statistics & Research Branch**
Principal Dr Chris Morris
Tel: 028 9052 2280
Email: chris.morris@dsdni.gov.uk

**Social Welfare Statistics & Consultancy Branch**
Principal: Michelle Crawford
Tel: 028 9052 2061
Email: michelle.crawford@dsdni.gov.uk

**Economics**
Principal: Noel McNally
Fax: 028 9025 1937
Email: noel.mcnally@dsdni.gov.uk

**Corporate Policy and Planning Branch**
Principal: Robert Breakey
Tel: 028 9082 9498
Email: robert.breakey@dsdni.gov.uk

**Corporate Improvement Team**
Principal: Karen Robinson
Tel: 028 9082 9486
Email: karen.robinson@dsdni.gov.uk

**Departmental Record Office**
Principal: Michael Hillis
Tel: 028 9052 0504
Email: michael.hillis@dsdni.gov.uk

### Urban Regeneration and Community Development Division

Deputy Secretary: John McGrath
Tel: 028 9082 9044
Email: john.mcgrath@dsdni.gov.uk

**Belfast City Centre Regeneration Directorate**
Director: Jackie Johnston
Tel: 028 9027 7685
Email: jackie.johnston@dsdni.gov.uk

**Belfast Regeneration Office**
Director: Frank Duffy
Email: frank.duffy@dsdni.gov.uk

**Urban Regeneration Strategy Directorate**
Director: Linda McHugh
Tel: 028 9082 9018
Email: linda.mchugh@dsdni.gov.uk

**North West Development Office**
Director: Declan O'Loan
Email: declan.o'hare@dsdni.gov.uk

**Regional Development Office**
Director: Henry Johnston
Fax: 028 9025 1902
Email: henry.johnston@dsdni.gov.uk

**Voluntary and Community Unit**
Director: Dave Wall
Tel: 028 9082 9017
Fax: 028 9082 9431
Email: dave.wall@dsdni.gov.uk

### Resources, Housing and Social Security Group

Deputy Secretary: Derek Baker
Tel: 028 9082 9001
Fax: 028 9082 9549
Email: derek.baker@dsdni.gov.uk

### Financial Management Directorate

Director: John Deery
Tel: 028 9082 9016
Fax: 028 9082 9516
Email: john.deery@dsdni.gov.uk

**Finance & Planning Unit**
Principal: Stephen Boyd
Tel: 028 9082 9506
Fax: 028 9082 9516
Email: stephen.boyd@dsdni.gov.uk

**Decision Making & Appeals Service**
Deputy Principal: Roisin McRory
Tel: 028 9037 6288
Fax: 028 9058 2300
Email: roisin.mcrory@dsdni.gov.uk

### Housing Division

Director: David Crothers
Fax: 028 9091 0084
Email: david.crothers@dsdni.gov.uk

**Housing Management**
Principal: Brendan Devlin
Tel: 028 9091 0058
Email: brendan.devlin@dsdni.gov.uk

**Housing Finance**
Principal: Patrick Anderson
Email: patrick.anderson@dsdni.gov.uk

**Housing Associations Branch**
Principal: Billy Graham
Tel: 028 9051 8382
Email: billy.graham@dsdni.gov.uk

**Housing Policy**
Principal: Jerome Burns
Tel: 028 9091 0062
Email: jerome.burns@dsdni.gov.uk

## Department for Social Development Organisation Chart

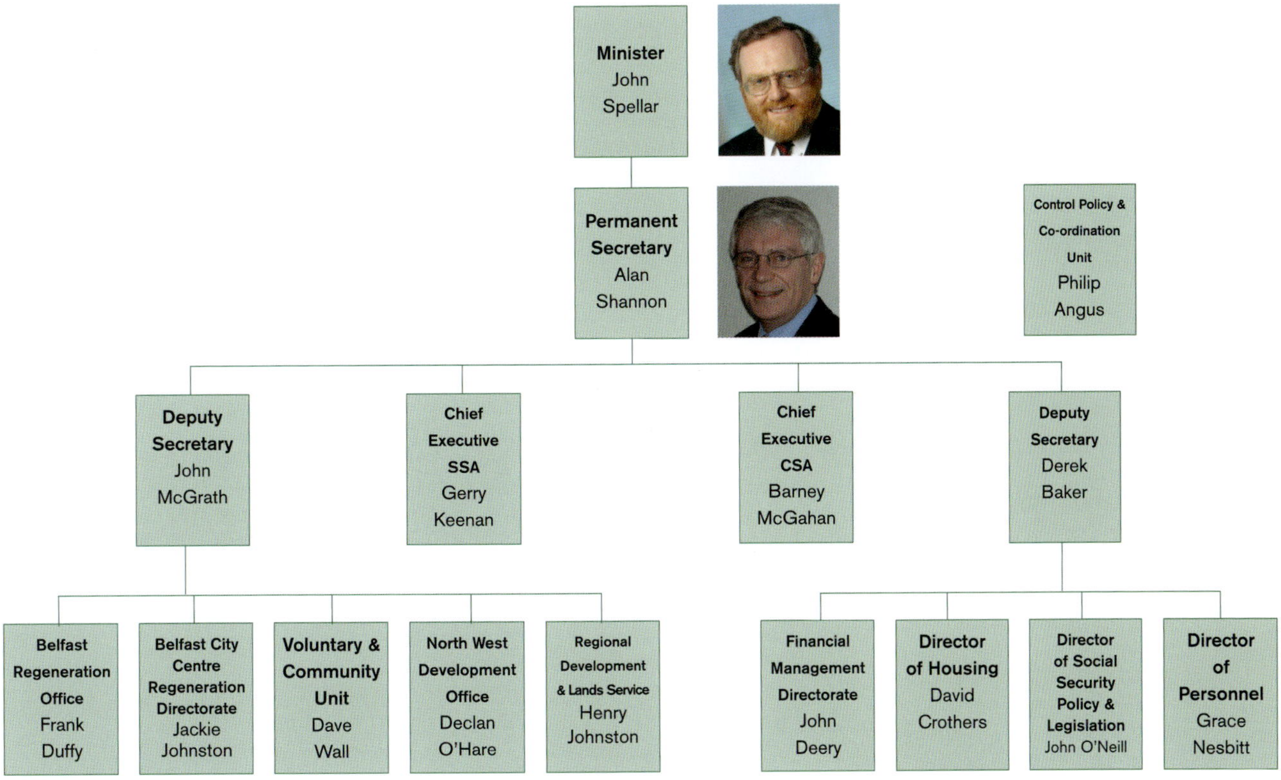


### Social Security Policy and Legislation Division
Director: John O'Neill
Fax: 028 9052 3202
Email: john.oneill@dsdni.gov.uk

### Personnel Division
Director: Grace Nesbitt
Tel: 028 9082 9006
Fax: 028 9082 9555
Email: grace.nesbitt@dsdni.gov.uk
Establishment Officer: Rosaleen Carlin
Tel: 028 9082 9505
Email: rosaleen.carlin@dsdni.gov.uk

### Child Support Agency
Chief Executive: Barney McGahan
Fax: 028 9089 6850
Email: barney.mcgahan@dwp.gsi.gov.uk
Director of Resources: John Canavan
Fax: 028 9089 6850
Email: john.canavan@dwp.gsi.gov.uk

Director NICSAC Operations:
Mary Quinn
Email: mary.quinn@dwp.gsi.gov.uk

Director EBU Field Operations:
Martin Johnston
Email: martin.johnston@dwp.gsi.gov.uk

Operations Manager (NI): Eilish O'Neill
Email: eilish.o'neill@dwp.gsi.gov.uk

Director of Business Development:
Chris Matthews
Tel: 028 9033 9200
Email: chris.matthews@dwp.gsi.gov.uk

Personnel Officer: Jayne Forster
Email: jayne.forster@dwp.gsi.gov.uk

Financial Controller: Jeff Glass
Email: jeff.glass@dwp.gsi.gov.uk

### Social Security Agency
Chief Executive: Gerry Keenan
Tel: 028 9082 9003

Finance Support
Principal: Alan Harvey
Tel: 028 9052 2007

### Human Resources Directorate
Director: Grace Nesbitt
Tel: 028 9082 9006

Personnel Officer
Principal: Margaret Stitt
Tel: 028 9081 9336

Training and Development Unit
Principal: Catherine McCallum
Tel: 028 9054 3649

### Business Development Directorate
Director: Tommy O'Reilly
Tel: 028 9082 9007

Contract and Service Management
Principal: Catherine Houston
Tel: 028 9037 6054

ICT Services
Principal: David McCalmont
Tel: 028 9037 6007

Strategy Unit
Principal: John O'Neill
Tel: 028 9037 6088

Programme Management Office
Principal: Janice Hatchell
Tel: 028 9082 9159

Accommodation Services
Principal: Jennifer Anthony
Tel: 028 9037 6344

Business Impact and Service Delivery
Delivery and Modernisation
Principal: Colin McRoberts
Tel: 028 9037 6020

## Finance and Planning Directorate

Director: Heather Cousins
Tel: 028 9082 9008

Financial Accounting Branch
Principal: Miriam Montgomery
Tel: 028 9082 9346

Planning Branch
Principal: Alison Hanna
Tel: 028 9082 92017

Finance Support
Principal: Alan Harvey
Tel: 028 9052 2007

Financial Management
Principal: Maurice Dowling
Tel: 028 9082 9345

## Operations Directorate

Director: Bryan Davis
Tel: 028 9082 9074

Belfast Benefit Centre
Principal: Mervyn Adair
Tel: 0845 3771025

## Working Age Services

Assistant Director: John Nevin
Tel: 028 9082 9020

**West District**
Principal: Rene Murray
Tel: 028 71319697
**South District**
Principal: Roger Matthews
Tel: 028 8754 3314
**North District**
Principal: Tom Wilson
Tel: 028 9442 6437
**East Down District**
Principal: John Sinnamon
Tel: 028 9054 5664
**Belfast West & Lisburn District**
Principal: Michael McGinn
Tel: 028 9054 4415
**Belfast North & East Antrim**
Principal: Jim Harvey
Tel: 028 9054 3265
**Operations Support**
Principal: Lyzan Martin
Tel: 028 9082 9240

Jobs and Benefits Project
Principal: Geraldine Brereton
Tel: 028 9037 6163

## MSS/IPSU/CPOU/DMU/IBB/ACM

Principal: Malcolm Beattie
Tel: 028 9033 6426
Pensions/Benefit Security
Assistant Director: David McCurry
Tel: 028 9082 9020

Benefit Security Services
Principal: Gerry Boyle
Tel: 028 9054 4604

Programme Protection Group
Tel: 028 7034 1085

Fraud Policy and Assurance Group
Principal: Tom Quinn
Tel: 028 9054 1524

Retirement Pensions/ Bereavement
Benefit and Pensions Mod Projects
Principal: Vacant

Pensions Centre
Principal: Brian Doherty
Tel: 028 7127 4610
Disability and Carers' Service
Assistant Director: Anne Flanagan
Tel: 028 9082 9009

Customer Services and Communications and Marketing
Principal: Margaret Boyle
Tel: 028 9082 9451

Payment Modernisation Programme
Principal: Janet Uhlemann
Tel: 028 9037 6225

Disability & Carers' Unit/Business Transformation Team
Principal: Mickey Kelly
Tel: 028 9033 6940

Quality & Change Support
Principal: Liz McKenna
Tel: 028 9082 9158

Medical Support Services
Director: Terry Dixon
Tel: 028 9054 2128

## Agencies, Non Departmental Public Bodies and other organisations within DSD

**Appeals Service**
Cleaver House, 3 Donegall Square North, Belfast, BT1 5GA
Tel: 028 9056 850
Fax: 028 9051 8516
Web: www.dsdni.gov.uk/appeals-service

**Charities Advisory Committee**
Treasury and Management Branch
4th Floor, Churchill House
Victoria Square, Belfast, BT1 4QW
Tel: 028 9056 9650
Secretary: Trevor Campbell

**Child Support Agency**
Great Northern Tower
17 Great Victoria Street
Belfast, BT2 7AD
Tel: 028 9089 6666
Fax: 028 9089 6777
Chief Executive: Barney McGahan

**Disability Living Allowance Advisory Board for Northern Ireland**
Castle Court, Royal Avenue
Belfast, BT1 1DS
Tel: 028 9033 6916
Fax: 028 9054 2112

**Laganside Corporation**
Clarendon Building, 15 Clarendon Road, Belfast, BT1 3BG
Tel: 028 9032 8507
Fax: 028 9033 2141
Web: www.laganside.com
Email: info@laganside.com
Chief Executive: Kyle Alexander

**Northern Ireland Housing Executive**
The Housing Centre
2 Adelaide Street, Belfast, BT2 8GA
Tel: 028 9024 0288
Fax: 028 9043 9803
Web: www.nihe.gov.uk
Chief Executive: Paddy McIntyre

**Rent Assessment Panel**
Housing Policy Branch
2nd Floor, Andras House
60 Great Victoria Street
Belfast, BT2 7BB
Tel: 028 9091 0050
Fax: 028 9091 0060
Rent Officer: Joan McCrum

**Social Security Agency**
Churchill House
Victoria Square, Belfast, BT1 4SS
Tel: 028 9056 9100
Fax: 028 9056 9178
Web: www.ssa.gov.uk
Email: customerservice.unit@dsdni.gov.uk
Chief Executive: Gerry Keenan

## Other Government Organisations

In addition to the 11 government departments, there exists in Northern Ireland a substantial number of other organisations within the public sector with responsibility for delivering public services. These fall into a number of different categories:

**Agencies**

Agencies tend to be organisations responsible for delivering specific and often customer-facing public services, operating at 'arm's length' from government. Their day-to-day work is involved in delivering that service, the general policy framework under which they operate is set by the relevant department. They are usually run by a Chief Executive and management team, and report to the minister of the relevant department, rather than an appointed Board. Examples of government agencies are Social Security Agency, Health Estates Agency or Business Development Service.

**Non-Departmental Public Bodies**

Non-Departmental Public Bodies (NDPBs) are attached to a sponsoring government department but are not part of that department. They are, however, the responsibility of the Minister of the department they are attached to. There are three categories of non-departmental public bodies: executive NDPBs, advisory NDPBs and tribunal NDPBs. NDPBs are usually accountable to an appointed Board.

**Executive NDPBs**

Executive bodies are public organisations whose duties include executive, administrative, regulatory or commercial functions. Operating within broad policy guidelines set by departmental ministers they are to varying degrees independent of government in the execution of their day-to-day responsibilities, employ their own staff and have their own budget.

Examples of Executive NDPBs in Northern Ireland include the Northern Ireland Housing Executive, Fire Authority for Northern Ireland or Invest Northern Ireland.

**Advisory NDPBs**

These bodies provide an advisory function to government ministers or departments – examples are the Health and Social Services Councils, the Water Council and the Waste Management Advisory Board. Members of these organisations often contribute on a voluntary basis, in addition to their 'day-job'.

**Tribunal NDPBs**

These organisations have jurisdiction in a specified field of law, for example, Mental Health Review Tribunal, Rent Assessment Panel, Fair Employment Tribunal.

## An A-Z Guide to Government Agencies and other Public Bodies

Agricultural Research Institute of Northern Ireland
Large Park
Hillsborough, BT26 6DR
Tel: 028 9268 2484
Fax: 028 9268 9594
Web: www.arini.ac.uk
Director: Dr Sinclair Mayne
Relevant department: Department of Agriculture and Rural Development

Agricultural Wages Board
Agricultural Wages Secretariat
Room 910, Dundonald House
Upper Newtownards Road
Belfast, BT4 3SB
Tel: 028 9052 0813
Fax: 028 9052 4266
Relevant department: Department of Agriculture and Rural Development

Altnagelvin Hospitals HSS Trust
Glenshane Road
Londonderry, BT47 6SB
Tel: 028 7134 5171
Fax: 028 7161 1222
Chairman: Denis Desmond CBE
Chief Executive: Stella Burnside
Relevant department: Department of Health, Social Services and Public Safety

Appeals Service
Cleaver House
3 Donegall Square North
Belfast, BT1 5GA
Tel: 028 9051 8501
Fax: 028 9051 8516
Web: www.dsdni.gov.uk/appeals-service
Relevant department: Department for Social Development

Armagh and Dungannon HSS Trust
St Luke's Hospital
Armagh, BT61 7NQ
Tel: 028 3752 2381
Fax: 028 3752 6302
Web: www.adhsst.n-i.nhs.uk
Chairperson: Deirdre Dorman
Chief Executive: Pauline Stanley
Relevant department: Department of Health, Social Services and Public Safety

Arts Council of Northern Ireland
MacNeice House
77 Malone Road
Belfast, BT9 6AQ
Tel: 028 9038 5200
Fax: 028 9066 1715
Web: www.artscouncil-ni.org
Email: info@artscouncil-ni.org
Chief Executive: Roisin McDonough
Relevant department: Department of Culture, Arts and Leisure

Belfast City Hospital HSS Trust
51 Lisburn Road
Belfast, BT9 7AB
Tel: 028 9032 9241
Fax: 028 9032 6614
Chairperson: Joan Ruddock OBE
Chief Executive: Quentin Coey
Relevant department: Department of Health, Social Services and Public Safety

Belfast Education and Library Board
40 Academy Street
Belfast, BT1 2NQ
Tel: 028 9056 4000
Fax: 028 9033 1714
Chairperson: Carmel McKinney
Chief Executive: David Cargo
Relevant department: Department of Education / Department of Culture, Arts and Leisure

Business Development Service
Craigantlet Buildings, Stoney Road
Belfast, BT4 3SX
Tel: 028 9052 7406
Fax: 028 9052 7270
Web: www.bdsni.gov.uk
Chief Executive: Ray Long
Relevant department: Department of Finance and Personnel

Causeway HSS Trust
8E Coleraine Road
Ballymoney, BT53 6BP
Tel: 028 2766 6600
Fax: 028 2766 1201
Chairperson: Jean Jefferson
Chief Executive (Acting): Alan Braiden
Relevant department: Department of Health, Social Services and Public Safety

Central Services Agency
25-27 Adelaide Street, Belfast, BT2 8FH
Tel: 028 9032 4431
Fax: 028 9023 2304
Web: www.centralservicesagency.com
Email: chiefexec@csa.n-i.nhs.uk
Chairman: Professor John Frances Fulton
Chief Executive: Stephen Hodkinson
Relevant department: Department of Health, Social Services and Public Safety

Charities Advisory Committee
3rd Floor, Lighthouse Building
1 Cromac Place
Gasworks Business Park
Belfast, BT7 2JB
Tel: 028 9082 9000
Secretary: Trevor Campbell
Relevant department: Department for Social Development

Child Support Agency
Great Northern Tower
17 Great Victoria Street
Belfast, BT2 7AD
Tel: 028 9089 6666
Fax: 028 9089 6777
Chief Executive: Barney McGahan
Relevant department: Department for Social Development

Community Relations Council
6 Murray Street, Belfast, BT1 6DN
Tel: 028 9022 7500
Fax: 028 9022 7551
Chief Executive: Dr Duncan Morrow
Relevant department: OFMDFM

Coleraine Harbour
Harbour Office, 4 Riversdale Road
Coleraine, BT52 1XA
Tel: 028 7034 2012
Relevant department: Department for Regional Development

Comhairle na Gaelscolaíochta
Teach an Gheata Thiar
4 Stráid na Banríona
Béal Feirste, BT1 6ED
Guthán: 028 9032 1475
Facs: 028 9032 4475
Web: www.comhairle.org
R-Phost: eolas@comhairle.org
Príomhfheidhmeannach: Seán Ó Coinn

Compensation Agency
Royston House, 34 Upper Queen Street
Belfast, BT1 6FX
Tel: 028 9024 9944
Fax: 028 9024 6956
Web: www.compensationni.gov.uk
Chief Executive: Anne McCleary
Relevant department: NIO

Construction Industry Training Board
Nutts Corner Training Centre
17 Dundrod Road, Crumlin, BT29 4SR
Tel: 028 9082 5466
Fax: 028 9082 5693
Chief Executive: Allan McMullen
Relevant department: Department for Employment and Learning

Council for Catholic Maintained Schools
160 High Street, Holywood, BT18 9HT
Tel: 028 9042 6972
Fax: 028 9042 4255
Chief Executive: Donal Flanagan
Relevant department: Department of Education

Council for Nature Conservation and the Countryside
Waterman House, 5-33 Hill Street
Belfast, BT1 2LA
Tel: 028 9054 3076
Fax: 028 9054 3076
Chairman: Adrian Darby OBE
Relevant department: Department of the Environment

Craigavon and Banbridge Community HSS Trust
Bannvale House, 10 Moyallen Road
Gilford, BT63 5JX
Tel: 028 3883 1983
Fax: 028 3883 1993
Chairman: Joseph Graham Martin
Chief Executive: Glenn Houston
Relevant department: Department of Health, Social Services and Public Safety

Craigavon Area Hospital HSS Trust
68 Lurgan Road, Portadown
Craigavon, BT63 5QQ
Tel: 028 3833 4444
Chairperson: Mrs E McClurg OBE
Chief Executive: John Templeton
Relevant department: Department of Health, Social Services and Public Safety

Criminal Justice Inspection Northern Ireland
14 Great Victoria Street
Belfast, BT2 7BA
Tel: 028 9025 8000
Fax: 028 9025 8033
Chief Inspector: Kit Chivers

Disability Living Allowance Advisory Board for Northern Ireland
Castle Court, Royal Avenue
Belfast, BT1 1DS
Tel: 028 9033 6916
Fax: 028 9054 2112
Relevant department: Department for Social Development

Distinction and Meritorious Service Awards Committee
Room 214, Castle Buildings, Stormont
Belfast, BT4 3SJ
Tel: 028 9052 2817
Secretary: John Nesbitt
Relevant department: Department of Health, Social Services and Public Safety

Down Lisburn HSS Trust
Lisburn Health Centre
25 Linenhall Street, Lisburn, BT28 1LU
Tel: 028 9266 5181
Chairperson: Denise Fitzsimmons
Chief Executive: John Compton
Relevant department: Department of Health, Social Services and Public Safety

Drainage Council
c/o Alan Morton
The Secretary, Rivers Agency
Hydebank, 4 Hospital Road
Belfast, BT8 8JP
Tel: 028 9025 3357
Chairman: Dr Robert Myers
Relevant department: Department of Agriculture and Rural Development

Driver and Vehicle Licensing Northern Ireland (DVLNI)
County Hall, Castlerock Road
Coleraine, BT51 3TA
Web: www.doeni.gov.uk/dvlni
Email: dvlni@doeni.gov.uk
Chief Executive: Brendan Magee
Tel: 028 7034 1461
Relevant department: Department of the Environment

Driver Licensing Division:
Tel: 028 7034 1469
Fax: 028 7034 1398

Vehicle Licensing Division:
Tel: 028 7034 1461
Fax: 028 7034 1422

Vehicle Licensing Central Office
Telephone Re-Licensing Section
Tel: 028 7034 1514

Sale of Mark Section
Tel: 028 7034 1244

Commercial Operator Licensing:
148-158 Corporation Street
Belfast, BT1 3DH
Tel: 028 9025 4100
Fax: 028 9025 4086

## DVLNI Local Offices

Opening hours for all local offices:
9.15am – 4.00pm

**Armagh**
Dobbin Centre, Dobbin Lane
Armagh, BT61 7QP
Tel: 028 3752 7305
Contact: Jill Kane

**Ballymena**
County Hall, Galgorm Road
Ballymena, BT42 1H
Tel: 028 2565 3333
Contact: Ronnie Rowe

**Belfast**
Royston House, Upper Queen Street
Belfast, BT1 6FA
Tel: 028 9054 2042
Contact: Christine Clark

**Coleraine**
County Hall, Castlerock Road
Coleraine, BT51 3TA
Tel: 028 7034 1417
Contact: Clare Wilson

**Downpatrick**
Rathkeltair House, Market Street
Downpatrick, BT30 6AJ
Tel: 028 4461 2211
Contact: Mary Keenan

**Enniskillen**
County Buildings, East Bridge Street
Enniskillen, BT74 7B
Tel: 028 6634 6555
Contact: Kate Charity

**Londonderry**
Orchard House, 40 Foyle Street
Londonderry, BT48 6AT
Tel: 028 7131 9900
Contact: Terence Healey

**Omagh**
Boaz House, 15 Scarffes Entry
Omagh, BT78 1JE
Tel: 028 8225 4700
Contact: Annie Alexander

Driver and Vehicle Testing Agency (DVTA)
Balmoral Road, Belfast, BT12 6QL
Tel: 028 9068 1831
Fax: 028 9066 5520
Web: www.doeni.gov.uk/dvta
Chief Executive: Stanley Duncan
Relevant department: Department of the Environment

## DVTA Local Offices

**Armagh**
47 Hamiltonsbawn Road
Armagh, BT60 1HW
Tel: 028 3752 2699

**Ballymena**
Pennybridge Industrial Estate
Larne Road, Ballymena, BT42 3E
Tel: 028 2565 6801

**Belfast**
Balmoral Road, Belfast, BT12 6QL
Tel: 028 9068 1831

**Coleraine**
2 Loughan Hill Industrial Estate
Gateside Road, Coleraine, BT52 2NJ
Tel: 028 7034 3819

**Cookstown**
Sandholes Road, Cookstown, BT80 9AR
Tel: 028 8676 4809

**Craigavon**
3 Diviny Drive, Carn Industrial Estate
Craigavon, BT63 5RY
Tel: 028 3833 6188

**Downpatrick**
Cloonagh Road, Flying Horse Road
Downpatrick, BT30 6D
Tel: 028 4461 4565

**Enniskillen**
Chanterhill, Enniskillen, BT74 6DE
Tel: 028 6632 2871

**Larne**
Ballyboley Road, Ballyloran
Larne, BT40 2SY
Tel: 028 2827 8808

**Lisburn**
Ballinderry Industrial Estate
Ballinderry Road, Lisburn, BT28 2S
Tel: 028 9266 3151

**Londonderry**
New Buildings Industrial Estat
Victoria Road, Londonderry
Tel: 028 7134 3674

**Mallusk**
Commercial Wa
Hydepark Industrial Estate
Newtownabbey, BT36 8YY
Tel: 028 9084 2111

**Newry**
51 Rathfriland Road, Newry, BT34 1LD
Tel: 028 3026 2853

**Newtownards**
Jubilee Road, Newtownards, BT23 4XP
Tel: 028 9181 3064

**Omagh**
Gortrush Industrial Estate, Derry Road,
Omagh, BT78 5EJ
Tel: 028 8224 2540

Eastern Health and Social Services Board
Champion House, 12-22 Linenhall Street
Belfast, BT2 8BS
Tel: 028 9032 1313
Fax: 028 9055 3681
Chairman: David Russell
Chief Executive: Paula Kilbane
Relevant department: Department of Health, Social Services and Public Safety

Eastern Health and Social Services Council
1st Floor, McKelvey House
25-27 Wellington Place
Belfast, BT1 6GQ
Tel: 028 9032 1230
Fax: 028 9032 1750
Chairperson: Patricia McMillan
Relevant department: Department of Health, Social Services and Public Safety

Economic Research Institute for Northern Ireland (ERINI)
22-24 Mount Charles, Belfast, BT7 1NZ
Tel: 028 9026 1803
Fax: 028 9033 0054
Director: Victor Hewitt

### Enterprise Ulster

The Close, Ravenhill Reach
Belfast, BT6 8RB
Tel: 028 9073 6400
Fax: 028 9073 6404
Web: www.enterpriseulster.co.uk
Chief Executive: Joe Eagleson
Relevant department: Department for Employment and Learning

### Environment and Heritage Service

Chief Executive: Richard Rogers
Web: www.ehsni.gov.uk
Relevant department: Department of the Environment

*Natural Heritage, Waste Management, Regional Operations, Information and Education*
Commonwealth House, 35 Castle Street
Belfast, BT1 1GU
Tel: 028 9025 1477
Fax: 028 9054 6660

*Historic Buildings and Monuments*
5-33 Hill Street, Belfast, BT1 2LA
Tel: 028 9054 3145

Water Management, Drinking Water, Air and Environmental Quality
Calvert House, 23 Castle Place
Belfast, BT1 1FF
Tel: 028 9025 4754

### Equality Commission for Northern Ireland

Equality House
7-9 Shaftesbury Square
Belfast, BT2 7DP
Tel: 028 9050 0600
Fax: 028 9033 1544
Web: www.equalityni.org
Email: information@equalityni.org
Chief Executive: Evelyn Collins
Chief Commissioner: Joan Harbison
Relevant department: OFMDFM

### Fire Authority for Northern Ireland

Brigade Headquarters, 1 Seymour Street
Lisburn, BT27 4SX
Tel: 028 9266 4221
Fax: 028 9267 7402
Web: www.nifb.org.uk
Chairman: William Gillespie
Chief Fire Officer: Colin Lammey
Relevant department: Department of Health, Social Services and Public Safety

### Fisheries Conservancy Board

1 Mahon Road, Portadown, BT62 3EE
Tel: 028 3833 4666
Fax: 028 3833 8912
Web: www.fcbni.com
Chief Executive: Karen Simpson
Relevant department: Department of Culture, Arts and Leisure

### Food Safety Promotion Board

7 Eastgate Avenue, Eastgate
Little Island, Cork
Tel: 00 353 21 230 4100
Fax: 00 353 21 230 4111
Web: www.safefoodonline.com
Chief Executive: Martin Higgins
Relevant department: Department of Health, Social Services and Public Safety

### Food Standards Agency

FOOD STANDARDS AGENCY
NORTHERN IRELAND

Unit 10B Clarendon Road
Belfast, BT1 3BG
Tel: 028 9041 7700
Fax: 028 9041 7726
Email: infofsani@foodstandards.gsi.gov.uk
Web: www.food.gov.uk
Director: Morris McAllister

The Food Standards Agency (FSA) is a non-ministerial UK department set up in 2000. It answers to a board appointed to protect public interest. The FSA has offices in Belfast, Aberdeen, Cardiff and London.

The FSA has three core aims:

- Put the consumer first
- Be open and accessible
- Be an independent voice

FSANI is the central competent authority for food standards. Its roles and responsibilities include:

- Advising Ministers on food safety and standards issues
- Developing policy and proposing legislation
- Auditing district councils' food enforcement activities
- Auditing meat hygiene enforcement by DARD veterinary service
- Giving the public advice on diet and nutrition issues

### Foras na Gaeilge

7 Merrion Square, Dublin 2
Tel: 00 353 1 639 8400
Fax: 00 353 1 639 8401
Web: www.gaeilge.ie
Email: eolas@forasnagaeilge.ie
Chief Executive: Seosamh MacDonncha
Chairperson: Maighread Uí Mhairtin
Relevant department: Department of Culture, Arts and Leisure

### Forensic Science Northern Ireland

151 Belfast Road
Carrickfergus, BT38 8PL
Tel: 028 9036 1888
Fax: 028 9036 1900
Web: www.fsni.gov.uk
Email: forensic.science@fsni.gov.uk
Chief Executive: Michael Walker
Relevant department: Northern Ireland Office

### Forest Service

Dundonald House
Upper Newtownards Road
Belfast, BT4 3SB
Tel: 028 9052 4480
Fax: 028 9052 4570
Web: www.forestserviceni.gov.uk
Chief Executive: Malcolm Beatty
Relevant department: Department of Agriculture and Rural Development

### Foyle HSS Trust

Riverview House, Abercorn Road
Londonderry, BT48 6FB
Tel: 028 7126 6111
Fax: 028 7126 0806
Chairman: Anthony Jackson
Chief Executive: Elaine Way
Relevant department: Department of Health, Social Services and Public Safety

### Foyle, Carlingford and Irish Lights Commission

The Loughs Agency
22 Victoria Road, Waterside
Londonderry, BT47 2AB
Tel: 028 7134 2100
Fax: 028 7134 2720
Web: www.loughs-agency.org
Email: general@loughs-agency.org
Relevant department: Department of Agriculture and Rural Development

## General Consumer Council

Elizabeth House
116 Holywood Road
Belfast, BT4 1NY
Tel: 028 9067 2488
Fax: 028 9065 7701
Web: www.gccni.org.uk

Chief Executive
Eleanor Gill

The General Consumer Council carries out research, publishes reports, influences decision makers and campaigns for a fair deal for consumers. It deals with complaints about electricity, gas, coal, and passenger transport.

Relevant department: Department of Enterprise, Trade and Investment

## General Council of the Bar of Northern Ireland

PO Box 414, Royal Courts of Justice, Chichester Street, Belfast, BT1 3JP
Tel: 028 9056 2349
Web: www.barlibrary.com

## General Teaching Council for Northern Ireland

4th Floor, Albany House
73-75 Great Victoria Street
Belfast, BT2 7AF
Tel: 028 9033 3390
Chairman: Dr Robert Rodgers
Relevant department: Department of Education

## Green Park Healthcare HSS Trust

20 Stockman's Lane, Belfast, BT9 7JB
Tel: 028 9066 9501
Web: www.greenpark.n-i.nhs.uk
Chairman: Ian Doherty
Chief Executive: Hilary Boyd
Relevant department: Health etc

## Health and Safety Executive for Northern Ireland

83 Ladas Drive, Belfast, BT6 9FR
Tel: 028 9024 3249
Web: www.hseni.gov.uk
Chief Executive: Jim Keyes
Relevant department: Department of Health, Social Services and Public Safety

## Health Estates Agency

Stoney Road, Dundonald
Belfast, BT16 1US
Tel: 028 9052 0025
Web: www.dhsspsni.gov.uk/hea
Chief Executive: John Cole
Relevant department: Department of Health, Social Services and Public Safety

## Health Promotion Agency for Northern Ireland

18 Ormeau Avenue, Belfast, BT2 8HS
Tel: 028 9031 1611
Fax: 028 9031 1711
Web: www.healthpromotionagency.org.uk
Chairperson: Alice Quinn
Chief Executive: Dr Brian Gaffney
Relevant department: Department of Health, Social Services and Public Safety

## Historic Buildings Council Secretariat

5-33 Hill Street, BT1 2LA
Tel: 028 9054 3076
Chairman: Ian McQuiston
Relevant department: Department of the Environment

## Historic Monuments Council

5-33 Hill Street, BT1 2LA
Tel: 028 9054 3037
Chairman: Richard Black
Relevant department: Department of the Environment

## Homefirst HSS Trust

The Cottage, 5 Greenmount Avenue
Ballymena, BT43 6DA
Tel: 028 2563 3700
Chairman: Bob Ferguson
Chief Executive: Norma Evans
Relevant department: Department of Health, Social Services and Public Safety

## Independent International Commission on Decommissioning

Rosepark House, Upper Newtownards Road, Belfast, BT4 3NR
Tel: 028 9048 8600
Chairman: John de Chastelain

## Integrated Education Fund

41 University Street, Belfast, BT7 1FY
Tel: 028 9033 0031
Fax: 028 9033 0061
Web: www.ief.org.uk
Director: Tina Merron
Relevant department: Department of Education

## Inter*Trade*Ireland

Old Gasworks Business Park
Kilmorey Street, Newry, BT34 2DE
Tel: 028 3083 4100
Web: www.intertradeireland.com
Email: info@intertradeireland.com
Chief Executive: Liam Nellis
Relevant department: Department of Enterprise, Trade and Investment

## Invest Northern Ireland

Goodwood House, 44-58 May Street
Belfast, BT1 4NN
Tel: 028 9023 9090
Web: www.investni.com
Chief Executive: Leslie Morrison
Relevant department: Department of Enterprise, Trade and Investment

## Iontaobhas na Gaelscolaiochta

199 Bothár na bhFal,
Béal Feirste, BT12 6FB
Guthán: 028 9024 1510
Príomhfheidhmeannach: Pilib Ó Runaidh
Relevant department: Department of Education

## Labour Relations Agency

Head Office
2-8 Gordon Street
Belfast, BT1 2LG
Tel: 028 9032 1442
Fax: 028 9033 0827

Regional Office
1-3 Guildhall Street
Londonderry, BT48 6BJ
Tel: 028 7126 9639
Fax: 028 7126 7729

Chief Executive
Willam Patterson

The Labour Relations Agency promotes the improvement of employment relations in Northern Ireland by providing impartial and independent services for promoting good employment practices and preventing and resolving disputes.

Relevant department: Department for Employment and Learning

### Laganside Corporation
Clarendon Building, 15 Clarendon Road
Belfast, BT1 3BG
Tel: 028 9032 8507
Web: www.laganside.com
Email: info@laganside.com
Chief Executive: Kyle Alexander
Relevant department: Department for Social Development

### Land Registers of Northern Ireland
Lincoln Building
27-45 Great Victoria Street
Belfast, BT2 7SL
Tel: 028 9025 1515
Web: www.lrni.gov.uk
Chief Executive: Patricia Montgomery
Relevant department: Department of Finance and Personnel

### Law Reform Advisory Committee for Northern Ireland
Lancashire House, 5 Linenhall Street
Belfast, BT2 8AA
Tel: 028 9054 2900
Web: www.olrni.gov.uk
Secretary: Clare Irvine
Email: clare.irvine@dfpni.gov.uk
Relevant department: Department of Finance and Personnel

### Learning and Skills Advisory Board
Chairman: Bill McGinnis
c/o Department for Employment and Learning
Adelaide House, Adelaide Street
Belfast, BT2 8FD
Tel: 028 9025 7777
Web: www.del.gov.uk
Relevant department: Department for Employment and Learning

### Library and Information Services Council Northern Ireland
PO Box 1231, Belfast, BT8 6AL
Tel: 028 9070 5441
Web: www.liscni.co.uk
Executive Officer: Mairead Gilheany
Relevant department: Department of Agriculture and Rural Development

### Livestock and Meat Commission for Northern Ireland
Lissue House, 31 Ballinderry Road
Lisburn, BT28 2SL
Tel: 028 9263 3000
Web: www.lmcni.com
Chief Executive: David Rutledge
Relevant department: Department of Agriculture and Rural Development

### Local Government Staff Commission
Commission House
18-22 Gordon Street, Belfast, BT1 2LG
Tel: 028 9031 3200
Web: www.lgsc.org.uk
Email: info@lgsc.org.uk
Chief Executive: Adrian Kerr
Relevant department: Department of the Environment

### Londonderry Port and Harbour
Harbour Office, Port Road, Lisahally
Londonderry, BT47 6FL
Tel: 028 7186 0555
Web: www.londonderryport.com
Email: info@londonderry-port.co.uk
Chief Executive: Brian McGrath
Relevant department: Department for Regional Development

### Mater Infirmorum HSS Trust
45-51 Crumlin Road, Belfast, BT14 6AB
Tel: 028 9080 2338
Fax: 028 9074 9784
Web: www.n-i.nhs.uk/mater
Chairperson: Lady McCollum
Chief Executive: Sean Donaghy
Relevant department: Department of Health, Social Services and Public Safety

### Mental Health Commission
Elizabeth House, 118 Holywood Road
Belfast, BT4 1NY
Tel: 028 9065 1157
Email: mhc@dhsspsni.gov.uk
Chairperson: Marian O'Neill
Acting Chief Executive: Stephen Jackson
Relevant department: Department of Health, Social Services and Public Safety

### Mental Health Review Tribunal
Room 11 Annex 6, Castle Buildings
Stormont, Belfast, BT4 3SQ
Tel: 028 9052 3388
Fax: 028 9052 0683
Chairman: Fraser Elliott QC
Secretary: Esther Clarke/Alison Bray
Relevant department: Department of Health, Social Services and Public Safety

### Museums and Galleries of Northern Ireland (MAGNI)
Ulster Museum
Botanic Gardens, Belfast, BT9 5AB
Tel: 028 9038 3000
Fax: 028 3083 3003
Web: www.magni.org.uk
Chief Executive: Tim Cooke
Relevant department: Department of Culture, Arts and Leisure

### NI-CO
25-27 Franklin Street
Belfast, BT2 8DS
Tel: 028 9034 7750
Fax: 028 9024 9730
Web: www.nico.org.uk
Chief Executive: Rupert Haydock

NI-CO was established by Government in 1992 to market the skills and expertise of Northern Ireland overseas. Boasting a portfolio of over 150 projects in 40 different countries, NI-CO is today recognised as one of the leading providers of technical assistance in Europe.

### Newry and Mourne HSS Trust
5 Downshire Place, Downshire Road
Newry, BT34 1DZ
Tel: 028 3026 0505
Fax: 028 3026 9064
Chief Executive: Eric Bowyer
Relevant department: Department of Health, Social Services and Public Safety

### North and West Belfast HSS Trust
Glendinning House, 6 Murray Street
Belfast, BT1 6DP
Tel: 028 9032 7156
Fax: 028 9082 1285
Chairman: Patrick McCartan
Chief Executive: Richard Black
Relevant department: Department of Health, Social Services and Public Safety

### North Eastern Education and Library Board
County Hall, 182 Galgorm Road
Ballymena, BT42 1HN
Tel: 028 2565 3333
Fax: 028 2564 6071
Chairperson: J Christie
Chief Executive: Gordon Topping
Relevant department: Department of Education / Department of Culture, Arts and Leisure

Northern Health and Social Services Board
County Hall, 182 Galgorm Road
Ballymena, BT42 1HN
Tel: 028 2565 3333
Fax: 028 2565 2311
Chairman: Michael Wood
Chief Executive: Stuart Macdonnell
Relevant department: Department of Health, Social Services and Public Safety

Northern Health and Social Services Council
8 Broadway Avenue
Ballymena, BT43 7AA
Tel: 028 2565 5777
Fax: 028 2565 5112
Chairman (Acting): Thomas Creighton
Chief Officer: Noel Graham
Relevant department: Department of Health, Social Services and Public Safety

Northern Ireland Ambulance HSS Trust
Knockbracken Healthcare Park
Saintfield Road, Belfast, BT8 8SG
Tel: 028 9040 0999
Fax: 028 9040 0900
Web: www.niamb.co.uk
Chairman: Doug Smyth
Chief Executive: Liam McIver
Relevant department: Department of Health, Social Services and Public Safety

Northern Ireland Authority for Energy Regulation
Brookmount Buildings, 42 Fountain Street
Belfast, BT1 5EE
Tel: 028 9031 1575
Fax: 028 9031 1740
Web: www.ofreg.nics.gov.uk
Chairman: Douglas McIldoon

Northern Ireland Blood Transfusion Service Agency
Belfast City Hospital Complex
51 Lisburn Road, Belfast, BT9 7TS
Tel: 028 9053 4662
Fax: 028 9043 9017
Web: www.nibts.org
Email: chiefexec@nibts.n-i.nhs.uk
Chairman: Stephen Costello
Chief Executive: Dr Morris McClelland
Relevant department: Department of Health, Social Services and Public Safety

Northern Ireland Building Regulations Advisory Committee
Building Regulations Unit
Office Estates and Building Standards Division
Department of Finance and Personnel
3rd Floor, Lancashire House
3 Linenhall Street, Belfast, BT2 8AA
Tel: 028 9054 2933
Fax: 028 9054 7866
Relevant department: Department of Finance and Personnel

Northern Ireland Commissioner for Children and Young People (NICCY)
Millennium House
17-25 Great Victoria Street
Belfast, BT2 7BN
Tel: 028 9031 1616
Web: www.niccy.org
Commissioner for Children and Young People: Nigel Williams
Relevant department: OFMDFM

Northern Ireland Council for Curriculum, Examinations and Assessment
29 Clarendon Road, Clarendon Dock
Belfast, BT1 3BG
Tel: 028 9026 1200
Fax: 028 9026 1234
Web: www.ccea.org.uk
Email: info@ccea.org.uk
Chief Executive: Gavin Boyd
Relevant department: Department of Education

Northern Ireland Council for Integrated Education
13-19 University Road, Belfast, BT7 1NA
Tel: 028 9023 6200
Fax: 028 9023 6237
Web: www.nicie.org
Email: info@nicie.org
Chief Executive Officer: Michael Wardlow
Relevant department: Department of Education

Northern Ireland Court Service
21st Floor, Windsor House
9-15 Bedford Street
Belfast, BT2 7LT
Tel: 028 9032 8594
Fax: 028 9032 8494
Web: www.courtsni.gov.uk
Relevant department: Northern Ireland Office

Northern Ireland Events Company
Redwood House, 66 Newforge Lane
Belfast, BT9 5NT
Tel: 028 9066 6661
Fax: 028 9066 8040
Web: www.nievents.co.uk
Email: info@nievents.co.uk
Chief Executive: Janice McAleese
Relevant department: Department of Culture, Arts and Leisure

Northern Ireland Fishery Harbour Authority
3 St Patrick's Avenue
Downpatrick, BT30 6DW
Tel: 028 4461 3844
Fax: 028 4461 7128
Web: www.nifha.fsnet.co.uk
Email: info@nifha.fsnet.co.uk
Chief Executive: Chris Warnock
Relevant department: Department of Agriculture and Rural Development

Northern Ireland Guardian Ad Litem Agency
Centre House, 79 Chichester Street
Belfast, BT1 4JE
Tel: 028 9031 6550
Fax: 028 9031 9811
Web: www.nigala.n-i.nhs.uk
Email: admin@nigala.n-i.nhs.uk
Chairman: Jim Currie
Chief Executive: Ronnie Williamson
Relevant department: Department of Health, Social Services and Public Safety

Northern Ireland Higher Education Council
Adelaide House, 39-49 Adelaide Street
Belfast, BT2 8FD
Tel: 028 9025 7777
Fax: 028 9025 7778
Chairman: Tony Hopkins
Relevant department: Department for Employment and Learning

Northern Ireland Housing Executive
The Housing Centre, 2 Adelaide Street
Belfast, BT2 8GA
Tel: 028 9024 0588
Fax: 028 9043 9803
Web: www.nihe.gov.uk
Chief Executive: Paddy McIntyre
Relevant department: Department for Social Development

### Northern Ireland Human Rights Commission

Temple Court, 39 North Street
Belfast, BT1 1NA
Tel: 028 9024 3987
Fax: 028 9023 7844
Web: www.nihrc.org
Chief Commissioner:
Professor Brice Dickson
Chief Executive: Paddy Sloan

### Northern Ireland Industrial Court

Room 203, Adelaide House
39-49 Adelaide Street
Belfast, BT2 8FD
Tel: 028 9025 7676
Web: www.delni.gov.uk/er
Senior Case Manager: Joanna Calixto
Relevant department: Department for Employment and Learning

### Northern Ireland Local Government Officers Superannuation Committee

Templeton House, 411 Holywood Road
Belfast, BT4 2LP
Tel: 028 9076 8025
Fax: 028 9076 8790
Web: www.nilgosc.org.uk
Email: info@nilgosc.org.uk
Chairman: John Galbraith
Relevant department: Department of the Environment

### Northern Ireland Medical and Dental Training Agency

5 Annadale Avenue, Belfast, BT7 3JH
Tel: 028 9049 2731
Fax: 028 9064 2279
Web: www.nicpmde.com
Email: nicpmde@nicpmde.gov.uk
Chairman: Dr Don Keegan
Chief Executive: Dr JR McCluggage
Relevant department: Department of Health, Social Services and Public Safety

### Northern Ireland Museums Council

6 Crescent Gardens, Belfast, BT7 1NS
Tel: 028 9055 0215
Fax: 028 9055 0216
Web: www.nimc.co.uk
Email: info@nimc.co.uk
Director: Chris Bailey
Relevant department: Department of Culture, Arts and Leisure

### Northern Ireland Policing Board

Northern Ireland PolicingBoard Defining the future

Waterside Tower
31 Clarendon Road
Clarendon Dock
Belfast, BT1 3BG
Tel: 028 9040 8500
Fax: 028 9040 8525
Email: information@nipolicingboard.org.uk
Web: www.nipolicingboard.org.uk

Chairman
Professor Desmond Rea

The Northern Ireland Policing Board was created on 4 November 2001 and is tasked with securing the maintenance, effectiveness and efficiency of the Police Service of Northern Ireland. It draws its legislative powers from the Police (NI) Acts 2000 & 2003. Its key responsibility is to hold the Chief Constable to account for his actions and those of his staff - this means that the Chief Constable is answerable to the Board on any aspect of policing in Northern Ireland.

### Northern Ireland Practice and Education Council for Nursing and Midwifery

Centre House, 79 Chichester Street
Belfast, BT1 4JE
Tel: 028 9023 8152
Fax: 028 9023 3298
Chief Executive: Ms Paddie Blaney
Relevant department: Department of Health, Social Services and Public Safety

### Northern Ireland Prison Service

Dundonald House
Upper Newtownards Road
Belfast, BT4 3SU
Tel: 028 9052 5065
Fax: 028 9052 5160
Email: info@niprisonservice.gov.uk
Web: www.niprisonservice.gov.uk
Director General: Peter Russell
Relevant department: NIO

### Northern Ireland Regional Medical Physics Agency

Musgrave and Clarke House
Royal Hospitals Site, Grosvenor Road
BT12 6BA
Tel: 028 9063 4430
Fax: 028 9031 3040
Web: www.medicalphysics.n-i.nhs.uk
Chairman: Professor David Walmsley
Chief Executive: Professor Peter Jaritt
Relevant department: Department of Health, Social Services and Public Safety

### Northern Ireland Social Care Council

7th Floor Millennium House
19-25 Great Victoria Street
Belfast, BT2 7AQ
Tel: 028 9041 7600
Fax: 028 9041 7601
Web: www.niscc.info
Chief Executive: Brendan Johnston
Chairman: Jeremy Harbison
Relevant department: Department of Health, Social Services and Public Safety

### Northern Ireland Statistics and Research Agency

McAuley House, 2-14 Castle Street
Belfast, BT1 1SA
Tel: 028 9034 8100
Fax: 028 9034 8106
Web: www.nisra.gov.uk
Chief Executive: Norman Caven
Relevant department: Department of Finance and Personnel

### Northern Ireland Tourist Board

St Anne's Quarter, North Street
Belfast, BT1 1NB
Tel: 028 9023 1221
Fax: 028 9024 0960
Web: www.nitb.com
Chief Executive: Alan Clarke
Relevant department: Department of Enterprise, Trade and Investment

### Northern Ireland Transport Holding Company

Chamber of Commerce House
22 Great Victoria Street
Belfast, BT2 7LX
Tel: 028 9024 3456
Fax: 028 9043 8717
Web: www.translink.co.uk/nithco
Email: nithc@dialstart.net
Chairperson: Dr Joan Smyth
Corporate Director: Jim Aiken
Relevant department: Department for Regional Development

North/South Language Body

The North/South Language Body is a single body composed of two separate and largely autonomous agencies, the Ulster Scots Agency and Foras na Gaeilge – their contact details are listed separately.

OFCOM

Landmark House, The Gasworks
Ormeau Road, Belfast, BT7 2JD
Tel: 028 9041 7500
Fax: 028 9041 7533
Director Northern Ireland: Denis Wolinsky

Office of the Commissioner for Public Appointments (Northern Ireland)

Room E5.20, Castle Buildings
Stormont Estate
Upper Newtownards Road
Belfast, BT4 3SR
Tel: 028 9052 8187
Fax: 028 9052 2522
Web: www.ocpa.gov.uk
Relevant department: OFMDFM

Ordnance Survey of Northern Ireland

Colby House, Stranmillis Court
Malone Lower, Belfast, BT9 5BJ
Tel: 028 9025 5755
Fax: 028 9025 5700
Web: www.osni.gov.uk
Email: osni@osni.gov.uk
Chief Executive: Mick Cory
Relevant department: Department of Culture, Arts and Leisur

Parades Commission

Windsor House, 9-15 Bedford Street
Belfast, BT2 7EL
Tel: 028 9089 5900
Fax: 028 9032 2988
Web: www.paradescommission.com
Email: info@paradescommission.org
Chairman: Sir Anthony Holland
Commission Secretary: Andrew Elliott

Pig Production Development Committee

c/o Farm Policy Division
Room 910, Dundonald House
Upper Newtownards Road
Belfast, BT4 3SB
Tel: 028 9052 4873
Fax: 028 9052 4266
Relevant department: Department of Agriculture and Rural Development

Planning Appeals Commission

Park House, 87-91 Great Victoria Street
Belfast, BT2 7AG
Tel: 028 9024 4710
Fax: 028 9031 2536
Web: www.pacni.gov.uk
Email: info@pacni.gov.uk
Chief Commissioner: John Warke
Relevant department: OFMDFM

Planning Service

Millennium House, 17-25 Great Victoria Street, Belfast, BT2 7BN
Tel: 028 9041 6700
Fax: 028 9041 6983
Web: www.planningni.gov.uk
Chief Executive: David Ferguson
Tel: 028 9054 0649
Relevant department: Department of the Environment

**Planning Service Regional Offices**

*Ballymena*
County Hall, 182 Galgorm Hall,
Ballymena, BT42 1QF
Tel: 028 2565 3333
Fax: 028 2566 2127
Divisional Planning Manager:
Helena O'Toole

*Belfast*
Bedford House, 16-22 Bedford Street
Belfast, BT2 7FD
Tel: 028 9025 2800
Fax: 028 9025 2828
Divisional Planning Manager: Vacant

*Coleraine*
County Hall, Castlerock Road
Coleraine, BT51 3HS
Tel: 028 7034 1300
Fax: 028 7034 1434
Divisional Planning Manager:
Mary McIntyre

*Craigavon*
Marlborough House, Central Way
Craigavon, BT64 1AD
Tel: 028 3834 1144
Fax: 028 3834 1065
Divisional Planning Manager:
Hilary Heslip

*Downpatrick*
Rathkeltair House, Market Street
Downpatrick, BT30 6EJ
Tel: 028 4461 2211
Fax: 028 4461 8196
Divisional Planning Manager:
Clifford McIlwaine

*Enniskillen*
County Buildings, 15 East Bridge Street
Enniskillen, BT74 7BW
Tel: 028 6634 6555
Fax: 028 6634 6550
Divisional Planning Manager:
Brian Hughes

*Londonderry*
Orchard House, 40 Foyle Street
Londonderry, BT48 6AT
Tel: 028 7131 9900
Fax: 028 7131 9777
Divisional Planning Manager:
Mary McIntyre

*Omagh*
County Hall, Drumragh Avenue
Omagh, BT79 7AE
Tel: 028 8225 4000
Fax: 028 8225 4009
Divisional Planning Manager:
Brian Hughes

Police Ombudsman

police Ombudsman FOR NORTHERN IRELAND

Police Ombudsman for Northern Ireland
New Cathedral Buildings
St Anne's Square
11 Church Street
Belfast, BT1 1PG
Tel: 028 9082 8600 / 0845 601 2931
Fax: 028 9082 8659
Email: info@policeombudsman.org
Web: www.policeombudsman.org

Police Ombudsman
Mrs Nuala O'Loan

The Police Ombudsman's Office deals with complaints from the public about the conduct of police officers in Northern Ireland. You do not have to pay for this service.

Relevant Department: Northern Ireland Office

## Police Service of Northern Ireland

PSNI Headquarters
65 Knock Road
Belfast BT5 6LE
Tel: 028 90650222
Web: www.psni.police.uk

Chief Constable
Hugh Orde

Making Northern Ireland Safer for Everyone Through Professional, Progressive Policing.

## Port of Belfast

Belfast Harbour Commissioners
Harbour Office, Corporation Square
Belfast, BT1 3AL
Tel: 028 9055 4422
Fax: 028 9055 4411
Email: info@belfast-harbour.co.uk
Web: www.belfast-harbour.co.uk
Chief Executive: John Doran
Relevant department: Department for Regional Development

## Probation Board for Northern Ireland

80-90 North Street, Belfast, BT1 1LD
Tel: 028 9026 2400
Fax: 028 9026 2470
Email: info@pbni.org.uk
Web: www.pbni.org.uk
Chairman: Vacant
Chief Executive: Noel Rooney
Relevant department: Northern Ireland Office

## Public Record Office of Northern Ireland

66 Balmoral Avenue, Belfast, BT9 6NY
Tel: 028 9025 1318
Fax: 028 9025 5999
Web: www.proni. gov.uk
Email: proni@dcalni.gov.uk
Chief Executive: Dr Gerry Slater
Relevant department: Department of Culture, Arts and Leisure

## Rate Collection Agency

Oxford House, 49-55 Chichester Street
Belfast, BT1 4HH
Tel: 028 9052 2252
Web: www.ratecollectionagencyni.gov.uk
Chief Executive: Arthur Scott
Relevant department: Department of Finance and Personnel

## Rent Assessment Panel

Housing Policy Branch
2nd Floor, Andras House
60 Great Victoria Street
Belfast, BT2 7BB
Tel: 028 9091 0050
Rent Officer: Joan McCrum
Relevant department: Department for Social Development

## Rivers Agency

Hydebank, 4 Hospital Road
Belfast, BT8 8JP
Tel: 028 9025 3355
Chief Executive: John Hagan
Tel: 028 9025 3440
Web: www.riversagencyni.gov.uk
Relevant department: Department of Agriculture and Rural Development

## Roads Service

Clarence Court
10-18 Adelaide Street
Belfast, BT2 8GB
Tel: 028 9054 0540
Web: www.roadsni.gov.uk
Chief Executive: Malcom McKibben
Relevant department: Department for Regional Development

**Roads Service Regional Offices**

*Eastern Division*
Hydebank, 4 Hospital Road
Belfast, BT8 8JL
Tel: 028 9025 3000
Divisional Manager: Joe Drew

*Northern Division*
County Hall, Castlerock Road
Coleraine, BT51 3HS
Tel: 028 7034 1300
Divisional Manager: Dr Andrew Murray

*Southern Division*
Marlborough House, Central Way
Craigavon, BT64 1AD
Tel: 028 3834 1144
Divisional Manager: John White

*Western Division*
County Hall, Drumragh Avenue
Omagh, BT79 7AF
Tel: 028 8225 4111
Divisional Manager: Pat Doherty

## Ordnance Survey of Northern Ireland

Mick Cory CEO

Colby House, Stranmillis Court
Belfast, BT9 8BJ
Tel: 028 9025 5755
Fax: 028 9025 5700

Ordnance Survey of Northern Ireland (OSNI) is an Executive Agency within the Department of Culture, Arts and Leisure. It is the official Government organisation responsible for supplying mapping and geographic information services for NI and for co-ordinating the implementation of Mosaic - a Geographical Information Strategy, which includes the definitive address database for Northern Ireland.

OSNI's work captures and records data about place and location, it defines direction, distance, area and height and provides a unique record of Northern Ireland's landscape and environment.

OSNI provides maps in paper and digital form aerial imagery, geographically referenced address, boundary, road and data needed by the economy and society. OSNI's customers are in the public and private sectors and also include local utilities, emergency services, engineers, architects, walkers and tourists.

OSNI's dedicated Geographic Information Systems (GIS) Support team provides support for existing users of OSNI data, enabling them to get maximum value for money and to utilise the full intelligence of mapping and address data. They also encourage the uptake of GIS by educating potential users of the applications of GIS for their organisation. OSNI is striving to be a leading public service organisation, which plays a key role in underpinning the economy of Northern Ireland.

**Contact Details**
OSNI General Enquiries
028 9025 5755
OSNI Services
Digital Data Supply: 028 9025 5721
Copyright/IPR: 028 9025 5722
Paper Map Sales: 028 9025 5769
GIS Support Unit: 028 9025 5737
Aerial Photography &
Historical Maps: 028 9025 5743
***www.osni.gov.uk***

mosaic

information on location

Many parts of Government have Geographic Information Systems (GIS) under development.

Mosaic is the brand name for the implemenation of the Geographic Information (GI) Strategy for Northern Ireland, an initiative being progressed by the Department of Culture, Arts and Leisure, through its Agency, Ordnance Survey of Northern Ireland.

Mosaic has been established to share best practice in developing GI and GIS within Government, and also to help Government share information being created from these projects, both within Government and with the Citizen.

A number of sectoral groups have been established:

- Culture & Heritage
- Education & Awareness
- Statistics
- Land & Property
- Utilities & Networks
- Environment & Agriculture
- Transport
- Health & Social Improvement
- Public Safety & Emergency Services

To join a sectorial group, or to find out more information about Mosaic, email: **info@mosaic-ni.gov.uk**

FURTHER INFORMATION

For further information contact MOSAIC, Colby House, Stranmillis Court, Malone Lower, Belfast, BT9 5BJ

Royal Group of Hospitals and Dental Hospital HSS Trust
Grosvenor Road, Belfast, BT12 6BA
Tel: 028 9024 0503
Fax: 028 9024 0899
Chairperson: Anne Balmer
Chief Executive: William McKee
Relevant department: Department of Health, Social Services and Public Safety

Rural Development Council
17 Loy Street, Cookstown, BT80 8PZ
Tel: 028 8676 6980
Fax: 028 8676 6922
Web: www.rdc.org.uk
Email: info@rdc.org.uk
Chief Executive: Martin McDonald
Relevant department: Department of Agriculture and Rural Development

Social Security Agency
Churchill House, Victoria Square
Belfast, BT1 4SS
Tel: 028 9056 9100
Fax: 028 9056 9178
Web: www.ssani.gov.uk
Chief Executive: Gerry Keenan
Relevant department: Department for Social Development

South and East Belfast HSS Trust
Knockbracken Healthcare Park
Saintfield Road, Belfast, BT8 8BH
Tel: 028 9056 5656
Fax: 028 9056 5813
Chairman: Robin Harris
Chief Executive: Patricia Gordon
Relevant department: Department of Health, Social Services and Public Safety

South Eastern Education and Library Board
Grahamsbridge Road, Dundonald
Belfast, BT16 2HS
Tel: 028 9056 6200
Fax: 028 9056 6266
Chairperson: R Gibson
Chief Executive: Mr Jackie Fitzsimons
Relevant department: Department of Education / Department of Culture, Arts and Leisure

Southern Education and Library Board
3 Charlemont Place, The Mall
Armagh, BT61 9AX
Tel: 028 3751 2200
Fax: 0287 3751 2490
Chairman: M Alexander
Chief Executive: Helen McClenaghan
Relevant department: Department of Education / Department of Culture, Arts and Leisure

Southern Health and Social Services Board
Tower Hill, Armagh, BT61 9DR
Tel: 028 3741 0041
Fax: 028 3741 4550
Chairman: Fionnuala Cook OBE
Chief Executive: Colm Donaghy
Relevant department: Department of Health, Social Services and Public Safety

Southern Health and Social Services Council
Quaker Buildings, High Street
Lurgan, BT66 8BB
Tel: 028 3834 9900
Fax: 028 3834 9858
Chairperson: Roisin Foster
Relevant department: Department of Health, Social Services and Public Safety

Sperrin Lakeland HSS Trust
Strathdene House
Tyrone and Fermanagh Hospital
Omagh, BT79 0NS
Tel: 028 8283 5285
Fax: 028 8283 5286
Chairman: Richard Scott
Chief Executive: Hugh Mills
Relevant department: Department of Health, Social Services and Public Safety

Sports Council for Northern Ireland
House of Sport, Upper Malone Road
Belfast, BT9 5LA
Tel: 028 90381222
Fax: 028 9068 2757
Web: www.sportni.net
Email: info@sportni.net
Chief Executive: Eamon McCartan
Relevant department: Department of Culture, Arts and Leisure

Staff Commission for Education and Library Boards
Forestview, Purdy's Lane
Belfast, BT8 7AR
Tel: 028 9049 1461
Fax: 028 9049 1744
Web: www.staffcom.org.uk
Email: info@staffcom.org.uk
Chairman: Professor Bernard Cullen
Chief Executive: Patricia Weir
Relevant department: Department of Education

Strategic Investment Board
Castle Buildings, Level 5, Block A
Belfast, BT4 3SR
Tel: 028 9052 8666
Fax: 028 9052 2432
Chief Executive: David Gavaghan

Tourism Ireland Limited
Beresford House, 2 Beresford Road
Coleraine, BT52 1GE
Tel: 028 7035 9200
Fax: 028 7032 6932
Chief Executive: Paul O'Toole
Relevant department: Department of Enterprise, Trade and Investment

Ulster Community and Hospitals HSS Trust
39 Regent Street
Newtownards, BT23 4AD
Tel: 028 9181 6666
Fax: 028 9182 0140
Chairperson: Siubhan Grant
Chief Executive: Jim McCall
Relevant department: Department of Health, Social Services and Public Safety

Ulster Scots Agency
Franklin House
10-12 Brunswick Street
Belfast, BT2 7GE
Tel: 028 9023 1113
Fax: 028 9023 1898
Email: info@ulsterscotsagency.org.uk
Web: www.ulsterscotsagency.com
Chief Executive: George Patton
Acting Chair: Jim Devenney
Relevant department: Department of Culture, Arts and Leisure

Ulster Supported Employment Limited
182-188 Cambrai Street
Belfast, BT13 3JH
Tel: 028 9035 6600
Fax: 028 9035 6611
Web: www.usel.co.uk
Email: info@usel.co.uk
Chief Executive: Mitchell Wylie
Relevant department: Department for Employment and Learning

United Hospitals HSS Trust
Bush House, 45 Bush Road
Antrim, BT41 2QB
Tel: 028 9442 4673
Fax: 028 9442 4675
Chairman: Raymond Milnes
Chief Executive: Bernard Mitchell
Relevant department: Department of Health, Social Services and Public Safety

Valuation and Lands Agency
Queen's Court
56-66 Upper Queen Street
Belfast, BT1 6FD
Tel: 028 9025 0700
Fax: 028 9054 3750
Web: www.vla.nics.gov.uk
Chief Executive: Nigel Woods
Relevant department: Department of Finance and Personnel

Warrenpoint Harbour
Warrenpoint Harbour Authority
Warrenpoint, BT34 3JR
Tel: 028 4177 3381
Fax: 028 4175 2875
Web: www.warrenpointharbour.co.uk
Email: info@warrenpointharbour.co.uk
Chief Executive: Quintin Goldie
Relevant department: Department of Culture, Arts and Leisure

Waste Management Advisory Board for Northern Ireland
Waterman House, 5-33 Hill Street
Belfast, BT1 2LA
Tel: 028 9054 3086
Fax: 028 9054 3106
Chairperson: Professor Deborah Boyd
Relevant department: Department of the Environment

Water Appeals Commission
Park House, 87-91 Great Victoria Street
Belfast, BT2 7AG
Tel: 028 9024 4710
Fax: 028 9031 2536
Web: www.pacni.gov.uk
Relevant department: Office of the First Minister and Deputy First Minister

Water Council
Water Service Strategic Policy Branch
Room 1.08, 34 College Street
Belfast, BT1 6DR
Tel: 028 9054 1158
Fax: 028 9054 1156
Web: www.watercouncilni.gov.uk
Email: secretary@watercouncilni.gov.uk
Relevant department: Department for Regional Development

Water Service
Northland House, 3 Frederick Street
Belfast, BT1 2NR
Tel: 028 9024 4711
Fax: 028 9032 4888
Web: www.waterni.gov.uk
Email: waterline@waterni.gov.uk
Chief Executive: Katharine Bryan
Relevant department: Department for Regional Development

**Eastern Division**
34 College Street, Belfast, BT1 6DR
Tel: 028 9032 8161
Fax: 028 9035 4828

**Northern Division**
Academy House
121a Broughshane Street
Ballymena, BT43 6BA
Tel: 028 2565 3655
Fax: 028 2566 3131

**Southern Division**
Marlborough House, Central Way
Craigavon, BT64 1AD
Tel: 028 3834 1100
Fax: 028 3832 0555

**Western Division**
Belt Road, Altnagelvin
Londonderry, BT47 2LL
Tel: 028 7131 2221
Fax: 028 7131 0330

Western Education and Library Board
1 Hospital Road, Omagh, BT79 0AW
Tel: 028 8241 1411
Fax: 028 8241 1400
Chairperson: Harry Mullan
Chief Executive: Barry Mulholland
Relevant department: Department of Education / Department of Culture, Arts and Leisure

Western Health and Social Services Board
15 Gransha Park, Clooney Road
Londonderry, BT47 6FN
Tel: 028 7186 0086
Fax: 028 7186 0311
Chairperson: Karen Meehan
Chief Executive: Steven Lindsay
Relevant department: Department of Health, Social Services and Public Safety

Western Health and Social Services Council
Hilltop, Tyrone and Fermanagh Hospital
Omagh, BT79 0NS
Tel: 028 8225 2555
Fax: 028 8225 2544
Chairman: Patrick McGowan
Chief Officer: Maggie Reilly
Relevant department: Department of Health, Social Services and Public Safety

Youth Council for Northern Ireland
Forestview, Purdy's Lane
Belfast, BT8 7AR
Tel: 028 9064 3882
Fax: 028 9064 3874
Web: www.youthcouncil-ni.org.uk
Chief Executive: David Guilfoyle
Relevant department: Department of Education

Youth Justice Agency of Northern Ireland
41-43 Waring Street
Belfast, BT1 2DY
Tel: 028 9031 6400
Fax: 028 9031 6402
Web: www.youthjusticeagencyni.gov.uk
Chief Executive: Dr Bill Lockhart OBE

BALLYMONEY
BOROUGH COUNCIL

FORWARD

Cookstown
DISTRICT COUNCIL

Omagh
DISTRICT COUNCIL

GLORIA PRISCA NOVATUR
Carrickfergus

DUNGANNON
& SOUTH TYRONE
Borough Council

MOYLE
DISTRICT
COUNCIL

FERMANAGH
DISTRICT COUNCIL

The Answer is Ards

MAGHERAFELT
DISTRICT COUNCIL

Falce Marique Potens
Larne Borough Council

COLERAINE
BOROUGH COUNCIL

Antrim
borough council

CRAIGAVON
Borough Council

VITA VERITAS VICTORIA
DERRY CITY COUNCIL

BALLYMENA
BOROUGH COUNCIL
POST PRAELIA PRAEMIA

NEWRY & MOURNE
AN tIÚR & MORNA

Castlereagh

Newtownabbey
BOROUGH COUNCIL

BELFAST
CITY COUNCIL

North Down
Borough Council

EX IGNE RESURGAM
LISBURN
CITY COUNCIL

Armagh
City and District Council...

Strabane
District Council
COMHAIRLE CEANTAIR
AN tSRATHA BÁIN

BOROUGH COUNCIL
LIMAVADY
Comhairle Bhuirg
Léim an Mhadaidh

HISTORIC DISTRICT
DOWN
DISTRICT COUNCIL

BANBRIDGE
DISTRICT COUNCIL

# Chapter 4

# Local Government and Administration

## An Overview of Northern Ireland Local Government

Along with Westminster and the Stormont Executive, Northern Ireland has a third tier of government, in the form of its 26 councils, which are involved in policy and decision-making, and more particularly the direct delivery of a range of services at a local level. These 26 Local Government Districts (LGDs) are subdivided into a number of District Electoral Areas (DEAs), usually between three and five (although Belfast has nine). Each of these DEAs returns a number of councillors who collectively comprise the council and act as a single-tier local authority. Local government elections are held once every four years, with councillors elected by proportional representation. The last local government elections were held on the same day as the last General Election, 7 June 2001.

### Recent History

Northern Ireland's present system of local government dates from the 1970s. In the context of the then civil rights movement and continuing general upheaval it was decided to reorganise the administration of key services at local level, and to review the geographical boundaries of local authorities. In response to the Macrory Report, the Local Government (Northern Ireland) Act 1972 sought to address claims of political bias in various areas of service provision. It produced a significant change in the roles and responsibilities of councils, most notably a diminution in their control of education and health care. Housing provision had already been transferred to a newly appointed housing authority, the Northern Ireland Housing Executive, in 1970.

Education, libraries and health were to be administered by area boards of appointed members, not directly accountable to councils. Local authorities retained responsibility for refuse collection, leisure and recreation facilities, building control, cemeteries and tourist amenities while nominating a number of elected members to the appointed health and education and library boards.

Local authorities also retained an important consultative role in matters such as planning, roads and housing, and were encouraged to offer leadership and support to local economic development.

### Cities, Boroughs and Districts

A Local Government District may be a borough, city or district council. Belfast, Derry, Armagh, and Lisburn all have city councils (although Armagh is officially a 'City and District' Council); the other 22 are either borough or district councils. Whilst Newry attained city status the council area remains known as Newry and Mourne District Council. A mayor and deputy mayor head city and borough councils, while chairpersons head district councils, the office-bearers in both cases being elected at the council's Annual General Meeting.

All Northern Ireland's councils are described in the Local Government Act as District Councils but the following have attained Borough status:

- Antrim
- Ards
- Ballymena
- Ballymoney
- Newtownabbey
- North Down
- Craigavon
- Larne
- Limavady
- Carrickfergus
- Castlereagh
- Coleraine

Where a council has a City or Borough status it has two other ceremonial privileges. It may:

- Designate up to one quarter of its members as aldermen;
- Confer the freedom of the City or Borough.

The mayor or chairperson of the council has a high profile within the council area, performing ceremonial duties and often playing a key role in promoting the area and welcoming visiting dignitaries.

Councils vary considerably in size, with Belfast being the largest by far in terms of population, followed by Lisburn, Derry, Craigavon and Newry & Mourne. In contrast, Moyle, Ballymoney and Larne are among the smallest. There is also considerable variation in the geographical area covered by the councils, with Belfast, Castlereagh and North Down among the smallest and Fermanagh the largest followed by Omagh and Strabane. *(Details of the main characteristics of the councils are listed in the table below).*

## Principal Characteristics of Local Government in Northern Ireland

Area, Population and Rates Revenue of Local Authorities

| Council | Area (Km2) | % of Total | Population | % of Total | Rates Revenue | % of Total |
|---|---|---|---|---|---|---|
| Antrim | 576 | 4.1 | 48, 366 | 2.9 | 7,082,577 | 2.8 |
| Ards | 376 | 2.7 | 73, 244 | 4.3 | 8,698,274 | 3.5 |
| Armagh | 670 | 4.7 | 54, 263 | 3.2 | 6,730,026 | 2.7 |
| Ballymena | 632 | 4.5 | 58, 610 | 3.5 | 7,902,590 | 3.2 |
| Ballymoney | 418 | 2.9 | 26, 894 | 1.6 | 2,718,770 | 1.1 |
| Banbridge | 452 | 3.2 | 41, 392 | 2.5 | 4,997,762 | 2.0 |
| Belfast | 114 | 0.8 | 277, 391 | 16.5 | 65,045,172 | 26.1 |
| Carrickfergus | 81 | 0.6 | 37, 659 | 2.2 | 5,451,343 | 2.2 |
| Castlereagh | 85 | 0.6 | 66, 488 | 3.9 | 7,698,484 | 3.1 |
| Coleraine | 485 | 3.4 | 56, 315 | 3.3 | 8,296,261 | 3.3 |
| Cookstown | 622 | 4.4 | 32, 581 | 1.9 | 3,300,216 | 1.3 |
| Craigavon | 378 | 2.7 | 80, 671 | 4.7 | 11,302,591 | 4.5 |
| Derry | 387 | 2.7 | 105, 066 | 6.2 | 16,830,944 | 6.7 |
| Down | 646 | 4.6 | 63, 828 | 3.8 | 8,057,339 | 3.2 |
| Dungannon | 783 | 5.5 | 47, 735 | 2.8 | 4,552,512 | 1.8 |
| Fermanagh | 1875 | 13.3 | 57, 527 | 3.4 | 5,938,073 | 2.4 |
| Larne | 335 | 2.4 | 30, 832 | 1.8 | 5,015,743 | 2.0 |
| Limavady | 585 | 4.1 | 32, 422 | 1.9 | 3,540,049 | 1.4 |
| Lisburn | 446 | 3.2 | 108, 694 | 6.4 | 13,787,637 | 5.5 |
| Magherafelt | 572 | 4.1 | 39, 780 | 2.4 | 3,515,675 | 1.4 |
| Moyle | 479 | 3.4 | 15, 933 | 0.9 | 2,075,711 | 0.8 |
| Newry and Mourne | 902 | 6.4 | 87, 058 | 5.2 | 11,851,749 | 4.7 |
| Newtownabbey | 150 | 1.1 | 79, 995 | 4.7 | 13,204,811 | 5.3 |
| North Down | 81 | 0.6 | 76, 323 | 4.5 | 12,374,235 | 4.9 |
| Omagh | 1130 | 7.9 | 47, 952 | 2.8 | 6,032,075 | 2.4 |
| Strabane | 861 | 6.1 | 38, 248 | 2.3 | 3,665,041 | 1.5 |
| Total: | 14135 | 100 | 1, 685, 267 | 100 | 249,665,673 | 100 |

Source: NISRA Northern Ireland 2001 Census Key Statistics

**Councils Political Control**

| Council | Unionist | Nationalist | Other | Total |
|---|---|---|---|---|
| Antrim | 13 | 6 | - | 19 |
| Ards | 17 | - | 6 | 23 |
| Armagh | 11 | 11 | - | 22 |
| Ballymena | 18 | 4 | 2 | 24 |
| Ballymoney | 13 | 3 | - | 16 |
| Banbridge | 12 | 3 | 2 | 17 |
| Belfast | 24 | 23 | 4 | 51 |
| Carrickfergus | 10 | - | 7 | 17 |
| Castlereagh | 15 | 2 | 6 | 23 |
| Coleraine | 17 | 4 | 1 | 22 |
| Cookstown | 5 | 10 | 1 | 16 |
| Craigavon | 13 | 11 | 2 | 26 |
| Derry | 6 | 23 | 1 | 30 |
| Down | 8 | 14 | 1 | 23 |
| Dungannon | 9 | 12 | 1 | 22 |
| Fermanagh | 9 | 13 | 1 | 23 |
| Larne | 9 | 2 | 4 | 15 |
| Limavady | 6 | 8 | 1 | 15 |
| Lisburn | 19 | 7 | 4 | 30 |
| Magherafelt | 5 | 10 | 1 | 16 |
| Moyle | 6 | 5 | 4 | 15 |
| Newry and Mourne | 5 | 22 | 3 | 30 |
| Newtownabbey | 17 | 3 | 5 | 25 |
| North Down | 15 | - | 10 | 25 |
| Omagh | 5 | 14 | 2 | 21 |
| Strabane | 5 | 11 | - | 16 |
| Total: | 292 | 221 | 69 | 582 |

## Roles and Functions of Local Government

Local councils are responsible for a wide range of functions including a number of key services delivered directly to individual households and workplaces. In addition the council is involved in numerous other roles locally although not always as the central player.

With twenty-six local councils in Northern Ireland, local government is a sizeable employer, with over 9,000 employees. The expansion of local government in recent years has seen its role grow in such areas as economic development, tourism, community development/relations, culture and the arts.

In addition to their established functions, the Northern Ireland Office has in recent times requested councils to develop Community Safety Strategies to enhance the safety of local communities in their area. Under this initiative local councils will work with the police in areas such as drug and alcohol abuse, the provision of youth clubs and other social amenities, with the objective of reducing the potential for crime. Local councils also play a central role in the new police partnership boards, involving a partnership approach with the police at local level.

Local councils also play a key role in dispensing the EU Special Peace and Reconciliation Funds, better known as Peace II. Local Strategy Partnerships (LSPs) were formed with strong representations from the district councils and their role and remit will continue to develop as funding decision makers under the auspices of Peace II. *(Full details of the membership of LSPs is included in Chapter 9, beginning at page 439)*

Local councils are also aiming to improve local environmental performance particularly in the area of waste management.
In the context of diminishing landfill capacity and restrictions on construction of new incineration plants local authorities are under unprecedented pressure to reduce the overall volume of waste produced and to recycle as much of this as possible. Ever more stringent environmental legislation will continue to add to these pressures.

The roles and functions conferred on the council by the Local Government Act (N.I.) 1972 and other legislation fall into three types:

- A direct role in which the council is responsible within its own area for the provision and management of certain services;
- A representative role where local authority nominees sit as representatives on a range of statutory bodies;
- A consultative role through which the council reflects the views of the community on the operation of certain regional services.

### Representative Role

The representative role relates to the appointment of councillors to a range of statutory bodies such as the Health and Social Services Area Boards and Councils and the Education and Library Boards. The status of the persons so appointed depends upon the legal provisions contained in the appropriate statute. They are in no sense delegates but are entirely free to exercise their own judgement although in practice they tend to represent their Council Area which is part of a wider area covered by the relevant board.

### Consultative Role

The consultative role relates to services provided by a government department or other public body in connection with Planning, Roads, Conservation (including water supply and sewerage services) and Housing.

As the locally elected political forum the council is seen as providing a useful consultative sounding board for administrative decisions although local authorities have no rights of decision.

Community concerns or views on proposed administrative decisions are often brought to bear when statutory authorities consult local councils. The consultative role of the local authority is particularly important in the arena of planning where there is no third party right of appeal and in housing where the Northern Ireland Housing Executive - which covers all of Northern Ireland - needs a robust input at the local level.

## Roles and Functions of Local Government

| Direct Service Provision |
|---|
| Advice and Information Services |
| Arts and Entertainment |
| Building Regulations |
| Burial Grounds and Crematoria |
| Civic Ceremonials |
| Community Services |
| Dog Control |
| Economic Development |
| Harbours |
| Health Inspection |
| Leisure and Community Centres |
| Licensing |
| Markets and Fairs |
| Museums and Art Galleries |
| Parks and Open Spaces |
| Pollution Control |
| Public Conveniences |
| Recreation Grounds and Services |
| Refuse Collection and Disposal |
| Street Cleansing |
| Tourism Development |
| **Representative Role** |
| Education and Library Boards |
| Health and Social Services Area Councils |
| Health and Social Services Boards |
| **Consultative Role** |
| Planning |
| Roads |
| Housing Council |
| Infrastructure/Utilities |
| Electricity |
| Water |

## The Role of the Department of the Environment

### Local Government Division

Although local authorities interact with numerous government departments in the course of carrying out their functions, the Department of the Environment is the central government department responsible for local government issues. Its key objectives in this area are to maintain and strengthen the links between central and local government, and to assist district councils to carry out their functions efficiently and effectively, in the interests of the ratepayer. It has a general supervisory role in relation to the affairs of district councils and exercises a number of statutory controls over certain financial and administrative matters.

### Financial Role

The Department provides direct support to the 26 district councils by way of General Exchequer Grant. This grant consists of a "derating element" and a "resources element", and its objectives are twofold:

(1) To compensate all district councils for loss of rate income due to the statutory derating of certain properties; and
(2) To provide additional finance to those councils whose rateable value per head of population falls below a standard determined each year by the Department.

The Department also regulates and determines the rates of allowances payable to councillors and provides guidance on a wide range of issues of interest to councillors and officials.

### Audit Function

The Department has statutory powers, under the Local Government Act (NI) 1972, to request information, reports and returns from councils and can order inquiries or investigations into any matter relating to the functions of a council. Where a council fails to discharge any of its functions, the Department can direct it to take specified action. If a council fails to comply with such a direction, the Department can empower its officials to exercise the functions of the council.

The Department of the Environment must also consult with the local council on:

- Applications for planning approval and on the Area Plan which is produced for its area;
- Roads and car parks in the area to ensure that the views of as many local residents are obtained as possible;
- Water and sewerage to ensure the area's requirements are met;
- Environmental issues, listed buildings and Areas of Special Scientific Interest.

*(More detailed information on the responsibilities of the Department of the Environment is set out in Chapter 3 'Central Government Departments and Agencies')*

## Future Outlook for Local Government

The first Northern Ireland Assembly embarked on a major Review of Public Administration, under the auspices of the Office of the First Minister and Deputy First Minister (OFMDFM) which may change significantly the role of local authorities in the medium term.

Although it will be several years before the Review's findings are implemented, it is widely expected that the result will be fewer local authorities but with enhanced responsibilities. Indeed, the consultation document launched by the Review Team in late 2003 puts forward a number of high-level models for future systems of public administration, the principal differentiator between which is the enhanced role local government may assume.

The Review of Public Administration may also have implications for where local authorities fit into the overall political and governmental framework of Northern Ireland.

## A-Z Guide to Northern Ireland's 26 Local Authorities

What follows is a comprehensive profiling of all of Northern Ireland's 26 local authorities.

Each summary profile contains:

- central contact information
- list of members
- simple diagram of local authority
- list of senior council officers

These are listed in an easy-to-use A-Z format.

## ANTRIM BOROUGH COUNCIL

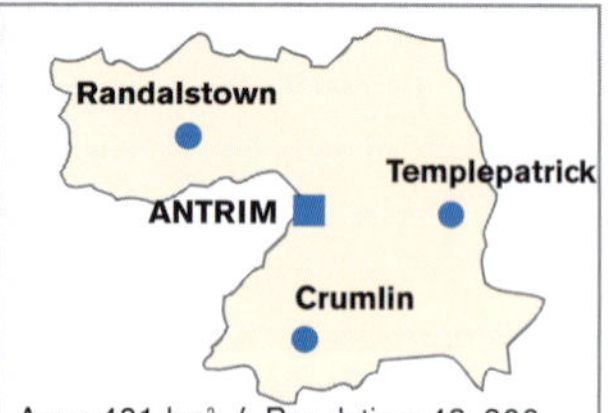


Area: 421 km² / Population: 48, 366

**The Steeple**
**Steeple Road**
**Antrim, BT41 1BJ**
Tel: 028 9446 3113
Fax: 028 9446 4469
Email: admin@antrim.gov.uk
Web: www.antrim.gov.uk

The main population centres in the Borough of Antrim include Antrim town, Crumlin, Randalstown and Templepatrick. The borough enjoys an excellent communications infrastructure, with the M2 motorway running north to Ballymena, and south to Belfast, some 18 miles away. The borough is also home to Belfast International Airport (Aldergrove).

### Elected Members and Council Committees

Mayor: Bobby Loughran (SDLP)
Deputy Mayor: Drew Ritchie (UUP)

| Councillor | Party | Councillor | Party |
|---|---|---|---|
| Thomas Burns | SDLP | Martin McManus | SF |
| Wilson Clyde | DUP | Martin Meehan | SF |
| Adrian Cochrane-Watson | UUP | Paul Michael | UUP |
| Samuel Dunlop | DUP | Stephen Nicholl | UUP |
| Brian Graham | DUP | Mervyn Rea | UUP |
| William Harkness | DUP | Drew Ritchie | UUP |
| Oran Keenan | SDLP | John Smyth | DUP |
| Bobby Loughran | SDLP | Roy Thompson | UUP |
| Paddy Marks | UUP | Edgar Wallace | UUP |
| Donovan McClelland | SDLP | | |

### Senior Officers

Chief Executive: David McCammick
Director of Development & Leisure Services: Geraldine Girvan
Recreation: Ivor McMullan
Economic Development Officer: Alan Liddle
Director of Environmental Services: Vacant
Building Services: Reggie Hillen
Environmental Health: Ian Suiter
Director of Corporate Services: Neill Cauwood
Finance: John Balmer

### Council Contact Details

| | |
|---|---|
| Chief Executive's Office | 028 9446 3113 |
| Administration | 028 9446 3113 |
| Public Relations | 028 9448 1303 |
| Building Control | 028 9448 1321 |
| Environmental Health | 028 9448 1319 |

## ARDS BOROUGH COUNCIL

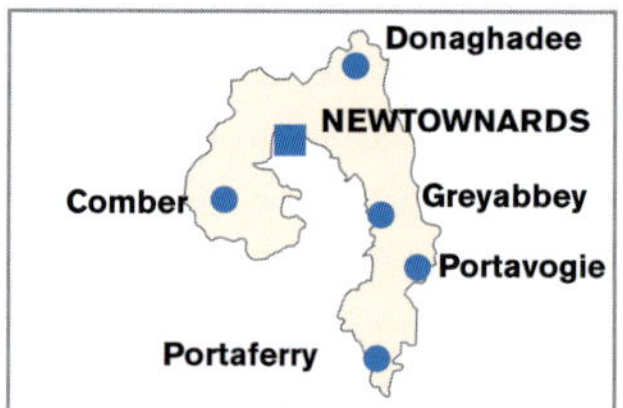


Area: 363 km² / Population: 73,244

**Council Offices**
**2 Church Street**
**Newtownards, BT23 4AP**
Tel: 028 9182 4000
Fax: 028 9181 9628
Email:
ards@ards-council.gov.uk
Web:
www.ards-council.gov.uk

The Ards Borough, situated southeast of Belfast on the shores of Strangford Lough is designated as an area of outstanding natural beauty and special scientific interest. It is the third fastest growing local government district in Northern Ireland with a population of 73,244.

The area administered by the council covers approximately 140 square miles, with its 90 miles of coastline being one of the longest in local government control. The borough's main town is Newtownards, with Comber and Donaghadee the other main centres of population.

### Elected Members

Mayor: Hamilton Gregory (DUP)
Deputy Mayor: Angus Carson (UUP)

| Councillor | Party | Councillor | Party |
|---|---|---|---|
| Angus Carson | UUP | Wilbert Magill | Ind |
| Linda Cleland | All | Jim McBriar | All |
| Margaret Craig | DUP | Alan McDowell | All |
| Robin Drysdale | DUP | Danny McCarthy | Ind |
| George Ennis | DUP | Kieran McCarthy | All |
| Ronnie Ferguson | UUP | William Montgomery | DUP |
| Robert Gibson | UUP | Jim Shannon | DUP |
| David Gilmore | DUP | John Shields | UUP |
| Hamilton Gregory | DUP | Philip Smith | UUP |
| Thomas Hamilton | UUP | David Smyth | UUP |
| Hamilton Lawther | DUP | Terence Williams | DUP |
| Jeff Magill | UUP | | |

### Senior Officers

Chief Executive: Ashley Boreland
Director of Corporate Services: David Clarke
Director of Development: Derek McCallan
Director of Environmental Services: John Rea
Director of Leisure Services: Archie Walls
Chief Building Control Officer: Robert Shields

### Council Contact Details

| | |
|---|---|
| Chief Executive's Office | 028 9182 4004 |
| Borough Inspector's Office | 028 9182 4005 |
| Leisure Services | 028 9182 4018 |
| Public Relations | 028 9182 4021 |
| Economic Development | 028 9182 4025 |
| Building Control | 028 9182 4033 |
| Refuse Collection | 028 9182 4014 |

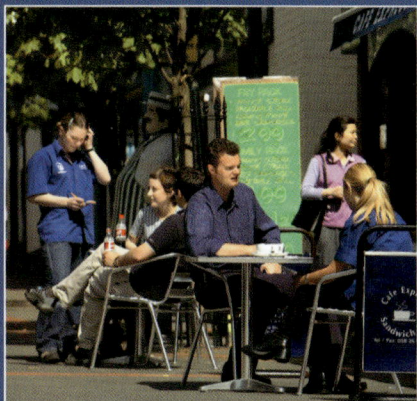

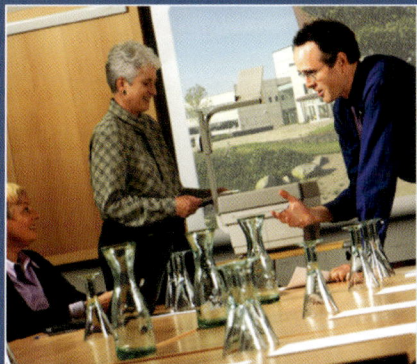

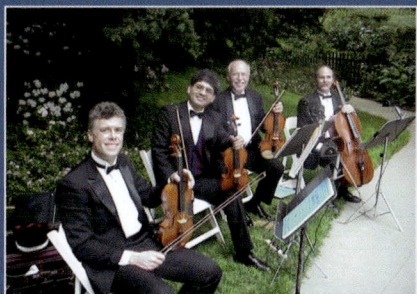

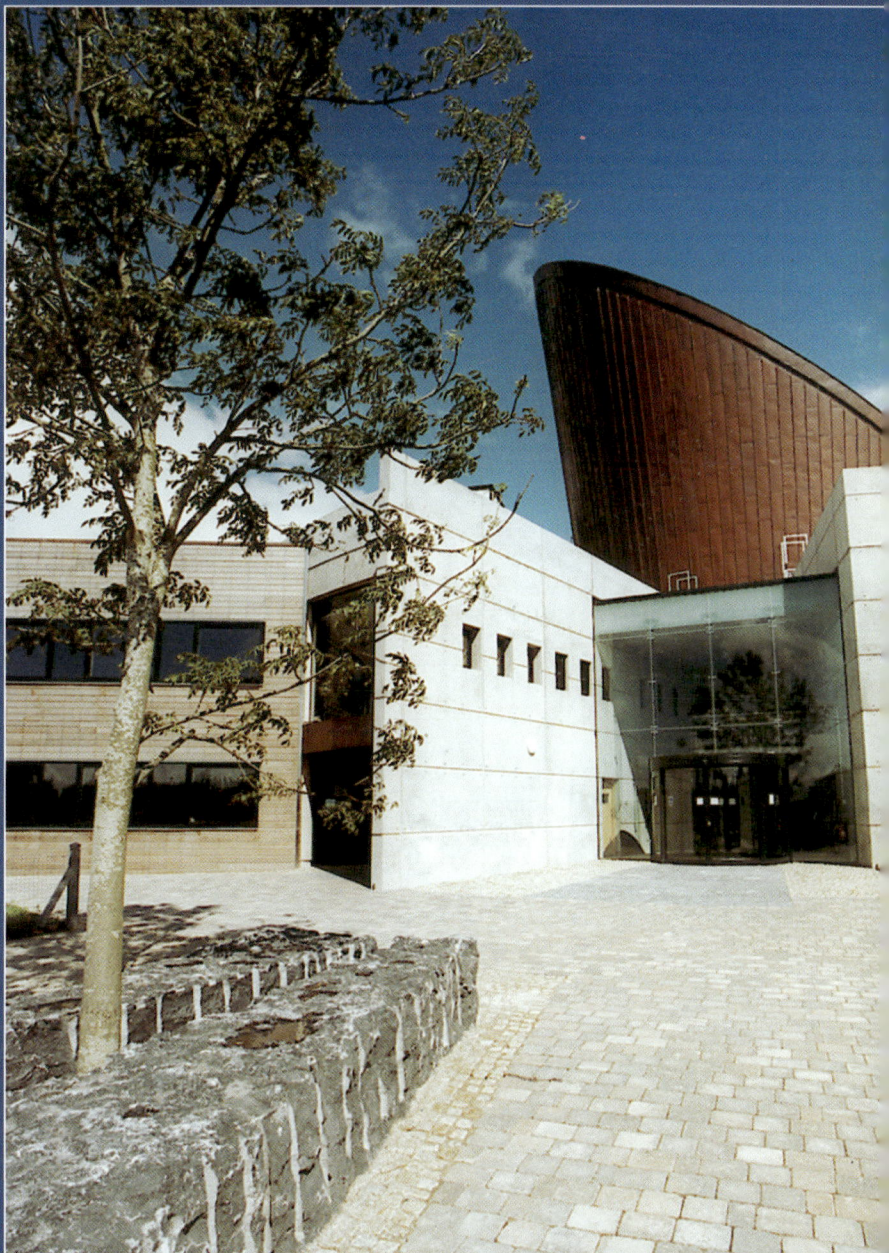

## ARMAGH CITY & DISTRICT COUNCIL

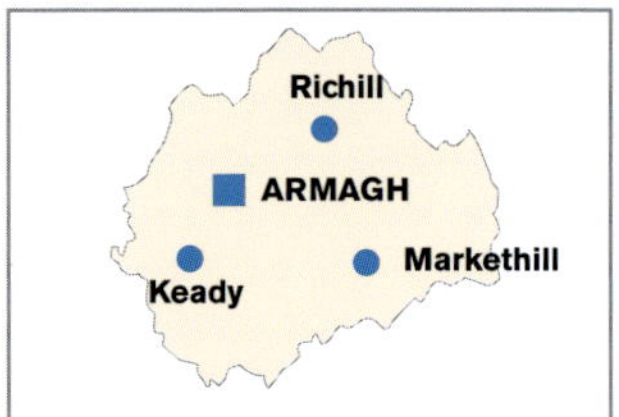


Area: 673 km² / Population: 54,263

**Council Offices**
**The Palace Demesne**
**Armagh**
**BT60 4EL**
Tel: 028 3752 9600
Fax: 028 3752 9601
Web: www.armagh.gov.uk

Armagh City and District Council lies in the south east of Northern Ireland 40 miles south of Belfast. It is essentially a rural district, the largest centre of population being Armagh City, the ecclesiastical capital of Ireland which hosts the two impressive hilltop Cathedrals of the Church of Ireland and Roman Catholic Churches. The area is rich in culture and heritage, making it an attractive location for tourism. The public sector is the main source of employment.

### Elected Members

Mayor: Eric Speers (UUP)
Deputy Mayor: John Campbell (SDLP)

| Councillor | Party | Councillor | Party |
|---|---|---|---|
| Paul Berry | DUP | William Irwin | DUP |
| Heather Black | DUP | Tommy Kavanagh | SDLP |
| Pat Brannigan | SDLP | James McKernan | SDLP |
| Anna Brolly | SDLP | Pat McNamee | SF |
| John Campbell | SDLP | Sylvia McRoberts | UUP |
| Tom Canavan | SDLP | Pat O'Rawe | SF |
| Jimmy Clayton | UUP | Cathy Rafferty | SF |
| Paul Corrigan | SF | Charles Rollston | UUP |
| Evelyn Corry | UUP | Eric Speers | UUP |
| Brian Cunningham | SF | Jim Speers | UUP |
| Freda Donnelly | DUP | Robert Turner | UUP |

### Senior Officers

Chief Executive: Victor Brownlees
Executive Manager and PA: Wendy Geary
Strategic Director of Corporate Services: Roger Wilson
Director of Environment, Health, and Recreation Services: John Briggs
Head of Environmental Health & Protection: Anne Donaghy
Head of Finance: Stephen Hyde
Head of Operational Services: David McKee
Head of Recreation and Leisure: Gerard Houlahan
Head of Regeneration and Development: Sharon O'Gorman
Chief Building Control Officer: Phillip Beattie

### Council Contact Details

| | |
|---|---|
| Corporate Administrative Services | 028 3752 9605 |
| Clerk and Chief Executive Secretariat | 028 3752 9603 |
| Member Services | 028 3752 9649 |
| Registration of Births, Deaths and Marriages | 028 3752 9615 |
| Regeneration and Development | 028 3752 9642 |
| Environmental Health | 028 3752 9626 |
| Building Control | 028 3752 9616 |
| Recreation and Leisure | 028 3752 9636 |

## BALLYMENA BOROUGH COUNCIL

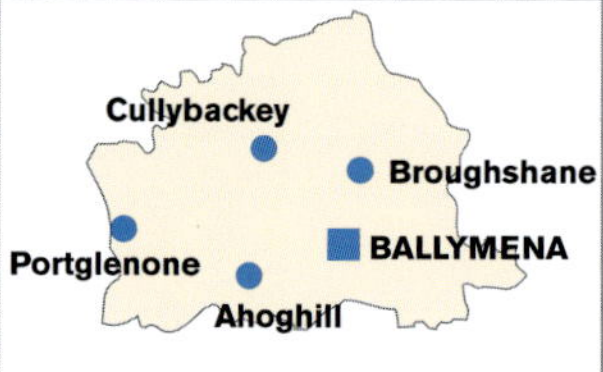


Area: 630km² / Population: 58, 610

**Ardeevin**
**80 Galgorm Road**
**Ballymena, BT42 1AB**
Tel: 028 2566 0300
Fax: 028 2566 0400
Email: info@ballymena.gov.uk
Web: www.ballymena.gov.uk

Ballymena Borough Council is located at the heart of one of Northern Ireland's most fertile and prosperous farming regions. Ballymena town is 27 miles north of Belfast and 22 miles from the Port of Larne. The present borough of Ballymena was created in 1973 and covers 200 square miles. Over half of the borough's total population of 58,610 live in the town of Ballymena, which is the regional administrative centre for many organisations in the north-eastern part of Northern Ireland, including the Health and Social Services Board, Education and Library Board and government departments such as Inland Revenue and Social Security. Other population centres include the smaller towns and villages of Kells, Cullybackey, Portglenone, Broughshane and Ahoghill. Among the many visitor attractions in the area is the unique ECOS environmental centre.

### Elected Members

Mayor: Hubert Nicholl (DUP)
Deputy Mayor: Lexie Scott (UUP)

| Councillor | Party | Councillor | Party |
|---|---|---|---|
| Elizabeth Adger | DUP | Seamus Laverty | SDLP |
| James Alexander | DUP | PJ McAvoy | SDLP |
| Neil Armstrong | UUP | Joseph McKernan | UUP |
| Peter Brown | UUP | William McNeilly | UUP |
| Martin Clarke | DUP | Maurice Mills | DUP |
| James Currie | UUP | Thomas Nicholl | DUP |
| David Clyde | UUP | Hubert Nicholl | DUP |
| Samuel Gaston | DUP | Declan O'Loan | SDLP |
| Roy Gillespie | DUP | Lexie Scott | UUP |
| Margaret Gribben | SDLP | Robin Stirling | DUP |
| Samuel Hanna | DUP | David Tweed | DUP |
| James Henry | Ind | William Wright | Ind |

### Senior Officers

Town Clerk and Chief Executive: Mervyn Rankin
Executive Manager and PA: Mary Magill (Acting)
Director of Building Control Services: Maurice Watterson
Director of Development, Leisure and Cultural Services: Ronnie McBride
Director of Environmental Health Services: Alex Kinghorn
Director of Finance and IT Services: Victor Benson
Director of Personnel, Policy and Operational Services: Rodger McKnight

### Council Contact Details

| | |
|---|---|
| Council Head Office – Ardeevin | 028 2566 0300 |
| Births, Deaths and Marriages | 028 2566 0352 |
| Building Control | 028 2566 0409 |
| Economic Development | 028 2563 3930 |
| Environmental Health | 028 2566 0372 |

## BALLYMONEY BOROUGH COUNCIL

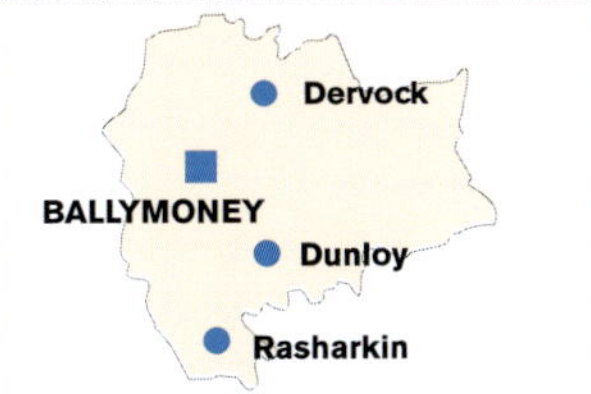


Area: 416 km² / Population: 26, 894

**Borough Offices**
**Riada House**
**14 Charles Street**
**Ballymoney, BT53 6DZ**
Tel: 028 2766 0200
Fax: 028 2766 0222
Email: info@ballymoney.gov.uk
Web:
www.ballymoney.gov.uk

Ballymoney Borough Council is one of the smallest local authority areas accounting for 3 per cent of Northern Ireland's land mass. The borough is bordered to the west by the Lower River Bann, to the north and east by Coleraine and Moyle Councils and to the south by Ballymena. Approximately one third of the borough's 26,000 inhabitants live in or near the town of Ballymoney, which is the main administrative, commercial and educational centre for the area. Satellite villages within the borough include: Ballybogey, Cloughmills, Dervock, Dunloy, Loughguile, Rasharkin, and Stranocum.

### Elected Members

Mayor: Cecil Cousley (DUP)
Deputy Mayor: Ian Stevenson (DUP)

| Councillor | Party | Councillor | Party |
|---|---|---|---|
| Frank Campbell | DUP | William Logan | UUP |
| Harry Connolly | SDLP | Malachy McCamphill | SDLP |
| Cecil Cousley | DUP | Philip McGuigan | SF |
| John Finlay | DUP | Thomas McKeown | UUP |
| Joseph Gaston | UUP | James Simpson | UUP |
| Robert Halliday | DUP | Ian Stevenson | DUP |
| William Johnston | UUP | Mervyn Storey | DUP |
| Bill Kennedy | DUP | Robert Wilson | DUP |

### Senior Officers

Chief Executive: John Dempsey
PA: Karen Wilson, Pauline McLaughlin
Director of Financial and Administrative Services: Iris McCleery
Director of Health and Environmental Services: John Michael
Director of Leisure and Amenities: John Paul
Chief Building Control Officer: Joe Martin

### Council Contact Details

| | |
|---|---|
| Building Control | 028 2766 0251 |
| Ballymoney Town Hall | 028 2766 2256 |
| Dog Control | 07775 938003 |
| Drumaheglis Marina & Caravan Park | 028 2766 6468 |
| Health & Environmental Services | 028 2766 0280 |
| Joey Dunlop Leisure Centre | 028 2766 0260 |
| Leisure & Amenities | 028 2766 0200 |
| Rasharkin Community Centre | 028 2957 1990 |
| Registrar of Births, Deaths and Marriages | 028 2766 0200 |
| Tourist Information | 028 2766 0200 |
| Waste Disposal & Civic Amenity Site | 028 2766 5169 |

## BANBRIDGE DISTRICT COUNCIL

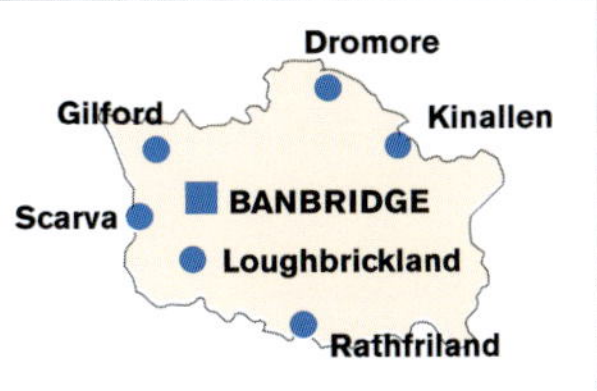


Area: 451 km² / Population: 42, 400

**Civic Building**
**Downshire Road**
**Banbridge, BT32 3JY**
Tel: 028 4066 0600
Fax: 028 4066 0601
Email:
info@banbridge.gov.uk
Web: www.banbridge.gov.uk

Banbridge District Council is situated in the north west of County Down adjacent to the main Belfast to Dublin road. It stretches from Dromore in the north to Rathfriland in the south and from Gilford in the west to Ballyward in the east. The district has a population of over 41,000 representing over 2.4 per cent of the population of Northern Ireland. The latest 2001 Census figures show that the Banbridge district is one of the fastest growing areas in Northern Ireland.

The main town is Banbridge, followed by Dromore, Rathfriland and Gilford. Approximately half of the population live in rural areas and small villages.

### Elected Members

Chairman: Ian Burns (UUP)
Vice-Chairman: John Hanna (UUP)

| Councillor | Party | Councillor | Party |
|---|---|---|---|
| Joan Baird | UUP | William Martin | UUP |
| Norah Beare | DUP | Pat McAleenan | SDLP |
| Derick Bell | UUP | Malachy McCartan | Ind |
| Ian Burns | UUP | Catherine McDermott | SDLP |
| Seamus Doyle | SDLP | Jim McElroy | DUP |
| John Hanna | UUP | Wilfred McFadden | DUP |
| David Herron | DUP | Frank McQuaid | All |
| Stephen Herron | DUP | Paul Rankin | DUP |
| John Ingram | UUP | | |

### Senior Officers

Chief Executive: Robert Gilmore
Executive Manager and PA: Eleanor McLoughlin
Director of Corporate Services: Pat Cumiskey
Director of Development: Liam Hannaway
Director of Environmental Services: Ken Forbes
Director of Leisure Services: Mike Reith
Head of Building & Technical Services: William Frazer

### Council Contact Details

| | |
|---|---|
| Chief Executive/Member Services | 028 4066 0602 |
| Corporate Services Finance Office | 028 4066 0607 |
| Human Resource Management | 028 4066 0608 |
| Registration of Births,Deaths & Marriages | 028 4066 0614 |
| Community Relations/Development | 028 4066 0643 |
| Sports Development | 028 4066 0637 |
| Development/General Office | 028 4066 0609 |
| Economic Development | 028 4066 0635 |
| Heritage & Genealogy | 028 4062 6369 |
| Tourism | 028 4066 0609 |
| Town Centre Development | 028 4066 2668 |

# BELFAST CITY COUNCIL

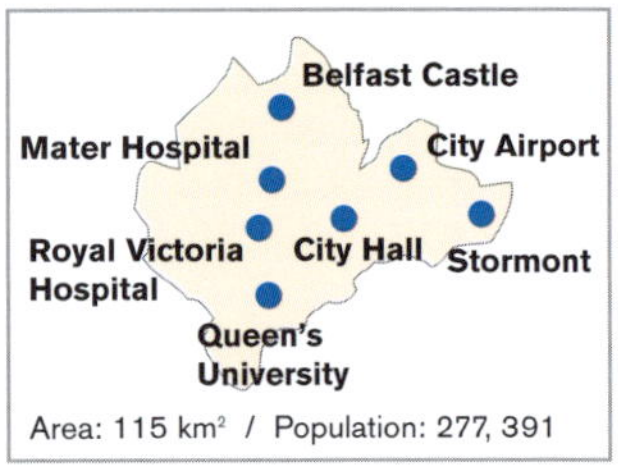


**City Hall**
**Belfast, BT1 5GS**
Tel: 028 9032 0202
Fax: 028 9027 0232
Textphone: 028 9027 0405
Web: www.belfastcity.gov.uk

Belfast City Council has local authority responsibility for Northern Ireland's largest population. Over 700,000 people live in the Greater Belfast Metropolitan area with 277,391 located within the Belfast City Council area.

Belfast City Council is by far the largest of the twenty-six district councils in Northern Ireland. It is responsible for the large scale delivery of key services, refuse collection and disposal, street cleansing, building control and environmental health, community development, indoor and outdoor leisure, parks and recreational facilities, tourism and economic development.

## Elected Members

Lord Mayor: Tom Ekin (ALL)
Deputy Lord Mayor: Joe O'Donnell (SF)
High Sheriff: Ruth Patterson (DUP)

| Councillor | Party | Councillor | Party |
|---|---|---|---|
| Ian Adamson | UUP | Fra McCann | SF |
| David Alderdice | All | Patrick McCarthy | SDLP |
| Alex Attwood | SDLP | Nelson McCausland | DUP |
| David Browne | UUP | Margaret McClenaghan | SF |
| Michael Browne | SF | Frank McCoubrey | Ind |
| Wallace Browne | DUP | Chris McGimpsey | UUP |
| Jim Clarke | UUP | Michael McGimpsey | UUP |
| Margaret Clarke | UUP | Elaine McMillen | DUP |
| Patrick Convery | SDLP | Catherine Molloy | SDLP |
| Margaret Crooks | UUP | Marie Moore | SF |
| Alan Crowe | UUP | Martin Morgan | SDLP |
| Ian Crozier | DUP | Robin Newton | DUP |
| Máire Cush | SF | Carál Ní Chuilln | SF |
| Nigel Dodds | DUP | Eoin O'Broin | SF |
| Thomas Ekin | All | Joseph O'Donnell | SF |
| Reg Empey | UUP | Gerard O'Neill | SF |
| David Ervine | PUP | Peter O'Reilly | SDLP |
| Carmel Hanna | SDLP | Ruth Patterson | DUP |
| Tom Hartley | SF | Jim Rodgers | UUP |
| Billy Hutchinson | PUP | Eric Smyth | DUP |
| Danny Lavery | SF | Hugh Smyth | PUP |
| Naomi Long | All | Robert Stoker | UUP |
| Alban Maginness | SDLP | Harry Toan | DUP |
| Alex Maskey | SF | Margaret Walsh | SDLP |
| Paul Maskey | SF | Sammy Wilson | DUP |
| Chrissie McAuley | SF | | |

## Senior Officers

Chief Executive: Peter McNaney
Assistant Chief Executive: Robert Wilson
Director of Client Services: Mervyn Elder
Director of Contract Services: Heather Louden
Director of Corporate Services: Trevor Salmon
Director of Development: Marie-Thérèse McGivern
Director of Health and Environmental Services: William Francey
Director of Legal Services: Ciaran Quigley
Head of Corporate Communications: Eamon Deeny
Head of Committee and Members' Services: Liam Steele
Acting Head of Civic Buildings & Property Care: David Cartmill
Head of Human Resources: Stanley Black
Head of Financial Services: Fred Maguire
Head of Business Improvement: John Millar
Head of Information Services Belfast (ISB): Tom Orr
Head of Economic Initiatives: Shirley McCay
Head of Environmental Health: Andrew Hassard
Head of Waste Management: Tim Walker
Head of Building Control: Trevor Martin
Head of Parks and Amenities: Maurice Parkinson
Head of Finance & Business Support: Mark McBride
Head of Cleansing: Sam Skimin
Head of Grounds Maintenance: Jim Kennedy
Head of Operational Services: George Wright

## Council Contact Details

| | |
|---|---|
| Arts and Heritage Unit | 028 9027 0461 |
| Chief Executive's Department | 028 9027 0202 |
| City Hall | 028 9032 0202 |
| Client Services Department | 028 9032 0202 |
| Committee Services | 028 9027 0465 |
| Community Development | 028 9027 0417 |
| Complaints Central Helpline | 028 9027 0270 |
| Consumer Advice Centre | 028 9032 8260 |
| Contract Services Department | 028 9032 0202 |
| Economic Development Unit | 028 9027 0482 |
| Equality Officer (Freefone) | 0800 0855 412 |
| Grounds Maintenance Head Office | 028 9037 3031 |
| Health & Environmental Services Department | 028 9032 0202 |
| Human Resources Section | 028 9032 0202 |
| Lord Mayor's Unit | 028 9027 0215 |
| Press and Media | 028 9027 0221 |
| Refuse Collection Customer Contact Centre | 028 9027 0230 |
| Registration of Births, Deaths & Marriages | 028 9027 0274 |
| Smoke Hotline | 028 9027 0420 |
| St George's Market | 028 9043 5704 |
| Tourism Development Unit | 028 9027 0426 |
| Ulster Hall | 028 9032 3900 |
| Waste Management (Complaints/Enquiries) | 028 9027 0656 |
| Waterfront Hall | 028 9033 4400 |
| Zoological Gardens | 028 9077 4625 |
| Zoological Gardens Information Line | 028 9077 6277 |

## CARRICKFERGUS BOROUGH COUNCIL

**Museum and Civic Centre**
**11 Antrim Street**
**Carrickfergus BT38 70G**
Tel: 028 9335 8000
Fax: 028 9336 6676
Email: info@carrickfergus.org
Web: www.carrickfergus.org

Carrickfergus is located along the coast in southeast Antrim with its main settlement, the town of Carrickfergus located on the northern shore of Belfast Lough some 10 miles from Belfast. Other significant settlements in the borough include Greenisland and Whitehead. Carrickfergus has a long history and came to prominence in Norman times. Its harbour area boasts possibly Ireland's best preserved Norman Keep, one of Northern Ireland's main tourist attractions.

### Elected Members

Mayor: David Hilditch (DUP)
Deputy Mayor: Eric Ferguson (UUP)

| Councillor | Party | Councillor | Party |
|---|---|---|---|
| William Ashe | DUP | Eric Ferguson | UUP |
| May Beattie | DUP | William Hamilton | Ind |
| Roy Beggs | UUP | David Hilditch | DUP |
| James Brown | Ind | James McClurg | DUP |
| Robert Cavan | All | Noreen McIlwrath | All |
| Terence Clements | DUP | Patricia McKinney | DUP |
| Janet Crampsey | All | Sean Neeson | All |
| Stewart Dickson | All | Gwen Wilson | UUP |
| Darin Ferguson | UUP | | |

### Senior Officers

Town Clerk & Chief Executive: Alan C Cardwell
Director of Building Services: Stephen J Johnston
Director of Development Services:John D McCormick
Director of Environmental Services: Alan Barkley
Best Value Officer: Norman Neill
Community Relations Officer: Colin Ellis
Countryside Officer: Neil Luney
District Policing Partnership Manager: Daniel Sweeney
Economic Development Officer: Alan Braithwaite
Enforcement Officer: Alan Reid
Health and Safety Officer: John MacIntyre
Waste Management Officer: Jean Stewart

### Council Contact Details

| | |
|---|---|
| Town Hall | 028 9335 1604 |
| Heritage Centre | 028 9336 6455 |
| Carrickfergus Leisure Centre | 028 9335 1711 |
| Andrew Jackson Centre | 028 9336 6455 |
| Carrickfergus Marina | 028 9336 6666 |
| Sullatober Depot | 028 9335 1192 |

## CASTLEREAGH BOROUGH COUNCIL

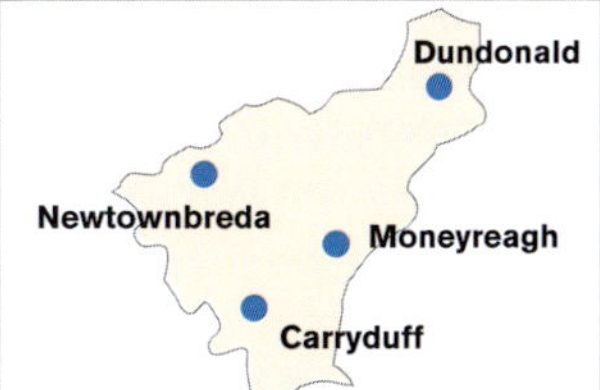


**Civic and Administrative Offices, Bradford Court**
**Upper Galwally**
**Castlereagh, BT8 6RB**
Tel: 028 9049 4500
Fax: 028 9049 4515
Email:
council@castlereagh.gov.uk
Web: www.castlereagh.gov.uk

Castlereagh Borough Council covers much of the southern and eastern outskirts of Belfast, including the suburbs of Newtownbreda, Knock and Stormont, as well as the satellite town of Carryduff and the villages of Moneyreagh and Crossnacreevy. Covering over 32.6 sq miles, the borough has a rapidly expanding population currently in excess of 66,000.

### Elected Members

Mayor: Joanne Bunting (DUP)
Deputy Mayor: David Drysdale (UUP)

| Councillor | Party | Councillor | Party |
|---|---|---|---|
| John Beattie | DUP | Barbara McBurney | UUP |
| Joanne Bunting | DUP | Kim Morton | Ind |
| Michael Copeland | UUP | John Norris | DUP |
| David Drysdale | UUP | Peter Osborne | All |
| Sara Duncan | All | Geraldine Rice | All |
| Claire Ennis | DUP | Iris Robinson | DUP |
| Francis Gallagher | Ind | Peter Robinson | DUP |
| Cecil Hall | UUP | Mark Robinson | DUP |
| Brian Hanvey | SDLP | Thomas Sandford | PUP |
| Michael Henderson | UUP | Vivienne Stevenson | DUP |
| Rosaleen Hughes | SDLP | Jim White | DUP |
| Michael Long | All | | |

### Senior Officers

Chief Executive: Adrian Donaldson
Director of Administration & Community Services: Joan McCoy
Director of Finance and Leisure Services: Edward Patterson
Director of Technical Services: Edwin Campbell
Building Control Manager: Gordon Bratten
Environmental Health Manager: Heather Moore
Borough Inspector: Tom Duke
Community Relations Officer: Cathy Clarke
Countryside Officer: Anne McFetridge
Economic Development Officer: Clare Jamison
Financial/Management Accountant: John Brewster
Human Resources Manager: Samantha Rea
Corporate Marketing & PR Manager: Jill Simpson
Tourism Officer: Jill Simpson

### Council Contact Details

| | |
|---|---|
| Headquarters | 028 9049 4500 |
| Registrar of Births, Deaths and Marriages | 028 9079 8405 |
| Belvoir Activity Centre | 028 9064 2174 |
| Dundonald International Ice Bowl | 028 9080 9100 |
| Lough Moss Centre | 028 9081 4884 |
| The Robinson Centre | 028 9070 3948 |

## COLERAINE BOROUGH COUNCIL

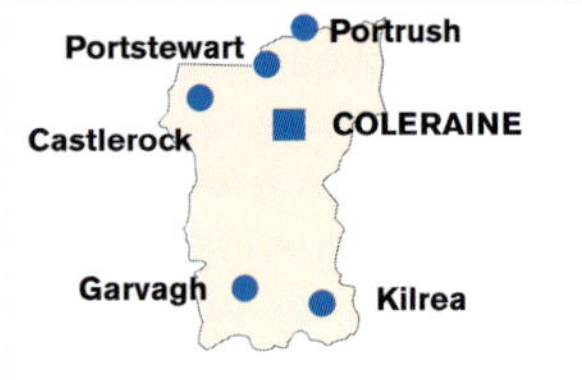


Area: 300 km² / Population: 56, 315

**Cloonavin**
**66 Portstewart Road**
**Coleraine BT52 1EY**
Tel: 028 7034 7034
Fax: 028 7034 7026
Web:
www.colerainebc.gov.uk

Coleraine Borough Council is situated on Northern Ireland's north coast, covering an area of 300 square kilometres. It has a population of 56,315 people, with 23,500 living in Coleraine town. The borough is the most popular tourist destination in Northern Ireland, embracing Portrush and Portstewart, two of Northern Ireland's busiest holiday resorts. The three towns together form an economic and social trio known as the "Triangle".

### Elected Members

Mayor: Robert McPherson (UUP)
Deputy Mayor: James McClure (DUP)

| Councillor | Party | Councillor | Party |
|---|---|---|---|
| Christine Alexander | Ind | Elizabeth Johnston | UUP |
| Pauline Armitage | UKUP | William King | UUP |
| David Barbour | UUP | Billy Leonard | SF |
| Toye Black | UUP | David McClarty | UUP |
| Maurice Bradley | DUP | James McClure | DUP |
| Olive Church | UUP | Gerry McLaughlin | SDLP |
| William Creelman | DUP | Adrian McQuillan | DUP |
| John Dallat | SDLP | Robert McPherson | UUP |
| Timothy Deans | DUP | Eamon Mullan | SDLP |
| Phyllis Fielding | DUP | Desmond Stewart | DUP |
| Norman Hillis | UUP | James Watt | UUP |

### Senior Officers

Town Clerk and Chief Executive: Wavell Moore
Director of Corporate Services: David Bell
Director of Environmental Health: Kieran Doherty
Director of Leisure Services: Jim Curry
Head of Development Services: Moira Mann
Director of Technical Services: Dessie Wreath
Principal Building Control Officer: David Robinson
Environment Officer: Jim Allen
Corporate Marketing Officer: Clair Balmer, Elaine Moore
DPP Manager: Suzanne Crozier
Economic Development Officer: Linda McGuinness
Registrar of Births, Deaths and Marriages: Gwyneth Kerr

### Council Contact Details

| | |
|---|---|
| Town Clerk & Chief Executive's Dept | 028 7034 7034 |
| Administration | 028 7034 7034 |
| Registration of Births, Deaths & Marriages | 028 7034 7021 |
| Economic Development | 028 7034 7045 |
| Tourism & Marketing | 028 7034 7044 |
| Environmental Health Dept | 028 7034 7171 |
| Technical Services Dept | 028 7034 7272 |

## COOKSTOWN DISTRICT COUNCIL

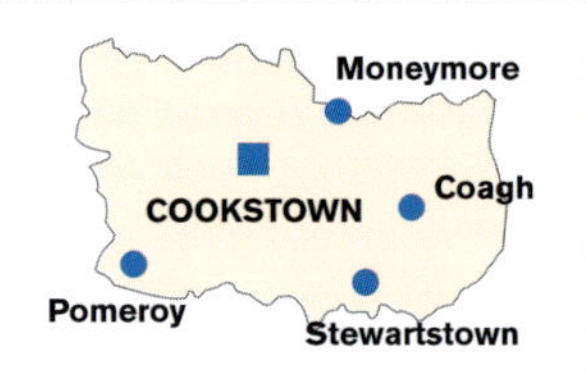


Area: 378 km² / Population: 32, 581

**12 Burn Road**
**Cookstown, BT80 8DT**
Tel: 028 8676 2205
Fax: 028 8676 4360
Email:
info@cookstown.gov.uk
Web:
www.cookstown.gov.uk

Cookstown District Council is an area of almost 378 sq. km with an approximate population of 32,000. The main settlement Cookstown, with an population of around 11,000 is the principal administrative and commercial centre for the district. It is noted for its very long and wide main thoroughfare. Other centres include Coagh, Moneymore, Pomeroy and Stewartstown.

### Elected Members

Chairman: Trevor Wilson (UUP)
Vice-Chairman: Pearse McAleer (SF)

| Councillor | Party | Councillor | Party |
|---|---|---|---|
| Mary Baker | SDLP | Ian McCrea | DUP |
| Seamus Campbell | SF | James McGarvey | SDLP |
| Peter Cassidy | SDLP | Patsy McGlone | SDLP |
| Sam Glasgow | UUP | Michael McIvor | SF |
| Walter Greer | UUP | John McNamee | SF |
| Dessie Grimes | SF | Oliver Molloy | SF |
| Pearse McAleer | SF | Sam Parke | Ind |
| Anne McCrea | DUP | Trevor Wilson | UUP |

### Senior Officers

Chief Executive: Michael McGuckin
Director of Corporate Services: Ivor Paisley
Director of Operational Services: Derek Duncan
Director of Building Control: Trevor McAdoo
Director of Environmental Health: Mark Kelso
Director of Development: Adrian McCreesh
Arts and Cultural Development: Linda McGarvey
Corporate Marketing Officer: Susan McCleary
District Policing Partnership Manager: Phillip Moffet
Dog Warden/Enforcement Officer: Noel Newell
Economic Development Officer: Fiona McKeown
Registrar of Births, Marriages and Deaths: Sandra Matchett
Sports Development Officer: Oliver McShane
Tourism Officer: Denise Campbell

### Council Contact Details

| | |
|---|---|
| Council Services | 028 8676 2205 |
| Cookstown Leisure Centre | 028 8676 3853 |
| Dog Warden | 028 8676 2205 |
| The Burnavon (Arts Centre) | 028 8676 9949 |
| Tourist Information | 028 8676 6727 |
| Waste Disposal Site | 028 8675 1153 |

## CRAIGAVON BOROUGH COUNCIL

Area: 378km² / Population: 80, 671

**Civic Centre**
**Lakeview Road**
**Craigavon , BT64 1AL**
Tel: 028 3831 2400
Fax: 028 3831 2444
Email: info@craigavon.gov.uk
Web: www.craigavon.gov.uk

Craigavon is based largely on the long established towns of Lurgan and Portadown. The third major centre of population is the area of Brownlow, which is situated between the two towns. There is also rural hinterland featuring a number of picturesque villages and hamlets including Waringstown, Magheralin, Donacloney and Derrymacash. Craigavon has a wealth of leisure facilities and is developing its 'lifestyle' brand.

### Elected Members

Mayor: David Simpson (DUP)
Deputy Mayor: Ignatius Fox (SDLP)

| Councillor | Party | Councillor | Party |
|---|---|---|---|
| Sydney Anderson | Ind | Patricia Mallon | SDLP |
| Jonathan Bell | DUP | Mary McAlinden | SDLP |
| Sydney Cairns | UUP | Nuala McAlinden | SDLP |
| Alan Carson | DUP | Tony Elliott | SDLP |
| Kieran Corr | SDLP | Brian McKeown | SF |
| Fred Crowe | UUP | Stephen Moutray | DUP |
| Meta Crozier | UUP | Francie Murray | SF |
| Ignatius Fox | SDLP | John O'Dowd | SF |
| Samuel Gardiner | UUP | George Savage | UUP |
| Arnold Hatch | UUP | David Simpson | DUP |
| David Jones | Ind | Robert Smith | DUP |
| Dolores Kelly | SDLP | Woolsey Smith | DUP |
| Maurice Magill | SF | Kenneth Twyble | UUP |

### Senior Officers

Chief Executive: Francis Rock
Director of Building Control Services: Robert Colvin
Director of Development: Vacant
Director of Environmental Services: Lorraine Crawford
Head of Environmental Services: Colin Kerr
Director of Finance and Corporate Services: David Pepper
Director of Leisure Services: Ross Miller
Economic Development Officer: Nicola Wilson
Human Resources Manager: Vacant
PR Officer: Pauline Nixon Black
Tourism Officer: Brian Johnston

### Council Contact Details

| | |
|---|---|
| Administration & Finance | 028 3831 2400 |
| Building Control, Craigavon | 028 3831 2500 |
| Chief Executive | 028 3831 2402 |
| Development | 028 3831 2581 |
| Environmental Health and Dog Warden | 028 3831 2521 |
| Leisure Services | 028 3831 2563 |
| Refuse Collection and Street Cleaning | 028 3833 9031 |

## DERRY CITY COUNCIL

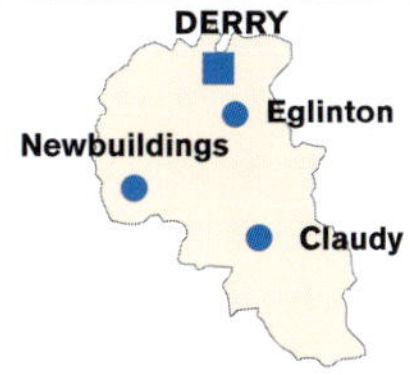


Area: 381 km² / Population: 105, 066

**98 Strand Road**
**Derry, BT48 7NN**
Tel: 028 7136 5151
Fax: 028 7126 5448
Email:
townclerk@derrycity.gov.uk
Web: www.derrycity.gov.uk

Derry City Council is one of the largest District Councils serving a population of 105,066; 85,300 of whom live within the urban area.

Derry City Council's area is located between the Sperrin Mountains and the Donegal Hills with the city straddling the River Foyle. Derry is recognised as the regional city of the north west of Ireland, whose natural hinterland includes the neighbouring districts of Strabane, Limavady and parts of Donegal.

### Elected Members

Mayor: Gearóid óhEára (SF)
Deputy Mayor: Alderman Joe Miller (DUP)

| Councillor | Party | Councillor | Party |
|---|---|---|---|
| Peter Anderson | SF | Tony Hassan | SF |
| Mary Bradley | SDLP | William Hay | DUP |
| Gregory Campbell | DUP | John Kerr | SDLP |
| Sean Carr | SDLP | Gerry MacLochlainn | SF |
| Jim Clifford | SDLP | Kathleen McCloskey | SDLP |
| Thomas Conway | SDLP | Jim McKeever | SDLP |
| Annie Courtney | Ind | Maeve McLaughlin | SF |
| Cathal Crumley | SF | Joe Miller | DUP |
| Gerard Diver | SDLP | William O'Connell | SDLP |
| Lynn Fleming | SF | Barney O'Hagan | SF |
| Paul Fleming | SF | Gearóid óhEára | SF |
| Shaun Gallagher | SDLP | William Page | SF |
| Mildred Garfield | DUP | Helen Quigley | SDLP |
| Ernest Hamilton | UUP | Pat Ramsey | SDLP |
| Mary Hamilton | UUP | Martin Reilly | SDLP |

### Senior Officers

Town Clerk and Chief Executive: Anthony McGurk
City Treasurer: Joseph Campbell
Deputy Town Clerk and Chief Environmental Health Officer: John Meehan
Director of City Marketing: Gerard Henry
City Secretary and Solicitor: Damian McMahon
Chief Building Control Officer: Robert White
Director of Recreation and Leisure: James Sanderson
Economic Development Officer: Mark Lusby

### Council Contact Details

| | |
|---|---|
| Airport (City of Derry) | 028 7181 0784 |
| Building Control | 028 7137 6521 |
| Client Services Department | 028 7137 6536 |
| Council Offices | 028 7136 5151 |
| Economic Development | 028 7137 6532 |
| Environmental Health | 028 7136 5151 |
| Marketing/Communications/PR | 028 7137 6504 |
| Town Clerk & Chief Executive's Department | 028 7137 6507 |

## DOWN DISTRICT COUNCIL

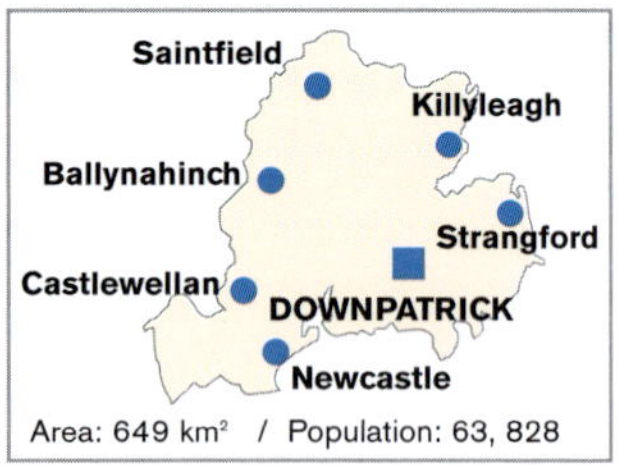


**24 Strangford Road**
**Downpatrick**
**BT30 6SR**
Tel: 028 4461 0800
Fax: 028 4461 0801
Email:
council@downdc.gov.uk
Web: www.downdc.gov.uk

Down district covers a large geographical area to the south east of the Province, including the Mourne Mountains, Northern Ireland's highest mountain range. The district's main population centres include the historic town of Downpatrick and the popular seaside resort of Newcastle. Downpatrick is well connected through public transport to the district's other main centres of population; Newcastle, Castlewellan, Ballynahinch, Saintfield, Crossgar and Killyleagh, and has traditionally been the administrative and service centre for the South Down region.

### Elected Members

Chairman: Robert Burgess (UUP)
Vice-Chairman: Carmel O'Boyle (SDLP)

| Councillor | Party | Councillor | Party |
|---|---|---|---|
| Raymond Blaney | GP | Anne McAleenan | SDLP |
| Peter Bowles | UUP | Eamonn McConvey | SF |
| Francis Braniff | SF | Francis McDowell | SF |
| Robert Burgess | UUP | John McIlheron | UUP |
| Willie Clarke | SF | Carmel O'Boyle | SDLP |
| Albert Colmer | UUP | Eamonn O'Neill | SDLP |
| Peter Craig | SDLP | Edward Rea | UUP |
| Dermot Curran | SDLP | Margaret Ritchie | SDLP |
| William Dick | DUP | Patrick Toman | SDLP |
| John Doris | SDLP | Anne Trainor | Ind |
| Gerry Douglas | UUP | Jim Wells | DUP |
| Peter Fitzpatrick | SDLP | | |

### Senior Officers

Clerk and Chief Executive: John McGrillen
Director of Corporate Services: Norman Stewart
Director of Cultural and Economic Development: Sharon O'Connor
Director of Recreation and Technical Services: Frank Cunningham
Group Chief Building Control Officer: John Dumigan
Business Improvement Manager: Stephen Wright
Principal Environmental Health Officer: Tony McCrory
Marketing Manager: Veronica Keegan
Registrar of Births, Deaths and Marriages: Helen Matthews

### Council Contact Details

| | |
|---|---|
| Licensing | 028 4461 0808 |
| Food Hygiene, Office Safety | 028 4461 0824 |
| District Building Control Offices | 028 4461 0829 |
| Births, Deaths & Marriages | 028 4461 0825 |
| Economic Development | 028 4461 0855 |
| Tourism Development | 028 4461 0856 |

## DUNGANNON & SOUTH TYRONE BOROUGH COUNCIL

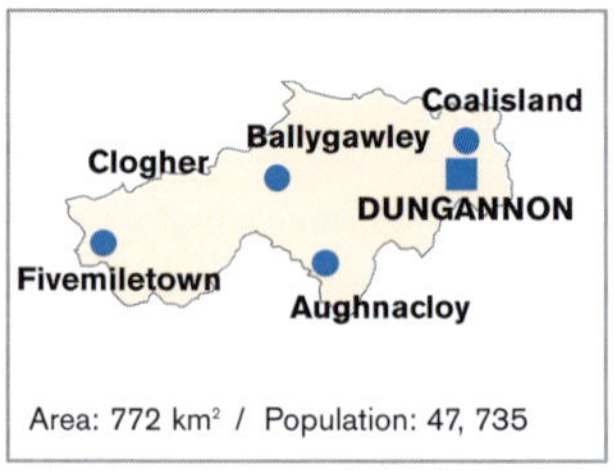


**Circular Road**
**Dungannon**
**BT71 6DT**
Tel: 028 8772 0300
Fax: 028 8772 0368

Email: reception.info
@dungannon.gov.uk
Web:
www.dungannon.gov.uk

The Borough of Dungannon and South Tyrone covers an area stretching from the shores of Lough Neagh in the east, through the Clogher Valley to Fivemiletown at the Fermanagh border. The Borough touches the border with County Monaghan and reaches up to the foothills of the Sperrins. Some 48,000 inhabitants live in the Borough area, an essentially rural area, but with a strong industrial base. Its central position means that it is an ideal location for industries such as Tyrone Crystal, Powerscreen, Tyrone Brick and Moy Park.

### Elected Members

Mayor: Robert Mulligan (UUP)
Deputy Mayor: Johnston McIlwrath (DUP)

| Councillor | Party | Councillor | Party |
|---|---|---|---|
| Norman Badger | UUP | Jim Hamilton | UUP |
| Roger Burton | DUP | Derek Irwin | UUP |
| Jim Canning | Ind | Anthony McGonnell | SDLP |
| Jim Cavanagh | SDLP | Sean McGuigan | SF |
| Walter Cuddy | UUP | Johnston McIlwrath | DUP |
| Vincent Currie | SDLP | Larry McLarnon | SF |
| Patsy Daly | SDLP | Ken Maginnis | UUP |
| Desmond Donnelly | SF | Francie Molloy | SF |
| Seamus Flanagan | SF | Barry Monteith | SF |
| Phelim Gildernew | SF | Maurice Morrow | DUP |
| Michael Gillespie | SF | Robert Mulligan | UUP |

### Senior Officers

Chief Executive: William Beattie
Head of Finance: Paula Kerr
Director of Building Control: Jim McClelland
Director of Development: Iain Frazer
Director of Environmental Health: Alan Burke
Director of Technical Services: Robert McMinn
Economic Development Officer: Vinny Beggs
Marketing and Events Officer: Emma Cox
Public Relations Officer: Emma Heatherington
Tourism Officers: Libby McClean, Genevieve Bell

### Council Contact Details

| | |
|---|---|
| Council Offices | 028 8772 0300 |
| Chief Executive's Department | 028 8772 0303 |
| Finance and Administration | 028 8772 0324 |
| Registrar Births, Deaths and Marriages | 028 8772 0329 |
| Building Control | 028 8772 0357 |
| Environmental Health | 028 8772 0367 |
| Technical Services | 028 8772 0390 |
| Economic Development | 028 8772 8601 |

## FERMANAGH DISTRICT COUNCIL

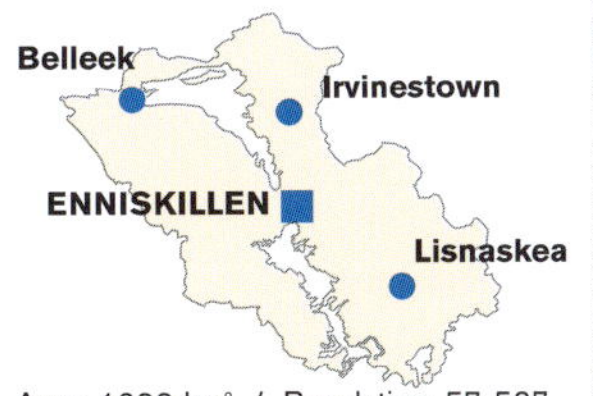

Area: 1699 km² / Population: 57, 527

**Town Hall**
**Enniskillen**
**BT74 7BA**
Tel: 028 6632 5050
Fax: 028 6632 2024
Email: fdc@fermanagh.gov.uk
Web:
www.fermanagh.gov.uk

Located in the south west of Northern Ireland, Fermanagh District Council is unique as a local authority in Northern Ireland as its boundaries are also those of the County of Fermanagh. Fermanagh is a county renowned for its lakeland scenery and tourism appeal. Often referred to as the lakeland county, tourism spending of almost £20 million per annum is a significant contributor to the local economy. Enniskillen is the principal town in Fermanagh with a well-developed and thriving town centre, which contains the greatest concentration of shopping and business activity in the district. Other significant settlements include Irvinestown, Lisnaskea and Kesh.

### Elected Members

Chairman: Gerry McHugh (SF)
Vice-Chairman: John O'Kane (SDLP)

| Councillor | Party | Councillor | Party |
|---|---|---|---|
| Harold Andrews | UUP | Bert Johnston | DUP |
| Frank Britton | SDLP | Davy Kettyles | Ind |
| Joe Cassidy | SF | Bertie Kerr | UUP |
| Pat Cox | SF | Ruth Lynch | SF |
| Joe Dodds | DUP | Robin Martin | SF |
| Tom Elliott | UUP | Brian McCaffrey | SF |
| Wilson Elliott | UUP | Gerry McHugh | SF |
| Raymond Ferguson | UUP | Fergus McQuillan | SDLP |
| Gerry Gallagher | SDLP | Cecil Noble | UUP |
| Patrick Gilgunn | SF | John O'Kane | SDLP |
| Stephen Huggett | SF | Thomas O'Reilly | SF |
| Robert Irvine | UUP | | |

### Senior Officers

Chief Executive: Rodney Connor
Director of Building Control: Desmond Reid
Director of Development: Peter Thompson
Director of Environmental Health: Robert Forde
Director of Environmental Services: Robert Gibson
Director of Finance and IT: Brendan Hegarty
Director of Technical Services: Gerry Knox
Head of Administration: David Phair
Policy Development Officer: Margaret McMahon
Registrar of Births, Deaths and Marriages: Lillian Thornton
Executive Officer, Sports & Recreation: Keith Collen

### Council Contact Details

All Council departments can be contacted via Town Hall on 028 6632 5050

## LARNE BOROUGH COUNCIL

Area: 336 km² / Population: 30, 832

**Smiley Buildings**
**Victoria Road**
**Larne, BT40 1RU**
Tel: 028 2827 2313
Fax: 028 2826 0660
Email: admin@larne.gov.uk
Web: www.larne.gov.uk

Larne Borough lies on the east coast of Northern Ireland between the Glens of Antrim and the Antrim plateau. Larne is the starting point of the world-famous Antrim Coast Road with its 36 miles of spectacular limestone coastline. Two-thirds of the borough is designated an Area of Outstanding Natural Beauty (AONB), one of the highest percentages of such designation in any of the 26 councils in Northern Ireland. The borough covers an area of approximately 131 sq miles, with a population of over 30,000. This figure includes the nearly 20,000 strong population of Larne town. After Larne Town, the next biggest population centres are Ballycarry, Glenarm and Carnlough.

### Elected Members

Mayor: Robert Craig (Ind)
Deputy Mayor: Geraldine Mulvenna (All)

| Councillor | Party | Councillor | Party |
|---|---|---|---|
| Roy Beggs | UUP | Jack McKee | Ind |
| Roy Craig | Ind | Gregg McKeen | DUP |
| Joan Drummond | UUP | John Mathews | All |
| Brian Dunn | UUP | Gerardine Mulvenna | All |
| Winston Fulton | DUP | Daniel O'Connor | SDLP |
| Robert Lindsay Mason | Ind | Rachel Rea | DUP |
| Bobby McKee | DUP | Martin Wilson | SDLP |

There is currently a vacancy on the Council following the death of Councillor David Fleck.

### Senior Officers

Chief Executive: Colm McGarry
Director of Building Services: Geraldine McGahey
Director of Corporate Services: Trevor Clarke
Director of Environmental Services: Morris Crum
Head of Building Control: Mark Hamill
Head of Environmental Health Unit: Bob Cameron
Economic Development: Ken Nelson
Financial Controller: Helen Gault
Press Officer: Lorraine Hunter
Technical Services: George Drury

### Council Contact Details

| | |
|---|---|
| Building Control Service | 028 2827 2313 |
| Council Depot | 028 2826 2307 |
| Larne Leisure Centre | 028 2826 0478 |
| Tourist Information Centre | 028 2826 0088 |
| Carnfunnock Country Park | 028 2827 0541 |
| Browns Bay Caravan Site | 028 9338 2497 |
| Larne Museum | 028 2827 0824 |
| Redlands Recycling Centre | 028 2826 7880 |

## LIMAVADY BOROUGH COUNCIL

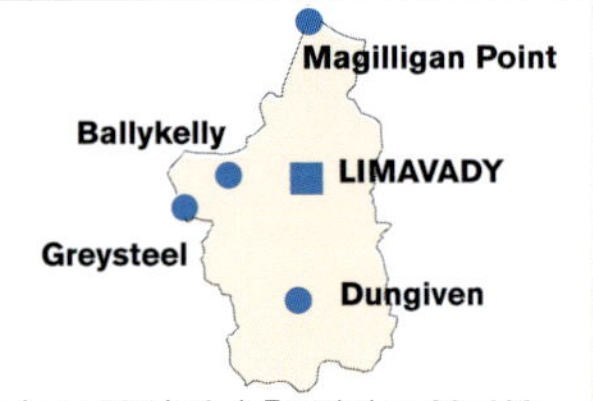


Area: 586 km² / Population: 32, 422

**7 Connell Street**
**Limavady, BT49 0HA**
Tel: 028 7772 2226
Fax: 028 7776 5241
Email: info@limavady.gov.uk
Web: www.limavady.gov.uk

Limavady Borough Council is one of Northern Ireland's smallest local authorities, located in the picturesque north of County Derry. Limavady town is by far the largest population centre, followed by Ballykelly and Dungiven. The area is well served by an extensive road network and is easily accessible from City of Derry Airport and Lisahally Deep Water port, which are within ten miles. A recent addition to the borough's infrastructure has been the introduction of a car ferry service between Magilligan Point and Greencastle in Co. Donegal. The borough stretches from the Sperrin Mountains in the south to Benone beach, a seven-mile strand of golden sand on the Atlantic coast.

### Elected Members

Mayor: Jack Rankin (UUP)
Deputy Mayor: Michael Coyle (SDLP)

| Councillor | Party | Councillor | Party |
|---|---|---|---|
| Anne Brolly | SF | Boyd Douglas | UUAP |
| Brian Brown | Ind | Dessie Lowry | SDLP |
| Michael Carten | SDLP | Martin McGuigan | SF |
| Brenda Chivers | SF | Gerard Mullan | SDLP |
| Michael Coyle | SDLP | Jack Rankin | UUP |
| Leslie Cubitt | DUP | George Robinson | DUP |
| Jack Dolan | UUP | Edwin Stevenson | UUP |
| Marion Donaghy | SF | | |

### Senior Officers

Chief Executive: John Stevenson
Chief Environmental Health Officer: Noel Crawford
Chief Finance and Administrative Officer: Eamon McCotter
Chief Recreation/Tourism Officer: Sam McGregor
Chief Technical Services Officer: Victor Wallace
District Chief Building Control Officer: Jim Mullan
Community Relations Officer: Steven Bell
Corporate Policy Officer: Chris Kane
Countryside Recreation Officer: Richard Gillen
District Policing Partnership Manager: Linda McKee
Dog Warden/Enforcement Officer: Tom Keogh
Economic Development Officer: Dermot McNally
Registrar of Births, Deaths and Marriages: Monica Anderson
Sports Development Officer: Ollie Mullan
Tourism Development Officer: Clare Quinn

### Council Contact Details

| | |
|---|---|
| Town Clerk & Chief Executive | 028 7776 0300 |
| General Enquiries | 028 7772 2226 |
| Building Control | 028 7776 0301 |
| Economic Development | 028 7776 0311 |
| Environmental Health | 028 7776 0302 |
| Finance and Administration | 028 7772 2226 |
| Registration of Births, Deaths & Marriages | 028 7772 2226 |

## LISBURN CITY COUNCIL

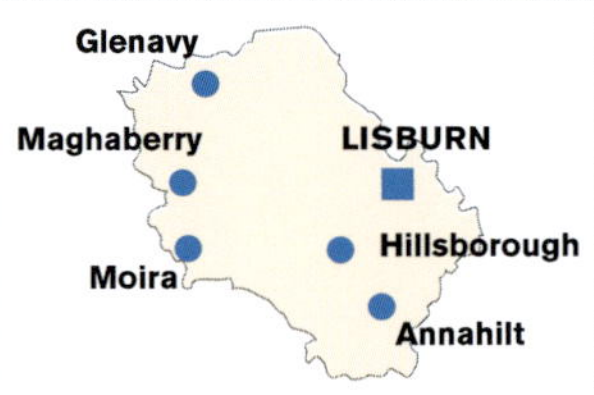


Area: 455 km² / Population: 108, 694

**Lagan Valley Island**
**The Island**
**Lisburn, BT27 4RL**
Tel: 028 9250 9250
Fax: 028 9250 9208
Email:enquiries@lisburn.gov.uk
Web: www.lisburncity.gov.uk

Lisburn was awarded City status in the Queen's Golden Jubilee City Status competition in 2002. Lisburn Borough Council became Lisburn City Council in August 2002. The City of Lisburn area has a population of 108,694. Lisburn City Council covers 455 square kilometres of southwest Antrim and northwest Down stretching from Glenavy and Dundrod in the north to Dromore and Hillsborough in the south, and from Drumbo in the east to Moira in the west. The City of Lisburn has a significant and growing industrial and commercial base.

### Elected Members

Mayor: Cecil Calvert (DUP)
Deputy Mayor: Bill Gardiner-Watson (UUP)

| Councillor | Party | Councillor | Party |
|---|---|---|---|
| David W Archer | UUP | Samuel Johnston | UUP |
| T David Archer | UUP | Harry Lewis | UUP |
| James Baird | UUP | Patricia Lewsley | SDLP |
| Billy Bell | UUP | Joseph Lockhart | UUP |
| Paul Butler | SF | Trevor Lunn | All |
| Cecil Calvert | DUP | William McDonnell | SDLP |
| Betty Campbell | All | Gary McMichael | Ind |
| Seamus Close | All | Lorraine Martin | DUP |
| Jonathan Craig | DUP | Peter O'Hagan | SDLP |
| Ronnie Crawford | UUP | Edwin Poots | DUP |
| Ivan Davis | UUP | Samuel Paul Porter | DUP |
| Jim Dillon | UUP | Sue Ramsey | SF |
| Ned Falloon | UUP | James Tinsley | DUP |
| Micheal Ferguson | SF | William Ward | UUP |
| Bill Gardiner-Watson | UUP | Veronica Willis | SF |

### Senior Officers

Chief Executive: Norman Davidson
Director of Corporate Services: David Briggs
Director of Environmental Services: Colin McClintock
Director of Leisure Services: Jim Rose
Marketing Managers: Alison Goddard/Claire Bethel

### Council Contact Details

| | |
|---|---|
| Births, Deaths & Marriages | 028 9250 9263 |
| Chief Executive's Office | 028 9250 9208 |
| Corporate Services Department | 028 9250 9270 |
| Economic Development | 028 9250 9487 |
| Environmental Services | 028 9250 9380 |
| Good Relations | 028 9250 9491 |
| Human Resources | 028 9250 9302 |
| Island Arts Centre | 028 9250 9502 |
| Leisure Services | 028 9250 9565 |
| Lisburn DPP | 028 9250 9279 |
| Marketing & Communications Unit | 028 9250 9221 |

## MAGHERAFELT DISTRICT COUNCIL

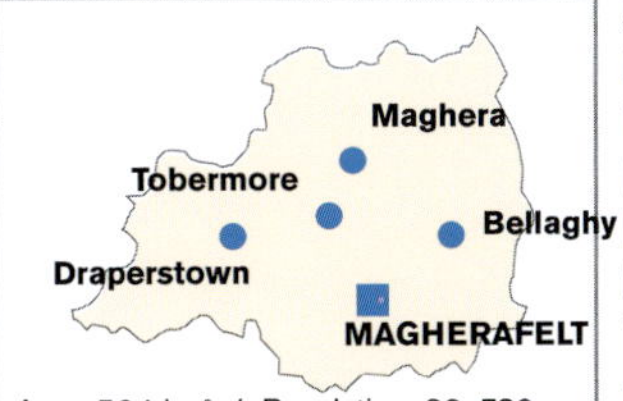


Area: 564 km² / Population: 39, 780

**50 Ballyronan Road**
**Magherafelt, BT45 6EN**
Tel: 028 7939 7979
Fax: 028 7939 7980
Email:
info@magherafelt.gov.uk
Web:
www.magherafelt.gov.uk

Magherafelt is one of Northern Ireland's smaller local authorities by population. Magherafelt town is the principal settlement followed by Maghera, and the villages of Bellaghy, Castledawson, Draperstown and Tobermore. The majority of people in the district live outside the towns, in smaller settlements and the open countryside.

### Elected Members

Chairman: Patrick Groogan (SF)
Vice-Chairman: Robert Montgomery (Ind)

| Councillor | Party | Councillor | Party |
|---|---|---|---|
| Thomas Catherwood | DUP | Rev William McCrea | DUP |
| Patrick Groogan | SF | Patrick McErlean | SDLP |
| Oliver Hughes | SF | Sean McPeake | SF |
| John Junkin | UUP | Robert Montgomery | Ind |
| Sean Kerr | SF | Hugh Mullan | SF |
| Kathleen Lagan | SDLP | Seamus O'Brien | SF |
| Joseph McBride | SDLP | Seamus O'Neill | SF |
| Paul McLean | DUP | George Shiels | UUP |

### Senior Officers

Chief Executive: John McLaughlin
Director of Finance and Administration: JJ Tohill
Director of Operational Services: Jackie Johnston
Chief Environmental Health Officer: Clifford Burrows
District Chief Building Control Officer: Ian Glendinning
Head of Leisure Services: Lawrence Hastings
Arts and Events Officer: Michael Browne
Community Relations Officer: Sean Henry
Corporate Marketing Officer: Florence Wilson
Economic Development Officer: Michael Brown
Finance Officer: Albert Hogg
Licensing Officer: Anne Boyle
Personnel Officer: Florence Wilson
Registrar of Births, Deaths and Marriages: Margaret Barnes
Tourism Officer: Michael Brown
Sports Development Officer: Nick Hastings
Waste Management Officer: Jackie Johnston

### Council Contact Details

| | |
|---|---|
| Council Offices | 028 7939 7979 |
| Greenvale Leisure Centre | 028 7963 2796 |
| Maghera Leisure Centre | 028 7954 7400 |
| Sperrins Tourism Ltd | 028 8674 7700 |
| Tobermore Driving Range | 028 7964 5406 |
| Waste Disposal Site | 028 7938 6874 |
| Director of Environment Health (Emergencies) | 028 7963 2845 |

## MOYLE DISTRICT COUNCIL

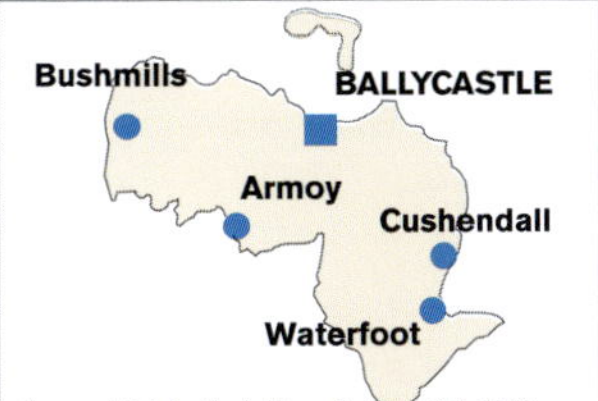


Area: 494 km² / Population: 15,933

**Sheskburn House**
**7 Mary Street**
**Ballycastle, BT54 6QH**
Tel: 028 2076 2225
Fax: 028 2076 2515
Email:
info@moyle-council.org
Web:
www.moyle-council.org

Moyle District Council is Northern Ireland's smallest local authority covering the north east of County Antrim, embracing the 'Glens of Antrim' and is one of the major tourism destinations in Northern Ireland. It is designated an Area of Outstanding Natural Beauty, and includes the Giant's Causeway, the most visited tourist attraction in Northern Ireland.

### Elected Members

Chairman: George Hartin (DUP)
Vice-Chairman: Michael Molloy (SDLP)

| Councillor | Party | Councillor | Party |
|---|---|---|---|
| Madeline Black | SDLP | Theo Laverty | SDLP |
| Christine Blaney | SDLP | David McAllister | DUP |
| Seamus Blaney | Ind | Catherine McCambridge | SDLP |
| Monica Digney | SF | Price McConaghy | Ind |
| William Graham | UUP | Randal McDonnell | Ind |
| Helen Harding | UUP | Robert McIlroy | UUP |
| George Hartin | DUP | Oliver McMullan | Ind |
| Gardiner Kane | DUP | Michael Molloy | SDLP |

### Senior Officers

Chief Executive: Richard Lewis
Director of Administration and Finance: Moira Quinn
Director of District Services: Peter Mawdsley
Chief Building Control Officer: David Kelly
Development Manager: Esther Mulholland
Human Resources Manager: Sandra Kelly
Tourism Development: Recreation Manager: Kevin McGarry
Arts Officer: Pauline Russell
Community Relations Officer: Ryan Moore
Countryside Officer: Michael McConaghie
Economic Development Officer: Marc McGerty
Finance Officer: Anne Dickson
Registrar of Births, Deaths and Marriages: Imelda McCauley
Senior Environmental Health Officer: Alan Wilson
Sports Development Officer: Damien McAfee
Technical Services Manager: Tony Stuart
Tourism Officer: Fiona Campbell

### Council Contact Details

| | |
|---|---|
| Bushmills Centre | 028 2073 2134 |
| Camping & Caravan Parks | |
| Cushendall | 028 2177 1699 |
| Cushendun | 028 2176 1254 |
| Giants Causeway Centre | 028 2073 1855 |
| Sheskburn Recreation Centre | 028 2076 3300 |
| Tourist Offices | 028 2076 2024 |

## NEWRY & MOURNE DISTRICT COUNCIL

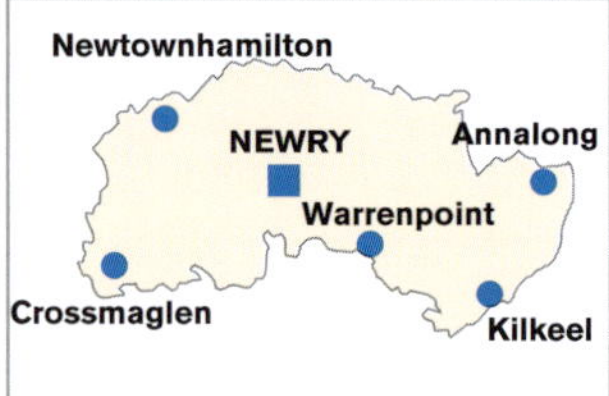

Area: 890 km² / Population: 87, 058

O'Hagan House
Monaghan Row
Newry, BT35 8DJ
Tel: 028 3031 3031
Fax: 028 3031 3077

Newry and Mourne District is situated in the south of Northern Ireland and borders the Republic of Ireland. The main settlements in the area are Newry, the towns of Warrenpoint and Kilkeel, and the villages of Camlough, Newtownhamilton, Annalong, Bessbrook, Crossmaglen, and Rostrevor. Predominantly rural in character, the district includes the newly designated City of Newry, which lies on the main transport route between Belfast and Dublin.

### Elected Members

Chairman: Henry Reilly (UUP)
Vice Chairman: John Feehan (SDLP)

| Councillor | Party | Councillor | Party |
|---|---|---|---|
| PJ Bradley | SDLP | Breandan Lewis | SF |
| Colman Burns | SF | Elena Martin | SF |
| William Burns | DUP | Marian Mathers | SF |
| Paul McKibbin | SDLP | John McArdle | SDLP |
| Michael Carr | SDLP | Jimmy McCreesh | SF |
| Charlie Casey | SF | Packie McDonald | SF |
| Michael Cole | SDLP | Pat McElroy | SDLP |
| Martin Cunningham | SF | Pat McGinn | SF |
| Brendan Curran | SF | Andy Moffett | UUP |
| John Fee | SDLP | Mick Murphy | SF |
| John Feehan | SDLP | Josephine O'Hare | SDLP |
| Frank Feeley | SDLP | Jack Patterson | Ind |
| Isaac Hanna | UUP | Henry Reilly | UUP |
| Terry Hearty | SF | Michael Ruane | SF |
| Danny Kennedy | UUP | Anthony Williamson | Ind |

### Senior Officers

Chief Executive: Thomas McCall
Director of Administration: Edwin Curtis
Assistant Director of Administration: Eileen McParland
Assistant Director of Administration: Carmel McKenna
Assistant Director of Administration (Equality): Regina Mackin
Director of Finance: Robert Dowey
Purchasing Officer: David Barter
Director of Technical and Leisure Services: Jim McCorry
Director of District Development: Gerard McGivern
Director of Environmental Health: Hugh O'Neill
Director of Building Control: Fulton Somerville
Senior Building Control Surveyor: David Shanks
Licensing Officer: Fintan Quinn

### Council Contact Details

| | |
|---|---|
| Administration/Equality/ Personnel | 028 3031 3031 |
| Arts Centre | 028 3031 3180 |
| Building Control | 028 3031 3000 |
| District Development Dept | 028 3031 3233 |
| Technical and Leisure Services Dept | 028 3031 3233 |
| Environmental Health Dept | 028 3031 3100 |
| Finance Department | 028 3031 3031 |

## NEWTOWNABBEY BOROUGH COUNCIL

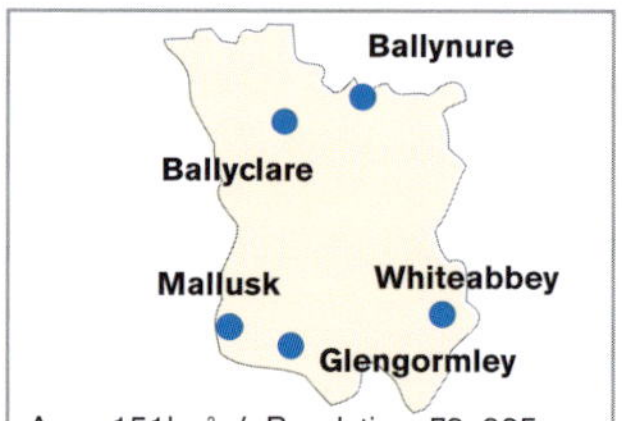

Area: 151km² / Population: 79, 995

**Mossley Mill**
**Newtownabbey, BT36 5QA**
Tel: 028 9034 0000
Fax: 028 9034 0200
Email:
info@newtownabbey.gov.uk
Web:
www.newtownabbey.gov.uk

Newtownabbey is the fifth largest local authority in Northern Ireland and combines a large urban area with a rural hinterland. Newtownabbey is part of greater North Belfast fringing Belfast Lough, Cave Hill and Carnmoney, but stretches into rural South Antrim and incorporates the busy market town of Ballyclare. Newtownabbey is situated directly north and east of Belfast and has benefited greatly from several large businesses relocating from Belfast city centre. Its close proximity to Northern Ireland's main airports and ports has made it an attractive location for inward investment. The borough hosts the University of Ulster campus at Jordanstown.

### Elected Members

Mayor: Alderman Ted Turkington (UUP)
Deputy Mayor: William DeCourcy (DUP)

| Councillor | Party | Councillor | Party |
|---|---|---|---|
| Fraser Agnew | UUAP | John Mann | DUP |
| James Bingham | UUP | Briege Meehan | SF |
| Janet Crilly | UUP | Noreen McClelland | SDLP |
| William DeCourcy | DUP | Tommy McTeague | SDLP |
| Lynn Frazer | All | Vera McWilliam | UUP |
| Barbara Gilliland | UUP | Ken Robinson | UUP |
| Paul Girvan | DUP | Victor Robinson | DUP |
| Nigel Hamilton | DUP | Vi Scott | UUP |
| Ivan Hunter | UUP | Arthur Templeton | DUP |
| Pamela Hunter | DUP | Edward Turkington | UUP |
| Roger Hutchinson | Ind | Dineen Walker | DUP |
| Tommy Kirkham | Ind | Billy Webb | NRA |
| Mark Langhammer | Lab | | |

### Senior Officers

Chief Executive: Norman Dunn
Deputy Chief Executive and Head of Development Services: Hilary Brady
Head of Central Services: Neal Willis
Head of Leisure: Stephen Montgomery
Head of Environmental Services: Hugh Kelly
Economic Development Manager: Jacqui O'Neill
Marketing Manager: Tracey White
Registrar of Births, Deaths and Marriages: Barbara Blaney

### Council Contact Details

| | |
|---|---|
| Arts Development | 028 9034 0063 |
| Births, Deaths & Marriages | 028 9034 0180 |
| Building Control | 028 9034 0140 |
| Economic Development | 028 9034 0072 |
| Marketing & Public Relations | 028 9034 0028 |

## NORTH DOWN BOROUGH COUNCIL

**Town Hall**
**The Castle**
**Bangor, BT20 4BT**
Tel: 028 9127 0371
Fax: 028 9127 1370
Email: enquiries@northdown.gov.uk
Web: www.northdown.gov.uk

The Borough of North Down is situated on the southern shores of Belfast Lough. The main town of the Borough, Bangor, which is Northern Ireland's third largest town, functions as a service and administrative centre as well as a market town and seaside resort. There are also several villages, Crawfordsburn, Groomsport, Helen's Bay, Conlig and Seahill. Although North Down is ranked as the least deprived local government district in Northern Ireland (sometimes known colloquially as the "gold coast") there are some pockets of high unemployment and relative social deprivation.

### Elected Members

Mayor: Valerie Kinghan (UKUP)
Deputy Mayor: John Montgomery (DUP)

| Councillor | Party | Councillor | Party |
|---|---|---|---|
| Alan Chambers | Ind | Bill Keery | UKUP |
| Ruby Cooling | DUP | Valerie Kinghan | UKUP |
| Irene Cree | UUP | Austen Lennon | Ind |
| Leslie Cree | UUP | Ellie McKay | UUP |
| Roy Davies | UUP | John Montgomery | DUP |
| Roberta Dunlop | UUP | Susan O'Brien | All |
| Gordon Dunne | DUP | Denis Ogborn | Ind |
| Alexander Easton | DUP | Diana Peacock | UUP |
| Stephen Farry | All | Marion Smith | UUP |
| Marsden Fitzsimons | All | Patricia Wallace | NIWC |
| Alan Graham | DUP | Anne Wilson | All |
| Ian Henry | UUP | Brian Wilson | Ind |
| Tony Hill | All | | |

### Senior Officers

Chief Executive: Trevor Polley
Director of Amenities and Technical Services: Jackie Snodden
Head of Policy Unit: John Thompson
Director of Leisure, Tourism and Community Services: Stephen Reid
Director of Environmental Services: Graham Yarr
Director of Corporate Services: Ken Webb
Chief Building Control Officer: Michael McGlennon
Chief Finance Officer: Claire Escott
Corporate Communications Officer: Claire Jackson
Economic Development Officer: Nick Rogers

### Council Contact Details

| | |
|---|---|
| Town Hall, Bangor | 028 9127 0371 |
| Borough Inspector | 028 9127 0371 |
| Building Control | 028 9127 0371 |
| Borough Inspector (after hours) | 028 9146 7975 |
| Registration of Births, Deaths Marriages | 028 9127 0371 |

## OMAGH DISTRICT COUNCIL

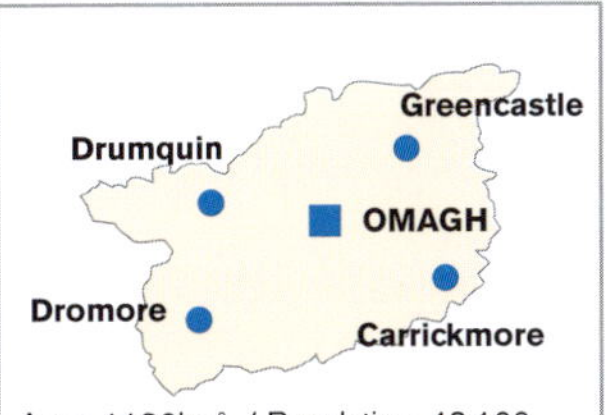


**The Grange**
**Mountjoy Road**
**Omagh, BT79 7BL**
Tel: 028 8224 5321
Fax: 028 8224 3888
Email: info@omagh.gov.uk
Web: www.omagh.gov.uk

The district of Omagh covers an area of almost 113,000 hectares (440 sq miles) making it the second largest district council area in Northern Ireland. The market town of Omagh is at the centre of the region with the rest of the Omagh district primarily rural in character. Approximately 20,000 people live in Omagh town. The next largest centres are Fintona and Dromore. Omagh town (with the exception of Derry City) is now the largest in the west of Northern Ireland.

Despite making the international headlines following the Omagh bomb atrocity, in which 29 people were killed, the people of the area have pulled together under the leadership of the local authority and the area is recovering.

### Elected Members

Chairman: Sean Clarke (SF)
Vice Chairman: Thomas Buchanan (DUP)

| Councillor | Party | Councillor | Party |
|---|---|---|---|
| Sean Begley | SF | Barry McElduff | SF |
| Thomas Buchanan | DUP | Patrick McGowan | Ind |
| Joe Byrne | SDLP | Reuben McKelvey | UUP |
| Sean Clarke | SF | Johnny McLaughlin | Ind |
| Damien Curran | SF | Liam McQuaid | SDLP |
| Josephine Deehan | SDLP | Gerry O'Doherty | SDLP |
| Oliver Gibson | Unionist | Allan Rainey | UUP |
| Peter Kelly | SF | Seamus Shields | SDLP |
| Barney McAleer | SF | Patrick Watters | SF |
| Michael McAnespie | SF | Robert Wilson | UUP |
| Patrick McDonnell | SDLP | | |

### Senior Officers

Chief Executive: Danny McSorley
Chief Client Services Officer: Kevin O'Gara
Chief Environmental Health Officer: Gerry Harte
Chief Finance Officer: Joan McCaffrey
District Chief Building Control Surveyor: Sean Kelly
Head of Arts and Tourism: Frank Sweeney
Head of Development: Alison McCullagh
Head of Personnel/Training: Rosemary Rafferty
Equality Officer: Elizabeth Beattie
Licensing Officer: Gerry Donnelly
PR Officer: Elizabeth Harkin

### Council Contact Details

| | |
|---|---|
| Council Offices | 028 8224 5321 |
| Strathroy | 028 8224 3725 |
| Hospital Road | 028 8224 4426 |

## STRABANE DISTRICT COUNCIL

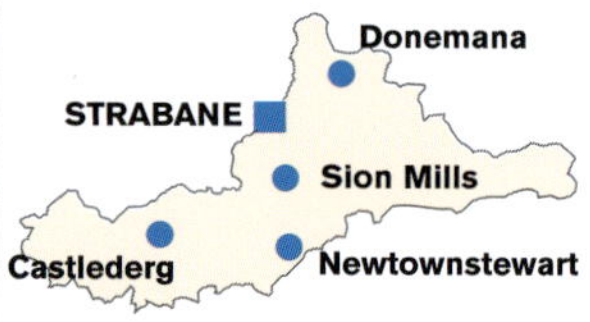


Area: 922 km² / Population: 38, 248

**47 Derry Road**
**Strabane, BT82 8DY**
Tel: 028 7138 2204
Fax: 028 7138 1348
Email:
info@strabanedc.com
Web: www.strabanedc.com

With an area covering some 922 km² of countryside, Strabane District is one of the largest council areas in Northern Ireland. Located on the border between counties Tyrone and Donegal and 20 miles south of Derry, Strabane is at the centre of the North West region of Northern Ireland. Strabane is the district's main town but there are also a substantial number of smaller towns and settlements, including Castlederg, Newtownstewart, Plumbridge and Sion Mills.

### Elected Members

Chairman: Jarlath McNulty (SF)
Vice-Chairman: Ann Bell (SDLP)

| Councillor | Party | Councillor | Party |
|---|---|---|---|
| Ivan Barr | SF | Tom McBride | SDLP |
| Ann Bell | SDLP | Eamon McGarvey | SF |
| Allan Bresland | DUP | Claire McGill | SF |
| Daniel Breslin | SF | Charlie McHugh | SF |
| John Donnell | DUP | Brian McMahon | SF |
| James Emery | UUP | Eugene McMenamin | SDLP |
| Derek Hussey | UUP | Bernadette McNamee | SDLP |
| Thomas Kerrigan | DUP | Jarlath McNulty | SF |

### Senior Officers

Chief Executive: Philip Faithful
Head of Finance: Maureen Henebery
Head of Culture, Arts and Leisure: Karen McFarland
Chief Building Control Officer: John Stewart
Chief Environmental Health Officer: Paddy Cosgrove
Chief Technical Services Officer: Malcolm Scott
Business Manager: Sharon Maxwell
Arts and Events Officer: Jean Smith
Client Services Officer: Liam Donnelly
Community Relations Officer: Shirley McAnenna
Corporate Policy Officer: Grace Nicholl
DPP Manager: Rachelle Harkin
Economic Development Officer: Geraldine Stafford
Human Resources Officer: Paula Donnelly
Leisure Services Manager: Fionnuala O'Kane
Strabane LSP Project Officer: Patrick O'Doherty
Tourism Officer: Phillip McShane

### Council Contact Details

| | |
|---|---|
| Administration | 028 7138 2204 |
| Arts and Culture | 028 7138 2204 |
| Building Control | 028 7138 2204 |
| Cemeteries Administration | 028 7138 2204 |
| Community Development | 028 7138 2204 |
| Environmental Health | 028 7135 1355 |
| Technical Services | 028 7138 2771 |

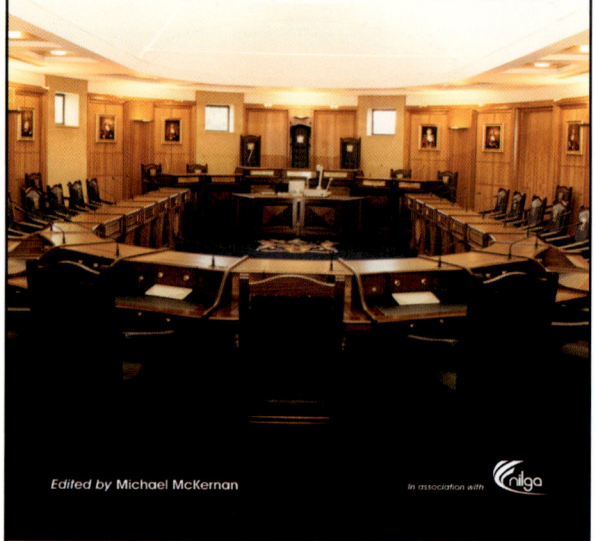

## Local Government Elections

Since Northern Ireland's local government structure was reformed in 1973 there have been 8 local government elections across the 26 Local Government Districts (LGDs). Results for the main parties have tended to correspond with overall performance in other elections although independents have featured more strongly.

Turnout for local elections is generally around 50–60 per cent, which is significantly lower than UK government elections, and also lower than the Assembly elections in 1998. This is probably reflective of the fact that the responsibilities of local authorities include areas such as waste disposal, cemeteries and parks, which although vital in everyday life, go largely unnoticed in comparison with mainstream political issues. Nevertheless the parties and candidates fiercely contest the elections, although issues raised at the hustings are matters over which they actually have little authority.

However, turnout for the 2001 local government election, at 66 per cent, was significantly higher than usual. This was largely due to the fact that Westminster elections were held on the same day.

**2001 Local Government Election**

Turnout: 66%

| | Votes | % votes | seats | % seats |
|---|---|---|---|---|
| UUP | 181336 | 22.9 | 154 | 26.5 |
| DUP | 169477 | 21.4 | 131 | 22.5 |
| SDLP | 153424 | 19.4 | 117 | 20.1 |
| SF | 163269 | 20.7 | 108 | 18.5 |
| All | 40443 | 5.1 | 28 | 4.8 |
| PUP | 12661 | 1.6 | 4 | 0.7 |
| Others | 70247 | 8.9 | 40 | 6.9 |
| **Total** | **790857** | **100** | **582** | **100** |

## Local Government Associations & Representative Groups

With the existence of 26 local authorities in Northern Ireland, there are many opportunities for the sector to work collectively across different areas. Some of the main representative local government organisations are listed below.

### Best Value Forum

Chairman: Ashley Boreland
Ards Borough Council, Council Offices
2 Church Street, Newtownards, BT23 4AP
Tel: 028 9182 4017 / Fax: 028 9181 9628

### Emergency Management Group

Chairman: Mervyn Rankin
c/o Ballymena Borough Council
80 Galgorm Road, Ballymena, BT42 1AB
Tel: 028 2566 0300 / Fax: 028 2566 0400

### Local Economic Development (Northern Ireland) Forum

Contact: Liam Hannaway
Banbridge District Council
Downshire Road, Banbridge, BT32 3JY
Tel: 028 4066 0600

### Local Government Staff Commission for Northern Ireland (LGSC)

Commission House
18-22 Gordon Street, Belfast, BT1 2LG
Tel: 028 9031 3200 / Fax: 028 9031 3151
Chief Executive: Adrian Kerr

### National Association of Councillors (NAC)

Chairman: Bertie Mongomery
c/o Magherafelt District Council
Council Offices
50 Ballyronan Road, Magherafelt, BT45 6EN
Tel: 028 7939 7979

### Northern Ireland Joint Council for Local Government Services (NIJC)

Secretary: Linda Leahy
Local Government Staff Commission for Northern Ireland
Tel: 028 9031 3200
Email: nijc@lgsc.org.uk

### Northern Ireland Local Government Association (NILGA)

Philip House
123 York Street, Belfast, BT15 1AB
Tel: 028 9024 9286 / Fax: 028 9023 3328
Chief Executive: Heather Moorhead
President: Cllr Francie Molloy

### Northern Ireland Local Government Officers Superannuation Committee (NILGOSC)

411 Holywood Road
Belfast, BT4 2LP
Tel: 028 9076 8025 / Fax: 028 9076 8790
Web: www.nilgosc.org.uk
Email: info@nilgosc.org.uk
Chairman: John Galbraith

### Society of Local Authority Chief Executives (SoLACE)

Chairman: Warll Moore
Coleraine Borough Council
Cloonavin, 66 Portstewart Road
Coleraine, BT52 1EY
Tel: 028 7034 7034 / Fax: 028 7034 7026

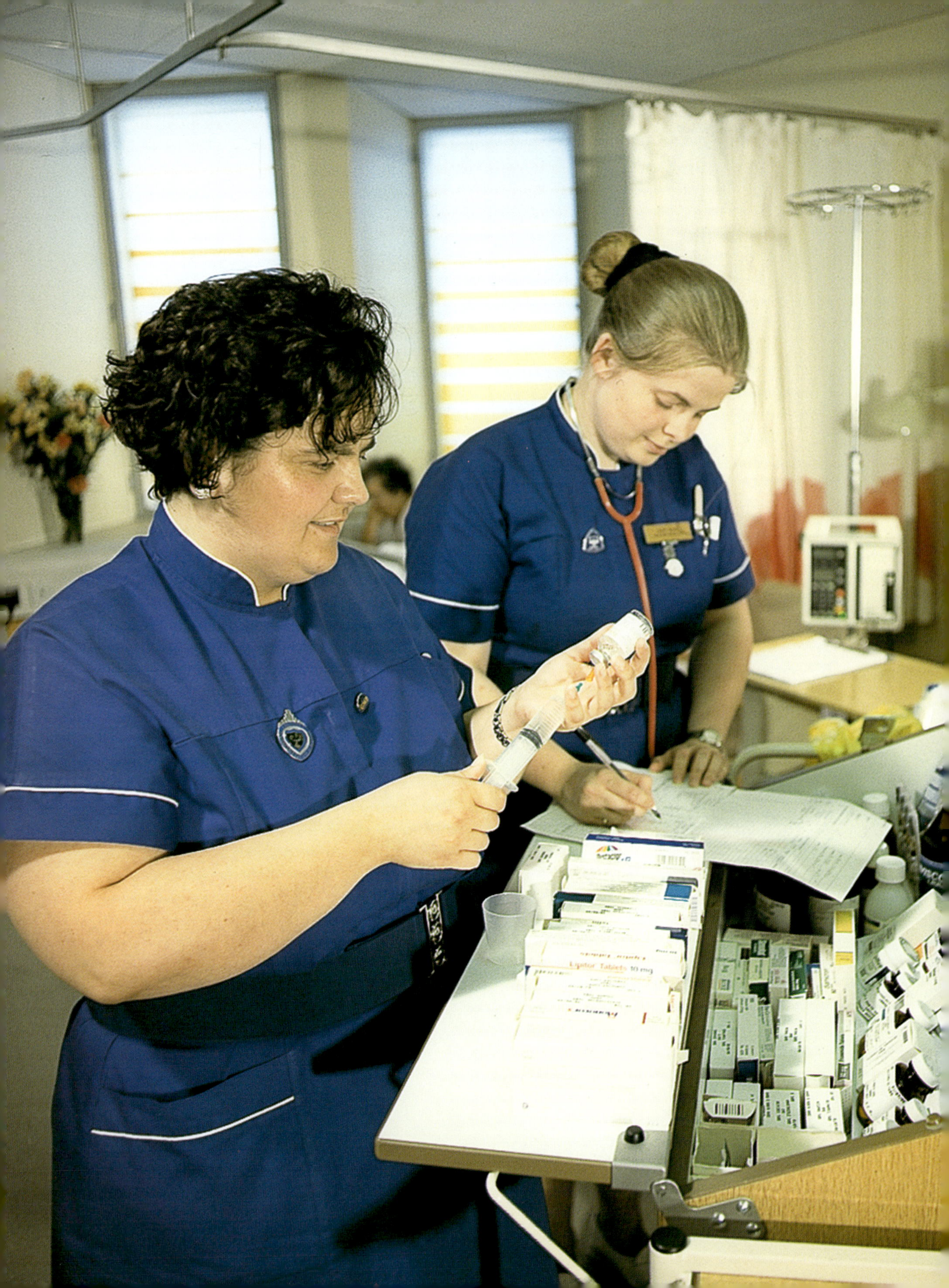

# Chapter 5

# Health, Social Services and Housing in Northern Ireland

# Overview of Health in Northern Ireland

The administration and delivery of health services is a hugely challenging undertaking in Northern Ireland as elsewhere. Surveys show it is something the general public cares deeply about and in recent years has become an increasingly important priority for government. In Northern Ireland the Department of Health Social Services and Public Safety is by far the government's biggest spending Department with an allocation in excess of £3.2bn.

Yet long waiting lists, hospital bed shortages, cancelled operations and reports of hospital 'superbugs' have become a familiar element of daily news coverage in Northern Ireland. It is no surprise therefore that, alongside public concern about the state of the health service in Northern Ireland there has been a steady growth in public investment in health with further significant increases promised.

This chapter sets out the main structures for the provision of healthcare, social services and housing in Northern Ireland, the challenges facing the current system and detailed insight into the government's plans for improvement in the provision of local health care services. It begins with a status-take on health in Northern Ireland and an overview of some of the inequalities and problems.

## Life Expectancy

Despite improvements in the last century, in comparison to the rest of Europe Northern Ireland's health record remains consistently poor. Whilst life expectancy rates have improved significantly, Northern Ireland lags behind European life expectancy norms and continues to lead the rankings in international league tables of the major diseases including cancer and coronary heart disease.

**Table 5.1 Life Expectancy Rates in Northern Ireland Expectation of Life**

| | At Birth | | At Age 1 Year | | At Age 65 Years | |
|---|---|---|---|---|---|---|
| Period | Male | Female | Male | Female | Male | Female |
| 1900-02 | 47.1 | 46.7 | - | - | 10.5 | 10.4 |
| 1950-52 | 65.5 | 68.8 | 67.5 | 70.3 | 12.1 | 13.5 |
| 1975-77 | 67.5 | 73.8 | 67.9 | 74.1 | 11.8 | 15.3 |
| 1985-87 | 70.9 | 77.1 | 70.6 | 76.8 | 13.2 | 16.9 |
| 1999-01 | 74.8 | 79.8 | 74.3 | 79.2 | 15.3 | 18.5 |
| 2000-02 | 75.2 | 80.1 | 74.6 | 79.5 | 15.6 | 18.7 |

Source: NISRA

The overall gradual improvements in life expectancy conceal a clear pattern of difference that exists between the life expectancy of those in high-income groups against those in lower socio-economic brackets. Nonetheless life expectancy in Northern Ireland is expected to continue to improve in the period ahead. Life expectancy for a baby boy born in 2010 will be 76.8 and for a baby girl 81.3 according to the latest government projections.

## Infant Mortality

Deaths in the first year of life are often regarded as a fair reflection of the overall health status of a population.

Infant mortality rates have been falling gradually for many years and are now at a level of 5.3 per 1000 births (2003 figures). The actual number of deaths is small, and slight fluctuations year on year can affect the rate. It is worth noting that multiple births are a risk factor for infant deaths and these have been increasing, mainly due to increased use of fertility treatments. Also the age of the mother is a risk factor and proportionately more babies are now being born to older mothers. The main causes of death in infancy are conditions associated with premature birth, low birth weight and congenital malformations. However Northern Ireland continues to experience levels of infant mortality above the European average.

## Main Causes of Death and Ill Health

Heart disease, cancer and respiratory disease account for 65 per cent of all adult deaths with suicides, accidents, strokes and other causes accounting for the remaining 35 per cent. Long standing illness is recognised as a measure of poor health in the community. It was found in the 2003/04 Continuous Household Survey that 33 per cent of men and 37 per cent of women in Northern Ireland had a long-standing illness.

It should be noted that the level of long-standing illness is much higher among lower income groups (61% among those with a gross household income of £5,210-£10,430). In the highest income bracket (over £31,290), just 20% reported a long-standing illness.

**Table 5.2 Main Causes of Death 2003**

| | |
|---|---|
| Circulatory Diseases | 39% |
| Cancer | 26% |
| Respiratory Diseases | 14% |
| External Causes (eg Accidents) | 3% |
| Other Causes | 18% |

Source: NISRA

### Heart Disease and Cancer

Heart disease and cancer continue to be the major causes of death in adults. Heart disease is the second most frequent cause of death in Northern Ireland. Statistics in relation to cancer show that:

- More than one in four of the population will die from a form of cancer during their lifetime;
- Men have a one in six chance and women a one in eight chance of dying from cancer before the age of 75;
- 800 people are killed by lung cancer each year which accounts for one quarter of cancer deaths in the under 75s;
- Breast cancer accounts for one in three cancer cases amongst women.

In the past pneumonia has often been found to be a major cause of death in Northern Ireland. However in many cases pneumonia is a complication of an underlying condition such as cancer, stroke or dementia, which are the real cause of death.

The concept of potential years of life lost (PYLL) is used to measure the contribution made by specific causes of death before age 75. The two main contributors to PYLL are cancer and coronary heart disease.

Another significant contributor in Northern Ireland is suicide where although the number of deaths is low relative to the number caused by diseases, the contribution to years of life lost is high because suicide often occurs at a young age. Suicide in Northern Ireland is high in comparison to European norms and its incidence is concentrated among males – particularly in younger age groups. Of 132 suicides occuring in Northern Ireland in 2003, 104 were by men.

**Smoking and Obesity**

Smoking is identified as the single greatest cause of premature death and is estimated to cause approximately 3,000 deaths per annum in Northern Ireland. Compared to other members of the European Union Northern Ireland has the second highest percentage of 13 year olds reported to smoke daily and the fourth highest rate of 14 year olds.

Although overall smoking rates have fallen over the last fifteen years, this has not occurred to the same extent among the less well off where the levels of smokers remain at their highest.

The figures show that among men in professional occupations, 17 per cent smoke compared with 30 per cent of those who have unskilled manual jobs. For women the figures are 12 per cent and 34 per cent respectively. 24 per cent of employed men smoke compared to 49 per cent of unemployed men and 26 per cent of employed women smoke as opposed to 45 per cent who are unemployed.

Obesity is a growing healthcare challenge in Northern Ireland. Surveys show that obesity is an increasing trend with predictions that by 2010, 23 per cent of women and 22 per cent of men will be obese. The rate of obesity amongst children is also increasing. It is estimated that over 450 deaths are caused, and 260,000 working days, at a cost to the economy of £500 million, are lost through the effects of obesity in Northern Ireland each year.

**Alcohol and Drugs**

Whilst the dangers associated with drugs misuse have a higher public profile, the level and effects of alcohol abuse in Northern Ireland is much more significant in terms of the overall wellbeing of the population.

It is estimated that there are over 730 deaths per annum in Northern Ireland attributable to excess alcohol consumption. Statistics show that 81 per cent of men and 73 per cent of women are currently consumers of alcohol in Northern Ireland, and that 33 per cent of men and 11 per cent of women drink in excess of recommended limits.

Statistics also reveal that in 2002-03 41% of all 20-24 year olds, have, at some stage, taken drugs – the figures are 44% for males and 38% for women. Of those that have taken drugs, 52% had done so for the first time by the age of 18, illustrating the extent of the problem among teenagers.

Drugs misuse is often associated with aspects of deprivation, and lack of educational and employment prospects with their resultant negative social consequences. Drug misuse is also associated with crime, which has high costs for society affecting both victims and the community.

Drug misusers place additional burdens on the health, social services and social security systems. It is estimated that the costs of enforcement, prevention, treatment and rehabilitation are £8 million per annum whilst it is estimated that drug misuse itself results in additional costs of £300-£500 million per annum to society in Northern Ireland.

**Accidents and Road Traffic Incidents**

Accidents and road traffic incidents are a major cause of death in Northern Ireland. There is a significant statistical link between the nature of some accidents and socio-economic status.

It is estimated that there are over 350 deaths and 150,000 injuries per annum equating to the loss of 180,000 working days and a cost to the economy of £370 million through accidental death and injury costs in Northern Ireland.

**Disability**

17 per cent of adults in Northern Ireland in comparison to 14 per cent in Britain have a disability. The violence of 'the Troubles' resulting in many permanent injuries to victims is a significant factor in Northern Ireland's very high rate of disability. Lower income, social exclusion and limited access to services and transport are some of the additional challenges facing the disproportionately high disabled population.

**Mental Health**

Overall Northern Ireland's Chief Medical Officer has estimated that up to 300,000 of Northern Ireland's population will at any one time experience poor mental health. Increasingly the link between mental health and emotional well-being and chronic physical disease is being accepted.

People who are unemployed are twice as likely to experience a mental health problem than those in employment and 60 per cent of women in the lowest social class group are likely to experience a form of neurotic disorder in comparison to those in the professional group.

Statistics from the 2001 Health and Social Well Being Survey indicated that 21 per cent of the population aged 16+ considered themselves to be depressed and a similar percentage had a potential psychiatric disorder.

### Children's Health

The differential in health status across social class can be seen in children from birth onwards. Babies in the lower socio-economic groups are more likely to have a low birth weight and die in infancy than the children of more affluent families. Infant mortality rates are nearly 50 per cent higher in the most deprived areas, compared to the least deprived. The proportion of children living in conditions of poverty is significantly higher, and over a quarter of children come from households dependent on Jobseeker's Allowance or Income Support.

In households where the household head has a professional occupation just 3% of children have a limiting long-standing illness. Where the head of household has an unskilled manual job, this is five times higher at 15%.

Inequalities in health continue to be evident throughout childhood and in young adults. Rates of accidental injury and oral health provide clear examples of this. Accidents are a major cause of death and disability among children and young people. Children from less affluent areas are 15 times more likely to die in a house fire, 7 times more likely to die as a result of a road traffic accident, and 5 times more likely to be injured as pedestrians. These figures are of particular concern given that the vast majority of accidents are preventable.

The Westminster Government has placed children at the centre of its anti-poverty strategy and in Northern Ireland a Children's Commissioner has been appointed to help focus policy more tellingly on the interests and needs of children.

### Dental Health

Although there has been a gradual improvement in oral health over the past 5 years, the most recent surveys indicate that the general level of oral health in Northern Ireland is still considerably worse than in Britain and the rest of Ireland, particularly amongst children. Dental Health is poorer among those people in lower socio-economic groups with just 40% of unskilled manual workers having regular dental check-ups compared to 64% among the professional class. Children in schools in the North and West of Belfast experience more tooth decay than those in other parts of the greater Belfast area. This is one of the reasons for the introduction of fluoride to the water supply.

### Elderly People

People of retirement age account for nearly 16 per cent of the population of Northern Ireland; a figure which is expected to continue to rise in line with greater life expectency. Smaller families, the growth of the number of women in the workplace and a more mobile population has resulted in an ageing population with rising rates of long-standing illness. It is acknowledged that there is a direct relationship between low income in the elderly and reported levels of disability.

## Factors Determining Health in Northern Ireland

The social, cultural, economic and physical environment determines the extent to which a population experiences relatively good or poor health. Many complex and interrelated factors have a role in determining health; these include:

- Disadvantage and social exclusion;
- Poverty;
- Unemployment;
- Low educational achievement;
- Poor social and community environment;
- Living conditions;
- Working conditions;
- The wider environment;
- Individual behaviour and lifestyle.

## Disadvantage and Poverty

Disadvantage takes many forms, all tending to concentrate on the same cohort of people, having a long-term detrimental effect on their health. Poverty is acknowledged as the greatest risk factor for health. All the evidence points to quality of health having a strong correlation with levels of income. Recent research shows that 24 per cent of households in Northern Ireland live in poverty, a rise of 3 per cent since 1990. Over 40 per cent of single parents, 19 per cent of single pensioners and 18 per cent of couples with children in Northern Ireland have been defined as living in 'absolute' poverty.

## Unemployment

Unemployment is often the link between poverty, social exclusion and poor mental and physical health. Whilst levels of unemployment in Northern Ireland have fallen sharply, halving since the early 1990s, there are still approximately 300,000 economically inactive people of working age, which is disproportionately high relative to the UK average.

## Educational Attainment

There are strong links between levels of educational attainment and deprivation with the most deprived areas showing the lowest rates of educational achievement. According to the Department of Education almost a fifth of the workforce has no formal qualifications and 24% of the population of Northern Ireland has literacy or numeracy problems.

## Housing and Homelessness

Homelessness is becoming an increasing problem in Northern Ireland and there is a strong link between homelessness and ill health. There were 17,150 homeless households in Northern Ireland in 2003. This figure was a significant increase on the previous year's total indicating the growing nature of the problem. Northern Ireland has persistently high levels of homelessness running at rates some 50% above the United Kingdom average.

Housing condition is a major contributor to the quality of health. The most recent survey of housing stock in Northern Ireland by the Housing Executive showed a high level of unfitness including many tenants without central heating. Issues in the wider environment also affect health and well being both directly and indirectly, including air and water quality.

### Impact of Gender
The differences in men and women's health are striking, particularly once they reach middle and older age groups. Death rates are much higher in men in middle age and old age than in women in the same age groups, although this gap narrows in the over 80s. However, older women are far more likely than older men to report long-standing sickness and disability. Coronary heart disease is the cause of death in 1 in 3 males and 1 in 4 females, a major cause of mortality.

### Geographical Factors
Inequalities are also evident on comparison of geographical locations. About 2000 lives could be preserved each year if those living in the council districts with the highest death rates had the health status of those in the districts with the lowest death rates. The electoral wards with the highest death rates are also those with the highest levels of deprivation. This correlation is particularly striking for deaths from coronary heart disease.

### Ethnic Minorities
Ethnic groups also suffer from inequalities in health compounded by difficulties accessing services including health and social care, education and language support. Northern Ireland has a number of ethnic minorities, the largest of which is the Chinese community, with approaching 10,000 people.

The Travelling Community is recognised as an ethnic group having poorer than average health status. Average life expectancy for a traveller is typically 15 years less than that of a member of the settled community. Only one in 10 of the Traveller population is over 40 years old and only one in 100 over 65. Infant mortality rates in travellers are three times higher than the general population.

### Teenage Parenthood
Northern Ireland has one of the highest rates of teenage pregnancy in Western Europe with 7% of all births in 2003 being to mothers aged under 20.

Teenage parenthood is recognised as both a cause and a consequence of disadvantage. Evidence demonstrates that levels of teenage pregnancy correlate with those areas of high deprivation.

## Department of Health, Social Services and Public Safety
In Northern Ireland responsibility for health policy and provision falls under the Department of Health, Social Services and Public Safety. The stated mission of the department is 'to improve people's health and social well-being'. 1000 staff are directly employed by the department, 2000 by the Fire Authority and over 40,000 other staff within the health and social services sector. The annual budget for DHSSPS at over £3 billion is by far the biggest of any government department in Northern Ireland. The department has three main areas of responsibility:

- **Health and Personal Social Services**
  Including policy, finance and legislation for hospitals, family practitioner services and community health and social services;

- **Public Health**
  Including policy, legislation and administrative action to promote and protect the health of the population; and

- **Public Safety**
  Including responsibility for policy and legislation for the Fire Services, Food Safety and emergency planning.

*(For further information about departmental organisation and personnel see Chapter 3 Central Government Departments and Agencies).*

## Structure of the Department
The Department of Health, Social Services and Public Safety is structured into five professional groups each led by a Chief Professional Officer. These are:

### Public Health, Medical and Allied Group
The Public Health, Medical and Allied Group led by the Chief Medical Officer Dr Henrietta Campbell is responsible for business relating to public health, including the Investing for Health initiative; health protection; health promotion; and smoking, drugs and alcohol related strategies. The Group also provides medical services for the department, the Northern Ireland Civil Service and the Prison Service.

### Social Services Inspectorate
Led by the Chief Inspector, the Social Services Inspectorate advises ministers, departments and government agencies on matters relating to social care. The Inspectorate is responsible for the completion of an annual inspection programme across a range of services and providers on behalf of the Department of Health, Social Services and Public Safety and the Northern Ireland Office. Policy development for social work, social care training and education, including postgraduate social work bursaries and other training support funding linked to the HPSS Training Strategy is the responsibility of the Social Services Inspectorate.

**Social Services Analysis Branch**
(SSAB) is responsible for providing management information, methodological and analytical support to help shape, develop and inform the work of the Social Services Inspectorate. This includes supporting the inspectorate in their inspection work, evaluations and monitoring exercises and other SSI projects including the Annual Report of the Chief Inspector. SSAB publish 'Key Indicators for Personal Social Services' in the form of an annual publication.

## Nursing and Midwifery Advisory Group
The Group led by the Chief Nursing Officer Miss Judith Hill is responsible for advising on all aspects of policy affecting nursing, midwifery, health visiting, education and services.

## Dental Services Group
Led by the Chief Dental Officer Doreen Wilson, the Group provides advice on oral health, and delivers direct dental services to the Prisons and Young Offenders Centres. The Chief Dental Officer advises the Minister and the Department on all aspects of dental policy affecting Northern Ireland. The Chief Dental Officer's primary responsibility is to promote and improve the oral health of the population.

## Pharmaceutical Advice and Services Group
The Chief Pharmaceutical Officer Dr Norman Morrow is responsible for advising in regard to medicines and pharmaceutical services and has responsibility for medicines legislation relating to both human and veterinary medicines.

The group also has responsibility for the inspection of premises and the enforcement of human and veterinary medicines under the Medicines Act, Misuse of Drugs Act, Pharmacy (Northern Ireland) Order and Poisons (Northern Ireland) Order.

**Northern Ireland Medicines Governance Project**
The Northern Ireland Medicines Governance Projects aims to provide a dedicated medicines risk management function throughout the acute hospital Trusts in Northern Ireland.

## Planning and Resources Group
The group negotiates and manages financial resources, departmental staffing policy and resources, information and analysis and ICT support and development for the department and the health and social services bodies.

The Planning and Resources group also has responsibility for public safety policies, including ambulance services, fire services and emergency planning, publication of the regional strategy for health and social well-being, and overall co-ordination of New TSN, Equality and Human Rights.

## Strategic Planning and Modernisation Group
The Group is responsible for strategic management and planning issues for the Health and Personal Social Services (HPSS). It provides ICT support and development for the Department and the HPSS, manages the Strategic Capital Development Programme and provides strategic direction on Human Resources, including public appointments to HPSS bodies. It is responsible for policy and strategic development of a range of modernisation issues, including the Review of HPSS organisational structures, and the HPSS Service Improvement Programme.

## Health Service Expenditure
Table 5.3 sets out the planned public expenditure on health in Northern Ireland over the next three years.

**Table 5.3 Department of Health, Social Services and Public Safety Planned Expenditure 2004/05 - 2006/07**

| **Objective A** | **2004-05 £m** | **2005-06 £m** | **2006-07 £m** |
|---|---|---|---|
| Policy Development | 35.2 | 36.5 | 40.3 |
| **Total Objective A** | 35.2 | 36.5 | 40.3 |
| **Objective B** | | | |
| Community Health | 2024.1 | 2182.1 | 2376.0 |
| Personal Social Services | 719.8 | 772 | 827.4 |
| Family Health Service | 281.4 | 320.3 | 359.0 |
| Training Bursaries & Further Education & Research | 70.2 | 74.2 | 77.5 |
| Other Centrally Financed Services & Welfare Foods | 42.9 | 44.3 | 45.4 |
| Grants to Voluntary Bodies | 7.4 | 8.0 | 8.7 |
| N/S Body - Food Safety Promotion | 1.7 | 1.7 | 1.7 |
| Foods Standards Agency | 2.6 | 2.7 | 2.8 |
| **Total Objective B** | **3150.1** | **3405.3** | **3698.5** |
| Objective C | | | |
| Fire Service | 62.5 | 64.1 | 74.8 |
| **Total Objective C** | **62.5** | **64.1** | **74.8** |
| Total DEL* | **3247.8** | **3505.9** | **3813.6** |
| EU Peace Programme | 0.07 | 0.0 | 0.0 |
| **Total DHSSPS** | **3248.5** | **3505.9** | **3813.6** |
| % Increase | 6.8 | 7.9 | 8.8 |

DEL* = Department Expenditure Limit

Source DFP

## Other Health Sector Agencies and Organisations

In addition to the regular health service delivery structures of Trusts, Boards and Councils, there are a number of Departments, public bodies and executive agencies charged with a range of specialist or support functions in the health sector. These are detailed below.

**Central Services Agency**
25-27 Adelaide Street, Belfast, BT2 8FH
Tel: 028 9032 4431 / Fax: 028 9023 2304
Web: www.centralservicesagency.n-i.nhs.uk
Chief Executive: Stephen Hodkinson
Chairman: Prof. S Fulton

The Central Services Agency provides support services to the Department of Health, health boards, trusts and agencies. The Agency is made up of seven core business units as follows:

- Finance directorate
- Human Resources
- Family practitioner services
- Regional supplies service
- Nicare
- Research and development
- Legal services
- Counter fraud unit (CFU)
- Equality unit

**Occupational Health Service (OHS)**
Musgrave Park Hospital, Stockman's Lane, Belfast, BT9 7JB
Tel: 028 9090 2000

The service provides comprehensive occupational health and medical advisory services to Northern Ireland government departments and agencies.

**Food Standards Agency Northern Ireland**
Unit 10B, Clarendon Road Belfast, BT1 3BG
Tel: 028 9041 7700 / Fax: 028 9041 7726
Web: www.food.gov.uk
Director: Morris McAllister

The Food Standards Agency is a UK-wide non-Ministerial government department, with offices in Belfast (FSANI), Aberdeen, Cardiff and London. It provides policy advice to ministers on food safety, food standards and aspects of nutrition and prepares draft legislation. The Agency also represents the UK in negotiations in the EU. FSANI is responsible for providing impartial accurate advice on a balanced diet. This includes:

- monitoring and surveillance of the nutrient content of food and the nutrient content of the diet;
- drafting and producing legislation relating to nutritional aspects of food, including labelling and claims, dietary supplements sold as food, fortified foods and functional foods;
- providing practical guidance in relation to nutritional aspects of the food chain, including production and catering;
- commissioning research on food and diet appropriate to its responsibility for the above issues.

**Health Estates**
Stoney Road, Dundonald, Belfast, BT16 1US
Tel: 028 9052 0025 / Fax: 028 9052 3900
Web: www.dhssni.gov.uk/hpss/hea
Chief Executive: Ronnie Browne

The Northern Ireland Health and Social Services Estates Agency, known as Health Estates is the Agency which determines policy on estate issues relating to the delivery of health and social care.

The Agency's task is to provide professional and technical advice, guidance and support on estates matters at both a strategic and operational level to the various bodies charged with the responsibility for the Health and Social Services estate in Northern Ireland.

**The Northern Ireland Blood Transfusion Service Agency**
Belfast City Hospital Complex, Lisburn Road, Belfast, BT9 7TS
Tel: 028 9032 1414 / Fax: 028 9043 9017
Web: www.nibts.org
Chairman: Steven Costello
Chief Executive/ Medical Director: Dr Morris McClelland

The Northern Ireland Blood Transfusion Service, is an independent agency of the Health and Personal Social Services. It is responsible for the collection, testing and distribution of over 75,000 blood donations each year. The Service operates three mobile units at around 300 locations throughout the province. Including headquarters, located on the site of Belfast City Hospital, a total of almost 1,000 donation sessions are held each year.

The NIBTS exists to fully supply the needs of all hospitals and clinical units in the province with safe and effective blood and blood products and other related services.

**The Northern Ireland Guardian Ad Litem Agency**
Centre House, 79 Chichester Street, Belfast, BT1 4JE
Tel: 028 90 9031 6550 / Fax: 028 90 9031 9811
Web: www.nigala.n.-i.nhs.uk
Chairman: Mr Jim Currie
Chief Executive: Ronnie Williamson

The Northern Ireland Guardian Ad Litem Agency maintains a register of guardians ad litem who are independent officers of the court experienced in working with children and families. Under the Children (NI) Order 1995, a guardian ad litem is appointed to safeguard the interests of children who are the subject of court proceedings.

**The Northern Ireland Health Promotion Agency**
18 Ormeau Avenue, Belfast, BT2 8HS
Tel: 028 9031 1611 / Fax: 028 9031 1711
Web: www.healthpromotionagency.org.uk
Chairperson: Alice Quinn
Chief Executive: Dr Brian Gaffney

The Health Promotion Agency provides a regional focus for health promotion. Its mission is 'to make health a top priority for everyone in Northern Ireland.' Its statutory functions include:

- Advising the Department (DHSSPS) on matters relating to health promotion:
- Undertaking health promotion activity;
- Planning and carrying out regional or local actions in co-operation with HSS Boards, District Councils, Education and Library Boards, voluntary organisations and other key interests;
- Sponsoring research and evaluation;
- Assisting the provision of training;
- Providing a regional centre of information and advice on health promotion;
- Making grants to and otherwise supporting voluntary organisations.

**The Northern Ireland Regional Medical Physics Agency**
Musgrave and Clarke House, Royal Victoria Hospital
Belfast, BT12 6BA
Tel: 028 9063 4430 / Fax: 028 9031 3040
Web: www.medicalphysics.n-i.nhs.uk
Chairman: Professor D.G Walmsley
Chief Executive: Professor Peter Smith

The Agency provides scientific measurement and control of high technology equipment in the application of physics and engineering to health care provided by HPSS bodies. Although most of its work is the provision of services for the health trusts. It also carries out work on behalf of clients outside the HPSS sector. Its main service groupings are:-

- Clinical Engineering and Physiological Sciences;
- Radiation Protection and Imaging;
- Radioisotopes;
- Radiotherapy Physics.

**The Mental Health Commission for Northern Ireland**
Elizabeth House, 118 Holywood Road, Belfast, BT4 1NY
Tel: 028 9065 1157 / Fax: 028 9047 1180
Chairperson: Marian O'Neill
Acting Chief Executive: Stephen Jackson

The Mental Health Commission for Northern Ireland is an independent body whose role is to review the care and treatment of persons suffering from mental disorder.

The Commission has a duty to ensure that no patient is either improperly detained or received into guardianship and that patients' rights are not infringed. The Commission visits and interviews patients and relatives in hospital and in the community and has the power to refer cases to the Mental Health Review Tribunal. The Commission has 15 members, including 5 lay people drawn from a cross section of relevant professions.

**The Northern Ireland Medical and Dental Training Agency**
*(formerly Northern Ireland Council for Postgraduate Medical and Dental Education)*
5 Annadale Avenue, Belfast, BT7 3JH
Tel: 028 9049 2731 / Fax: 028 9064 2279
Chairman: Dr Harry McGuigan
Vice Chairman: Dr John Jenkins
Chief Executive: Jack McCluggage

The core function of the Agency is the provision and development of postgraduate and continuing medical and dental education within Northern Ireland. The Chief Executive/Postgraduate Dean supported by the Director of General Practice Education holds overall responsibility for this provision. The business of the Agency falls largely into three functional areas: Hospital Medicine, General Practice and Dentistry. The Council oversees the postgraduate and medical education of doctors and dentists and is responsible for the development and delivery of vocational training and continuing medical education for GPs and dentists.

**The Northern Ireland Social Care Council (NISCC)**
7th Floor, Millennium House
19-25 Great Victoria Street, Belfast, BT2 7AQ
Web: www.niscc.info
Tel: 028 9041 7600 / Fax: 028 9041 7601
Chief Executive: Brendan Johnston
Chairman: Dr Jeremy Harbison

Northern Ireland Social Care Council is responsible for raising standards in the Northern Ireland social care work force. There are currently around 30,000 social care workers in Northern Ireland.

**The Northern Ireland Practice and Education Council for Nursing and Midwifery**
Centre House, 75 Chichester Street, Belfast
Tel: 028 9023 8152 / Fax: 028 9033 3298
Web: www.nipec.n-i.nhs.uk
Chairman: Mrs Maureen Griffith
Chief Executive: Ms Paddie Blaney

The role of the Council is to support the professional development of the nursing and midwifery professions in areas of best practice, education and performance so that the public in Northern Ireland can be provided with a high standard of nursing and midwifery care.

**The Fire Authority for Northern Ireland (FANI)**
Brigade HQ, 1 Seymour Street, Lisburn, BT27 4SX
Tel: 028 9266 4221 / Fax: 028 9267 7402
Chairman: William F Gillespie
Chief Executive: Colin Lammey

The Authority is responsible for the provision of regional fire services, ensuring their compliance with national fire cover standards and implementing the department's fire safety policy. The Northern Ireland Fire Brigade serves the 1.7 million people of Northern Ireland over 5,500 sq. miles. The Fire Authority is composed of 17 members, appointed by the head of the Department of Health, Social Services and Public Safety.

The role of the Fire Authority is to determine detailed strategic policy for the Fire Brigade and carries out an overseeing role via reports presented at monthly meetings.

The Brigade is divided into four Operational Command Areas, with Brigade Headquarters situated in Lisburn, Co. Antrim.

*Operational Command Area*
Headquarters are based in Ballymena, Belfast, Londonderry and Portadown. The Northern Ireland Fire Brigade also has a training centre based in Boucher Crescent, Belfast.

# Administration and Delivery of Healthcare Services

## Structure of Health and Social Services in Northern Ireland

### The HSS Boards

Under the Department of Health are the four Health and Social Services Boards, which act as agents of the department. The regional Boards carry out the bulk of all public expenditure on health in Northern Ireland.

Health Boards purchase healthcare services from Northern Ireland's Trusts and at local level from General Practitioner centres. There are 19 trusts of varying sizes, the larger of which cover several major hospitals.

Under the plans announced in the department's Corporate Plan and under the Investing for Health strategy Wellbeing Investment Plans (HWIP) are the arrangements by which the four HSS Boards will secure effective health and social services for their local populations, improve health and social well being and reduce inequalities.

These plans, which became effective in 2002, are the key planning and accountability documents for the HPSS and consist of three main elements:

- HSS Boards' plans for commissioning services in their local areas;
- HSS Boards' plans to deliver on the Investing for Health Strategy of the department and reduce inequalities;
- HSS Boards' plans to deliver on the major underpinning themes of the Programme for Government.

The Health and Well Being and Investment Plans will act as the single vehicle for all local HPSS planning. It is expected that health improvement planning will be done on a three year cycle rolling forward annually.

It is considered quite possible that there will be radical change to the existing Health Board structures in the context of the Government's major review of public administration. There is a general view that there are too many different bodies covering relatively small administrative units.

### Investing for Health Partnerships

Each Health and Social Services Board will have responsibility for developing an Investing for Health Partnership in their area bringing together different organisations in partnership to ensure that actions to improve health are properly coordinated, and an action plan agreed to improve the health of the local population in line with the Investing for Health Strategy.

The purpose of the Partnerships is to identify opportunities to improve the health of the people in the area by addressing the social, cultural, economic and environmental determinants of health.

Members of these local partnerships will include representatives from voluntary, community and statutory organisations in the locality, including those from District Councils, the Housing Executive, Education and Library Boards and HSS Trusts. Where applicable, members of the business community will also be invited to participate.

District Councils will have a key role in the Investing for Health Partnerships, presenting concerns particularly relevant to their locality and in respect to many of their statutory functions including environmental health, consumer protection, building control, waste management, community services and local economic development planning which have a direct bearing on health and the determinants of health. The councils' participation in the Investing for Health Partnerships led by the Health Boards will also ensure that health issues are considered in local strategic planning processes and considered by other statutory bodies.

The Investing for Health Partnerships is run in parallel with existing networks such as Health Action Zones, Healthy Cities, Child Care Partnerships and Peace and Reconciliation Partnerships.

## Local Health and Social Care Groups

New primary care arrangements were put in place in April 2002 following consultation on the proposals set out in the paper 'Building the Way Forward in Primary Care'. Under the new arrangements Local Health and Social Care Groups have been created to provide a framework to help primary care professionals improve health and well-being.

## The HSS Trusts

HSS Trusts after GPs are the main deliverers of healthcare services to the general public. They are accountable to the department in relation to the capital, income, workforce, estate and all other resources at their disposal and will be accountable for the effectiveness of their relationships with users, carers and the wider community. Each of the HSS Trusts produces a Trust Delivery Plan (TDP) illustrating how the Trust intends to use their resources to deliver in line with planning goals set by the Minister for Health.

The Trusts will work in partnership with the Boards to implement the HWIPs and are required to produce an implementation plan, which will:

- Demonstrate how the HWIP is to be effected within the Trust;
- Identify the consequences and risks to the Trust in relation to current and future clinical support services, funding sources (both capital and revenue) costs, human resources, capital assets and information and management technology.

## Health and Social Services Councils

Health Councils were established in 1982 to shadow the areas covered by each of the Health Boards and report independently on the quality of healthcare delivery. The Councils regularly consult with the general public to monitor healthcare from the perspective of the consumer and make recommendations on how services might be improved. Councils have an important role in representing their local area population and influencing the policies of the Health Boards. In relation to the Health Wellbeing Investment Plans the role of Councils will be to:

- Contribute to the development of HWIPs and closely monitor their outcomes;
- Report on the practical difference achieved by the HWIP from the perspective of the local population;
- Promote greater participation and involvement of the local community in the Investing for Health strategy.

## Health and Social Services Boards (HSSBs)

Northern Ireland is served by 4 Health and Social Services Boards, each representing a geographical area and its population. Originally the Boards had responsibility for all health and social services provided within their area, including hospitals, clinics, social services centres. Towards the end of the 1980s central government initiated a series of reforms to the National Health Service (NHS), which affected the way services were provided in Britain and in Northern Ireland.

The Health and Social Services Boards work under government policies and guidelines, overseen by the Department for Health, Social Services and Public Safety. The role of the Boards is primarily to improve the health and wellbeing of the people who live in their area. This involves an assessment of the health and social services needed by local people, and arrangements for the provision of those services.

Assessment takes place in consultation with 'stakeholders' in the health sector. Stakeholders are organisations and groups which have an interest in the health sector, and include elected representatives of local councils, professional organisations, voluntary groups, statutory bodies, HSS Trusts, primary healthcare professionals (such as GPs) and representatives of the local community.

From this consultation a plan is devised for the procurement of the services required. This is achieved by purchasing, or 'commissioning' health and social services, principally from 3 sources: Health and Social Services Trusts, voluntary organisations and private sector organisations. Boards negotiate Service Level Agreements with service providers, essentially contracts to provide services to patients.

Health and Social Services Boards are also required to evaluate all services provided, in order to ensure that they are meeting the needs of the population. This includes monitoring services provided in hospitals and in the community.

Health and Social Services Boards have responsibilities relating to the areas of family health and childcare. Boards manage the registration, inspection and monitoring of residential and nursing homes, including those for children and the elderly. They also have a role in overseeing arrangements for the delivery of health services to families by GPs, dentists, opticians and pharmacists.

Other services provided by Boards include the control of infectious diseases and the monitoring of the statutory functions delegated to Trusts.

**Board Structure**
Each Health and Social Services Board is composed of both executive and non-executive directors, and holds a public meeting every month. Geographical divisions between the Boards coincide with local government boundaries, so that each Board covers a number of local government districts.

Each local authority nominates at least one representative to sit on the appropriate Board. Other members of the Boards are Government nominees, as well as some senior executives employed by the Boards themselves.

**Table 5.4**
**Northern Ireland: Population by Health Board**
**2003**

| | Male | Female | Total |
|---|---|---|---|
| Eastern | 318,587 | 345,324 | 663,911 |
| Northern | 212,847 | 219,987 | 432,834 |
| Southern | 158,459 | 160,567 | 319,026 |
| Western | 142,929 | 143,928 | 286,857 |
| Total | 832,822 | 869,806 | 1,702,628 |

Source NISRA

The Eastern Board is by far the largest in terms of population, with over twice as many people as the smallest, the Western Board. It should be noted that the population of the Eastern Board has been decreasing over time, while those of the other Boards have been increasing.

## Health and Social Services Boards

### Eastern Health and Social Services Board

EHSSB

12-22 Linenhall Street
Belfast, BT2 8BS
Tel: 028 9032 1313
Minicom: 028 9032 4980
(for people who are deaf or who have hearing problems)

Email: Enquiry@ehssb.n-i.nhs.uk
Web: www.ehssb.n-i.nhs.uk

The Eastern Board 'commissions' or arranges a comprehensive range of health and social services for the 670,000 people who live within its area.

The area served by the Board includes the City Council areas of Belfast and Lisburn, the Borough Council areas of Ards, Castlereagh and North Down, and the Down District Council area.

The Board each year deploys its annual funding from government of around £1 billion to ensure that hospital services, family health services provided by professionals such as GPs and a wide array of community social services are all available to people.

*Board Structure*
The Board consists of non-executive Board members, executive Board members and a senior management team. A team of directors leads the Board:

*Executive Directors:*
Chief Executive: Dr Paula Kilbane
Tel: 028 9032 1313
Medical Director of Primary Care: Dr Stanton Adair
Tel: 028 9055 3782
Director of Planning and Contracting: Anne Lynch
Tel: 028 9055 3900
Director of Finance: Angela Paisley
Tel: 028 9055 3911
Director of Social Services: Hugh Connor
Tel: 028 9055 3964
Director of Public Health: Dr David Stewart
Tel: 028 9055 3940

The main providers of care within the EHSSB area are:

Royal Hospitals HSS Trust, Belfast City Hospital HSS Trust Mater Hospital HSS Trust, Green Park Healthcare HSS Trust, Down Lisburn HSS Trust, Ulster Community and Hospitals HSS Trust, North and West Belfast HSS Trust, South and East Belfast HSS Trust, Northern Ireland Ambulance Service HSS Trust.

*Family Health Services*
Within the Eastern Health and Social Services Board's area there are currently 146 medical practices, employing approximately 400 doctors. Chemists, opticians and dentists also provide health services.

## Northern Health and Social Services Board

County Hall, 182 Galgorm Road
Ballymena, BT42 1QB
Tel: 028 2566 3333
Fax: 028 2565 2311
Web: www.nhssb.n-i.nhs.uk
Chief Executive: Stuart MacDonnell
Chairman: Michael Wood

The Northern Health and Social Services Board serves the district council areas of Antrim, Ballymena, Ballymoney, Carrickfergus, Coleraine, Cookstown, Larne, Magherafelt, Moyle and Newtownabbey, which include around 430,000 people. It is Northern Ireland's second largest health board with an expenditure in 2002/03 of £563.2m.

*Executive Board Members*
Director of Finance: Wilson Matthews
Director of Nursing & Consumer Services: Elizabeth McNair
Director of Public Health: Professor John Watson
Director of Social Services: Mary Wilmont

*Senior Management Team*
Director, Dental Services: A Millen
Director of Social Services: Mary Wilmont
Director, Service, Performance and Development: Ian Deboys
Director, Strategic Planning and Commissioning: Ed McClean
Director, Pharmaceutical Services: Dr D Morrison
Director of Primary Care: W Boyd
Head of Information Services: George McGuigan

*Health and Social Services Trusts*
The Northern Board covers three Health and Social Services Trusts:

*Causeway Health and Social Services Trust*
Providing both health and social care services in the local council areas of Ballymoney, Coleraine and Moyle

*Homefirst Community Trust*
Providing health and social care services in the local council areas of Antrim, Ballymena, Carrickfergus, Cookstown, Larne, Magherafelt and Newtownabbey.

*United Hospitals Trust*
Provides services at Antrim, Braid Valley, Mid Ulster, Moyle and Whiteabbey hospitals.

## Southern Health and Social Services Board

Southern Health & Social Services Board

Tower Hill
Armagh, BT61 9DR
Tel: 028 3741 0041
Fax: 028 3741 4550
Web: www.shssb.org

The Southern Health and Social Services Board serves a population of 320,000 in the District Council Areas of Armagh, Banbridge, Craigavon, Dungannon and Newry and Mourne.

*Expenditure*
In the year ending 31st March 2004, the Southern Board's total revenue expenditure was £475 million on various services.

*Health Trusts*
Armagh and Dungannon HSS Trust
Craigavon and Banbridge Community HSS Trust
Craigavon Area Hospital Group Trust
Newry and Mourne HSS Trust

*Board Members*
Chairwoman: Fionnuala Cook OBE
Chief Executive: Mr Colm Donaghy
Director of Public Health: Dr Anne-Marie Telford
Director of Finance: Mr Sean McKeever
Director of Social Services: Mr Brian Dornan
Director of Planning and Performance Management: Mrs Mairead McAlinden
Director of Primary Care: Mr Eddie Ritson

*Non-Executive Directors*
Mrs Margaret Campbell
Mrs Margaret Martin
Mr Gordon Myers
Mr Paul McCreesh
Mrs Eimer Cleland
Mrs Roberta Brownlee

*Associate Board Members*
Mr Edwin Graham - Chair, Craigavon and Banbridge Health and Social Care Group, Tel: 028 3834 3869

Ms Cathy McPhillips - Chair, Armagh and Dungannon Health and Social Care Group, Tel: 028 8771 3860

Mrs Teresa Ross - Chair, Newry and Mourne Local Health and Social Care Group, Tel: 028 3026 6875

## Western Health and Social Services Board

15 Gransha Park, Clooney Road
Derry, BT47 6FN
Tel: 028 7186 0086
Fax: 028 7186 0311
Web: www.whssb.org
Chief Executive: Steven Lindsay
Chairman: Karen Meehan

The Western Health and Social Services Board covers the District Council areas of Derry, Limavady, Strabane, Omagh and Fermanagh. The Board serves a population of 284,000 over an area of almost 5,000 sq kms from Limavady in the North to the Enniskillen area in the South. It is the smallest of the four Boards in terms of the population it serves and population density is low, at around 58 persons per square kilometre.

*Non-Executive Directors*
Mr Edward Turner
Dr Aine Downey
Mrs Bernadette Grant
Mr Vincent Lusby
Mr Ryan Williams

*Executive Directors*
Chief Executive: Mr Steven Lindsay
Director of Social Care: Mr Dominic Burke
Director of Finance and Information: Mr Peter McLaughlin

## Health and Social Services Trusts

Details of Northern Ireland's Health and Social Services Trusts (HSS Trusts) are set out below in an A-Z format for ease of reference. The trusts are essentially providers of healthcare operating under contract to the regional Health and Social Services Boards, and are primarily appointed bodies. Each Health and Social Services Trust is required to ensure that income is sufficient to cover expenditure, referred to as the 'break-even' duty. HSS Trusts are among Northern Ireland's biggest employers.

### Altnagelvin Hospitals Trust

Glenshane Road, Derry, BT47 6SB
Tel: 028 7134 5171
Fax: 028 7161 1222
Chairman: Denis Desmond CBE
Web: www.altnagelvin.n-i.nhs.uk
Chief Executive: Stella Burnside

The Trust provides a range of acute hospital services; Altnagelvin is the major hospital in the north-west and is the largest acute hospital in the north of Ireland, providing a designated cancer unit, and offering the most comprehensive and complex range of services of any hospital outside Belfast. The hospital has an extensive 10-year investment plan to develop the quality of its accommodation and services. Plans have recently been announced for a major development programme at Altnagelvin Hospital, which will remodernise all areas of the hospital over the next decade.

*Management*
Director of Nursing: Irene Duddy
Medical Director: Geoff Nesbitt
Director of Business Services: Raymond McCartney

*Altnagelvin Hospital, Derry*

*Acute Hospital Services within the Altnagelvin Hospitals Trust*
Altnagelvin Area Hospital
Acute Hospital Services
488 Inpatient Beds
54 Day Case Beds

Ward 5, Waterside Hospital
Slow Stream Rehabilitation
18 Inpatient Rehabilitation Beds for elderly people

Spruce House, Gransha Park
Care of the Young Physically Disabled
17 In patient beds.

### Armagh and Dungannon HSS Trust

St Luke's Hospital, Loughgall Road
Armagh, BT61 7NQ
Tel: 028 3752 2381
Fax: 028 3752 6302
Web: www.adhsst.n-i.nhs.uk
Chairman: Mrs Deirdre Dorman
Chief Executive: Pauline Stanley

Armagh and Dungannon Health and Social Services Trust shares its service boundaries with those of Armagh City and District Council and Dungannon and South Tyrone Borough Council. The combined population of the area is 103,000 and represents 33% of the population in the Southern Health and Social Services Board. The Trust employs a total of 2,651 employees including 892 home helps. Expenditure on the provision of services across the Trust's nine programmes of care for the year ending 31st March 2003 was £70.7m.

*Management*
Director of Social Services: Carmel Rooney
Director of Finance: Stephen McNally
Medical Director: Dr Cathal Cassidy
Director of Planning and Performance Management: Patrick McCabe
Director of Mental Health Services: Kevin Toal
Director of Personnel: Gordon Wells
Director of Healthcare Services and Nursing: Angela McVeigh
Director of Personnel Services: Heather Ellis
Director of Estates: Brian Quinn

*Main Facilities within the Armagh and Dungannon HSS Trust*
Mullinure Hospital
Armagh Community Hospital
South Tyrone Hospital

### Belfast City Hospital HSS Trust

51 Lisburn Road, Belfast, BT9 7AB
Tel: 028 9032 9241
Fax: 028 9032 6614
Web: www.n-i.nhs.uk/trusts/bch
Chairman: Joan Ruddock OBE
Deputy Chairman: Mr W F I McKay
Chief Executive: Quentin Coey

*Belfast City Hospital*

*Management*
Deputy Chairman: Mr W F I McKay
Medical Director: Dr K J Fullerton
Director of Finance: Mr J Copeland
Director of Nursing: Mrs A McCabe
Director of Operational Support: Mr A Brown
Director of Planning: Miss PA Haines
Director of Personnel: Mr MC Barkley

Main Facilities within the Belfast City Hospital Trust
Belfast City Hospital
Belvoir Park Hospital

### Causeway HSS Trust

8E Coleraine Road
Ballymoney, BT53 6BP
Tel: 028 2766 6600
Fax: 028 2766 1201
Web: www.chsst.n-i.nhs.uk
Chairperson: Jean Jefferson
Chief Executive: Alan Braiden (Acting)

The Causeway Trust covers a population of approximately 100,000 people in the most northerly parts of Antrim and East Londonderry. Its main facility is the recently built Causeway Hospital in Coleraine. The Trust has an operating budget of around £88m.

*Management*
Director of Child and Community Care Services: Jim Loughrey
Director of Finance: Neil Guckian
Director of Acute Hospital Services: Alan Braiden
Director of Medical Services: Mike Ledwith
Director of Nursing and Quality Services: Linda Marshall
Director of Human Resources: Jacinta Melaugh
Director of Business and Corporate Services: Nevin Oliver

*Acute Facilities within the Causeway HSS Trust*
Causeway Hospital, Coleraine

## Craigavon Area Hospital Group HSS Trust

68 Lurgan Road, Craigavon, BT63 5QQ
Tel: 028 3833 4444
Chairman: E McClurg
Chief Executive: J Templeton

The Craigavon Area Hospital Group Trust incorporates services across four main locations – Craigavon Area Hospital, Lurgan Hospital, South Tyrone Hospital and Banbridge and Dungannon Polyclinic.

The Trust provides services to all four of the Northern Ireland Health and Social Services Boards but the SHSSB is the main purchaser and user of Trust services. The Trust was also contracted to provide services to the patients of the 18 GP practices within the Southern Board area and to 30 GP practices outside the area. The Trust has a major £80m development plan for the Craigavon Hospital Site. The Trust has a annual budget of around £85m.

*Management*
Director of Medical Services/Deputy Chief Executive: Dr Caroline Humphrey
Business Planning and Contracts: Mr D Herron
Estates: Mr PC Legge
Nursing and Quality: Mr John Mone
Human Resources: Mrs M Richardson
Finance: Mr LA Stead

*Craigavon Area Hospital*

*Main Facilities within the Craigavon Area Hospital Group Trust*
South Tyrone Hospital
Craigavon Area Hospital
Lurgan Hospital
Banbridge Polyclinic

## Craigavon and Banbridge Community HSS Trust

Bannvale House
10 Moyallen Road Gilford, BT63 5JX
Tel: 028 3883 1983
Fax: 028 3883 1993
Web: www.n-i.nhs.uk/trusts/cbc
Chairman: Joseph Graham Martin
Chief Executive: Glenn Houston

The Craigavon and Banbridge Community Health and Social Services Trust covers a largely rural area, the principal towns of which are Banbridge, Lurgan and Portadown. The population of the Trust area is approximately 119,600 representing 38% of the Southern Board's population.

Almost half of the Trust's annual expenditure relates to services for the elderly with around one quarter dedicated to services relating to mental health and learning disability.

*Management*
Director of Child and Family Care: Louise Boyle
Director of Mental Health and Disability: Rosaleen Moore
Director of Planning and Information: Martin Kelly
Director of Human Resources: Kieran Donaghy
Director of Finance: Ronnie Crozier
Director of Elderly and Primary Care: Roisin Burns

## Down Lisburn HSS Trust

Lisburn Health Centre
25 Linenhall Street, Lisburn, BT28 1LU
Tel: 028 9266 5181
Fax: 028 9266 5179
Web: www.dlt.n-i.nhs.uk
Chairman: Denise Fitzsimmons
Chief Executive: John Compton

Down Lisburn Trust serves a population of around 180,000 people across counties Antrim and Down. The Trust's population varies between urban (including parts of Belfast) and rural and includes both areas of considerable deprivation as well as areas of relative wealth. The annual income of the Trust is approximately £125m.

*Management*
Director of Finance: Paul Simpson
Director for Social Work: Kate Thompson
Director for Acute Services and Nursing: Alan Finn
Director of Disability and Mental Health and Support Services: Sean O'Rourke
Director of Human Resources: Alan Best
Director of Planning and Performance: John Simpson
Director of Corporate Affairs: Paul McBrearty
Medical Director: Dr Noeleen Devaney

*Acute Facilities within the Down Lisburn HSS Trust*
Downe Hospital, Lagan Valley Hospital, Downpatrick Maternity Hospital

## Foyle HSS Trust

Riverview House, Abercorn Road
Derry, BT48 6SB
Tel: 028 7126 6111
Fax: 028 7126 0806
Web: www.foyletrust.n-i.nhs.uk
Chairman: Anthony Jackson
Chief Executive: Elaine Way

*Management*
Medical Director: Dr Artie O'Hara
Director of Healthcare: Phil Mahon
Director of Social Care: John Doherty
Director of Finance: Lesley Mitchell
Director of Business Services: Joe Lusby
Director of Personnel: Nuala Sheerin

Foyle Trust provides community health and social care services to cover 165,000 people in the council areas of Derry City, Limavady and most of Strabane.

The total annual budget of the Trust is around £80 million, including income from Westcare Business Services is part of Foyle HSS Trust, and operates as a trading agency providing common support services to the Western Health and Social Services Board and to the Trusts in the Western Board area.

*Major Facilities within Foyle Trust:*
Gransha Hospital

## Green Park HSS Trust

20 Stockmans Lane, Belfast, BT9 7JB
Tel: 028 9090 2000
Fax: 028 9090 2222
Web: www.greenpark.n-i.nhs.uk
Chairman: Ian Doherty
Chief Executive: Hilary Boyd

*Management*
Director of Corporate Planning and Deputy Chief Executive: Brian Sore
Medical Director: Dr Denis Connolly
Director of Finance: Colin Bradley
Director of Nursing and Clinical Effectiveness: Patricia O'Callaghan
Director of Human Resources: Therese McKernan
Director of Support Services: Colin Cairns

*Major Facilities within the Greenpark HSS Trust*
Musgrave Park Hospital
Forster Green Hospital

## Homefirst Community HSS Trust

The Cottage, 5 Greenmount Avenue
Ballymena, BT43 6DA
Tel: 028 2563 3700
Fax: 028 2563 3733
Web: www.homefirst.n-i.nhs.uk
Chairman: Bob Ferguson
Chief Executive: Norma Evans

Homefirst Community Trust is the largest Community Trust in Northern Ireland employing in excess of 5,300 staff and providing a range of services to the population of around 327,000 people in the local authority areas of Antrim, Ballymena, Carrickfergus, Cookstown, Larne, Magherafelt and Newtownabbey.

*Management*
Executive Director, Finance: Harold Sharp
Executive Director, Nursing, Dental & Governance: Hazel Baird
Director Social Care and Disability Services: Rosemary Simpson
Director Planning & Information: Martin Sloan
Director Personnel: William Day
Director Mental Health Services: Glenn Houston
Executive Medical Director: Dr Michael Mannion
Executive Director Social Work and Director Child Care Services: Brenda Smyth
Acting Director Child Health & Allied Health Services: Joan Stephenson

## Mater Infirmorum Hospital HSS Trust

45-51 Crumlin Road, Belfast, BT14 6AB
Tel: 028 9074 1211
Fax: 028 9074 1342
Web: www.n-i.nhs.uk/mater
Chairman: Lady McCollum
Chief Executive: Sean Donaghy

The Mater Trust is an acute hospital providing services to North Belfast and surrounding areas. It employs over 1,000 staff. The Mater Hospital provides a range of services including acute in- patient, A & E, day procedures, mental illness and maternity.

*Board Members*
Director of Finance: Larry O'Neill
Director of Nursing and Quality: Mary Hinds
Director of Corporate Development: Joan Pedan
Medical Director: Colm Harvey

*Acute Facilities within the Mater Infirmorum Hospital HSS Trust*
Mater Infirmorum Hospital

## Newry and Mourne HSS Trust

5 Downshire Place, Downshire Road
Newry, BT34 1DZ
Tel: 028 3026 0505
Fax: 028 3026 9064
Web: www.n-i.nhs.uk/trusts/newry
Chairman: Sean Hogan
Chief Executive: Eric Bowyer

The Newry and Mourne HSS Trust provides a wide range of hospital community health and social services to the 86,000 population of the Newry and Mourne area. Over 1700 staff are employed by the Trust.

*Management*
Director of Finance and Planning: Martin Dillon
Medical Director: Dr P Loughran
Director of Nursing and Community Health: Joan O'Hagan
Director of Social Services: J Flynn
Director of Personal and Operational Services: M Ferris
Director of Community Medical and Preventative Services: Dr M Hollinger
Director of Professions Allied to Medicine: L Cavan
General Practitioner Advisor: Dr A Mulholland

*Acute Facilities within the Newry and Mourne HSS Trust*
Daisy Hill Hospital

## North and West Belfast HSS Trust

Glendinning House, 6 Murray Street
Belfast, BT1 6DP
Tel: 028 9032 7156
Fax: 028 9082 1285
Web: www.nwb.n-i.nhs.uk
Chairperson: Pat McCartan
Chief Executive: Richard Black

The North and West Belfast HSS Trust provides health and social care services to 145,000 people, providing specialist services for people with learning disabilities at Muckamore Abbey Hospital. These services are provided to all four health and social services boards in Northern Ireland. The Trust also provides the Eastern Board with community nutrition and dietetic services, the child health information system, family planning services, services for people travelling abroad and services relating to sexual health and AIDS.

*Management*
Director of Nursing: Brenda Connolly
Director of Finance: Peter Harvey
Director of Medical Services (Hospitals): Dr Caroline Marriott
Director of Medical Services (Community): Dr Robin McKee
Director of Human Resources & Corporate Affairs: Eamonn Molloy
Director of Planning/Deputy Chief Executive: Paul Ryan
Director of Hospital Services: Mirian Somerville

*Main Facilities within the Trust*
Muckamore Abbey

## Northern Ireland Ambulance Service HSS Trust

Site 30, Knockbracken Healthcare Park
Saintfield Road
Belfast, BT8 8SG
Tel: 028 9040 0999
Fax: 028 9040 0900
Web: www.niamb.co.uk
Chairman: Doug Smyth
Chief Executive: Paul McCormick

Northern Ireland Ambulance Service has, since 1995, provided pre-hospital emergency care and patient transport services for the entire population of Northern Ireland.

## Royal Group of Hospitals and Dental Hospital HSS Trust

Grosvenor Road, Belfast, BT12 6BA
Tel: 028 9024 0503
Fax: 028 9024 0899
Web: www.royalhospitals.org
Chairman: Dr Anne Balmer
Chief Executive: William McKee

The Royal Group of Hospitals and Dental Hospital HSS Trust is a hospital complex on a 70-acre site in Belfast. Many, if not most of Northern Ireland's regional speciality healthcare services are provided by the Trust. The Royal Group of Hospitals comprises the Royal Victoria Hospital; the Royal Jubilee Maternity Service; Royal Belfast Hospital for Sick Children and the Dental Hospital. The Royal Group has over 20% of all acute beds in Northern Ireland and has over 6,000 staff.

*Management*
Medical Director: Michael McBride
Director of Nursing and Patient Services: Deirdre O'Brien
Director of Finance: Wendy Galbraith
Director of Organisational Development: Hugh McCaughey

*Main Facilities within the Royal Group of Hospitals and Dental Hospital HSS Trust*
The Royal Victoria Hospital; Royal Jubilee Maternity Hospital; Royal Belfast Hospital for Sick Children; Dental Hospital.

## South and East Belfast HSS Trust

Knockbracken Healthcare Park
Saintfield Road, Belfast, BT8 8BH
Tel: 028 9056 5656
Fax: 028 9056 5813
Web: www.sebt.n-i.nhs.uk
Chairman: Robin Harris
Chief Executive: Patricia Gordon
The Trust has an annual budget of around £135m.

South and East Belfast Trust provides health and social care services for around 205,000 people in the South and East Belfast and Castlereagh areas.

*Management*
Executive Director of Medical Services: Dr Paul Bell
Executive Director of Finance: Norman Carson
Executive Director of Social Services: Stephen O'Brien
Executive Director of Nursing: Ray Magee

*Acute Facilities within the South and East Belfast HSS Trust*
Acute Psychiatric at the Knockbracken Healthcare Centre Park

## Sperrin Lakeland HSS Trust

Strathdene House
Tyrone and Fermanagh Hospital
Omagh, BT79 0NS
Tel: 028 8283 5285
Fax: 028 8283 5286
Web: www.sperrin-lakeland.org
Chairman: Richard Scott
Chief Executive: Hugh Mills

The Sperrin Lakeland Health and Social Care Trust covers the three District Council Areas of Fermanagh, Omagh and Strabane (part). It provides services to around 118,000 people spread over a wide area including some of Northern Ireland's remotest locations. The Trust has an annual budget of around £115m. The Trust is at the heart of a major struggle where a very strong lobby exists against the proposed downgrading of Tyrone County hospital and the new hospital planned for Enniskillen.

*Management*
Medical Director: Dr Diana Cody
Director of Mental Health & Elderly Services: Gabriel Carey
Director of Acute Hospital Services: Eugene Fee
Director of Finance: Colm McCauley

*Main Facilities within the Sperrin Lakeland HSS Trust*
Erne Hospital
Tyrone County Hospital

## Ulster Community and Hospitals Trust

39 Regent Street
Newtownards, BT23 4AD
Tel: 028 9181 6666
Fax: 028 9182 0140
Web: www.ucht.n-i.nhs.uk
Chairman: Siubhan Grant
Chief Executive: Jim McCall

Ulster Community and Hospitals Trusts provide a comprehensive range of hospital community health and social services. It is one of the largest HSS Trusts in Northern Ireland with an annual budget of around £160m.

*Acute Facilities within the Ulster Community and Hospitals Trust*
Ulster Hospital

## United Hospitals HSS Trust

Bush House, 45 Bush Road
Antrim, BT41 2QB
Tel: 028 9442 4655
Fax: 028 9442 4654
Web: www.unitedhospitals.org
Chairman: Raymond Milnes
Chief Executive: Bernard Mitchell

*Acute Facilities within the United Hospitals HSS Trust*
Antrim Hospital
Whiteabbey Hospital
Mid Ulster Hospital

## Health and Social Services Councils

Northern Ireland has four Health and Social Services Councils; one shadowing each of the four Health and Social Services Boards.

The principal function of each Council is to represent the interests of the general public in all areas of health and social services. This includes providing advice, information and support on a wide range of related issues, and guidance for those considering making a complaint about a service. Councils also work with local groups to monitor services, and to encourage people to put forward their opinions on health and social services, partly by carrying out surveys to gauge opinion. Councils represent the public by participating in consultations about health and social services, and acting to improve services. Councils also visit health and social services facilities, to ensure that the public is being effectively provided for.

A Work Programme for each of the Councils is drawn up in conjunction with the Health Board being shadowed, and an annual report is published. The Councils are funded by their respective Boards but are autonomous. Councils have the right of consultation on developments and changes to services provided by Health and Social Services Boards, as well as the right to have formal meetings with Boards. They are also entitled to visit and inspect health and social service facilities.

Each Health and Social Services Council is composed of representatives from local councils, voluntary organisations and other interested groups. The Eastern Council has 30 members as the Eastern Board represents more people than any other Board. The Northern, Southern and Western Boards each have 24 members. A team of full-time staff support the councils. Membership comprises approximately:

- 40% district councillors;
- 30% voluntary/community nominations;
- 30% individuals with an interest in health and social care.

The Councils have a statutory duty to publish and distribute an annual report giving details of their performance during the preceding year.

The Councils must also adhere to a Code of Practice on Openness in the HPSS. Members must abide by a Code of Conduct, covering issues such as impartiality, financial accountability, confidentiality, non-discriminatory practices, casual gifts, hospitality and declaration of interests.

Each council maintains an up to date register of members' interests, which is open to the public for inspection. The Councils also have a procedure to enable members of the public to make complaints. The Ombudsman can ultimately investigate complaints about the Councils.

In recent years some of the Councils have expressed frustration at their inability to effect change in healthcare delivery performance even where clear performance issues have been identified and targeted. Details of each of the four Health and Social Services Councils follow.

**Eastern Health and Social Services Council**
1st Floor McKelvey House
25-27 Wellington Park
Belfast, BT1 6GQ
Tel: 028 9032 1230
Fax: 028 9032 1750
Web: www.ehssc.org
Chair: Patricia McMillan

Chief Officer: Jane Graham
Senior Managers: Raymond Newman, Sean Brown

**Northern Health and Social Services Council (NHSSC)**
8 Broadway Avenue
Ballymena, BT43 7AA
Tel: 028 2565 5777
Fax: 028 2565 5112
Web: www.nhssc.org
Chairperson: Mr Thomas Creighton (Acting)
Chief Officer: Noel Graham

**Southern Health and Social Services Council**
Quaker Buildings, High Street
Lurgan, BT66 8BB
Tel: 028 3834 9900
Fax: 028 3834 9858
Chairperson: Mrs Roisin Foster
Chief Officer: Stella Cunningham

**Western Health and Social Services Council**
Hilltop, Tyrone and Fermanagh Hospital
Omagh, BT79 0NS
Tel: 028 8225 2555
Fax: 028 8225 2544
Chairman: Patrick McGowan
Chief Officer: Maggie Reilly

## Local Health and Social Care Groups

Local Health and Social Care Groups (LHSCGs), which are committees of Health and Social Services Boards, bring together providers of local primary and community services under a management board whose membership is drawn from representatives of primary care professionals, the community and services users, as well as Health and Social Services Boards and Trusts. While others may be co-opted onto the management boards, the core membership comprise the following:

**Table 5.5 Local Health and Social Care Groups Membership Core**

| | |
|---|---|
| Local Community Trusts HSS Boards* | 5 |
| Local Acute Trusts | 1 |
| GPs | 5 |
| Nurses | 1 |
| Community/Service Users | 2 |
| Social Workers | 1 |
| Community Pharmacists | 1 |
| Allied Health Professionals | 1 |
| LHSCG Manager | 1 |

* (Must include 1 Nurse, 1 Social Worker & 1 Allied Health Professional)

There are 15 LHSCGs based around GP practices and representing natural communities. There are six groups in the Eastern Board area, four in the Northern Board, three in the Southern Board and two in the Western Board area, covering populations ranging between 60,000 to 200,000.

LHSCGs are responsible for the planning and delivery of primary and community care and for contributing to their Health and Social Services Boards' commissioning decisions seeking to reflect the local dimension. Ultimately they will assume greater responsibility for the commissioning of services which will involve delegated budgets. Key tasks for the LHSCGs include:

- Identifying local health and social care needs and setting objectives to meet them;
- Contributing to Heath and Wellbeing Investment Plans;
- Taking steps to promote equality of opportunity and reduce inequalities in health and social care and in access to services, consistent with the existing Targeting Social Need Policy;
- Looking for ways to improve and develop primary care services at local levels while taking account of local and national priorities;
- Contributing to efforts to reduce waiting lists and waiting times for treatment;
- Complying with HPSS quality standards and guidelines for services;
- Working across health and social services boundaries and in partnership with other organisations to meet their communities' needs: and
- Ensuring value for money in the use of resources available.

**Table 5.6 Local Health and Social Care Groups Membership**

| LHSCGs | GPs (No of) | Dentists (No of) | Opticians Optometrist practices | Pharmacists Community practices |
|---|---|---|---|---|
| Ards | 40 | 22 | 12 | 20 |
| North Down | 37 | 45 | 12 | 19 |
| Down | 33 | 22 | 9 | 21 |
| Lisburn | 56 | 38 | 16 | 28 |
| North & West Belfast | 129 | 89 | 14 | 62 |
| South & East Belfast | 132 | 128 | 40 | 71 |
| Antrim/Ballymena | 69 | 44 | 11 | 20 |
| Causeway | 63 | 41 | 15 | 28 |
| East Antrim | 75 | 57 | 16 | 37 |
| Mid Ulster | 43 | 27 | 9 | 24 |
| Southern | 79 | 26 | 16 | 44 |
| Northern | 107 | 35 | 14 | 44 |
| Newry & Mourne | 60 | 38 | 8 | 29 |
| Craigavon & Banbridge | 79 | 48 | 13 | 31 |
| Armagh & Dungannon | 66 | 61 | 10 | 29 |

## Local Health and Social Care Groups (LHSCGs)

**Antrim & Ballymena LHSCG**
County Hall
182 Galgorm Road
Ballymena, BT42 1QB
Tel: 028 2566 7657

**Ards LHSCG**
Ards Hospital, Church Street
Newtownards, BT23 4AS
Tel: 028 9181 0222

**Armagh & Dungannon LHSCG**
Milford Building, Tower Hill
Armagh, BT61 9DR
Tel: 028 3741 4543

**Causeway LHSCG**
9 Newal Road
Ballymoney, BT53 6HB
Tel: 028 2766 8370

**Craigavon & Banbridge LHSCG**
80-82 High Street
Lurgan, BT66 8BB
Tel: 028 3834 3869

**Down LHSCG**
Corncrane Building
Lower Square
Castlewellan, BT31 9DX
Tel: 028 4377 2082

**East Antrim LHSCG**
Whiteabbey Hospital
Doagh Road
Newtownabbey, BT37 9RH
Tel: 028 9055 2242

**Lisburn LHSCG**
1st Floor
Lisburn Squre House
1-4 Haslem's Lane
Lisburn, BT27 1TW
Tel: 028 9267 7272

**Mid Ulster LHSCG**
Manor House, High Street
Moneymore
Tel: 028 8674 8761

**Newry & Mourne LHSCG**
WIN Business Park
Canal Quay
Newry, BT35 6PH
Tel: 028 3026 6875

**North & West LHSCG**
Howard Building
Twin Spires Centre
155 Northumberland Street
Belfast, BT13 2JF
Tel: 028 9024 4500

**North Down LHSCG**
Bangor Community Hospital
Castle Street
Bangor, BT20 3TS
Tel: 028 9147 5109

**Northern LHSCG**
23A Bishop Street
Londonderry, BT48 6PR
Tel: 028 7136 9500

**South & East LHSCG**
1 Cromac Quay
Belfast, BT7 7JA
Tel: 028 9043 4248

**Southern LHSCG**
Trillick Enterprise Centre
Main Street, Trillick
Co Tyrone, BT78 3ST
Tel: 028 8956 1989

# A-Z of Hospitals and Hospices in Northern Ireland

## Hospitals A-Z

**Alexander Gardens Day Hospital**
Old See House
603 Antrim Road, BT15
Tel: 028 9077 4391

**Altnagelvin Hospital**
Glenshane Road
Londonderry, BT47 6SB
Tel: 028 7134 5171

**Antrim Hospital**
45 Bush Road
Antrim, BT41 2RL
Tel: 028 9442 4000

**Ards Hospital**
Church Street
Newtownards, BT23 4AS
Tel: 028 9181 2661

**Bangor Hospital**
Castle Street
Bangor, BT20 4TA
Tel: 028 9147 5140

**Belfast City Hospital**
Lisburn Road
Belfast, BT9 7AB
Tel: 028 9032 9241

**Belvoir Park Hospital**
Hospital Road
Belfast, BT8 8JR
Tel: 028 9069 9069

**Braid Valley Hospital**
Cushendall Road
Ballymena, BT43 6HH
Tel: 028 2563 5200

**Causeway Hospital**
4 Newbridge Road
Coleraine, BT52 1HS
Tel: 028 7032 7032

**Craigavon Area Hospital**
68 Lurgan Road
Portadown, BT63 5QQ
Tel: 028 3833 4444

**Daisy Hill Hospital**
5 Hospital Road
Newry, BT35 8DR
Tel: 028 3083 5000

**Dalriada Hospital**
1A Coleraine Road
Ballycastle, BT54 6EY
Tel: 028 2076 3793

**The Dental Hospital (RVH)**
Grosvenor Road, Belfast
Tel: 028 9024 0503

**Downshire Hospital**
Ardglass Road
Downpatrick, BT30 6RA
Tel: 028 4461 3311

**Downe Hospital**
Pound Lane
Downpatrick, BT30 6JA
Tel: 028 4461 3311

**Erne Hospital**
Cornagrade Road
Enniskillen, BT74 6AY
Tel: 028 6638 2000

**Forster Green Hospital**
110 Saintfield Road
Belfast, BT8 4HD
Tel: 028 9094 4444

**Gransha Hospital**
Clooney Road
Londonderry, BT47 6TF
Tel: 028 7186 0261

**Holywell Hospital**
60 Steeple Road
Antrim, BT41 2RJ
Tel: 028 9446 5211

**Lagan Valley Hospital**
39 Hillsborough Road
Lisburn, BT28 1JP
Tel: 028 9266 5141

**Lurgan Hospital**
100 Sloan Street
Lurgan, BT66 8NX
Tel: 028 3832 3262

**Mater Infirmorum Hospital**
47-51 Crumlin Road
Belfast, BT14 6AB
Tel: 028 9074 1211

**Mid Ulster Hospital**
59 Hospital Road
Magherafelt, BT45 5EX
Tel: 028 7963 1031

**Mourne Hospital**
Newry Street
Kilkeel, BT34 4DP
Tel: 028 4176 2626

**Moyle Hospital**
Gloucester Avenue
Larne, BT40 1RP
Tel: 028 2827 5431

**Muckamore Abbey Hospital**
1 Abbey Road, Muckamore
Antrim, BT41 4SH
Tel: 028 9446 3333

**Musgrave Park Hospital**
Stockman's Lane
Belfast, BT9 7JB
Tel: 028 9090 2000

**Northwest Independent Hospital**
Churchill House, Ballykelly
Limavady, BT49 9HS
Tel: 028 7776 3090

**Robinson Memorial Hospital**
23 Newal Road
Ballymoney, BT53 6HB
Tel: 028 2766 0322

**Royal Belfast Hospital for Sick Children (RVH)**
Grosvenor Road
Belfast, BT12 6BA
Tel: 028 9024 0503

**Royal Maternity Hospital (RVH)**
Grosvenor Road
Belfast, BT12 6BA
Tel: 028 9024 0503

**Royal Victoria Hospital (RVH)**
Grosvenor Road
Belfast, BT12 6BA
Tel: 028 9024 0503

**St Luke's Hospital**
Loughgall Road
Armagh, BT61 7NQ
Tel: 028 3752 2381

**Shaftesbury Square Hospital**
116-120 Great Victoria Street
Belfast, BT2 7BG
Tel: 028 9032 9808

**South Tyrone Hospital**
Carland Road
Dungannon, BT71 4AU
Tel: 028 8772 2821

**Thompson House Hospital**
19-21 Magheralave Road
Lisburn, BT28 3BP
Tel: 028 9266 5646

**Ulster Hospital**
Upper Newtownards Road
Dundonals, BT16 1RH
Tel: 028 9048 4511

**Whiteabbey Hospital**
Doagh Road
Newtownabbey, BT37 9RH
Tel: 028 9086 5181

**Woodstock Lodge**
1 Woodstock Link
Belfast, BT6 8DD
Tel: 028 9073 7500

## Hospices A-Z

**Foyle Hospice**
61 Culmore Road
Derry, BT48 8JE
Tel: 028 7135 1010

**Northern Ireland Hospice Care**
74 Somerton Road
Belfast, BT15 3LH
Tel: 028 9078 1836

**Northern Ireland Children's Hospice**
Horizon House
18 O'Neill Road
Newtownabbey
BT36 6WB
Tel: 028 9077 7635

**Southern Area Hospice Services**
St John's House
Courtenay Hill
Newry, BT34 2EB
Tel: 028 3026 7711

**Marie Curie Centre**
1 Kensington Road
Belfast, BT5 6OD
Tel: 028 9088 2000

## North/South, East/West and International Co-operation on Health

### North/South

The Belfast Agreement introduced new arrangements for co-operation on health issues. The North/South Ministerial Council provides a structure for Ministers of all departments throughout Ireland to facilitate the exchange of information, discussion and consultation with a view to cooperating on matters of mutual interest. While agreement may be reached on the adoption of common policies in areas where there is a mutual cross-border and all-island benefit, decisions would be taken on implementation separately in each jurisdiction. Where appropriate, decisions on policies and action at an all-island and cross-border level would be implemented by the new cross-border implementation bodies. Six cross-border implementation bodies have been established, including the Food Safety Promotion Board.

**The Food Safety Promotion Board**

The key function of the Food Safety Promotion Board is to ensure that producers, processors, distributors, caterers and general public take responsibility for the provision of safe food. Other functions include microbiological surveillance of food borne diseases, and promotion of scientific co-operation. The Board also aims to develop a strategy for the island of Ireland for the delivery of specialised laboratory services.

The Board consults widely where appropriate and works closely with the Food Standards Agency in Northern Ireland, and the Food Safety Authority of Ireland (FSAI) in the South. Further information on the Food Safety Promotion Board, including contact details can be found on page 57.

**Practical North/South Co-operation under Health**

The North/South Ministerial Council (NSMC) has identified health as one of the six additional areas for co-operation and collaboration. Five specific areas have been highlighted for co-operation under Health:

- Accident and Emergency services;
- Planning for Major Emergencies;
- Co-operation on High Technology Equipment;
- Cancer Research;
- Health Promotion.

The NSMC agreed to share information and discuss opportunities for co-operation in relation to health promotion on an all Ireland basis, and to collaborate on public information campaigns, particularly major media campaigns. The NSMC also aims to examine the scope for research and public information and education in the areas of heart disease, cancer and smoking.

However, recent decisions taken in relation to acute hospitals provisions in Northern Ireland have placed no reliance on the availability of acute facilities south of the border. While hospitals in Cavan, Monaghan and Sligo are of 'additional benefit' to populations living near the border they have not been factored into the plan that resulted in the decision to build a new acute hospital north of Enniskillen.

**The Institute of Public Health in Ireland**
5th Floor, Bishop's Square
Redmond's Hill, Dublin 2
Tel: 01478 6300 / Fax: 01 478 6317
Web: www.publichealth.ie
Director: Dr Jane Wilde

The Institute of Public Health in Ireland, whose establishment predated the Belfast Agreement, works to promote North/South co-operation on public health in the following areas:

- tackling health inequalities;
- strengthening partnerships for health;
- contributing to public health information and surveillance;
- develop public health capacity and leadership;
- networking internationally and nationally.

Under the remit of the Investing for Health strategy the Institute of Public Health will enhance its capacity to include the comparative monitoring of trends in health, the determinants of health, and health inequalities North and South, and relative to other EU countries, and highlighting new areas of concern as they emerge. The Institute advises on the methodology for health equity impact assessments, and disseminates information from international research and experience throughout Ireland.

**CAWT (Co-operation and Working Together)**

A major cross-border health initiative known as CAWT, Co-operation and Working Together, is aimed at improving the health and social well being of people in border areas.

- CAWT is made up of NWHB (RoI), NEHB (RoI), SHSSB (NI), WHSSB (NI) and 7 Trusts.
- Objective is improvement of health and social well being of border area population.
- Population Health Profile – first time comprehensive health and social care information is available on the border area as a region.

**European and International Programmes**

European and international money has also been used to support cross-border programmes in the voluntary and community sector, for example in the area of early years and family support. Another area to be addressed is the development of common data systems to allow meaningful comparisons to be made on a North/South basis.

**East/West Co-operation in Health**

The British-Irish Council provides a structure for co-operation between Britain and Ireland on health matters. It has identified a range of areas for co-operation, including social exclusion, drug misuse, the environment, transport and other issues in health and education.

A Concordat provides a more specific framework for co-operation between the Department of Health in England and departments concerned with health and social care in each of the devolved administrations. DHSSPS is also included in discussions, which feed in to the European Health Council.

There are a number of Joint Committees, which advise Health Departments such as the Joint Committee on Vaccination and Immunisation and the National Screening Committee.

**Joint Ministerial Committee**
There is a joint Ministerial committee on health issues, providing an opportunity for the separate administrations to share information, experience and best practice on a wide range of policy issues. These include developing common measures of performance, learning from each other's experiences and sharing ideas on incentives.

**Inter-Departmental Group on Tobacco**
An interdepartmental group on tobacco was convened at the time of publication of the White Paper 'Smoking Kills' (December 1998). The membership of this group includes representatives from DHSSPS and the health departments in London, Edinburgh and Dublin. The purpose of the group is to provide strategic direction and share information on action against tobacco.

**Anti-Drugs Co-ordination**
Strong links exist between the devolved administrations and the Anti Drugs Co-ordination Unit in the Cabinet Office. There is frequent contact on a range of issues relating to drug misuse, including progress with the implementation of strategies for action.

**Food Standards Agency Northern Ireland**
Unit 10B, Clarendon Road Belfast, BT1 3BG
Tel: 028 9041 7700
Web: www.food.gov.uk
Director: Morris McAllister

The Food Standards Agency is a UK-wide non-Ministerial government department, with offices in Belfast (FSANI), Aberdeen, Cardiff and London. It provides policy advice to ministers on food safety, food standards and aspects of nutrition and prepares draft legislation. The Agency also represents the UK in negotiations in the EU. FSANI is responsible for providing impartial accurate advice on a balanced diet. This includes:

- monitoring and surveillance of the nutrient content of food and the nutrient content of the diet;
- drafting and producing legislation relating to nutritional aspects of food, including labelling and claims, dietary supplements sold as food, fortified foods and functional foods;
- Providing practical guidance in relation to nutritional aspects of the food chain, including production and catering;
- Commissioning research on food and diet appropriate to its responsibility for the above issues.

FSANI works in partnership with a range of departments, agencies and stakeholder groups to exercise its role.

The Agency exercises its role in partnership with the Food Safety Promotion Board, so combining an East/West with a North/South dimension.

## International Co-operation
Northern Ireland is one of the 51 members of the European Region of the World Health Organisation. The health policy framework for Europe, Health 21, sets 21 targets for health action, including closing the health gap between and with countries and multi-sectoral responsibility for health. World Health Organisation initiatives in Northern Ireland include:

- Healthy Cities;
- Health Promoting Schools;
- Health Promoting Hospitals.

The Health Promotion Agency has recently been designated as a Collaborating Centre for Training and Research in Communications and Information Technology in health promotion and disease prevention by the World Health Organisation.
Currently under development is a new EU Public Health Strategy and Action Plan and relationships are being developed with the National Cancer Institute in the United States with the objective of improving research and improving patient care. The Institute of Public Health in Ireland is working with leaders in Public Health in the US to develop a groundbreaking Creative Public Health Leadership course in Ireland.

**Public Finance Initiative / Public-Private Partnership**
The Public Finance Initiative (PFI), now known as Public-Private Partnership (PPP), was announced as a necessary and desirable way of raising finance for projects, by bringing private sector funding and skills to bear on long-term health infrastructural investment. Since its introduction in 1998, many schemes have been initiated using the PPP approach for funding. These have included management and disposal of clinical waste, equipment leasing and a new renal unit.

There is a considerable amount of public debate about the area of Public-Private Partnerships (PPPs), in no small part due to the perceived problems with privatisation in other areas. Opponents of PPP are concerned that private finance will put undue pressure on services to be profitable, rather than concentrate on serving the health needs of the population, and that services will suffer. A further criticism of PPP is that it is a very complex, drawn-out process which can cost the client more in the long term. However, advocates argue that it is vital to draw in private sector finance, as public money is not available in sufficient quantities. PPP also passes most of a project's risks to the private sector, protecting the public purse from some of the spectacular cost overruns that have occurred on major health projects in the past. Nonetheless, public-private finance is still in relatively early development, and whilst government is confident about the benefits it could bring, it remains to be seen how the policy will ultimately contribute in the long-term to health service provision in Northern Ireland.

As part of the Government's reinvestment and reform Initiative a new body – the Strategic Investment Board was established to bring new expertise and speedier delivery to public sector infrastructural developments. The SIB is now heavily engaged in major health sector projects.

## Key Issues in Health in Northern Ireland

Health has risen steadily as a priority on the Government and public policy agenda in recent years. There has been growing concern that despite increased investment, the quantity and quality of health service delivery is not meeting public expectations. At its most visible Northern Ireland's health service is struggling in terms of long waiting lists for non-emergency surgery and insufficient hospital beds to accommodate demand, particularly in winter or whenever there is a serious flu epidemic. The Government has responded with a major 'Investing for Health' strategy initiative and is in the final stages of reconfiguring the structure administration and processes for delivering healthcare effectively.

**Health Definitions**

**Acute Services/Secondary Care**

Treatment and health care provided by hospitals. Of particular importance in hospital restructuring is the provision of accident and emergency services.

**Acute Trusts**
Trusts providing acute hospital care only

**Community Care Services**
Health or social care provided outside hospital

**Community Trusts**
Trusts providing Community Health and social services, but not acute hospital services

**Primary Care**
Health services provided by the GP, dentist, chemist, optician. Includes family and community health services and major components of social care outside of hospitals, which may be accessed by individuals on their own behalf.

**Social Care**
Social care encompasses services provided to help people to cope with many types of personal hardship including:

- Physical or sensory disability;
- Protection of vulnerable children

## Investing for Health Initiative

The Investing for Health Initiative falls under 'Working for a Healthier People', one of the Devolved Government's five overarching priorities in its Programme for Government under devolution.

The aim of the Investing for Health initiative is the development of a long term plan for the improvement of health care in Northern Ireland and by tackling the causes of poor health to individuals such as poor living conditions and social and economic disadvantage, thus pre empting the need for medical care. The Investing for Health initiative is an attempt by the department to shift the emphasis in healthcare from the treatment of ill health to its prevention by tackling the factors that adversely affect health. The DHSSPS has the lead responsibility for the Investing in Health framework.

Under the terms of the Investing for Health strategy the DHSSPS has undertaken a review of public health functions in Northern Ireland. The aim of the review is to ensure that the department has all the components in place to respond to the health challenges facing Northern Ireland.

## Developing Better Services - Acute Hospital Provision

The issue of rationalisation of hospital services has been debated widely, with many interpreting the terms as simply 'cutting back' on services. In August 2001 the report compiled by Chairman of the Acute Hospitals Review Group, Dr Maurice Hayes, was published, which made some far-reaching and controversial recommendations for change. As a general finding, Dr Hayes reported that in the process of conducting a major consultation exercise all round Northern Ireland he had experienced considerable public dissatisfaction with the current provision of hospital services. Dr Hayes concluded that maintaining the status quo was therefore 'not an option'. The main recommendations of the report are set out below.

**Acute Hospitals**

Acute Hospitals are those capable of providing comprehensive accident and emergency services. Prior to devolution the Department of Health had been proposing to close seven of Northern Ireland's existing acute hospitals, centralising acute services to six main hospitals. The original six to retain acute services under the Hayes recommendations were:

- Royal Victoria Hospital (RVH) — Belfast
- City Hospital — Belfast
- Ulster Hospital (Dundonald) — Belfast
- Antrim Area Hospital — Antrim
- Craigavon Area Hospital — Craigavon
- Altnagelvin — Derry

The Hayes report recommended that three more hospitals retain acute services, in addition to the six mentioned above. They were:

- Causeway Hospital — Coleraine
- Daisy Hill Hospital — Newry
- A New South West Hospital (to be built) — Enniskillen

The hospitals that would lose their existing accident and emergency services would be:

- Mater Hospital — Belfast
- Tyrone County Hospital — Omagh
- Lagan Valley — Lisburn
- Whiteabbey — Newtownabbey
- South Tyrone hospital, where the earlier decision had already been implemented.

In addition the Downe hospital in Downpatrick would lose its maternity services. Inevitably, there were strong feelings about the downgrading of hospitals, and many argued that residents in areas served by them would be disadvantaged and possibly endangered by the reduction of services. Supporters of South Tyrone Hospital were particularly angry that the proposal was implemented so quickly in their area. In Tyrone public anger at the decision to downgrade Omagh Hospital was reflected in the election of a local GP as an independent Omagh Hospital candidate in the 2003 Assembly elections.

The Hayes report also made radical recommendations on the existing NHS structures in Northern Ireland. It recommended that the four existing Health Boards be unified into one large single Board, and that the hospitals of Northern Ireland be further grouped into 3 'super' trusts, comprised as follows:

- **Greater Belfast,** including: RVH, City Hospital, Musgrave Park, Mater Hospital, Ulster Hospital, Whiteabbey Hospital, Lagan Valley, Downe Hospital
- **Northern,** including: Altnagelvin, Antrim Hospital, Causeway,
- **Southern,** including: Craigavon Area Hospital, Daisy Hill, 'New' South-West Hospital (Enniskillen)

The report also called for much higher numbers of professional staff, in particular aiming for an increase of 100% in hospital consultants and a 25% increase in the number of general practitioners. A rotation system for doctors, between acute and local hospitals, was also recommended, as was a higher level of investment in the ambulance service. If implemented its recommendations could take 15 years to fulfilment.

**Developing Better Services**

Following an extensive consultation on 'Developing Better Services: Modernising Hospitals and Reforming Structures' which took forward most of the thinking in the Hayes Report, the government announced its proposed hospital reforms.

The present configuration of fifteen acute hospitals would be replaced by a network of nine acute hospitals supported by seven local hospitals, two with enhanced services. The nine acute hospitals were those already identified by Hayes including a new South-Western acute hospital to be located north of Enniskillen. The Mater would also retain acute status into the medium-term at least. The main 'local' hospitals would be Musgrave Park (Belfast), Whiteabbey, Mid-Ulster (Magherafelt), Lagan Valley (Lisburn), the Downe (Downpatrick - to be rebuilt), South Tyrone (Dungannon) and Tyrone County (Omagh). A new feature of the healthcare system would be 'protected elective centres', essentially surgical units dedicated solely to reduce waiting lists for planned surgery (Northern Ireland has among the longest waiting lists in Europe). Two centres, one at Lagan Valley and one West of the Bann would operate free from the pressures of day-to-day urgencies.

The decisions in 'Developing Better Services' would be backed by a major investment programme of around £1.2 billion, delivering a major upgrade and re-configuration of hospital services.

## Private Healthcare

The NHS dominates healthcare in Northern Ireland although there is also a private sector presence in what is a growing health 'market'. The main players in the private market include BUPA, PPP, Norwich Union and WPA who all offer a range of different levels of private health insurance to individuals and to groups. For those who can afford it, private medical treatment guarantees immediate access to healthcare and it is this instant access rather than the actual treatment delivered that is often the key selling point. Medical insurance is also available, offering financial protection against illness and injury, although some people with poorer health, who are less affluent, are unable to afford it.

The main private sector hospital in Northern Ireland is the Ulster Independent Clinic in South Belfast, which, in addition to a wide range of healthcare treatment allows individuals (appropriately insured) to undergo operations without waiting and via their choice of surgeon.

NHS consultants are free to operate a private practice as well as carry out their salaried NHS work. Many such consultants have private consulting rooms in their homes although some operate 'privately' within NHS facilities. Government is anxious to introduce a new 'contract' for consultants which, it is hoped, will lead to more efficient working and use of resources. A similar practice operates within dentistry; a dentist may offer the same service privately or on the NHS, with waiting times and costs differing greatly. Unlike the problems sometimes experienced in Britain, NHS dental services are widely available in Northern Ireland, although as there are sometimes long waiting times for non-emergency NHS treatment, the private sector is growing.

This system has attracted much criticism on grounds of equity. It is argued that a two-tier health service is evolving with a high-quality instant service for those who can afford it and a lower quality service with long waiting lists for those who cannot. In addition, there are controversial regional disparities, whereby some treatments are available on the NHS (i.e. free) in some regions and not in others, which affects Northern Ireland adversely. An example is IVF (in-vitro fertilisation), a fertility treatment that is available on the NHS in various parts of the UK, but not in Northern Ireland. Northern Ireland tends to suffer from significantly less financial support for some treatments, which are not considered essential.

**Ulster Independent Clinic**
245 Stranmillis Road, Belfast, BT9 5FJ
Tel: 028 9066 1212 / Fax: 028 9038 1704

**BUPA Health Screening Centre**
83-85 Great Victoria Street, Belfast
Tel: 028 90 232 723 / Fax:028 90 238 1233

## Complementary Medicine

Complementary medicine is a growing sector in Northern Ireland, including reflexology, Chinese medicine, homeopathy, acupuncture, chiropractic and hypnotherapy. These are not widely (if at all) available on the NHS so patients have to pay.

# Housing in Northern Ireland

Until the reorganisation of local government in the early 1970s, responsibility for housing in Northern Ireland was held by local councils. In 1971 the Northern Ireland Housing Executive (NIHE) was created to take on this responsibility, under the then Department of the Environment. The NIHE was unique in that it was the UK's first comprehensive housing authority, with a wide range of powers and responsibilities beyond that of managing the public rented housing sector. Since the establishment of a new configuration of government departments, under the Belfast Agreement, the Department for Social Development now has overall control over housing and housing policy in Northern Ireland.

**Table 5.7**

**The Housing Market in Northern Ireland**

| | 1992 | % | 2004 | % |
|---|---|---|---|---|
| Owner Occupancy | 363, 500 | 62.7 | 494,200 | 72.8 |
| NIHE | 155,500 | 26.8 | 94,600 | 13.9 |
| Housing Association | 10,500 | 1.8 | 21,000 | 3.1 |
| Private Rented | 19,500 | 3.4 | 34,600 | 5.1 |
| Vacant | 31,000 | 5.3 | 34,800 | 5.1 |
| Total | 580,000 | 100 | 679,200 | 100 |

Northern Ireland Housing Statistics 2003-04, DSD

## Housing Policy

Responsibility for housing policy falls to the Housing Division within the Department for Social Development (DSD). The Division works closely with the Northern Ireland Housing Executive (NIHE) and the Registered Housing Associations (RHA). The Housing Division holds regulatory powers over these organisations, as well as overseeing that section of the private rented sector, which is controlled by the Rent (Northern Ireland) Order 1978. The Division also appoints the Board of the Northern Ireland Housing Executive and the Rent Assessment Panels.

The draft programme for Government published by the devolved administration in September 2002 gave housing a degree of priority but clearly behind that attached to health, education and infrastructure. The suspension of the devolved administration has not had a beneficial effect on housing, slowing policy development and the legislative process. The period of suspension has also coincided with a marked slow-down in the Northern Ireland housing market following a period of rapid growth.

New house prices rose throughout 2003 and 2004, although more slowly than in 2000. The vast majority of new dwellings started were commissioned by the private sector, with over a third being detached. There has been a marked increase in repossessions recently and there are some other indications that the local housing market is beginning to slow down.

### The Northern Ireland Housing Executive

The Housing Centre
2 Adelaide Street, Belfast, BT2 8PB
Tel: 028 9024 0588 / Fax: 028 9043 9803
Chief Executive: Paddy McIntyre

The Chief Executive, Paddy McIntyre, is the accounting officer and chief officer in the Housing Executive and reports directly to the Board. He is responsible for setting the organisation's strategic direction and objectives and for ensuring performance is maintained.

The team of Central Directors report to the Chief Executive and decide on operational issues delegated by the Board as well as referring matters to it for approval. They are:

| | |
|---|---|
| Stuart Cuddy | Director of Corporate Services/Deputy Chief Executive |
| John Wilson | Director of Finance |
| Mike Shanks | Director of Development |
| Colm McCaughley | Director of Housing and Regeneration |
| Maureen Taggart | Director of Personnel and Management Services |
| John McPeake | Director of Design and Property Services |
| Imelda McGrath | Head of Information and Secretariat |

The Northern Ireland Housing Executive is a non-departmental public body established under the Housing Executive (Northern Ireland) Act, 1971. Since then it has built over 90,000 new homes, housed more than 500,000 people, improved 350,000 homes in the private sector, and sold over 100,000 homes to sitting tenants.

Its primary responsibilities cover a wide range of issues relating to housing and its provision in Northern Ireland. The NIHE assesses housing conditions and requirements, and devises strategies to address them. It also seeks to improve the condition of housing stock where practical, and to demolish unfit housing. The NIHE manages its own housing stock and provides information and advice on housing issues. It works with the Housing Council, and with the 26 local district councils, and acts as the Home Energy Conservation Authority in Northern Ireland to encourage energy efficiency within the residential sector.

The Housing Executive Headquarters is located in central Belfast. Five area offices are located in principal towns around Northern Ireland with a further 37 district offices and 12 grants offices providing a range of housing services at the local level.

During 2003/04 the Housing Executive:

- Contributed over £430m to the economy;
- Administered a Housing Benefit budget of over £359m;
- Help 1,245 households homeless due to intimidation;
- Approved almost 9,830 private sector grant applications;
- Launched the £40m Home Improvement Grants Scheme;
- Managed a housing stock of 102,850 dwellings.

**Housing Board**

Responsibility for general policy, management and operation of the Housing Executive lies with the Housing Board. The ten person Board, including the Chairman meets every month and decides on all important matters affecting the Housing Executive. Seven members of the Board are appointed by the Minister for Social Development, and the remaining three are nominated by the Northern Ireland Housing Council. At least one member must be female.

**Members of the Board**

Chairman: Brian Rowntree    Vice Chairman: Anne Henderson
John Shields, Bobby McKee, Alistair Joynes, Brendan Mackin
Liam McQuaid, Ciaran Brolly

**Housing Council Members**

| | |
|---|---|
| Cllr B Loughran | Antrim Borough Council |
| Ald J Shields | Ards Borough Council |
| Cllr J Speers (Chair) | Armagh City & District Council |
| Cllr J McKernan | Ballymena Borough Council |
| Cllr B Kennedy | Ballymoney Borough Council |
| Cllr J Baird | Banbridge District Council |
| Cllr S Wilson | Belfast City Council |
| Cllr B J Crampsey (Vice Chair) | Carrickfergus Borough Council |
| Cllr B McBurney | Castlereagh Borough Counci |
| Ald P E A Armitage | Coleraine Borough Council |
| Cllr P McGlone | Cookstown District Council |
| Ald S Gardiner | Craigavon Borough Council |
| Cllr T Hassan | Derry City Council |
| Cllr A McAleenan | Down District Council |
| Cllr B Monteith | Dungannon & South Tyrone BC |
| Cllr R Martin | Fermanagh District Council |
| Cllr R McKee | Larne Borough Council |
| Ald M Carten | Limavady Borough Council |
| Cllr W J Dillon | Lisburn Borough Council |
| Cllr P McErlean | Magherafelt District Council |
| Cllr D McAllister | Moyle District Council |
| Cllr B Curran | Newry & Mourne District Council |
| Cllr D Walker | Newtownabbey Borough Council |
| Cllr I Cree | North Down Borough Council |
| Cllr L McQuaid | Omagh District Council |
| Cllr T Kerrigan | Strabane District Council |

**Northern Ireland Housing Council**

The Housing Council was established by the Housing Executive Act (Northern Ireland) 1971. The Council is consulted by the Housing Executive and the DSD on all matters that affect housing policy in Northern Ireland. The Housing Executive meets once a month with the Housing Council, explaining operations and strategy. The Housing Council is made up of one representative from each of the 26 District Councils in Northern Ireland. There are three Housing Council members on the Board of the Housing Executive who are appointed for a one-year period. The current membership of the Housing Council is set out below left.

## Housing Executive Area Offices

### Belfast

32-36 Great Victoria Street, Belfast, BT2 7BL
Tel: 028 9031 7000
Manager: Maurice Johnson

### Homeless Advice Centre

32-36 Great Victoria Street, Belfast, BT2 7BL
Tel: 028 9031 7000
Manager: Des Marky

### Private Sector Housing Benefit

32-36 Great Victoria Street, Belfast, BT2 7BL
Tel: 028 9031 7000
Manager: Helen Walkers

### North East

Twickenham House, Mount Street, Ballymena, BT43 6BP
Tel: 028 2564 4211
Contact: Frank O'Connor

### South

Marlborough House, Central Way, Craigavon, BT64 1AJ
Tel: 028 3834 1188
Manager: Eamon McKeown

### South East

Strangford House, 28 Court Street,Newtownards, BT23 7NX
Tel: 028 9182 0600
Manager: Stephen Graham

### West

Richmond Chambers, The Diamond, Derry, BT48 6QP
Tel: 028 7137 2000
Manager: Sean Mackie

## NI Housing Executive District Offices

### Antrim
48 High Street, Antrim, BT41 4AN
Tel: 028 9442 8142
Manager: Patsy Smyth
Covers: Antrim Town, Crumlin, Randalstown, Templepatrick, Toome

### Armagh
48 Dobbin Street, Armagh, BT61 7QQ
Tel: 028 3752 3379
Manager: Joyce Dobbin
Covers: Armagh, Benburb, Charlemont, Keady, Loughgall, Markethill, Poyntzpass, Richhill, Tandragee

### Ballycastle
Fleming House, Coleraine Road
Ballycastle, BT54 6EY
Tel: 028 2076 2014
Manager: Gerry McCloskey
Covers: Ballycastle, Armoy, Cushendun, Bushmills, Cushendall, Waterfoot

### Ballymena
Twickenham House
Mount Street, Ballymena, BT43 6BP
Tel: 028 2564 4211
Manager: Christine Marks
Covers: Ballymena Town, Ahoghill, Broughshane, Cullybackey, Galgorm, Kells, Portglenone, Straid

### Ballymoney
50-54 Main Street
Ballymoney, BT53 6AL
Tel: 028 2766 3442
Manager: Mairead Myles-Davey
Covers: Ballymoney Town, Cloughmills, Dunloy, Rasharkin

### Banbridge
56 Bridge Street, Banbridge, BT32 3JU
Tel: 028 4066 2721
Manager: Angus Hannaway
Covers: Banbridge Town, Dromore, Gilford, Rathfriland

### Bangor
2 Alfred Street, Bangor, BT20 5DH
Tel: 028 9127 0761
Manager: Robert Mahaffy
Covers: Bangor, Conlig, Groomsport, Holywood

### Belfast 1
9 Upper Queen Street, Belfast, BT1 6FB
Tel: 028 9032 8282
Manager: Gary Ballintine
Covers: West Belfast, Hannahstown, Upper Falls

### Belfast 2
Laganview House, 95 Ann Street
Belfast, BT1 3HF
Tel: 028 9032 4558
Manager: Mr Richard Williamson
Covers: East Belfast

### Belfast 3
Murray House, Murray Street
Belfast, BT1 6DN
Tel: 028 9032 3642
Manager: Malachy McKinney
Covers: West Belfast, Lower Falls, Clonard, Divis

### Belfast 4
10-16 Hill Street, Belfast, BT1 2LA
Tel: 028 9024 1525
Manager: Sean McKenna
Covers: North Belfast, Whitewell, Shore Road

### Belfast 5
83-87 Shankill Road, Belfast, BT13 1FD
Tel: 028 9032 9442
Manager: Gordon Reilly
Covers: West Belfast, Shankill, Woodvale, Glencairn

### Belfast 6
1st Floor, Spencer House
71 Royal Avenue, Belfast, BT1 1FE
Tel: 028 9032 6477
Manager: Ivan Kelly
Covers: North Belfast, Ardoyne, Glenbryn, Oldpark

### Belfast 7
Law Society House, 96 Victoria Street
Belfast, BT1 3GN
Tel: 028 9024 8312
Manager: Liam Kinney
Covers: South Belfast, Ormeau, Donegall Road, Taughmonagh

### Brownlow (Craigavon)
16 Legahory Centre
Craigavon, BT65 5BE
Tel: 028 3832 6417
Manager: Paul Hughes
Covers: Brownlow, Craigavon Central area, Derrymagh, Derrytrasna

### Carrickfergus
19 High Street
Carrickfergus, BT38 7AN
Tel: 028 9335 1115
Manager: Aisling Marks
Covers: Carrickfergus Town, Greenisland, Whitehead

### Castlereagh
30 Church Road, Dundonald, BT16 0LN
Tel: 028 9048 5237
Manager: Paul Carland
Covers: Castlereagh area, Newtownards, Carryduff, Moneyreagh

### Coleraine
19 Abbey Street, Coleraine, BT52 1DU
Tel: 028 7035 8111
Manager: Joan Baird
Covers: Coleraine Town, Castlerock, Kilrea, Portrush, Portstewart

### Cookstown
15 Morgan's Hill Road
Cookstown, BT80 8HA
Tel: 028 8676 2004
Manager: Oonagh McElvenney
Covers: Cookstown, Moneymore, Pomeroy, Stewartstown

### Dairy Farm (Lisburn)
Stewartstown Road, Belfast, BT17 0SB
Tel: 028 9061 1199
Manager: Danny Cochrane
Covers: Poleglass, Twinbrook

### Downpatrick
51 John Street, Downpatrick, BT30 6HS
Tel: 028 4461 3551
Manager: Owen Brady
Covers: Downpatrick, Ardglass, Ballynahinch, Castlewellan, Killyleagh, Newcastle, Saintfield

### Dungannon
Ballygawley Road, Dungannon, BT70 1EL
Tel: 028 8772 3000
Manager: John Quigley
Covers: Dungannon Town, Aughnacloy, Ballygawley, Coalisland, Fivemiletown, Moy

### Fermanagh
Riverview House, 15 Head Street
Enniskillen, BT74 7DA
Tel: 028 6632 5770
Manager: Michael Callaghan
Covers: Fermanagh County, Belleek, Irvinestown, Kesh, Lisbellaw

### Larne
Sir Thomas Dixon Buildings,
47 Victoria Road, Larne, BT40 1RU
Tel: 028 2827 4426
Manager: Phylis Graig

Limavady
33 Catherine Street, Limavady, BT49 9DA
Tel: 028 7776 2711
Manager: John Donnell
Covers: Limavady Town, Ballykelly, Bellarena, Dungiven

Lisburn
29 Antrim Street, Lisburn, BT28 1AU
Telephone 028 9266 5222
Manager: Jill England
Covers: Lisburn City, Aghalee, Drumbo, Glenavy, Hillsborough, Moira

Londonderry 1
Ulster Bank Buildings
Waterloo Place, Derry, BT48 6BS
Tel: 028 7126 6227
Manager: Sam McPherson
Covers: Bogside, Brandywell, Creggan, Rosemount

Londonderry 2
2 Glendermott Road
Waterside, Derry, BT47 1AU
Tel: 028 7131 1490
Manager: Avril McAllister
Covers: Waterside, Claudy, Eglinton

Londonderry 3
14 Collon Terrace, Derry, BT48 7QP
Tel: 028 7137 3683
Manager: Walter Mullan
Covers: Culmore Road, Ballymcgroarty, Shantallow

Lurgan (Craigavon)
122 Hill Street, Lurgan, BT66 6BH
Tel: 028 3832 6417
Manager: Paul Hughes
Covers: Lurgan Town

Magherafelt
3 Ballyronan Road
Magherafelt, BT45 6BP
Tel: 028 7963 1121
Manager: Michael Dallat
Covers: Magherafelt, Bellaghy, Draperstown, Maghera, Tobermore

Newry
35-45 Boat Street, Newry, BT34 2DB
Tel: 028 3026 7331
Manager: Jan Sweeney
Covers: Newry City, Bessbrook, Crossmaglen, Hilltown, Rostrevor, Warrenpoint, Annalong, Kilkeel

Newtownabbey 1
Rantalard House, Rathcoole Drive
Rathcoole, Newtownabbey, BT37 9AG
Tel: 028 9036 5911
Manager: Keery Irvine
Covers: Bawnmore, Rathcoole, Whiteabbey

Newtownabbey 2
2 Ballyearl Drive, New Mossley
Newtownabbey, BT36 5XJ
Tel: 028 9084 3711
Manager: Brian Newman
Covers: Ballyclare, Glengormley, Monkstown, New Mossley

Newtownards
2-32 Frederick Street
Newtownards, BT23 4LR
Tel: 028 9181 6979
Manager: Michael Taylor
Covers: Newtownards, Ballygowan, Comber, Portaferry, Portavogie

Omagh
Riverston House, 7 Holmview Terrace
Omagh, BT79 0AH
Tel: 028 8224 7701
Manager: Ivan Armstrong
Covers: Omagh, Dromore, Fintona, Sixmilecross

Portadown
41 Thomas Street, Portadown, BT62 3AF
Tel: 028 3836 1895
Manager: Bob Smyth
Covers: Portadown Estates

Strabane
48 Railway Road, Strabane, BT82 8EH
Tel: 028 7138 2637
Contact: Seamus Kelly
Covers: Strabane, Donemana, Castlederg, Newtownstewart, Sion Mills

## Home Improvement Grant Offices

Ballyclare
141 Mill Road, Ballyclare, BT39 9DZ
Tel: 028 9335 2849

Ballymena
Twickenham House, Mount Street
Ballymena, BT43 6BP
Tel: 028 2565 3399

Belfast
32-36 Great Victoria Street
Belfast, BT2 7BA
Tel: 028 9031 7000

Craigavon
Marlborough House, Central Way
Craigavon, BT64 1AJ
Tel: 028 3834 1188

Fermanagh
Riverview House, 15 Head Street
Enniskillen, BT74 7DA
Tel: 028 6632 5770

Lisburn
46 Graham Gardens, Lisburn, BT28 1XE
Tel: 028 9266 5222

Londonderry
Richmond Chambers
The Diamond, Derry, BT48 6QP
Tel: 028 7137 2000

Newry
35-45 Boat Street, Newry, BT34 2DB
Tel: 028 3026 7331

Newtownards
Strangford House, 28 Court Street
Newtownards, BT23 7NX
Tel: 028 9182 0600

Omagh
McAllister House, Woodside Avenue
Omagh, BT79 7BP
Tel: 028 8224 6111

**Housing in Multiple Occupation Units**
32-36 Great Victoria Street
Belfast, BT2 7BL
Tel: 028 9031 7000

19 Abbey Street, Coleraine, BT52 1DU
Tel: 028 7035 8111

## After Hours Homeless Service

| | |
|---|---|
| *Armagh* | Tel: 028 3752 2381 |
| *Banbridge* | Tel: 028 3833 4444 |
| *Belfast Inner & Greater* | Tel: 028 9056 5444 |
| *Co Antrim* | Tel: 028 9446 8833 |
| *Co Down (East, Mid & North)* | Tel: 028 9056 5444 |
| *Coleraine* | Tel: 028 9446 8833 |
| *Craigavon* | Tel: 028 3833 4444 |
| *Derry* | Tel: 028 7134 5171 |
| *Dungannon* | Tel: 028 3752 2381 |
| *Enniskillen* | Tel: 028 6638 2000 |
| *Magherafelt* | Tel: 028 9446 8833 |
| *Newry & Mourne* | Tel: 028 3083 5000 |
| *Omagh* | Tel: 028 8283 3100 |

**Emergency Repairs – After Hours**

| | |
|---|---|
| *Belfast* | Tel: 028 9024 6111 |
| *Derry* | Tel: 028 7126 2628 |

## Housing Associations

There are approximately 39 officially registered Housing Associations in Northern Ireland. These are independent not-for-profit organisations, often community-based, which provide good quality affordable housing for people in housing need.

Although many of the associations are locally focused serving a particular locality, some of the larger associations operate throughout Northern Ireland. Others specialise in a particular kind of accommodation provision e.g. supported housing for the elderly. All are funded by the Department for Social Development.

Housing Associations have around 25,000 social housing units under management. This accounts for around 18% of social housing – the remainder accounted for by the Northern Ireland Housing Executive. These proportions are likely to change significantly going forward as responsibility for social housing new build now rests exclusively with housing associations (no longer the responsibility of NIHE) while at the same time, the Housing Executive social housing stock will continue to decline through house sales to tenants.

One of the challenges facing Housing Associations is to project manage and complete new social housing at the rate targeted to meet priority housing need and to make inroads on existing waiting lists. This will be a significant task for what are in amany cases relatively small organisations with limited project management resources. Table 5.8 indicates the main players in the Housing Association sector in terms of scale.

## Housing Associations A-Z

**Table 5.8 Housing Associations with more than 500 Units of Accommodation, March 2003**

| | Total Units |
|---|---|
| BIH | 3,730 |
| Fold | 3,426 |
| Oaklee | 3,266 |
| North and West | 2,220 |
| Clanmill | 1,482 |
| Habinteg | 1,486 |
| SHAC | 1,045 |
| South Ulster | 658 |
| Presbyterian | 624 |
| Ulidia | 566 |
| **Total** | **18,503** |
| **Total Housing Association Stock** | **29,297** |

Source: DSD, Housing Association Branch

### Abbeyfield UK(NI) Ltd
3 Grand Parade, Belfast, BT5 5HG
Tel: 028 9040 2045
Fax: 028 9070 3776
Chief Executive: Geraldine Gilpin
Chairman: Celia Worthington

### Abode
2A Wesley Court
Carrickfergus, BT38 8HS
Tel: 028 9336 0973
Fax: 028 9336 1472
Chief Executive: Mary Green
Chairman: Waltham Balmer

### Ark Housing Association
9 Stranmillis Road, Belfast, BT9 5AF
Tel: 028 9068 1808
Fax: 028 9066 4524
Director: Tony Ruddy
Chairman: Oliver Magill

### Ballynafeigh Housing Association
70 Kimberley Street, Belfast, BT7 3DY
Tel: 028 9049 1569
Fax: 028 9064 3068
Director: Paul O'Neill
Chairman: Duncan Graham

### Belfast Community Housing Association Ltd
Neilly House, Bellsbridge Office Park
100A Ladas Drive
Belfast, BT6 9FH
Tel: 028 9046 3686
Fax: 028 9046 0788
Chief Executive: Dermot Curran
Chairman: David Scholes

### BIH Housing Association Ltd
Russell Court
Claremont Street, Belfast, BT9 6JX
Tel: 028 9032 0485
Fax: 028 9033 0402
Chief Executive: Jean Fulton
Chairman: Donal MacRandal

### Broadway
Bedeque House, 3 Annesley Street
Belfast, BT14 6AU
Tel: 028 9074 2984
Chairman: Dr Cooper

### Choice
95A Finaghy Road South
Belfast, BT10 0BY
Tel: 028 9030 8140
Fax: 028 9030 6929
Chief Executive: Mr Arthur Canning
Chairman: Robert Moore

### Clanmil Housing
Northern Whig House
Waring Street, Belfast, BT1 2DX
Tel: 028 9087 6000
Fax: 028 9087 6001
Chief Executive: Clare McCarty
Chairman: Geraldine Rice

### Clonard
c/o Carlisle Memorial Centre
88 Clifton Street
Belfast, BT13 1AB
Tel: 028 9031 1156
Fax: 028 9031 1264
Secretary: Thelma Armstrong

### Connswater Housing
2 Severn Street, Belfast, BT4 1FB
Tel: 028 9045 6596
Fax: 028 9045 5639
Director: Jacqueline Locke
Chairman: Rev James McAllister

### Coral Crescent
13 Atlantic Avenue, Antrim, BT41 4LS
Tel: 028 9442 8364
Chief Executive: Liam Magill

### Co-Ownership Housing

Co-Ownership Housing

*Creating **Homes** - Building **Communities***

Murray House, Murray Street
Belfast, BT1 6DN
Tel: 028 9032 7276
Fax: 028 9033 0720
Email: nicha@co-ownership.org
Web: www.co-ownership.org

Chief Executive:
Alan Crowe

NICHA operates a form of Do It Yourself Shared Ownership (DIYSO) scheme called Co-Ownership throughout Northern Ireland. On an individual level Co-Ownership provides a low cost route into home ownership for people who could not afford to buy a home of their own otherwise. On a regional level it plays an important role in creating balanced and sustainable communities through tenure diversification as well as an active role in urban and rural regeneration initiatives.

Purchasers start with a 50%, 62.5% or 75% share in the property of their choice, and may increase their share at any time.

18,000 homes have been purchased through Co-Ownership to date.

### Corinthian

95A Finaghy Road South
Belfast, BT10 0BY
Tel: 028 9030 8019
Chief Executive: Arthur Canning
Chairman William Gibney

### The Covenanter Residential Association Ltd

Cameron House, 98 Lisburn Road
Belfast, BT9 6AG
Tel: 028 9066 4875
Contact: Valerie McKay
Chairman: John Reid

### Craigowen

Glencraig Village Community
Craigavad, Holywood, BT18 ODB,
Tel: 028 9042 3396
Fax: 028 9042 8199

### Donacloney Housing Association Ltd

38 Main Street, Donacloney
Craigavon, BT66 7LR
Tel: 028 3888 1307
Fax: 028 3888 1307
Chairman: George Savage

### Dungannon & District Housing Association Ltd

27 Market Square
Dungannon, BT70 1JD
Tel: 028 8772 2121
Fax: 028 8775 3870
Director: Maura McNally
Chairman: John Gill

### Filor Housing Association Ltd

282-290 Crumlin Road,
Belfast, BT14 7EE
Tel: 028 9035 1131
Fax: 028 9074 1755
Acting Chief Executive: Dermot Leonard

### Flax Housing Association

Unit 9, Flax Centre, Ardoyne Avenue,
Belfast, BT14 7DA
Tel: 028 9059 2110
Director: John Donaghey
Chairman: Father Miles Kavanagh

### Fold Housing Association

3 Redburn Square
Holywood, BT18 9HZ
Tel: 028 9042 8314
Fax: 028 9042 8167
Chief Executive: Mr B G Coulter
Chairman: Mr W Cameron

### Gosford Housing Association

6 Georges Street, Armagh, BT60 1BY
Tel: 028 3752 8272
Manager: Michael Hermin
Chairman: Gordon Bratten

### Grove Housing Association Ltd

171 York Road, Belfast, BT15 3BH
Tel: 028 9077 3330
Fax: 028 9077 6661
General Manager: Vacant
Chairman: David Brown

### Habinteg Housing Association (Ulster) Ltd

Alex Moira House, 22 Hibernia Street
Holywood, BT18 9JE
Tel: 028 9042 7211
Fax: 028 9042 8069
Chief Executive: David Duly
Chairman: George Harkness

### Hearth Housing Association

66 Donegall Pass, Belfast, BT7 1BU
Tel: 028 9053 0121
Fax: 028 9053 0122
Director: Marcus Patton
Chairman: Karen Latimer

### Larne & District Housing Association

1st Floor, 93 Main Street
Larne, BT40 1HJ
Tel: 028 2827 6431
Fax: 028 2827 9481
Director: Marie Kyle
Chairman: Hazel Bell

### Newington Housing Association (1975) Ltd

300-302 Limestone Road,
Belfast, BT15 3AR
Tel: 028 9074 4055
Fax: 028 9074 7624
Director: Gary Dugan
Chairperson: Peter Privilege

### North & West Housing Ltd

18 Magazine Street, Derry, BT48 6HH
Tel: 028 7126 3819
Fax: 028 7126 3362
Chief Executive: Gerry Kelly
Chairman: Joe Cowan

### Oaklee Housing Association Ltd

Leslie Morrell House
37-41 May Street, Belfast, BT1 4DN
Tel: 028 9044 1300
Fax: 028 9044 1346
Chief Executive: Ian Elliott
Chairman: Jack Allen

### Open Door Housing Association (NI) Ltd

10-14 Commercial Court
Belfast, BT1 2NB
Tel: 028 9024 3785
Fax: 028 9023 5336
Managing Director: Austin Herron
Chairman: Brendan Mackin

Presbyterian Housing Association (NI) Ltd
7A Weavers Court, Linfield Road
Belfast, BT12 5GH
Tel: 028 9050 7755
Fax: 028 9050 7756
Director: John Tinman
Chairman: Alistair Giffen

Rural Housing Association Ltd
64A Derry Road, Omagh, BT78 5DY
Tel: 028 8224 6118
Fax: 028 8224 6120
Web: www.ruralhousing.co.uk
Chief Executive: Mr Paddy McGurk
Chairman: Alistair McKane

SHAC Housing
29 Bedford Street, Belfast, BT2 7EJ
Tel: 028 9024 6811
Fax: 028 9033 3724
Chief Executive: Ray Cashel
Chairperson: Mark McLean

South Ulster Housing Association Ltd
20-22 Carleton Street
Portadown, BT62 3EN
Tel: 028 3833 9795
Fax: 028 3835 0944
Chairman: Brian Cassells
Director: Sam Preston

St Matthews Housing Association Ltd
58 Harper Street, Belfast, BT5 4EN
Tel: 028 9045 1070
Fax: 028 9045 4205
Chairman: Patrick Devlin
Director: Michael McKeever

Triangle Housing Association Ltd
60 Eastermeade Gardens
Ballymoney, BT53 6BD
Tel: 028 2766 6880
Fax: 028 2766 2994
Chief Executive: Edna Dunbar
Chairperson: Oonagh Boyle

Ulidia Housing Association Ltd
20 Derryvolgie Avenue
Belfast, BT9 6FN
Tel: 028 9038 2288
Fax: 028 9038 2738
Chief Executive: John Gartland
Chairman: Liz Millen

Wesley
2 Wesley Court
Carrickfergus, BT38 8HS
Tel: 028 9336 3558
Fax: 028 9335 5319
Chief Executive: Lawrence McAdams
Chairman: Mr H. Hughes

Woodvale & Shankill Housing Association Ltd
91 Woodvale Road, Belfast, BT13 3BP
Tel: 028 9074 1618
Fax: 028 9035 1922
Chief Executive: Jim Smyth
Chairman: Roy Baillie

## Northern Ireland Federation of Housing Associations

38 Hill Street, Belfast, BT1 2LB
Tel: 028 9023 0446
Fax: 028 9023 8057

NIFHA is the umbrella organisation for the Housing Association sector providing a range of representational and other services for its members.

**Membership of NIHFA Council**

*Chairperson*
Mr Arnold Hatch — South Ulster

*Vice Chairperson*
Arthur Canning — Choice

| | |
|---|---|
| Alan Crowe | NI Co-Ownership |
| Mr W Cameron | Fold |
| David Duly | Habinteg |
| Edna Dunbar | Triangle |
| Ian Elliott | Oaklee |
| Mr E Holmes | Glenall |
| Mr J Patterson | Flax |
| Rev James McAllister | Connswater |
| Paddy McGurk | Rural |
| Mrs M Mitchell | Ulster Provident |
| Marcus Patton | Hearth |
| Mr D Rankin | Clanmil |
| Mr R Roulston | Ulidia |
| John Tinman | Presbyterian |
| Ray Cashel | SHAC |
| Jean Fulton | BIH |
| John Gill | Dungannon & District |
| Mr P Howard | Abbeyfield |

# Chapter 6

# Education and Training in Northern Ireland

## Introduction

Children in Northern Ireland are legally obliged to attend school between the ages of 5 and 16. The system has three learning levels: primary, secondary and tertiary. In addition to this are pre-school/nursery and higher/adult education. Most children in Northern Ireland begin primary school at the age of 4. Primary education is geared toward completion of the UK Government's Key Stages 1 and 2, a curriculum designed to ensure basic standards of literacy and numeracy, as well as some initial science and a foreign language. While in their last year at primary school, many pupils take the '11 plus' exam.

According to their performance in the 11 plus, children progress to one of a variety of educational institutions in second level education. The most academically able children (according to the examination) for the most part attend a grammar school. These schools are generally focused towards academic results, normally A-levels, traditionally seen as the passport to a university place. Most of the remainder of children, i.e. who do not attain a high enough grade in the examination, or the majority who do not actually sit it, attend comprehensive or secondary intermediate schools, which tend to be more vocational in their outlook. A smaller proportion of these pupils go on to attain A-levels and move onward to university, although many study for more vocational qualifications such as GNVQs, which are increasingly becoming a route to a university education.

Whilst different types of secondary school each have their own priorities, all are obliged to follow the curriculum (key stages 3 and 4) formulated by the UK Department of Education. This tries to ensure that pupils leave school with certain basic levels of literacy and numeracy, as well as studying science and at least one foreign language.

A small percentage of children leave school with no qualifications, and some leave directly after taking their GCSE exams. However the majority stay on to undertake further qualifications. As well as secondary schools, many colleges of higher and further education offer both academic and vocational qualifications. Students can resit GCSEs and study for A-levels, BTECs, HNCs (Higher National Certificates) and HNDs (Higher National Diplomas) in a wide range of subjects. This can then lead to university, or alternatively provides a vocational qualification which is useful in preparation for the workplace.

Alongside traditional, formal education there is also the Open University, offering part-time university education, and numerous colleges providing nighttime and daytime classes for many thousands of part-time students. Despite this flexibility, however, there remain a number of perceived deficiencies in the system of education in Northern Ireland. Many educationalists regard the selection system as being unsatisfactory while others see the religious segregation of the pupil population as the big weakness in the system. In addition there are concerns about pupil teacher ratios and the level of resources allocated to education. Some of the key issues facing the sector are discussed later in this chapter.

## Structure of the Northern Ireland Education System

The structure of the education system in Northern Ireland is complex, with ten Statutory Bodies involved in the management and administration of the system, including:

- The Department of Education;
- The Education and Library Boards (5);
- The Council for Catholic Maintained Schools;
- The Northern Ireland Council for the Curriculum, Examinations and Assessment (CCEA);
- The Staff Commission for Education and Library Boards;
- The Youth Council for Northern Ireland.

There are also a number of voluntary bodies involved in the administration of the education system, including the Northern Ireland Council for Integrated Education, Comhairle na Gaelscolaiochta, (the council for Irish-medium schools) the Transferor Representatives Council which brings together representatives of the Transferor Churches (Church of Ireland, Presbyterian and Methodist) and the Association of Governing Bodies which represents the voluntary grammar schools.

The roles and functions of these bodies are described in detail in the relevant sections below. However, here follows a brief overview of the main responsibilities of the Department, the Education and Library Boards (ELBs) and the Council for Catholic Maintained Schools (CCMS) to provide a context for the later material.

### The Department of Education

The Department of Education is responsible for the central administration of education and related services in Northern Ireland. Its primary duties are to promote the education of young people in Northern Ireland and to secure the effective execution of its policy in relation to the provision of the education service. The structure, functions and senior personnel of the Department of Education are set out in detail in Chapter 3, Government Departments and Agencies.

### Education and Library Boards

There are five Education and Library Boards (ELBs), which are the local education authorities and library authorities for their areas. ELBs have a statutory responsibility to ensure that there are sufficient schools of all kinds to meet the needs of their area; to provide all the finance for the schools under their management; and to equip, maintain and meet other running costs of maintained schools. ELB expenditure is funded at 100 per cent by the Department.

### Enrolments in Educational Institutions

Table 6.1 shows the current levels of educational provision in Northern Ireland in terms of numbers and categories of educational institution, along with associated student numbers.

**Table 6.1: Educational Attendance by Type of Institution 2003/04**

| Education Type | Number | Number of Students |
|---|---|---|
| NURSERY | 100 | 6,238 |
| PRE-SCHOOL* | 383 | 5,913 |
| PRIMARY | 892 | 171,561 |
| SECONDARY (Excl Grammar) | 163 | 92,047 |
| GRAMMAR (Years 8-14) | 70 | 63,347 |
| SPECIAL | 47 | 4,834 |
| INDEPENDENT | 17 | 835 |
| HOSPITAL | 3 | 298 |

Source: NISRA

*Pre-school = Voluntary and private pre-school centres

In addition there are 16 Further Education (FE) Colleges, and 2 Universities: the traditional red-brick Queen's University of Belfast, and the more recent University of Ulster, split between campuses at Jordanstown, Coleraine, Derry and Belfast. The number of students attending Northern Ireland's educational institutions has increased gradually, in most categories, in recent years as illustrated in table 6.2

Although the increases in attendance in the primary and secondary sectors are largely a function of population growth, the recent rapid expansion of third level attendances reflects the policy continued by successive governments, of opening up third level opportunities to as many as possible.

## Main Categories of School in Northern Ireland

There are a number of types of school in Northern Ireland, differing in the level of government control, as well as management structures. The main types are detailed below:

### Controlled Schools

In terms of the religious divide in Northern Ireland's education system, controlled schools are essentially Protestant in terms of staffing, management and pupil intake. Controlled schools are managed by ELBs, who act as the employer, through Boards of Governors. Primary and secondary school Boards of Governors consist of representatives of transferors (the main Protestant Churches) along with representatives of parents, teachers and ELBs. Nursery, grammar and special school Boards of Governors consist of representatives of the latter three categories. Within the controlled sector there is a small number of controlled integrated schools.

### Maintained Schools

These schools are largely regarded as Catholic schools. Whilst they have a relatively close relationship with their local Education and Library Board, they are also aligned with the Council for Catholic Maintained Schools (CCMS), which is the employing authority for teaching staff, The ELB is the employing authority for non-teaching staff.

### Voluntary (Maintained)

This type of voluntary school is managed by Boards of Governors which consist of members nominated by trustees (mainly Roman Catholic), along with representatives of parents, teachers and ELBs. Voluntary schools vary in the rates of capital grant to which they are entitled, depending on the management structures they have adopted. A majority are entitled to capital grants at 100 percent.

### Voluntary (Non-Maintained)

These are mainly voluntary (Catholic and Protestant) grammar schools, managed by Boards of Governors which consist of persons appointed as provided in each school's scheme of management, along with representatives of parents and teachers and, in most cases, members appointed by the Department or ELBs.

Grant-Maintained Integrated Schools

In recent years a number of grant-maintained integrated schools have been established at primary and post-primary levels. The practical operation of all schools has increasingly become a matter for Boards of Governors. They are responsible for the delivery of the curriculum, admission of pupils, and in the case of schools with delegated budgets, for the management of their own financial affairs, including staff matters.

### Irish Medium Schools

There are currently 18 grant-aided Irish Medium schools and 12 units (10 primary and 2 secondary) catering for over 2,000 pupils. This means that over 90% of all those being educated through the medium of Irish are in fully grant-aided schools.

### Independent Schools

In addition to the public system of free education, there are also independent schools. These schools do not necessarily follow the Northern Ireland Curriculum and do not receive grant-aid from the Department. Some of these schools charge fees which are payable directly to the school by parents.
Independent school look after their own day-to-day affairs but are subject to inspection to ensure they maintain acceptable standards of education appropriate for the number, ages and sex of the pupils attending the school.

## Pre-School Education

Pre-school education is broken down into nursery and reception classes, provided by the state and by the independent sector. In recent years there has been much debate on the levels and funding of pre-school provision. In 1995/96 there were 10,785 children in funded places. Currently there are 17,878 children in funded places (11,931 in nursery classes, 1,990 in reception classes and 3,957 in voluntary/private pre-school education centres). This is a significant increase but may still leave as many as 7,000 children with no funded provision at all.

## Primary Education

Primary education is normally organised on the basis of a delivery period of seven years. Despite its informal appearance primary education is carefully structured against a detailed curriculum. Primary education is dominated by two categories of school: Controlled State Schools and Catholic Maintained Schools. Together they account for 95 per cent of all primary school enrolments. The remainder is accounted for by integrated primary schools.

## Primary Curriculum

The Northern Ireland Curriculum, which was established by the Education Reform (Northern Ireland) Order 1989, sets out the minimum educational entitlement for pupils aged 4 to 16 years. The Order was amended in 1993 and in 1996.

The 1989 Order requires schools to provide a curriculum for all pupils which:

- Promotes the spiritual, moral, cultural, intellectual and physical development of pupils at the school and thereby of society;
- Prepares pupils for the opportunities and experiences of adult life.

The Northern Ireland Curriculum was introduced on a phased basis from 1990. It was reviewed in 1994 and the revised Northern Ireland Curriculum was introduced in September 1996.

The curriculum is defined in terms of four key stages which cover the 12 years of compulsory schooling. Primary education incorporates Key Stages 1 and 2 as follows:

- Key Stage 1 covers school years 1-4 for pupils aged 4-8;
- Key Stage 2 covers school years 5-7 for pupils aged 8-11.

The Curriculum does not constitute the whole curriculum for schools. Schools can develop additional curriculum elements to express their particular ethos.

### Key Stages 1 and 2

The curriculum for Key Stages 1 and 2 includes:

- English;
- Mathematics;
- Science and Technology;
- History and Geography (known as the Environment and Society Area of Study);
- Art and Design, Music and Physical Education (known as the Creative and Expressive Area of Study);
- Religious Education;
- Irish, in Irish speaking schools only; and
- Four educational cross-curricular themes (Education for Mutual Understanding, Cultural Heritage, Health Education and Information Technology). The educational themes are not separate subjects but are woven through the main subjects of the curriculum.

### Content

Each subject in the Northern Ireland Curriculum is defined within the Programmes of Study and Attainment Targets. There may be different numbers of Attainment Targets in each subject.

### Programmes of Study

The Programmes of Study set out the opportunities which should be offered to all pupils, in terms of the knowledge, skills and understanding at each key stage. Teachers use the programmes of study as a basis for planning schemes of work.

### Attainment Targets

Attainment Targets define the expected standards of pupil performance in particular aspects of a subject in terms of Level Descriptions. These provide the basis for making judgements on pupils' attainment at the end of each key stage.

## Level Descriptions

There are eight levels in each attainment target. For each level there is a Level Description indicating the type and range of attainment that a pupil working at that level should demonstrate. At the end of Key Stage 1, it is expected that the majority of pupils will be working at Level 2. At the end of Key Stage 2, it is expected that pupils will be working at either Level 3 or 4.

**Table 6.2: Schools - Number of Pupils**

| | 1990/91 | 1996/97 | 1999/00 | 2000/01 | 2001/02 | 2003/04 |
|---|---|---|---|---|---|---|
| Nursery | | | | | | |
| - Full-time | 2,702 | 2,983 | 3,277 | 3,304 | 3,381 | 3,712 |
| - Part-time | 2,224 | 2,513 | 2,675 | 2,661 | 2,712 | 2,526 |
| Nursery classes (primary schools) | | | | | | |
| - Full-time | 1,729 | 1,901 | 2,629 | 3,225 | 3,529 | 3,831 |
| - Part-time | 838 | 1,125 | 1,418 | 2,741 | 3,483 | 3,945 |
| Primary - Reception | 2,084 | 2,499 | 2,318 | 1,963 | 1,445 | 995 |
| Primary - Years 1-7 | 181,233 | 181,284 | 172,591 | 169,700 | 167,883 | 162,790 |
| Grammar Preparatory - Reception | 23 | 45 | 12 | 27 | 29 | 49 |
| Grammar Preparatory - Years 1-7 | 3,641 | 3,354 | 3,011 | 2,791 | 2,670 | 2,557 |
| Secondary (excluding Grammar) | 86,667 | 90,746 | 92,603 | 92,979 | 92,760 | 92,047 |
| Grammar - Years 8-14 | 54,479 | 61,997 | 62,361 | 62,574 | 62,743 | 63,347 |
| Special Schools | 3,983 | 4,680 | 4,688 | 4,674 | 4,710 | 4,834 |
| Hospital Schools | 234 | 178 | 173 | 171 | 246 | 298 |
| Independent Schools | 1,023 | 925 | 1,243 | 1,255 | 1,072 | 835 |
| **Total All Schools** | **340,880** | **354,230** | **348,999** | **348,065** | **346,663** | **341,766** |

Source: Department of Education

## Secondary Education

### Northern Ireland Curriculum

The Northern Ireland Curriculum sets out the educational entitlement for pupils aged 11 to 16 years. Second level education is defined as covering key stages 3 and 4 as follows:

- Key Stage 3, covers school years 8-10 for pupils aged 12-14;
- Key Stage 4, covers school years 11-12 for pupils aged 15-16.

The curricular requirements for Key Stages 3 and 4 are:

**Key Stage 3**

- English;
- Mathematics;
- Science, Technology and Design;
- History and Geography (known as the Environment and Society Area of Study);
- Art and Design, Music and Physical Education (known as the Creative and Expressive Area of Study);
- French or German or Italian or Spanish or Irish (known as the Modern Languages Area of Study);
- Religious Education;
- Six educational themes (Education for Mutual Understanding, Cultural Heritage, Health Education, Information Technology, Economic Awareness and Careers Education).

**Key Stage 4**

- English;
- Mathematics;
- Science;
- A course in one of History, Geography, Business Studies, Home Economics, Economics, Politics or an appropriate modular provision;
- Physical Education;
- Religious Education;
- An approved course in a modern language; and
- Six educational themes (Education for Mutual Understanding, Cultural Heritage, Health Education, Information Technology, Economic Awareness and Careers Education).

As with primary education the content of each subject in the Northern Ireland Curriculum at Key Stage 3 and 4 is defined in a Statutory Order and each Order consists of Programmes of Study and Attainment Targets.

At the end of Key Stage 3, it is expected that the majority of pupils will be working at either Level 5 or 6.

## Third Level Education

In terms of institutions, tertiary level education in Northern Ireland consists of the two main universities (Queen's University, Belfast and the University of Ulster), two teacher-training colleges (St Mary's and Stranmillis) and 16 Further Education Colleges, as well as specialist centres for agriculture. Several thousand people in Northern Ireland are also enrolled in the Open University. Participation in third-level education has grown steadily in recent years in Northern Ireland, across both the university and FE sectors, with the number of students approximately doubling over a twenty-year period. Additionally, the number of students availing of full-time undergraduate study opportunities outside Northern Ireland has also doubled.

Details of Northern Ireland's two universities are set out below, including faculty and departmental listings and names of senior university personnel.

**Table 6.3: Higher Education Enrolments (NI Domiciled Students)**

| | 1990/91 | 1993/94 | 1996/97 | 2000/01 | 2001/02 | 2002/03 |
|---|---|---|---|---|---|---|
| Full-Time Undergraduates | 24,617 | 31,331 | 34,940 | 40,171 | 40,944 | 42,713 |
| Part-Time Undergraduates | 5,949 | 7,276 | 15,079 | 22,865 | 23,164 | 22,617 |
| Full-Time Post Graduates | 2,186 | 2,871 | 3,382 | 4,078 | 4,047 | 4,107 |
| Part-Time Post Graduates | 3,485 | 4,620 | 5,650 | 6,934 | 6,982 | 7,153 |
| **Total** | **36,237** | **46,098** | **59,051** | **74,048** | **75,137** | **76,590** |

Source: Department of Education

### Queen's University Belfast

Queen's University Belfast

University Road
Belfast
BT7 1NN
Tel: 028 9024 5133
Fax: 028 9024 7895
Web: www.qub.ac.uk

Queen's University gives Northern Ireland an international profile through world-class research and teaching, making a major contribution to economic, social and cultural development.

Queen's was founded in 1845 as Queen's College, part of the National University of Ireland. In 1908 it became a university in its own right. It offers a comprehensive range of courses across five faculties, Humanities, Science and Agriculture, Medicine, Engineering, and Legal, Social and Educational Sciences. The University has a particularly strong profile in professional education including law, medicine, accountancy, engineering and architecture. Queen's has a total of 25,000 students, and the University awards some 3,000 degrees and 1,200 higher degrees annually.

Queen's University is one of Northern Ireland's biggest employers, employing 3,500 staff including 1,600 teaching and research staff.

**Senior Officers of the University**

| | |
|---|---|
| Chancellor: | Senator George Mitchell |
| Pro-Chancellors: | Brenda McLaughlin<br>Christopher Gibson |
| President and Vice Chancellor: | Professor Peter Gregson |
| Pro-Vice-Chancellors: | Professor Ken Brown (Academic Planning & Resources)<br>Professor Robert J Crawford (Research and Development)<br>Professor K L Bell (Students and Learning)<br>Professor F G McCormac (Community and Communications) |
| Hon Treasurer: | Teresa Townsley |
| Registrar: | James P J O'Kane |

**Academic Units**

*Faculty of Engineering*

Schools: Aeronautical Engineering, Architecture, Chemical Engineering, Civil Engineering, Computer Science, Electrical and Electronic Engineering, Environmental Planning, Mechanical and Manufacturing Engineering, Northern Ireland Technology Centre.

*Faculty of Medicine and Health Sciences*

Schools: Dentistry, Medicine, Nursing and Midwifery, Medicine Research Office.

*Faculty of Humanities*

Schools: English, History, Languages, Literatures and Arts, Music, Philosophical Studies, Anthropological Studies, Institutes: Irish Studies, Theology, Byzantine Studies.

*Faculty of Legal, Social and Educational Sciences*
Schools: Law, Management and Economics, Politics and International Studies, Social Work, Sociology and Social Policy
Institutes: Governance, Graduate School of Education, University Colleges: Stranmillis, St Mary's, Institute of Lifelong Learning, Armagh Outreach Campus.

*Faculty of Science and Agriculture*
Schools: Agriculture and Food Science, Archaeology and Palaeoecology, Biology and Biochemistry, Chemistry, Geography, Mathematics and Physics, Pharmacy, Psychology. Gibson Institute, QUESTOR Centre

*Academic Units outside the faculty structure*
Centres: Migration Studies, Canadian Studies, Polymer Processing Research, Institute of Professional Legal Studies

### Table 6.4: Student Numbers (QUB) 2002/03

| | Undergraduates | | Postgraduates | | Total |
|---|---|---|---|---|---|
| | Full Time | Part Time | Full Time | Part Time | |
| Faculty of Engineering | 2,598 | 134 | 454 | 275 | 3,461 |
| Faculty of Humanities | 1,784 | 170 | 170 | 197 | 2,321 |
| Faculty of Legal, Social & Educational Sciences | 2,738 | 1,345 | 751 | 938 | 5,772 |
| Faculty of Medicine & Health Sciences | 2,637 | 1,408 | 169 | 276 | 4,490 |
| Faculty of Science & Agriculture | 2,542 | 105 | 425 | 584 | 3,656 |
| Extra Mural Studies | – | 2,335 | – | – | 2,335 |
| Stranmillis University College | 953 | 264 | 40 | 118 | 1,375 |
| St Mary's University College | 944 | 51 | 18 | 134 | 1,147 |
| **Total** | **14,196** | **5,812** | **2,027** | **2,522** | **24,557** |

## University of Ulster

The University of Ulster is a major UK university with an international profile for academic and research excellence and is a significant contributor to the region's economic development.

The University of Ulster has four campuses.

**Belfast Campus**
York Street, Belfast, BT15 1ED

**Coleraine Campus**
Cromore Road, Coleraine, BT52 1SA

**Jordanstown Campus**
Shore Road, Newtownabbey, BT37 0QB

**Magee Campus**
Northland Road, Londonderry, BT48 7JL

Tel: 08 700 400 700
Web: www.ulster.ac.uk

The University is one of Northern Ireland's largest and most influential institutions with an annual turnover in excess of £130 million and contributes approximately £265 million a year to the local economy through salaries, contracts, visiting students and the hosting of major events. It is a major contributor to the research and development capacity of the region supporting local business and industry.

The course profile covers arts, business and management, engineering, information technology, life and health sciences and social sciences. Courses have a strong vocational element and the majority offer a period of industrial or professional placement. Annually more than 2,800 students undertake periods of placement in the public and private sectors throughout the UK and overseas.

Committed to social inclusion and widening access it is one of the most successful universities in the UK at attracting students with non-traditional backgrounds and qualifications. Nearly 40% of full-time undergraduate entrants are from the three lower social groups, compared to the UK average of 25%.

High standards in teaching and research have been repeatedly achieved. This is demonstrated by the last eleven teaching quality assessments receiving 'excellent' graded scores of 22 or higher and by the awarding of two 5*s together with many other high grades in the most recent Research Assessment Exercise.

Collaboration in exploiting knowledge and technology is promoted by the University's Office of Innovation and Enterprise (http://www.ulster.ac.uk/oie). The Office provides dedicated support to the business community seeking expertise and resources. UUTech Limited, a University-owned company, provides incubation support and consultancy for new spin-out companies in innovation centres and research parks across the campuses and facilitates the commercialisation of intellectual property for existing and new start-up companies.

**Senior Officers of the University**

President and Vice-Chancellor: Professor P G McKenna DL BSc PhD DSc LLD MRIA CBiol FIBiol FIBMS FRSA

Pro-Vice-Chancellor (Quality Assurance & Enhancement): Professor D McAlister BSc MSc DipHealthEcon

Pro-Vice-Chancellor (Research): Professor B Hannigan BA(Mod) PhD FIBMS

Pro-Vice-Chancellor (Student Support): Professor J M Allen BSc PhD CBiol FIBiol

Pro-Vice-Chancellor (Teaching and Learning): Professor R R Barnett BSc PhD

Provost (Jordanstown and Belfast campus): Professor W Clarke BSc MSc MCIM FCIM

Provost (Coleraine campus): Professor P Roebuck CBE BA PhD FRHistsS

Provost (Magee campus): Professor T Fraser MA PhD FRHistsS FRSA

Director of Development: Ms N E R Taggart BA

Director of Finance: Mr P Hope BA MBA FCA

Director of Human Resources: Mr R Magee BA PGDip MCIPD

Director of Information Services: Mr N Macartney BA MA DipLib CertEd

Director of Physical Resources: Mr P P G Donnelly DipQS MRICS MBIFM

Director of Planning and Governance Services: Ms I I Aston BSc

Director of Public Affairs: Mr B Kelleher BA DipEd

**Student Numbers**

Table 6.5 sets out total student population 2001/02 to 2003/04, whilst Table 6.6 shows Total Student Population by Faculty.

**Table 6.5: Student Population by Campus (UU)**

| | 2001/02 | 2002/03 | 2003/04 |
|---|---|---|---|
| **Jordanstown** | | | |
| Full-time | 7,798 | 8,328 | 8,584 |
| Part-time | 4,513 | 4,697 | 5,309 |
| Campus total | 12,311 | 13,025 | 13,893 |
| **Coleraine** | | | |
| Full-time | 3,919 | 4,144 | 4,223 |
| Part-time | 1,012 | 1,044 | 1,464 |
| Campus total | 4,931 | 5,188 | 5,687 |
| **Belfast** | | | |
| Full-time | 908 | 923 | 1,045 |
| Part-time | 146 | 181 | 168 |
| Campus total | 1,054 | 1,104 | 1,213 |
| **Magee** | | | |
| Full-time | 2,064 | 2,559 | 2,645 |
| Part-time | 860 | 836 | 806 |
| Campus total | 2,924 | 3,395 | 3,451 |
| **Total** | | | |
| Full-time | 14,689 | 15,954 | 16,497 |
| Part-time | 6,531 | 6,758 | 7,747 |
| **University Total** | **21,220** | **22,712** | **24,244** |

**Table 6.6: Total Student Population by Faculty (UU) 2003/04**

| Faculty | Full Time | Part Time | Total |
|---|---|---|---|
| Arts | 2,711 | 488 | 3,199 |
| Business & Management | 3,222 | 2,195 | 5,417 |
| Engineering | 4,219 | 813 | 5,032 |
| Life & Health Sciences | 3,951 | 2,740 | 6,691 |
| Social Sciences | 2,394 | 1,511 | 3,905 |
| **Total** | **16,497** | **7,747** | **24,244** |

Note figures include 1037 e-learning students

**Faculty and Departments**

*Faculty of Arts*
Academy for Irish Cultural Heritages, Cultural Development, Institute of Ulster Scots Studies, School of Art and Design, School of History and International Affairs, School of Languages and Literature, School of Media and Performing Arts, Research Graduate School

*Faculty of Business and Management*
Business Institute, Northern Ireland Centre For Entrepreneurship (Nicent), School of Accounting, School of Business Organisation and Management, School of Business, Retail and Financial Services, School of Hotel, Leisure and Tourism, School of International Business School of Marketing, Entrepreneurship and Strategy, Research Graduate School

*Faculty of Engineering*
School of the Built Environment, School of Computing and Information Engineering, School of Computing and Intelligent Systems, School of Computing and Mathematics, School of Electrical and Mechanical Engineering, Research Graduate School

*Faculty of Life and Health Sciences*
Faculty of Life and Health Sciences, Virtual School, Institute for Postgraduate Medicine and Primary Care, School of Applied Medical Sciences and Sports Studies, School of Biological and Environmental Sciences, School of Biomedical Sciences, School of Nursing, School of Psychology, School of Rehabilitation Sciences, Research Graduate School

*Faculty of Social Sciences*
Research Graduate School (Social Sciences), School of Communication, School of Economics and Politics, School of Education, School of Law School of Policy Studies, School of Sociology and Applied Social Studies, Research Graduate School

### The Open University

The Open University in Ireland
40 University Road
Belfast, BT7 1SU
Tel: 028 9024 5025
Fax: 028 9023 0565
Evening Advice: 0870 333 1444
Regional Director: Dr Rosemary Hamilton

The Open University is the UK's largest university, with over 200,000 full and part-time students. It is established throughout the UK and Ireland, and is ranked amongst the top UK universities for the quality of its teaching. Over 30% of students starting courses have qualifications below mainstream university requirements, but 70% of all students pass their courses each year. The majority of Open University students are part time, and although students can enter at the age of 18, two thirds are aged between 25 and 44.

## University Colleges

Northern Ireland has two major centres for teacher training, St Mary's College and Stranmillis College. Both are attached to Queen's University, Belfast.

### St Mary's University College

ST. MARY'S UNIVERSITY COLLEGE
A COLLEGE OF THE QUEEN'S UNIVERSITY OF BELFAST

191 Falls Road, Belfast, BT12 6FE
Tel: 028 9032 7678
Fax: 028 9033 3719
Web: www.stmarys-belfast.ac.uk
Principal: Very Rev Professor Martin O'Callaghan

**A Place with a mission**

Our purpose is to make a distinctive contribution, in the Catholic tradition, to higher education in Northern Ireland. St Mary's is an academic community committed to the search for meaning and value in the intellectual life, to academic excellence and to individual attention for our students.

We work for the development of the whole person in a Christian, values-sensitive environment in preparation for a lifetime of learning, leadership and service.

We want the college to be a religious, educational, cultural and social resource for the local community and to show concern for the world's poor and powerless.

*St Mary's University College*

We provide courses for the education of teachers (in English and in Irish) and courses in liberal arts. We offer students on these courses high quality learning, teaching and support.

We aim to increase access to higher education for students from every background.

We emphasize economic regeneration and social development as an important way of facilitating conflict resolution and peace in Ireland. In order to promote our vision we work with a wide range of partners including local communities, particularly those nearest the college in West and North Belfast.

We are committed to a rich international dimension in our teacher education and liberal arts courses.

The college has partnerships with forty Universities in Europe, the United States of America and South Africa. Over one thousand full-time students and three hundred part-time students attend St Mary's University College.

### Stranmillis University College

Stranmillis Road, Belfast, BT9 5DY
Tel: 028 9038 1271
Fax: 028 9066 4423
Web: www.stran.ac.uk
Principal: Professor Richard McMinn

Stranmillis College is a multi-professional institution engaged not only in undergraduate and postgraduate teacher education but also the provision of pre-service and in-service training. The college, which has an enrolment of around 700 full-time students, offers a range of consultancy services to Northern Ireland schools, Education and Library Boards and other education agencies.

## Further Education Sector

Northern Ireland has a network of 16 institutions of Further Education (with approximately 400 out centres) providing a range of courses of a technical or commercial nature as well as a wide range of general educational and recreational classes. Higher education courses have also been franchised from universities to colleges of further education. Part-time courses usually relate to employment and some apprentices are given day release to attend these courses. Colleges also provide courses of training for unemployed young people as part of the New Deal Programme. The Department for Employment and Learning directly funds further education colleges, whilst allowing institutions to become self-standing incorporated bodies. Details of Northern Ireland's Further Education Colleges are set out below:

### Armagh College of Further & Higher Education

College Hill, Armagh, BT617HN
Tel: 028 3752 2205
College Director: Paul Little
Web: www.armaghcollege.ac.uk

### Belfast Institute of Further & Higher Education

The Gerald Moag Campus
125-153 Millfield
Belfast, BT1 1HS
Tel: 028 9026 5000
Fax: 028 9026 5451
Email: information@belfastinstitute.ac.uk
Web: www.belfastinstitute.ac.uk

Director
Brian Turtle

Belfast Institute of Further and Higher Education is the largest educational establishment in Northern Ireland. With over 44,000 enrolments, it is one of the largest providers of further and higher education in these islands.

The Institute delivers university degree and equivalent courses to nearly 5,000 students. Courses include Higher National Certificates and Diplomas, degrees, post-graduate qualifications and a range of professional awards.

Almost 20,000 students attend our 1200 further education courses including National Vocational Qualifications, Advanced Vocational Certificates in Education, 'A' Levels and GCSEs, and a wide range of similar qualifications that can be matched to national award standards.

### Castlereagh College of Further & Higher Education

16 Montgomery Road
Belfast, BT6 9JD
Tel: 028 9079 7144
Fax: 028 9040 1820
Email: enquiry@castlereagh.ac.uk
Web: www.castlereagh.ac.uk

Principal and
Chief Executive
Muriel W. Shankey

Castlereagh College is a progressive and responsive college of Further and Higher Education offering a wide range of full and part-time programmes.
The College has an excellent reputation for academic success, quality education as well as the development and delivery of training programmes for businesses in Northern Ireland

### Causeway Institute of Further & Higher Education

Coleraine Road, Ballymoney, BT53 6BP
Tel: 028 2766 0401
Fax: 028 2766 4529
Web: www.causeway.ac.uk
College Director: Ian Williams

### East Antrim Institute of Further & Higher Education

400 Shore Road
Newtownabbey, BT37 9RS
Tel: 028 9085 5000
Fax: 028 9086 2076
Web: www.eaifhe.ac.uk
College Director: John Blayney

### East Down Institute of Further & Higher Education

Market Street, Downpatrick, BT30 6ND
Tel: 028 4461 5815
Fax: 028 4461 5817
Web: www.edifhe.ac.uk
College Director: Tom L Place

### East Tyrone College of Further & Higher Education

Circular Road, Dungannon, BT71 6BQ
Tel: 028 8772 2323
Fax: 028 8775 2018
Web: www.etcfhe.ac.uk
College Director: Tony Dardis

### Fermanagh College

1 Dublin Road, Enniskillen, BT74 6AE
Tel: 028 6632 2431
Fax: 028 6632 6357
Web: www.fermanaghcoll.ac.uk
College Director: Brian Rouse

### Limavady College of Further & Higher Education

Main Street, Limavady, BT49 0EX
Tel: 028 7776 2334
Fax: 028 7776 1018
Web: www.limavady.ac.uk
College Director: Dr Anne Heaslett

**Table 6.7: Further Education Colleges - Enrolments**

| | 1990/91 | 1996/97 | 2001/02 |
|---|---|---|---|
| All Vocational Students | | | |
| - Full-time | 18,065 | 25,033 | 25,163 |
| - Part-time | 53,356 | 60,069 | 67,253 |
| Students on non-vocational courses | 53,505 | 59,087 | N/A |

Source: Department of Education

### Lisburn Institute of Further & Higher Education

Castle Street, Lisburn, BT27 4SU
Tel: 028 9267 7225
Fax: 028 9267 7291
Web: www.liscol.ac.uk
College Director: Alister J McReynolds

### Newry & Kilkeel Institute of Further & Higher Education

Patrick Street, Newry, BT35 8DN
Tel: 028 3026 1071
Fax: 028 3025 9679
Web: www.nkifhe.ac.uk
College Director: Raymond J Mullan

### North Down & Ards Institute of Further & Higher Education

Castle Park Road, Bangor, BT20 4TF
Tel: 028 9127 6600
Fax: 028 9127 6601
Web: www.ndai.ac.uk
College Director: Brian Henry

### North East Institute of Further & Higher Education

Magherafelt Site
22 Moneymore Road
Magherafelt, BT45 6AE
Tel: 028 7963 2462
Fax: 028 7963 3501
Web: www.nei.ac.uk
College Director: Mr Trevor Neillands

### North West Institute of Further & Higher Education

Strand Road, Londonderry, BT48 7AL
Tel: 028 7126 6711
Fax: 028 7126 0520
Web: www.nwifhe.ac.uk
College Director: Seamus Murphy

### Omagh College of Further Education

2 Mountjoy Road, Omagh, BT79 7AH
Tel: 028 8224 5433
Fax: 028 8224 1440
Web: www.omagh.ac.uk
College Director: Victor Refaussé

### Upper Bann College of Further & Higher Education

Lurgan Road, Portadown, BT63 5BL
Tel: 028 3839 7777
Fax: 028 3839 7751
Web: www.ubifhe.ac.uk
College Director: Jim Crooks

## Other Colleges

### College of Agriculture, Food and Rural Enterprise (CAFRE)

**Greenmount Campus**
22 Greenmount Road, Antrim, BT41 4PU
Tel: 028 9442 6601
Fax: 028 9442 6606
Email: enquiries@dardni.gov.uk
College Director: John Fay

**Enniskillen Campus**
Levaghy, Enniskillen, BT74 4GF
Tel: 028 6634 4853
Fax: 028 6634 4888
Principal: Seamus McAlinney

**Loughry College**
Cookstown, Co Tyrone, BT80 9AA
Tel: 0800 216139 (Freephone)
Fax: 028 8676 1043
Web: www.loughry.ac.uk
College Director: John Fay

## Further and Higher Education Organisations

### The Association of Northern Ireland Colleges

Unit 3 The Sidings Office Park
Antrim Road
Lisburn, BT28 3AJ
Tel: 028 9262 7512
Fax: 028 9262 7594
Email: info@anic.ac.uk
Web: www.femeansbusiness.com

Chief Executive
John D'Arcy

The Association of Northern Ireland Colleges (ANIC) represents the 16 colleges of further and higher education in Northern Ireland and is the central point of contact for FE and lifelong learning issues in Northern Ireland.

ANIC was set up in 1998 to represent the newly independent F&HE Colleges and provides information about the role and activities of the FE sector in supporting learning, training and economic development in Northern Ireland.

### Department for Employment and Learning (DEL)

The Department for Employment and Learning is responsible for the policy, strategic development and financing of the statutory Further Education sector with advice from the Learning and Skills Advisory Board. DEL is also responsible for curriculum and qualification below degree level, with a key focus on the development of adult literacy.

**Higher Education**

Higher Education Branch is responsible for the formulation, development and oversight of the implementation of higher education policy in accordance with Northern Ireland needs (taking account of developments in the rest of the United kingdom) and for the funding of two universities (Queen's University Belfast and the University of Ulster) and the two university colleges (Stranmillis University College and St Mary's University College). The main functions of the branch are:

- to promote high standards of teaching;
- to promote high standards of research and encourage enterprise and innovation;
- to promote and support productive interaction between higher education and industry and commerce and encourage the transfer of knowledge;
- to encourage increased access, support lifelong learning, and maximise achievement for all who can benefit from higher education;
- to fund the universities and teacher training colleges and promote the effective financial management, accountability and value for money of public funds in the higher education sector;
- to formulate higher education policy in Northern Ireland and provide advice to Ministers and officials.

**Further Education**

The Further Education Division of DEL is responsible for the policy, strategic development and financing of the statutory Further Education Sector with advice from the Learning and Skills Advisory Board. It also provides support to a small number of non-statutory further education providers. The Division is also responsible for curriculum and qualification below degree level, with a key focus on the development of adult literacy.

Further Education is defined in legislation as full-time and part-time education (other than Higher Education) for persons over compulsory school age. Key strategic objectives set out for the sector are:

- to support regional economic development and, in particular, to provide the skills necessary for the knowledge-based economy;
- to increase participation and widen access to those previously under-represented in the sector; and,
- to improve the quality of provision and enhance standards of performance.

The Department of Education's Education and Training Inspectorate provides for inspections of FE colleges in relation to the quality of teaching and learning.

The Further Education Division also provides support to and has formal compacts with a small number of non-statutory further education bodies.

- Workers' Education Association (WEA) - provides a range of adult education opportunities throughout Northern Ireland;
- Educational Guidance Service for Adults (EGSA) - provides adults with an independent source of advice and guidance on accessing learning opportunities;
- Ulster People's College provides community and personal development programmes.

**Lifelong Learning**

Lifelong Learning Division is responsible for the policy, strategic development and financing of the statutory further education sector as well as supporting a small number of non-statutory further education bodies.

Student Support is divided into two sections with students wishing to undertake either undergraduate or postgraduate study.

**Essential Skills**

The Essential Skills for Living Strategy marks a radical new approach to literacy and numeracy in Northern Ireland. The Strategy plans the introduction of a regional curriculum, accreditation for adult learners and improved tutor qualifications. It sets targets for building capacity, engaging new learners and suggests ways in which these might be achieved.

**Qualifications and National Occupational Standards**

The Department collaborates with the other administrations and their respective Regulatory Authorities throughout the UK to support the development of National Occupational Standards as the basis for high quality vocational qualifications and to ensure the establishment of a coherent and well-regulated framework of national qualifications. The Council for the Curriculum, Examinations and Assessment (CCEA) is the main regulatory authority for qualifications in Northern Ireland, however the regulation of National Vocational Qualifications (NVQs) falls within the remit of the Qualifications and Curriculum Authority (QCA).

Learning and Skills Development Agency Northern Ireland

Unit 202
20 Adelaide Street
Belfast, BT2 8GB
Tel: 028 9051 7014
Fax: 028 9051 7164
Director: Trevor Carson

The Learning and Skills Development Agency (LSDA) was created in 2003 to create a strategic national resource, supporting the development of policy and assisting in its implementation, across all further education providers in Northern Ireland. The agency has prioritised widening and increasing participation, enhancing quality, making further education relevant to industry and the 16-19 curriculum on its agenda for effecting change to the further education sector.

## Library Service

The five Education and Library Boards provide library services in Northern Ireland, under the auspices of the Department of Education. As well as fixed libraries in main population centres, library provision includes mobile library services to homes, hospitals and schools. A list of the main public libraries is set out below.

### Public Libraries

Andersonstown Library
Slievegallion Drive
Belfast, BT11 8JP
Tel: 028 9050 9200

Antrim Library
41 Church Street
Antrim, BT41 4BE
Tel: 028 9446 1942

Ardoyne Library
446-450 Crumlin Road
Belfast, BT14 7GH
Tel: 028 9050 9202

Armagh City Library
Market Street
Armagh, BT61 7BU
Tel: 028 3752 4072

Armagh Public Library
43 Abbey Street
Armagh, BT61 7DY
Tel: 028 3752 3142

Ballee Library
2 Neighbourhood Centre
Ballee Drive
Ballymena, BT42 2SX
Tel: 028 2564 5761

Ballycastle Library
5 Leyland Road
Ballycastle, BT54 6DP
Tel: 028 2076 2566

Ballyclare Library
School Street
Ballyclare, BT39 9BE
Tel: 028 9335 2269

Ballyhackamore Library
1 Eastleigh Drive
Ballyhackamore
Belfast, BT4 3DX
Tel: 028 9050 9204

Ballymacarrett Library
19-35 Templemore Avenue
Belfast, BT5 4FP
Tel: 028 9050 9207

Ballymena Library
5 Pat's Brea
Ballymena, BT43 5AX
Tel: 028 2563 3950

Ballymoney Library
Rodden Foot, Queen Street
Ballymoney, BT53 6JB
Tel: 028 2766 3589

Ballynahinch Library
Main Street
Ballynahinch, BT24 8DN
Tel: 028 9756 6442

Banbridge Library
Scarva Street
Banbridge, BT32 3AD
Tel: 028 4062 3973

Bangor Branch Library
80 Hamilton Road
Bangor, BT20 4LH
Tel: 028 9127 0591

Bellaghy Library
20 Castle Street
Bellaghy, BT45 8LA
Tel: 028 7938 6627

Belvoir Park Library
Drumart Square
Belfast, BT8 7EY
Tel: 028 9064 4331

Bessbrook Library
12 Church Road
Bessbrook, BT35 7AQ
Tel: 028 3083 0424

Braniel Library
Glen Road
Castlereagh, BT5 7JH
Tel: 028 9079 7420

Broughshane Library
Main Street
Broughshane, BT42 4JW
Tel: 028 2586 1613

Brownlow Library
Brownlow Road, Brownlow
Craigavon, BT65 5DP
Tel: 028 3834 1946

Bushmills Library
44 Main Street
Bushmills, BT57 8QA
Tel: 028 2073 1424

Carnlough Library
Town Hall, Harbour Road
Carnlough, BT44 0EQ
Tel: 028 2888 5552

Carrickfergus Library
2 Joymount Court
Carrickfergus, BT38 7DN
Tel: 028 9336 2261

Carryduff Library
Church Road
Carryduff, BT8 8DT
Tel: 028 9081 3568

Castlederg Library
1A Hospital Road
Castlederg, BT81 7BU
Tel: 028 8167 1419

Castlerock Library
6 Sea Road, Castlerock
Tel: 028 7084 8463

Castlewellan Library
Main Street
Castlewellan, BT31 9DA
Tel: 028 4377 8433

Central Library
Royal Avenue
Belfast, BT1 1EA
Tel: 028 9050 9150

Chichester Library
Salisbury Avenue
Belfast, BT15 5EB
Tel: 028 9050 9210

Cloughfern Library
2a Kings Crescent
Newtownabbey, BT37 0DH
Tel: 028 9085 4789

Coalisland Library
The Cornmill, Lineside
Coalisland, BT71 4LT
Tel: 028 8774 0569

Coleraine Library
Queen Street
Coleraine, BT52 1BE
Tel: 028 7034 2561

Colin Glen Library
Colin Glen Centre
Stewartstown Road
Dunmurry
Belfast, BT17 0AW
Tel: 028 9043 1266

Comber Library
5 Newtownards Road Comber,
BT23 5AU
Tel: 028 9187 2610

Cookstown Library
Burn Road
Cookstown, BT80 8DJ
Tel: 028 8676 3702

Craigavon Divisional Library
24-26 Church Street
Portadown, BT62 3LQ
Tel: 028 3833 6122

Cregagh Library
409-413 Cregagh Road
Belfast, BT6 0LF
Tel: 028 9040 1365

Creggan Library
Central Drive
Londonderry, BT48 9QH
Tel: 028 7126 6168

Crossmaglen Library
The Square
Crossmaglen, BT35 9AA
Tel: 028 3086 1951

Crumlin Library
Orchard Road
Crumlin, BT29 4SD
Tel: 028 9442 3066

Cullybackey Branch Library
153 Tobar Park
Cullybackey, BT42 1NW
Tel: 028 2588 1878

Cushendall Library
Mill Street
Cushendall, BT44 0RR
Tel: 028 2177 1297

Derry Central Library
35 Foyle Street
Londonderry, BT48 6AL
Tel: 028 7127 2300

Donaghadee Library
Killaughey Road
Donaghadee, BT21 0BL
Tel: 028 9188 2507

Downpatrick Library
79 Market Street
Downpatrick, BT30 6LZ
Tel: 028 4461 2895

Draperstown Library
The Square, High Street
Draperstown, BT45 7AD
Tel: 028 7962 8249

Dromore Library
Town Hall, Market Square
Dromore, BT25 1AW
Tel: 028 9269 2280

Dundonald Library
16 Church Road, Dundonald
Belfast, BT16 2LN
Tel: 028 9048 3994

Dungannon Library
Market Square
Dungannon, BT70 1JD
Tel: 028 8772 2952

Dungiven Library
74 Main Street
Dungiven, BT47 4LD
Tel: 028 7774 1475

Dunmurry Library
Upper Dunmurry Lane
Dunmurry, BT17 0AA
Tel: 028 9062 3007

Enniskillen Library
Halls Lane
Enniskillen, BT74 7DR
Tel: 028 6632 2886

Falls Road Library
49 Falls Road
Belfast, BT12 4PD
Tel: 028 9050 9212

Finaghy Library
13 Finaghy Road South
Belfast, BT10 0BW
Tel: 028 9050 9214

Fintona Library
112 Main Street
Fintona, BT78 2AE
Tel: 028 8284 1774

Fivemiletown Library
Main Street
Fivemiletown, BT75 0PG
Tel: 028 8952 1409

Garvagh Library
Bridge Street
Garvagh, BT51 5AF
Tel: 028 2955 8500

Gilford Library
Main Street
Gilford, BT63 6HY
Tel: 028 3883 1770

Gilnahirk Library
Gilnahirk Rise
Belfast, BT5 7DT
Tel: 028 9079 6573

Glengormley Library
40 Carnmoney Road
Glengormley, BT36 6HP
Tel: 028 9083 3797

Greenisland Library
17 Glassillan Grove
Greenisland, BT38 8TE
Tel: 028 9086 5419

Greystone Library
Greystone Road
Antrim, BT41 1JW
Tel: 028 9446 3891

Holywood Arches Library
4 Holywood Road
Belfast, BT4 1NT
Tel: 028 9050 9216

Holywood Library
86-88 High Street
Holywood, BT18 9AE
Tel: 028 9042 4232

Irvinestown Library
Main Street
Irvinestown, BT94 1GL
Tel: 028 6862 1383

Keady Library
1 Bridge Street
Keady, BT60 3SY
Tel: 028 3753 1365

Kilkeel Library
49 Greencastle Street
Kilkeel, BT34 4BH
Tel: 028 4176 2278

Killyleagh Library
High Street
Killyleagh, BT30 9QF
Tel: 028 4482 8407

Kilrea Library
27 The Diamond
Kilrea, BT51 5QJ
Tel: 028 2954 0630

Larne Library
36 Pound Street
Larne, BT40 1SQ
Tel: 028 2827 7047

Laurelhill Community Library
22 Laurelhill Road
Lisburn, BT28 2UH
Tel: 028 9266 4596

Ligoniel Library
53-55 Ligoniel Road
Belfast, BT14 8BW
Tel: 028 9050 9221

Limavady Library
5 Connell Street
Limavady, BT49 0EA
Tel: 028 7776 2540

Linenhall Library
17 Donegall Square North
Belfast, BT1 5GB
Tel: 028 9032 1707

Lisburn Library
29 Railway Street
Lisburn, BT28 1XP
Tel: 028 9260 1749

Lisburn Road Library
440 Lisburn Road
Belfast, BT9 6GR
Tel: 028 9050 9223

Lisnaskea Library
Drumhaw
Lisnaskea, BT92 0GT
Tel: 028 6772 1222

Lurgan Library
Carnegie Street
Lurgan, BT66 6AS
Tel: 028 3832 3912

Maghera Library
1 Church Street
Maghera, BT46 5EA
Tel: 028 7964 2578

Magherafelt Library
The Bridewell
6 Church Street
Magherafelt, BT45 6AN
Tel: 028 7963 2278

Moira Library
Backwood Road
Moira, BT67 0LJ
Tel: 028 9261 9330

Moneymore Library
8 Main Street
Moneymore, BT45 7PD
Tel: 028 8674 8380

Monkstown Library
Bridge Road
Monkstown, BT37 0EG
Tel: 028 9085 3138

Moy Library
The Square, Moy, BT71 7SG
Tel: 028 8778 4661

Newcastle Library
141/143 Main Street
Newcastle, BT33 0AE
Tel: 028 4372 2710

Newry Public Library
79 Hill Street
Newry, BT34 1DG
Tel: 028 3026 4683

Newtownards Library
Regent Street
Newtownards, BT23 4AB
Tel: 028 9181 4732

Newtownbreda Library
Saintfield Road
Belfast, BT8 4HL
Tel: 028 9070 1620

Newtownstewart Library
2 Main Street
Newtownstewart, BT78 4AA
Tel: 028 8166 1245

O'Fiaich Memorial & Archive
15 Moy Road
Armagh, BT61 7LY
Tel: 028 3752 2981

Oldpark Library
46 Oldpark Road
Belfast, BT14 6FS
Tel: 028 9050 9226

Omagh Library
1 Spillars Place
Omagh, BT78 1HL
Tel: 028 8224 4821

Ormeau Library
247 Ormeau Road
Belfast, BT7 3GG
Tel: 028 9050 9228

Poleglass Library
14 Good Shepherd Road
Belfast, BT19 0LD
Tel: 028 9062 9740

Portadown Library
24-26 Church Street
Portadown, BT62 3LQ
Tel: 028 3833 6122

Portaferry Library
47 High Street
Portaferry, BT22 1QT
Tel: 028 4272 8194

Portglenone Library
19 Townhill Road,
Portglenone, BT44 8AD
Tel: 028 2582 2228

Portstewart Library
Town Hall, The Crescent
Portstewart, BT55 7AB
Tel: 028 7083 2712

Randalstown Library
34 New Street
Randalstown, BT41 3AF
Tel: 028 9447 2725

Rathcoole Library
2 Rosslea Way, Rathcoole
Newtownabbey, BT37 9BJ
Tel: 028 9085 1157

Rathfriland Library
John Street
Rathfriland, BT34 5QH
Tel: 028 4063 0661

Richhill Branch Library
1 Maynooth Road
Richhill, BT61 9PE
Tel: 028 3887 0639

Saintfield Library
17 Fairview
Saintfield, BT24 7AD
Tel: 028 9751 0550

Sandy Row Branch Library
127A Sandy Row
Belfast, BT12 5ET
Tel: 028 9050 9230

Shankill Road Library
298 Shankill Road
Belfast, BT13 2BN
Tel: 028 9050 9232

Shantallow Library
92 Racecourse Road
Londonderry, BT48 8DA
Tel: 028 7135 4185

Sion Mills Library
Church Square
Sion Mills, BT82 9HD
Tel: 028 8165 8513

Skegoneill Library
Skegoneill Avenue
Belfast, BT15 3JN
Tel: 028 9050 9244

Strabane Library
1 Railway Road
Strabane, BT82 8AN
Tel: 028 7188 3686

Strathfoyle Library
22 Temple Road, Strathfoyle
Londonderry, BT47 6TJ
Tel: 028 7186 0385

Suffolk Library
57 Stewartstown Road
Belfast, BT11 9JP
Tel: 028 9050 9234

Tandragee Library
Market Street
Tandragee, BT62 2BP
Tel: 028 3884 0694

Templepatrick Library
23 The Village
Templepatrick, BT39 0AA
Tel: 028 9443 2953

Tullycarnet Library
Kinross Avenue
Belfast, BT5 7GF
Tel: 028 9048 5079

Waringstown Library
47 Main Street
Waringstown, BT66 7QH
Tel: 028 3888 1077

Warrenpoint Library
Summer Hill
Warrenpoint, BT34 3JB
Tel: 028 4175 3375

Waterside Library
The Workhouse
23 Glendermott Road
Londonderry, BT47 6BG
Tel: 028 7134 2963

Whitehead Library
17B Edward Road
Whitehead, BT38 9RU
Tel: 028 9335 3249

Whiterock Library
195 Whiterock Road
Belfast, BT12 7FW
Tel: 028 9050 9236

Whitewell Library
Ballygolan Primary School
Serpentine Road, Belfast
Tel: 028 9050 9242

Woodstock Library
358 Woodstock Road
Belfast, BT6 9DQ
Tel: 028 9050 9239

## Key Issues Facing Northern Ireland Education

This section of the Yearbook addresses five of the key issues facing the education sector in Northern Ireland:

- Integrated education and religion;
- Selection procedure - Post Primary Review Team;
- Pupil Teacher Ratios;
- Investment in Education;
- Student finance/University fees

### Integrated Education and Religion

Many commentators agree that Northern Ireland's most fundamental problem is that of sectarian division between Protestants and Catholics. Despite the fact that the divisions date back for centuries, prejudices are passed from generation to generation and preserved by the fact that the two communities are segregated in many areas of everyday life, including education. There is a growing belief that integrated education could be a major contributor to breaking the cycle of prejudice.

The establishment of a set of schools designed specifically to facilitate the education of pupils from Roman Catholic and Protestant backgrounds side by side has been one of the major developments in Northern Ireland education over the last twenty years. There has been steady growth in integrated education during this period.

The first planned integrated school, Lagan College, opened in 1981, the second in 1985, and by 1995, this new sector had grown to have a total enrolment of 5,816 pupils. In the last five years this number has risen to 15,770 pupils, 4.6 per cent of the total primary/post-primary enrolment in Northern Ireland. Table 6.9 lists all of the major existing schools and shows how numbers have grown steadily.

Integrated education is popular, but it is not yet available everywhere due to financial and logistical difficulties, particularly in getting new schools established. It may therefore be some time before the sector realises its full potential. In 2000/01 some 1140 applications for places in integrated education had to be turned away due to lack of places.

**Table 6.8 Integrated Schools in Northern Ireland**

| Opened | Location | Enrolment | School/College |
|---|---|---|---|
| 1981 | Belfast | 1020 | Lagan College |
| 1985 | Belfast | 212 | Forge CIPS |
| 1985 | Belfast | 721 | Hazelwood College |
| 1985 | Belfast | 456 | Hazelwood IPS |
| 1986 | Newcastle | 211 | All Children's CIPS |
| 1987 | Banbridge | 411 | Bridge IPS |
| 1987 | Portrush | 184 | Mill Strand IPS |
| 1988 | Dungannon | 217 | Windmill IPS |
| 1989 | Ballymena | 335 | Braidside IPS |
| 1989 | Enniskillen | 235 | Enniskillen IPS |
| 1990 | Omagh | 239 | Omagh IPS |
| 1990 | Portadown | 223 | Portadown IPS |
| 1991 | Craigavon | 410 | Brownlow CIC |
| 1991 | Garvagh | 41 | Carhill CIPS |
| 1991 | Larne | 199 | Corran IPS |
| 1991 | Derry | 460 | Oakgrove IPS |
| 1992 | Carrickfergus | 229 | Acorn IPS |
| 1992 | Derry | 852 | Oakgrove IC |
| 1993 | Belfast | 211 | Cranmore IPS |
| 1993 | Belfast | 348 | Loughview IPS |
| 1993 | Armagh | 240 | Saints & Scholars IPS |
| 1994 | Enniskillen | 341 | Erne IC |
| 1994 | Newcastle | 500 | Shimna IC |
| 1995 | Dungannon | 489 | IC Dungannon |
| 1995 | Crossgar | 213 | Cedar IPS |
| 1995 | Omagh | 563 | Drumragh IC |
| 1995 | Loughbrickland | 488 | New-Bridge IC |
| 1995 | Portaferry | 84 | Portaferry CIPS |
| 1996 | Lambeg | 69 | Hilden CIPS |
| 1996 | Coleraine | 527 | North Coast IC |
| 1996 | Derriaghy | 206 | Oakwood IPS |
| 1996 | Antrim | 111 | Rathenraw CIPS |
| 1996 | Ballymena | 677 | Slemish IC |
| 1997 | Castlewellan | 42 | Annsborough CIPS |
| 1997 | Whitehead | 500 | Ulidia IC |
| 1997 | Carrowdore | 466 | Strangford |
| 1997 | Belfast | 799 | Malone IC |
| 1998 | Bangor | 498 | Bangor Central CIPS |
| 1998 | Kircubbin | 126 | Kircubbin CIPS |
| 1998 | Rostrevor | 88 | Kilbroney CIPS |
| 1998 | Holywood | 446 | Priory CIC |
| 1998 | Downpatrick | 304 | Down Academy CIC |
| 1998 | Lisburn | 891 | Forthill CIC |
| 1999 | Magherafelt | 163 | Spires IPS |
| 2000 | Saintfield | 97 | Millennium IPS |
| 2001 | Carlough | 27 | Carnlough CIP |
| 2002 | Magherafelt | 115 | Sperrin IC |
| 2003 | Glengormley | 185 | Glengormley CIPS |
| 2003 | Maine | 17 | Maine IPS |
| 2003 | Antrim | 136 | Round Tower CIPS |
| 2004 | Armagh | 50 | Armagh IC |
| 2004 | Holywood | 172 | Glencraig CIPS |
| 2004 | Groomsport | 21 | Gloomsport CIPS |
| 2004 | Ballynahinch | 12 | Drumlins IPS |
| 2004 | Ballycastle | 18 | Lir IP |
| 2004 | Cookstown | 17 | Phoenix IPS |
| 2004 | Limavady | 25 | Roe Valley IPS |

## Selection Procedure: Post Primary Review

The process of selection (currently the 11-plus examination) is at the heart of the Northern Ireland education system. Essentially it is the case that all children are placed in either Grammar or Secondary schools based on a test taken during their seventh year at school, when they are ten or eleven years of age. It is widely accepted that this placement, coupled with the educational provision available thereafter, fundamentally affects each child's future prospects and the nature of society as a whole. In September 2000, following a major, wide ranging study, the report titled 'The Effects of the Selective System of Secondary Education in Northern Ireland' was published. It looked at the current system and considered possible alternatives.

**Five main models came to the fore:**

- A system of delayed selection, perhaps at age 14 (a number of pupils in the Craigavon region already participate in this system under the Dickson Plan for secondary education);
- A system of all-through comprehensive schools, like that currently in operation in Scotland;
- A system using common primary and lower secondary schools, followed by differentiated upper secondary schools, as currently operated in France, Italy and other European countries;
- A system of differentiated post-primary schools with distinctive academic and vocational/technical routes;
- The status quo: selection at 11 years and a system of grammar and secondary schools.

## The Current System

Significant strengths in the current selective system in Northern Ireland were identified including:

- The high academic standards achieved in grammar schools;
- The supportive environment provided in secondary schools for pupils who may not succeed in grammar schools;
- Secondary schools tend to draw their enrolment from more localised areas, possibly providing opportunities to strengthen the links between local communities and these schools.

Significant weaknesses in the current selective system in Northern Ireland were identified including:

- The perception that testing is unfair and places undue pressure on young children; this concern is shared by teachers, parents and society more generally;
- Primary teachers in some cases feel obliged to focus curricular attention narrowly on the requirements of the selection test, partly to assist each child in achieving their highest score and also because they feel they are judged in the public mind on the basis of their school's overall transfer test performance;

- Rather than simply identifying all the children suited to grammar schooling the testing procedure enables the grammar schools to admit only the pupils with high scores, possibly leaving many children, who have academic ability behind. Secondary schools, who then cater for the 'failures' are in turn accorded a lesser status than grammar schools in the eyes of most people. Teachers in secondary schools argue that they have to rebuild the self-confidence and esteem of many pupils who arrive in their schools with a sense of failure;
- In spite of the grading system which is designed so as not to label children as having passed or failed, this is still how results are generally interpreted;
- Increasingly parents feel obliged to pay for out-of-school coaching, and not all parents can afford to do so.

## Success and Failure

With regard to the current system, the report concluded that the most important factor for a pupil achieving a high GCSE score is achieving a place in a grammar school.

The original purpose of the transfer test procedure was to identify pupils, from any background, not just those most financially advantaged, deemed able to cope with the academic curriculum provided in grammar schools. However, the current performance patterns may imply that a higher proportion of pupils should have the opportunity to experience a grammar school education or equivalent. Interviews with pupils in both grammar and secondary schools indicated a strong difference in aspirations. The vast majority of those in grammar were planning to enter higher education whereas only a minority of those in secondary schools aspired to do so.

Table 6.9 shows how Northern Ireland compares with Scotland and England/Wales in terms of the spread of exam performance. Proportionately Northern Ireland has more high and low achieving schools, whereas the distribution in England/Wales and, even more so, Scotland shows a more even spread.

**Table 6.9: Examination Performance Comparison Across the UK (Percentage of Schools)**

| 5+ GCSE grades (A*-C or equivalent) | Northern Ireland | England/Wales | Scotland |
|---|---|---|---|
| 0 to 20% of pupils | 17 | 11 | 3 |
| 21 to 40% of pupils | 37 | 43 | 12 |
| 41 to 60% of pupils | 13 | 31 | 38 |
| 61 to 80% of pupils | 3 | 13 | 34 |
| 81 to 100% of pupils | 31 | 3 | 14 |
| Total | 100 | 100 | 100 |

On the government's behalf the Independent Review Body on Post-Primary Education produced a major report called 'Education for the 21st Century'. The Review Body, chaired by Gerry Burns, made four key recommendations, which, if implemented, could mean fundamental reorganisation of Northern Ireland's educational system.
They were:

- Abolition of the transfer test (the 11 plus);
- The ending of selection on academic grounds;
- The development of a 'Pupil Profile' assessment system;
- The creation of a 'collegiate system' of schools across Northern Ireland.

The Burns report called the 11 plus 'divisive' and argued that the exam leads to inequality of opportunity.

## Response to the Post Primary Review Group Recommendations

The Review Group report (commonly referred to as the Burns report) published in October 2001 stirred a major debate including all of the interested players from political parties through all kinds of educational organisations, churches, business groups and trade unions. A major consultative exercise was completed in September 2002.

The consultative exercise was unprecedented in scale (proposals communicated to every household in Northern Ireland) and yielded over 1300 written responses, including over 500 from schools and 200,000 completed household response forms.

The Northern Ireland Assembly and the Education Committee divided along traditional lines on the issue with the nationalist parties broadly in support of the Burns proposals and unionist parties generally opposed. Overall there was overwhelming support for the objectives of the Burns Report and general acceptance that the 11+ transfer test should be abolished. However, some of the support for abolition was conditional on a suitable alternative means of academic selection being found.

The many educational interests were divided on the broader principle of academic selection. Although there was support from all five Education and Library Boards, two-thirds of schools, CCMS and NICIE, there was opposition from the Governing Bodies Association, voluntary grammar schools and two-thirds of household respondents.

There was broad support for the concept of pupil profiles but uncertainty about the extent to which it would be used for admission purposes. There was widespread opposition to the system of collegiates as proposed in the Burns Report although there was support for greater collaboration and networking between schools.

In April 2003 a further Working Group was formed, under the chairmanship of Steve Costello, with the aim to take forward the responses to the consultation on the Burns Report. The details of the report of the consultation group (the Costello Report) were made public in January 2004 and indicated that the 11+ test would not remain beyond 2008, and that any selection on the basis of academic ability would not be allowed from then on. The report did not provide the detailed alternative to academic selection at age 11 but suggested that schools may be able to look at factors such as family connections and limited geography in deciding which pupils to admit. Much of the process will depend on enabling parents to arrive at an 'informed choice' based on pupil profiles. The detailed design of a future scheme has yet to be finalised.

## Pupil-Teacher Ratios

Pupil/teacher ratio is an issue close to the hearts of parents and teachers. Parents value lower class sizes. Governments are always keen to show how they have succeeded in reducing the pupil-teacher ratios.

Unfortunately, the ratio figures can be quite misleading. The following table indicates that the ratio in primary schools is about twenty pupils to each teacher. However to reach this figure all teachers will have been included, many of whom have no class duties. 'Floating teachers' such as many principals, vice-principals, supply teachers, reading recovery and special needs teachers give the impression of lower ratios than may often actually be the case.

**Table 6.10 Pupil Teacher Ratios**

| | Ratio 2001/02 | Ratio 2002/03 | Ratio 2003/04 |
|---|---|---|---|
| Nursery | 24.4 | 24.1 | 25.2 |
| Primary | 19.9 | 19.7 | 20.0 |
| Secondary | 13.8 | 13.8 | 14.1 |
| Grammar | 15.3 | 17.2 | 15.2 |
| Special | 5.9 | 6.0 | 5.9 |
| **All Schools** | **16.5** | **16.4** | **16.6** |

Source: NISRA

The reality in the classroom is usually higher, and in some cases significantly higher, than indicated in the table. Nonetheless parents who look around may be surprised to find relatively low pupil-teacher ratios in certain schools or subjects as there can be considerable class-to-class variation against average ratios. However overall, Northern Ireland enjoys pupil-teacher ratios which are significantly below the UK average in both primary and secondary education.

## Investment in Education

There is a general consensus that for many years education in Northern Ireland (and perhaps in the UK as a whole) had been an area of under-investment. The Northern Ireland Executive prioritised this area, and planned capital expenditure in 2002/2003 was £108.9 million. However, it is accepted that even these substantial sums will not bring Northern Ireland's ageing educational infrastructure up to modern standards. The problem is particularly acute in terms of outdated school buildings, many in a poor state of repair. A high percentage of Northern Ireland's classrooms are temporary or mobile buildings.

As in other sectors, one possible solution to the infrastructural deficit is PFI, or as it is now known, PPP (Public-Private Partnerships), whereby private sector capital can create the necessary infrastructure and effectively lease it to the Department or Education and Library Board as the client. This approach has both supporters and opponents.

Those in favour of PPP argue that it is the only way of ensuring that necessary investment actually happens and all the construction and operational risks pass to the private sector developer or facilities manager.

Opponents contend that the process is complex and unwieldy, and that in order to give the private sector a good return on their investment, it *must* cost the taxpayer more in the long term. The Treasury has developed public sector comparators which allow the public sector client to judge to some extent how the PPP proposition looks in terms of overall value against the alternative approach.

Nonetheless, while the debate continues, Northern Ireland's educational authorities have been steadily adopting the PPP approach to a number of key projects including:

- Rebuilding of the main campus for Belfast Institute of Further & Higher Education (capital approximately £40 million);
- Secondary schools: Balmoral High School, Wellington College, Drumglass, St Genevieve's.

However, even with this PPP activity Northern Ireland's educational estate will require sustained investment in buildings and equipment in coming years. It is possible that much of the 'catching up' that is essential can be achieved under the Reinvestment and Reform Initiative (RRI) which allows the Northern Ireland government to borrow considerable low cost funds for infrastructural development.

## Student Finance

The funding of third level education has become a major issue across the UK. A new Higher Education Bill is to be introduced which will see the introduction of 'top-up' fees for university places. Top-up fees, or differential fees, would enable, by law, universities to set their own level of tuition fees. At present universities charge £1,150 a year to undergraduates, a rate set by government. The new proposals would mean that universities could charge nearer the real cost of studying, which is estimated to be around an average figure of £5,000 in the UK. However, depending on the institution, department and course, it could be higher than this. To meet these higher fee levels the government would make more loans available to help students pay fees up front.

Most universities are in favour of top-up fees as they claim that they are seriously under-funded. In Northern Ireland Queen's University Belfast is in favour of top-up fees and the University of Ulster against their introduction.

Funding of third level education was an issue for the first Northern Ireland Assembly. The then Minster for Employment and Learning Dr Sean Farren announced a £65 million student finance package, which included the restoration of means-tested grants, the application of some fee exemptions and the establishment of a further 1,000 new university places.

Whatever the outcome of the top-up fees controversy students are increasingly having to work during their education in order to fund their studies. Statistics suggest that in Britain around 80 per cent of students are working part-time. On average a student in Northern Ireland works 17.7 hours per week in addition to studying full-time.

# Delivery of Northern Ireland's Education Service

## Department of Education

The education system in Northern Ireland is administered by the Department of Education (NI), one of the ten departments devolved under the new arrangements for the government of Northern Ireland.

The Department's stated aim and objective is:

'To provide for the education and development of all our young people to the highest possible standards, with equal access for all.'

**Contact:**
Rathgael House
Balloo Road, Bangor, BT19 7PR
Tel: 028 9127 9279 / Fax: 028 9127 9100
Email: deni@nics.gov.uk
Web: www.deni.gov.uk

Statistics and Research Branch
Rathgael House
Balloo Road, Bangor, BT19 7PR
Tel: 028 9127 9311 / Fax: 028 9127 9594
Email: nicola.wilson@deni.gov.uk

Contact: Nicola Wilson

Further detailed information about the Department, including organisational structure and senior officials is set out in Chapter 3.

## Overview of Education and Library Boards

The Education and Library (NI) Order 1972 took control of the provision of education and library services from local authorities, and placed it under the direction of new Education and Library Boards. Five new Boards were established in 1973 to cover Northern Ireland: Belfast, North Eastern, Western, Southern and South Eastern.

### Functions, Duties, Powers and Services

Within the public education system, Education and Library Boards have statutory responsibility for primary and secondary education within their respective areas. The system of education is divided into three stages:

- Primary Education: for pupils aged 5-11 in Key Stages 1 and 2;
- Secondary Education: for pupils aged 11-18 in Key Stages 3 and 4 and post-16 studies;
- Further Education: for people over compulsory school age.

Each Board must also have regard for the need for pre-school education. Boards are responsible for the provision of a youth service and library services to schools and the public.

The principal duties of each Board are:

- To contribute to the spiritual, moral, cultural, intellectual and physical development of the community;
- To ensure that there are sufficient schools for providing primary and secondary education;
- To secure special education provision for those children who have been identified as having special educational needs;
- To provide a comprehensive and efficient library service for people who live, work or undertake courses of study within its area;
- To secure the provision for their respective areas of adequate facilities for recreational, social, physical, cultural and youth service activities and for services ancillary to education.

Each Education and Library Board has 32-35 members, appointed by the Minister responsible for the Department of Education in Northern Ireland and representative of the following:

- Each Local Government District in the Board's area;
- Transferors' interests;
- Trustees of maintained schools;
- Those with an interest in the services provided by the Board.

## Education and Library Boards

Belfast Education and Library Board
40 Academy Street
Belfast, BT1 2NQ
Tel: 028 9056 4000
Fax: 028 9033 1714
Chairperson: Carmel McKinney
Chief Executive: David Cargo

Belfast Education and Library Board is the local education and library authority for the area served by Belfast City Council, covering, according to the 2001 census figures a population of 277,391. Approximately 65,000 children are enrolled in 178 schools in the Belfast Area. The Board provides 21 libraries, library services to hospitals and homes, a schools' library service, a teachers' reference library and the Northern Ireland Schools' Video Library.

The Board provides music tuition through the School of Music. It also provides a comprehensive youth service through the operation of 53 controlled youth organisations, and support for over 350 voluntary youth organisations. It also maintains two outdoor centres at Delamont and Drumalla, which are used extensively by people from a wide range of schools and youth organisations. Specialist resource and teachers' centres are located in Mountcollyer and Ulidia.

**Expenditure**
During the financial year 2001-2002, Belfast Education and Library Board spent a total of £230.9 million, the main portion of this going to schools (£154.5 million). A further £12 million went to other education services, bringing the total spent on education to £166.5 million. The remaining £8.4 million was split between Culture, Arts and Leisure, and Further and Higher Education.

North Eastern Education and Library Board
County Hall, 182 Galgorm Road
Ballymena, BT42 1HN
Tel: 028 2565 3333
Fax: 028 2564 6071
Web: www.neelb.org.uk
Chairperson: Joan Christie
Chief Executive: Gordon Topping

The North Eastern Education and Library Board is the local education and library authority for most of County Antrim and the eastern part of County Londonderry, comprising the Local Government Districts of Antrim, Ballymena, Ballymoney, Carrickfergus, Coleraine, Larne, Magherafelt, Moyle and Newtownabbey.

The population of the Board's area in the 2001 census was 394,384. (The 2003 mid-year population estimate was 399,477). Latest school enrolment figures from 2002/03 indicate that 75,184 children are enrolled in schools within the Board's area. This includes 2,847 children in 17 nursery schools (and 32 nursery units located within primary schools); 36,275 in 211 primary schools; 18,389 in 34 secondary schools; 976 in 11 special schools and 4,666 in 5 grammar schools. There are also 9,111 pupils attending 11 voluntary grammar schools and 999 pupils in 5 grant maintained integrated schools, and 1,657 pupils in 2 grant maintained post-primary schools. 104 pupils attend 4 Grant Maintained nursery units. There are 37 branch libraries, 9 public service mobile libraries and 4 schools' mobile libraries in the area. There are also 33 controlled youth clubs and 534 voluntary youth organisations.

The Board is the employing authority of approximately 11,000 people in full-time and part-time capacities.

South Eastern Education and Library Board
Grahamsbridge Road, Dundonald
Belfast, BT16 2HS
Tel: 028 9056 6200
Fax: 028 9056 6266
Web: www.seelb.org.uk
Chairperson: Cllr Robert Gibson
Chief Executive: Mr Jackie Fitzsimons

**Library Headquarters**
Windmill Hill
Ballynahinch, BT24 8DH
Tel: 028 9756 6400
Fax: 028 9756 5072

The South Eastern Education and Library Board covers much of County Down, including the Local Government Districts of Ards, Castlereagh, Lisburn and North Down. The population of the Board's area in 2001 was 388,577. School enrolment figures indicate that at October 2001 there were 66,700 children attending schools in the area. The Board is responsible for 18 nursery schools, 41 nursery/pre-school units, 163 primary schools, 29 secondary schools, 10 grammar schools, 11 special schools and 24 special units. The Board also provides or supports 31 public library service points, 3 outdoor education centres, 18 controlled youth centres, 2 resource centres and a music centre.

**Expenditure**
During the financial year ending 31 March 2003, the South Eastern Board spent a total of £264.5 million. The majority went on schools, with smaller amounts spent on library and other services.

**Structure of the Board**
The work of the Board is carried out through a committee structure; the committees being as follows:

- Audit Committee
- Chairmen's Committee
- Committee for the Management of Schools
- Education Committee
- Expulsions Committee
- Finance and Property Services Committee
- General Purposes Committee
- Library and Information Committee
- Teaching Appointments Committee
- Youth Committee

Southern Education and Library Board
3 Charlemont Place, The Mall
Armagh, BT61 9AX
Tel: 028 3751 2200
Fax: 028 3751 2490
Web: www.selb.org
Chairperson: Mrs M Alexander
Chief Executive: Helen McClenaghan

The Southern Education and Library Board is the local authority for education and library services in the Armagh, Banbridge, Cookstown, Craigavon, Dungannon and Newry and Mourne Local Government Districts.

The population of the area is estimated at 332,000 including 75,000 pupils. To serve this population the Board provides or maintains 18 nursery, 238 primary, 36 secondary, 3 grammar and 6 special schools. It also provides 23 public libraries, 12 youth centres and 3 outdoor education centres. Services are also offered to a further 12 voluntary grammar schools and 8 grant maintained integrated schools in the area, along with 448 voluntary youth clubs. The Board is the employer of 7,844 staff. It is required by law to have 2 statutory committees: the Library Committee and the Teaching Appointments Committee. It also has a number of other committees through which much of its detailed work is carried out:

- Education Committee;
- Services Committee;
- Direct Service Committee;
- Committee for Peripatetic Teachers;
- Teachers' Staffing Committee;
- Audit Committee;
- Special Education Committee;
- Consultants' Selection Panel;
- Membership Committee;
- Special Business Committee;
- Policy Committee;
- Best Value Committee;
- Remuneration Committee.

**Expenditure**
During the financial year 2002/2003, the revenue budget for the Board was £225 million. The majority of this was delegated to schools, with smaller amounts going to various other areas.

Western Education and Library Board
1 Hospital Road
Omagh, BT79 0AW
Tel: 028 8241 1411
Fax: 028 8241 1400
Web: www.welbni.org
Chairperson: Harry Mullan
Chief Executive: Barry Mulholland

The Western Education and Library Board is the local authority for the provision of education, library and youth services in the District Council areas of Derry, Fermanagh, Limavady, Omagh and Strabane.

The area has a population of 282,000. There are over 63,000 pupils attending schools and over 137,000 registered library users. The Board provides or maintains 12 nursery, 194 primary, 10 special, 36 secondary/high, 4 grammar schools and 16 public libraries. In addition, services are provided to 10 voluntary grammar and 6 grant-maintained integrated schools. The Board also makes extensive provision for youth facilities and over 400 registered youth groups are supported.

The Board has 32 members. The activities of the Board are managed through the Education, Library, Services, Finance and Youth Committees. The Board also has a Teaching Appointments Committee and an Audit Committee.

The Western Board also has a responsibility, on behalf of the five Education and Library Boards, for the Classroom 2000 Project, which has as its purpose the design, development and operation of an ICT infrastructure to support the curricular, management and information needs of the major bodies within the education service in Northern Ireland.

**Expenditure**
During the financial year ending 31 March 2003, the Western Board's total expenditure was £277.9m. This was largely made up by a departmental grant, as well as funding from other sources. The majority of expenditure was on schools, with smaller amounts spent on library and other services.

## Other Agencies and Organisations in Education

Staff Commission for Education and Library Boards
Forestview
Purdy's Lane, Belfast, BT8 7AR
Tel:028 9049 1461
Fax: 028 9049 1744
Chairman: Prof Bernard Collen

The Staff Commission oversees recruitment, promotion, training and terms and conditions of employment for people working in Education and Library Boards.

Council for the Curriculum, Examinations and Assessment (CCEA)
Clarendon Dock, 29 Clarendon Road
Belfast, BT1 3BG
Web: www.ccea.org.uk
Tel: 028 9026 1200
Fax: 028 9026 1234
Chairman: Dr Alan Lennon
Chief Executive: Gavin Boyd

CCEA has vresponsiblity for pupils' assessment and conducting public examinations, including amongst others the 11 plus, GCSEs and A-Levels.

Council for Catholic Maintained Schools (CCMS)
160 High Street, Holywood, BT18 9HT
Tel: 028 9042 6972
Fax: 028 9042 4255
Chairman: Most Rev J McAreavey DD, Bishop of Dromore
Chief Executive: Donal Flanagan

CCMS manages, on behalf of the voluntary maintained (Catholic) sector, staff recruitment and appointments and maintenance and finance. CCMS also has a strong input into the curriculum for these schools.

Northern Ireland Higher Education Council
Adelaide House, 39-49 Adelaide Street
Belfast, BT2 8FD
Tel: 028 9025 7777
Fax: 028 9025 7778
Chairman: Tony Hopkins CBE

The Northern Ireland Higher Education Council (NIHEC) provides advice to the Department of Employment and Learning on the planning and funding of higher education in Northern Ireland.

## Employment and Training in Northern Ireland

The Department of Employment and Learning (DEL) manages a range of training and employment measures and programmes in Northern Ireland. These programmes range from a public employment service delivered through a network of 35 JobCentres/Jobs and Benefits Offices through to modern apprenticeship schemes. The programmes are profiled below and further information is available from:

### Department for Employment and Learning

Adelaide House, 39-49 Adelaide Street
Belfast, BT2 8FB
Tel: 028 9025 7793
Fax: 028 9025 7795
Web: www.delni.gov.uk

The aim of the Department for Employment and Learning is 'to promote a culture of lifelong learning and to equip people for work in a modern economy.' The Department's Management Development Branch exists to further this aim through its support measures for Northern Ireland's businesses and organisations. These support measures include:

A range of entry into management initiatives:

- The Business Education Initiative (BEI);
- The Premiere 2 - Management Development Programme;
- The Rapid Advancement Programme (RAP).

Programmes aimed at developing existing managers:

- Management and Leadership Development Programme;
- Leaders for Tomorrow.

Further detailed information about the Department of Employment and Learning organisation is set out in Chapter 3.

**Investors In People**

The Department for Employment and Learning is responsible for the delivery of Investors in People in Northern Ireland. The aim of the Centre is to promote awareness of the Investors in People Standard in Northern Ireland and to encourage and support organisations to achieve and maintain the Standard. The Investors in People Standard is a business improvement tool that helps organisations to compete and succeed through improved people performance.

**Modern Apprenticeships**

Modern Apprenticeships were launched by government in response to employer demand, to enhance the status of apprenticeships and improve the supply into industry of young people with advanced occupational skills and broader key skills. The approach, a further development of the NVQ approach to training, was introduced throughout Great Britain from September 1995 and now covers most skill sectors there.

In Northern Ireland, consultation with interested parties showed widespread support for a similar approach. Accordingly, in July 1996, Modern Apprenticeships were introduced here, initially on a pilot basis. The pilots proved successful and there was commitment to the further development and application of Modern Apprenticeships throughout the province, in particular the concept of direct employer involvement in the delivery of training based on the principles of cost sharing between employers, young people and government.

Modern Apprenticeships are now an integral part of the Department's Jobskills programme and have steadily increased in popularity with both young people and employers during recent years. Intake into training has almost doubled over the past two years. Around 5,500 young people in Northern Ireland, ranging in experience from first year to fourth year, are currently following a Modern Apprenticeship and over 2,000 local employers are participating in the programme.

Employers, both public and private sector, have a key role within New Deal and can:

- take the opportunity New Deal offers to help their organisations drawing on this source of potential recruits;
- offer people permanent jobs through New Deal,
- obtain a financial subsidy.

### Training Organisations

Abbey Training Services
Lennie House, 314 Antrim Road
Glengormley, Newtownabbey, BT36 8EH
Contact: Jarlath McCamphill
Tel: 028 9084 0527

Advance Training & Development
50 Railway Street, Lisburn, BT28 1XP
Contact: Colleen Dalzell
Tel: 028 9266 6094

Armagh College
Lonsdale Street, Armagh, BT61 7HN
Contact: Sarah Mallon
Tel: 028 3751 2818

Austins Quality Training Services
The Diamond, Derry, BT48 6HR
Contact: Ana McColgan
Tel: 028 7126 9324

BCW Training Ltd
Unit 18, Leyland Road Industrial Estate
Ballycastle, BT54 6EZ
Contact: Jacinta Hill
Tel: 028 2076 2902

Belfast Central Training Ltd
98/102 Donegall Street
Belfast, BT1 2GW
Contact: John Savage
Tel: 028 9032 4973

Belfast Centre of Learning,
H J O'Boyle Belfast
1A Rossmore Avenue, Belfast, BT7 3HB
Contact: Francis Tumelty
Tel: 028 9064 6446

Belfast College of Training & Education Ltd
Franklin House, 12 Brunswick Street
Belfast, BT2 7GE
Contact: Collette Steele
Tel: 028 9023 2186

Belfast Institute
Millfield Building, Belfast, BT1 1HS
Contact: Christina McCool
Tel: 028 9026 5000

Blackwater House (STC)
Riverpark, Blackwater Road
Mallusk, BT36 4TZ
Contact: Pamela Morgan
Tel: 028 9034 2400

Brookfield Business School
Brookfield Business Centre
333 Crumlin Road, Belfast, BT14 7EA
Contact: Deborah Stewart
Tel: 028 9075 1293

**Castlereagh College**
Montgomery Road
Belfast, BT6 9JD
Contact: Isobel McClean
Tel: 028 9070 8228

**Causeway Institute**
2 Coleraine Road
Ballymoney, BT53 6BP
Contact: Carolyn Taggart
Tel: 028 2766 0404

**CITB (STC)**
17 Dundrod Road
Crumlin, BT29 4SR
Contact: Karen Hunter / Katrina Carlin
Tel: 028 9082 4200/4204

**Clanrye Employment & Training Services**
The Abbey, Abbey Yard
Newry, BT34 2EG
Contact: Liam Devine
Tel: 028 3026 7121

**Coalisland Training Services Ltd**
51 Dungannon Road
Coalisland, BT71 4HP
Contact: Richard Thornton
Tel: 028 8774 8512

**Centre for Technology**
11 Greystone Road
Limavady, BT49 0ND
Contact: Robert Roddy
Tel: 028 7776 2745

**Conservation Volunteers**
Dendron Lodge
Clandeboye Estate
Bangor, BT19 1RN
Contact: Linda Wilson
Tel: 028 9185 2817

**Cookstown Training**
New Generation Tech Centre
T5 Cookstown Enterprise Centre, Derryloran Estate
Sandholes Road
Cookstown, BT80 9LU
Contact: Geraldine McIvor
Tel: 028 8676 1145

**Craft Recruitment & Training**
Mopack Business Complex
Ballycolman Road
Strabane, BT82 9PH
Contact: Marie Nealis
Tel: 028 7188 0044

**CTRS Community Training**
New Hope Centre, Erne Road
Enniskillen, BT74 6NN
Contact: Yvonee Fallis
Tel: 028 6632 8073

**Customized Training Services**
Units 11 & 12
3-5 Main Street
Strabane, BT82 8AR
Contact: Ms Carmel Boyce
Tel: 028 7138 2260

**Dairy Farm Training (People 1st)**
Unit 18, Dairy Farm Centre
Stewartstown Road
Belfast, BT17 0AW
Contact: Ronan Heenan
Tel: 028 9061 8452

**DARD**
22 Greenmount Road
Antrim, BT41 4PU
Contact: Marie McAuley
Tel: 028 9442 6674

**Derry Youth & Community Workshop Ltd**
6 Society Street
Derry, BT48 6PJ
Contact: Phyliss Kennedy
Tel: 028 7126 8891

**East Antrim Institute**
400 Shore Road
Newtownabbey, BT37 9RS
Contact: Mark Sault
Tel: 028 9085 0000

**East Down Institute**
Market Street
Downpatrick, BT30 6ND
Contact: Jacqueline Doran
Tel: 028 4461 1517

**East Tyrone College**
Circular Road
Dungannon, BT71 6BQ
Contact: AJ Dardis
Tel: 028 8772 2323

**Electrical Training Trust (STC)**
Unit 4, Ballymena Business Development, Fenaghy Road
Ballymena, BT42 1FL
Contact: Claire Alexander
Tel: 028 2565 0750

**Engineering Training Council (STC)**
Interpoint, 20-24 York Street
Belfast, BT15 1AQ
Contact: Sylvia Law
Tel: 028 9032 9878

**Fermanagh College**
Fairview, Dublin Road
Enniskillen, BT74 6AE
Contact: Dermot Dolan
Tel: 028 6632 2431

**Fermanagh Training Ltd**
Skills Centre
Killyhevlin Industrial Estate
Dublin Road
Enniskillen, BT74 4EJ
Contact: Margaret McManus
Tel: 028 6632 4860

**Food & Drink Training Council (STC)**
4B Weavers' Court
Linfield Road
Belfast, BT12 5GH
Contact: Wendy Kelly
Tel: 028 9032 9269

**Graham Training**
40-44 Railway Street
Lisburn, BT28 1XP
Contact: Patricia Moley
Tel: 028 9266 5100

**H J O'Boyle Training Ltd**
15A English Street
Downpatrick, BT30 6AB
Contact: Francis Tumelty
Tel: 028 4461 6438

**Hastings Hotel Group (STC)**
Midland Building
Whitla Street
Belfast, BT15 1NA
Contact: Patricia Fitzpatrick
Tel: 028 9075 1066

**Impact Training (NI) Limited**
16 Lanark Way
Belfast, BT13 3BH
Contact: Ms Sarah Cairns
Tel: 028 9033 9910

**Jennymount Training Services / Hair Academy**
10-12 Rosemary Street
Belfast, BT1 1QD
Contact: Eileen Kane
Tel: 028 9043 5414

**JTM Training and Employment**
29-31 Church Street
Ballymena, BT43 6BD
Contact: Patricia Cathcart
Tel: 028 2565 6567

**JTM Training and Employment**
24 The Diamond
Coleraine, BT52 1PD
Contact: Patricia Cathcart
Tel: 028 7035 6677

**Lagan Consulting**

Lagan Consulting
www.laganconsulting.com

TSL House
38 Bachelors Walk
Lisburn, BT28 1XN
Tel: 028 9262 8777
Web: laganconsulting.com
Contact: Owen McQuade

Specialist trainers in public affairs and stakeholder management.

**Larne Skills Development Ltd**
Larne Business Centre
Bank Road
Larne, BT40 3AW
Contact: Ruth Dillon
Tel: 028 2827 3337

**Lets Training & Employment Ltd**
100 Hill Street
Lurgan, BT66 6BQ
Contact: Myles Haughey
Tel: 028 3832 7307

**The Link Works**
11 Sugar Island
Newry, BT35 6HT
Contact: Wendy Connor
Tel: 028 3026 2777

**Lisburn Institute**
39 Castle Street
Lisburn, BT27 4SU
Contact: Grainne McCartan
Tel: 028 9267 3437

**Lisburn YMCA**
28 Market Square
Lisburn, BT28 1AG
Contact: Sandra Walsh
Tel: 028 9267 0918

**Loughview Training Services**
1 Ballyclare Road
Glengormley, BT36 5EX
Contact: Julie Hughes
Tel: 028 9080 1010

**Momentum (STC)**
NiSoft House
Ravenhill Business Park
Ravenhill Road
Belfast, BT6 8AW
Contact: Laurence Downey
Tel: 028 9045 0101

**Network Personnel**
80-82 Rainey Street
Magherafelt, BT45 5AJ
Contact: Ann McBride
Tel: 028 7963 1032

**Newry & Kilkeel Institute**
Patrick Street
Newry, BT35 5DL
Contact: Libby McCreesh
Tel: 028 3026 4721

**NIE Powerteam**
Nutts Corner, Dundrod Road
Crumlin, BT29 4SR
Contact: Helen Gallagher
Tel: 028 9068 8249

**North City Training**
275 Antrim Road
Belfast, BT15 2GZ
Contact: Richard Henderson
Tel: 028 9074 5408

**North Down and Ards**
Victoria Avenue
Newtownards, BT23 7ED
Contact: Jennifer Palmer
Tel: 028 9127 6600

**North Down Training**
4-6 Conway Square
Newtownards, BT23 4DD
Contact: Nigel Finch
Tel: 028 9182 2880

**North East Institute**
Jobskills Department
Farm Lodge Building Ballymena, BT43 7DF
Contact: Ruth Wylie
Tel: 028 2565 6561

**Omagh College**
Training Office, Woodside Avenue, Omagh, BT79 7BP
Contact: Jennifer Barton
Tel: 028 8225 4954

**Oriel Training Services**
Unit 1, 35A Main Street
Randalstown, BT41 3AB
Contact: Leanne Karney
Tel: 028 9447 8860
Tel: 028 9446 2620

**Paragon Services (NI) Ltd**
Unit HG2
Twinspires Complex
North Howard Street
Belfast, BT13 2JS
Contact: Anita Fitzsimons
Tel: 028 9024 2535

**Parity Training Ltd**
Blackstaff Chamber
2 Amelia Street
Belfast, BT2 7GS
Contact: Victoria Allen
Tel: 028 9024 0780

**Printing & Packaging (STC)**
c/o Graham & Heslip Ltd
96 Beechill Road
Belfast, BT8 4QM
Contact: Rosie Mitten
Tel: 028 4176 5516

**Protocol Skills (Belfast)**
3rd Floor
Scottish Legal House
65-67 Chichester Street
Belfast, BT1 4JD
Contact: Lynn Gabby
Tel: 028 9033 0331

**Protocol Skills (Derry, Dungannon, Cookstown)**
1st Floor
50-54a Waterloo Street
Londonderry, BT48 6BU
Contact: Moya McDevitt
Tel: 028 7137 3002

**Protocol Skills (Newry)**
2 Marcus Street
Newry, BT34 1AZ
Contact: Celine Cunningham
Tel: 028 3026 4440

**Rutledge Joblink Antrim**
12 High Street
Antrim, BT41 4AN
Contact: Sheila Hogg
Tel: 028 9448 7848

**Rutledge Joblink Bangor (Appello)**
Market House
3 Market Street
Bangor, BT20 4SP
Contact: Tracey Eisen
Tel: 028 9127 3474

**Rutledge Joblink Belfast**
2nd Floor
86 Great Victoria Street
Belfast, BT2 7BD
Contact: Tracey Eisen
Tel: 028 9024 6888

**Rutledge Joblink Braid (Ballymena)**
48-50 Linenhall Street
Ballymena, BT43 5AL
Contact: Sheila Hogg
Tel: 028 2563 1800

**Rutledge Joblink Limavady**
42 Catherine Street
Limavady, BT49 9DB
Contact: Patricia Frederick
Tel: 028 7772 2174

**Rutledge Joblink Magherafelt**
11A Meeting Street
Magherfelt, BT45 6BN
Contact: Brena Hasson
Tel: 028 7963 4666

**Rutledge Joblink NE (Coleraine)**
Market Court
57-59 New Row
Coleraine, BT52 1EJ
Contact: Sam McCartney
Tel: 028 7035 2434

**Rutledge Joblink Omagh**
2nd Floor, Anderson House,
Market Street
Omagh, BT78 1EE
Contact: Nathan Flatman
Tel: 028 8224 0999

**Rutledge Joblink Strabane**
Abercorn House
2 Railway Street
Strabane, BT82 9EF
Contact: Monica Langan
Tel: 028 7035 2434

**Rutledge Joblink (Waterloo House)**
48 Waterloo Street
Londonderry, BT48 6HF
Contact: Collum McCaughan
Tel: 028 7137 0300

**Seven Towers Training Ltd**
56 Henry Street
Ballymena, BT42 3AH
Contact: Kim Alexander
Tel: 028 2564 4003

**Shantallow Training Services**
10 Northland Road
Derry, BT48 7GD
Contact: Glen McElwee
Tel: 028 7135 1190

**Shorts Bombardier**
Interpoint, 20-24 York Street
Belfast, BT15 1AW
Contact: Helen Savage
Tel: 028 9046 8338

**Southern ITEC**
52 Armagh Road
Newry, BT35 6DP
Contact: Ms Sharon Toner
Tel: 028 3026 8131

**Sperrin Lakeland**
Tyrone County Hospital
Hospital Road
Omagh, BT79 0AP
Contact: Ms Esme Hill
Tel: 028 82 245211

**Springvale Training Ltd**
200 Springfield Road
Belfast, BT12 7GB
Contact: Mary Lyons
Tel: 028 9024 2362

**Strabane Training Services**
Ballycolman Industrial Estate
Strabane, BT82 9PH
Contact: Jolene Atkinson
Tel: 028 7138 2438

**Sureskills**

SureSkills

Callender House
58-60 Upper Arthur Street
Belfast, BT1 4GP
Tel: +44 (0) 28 9093 5555
Fax: +44 (0) 28 9093 5566
Email: niinfo@sureskills.com
Web: www.sureskills.com

General Manager Pauline Thompson

SureSkills is widely recognised as the premier training solutions organisation in Ireland, delivering over 25,000 days of authorised and customised programmes each year to both the private and public sectors. Training is delivered in our state of the art training centres in Belfast and Dublin and where required, on-site at the customer's premises.

**Swan Training Services**
165-169 Albertbridge Road
Belfast, BT5 4PS
Contact: Jane Courtney
Tel: 028 9073 1030

**Tourism Training Trust (STC)**
Caernarvon House
19 Donegall Pass
Belfast, BT7 1DQ
Contact: Roisin McKee
Tel: 028 9032 0625

**Training Direct (North West Institute)**
Springtown Industrial Estate
Londonderry, BT48 0LY
Contact: Suzanne Currie
Tel: 028 7127 6222

**Training for Business**
Unit 22
Greenbank Industrial Estate
Warrenpoint
Newry, BT34 2QU
Contact: Mr Robert Barton
Tel: 028 3026 6924

**Transport Training Services (STC)**
15 Dundrod Road
Crumlin, BT29 4SS
Contact: Mr Sean McCullagh
Tel: 028 9082 5653

**Tyrone Training Services**
38 Gortin Road
Omagh, BT79 7HX
Contact: Heather Managh
Tel: 028 8224 9999

**Upper Bann Institute**
Portadown Campus
36 Lurgan Road
Portadown, BT63 5BL
Contact: Rosemary Muldrew
Tel: 028 3839 7855

**Wade Training Ltd, (Armagh & Portadown)**
33 Castle Street
Portadown, BT62 1BB
Contact: Orla Waterson
Tel: 028 3833 7000

**Wholesale & Retail Training Council (STC)**
10 Hydepark Road, Mallusk,
Newtownabbey, BT36 4PY
Contact: Jacqueline King
Tel: 028 9084 5830

**Workforce**
90-120 Springfield Road
Belfast, BT12 7AJ
Contact: Tara Toland
Tel: 028 9024 7016

**Workscene Training Organisation**
Curran House
Twin Spires House
155 Northumberland Street
Belfast, BT13 2JF
Contact: Paul Wilson
Tel: 028 9031 1787

WILSON

# Chapter 7

# The Northern Ireland Economy

# Overview of The Northern Ireland Economy

## Introduction

The Northern Ireland economy is a relatively small regional economy within the United Kingdom and in an overall European context Northern Ireland is a peripheral and less favoured economic area.

Although Northern Ireland was traditionally (at least until the 1970s) the most industrialised part of the island of Ireland, it has gradually been overtaken economically by the adjacent Republic of Ireland economy, which has enjoyed a sustained boom over the last decade. It has also generally lagged behind the overall economic performance of the UK, although in recent years with economic growth more rapid than the UK overall, Northern Ireland has overtaken one or two of the poorer regions of Great Britain.

Table 7.1 gives a good snapshot of Northern Ireland's economic situation in the UK regional context. Of the 12 UK regions analysed Northern Ireland tends to be towards the lowest in terms of economic performance across a range of indicators.

**Table 7.1 Northern Ireland Economy Position in UK Regional League Table**

| Indicator | Rank in 2004 |
|---|---|
| Working age population as % of total pop | 4 |
| Participation rate | 9 |
| Unemployment rate | 11 |
| % employment in manufacturing | 8 |
| % employment in private services | 12 |
| Self employment % of total employment | 4 |
| GVA per person | 10 |
| GVA per manufacturing employee | 8 |
| GVA per private services employee | 11 |
| Average earnings | 12 |
| Disposable income per head | 11 |
| Consumers expenditure per head | 10 |
| House prices | 10 |

Source: RF/OEF Regional Outlook 2004

The Northern Ireland economy has some unique characteristics that present structural challenges for the future. These include:

- A relatively small industrial and manufacturing base;
- An over-dependence on the public sector for employment and wealth;
- Traditional industries – shipbuilding, engineering, textiles and agriculture, all in crisis or long term decline;
- Difficulty attracting quality international investment and tourism revenue;
- Arguably, an introspective culture, which results in low levels of entrepreneurship, export focus and uptake of private equity.

However, because these structural difficulties are fully recognised and considerable efforts deployed to counter them, Northern Ireland has exhibited an impressively resilient economic long-term performance. It does not 'collapse' in the manner of some other economies in times of international cyclical downturn nor does it enjoy spectacular growth even when all western economies are experiencing a boom. To some extent however this resilience is a function of the dominance of the public sector and public expenditure in the local economy which tends to remain steady across the economic cycle.

Although performance has certainly improved over recent years, Northern Ireland is not a major exporter in terms of exporting beyond the British Isles and continues to depend heavily on the rest of the United Kingdom as its key export market. The authorities, including the Department of Enterprise, Trade and Investment and its main economic development agency Invest NI, have set an ambitious vision for the Northern Ireland economy. The vision is to make Northern Ireland a knowledge-based economy and an exemplar location for starting and growing a successful business.

## Economic Vision

Northern Ireland does not currently have a detailed economic plan although a number of strategic documents have been produced in recent years. These include the Government's Strategy 2010 document – which drew support and criticism in equal measure – and the output of the government-sponsored Economic Development Forum. At time of going to print the Department of Enterprise, Trade and Investment is consulting on a draft Economic Vision – setting out the fundamentals and imperatives of future economic development in Northern Ireland. Once finalised, the Vision will be the cornerstone document against which all departmental, crosscutting and sectoral strategies and plans should be consistent.

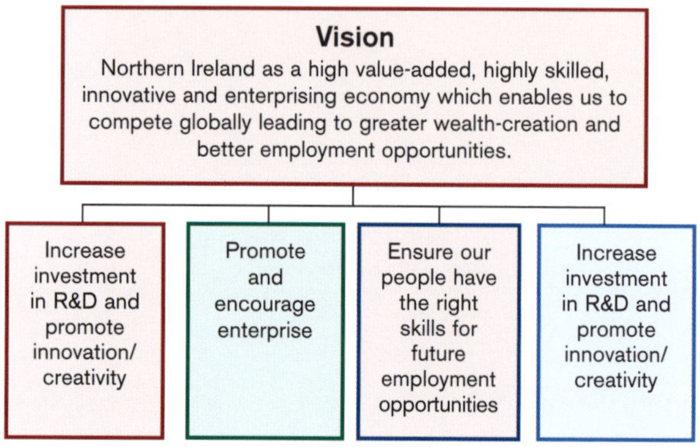

Vision
Northern Ireland as a high value-added, highly skilled, innovative and enterprising economy which enables us to compete globally leading to greater wealth-creation and better employment opportunities.
Increase investment in R&D and promote innovation/ creativity
Promote and encourage enterprise
Ensure our people have the right skills for future employment opportunities
Increase investment in R&D and promote innovation/ creativity


The draft Vision describes an ideal economy which should be reached through prioritisation of key drivers such as innovation, entrepreneurship, skills and investment.

## Economic Growth

Northern Ireland accounts for around 2.3 per cent of the UK Gross Domestic Product (GDP) and does not vary greatly around this figure. In recent years Northern Ireland GDP has grown at rates that have been slightly above the UK average. *(Although the size and growth of the economy has traditionally been measured in terms of GDP or GNP (Gross National Product) statisticians have moved to Gross Value Added (GVA), a broadly similar measure).*

Table 7.2 below indicates that Northern Ireland not only accounts for a small share of the UK GVA but also that per capita GVA in Northern Ireland lags behind the UK average by a considerable margin. Historically Northern Ireland GDP per capita has hovered around 75 per cent of the UK average although this improved noticeably in the later 1990s (possibly but not indisputably coinciding with the 'peace process') reaching a peak of 81.5% in 1995). The latest estimate of Northern Ireland per capita GDP as a proportion of UK is 79%.

Remarkably Northern Ireland has continued to have one of the fastest rates of economic growth of any UK region in the past years, although it still has one of the highest rates of unemployment and certainly the highest rate of economic inactivity. Yet, coming from a low base, growth in employment has risen faster in Northern Ireland in recent years than any other UK region.

**Table 7.2 Northern Ireland Economic Growth 1999-2002**

**£ million**

| | 1999 | 2000 | 2001 | 2002 |
|---|---|---|---|---|
| Gross Value Added | 17,746 | 18,514 | 19,414 | 20,497 |
| GVA per head (£s) | 10,569 | 11,001 | 11,492 | 12,081 |
| GVA as % of UK | 2.3 | 2.3 | 2.3 | 2.3 |
| GVA per head as % of UK | 79 | 79 | 79 | 79 |

Source: Office for National Statistics

Although GDP per capita is well below the UK average, it is no longer the lowest of the UK regions, with the North East of England now slightly lower.

## Sectoral Composition of Gross Value Added (GVA)

The Services sector is by far the most important economic sector in Northern Ireland contributing almost 70% of Gross Value Added. While this high figure is in line with other developed Western economies and clearly slows the transition of Northern Ireland toward becoming a knowledge-based economy it includes a predominance of public sector services activity. The public sector contributes around 60% of GVA in Northern Ireland, a figure that is extremely high by EU or OECD standards and which some economists would argue is unsustainable. Manufacturing, although in decline has, through productivity improvements, held on to around 20% of GVA while the contribution from agriculture has continued to fall - now only 2%. (See table 7.3).

**Table 7.3 Origins of Gross Value Added (GVA) by Industrial Sector**

| Sector | % |
|---|---|
| Services | 68 |
| Manufacturing | 20.5 |
| Construction | 7 |
| Agriculture | 2 |
| Electricity, Gas and Water | 2 |
| Mining and Quarrying | 0.5 |

Source: Northern Ireland Annual Abstract of Statistics

## Current Growth Forecast

Table 7.4 below indicates the latest Invest NI forecast for the Northern Ireland economy in an international context. However, growth forecasting can vary from expert to expert. The 3.1% forecast for the UK looks ambitious. Other forecasts for Northern Ireland growth in 2004 includes First Trust Bank at 3.0% and PricewaterhouseCoopers at 3.1% in 2004, falling to 2.6% in 2005.

**Table 7.4 Economic Growth Forecast 2004 Real Annual Growth %**

| | |
|---|---|
| USA | 4.7 |
| Republic of Ireland | 4.6 |
| United Kingdom | 3.1 |
| Northern Ireland | 3.0 |
| France | 2.1 |

Source: Invest NI Quarterly Economic Commentary 2004

## Comparisons with Republic of Ireland

Although Northern Ireland GDP performance compares favourably with other regions of the UK, the comparison with the neighbouring economy of the Irish Republic is quite interesting.

Only 10 years ago Northern Ireland was regarded as being more prosperous as a region than its southern neighbour, although both were acknowledged to be Objective 1 regions of the European Union (regions eligible for financial support from Europe where GDP per capita was below 75 per cent of the EU average). At that time Northern Ireland had just under half of the population of the Republic and about half of the Republic's gross domestic product in absolute terms.

With the sustained boom in the Republic and the slower growth in Northern Ireland, the province's GDP as a proportion of Republic of Ireland GDP has fallen from approximately 50 per cent in 1992 to 30 per cent in 1999 to around 25% in 2003. This general trend is predicted to continue, although much less dramatically. It is estimated therefore that Northern Ireland's share of all-island GDP is currently under 20 per cent.

Although Northern Ireland has lost its Objective 1 status, the Republic despite its 'wealth' being recognised as now being well over the EU average has retained Objective 1 status for its border, midlands and western region.

## Labour Force, Employment and Unemployment

At June 2003 there were an estimated 681,370 employee jobs in Northern Ireland – the highest figure on record. Despite record employment and a low rate of unemployment Northern Ireland's unemployment was still among the highest for any UK region.

The dominance of the public sector is reflected in the composition of Northern Ireland's employees. The numbers employed in health, education and public administration combined are over twice the number employed in manufacturing. As with many developed economies the service sector's share of employment has grown steadily.

**Table 7.5 Northern Ireland Employee Jobs by Standard Industrial Classification 1999-2004**

| Standard Industrial Classification 2003 | June 1999 | June 2004 |
|---|---|---|
| Agriculture, hunting, forestry and fishing | 15,450 | 14,820 |
| Mining and quarrying | 2,000 | 2,070 |
| Manufacturing | 105,170 | 88,920 |
| Electricity, gas and water supply | 3,440 | 2,810 |
| Construction | 31,290 | 36,240 |
| Wholesale and retail trade; repairs | 102,530 | 117,190 |
| Hotels and restaurants | 35,790 | 40,160 |
| Transport, storage and communication | 25,210 | 27,360 |
| Financial intermediation | 14,250 | 16,830 |
| Real estate, renting and business activities | 45,260 | 61,070 |
| Public administration and defence | 58,160 | 63,990 |
| Education | 64,720 | 70,430 |
| Health and social work | 93,550 | 107,890 |
| Other service activities | 27,160 | 31,590 |
| Services | 466,650 | 536,510 |
| **All Sections** | **624,000** | **681,370** |

Source NISRA

In contrast to the rise in employment in the services sector, the number employed in manufacturing has decreased significantly in recent years. This decrease in manufacturing employment has, however, not been as dramatic as for the UK as a whole and shows that despite a downturn in many of Northern Ireland's traditional industries the overall manufacturing base, although small, is proving quite resilient.

Although there has been a stabilising effect from a large public sector this is now recognised by some commentators as being both unsustainable and acting as a barrier to accelerating economic growth.

### Employment

Northern Ireland's employment growth over the last number of years compares favourably with the UK.

Total employment in Northern Ireland is expected to grow faster between 2001-2010 than the UK as a whole in each year of the forecast period. This growth rate is expected to result in an extra 40,000 jobs by the end of the decade.

Salary costs are also significantly lower in Northern Ireland – which enhance the region's overall competitiveness in attracting investment with significant labour requirements.

**Table 7.6 Employee Jobs 2004 Northern Ireland**

| | Total | % change since last year |
|---|---|---|
| Manufacturing | 89,080 | -4.10% |
| Construction | 36,350 | +3.20% |
| Services | 537,910 | +2.80% |
| Other | 19,710 | -0.01% |
| Total | 683,050 | +1.80% |

Source DETI, Quarterly Employment Survey Supplement for June 2004

**Table 7.7 Working Age Economic Activity Rates UK and NI 2004**

| Year | UK | NI |
|---|---|---|
| 1996 | 78.4 | 71.9 |
| 1997 | 78.6 | 73.3 |
| 1998 | 78.3 | 72.8 |
| 1999 | 78.7 | 72.6 |
| 2000 | 78.9 | 70.1 |
| 2001 | 78.6 | 71.9 |
| 2002 | 78.6 | 71.6 |
| 2003 | 78.7 | 72.9 |
| 2004 | 78.5 | 70.5 |

Source NI Labour Force Survey

### Unemployment

Unemployment is currently running at its lowest level since records began and has fallen steadily from a peak of 17.2% in 1986 to 4.9% in August 2004, compared with the current EU (25) average of 9%. However, some economists have warned that the official unemployment figure for Northern Ireland is misleading and much understated. This is because Northern Ireland – uniquely as a region has a very high level of compulsory early retirement as well as a uniquely high proportion of people of working age in receipt of invalidity benefit. This is borne out by Table 7.7 above showing Northern Ireland's comparatively low participation rate.

## Public Expenditure in Northern Ireland

The public sector is by far the most important employer in Northern Ireland. In addition to those employed directly a large number of private sector companies rely solely on the public sector for their customer base and are therefore dependant on the public sector for their employment. Public sector employment is set to rise further as a proportion of total employment given the proposed budgetary increases in the comparatively labour-intensive public services sector.

Public Expenditure accounts for a disproportionately high share of value-added (around 60% compared to around 40% in the UK and the Republic of Ireland). Tables 7.9 and 7.10 indicate the planned budget for the next three years. The most substantial increases are in health education and infrastructure and the overall level of spending in 2007/8 is expected to be some 29% higher than in 2003/04.

**Table 7.8 Identifiable Public Expenditure per head: UK = 100**

| | 1987/88 | 1991/92 | 1995/96 | 1999/00 | 2002/03 |
|---|---|---|---|---|---|
| England | 96 | 97 | 96 | 96 | 96 |
| Scotland | 122 | 115 | 117 | 118 | 116 |
| Wales | 109 | 107 | 114 | 113 | 115 |
| Northern Ireland | 146 | 137 | 131 | 133 | 129 |

Source NISRA

**Table 7.9 - Proposed Current Expenditure (£m)**

| | Outturn 2003-04 | Plans 2004-05 | 2005-06 | % | 2006-7 | % | 2007-8 | % |
|---|---|---|---|---|---|---|---|---|
| Agriculture & Rural Development | 215.4 | 236.2 | 245.1 | 3.8 | 229.6 | -6.3 | 235.0 | 2.4 |
| Culture, Arts and Leisure | 92.2 | 91.0 | 96.7 | 6.4 | 95.7 | -1.0 | 98.3 | 2.7 |
| Education | 1419.8 | 1447.6 | 1526.5 | 5.5 | 1556.9 | 2.0 | 1614.6 | 3.7 |
| Employment & Learning | 566.8 | 623.8 | 640.1 | 2.6 | 665.7 | 4.0 | 700.6 | 5.2 |
| Enterprise, Trade & Investment | 179.6 | 209.2 | 216.3 | 3.4 | 217.4 | 0.5 | 217.7 | 0.1 |
| Finance & Personnel | 136.5 | 144.9 | 174.0 | 20.1 | 181.5 | 4.3 | 180.0 | -0.8 |
| Health, Social Services & Public Safety | 2821.4 | 3048.4 | 3,26.1 | 9.1 | 3543.6 | 6.5 | 3754.0 | 5.9 |
| Environment | 115.7 | 131.0 | 128.5 | -1.9 | 125.2 | -2.6 | 130.1 | 3.9 |
| Regional Development | 339.7 | 350.4 | 364.6 | 4.0 | 379.7 | 4.1 | 392.7 | 3.4 |
| Social Development | 304.7 | 443.8 | 449.5 | 1.3 | 470.7 | 4.7 | 482.3 | 2.5 |
| OFMDFM | 40.4 | 56.4 | 60.3 | 7.0 | 66.2 | 9.6 | 67.1 | 1.5 |
| Northern Ireland Assembly | 32.7 | 47.2 | 47.3 | 0.1 | 47.3 | 0.0 | 47.3 | 0.0 |
| Other Departments | 6.8 | 11.7 | 13.2 | 13.0 | 13.2 | 0.3 | 13.2 | -0.1 |
| Central Funds | 0.0 | 18.0 | 5.0 | -72.2 | 6.0 | 20.0 | 26.0 | 333.3 |
| Total Planned Allocations | 6271.7 | 6859.6 | 7293.3 | 6.3 | 7598.7 | 4.2 | 7958.9 | 4.7 |

Source DFP

**Table 7.10 - Proposed Capital Investment (£m)**

| | Outturn 2003-04 | Plans 2004-05 | 2005-06 | % | 2006-7 | % | 2007-8 | % |
|---|---|---|---|---|---|---|---|---|
| Agriculture & Rural Development | 29.2 | 28.6 | 73.1 | 156 | 49.4 | -32.4 | 35.2 | -28.9 |
| Culture, Arts and Leisure | 6.6 | 9.3 | 20.7 | 122.4 | 13.1 | -37 | 12.9 | -1.5 |
| Education | 128 | 174.8 | 208.1 | 19.1 | 192.1 | -7.6 | 248.4 | 29.3 |
| Employment & Learning | 39.6 | 49.5 | 83.9 | 69.5 | 46.9 | -44.1 | 34.8 | -25.7 |
| Enterprise, Trade & Investment | 31.2 | 66.2 | 45.2 | -31.8 | 59.8 | 32.4 | 39.8 | -33.4 |
| Finance & Personnel | 41.5 | -6.1 | 25.9 | -526.5 | 28.1 | 8.4 | 28.1 | 0 |
| Health, Social Services & Public Safety | 124.1 | 118.7 | 173.4 | 46.1 | 188.1 | 8.4 | 208.8 | 11 |
| Environment | 7.3 | 12.7 | 14.3 | 12.8 | 11.2 | -21.7 | 6.2 | -44.7 |
| Regional Development | 246.4 | 379.8 | 468.2 | 23.3 | 407.4 | -13 | 422.5 | 3.7 |
| Social Development | 158.4 | 95.5 | 119.4 | 25 | 129.1 | 8.2 | 131.3 | 1.7 |
| OFMDFM | -2.8 | 0.7 | 6.9 | 848.8 | 4.8 | -29.7 | 10.7 | 121.7 |
| Northern Ireland Assembly | 0 | 2 | 2 | 0 | 2 | 0 | 2 | 0 |
| Other Departments | 0.2 | 0.2 | 0.2 | 0 | 0.2 | 0 | 0.2 | 0 |
| Central Funds | 0 | 15 | 16 | 6.7 | 23 | 43.8 | 19 | -17.4 |
| Total Planned Allocations | 809.7 | 946.8 | 1,257.30 | 32.8 | 1,155.20 | -8.1 | 1,199.90 | 3.9 |

Source DFP

## Trade and Exports From Northern Ireland

The recent export performance of the Northern Ireland Economy has been quite positive. Between 1996/97 and 2001/02 manufacturing exports from Northern Ireland increased by some 45% in real terms. More recently exports have levelled off with a slight decline in exports to the EU and rest of the World. The Irish Republic has also become a growing and increasingly important market for Northern Ireland exports. However Northern Ireland is still heavily dependant on Great Britain as its key export market, still accounting for almost half of all Northern Ireland exports. The equivalent figure for Republic of Ireland exports to Great Britain is 19%.

**Table 7.11 % Share of Total Sales by Broad Destination, 1991/92-2002/03**

| | 1995/96 | 1999/00 | 2002/03 |
|---|---|---|---|
| Northern Ireland | 32.4 | 27.4 | 27.9 |
| Great Britain | 32.6 | 32.9 | 32.5 |
| Republic of Ireland | 7.9 | 9.0 | 10.2 |
| Rest of EU | 14.1 | 11.5 | 11.4 |
| Rest of World | 13.0 | 19.2 | 18.0 |
| Total Sales | 100.0 | 100.0 | 100.0 |

Source DETI

Although there was growth across a number of sectors, most of the growth in external and export markets has been driven by a small number of large firms in key sectors including transport equipment, food, drink and tobacco, and electrical and optical equipment. The majority of these industrial sectors in Northern Ireland are heavily reliant on external markets for their sales. In seven of the twelve broad industrial sectors, external sales account for more than half of total sales.

There are ongoing difficulties in other key sectors, most notably the textiles and clothing sector and the meat processing and dairy sector, which have been hit by a number of crises in recent years to the detriment of their sectoral export performance.

**Table 7.12 Value of Exports by Industrial Sector 2002-03**

| Industrial Sector | Value £m | % of total |
|---|---|---|
| Food, drink & tobacco | 751 | 18.6 |
| Electrical & optical equipment | 1,058 | 26.1 |
| Transport equipment | 572 | 14.1 |
| Other machinery & equipment | 375 | 9.3 |
| Rubber & plastics | 279 | 6.9 |
| Textiles, clothing & leather | 153 | 3.8 |
| Other non-metallic mineral products | 101 | 2.5 |
| Chemicals & man-made fibres | 339 | 8.4 |
| Metals & fabricated metal products | 160 | 4 |
| Paper & printing | 81 | 2 |
| Other manufacturing | 100 | 2.5 |
| Wood & wood products | 77 | 1.9 |
| **Total** | **4,046** | **100** |

Source DETI

## Northern Ireland Competitiveness and Productivity

Since 1995 manufacturing output has increased significantly in Northern Ireland. Although the food, drink and tobacco sub-sector has experienced the most significant growth there have been significant reverses in textiles, engineering, the ICT sector and aerospace. The Northern Ireland engineering sector accounts for half of all Northern Ireland's manufacturing exports.

In textiles Northern Ireland's difficulty has been sustaining competitiveness against low-wage economies and there have been significant job losses as a result, particularly in the lower value-added parts of the sector.

**Table 7.13 Index of Manufacturing Productivity**
Annual Averages (Base year 1995 = 100)

| | Northern Ireland | United Kingdom |
|---|---|---|
| 1998 | 79.8 | 86.5 |
| 1999 | 90.6 | 90.6 |
| 2000 | 100.0 | 96.5 |
| 2001 | 106.6 | 100.0 |
| 2002 | 111.0 | 101.7 |
| 2003 | 119.1 | 106.5 |

Source NISRA Annual Abstract of Statistics

A major study by cross-border trade body Inter*Trade*Ireland found that competitiveness in Northern Ireland lagged significantly behind that of the Republic of Ireland in some sectors, although was ahead in some also.

Under one key measure 'value added per employee' the Irish Republic registered over twice the real value added for each industrial employee. However the booming economy of Ireland is not 'necessarily' the most reasonable comparator for Northern Ireland. Against the United Kingdom as a whole, Northern Ireland's productivity has been improving much more rapidly. Table 7.13 shows the improvement in NI and UK productivity as an index (however in absolute numbers UK productivity – indexed from a higher base is still well ahead).

**Table 7.14 GDP Per Hour Worked 1996-2002 (UK = 100)**

| | 1996 | 1998 | 2000 | 2002 |
|---|---|---|---|---|
| France | 132.8 | 132.4 | 132.3 | 131.7 |
| Germany | 124.0 | 119.7 | 119.8 | 116.4 |
| Japan | 89.4 | 86.9 | 87.6 | n/a |
| USA | 122.7 | 120.3 | 121.2 | 119.4 |
| G7 | 114.3 | 112.2 | 112.7 | n/a |
| UK | 100.0 | 100.0 | 100.0 | 100.0 |
| NI | 86.2 | 84.7 | 82.3 | 84.4 |

Source DETI

## Inward Investment

Northern Ireland continues to attract significant inward investment, which accounts for a very high proportion of manufacturing and industrial value added and employment.

Invest NI reported that 32 inward investment projects were secured in 2003/04 offering a total investment within Northern Ireland of £167m.

Table 7.15 shows the number of foreign owned companies operating in Northern Ireland and their home country location. The number of foreign-owned companies operating in Northern Ireland increased by over 60% between 1996 and 2003, to nearly 637. The majority of the companies are from the Republic of Ireland and the US.

**Table 7.15 Number of foreign owned companies operating in Northern Ireland by country of ownership, 1996 to 2002**

| Country | 1996 | 1998 | 2000 | 2003 |
|---|---|---|---|---|
| Republic of Ireland | 100 | 123 | 165 | 232 |
| United States of America | 71 | 111 | 146 | 154 |
| France | 23 | 23 | 36 | 47 |
| Netherlands | 17 | 30 | 26 | 41 |
| Germany | 17 | 22 | 26 | 37 |
| Denmark | 13 | 12 | 12 | 13 |
| Japan | 11 | 15 | 14 | 12 |
| Switzerland | 10 | 5 | 7 | 12 |
| Canada | 8 | 9 | 10 | 8 |
| Australia | 7 | 6 | 5 | 9 |
| South Korea | 6 | 8 | 7 | 6 |
| Sweden | 4 | 2 | 3 | 8 |
| Finland | 3 | 3 | 5 | 9 |
| Belgium | 3 | 5 | 3 | 3 |
| South Africa | 2 | 2 | 3 | 3 |
| Portugal | 1 | 1 | 4 | 1 |
| Norway | 1 | 1 | 9 | 4 |
| Channel Islands | 0 | 5 | 5 | 6 |
| Isle of Man | 0 | 4 | 3 | 1 |
| Other Countries | 7 | 2 | 4 | 25 |
| **All foreign owned companies** | **304** | **389** | **497** | **631** |

Source NISRA

Though continuing to be important, future economic growth and employment opportunities cannot be dependent on Foreign Direct Investment (FDI). The focus will therefore be on targeted FDI which provides wider economic benefits to the NI economy e.g. through the introduction of new products/processes, improved management practices, new technology and skills training. Indigenous businesses, and particularly those in high value added/niche markets, will become increasingly important to the economy.

- The UK is the second largest recipient of overseas direct investment (FDI) globally. Only the US has a larger stock. The UK holds 22.5% of all ODI in the EU and 9% worldwide.
  *Source UNCTAD, World Investment Report 2003*
- Over the past six years, Northern Ireland has become increasingly successful in attracting foreign investors and Foreign Direct Investment has increased. Nearly three-quarters of foreign investors in Northern Ireland have already reinvested or are gearing up to invest more.
- Investments from ICT, service and technology sectors have increased from 29% in 1994 to account for 83% of all FDI into Northern Ireland in 2003/04, reflecting Northern Ireland's knowledge-led economy.

Principal responsibility for winning inward direct investment lies with the Government's leading economic development agency Invest NI. The Agency pointed to prevailing economic circumstances in which investment decisions were being delayed, as a constraint on FDI at present.

## Innovation, Research and Development in Northern Ireland

As might be expected, R&D expenditure in Northern Ireland is concentrated in a small number of large companies. The ten biggest R&D spenders in 1999 accounted for 59 per cent of civil expenditure and five companies have appeared in the top ten in each of the three surveys.

Northern Ireland has relatively low levels of Innovation and Research and Development activity. Research and Development business expenditure per employee is below that for the United Kingdom as a whole.

This shortcoming in the local economy has been recognised by Government, the Economic Development Forum and by Invest NI. As a result the authorities have produced a Regional Innovation Strategy entitled 'think/create/innovate'. The key aim of the strategy is to enhance regional innovation by coordinating the research and education sector with business and government in a new partnership. This is intended to result in a monitor of all R&D activity in Northern Ireland and the wider dissemination of information to all relevant parties.

Improving innovation is one of four priority areas for Invest NI's corporate plan and a number of milestones were reached by the agency in the past – including the leveraging of £23m of private sector investment in R&D (target £20m) through Invest NI's main programme at a cost of £15m. Also the agency established 17 centres of Research Excellence and increased participation in Research and Development programmes by 7.9%. One of the primary purposes of the Centre of Research Excellence is to facilitate collaboration.

## Economic Prospects

There are few professional forecasts available in the UK (at a regional level) relating to the future of the Northern Ireland economy. About the best available is produced between the new economic research agency (ERINI) and Regional Forecast Consultants (Dr Graham Gudgin) who provide an expert forecast for all regions in the United Kingdom.

In recent years the forecast has pointed out that despite its well-publicised difficulties the Northern Ireland economy, taken as a region, has been one of the star performers in the United Kingdom.

Despite its outlying location, Northern Ireland's economic growth has been rapid and close to that of the South-East of England. It has easily outpaced growth in all the northern regions of the UK. Given Northern Ireland's structural disadvantages this is primarily explained by competitive advantages such as low wages and a high level of government subsidies and spending.

The Gudgin forecast (see Table 7.17 below) sees little medium term change in these fundamentals and therefore concludes that steady growth is set to continue. By UK standards the overall performance projected, while continuing to lag behind the forecast for the rapidly growing Republic of Ireland economy, is creditable in the context of the United Kingdom.

However there are dissenting voices both in business and academia who argue that Northern Ireland's positive economic outlook is projected on the back of ever continuing and ultimately unsustainable real increases in public expenditure - effectively subsidisation of Northern Ireland by the UK as a whole.

The public expenditure plans for Northern Ireland over the next three years indicate substantial real increases in spending (current and capital) - see page 283. By 2007-08 there will be a net increase of nearly 30% (or around £2 billion) against current levels. This very significant additional injection into the Northern Ireland economy will bolster overall economic performance even if the decline in manufacturing and other key sectors continues.

There is even the prospect that with the re-establishment of devolved government, the investment in public infrastructure may be expanded further. Under the Reinvestment and Reform Initiative a devolved administration would have access to very substantial low-cost finance for infrastructural investment. The local parties have indicated their intention to invest heavily to overcome the infrastructural deficit and bring Northern Ireland infrastructure up to European standards. Should this happen the province could enjoy a medium-term economic boom.

However, in the long run the overdependence on public expenditure will have to be corrected. There is a growing view that the local economy has a few years grace to get the private sector into a rapid growth cycle through greater entrepreneurship and innovation before reality eventually re-asserts itself. Failure to kick-start greater private sector wealth creation will manifest itself in the form of a very weak economy after the next few years.

**Table 7.16: Projected GDP Growth (%) 2004-05**

| | 2003 | 2004 | 2005 |
|---|---|---|---|
| OECD | 2.1 | 3.5 | 3.1 |
| US | 3.1 | 4.5 | 3.9 |
| Eurozone | 0.5 | 1.8 | 2.2 |
| Republic of Ireland | 3.7 | 5.0 | 5.5 |
| United Kingdom | 2.2 | 3.5 | 2.8 |
| Northern Ireland | 2.5 | 3.0 | 3.0 |

Source First Trust Economic Outlook, Sept. 2004

**Table 7.17: Economic Prospects**
**Northern Ireland Forecasts**

| | 2002 | 2003 | 2004 | 2005 | 2006 | 2007 |
|---|---|---|---|---|---|---|
| Employment Change (thousands) | 14 | 11 | 16 | 14 | 8 | 3 |
| Total GVA (annual growth % pa) | 3.2 | 3.6 | 4.6 | 3.8 | 2.8 | 2.7 |
| Unemployment Rate (% of work-force) | 4.5 | 4.2 | 3.8 | 3.6 | 3.7 | 3.9 |

Source R/FOEF Economic Outlook Autumn 2004

# Sectoral Analysis of The Northern Ireland Economy

## Agriculture and Food Sector

Agriculture, forestry and fishing are important industries in the local economy. The sector accounts for around 4.5 per cent of regional Gross Domestic Product (GDP) and 4.8 per cent of total employment. Proportionately, agriculture's contribution to employment in Northern Ireland is the highest of all UK regions and only in East Anglia does it provide a greater share of regional GDP.

There are around 28,500 active, mostly family-run, farm businesses in Northern Ireland, the number of which have been declining at a rate of nearly 2 per cent per year for the past ten years. Although the average size of farms is more than twice the average size of European farms it is half the size of farms in the United Kingdom.

Because of the downward trend in the number of farms the average farm size has increased gradually. Three-fifths of farm businesses own the land which they farm and the remainder are a mixture of owned land, and land which is leased on a short-term lettings basis.

**Table 7.18: Key facts about Agriculture**

| | NI | UK | ROI |
|---|---|---|---|
| Gross Value Added (GVA) Agriculture as % of total GVA | 2.5[1] | 0.8[1] | 3.2[3] |
| **Employment** Agriculture employment | 34[2] | 390[2] | 121[2] |
| As % of total Civil employment | 4.8[2] | 1.4[2] | 6.9[2] |
| **Land Use** As % of total Civil area | 78.7[1] | 70.4[1] | 63.1[2] |
| **Farms** Number ('000) | 28.5[1] | 232[2] | 142[2] |
| Average agricultural area (ha) | 37.4[2] | 71.6[2] | 31.4[2] |

Note 1 2002, Note 2 2001, Note 3 2000

Source DARD

There was a sharp fall in farm income in recent years. The sharp decline in income was due to several factors: a fall in the average producer milk price; and the consequences of adverse weather conditions particularly 2002, which led to reduced volumes of output and increased input costs. Also the damage done by the outbreak of foot and mouth disease which had proved devastating in Britain.

Although figures are not yet available for 2004 there are indications that there has been a rise in farm incomes due to the strengthening of the Euro against Sterling. Agreement was reached in 2003 on further CAP reform, which requires member states to break the link between agricultural subsidies and production. As reform of the CAP unfolds it will continue to have a significant impact on farm incomes. There are approximately 400 food processors in Northern Ireland, employing around 19,000 people and generating approximately 20 per cent of the manufacturing sector's total external sales. This continues to be a vitally important sector for the local economy and is the subject of a major strategic review by government.

**Table 7.19: Number of Farmers and Workers Northern Ireland 1989-2003**

| | 1989 | 1996 | 2003 |
|---|---|---|---|
| Total full-time farmers | 27,097 | 22,710 | 19,265 |
| Total part-time farmers | 15,864 | 17,204 | 14,728 |
| Total Farmers | 42,961 | 39,914 | 33,993 |

Source DARD

**Table 7.20: Farm Numbers Northern Ireland 1997-2003**

| Farm business type | 1997 | 1999 | 2001 | 2003 |
|---|---|---|---|---|
| Cereals | 544 | 631 | 537 | 457 |
| General cropping | 443 | 372 | 311 | 295 |
| Horticulture | 402 | 370 | 331 | 322 |
| Pigs & poultry | 846 | 591 | 523 | 510 |
| Dairy | 5,233 | 5,039 | 4,741 | 4,425 |
| Cattle & sheep (LFA) | 16,955 | 16,891 | 16,061 | 15,700 |
| Cattle & sheep (lowland) | 4,860 | 4,985 | 4,850 | 4,589 |
| Mixed | 1,567 | 1,305 | 1,067 | 1,058 |
| Others | 1,268 | 1,048 | 1,397 | 925 |
| | 32,118 | 31,232 | 29,818 | 28,281 |

Source DARD

**Table 7.21: Farm Enterprises: Numbers and Average Size Northern Ireland 1981-2003**

| | 1981 | 1991 | 2003 |
|---|---|---|---|
| Dairy Cows | 1981 | 1991 | 2003 |
| Number | 270,459 | 274,058 | 290,145 |
| Beef Cows | | | |
| Number | 231,258 | 285,515 | 295,447 |
| Total Cattle | 1,544,553 | 1,655,727 | 1,685,254 |
| Ave. herd size | 42.8 | 55.5 | 69.3 |
| Sheep & Lambs | | | |
| Number | 1,283,769 | 2,889,429 | 2,241,112 |
| Ave. flock size | 129.5 | 215.0 | 252.4 |
| Total Pigs | | | |
| Number | 729,462 | 684,209 | 433,689 |
| Ave. herd size | 91.6 | 204.6 | 794.3 |
| Poultry | | | |
| Number | 12,209,044 | 12,079,343 | 18,525,370 |
| Ave. flock size | 1,601 | 3,706 | 9,356 |

Source DARD

## Agriculture and Food Agencies

Livestock & Meat Commission for Northern Ireland
31 Ballinderry Road, Lisburn, BT28 2SL
Tel: 028 9263 3000
Fax: 028 9263 3001
Chief Executive: David Rutledge

Food Standards Agency

FOOD STANDARDS AGENCY
NORTHERN IRELAND

Unit 10B Clarendon Road
Belfast, BT1 3BG
Tel: 028 9041 7700
Fax: 028 9041 7726
Email: infofsani@foodstandards.gsi.gov.uk
Web: www.food.gov.uk
Director: Morris McAllister

The Food Standards Agency is a non-ministerial UK department set up in 2000. It has a non-executive board appointed to protect public interest.

The FSA has offices in Belfast (FSANI), Aberdeen, Cardiff and London and has three core aims:

- Put the consumer first
- Be open and accessible
- Be an independent voice

FSANI's functions include food safety and standards. Its roles and responsibilities include:

- Commissioning research
- Setting standards for enforcement of legislation
- Monitoring performance of enforcement authorities

The Agency has the power to issue, revoke and suspend licences approvals and authorisations for food businesses.

## Major Agricultural and Food Companies

Armaghdown Creameries Ltd
30 Rathfriland Road
Banbridge, BT32 4LN
Tel: 028 4066 2742
Fax: 028 4066 2443
Principal Activity: dairy products
Chief Executive: David Graham

Ballyrashane Co-op Society Ltd
18 Creamery Road, Coleraine, BT52 2NE
Tel: 028 7034 3265
Fax: 028 7035 1653
Principal Activity: milk and dairy products
Managing Director: Francis Kerr

Dairy Produce Packers Ltd
Millburn Road, Coleraine, BT52 1QZ
Tel: 028 7035 6231
Fax: 028 7035 6412
Principal Activity: dairy products
Chief Executive: Alan McMinn

Dale Farm Dairies Ltd
Pennybridge Industrial Estate
Larne Road, Ballymena, BT42 3HB
Tel: 028 2564 5161
Fax: 028 2565 1108
Principal Activity: dairy products
Chief Executive: Neville Cruikshanks

Fane Valley Co-op
Alexander Road, Armagh, BT61 7JF
Tel: 028 3752 2344
Fax: 028 3751 0511
Principal activity: milk and dairy products
Chief Executive: David Graham

Fayrefields Food Ireland
123-127 York Street, Belfast, BT15 1AB
Tel: 028 9024 7448
Fax: 028 9032 6375
Principal activity:
dairy produce distributors
Chief Executive: David Graham

Glanbia Cheese Ltd
35 Steps Road, Magheralin
Craigavon, BT67 0QY
Tel: 028 9261 1274
Fax: 028 9261 2464
Principal Activity: dairy products
Chief Executive: Conor Donovan

Golden Cow Dairies Ltd
25-29 Artabrackagh Road
Portadown, Craigavon, BT62 4HB
Tel: 028 3833 8411
Fax: 028 3835 0292
General Manager: Eamon Rice

Lakeland Dairies (Omagh) Ltd
46 Beltany Road, Omagh, BT78 5NF
Tel: 028 8224 6411
Fax: 028 8225 6496
General Manager: Michael Hanley

Leckpatrick Dairies Ltd.
10 Rossdowney Road
Londonderry, BT47 6NS
Tel: 028 7131 1300
Fax: 028 7134 2723
Principal Activity: dairy product manufacturers and distributors
Managing Director: Kieran Mulgrew

United Dairy Farmers
456 Antrim Road, Belfast, BT15 5GD
Tel: 028 9037 2237
Fax: 028 9037 2222
Principal Activity: milk collection and sale
Chief Executive: David Dobbin

## Meat and Poultry Processing

ABP Lurgan Ltd
Unit 33, Annesborough Industrial Estate
Annesborough Road, Lurgan, BT67 9JD
Tel: 028 3832 3622
Fax: 028 3832 3944
Principal Activity: abattoir
Managing Director: John Corr

ABP Newry
Greenbank Industrial Estate
Warrenpoint Road, Newry, BT34 2PD
Tel: 028 3026 3211
Fax: 028 3026 1321
Principal Activity: meat processing
General Manager: Colin Duffy

Crossgar Poultry Ltd
11 Kilmore Road
Crossgar, Downpatrick, BT30 9HJ
Tel: 028 4483 0301
Fax: 028 4483 0724
Principal Activity: poultry processing
Chief Executive: Gerald Bell

Dungannon Meats Ltd
Granville Industrial Estate
Dungannon, BT70 1NJ
Tel: 028 8775 3338
Fax: 028 8775 3790
Chief Executive: Wilson Graham

Foyle Food Group
Lisahally, Campsie, Derry, BT47 6TJ
Tel: 028 7186 0691
Fax: 028 7186 0700
Principal Activity: meat processing
Chief Executive: Robert Watson

Henry Denny & Sons Ltd
6 Corcrain Road, Portadown
Craigavon, BT62 3UF
Tel: 028 3833 2411
Fax: 028 3833 4913
Principal Activity: pork processing
Chief Executive: Gareth Fitzgerald

Linden Foods
Granville Industrial Estate
Dungannon, BT70 1NJ
Tel: 028 8772 4777
Fax: 028 8772 4714
Principal Activity: meat processors
Managing Directors: Richard Moore
Gerry Maguire

Moy Park Ltd
The Food Park
39 Seagoe Industrial Estate
Craigavon, BT63 5QE
Tel: 028 3835 2233
Fax: 028 3836 8011
Principal Activity: poultry processing
Chief Executive: Trefor Campbell

O'Kane Poultry Ltd
170 Larne Road
Ballymena, BT42 3HA
Tel: 028 2564 1111
Fax: 028 2566 0680
Principal Activity: poultry processing
Chief Executive: Billy O'Kane

Omagh Meats Ltd
52 Doogary Road, Omagh, BT79 0BQ
Tel: 028 8224 3201
Fax: 028 8224 3013
Principal Activity: meat processing
Managing Director: Wayne Acheson

## Drinks Companies

Bass Ireland Ltd
Ulster Brewery, Glen Road
Belfast, BT11 8BY
Tel: 028 9030 1301
Fax: 028 9062 4884
Principal Activity: brewing
Managing Director: Steve McAllister

Bushmills Distillery Ltd
2 Distillery Road, Bushmills, BT57 8XH
Tel: 028 2073 1521
Fax: 028 2073 1339
Principal Activity: whiskey manufacture
Managing Director: Gill Jefferson

Cantrell & Cochrane Ltd
468-472 Castlereagh Road
Belfast, BT5 6RG
Tel: 028 9079 9335
Fax: 028 9070 7206
Principal Activity: soft drinks manufacturer
Managing Director: Colin Gordon

Coca-Cola HBC Ltd
The Green, Lambeg
Lisburn, BT27 5SS
Tel: 028 9267 4231
Fax: 028 9267 1049
Principal Activity:
drinks bottling and distribution
Executive Director: John Barrett

Diageo Ltd NI
Apollo Road, Adelaide Industrial Estate
Belfast, BT12 6PJ
Tel: 028 9066 1611
Fax: 028 9066 9889
Principal Activity: drinks distribution
Commercial Director (Acting):
Michael McCann

Dillon Bass Ltd
Hawthorne Park, 41A Stockman's Way
Belfast, BT9 7ET
Tel: 028 9038 2233
Fax: 028 9038 2266
Principal Activity: wine and spirit
marketing and distribution
Managing Director: Peter Gallogly

James E McCabe Ltd
Carn Industrial Estate
Portadown, BT63 5QL
Tel: 028 3833 3102
Fax: 028 3833 5916
Principal Activity: wine and spirit retailers
Managing Director: John O'Hare

## Other Processing

Cuisine de France
Unit 5, Blaris Industrial Estate
Old Hill Road, Lisburn, BT27 5QB
Tel: 028 9260 3222
Fax: 028 9260 3072
Principal Activity: bakery products
Managing Director: Hugo Kane

Farmlea Foods Ltd
Farmlea House, 23 Shore Road
Holywood, BT18 9HX
Tel: 028 9042 7222
Fax: 028 9042 7538
Principal Activity: food brokers
Managing Director: Arthur Richmond

Hilton Food Group
Derryloran Industrial Estate
Sandholes Road, Cookstown, BT80 9LU
Tel: 028 8676 2106
Fax: 028 8676 2327
Principal Activity: fresh food distributors
Managing Director: Tracey Acheson

Gallaher Ltd
201 Galgorm Road
Ballymena, BT42 1HS
Tel: 028 2564 6666
Fax: 028 2566 5210
Principal Activity: tobacco products
General Manager: Adrian Goodrich

Irwins Bakery Ltd
5 Diviny Drive
Portadown, Craigavon, BT63 5WE
Tel: 028 3833 2421
Fax: 028 3833 3918
Principal Activity: bakery products
Managing Director: Brian Irwin

John Thompson & Sons
35-39 York Road, Belfast, BT15 3GW
Tel: 028 9035 1321
Fax: 028 9035 1420
Principal Activity: animal feedstuff
manufacturer
Managing Director: John McCauley

Tayto
Tandragee Castle
Tandragee, Craigavon, BT62 2AB
Tel: 028 3884 1466
Fax: 028 3884 0085
Principal Activity: snack food
manufacturer
Chief Executive: Paul Allen

## Energy and Environment Sector

### Energy Policy in Northern Ireland

Northern Ireland has historically faced a number of fundamental challenges in terms of energy supply: lack of indigenous resources has meant over-dependence on fuel imports. This coupled with lack of interconnection with adjacent energy grids has resulted in above average system costs and comparatively high prices for final energy users. In recent years however there has been the development of interconnection with Great Britain (electricity and gas) and the Republic of Ireland (electricity), which has helped negate the inherent disadvantages of a small isolated system.

### Strategic Framework for Energy

In 2003 the Department of Enterprise, Trade and Investment produced a draft energy strategy for Northern Ireland, followed by a strategic framework document in 2004. This strategy seeks to set out future priorities for the development of the energy market and infrastructure in Northern Ireland. The responses to DETI's draft strategy covered the key strategic issues facing the energy sector and energy users in Northern Ireland: electricity prices; the all-island energy market; energy efficiency; fuel poverty; renewable energy; security of supply and energy and the environment.

The DETI Strategic Framework for Energy stages 'Our vision is for a competitive, sustainable, reliable energy market at the minimum cost necessary'. There are four policy goals:

- Reducing energy costs;
- Building competitive markets;
- Enhancing sustainability in energy;
- Reliable energy supplies;

Although the strategy lists proposed actions under each policy goal, the document has been criticised for having a lack of specificity or prioritisation – given the fact that Northern Ireland's major energy challenges have been understood for many years.

### Electricity

The electricity market in Northern Ireland has a number of competing suppliers including Viridian Group's marketers, Energia, ESB Independent Energy and renewable energy company, Airtricity. At present 35% of the market is open to competition with around 7,000 customers eligible to choose their electricity supplier. During 2004 there will be a phased opening of the market for non-domestic customers and the market must be fully open to all customers in 2007.

### Natural Gas Market

Natural gas was introduced to Northern Ireland in 1992 and since then Phoenix Natural Gas has invested around £170m in its network in the greater Belfast area. The natural gas market is now partially open with only the very large users of natural gas able to choose their supplier, although at present there is no natural gas being supplied by a supplier other than Phoenix Natural Gas. From 1st January 2005 all customers will be able to choose their supplier and by this date there will be an estimated 80,000 natural gas customers in Northern Ireland (7,000 business and 73,000 domestic).

### Investment in Energy Infrastructure

Investment in Northern Ireland energy infrastructure has seen the development of two new power stations: a new 600 MW combined cycle gas turbine (CCGT) plant at Ballylumford which came on line in late 2003 and the new Coolkeeragh power station in the North West, (now owned 100% by ESB), a 400 MW CCGT which will come on stream in March 2005. The Coolkeeragh project is also part of the extension of the natural gas network from greater Belfast to the North West. Bord Gáis Eireann is building the transmission line to supply the new gas fired power station and plans to distribute natural gas to towns along the pipeline route. BGE is also planning to interconnect the gas networks North and South on the Eastern Dublin/Belfast corridor.

### Sustainable Energy

DETI's energy strategy, in line with UK energy policy, seeks to put mechanisms in place to support increased renewable energy sources. By 2012, 12% of total electricity consumed is to come from renewable sources. One important initiative to help achieve this in Northern Ireland is Action Renewables. This is a joint initiative between Viridian Group and DETI to raise awareness of renewable forms of energy and increase the deployment of such technologies in Northern Ireland at all levels from domestic to industrial customers.

For the foreseeable future, wind is the largest source of renewable energy in Northern Ireland. There are two large scale developers, B9 and Airtricity, active in the local market and many small scale individual wind farm developments.

In addition to increasing the amount of renewable forms of energy, any sustainable energy strategy also has a strong element of using energy more efficiently. In Northern Ireland energy users are supported by the initiatives of Invest NI and the Carbon Trust, a non-profit making company set up by the Government to promote sustainable energy use.

### Climate Change

International concern about climate change - attributed to the ever increasing emissions of greenhouse gases into the atmosphere - has led to the Kyoto agreement under which the UK has signed up to significant reductions in emissions.

## Major Energy Organisations/ Companies

### Action Renewables

Woodchester House, 50 Newforge Lane
Belfast, BT9 5NW
Tel: 028 9068 5061
Fax: 028 9068 5035
Web: www.actionrenewables.org
Director: Dr Andy McCrea MBE

### AES Kilroot Power Station

Larne Road Carrickfergus, BT38 7LX
Tel: 028 9335 1644
Fax: 028 9335 1086
Managing Director: Shane Lynch

### Airtricity Energy Supply Ltd

2nd Floor, 83-85 Great Victoria Street
Belfast, BT2 7AF
Tel: 028 9043 7470
Chief Executive Officer: Mark Ennis

### B9 Energy Services Ltd.

Willowbank Road
Millbrook Industrial Estate
Larne, BT40 2SF
Tel: 028 2836 3900
Fax: 028 2826 3901
Managing Director: Michael Harper

### Carbon Trust

CARBON TRUST
Making business sense of climate change

Unit 9, The Innovation Centre
Northern Ireland Science Park
Queen's Island
Belfast, BT3 9DT
Tel: 028 9073 7910
Fax: 028 9073 7911
Email: ctni@thecarbontrust.co.uk
Web: www.thecarbontrust.co.uk

Manager
Northern Ireland
Geoff Smyth

The Carbon Trust - an independent company set up by Government - works with UK business and the public sector to cut carbon emissions and develop commercial low carbon technologies.

### Coolkeeragh ESB

COOLKEERAGH ESB

Coolkeeragh ESB Ltd
PO Box 217
2 Electra Road
Maydown, Londonderry BT47 6XU
Tel: 028 7186 4700
Fax: 028 7186 4701
Web: www.coolkeeragh.com
Email: ccgt@coolkeeragh.co.uk

Coolkeeragh ESB Ltd, is a joint venture between Coolkeeragh Power and ESB International, which has constructed the new 400 MW natural gas combined cycle electrical power station at Coolkeeragh in the Northwest. The station will use the most advanced and environmentally friendly technology to deliver efficient and competitive power to Northern Ireland

### DCC Energy Ltd

Airport Road West, Sydenham
Belfast, BT3 9ED
Tel: 028 9073 2611
Chief Executive: Sam Chambers

### Energia

energia

Energia House
62 Newforge Lane
Belfast, BT9 5NF
Tel: 028 9068 5900
Fax: 028 9068 5902
Email: sales@energia.ie
Web: www.energia.ie
Principal Activity: energy supply

Head of Sales
and Marketing
John Mawhinney

Energia provide energy solutions switched on to today's business needs.

Energia operate throughout Ireland with Offices in Belfast, Dublin, Cork, Galway and Omagh and is a member of the Viridian Group.

### Energy Saving Trust NI

Enterprise House, 55-59 Adelaide Street
Belfast, BT2 8FE
Tel: 028 9072 6006
Head of EST NI: Noel Williams

### ESB Independent Energy

ESB Independent Energy

ESB Independent Energy
33 Clarendon Dock
Laganside
Belfast, BT1 3BG
LoCall: 0845 309 8138
Web: www.esbie.co.uk
Email: info@esbie.ie

ESB Independent Energy is a subsidiary company of the ESB Group and one of the largest suppliers in the liberalised electricity market in Northern Ireland. Offering customers a unique combination of competitive price and premium service their offering is based on understanding the business, energy usage patterns and the needs of their customers.

### Invest Northern Ireland

Regional Environment & Energy Unit
17 Antrim Road
Lisburn, BT28 3AL
Tel: 028 9262 3028
Fax: 028 9262 3103
Web: www.investni.com
Energy and Environment
Manager: Dan Sinton

### NIE Electricity Infrastructure

120 Malone Road, Belfast, BT9 5HT
Tel: 028 9066 1100
Managing Director: Laurence MacKenzie

### Northern Ireland Authority for Energy Regulation

Brookmount Buildings
42 Fountain Street, Belfast, BT1 5EE
Tel: 028 9031 1575
Chairman: Douglas McIldoon

### Phoenix Natural Gas Limited

197 Airport Road West, Belfast, BT3 9ED
Tel: 0845 4555 555
Chief Executive: Peter Dixon

### Premier Power Limited

Islandmagee, Larne, BT40 3RS
Tel: 028 9338 1100
Principal Activity: power generation
Chief Executive Officer: Jeff Baillie

### Viridian Group PLC

Danesfort, 120 Malone Road
Belfast, BT9 5HT
Tel: 028 9066 8416
Fax: 028 9068 9128
Group Chief Executive: Dr Patrick Haren

## Manufacturing Industry

### Manufacturing in Northern Ireland

Manufacturing in Northern Ireland which employs around 88,000 people is - by the standards of western European countries - a relatively small part of the economy. It is also in long-term decline in terms of numbers employed and share of overall GDP. Traditional local industries of shipbuilding, engineering and textiles have been in sharp decline in recent years. However, among all the bad news Northern Ireland's manufacturing productivity has improved significantly year on year and the sector boasts a number of export leaders in their particular industrial market sub-sector.

Following a decade of relative stability in the manufacturing sector in Northern Ireland throughout the 1990s, the new millennium saw a decline in manufacturing jobs. In 2003 there were 92,760 people employed in manufacturing compared to nearly 107,000 in 1998. In the year to Q3 2003, manufacturing output dropped by 3 per cent and nearly 5,000 employees lost their jobs. In 2003 a further 4,500 redundancies were announced in manufacturing with just over half of these in the textiles sector.

In recent years continuing strength of the pound has had a huge impact on exports to the eurozone and many manufacturing companies have faced unprecedented pressure on margins, having to absorb price reductions to remain competitive. Many Northern Ireland companies however are overcoming the difficulty of the weak euro by finding new international markets outside the eurozone. Indeed, exports from Northern Ireland manufacturing companies to 'Rest of The World' markets have grown in recent years. However the experience in recent years has varied considerably across individual sectors.

The past decade has also seen a structural change in the make-up of the manufacturing sector. Over the period 1995-2000, NI manufacturing output increased by 29 per cent. The biggest sectoral increase over this period was in engineering and allied industries (an increase of 78 per cent). The largest decrease (approximately 16 per cent) occurred in the leather, textile and textile products industries.

### Engineering Sector

Traditionally engineering has been a vital sector of the economy employing over 30,000 people and accounting for a quarter of all manufacturing jobs. Large companies dominate, although there are many active small businesses in the sector. Despite a worldwide shift from manufacturing into services the engineering sector continues to perform quite strongly in Northern Ireland. The key sub-sectors in engineering are aerospace, the automotive sector and shipbuilding.

The aerospace sector was hit hard by the aftermath of 9/11 and the slow down in international travel. Shorts, the biggest player in the Northern Ireland aerospace sector, which in buoyant economic conditions employed over 6,000 people, have announced significant job losses recently.

A cluster of aerospace-related manufacturing companies has grown around Shorts. Local companies now manufacture aircraft seats, while RFD/Beaufort in Dunmurry are world leaders in the design and production of life rafts and other life-saving equipment for aircrafts. RFD has expanded in recent years with acquisitions in the US, Italy and Australia.

*Finlay Blockmaking Plant, Co Tyrone*

In the automotive sector the Visteon plant in Belfast, previously the automotive components division of Ford Motor Company employs 600 people in automotive systems manufacture. The Montupet plant at Dunmurry on the outskirts of Belfast employs a similar number in the production of aluminium and alloy engine blocks and wheels for the major European motor manufacturers. In Craigavon Nacco Materials Handling has over 800 employees producing forklift trucks for worldwide markets. After a financial crisis, quarry equipment manufacturer Powerscreen has now recovered and continues to service markets worldwide.

Extreme difficulties continue for Belfast shipyard Harland and Wolff owned by Norwegian shipping company Fred Olsen Energy. The yard continues to fight for its survival with employment reduced to an all time low of around 150. It has now gone beyond the point where it can actually recover its ship building capability and has planned its future around marine maintenance and other engineering services. Founded in 1861 Harland & Wolff has dominated the east of Belfast, both physically and economically. It was famed for building the Titanic Cruise Liner and at its peak employed 35,000 people.

### Chemicals and Plastics

Northern Ireland has been a base for the manufacture of chemicals since the mid 1950s. It currently employs around 10,500 people. During the 1960s and 1970s Northern Ireland had a significant chemical sector, which was dominated by the manufacture of man made fibres. ICI, Courtaulds, Monsanto, DuPont and British Enkalon had major plants in Northern Ireland.

There were also a number of smaller plants supplying process chemicals and services to these plants including a large BOC plant at Maydown. The recession in the man-made fibres sector in the early 1980s saw the closure of all these plants except DuPont which still operates on its Maydown site, although now with only two plants. There are now no upstream polymer companies in Northern Ireland and any plastic and polymers manufacturing is in the lower value extrusion segment of the industry.

**Electrical and Electronics**

The electrical and electronics sector employs over 11,000 people in Northern Ireland, equivalent to around 12 per cent of manufacturing employment. UK and Northern Ireland electronics companies have the lowest operating costs in Europe. Operating costs, particularly labour related costs account on average for approximately 57 per cent of core costs for this sector. Therefore, the Belfast area is particularly attractive to electronics companies seeking a base within the European Union. The information and communications technologies sub sector's share of overall output from the sector is expected to grow by almost 50 per cent over the next ten years.

Northern Ireland is the base for several leading electronics companies including AVX, Seagate Technologies and Nortel Networks. There is also a growing number of local companies operating in specialist niches within the electronics sector. Many of these companies have been spun out of Northern Ireland's two universities, which have internationally renowned electronics research centres. The focus of the centres has been on the information and communication technologies (ICT) sub-sectors.

The ICT sub-sector is expected to dominate the electronics sector within the next five years, in contrast to the consumer electronics sector, which is not expected to grow at the same pace. Northern Ireland is a world leader in Digital Signal Processing (DSP) with Queen's University renowned for developing this important technology, which powers nearly every sector of the electronics industry. Queen's is one of a few universities in the UK that has its own silicon fabrication facilities.

Northern Ireland also has a growing community of software development companies - represented by the Software Industry Federation, Momentum. Companies such as Kainos, Lagan Technologies and Northbrook are leaders in niche software markets.

**Textiles and Apparel**

Textiles manufacturing has a 300-year history in Northern Ireland, originating in the world famous Irish linen industry. The industry now comprises businesses in fibres and yarns, threads, fabric (woven, non-woven and knitted), garments, hosiery, carpets, household furnishings and industrial textiles.

Sadly, after shipbuilding, textiles in Northern Ireland is probably the traditional sector in most serious long-term decline. In recent years there has been a spate of closures collapsing the total employed (textiles and apparel) to around 6,500 people.

The sector has experienced a period of intense competitive pressure over the past five years, and this has changed the landscape of the industry considerably. The drivers for this have been the consumer demand for a wider choice of well-designed clothing and household goods at lower cost, coupled with the globalisation of the industry.

Manufacturing hubs have developed rapidly in Eastern Europe, Turkey and the Far East, and many of the large publicly owned companies have uprooted to sources of cheaper production. Companies in Northern Ireland servicing the volume high street market have had to re-examine how and where they do business to compete. Excellent design, efficient customer service, IT expertise and balancing home production with offshore sourcing have been the survival tactics of companies such as bedding company Bedeck, which has experienced an average 10% growth year on year over the past decade.

Other companies have concentrated on niche markets where products are differentiated either by design, quality and branding or by innovation. Glenaden Shirts, a former Coats Viyella plant manufacturing solely for M&S, underwent a management buyout several years ago. The new company very successfully targeted the luxury market by producing for some of the world's most prestigious brand names and launching its own premium brand.

Irish Linen, once seen as the most traditional of fabrics, has also reinvented itself with new treatments and blends to improve performance, including Irish Linen & Lycra®, the result of collaboration between the Irish linen industry, INVISTA (formerly DuPont Textiles & Interiors), University of Ulster and Invest NI.

The Northern Ireland Textiles and Apparel Association (NITA), the industry's representative body in Northern Ireland, has supported its members in refashioning their businesses. It has run a number of programmes in partnership with Invest NI to promote the use of branding, encourage product development and improve business competitiveness.

**Life Sciences**

The life sciences industry employs almost 4,000 people in some 50 organisations, operating in a range of activities across the industry. There is a growing network of sub contract services ranging from custom synthesis, pharmacology and bio-analytical services to packaging and sterilisation. The sector has also increasing research and development capability in Northern Ireland. There are now several research centres focusing on activities in the sector.

**Major Manufacturing Company Listings**

What follows below is a list of manufacturing companies - which are located in Northern Ireland across the main sectors. The list is by no means exhaustive although it does include nearly all of the larger undertakings.

## Manufacturing Companies: General

### 3M Industrial Tapes
5-7 Balloo Drive, Bangor, BT19 7PB
Tel: 028 9127 8200
Fax: 028 9145 1072
Principal Activity: industrial tape manufacture
Plant Manager: Jon Nixon

### Acheson & Glover Ltd
127 Crievehill Road
Fivemiletown, BT75 0SY
Tel: 028 8952 1275
Fax: 028 8952 1886
Principal Activity: bricks
Managing Director: Raymond Acheson

### John Finlay Ltd
Tullyvannon, Ballygawley
Dungannon, BT70 2HW
Tel: 028 8556 8666
Fax: 028 8556 8447
Principal Activity: concrete products
Managing Director: Phil Gray

### Quinn Group Ltd
Head Office, Derrylin
Enniskillen, BT92 9AU
Tel: 028 6774 8866
Fax: 028 6774 8800
Principal Activity: concrete products
Managing Director: Sean Quinn

### RJ Hall & Sons Ltd
Homebright House
Hillview Industrial Estate
Belfast, BT14 7BT
Tel: 028 9035 1707
Fax: 028 9075 3833
Principal Activity: brushes
Managing Director: Max Crosby Brown

### Readymix Northern Ireland
RMC House, Upper Dunmurry Lane
Belfast, BT17 0AJ
Tel: 028 9061 6611
Fax: 028 9061 9969
Principal Activity: concrete
Managing Director: Joe Doyle

### Teleflex Medical
Portadown Road, Lurgan
Craigavon, BT66 8RD
Tel: 028 3832 5771
Fax: 028 3832 4306
Principal Activity: medical devices
Managing Director: Gerry McCaffery

### Tyrone Crystal Ltd
Killybrackey
Dungannon, BT71 6TT
Tel: 028 8772 5335
Fax: 028 8772 6260
Principal Activity: crystal manufacturing
Managing Director: Peter Nunn

### Thales Air Defence Limited
Alanbrooke Road
Belfast, BT6 9HB
Tel: 028 9046 5200
Fax: 028 9046 5201
Web: www.thales-ad.co.uk
Principal Activity: defence manufacture
Managing Director: Miller Crawford

### Wrightbus
Galgorm Industrial Estate
Finaghy Road, Ballymena, BT42 1PY
Tel: 028 2564 1212
Fax: 028 2564 9703
Principal Activity: coaches
Managing Director: Jeff Wright

## Manufacturing Companies: Engineering

### Arntz Belting Co Ltd
Pennyburn Pass, Londonderry, BT48 0AE
Tel: 028 7126 1221
Fax: 028 7126 3386
Principal Activity: fan belts
Managing Director: Robert Moore

### Bombardier Aerospace
Airport Road, Belfast, BT3 9DZ
Tel: 028 9045 8444
Fax: 028 9073 3396
Principal Activity: aircraft equipment
Vice President: Michael Ryan

### BE Aerospace
2 Moor Road, Kilkeel
Newry, BT34 4NG
Tel: 028 4176 2471
Fax: 028 4176 4297
Principal Activity: aircraft seats

### Copeland Ltd
Ballyray Industrial Estate
Sandholes Road, Cookstown, BT80 9DG
Tel: 028 8676 0100
Fax: 028 8676 0110
Principal Activity: compressors
Plant Director: Declan Billington

### Crane Stockham Valve Ltd
Alexander Road
Belfast, BT6 9HJ
Tel: 028 9070 4222
Fax: 028 9040 1582
Principal Activity: valves
Commercial Director: Paul Clarke

### Denman International
Balloo Industrial Estate
Balloo Drive, Bangor, BT19 2QY
Tel: 028 9147 4822
Principal Activity: injection moulding
Managing Director: John Rainey

### FG Wilson Engineering Ltd
Old Glenarm Road, Larne, BT40 1EJ
Tel: 028 2826 1000
Fax: 028 2826 1111
Principal Activity: generators
Chief Executive Officer: Dr Mark Sweeney

### Fisher Engineering Ltd
Main Street, Ballinamallard
Enniskillen, BT94 2FY
Tel: 028 6638 8521
Fax: 028 6638 8706
Principal Activity: steelwork
Managing Director: Ernie Fisher

### John Crane UK Ltd
66-96 Queen Street
Ballymena, BT42 2BE
Tel: 028 2565 3569
Fax: 028 2564 1002
Principal Activity: mechanical seals & couplings
General Manager: Hubert Dunlop

### Glen Electric Ltd
Greenbank Industrial Estate
Rampart Road, Newry, BT34 2QU
Tel: 028 3026 4621
Fax: 028 3026 6122
Principal Activity: electrical products
Managing Director: Brian McLoran

### Harland & Wolff SHI Ltd
Queens Island, Belfast. BT3 9DE
Tel: 028 9045 8456
Fax: 028 9045 8515
Principal Activity: Marine Maintenance
Chief Executive Officer: Robert J Cooper

### Heyn Engineering
1 Corry Place, Belfast Harbour Estate
Belfast, BT3 9AH
Tel: 028 9035 0022
Fax: 028 9035 0012
Principal Activity: engineering
Managing Director: Alec Toland

Langford Lodge Engineering Co
97 Largy Road, Crumlin, BT29 4RT
Tel: 028 9445 2451
Fax: 028 9445 2161
Principal Activity: precision engineering
Managing Director: Gary McAreavey

Mivan Ltd
Newpark, Greystone Road
Antrim, BT41 2QN
Tel: 028 9448 1000
Fax: 028 9448 1015
Principal Activity: ship outfitting/fitting
Chief Executive: Ivan McCabrey

Montupet UK Ltd
The Cutts, Dunmurry, Belfast, BT17 9HN
Tel: 028 9030 1049
Fax: 028 9030 3030
Principal Activity: aluminium components
Managing Director: Phillipe Bonnell

Munster Simms
Old Belfast Road, Bangor
Tel: 028 9127 0531
Fax: 028 9146 6421
Managing Director: Brian Batchelor

NACCO Materials Handling Ltd
Carn Industrial Estate
Portadown, Craigavon, BT63 5RH
Tel: 028 3835 4499
Fax: 028 3833 9977
Principal Activity: forklift trucks
Managing Director: Alan Little

RFD Beaufort
Kingsway
Dunmurry, Belfast, BT17 9AF
Tel: 028 9030 1531
Fax: 028 9062 1765
Principal Activity: life rafts
Managing Director: Uel McChesney

Rotary Group Ltd
5 Trench Road
Mallusk, Newtownabbey, BT36 4XA
Tel: 028 9083 1200
Fax: 028 9083 1201
Principal Activity: electrical mechanical & ventilation engineers
Managing Director: Thomas Jennings

Ryobi Aluminium Casting (UK) Ltd
5 Meadowbank Road
Troperslane Industrial Estate
Carrickfergus, BT38 8YF
Tel: 028 9335 1043
Fax: 028 9335 5644
Principal Activity: aluminium castings
Managing Director: John Hughes

Sanmina-Sci
19a Ballinderry Road, Lisburn, BT28 2SA
Tel: 028 9267 7634
Fax: 028 9266 0258
Principal Activity: sheet metal parts
Managing Director: David Farrell

Schlumberger Ltd
Cloughfern Avenue
Doagh Road, Monkstown
Newtownabbey, BT37 0UH
Tel: 028 9036 4444
Fax: 028 9085 2766
Principal Activity: manufacture oil well equipment
Managing Director: Pat Bixenman

SDC Trailers Ltd
116 Deerpark Road
Toomebridge, Co Antrim, BT41 3SS
Tel: 028 7965 0765
Fax: 028 7965 0042
Principal Activity: commercial trailers
Managing Director: Don Campbell

Seagoe Technology
Church Road, Seagoe, Portadown
Craigavon, BT63 5HU
Tel: 028 3833 3131
Fax: 028 3833 3042
Principal Activity: storage heaters
Managing Director: Neil Stewart

Sperrin Metal Products Ltd
Cahore Road, Draperstown
Magherafelt, BT45 7AP
Tel: 028 7962 8362
Fax: 028 7962 8972
Principal Activity: shelving systems
Director: Patrick Gormley

Visteon
Belfast Plant
Finaghy Road North, Belfast, BT11 9EF
Tel: 028 9060 8300
Fax: 028 9060 8490
Principal Activity: car parts
Plant Manager: Kevin Gaffney

## Manufacturing Companies: Electronics

AVX Ceramics Ltd
Hillmans Way, Ballycastle Road
Coleraine, BT52 2ED
Tel: 028 7034 4188
Fax: 028 7035 5527
Principal Activity: electrical components
Vice President: Martin McGuigan

Elite Electronic Systems Ltd
Lackaboy Industrial Estate
Killyvilly, Enniskillen, BT74 4RL
Tel: 028 6632 7172
Fax: 028 6632 5668
Principal Activity: PCB's electronics manufacturer
Managing Director: Ron Balfour

Fujitsu Telecommunications (Ireland)
10 Antrim Technology Park
Belfast Road, Muckamore
Antrim, BT41 1QS
Tel: 028 9442 8394
Fax: 028 9442 8395
Principal Activity: telecommunications equipment manufacture
General Manager: Peter Bowman

Irlandus Circuits
Annesborough Industrial Estate
Craigavon, BT67 9JJ
Tel: 028 3832 6211
Fax: 028 3832 4037
Principal Activity: printed circuit boards
Joint Managing Directors: Roy Adair, Sean Ritchie

Nitronica Ltd
Antrim Road, Ballynahinch, BT24 8AN
Tel: 028 9756 6200
Fax: 028 9756 6256
Principal Activities: Telecommunications
Managing Director: John Mellon

Nortel Networks
Doagh Road, Newtownabbey, BT36 6XA
Tel: 028 9036 5111
Fax: 028 9036 5285
Principal Activity: telecommunications equipment
Managing Director: Chris Conway

Partsnic UK Company Ltd
1 Sloefield Drive
Carrickfergus, BT38 8GD
Tel: 028 9336 0338
Fax: 028 9336 2223
Principal Activity: electronics components
Managing Director: S E Kim

### Seagate Technology
1 Disc Drive
Springtown Industrial Estate
Londonderry, BT48 0BF
Tel: 028 7127 4000
Fax: 028 7127 4202
Principal Activity: electronic & computer equipment
Managing Director: John Spangler

### Sintec Europe
72 Silverwood Road
Lurgan, Craigavon, BT66 6NB
Fax: 028 3832 3297
Principal Activity: sub contract manufacturer for electronics

## Manufacturing Companies: Textiles and Clothing

### Adria Ltd
Beechmount Avenue
Strabane, BT82 9BG
Tel: 028 7138 2568
Fax: 028 7138 2910
Principal Activity: ladies hosiery/socks
Managing Director: David Taylor

### Carpets International
7 Saintfield Road, Killinchy
Newtownards, BT23 6RJ
Tel: 028 9754 1441
Principal Activity: carpet yarns
(Re-opened in late 2003)

### Coats Barbour Ltd
Hilden Mill, Hilden, Lisburn, BT27 4RR
Tel: 028 9267 2231
Fax: 028 9267 8048
Principal Activity: thread manufacturer
Managing Director: Sherwell Fernando

### Desmond & Sons Ltd
Drumahoe, Londonderry, BT47 35D
Tel: 028 7129 5000
Fax: 028 7129 5005
Principal Activity: clothing manufacturer
Managing Director: Denis Desmond

### Ferguson Irish Linen
54 Scarva Road, Banbridge, BT32 3AU
Tel: 028 4062 3491
Fax: 028 4062 2453
Principal Activity: textiles
Managing Director: Dr David Neilly

### Interface Europe
Silverwood Industrial Estate
Lurgan, Craigavon, BT66 6LN
Tel: 028 3831 2600
Fax: 028 3831 2666
Principal Activity: Carpet tiles
General Manager: Tony McConville

### Magee Clothing Ltd
Millennium Park
Ballymena, BT42 4QJ
Tel: 028 2564 6211
Fax: 028 2564 5111
Principal Activity: men's clothing
Managing Director: Lynn Temple

### O'Neill Irish International Sports
Unit 1, Dublin Road Industrial Estate
Strabane, BT82 9EA
Tel: 028 7188 2320
Fax: 028 7188 2902
Principal Activity: sports manufacture
Managing Director: Kieran Kennedy

### Regency Spinning Ltd
Comber Road Industrial Estate
Comber, Newtownards, BT23 4RX
Tel: 028 9181 8836
Fax: 028 9182 0569
Principal Activity: textiles manufacture
Manager: Jim Johnson

### Ulster Weavers Home Fashions
Maldon Street
Donegall Road, Belfast, BT12 6NZ
Tel: 028 9032 9494
Fax: 028 9032 6612
Principal Activity: textile manufacturers
Managing Director: Dr Ian McMorris

### Huhtamaki Lurgan Ltd
Inn Road, Lurgan, Craigavon, BT66 7JW
Tel: 028 3832 7711
Fax: 028 3832 1782
Principal Activity: moulded fibre products
Managing Director: Steve Chapman

### William Clark & Sons Ltd
72 Upperlands
Maghera, BT46 5RZ
Tel: 028 7964 2214
Fax: 028 7954 7257
Principal Activity: textile manufacture
Managing Director: Richard Semple

## Manufacturing Companies: Chemicals and Plastics

### BOC Gases Ltd
Prince Regent Road
Castlereagh, Belfast, BT5 6RW
Tel: 028 9040 1441
Fax: 028 9040 1379
Principal Activity: medical & industrial gases
Operations Manager: Peter Loade

### Brett Martin Ltd
24 Roughfort Road
Mallusk, Newtownabbey, BT36 4RB
Tel: 028 9084 9999
Fax: 028 9083 6666
Principal Activity: PVC plastic sheeting
Managing Director: Lawrence Martin

### Creative Composites Ltd
Blaris Industrial Estate
Altona Road, Lisburn, BT27 5QB
Tel: 028 9267 3312
Fax: 028 9260 7381
Principal Activity: reinforced plastic
Managing Director: Roy Kelly

### Dessian Products Ltd
9 Apollo Road
Adelaide Industrial Estate
Belfast, BT12 6HP
Tel: 028 9038 1118
Fax: 028 9066 0741
Principal Activity: uPVC windows
Managing Director: Alan McGaughey

### Glentronics Ltd
64 Mallusk Road
Newtownabbey, BT36 4QE
Tel: 028 9034 2090
Fax: 028 9034 2147
Principal Activity: injection moulding
Managing Director: Jeremy Brassington

### Invista UK Ltd
PO Box 15, Maydown Works
Londonderry, BT47 6TH
Tel: 028 7186 0860
Fax: 028 7186 4222
Principal Activity: manmade fibres
Site Manager: Pat Carroll

### Michelin Tyre plc
Ballymena Factory
190 Raceview Road
Ballymena, BT42 4HZ
Tel: 028 2566 3600
Fax: 028 2566 3760

Polypipe (Ulster) Ltd
Dromore Road
Lurgan, Craigavon
BT66 7HL
Tel: 028 3888 1270
Fax: 028 3888 2344
Principal Activity: plastic pipe fittings
Managing Director: Henry White

## Manufacturing Companies: Life Sciences

Norbrook Laboratories Ltd
Station Works
Camlough Road, Newry, BT35 6JP
Tel: 028 3026 4435
Fax: 028 3026 1721
Principal Activity: veterinary pharmaceutical manufacturer
Managing Director:
Dr Edward Haughey

PDMS Ltd
22 Seagoe Industrial Estate
Craigavon, BT63 5UA
Tel: 028 3836 3363
Fax: 028 3836 3300
Principal Activity: pharmaceutical development and manufacturing
Managing Director: Graham McBurney

Perfecseal Ltd
Springtown Industrial Estate
Londonderry, BT48 0LY
Tel: 028 7128 7000
Fax: 028 7128 7401
Principal Activity: medical packaging
General Manager: Keith McCracken

Randox Laboratories Ltd
55 Diamond Road
Crumlin, BT29 4QT
Tel: 028 9442 2413
Fax: 028 9445 2912
Principal Activity: clinical diagnostic reagents
Managing Director:
Dr Peter Fitzgerald

Tyco Healthcare
20 Garryduff Road
Ballymoney, BT53 7AP
Tel: 028 2766 3234
Fax: 028 2766 4799
Principal Activity: syringes
Plant Manager: Rodney Crooks

## Information and Communications Technology (ICT) Sector

Northern Ireland has now a sizeable information and communications technology sector (ICT), with several large multi-nationals and a cluster of local IT and software companies.

The sector employs around 7,500 people, which has reduced over recent years from its peak of 10,000 in 2001. Although recent times have seen a fall in employment numbers the current level is still over twice the 1997 level of 3,000 people employed in the sector.

The importance of the sector has been fully recognised by policy makers: in the Government's Strategy 2010 blueprint for Northern Ireland's economic future, specific targets are established for growth in turnover in the various high-tech sub-sectors while an overall target to make high-tech industry account for up to 6 per cent of total employment by 2010 has been established.

With the bursting of the 'dotcom bubble' the excessive valuations seen in this sector have now retreated to more realistic levels. The telecommunications sector has been hit particularly hard, with providers taking on significant levels of debt to pay for third generation network licences. The arrival of real competition has extended customer choice and imposed downward pressure on prices. The mobile market has now reached saturation in Northern Ireland with all the main UK mobile operators present.

Although the last two years have been difficult for the technology sector across the globe, the software sector in Northern Ireland remains a key sector for economic growth. The Northern Ireland software and IT sector now consists of over 200 organisations across a wide range of activities including systems development, Internet products and services, financial services applications, telecommunications related products and services, management information systems and manufacturing systems development.

The sector includes inward investors such as Northbrook Technology and several indigenous companies such as B.I.C. Systems. This local 'cluster' of software and IT companies is growing and these companies are exporting a wide range of products and services to markets worldwide. Northern Ireland's universities and technical colleges produce around 1,000 IT graduates each year to meet the growing demands of the sector.

## IT and Software Companies

Aepona
Interpoint Building
20-24 York Street, Belfast, B15 1AQ
Tel: 028 9026 9100
Fax: 028 9026 9111
Managing Director: Liam McQuillan

B.I.C. Systems

B·I·C Systems
www.bicsystems.com
A company of BT

Sydenham Business Park
201 Airport Road West
Belfast, BT3 9ED
Tel: 028 9053 2200
Fax: 028 9056 0056
Email: info@bicsystems.com
Web: www.bicsystems.com

CEM Systems
Unit 4, Ravenhill Business Park
Ravenhill Road, Belfast, BT6 8AW
Tel: 028 9045 6767
Fax: 028 9045 4535
Web: www.cemsys.com
General Manager: Richard Fulton

Claritas Software
7 Springrowth House, Ballinske Road
Springtown, Derry, BT48 0MA
Tel: 028 7129 1111
Fax: 028 7129 1110
Web: www.claritassoftware.com
Managing Director: Plunkett Devlin

Consilium Technologies
Consilium House, Technology Park
Belfast Road, Antrim, BT41 1QS
Tel: 028 9448 0000
Fax: 028 9448 0001
Web www.task.co.uk
Director: Colin Reid

### Fujitsu Telecommunications Software Ireland (FTSI)
10 Antrim Technology Park, Belfast Road
Antrim, BT41 1QS
Tel: 028 9442 8394
Fax: 028 9442 8395
General Manager: Peter Bowman

### Kainos Software
Kainos House
4-6 Upper Crescent Street
Belfast, BT7 1NZ
Tel: 028 9023 6868
Fax: 028 9057 1101
Managing Director: Brendan Mooney

### Lagan Technologies
Lagan Court, 20 Wildflower Way
Belfast, BT12 6TA
Tel: 028 9050 9300
Fax: 028 9050 9339
Web: www.lagan.com
Managing Director: Des Speed

### Liberty Information Technologies
Clarendon House, 9-21 Adelaide Street
Belfast, BT2 8DJ
Tel: 028 9044 5500
Fax: 028 9044 5511
Web: www.liberty-it.co.uk
Managing Director: Gordon Bell

### Northbrook Technology of Northern Ireland
9 Lanyon Place,
Belfast, BT1 3LZ
Tel: 028 9034 6500
Web: www.northbrooktechnology.com
Managing Director: Bro McFerron

### Parity Solutions Ltd
Unit 1, Technology Park
Belfast Road, Antrim, BT41 1QS
Tel: 028 9446 4901
Fax: 028 9446 0702
General Manager: John Connelly

### Singularity
100 Patrick Street, Derry, BT48 7EL
Tel : 028 7126 7767
Fax : 028 7126 8085
Web: www.singularity.co.uk
Managing Director: Padraig Canavan

### Sx3 (Service & Systems Solutions) Ltd
Hillview House, 61 Church Road
Newtownabbey, BT36 7SS
Tel: 028 9068 8000
Fax: 028 9066 3579
Managing Director: Jeff Neville

## Telecommunications Companies

### BT NI
Riverside Tower, 5 Lanyon Place
Belfast, BT1 3BT
Tel: 028 9032 2327
Managing Director: Bill Murphy

### Cable & Wireless
Post Quarry Corner
Upper Newtownards Road
Belfast, BT16 1UD
Tel: 028 9055 5000
Fax: 028 9055 5111
Sales Director: Barry Moylan

### Clarity Telecom
1st Floor, 103-113 Ravenhill Road
Belfast, BT6 8DR
Tel: 028 9045 5022
Fax: 028 9046 9560
Managing Director: Paul Graham

### Energis
Sydenham Business Park
9 Heron Avenue, Belfast, BT3 1LF
Tel: 028 9095 9595
Chief Executive: John Pluthero

### ntl:
ntl:
smarter solutions
better business

209 Airport Road West
Belfast Harbour Industrial Estate
Belfast, Northern Ireland, BT3 9EZ
Tel: 0800 052 0158
Email: celticsalesteam.nireland@ntl.com
Web: www.ntl.com/business

Area Sales Director
Northern Ireland
David Armstrong

ntl is a leading provider of communications services and a trusted partner to both businesses and public sector organisations. Delivering competitive solutions, from individual and bundled voice, data and internet products to fully managed communications networks.

### Opal
OPAL
TELECOM

Unit 14, Arches Retail Park
East Bread Street
Belfast, BT5 5AP
Tel: 0800 083 2988
Fax: 0845 330 5265
Email: enquiries@opaltelecom.co.uk
Web: www.opaltelecom.co.uk

Sales & Marketing
Director
Aiden Dermody

Opal Telecom, the UK's leading business telecoms provider, has arrived in Northern Ireland. A wholly owned subsidiary of The Carphone Warehouse, we are now the new and exciting alternative to current carriers and invite you to enjoy more choice, better value and all the business benefits of working with a company that truly understands your needs.

Orange

Quay Gate House
15 Scrabo Street
Belfast, BT5 4BD
Tel: 0870 376 8888
Fax: 028 9073 6601
Email: media.centre@orange.co.uk
Web: www.orange.co.uk

Eric Carson
General Manager
Orange
in Northern Ireland

Orange is Northern Ireland's best performing mobile network with more transmitters in more places than anyone else and covering more than 99% of the population.

Orange launched in Northern Ireland in 1998 as part of a £200 million investment. Today more than 1 in 5 people in Northern Ireland are Orange customers. The company employs around 90 people locally, mainly through 8 Orange Shops.

Orange has launched its 3G network which will offer mobile broadband services. 3G coverage is available in Belfast and Derry and will extend across the main provincial towns. When customers move outside 3G coverage their 3G device will switch seamlessly to the high speed GPRS service which is available on Orange's existing network.

The future's bright, the future's Orange.

Vodafone

16 Wellington Park
Belfast, BT9 6DJ
Tel: 0800 052 5200
Web: www.vodafone.co.uk
Managing Director: David Hughes

# Transport and Tourism

## Transport

Although a large proportion of the population lives within the greater Belfast area, the rest of Northern Ireland's population is relatively dispersed. Unlike the rest of the UK the population is not concentrated in towns and villages but tends to be scattered throughout the countryside. Therefore road transport is central to most people's daily life. This is reflected in the number of vehicles licensed for use in Northern Ireland's roads which now stands at over 850,000. In the year 2003 there were over 87,506 new registrations for private cars.

Translink is the major provider of public transport services in Northern Ireland, through Citybus, Ulsterbus and Northern Ireland Railways (NIR). At the end of 2003/04 there were 1,240 Ulsterbuses and over 240 Citybuses on the roads. NIR operates a fully integrated rail network covering 211 miles of track services to Derry and Portrush in the north-west; Larne, Belfast and Bangor along the eastern seaboard; Newry in the south and onwards to Dublin, in the Republic of Ireland. Translink is also one of Northern Ireland's largest employers.

There are three main regional airports in Northern Ireland, the biggest being Belfast International which was the ninth busiest commercial airport in the UK in 2002.

Northern Ireland has four main seaports, which in order of importance are: Belfast, Larne, Warrenpoint and Derry. The Port of Belfast benefits from a safe, accessible, deepwater harbour, which is ideally placed to service middle corridor routes across the Irish Sea Ports in the North-West of England such as Heysham and Liverpool.

The designation of Liverpool as channel tunnel rail freight hub with a quayside rail link facilitates access to the European rail network and rapid onward transit of goods to the continent. Heysham and Liverpool also offer links to Great Britain's extensive motorway network and its centres of population and manufacturing.

*(For further information on Translink and the Northern Ireland transport system see Chapter 14, 'A Visitors Guide to Northen Ireland').*

## Tourism

Northern Ireland's image abroad plays a key role in determining visitor numbers and revenue from tourism.

Since the commencement of the peace process, Northern Ireland tourism – which had been in the doldrums for many years – has been developing rapidly. Visitor numbers are currently running at record levels. Responsibility for the development of the tourism industry is shared by the Northern Ireland Tourist Board (NITB), who have responsibility for tourism strategy, research and product development and Invest NI who support the physical development of the sector.

The Northern Ireland Tourist Board has produced a strategic framework for action to be delivered across ten programme areas. Four programmes relate to attracting visitors, four relate to business (product) enhancement and two relate to communication. Business tourism has been identified as a priority or 'winning theme' within the strategy. Visitors from Great Britain (Northern Ireland's main market) increased by 16% in the last year reported.

**Northern Ireland Tourist Board**
Research and Intelligence Department
St Anne's Court,
59 North Street,
Belfast, BT1 1NB
Tel: 028 9023 1221
Fax: 028 9024 0960
Web: www.nitb.com

## Public Road and Rail Transport

Translink Ltd
Central Station, East Bridge Street
Belfast, BT1 3PB
Tel: 028 9089 9400
Fax: 028 9089 9401
Principal Activity: public transport
Managing Director: Keith Moffatt

## Sea Transport Companies

Belfast Freight Ferries Ltd
Victoria Terminal 1, Dargan Road
Belfast, BT3 9LJ
Tel: 028 9077 0112
Fax: 028 9078 1217
Principal Activity: shipping/RORO
Secretary: Claire Jenkins

G Heyn & Sons Ltd
1 Corry Place, Belfast Harbour Estate
Belfast, BT3 9AH
Tel: 028 9035 0000
Fax: 028 9035 0011
Principal Activity: shipping agents
Managing Directors:
Michael Maclaren, David Clarke

Londonderry Port & Harbour
Harbour Office, Port Road
Lisahally, Londonderry, BT47 6FL
Tel: 028 7186 0555
Fax: 028 7186 1168
Principal Activity: pilotage, storage, cranes
Chief Executive: Brian McGrath

Norse Merchant Ferries
Victoria Terminal 2
Westbank Road, Belfast, BT3 9JN
Tel: 028 9077 9090
Fax: 028 9077 5520
Web: www.norsemerchant.com
Principal Activity: sea transport
General Manager: Liam Higgins

Port of Belfast

Harbour Office, Corporation Square
Belfast, BT1 3AL
Tel: 028 9055 4422
Fax: 028 9055 4411
Email: info@belfast-harbour.co.uk
Web: www.belfast-harbour.co.uk
Principal Activity: Port Authority

Chief Executive
John Doran

The Port of Belfast is a major maritime gateway linking Ireland's exporters and importers with Great Britain, Europe and onward to worldwide markets.

The Port handles over 60% of Northern Ireland's seaborne trade and more than 20% for the island of Ireland as a whole. It is Ireland's busiest ferry port, used by 1.75 million passengers each year.

Port of Larne
9 Olderfleet Road, Larne
Northern Ireland, BT40 1AS
Tel: 028 2887 2100
Fax: 028 2887 2209
Website: www.portoflarne.co.uk
Email: info@portoflarne.co.uk

P&O European Ferries
Larne Harbour, Larne, BT40 1AQ
Tel: 028 2887 2200
Fax: 028 2887 2129
Principal Activity: sea transport

Sea-Truck Ferries
Ferry Terminal, The Docks
Warrenpoint, Newry, BT34 3JR
Tel: 028 4175 4400
Principal Activity: ferry service
Director: Kevin Hobbs

Stena Line
Passenger Terminal
Corry Road, Dock Street
Belfast, BT3 9SS
Tel: 028 9088 4089
Principal Activity: transport ferry service
Port Service Manager: Billy Wicks

Warrenpoint Harbour Authority
The Docks, Warrenpoint
Newry, BT34 3JR
Tel: 028 4177 3381
Fax: 028 4175 2875
Principal Activity: harbour authority
Chief Executive: Quentin Goldie

## Air Transport Companies

Belfast City Airport
Sydenham By-Pass
Belfast, BT3 9JH
Tel: 028 9093 9093
Fax: 028 9093 5007
Principal Activity: airport operator
Chief Executive: Brian Ambrose

Belfast International Airport
Belfast, BT29 4AB
Tel: 028 9442 2888
Fax: 028 9445 2096
Principal Activity: airport operator
Managing Director: Albert Harrison

bmi - British Midland
Suite 2, Fountain Centre
College Street, Belfast, BT1 6ET
Tel: 028 9024 1188
Principal Activity: airline

City of Derry Airport
Airport Road, Derry, BT47 3PY
Tel: 028 7181 0784
Fax: 028 7181 1426
Principal Activity: airport
Airport Manager: Seamus Devine

FlyBe
City Airport, Belfast, BT3 9JH
Tel: 08705 676 676
Principal Activity: air transport
Manager: Andrea Hayes

## Distribution Companies

Royal Mail Northern Ireland Ltd
20 Donegall Quay
Belfast, BT1 1AA
Tel: 0845 774 0740
Fax: 0870 241 5967
Principal Activity: postal delivery
Managing Director:
Michael Kennedy

Montgomery Transport Ltd
607 Antrim Road
Newtownabbey, BT36 4RF
Tel: 028 9084 9321
Principal Activity:
transport haulage company
Managing Director: Harold Montgomery

## Tradeable Services Sector

The government has identified the tradeable services sector as a key growth sector for the Northern Ireland economy going forward. It incorporates a very wide range of activities.

### Financial Services in Northern Ireland

Employment in the financial services sector in Northern Ireland has grown over the past decade. Most of this growth has been in the non-traditional area of financial services including real estate renting and business activities sub-sector. The traditional side of the financial services sector, financial intermediation which includes mainstream retail banking has seen a decline in employment numbers over the same period. Much of this however has been a result of productivity improvements.

Some economic commentators suggest that most national economies can only support one physical centre for international financial activity. This is clearly the case for the UK with London being the main centre for international services and the other regional centres, including Belfast, focusing on provides financial services for their own region.

Bank mergers in the 1970s in Northern Ireland and RoI had led to the creation of two Northern-based clearing banks and two clearing banks headquartered in Dublin. In Northern Ireland there are the Ulster Bank (owned by Royal Bank of Scotland) and the Northern Bank (wholly owned by the National Australia Bank) and in RoI there are the Bank of Ireland and Allied Irish Bank (AIB). All the four main banks have operations north and south, with AIB having a Northern Ireland subsidiary called First Trust Bank.

Competition in the financial services sector has increased over the last five years with the introduction of legislation facilitating the deregulation of the sector and many building societies becoming banks. In recent years several of the RoI banks and building societies have entered the Northern Ireland market.

The small scale of the Northern Ireland market is illustrated by the fact that Ulster Bank now carries out the bulk of its business, by value, in the Irish Republic. Northern Bank is currently on the market with a number of international buyers expressing interest in its acquisition.

Recent years have seen several large international financial services companies develop operations in Northern Ireland. With the Northern Ireland financial services sector being largely companies headquartered outside Northern Ireland with regional offices, local demand will determine the demand for their services rather than broad international developments. Northern Ireland is the only part of the UK that shares a land border with a Euro participant and the Banking and Financial Services sector in Northern Ireland deals readily in Euros.

Financial services have grown strongly in recent years, at a time when the rest of the UK is experiencing some concentration in the sector. The major driver of local growth has been call-centres and while there are issues over the long-term value of some call-centre operations, investment from blue-chip companies like Halifax, Abbey National and Prudential has served to position Northern Ireland as a leading call centre location particularly for the financial services sector.

### Construction and Property

Up to 36,000 people are employed in the construction industry in Northern Ireland which, although employment levels tend to fluctuate, contributes 8 per cent of GDP. The representative body for the construction industry in Northern Ireland is the Construction Employers Federation. One of the main players is the Construction Industry Training Board (CITB), which ensures that the industry is properly staffed and trained. There has been something of a boom in private house building in recent years (although a slow down in public sector house building) and a number of major development projects including at Laganside and Victoria Square are underway in Belfast.

The planned expansion of public investment in major infrastructural projects over the next few years should boost the local construction sector in the medium term.

### Retailing

The Northern Ireland retail sector has developed considerably with the arrival of many of the large UK retailers previously reluctant to enter the local market during years of political instability. Retailers Tesco, Sainsbury's and Safeway (now part of the Morrison's chain) are now among Northern Ireland's largest employers.

*Queen's Arcade, Belfast*

Some major new retail developments have been completed (Debenhams, Craigavon) or are at the planning stage (John Lewis, Sprucefield), although there is growing concern at how the major out-of-town developments are impacting the traditional town centre high streets in terms of footfall and sales.

The Northern Ireland retail sector is also benefitting from a considerable influx of shoppers from South of the border who find that many items are cheaper to buy in Northern Ireland regardless of the currency differential.

## Financial Services

### Allianz

Allianz

Allianz House
21 Linenhall Street
Belfast, BT2 8AB
Tel: 028 9089 5600
Fax: 028 9043 4222
Web: www.allianz-ni.co.uk

Head of Allianz
Northern Ireland
Adrian Toner

Allianz Northern Ireland is a leading local insurer and part of the Allianz global network. As part of this network, Allianz Northern Ireland enjoys unrivalled access to risk and product knowledge. Working with a network of over one hundred brokers and intermediaries, the company has established itself as market leader in all lines of personal and commercial insurance, providing an efficient and comprehensive service to the local business community.

### AXA Insurance

AXA INSURANCE

Windsor House
9-15 Bedford Street
Belfast, BT2 7FT
Tel: 028 9033 3222
Fax: 028 9024 2864
Principal Activity: Insurance Services

Branch Manager
Tim Scott

AXA Insurance is one of Northern Ireland's leading personal and commercial motor insurers and is part of the Global AXA Group. The company is a major player in the drive to improve road safety through its involvement in major campaigns such as 'Thump' and 'Damage' with the DOE, and the 'Roadsafe Roadshows' aimed at young drivers.

### Bank of Ireland

4-8 High Street, Belfast, BT1 2BA
Tel: 028 9024 4901
Fax: 028 9023 4388
Principal Activity: banking services
Chief Executive: David Magowan
Senior Manager: Bernard Rooney

### Bank of Scotland (Ireland) Ltd

10-15 Donegal Square North
Belfast, BT1 5GB
Tel: 028 9033 0033
Fax: 028 9033 0030
Principal Activity: financial services
Regional Manager: Hugh Donnelly

### Cunningham Coates Ltd

19 Donegall Street, Belfast, BT1 2HA
Tel: 028 9032 3456
Fax: 028 9023 1479
Principal Activity: stockbrokers
Chief Operating Officer:
Jonathan Cunningham

### Edward Jones Investments

2 Malone Road
Belfast, BT9 5BN
Tel: 028 9068 7715
Fax: 028 9068 2580
Principal Activity: stockbrokers
Managing Director: Patrick Mahony

### First Trust

PO Box 123
First Trust Centre, 92 Ann Street,
Belfast, BT1 3AY
Web: www.firsttrustbank.co.uk
Tel: 028 9032 5599
Managing Director: Dennis Licence

### Northern Bank Ltd

PO Box 183
14 Donegall Square West
Belfast, BT1 6JS
Tel: 028 9024 5277
Fax: 028 9089 3245
Principal Activity: banking services

### HBOS

Donegall Square North
Belfast, BT1 5GL
Tel: 0845 720 3040
Fax: 028 9027 8233
Principal Activity: financial services
Branch Manager: Jim Porter

### HFC Bank plc

44-46 High Street
Belfast, BT1 2BF
Tel: 028 9032 4400
Fax: 028 9032 4300
Principal Activity: financial services
Manager: Paul Graham

### HSBC

4th Floor, 5 Donegall Square South
Belfast, BT1 5JP
Tel: 0845 740 4404
Principal Activity: financial services

### Lombard & Ulster Group Ltd

11-16 Donegall Square East
Belfast, BT1 5UD
Tel: 028 9027 6276
Fax: 028 9027 6279
Principal Activity: financial services
Area Director: James Conn

### Open+Direct

Royston House
34 Upper Queen Street
Belfast, BT1 6FD
Tel: 028 9026 0900
Fax: 028 9026 0978
Managing Director: Sam Downey

### Progressive Building Society

PROGRESSIVE
BUILDING SOCIETY

Progressive Building Society
12/14 Chichester Street
Belfast, BT1 4LA
Tel: 028 9032 0573
Fax: 028 9024 2035

33/37 Wellington Place
Belfast, BT1 6HH
Tel: 028 9082 1821
Fax: 028 9043 9421
Chief Executive: William Webb

Your Homegrown Society - with branches and agents across the Province.

Prudential Assurance Co Ltd
Beacon House, 27 Clarendon Road
Belfast, BT1 3PD
Tel: 0845 720 0000
Fax: 028 9089 6000
Principal Activity: insurance

Royal Sun Alliance Insurance Plc
Sun Alliance House, 42 Queen Street
Belfast, BT1 6HL
Tel: 028 9024 4433
Fax: 028 9026 2357
Principal Activity: insurance
Chief Executive: Andy Haste

Ulster Bank

Registered office
Ulster Bank Group
Head Office
11-16 Donegall Square East
Belfast, BT1 5UB
Tel: 028 9027 6000
Fax: 028 9027 5507
Email: webmaster@ulsterbank.com
Web: www.ulsterbank.com

Group Chief Executive
Cormac McCarthy

Ulster Bank Group is a wholly owned subsidiary of the Royal Bank of Scotland Group, the 2nd largest bank in Europe and the 5th largest in the world by market capitalisation. Following the acquisition of First Active in January 2004, the enlarged Ulster Bank Group consists of 265 branches, more than 1.4 million customers and approximately 5,100 staff.

Willis
78-86 Dublin Road, Belfast, BT2 7BY
Tel: 028 9024 2131
Fax: 028 9032 1087
Principal Activity: insurance
Managing Director: Jim Halliday

Zurich Insurance
7 Upper Queen Street
Belfast, BT1 6QD
Tel: 028 9024 5222
Fax: 028 9023 2435
Principal Activity: insurance
Area Manager (NI): James Shields

## Construction and Property Companies

Ardmac Performance Contracting Ltd
Unit 15 Annesborough Industrial Estate
Craigavon, BT67 9JD
Tel: 028 3834 7093
Fax: 028 3834 1604
Principal Activity: interior
Managing Director: Roy Miller

B Mullan & Sons (Contractors)
Bovally House, 11-13 Anderson Avenue
Limavady, BT49 0TF
Tel: 028 7772 2337
Fax: 028 7776 4780
Principal Activity: stone, asphalt
Managing Director: Sean Mullan

Farrans (Construction) Ltd
99 Kingsway
Dunmurry, Belfast, BT17 9NU
Tel: 028 9061 1122
Fax: 028 9062 9753
Principal Activity: construction
Managing Director: John Gillivray

Felix O'Hare & Co Ltd
88 Chancellors Road
Newry, BT35 8NG
Tel: 028 3026 1134
Fax: 028 3026 1397
Principal Activity: builders
Managing Director: John Parr

Gilbert Ash (NI) Ltd
47 Boucher Road
Belfast, BT12 6HR
Tel: 028 9066 4334
Fax: 028 9066 3634
Principal Activity: building contractors
Managing Director: Eddie O'Neill

Graham Construction
Lagan Mills
Dromore, BT25 1AS
Tel: 028 9269 2291
Fax: 028 9269 3412
Principal Activity: building contractors
Managing Director: Michael Graham

J Kennedy & Co (Contractors) Ltd
1 Letterloan Road
Macosquin, Coleraine, BT51 4PP
Tel: 028 7035 2211
Fax: 028 7035 6308
Principal Activity: builders
Manager: Danny Kennedy
Chief Executive: Chris Kennedy

Lagan Holdings Ltd
19 Clarendon Road
Clarendon Dock, Belfast, BT1 3BG
Tel: 028 9026 1000
Fax: 028 9026 1010
Principal Activity: quarrying civil engineering & construction group
Managing Director: Michael Lagan

Mivan Construction Ltd
Newpark, Greystone Road
Antrim, BT41 2QN
Tel: 028 9448 1000
Fax: 028 9448 1015
Principal Activity: construction
Managing Director: Dr Ivan McCabrey

PJ Conway (Contractors) Ltd
58 Moneymore Road
Magherafelt, BT45 6HG
Tel: 028 7963 2001
Fax: 028 7963 3038
Principal Activity: building contractors
Proprietor: Patrick Conway
Managing Director: Trevor Simpson

Redland Tile & Brick Ltd
61 Largy Road, Crumlin, BT29 4RR
Tel: 028 9442 2791
Fax: 028 9442 2165
Principal Activity: roofing services
Sales Manager: Billy Wright

RJ Maxwell & Son Ltd
209 Bushmills Road
Coleraine, BT52 2BX
Tel: 028 7034 3281
Fax: 028 7035 3346
Principal Activity: civil engineering
Managing Director: Willy McNabb

Northern Ireland
## TOP 100 BUSINESSES

## 1-20

| RANK | COMPANY | TOWN | ACCOUNTS DATE | TURNOVER (000's) | | PRE-TAX PROFIT (000's) | |
|---|---|---|---|---|---|---|---|
| | | | | Current | Previous | Current | Previous |
| 1 | **Viridian Group Plc** | Belfast | 31/3/03 | 781000 | 730000 | 78400 | -7500 |
| 2 | **Glen Electric Ltd** | Newry | 31/3/03 | 618000 | 578000 | 29000 | 20800 |
| 3 | **Short Bros Plc** | Belfast | 31/1/03 | 431000 | 451000 | 29800 | 53000 |
| 4 | **FG Wilson (Eng) Ltd** | Larne | 31/12/02 | 284000 | 307000 | 5279 | 35600 |
| 5 | **Moy Park Ltd** | Craigavon | 31/12/02 | 266000 | 242000 | 3911 | 3875 |
| 6 | **Charles Hurst Ltd** | Belfast | 31/12/02 | 261000 | 215000 | 7312 | 4821 |
| 7 | **John Henderson (Hldg) Ltd** | N'abbey | 31/12/02 | 255699 | N/A | 6230 | N/A |
| 8 | **Warner Chilcott Plc** | Craigavon | 30/9/03 | 254200 | 201562 | 68459 | 101091 |
| 9 | **United Dairy Farmers** | Belfast | 31/3/03 | 251000 | 247000 | 3217 | 1307 |
| 10 | **SHS Group Ltd** | N'abbey | 31/12/02 | 235000 | 183000 | 22900 | 17500 |
| 11 | **DCC Energy Ltd** | Belfast | 31/3/03 | 233000 | 206000 | 3985 | 2410 |
| 12 | **Dunnes Stores (Bangor) Ltd** | Newry | 31/1/03 | 219000 | 218000 | 40900 | 24100 |
| 13 | **J&J Haslett Ltd** | Belfast | 31/12/02 | 213000 | 214000 | 2264 | 2778 |
| 14 | **Isaac Agnew (Holdings) Ltd** | N'abbey | 31/12/02 | 201000 | 168000 | 6645 | 4701 |
| 15 | **Hilton Food Group Ltd** | Cookstown | 31/12/02 | 200000 | 157000 | 4540 | 4932 |
| 16 | **Farmlea Foods Ltd** | Holywood | 31/12/02 | 188000 | 149000 | 2647 | 2980 |
| 17 | **Lagan Cement Group** | Belfast | 31/3/03 | 180000 | 135000 | 10800 | 10600 |
| 18 | **Farrans Ltd** | Belfast | 31/12/02 | 169000 | 172000 | 4483 | 4980 |
| 19 | **Premier Power Ltd** | Larne | 31/12/02 | 151000 | 178000 | 42300 | 30900 |
| 20 | **Diageo Northern Ireland** | Belfast | 30/6/03 | 147659 | 67464 | 13139 | 6377 |

# Top 100 Businesses

**Ulster Business Top 100**

The following tables set out Northern Ireland's top 100 businesses including information relating to their turnover, profit and employment. There is no perfect way to rank businesses by size but the best proxy is turnover. The information below was compiled in August 2004 by Ulster Business Magazine. Obviously there has been some change since then, including the closure of Desmonds and TK/ECC.

## listings for 2004

Data compiled by D&B

| NET WORTH (000's) | EMPL. | DATE STARTED | LINE OF BUSINESS | OWNERSHIP | RANK |
|---|---|---|---|---|---|
| 203000 | 2732 | 1998 | Electricity Service | - | 1 |
| 341000 | 5402 | 1973 | Heating Appliance Manufacturers | - | 2 |
| 176000 | 6553 | 1909 | Aircraft Manufacturers | Bombardier Inc | 3 |
| 93200 | 2089 | 1966 | Electricity generating equipment | Caterpillar Inc | 4 |
| 25300 | 3818 | 1961 | Poultry Product Manufacturers | Osi Industries | 5 |
| 26900 | 798 | 1938 | Car Dealers | Lookers Plc | 6 |
| 26744 | 1378 | 1990 | Grocery Wholesalers | - | 7 |
| -193343 | 1692 | 1991 | Pharmaceutical Manufacturers | - | 8 |
| 21900 | 874 | 1995 | Milk and Dairy Products | - | 9 |
| 22300 | 340 | 1975 | Grocery Wholesalers | - | 10 |
| 6506 | 362 | 1978 | Gas & Oil Suppliers | DCC Plc | 11 |
| 164000 | 3335 | 1971 | Drapery, grocery & hardware retailers | Dunnes Stores Ltd | 12 |
| 6102 | 521 | 1854 | Grocery Wholesalers | Bwg Foods Holdings Ltd | 13 |
| 25400 | 706 | 1931 | Car dealers | - | 14 |
| 8052 | 458 | 1998 | Fresh Food Distributors | - | 15 |
| 4026 | 100 | 1977 | Food Brokers | SHS Group Ltd | 16 |
| 71800 | 920 | 1960 | Quarrying & Construction | - | 17 |
| 45700 | 1001 | 1941 | Construction | CRH Plc | 18 |
| 65700 | 215 | 1991 | Electricity generation and suppliers | BG Group Plc | 19 |
| 52051 | 194 | 1956 | Wine and Spirits Wholesalers | Diageo Plc | 20 |

1-20

Northern Ireland
## TOP 100 BUSINESSES

# 21-40

| RANK | COMPANY | TOWN | ACCOUNTS DATE | TURNOVER (000's) | | PRE-TAX PROFIT (000's) | |
|---|---|---|---|---|---|---|---|
| | | | | Current | Previous | Current | Previous |
| 21 | **Sangers Northern Ireland** | Belfast | 30/9/02 | 146000 | 130000 | 2218 | 2084 |
| 22 | **Desmond & Sons Ltd** | L'derry | 31/12/02 | 145028 | 128369 | 8196 | 8854 |
| 23 | **Musgrave SuperValu** | Belfast | 31/12/02 | 140745 | 126040 | -3701 | -7905 |
| 24 | **Coca-Cola Bottlers** | Lisburn | 31/12/02 | 137000 | 124000 | 8764 | 5201 |
| 25 | **Rotary Ltd** | N'abbey | 30/9/03 | 116000 | 110000 | 6644 | 6407 |
| 26 | **Quinn Manufacturing** | Enniskillen | 31/12/02 | 113000 | 101000 | 10300 | 7845 |
| 27 | **Foyle Food Group Ltd** | L'derry | 31/12/02 | 110000 | 117000 | 1912 | 2970 |
| 28 | **Maxol Oil Ltd** | Belfast | 31/12/02 | 110000 | 107400 | -439 | -600 |
| 29 | **Donnelly Bros Garage** | Dungannon | 31/3/03 | 109000 | 79200 | 1393 | 1107 |
| 30 | **AES (NI) Ltd** | Carrickfergus | 31/12/02 | 104000 | 128000 | 24700 | 26500 |
| 31 | **John Kelly Ltd** | Belfast | 31/3/03 | 102984 | 89500 | 876 | 1031 |
| 32 | **McLaughlin & Harvey** | N'abbey | 31/12/03 | 98400 | 76400 | 3517 | 3133 |
| 33 | **O'Kane Poultry Ltd** | Ballymena | 27/4/02 | 97400 | 87800 | 70 | 105 |
| 34 | **Thales Air Defence** | Belfast | 31/12/03 | 97100 | 109000 | 13800 | 15600 |
| 35 | **Lindsay Cars Ltd** | Lisburn | 31/12/02 | 96700 | 94300 | 449 | -224 |
| 36 | **Fane Valley Co-Op** | Armagh | 30/9/02 | 93400 | 79900 | 10400 | 1174 |
| 37 | **Fayrefield Foods Ireland** | Belfast | 31/12/02 | 93300 | 114000 | 421 | 243 |
| 38 | **Linden Foods Ltd** | Dungannon | 30/9/02 | 86800 | 64200 | 601 | 1402 |
| 39 | **David Patton & Sons (NI)** | Ballymena | 30/11/02 | 83200 | 98900 | 2660 | 1976 |
| 40 | **Brett Martin Ltd** | N'abbey | 31/12/02 | 79800 | 76100 | 1976 | 3745 |

# Top 100 Businesses

# listings for 2004

Data compiled by D&B

| NET WORTH (000's) | EMPL. | DATE STARTED | LINE OF BUSINESS | OWNERSHIP | RANK |
|---|---|---|---|---|---|
| 6944 | 229 | 1830 | Pharmaceutical Supplies Wholesalers | Alchem Plc | 21 |
| 46185 | 1,895 | 1885 | Textile Manufacturers | - | 22 |
| 9896 | 336 | 1997 | Grocery Wholesalers | Musgrave Investments | 23 |
| 16500 | 492 | 1939 | Soft drinks manufacturers and bottlers | Molino Beverages Holdings | 24 |
| 28500 | 1412 | 1988 | Elec/Mech/Vent engineers | - | 25 |
| 107000 | 787 | 1973 | Quarrymasters | - | 26 |
| 10900 | 627 | 1975 | Abattoirs and meat processors | - | 27 |
| 6503 | 124 | 1918 | Petrol and Oil distributors/retailers | Mullen Bros | 28 |
| 4023 | 251 | 1925 | New and used car dealers | - | 29 |
| -89200 | 113 | 1992 | Electrical Supply | Aes Global Power Holdings | 30 |
| 10474 | 135 | 1875 | Coal and Oil importers and distributors | Tedcastles (Group) Ltd | 31 |
| 13100 | 226 | 1993 | Building Contractors | - | 32 |
| 10800 | 878 | 1931 | Poultry breeders and processors | - | 33 |
| 73500 | 586 | 1993 | Missile system manufacturers | Thales | 34 |
| 4010 | 438 | 1962 | Car dealers | - | 35 |
| 29900 | 0 | 1920 | Milk and Dairy Products | - | 36 |
| 1791 | 24 | 1992 | Dairy produce distributors | - | 37 |
| 7405 | 232 | 1982 | Meat processors | Asarin Ltd | 38 |
| 13600 | 373 | 1912 | Construction | - | 39 |
| 24900 | 671 | 1960 | Plastic building product manufacturers | - | 40 |

21-40

Northern Ireland
## TOP 100 BUSINESSES

# 41-60

| RANK | COMPANY | TOWN | ACCOUNTS DATE | TURNOVER (000's) Current | TURNOVER (000's) Previous | PRE-TAX PROFIT (000's) Current | PRE-TAX PROFIT (000's) Previous |
|---|---|---|---|---|---|---|---|
| 41 | **W&R Barnett Ltd** | Belfast | 31/3/03 | 79000 | 78100 | 7422 | 6753 |
| 42 | **Musgrave Distribution** | Belfast | 31/12/02 | 77800 | 75100 | 2164 | 1898 |
| 43 | **Shell Northern Ireland** | Belfast | 31/12/02 | 76200 | 98100 | 851 | -1861 |
| 44 | **Gilbert-Ash NI Ltd** | Belfast | 31/12/03 | 76023 | 55325 | 1524 | 1105 |
| 45 | **John Thompson & Sons** | Belfast | 31/7/02 | 74600 | 63700 | 2688 | 2099 |
| 46 | **Ulsterbus Ltd** | Belfast | 30/3/03 | 73830 | 69650 | 2381 | 1465 |
| 47 | **Dairy Produce Packers** | Coleraine | 31/12/02 | 72100 | 64200 | 7995 | 1149 |
| 48 | **Bass Ireland Ltd** | Belfast | 28/12/02 | 71100 | 70500 | -622 | 5666 |
| 49 | **NI Co-Op Society** | Carrickfergus | 12/1/02 | 69500 | 88200 | 500 | 1220 |
| 50 | **Ulster Carpet Mills** | Craigavon | 31/3/03 | 68500 | 53100 | 1623 | 1465 |
| 51 | **John Graham (Dromore)** | Dromore | 31/3/03 | 67700 | 54300 | 789 | -716 |
| 52 | **TK-ECC Ltd** | Belfast | 31/3/03 | 66700 | 52700 | -20000 | -17700 |
| 53 | **J P Corry Group Ltd** | Belfast | 31/3/03 | 67600 | 71200 | 1901 | -1649 |
| 54 | **BE Aerospace (UK) Ltd** | Newry | 31/12/02 | 64300 | 67400 | -16300 | 8929 |
| 55 | **Nicholls (Fuel Oils) Ltd** | L'derry | 31/5/03 | 63000 | 48100 | 206 | 1434 |
| 56 | **Philip Russell Ltd** | Belfast | 30/6/03 | 62800 | 63300 | 483 | 891 |
| 57 | **Norbrook Laboratories** | Newry | 2/8/02 | 62800 | 59600 | 527 | 3992 |
| 58 | **James E McCabe Ltd** | Craigavon | 31/12/02 | 62600 | 62500 | 4517 | 3907 |
| 59 | **Mivan Group Holding** | Antrim | 31/12/03 | 61843 | 50511 | 2494 | 2007 |
| 60 | **Powerscreen International** | Dungannon | 31/12/02 | 61200 | 56300 | 11700 | 3658 |

# Top 100 Businesses

# listings for 2004

Data compiled by D&B

| NET WORTH (000's) | EMPL. | DATE STARTED | LINE OF BUSINESS | OWNERSHIP | RANK |
|---|---|---|---|---|---|
| 77300 | 200 | 1924 | Commodity trading, handling, services | - | 41 |
| 12700 | 205 | 1983 | Cash and carry wholesale distributors | Musgrave Group Plc | 42 |
| -958 | 41 | 1983 | Fuel oil distributors | N.V. Koninklijke Nederlands | 43 |
| 7226 | 145 | 1900 | Building Contractors | Ards Holdings Ltd | 44 |
| 10500 | 153 | 1880 | Animal Feedstuff manufacturer | - | 45 |
| 35051 | 2,233 | 1966 | Transport Co | NI Transport Holdings | 46 |
| 11900 | 334 | 1944 | Processed cheese manufacturers | Kerry Group Plc | 47 |
| 30300 | 358 | 1897 | Brewers | Adolph Coors Company | 48 |
| 2732 | 0 | 1899 | Grocery Retailer | Co-Operative Group Ltd | 49 |
| 32000 | 1533 | 1938 | Carpet Manufacturers | - | 50 |
| 9021 | 372 | 1955 | Building and civil engineering contractors | - | 51 |
| 486 | 744 | 1979 | Air bag and seat belt manufacturers | Takata Corp | 52 |
| 7318 | 465 | 1996 | Builders Merchants | - | 53 |
| -4206 | 609 | 1985 | Aircraft seating/accessory manufacturers | BE Aerospace Inc | 54 |
| 4799 | 125 | 1962 | Fuel Distributors | - | 55 |
| 2617 | 379 | 1968 | Off Licence and Pub proprietors | - | 56 |
| 18900 | 736 | 1969 | Veterinary pharmaceutical manufacturers | - | 57 |
| 25100 | 229 | 1919 | Wine and spirit retailers | - | 58 |
| 21083 | 826 | 1981 | Construction | - | 59 |
| 15700 | 64 | 1966 | Portable screening mfrs and wholesalers | Terex Corporation | 60 |

## 41-60

Northern Ireland
## TOP 100 BUSINESSES

# 61-80

| RANK | COMPANY | TOWN | ACCOUNTS DATE | TURNOVER (000's) Current | TURNOVER (000's) Previous | PRE-TAX PROFIT (000's) Current | PRE-TAX PROFIT (000's) Previous |
|---|---|---|---|---|---|---|---|
| 61 | **Daewoo Electronics** | Antrim | 31/12/02 | 61000 | 56600 | 993 | 86 |
| 62 | **Wrightbus Ltd** | Ballymena | 30/9/03 | 59863 | 51535 | 3485 | 1047 |
| 63 | **Cuisine de France** | Lisburn | 31/7/02 | 58900 | 50600 | 950 | 768 |
| 64 | **SDC Trailers Ltd** | Antrim | 31/3/03 | 58500 | 55600 | 1498 | 3371 |
| 65 | **Montupet UK Ltd** | Belfast | 31/12/01 | 56370 | 32497 | 2275 | 1196 |
| 66 | **Belfast Telegraph** | Belfast | 31/12/01 | 56030 | 53858 | 21258 | 22058 |
| 67 | **Humax Electronics** | N'ards | 31/12/03 | 55600 | 83700 | 61 | -351 |
| 68 | **Dale Farm Ingredients Ltd** | Belfast | 31/3/03 | 55100 | 56600 | 39 | 5 |
| 69 | **Haldane Shiells & Co** | Newry | 31/12/02 | 53300 | 51500 | 1182 | 1220 |
| 70 | **The Cornerstone Group Ltd** | Ballymena | 30/9/02 | 52800 | 39400 | 1227 | 2513 |
| 71 | **Henry Group (NI) Ltd** | Magherafelt | 31/3/03 | 51400 | 45500 | 729 | 613 |
| 72 | **Readymix (NI) Ltd** | Belfast | 31/12/02 | 51200 | 53000 | 4250 | 3729 |
| 73 | **W&G Baird Holdings** | Antrim | 31/12/02 | 51100 | 51700 | 44 | 2160 |
| 74 | **L Stanley Ltd** | Belfast | 27/4/03 | 51100 | 32900 | 2088 | 9126 |
| 75 | **Balcas Ltd** | Enniskillen | 30/1/03 | 50400 | 49000 | 562 | -30 |
| 76 | **Haldane Fisher Ltd** | Newry | 31/12/02 | 49200 | 48600 | 1147 | 1050 |
| 77 | **Bavarian Garages (NI)** | Belfast | 31/12/02 | 47500 | 36900 | 2933 | 2346 |
| 78 | **Ulster Television Plc** | Belfast | 31/12/02 | 47300 | 43000 | 11300 | 11900 |
| 79 | **Murdock Group Ltd** | Newry | 31/12/02 | 47000 | N/A | 1195 | N/A |
| 80 | **Mivan** | Antrim | 31/12/02 | 46800 | 33700 | 2788 | 1574 |

# Top 100 Businesses

# listings for 2004

Data compiled by D&B

| NET WORTH (000's) | EMPL. | DATE STARTED | LINE OF BUSINESS | OWNERSHIP | RANK |
|---|---|---|---|---|---|
| 9733 | 736 | 1989 | Video recorder manufacturers | Daewoo Electronics Co. Ltd | 61 |
| 6349 | 708 | 1946 | Coach manufacturers | - | 62 |
| 4876 | 103 | 1989 | Frozen food suppliers (bakery products) | IAWS Group Plc | 63 |
| 6606 | 314 | 1978 | Commercial Vehicle trailer mfrs | Retlan Manufacturing Ltd | 64 |
| 32291 | 1,029 | 1990 | Aluminium Casting Manufacturers | Montupet SA | 65 |
| 25427 | 556 | 1861 | Newspaper Publishers | TIH Ltd | 66 |
| 2363 | 154 | 1997 | Digital satellite receiver manufacturers | - | 67 |
| 150 | 12 | 1984 | Dairy Product distributors | United Dairy Farmers | 68 |
| 14200 | 417 | 1946 | Timber importers | - | 69 |
| 8194 | 647 | 1999 | Holding company for Wright Group | - | 70 |
| 8038 | 509 | 1985 | Building contractors | - | 71 |
| 4013 | 543 | 1996 | Ready mix concrete mfrs, stone quarriers | Readymix-Huddersfield Ltd | 72 |
| 16600 | 611 | 1882 | Commercial printers | - | 73 |
| 141000 | 176 | 1958 | Operation of licensed betting offices | - | 74 |
| 11500 | 662 | 1962 | Timber merchants | - | 75 |
| 601 | 373 | 1860 | Builders Merchants | - | 76 |
| 2920 | 155 | 1979 | Car dealers | Isaac Agnew (Holdings) Ltd | 77 |
| -22100 | 315 | 1959 | NI TV Contractor to ITC | - | 78 |
| 8204 | 251 | 1991 | Building/timber merchants | - | 79 |
| 7905 | 457 | 1975 | Construction | Mivan Group Holding Ltd | 80 |

61-80

Northern Ireland
## TOP 100 BUSINESSES

# 81-100

| RANK | COMPANY | TOWN | ACCOUNTS DATE | TURNOVER (000's) Current | TURNOVER (000's) Previous | PRE-TAX PROFIT (000's) Current | PRE-TAX PROFIT (000's) Previous |
|---|---|---|---|---|---|---|---|
| 81 | **Harland & Wolff Group** | Belfast | 31/12/02 | 46585 | N/A | -41 | N/A |
| 82 | **Adria Ltd** | Strabane | 31/12/02 | 45200 | 41000 | 159 | 1562 |
| 83 | **Clearway Disposals Ltd** | Craigavon | 31/12/02 | 44300 | 37300 | 4083 | 1108 |
| 84 | **Leckpatrick Dairies Ltd** | L'derry | 31/12/02 | 43851 | 73505 | 7407 | -2962 |
| 85 | **Bettercare Group Ltd** | Belfast | 30/9/02 | 41000 | 38000 | 472 | 173 |
| 86 | **Lurgan Chilling Ltd** | Craigavon | 31/3/03 | 40800 | 34100 | 1110 | 783 |
| 87 | **Grafton Recruitment Int.** | Belfast | 31/3/03 | 40800 | 36200 | 1186 | 408 |
| 88 | **Savilles Auto Village** | Lisburn | 30/11/02 | 39100 | 38000 | 490 | 523 |
| 89 | **Dillon Bass Ltd** | Belfast | 31/12/02 | 39100 | 37300 | 27 | 25 |
| 90 | **Ashton Centre Development Ltd** | Belfast | 31/1/02 | 38900 | N/A | 1752 | N/A |
| 91 | **Brooks Group (UK) Ltd** | Belfast | 31/12/02 | 38900 | 52800 | 2454 | -1281 |
| 92 | **Sanmina-Sci Enclosure Systems** | Lisburn | 28/9/02 | 38400 | 46100 | -455 | -9578 |
| 93 | **Ballyrashane Co-operative** | Coleraine | 31/12/02 | 37200 | 32700 | 523 | 82 |
| 94 | **WFB Baird & Co. Ltd** | Craigavon | 30/4/02 | 37200 | 32300 | -1024 | -1455 |
| 95 | **H&J Martin Ltd** | Belfast | 31/12/02 | 36500 | 25000 | 450 | 389 |
| 96 | **John Hogg & Co Ltd** | Holywood | 30/4/03 | 35900 | 73000 | 1505 | 3086 |
| 97 | **Howden Power Ltd** | Belfast | 31/12/02 | 35500 | 35400 | 275 | 1152 |
| 98 | **JP Corry (NI) Ltd** | Belfast | 31/3/03 | 34800 | 34500 | 1060 | 758 |
| 99 | **Northern Ireland Railways Co. Ltd** | Belfast | 30/3/03 | 34800 | 28700 | -1101 | -2816 |
| 100 | **Macnaughton Blair & Co. Ltd** | Belfast | 31/12/02 | 34500 | 32700 | 2327 | 1777 |

# Top 100 Businesses

# listings for 2004

Data compiled by D&B

| NET WORTH (000's) | EMPL. | DATE STARTED | LINE OF BUSINESS | OWNERSHIP | RANK |
|---|---|---|---|---|---|
| 233 | N/A | 2001 | Marine Engineering | - | 81 |
| 7774 | 1111 | 1961 | Hosiery and sock manufacturers | AP Galgorm Ltd | 82 |
| 8019 | 142 | 1964 | Scrap and waste disposal contractors | - | 83 |
| 11950 | 113 | 1901 | Dairy product mfrs & distributors | Golden Vale | 84 |
| 11900 | 1947 | 1996 | Nursery home proprietors | - | 85 |
| 2026 | 100 | 1990 | Abattoir | Anglo Beef Processors (UK) | 86 |
| 2427 | 337 | 1998 | Holding Company | - | 87 |
| 1603 | 157 | 1969 | Motor vehicle sales and repair | Lookers Plc | 88 |
| 61 | 26 | 1990 | Wine and spirit marketing and distribution | Bow Street Investments Ltd | 89 |
| 77100 | 127 | 1988 | Development agency | - | 90 |
| 13800 | 190 | 1996 | Timber importers and builders merchants | Wolseley Plc | 91 |
| -2802 | 359 | 1969 | Sheet metal manufacturers | Sanmina-Sci Corporation | 92 |
| 8223 | 189 | 1896 | Milk processors and milk product mftrs | - | 93 |
| 175 | 108 | 1912 | Linen manufacturers | - | 94 |
| 3244 | 88 | 1839 | Building and civil engineering contractors | H&J Martin Holdings Ltd | 95 |
| 18100 | 580 | 1890 | Holding comps | - | 96 |
| 28200 | 254 | 1881 | Industrial fan manufacturers | Charter Plc | 97 |
| 5619 | 223 | 1814 | Timber importers and builders merchants | JP Corry Group Ltd | 98 |
| 6191 | 762 | 1967 | Railway undertaking | Northern Ireland Transport | 99 |
| -3732 | 242 | 1908 | Buliders Merchants | Grafton Group (UK) Plc | 100 |

# 81-100

*Doing Business in Belfast's Waterfront Hall*

A Guide to Doing Business in Northern Ireland

# Chapter 8

Blues wary of upset
This is the new Skoda.

## Business Environment

This section of the Northern Ireland Yearbook 2005 is aimed primarily at individuals or groups considering going into business for the first time and people and organisations based outside Northern Ireland who are thinking of developing business opportunities within Northern Ireland. It sets out a detailed description of the environment for business in Northern Ireland as well as the main practical considerations such as company registration, regulations, compliance, employment and taxation.

## The Northern Ireland Economic Environment

The estimated population of Northern Ireland as at June 2003 was 1.7m. With an area of approximately 14,000 sq km it has a population density of 125 persons per square km. The population of some of Northern Ireland's main towns and cities in 2002 was: Belfast 340,400; Lisburn 109,400; Londonderry 106,200; Newry 88,500; Bangor/North Down 77,000; Ballymena 59,000; Armagh 55,000.

Northern Ireland is part of the United Kingdom and is governed by the UK tax and business regime. The currency is sterling Northern Ireland is an increasingly attractive location for those seeking to establish a new branch of an existing business or those seeking to build a completely new enterprise. It is characterised by a youthful and well-educated population, a low cost base and one of the most technologically advanced network infrastructures in Europe as the following tables show. *(Further analysis of the Northern Ireland economy and its key sectors is set out in Chapter 7).*

**Table 8.1: United Nations Population Comparison**

| Country | % Aged 0-39 |
|---|---|
| Sweden | 50.4 |
| Germany | 49.0 |
| United Kingdom | 53.2 |
| **Northern Ireland** | **58.2** |

Source: United Nations Statistics Division 2002

Throughout the 1990s, Northern Ireland enjoyed the fastest economic growth of any region of the United Kingdom. In 1999 GDP was £17,003 million ($24,707 million). During the period 1990-1999 Northern Ireland's GDP increased 1% per annum faster than the UK average. It can also be seen (Table 8.2 below) that the Northern Ireland economy in line with western European economies is increasingly dependant on the services sector. This now accounts for almost 70% of total GVA (Gross Value Added).

**Table 8.2: Origins of GVA by Industrial Sector**

| Sector | % of total |
|---|---|
| Services | 68.0 |
| Manufacturing | 20.5 |
| Construction | 7.0 |
| Agriculture | 2.0 |
| Electricity, Gas, Water | 2.0 |
| Mining and Quarrying | 0.5 |
| **Total** | **100** |

Source: Northern Ireland Annual Abstract of Statistics 2003

Traditionally a very inward looking economy, Northern Ireland has developed an increasing export focus, with exports in 2002-2003 accounting for almost 40% of total sales by Northern Ireland companies. £20m of manufactured goods are sold outside of Northern Ireland daily with 72% of all manufacturing sales to customers outside Northern Ireland.

**Table 8.3: Major Export Markets 2001/02 - 2002/03**

| | Total Exports £m |
|---|---|
| Republic of Ireland | 1,039 |
| North America | 891 |
| Asia | 398 |
| Rest of EU | 328 |
| Rest of Europe | 281 |
| German | 273 |
| France | 233 |
| Netherlands | 222 |
| Belgium | 112 |
| Middle East | 101 |
| Africa | 74 |
| Central & South America | 66 |
| Australia & New Zealand | 28 |
| **Total** | **4,046** |

Source: NISRA / DETI

Latest figures show that manufacturing output in Northern Ireland has increased during 2004, but at a slower rate than the UK as a whole. Over the past five years, total manufacturing sales from Northern Ireland have increased by 12.5%. Manufacturing productivity has shown an upward trend in recent years, due to manufacturing output remaining fairly steady, while the number of jobs in manufacturing fell.

The UK is the second largest recipient of Foreign Direct Investment globally and holds 22.5% of all FDI stock in the EU and 9% worldwide. Northern Ireland has captured a proportional share of this investment.

## Northern Ireland Labour Force

The Northern Ireland labour force is well trained and educated and although unemployment is low there are no significant skills shortages.

Unemployment, which is currently at its lowest level since records began - has fallen steadily from a peak of 17.2% in 1986 to 4.7% for the period June-August 2004, compared with the current EU25 average of 9%. Between 1998-2003 employee jobs in Northern Ireland increased by 8.9% compared to an increase of 5.7% in the UK as a whole.

It is worth noting that rates of unemployment vary significantly across Northern Ireland, being highest in the local government areas of Derry and Strabane, in the west.

During 2003 the average weekly wage in Northern Ireland was £404 with the highest-paid group (managers) earning, on average £599 per week and the lowest-paid group (sales/customer service staff) earning £239 per week. Average public sector earnings were £463 per week compared with £371 in the private sector.

In addition to relatively low cost labour by western standards, Northern Ireland is also a stable environment in terms of its industrial relations, with a lower incidence of industrial disputes than its European neighbours (see Table 8.4 below).

**Table 8.4: International Comparisons of Labour Disputes 2001**

| Country | No of days* |
|---|---|
| France | 83 |
| Ireland | 82 |
| Italy | 66 |
| EU Average | 43 |
| Finland | 30 |
| Scotland | 29 |
| USA | 9 |
| Switzerland | 6 |
| **Northern Ireland** | **1** |

*not worked per 1,000 employees

Source: UK National Statistics

Levels of staff absenteeism due to sickness in Northern Ireland are the lowest in the United Kingdom (see Table 8.5 below).

**Table: 8.5: Levels of Sickness across UK Countries**

| Country | No of days* |
|---|---|
| Scotland | 3 |
| England | 3 |
| Wales | 2.7 |
| Northern Ireland | 2.1 |

*not worked per 1,000 employees

Source: UK National Statistics

## Education of Labour Force

There are a total of 341,300 pupils in Northern Ireland schools (02/03), with approximately 21,000 school teachers and a ratio of 17 pupils per teacher (see Table 8.6 below).

**Table: 8.6: Pupil/Teacher Ratios 2002-03**

| | Primary | Secondary |
|---|---|---|
| Northern Ireland | 19.7 | 14.4 |
| Republic of Ireland | 18.4 | 15.8 |
| United Kingdom | 22.6 | 17 |

Source: NISRA

Pupil/teacher ratios, which are generally regarded to some degree as a measure of the quality of education a child receives, although marginally higher in Northern Ireland than the Republic of Ireland for primary education, are otherwise lower than both the United Kingdom and the Republic of Ireland.

On average students in Northern Ireland obtain higher grades on standardised exams than they do elsewhere in the UK. In 2002 almost 59% of Northern Ireland's students achieved 5 or more GCSE grades A*-C, compared with the UK average of 52.5%. The number of students applying to Northern Ireland's universities has increased by 9% since June 2003.

# Infrastructure and Utilities

## Electricity

The electrical power system is 3-phase AC operating at 50Hz with transmission systems of 275kV and 110kV serving a wide distribution network of 33kV and 11kV. Low voltage supplies are 230/400 volts although many large factories take supply at 11kV or 33kV. A range of tariffs is available although most large companies are charged on the basis of an Electricity Purchase Agreement. Rates vary considerably depending on the pattern of usage and voltage of supply. However, as a guide, most large companies pay an average price between 3.3p and 9.2p per kWh.

The Northern Ireland electrical grid has been strengthened considerably in recent years by physical interconnection with both the Republic of Ireland grid and Great Britain, through the North/South and Moyle interconnectors.

As the electricity market in Northern Ireland continues to open, more and more businesses with smaller electricity requirements will be free to choose their electricity supplier. This will introduce greater competition to the market and exert a downward pressure on electricity prices, which have previously been disproportionately high.

## Gas

Until relatively recently when a gas pipeline was built across the Irish sea, Northern Ireland had no natural gas network. Phoenix Natural Gas commenced supplying its first major customers in Belfast in January 1997. To date there are over 3,000 industrial and commercial customers using natural gas. Natural gas is, however, currently only available in the Greater Belfast and surrounding area although there are plans to extend the network significantly both northwest and south over the next few years. Work to bring natural gas to the North West is at an advanced stage, and the pipeline should be complete in time to bring gas to the new combined-cycle gas turbine power station currently under construction at Coolkeeragh, Derry and due to come on stream in 2005. The North-West pipeline should also facilitate the extension of natural gas to many towns along its route eg Ballymena, Coleraine, Limavady. The proposed North/South gas pipeline is scheduled to be built in 2006 and this will make natural gas available to homes and businesses along the North/South corridor, including the towns/cities of Newry, Banbridge, Armagh, Craigavon and Antrim.

Contract customers, using above 25,000 therms (732,000 kWh) per annum, can expect to pay up to 1.65p per kWh depending upon the size of load, load factor, contract duration etc. For large customers with equipment capable of firing on alternative fuels, 'interruptible supply' contracts are available at prices below the 1.4p per kWh level.

### Telecoms

Northern Ireland has an advanced resilient, digital telecommunications network that provides high-speed voice and data connections. It was the first region in the UK to develop a fully fibre-optic infrastructure, and is part of a UK network that supplies greater bandwidth than the rest of Europe combined.

Northern Ireland is the leading region of the UK in terms of broadband roll-out. It is expected that by 2005 Northern Ireland will have 100% broadband coverage.

**Table 8.7: Rate for a Three-Minute Trunk Call at Peak Hours - U.S.$**

| From | Northern Ireland | Republic of Ireland | Germany | USA |
|---|---|---|---|---|
| Northern Ireland (ntl) | 0.14 | 0.23 | 0.23 | 0.14 |
| Republic of Ireland | 0.25 | n/a | 0.74 | 0.58 |
| Germany | 0.39 | 0.39 | 0.39 | 0.39 |
| USA | 0.24 | 0.45 | 0.45 | n/a |

Source - Tarrifica PBI Media. January 2004

### Water

For industry, metered water costs are made up of two separate charges. The first is a volumetric charge for each cubic metre of water registered on the meter, the second is a yearly standing charge which depends on the internal diameter of the metre supply pipe, (e.g. 41-50mm equates to £289 per annum).
Domestic customers are not currently charged directly for water, although plans have been developed for this to be introduced in the future. Opposition to these plans is fierce in many quarters.

## Property and Accommodation

New, purpose built and fitted out office space is available throughout Northern Ireland from £12.50 per square foot in the greater Belfast area. Belfast currently offers the lowest net-rent of any large city in the UK. (see Table 8.8 below)

**Table 8.8: Cost of Office Space per Sq Foot by Location**

| Region | City | Cost per sq foot (£) |
|---|---|---|
| UK and Ireland | Belfast | 12.00 |
| | Dublin | 36.42 |
| | Glasgow | 23.00 |
| | London (City) | 50.00 |
| | London (West End) | 67.50 |
| | Manchester | 24.00 |

Source: CB Richard Ellis (Aug 2004) and Lands Agency (2003)

Specialist incubator units at the Northern Ireland Science Park and the University of Ulster Science and Research Park provide state-of-the-art accommodation and support during the start-up phase for knowledge-based industries.

New business parks such as Invest NI's Global Point International Business Park have flexible leasing at costs that are among the lowest in Europe. Invest Northern Ireland's Speculative Build Initiative will involve the private sector in the provision of property of up to 30,000 sqft (sub divisible into units of 5000 sqft) at a number of locations throughout Northern Ireland. These units are primarily suitable for companies operating in the Information, Communication and Telecoms sectors.

## Transport Connections

### Road Network

As of April 2004 there were 24,880 kilometres of public roads in Northern Ireland, of which just 1% is motorway or dual carriageway. Traffic congestion is minimal, compared to main routes in Britain, although larger towns and cities do experience problems during the conventional morning and evening rush hours.

### Seaports

Over 80 international shipping lines operate out of Northern Ireland's 5 commercial seaports. 90% of Northern Ireland's total trade, and almost 50% of the Republic of Ireland's freight traffic, leaves through these ports. There are 150 sailings a week to destinations including the United Kingdom, the USA, Continental Europe and the rest of the world. 8,800 ships carrying 17million tonnes of cargo leave Belfast port each year. Over 60% of Northern Ireland's sea borne trade is shipped through the Port of Belfast. The Port of Londonderry at Lisahally is the United Kingdom's most westerly port and has a capacity for 30,000 tonne vessels.

### Airports

Serving almost 4 million passengers a year during 2003, Belfast International Airport is the principal gateway to the north of Ireland. It was the tenth largest UK airport by passenger numbers during 2003. It is the most technically advanced airport in Ireland and the fifth largest regional air cargo centre in the UK. Airfreight services are currently provided by regular scheduled passenger aircraft and an increasing number of dedicated freighter aircraft. Leading companies operating services from the 24-hour centre at Belfast International Airport are DHL and TNT, while Royal Mail also has a large presence there.

Belfast City Airport has opened a new £21 million terminal as a result of rapidly growing passenger traffic. Almost 2 million passengers passed through the terminal during 2003. The City of Derry airport serves the entire North-West region of Ireland. Located 7 miles from the city of Derry it is within easy reach of Donegal. *(Further details of Northern Ireland's sea crossings and connections and airline services are set out in Chapter 13. A Visitors Guide to Northern Ireland).*

## Formation and Registration of Companies in Northern Ireland

Forming a company in Northern Ireland is an uncomplicated process, although all companies registered in Northern Ireland are required to register with Companies House, submit accounts and annual returns and follow general procedures relating to registration.

Business entities may be incorporated or unincorporated. Incorporated bodies have a legal status separate from that of their owners and may sue and be sued in their own name. Incorporated bodies include private limited companies, public limited companies and unlimited companies. An unincorporated body may be a sole proprietorship or a partnership.

Below is an outline of some of the steps involved in the process of registering a company in Northern Ireland, along with details of different types of company. Detailed information and advice on all aspects of company formation may be obtained from:

**Companies Registry**
1st Floor, Waterfront Plaza
Laganbank Road
Belfast, BT1 3BS
*(office is open to callers 10am-4pm Monday-Friday, except bank holidays)*
Tel: 0845 604 8888 / Fax: 028 9090 5291
Web: www.companiesregistry-ni.gov.uk

### Registering a Company

There are four main types of company:

- Private company limited by shares - members' liability is limited to the amount unpaid on shares they hold;
- Private company limited by guarantee - members' liability is limited to the amount they have agreed to contribute to the company's assets if it is wound up;
- Private unlimited company - there is no limit to the members' liability;
- Public limited company (PLC) - the company's shares may be offered for sale to the general public and members' liability is limited to the amount unpaid on shares held by them.

A limited company has the fundamental advantage of being a legal entity separate from its members. An unlimited company lacks the advantage that most people seek from incorporation - that of the limited liability of its members.

Limited liability companies have the advantage that the member's liability to contribute to the debts of the company have a fixed limit, which is always clear. The limit is set by issuing shares, (a company limited by shares) or by taking guarantees (a company limited by guarantee) from the members that they will contribute up to a fixed amount to the debts of the company when it is wound up or when it needs money in particular circumstances (not yet available as an option in Northern Ireland).

The Companies Act generally allows one or more persons to form a company for any lawful purpose by subscribing to its memorandum of association. However, a public company or an unlimited company must have at least two subscribers.

### Company Formation

Ready-made companies are available from company formation agents (see list on page 327) but those seeking to register a new company must submit the following documents, together with appropriate registration fee (standard fee is £35):

- Form 21: summary of a companies officers, registered company address etc;
- Form 23: declaration of compliance;
- Memorandum of Association;
- Articles of Association;

#### Form 21

Form 21 gives details of the first director(s), secretary and the address of the intended registered office. The company's directors must give their date of birth, occupation and details of other directorships they have held within the last five years. Each director appointed and each subscriber (or their agent) must sign and date the form. Form 21 is available from the Companies Register in Belfast or from any of the company registration agents for which details are given below.

#### Form 23

Form 23 is a statutory declaration of compliance with all the legal requirements relating to the incorporation of a company. It must be signed by a solicitor who is forming the company, or by one of the people named as director or company secretary on Form 21. It must be signed in the presence of a commissioner for oaths, a public notary, a JP or a solicitor.

Form 23 must be signed and dated after all other documents are signed and dated, as Form 23 confirms that all other documentation is complete. Form 23 is available from the Companies Registry in Belfast, or online.

All company formation documents are checked, including checks of prospective officers against the disqualified directors' register. The documents are retained by the Registrar and are available for public inspection.

#### The Memorandum of Association and Registration

It is essential that a company has a memorandum of association to specify its constitution and objects.
The memorandum of every company must state:

- The name of the company;
- Where the registered office of the company is to be situated;
- The objects of the company (the object of a company may simply be to carry on business as a general commercial company.);

Other clauses in the Memorandum depend on the type of company being incorporated. Details of what should be included can be obtained from Companies Registry.

### Articles of Association

The Articles of Association is a document setting out the rules for the running of the company's internal affairs. All companies that are limited by guarantee or unlimited must register articles. Different articles are required for different types of companies. Details can be found on the Companies Registry website www.companiesregistry-ni.gov.uk.

## Company Names

The choice of name for a company is of considerable importance and is subject to a number of restrictions, briefly:

- The company being registered can't have the same name as another company;
- The use of certain words is restricted;
- Names likely to cause offence are not allowed.

If a name chose is too similar to a name already registered, an objection can be made within 12 months of the incorporation of the similar name and it may be directed to be changed by law. The name of a public company must end with the words 'public limited company'. In the case of a company limited by shares or guarantee the company must have 'limited' as its last word unless exempted under the Companies Act 1986.

A company may not be registered by any name, unless with the approval of the Secretary of State, which would give the impression that the company is connected in any way with government or the local authority. If a company goes into insolvent liquidation a person who was acting as a director of the insolvent company is not permitted to act as a director of a new company with the same or a similar name. This restriction lasts for five years and aims to prevent the misuse of limited liability companies by putting one into liquidation, leaving the debts behind and starting another.

### Effect of Registration

Following registration of a company's memorandum, the registrar of companies will give a certificate that the company is incorporated and in the case of a limited company that it is limited. The certificate may be signed by the registrar or authenticated by his official seal. From the date of incorporation contained in the certificate the subscribers of its memorandum shall be a body corporate by the name contained in the memorandum.

### Location of Registered Office

A company registered in Northern Ireland is required to have a registered office located in Northern Ireland. Any change to the registered address should be notified to Companies Registry on Form 295. Smaller companies frequently use their accountant's office as their registered address.

### Publication of the Company Name

The name and address of a company must be present on company letterheads and other documentation. The name of the company must be displayed outside every place of business including the registered office. Under the terms of the Companies Act 1986 there is a requirement to state the company's name, place of registration, registered number and the address of its registered office on all business letters, notices and official publications, bills of exchange, promissory notes, endorsements, cheques, orders for money or goods, invoices, receipts and letters of credit. Failure to do so may leave the company and officers liable to a fine and may lead to personal liability for a director or agent.

## Companies Incorporated Outside Northern Ireland

In the case where a company, which is incorporated outside Northern Ireland, wishes to establish a presence within Northern Ireland, the company must be registered and give similar details as indigenous companies.

## Partnerships

A partnership has many fewer formalities to be complied with than a limited company, however, the members of a partnership are liable for all the debts incurred by the business they run. If large losses are made they must contribute their own money to clear the debts of the business. In practice with small businesses there may be little distinction between partnership and limited status, as banks will not lend money without first securing guarantees from those running the business so that if the company cannot pay its debts, the personal assets of those in charge will meet such debts.

### Limited Partnerships

A limited partnership consists of:

- One or more persons called general partners, who are liable for all the debts and obligations of the firm; and
- One or more persons called limited partners, who contribute a sum or sums of money as capital, or property valued at a stated amount. Limited partners are not liable for the debts and obligations of the firm beyond the amount contributed.

A limited partnership must be registered under the Limited Partnership Act. To register as a limited partnership a statement signed by all the Partners must be delivered to Companies House.

### Limited Liability Partnerships

A limited liability partnership is an alternative corporate vehicle providing the benefits of limited liability but allowing members the flexibility of organising their internal structure as a traditional partnership. Any new or existing firm of two or more persons will be able to incorporate as a limited liability partnership. Incorporation of a limited liability partnership will be by registration at Companies House through a similar process to registration of a company. Limited liability partnerships have similar disclosure requirements to a company including the filing of accounts. Limited liability partnerships will also be required to:

- File an annual return;
- Notify any changes to the limited liability partnership's membership;
- Notify any changes to the members names and residential addresses;
- Notify any change to their registered office address.

The Limited Liability Partnership (LLP) trading form has not yet been introduced to Northern Ireland, although it is available in the rest of the United Kingdom. It is expected to be introduced to Northern Ireland during 2005.

### Joint Ventures

An overseas company may form a base in Northern Ireland by joining an established company. Such joint ventures are usually as a limited company or as a partnership.

## Accounts and Audit

Every company has a duty to keep accounting records sufficient to show and explain the company's transactions and should disclose with reasonable accuracy at any time the financial position of the company. Directors must ensure that the balance sheet and profit and loss account is compliant with their obligations under the terms of the Companies Act. Accounting records should contain day to day entries of all sums of money received and expended by the company and the matters in respect of which the receipt and expenditure takes place, and a record of the assets and liabilities of the company.

A company's accounting records may be held at its registered office or such other place as the directors may think fit, and should be open to inspection by the company's officers at all times. A private company should keep its accounting records for three years from the date upon which they were made.

### Annual Accounts

The directors of every company have a duty to prepare a set of accounts for each financial year. These accounts must include a profit and loss account, a balance sheet signed by a director, an auditors report signed by the auditor, notes to the accounts, and if relevant, group accounts.
Small and medium sized enterprises (SMEs) may abbreviate the accounts they submit to Companies Registry. All limited and public limited companies must submit their accounts to the Registrar. Unlimited companies need only deliver accounts to the Registrar if during the period covered by the accounts, the company was:

- A subsidiary or a parent of a limited undertaking;
- A banking or insurance company;
- A qualifying company within the meaning of the Partnerships and Unlimited Companies (Accounts) Regulations 1993;
- Operating a trading stamp scheme.

Whilst accountants may prepare the company accounts it is the responsibility of the director to ensure that accounts are filed on time. Late filing penalties are enforced against those companies whose accounts are late. These penalties are shown below:

**Table 8.9: Penalties for Late Filing of Company Accounts**

| Length of Delay | Private Company | Public Company |
|---|---|---|
| 3 months or less | £100 | £500 |
| 3 months 1 day to 6 months | £250 | £1000 |
| 6 months 1 day to 12 months | £500 | £2000 |
| More than 12 months | £1000 | £5000 |

## Qualification of a Company as Small or Medium Sized

Companies qualifying as small or medium may prepare and deliver abbreviated accounts to the Registrar. Certain small companies with a turnover of less than £5.6 million (the gross income limit for charitable companies is £90,000) and assets of less that £2.8 million can claim exemption from audit.

Public companies and certain companies in the regulated sectors cannot qualify as small or medium sized. For other companies, the size of the company (and in the case of a parent company the size of the group headed by it) in terms of its turnover and balance sheet total (meaning the total of the fixed and current assets) determines whether it is classed as small or medium.

To be classified as a small company at least two of the following conditions must be met:

- Annual turnover must be £5.6m or less;
- The balance sheet total must be £2.8m or less;

To be a medium sized company at least two of the following conditions must be met:

- Annual turnover must be £22.8m or less;
- The balance sheet total must be £11.4m or less:

If the company is a parent company it cannot qualify as a small or medium sized enterprise unless the group headed by it is also small or medium sized.

The abbreviated accounts of a small company must include:

- The abbreviated balance sheet and notes;
- A special auditor's report unless the company is also claiming audit exemption.

The abbreviated accounts of a medium company must include:

- The abbreviated profit and loss account;
- The full balance sheet;
- A special auditor's report;
- The directors' report;
- Notes to the accounts.

The special auditor's report should state that in the auditor's opinion the company is entitled to deliver abbreviated accounts and that they have been properly prepared in accordance with requirements of the Companies Act.

## Company Governance

### Company Officers

Every company must have formally appointed company officers at all times. All company officers have wide responsibilities in law. A private company must have at least:

- One director;
- One secretary - formal qualifications are not required.

A company's sole director cannot also be the company secretary. A public company must have at least:

- Two directors;
- One secretary - formally qualified.

After incorporation Companies Registry must be notified about:

- The appointment of a new officer - use Form 296;
- An officer's resignation from the company - use Form 296;
- Changes in an officer's name or address or any of the other details originally registered on Form 21 - use Form 296.

#### Company Directors

Anyone of good standing may act as a company director subject to a few exceptions. Every company director has personal responsibility to ensure that statutory documents are delivered to the Companies Registry particularly:

- Accounts (only for limited companies);
- Annual returns (Form 363);
- Notice of change of directors or secretaries or their details (Forms 296);
- Notice of change of registered office (Form 295).

There is no minimum age limit for the director of a company in Northern Ireland.

#### Company Secretaries

The company secretary of a public limited company must be qualified. However the company secretary of a private limited company requires no formal qualifications.

### Winding Up

Private companies which have not traded or otherwise carried on business for at least 3 months may apply to Companies Registry to be removed from the Register of Companies. Further details are available from Companies Registry.

### Off-the-Shelf Companies

Ready-made companies may be acquired from enterprises, which register a number of companies and hold them dormant until they are purchased. This may save time where a company is needed quickly for a particular enterprise. These ready-made companies are formed with the objects of a general commercial company having the power to carry on any trade or business.

#### Company Formation Agents

Business World Enterprise Centre Ltd
69 Canal Street, Newry, BT35 6JF
Tel: 028 4177 3542

Company Business Solutions
99 Skegoneill Avenue, Belfast, BT15 3JR
Tel: 028 9059 3810

Company Registration Agents
138 University Street, Belfast, BT7 1HH
Tel: 028 9032 9984

The Company Shop
79 Chichester Street, Belfast, BT1 4JE
Tel: 028 9055 9955

Company Solutions Europe Ltd
4 Lower Crescent, Belfast, BT7 1NR
Tel: 028 9032 9073

Comperia Ltd
26 Donard Avenue, Newtownards, BT23 4NF
Tel: 028 9181 0284

## Taxation of Businesses in Northern Ireland

### Corporation Tax

Corporation tax is based on the total profits, income and capital gains, arising in an accounting period. The Corporation tax year runs from 1 April to 31 March. Where an organisation has an accounting period not coinciding with the corporation tax year, and the rate of tax varies from one year to the next, the company's profits are distributed pro rata over the two years.

The Corporation Tax Self Assessment (CTSA) regime applies in respect of all accounting periods ending after 30 June 1999. Under CTSA, companies compute their own tax and larger organisations are required to make payments on account. A company is required to complete a detailed tax return (CT600) in respect of each accounting period. The return contains a section requiring a computation of corporation tax and a self-assessment of liability. The return must usually be filed within twelve months of the end of the accounting period. Penalties of up to £1000 may be imposed for failure to submit a return and should the failure continue beyond six months, liability may increase to a tax related penalty of up to 20 per cent.

Under the terms of the Corporation Tax Self Assessment scheme a company's self-assessment stands unless amended by the company concerned or by the Inland Revenue. Where a company fails to make a return, the Inland Revenue will determine the tax due.

#### Payment of Corporation Tax

Corporation tax must be paid no later than nine months and one day from the end of the company's accounting period. This due and payable date predates the date for filing a return. Under self-assessment large companies must operate a quarterly account.

Where quarterly payments on account are to be made, they fall due as follows: six months and 14 days from the start of the accounting period; nine months and 14 days from the start of the accounting period; twelve months and 14 days from the start of the accounting period; and three months and 14 days from the end of the accounting period.

Interest on tax paid late runs from the due and payable date with respect to the final liability. The rate of interest on underpaid tax is currently 5% and the interest on overpaid tax 3.75 per cent. During the period leading up to the due date different rates apply. Under CTSA interest on overdue tax is deductible when computing accessible profits and interest on overpaid tax is taxable.

#### Tax Audits

The Inland Revenue has one year from the due filing date to commence an enquiry into a company's return. Where errors are discovered during the period of the enquiry the return may be corrected. However, once the period of the enquiry has expired, the return stands, unless deficiencies emerge of which the Inland Revenue could not reasonably have been made aware on the basis of the information available at the time.

**Appeal Procedures**
Where disputes arise over a self-assessment, assessment or determination and resolution cannot be achieved with the local tax office, an appeal is heard before the General or Special Commissioners.

**Rates of Corporation Tax**
The current rates of corporation tax are set out in Table 8.10 below. The levels may be reduced for certain companies, especially if there are other companies under the same control. If two companies are under the same control the thresholds will be halved for each company. The UK has among the lowest corporate tax rates in Europe, which helps make Northern Ireland a more competitive business location.

**Table 8.10: Table Corporation Tax (2004-05)**

| Taxable Profits (£) | Tax Rate (%) |
|---|---|
| 0 - 10,000 | 0 |
| 10,001 - 50,000 | 0-19 (marginal relief) |
| 50,001 - 300,000 | 19 |
| 300,001 - 1.5m | 19-30 (marginal relief) |
| Over 1.5m | 30 |

## Capital Gains Tax
Capital Gains Tax (CGT) may have to be paid if an asset is disposed or a sum of money is received in respect of an asset. CGT is only paid on disposal of an asset if a 'chargeable gain' has been made. A gain is typically made if the asset is worth more on disposal than it was on acquisition. For the purposes of capital gain, an asset can be shares, property or the goodwill of a business, but doesn't normally include the sale of a person's own home. There is a range of exemptions and reliefs from CGT – details are available from Inland Revenue. Limited companies pay corporation tax on any capital gains as they are treated as part of the company's taxable profit.

**Table 8.11: Assets Eligible for Deductions in lieu of Depreciation**

| Asset | Deduction |
|---|---|
| Industrial Buildings (factories & workshops but not commercial or retail premises) | 4% per annum straight line |
| Hotels | 4% per annum straight line |
| Plant and Machinery (including furniture on a reducing balance and office equipment) | 25% per annum |
| Agricultural Buildings and Works | 4% per annum straight line |
| Mineral Extraction | 25% or 10% on a reducing balance |
| Scientific Research | 100% in the year of expenditure |
| Patent Rights | 25% per annum on a reducing balance |

## Depreciation and Capital Allowances
Depreciation of capital assets is not an allowable deduction. Deductions in lieu of depreciation are granted in respect of capital expenditure on certain classes of assets. These deductions known as capital allowances apply as per Table 8.11 bottom left.

A 'first year allowance' of 40% is available to most small and medium sized enterprises (SMEs) resident in Northern Ireland for expenditure on plan and machinery. This allowance may be increased to 100% in certain circumstances. Expenditure on certain designated energy saving plant and machinery also qualifies for a 100% allowance for all companies. The plant and machinery must be used in Northern Ireland by the SME claiming the allowance.

The Finance Act 2002 allows companies to benefit from tax relief on the acquisition cost of intellectual property, goodwill and other tangible assets. This relief applies to companies only, not to sole traders or partnerships.

## Research and Development Tax Credits
Research and development tax credits were introduced for small companies with effect from 1 April 2000. Qualifying companies may claim 150% of qualifying revenue research and development expenditure against taxable profits or potentially claim 16% of the 150% as a repayment. This was extended to include large companies from 2002.

## Personal Taxation
The higher tax band in Northern Ireland, at 40% is one of the lowest in the EU (see Table 8.12 below).

**Table 8.12: EU Personal Tax (Higher) Rates 2003**

| Country | % Rate |
|---|---|
| Netherlands | 52 |
| Belgium | 50 |
| France | 50 |
| Germany | 48 |
| Austria | 50 |
| Italy | 45 |
| Ireland | 42 |
| Spain | 45 |
| Portugal | 40 |
| **Northern Ireland** | 40 |

Source: Invest UK "Key Facts" March 2003

In the UK, income becomes liable for taxation if it falls within one of the four schedules listed in Table 8.13 below.

**Table 8.13 Income Tax Schedules**

| Schedule | Description |
|---|---|
| Schedule A | Rental income from land and property in the UK |
| Schedule D | |
| Case I | Income from trade |
| Case II | Income from a profession or vocation |
| Case III | Interest, annuities or other annual payments |
| Case IV | Income from foreign securities |
| Case V | Income from foreign possessions |
| Case VI | Miscellaneous income |
| Schedule E | Income from employment and pensions (repealed for accounting periods after 5 April 2003 - income now called 'Employment Income') |
| Schedule F | Dividends and distributions from other UK companies |

Each schedule and case has its own rules for computing income and deductions. The computed income is then aggregated to produce an individual's total income, which is taxable. The tax year commences on the 6 April and ends on the following 5 April. The income assessable in any tax year is the income of that year.

A self-assessment system was introduced on 6 April 1996 for taxpayers whose liability is not satisfied solely by deductions under PAYE. The Inland Revenue sends tax returns to these taxpayers shortly after the end of the tax year. Taxpayers may choose between self-assessments in which case they must complete the return and calculate their own tax payable and file by 31 January, or leaving it up to the Inland Revenue to compute tax payable, in which case completed returns must be filed by 30 September. Interest and penalty charges will be incurred if the return is not filed on time.

The Inland Revenue has been trying to move the tax return process on-line but the response from taxpayers has not been as enthusiastic as had been hoped.

## PAYE System

Employers on a cumulative basis deduct tax and National Insurance contributions under the PAYE (Pay As You Earn) system. Deductions are made according to a code number (taxcode) for each employee issued by the Inland Revenue.

The taxcode takes into account the employees' allowances, benefits and credits, so that the correct amount of tax should have been deducted by the end of the tax year.

PAYE income tax and primary employee's National Insurance Contributions (NIC) deductions must be applied to virtually all payments of income assessable to Schedule E tax and /or NIC. Deductions cannot be made from payments in kind but a suitable adjustment is made to the employee's PAYE code number to allow for the tax due.

Every employer with a sufficient tax presence in the United Kingdom is obliged to operate PAYE. Special rules apply if the employee is not resident or ordinarily resident in the UK.

Tax and National Insurance Contributions must be paid to the Inland Revenue by the 19th of each month. Employers collecting less than £1,500 per month may apply for quarterly accounting.

At the end of the tax year the employer must provide a certificate of pay and tax deducted (P60) to each employee and a return of deductions in respect of all employees to the Inland Revenue, together with the payment of any balance of deductions outstanding. These returns and payments must be submitted to the Inland Revenue by 19 May of the following tax year. Interest is charged on late payment of end of year balances and penalties are imposed for late filing of returns.

## Income Tax

For the income tax year 2004-2005 the income tax bands after allowances are as follows:

**Table 8.14: Income Tax Bands**

| | |
|---|---|
| Basic Personal Allowance | £4,745 |
| Starting Rate £0-£2,020 | 10% |
| Basic Rate £2,021-£31,400 | 22% |
| Higher Rate £31,401+ | 40% |

Income tax is computed by aggregating income under the various schedule and cases and subjecting the result (total income) to tax at three progressive rates, after deducting personal and other allowance and deductions. The names of the various income tax rates used in the United Kingdom are listed below:

**Table 8.15: UK Income Tax Rates**

| | |
|---|---|
| Lower Rate | 10% |
| Savings Rate | 20% |
| Basic Rate | 22% |
| Higher Rate on Dividends | 32.5% |
| Discretionary Trusts | 34% |
| Higher Rate | 40% |

## Inland Revenue

Regional Office Floor 5
Millennium House
17-25 Great Victoria Street
Belfast, BT2 7BN
Web: www.inlandrevenue.gov.uk
Director: Tina Gallagher

The Chancellor has announced that Inland Revenue and Customs and Excise are merging to create one new organisation - HM Revenue and Customs, during 2005. Exact dates and other details are not yet clear as they are subject to further legislation.

**National Helplines**
*New Employer:* 0845 607 0143
(For registration & advice on PAYE, NI, SSP, SMP)
Open: 8am-8pm Mon-Fri, 8am-4pm Sat/Sun

*Existing Employers:* 0845 714 3143
(For advice on PAYE, NI, SSP, SMP)
Open: 8am-8pm Mon-Fri, 8am-5pm Sat/Sun

*Self Assessment:* 0845 900 0444
Open: 8am-8pm Mon-Sun

*Self Employed:* 0845 915 4655
(Class 2 National Insurance queries)
Open: 8am-5pm Mon-Fri

*Newly Self-Employed:* 0845 915 4515
(Registration & Advice)
Open: 8am-8pm Mon-Fri, 8am-4pm Sat/Sun

*Construction Industry Scheme:*
Contractors: 0845 733 5588
8am-8pm Mon-Fri, 8am-5pm Sat/Sun

*Sub Contractors:* 0845 300 0581
8am-8pm Mon-Sun

## Local Enquiry Centres

Offices are open 8.30am – 5pm Monday to Friday unless stated otherwise

**Belfast**
Beaufort House
31 Wellington Place, BT1 6GB
Tel: 0845 302 1469

**Lisburn**
Moira House
121 Hillsborough Road, BT28 1LA
Tel: 028 9266 5230

For offices listed below please call 0845 302 1481

**Antrim**
Open 9am - 4.30pm, Mon - Fri
12-14 Castle Street , BT41 4JE

**Ballymena**
Kilpatrick House
38-54 High Street, BT43 7DQ

**Banbridge**
Bridgewater House,
25 Castlewellan Road, BT32 4AX

**Coleraine**
Fern House
1A Adelaide Avenue, BT52 1LT

**Craigavon**
Marlborough House
Central Way, BT64 1AT

**Enniskillen**
Abbey House
Head Street, BT74 7DB

**Londonderry**
Foyle House
Duncreggan Road, BT48 0AA

**Newry**
Downshire House,
22-23 Merchant's Quay, BT35 6AH

**Employer Queries**
If your reference starts with:-
916 – call 028 2563 3052
925 – call 028 9053 2413
953 – call 028 9260 6072

## Other Useful Numbers

**Tax Credits/Child Benefit Helpline**
0845 603 2000
Open: 8am-8pm Mon-Sun

**Enforcement and Insolvency Service**
Olivetree House
23 Fountain Street
Belfast, BT1 5EA
Tel: 028 9053 2730

**National Insurance Contributions**
Tel: 0845 302 1479

**Director's Office**
Floor 5 Millennium House
17-25 Great Victoria Street,
Belfast, BT2 7BN
Tel: 028 9093 9700

**National Minimum Wage Helpline**
0845 650 0207

**Capital Taxes Office**
Dorchester House
52-58 Great Victoria Street
Belfast, BT2 7BB
Tel: 028 9050 5353

**Business Support Team**
Tel: 028 9053 2755

**Confidential Information**
Tel: 028 9053 2706
Open: 9am-5pm Mon-Fri

**Stamp Office**
Dorchester House
52-58 Great Victoria Street
Belfast, BT2 7BB
Tel: 028 9050 5312
028 9050 5314 / 028 9050 5316

## National Insurance

National Insurance is a significant labour cost in the United Kingdom and can add up to 10% to salary costs. Social Security Taxes in the form of National Insurance Contributions are payable by individuals and employers. There are six classes of contributions. The greatest share of revenue is raised by Class One contributions, paid by employers and employees. For employees, NICs are payable at a single rate of 11% on the excess of gross earnings (excluding most benefits in kind) over £91 per week (equivalent to £4,732 per year). However, once gross earnings exceed £31,720 per year, the upper earnings limit, a further 1% is payable on the excess. No NICs are payable if earnings do not exceed the lower earnings limit (LEL). Employers' contributions are 12.8% of an employee's weekly earnings above £91 per week.

## Value Added Tax (VAT)

VAT is a tax which VAT registered businesses charge when they supply their goods and services in the UK or the Isle of Man, but there are some exceptions. It is also a tax on goods, and some services, that are imported or acquired from outside the UK.

VAT does not apply to certain services. These include loans of money, some property transactions, insurance and certain types of education and training. Supplies, which are exempt from VAT, do not form part of taxable turnover.

There are three rates of VAT in the UK:

- 17.5% (standard rate);
- 5% (reduced rate);
- 0% (zero rate).

Businesses are likely to have to register for and charge VAT if:

- Taxable turnover reaches or is likely to reach a set limit, known as the VAT registration threshold;
- A business has been taken over as a going concern; or
- Goods are acquired from other European Community countries.

Most businesses have to register for VAT once sales reach £58,000 per year. But businesses may opt to register for VAT if taxable turnover is less than this. Turnover is the amount of money going through the business, not just the profit.

The VAT which registered businesses charge and collect from customers is payable to Customs & Excise and is know as 'output tax'. The VAT which businesses are charged by their suppliers is called 'input tax' and can normally be reclaimed from Customs, although there are some exceptions.

Most businesses collect more VAT than they pay to their suppliers, and therefore pay the surplus VAT to Customs. However, if a business's input tax is more than its output tax, the difference will be refunded.

Contact Inland Revenue's Northern Ireland Business Support Team for information on the steps required to register VAT and organise tax and National Insurance payments.

## HM Customs and Excise

Customs & Excise is the UK Government department responsible for the collection and administration of VAT and excise duties as well as looking after Import & Export formalities. The Chancellor has announced that Inland Revenue and Customs and Excise are merging to create one new organisation - HM Revenue and Customs, during 2005. Exact dates and other details are not yet clear as they are subject to further legislation. HM Customs & Excise provides a range of support services for businesses that may need advice or assistance in operating any of these regimes.

- The National Enquiry Service deals with all general telephone enquiries via a single telephone number - 0845 010 9000. This service is available Monday to Friday from 8am to 8pm;
- If the enquiry is more complex, or a written response is required, the Written Enquiry Service may be contacted at the address below or by e-mail to enquiries.ni@hmce.gsi.gov.uk;
- The local Business Support Team offers support for businesses in Northern Ireland. This support can take the form of a one to one consultation for a single business or a seminar for a group of businesses with a common interest, such as cross border trade. The Business Support Team may be contacted at the address below or by telephone on 028 9056 2600;
- The Customs & Excise Website www.hmce.gov.uk contains further information and visitors to the site may download a wide range of information notices and leaflets.

All Customs & Excise support services are provided free of charge.

**HM Customs and Excise**
Custom House, Custom House Square
Belfast, BT1 3ET
Tel: 028 9056 2600
Email: ni@hmce.gov.uk
Web: www.hmce.gov.uk

**Registration & Deregistration**
Tel: 0845 711 2114 / Fax: 028 3026 4165

**Debt Management**
Tel: 028 9056 2600 / Fax: 028 9056 2975

**Belfast International Airport:** Tel: 028 9442 3439

**Complaints and Suggestions**
Tel: 028 9056 2618 / Fax: 028 9056 2970

**Customs Confidential:** Tel: 0800 59 5000

**National Advice Service:** Tel: 0845 010 9000

Text-phone for the deaf or hard of hearing: 0845 000 0200

### Importing and Exporting

If a business involves importing or exporting goods, there are certain requirements, which must be complied with, such as declaration of imports and exports to Customs & Excise and payment of any duties or VAT due.

Some imported goods are also liable to duties; further information on those goods affected is available from Customs and Excise.

With the establishment of the internal market across the European Union import/export procedures have been greatly simplified. However, there are numerous compliance requirements relating to trade with non-EU member states.

## Employment of Staff in Northern Ireland

The employment of staff for business in Northern Ireland entails much more than the payment of salary and overhead costs. Employers will need to be aware of a plethora of legal employment requirements and regulations across a range of headings. Some of the regulation derives from the Social Chapter of the European Union and is governed by European Directives. The remainder comes from the particular requirements deemed necessary for Northern Ireland in terms of ensuring fairness and equality in the employment sphere.

## Overview of Employment Legislation

Below is an outline of some of the current legislation governing employment rights and obligations which employers and employees in Northern Ireland should be aware of. Further details, may be obtained from:

**The Equality Commission for Northern Ireland**
Equality House, 7 - 9 Shaftesbury Square
Belfast, BT2 7DP
Tel: 028 9050 0600 / Fax : 028 9024 8687
Textphone : 028 9050 0589
Web: www.equalityni.org
Email : information@equalityni.org

**Disability Discrimination Act 1995 (DDA)**

This Act introduced new rights for disabled people in the areas of employment and access to goods, facilities, services and premises. The Act makes it unlawful for employers to discriminate against disabled employees or disabled job applicants in any aspect of employment. The Act also places a duty on employers to make reasonable adjustments if employment arrangements, or the workplace itself, place a disabled person at a substantial disadvantage compared to a non-disabled person.

**Equality (Disability, etc.) (Northern Ireland) Order 2000**

The Order expanded the duties and powers of the Equality Commission for Northern Ireland in relation to disability matters. It made provision for the ECNI to take a more proactive role in the promotion of the equalisation of opportunities for disabled people and the elimination of discrimination against them.

**Fair Employment and Treatment (Northern Ireland) Order 1998 (FETO)**

This Order makes it unlawful to discriminate against someone on the ground of religious belief or political opinion. The 1998 Order was amended in December 2003 to meet the requirements of the EU Employment Framework Directive. The Order defines discrimination as the less favourable treatment of a person on grounds of religious belief or political opinion and includes indirect discrimination. The Order outlaws discrimination by employers against members of their existing workforce and in the recruitment of new employees. Employers are also liable for acts of discrimination committed by their employees in the course of their employment.

**Sex Discrimination (Northern Ireland) Order 1976 (SDO)**

This Order makes it unlawful to discriminate against an individual on the grounds of his or her sex in the fields of employment, training, education, the provision of goods, facilities and services, and the disposal and management of premises. The Order also makes it unlawful to discriminate against married persons in employment; on grounds of gender reassignment in employment and training; and prohibits discrimination against contract workers.

**Equal Pay Act (NI) 1970**

Equal Pay legislation, provides for equal pay between men and women by giving a woman the right to equality in the terms of her contract of employment where she is employed on: like work to that of a man; work rated as equivalent to that of a man, or work of equal value to that of a man.

The Act applies equally to men and women of all ages and its purpose is to eliminate discrimination between men and women in pay and other terms of their contracts of employment such as piecework, output and bonus payments, holidays, free accommodation and sick leave.

**Race Relations (NI) Order 1997 (RRO)**

This order outlaws discrimination on grounds of colour, race, nationality or ethnic or national origin. The Irish Traveller community is specifically identified in the Order as a racial group against which racial discrimination is unlawful.

**Employment Equality (Sexual Orientation) Regulations (NI) 2003**

This legislation makes it unlawful for employers and others to discriminate on grounds of sexual orientation in the areas of:

- Employment
- Vocational training, including further and higher education.

These Regulations apply only to employment and training and do not extend to goods, facilities and services.

**Northern Ireland Act 1998**

Section 75 and Schedule 9 provisions within the Northern Ireland Act 1998 place a statutory obligation on public authorities (government departments, most non-departmental public bodies, District Councils and other bodies including UK departments designated by the Secretary of State) to carry out their functions relating to Northern Ireland with due regard to the need to promote equality of opportunity between:

- persons of different religious belief, political opinion, racial group, age, marital status or sexual
- orientation,
- men and women generally;
- persons with a disability and persons without, and
- persons with dependants and persons without.

In addition public authorities must have regard to the desirability of promoting good relations between persons of different religious belief, political opinion, or racial group.

**Working Time (NI) Regulations 1998**
These regulations set working hours of 48 hours per week. Employees may choose to work in excess of this, but must not be forced to do so.

**Employment Rights (NI) Order 1996**
This order sets out the notice that employees must provide to their employer when leaving his/her employment. Details are as follows:

| *Length of Service* | *Notice* |
|---|---|
| One month | 1 week |
| 2-3 year | 2 week |
| 3-4 years | 3 weeks |
| 12 years or more | up to 12 weeks |

**Employment Rights (NI) Order 1996**
This Order sets out the regulations for employees regarding annual leave and public holidays. This also sets out an employee's rights in relation to unfair dismissal.

**Minimum Wage (NI) Act 1998**
The minimum hourly rate is currently £4.85 per hour (aged 22+), £4.10 per hour (aged 18-21) or £3.00 per hour (aged 16 and 17). The minimum rate for agricultural workers aged 19 and over is £5.09 per hour.

**Human Rights Act 1998**
Article 8 confers the right to respect for family and private life.

**Public Interest Disclosure (NI) Order 1998**
Provides protection for workers who are dismissed or victimised as a result of making certain disclosures.

## Public Holidays
Public holidays include bank holidays, holidays by Royal Proclamation and 'common law holidays'. There is no statutory entitlement to bank or other public holidays, these are days where an employee may receive paid or unpaid leave depending on the terms of their contract. Where employees work on a public holiday to which they are entitled under the terms of their contracts, compensation for doing so is a matter for resolution under the terms of their contract.

Bank holidays in Northern Ireland include the Easter holidays, traditional "12th" holiday of the 12th and 13th July, the August Bank Holiday, 25th and 26th December, 1st January, and May Day.

## Annual Leave
Annual leave is usually accrued over 'leave years' from the date of employment or the date of the commencement of the organisation's leave year. If an employee joins an organisation during the course of the leave year their annual leave entitlement is calculated pro rata to the full leave year. Under the terms of the Working Time Regulations (Northern Ireland) 1998 entitlement to statutory leave for part years is proportionate to the amount of leave year that the employee works.

Employees are entitled to a minimum of four weeks' paid annual leave per year, which may include bank holidays.

## Holidays and Holiday Pay
Entitlement to holidays and holiday pay for most workers is determined by their contract of employment subject to the minimum conditions of the Working Time Regulations (Northern Ireland) 1998. Most employees have the statutory right to receive from their employers a written statement of employment details; although not a contract in itself this statement provides evidence of many of the terms of the contract. These must include provisions relating to holidays, including public holidays and holiday pay.

**Restrictions on Taking Holidays**
Restrictions on the taking of annual leave may be stated in the contract of employment, implied from custom and practice or incorporated into individual contracts from a collective agreement between the employer and trade unions.

## Maternity Leave
Maternity rights are set out in the Employment Relations (Northern Ireland) Order 1996 and the Maternity and Parental Leave Regulations (Northern Ireland) 1999.

- Pregnant employees are entitled to 26 weeks of ordinary maternity leave;
- Women who have completed 26 weeks service with their employer are entitled to take 26 weeks additional unpaid maternity leave commencing at the end of ordinary maternity leave.

The rate of statutory maternity pay for the first six weeks is 90% of the woman's average weekly earnings. For the remaining twenty weeks, a standard rate of statutory maternity pay is payable of £102.80 per week, or 90% of the woman's average weekly earnings, whichever is lower. Employers recover statutory maternity pay from the income tax and National Insurance Contributions they pay to the Inland Revenue.

Fathers are entitled to 2 weeks paid paternity leave, the payments for which can be claimed back from the government.

One member of a couple – or an individual – who adopts a child is entitled to adoption leave and pay.

## Parental Leave
Parental leave is a new entitlement. Parents may use this entitlement to spend more time with their children. Employees qualify for this entitlement following one year's service with the employer. Parents can take 13 weeks' unpaid parental leave for each child born or adopted on or after 15 December 1999. This leave can be taken until the child's fifth birthday or until five years after the adoption of a child. Parents of disabled children born on or after 15 December 1994 can take 18 weeks unpaid leave until the child's 18th birthday.

### Other Time Off
All employees have the right to take a reasonable period of time off work (not necessarily paid) to deal with an emergency involving a dependant and not be victimised or dismissed for doing so. Employees must also be released to attend jury service or for public duties eg as a member of an education and library board.

### Flexible Working
Parents of children under the age of 6, or of disabled children under the age of 18 must have requests for flexible working (including job-sharing, term-time working and flexitime) seriously considered by their employers. The request may be refused if there is a clear business reason why the work pattern cannot be accommodated.

### Sick Pay
Staff who are unable to work for four days or more due to illness are entitled to a minimum level of sick pay. The rate for the 2004/05 tax year is £66.15 per week. All full and part-time employees are entitled to statutory sick pay, provided they earn more than the National Insurance Lower Earnings Limit (£79 per week for 2004/05). Statutory sick pay is payable for up to 28 weeks for any one period of sickness or series of linked periods of sickness.

### Rest Breaks and Night Working
Workers must have a minimum of a 20 minute rest break in each shift lasting more than 6 hours. Staff have a right to 11 hours' rest between each working day. Staff shouldn't be forced to work more than 6 days out of every 7 or 12 days out of every 14. (Different limits apply for young workers aged between 16 and 18).

Night workers (people who regularly work at least three hours during night time which is classed as between 11pm and 6am) shouldn't average more than 8 hours in each 24 hour period. Workers must be offered a free health assessment before they begin working at night, and repeated at least once a year.

### Disability Issues
Issues relating to disability are legislated for under the Disability Discrimination Act 1995 which makes it unlawful to discriminate against disabled persons in connection with employment, the provision of goods, facilities and services. For businesses and organisations it is unlawful to treat disabled people less favourably than other people for a reason related to their disability. Organisations are required to make reasonable adjustments for disabled people, such as providing extra help or making changes to the way they provide their services and may have to make reasonable adjustments to the physical features of their premises to overcome physical barriers to access.

## Other Regulation of Business in Northern Ireland
In addition to the regulation of fundamental business concerns such as employment, taxation and governance, businesses are subject to extensive regulation in many other areas.
Depending on the nature of the business being started it may be affected by legislation and regulations regarding:

- Planning and Building Control;
- Health and safety;
- Fire precautions;
- Environmental protection;
- Intellectual property;
- Fair trading;
- Data protection;
- Licensing;
- Insurance.

### Planning Permission, Buildings/Premises
All development activity on a site or premises is subject to planning regulations overseen by the Planning Service. This can include as small a matter as installation of external signage right through to refurbishment and new build. The Planning Service has a network of regional offices *(full details are listed in Chapter 3).*

In addition to planning authorisations all developments require building control approvals. Building control is a function of the Department of the Environment with local offices organised through local councils. Further information is available from the Building Control department of the relevant local authority.

### Health and Safety
Company directors are responsible for the effect their business may have on the health and safety of employees and members of the public and may need to register with the Health & Safety Executive (HSE) or Local Authority. Further information is available from the Health and Safety Executive. Depending on the activities a company is engaged in and the extent of the danger it may present to staff and the public there are exacting procedures, which are legally binding. Larger businesses are required to produce a Health and Safety Policy statement.

**Health & Safety Executive for Northern Ireland (HSENI)**
83 Ladas Drive, Belfast BT6 9FR
Tel: 028 9024 3249 / Fax: 028 9023 5383
Web: www.hseni.gov.uk

### Fire Precautions
All business premises are required to have adequate levels of protection against fire hazard. This includes the installation (and regular checking) of equipment such as fire extinguishers and blankets. Staff should be trained to combat fire - a clear fire drill should be established and in larger premises a fire alarm system must be installed. Certain businesses may require a fire certificate, particularly if the business is a guest house, hotel or residential nursing home.

## Environmental Protection

There are environmental regulations that may apply to a business if it:

- Uses refrigeration or air-conditioning equipment, fire equipment or solvents for cleaning;
- Produces, imports, exports, stores, transports, treats, disposes of or recovers waste;
- Produces, imports or exports packaging;
- Produces packaging waste.

For more information contact:

**Environment and Heritage Service**
Tel: 028 9054 0540
Web: www.ehsni.gov.uk
Email: ehs@doeni.gov.uk

**Environmental Protection**
Headquarters, Calvert House, 23 Castle Place, Belfast BT1 1FY
Tel: 028 9025 4754

**Information and Education**
Commonwealth House, 35 Castle Street, Belfast BT1 1GU
Tel: 028 9054 6533

**Industrial Pollution & Radiochemical**
Inspectorate, Calvert House, 23 Castle Place, Belfast BT1 1FY
Tel: 028 9025 4754

## Intellectual Property

'Intellectual property' describes things such as business names, patents and inventions. Businesses should protect their own company name and logo, along with any inventions, product designs or copyrights and must also respect other people's intellectual property rights. The Patent Office can provide useful information and advice.

Tel: 08459 500 505.
Web: www.patent.gov.uk
Web: www.intellectual-property.gov.uk

## Fair Trading

The Office of Fair Trading (OFT) is responsible for protecting consumers by promoting effective competition, removing trading malpractice and publishing appropriate guidance. The OFT also issues consumer credit licences. More information is available by contacting The Office of Fair Trading:

Web: www.oft.gov.uk or
Tel: 08457 224499.
Email: enquiries@oft.gsi.gov.uk

## Data Protection/Freedom of Information

The Data Protection Act gives an individual the right to access personal information held by an organisation, of which that individual is the subject eg medical records. The Freedom of Information Act enables people to access any information held by/on behalf of public bodies, but which may not be about that individual eg details of the management structure of a public sector organisation. All organisations have obligations under both these pieces of legislation in regard to the way information is stored, shared and made available.

Further information is available from:

**Information Commissioner's Office Northern Ireland**
Room 101, Regus House
33 Clarendon Dock
Belfast, BT1 3BG
Tel: 028 9051 1270 / Fax: 028 9051 1584
Web: www.informationcommissioner.gov.uk

## Licensing

Most business sectors are specifically regulated and participants are often individually licensed to engage in particular activities. For example, a licence is required to run a hotel, a guesthouse, or a mobile shop. Companies should always check whether the business requires a licence to trade.

## Insurance

### Employers' Liability Insurance

All employers are required to take out Employers' Liability Insurance to cover the consequences of possible accidents in the workplace. The lower limit for cover is £5m. Depending on the nature of the business directors or staff may also wish to investigate personal indemnity insurance.

A valid certificate of Public Liability Insurance should be displayed at each business premises and should be retained even after it expires. This insurance should cover all employees, including contract staff and casual workers.

### Public Liability Insurance

While not a legal requirement, public liability insurance covers damages payments and any legal costs to members of the public for death or injury caused on business premises or as a result of business activities.

### Professional Indemnity Insurance

Professional Indemnity Insurance cover protects firms which provide advice in a professional capacity eg as a managment or IT consultant. If a business is proved to have been negligent in the professional advice it has given, professional indemnity insurance offers cover against damages.

*(A list of leading insurance companies is included in the business services listings, which follow later in this chapter).*

## Sources of Support for Business

There are a number of organisations within Northern Ireland offering various types of support to businesses at all levels. Some of these are listed below, together with details of the network of local enterprise agencies. Details on the support offered may be obtained by contacting the organisations directly.

### Belfast First Stop Business Shop Ltd

14 Wellington Place
Belfast, BT1 6GE
Tel: 028 9027 8399
Fax: 028 9027 8398
Email: info@firststopshop.co.uk
Web: www.firststopshop.co.uk

The First Stop Shop provides a free information, advisory and signposting service for potential and existing businesses.

Services Include:

- Business Information
- Advice & Counselling
- Assistance with Market Research
- Health & Safety Advice
- Signposting to further sources of help.

### The International Fund for Ireland

PO Box 200, Belfast, BT4 2QY
Tel: 028 9076 8832
Fax: 028 9076 3313

The International Fund for Ireland was established as an independent, international organisation by the British and Irish governments in 1986. The Fund promotes economic regeneration and reconciliation, through economic projects, and targets its resources at the most disadvantaged areas in Northern Ireland and the six southern border counties. Some initiatives include:

*Business Enterprise & Technology Programme* – aims to create conditions within which enterprise and business opportunities can develop, particularly in the sphere of local economic development.

*Tourism Programme* – aims to encourage economic regeneration by stimulating private sector investment in the provision and upgrading of tourist amenities and through supporting tourism marketing initiatives and staff development. *Radiane (Research and Development between Ireland and North America or Europe)* – seeks to stimulate, promote and provide financial support for product and process development joint ventures. The programme operates between manufacturing or internationally tradeable services companies located in Northern Ireland or the six southern border counties and partner companies in the United States of America, Canada or the European Union.

*The Flagship Programme* – supports a limited number of major projects with the potential to make a significant contribution to the economic and social revitalisation of their area and which have a symbolic significance for the island as a whole.

**Investment Companies**

The Fund's two Investment Companies, Enterprise Equity (NI) Ltd based in Belfast and Enterprise Equity (Irl) Ltd in Dundalk, were established with the objective of encouraging business development through the investment of new equity in well managed, innovative companies in Northern Ireland and the six Southern border counties. They provide venture capital on normal commercial criteria to new and expanding businesses.

### Investment Belfast

Investment Belfast Ltd
Fifth Floor
40 Linenhall Street
Belfast, BT2 8BA
Tel: +44 (0)28 9033 1136
Fax: +44 (0)28 9033 1137
Web: www.investmentbelfast.com

### Inter*Trade*Ireland

The Old Gasworks Business Park
Kilmorey Street
Newry, BT34 2DE
Tel: 028 3083 4100
Fax: 028 3083 4155
Email: info@intertradeireland.com
Web: www.intertradeireland.com

Chief Executive
Liam Nellis

Inter*Trade*Ireland was established in 1999 as part of the Belfast Agreement between the Government of Ireland and the Government of the United Kingdom of Great Britain and Northern Ireland. Inter*Trade*Ireland's mission is to expand cross-border trade and business on the island of Ireland.

Inter*Trade*Ireland provides a range of funding opportunities and business support initiatives on a cross-border basis. Some of the programmes administered by Inter*Trade*Ireland include:

**Acumen:** Concentrates on stimulating cross-border trade by assisting SMEs North and South by providing tailored consultancy and sales salary support.

**Focus:** An all-island sales and marketing initiative emphasising the promotion of all-island trade - identifying new market opportunities and delivering cross-border sales.

**Go Source** (www.Go-Source.com): An online directory aimed at suppliers interested in tackling the all-island €13bn public procurement market.

**Supplier Education Programme:** Provides guidance to SMEs in Northern Ireland and the Republic in the area of bidding for and servicing public sector contracts.

### Invest Northern Ireland

In 2002 a new agency, Invest Northern Ireland was established to co-ordinate industrial development efforts.

The agency falls under the auspices of the Department of Enterprise, Trade and Investment, which is the principal department responsible for providing business support for the private sector in Northern Ireland.

Invest Northern Ireland was formed to draw together the activities previously carried out by the Industrial Development Board (IDB), Local Enterprise Development Unit (LEDU), Industrial Research and Technology Unit (IRTU), and certain functions of the Northern Ireland Tourist Board (NITB) and the Business Support Division of DETI.

**Invest Northern Ireland**
Goodwood House, 44-58 May Street
Belfast BT1 4NN
Tel: 028 9023 9090
Fax: 028 9054 0490
Email: info@investni.com
Web: www.investni.com
Chief Executive: Leslie Morrison
Chairman: Prof Fabian Monds

**Invest Northern Ireland**
Upper Galwally, Belfast, BT8 6TB

**Invest Northern Ireland**
17 Antrim Road, Lisburn BT28 3AL

**North Western Local Office** *covers Coleraine, Limavady, Derry and Magherafelt.*
Building 1, Ulster Science and Technology Park
Buncrana Road
Londonderry, BT48 0JB
Tel: 028 7126 7257
Fax: 028 7126 6054
E-mail: nwlo@investni.com
Regional Manager: Kevin Helferty

**North Eastern Local Office** *Antrim, Ballymena, Ballymoney, Carrickfergus, Larne and Moyle.*
Clarence House, 86 Mill Street
Ballymena, BT43 5AF
Tel: 028 2564 9215
Fax: 028 2564 8427
E-mail: nelo@investni.com
Regional Manager: George McKinney

**Eastern Local Office** *covers Ards, Belfast, Castlereagh, Lisburn, Newtownabbey and North Down.*
Goodwood House, 44-58 May Street
Belfast, BT1 4NN
Tel: 028 9023 9090
Fax: 028 9054 5000
E-mail: info@investni.com
Regional Manager: Maurice Patterson

**Southern Local Office** *covers Armagh, Banbridge, Craigavon, Down and Newry and Mourne.*
6-7 The Mall, Newry, BT34 1BX
Tel: 028 3026 2955
Fax: 028 3026 5358
E-mail: slo@investni.com
Regional Manager: Mark Bleakney

**Western Local Office** *covers Dungannon, Omagh, Fermanagh, Cookstown and Strabane.*
Kevlin Buildings, 47 Kevlin Avenue
Omagh, BT78 1ER
Tel: 028 8224 5763
Fax: 028 8224 4291
E-mail: wlo@investni.com
Regional Manager: Patricia Devine

### Northern Ireland Business Start Programme

The Northern Ireland Business Start Programme provides a package of support to anyone interested in setting up a business. The Programme has three key components:

**Business advisory service** – provides the services of an expert business advisor on a one-to-one basis.

**Training course** - comprises 10 modules focused particularly on sales and marketing, financial management, legal and statutory issues, ICT and general business practices.

**Financial planning service** – explores all potential sources of funding including access to programme grant support and small business loans which are available under the programme.

For further information on the Northern Ireland Business Start Programme contact any Local Enterprise Agency. A full list of Local Enterprise Agencies is included in this chapter, beginning on the next page,

### Peace II

The European Union has allocated substantial funding for the purposes of helping sustain the 'peace' in Northern Ireland. Two of the five priorities under Peace II are 'Economic Renewal' and 'Locally Based Regeneration and Development Strategies' and there is an extensive list of measures within each of these priorities, under which funding may be allocated. It is worth noting that not all measures are currently taking applications, details of which measures are currently 'open' may be obtained from the Special EU Programmes Body. *(For further information on Peace II and a full list of priority and measures, see Chapter 12).*

### Prince's Trust

Block 5, Jennymount Court
North Derby Street
Belfast, BT15 3HN
Tel: 028 9074 5454
Fax: 028 9074 8416

The Prince's Trust offers support and guidance to young people, aged between 14-30 who may be interested in starting their own business.

## Local Enterprise Agencies

### Belfast

Argyle Business Centre Ltd
39 North Howard Street
Belfast, BT13 2AP
Tel: 028 9023 3777/Fax: 028 9031 3446
E-mail: admin@abc-ni.co.uk
Web: www.abc-ni.co.uk
Manager: Frank Hamill

Brookfield Business Centre
333 Crumlin Road Belfast, BT14 7EA
Tel: 028 9074 5241/Fax: 028 9074 8025
E: bob.mcneill@brookfieldcampus.com
Web: www.flaxtrust.com
Manager: Bob McNeill

Castlereagh Enterprises Ltd
Dundonald Enterprise Park
Enterprise Drive Carrowreagh Road
Dundonald, Belfast, BT16 1QT
Tel: 028 9055 7557/Fax: 028 9055 7558
E-mail: enterprise@castlereagh.com
Web: www.castlereagh.com
Manager: Jack McComiskey

East Belfast Enterprise Park Ltd
308 Albertbridge Road Belfast, BT5 4GX
Tel: 028 9045 5450/Fax: 028 9073 2600
E-mail: info@eastbelfast.org
Web: www.eastbelfast.org
Manager: Roisin Boyle

Farset Enterprise Park Ltd
638 Springfield Road Belfast, BT12 7DY
Tel: 028 9024 2373/Fax: 028 9043 8967
E-mail: admin@farset.com
Web: www.farset.com
Manager: William Bradley

Glenwood Enterprises Ltd
Glenwood Business Centre
Springbank Industrial Estate
Pembroke Loop Road
Poleglass, Belfast, BT17 0QL
Tel: 028 9061 0311/Fax: 028 9060 0929
E-mail: office@glenwoodbc.com
Web: www.glenwoodbc.com
Manager: Eamon Foster

Investment Belfast
40 Linenhall Street Belfast, BT2 8BA
Tel: 028 9033 1136/Fax: 028 9033 1137
E-mail: info@investmentbelfast.co.uk
Web: www.investmentbelfast.co.uk
Chief Executive: Brendan Mullan

Laganside Corporation
Clarendon Building, 15 Clarendon Road
Belfast, BT1 3BG
Tel: 028 9032 8507/Fax: 028 9033 2141
E-mail: info@laganside.com
Web: www.laganside.com
Chief Executive: Kyle Alexander

North City Business Centre Ltd
2 Duncairn Gardens, Belfast, BT15 2GG
Tel: 028 9074 7470/Fax: 028 9074 6565
E-mail: mailbox@north-city.co.uk
Web: www.north-city.co.uk
Centre Manager: Michael McCorry

Ormeau Business Park
8 Cromac Avenue Belfast, BT7 2JA
Tel: 028 9033 9906/Fax: 028 9033 9937
E-mail: info@ormeaubusinesspark.com
Web: www.ormeaubusinesspark.com
Development Officer: Patricia McNeil

ORTUS: The West Belfast Enterprise Board
Twin Spires Centre
155 Northumberland Street
Belfast, BT13 2JF
Tel: 028 9031 1002/Fax: 028 9031 1005
E-mail: hq@ortus.org
Web: www.ortus.org
Manager: Seamus O'Prey

Townsend Enterprise Park Ltd
28 Townsend Street, Belfast, BT13 2ES
Tel: 028 9089 4500/Fax: 028 9089 4502
E-mail: admin@townsend.co.uk
Web: www.townsend.co.uk
Manager: George Briggs

Work West Enterprise Agency
301 Glen Road, Andersonstown,
Belfast, BT11 8BU
Tel: 028 9061 0826 /Fax:028 9062 2001
E-mail: info@workwest.co.uk
Web: www.workwest.co.uk
Manager: Claire Ferris

### Co Antrim

Acorn the Business Centre
2 Riada Avenue, Garryduff Road
Ballymoney, BT53 7LH
Tel: 028 2766 6133/Fax: 028 2766 5019
E-mail: enquiries@acornbusiness.co.uk
Manager: Bobby Farren

Antrim Enterprise Agency
58 Greystone Road, Antrim, BT41 1JZ
Tel: 028 9446 7774/Fax: 028 9446 7292
E-mail: admin@antrimenterprise.com
Web: www.antrimenterprise.com
Manager: Jennifer McWilliams

Ballymena Business Development Centre Ltd
Galgorm Industrial Estate
62 Fenaghy Road, Galgorm
Ballymena, BT42 1FL
Tel: 028 2565 8616/Fax: 028 2563 0830
E-mail: bb.dc@virgin.net
Web: www.bbdc.co.uk
Manager: Melanie Christie

Carrickfergus Enterprise Agency
8 Meadowbank Road
Troopers Lane Industrial Estate
Carrickfergus, BT38 8YF
Tel: 028 9336 9528/Fax: 028 9336 9979
E-mail: carrickenterprise@dnet.co.uk
Web: www.ceal.co.uk
Business Development Officer:
Kelli Bagchus

Larne Enterprise Development Company (LEDCOM)
Ledcom Industrial Estate, Bank Road
Larne, BT40 3AW
Tel: 028 2827 0742/Fax: 028 2827 5653
E-mail: info@ledcom.org
Web: www.ledcom.org
Chief Executive: Ken Nelson

Lisburn Enterprise Organisation
Ballinderry Industrial Estate
Enterprise Crescent, Ballinderry Road
Lisburn, BT28 2BP
Tel: 028 9266 1160/Fax: 028 9260 3084
E-mail: centre@lisburn-enterprise.co.uk
Web: www.lisburn-enterprise.co.uk
Chief Executive: Aisling Owens

Mallusk Enterprise Park
2 Mallusk Drive
Newtownabbey, BT36 4GN
Tel: 028 9083 8860/Fax: 028 9084 1525
Chief Executive: Melanie Humphrey

Moyle Enterprise Co Ltd
61 Leyland Rd, Ballycastle, BT54 6EZ
Tel: 028 2076 3737/Fax: 028 2076 9690
E-mail: moyle.enterprise@dnet.co.uk
Web: www.moyle-enterprise.com
Manager: Colette McMullan

## Co Armagh

Armagh Business Centre
2 Loughgall Road, Armagh, BT61 7NJ
Tel: 028 3752 5050/Fax: 028 3752 6717
Manager: Anna Logan

Craigavon Industrial Development Organisation Ltd (CIDO)
Carn Industrial Estate
Craigavon, BT63 5RH
Tel: 028 3833 3393/Fax: 028 3835 0390
Web: www.cido.co.uk
Chief Executive: Jim Smith

CIDO Business Complex
Charles St, Lurgan, BT66 6HG
Tel: 028 3834 7020/Fax: 028 3834 7052
Chief Executive: Jim Smith

## Co Derry

Coleraine Enterprise Agency Ltd
Unit 7, Loughanhill Industrial Estate
Coleraine, BT52 2NR
Tel: 028 7035 6318/Fax: 028 7035 5464
Web: www.coleraine-enterprise.co.uk
Manager: Ray Young

Creggan Enterprises Ltd
Rath Mor Centre, Blighs Lane
Derry, BT48 0LZ
Tel: 028 7137 3170/Fax: 028 7137 3004
Chairperson: Eddie Clements

Dunamanagh & District Community Association Ltd
2a Lisnarragh Road
Dunamanagh, BT82 0QL
Tel: 028 7139 7097
Business Manager: Albert Allen

Eurocentre West Ltd
Unit 25B Pennyburn Industrial Estate,
Buncrana Road, Derry, BT48 0LU
Tel: 028 7136 4015/Fax: 028 7726 6032
E-mail: fdecw@aol.com
Contact: Denis Feeney

Glenshane Business Park
50 Legavallon Rd, Dungiven, BT47 4QL
Tel: 028 7774 2474/Fax: 028 7774 2393
Manager: Mairead McCormick Kelly

Glenshane Enterprise Centre
414a Ballyquann Rd
Dungiven, BT47 4NQ
Tel: 028 7774 2494 /Fax: 028 7774 2393
Manager: John McNicholl

Limavady Small Business Agency
Aghanloo Industrial Estate
Aghanloo Road, Limavady, BT49 0HE
Tel: 028 7776 5655
Fax: 028 7776 5707
Web: www.lysba.com
Manager: Martin Devlin

Maghera Development Association
10B Coleraine Rd, Maghera, BT46 5BN
Tel: 028 7964 5425/Fax: 028 7964 5425
Manager: Breige Church

Noribic Ltd
North West Institute for Further & Higher Education
Strand Road, Derry, BT48 7BY
Tel: 028 7126 4242
E-mail: noribic@nwifhe.ac.uk
Web: www.noribic.com
Chief Executive: Barney Toal

North West Enterprises
16C Queen Street
Londonderry, BT48 7ED
Tel: 028 7127 9191/Fax: 028 7137 1867
Manager: John McGowan

Roe Valley Enterprises Ltd
Aghanloo Industrial Estate, Aghanloo Road, Limavady, BT49 0HE
Tel: 028 7776 2323/Fax: 028 7776 5707
Web: www.lysba.com
Manager: Martin Devlin

Workspace (Draperstown) Ltd
The Business Centre, 7 Tobermore Road
Draperstown, BT45 7AG
Tel: 028 7962 8113/Fax: 028 7962 8975
E-mail: info@workspace.org
Web: www.workspace.org.uk
Chief Executive: Brian Murray

## Co Down

Ards Business Centre Ltd
Jubilee Rd, Newtownards, BT23 4YH
Tel: 028 9181 9787/Fax: 028 9182 0625
E-mail: info@ardsbusiness.co.uk
Web: www.ardsbusiness.co.uk
Chief Executive: Margaret Patterson

Banbridge District Enterprises Ltd
Scarva Road Industrial Estate
Banbridge, BT32 3QD
Tel: 028 4066 2260/Fax: 028 4066 2325
E-mail: info@bdelonline.com
Web: www.bdelonline.com
Manager: Ciaran Cunningham

Down Business Centre
46 Belfast Road, Downpatrick, BT30 9UP
Tel: 028 4461 6416/Fax: 028 4461 6419
E-mail: business@downbc.co.uk
Web: www.downbc.co.uk
Chief Executive: Janice Symington

Newry and Mourne Enterprise Agency
Enterprise House, Win Business Park,
Canal Quay, Newry, BT35 6PH
Tel: 028 3026 7011/Fax: 028 3026 1316
E-mail: nmcoop@dial.pipex.com
Web: www.nmea.net
Manager: Conor Patterson

North Down Development Organisation Ltd
Enterprise House, Balloo Avenue
Balloo Industrial Estate
Bangor, BT19 7QT
Tel: 028 9127 1525/Fax: 028 9127 0080
E-mail: mail@nddo.u-net.com
Web: www.nndo.u-net.com
Chief Executive: Lynne Vance

## Co Fermanagh

Belcoo Enterprises Ltd
Railway Road, Belcoo, BT93 5FJ
Tel: 028 6638 6377/Fax: 028 6638 6377
Chairman: Harold Johnston

Fermanagh Enterprise Ltd
Enniskillen Business Centre
Lackaghboy Industrial Estate
Tempo Rd, Enniskillen, BT74 4RL
Tel: 028 6632 3117
Fax: 028 6632 7878
E-mail: info@fermanaghenterprise.net
Web: www.fermanaghenterprise.com
Manager: John Treacy

Irvinestown Trustee Enterprise Co
Irvinestown Business Park
Old Market Yard, Mill St
Irvinestown, BT94 1GR
Tel: 028 6862 1977/Fax: 028 6862 8414
Manager: Jenny Irvine

Kesh Development Association Charitable Trust
Mantlin Road, Kesh, BT93 1TU
Tel: 028 6863 2158/Fax: 028 6863 2158
E-mail: dev@kesh.org.uk
Manager: Glenn Moore

**Lisnaskea Community Enterprise Centre Ltd**
Drumbrughas North, Lisnaskea, BT92 0PE
Tel: 028 6772 1081/Fax: 028 6772 1088
Manager: Brian Cosgrove

**Rosslea Enterprises Ltd**
Rosslea Enterprise Centre, Liskilly
Rosslea, BT92 7FH
Tel: 028 6775 1851
Contact: Jane Collins

**South West Fermanagh Development Organisation Ltd**
Teemore Business Complex
Teemore, Derrylin, BT92 9BL
Tel: 6774 8893 / Fax: 6774 8493
E-mail: teemorecomplex@hotmail.com
Web: www.shannon-erne.co.uk
Contact: James McBarron

## Co Tyrone

**Acumen Cross-Border Support Agency**
Unit B4, Omagh Business Complex
Great Northern Road
Omagh, BT78 5LU
Tel: 028 8225 0404/Fax: 028 8225 0416
E: info@acumenprogramme.com
W: www.acumenprogramme.com
Director: Willie Maxwell

**Castlederg and District Enterprises Company Ltd**
Drumquin Rd
Castlederg, BT81 7PX
Tel: 028 8167 0414/Fax: 028 8167 0731
Director: Gerald Sproule

**Coalisland and District Development Association Ltd**
51 Dungannon Road
Coalisland, BT71 4HP
Tel: 028 8774 7215/Fax: 028 8774 8695
Chief Executive: Pat McGirr

**Cookstown Enterprise Centre Ltd**
Derryloran Industrial Estate
Sandholes Road, Cookstown, BT80 9LU
Tel: 028 8676 3660/Fax: 028 8676 3160
E: info@cookstownenterprise.com
W: www.cookstownenterprise.com
Chief Executive: Jim Eastwood

**Dungannon Enterprise Centre Ltd**
2 Coalisland Road
Dungannon, BT71 6JT
Tel: 028 8772 3489/Fax: 028 8775 2200
E: admin@dungannonenterprise.com
W: www.dungannonenterprise.com
Centre Manager: Brian McAuley

**Omagh Enterprise Co Ltd**
Omagh Business Complex
Gortrush Industrial Estate
Great Northern Road
Omagh, BT78 5LU
Tel: 028 8224 9494/Fax: 028 8224 9451
E: info@oecl.co.uk
W: www.oecl.co.uk
Manager: Nicholas O'Shiel

**Strabane Enterprise Agency Ltd**
Orchard Road Industrial Estate
Orchard Road, Strabane, BT82 9FR
Tel: 028 7138 2518/Fax: 028 7188 4531
E-mail: info@ceagency.co.uk
Chief Executive: Christina Mulle

## Business Services Listings

What follows below are listings of business services providers. They inlude: Legal Advisors, Economic and Financial Advisors, IT Consultants, Recruitment Agencies and several other categories of service providers.

**Legal Advisors**

Arthur Cox
Capital House, 3 Upper Queen Street
Belfast, BT1 6PU
Tel: 028 9023 0007

Bernard Campbell & Co Solicitors
91-93 Victoria Street, Belfast, BT1 4PB
Tel: 028 9023 2008

Bigger & Strahane Solicitors
Sinclair House, 89 Royal Avenue
Belfast, BT1 1EX
Tel: 028 9032 5229

C&H Jefferson Solicitors
Norwich Union House, 7 Fountain Street
Belfast, BT1 5EA
Tel: 028 9032 9545

Campbell Stafford Solicitors
41 Fitzwilliam Street, University Road
Belfast, BT9 6AW
Tel: 028 9023 0808

Carson McDowell Solicitors
Murray House, 4-5 Murray Street
Belfast, BT1 6DN
Tel: 028 9024 4951

Cleaver Black
54 Lisburn Road, Belfast, BT9 6AF
Tel: 028 9032 2904

Cleaver Fulton Rankin
50 Bedford Street, Belfast, BT2 7FW
Tel: 028 9024 3141

Comerton & Hill
8th Floor, 14 Great Victoria Street
Belfast, BT2 7BA
Tel: 028 9023 4629

Cooper Wilkinson
Imperial Buildings
38-40 Queen Elizabeth Road
Enniskillen, BT74 7BY
Tel: 028 6632 2615

Culbert & Martin Solicitors
Scottish Provident Building
7 Donegall Square West
Belfast, BT1 6JH
Tel: 028 9032 5508

Cunningham & Dickey Solicitors
68 Upper Church Lane
Belfast, BT1 4LG
Tel: 028 9024 5896

Deery McGuinness & Co Solicitors
181 Victoria Street, Belfast, BT1 4PE
Tel: 028 9023 3268

Desmond J Doherty & Co
Clarendon Chambers
7 Clarendon Street
Londonderry, BT48 7EP
Tel: 028 7128 8870

Diamond Heron Solicitors
Diamond House, 7-19 Royal Avenue
Belfast, BT1 1FB
Tel: 028 9024 3726

Donnelly & Kinder Solicitors
Claims Exchange Building
11 Victoria Street
Belfast, BT1 3GA
Tel: 028 9024 4999

Donnelly & Wall
Callender House
58-60 Upper Arthur Street
Belfast, BT1 4GP
Tel: 028 9023 3157

Edwards & Co
28 Hill Street, Belfast, BT1 2LA
Tel: 028 9032 1863

EJ Lavery & Co Solicitors
1-3 Hightown Road
Glengormley, BT36 7TZ
Tel: 028 9084 3436

Elliott Duffy Garrett
Royston House, 34 Upper Queen Street
Belfast, BT1 6FD
Tel: 028 9024 5034

Falls & Hanna
125 Main Street
Fivemiletown, BT75 0PG
Tel: 028 8952 1234

Flynn & McGettrick
9 Clarence Street, Belfast, BT2 8DX
Tel: 028 9024 4212

Francis Hanna & Co
75-77 May Street, Belfast, BT1 3JL
Tel: 028 9024 3901

Francis J Irvine & Company Solicitors
42 Dublin Road, Belfast, BT2 7HN
Tel: 028 9024 6451

Hewitt & Gilpin
Thomas House
14-16 James Street South
Belfast, BT2 7GA
Tel: 028 9057 3573

James Doran & Co Solicitors
19-21 Cornmarket, Belfast, BT1 4DB
Tel: 028 9024 0440

JG O'Hare & Co Solicitors
St George's Building, 37-41 High Street
Belfast, BT1 2AB
Tel: 028 9023 4800

Jones & Company Solicitors
Scottish Provident Building
7 Donegall Square West
Belfast, BT1 6JF
Tel: 028 9024 5471

Keenan Solicitors
54 Knockbreda Road, Belfast, BT6 0JB
Tel: 028 9049 3349

L'Estrange & Brett
Arnott House, 12-16 Bridge Street
Belfast, BT1 1LS
Tel: 028 90230426

McCartan Turkington Breen Solicitors
Chancery House, 88 Victoria Street
Belfast, BT1 3GN
Tel: 028 9032 9801

McCreery Turkington Stockman
Stockman House, 39-43 Bedford Street
Belfast, BT2 7EE
Tel: 028 9032 3040

McLaughlin & Co Solicitors
218 Woodstock Road
Belfast, BT6 9DL
Tel: 028 9080 7000

Mills Selig Solicitors
21 Arthur Street, Belfast, BT1 4GA
Tel: 028 9024 3878

Morgan & Murphy Solicitors
1st Floor, 42 Castle Street
Belfast, BT1 1HB
Tel: 028 9024 4545

Morrow & Wells Solicitors
57 Upper Arthur Street
Belfast, BT1 4GJ
Tel: 028 9023 3866

O'Reilly Stewart Solicitors
114-116 Royal Avenue
Belfast, BT1 1DL
Tel: 028 9032 1000

Paschal J O'Hare Solicitors
Donegall House
98-102 Donegall Street
Belfast, BT1 2GW
Tel: 028 9031 3613

Rosemary Connolly Solicitors
2 The Square
Warrenpoint, BT34 3JT
Tel: 028 4175 3121

Tughans Solicitors
30 Victoria Street
Belfast, BT1 3GS
Tel: 028 9055 3300

Wilson-Nesbitt Solicitors
Citylink Business Park, Albert Street
Belfast, BT12 4WA
Tel: 028 9032 3864

## Economic & Financial Advisors

### Accountants

Adrian Hall & Co.
4th Floor, Franklin House
12 Brunswick Street
Belfast, BT2 7GE
Tel: 028 9032 4250
Web: www.adrianhallco.co.uk

Arthur Boyd & Company
Franklin House, 12 Brunswick Street
Belfast, BT2 7GE
Tel: 028 9032 9255

ASM Horwath
Horwath House, 20 Rosemary Street
Belfast, BT1 1QD
Tel: 028 9024 9222
Web: www.asmhorwath.com
Email: asm@asmhorwath.com

BDO Stoy Hayward

BDO

BDO Stoy Hayward

Lindsay House
10 Callender Street
Belfast, BT1 5BN
Tel: 028 9043 9009
Fax: 028 9043 9010
Web: www.bdoni.com

Managing Partner
Stephen Prenter

BDO Stoy Hayward is the adviser of choice to growing businesses, public sector bodies, voluntary organisations and entrepreneurs. BDO Stoy Hayward has a total of 15 offices across the UK and is a member of BDO International, the world's fifth largest accountancy firm with 600 offices in 100 countries.
Key services include; management consultancy, marketing consultancy, corporate finance, audit, tax, forensic accounting, wealth management, business recovery services, property and people solutions

Deloitte

Deloitte.

19 Bedford Street
Belfast, BT2 7EJ
Tel: 028 9032 2861
Fax: 028 9023 4786
Web: www.deloitte.co.uk

Senior Partner
Paul Clarke

Deloitte is the UK's fastest growing Big 4 professional services firm with over 10,000 staff nationwide and a fee income of £1,246 million in 2003/2004.

Employing more than 160 people locally, Deloitte Belfast provides fully integrated services that include accounting, business advisory, audit, tax, management consulting, corporate finance and reorganisation services, offering our clients the best possible opportunities and services with access to our global capabilities and extensive network. Our clients include local plcs, subsidiaries of global organisations, locally owned businesses and public sector organisations.

FPM Chartered Accountants

FPM
CHARTERED ACCOUNTANTS

**Newry Office:**
Dromalane Mill
The Quays
Newry
Co Down BT35 8QS
Tel: 028 3026 1010
Fax: 028 3026 2345

**Dundalk Office:**
17A Francis Street
Dundalk
Co Louth
Tel: 00 353 42 938 8898
Fax: 00 353 42 938 8899

**Dungannon Office:**
25 Georges Street
Dungannon, Co Tyrone
BT70 1BT
Tel: 028 8775 0400
Fax: 028 8775 0445

**Web: www.fpmca.com**
**E-mail: info@fpmca.com**

FPM Chartered Accountants is a client-focused practice with specialist skills in accounts preparation, audit, tax planning, business consultancy, strategic planning, corporate finance, financial management, project management and forensic accounting.

Goldblatt McGuigan
Alfred House,19 Alfred Street
Belfast, BT2 8EQ
Tel: 028 9031 1113
Web: www.goldblattmcguigan.com

Grant Thornton
Water's Edge, Clarendon Dock
Belfast, BT1 3BH
Tel: 028 9031 5500
Fax: 028 9031 4036

Hanna Thompson & Co.
Century House, Enterprise Crescent
Lisburn, BT28 2BP
Tel: 028 9260 7355

Hassard McClements
32 East Bridge St
Enniskillen, BT74 7BT
Tel: 028 6632 0555

Helm Corporation Ltd
Commercial House, Demesne Court
88 Main Street, Moira, BT67 OLH
Tel: 028 9261 0930
Web: www.helm-corp.com
Email: helm@helm-corp.com

Henry Murray & Company
6 Edward Street, Lurgan, BT66 6DB
Tel: 028 3832 7744

Johnston Kennedy
18 Orby Link, Castlereagh Road
Belfast, BT5 5HW
Tel: 028 9070 5333

KPMG
Stokes House, College Square East
Belfast, BT1 6DH
Tel: 028 9024 3377
Fax: 028 9089 3893

M.B. McGrady & Co.
Rathmore House
52 St.Patrick's Avenue
Downpatrick, BT30 6DS
Tel: 028 4461 6321
Web: www.mbmcgrady.co.uk
Email: nfo@mbmcgrady.co.uk

McClureWatters
1 Lagan Quay, Belfast, BT1 3GP
Tel: 028 9023 4343
Fax: 028 9043 9077

McElholm & Company
28 Gortin Road, Omagh, BT79 7HX
Tel: 028 8224 4016

McKeague Morgan & Co
40 University Street, Belfast, BT7 1F2
Tel: 028 9024 2612

Moore Stephens
Scottish Provident Building
7 Donegall Square West
Belfast, BT1 6JH
Tel: 028 9032 9481
Fax: 028 9043 9185

Nichol Donnelly & Partners
222 Ormeau Road, Belfast, BT7 2FY
Tel: 028 9064 6262

O'Hare Finnegan Chartered Accountants
Wyncroft, 30 Rathfriland Road
Newry, BT34 1JZ
Tel: 028 3026 9933

Paul Hagerty and Co
11 The Square, Rostrevor, BT34 3AZ
Tel: 028 4173 9340
Fax: 028 4173 9342
Email: info@paulhagerty.co.uk
Web: www.paulhagerty.co.uk

PGM Chartered Accountants
405 Lisburn Road, Belfast, BT9 7EU
Tel: 028 9066 3111

S D Brown & Company Accountants
Carnegie Building, 25-27 Edward Street
Portadown, BT62 3NE
Tel: 028 3833 8913

Stevenson & Wilson
22 Broadway Avenue
Ballymena, BT43 7AA
Tel: 028 2564 7712

PricewaterhouseCoopers LLP

Waterfront Plaza
8 Laganbank Road
Belfast, BT1 3LR
Tel: 028 9024 5454
Fax: 028 9041 5600
Web: www.pwc.com/uk

Managing Partner
Stephen Kingon

PricewaterhouseCoopers is Northern Ireland's - and the world's - largest professional services organisation. With over 650 staff in Northern Ireland, PwC provides advisory services to 80 per cent of Northern Ireland's 'Top-100' companies, to Government Departments and Agencies and to more family-owned and owner-managed firms than any other advisor.

Our worldwide networks throughout 139 countries help clients compete successfully in global markets, while our regular surveys, research and economic analyses are acknowledged as key factors in stimulating foreign direct investment and contributing to Northern Ireland's economic competitiveness.

## Management Consultants

Abacus Partnership
28 Richmond Court, Lisburn, BT27 4QU
Tel: 028 9267 8582

ASM Horwath
20 Rosemary Street, Belfast, BT1 1QD
Tel: 028 9024 9222

Barklie & Logan Management Consultants
8 Cameron Park, Ballymena, BT42 1QJ
Tel: 028 2564 5447

BDO Stoy Hayward Management Consultants
Lindsay House, 10 Callender Street
Belfast, BT1 5BN
Tel: 028 9043 9009
Fax: 028 9043 9010

BearingPoint
Stokes House
17-25 College Square East
Belfast, BT1 6DH
Tel: 028 9089 3888

Blueprint Development Consultancy
Unit 2 Ormeau Business Park
8 Cromac Avenue, Belfast, BT7 2JA
Tel: 028 9024 4115
Fax: 028 9024 2115

CAM Benchmarking Ltd
9 Wellington Park, Belfast, BT9 6DJ
Tel: 028 9066 7722
Fax: 028 9068 3378

Capita Business Services Ltd
425 Holywood Road, Belfast, BT4 2PL
Tel: 028 9076 3910
Fax: 028 9076 1698
Web: www.capitaconsulting.co.uk

DTZ Pieda Consulting
Scottish Provident Building
7 Donegall Square West
Belfast, BT1 6JE
Tel: 028 9024 7623
Fax: 028 9024 7632

EPEC
Floral Buildings, 2-14 East Bridge Street
Belfast, BT1 3MQ
Tel: 028 9092 3475

Helm Corporation Limited
Commercial House, Demense Court
88 Main Street, Moira, BT67 0LH
Tel: 028 9261 0930
Fax: 028 9061 0931

Key Consulting Group
144 High Street, Holywood, BT18 9HS
Tel: 028 9042 3635

Level Seven
Curlew Pavilion, Portside Business Park
Airport Road West, Belfast, BT3 9ED
Tel: 028 9092 9777

McCann Consulting
30B East Bridge Street
Enniskillen, BT74 7BT
Tel: 028 6632 0443

Merc Partners
12B Clarendon Roa, Clarendon Dock
Belfast, BT1 3BG
Tel: 028 9072 5750
Fax: 028 9072 5751

Penna Consulting
405 Holywood Road, Belfast, BT4 2GU
Tel: 028 9076 4700
Fax: 028 9076 4701

PricewaterhouseCoopers
Waterfront Plaza, 8 Laganbank Road
Belfast, BT1 3LR
Tel: 028 9024 5454
Fax; 028 9041 5600

Vision Management Services
97E Queen Street
Ballymena, BT42 2BE
Tel: 028 2563 9695

Whitewater Consulting
313 Belmont Road
Belfast, BT4 2NE
Tel: 028 9076 9520

**Financial Advisers/Investment Consultants**

Aegis Insurance Services (NI) Ltd
229-235 Upper Newtownards Road
Belfast, BT4 3JF
Tel: 028 9065 5311

Aiken Kennedy Financial Planning
8-10 Graham Gardens
Lisburn, BT28 1XE
Tel: 028 9260 3175

AMG Financial Services
27 Hill Street, Ballymena, BT43 6BH
Tel: 028 2563 1377

Aon McMillen
31 Bedford Street, Belfast, BT2 7FP
Tel: 028 9024 2771
Fax: 028 9031 3644

Belgravia Associates
6 Belgravia Road, Bangor, BT19 6XJ
Tel: 028 9127 0244

Boyce Financial Services
24 High Street, Portadown, BT62 1HJ
Tel: 028 3833 4141

C&S Associates
14 Cromac Place, Belfast, BT7 2JB
Tel: 028 9072 6500

CRN Financial Advisors
20 Stranmillis Road, Belfast, BT9 5AA
Tel: 028 9066 0300

Capital Trust Financial Management
Capital House, 28 Lodge Road
Coleraine, BT52 1NB
Tel: 028 7035 8500

Census Financial Planning
437 Lisburn Road, Belfast, BT9 7EY
Tel: 028 9066 8700

Financial Solutions
26 Oldtown Street
Cookstown, BT80 8EF
Tel: 028 8676 5900

Forward Financial Planning
Regent Suite, Regent House
Regent Street
Newtownards, BT23 4AD
Tel: 028 9182 6767
Fax: 028 9182 6131

Foundation Financial Consulting
Banbridge Enterprise Centre
Scarva Road Industrial Estate
Banbridge, BT32 3OD
Tel: 028 4062 9966

Halliday Financial Guidance
32 Hamilton Road, Bangor, BT20 4LE
Tel: 028 9147 2634

Hanna Hillen Financial Services
11 Church Square
Banbridge, BT32 4AP
Tel: 028 4066 2848

Homelink Financial Services
61-63 High Street Bangor, BT20 5BE
Tel: 028 9127 1771

McClure Watters
Thomas House
14-16 James Street South
Belfast, BT2 7GA
Tel: 028 9023 4343

Medical and Dental Financial Management
41 Malone Road, Belfast, BT9 6RX
Tel: 028 9029 0000

Odyssey Financial Planning (Northern Ireland)
Unit 7 Boucher Plaza
4-6 Boucher Road
Belfast, BT12 6HR
Tel: 028 9024 3921

Pension & Financial Consultants Ltd
Victoria Buildings, 41 Belmore Street
Enniskillen, BT74 6AA
Tel: 028 6632 8080

SRG Financial Management Ltd.
73 Main Street, Larne, BT40 1HH
Tel: 028 2827 7357

Stockbrokers

Cunningham Coates
19 Donegall Street, Belfast, BT1 2HA
Tel: 028 9032 3456

DM Wright
15 The Diamond
Londonderry, BT48 6HS
Tel: 028 7126 3344
Fax: 028 7126 0738

Edward Jones Ltd
2 Malone Road, Belfast, BT9 5BN
Tel: 028 9068 7715

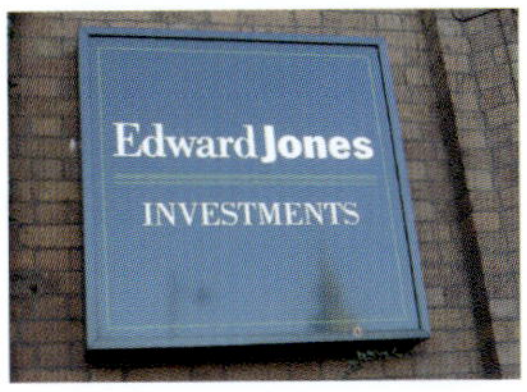


Rensburg Investment Management
St Georges House, 99-101 High Street
Belfast, BT1 2AG
Tel: 028 9032 1002

## Insurance Brokers

Abbey
8-10 Governor's Place
Carrickfergus, BT38 7BN
Tel: 028 9335 1525
Fax: 028 9336 2509

Allianz Northern Ireland
Allianz House, 21 Linenhall Street
Belfast, BT2 8AB
Tel: 028 9089 5600
Web: www.allianz-ni.gov.uk

Aon McMillen
31 Bedford Street, Belfast, BT2 7FP
Tel: 028 9024 2771
Fax: 028 9031 3644

Bartholomew & James
Metropolitan Building
29-31 Alfred Street
Belfast, BT2 8ED
Tel: 028 9024 1651
Fax: 028 9024 0441
Web: www.bartjames.co.uk

CJ Higgins
22 Mallusk Road
Newtownabbey, BT36 8PP
Tel: 028 9083 0830
Web: www.cjhiggins.co.uk

EPJ Morgan Insurance Brokers
29 Mill Street, Newry, BT34 1EY
Tel: 028 3026 5447
Fax: 028 3026 9738

Hughes & Company
Strangford House, 4 Jubilee Road
Newtownards, BT23 4WN
Tel: 028 9181 0081
Fax: 028 9181 8842

Marsh Ltd
16-20 Bedford House, Bedford Street
Belfast, BT2 7DX
Tel: 028 9055 6100
Fax: 028 9055 6166

Open + Direct
1 Regent Street, Newtownards
BT23 4AB
Tel: 08702 470 470
(There are also branches in Belfast, Coleraine, Dungiven, Londonderry and Magherafelt.)

S Rankin & Co
21-23 Bachelor's Walk
Lisburn, BT28 1XJ
Tel: 028 9267 6235
Fax: 028 9267 1289

Wallace Insurance Brokers
Whitehall Chambers, 43 New Row
Coleraine, BT52 1AE
Tel: 028 7032 5999
Fax: 028 7034 3641

Willis & Company
News Letter Building
55-59 Donegall Street
Belfast, BT1 2FH
Tel: 028 9032 9042
Fax: 028 9023 2362

## Leasing

Agnew Corporate
45 Mallusk Road
Newtownabbey, BT36 4PS
Tel: 028 9080 4408
Fax: 028 9034 1083

Bank of Scotland (Ireland) Limited
10-15 Donegall Square North
Belfast, BT1 5GB
Tel: 028 9044 2600
Fax: 028 9044 2692

Charles Hurst Business Solutions
62 Boucher Road, Belfast, BT12 6LR
Tel: 028 9038 3426
Fax: 028 9038 3425

CVC Direct
PO Box 30, Ballyclare, BT39 0BQ
Tel: 028 9443 2223
Fax: 028 9443 9220

DFC Ltd
380C Belmont Road, Belfast, BT4 2NF
Tel: 028 9076 1669
Fax: 028 9076 9779

Donnelly Brothers
2 Apollo Road, Boucher Road
Belfast, BT12 6HP
Tel: 028 9066 2000
Fax: 028 9066 1111

Fleet Financial NI Ltd.
7 Mallusk Drive, Mallusk
Newtownabbey, BT36 4GX
Tel: 028 9084 9777
Fax: 028 9084 9555

Hertz Lease
Musgrave Business Centre
45 Stockman's Way
Belfast, BT9 7ET
Tel: 028 9038 1800
Fax: 028 9038 2001

### Market Research

Market Research Northern Ireland Ltd (MRNI)
Elmwood House
44-46 Elmwood Avenue
Belfast, BT9 6AZ
Tel: 028 9066 1037
Fax: 028 9068 2007
Web: www.mrni.co.uk
Email: info@mrni.co.uk

Millward Brown Ulster
115 University Street, Belfast, BT7 1HP
Tel: 028 9023 1060
Fax: 028 9024 3887
Web: www.ums-research.com
Email: ask@uk.millwardbrown.com

Mintel
6 Citylink Business Park
Belfast, BT12 4HB
Tel: 028 9024 1849
Fax: 028 9024 2597
Web: www.reports.mintel.com
Email: irelandinfo@mintel.com

MORI-MRC
92-96 Lisburn Road, Belfast, BT9 6AG
Tel: 028 9050 0800
Fax: 028 9050 0801
Web: www.morimrc.ie
Email: info@morimrc.ie

Quadriga Consulting
99 Hillsborough Road
Lisburn, BT28 1JX
Tel: 028 9266 8968
Fax: 028 9266 8971
Web: www.quadrigaconsulting.com
Email: info@quadrigaconsulting.com

RES (Research and Evaluation Services)
City Link Business Park, Albert Street
Belfast, BT12 4HB
Tel: 028 9050 7777
Fax: 028 9050 7779
Web: www.res.nireland.com
Email: info@res.nireland.com

SMR (Social and Market Research)
3 Wellington Park, Belfast, BT9 6DJ
Tel: 028 9092 3362
Fax: 028 9092 3334
Web: www.smresearch.co.uk
Email: info@smresearch.co.uk

### IT Consultants

Advance Systems
Unit 10b, 80-82 Rainey Street
Magherafelt, BT45 5AJ
Tel: 028 7963 4455
Web: www.advance-systems.co.uk
Email: info@ advance-systems.co.uk

Amt-Sybex (NI) Ltd
Edgewater Office Park, Edgewater Rd
Belfast, BT3 9JQ
Tel 028 9078 1616
Fax 028 9078 1717
Web: www.amt-sybex.com
Email: info@amt-sybex.com

Applied Networks
Building 22B, Central Park
Mallusk, BT36 4FS
Tel: 028 9083 0683
Fax: 028 9083 6776
Email: info@applied-networks.com

Armada Solutions
Unit 4 Cookstown Enterprise Centre
Derryloran Industrial Estate
Cookstown, BT80 9LU
Tel: 028 8676 9941
Web: www.armada-solutions.com
Email: info@armada-solutions.com

B.I.C. Systems Ltd
Enterprise House
201 Airport Road West
Belfast, BT3 9ED
Tel: 028 9053 2200
Fax: 028 9056 0056
Web: www.bicsystems.com
Email: info@bicsystems.com

Biznet Solutions
133-137 Lisburn Road
Belfast, BT9 7AG
Tel 028 9022 3224
Fax 028 9022 3223
Web: www.biznet-solutions.com
Email: belfast@biznet-solutions.com

BT13
Unit 11 Mallusk Enterprise Park
Newtownabbey, BT36 4GN
Tel: 028 9084 3313
Email: info@bt13.com

Consilium Technologies Ltd
Consilium House, Antrim Technology Pk
Belfast Road, Antrim, BT41 1QS
Tel 028 9448 0000
Fax 028 9448 0001
Web: www.ctechs.co.uk
Email: info@ctechs.co.uk

Fujitsu
110-112 Holywood Road
Belfast, BT4 1NU
Tel: 028 9047 4200
Web: www.services.fujitsu.com

Gibson Computing & Co
218 Lisburn Enterprise Centre
Enterprise Crescent, Lisburn, BT28 2BP
Tel: 028 9266 9936
Fax: 028 9266 9914
Web: www.gibson-computing.co.uk
Email: enquiries@gibson-computing.co.uk

Harbinson Mulholland
IBM House, 4 Bruce Street
Belfast, BT2 7JD
Tel: 028 9044 5100
Fax: 028 9044 5101

Hewlett Packard
Rushmere House, 46 Cadogan Park
Belfast, BT9 6HH
Tel 028 9038 1381
Web www.compaq.co.uk

Horizon Open Systems
The Sidings Office Park, Antrim Road
Lisburn, BT28 3AJ
Tel: 028 9262 9636
Fax: 028 9262 9584
Web: www.hos.horizon.ie
Email: info@hos.horizon.ie

ICC Computers & Support NI Ltd
236 Upper Newtownards Road
Belfast, BT4 3EU
Tel: 028 9065 5788
Fax: 028 9065 3646
Email: sales@iccsupport.co.uk

Ion Technologies
1a Bryson St, Belfast, BT5 4ES
Tel 028 9045 5911
Web: www.iontechnologies.com

Kainos
4-6 Upper Crescent, Belfast, BT7 1NT
Tel: 028 9057 1100
Fax: 028 9057 1101
Web: www.kainos.com
Email: info@kainos.com

Lagan Technologies
20 Wildflower Way, Belfast, BT12 6TA
Tel 028 9050 9300
Web: www.lagan.com
Email: info@lagan.com

Liberty Information Technology Ltd
Clarendon House, 9-21 Adelaide Street
Belfast, BT2 8DJ
Tel 028 9044 5500
Fax: 028 9044 5511
Web: www.liberty-it.co.uk

MCS Micro Computer Solutions Ltd
25 Carn Road
Craigavon, BT63 5WG
Tel: 028 3839 3839
Fax: 028 3839 3838
Web: www.mcsgroup.co.uk
Email: sales@mcsgroup.co.uk

Memsis
Rose House, 2A Derryvolgie Avenue
Belfast, BT9 6FL
Tel: 028 9080 6999
Fax: 028 9080 6060
Web: www.memsis.com

NISAT
19 CIDO Business Complex
Carn Industrial Estate
Craigavon, BT63 5RH
Tel: 028 3833 1070

Nitec Solutions
Oakmont House
2 Queen's Road
Lisburn, BT27 4TZ
Tel: 028 9262 5000
Fax: 028 9262 5030
Web: www.nitec.com
Email: solutions@nitec.com

Parity Solutions Ltd.
Unit 1, Beecom House, Technology Park
Antrim, BT41 1QS
Tel 028 9446 4901
Fax 028 9446 0702
Web: www.parity.co.uk

Primus Knowledge Solutions
Falcon Road, Belfast, BT12 6SJ
Tel: 028 9087 2000
Fax: 028 9087 2001
Web: www.primus.com

Real Time Systems Ltd
Agar House, 31 Ballynahinch Road
Carryduff, BT8 8EH
Tel: 028 9081 7171
Fax: 028 9081 7172
Web: www.rtsl.com

Sherwood Systems
Ash Grove, Wildflower Way
Boucher Road, Belfast, BT12 6TA
Tel: 028 9066 8585
Fax: 028 9066 5547
Web: www.sherwoodsys.com
Email: info@sherwoodsys.com

Singularity Ltd
100 Patrick Street
Derry, BT48 7EL
Tel 028 7126 7767
Fax 028 7126 8085
Web: www.singularity.co.uk
Email: info@singularity.co.uk

Siemens Business Services
Unit 8 Enterprise House
Boucher Crescent
Belfast, BT12 6HU
Tel: 028 9066 4331

Sx3
Hillview House, 61 Church Road
Newtownabbey, BT36 7SS
Tel: 028 9085 9085
Fax: 028 9085 9086

t.i. solutions
Thomas Andrews House, Queen's Road
Queen's Island, Belfast BT3 9DU
Tel: 028 9053 4570
Fax: 028 9053 4577
Web: www.tisolutions.biz
Email: info@tisolutions.biz

Xperience
11 Altona Road, Lisburn, BT27 5QB
Tel: 028 9267 7533
Fax: 028 9267 2887
Web: xperience-group.com
Email: info@xperience-group.com

## Recruitment Consultants

ABC Recruitment Ltd
40 Frances Street
Newtownards, BT23 7DN
Tel: 028 9182 3333

Adecco
2-4 Adelaide Street, Belfast, BT2 8GA
Tel: 028 9024 4660

Advance Recruitment Services
80 High Street, Belfast, BT1 2BG
Tel: 028 9027 8278

Apple Recruitment Services
8 Bedford Street, Belfast, BT2 7FB
Tel: 028 9024 9747

Bell Recruitment Services
Shaftesbury House, Shaftesbury Square
1 Donegall Road
Belfast, BT12 5JJ
Tel: 028 9031 1211

Blueprint Appointments
143-147 Great Victoria Street
Belfast, BT1 4PE
Tel: 028 9032 3333

Bond Financial Services
Enterprise House
55-59 Adelaide Street, Belfast, BT2 8FE
Tel: 028 9072 6008

BrightWater Selection (Belfast) Ltd
51-53 Adelaide Street, Belfast, BT2 8FE
Tel: 028 9032 5325

Career Prospects
Park House, 87-91 Great Victoria Street
Belfast, BT2 7AG
Tel: 028 9058 9880

Cornerstone Recruitment
Albany House
73-75 Great Victoria Street
Belfast, BT2 7AF
Tel: 028 9058 0101

Diamond Recruitment
16 Donegall Square South
Belfast, BT1 5JF
Tel: 028 9055 8000

Direct Contract Staff
28 St Julian's Way, Omagh, BT79 7UN
Tel: 028 8224 9248

First Choice Selection Services Ltd
Sinclair House, 89 Royal Avenue
Belfast, BT1 1EX
Tel: 028 9031 3693

Flexiskills Recruitment
Washington House, 3rd Floor
14-16 High Street
Belfast, BT1 2BD
Tel: 028 9032 4436

Forde May Consulting
Barmoral House
77 Upper Lisburn Road
Belfast, BT10 0GY
Tel: 028 9062 8877

Grafton Recruitment Ltd
35-37 Queen's Square
Belfast, BT1 3FG
Tel: 028 9024 2824

Hays Montrose
Spencer House, 71 Royal Avenue
Belfast, BT1 1FE
Tel: 028 9031 5184

Industrial Temps
Park House, 87-91 Great Victoria Street
Belfast, BT2 7AG
Tel: 028 9032 2511

Jobfinder
405 Lisburn Road, Belfast, BT9 7EW
Tel: 028 9066 3377

Kennedy Recruitment
31-35 May Street, Belfast, BT1 4NG
Tel: 028 9033 0555

Key Staff Recruitment
36 University Street
Belfast, BT7 1FZ
Tel: 028 9024 0340

Lagan Recruitment
3rd Floor, Merrion Business Centre
58 Howard Street
Belfast, BT1 6PJ
Tel: 028 9043 7801

Tim Lewis Recruitment
Clarence Chambers
19-20 Donegall Square East
Belfast BT1 5HD
Tel: 028 9043 5835

Lynn Recruitment
48-50 Bedford Street
Belfast, BT2 7FG
Tel: 028 9023 4324

Manpower
50-56 Wellington Place
Belfast, BT1 6GF
Tel: 028 9023 6860

Merc Partners
12B Clarendon Dock, Clarendon Road,
Belfast, BT1 3BG
Tel: 028 9072 5750

MRI Worldwide
1st Floor, Hawarden House
163 Upper Newtownards Road
Belfast, BT4 3HZ
Tel: 028 9065 5992

MSL Search & Selection
20 Rosemary Street, Belfast, BT1 1QD
Tel: 028 9023 4444

Mydas Recruitment
Enterprise House, Balloo Avenue
Bangor, BT19 7QT
Tel: 028 9145 0107

Next Step Recruitment (NI) Ltd
18 Bradbury Place, Belfast BT7 1PN
Tel: 028 9024 3443

Nijobs.com
3rd Floor
Scottish Mutual Building
16 Donegall Square South
Belfast, BT1 5JH
Tel: 028 9043 4477

Optima Recruitment Europe Ltd
134A Great Victoria Street
Belfast, BT2 7BG
Tel: 028 9031 2626

Parity
Blackstaff Chambers, Amelia Street
Belfast, BT2 7GS
Tel: 028 9024 0780

Pertemps Savage Recruitment
Stokes House
17-25 College Square East
Belfast, BT1 6DD
Tel: 028 9023 6999

Precision
28 Campsie Industrial Estate
McLean Road, Eglinton
Londonderry, BT47 3XX
Tel: 028 7186 0135

Premiere People
Hampden House, 55 Royal Avenue
Belfast, BT1 1FX
Tel: 028 9023 5777

Recruitment Direct
1st Floor, Fanum House
108 Great Victoria Street
Belfast, BT2 7BE
Tel: 028 9058 0888

Reed Accountancy
1 Donegall Square West
Belfast, BT1 6JA
Tel: 028 9033 0604

Reed Employment
10 Ann Street, Belfast, BT1 4EF
Tel: 028 9033 0812

Reed Hospitality
9-11 Castle Lane, Belfast, BT1 5DA
Tel: 028 9031 3453

Riada Recruitment
90 Union Street, Coleraine, BT52 1QB
Tel: 028 7032 6600

Rutledge Recruitment & Training
54 Scotch Street, Armagh, BT61 7DF
Tel: 028 3752 7932

Sales Placement Contract People (NI) Ltd
2 Crescent Gardens, Belfast, BT7 1NS
Tel: 028 9033 9901

Select Recruitment (NI)
20 Adelaide Street, Belfast, BT2 8GD
Tel: 028 9023 2328

Spengler Fox
3rd Floor, Quay Gate House
15 Scrabo Street, Belfast, BT5 4BD
Tel: 028 9055 6000

Target Recruitment
303A Antrim Road
Glengormley, BT36 7AT
Tel: 028 9084 8897

Task Recruitment
90 Stranmillis Road, Belfast, BT9 5AD
Tel: 028 9066 3300

Tech Trade Recruiting Ltd
13-15 Wilson's Court
Belfast, BT1 4DQ
Tel: 028 9087 7883

TSL IT
58 Greystone Road, Antrim, BT41 1JZ
Tel: 028 9446 7774

Vanrath Financial Selection
6th Floor Lesley Suite
2-12 Montgomery Street
Belfast, BT1 4NX
Tel: 0870 774 1000

www.recruitni.com
Bank House, 135 Albertbridge Road
Belfast, BT5 4PS
Tel: 028 9073 8000

## Training Organisations

**Abbey Training Services**
Lennie House, 314 Antrim Road
Newtownabbey, BT36 8EH
Tel: 028 9084 0527

**BIC Systems**
Enterprise House
Sydenham Business Park
201 Airport Road West
Belfast, BT3 9ED
Tel: 028 9053 2200

**CITB - Construction Industry Training Board**
17 Dundrod Road, Crumlin, BT29 4SR
Tel: 028 9082 5466

**Conexus**
16 Montgomery Road, Belfast, BT6 9JD
Tel: 028 9070 8208

**DDA Training Services Ltd**
21 William Street
Dungannon, BT70 1DX
Tel: 028 8772 6342

**Edge Innovative Learning International Ltd**
Unit 18, North City Business Centre
Duncairn Gardens, Belfast, BT15 2GG
Tel: 028 9042 6425

**Elite Training**
4th Floor, Lindsay House
10 Callender Street, Belfast, BT1 5BN
Tel: 028 9031 6840

**Graham Training**
40-44 Railway Street
Lisburn, BT28 1XP
Tel: 028 9266 5100

**HMC Communications**
18 Shanrod Road, Katesbridge
Banbridge, BT32 5PG
Tel: 028 4067 1246

**ITS (Industry Training Services)**
Dowlands Business Park
89 Dowland Road, Limavady, BT49 OJT
Tel: 028 7772 2211

**Kennedy Training**
31-35 May Street, Belfast, BT1 4NG
Tel: 028 9033 0555

**Rutledge Joblink**
Market Court, 57-59 New Row
Coleraine, BT52 1EJ
Tel: 028 7035 2434

**Sureskills**
Callender House
58-60 Upper Arthur Street
Belfast, BT1 4GP
Tel: 028 9093 5555

## Other Business Services Providers

### Serviced Office Accommodation Providers

**Elmwood House Business Centre**
46 Elmwood Avenue, Belfast, BT9 6AZ
Tel: 028 9066 4941

**The Mount Business and Conference Centre**
2 Woodstock Link, Belfast, BT6 8DD
Tel: 028 9073 0188

**Premier Business Centres**
20 Adelaide Street, Belfast, BT2 8GB
Tel: 028 9051 7000

**Regus**
33 Clarendon Dock
Laganside, Belfast, BT1 3BW
Tel: 0845 301 0300

**Valley Business Centre**
67 Church Road
Newtownabbey, BT36 7LS
Tel: 028 9055 1600

**Wellington Park Business Centre**
3 Wellington Park, Belfast, BT9 6DJ
Tel: 028 9092 3333

## Printers

W&G Baird Ltd
Greystone Press
Caulside Drive, Antrim, BT41 2RS
Tel: 028 9446 3911

Dargan Press Ltd
5 Round Tower Centre
Dargan Crescent, Belfast, BT3 9JP
Tel: 028 9077 4478

Edenderry Print Ltd
Units 6-8 Agnew Street Industrial Estate
Belfast, BT13 1GB
Tel: 028 9074 0192
Fax: 028 9074 6345
Email: edenderryprint@btconnect.com

GPS Colour Graphics Ltd
Alexander Road, Belfast, BT6 9HP
Tel: 028 9070 2020
Fax: 028 9079 8463
Email: sales@gpscolour.co.uk

Graham & Heslip Ltd
Beechhill Industrial Estate
96 Beechill Road, Belfast, BT8 7QN
Tel: 028 9049 4949

Graham & Sons Ltd
51 Gortin Road, Omagh, BT79 7HZ
Tel: 028 8224 9222
Fax: 028 8224 9886

Impro Printing
41 Dargan Road, Belfast, BT3 9JU
Tel: 028 9077 7795
Email: sales@impro.co.uk

Impression Print and Design
53 Enterprise Crescent
Ballinderry Road, Lisburn, BT28 2BP
Tel: 028 9260 4432
Fax: 028 9262 9018

Johnston Printing Ltd
Mill Road, Kilrea, BT51 5RJ
Tel: 028 2954 0312
Fax: 028 2954 1070
Web: www.johnston-printing.co.uk

Limavady Printing Co Ltd
26C Catherine Street
Limavady, BT49 9BD
Tel: 028 7776 2051
Fax: 028 7776 2132
Web: www.limprint.com

Media Solutions Ireland
34 Waterloo Road, Lisburn, BT27 3NN
Tel: 028 9266 9980
Fax: 028 9266 9981
Web: www.mediasolutionsireland.com
Email: info@mediasolutionsireland.com

Minprint Media Solutions Ireland Ltd
401 Castlereagh Road
Belfast, BT5 6QP
Tel: 028 9070 5205
Fax: 028 9079 9030
Web: www.minprint.co.uk
Email: sales@minprint.co.uk

Nicholson & Bass Ltd
3 Nicholson Drive, Mallusk,
Michelin Road, Newtownabbey
BT36 4FB
Tel: 028 9034 2433
Fax: 028 9034 2066

Northern Whig
107 Limestone Road
Belfast, BT15 3AH
Tel: 028 9035 2233
Fax: 028 9035 2181

Peninsula Print & Design
Unit 2
Lansdowne Road
Newtownards, BT23 4NT
Tel: 028 9181 4125
Fax: 028 9181 4864
Web: www.peninsulaprint.co.uk

Universities Press (Belfast) Ltd
6 Alanbrooke Road, Belfast, BT6 9HF
Tel: 028 9070 4464
Fax: 028 9079 3295

## Signage

4 Corners
Unit 254 Lisburn Enterprise Centre
Ballinderry Road, Lisburn, BT28 2BP
Tel: 028 9266 4345
Web: www.4corners.org.uk
Email; info@4corners.org.uk

Alexander Boyd Displays
Lambeg Mills, Lambeg
Lisburn, BT27 5SX
Tel: 028 9030 1115

Autosign Graphix
Unit 73 Derriaghy Industrial Park
Dunmurry, Belfast, BT17 9HU
Tel: 028 9061 0282
Web: www.autosign.co.uk

Connswater Graphics
Unit 1 Dargan Court, Dargan Crescent
Belfast, BT3 9JP
Tel: 028 9077 7395
Fax: 028 9077 7065

Delta Sign Systems
Units 3-4A Carn Business Park
Carn Road, Portadown, BT63 5WG
Tel: 028 3835 0698
Fax: 028 3833 4487
Web: www.deltasignsystems.co.uk

DMB Graphics
55 Holly Hill, Dollingstown
Craigavon, BT66 7UB
Tel: 028 3834 9993

Exclaim
2 Ballyoran Lane, Dundonald, BT16 1XJ
Tel: 028 9041 0006
Fax: 028 9041 0044
Web: www.exclaim.co.uk

Gemini Graphics Ltd
21 Derryloran Industrial Estate
Cookstown, BT80 9LU
Tel: 028 8676 1292
Fax: 028 8676 5566
Web: www.thegeminigroup.co.uk

Gilmore Signs
41-45 Middlepath Street
Belfast, BT5 4BG
Tel: 028 9045 5419
Fax: 028 9045 8451

Impact Signs
East Belfast Enterprise Park
Unit 23, Belfast, BT5 4GX
Tel: 028 9073 9402
Fax: 028 9073 8040

PJ Display
6 Greenway Industrial Estate, Conlig
Newtownards, BT23 7SU
Tel: 028 9127 5616
Fax: 028 9127 5612

Riada Signs
Unit 4D
Ballybrakes Business Park
Ballymoney, BT53 6LW
Tel: 028 2766 2845
Fax: 028 2766 2228
Web: www.riadasigns.biz

Sign D Sign
172A Tate's Avenue, Belfast, BT12 6ND
Tel: 028 9023 6006
Fax: 028 9023 6856
Web: www.signdsign.biz

### Fulfilment & Direct Mail

AMA Communication Centre
Newtownards Road, Bangor, BT19 7TA
Tel: 028 9147 2525
Fax: 028 9147 2797
Web: www.andersonmanning.com
Email: info@andersonmanning.com

Community Telegraph
124 Royal Avenue, Belfast, BT1 1EB
Tel: 028 9026 4620
Fax: 028 9055 4582
Web: www.belfasttelegraph.co.uk

Mailroom Ltd
4 Fern Business Park, Blackstaff Road
Belfast, BT11 9DT
Tel: 028 9080 6600
Fax: 028 9080 6699
Email: info@mailroomltd.com

TDS Group
11 Kilbride Road, Doagh
Ballyclare, BT39 0QA
Tel: 028 9332 4405
Fax: 028 9334 1150
Web: www.thetdsgroup.com

Tricord Direct Mail
Trinity House, Lisburn, BT28 2YY
Tel: 028 9260 6966
Fax: 028 9260 6965
Web: www.tricord.co.uk
Email: info@tricord.co.uk

### Payroll Services

CJS Payroll Ltd
240-242 Upper Newtownards Road
Belfast, BT4 3EU
Tel: 028 9047 1754
Fax: 028 9047 1756
Email: cjs@cjspayroll.com
Web: www.cjspayroll.com

### Office Equipment & Supplies

Adelaide Office Supplies
31 Upper Dunmurry Lane
Belfast, BT17 0AA
Tel: 028 9061 8841

Banner Business Supplies Ltd.
2nd Floor, 12 Cromac place
Belfast, BT7 2JB
Tel: 0845 712 5926
Fax: 0845 712 5927

Craigavon Office Supplies
1 Moore's Lane, Lurgan, BT66 8DW
Tel: 028 3832 7231

Desk Warehouse
288 Beersbridge Road
Belfast, BT5 5DX
Tel: 028 9046 0055
Fax: 028 9058 0900
Web: www.deskwarehouse.co.uk

ED-CO
Hydepark House, 54 Mallusk Road
Newtownabbey, BT36 4WU
Tel: 028 9084 4023
Fax: 028 9084 0705
Web: www.edco.co.uk

Hodge Office Supplies Ltd
4 North Howard Street
Belfast, BT13 2AS
Tel: 028 9024 1812
Fax: 028 9024 6866

### Facilities Management

BCC
5 College Court
Belfast, BT1 6BS
Tel: 028 9024 9240
Fax: 028 9023 2834
Web: www.belfastcontractcleaners.co.uk

Maybin Support Services
4 Duncrue Crescent
Belfast, BT3 9BW
Tel: 028 9077 4799
Web: www.maybin.com

Mount Charles Catering Ltd.
Ascot House
24-31 Shaftesbury Square
Belfast, BT2 7DB
Tel: 028 9032 0070
Fax: 028 9024 5391
Web: www.mountcharles.com

Robinson Cleaning
Unit 5-7 Antrim Enterprise Agency
58 Greystone Road, Antrim, BT41 1JZ
Tel: 028 9442 9717
Fax: 028 9446 3336
Web: www.robinson-cleaning.co.uk

Serco Integrated Services
Mallusk Enterprise Park
Mallusk Drive
Newtownabbey, BT36 4GN
Tel: 028 9084 1851
Fax: 028 9083 9251
Web: www.serco-is.com

Printing Presses at the Andersonstown News Group

# Chapter 9

## The Media and Communications

## The Media in Northern Ireland

Northern Ireland is a veritable hotbed of media and communications activity. Over the period of the last 30 years of political instability the province has attracted highly disproportionate international media attention, which has created a degree of media and communications sophistication normally associated with much larger places.

Northern Ireland has a comparatively high level of newspaper readership despite having a relatively small market. Surveys have shown that almost three quarters of the adult population read at least one paid-for newspaper daily – nearly 900,000 readers a day. There are only four home-produced daily papers in Northern Ireland – one evening, two morning and one Sunday. Of these regional titles only the nationalist Irish News is genuinely local in ownership, being controlled by a local family business. Its unionist counterpart the News Letter was owned by the Trinity Mirror Group since 1996 although along with 6 other regional titles, including the Derry Journal, it has recently been sold to venture capital group 3i in a £46.3 million deal. The main evening newspaper, the Belfast Telegraph, which was formerly owned by the Canadian-based Thomson Regional Newspapers, was sold to the English-based Trinity Holdings in 1995 before being acquired by Tony O'Reilly's Dublin-based Independent Newspaper Group. The Belfast Telegraph has a monopoly on the popular evening paper market and this is reflected in that it is in its own right one of Northern Ireland's most profitable businesses.

In addition to the four local newspapers there are Northern Ireland and Irish editions of many of the British papers. British newspapers, broadsheet and tabloid, are widely read in Northern Ireland. There is also some readership of the leading Southern Irish papers who have been making efforts to increase circulation in Northern Ireland in recent years. Local newspapers are very popular in Northern Ireland with most publishing weekly. A list of the main local newspapers is included later in this chapter, beginning on page 451.

Just fewer than 23m people in the UK hold a television licence. Television is a dynamic industry, which continues to develop at a rapid rate. In addition to the five terrestrial channels, BBC1, BBC2, ITV, Channel 4 (S4C in Wales) and Channel 5, there are now hundreds more available on satellite, cable and digital – and a thriving independent production sector. The BBC is the UK's main public service broadcaster, run by a board of governors and funded by the licence fee. In addition to its two terrestrial channels, the corporation runs several digital services including BBC Knowledge and BBC Choice (both soon to be relaunched) and a news channel, BBC News 24.

ITV was made up originally of 15 regionally based television companies and GMTV, the national breakfast-time service, licensed by the ITC and funded through advertising. However there has been a significant ongoing merger and takeover activity greatly consolidating the independent sector. The ITV Network Centre commissions and schedules programmes and, as with the BBC, 25% of programmes must come from independent producers. There are over 1,500 independent production companies in the UK which generate over £1bn of programming.

Channel 4 and S4C (the fourth channel in Wales) were set up to provide programmes with a distinctive character and which appeal to interests not catered for by ITV and are also funded through advertising. S4C also has to provide a certain amount of Welsh language programming. Channel 4 has two digital services, FilmFour and E4, a youth entertainment channel.

Channel 5 began broadcasting in 1997 and now reaches about 80% of the population. It is advertising-funded and its remit is to show programmes of quality and diversity.

Satellite and cable services are funded mainly through subscriptions. The UK's largest supplier is BSkyB, with over 5m subscribers.

Digital television is expanding rapidly. It has been taken up by about a third of the population and offers the potential to access over 200 channels and other services including interactive TV and the Internet. The government expects all television transmissions to be digital sometime between 2006 and 2010. There are also several teletext services available through both the BBC and commercial TV which carry news, sport, travel, weather and other information and also offer subtitling.

BBC has a regional organisation in Northern Ireland, BBC NI, and in addition to showing network programmes has an autonomous news and current affairs department. The regional independent television company UTV, formerly known as Ulster Television, is the most popular of the two television stations and attracts around 43 per cent of the Northern Ireland television audience against 30 per cent for BBC. The BBC has also a local radio station (Radio Ulster) with bases in both Belfast and the north west (BBC Radio Foyle). Independent radio has also a strong foothold in the local radio market.

An increasing proportion of Northern Ireland households now receive the Southern Irish national broadcaster RTE and there is an estimated subscriber base of 80,000 cable multi-channel services subscribers and a fast rising subscriber base for satellite services.

Northern Ireland is well served by a growing community of communications professionals beyond those operating in the local media. Some of the world's largest communications organisations have Belfast offices in the fields of advertising, public relations and other communications services. A list of PR and advertising agencies is included later in this chapter beginning on page 366.

## Television and Radio

### BBC Northern Ireland

Broadcasting House, Ormeau Avenue
Belfast, BT2 8HQ
Tel: 028 9033 8000
Fax: 028 9033 8800
News: 028 9033 8806

Press Office
Tel: 028 9033 8226/906
Fax: 028 9033 8279
Web: www.bbc.co.uk

Governor for Northern Ireland:
Professor Fabian Monds

Senior Management Board BBC NI:
Controller: Anna Carragher
Head of Broadcast: Peter Johnson
Head of Public Affairs: Mark Adair
Head of Finance: Crawford MacLean
Head of News & Current Affairs:
Andrew Colman
Head of Marketing, Communications and Audiences : Kathy Bruce
Head of Resources: Stephen Beckett
Head of Programming and Production:
Mike Edgar
Head of Factual & Learning:
Kieran Hegarty
Head of Drama: Patrick Spence
Editor, Foyle: Ana Leddy

Editors BBC NI:
Editor Sport: Edward Smith
Editor Music: Declan McGovern
Editor Specialist Factual: (Acting)
Paul McGuigan
Editor Entertainment: Alex Johnston
Editor Broadcasting: Fergus Keeling
Editor Learning Unit: Jane Cassidy
Editor New Media: David Sims
Editor Newsgathering: Michael Cairns
Editor Radio: Noel Russel

News Correspondents:
Political Editor: Mark Davenport
Business Editor: James Kerr
Health Correspondent: Dot Kirby
Chief Security Editor:
Brian Rowan
Education & Arts Correspondent:
Maggie Taggart
Ireland Correspondents: Denis Murray
Ireland Producer: Kevin Kelly
Sport Producer: Padraig Coyle

Manager, Press Office: Una Carlin
Tel: 028 9033 8014
Fax: 028 9033 8279
Press Officer: Caroline Cooper
Press Officer: Kevin McAuley
Press Officer: Jeff Magill

### BBC Radio Foyle

(MW 792, FM 93.1)
8 Northland Road
Londonderry, BT48 7GD
Tel: 028 7137 8600
Fax: 028 7137 8666
Web: www.bbc.co.uk/northernireland
Managing Director: Ana Leddy
Head of News: Eimer O'Callaghan

### BBC Radio Ulster

(92.4/95FM)
Broadcasting House
Ormeau Avenue
Belfast, BT2 8HQ
Tel: 028 9033 8000
Fax: 028 9033 8804 (General)
Fax: 028 9033 8806 (News)
Web: www.bbc.co.uk
Head of News and Current Affairs:
Andrew Colman

### Belfast Citybeat

(FM 96.7)
Lamont Buildings, Stranmillis Road
Belfast, BT9 5DF
Tel: 028 9020 5967
Fax: 028 9020 0023
Web: www.citybeat.co.uk

### Cool FM

(Greater Belfast FM 97.4)
Kiltonga Industrial Estate, Belfast Road
Newtownards, BT23 4ES
Tel: 028 9181 7181
Fax: 028 9181 4974
Web: www.coolfm.co.uk
Managing Director: David Sloan

### Downtown Radio

Kiltonga Industrial Estate, Belfast Road
Newtownards, BT23 4ES
Tel: 028 9181 5555
Fax: 028 9181 8913 (General)
Fax: 028 9181 7878 (News)
Web: www.downtown.co.uk
Chairman: James Donnelly
Managing Director: David Sloan
News/Sports Editor: Harry Castles
Political Correspondent: Eamonn Mailie

All Northern Ireland AM 102.6, Derry FM 102.4, Limavady FM, Enniskillen & Omagh FM 96.6

### GMTV Northern Ireland

Macmillan Media bcb
Broadcast Centre
Venture Gate Building
32-36 Dublin Road
Belfast, BT2 7HN
Tel: 08703 502150
Web: www.mcmillanmedia.co.uk
Email: gmtv@mcmillanmedia.co.uk

### Q97.2FM Causeway Coast Radio

24 Cloyfin Road
Coleraine, Co Derry, BT52 2NU
Tel: 028 7035 9100
Fax: 028 7032 6666
Web: www.q972.fm
Managing Director: Frank McLaughlin
Station Manager: Damien Devenny
News Editors: Bob McCracken

### Q102.9 FM

The Riverside Suite
Old Waterside Railway Station
87 Rossdowney Street
Waterside
Derry, BT47 5FU
Tel: 028 7134 6666
Fax: 028 7131 1177
Managing Director: Frank McLaughlin
Station Manager: David Austin
News Editor: Roger Donnelly

### Ulster Television plc

Havelock House
Ormeau Road
Belfast, BT7 1EB
Tel: 028 9032 8122
Fax: 028 9024 6695

Newsroom:
Tel: 028 9026 2000
Fax: 028 9023 8381

Press Office:
Tel: 028 9026 2187
Fax: 028 9026 2219
Web: www.utvlive.com
Chairman: John B McGuckian
Group Chief Executive: John McCann
Head of News & Current Affairs:
Rob Morrison
Director of Television Programming:
Alan Bremner
News Editor: Chris Hagan
Political Correspondent: Ken Reid
Sports Editor: Adrian Logan
Producer of 'Kelly': Patricia Moore
Editor of 'Insight': Trevor Birney
Group Director of Engineering:
Bob McCourt
Head of Press & Public Relations:
Orla McKibbin

# Northern Ireland Newspapers

## Local Daily/Sunday Newspapers

### Belfast Telegraph

124–144 Royal Avenue
Belfast, BT1 1EB
Tel: 028 9026 4000
Fax: 028 9055 4506
Email: editor@belfasttelegraph.co.uk
Web: www.belfasttelegraph.co.uk
Managing Director: Derek Carvell

Editor: Ed Curran
Tel: 028 9026 4400
Deputy Editor: Jim Flanagan

News Editor: Paul Connolly
Tel: 028 9026 4420
Fax: 028 9055 4540
Email: newseditor@belfasttelegraph.co.uk
Deputy News Editor: Ronan Henry
Features Editor: Gail Walker
Political Correspondents: Noel McAdam,
Chris Thornton
Business Editor: Nigel Tilson
Business Correspondents:
Robin Morton, Paul Dykes
Agriculture Editor: Michael Drake
Education Correspondent:
Kathryn Torney
Health Correspondent: Nigel Gould
Sports Editor: John Laverty
Assistant Editors (Sports):
Graham Hamilton, John Taylor
Pictures Editor: Gerry FitzGerald
Commercial Director: John Leslie
Tel: 028 9026 4162
Fax: 028 9033 1332

Advertising Director: Simon Mann
Tel: 028 9026 4462
Fax: 028 9033 1332

Marketing Director: Richard McLean
Tel: 028 9026 4138
Fax: 028 9055 4523

Marketing Manager: Ramsey Fawell
Circulation & Resources: Roy Lyttle
Tel: 028 9026 4022

### Irish News

113-117 Donegall Street
Belfast, BT1 2GE
Tel: 028 9032 2226
Fax: 028 9033 7505 (News)
Fax: 028 9033 7508 (Advertising)
Email: newsdesk@irishnews.com
Web: www.irishnews.com

Chairman: James Fitzpatrick
Managing Director: Dominic Fitzpatrick
Editor: Noel Doran
Deputy Editor: Stephen O'Reilly
News Editor: Steven McCaffrey
Tel: 028 9033 7544
Features: Joanna Braniff
Assistant Editor: Fiona McGarry
Business Editor: Gary McDonald
Pictures Editor: Ann McManus
Political Correspondent: William Graham
Health Correspondent: Anne Madden
Travel Editor: James Stinson
Sports Editor: Thomas Hawkins
Derry Correspondent: Seamus McKinney
Tel: 028 7137 4455
Newry Correspondent:
Catherine Morrison
Tel: 028 3025 7788
Fax: 028 3025 1017
Marketing Manager: John Brolly
Tel: 028 9032 2226
Advertising Manager: Paddy Meehan
Tel: 028 9033 7516
Fax: 028 9033 7508
Deputy Advertising Manager:
Sean Higgins
Tel: 028 9033 7509
Fax: 028 9033 7508

### News Letter

46-56 Boucher Crescent
Belfast, BT12 6QY
Tel: 028 9068 0000
Fax: 028 9066 4412
Email: newsletter@mgn.co.uk
Web: www.news-letter.co.uk

Editor: Austin Hunter
Assistant Editor: Helen Greenaway
News Editors: Karen Quinn,
Jackie McKeown
Tel: 028 9068 0005
Political Correspondent:
Stephen Dempster
Business Correspondent:
Adrienne McGill
Farming Life: David McCoy
Travel & Tourism: Geoff Hill
Women's Editor: Sandra Chapman
Religious Correspondent: Billy Kennedy
Entertainment: Liz Kennedy
Sports Editor: Brian Millar
Pictures Editor: Brian Little

Advertising Manager: Shiona Rafferty
Tel: 028 9068 0000
Sales & Marketing Manager:
William Berkeley
Tel: 028 9068 0000

### Sunday Life

124-144 Royal Avenue
Belfast, BT1 1EB
Tel: 028 9026 4300
Email: betty.arnold@belfasttelegraph.co.uk
Web: www.sundaylife.co.uk

Editor: Martin Lindsay
Tel: 028 9026 4309
Deputy Editor and News Editor:
Martin Hill
Tel: 028 9026 4305
Women's Editor:
Tel: 028 9026 4315
Pictures Editor: Darren Kidd
Tel: 028 9026 4317
Sports Editor: Jim Gracey
Tel: 028 9026 4308

## Local Weekly Newspapers

### Andersonstown News
2 Hannahstown Hill
Belfast, BT17 0LT
Tel: 028 9061 9000
Fax: 028 9062 0602
Email: editorial@irelandclick.com
Web: www.irelandclick.com
Editor: Robin Livingstone

### Antrim Guardian
5 Railway Street
Antrim, BT41 4AE
Tel: 028 9446 2624
Fax: 028 9446 5551
Email: antrimguardian@macunlimited.net
Editor: Liam Heffron

### Antrim Times
22-24 Ballymoney Street
Ballymena, BT43 6AL
Tel: 028 2565 3300
Fax: 028 2564 1517
Web: www.mortonnewspapers.com
Editor: Dessie Blackadder

### Armagh Observer/Armagh – Down Observer (Part of Observer Group)
Ann Street
Dungannon, BT70 1ET
Tel: 028 8772 2557
Fax: 028 8772 7334
Email:
editor@observernewspapersni.com
Editor: Desmond Mallon

### Ballyclare Gazette
36 The Square
Ballyclare, BT39 9BB
Tel: 028 9335 2967
Fax: 028 9335 2449
Web: www.ulsternet-ni.co.uk
Editor: Raymond Hughes

### Ballymena Chronicle & Antrim Observer
(Part of the Observer Group)
Ann Street
Dungannon, BT70 1ET
Tel: 028 8772 2557
Fax: 028 8772 7334
Email: editor@observernewspapersni.com
Editor: Desmond Mallon

### Ballymena Guardian
83-85 Wellington Street
Ballymena, BT43 6AD
Tel: 028 2564 1221
Fax: 028 2565 3920
Editor: Maurice O'Neill

### Ballymena Times (Part of the Morton Group)
22-24 Ballymoney Street
Ballymena, BT43 6AL
Tel: 028 2565 3300
Fax: 028 2564 1517
Web: www.mortonnewspapers.com
Editor: Dessie Blackadder

### Ballymoney Times
(Part of the Morton Group)
6 Church Street
Ballymoney, BT53 6DL
Tel: 028 2766 6216
Fax: 028 2766 7066
Web: www.mortonnewspapers.com
Editor: Lyle McMullen

### Banbridge Chronicle
14 Bridge Street
Banbridge, BT32 3JS
Tel: 028 4066 2322
Fax: 028 4062 4397
Editor: Bryan Hooks

### The Banbridge Leader
(Part of the Morton Group)
25 Bridge Street
Banbridge, BT32 3JL
Tel: 028 4066 2745
Fax: 028 4062 6378
Web: www.mortonnewspapers.com
Editor: Damien Wilson

### Bangor Spectator Group
Spectator Buildings
109 Main Street
Bangor, BT20 4AF
Tel: 028 9127 0270
Fax: 028 9127 1544
Editor: Paul Flowers

### Belfast News
46-56 Boucher Crescent
Belfast, BT12 6QY
Tel: 028 9068 0000
Fax: 028 9066 4412
Email: newsletter@mgn.co.uk
Editor: Julie McClay

### Carrick Times (Part of the Morton Group)
19 North Street
Carrickfergus, BT38 7AQ
Tel: 028 9335 1992
Fax: 028 9336 9825
Email: edct@mortonnewspapers.com
Editor: Terence Ferry

### Carrickfergus Advertiser
31a High Street
Carrickfergus, BT38 7AN
Tel: 028 9336 3651
Fax: 028 9336 3092
Web: www.ulsternet-ni.co.uk
Editor: Raymond Hughes

### Coleraine Chronicle
20 Railway Road
Coleraine, BT52 1PD
Tel: 028 7034 3344
Fax: 028 7034 3606
Editor: John Fillis

### Coleraine Times (Part of the Morton Group)
71 New Row, Market Court
Coleraine, BT52 1EJ
Tel: 028 7035 5260
Fax: 028 7035 6186
Web: www.mortonnewspapers.com
Editor: David Rankin

### Community Telegraph
124-144 Royal Avenue
Belfast, BT1 1EB
Tel: 028 9026 4396
Fax: 028 9055 4585
Editor: Victoria Sloss

### County Down Spectator
109 Main Street
Bangor, BT20 4AF
Tel: 028 9127 0270
Fax: 028 9027 1544
Email: editor@spectatornews.co.uk
Editor: Paul Flowers

### Craigavon Echo
(Part of Morton Group, distributed free)
14 Church Street
Portadown, BT62 3LQ
Tel: 028 3839 5400
Fax: 028 3835 0203
Editor: David Armstrong

### The Democrat
(Part of the Observer Group Newspapers)
Ann Street
Dungannon, BT70 1ET
Tel: 028 8772 2557
Fax: 028 8772 7334
Editor: Desmond Mallon

### Derry Journal (Part of Trinity Mirror Group)
22 Buncrana Road
Derry, BT48 8AA
Tel: 028 7127 2200
Fax: 028 7127 2260
Web: www.derryjournal.com
Email: editorial@derryjournal.com
Editor-in-Chief: Patrick McArt

### Derry News
26 Balliniska Road
Springtown Industrial Estate
Derry, BT48 0LY
Tel: 028 7129 6600
Fax: 028 7129 6611
Email: editorial@derrynews.net
Editor: Joanne McCool

### Down Democrat
74 Market Street
Downpatrick, BT30 6LZ
Tel: 028 4461 6600
Fax: 028 4461 6221
Email: reception@downdemocrat.com
Web: www.downdemocrat.com
Editor: Terry McLaughlin

### Down Recorder
2-4 Church Street
Downpatrick, BT30 6EJ
Tel: 028 4461 3711
Fax: 028 4461 4624
Email: downrecorder@ni.com
Web: www.thedownrecorder.com
Editor: Paul Symington

### The Dromore Leader
(Part of the Morton Group)
30a Market Square
Dromore, BT25 1AW
Tel: 028 9269 2217
Fax: 028 9269 9260
Email: eddl@mortonnewspapers.com
Editor: Damien Wilson

### Dungannon News and Tyrone Courier
58 Scotch Street
Dungannon, BT70 1BD
Tel: 028 8772 2271
Fax: 028 8772 6171
Web: www.ulsternet-ni.co.uk
Editor: Ian Greer

### Dungannon Observer (Part of the Observer Group)
Ann Street
Dungannon, BT70 1ET
Tel: 028 8772 2557
Fax: 028 8772 7334
Editor: Desmond Mallon

### East Antrim Advertiser
(Part of Morton Group, free monthly)
8 Dunluce Street
Larne, BT40 1JG
Tel: 028 2826 0605
Fax: 028 2826 0255
Editor: Hugh Vance

### East Antrim Gazette
20 Main Street
Larne, BT40 1SS
Tel: 028 2827 7450
Fax: 028 2826 7333
Editor: Raymond Hughes

### East Antrim Guardian
5 Railway Street
Antrim, BT41 4AE
Tel: 028 9446 2624
Fax: 028 9446 5551
Editor: Liam Heffron

### East Antrim Times (Part of Morton Group)
8 Dunluce Street
Larne, BT40 1JG
Tel: 028 2827 2303
Fax: 028 2826 0255
Email: edit@mortonnewspapers.com
Web: www.mortonnewspapers.com
Editor: Hugh Vance

### The Examiner
Rathkeeland House
1 Blaney Road
Crossmaglen, BT35 2JJ
Tel: 028 3086 8500
Fax: 028 3086 8580
Email: examiner@btconnect.com
Editor: Gerry Murray

### Fermanagh Herald
30 Belmore Street
Enniskillen, BT74 6AA
Tel: 028 6632 2066
Fax: 028 6632 5521
Web: www.fermanaghherald.com
Editor: Pauline Leary

### Fermanagh News (Part of the Observer Group)
Ann Street
Dungannon BT70 1ET
Tel: 028 8772 2557
Fax: 028 8772 7334
Email: editor@observernewspapersni.com
Editor: Desmond Mallon

### Impartial Reporter
8-10 East Bridge Street
Enniskillen, BT74 7BT
Tel: 028 6632 4422
Fax: 028 6632 5047
Email: mcdaniel@impartialreporter.com
Web: www.impartialreporter.com
Editor: Denzil McDaniel

### Journal Extra (Part of Derry Journal, distributed free)
22 Buncrana Road
Derry, BT28 8AA
Tel: 028 7127 2200
Fax: 028 7127 2270
Editor: Patrick McArt

### LÁ
Teach Basit
2 Cnoc Bhaile Haine
Béal Feirste, BT17 0LT
Tel: 028 9060 5050
Fax: 028 9060 5544
Editor: Ciaran Pronntaigh

### The Lakeland Extra
8-10 East Bridge Street
Enniskillen, BT74 7BT
Tel: 028 6632 4422
Fax: 028 6632 5047
Web: www.impartialreporter.com
Editor: Denzil McDaniel

### Larne Gazette
20 Main Street
Larne, BT40 1SS
Tel: 028 2827 7450
Fax: 028 2826 0733
Editor: Raymond Hughes

### Larne Times (Part of Morton Group)
8 Dunluce Street
Larne, BT40 1JG
Tel: 028 2827 2303
Fax: 028 2826 0255
Web: www.mortonnewspapers.com
Editor: Hugh Vance

### The Leader
20 Railway Road
Coleraine, BT52 1PD
Tel: 028 7034 3344
Fax: 028 7034 3606
Editor: Linda Kelly

### Lisburn Echo (Part of Morton Group, distributed free)
12a Bow Street Lisburn, BT28 1BN
Tel: 028 9260 1114
Fax: 028 9260 2904
Web: www.mortonnewspapers.com
Editor: David Fletcher

### Londonderry Sentinel (Part of Morton Group)
Suite 3, Spencer House
Spencer Road, Derry, BT47 6AA
Tel: 028 7134 8889
Fax: 028 7134 1175
Email: edls@mortonnewspapers.com
Web: www.mortonnewspapers.com
Editor: William McClelland

## Lurgan & Portadown Examiner
(Part of Observer Group)
Ann Street
Dungannon, BT70 1ET
Tel: 028 8772 2557
Fax: 028 8772 7334
Editor: Desmond Mallon

## Lurgan Mail (Part of Morton Group)
4a High Street
Lurgan, BT66 8AW
Tel: 028 3832 7777
Fax: 028 3832 5271
Email: edlm@mortonnewspapers.com
Web: www.mortonnewspapers.com
Editor: Richard Elliott

## Mid-Ulster Echo (Part of Morton Group)
52 Oldtown Street
Cookstown, BT80 8EF
Tel: 028 8676 1364
Fax: 028 8676 4295
Web: www.mortonnewspapers.com
Editor: Mark Bain

## Mid-Ulster Mail (Part of Morton Group)
52 Oldtown Street
Cookstown, BT80 8EF
Tel: 028 8676 2288
Fax: 028 8676 4295
Email: edmm@mortonnewspapers.com
Web: www.mortonnewspapers.com
Editor: Mark Bain

## Mid-Ulster Observer (Part of Observer Group)
Ann Street, Dungannon, BT70 1ET
Tel: 028 8772 2557
Fax: 028 8772 7334
Editor: Desmond Mallon

## Morton Newspapers Limited
2 Esky Drive
Carn Industrial Estate Area
Portadown, BT63 5YY
Tel: 028 3839 3939
Fax: 028 3839 3940
Web: www.mortonnewspaper.com
Group Editor: David Armstrong

Morton is Northern Ireland's largest local newspapers group. Its main titles include: Antrim/Ballymena Times, Ballymoney/Coleraine Times, Carrickfergus/Larne/Newtownabbey Times, Roe Valley/Londonderry Sentinel, Lurgan Mail, Portadown Times, Castlereagh/Dromore/Ulster Star, Banbridge Leader, Tyrone Times, Magherafelt/ Cookstown Mid-Ulster Mail & Echo, Craigavon Echo, Lisburn Echo, North-West-free

## Mourne Observer & County Down News
Castlewellan Road
Newcastle, BT33 0JX
Tel: 028 4372 2666
Fax: 028 4372 4566
Email: mobserver@btinternet.com
Editor: Terence Bowman

## Newry Democrat
45 Hill Street
Newry, BT34 1UF
Tel: 028 3025 1250
Fax: 028 3025 1017
Email: info@newrydemocrat.com
Web: www.newrydemocrat.com
Editor: Caroline McEvoy

## The Newry Reporter
4 Margaret Street
Newry, BT34 1DF
Tel: 028 3026 7633
Fax: 028 3026 3157
Editor: Austin Smyth

## Newtownabbey Times (Part of the Morton Group)
14 Portland Avenue
Glengormley, BT36 8EY
Tel: 028 9084 3621
Fax: 028 9083 7715
Editor: Judith Watson

## Newtownards Chronicle & Co Down Observer
25 Frances Street
Newtownards, BT23 7DT
Tel: 028 9181 3333
Fax: 028 9182 0087
Email: news@ardschronicle
Editor: John Savage

## Newtownards Spectator
109 Main Street
Bangor, BT20 4AF
Tel: 028 9127 0270
Fax: 028 9127 1544
Email: editor@spectornews.co.uk
Editor: Paul Flowers

## North Belfast News
253-255 Antrim Road
Belfast, BT15 2GY
Tel: 028 9058 4444
Fax: 028 9058 4450
Web: www.irelandclick.com
Editor: John Ferris

## North West Echo
(Part of the Morton Group, distribution free)
Suite 3, Spencer House
Spencer Road
Derry, BT47 1AA
Tel: 028 7134 2226
Fax: 028 7134 1175
Web: www.mortonnewspapers.com
Editor: William McClelland

## Northern Constitution
20 Railway Road
Coleraine, BT52 1PD
Tel: 028 7034 3344
Fax: 028 7034 3606
Editor: John Fillis

## Northern Newspaper Group
20 Railway Street
Coleraine, BT52 1PD
Tel: 028 7034 3344
Fax: 028 7034 3606
Group Editor: Morris O'Neil

The group's main titles include: Coleraine Chronicle, Ballymena Guardian, Antrim Guardian, Newtownabbey Guardian, The Leader, Northern Constitution

## Observer Group
Ann Street
Dungannon, BT70 1ET
Tel: 028 8772 2557
Fax: 028 8772 7334
Group Editor: Desmond Mallon

The group's main titles include: Armagh/Down Observer, Dungannon Observer, Fermanagh News, Lurgan and Portadown Examiner, Mid-Ulster Mail.

## The Outlook
Castle Street
Rathfriland
Newry, BT34 5QR
Tel: 028 4063 0781
Fax: 028 4063 1022
Editor: Ruth Rodgers

## Portadown Times (Part of the Morton Group)
14A Church Street
Portadown, BT62 3LQ
Tel: 028 3833 6111
Fax: 028 3835 0203
Email: edpt@mortonnewspapers.com
Editor: David Armstrong

### Roe Valley Sentinel (Part of the Morton Group)
32A Market Street, Limavady, BT49 0AA
Tel: 028 7776 4090
Fax: 028 7772 2234
Web: www.mortonnewspapers.com
Editor: William McClelland

### Strabane Chronicle
15 Upper Main Street
Strabane, BT82 8AS
Tel: 028 7188 2100
Fax: 028 7188 3199
Web: www.strabanechronicle.com
Editor: Darach McDonald

### Strabane Weekly News
25-27 High Street, Omagh, BT78 1BA
Tel: 028 8224 2721
Fax: 028 8224 3549
Editor: Wesley Atchison

### Tyrone Constitution
25-27 High Street, Omagh, BT78 1BA
Tel: 028 8224 2721
Fax: 028 8224 3549
Editor: Wesley Atchison

### Tyrone Times (Part of the Morton Group)
Unit B, Butter Market Centre
Thomas Street, Dungannon, BT70 1HN
Tel: 028 8775 2801
Fax: 028 8775 2819
Editor: Clint Aiken

### Ulster Farmer (Part of the Observer Group)
Ann Street, Dungannon, BT70 1ET
Tel: 028 8772 3153
Fax: 028 8772 7334
Editor: Desmond Mallon

### Ulster Gazette and Armagh Standard
56 Scotch Street, Armagh, BT61 7DQ
Tel: 028 3752 2639
Fax: 028 3752 7029
Editor: Richard Stewart

### Ulster Herald Group
10 John Street, Omagh, BT78 1DN
Tel: 028 8224 3444
Fax: 028 8224 2206
Web: www.ulsterherald.com
Editor: Darach McDonald
Deputy Editor: Rosetta Donnelly

### Ulster Star
12A Bow Street
Lisburn, BT28 1BN
Tel: 028 9267 9111
Fax: 028 9260 2904
Editor: David Fletcher

## National Newspapers (Belfast Offices)

### Ireland on Sunday
3rd Floor, Embassy House
Herbert Park Lane, Ballsbridge, Dublin 4
Tel: 003531 637 5800
Email: paul.drury@irelandonsunday.com
Editor: Paul Drury

### Irish Examiner
Tel: 0035321 480 2153
Fax: 0035321 427 5477
Email: editor@examiner.ie
Editor: Tim Vaughan

### Irish Independent
(Sunday Independent and Evening Herald)
7 North Street
Belfast, BT1 1PA
Tel: 028 9032 9436
Fax: 028 9024 5726
Belfast Correspondent: John Devine

### Irish Times
Fanum House
110 Great Victoria Street
Belfast, BT2 7BE
Tel: 028 9032 3324
Fax: 028 9023 1469
Email: gmoriarty@irish-times.ie
Northern Editor: Gerry Moriarty

### The Mirror
415 Holywood Road
Belfast, BT4 2GU
Tel: 028 9056 8000
Fax: 028 9056 8005
Editor: Greg Harkin
News Editor: Joe Gorrod

### Sunday Business Post
80 Harcourt Street, Dublin 2
Tel: 003531 602 6000
Fax: 003531 679 6496
Email: sbpost@iol.ie
Editor: Gavin Daly

### Sunday Independent
90 Middle Abbey Street
Tel: 003531 705 5333
Fax: 003531 705 5779
Email: snews@unison.independent.ie
Editor: Vincent Doyle

### The Sunday Mirror
415 Holywood Road
Belfast, BT4 2GU
Tel: 028 9056 8000
Fax: 028 9056 8005
Editor: Christian McCashin

### Sunday People
415 Holywood Road
Belfast, BT4 2GU
Tel: 028 9056 8000
Fax: 028 9056 8005
Editor: Greg Harkin

### Sunday Tribune
15 Lower Baggot Street, Dublin 2
Tel: 003531 661 5555
Fax: 003531 631 4390
Email: pmurray@tribune.ie
Editor: Paddy Murray

### Sunday World
3-5 Commercial Court
Lower Donegall Street
Belfast, BT1 2NB
Tel: 028 9023 8118
Fax: 028 9023 6155
Editor: Jim McDowell

## News Agencies

### Press Association
Tel: 028 9024 5008
Fax: 028 9043 9246
E-mail: belfast@pa.press.net
Ireland Editor: Derick Henderson
Political Editor: Dan McGinn

### Reuters
2nd Floor
Fanum House, Great Victoria Street
Belfast, BT2 7BE
Tel: 028 9031 5253
Fax: 028 9023 4106
Correspondent: Alex Richardson

## Magazines and Periodicals

Northern Ireland has a small but vibrant magazines and periodicals publishing sector covering most areas of economic and social activity. In addition to numerous local offerings available some of the top-selling publications are national products originating in Britain or from the growing Dublin-based industry.

**Angling Ireland** (Monthly)
124 Low Road
Islandmagee
Larne, BT40 3RF
Tel: 028 9338 2610
Fax: 028 9338 2610
Web: www.anglingireland.com
Editor: Frank Quigley

**An Phoblacht** (Weekly)
535e Falls Road
Belfast, BT11 9AA
Tel: 028 9060 0279
Fax: 028 9060 0207
Web: www.irlnet.com/aprn
Editor: Martin Spain

**Auto Trader** (Weekly)
James House
Dargan Crescent
Belfast, BT3 9JP
Tel: 028 9037 0444
Fax: 028 9037 2828

**Belfast Magazine** (Monthly)
5 Churchill Street
Belfast, BT15 2BP
Tel: 028 9074 2255
Fax: 028 9035 1326
Web: www.glenravel.com
Editor: Joe Baker

**BNIL** (Bulletin of Northern Ireland Law) (Monthly)
SLS Legal Publications Ltd
School of Law
Queen's University
Belfast, BT7 1NN
Tel: 028 9033 5224
Fax: 028 9032 6308
Editor: Deborah McBride

**The Big List** (Fortnightly)
Flagship Media Group Ltd
48-50 York Street
Belfast, BT15 1AS
Tel: 028 9031 9008
Fax: 028 9072 7800
Web: www.thebiglist.co.uk
Editor: Gavin Bell

**Business Eye** (Monthly)
Buckley Publications
20 Kings Road
Belfast, BT5 6JJ
Tel: 028 9073 5859
Fax: 028 9073 5858
Web: www.businesseye.co.uk
Editor: Richard Buckley

**Business Ulster**
(Bimonthly with Ulster Tatler)
Ulster Journals Ltd
39 Boucher Road, Belfast
Tel: 028 9068 1371
Fax: 028 9038 1915
Email: ulstertatler@aol.com
Editor: Richard Sherry

**Carsport Magazine** (Monthly)
Greer Publications
5B Edgewater Business Park
Belfast Harbour Estate
Belfast, BT3 9JQ
Tel: 028 9078 3200
Fax: 028 9078 3210
Email: patburns@greerpublications.com
Editor: Patrick Burns

**Catering & Licensing Review** (Monthly)
Greer Publications
5B Edgewater Business Park
Belfast Harbour Estate
Belfast, BT3 9JQ
Tel: 028 9078 3200
Fax: 028 9078 3210
Email: kathyjensen@greerpublications.com
Editor: Kathy Jensen

**Church of Ireland Gazette** (Weekly)
C of I Publishing Co
3 Wallace Avenue
Lisburn, BT27 4AA
Tel: 028 9267 5743
Fax: 028 9266 7580
Web: www.gazette.ireland.anglican.org
Editor: Rev Canon Ian Ellis

**Club Review**
B101 Portview Trade Centre
Newtownards Road
Belfast, BT4 1RX
Tel: 028 9045 9864
Fax: 028 9045 9034
Email: info@media-marketing.net

**Constabulary Gazette** (Monthly)
Ulster Journals Ltd
39 Boucher Road
Belfast, BT12 6UT
Tel: 028 9066 3311
Fax: 028 9038 1915
Editor: Bob Catterson

**Equestrian** (Bi-monthly)
Mainstream Publications Ltd
139-140 Thomas Street
Portadown, BT62 3BE
Tel: 028 3833 4272
Fax: 028 3835 1046
Web: mainstreampublishing.co.uk
Managing Editor: Diane Wray

**Export & Freight** (8 times pa)
Four Square Media
The Mill House, 10 Main Street
Hillisborough, BT 6AE
Tel: 028 9268 8888
Fax: 028 9268 8866
Editor: Helen Beggs

**Extraction Industry Ireland** (Annual Review)
Mainstream Publications Ltd
139-140 Thomas Street
Portadown, BT62 3BE
Tel: 028 3833 4272
Fax: 028 3835 1046
Web: mainstreampublishing.co.uk
Editor: Karen McAvoy

**Farmers' Journal** (Impartial Reporter) (Weekly)
8-10 East Bridge Street
Enniskillen, BT74 7BT
Tel: 028 6632 4422/425
Fax: 028 6632 5047
Fax: 028 6632 5969 (Advertising)
Web: www.impartialreporter.com
Editor: Denzil McDaniel

**Farming Life (Newsletter)** (Weekly)
46-56 Boucher Crescent
Belfast, BT12 6QY
Tel: 028 9068 0033
Fax: 028 9066 4432
News Editor: David McCoy

**Farm Week** (Weekly)
Morton Newspapers Ltd
14 Church Street
Portadown, BT62 3QU
Tel: 028 3833 9421
Fax: 028 3835 0203
Web: www.mortonnewspapers.co.uk
Editor: Hal Crowe

**Food Technology & Packaging** (Quarterly)
Greer Publications
5B Edgewater Business Park
Belfast Harbour Estate
Belfast, BT3 9JQ
Tel: 028 9078 3200
Fax: 028 9078 3210
Editorial Contact: Kathy Jensen

### Fortnight (Monthly)
81 Botanic Avenue
Belfast, BT7 1JL
Tel: 028 9023 2353
Fax: 028 9023 2650
Web: www.fortnight.org
Editor: Malachi O'Doherty

### Funeral Times (Quarterly)
1 Annagh Drive
Carn Industrial Estate
Portadown, BT63 5WF
Tel: 028 3835 5060
Fax: 028 3833 6959
Editor: Ian Millen

### Getting Married in Northern Ireland
Mainstream Publications Ltd
139-140 Thomas Street
Portadown, BT62 3BE
Tel: 028 3833 4272
Fax: 028 3835 1046
Web: www.mainstreampublishing.co.uk
Editor: Catherine McGinn

### The Gown (Monthly during term)
C/o Students Union
Queen's University
University Road
Belfast, BT7 1PE
Tel: 028 9027 3106
Editor: Peter Cheney

### Guide to Industrial Estates (Quarterly)
Mainstream Publications Ltd
139-140 Thomas Street
Portadown, BT62 3BE
Tel: 028 3833 4272
Fax: 028 3835 1046
Web: www.mainstreampublishing.co.uk
Managing Editor: Gerald McAlinden

### Home Life Magazine (Monthly)
CIDO Business Complex
Charles Street, Lurgan, BT66 6HG
Tel: 028 3832 4000
Fax: 028 3832 5213
Editor: Margaret Kinsella

### Horizon Magazine (Monthly)
Unit 11
Broomfield Industrial Estate
333 Crumlin Road
Belfast, BT14 7EA
Tel: 028 9074 5573
Fax: 028 9074 5573
Editor: Eddie McAteer

### Industrial & Manufacturing Engineer (Quarterly)
Greer Publications
5B Edgewater Business Park
Belfast Harbour Estate
Belfast, BT3 9JQ
Tel: 028 9078 3200
Fax: 028 9078 3210
Editor: Vacant

### Ireland's Forecourt & Convenience Retailer
Penton Publications Ltd
Penton House
38 Heron Road
Sydenham Business Park
Belfast, BT3 9LE
Tel: 028 9045 7457
Fax: 028 9045 6611
Editor: Margaret Henderson

### Ireland's Homes, Interiors & Living (Monthly)
Unit 65, Dunlop Commercial Park
4 Balloo Drive
Bangor, BT19 7QY
Tel: 028 9147 3979
Fax: 028 9145 7226
Email: mckeenan@ihil.net
Lifestyle Editor: Samantha Blair
Publisher: Mike Keenan

### Ireland's Horse Trader (Bi-monthly)
Mainstream Publications Ltd
140 Thomas Street
Portadown, BT62 3BE
Tel: 028 3833 4272
Fax: 028 3835 1046
Web: www.mainstreampublishing.co.uk
Editor: Una McCann

### Ireland's Pets (Bi-monthly)
Mainstream Publications Ltd
140 Thomas Street
Portadown, BT62 3BE
Tel: 028 3833 4272
Fax: 028 3835 1046
Web: www.mainstreampublishing.co.uk
Editor: Debbie Orne

### Irish Farmers Journal
Northern Ireland Editorial Office
69 Ballyrainey Road
Newtownards, BT23 5AF
Tel: 028 9181 2054
Fax: 028 9182 0946
Editor: James Campbell

### Irish Country Sports and Country Life (Quarterly)
PO Box 62
Portadown, BT62 1XP
Tel: 028 3885 1326/
028 9048 3873
Fax: 028 3885 2237/
028 9048 0195
Editor: Albert Titterington

### Keystone (Construction Industry) (Bi-monthly)
Flagship Media Group Ltd
48-50 York Street
Belfast, BT15 1AS
Tel: 028 9031 9008
Fax: 028 9072 7800
Editor: Stephen Preston

### LÁ (Irish Language Newspaper) (Weekly)
Teach Basil
2 Cnoc Bhaile hAnnaidh
Béal Feirste, BT17 0LY
Tel: 028 9060 5050
Fax: 028 9060 5544
Web: www.nuacht.com
Eaghatoir: Ciarán Ó Pronntaigh

### Licensed Catering News (LCN) (Monthly)
8 Lowes Industrial Estate
31 Ballynahinch Road
Carryduff, BT8 8EH
Tel: 028 9081 5656
Fax: 028 9081 7481
Editor: Linda Brooks

### Methodist Newsletter
Edgehill Theological College
9 Lennoxvale, Belfast, BT9 5BY
Tel: 028 9032 0078
Fax: 028 9032 7000
Email: office@egehillcollege.org
Web: www.irishmethodist.org
Manager: Harold Baird

### Neighbourhood Retailer & Forecourt Technology (10 issues pa)
Penton Publications Ltd
Penton House
38 Heron Road
Sydenham Business Park
Belfast, BT3 9LE
Tel: 028 9045 7457
Fax: 028 9045 6611
Managing Editor: Margaret Henderson

### New Houses in Northern Ireland (Quarterly)
Mainstream Magazines Ltd
139-140 Thomas Street
Portadown, BT62 3BE
Tel: 028 3839 2000
Fax: 028 3835 1071
Web: mainstreampublishing.co.uk
Managing Editor: Karen McAvoy

### The Northern Builder Magazine (Quarterly)
Unit 22, Lisburn Enterprise Centre
Ballinderry Road Industrial Estate
Lisburn, BT28 2BP
Tel: 028 9266 3390
Fax: 028 9266 6242
Web: www.northernbuilder.co.uk
Editor: Alan Bailie

### Northern Farmer (The Irish News) (Weekly)
113-117 Donegall Street
Belfast, BT1 2GE
Tel: 028 9032 2226
Fax: 028 9033 7451
Editor: John Manley

### Northern Ireland Legal Quarterly
SLS Legal Publications Ltd
School of Law, Queen's University
Belfast, BT7 1NN
Tel: 028 9027 3597
Fax: 028 9032 6308
Editor: David Capper

### Northern Ireland Medicine Today (Monthly)
Penton Publications Ltd
Penton House
38 Heron Road
Sydenham Business Park
Belfast, BT3 9LE
Tel: 028 9045 7457
Fax: 028 9045 6611
Managing Editor: Bill Penton

### Northern Ireland Travel & Leisure News (Monthly)
Unit 1, Windsor Business Park
16-18 Lower Windsor Avenue
Belfast, BT9 7DW
Tel: 028 9066 6151
Fax: 028 9068 3819
Web: www.nitravelnews.com
Editor: Brian Ogle

### Northern Ireland Veterinary Today (Quarterly)
Penton Publications Ltd
Penton House
38 Heron Road
Sydenham Business Park
Belfast, BT3 9LE
Tel: 028 9045 7457
Fax: 028 9045 6611
Managing Editor: Bill Penton

### Northern Ireland Visitors' Journal (Annual)
Penton Publications Ltd
Penton House
38 Heron Road
Sydenham Business Park
Belfast, BT3 9LE
Tel: 028 9045 7457
Fax: 028 9045 6611
Managing Editor: Bill Penton

### Northern Woman (Monthly)
Greer Publications
5B Edgewater Business Park
Belfast Harbour Estate
Belfast, BT3 9JQ
Tel: 028 9078 3200
Fax: 028 9078 3210
Editor: Lyn Palmer

### Perspective (Bi-monthly)
Journal of the Royal Society of Ulster Architects
Ulster Journals Ltd.
39 Boucher Road
Belfast, BT12 6UT
Tel: 028 9066 3311
Fax: 028 9038 1915
Editor: Chris Sherry

### Plant & Civil Engineer (6 issues pa)
69 Glen Road
Comber, BT23 5QS
Tel: 028 9187 2656
Editor: Michael McRitchie

### Plumbing & Heating (Quarterly)
Mainstream Magazines Ltd
139-140 Thomas Street
Portadown, BT62 3BE
Tel: 028 3839 2000
Fax: 028 3835 1071
Web: www.mainstreampublishing.co.uk
Managing Editor: Jacqueline Farley

### The Presbyterian Herald (10 issues pa)
Church House, Fisherwick Place
Belfast, BT1 6DW
Tel: 028 9032 2284
Fax: 028 9024 8377
Web: www.presbyterianireland.org
Editor: Rev Arthur Clarke

### Property News (Monthly)
1 Annagh Drive
Carn Industrial Estate
Portadown, BT63 5RH
Tel: 028 3835 5060
Fax: 028 3833 6959
Editor: Graham Brown

### Recruitment (Weekly)
48-50 York Street
Belfast, BT15 1AS
Tel: 028 9031 9008
Fax: 028 9072 7800
Web: www.JobsNation.net
Editor: Stephen Preston

### Regional Film & Video (Monthly)
Flagship Media Group Ltd
48-50 York Street
Belfast, BT15 1AS
Tel: 028 9031 9008
Fax: 028 9072 7800
Web: www.4rfv.co.uk
Editor: Stephen Preston

### Retail Forecourt & Convenience Store (Bi-monthly)
8 Lowes Industrial Estate
31 Ballynahinch Road
Carryduff
Tel: 028 9081 5656
Fax: 028 90281 7481
Editor: Linda Brooks

### Retail Grocer (Monthly)
8 Lowes Industrial Estate
31 Ballynahinch Road
Carryduff, BT8 8EH
Tel: 028 9081 5656
Fax: 028 9081 7481
Editor: Linda Brooks

### Shelf Build, Extend & Renovate
Corry Home Building Ltd
96 Lisburn Road
Saintfield
Tel: 028 9751 0570
Fax: 028 9751 0576
Editor: Gillian Corry

### Specify (Construction Industry) (Bi-monthly)
Greer Publications
5B Edgewater Business Park
Belfast Harbour Estate
Belfast, BT3 9JQ
Tel: 028 9078 3200
Fax: 028 9078 3210
Editor: Emma Cowan

Ulster Architect Magazine (Monthly)
Addemo Press Ltd
182 Ravenhill Road
Belfast, BT6 8EE
Tel: 028 9073 1636
Fax: 028 9073 8927
Editor: Ann Davey Orr

Ulster Bride (Bi-Annual)
Ulster Journals Ltd
39 Boucher Road
Belfast, BT12 6UT
Tel: 028 9068 1371
Fax: 028 9038 1915
Editor: Pauline Roy

Ulster Business (Monthly)

Greer Publications
5B Edgewater Business Park
Belfast Harbour Estate
Belfast, BT3 9JQ
Tel: 028 9078 3200
Fax: 028 9078 3210
Web: www.ulsterbusiness.com

Editor
Russell Campbell

Published monthly, Ulster Business is Northern Ireland's best known business magazine. Highlighting the issues that are dominating the world of business in Northern Ireland, the magazine is very widely read by senior business people and policymakers all over Northern Ireland.

Ulster Farmer (Weekly)
Observer Newspapers
Ann Street
Dungannon, BT70 1ET
Tel: 028 8772 2557
Fax: 028 8772 7334
Editor: Desmond Mallon

Ulster Grocer (Monthly)
Greer Publications
5B Edgewater Business Park
Belfast Harbour Estate
Belfast, BT3 9JQ
Tel: 028 9078 3200
Fax: 028 9078 3210
Editor: Kathy Jensen

Ulster Homes (Quarterly)
Ulster Journals Ltd
39 Boucher Road
Belfast, BT12 6UT
Tel: 028 9068 1371
Fax: 028 9038 1915
Editor: Chris Sherry

Ulster Tatler Series (Monthly)
Ulster Journals Ltd, 39 Boucher Road
Belfast, BT12 6UT
Tel: 028 9068 1371
Fax: 028 9038 1915
Editor: Richard Sherry

Ulster Tatler Wine & Dine Guide (Annual)
Ulster Journals Ltd, 39 Boucher Road
Belfast, BT12 6UT
Tel: 028 9068 1371
Fax: 028 9038 1915
Editor: Walter Love

United News (Farming) (Monthly)
Greer Publications
5B Edgewater Business Park
Belfast Harbour Estate
Belfast, BT3 9JQ
Tel: 028 9078 3200
Fax: 028 9078 3210
Editor: Kathy Jensen

Wedding Journal (Quarterly)
Penton Publications Ltd
38 Heron Road
Sydenham Business Park
Belfast, BT3 9LE
Tel: 028 9045 7457
Fax: 028 9045 6611
Web: www.weddingjournalonline.com
Managing Editor: Tara Craig

Women's News (Monthly)
109-113 Royal Avenue
Belfast, BT1 1FF
Tel: 028 9032 2823
Fax: 028 9043 8788

## Publishers

Ambassador
Providence House
Ardenlee Street
Belfast, BT6 8QJ
Tel: 028 9045 0010
Fax: 028 9073 9659
Web: www.ambassador-productions.com
Director: Samuel Lowry

Appletree Press Ltd
14 Howard Street South
Belfast, BT7 1AP
Tel: 028 9024 3074
Fax: 028 9024 6756
Email: reception@appletree.ie
Web: www.appletree.ie

Beyond the Pale Publications
Unit 212, Conway Mall
5-7 Conway Street, Belfast, BT13 2DE
Tel: 028 9043 8630
Fax: 028 9043 9707
Web: www.btpale.com

Blackstaff Press
4C Heron Wharf
Sydenham Business Park
Belfast, BT3 9LE
Tel: 028 9045 5006
Fax: 028 9046 6237
Email: info@blackstaffpress.com
Web: www.blackstaffpress.com

bmf Publishing
TSL House
38 Bachelors Walk
Lisburn, BT28 1XN
Tel: 028 9262 8787
Fax: 028 9262 8789
Email: info@bmfbusinessservices.com
Web: www.bmfbusinessservices.com

BMG Publishing
5 Ballynahinch Road
Carryduff
Belfast, BT8 8DN
Tel: 028 9081 7333
Fax: 028 9081 744

Colourpoint Books
Colour House, Jubilee Business Park
21 Jubilee Road
Newtownards, BT23 4YH
Tel: 028 9182 0505
Fax: 028 9182 1900
Web: www.colourpoint.co.uk

### Creagh Media Publications
644 Antrim Road
Belfast, BT15 4EL
Tel: 028 9077 0776
Fax: 028 9077 2577

### GCAS Publications
Russell Court
38-52 Lisburn Road
Belfast, BT9 6AA
Tel: 028 9055 7700
Fax: 028 9024 5741
Web: www.gcasgroup.com
Managing Director: Robin Hetherington

### Greer Publications
5b Edgewater Business Park
Belfast Harbour Estate
Belfast, BT3 9JQ
Tel: 028 9078 3200
Fax: 028 9078 3210

### Guildhall Press
Unit 4, Community Service Units
Bligh's Lane
Derry, BT48 0LZ
Tel: 028 7136 4413
Fax: 028 7137 2949
Web: www.ghpress.com

### Laurel Cottage Ltd.
Cottage Publications / Ballyhay Books
15 Ballyhay Road
Donaghadee, BT21 0NG
Tel: 028 9188 8033
Fax: 028 9188 8063
Email: info@cottage-publications.com

### Linenhall Library
17 Donegall Square North
Belfast, BT1 5GB
Tel: 028 9032 1707
Fax: 028 9043 8586
Email: info@linenhall.com
Web: www.linenhall.com

### Local Directories
Commercial House
15 Merchants Quay
Newry, BT35 6AH
Tel: 028 3025 4718
Fax: 028 3025 4705
Web: www.localdirectories.net
Email: info@localdirectories.net

### Locksley Press Ltd
16 Coolsara Park
Lisburn, BT28 3BG
Tel/Fax: 028 9260 3195
Freephone: 0800 9178104

### Mainstream Publications Ltd
139-140 Thomas Street
Portadown, BT62 3BE
Tel: 028 3833 4272
Fax: 028 3835 1046
Web: www.mainstreampublishing.co.uk

### Mathematics Publishing Co
45 Blackstaff Road
Clough
Downpatrick, BT30 8SR
Tel: 028 4485 1211
Fax: 028 4485 1566

### Medical Communications Ltd
Ulster Bank Building
142-148 Albertbridge Road
Belfast, BT5 4GS
Tel: 028 9080 9090
Fax: 028 9080 9097

### N.I. Media Ltd
41-51 Royal Avenue
Belfast, BT1 1FB
Tel: 028 9058 5000
Fax: 028 9058 5001
Email: info@nimedia.net

### Outlook Press
Castle Street
Rathfriland, BT34 5QR
Tel: 028 4063 0202
Fax: 028 4063 1022

### Penton Publications Ltd
Penton House
38 Heron Road
Sydenham Business Park
Belfast, BT3 9LE
Tel: 028 9045 7457
Fax: 028 9045 6611
Email: info@pentonpublications.co.uk

### tSO Ireland (The Stationery Office)
16 Arthur Street
Belfast, BT1 4GD
Tel: 028 9023 8451
Fax: 028 9023 5401
Web: www.tso.com

### Ulster Historical Foundation
Balmoral Buildings
12 College Square East
Belfast, BT1 6DD
Tel: 028 9033 2288
Fax: 028 9023 9885
Email: enquiry@uhf.org.uk
Web: www.ancestryireland.co.uk

### Ulster Magazines Ltd
Crescent House
58 Rugby Road
Belfast, BT7 1PT
Tel: 028 9023 0425
Fax: 028 9023 6572

### Editoral Solutions
537 Antrim Road
Belfast, BT15 3BU
Tel: 028 9077 2300
Fax: 028 9078 1356
Email: info@editorialsolutions.com
Web: www.editorialsolutions.com

### WG Baird
Greystone Press, Caulfield Drive
Antrim, BT41 2RS
Tel: 028 9446 3911
Fax: 028 9446 6250
Email: wgbaird@wgbaird.com
Web: www.wgbaird.com

## Communications Services Providers

### Advertising Agencies

**Anderson Spratt Group Advertising**
Anderson House
409 Hollywood Road
Belfast, BT4 2GU
Tel: 028 9080 2000
Fax: 028 9080 2001
Web: www.asgh.com

**Ardmore Advertising & Marketing Ltd**
Ardmore House
Pavillions
Kinnegar Drive
Holywood, BT18 9JQ
Tel: 028 9042 5344
Fax: 028 9042 4823
Email: info@ardmore.co.uk
Web: www.ardmore.co.uk

**AV Browne Advertising Ltd**
46 Bedford Street
Belfast, BT2 7GH
Tel: 028 9032 0663
Fax: 028 9024 4279
Web: www.avb.co.uk

**Coey Advertising & Design**
Victoria Lodge
158 Upper Newtownards Road
Belfast, BT4 3EQ
Tel: 028 9047 1221
Fax: 028 9047 1509
Email: info@coeyadvertising.co.uk
Web: www.coeyadvertising.co.uk

**Concept Advertising & Marketing**
1A Wellington Park, Belfast, BT9 6DJ
Tel: 028 9066 7797
Fax: 028 9066 7745
Web: www.conceptadvertising.co.uk

**Design & Place Recruitment Advertising**
409 Holywood Road
Belfast, BT4 2GU
Tel: 028 9080 2010
Fax: 028 9080 2011
Web: www.andersonspratt.com

**Fire IMC Ltd**
10 Dargan Crescent, Duncrue Road
Belfast, BT3 9JP
Tel: 028 9077 4388
Fax: 028 9077 6906
Web: www.fireimc.com



**Fox Advertising**
1 Union Buildings, Union Place
Dungannon, BT70 1DL
Tel: 028 8772 2962
Fax: 028 8772 9719
E-mail: martin@fox-advertising.com

**GCAS Advertising Limited**
Russell Court
38-52 Lisburn Road
Belfast, BT9 6AA
Tel: 028 9055 7700
Fax: 028 9024 5741
Web: www.gcasgroup.com

**Higher Profile Advertising**
74 Ballycrochan Road
Bangor, BT19 6NF
Tel: 028 9127 1016
Fax: 028 9127 1016

**Jelly**
24 College Gardens
Belfast, BT9 6BS
Tel: 028 9066 3663
Fax: 028 9066 3600
Web: www.jellycommunications.com

**KR Graphics**
121 University Street
Belfast, BT7 1HP
Tel: 028 9033 3792
Fax: 028 9033 0549
Web: www.krgraphics.co.uk

**The Levy McCallum Advertising Agency**
10 Arthur Street
Belfast, BT1 4GD
Tel: 028 9031 9220
Fax: 028 9031 9221
Web: www.levymccallum.co.uk

**Lyle Bailie International**
31 Bruce Street
Great Victoria Street
Belfast, BT2 7JD
Tel: 028 9033 1044
Fax: 028 9033 1622
Email: directors@lylebailie.com
Web: www.lylebailie.com
Chief Executive: David Lyle
Executive Creative Director:
Julie Anne Bailie

Specialists in attitude and behaviour change.

**Main Line Marketing**
47e Oaks Road
Dungannon, BT71 4AS
Tel: 028 8772 7358
Fax: 028 8772 7358

Navigator Blue
The Baths, 18 Ormeau Avenue
Belfast, BT2 8HS
Tel: 028 9024 6722
Fax: 028 9023 1607
Web: www.navigatorblue.com

RLA Northern Ireland Limited
86 Lisburn Road
Belfast, BT9 6AF
Tel: 028 9066 4444
Fax: 028 9068 3497
Web: www.rla.co.uk

TDP Advertising
76 University Street
Belfast, BT7 1HE
Tel: 028 9032 2882
Fax: 028 9033 2727
Web: www.tdpadvertising.co.uk

Walker Communications
The Old Post Office
43 High Street
Holywood, BT18 9AB
Tel: 028 9042 5555
Fax: 028 9042 1222
Web: www.walkercommunications.co.uk

Weber Shandwick
425 Holywood Road
Belfast, BT4 2GU
Tel: 028 9076 1007
Fax: 028 9076 1941
Email: 028 9076 3490
Web: www.webershandwickdesign.com

Wyncroft International Communications
Wyncroft House
52 Warren Road
Donaghadee, BT21 0PD
Tel: 028 9188 8808
Fax: 028 9188 4411
Web: www.wyncroft.com

## Broadcasting and Studio Services

Audio Processing Technology Ltd
Unit 6 , Edgewater Road
Belfast, BT3 9JQ
Tel: 028 9037 1110
Fax: 028 9037 1137
Web: www.aptx.com

BBC Northern Ireland
Broadcasting House
25 Ormeau Avenue
Belfast, BT2 8HD
Tel: 028 9033 8000
Fax: 028 9033 8800
Web: www.bbc.co.uk

BBC Radio Foyle
8 Northland Road
Derry, BT48 7JD
Tel: 028 7137 8600
Fax: 028 7137 8666
Web: www.bbc.co.uk

Belfast Citybeat
Lamont Buildings, Stranmillis Road
Belfast, BT9 5DF
Tel: 028 9020 5967
Fax: 028 9020 0023
Web: www.citybeat.co.uk

Cool FM
Kiltonga Industrial Estate
Belfast Road
Newtownards, BT1 1RT
Tel: 028 9181 7181
Fax: 028 9181 4974
Web: www.coolfm.co.uk

CPR Recording Studio
3a Bingham Lane
Bangor, BT20 5DR
Tel: 028 9146 7631

Downtown Radio Ltd
Kiltonga Industrial Estate
Belfast Road
Newtownards, BT23 4ES
Tel: 028 9181 5555
Fax: 028 9181 8913
Web: www.downtown.co.uk

Duplitape
100 Duncairn Gardens
Belfast, BT15 2GN
Tel: 028 9074 7411
Fax: 028 9029 9001
Email: duplitape@enterprise.net

Elmstree Studio
12 Turmore Road, Newry, BT34 1PJ
Tel: 028 3026 5913
Fax: 028 3026 5913

EMS The Studio
12 Balloo Avenue, Bangor, BT19 7QT
Tel: 028 9127 4411
Fax: 028 9127 4412

Jingle Jangle
The Strand, 156 Holywood Road
Belfast, BT4 1NY
Tel: 028 9065 6769
Fax: 028 9067 3771

Komodo Recordings
79 Magheraconluce Road
Hillsborough, BT26 6PR
Tel: 028 9268 8285
Fax: 028 9268 9551

Q97.2FM
24 Cloyfin Road, Coleraine, BT52 2NU
Tel: 028 7035 9100
Fax: 028 7032 6666
Web: www.q972.fm

Q102.9FM
The Riverside Suite
The Old Waterside Railway Station
87 Rossdowney Road
Derry, BT47 6DH
Tel: 028 7134 6666
Fax: 028 7131 1177
Web: www.q102.fm

Radio Telefis Eireann
Fanum House ,Great Victoria Street
Belfast, BT2 7BE
Tel: 028 9032 6441
Fax: 028 9033 2222

Radio Valley
Lagan Valley Hospital
Hillsborough Road
Lisburn, BT28 1JP
Tel: 028 9267 1151
Fax: 028 9266 6100

Studio 2
69A Whitesides Hill
Craigavon, BT62 3RJ
Tel: 028 3884 1335

UTV plc
Havelock House, Ormeau Road
Belfast, BT7 1EB
Tel: 028 9032 8122
Fax: 028 9024 6695
Web: www.utvlive.com

## Television, Film and Video Production

**About Face Media**
Townsend Enterprise Park
Townsend Street
Belfast, BT13 2ES
Tel: 028 9089 4555
Fax: 028 9089 4502

**Acorn Film & Video Ltd**
13 Fitzwilliam Street
Belfast, BT9 6AW
Tel: 028 9024 0977
Fax: 028 9022 2309

**Another World Productions**
2nd Floor
11 Lismore House
23 Church Street
Portadown, BT62 3LN
Tel: 028 3833 2933
Fax: 028 3839 6941

**Arcom Interactive**
8 Tennyson Avenue, Bangor, BT20 3SS
Tel: 028 9185 9064
Fax: 028 9185 9064

**Brian Waddell Productions Ltd**
Strand Studios
5-7 Shore Road
Holywood, BT18 9HX
Tel: 028 9042 7646
Fax: 028 9042 7922

**Christian Communications Networks (Europe) Ltd**
646 Shore Road
Whiteabbey, BT37 0PR
Tel: 028 9085 3997
Fax: 028 9036 5536

**Extreme Film & TV Productions Ltd**
1 Church View
Holywood, BT18 9DP
Tel: 028 9080 9050
Fax: 028 9080 9051

**Macmillan Media bcb**

macmillan new media
broadcast centre belfast

Broadcast Centre
Venture Gate Building
32-36 Dublin Road
Belfast, BT2 7HN
Tel: 087 0350 2150
Fax: 028 9050 2151
Email: info@macmillanmedia.co.uk
Web: www.macmillanmedia.co.uk

Managing Director
Michael Macmillan

macmillan media is a leading UK and Ireland production company and is GMTV's news contractor for Northern Ireland, Assembly Broadcast Contractor and European video production provider to National Australia Bank.

**MGTV**
Victoria House
1A Victoria Road, Holywood, BT18 9BA
Tel: 028 9020 0060
Fax: 028 9059 2000
Email: info@mgtv.co.uk
Web: www.mgtv.co.uk

**Miracles Production**
200 Upper Newtownards Road
Belfast, BT4 3ET
Tel: 028 9047 3838
Fax: 028 9047 3839
Email: info@miraclesproduction.co.uk

**Northland Broadcast**
30 Chamerlain Street
Derry, BT48 6LR
Tel: 028 7137 2432
Fax: 028 7137 7132

**Nosedive Animation Studio**
Units 2-3, Laganside Studio
Ravenhill Business Park
Belfast, BT6 8AW
Tel: 028 9022 2410

**The Picturehouse**
The Strand
156 Holywood Road
Belfast, BT4 1NY
Tel: 028 9065 1111
Fax: 028 9067 3771

**Stirling Productions Ltd**
137 University Street
Belfast, BT7 1HP
Tel: 028 9033 3848
Fax: 028 9024 9583

**Straight Forward Film & Television Productions Ltd**
Building 2, Lesley Office Park
393 Holywood Road
Belfast, BT4 2LS
Tel: 028 9065 1010

**Tyndall PR Productions**
58 Edentrillick Road
Hillsborough, BT26 6PG
Tel: 028 9268 9444
Fax: 028 9268 9224

**Visionworks Television Ltd**
Vision House
56 Dongall Pass
Belfast, BT7 1BU
Tel: 028 9024 1241
Fax: 028 9024 1777
Email: production@visionworks.co.uk

**Westway Film Production Ltd**
42 Clarendon Street
Londonderry, BT79 4SW
Tel: 028 7130 8383
Fax: 028 7130 9393

## Public Relations/Public Affairs Consultancies

**Aiken PR**
418 Lisburn Road
Belfast, BT9 6GH
Tel: 028 9066 3000
Fax: 028 9068 3030
Web: aikenpr.co.uk

**Anderson Spratt Group Public Relations**
Holywood House, Innis Court,
High Street, Holywood, BT18 9HT
Tel: 028 9042 3332
Fax: 028 9042 7730
Web: www.andersonspratt.com

**Cactus PR & Communications Ltd**
38 Heron Road
Belfast, BT3 9LE
Tel: 028 9045 7700
Fax: 028 9045 6622
Web: pentonpublications.co.uk

**Carmah Communications**
39a Main Street
Bangor, BT20 5AF
Tel: 028 9127 5965
Fax: 028 9127 5284

Citigate Northern Ireland Ltd
157-159 High Street
Holywood, BT18 9HU
Tel: 028 9039 5500
Fax: 028 9039 5600
Web: www.citigateni.co.uk

Compton Communications
17 Station Road
Holywood, BT18 0BP
Tel: 028 9042 7949
Fax: 028 9042 8459
Email: john@comptoncom.co.uk

Crockard Communications

CROCKARD
COMMUNICATIONS

33a Belmont Road
Belfast, BT4 2AA
Tel: 028 9087 7290
Fax: 028 9065 1400
Email: mail@crockard.co.uk
Managing Director: Joanne Crockard

Crockard Communications has a wealth of experience providing a complete integrated communications service to blue-chip public and private organisations at executive level.

It specialises in media relations, website editorial and content management services and the production of customer/staff newspapers and magazines.

Davidson Cockcroft Partnership
Bamford House
91-93 Saintfield Road
Belfast, BT8 7HR
Tel: 028 9040 2296
Fax: 028 9040 2291

DCL (NI)
2 Donegall Square East
Belfast, BT1 5HB
Tel: 028 9033 9949
Fax: 028 9033 9959
Email: info@dclmedia.com

Doris Leeman Public Relations
27 Berwick View
Moira, BT67 0SX
Tel: 028 9261 1044
Fax: 028 9261 1979

GCAS Public Relations Ltd
Russell Court
38-52 Lisburn Road
Belfast, BT9 6AA
Tel: 028 9055 7777
Fax: 028 9023 0142

Inform Communications
13 University Street
Belfast, BT7 1FY
Tel: 028 9023 3550
Fax: 028 9033 1017
Email: info@informcommunications.com

Laird Public Relations Ltd
104 Holywood Road
Belfast, BT4 1NU
Tel: 028 9047 1282
Fax: 028 9065 6022

Lagan Consulting (Public Affairs)
TSL House
38 Bachelor's Walk
Lisburn, BT28 1XN
Tel: 028 9262 8777
Fax: 028 9262 8789
Email: info@laganconsulting.com
Web: www.laganconsulting.com

Specialist consultants in stakeholder management serving primarily those clients who have a substantive issues-based agenda.

Life Communications
46 Bedford Street
Belfast, BT2 7FF
Tel: 028 9024 8805
Fax: 028 9024 8806

Morrow Communications Ltd
Hanwood House
Pavillions Office Park
Kinnegar Drive
Holywood, BT18 9JQ
Tel: 028 9039 3837
Fax: 028 9039 3830

The PR Agency
721A Lisburn Road
Belfast, BT9 7GU
Tel: 028 9022 2422
Fax: 028 9022 2423
Email: info@thepragency.co.uk

## Event Management Organisations

bmf Business Services
TSL House, 38 Bachelor's Walk
Lisburn, BT28 1XN
Tel: 028 9262 8787
Fax: 028 9262 8789
Email: bmf@dnet.com

Class Acts Promotions
39 Wellington Park, Belfast, BT9 6DN
Tel: 028 9068 1041
Fax: 028 9068 7747

Creative Events
1 Dublin Road, Belfast, BT2 7HB
Tel: 028 9023 5001
Fax: 028 9023 5003
Email: info@creativeevents.co.uk

DCL Event Management (NI)
2 Donegall Square East
Belfast, BT1 5HB
Tel: 028 9033 9949
Fax: 028 9033 9959
Email: info@dclmedia.com

Event
One Weavers Court, Linfield Road,
Belfast, BT12 5GH
Tel: 028 9023 9323
Fax: 028 9023 9139
Email: info@eventexhibition.co.uk
Web: www.eventexhibition.co.uk

Happening Creative Communications
9 Wellington Park, Belfast, BT9 6DJ
Tel: 028 9066 4020
Fax: 028 9038 1257
Email: happening@happen.oco.uk

Mitchell Kane Associates
The Technology Centre
Townsend Street
Belfast, BT13 2ES
Tel: 028 9089 4504
Fax: 028 9089 4502

Morrow Communications Ltd
Hanwood House
Pavillions Office Park
Kinnegar Drive
Holywood, BT18 9JQ
Tel: 028 9039 3837
Fax: 028 9039 3830

Project Planning International
Montalto Estate, Spa Road
Ballynahinch, BT24 8PT
Tel: 028 9756 1993
Fax: 028 9756 5073

## Printers

**Dargan Press Ltd**
5 Round Tower Centre
Dargan Crescent
Belfast, BT3 9JP
Tel: 028 9077 4478
Fax: 028 9077 4771

**Dorman & Sons Ltd**
Unit 2, 2A Apollo Road
Boucher Road
Belfast, BT12 6HP
Tel:028 9066 6700
Fax: 028 9066 1881

**Graham & Heslip**
Beechhill Industrial Park
96 Beechill Road
Belfast, BT8 7QN
Tel: 028 9049 4949

**Graham & Sons Ltd**
51 Gortin Road
Omagh, BT79 7HZ
Tel: 028 8224 9222
Fax: 028 8224 9886

**Impro Printing**
41 Dargan Road
Belfast, BT3 9JU
Tel: 028 9077 7795

**Johnston Printing Ltd**
Mill Road
Kilrea, BT51 5RJ
Tel: 028 2954 0312
Fax: 028 2954 1070
Web: www.johnston-printing.co.uk

**LM Press Ltd**
47 High Street
Lurgan, BT66 8AH
Tel: 028 3832 2412
Fax: 028 3832 1820

**Limavady Printing Co Ltd**
26c Catherine Street
Limavady, BT49 9DB
Tel: 028 7776 2051
Fax: 028 7776 2132
Web: www.limprint.com

**Northern Whig**
107 Limestone Road
Belfast, BT15 3AH
Tel: 028 9035 2233
Fax: 028 9035 2181

**Nicholson & Bass Ltd**
3 Nicholson Drive
Michelin Road, Mallusk
Newtownabbey, BT36 4FB
Tel: 028 9034 2433

## Graphic Designers

**Ardmore Design**
Ardmore House
Pavillions, Kinnegar Drive
Holywood, BT18 9JQ
Tel: 028 9042 5344
Fax: 028 9042 4823
Web: www.ardmore.co.uk

**Darragh Neely Associates**
Ama Communication Centre
Newtownards Road, Bangor, BT19 7TA
Tel: 028 9151 6034
Fax: 028 9147 2797
Web: www.daraghneelyassociates.com

**GCAS Design**
Russell Court
38-52 Lisburn Road, Belfast, BT9 6AA
Tel: 028 9055 7700
Fax: 028 9024 5741
Email: design@gcasgroup.com
Web: www.gcasgroup.com

**IPR Communications Group**
27 Shore Road, Holywood, BT18 9HX
Tel: 028 9042 7094
Email: ipr@d-n-a.net

### KR Graphics
121 University Street, Belfast, BT7 1HP
Tel: 028 9033 3792
Fax: 028 9033 0549

### Leslie Stannage Design
71-75 Donegall Pass, Belfast, BT7 1DR
Tel: 028 9022 4455
Fax: 028 9022 4456

### Rocket
3 Pavillions Office Park
Kinnegar Drive, Holywood, BT18 9JQ
Tel: 028 9022 7700
www.rocket-design.com

### Slater Design
The Old Sorting Office
Strand Avenue, Holywood, BT18 9AA
Tel: 028 9042 1122
Fax: 028 9042 1133

### TDP Advertising
76 University Street, Belfast, BT7 1HE
Tel: 028 9032 2882
Fax: 028 9033 2727
Email: mail@tdpadvertising.co.uk
Web: www.tdpadvertising.co.uk

# New Media

## Internet Access Service Providers (ASPs)

*Note: The listing below is for Northern Ireland based Internet access providers who provide access to the Internet. Internet service providers (ISPs) offer access through leased lines and provide hosting and design services.*

### BT NI
Riverside Tower
5 Lanyon Place
Belfast, BT1 3BT
Tel: 0800 800 800 (Business Enquiries)
Tel: 028 9032 7327 (General Switchboard)
Web: www.bt.com

### Energis
1 Cromac Avenue
Belfast, BT7 2JA
Tel: 028 9095 9595
Fax: 028 9095 9401

### Firenet Internet
Knockmore Industrial Estate
Moira Road
Lisburn, BT28 2EJ
Tel: 028 9267 0600
Fax: 028 9267 0916
Web: www.firenet.uk.net

### The Internet Business
Holywood House
1 Innis Court
Holywood, BT18 9HF
Tel: 028 9042 4190
Fax: 028 9042 4709
Web: www.tibus.net

### Unite Solutions
121 University Street
Belfast, BT7 1HP
Tel: 028 9077 7338
Fax: 028 90733 0549
Web: www.unite.net

### UTV Internet Ltd
17 Ormeau Road, Belfast, BT7 1EB
Tel: 0845 2470000
Fax: 028 9020 1203
Web: www.utvinternet.com

## Website Hosting and Design

*Note: the above ISPs all offer web site development and design services as do most advertising agencies and some PR agencies. The listing below are companies whose main business is website design.*

### Aurion
Laganside Studios
Ravenhill Business Park
Belfast, BT6 8AW
Tel: 028 9045 5244
Fax: 028 9045 3157
Web: www.aurion.co.uk

### BizNet Solutions
133-137 Lisburn Road
Belfast
BT9 7AG
Tel: 028 9022 3224
Fax: 028 9022 3223
Web: www.biznet-solutions.com

### Memsis
Rose House, Derryvolgie Avenue,
Belfast, BT9 6FL
Tel: 028 9080 6999
Fax: 028 9080 6060
Web: www.memsis.com

### Networks
Russell Court
38-52 Lisburn Road
Belfast, BT9 6AA
Tel: 028 9055 7700
Fax: 028 9024 5741
Web: www.networksforyou.co.uk

### Revelations Internet.com
27 Shaftesbury Square
Belfast, BT2 7DB
Tel: 028 9032 0337
Fax: 028 9032 0432
Web: www.revelations.co.uk

### Sugarcube
Unit 17, The Innovation Centre
NI Science Park, Titanic Quarter
Belfast, BT3 3DT
Tel: 028 9073 7878
Fax: 028 9073 7879
Email: info@sugarcube.biz
Web: www.sugarcube.biz

### Vision Business Solutions
Suite 5, The Innovation Centre
NI Science Park, Queen's Road
Harbour Estate, Belfast, BT3 9DT
Tel: 028 9073 7860
Email: info@visionbusiness.com
Web: www.visionbusiness.com

# Other Media Organisations

### Institute of Public Relations (IPR)
C/o Claire Guiney (Affiliate member)
Public Relations Executive
The PR Agency
721A Lisburn Road
Belfast, BT9 7GU
Tel: 028 9022 2422
Email: claire@thepragency.co.uk

### Northern Ireland Film Commission
Alfred House, 21 Alfred Street,
Belfast, BT2 8ED
Tel: 028 9023 2444
Fax: 028 9023 9918
Web: www.niftc.co.uk

### Northern Ireland Government Affairs Group
Chairman: Glyn Roberts
C/o Northern Ireland Press and Parliamentary Officer
Federation of Small Buiness
20 Adelaide Street
Belfast, BT2 8GB
Tel: 028 9051 7024
Fax: 028 9051 7120

### OFCOM
Landmark House, The Gasworks
Ormeau Road, Belfast, BT7 2JD
Tel: 028 9041 7500
Fax: 028 9041 7533
Web: www.ofcom.org.uk
Director: Denis Wolinski

## Media and Communications Training

Northern Visions
23 Donegall Street Place
Belfast, BT1 2FF
Tel: 028 9024 5495
Fax: 028 9032 6608
Web: www.northernvisions.org

University of Ulster
School of Design and Communication
York Street
Belfast, BT15 1ED
Tel: 028 9032 8515
Fax: 028 9032 1048

University of Ulster
School of Media and Performing Arts
Cromore Road
Coleraine, BT37 0QB
Tel: 028 7032 4196
Fax: 028 7032 4964

Anderson Spratt Group Public Relations
Holywood House, Innis Court
High Street, Holywood, BT18 9HT
Tel: 028 9042 3332
Fax: 028 9042 7730

Macmillan Media
729 Lisburn Road
Belfast, BT9 7GU
Tel: 028 9050 2150
Fax: 028 9050 2151

## Photographic Libraries

Chris Hill Photographic
17 Clarence Street, Belfast, BT2 8DY
Tel: 028 9024 5038
Fax: 028 9023 1942
Web: www.scenicireland.com

Pacemaker Press
787 Lisburn Road, Belfast, BT9 7GX
Tel: 028 9066 3191
Fax: 028 9068 2111
Web: www.pacemakerpressintl.com

Esler Crawford Photography
37A Lisburn Road
Belfast, BT9 7AA
Tel: 028 9032 6999
Fax: 028 9033 1542
Web: www.eslercrawford.com

Roger Kinkead Photo Library
20 Lynden Gate
Portadown, BT63 5YH
Tel: 028 3839 4553

## Conference Venues

The conference market in Northern Ireland is worth an estimated £5-6million per annum equating to an approximate spend of £160 per delegate. Whilst the total UK conference market generates income of £6-7 billion, purpose built conference developments such as the Odyssey complex and the Waterfront Hall enable Northern Ireland to compete with other UK conference destinations, heightening the profile of Belfast and Northern Ireland as an attractive conference centre for international events, and generating greater economic revenue for the city. In fact, the European Society for Cystic Fibrosis Congress, the International Healthy Eater Conference and the International Council for Small Business Congress received more delegates when their events were held in Belfast than they had ever received in the past.

Below is a listing of some of Belfast and Northern Ireland's major conference venues. Almost all the venues listed offer a full range of audio-visual equipment (such as projectors, sound systems) as well as communications links (telephone and fax points, ISDN connection). Many of the larger venues have a dedicated Business Centre with a range of services, such as photocopying, available. For full details of exactly what facilities are offered by each venue, contact the venue directly.

Note: all delegate figures are for theatre style conferences (rows of chairs without tables).

### Belfast

Belfast Castle
Antrim Road
Belfast, BT15 5GR
Tel: 028 9077 6925
Fax: 028 9037 0228
Email: bcr@belfastcastle.co.uk
Contact: Brendan Toland, Manager

Max No of Delegates: 200

Part of the Belfast Castle Parks Group, Belfast Castle is situated 400 feet above sea level, on the slopes of Cavehill. Belfast Castle is located 2.5 miles from the City Centre and is in close proximity to both the province's main air and sea ports.

Belfast Waterfront Hall, Conference & Concert Centre
2 Lanyon Place
Belfast, BT1 3WH
Tel: 028 9033 4400
Fax: 028 9033 4467
Contact: Andrew Kyle, Sales & Marketing Manager

Max No of Delegates: 2,000
(Also many smaller venues within the Hall complex)

Belfast Waterfront Hall is a very large venue and offers all the advantages of a City Centre location. Belfast City Airport is a five-minute taxi ride away and Belfast International Airport about 25 minutes. There is a regular Seacat service between Belfast and Scotland and the Belfast to Dublin express train runs six times a day in both directions. Both the Seacat Terminal and Belfast Central Station are five minutes away.

Dukes Hotel
65-67 University Street
Belfast, BT7 1HL
Tel: 028 9023 6666
Fax: 028 9023 7177
Contact: Christine Cardwell, Reception Manager

Max No of Delegates: 150

A converted Victorian building, Dukes is less that a mile from the centre of Belfast and near to both main airports, sea and rail links.

Europa Hotel
Great Victoria Street, Belfast, BT2 7AP
Tel: 028 9027 1066
Fax: 028 9032 7800

Contact: Rosalyn Goldsborough
Events Manger

Max No of Delegates: 750
(Many smaller rooms also available)

Four-star international hotel situated in the centre of Belfast. Belfast City Airport is five minutes drive away from the Europa, and Belfast International Airport is 16 miles outside the City. The Central Railway Station is located one mile from the Hotel, whilst the Great Victoria Street Railway Station is located next to the Europa. The link road for the

M1 and M2 is half a mile from the Hotel and both the Seacat and Ferry Terminals are five minutes away.

### Express by Holiday Inn

Inex Conference Centre
106A University Street
Belfast, BT7 1HP
Tel: 028 9020 5000
Fax: 028 9020 5001
Contact: Theresa McGuiness, Conference Manager
Max No of Delegates: 120

Three star hotel located 15 minutes from Belfast City Airport, 45 minutes from the International Airport and 10 minutes from the Seacat terminal.

### Fitzwilliam International Hotel

Belfast International Airport
Belfast, BT29 4ZY
Tel: 028 9442 2033
Fax: 028 9442 3500
Contact: Laura Maxwell, Conference & Banqueting Co-ordinator

Max No of Delegates: 590

Three star hotel situated on the Belfast International Airport Complex, 50 metres from the main terminal and 17 miles from Belfast City Centre. The nearest train station is in Antrim (six miles away) and Larne, the nearest port, is 21 miles away.

### Glenavna House Hotel

588 Shore Road
Newtownabbey, BT37 0SN
Tel: 028 9086 4461
Fax: 028 9086 2531

Contact: Lorna McClenaghan, Conference and Banqueting Co-ordinator

Max No of Delegates: 220

Situated just 8 miles from Belfast city centre and easily accessed from airport and ferry terminals.

### Hilton Belfast *****

4 Lanyon Place
Belfast, BT1 3LP
Tel: 028 9027 7000
Fax: 028 9027 7277
Email: hilton.belfast@hilton.com
Web: www.hilton.co.uk/belfast

Hilton Belfast is Belfast City centre's only five star hotel and is located in the stylish Laganside riverfront area adjacent to the Waterfront Hall and close to the Odyssey Arena. 195 guest rooms, including an outstanding selection of suites and corner studios, 3 Executive floors, Executive Club Lounge and LivingWell Health Club with pool on-site. Hilton Belfast is only a short walk from a selection of chic bars, restaurants and the city centre's shopping.

### King's Hall Exhibition & Conference Centre

Balmoral, Belfast, BT9 6GW
Tel: 028 9066 5225
Fax: 028 9066 1264
Web: www.kingshall.co.uk
Contact: Lucy Fraser, Sales & Marketing Manager

Max No of Delegates: 5,500

The King's Hall offers a choice of up to five exhibition halls and an adjoining conference centre with a total of up to 10,000 square metres of space available. The conference centre offers a full range of telecommunications technology and audio-visual equipment.

### Lansdowne Hotel

657 Antrim Road, Belfast, BT15 4EF
Tel: 028 9077 3317
Fax: 028 9078 1588
Contact: Francis McGowan

Max No of Delegates: 280

The Lansdowne Hotel offers a full range of conference facilities for large or small parties. It is within close proximity to Belfast Castle, Fortwilliam Golf Course, Cavehill Country Park and Belfast Zoo, and is only 15 minutes drive from Belfast International Airport.

### Odyssey Arena

Queen's Quay, Belfast, BT3 9QQ
Tel: 028 9076 6000
Fax: 028 9076 6111
Web: www.odysseyarena.com
Email: info@odysseyarena.com
Contact: Lorraine McGoran, Marketing Manager

Max No of Delegates: 8,400
Odyssey Arena offers the potential to host a huge variety of events due to its large floor area, flexible seating configuration and full range of technical facilities. The venue is suitable for large conferences, with up to 8,500 participants, making it a unique venue within Northern Ireland.

### Park Avenue Hotel

158 Holywood Road, Belfast, BT4 1PB
Tel: 028 9065 6520
Fax: 028 9047 1417
Web: www.parkavenuehotel.com
Contact: Angela Reid, Conference Manager

Max No of Delegates: 500

Park Avenue is a family-run hotel, situated in East Belfast within very close proximity to Belfast City Airport, and close to main arterial routes into the city. The hotel offers a full range of conference facilities, along with 250 car parking spaces.

### Holiday Inn Belfast

22 Ormeau Avenue, Belfast, BT2 8HS
Tel: 0870 400 9005
Fax: 028 9062 6546
Web: www.belfast.holiday-inn.com

Max No of Delegates: 120

The Holiday Inn, located right in the centre of Belfast, offers a full range of conference facilities from its Academy Conference Centre. The hotel also has a Spirit Health Club with pool and gym.

Queen's University of Belfast
University Road
Belfast, BT7 1NN
Tel: 028 9033 5005
Fax: 028 9032 1005
Contact: Pauline Banna, Conference Manager

Max No of Delegates: 1,250

Situated in a tree-lined Victorian suburb in the fashionable side of Belfast, this well-established institution is one mile from the City Centre, close to all the mail air, rail and sea links. It offers major conference and residential facilities outside the main University terms. Smaller events can be accommodated all year round.

Radisson SAS
Cromac Place, Cromac Wood
Ormeau Road, Belfast, BT7 2JB
Tel: 028 9043 4065
Fax: 028 9043 4066
Contact: John Crossley
Conference and Banqueting Manager

Max No of Delegates: 150

The Radisson Hotel is within walking distance of Belfast's main commercial and shopping district.

Ramada Hotel
Shaw's Bridge, Belfast, BT8 7XP
Tel: 028 9092 3500
Fax: 028 9092 3600
Web: www.ramadabelfast.com
Contact: Nicola Webster-Hughes, Conference & Banqueting Manager

Max No of Delegates: 900

The Ramada Hotel is situated on the southern outskirts of Belfast and is one of the city's newer conference venues. It offers a full range of conference facilities, with The Grand Ballroom accommodating 900 people theatre style of 700 people banquet style.

Spires Conference & Exhibition Centre
Church House, Wellington Street
Belfast, BT1 6DW
Tel: 028 9032 2284
Fax: 028 9023 6609
Contact: Harry Orr, Building Manager

Max No of Delegates: 1150

Spires Conference & Exhibition Centre, built in 1905, is located in Belfast City Centre and is a suitable venue for both small and large events. Full on-site catering facilities are available.

Stormont Hotel
Upper Newtownards Road
Belfast, BT4 3LP
Tel: 028 9065 1066
Fax: 028 9048 0240
Contact: Joanne Stewart, Events Manager

Max No of Delegates: 500

Stormont Hotel is 4 miles from the City centre. Belfast City Airport is two miles from the Hotel and Belfast International Airport 45 minutes away.

The Wellington Park Hotel
21 Malone Road
Belfast
BT9 6RU
Tel: 028 9038 1111
Fax: 028 9066 5410
Contact: Malachy Toner, Conference and Banqueting Manager

Max No of Delegates: 350

Situated in the university area of South Belfast, Wellington Park is five minutes away from the City Centre.

## Co Antrim

Ballygally Castle Hotel
Coast Road
Ballygally, BT40 2QR
Tel: 028 2858 1066
Fax: 028 2858 3681
Contact: Stephen Meldrum

Max No of Delegates: 200

Three-star hotel situated 20 miles from Belfast on the Antrim coast road. Ballygally Castle Hotel is also situated 4 miles from Larne, which is serviced by both Northern Ireland Rail and ferry services from Cairnryan in Scotland. The hotel is 30 minutes drive from Belfast City Airport and is 25 minutes from Belfast International Airport.

Bushmills Inn
9 Dunluce Road, Bushmills, BT57 8QG
Tel: 028 2073 2339
Fax: 028 2073 2048
Web: www.bushmillsinn.com

Max No of Delegates: 40

Dunadry Hotel & Country Club
2 Islandreagh Drive
Dunadry, BT41 2HA
Tel: 028 9443 4343
Fax: 028 9443 389
Contact: Sheree Davis, Business Development Co-ordinator

Max No of Delegates: 400

Just a short 15 minute drive form Belfast City Centre, 18 miles from Belfast International Airport and 11 miles from Belfast City Airport, the hotel is easily accessible from all major transportation links.

Galgorm Manor
136 Fenaghy Road
Ballymena, BT42 1EA
Tel: 028 2588 1001
Fax: 028 2588 0080
Contact: Wendy Dickey, Events Organiser

Max No of Delegates: 500

Galgorm Manor offers a full range of conference and meeting facilities in a tranquil setting. Larger events can be held in The Great Hall, which is located within the grounds of the hotel.

Hilton Templepatrick****

Hilton
Templepatrick
Hotel & Country Club

Hilton Templepatrick
Castle Upton Estate
Templepatrick, BT39 0DD
Tel: 028 9443 5500
Fax: 028 9443 5511
Email: hilton.templepatrick@hilton.com
Web: www.hilton.co.uk/templepatrick

Hilton Templepatrick Hotel and Country Club four star hotel is located in the magnificent Castle Upton Estate. Situated only five minutes from Belfast International Airport and twenty minutes from the city centre. With 129 bedrooms featuring wonderful views, the best of local international cuisine and a host of leisure and conference facilities, Hilton Templepatrick Hotel and Country club is one of the most prestigious hotels in Northern Ireland.

Rosspark Hotel
20 Doagh Road
Kells, Ballymena, BT42 3LZ
Tel: 028 2589 1663
Fax: 028 2589 1477
Email: info@rosspark.com
Contact: Carol Sloan, Conference Manager

Max No of Delegates: 250

The Ross Park Hotel is situated 5 miles from Ballymena town, 21 miles from Belfast and 16 miles from Belfast International Airport. Centrally located in the heart of Co Antrim, the province's major ports are also within easy reach.

## Co Armagh

Armagh City Hotel
2 Friary Road, Armagh, BT60 2FR
Tel: 028 3751 8888
Fax: 028 3751 2777

Contact: Gary Hynes, Conference & Banqueting Manager

Max No of Delegates: 1,200

Armagh City Hotel is one of Northern Ireland's newest, and largest, conference venues and offers a full range of conference and banqueting facilities, with its Fisher Suite capable of accommodating 1200 delegates. Full range of audio-visual equipment is available.

Carngrove Hotel
2 Charlestown Road
Portadown, BT63 5PW
Tel: 028 3833 9222
Fax: 028 3833 2899
Contact: Bridget Currie, General Manager

Max No of Delegates: 300

Located on the outskirts of Portadown town, the two-star Carngrove Hotel is close to all local rail and motorway links, half an hour from Belfast City Airport and only 20 minutes from Belfast International Airport.

Craigavon Civic Centre
PO Box 66, Lakeview Road,
Craigavon, BT64 1AL
Tel: 028 3831 2400
Contact: Ian Bann, Facilities Manager

Max No of Delegates: 600

Market Place Theatre & Arts Centre
Market Street, Armagh, BT61 7AT

Contact: Sharon Kerr/Vincent McCann

Max No of Delegates: 397

Seagoe Hotel
Upper Church Lane
Portadown, BT63 5JE
Tel: 028 3833 3076
Fax: 028 3835 0210
Contact: Andrea Barron, Banqueting Coordinator

Max No of Delegates: 600

A three star hotel on the outskirts of Portadown. The hotel is 40 minutes from Belfast International Airport and 5 minutes from Portadown train station, which is on the main Belfast to Dublin line.

## Co Down

Canal Court Hotel
Merchant's Quay
Newry, BT35 8FC
Tel: 028 3025 1234
Contact: Aibhin Rush, Conference & Banqueting Manager

Max No of Delegates: 300

Clandeboye Lodge Hotel
10 Estate Road
Bangor, BT19 1UR
Tel: 028 9185 2500
Contact: Donna Wilson, Conference & Banqueting Co-ordinator

Max No of Delegates: 350

Culloden Hotel
Holywood, BT18 0EX
Tel: 028 9042 1066
Fax: 028 9042 6777
Contact: Allyson Hastings
Event Co-ordinator

Max No of Delegates: 500

Northern Ireland's first five-star hotel is situated in 12 acres of private parkland on the North Down coast. The Culloden is 6 miles from Belfast City centre where transport links to Belfast City Airport takes only 10 minutes (taxi) and rail links between Cultra and Belfast Central Station are a two minute walk from the hotel. The Culloden is 18 miles away from Belfast International Airport.

Marine Court Hotel
The Marina
Bangor, BT20 5ED
Tel: 028 9145 1100
Fax: 028 9145 1200
Contact: Martha Knapp

Max No of Delegates: 450

The three-star Marine Court Hotel, situated on Bangor's marina, is only 12 miles from Belfast City Centre.

Mourne Country Hotel
52 Belfast Road
Newry, BT34 1TR
Tel: 028 3026 7922
Contact: Donna Quail, Conference & Banqueting Manager

Max No of Delegates: 450

Old Inn
15 Main Street
Crawfordsburn, BT19 1JH
Tel: 028 9185 3255
Contact: Jill Graham, Conference & Events Manager

Max No of Delegates: 120

Slieve Donard Hotel
Newcastle
Co Down, BT33 0AH
Tel: 028 4372 1066
Fax: 028 4372 4830
Contact: Nora Hannah, Business Manager

Max No of Delegates: 1,000

The four-star Slieve Donard hotel is set in six-acres of Private Grounds. Newcastle is 30 miles from Belfast and approximately 85 miles from Dublin. A bus service, run by Europa Bus Centre, connects Newcastle and Belfast, with Belfast City Airport only a ten-minute drive away.

## Co Fermanagh

Hotel Carlton
2 Main Street, Belleek, BT93 3FX
Tel: 028 6865 8282
Fax: 028 6865 9005
Contact: Brian Hill, Conference & Banqueting Manager

Max No of Delegates: 120

Killyhevlin Hotel
Dublin Road
Enniskillen, BT74 76RW
Tel: 028 6632 3481
Fax: 028 6632 4726
Web: www.killyhevlin.com
Contact: David Morrison

Max No of Delegates: 300

Situated on the outskirts of Enniskillen, on the shores of Lough Erne, this four-star hotel is a two hour drive from Belfast International Airport.

Lusty Beg Island
Boa Island, Kesh, BT94 1NY
Tel: 028 6863 3300
Fax: 028 6863 2003
Web: www.lustybegisland.com
Contact: Arthur Cadden, General Manager

Max No of Delegates: 300

This unique venue is situated on an island in Lough Erne and is accessible by boat.

Manor House Country Hotel
Killadeas
Irvinestown, BT94 1NY
Tel: 028 6862 2200
Fax: 028 6862 1545
Contact: Sinead Stewart, Conferences Manager

Max No of Delegates: 400

Situated on the shores of Lower Lough Erne, four-star Manor House is a two hour drive from Belfast International Airport.

## Co Londonderry

Beech Hill Country House Hotel
32 Ardmore Road
Londonderry, BT47 3QP
Tel: 028 7134 9279
Contact: Crawford McIlwaine, General Manager

Max No of Delegates: 100

City Hotel
14-18 Quay's Quay
Derry, BT48 7AS
Tel: 028 7136 5800
Contact: Collette Brennan, Conference & Banqueting Manager

Max No of Delegates: 350

Everglades Hotel
Prehen Road
Derry, BT47 2NH
Tel: 028 7132 1066
Fax: 028 7134 9200
Contact: Hugh O'Doherty, Conference & Banqueting Manager

Max No of Delegates: 400

The four-star Everglades Hotel is situated in the Southern outskirts of Derry on the banks of the river Foyle.

Inn At The Cross
171 Glenshane Road
Derry, BT47 3EN
Tel: 028 7130 1480
Fax: 028 7130 1394
Contacts: Muriel or Ivan Millar, Hotel Proprietors.

Max No of Delegates: 300

Situated on the main Derry-Belfast Road (A6) in a country setting, the Inn at the Cross is approximately 3 miles from Derry City Centre.

Lodge Hotel & Travelstop
Lodge Road
Coleraine, BT52 1NF
Tel: 028 7034 4848
Fax: 028 7035 4555
Contact: Norma Wilkinson, General Manager

Max No of Delegates: 350

Millennium Forum
Newmarket Street
Londonderry, BT48 6EB
Tel: 028 7126 4426

Max No of Delegates: 1020

Radisson Roe Park
Roe Park
Limavady
Co Londonderry, BT49 9LB
Tel: 028 7772 2222
Fax: 028 7772 2313
Contact: Simone Martin, Event Co-ordinator

Max No of Delegates: 450

4-star hotel with outstanding conference facilities. Situated on the A2 Derry-Limavady Road, the venue is 16 miles from the City of Derry Airport and 45 miles from Belfast International Airport.

Tower Hotel
Butcher Street, Derry, BT48 6HL
Tel: 028 7137 1000
Fax: 028 7137 7123
Contact: Ian Hyland, General Manager

Max No of Delegates: 250

White Horse Hotel
68 Clooney Road
Londonderry, BT47 3PA
Tel: 028 7186 0606
Contact: Ruth Taylor, Conference & Banqueting Manager

Max No of Delegates: 450

## Co Tyrone

Fir Trees Hotel
Dublin Road, Strabane, BT82 9EA
Tel: 028 7138 2382
Contact: Christine O'Neill, Conference and Banqueting Manager

Max No of Delegates: 250

Glenavon House Hotel
52 Drum Road, Cookstown, BT80 8JQ
Tel: 028 8676 4949
Fax: 028 8676 4396
Contact: Paula Wilson, Director

Max No of Delegates: 400

Three-star Glenavon House is located just 30 miles from Belfast International Airport, set in 9 acres of mature grounds on the banks of the Ballinderry River.

Greenvale Hotel
57 Drum Road, Cookstown, BT80 8GS
Tel: 028 8676 2243
Contact: Paul Kelly, Conference and Banqueting Manager

Max No of Delegates: 280

Silver Birch Hotel
5 Gortin Road, Omagh, BT79 7DH
Tel: 028 8224 2520
Fax: 028 8224 9061
Contact: Louise McGeough, Receptionist

Max No of Delegates: 230

Situated on the outskirts of Omagh, the Silver Birch Hotel is on the B48 Gorton Road, one and a half hour's drive from both Belfast City and Belfast International Airports.

# Chapter 10

## Representative Groups and Associations

## Introduction

Northern Ireland has a vast number of representative groups and associations, large and small, commercial and not-for-profit, covering a wide spectrum of the economic and social life of its people. The main groups are listed A–Z below under appropriate categories. These listings have been extensively researched but they are by no means exhaustive.

Some organisations may fall into more than one categorisation due to the breadth of their activities.

## Business, Trade Associations and Representative Groups

Allied Trades Confederation Ltd.
Unit 16 Lisburn Enterprise Centre
Lisburn, BT28 2BP
Tel: 028 9263 4623
Contact: Margaret Martin

Anglo North Irish Fish Producers Organisation Limited
The Harbour, Kilkeel, BT34 4AX
Tel: 028 4176 2855
Fax: 028 4176 4904
Chief Executive: Alan McCulla

Armagh City Centre Management
The Palace Demesne
Armagh, BT60 4EL
Tel: 028 3752 9600
Fax: 028 3752 9601
Contact: Dawn Park

Arts and Business
53 Malone Road, Belfast, BT9 6RY
Tel: 028 9066 4736
Fax: 028 9066 4500
Director: Alice O'Rawe

Association of Consulting Engineers
c/o Taylor and Fegan, Riversedge
11 Ravenhill Road, Belfast, BT6 8DN
Tel: 028 9045 4401
Fax: 028 9045 8400
Secretary: Bill Taylor

Association of Northern Ireland Colleges
Unit 3, The Sidings Business Park
Antrim Road, Lisburn, BT28 3AJ
Tel: 028 9262 7512
Fax: 028 9262 7594
Web: www.anic.ac.uk
Chief Executive: John D'Arcy

Association for Residential Care
43 Marsden Gardens, Cavehill Road
Belfast, BT15 5FL
Tel: 028 9022 9020
Fax: 028 9020 9300
Manager: Siobhan Bogues

Bar Library
Royal Courts of Justice
91 Chichester Street, Belfast, BT1 3JQ
Tel: 028 9024 1523
Web: www.barlibrary.com
Chief Executive: Brendan Garland

Belfast City Centre Management Co.

Belfast City Centre Management

Second Floor, Sinclair House
95/101 Royal Avenue
Belfast, BT1 1FE
Tel: 028 9024 2111
Fax: 028 9023 0809
Email: info@belfastcentre.com
Web: www.belfastcentre.com

City Centre Manager
Joanne Jennings

BCCM was set up in January 2000 as a Company Limited by Guarantee, jointly core funded by BCC and BRO to provide a bridge between central and local government and the private sector, and to promote a cleaner, safer, more attractive and more accessible city centre.

British Association of Social Workers BASW (NI)
216 Belmont Road, Belfast, BT4 2AT
Tel: 028 9067 2247
Fax: 028 9065 6273
Web: www.basw.co.uk
Professional Officer:
Eileen Ashenhurst

British Council
2nd Floor, Norwich Union House
7 Fountain Street, Belfast, BT1 5EG
Tel: 028 9024 8220
Fax: 028 9023 7592
Web: www.britishcouncil.org
Director: Colm McGivern

British Dental Association
The Mount, 2 Woodstock Link
Belfast, BT6 8DD
Tel: 028 9073 5856
Contact: Dr Claudett Christie

British Medical Association
16 Cromac Place, Ormeau Road
Belfast, BT7 2JB
Tel: 028 9026 9666
Regional Service Co-ordinator:
Avril Campbell

### Chambers of Commerce

Chambers of Commerce represent the business community in Northern Ireland at a local level and are active in dealing with local issues which have implications for the commercial life of a locality. The Northern Ireland Chamber of Commerce and Industry and the regional Chamber of Commerce network currently represents more than 4000 businesses in Northern Ireland.

Members are drawn from every sector of the business community including senior management from major industrial sites, smaller scale retailers and service providers. As well as being an authentic voice for local business and undertaking the representational work, which that entails, local Chambers of Commerce are very active in charitable work in their respective areas

The Northern Ireland Chamber of Commerce and Industry
Chamber of Commerce House
22 Great Victoria Street
Belfast, BT2 7BJ
Tel: 028 9024 4113
Fax: 028 9024 7024
Web: www.northernirelandchamber.com
President: Lord Rana MBE

Antrim Borough Chamber of Commerce
c/o Unit 33b, Antrim Enterprise Agency
58 Greystone Road, Antrim, BT41 1JZ
Tel: 028 9446 7774
Fax: 028 9446 7292
Contact: Mr Douglas Stoddard

Armagh Chamber of Commerce
43 Thomas Street
Armagh City, BT61 7QD
Tel: 028 3752 3163
Fax: 028 3741 5111
Contact: Mr Godfrey Abbott

**Ballymena Chamber of Commerce**
c/o Michelin Tyre PLC
190 Raceview Road
Ballymena, BT42 4HZ
Tel: 028 2566 3657
Fax: 028 2566 3628
Contact: Mr Philip Brunt

**Ballymoney Chamber of Commerce**
c/o JF & H Dowds
2 Milltown Road, Ballymoney, BT53 6LE
Tel: 028 2766 2789
Fax: 028 2766 5905
Contact: Mr Johnny Dowds

**Bangor Chamber of Commerce**
c/o 65B Main Street
Bangor, BT20 5AF
Tel: 028 9146 0035
Fax: 028 9146 0035
Contact: Mr Evan Ward

**Belfast Chamber of Trade & Commerce**
Sinclair House, 95-101 Royal Avenue
Belfast, BT1 1FE
Tel: 028 9024 2111
Fax: 028 9023 0809
Web: www.belfastcentre.com
President: Mr Gerald Steinberg

**Belleek Chamber of Commerce**
Main Street, Belleek, BT93 3FX
Tel: 028 6865 8942
Contact: Mr Peter Clarke

**Carrickfergus Chamber of Commerce**
c/o Wadsworth Estate
Tower House, 33-35 High Street
Carrickfergus, BT38 7AN
Tel: 028 9336 0707
Fax: 028 9336 7368
Contact: Mr Peter Wadsworth

**Castlederg Chamber of Commerce**
c/o 11-12 The Diamond
Castlederg, BT81 7AR
Tel: 028 8167 1974
Fax: 028 8167 1974
Contact: Mr Gordon Speer

**Coleraine Borough Chamber of Commerce & Industry**
c/o 2 Abbey Street
Coleraine, BT52 1DS
Tel: 028 7034 4067
Fax: 028 7032 1416
Contact: Mr Chris McLean

**Cookstown Chamber of Commerce**
12 Lissan Road, Cookstown, BT80 8EN
Contact: Mr Raymond McGarvey

**Dromore Chamber of Commerce**
21 Princes Street, Dromore, BT25 1AY
Tel: 028 9269 9628
Contact: Ms Janice McCrudden

**Enniskillen Chamber of Commerce**
c/o Old Gate Lodge
Drumawill, Enniskillen, BT74 5QN
Tel: 028 6632 4595
Contact: Mrs Jennifer McCrea

**Fivemiletown Chamber of Commerce**
Four Ways Hotel, 41 Main Street
Fivemiletown, BT75 0PG
Tel: 028 8952 1260
Contact: Mr Eric Armstrong

**Holywood Chamber of Trade & Commerce**
c/o 44 Ballyholme Road
Bangor, BT20 5JS
Tel: 028 9146 0901
Contact: Mr Neil Kirkpatrick

**Kilkeel Chamber of Commerce**
c/o Special Occasions
8 Bridge Street, Kilkeel, BT34 4AD
Contact: Ms Mary Tremlett

**Lisburn Chamber of Commerce**
3A Bridge Street, Lisburn, BT28 1XZ
Tel: 028 9266 6297
Contact: Ms Ellen Hillen

**Lisnaskea Chamber of Commerce**
c/o Cedar Gables
Killynamph Road, Lisnaskea, BT92 0EE
Tel: 028 6772 1571
Contact: Mr Glen Charles

**Londonderry Chamber of Commerce**
1 St. Columb's Court
Bishop Street, Londonderry, BT48 6PL
Tel: 028 7126 2379
Fax: 028 7128 6789
Contact: Mr Richard Stirling OBE

**Magherafelt Chamber of Commerce**
c/o Meadow Lane Shopping Centre
Magherafelt
Tel: 028 7963 4081
Contact: Mr Paul Beacom

**Newcastle Chamber of Commerce**
c/o 51 Main Street
Newcastle, BT33 0AD
Tel: 028 4372 4903
Fax: 028 4372 4263
Contact: Mr Peter Law

**Newry Chamber of Commerce**
74 Hill Street, Newry, BT34 1BE
Tel: 028 3025 0303
Contact: Mr Peter Murray

**Omagh Chamber of Commerce**
c/o 2nd Floor, 33 Market Street
Omagh, BT78 1EE
Tel: 028 8225 9595
Contact: Mr Oliver Gormley

**Portadown Chamber of Commerce**
c/o High Street Mall
High Street, Portadown, BT62 1HX
Tel: 028 3836 2251
Contact: Ms Tracey Jackson

**Portrush Chamber of Commerce**
c/o 110 Dunluce Road
Portrush, BT56 8NB
Tel: 028 7082 2783
Fax: 028 7082 4524
Contact: Mr David Alexander

**Portstewart Chamber of Commerce**
c/o 17 Ballyleese Park
Portstewart, BT55 7QA
Tel: 028 7083 2960
Contact: Mr Peter Bayliss

**Roe Valley Chamber of Trade & Commerce**
c/o 29 Bell's Hill, Limavady, BT49 0DQ
Tel: 028 7776 2307
Contact: Mr Cyril Roulston

**Strabane Chamber of Commerce**
c/o Fir Trees Hotel
Dublin Road, Strabane, BT82 9EA
Tel: 028 7138 2382
Contact: Mr John Kelly

**Carrickfergus Gasworks Preservation Society**
44 Irish Quarter West
Carrickfergus, BT38 8AT
Tel: 028 90336 9575
Contact: Samuel Gault

**CBI (Confederation of British Industry)**
Scottish Amicable Building
11 Donegall Square South
Belfast, BT1 5JE
Tel: 028 9032 6658
Web: www.cbi.org.uk
Chairman: David Dobbin
Vice Chairman: Dr Ian McMorris
Director: Nigel Smyth

**CBI / IBEC Joint Business Council**
Also based at the address above and at the offices of the CBI counterpart in the Republic of Ireland, IBEC.
Contact: William Poole, Business Development Director

**Centre for Competitiveness**
The Innovation Centre, NI Science Park
Queen's Road, Belfast, BT3 9DT
Tel: 028 9073 7950
Web: www.cforc.org
Chief Executive: Bob Barbour

# Chapter 10: Representative Groups and Associations

### Chartered Institute of Marketing
The Mount Business Park
2 Woodstock Link, Belfast, BT6 8DD
Tel: 028 9073 5898
Regional Director: Mike Maguire

### Construction Employers Federation
143 Malone Road, Belfast, BT9 6SU
Tel: 028 9087 7143
Web: www.cefni.co.uk
Managing Director: Mr W A Doran

### Coal Advisory Service (NI)
Unit 18a Lowes Industrial Estate
31 Hillsborough Road, Carryduff
Belfast, BT8 8EH
Tel: 0845 7125300

### Construction Industry Training Board
Nutts Corner Training Centre
17 Dundrod Road, Crumlin, BT29 4SR
Tel: 028 9082 5466
Chief Executive: Allan McMullen

### Dairy UK (NI)
8 Ranfurly Avenue, Bangor, BT20 3SN
Tel: 028 9147 1300
Contact: Paul Archer

### East Belfast Traders Association
Unit 1a, 321 Beersbridge Road
Belfast, BT5 5DS
Tel: 028 9022 6464

### Electrical Contractors Association
25 Prospect Park, Bangor
Tel: 028 9147 9527
Web: www.eca.co.uk

### Engineering Employers Federation
2 Greenwood Avenue, Belfast, BT4 3JL
Tel: 028 9059 5050
Web: www.eef.org.uk
Director: Peter Bloch

### Federation of Master Builders
42a–44a New Row
Coleraine, BT52 1AF
Tel: 028 7034 0999
Web: www.fmb.org.uk
Administrator: Jim Morrison

### Federation for Ulster Local Studies
18 May Street, Belfast, BT1 4NL
Tel: 028 9023 5254
Fax: 028 9043 4086
Contact: Roddy Hegarty

### Federation of Small Businesses
20 Adelaide Street, Belfast, BT2 8GB
Tel: 028 9051 7024
Web: www.nireland.policy@fsb.org.uk
NI Press Officer: Glyn Roberts
Chairman: John Friel

### Federation of the Retail Licensed Trade
91 University Street, Belfast, BT7 1HP
Tel: 028 9032 7578
Web: www.ulsterpubs.com
Chief Executive: Nicola Jamison

The Federation represents around 1,100 pubs, hotels and restaurants in Northern Ireland.

### Freight Transport Association Ltd
109 Airport Road West
Belfast, BT3 9ED
Tel: 028 9046 6699
Web: www.fta.co.uk
Manager: Tom Wilson

### Institute of Directors
4 Royal Avenue, Belfast, BT1 1DA
Tel: 028 9023 2880
Web: www.iod.com
Chairman: Denis Rooney
Divisional Director: Linda Brown

### Institute of Export (NI Branch)
Contact: Robert Hamilton
Email: rhamilton@btclick.com

### Irish CHP Association (ICHPA)
c/o bmf Business Services, TSL House,
38 Bachelors Walk, Lisburn, BT28 1XN
Tel: 028 9262 8787
Fax: 028 9262 8789
Web: www.ichpa.ie

### Irish Linen Guild
Riverside Factory, Victoria Street,
Lurgan, BT67 9DU
Tel: 028 9268 9999
Web: www.irishlinen.co.uk
Contact: Andrew Lowden

### Lisburn City Centre Management
3A Bridge Street, Lisburn, BT28 1XZ
Tel: 028 9266 0625
Web: www.lisburnccm.co.uk
Centre Manager: Alan Jeffers

### Livestock & Meat Commission for Northern Ireland
Lissue House, 31 Ballinderry Road
Lisburn, BT28 2SL
Tel: 028 9263 3000
Web: www.lmcni.com
Chief Executive: David Rutledge

### Momentum
*(Formerly Northern Ireland Software Federation)*
Ni-Soft House, Ravenhill Business Park
Ravenhill Road, Belfast, BT6 8AW
Tel: 028 9045 0101
Contact: Ruth Walmsley

### National Farmers' Union
72 High Street
Newtownards, BT23 7HZ
Tel: 028 9181 4218
Group Secretary: Jane Lyness

### National Federation of Retail Newsagents
Yeoman House, 11 Sekforde Street
London, EC1R 0HF
Tel: 020 7253 4225

### National House Building Council
59 Malone Road, Belfast, BT9 6SA
Tel: 028 9068 3131
Regional Director: Tom Kirk

### Newry City Centre Management
O'Hagan House, Monaghan Row
Newry, BT35 8DJ
Tel: 028 3031 3031

### North Belfast Traders Association
Unit 3, North City Business Centre
Duncairn Gardens, Belfast, BT15 2GF

### Northern Ireland Aerospace Consortium
Northern Ireland Technology Centre
Cloreen Park, Malone Road
Belfast, BT9 5HN
Tel: 028 9027 4505
Chairperson: Dr Paul Madden

### Northern Ireland Agricultural Producers' Association
15 Molesworth Street
Cookstown, BT80 8NX
Tel: 028 8676 5700
Chairman: Alex Scullon

### Northern Ireland Bankers' Association
Stokes House
17–25 College Square East
Belfast, BT1 6DE
Tel: 028 9032 7551
Contact: Bill McAlister

### Northern Ireland Chamber of Trade
PO Box 444, Belfast, BT1 1DY
Tel: 028 9023 0444
Director: Joan Roberts

### Northern Ireland Childminding Association
16–18 Mill St, Newtownards, BT23 4LU
Tel: 028 9181 1015
Web: www.nicma.org
Director: Bridget Nodder

### Northern Ireland Council for Ethnic Minorities
Ascot House
24–31 Shaftesbury Square
Belfast, BT2 7DB
Tel: 028 9023 8645
Contact: Patrick Yu

### Northern Ireland Dyslexia Association
17a Upper Newtownards Road
Belfast, BT4 3HT
Tel: 028 9066 0111
Chairman: John Clarke

### Northern Ireland Fish Producers' Organisation
1 Coastguard Cottages, Harbour Road
Portavogie, Newtownards, BT22 1EA
Tel: 028 4277 1946
Email: nifpo@aol.com
Chief Executive: Richard James

### Northern Ireland Food & Drink Association
Quay Gate House, 15 Scrabo Street
Belfast, BT5 4BD
Tel: 028 9045 2424
Web: www.nifda.co.uk
Director: Michael Bell

### Northern Ireland Grain Trade Association (NIGTA)
Cuinne an Chaireil, 27 Berwick View
Moira, BT67 0SX
Tel: 028 9261 1044
Email: doris@leemanpr.demon.co.uk
Contact: Doris Leeman

### Northern Ireland Heritage Gardens Committee
PO Box 252, Belfast, BT9 6GY
Tel: 028 9066 8817
Contact: Belinda Jupp

### Northern Ireland Hotels Federation
Midland Building, Whitla Street
Belfast, BT15 1JP
Tel: 028 9035 1110
Chief Executive: Janice Gault

### NI Local Government Association (NILGA)
Philip House, 123 York Street
Belfast, BT15 1AB
Tel: 028 9024 9286
Chief Executive: Heather Moorhead

### Northern Ireland Master Butchers' Association
38 Oldstone Hill
Muckamore, BT41 4SB
Tel: 028 9446 5180
Secretary: Mr H Marquess

### Northern Ireland Master Plumbers' Association
c/o Mr W Crawford,
Crawford Sedgwick & Co,
38 Hill Street, Belfast, BT1 2LB
Tel: 028 9032 1731
Secretary: William Crawford

### Northern Ireland Meat Exporters Association
24 Ballydown Road
Banbridge, BT32 3RP
Tel: 028 4062 6338
Chief Executive: Cecil Mathers

### Northern Ireland Museums Council
6 Crescent Gardens, Belfast, BT7 1NS
Tel: 028 9055 0215
Director: Chris Bailey

### Northern Ireland Optometric Society
PO Box 28. Dromore, BT25 1VH
Tel: 028 9269 8077
Secretary: Liz Gillespie

### Northern Ireland Seafood Association
Quay Gate House, 15 Scrabo St
Belfast, BT5 4BD
Tel: 028 9045 2829
Web: www.niseafood.co.uk
Chief Executive: Dennis Law

### Northern Ireland Textile & Apparel Association
Riverside Factory
Victoria Street, Lurgan, BT67 9DU
Tel: 028 9268 9999
Contact: Andrew Lowden
Web: www.nita.co.uk

### Northern Ireland Timber Trade Association
13 Churchhill Drive
Carrickfergus, BT38 7LH
Tel: 028 9336 2784
Secretary: Mr T G Rankin

### Pharmaceutical Society
73 University Street, Belfast, BT7 1HL
Tel: 028 9032 6927
Chief Executive: Sheila Maltby

### Professional Craftsmen Association
14 Northland Row
Dungannon, BT71 6AP
Tel: 028 8772 5377
Chairman: Paul Devlin

### Retail Motor Industry Federation
107A Shore Road, Belfast, BT15 3BB
Tel: 028 9037 0137
Regional Manager: Noel Smyth

### Royal Life Saving Society
Trinity House, Lisburn, BT28 2YY
Tel: 028 9260 6969
Web: www.rlssdirect.co.uk

### Social Economy Agency
45–47 Donegall Street
Belfast, BT1 2FG
Tel: 028 9096 1115
Regional Manager: Eamonn Donnelly

### Ulster Archaeological Society
c/o Dept of Archaeology
Queen's University, Belfast, BT7 1NN
Tel: 028 9027 3186
Contact: John O'Neil

### Ulster Chemists' Association
73 University Street, Belfast, BT7 1HL
Tel: 028 9032 0787
President: Paula McDaid

### Ulster Farmers' Union
475 Antrim Road, Belfast, BT15 3DA
Tel: 028 9037 0222
Chief Executive: Clarke Black
President: John Gilliland OBE

### Ulster Launderers' Association
c/o Lilliput, The Cutts
Dunmurray, BT17 9HU
Tel: 028 9061 8555
Secretary: Geoff Woods

### Ulster GAA Writers Association
20 Stewartstown Park
Belfast, BT11 9GL
Tel: 028 9060 0833
Web: www.ulstergaawriters.com
Treasurer: Tony McGee

### YMCA National Council
Memorial House, Waring Street
Belfast, BT1 2EU
Tel: 028 9032 7757
Chief Executive: Stephen Turner

## Professional Institutes and Associations

### Architects Registration Board

8 Weymouth Street,
London, W1W 5BU
Tel: 020 7580 5861
Fax: 020 7436 5269
Web: www.arb.org.uk
Chief Executive: Robin Vaughan

### Association of Belfast Doctors on Call

The Old Casualty, 64 Crumlin Road
Belfast, BT14 6AG
Tel: 028 9074 4447
Fax: 028 9074 9999
Manager: Kerry Cavanan

### Association of Chartered Certified Accountants (ACCA)

29 Lincoln's Inn Fields
London, WC2A 3EE
Tel: 020 7396 7000
Fax: 020 7396 7070
Email: info@accaglobal.com
Chief Executive: Allen Blewitt

### Association of Consulting Engineers (NI Branch)

c/o Taylor and Fagan, Riveredge
11 Ravenhill Road, Belfast, BT6 8DN
Tel: 028 9045 4401
Fax: 028 9045 8400
Secretary: Bill Taylor

### Association of Southern Area Doctors on Call

Legahory Green, Craigavon, BT65 5BE
Tel: 028 8778 9713

### British Dental Association

The Mount, 2 Woodstock Link
Belfast, BT6 8DD
Tel: 028 9073 5856
Fax: 028 9073 5857
Contact: Dr Claudett Christie

### British Medical Association

16 Cromac Place, Cromac Wood,
Ormeau Road, Belfast, BT7 2JB
Tel: 028 9026 9666
Fax: 028 9026 9665
Email: info.belfast@bma.org.uk
Regional Service Co-ordinator:
Avril Campbell

### Chartered Institute of Building

PO Box 1268, Bangor, BT20 5DY
Tel: 028 9147 9883
Fax: 028 9147 9884
Contact: Trevor Patterson

### Chartered Institution of Building Surveyors

c/o The Caldwell Partnership
8 Lorne Street, Belfast, BT9 7DU
Tel: 028 9066 9456
Fax: 028 9066 2219
Honorary Secretary: Mark Taylor

### Chartered Institute of Housing

Carnmoney House
Edgewater Office Park
Belfast, BT3 9JQ
Tel: 028 9077 8222
Fax: 028 9077 8333
Email: ni@cih.org
Chief Executive: David Butler

### Chartered Institute of Management Accountants (CIMA)

26 Chapter Street
London SW1P 4NP
Tel: 020 7663 5441
Web: www.cimaglobal.com
Tel: 020 7663 5441

### Chartered Institute of Marketing

The Mount Business Centre
2 Woodstock Link, Belfast, BT6 8DD
Tel: 028 9073 5898
Fax: 028 9073 0199
Regional Director: Mike Maguire

### Chartered Institute of Personnel and Development

Weavers Court Business Park
Linfield Road, Belfast, BT12 5LA
Tel: 028 9051 7046
Web: www.cipd.co.uk
Vice Chairperson: Lynne Stephenson

### Chartered Institute of Public Finance and Accountancy

2nd Floor, Scottish Amicable Building
11 Donegal Square South
Belfast, BT1 5JE
Tel: 028 9026 6770
Fax: 028 9026 6771
Contact: David Nicholl

The Accountancy Institute, which represents in the main professional accountants operating in the public sector.

### Chartered Institute of Purchasing and Supply

Easton House, Easton on the Hill,
Stamford, Lincolnshire, PE9 3NZ
Tel: 01780 756 777
Contact: Sarah Lewithwaite

### Chartered Society of Physiotherapy (CSP)

Merrion Business Centre
58 Howard Street, Belfast, BT1 6PJ

### Chief Executives' Forum

Lancashire House, 5 Linenhall St
Belfast, BT2 8AA
Tel: 028 9054 2966
Fax: 028 9054 2970
Web: www.ceforum.org
Director: Alvin McKinley

The Chief Executives' Forum is the association of chief executive officers of public bodies in Northern Ireland. The Forum aims to support the democratic process by promoting excellence in public service and encourage innovation and development of leadership.

### The General Council of the Bar in Northern Ireland

Royal Courts of Justice, 91 Chichester Street, Belfast, BT1 3JP
Tel: 028 9056 2349
Fax: 028 9056 2350
Chief Executive: Brendan Garland

The Bar Council is responsible for the maintenance of the standards, honour and independence of the bar, and through its Professional Conduct Committee, receives and investigates any complaints against members of the Bar in their professional capacity.

### The Institute of Chartered Accountants in Ireland

11 Donegall Square South
Belfast, BT1 5JE
Tel: 028 9032 1600
Fax: 028 9023 0071
Director: Heather Briars

### Institution of Chemical Engineers

Irish Branch: Northern Section
School of Chemical Engineering
Queens University Belfast
Tel: 028 9027 4255
Fax: 028 90281753
Contact: Prof. Ronnie Magee

### Institution of Civil Engineers

c/o Construction Employers Federation
143 Malone Road, Belfast, BT9 6SU
Tel: 028 9087 7157
Fax: 028 9087 7155
Regional Secretary: Wendy Blundell

### The Law Society of Northern Ireland

Law Society House
98 Victoria Street
Belfast, BT1 3JZ
Tel: 028 9023 1614
Fax: 028 9023 2606
Web: www.lawsoc-ni.org

In 1922 a Royal Charter was granted to solicitors in Northern Ireland to permit the setting up of the Incorporated Law Society of Northern Ireland. Under the Solicitors (Northern Ireland) Order of 1976, the Law Society acts as the regulatory authority governing the education, accounts, discipline and professional conduct of solicitors in order to maintain the independence, ethical standards, professional competence and quality of services offered to the public.

The Society operates through an elected Council which is served by numerous Standing and Special Committees, all comprising practising solicitors. It takes an active interest in all issues connected with law and order and the administration of justice.

### Institution of Electrical Engineers IEE

Michael Faraday House, 6 Hills Way
Stevenage, SG1 2AY
Tel: 028 4461 6051
Web: www.iee.org
Regional Development Manager - Ireland: Patrick Gorman

### Institute of Financial Accountants

Burford House, 44 London Road
Sevenoaks, Kent, TN13 1AS
Tel: 01732 458 080
Fax: 01732 455 848
Email: mail@ifa.org.uk
Web: www.accountingweb.co.ukifa

### Institute of Management

PO Box 34, Newtownards, BT23 6ST
Tel: 028 9754 2451
Tel: 0207 497 0580 (London)
Web: www.inst-mgt.org.uk

### Institute of Management Services

Stowe House, Netherstowe, Lichfield
Staffordshire, WS13 6TJ
Tel: 01543 266 825
Fax: 01543 266 833
Email: admin@ims-stowe.fsnet.co.uk
Contact: Vivienne Phillips

The Institute operates through a network of regions throughout the UK and abroad, which work in conjunction with other professional institutes in their region.

### Institution of Mechanical Engineers

105 West George Street
Glasgow, G2 1QL
Tel: 0141 2217156
Regional Manager: Sandra Mulligan

### Institute of Ophthalmology

11–43 Bath Street, London, EC1V 9EL
Tel: 0207 608 6800
Fax: 0207 608 6851
Contact: Colin Bookbinder

### Institute of Psychiatry

De Crespigny Park, London, SE5 8AF
Tel: 0207 848 0140
Fax: 0207 701 9044
Web: www.iop.kcl.ac.uk

### Institute of Public Relations

The Old Trading House
15 Northburgh Street
London, EC1V OPR
Tel: 0207 253 5151
Fax: 0207 490 0588
Email: info@ipr.org.uk
Contact: Richard George

### Royal College of General Practitioners (NI)

44 Elmwood Avenue, Belfast, BT9 6AZ
Tel: 028 9066 7389
Fax: 028 9068 2155
Web: www.rcgp.org
Regional Manager: Valerie Fiddis

### Royal College of Midwives

58 Howard St, Belfast, BT1 6PJ
Tel: 028 9024 1531
Fax: 028 9024 5889
Web: www.rcm.org.uk
NI Board Secretary: Bredagh Hughes

### Royal College of Nursing

17 Windsor Avenue, Belfast, BT9 6EE
Tel: 028 9066 8236
Fax: 028 9038 2188
Director: Martin Bradley

### Royal Institute of Chartered Surveyors (NI Branch)

9/11 Corporation Square
Belfast, BT1 3AJ
Tel: 028 9032 2877
Fax: 028 9023 3465
Director: Ian Murray

### Royal Society of Ulster Architects

2 Mount Charles, Belfast, BT7 1NZ
Tel: 028 9032 3760
Fax: 028 9023 7313
Web: www.rsua.org.uk
Director: Frank McCloskey

### Royal Town Planning Institute (NI Branch)

2 Mount Charles, Belfast, BT7 1NZ
Tel: 028 9032 3760
Fax: 028 9023 7313
Chairman: Helen Harrison

### Society of Radiographers (SOR)

207 Providence Square
Mill St, London, SE1 2EW
Tel: 0207 740 7200

## Trades Unions

Northern Ireland has a variety of trades union organisations covering a wide spectrum of economic life. For the most part the unions are regional parts of UK-based national unions, or in quite a number of cases, all-island unions, or unions active throughout the British Isles. There are a few union organisations unique to Northern Ireland.

Generally, Northern Ireland has a reasonably good industrial relations record and relations between management and trades unions across the economic sectors are positive and professional. There has been a long-term decline in individual membership of trades unions but formal union-centred industrial relations procedures still operate in many workplaces.

**Irish Congress of Trade Unions (ICTU)**
3 Crescent Gardens, Belfast, BT7 1NS
Tel: 028 9024 7940
Fax: 028 9024 6898
Assistant General Secretary:
Peter Bunting

The Irish Congress of Trade Unions is the umbrella organisation of, and provides leadership for, the entire trades union movements in Ireland, North and South. It is organised on a regional basis, which includes a Northern Ireland section.

ICTU negotiates with government directly on national labour issues and carries out research on behalf of the union movement.

**AMICUS**
26-34 Antrim Road, Belfast, BT15 2AA
Tel: 028 9074 7871
Fax: 028 90748052
Regional Secretary: Peter Williamson

4 Foyle Road, Derry, BT48 7FR
Tel: 028 7126 1622
Fax: 028 7136 6025
Regional Secretary:
Peter Williamson

**Amalgamated Transport & General Workers Union (ATGWU)**
Transport House, 102 High Street
Belfast, BT1 2DL
Tel: 028 9023 2381
Fax: 028 9032 9904

56–58 Carlisle Road, Derry, BT48 6JW
Tel: 028 7126 4851
Regional Secretary: Brendan Hodgers

**Association of First Division Civil Servants (AFDCS)**
Room 3, Craigantlet Buildings
Stoney Road, Belfast, BT4 3SX

**Association of Teachers and Lecturers**
397a Holywood Road, Belfast, BT4 2LS
Tel: 028 9047 1412
Fax: 028 9047 1535
Office Administrator: Evelyn Rogers

**Association of University Teachers (AUT)**
c/o Dr S Lowry, Faculty of Science
University of Ulster
Coleraine, BT52 1SA
Tel: 028 7034 4141

**Bakers, Food & Allied Workers Union (BFAWU)**
80 High Street, Belfast, BT1 2BG
Tel: 028 9032 2767
Contact: John Halliday

**British Actors' Equity Association (EQUITY)**
114 Union St, Glasgow, G1 3QQ
Tel: 0141 248 2472
Fax: 0141 248 2472
Web: www.equity.org.uk
Secretary: Drew McFarland

**Broadcasting, Entertainment, Cinematograph & Theatre Union (BECTU)**
373–377 Clapham Road
London, SW9 9BT
Tel: 0207 346 0900
Fax: 0207 346 0901
General Secretary: Roger Bolton

**Communication Managers' Association (CMA)**
Royal Mail House, 20 Donegall Quay
Belfast, BT1 1AA
Tel: 028 9089 2288
Secretary: Bobby Smith

**Communication Workers' Union (CWU)**
2-8 Commercial Court, Belfast, BT1 2NB
Tel: 028 9032 1771
Fax: 028 9043 9390
Chairman: John McLoughlin

**Connect**
c/o Mr A Gibb, BT plc Riverside Tower
5 Lanyon Place, Belfast, BT1 3BT

**Counteract**
2-8 Commercial Court, Belfast, BT1 2NB
Tel: 028 9023 7023
Fax: 028 9031 3585
Web: www.counteract.org
Director: William Robinson

**National Farmers' Union**
72 High Street, Newtownards, BT23 7HZ
Tel: 028 9181 4218
Fax: 028 9181 1574
Group Secretary: Jane Lyness

**Prospect**
75–79 York Road, London, SE1 7AQ
Tel: 020 7902 6600
Fax: 020 7902 6667
Email: enquiries@prospect.org.uk
General Secretary: Paul Noon

**Fire Brigades' Union (FBU)**
14 Bachelors Walk, Lisburn, BT28 1XJ
Tel: 028 9266 4622
Contact: Tony Maguire

**GMB**
3–4 Donegal Quay, Belfast, BT1 3EA
Tel: 028 9031 2111
Fax: 028 90 312 333
Organiser: Bobby Carson

**Graphical Paper & Media Union**
Unit A, First Floor, Loughside Industrial Pk
Dargan Crescent, Belfast, BT3 9JP
Tel: 028 9077 8550
Fax: 028 9077 8552
Branch Secretary: Davy Edmont

**Irish Bank Officials Association (IBOA)**
92-93 St Stephen's Green, Dublin 2
Tel: 01 475 5908
Fax: 01 478 0567
Secretary: Larry Broderick

**Irish National Teachers Association (INTO)**
23 College Gardens, Belfast, BT9 6BS
Tel: 028 9038 1455
Fax: 028 9066 2803
Email: info@ni.into.ie
Northern Secretary: Frank Bunting

**National Association of Head Teachers**
Carnmoney House, Edgewater Office
Park, Belfast, BT3 9JQ
Tel: 028 9077 6633
Fax: 028 9077 4777
Email: fernt@naht.org.uk
Regional Officer: Fern Turner

**National Association for Probation Officers (NAPO)**
c/o Ms E Richardson, PBNI
80/90 Great Patrick St
Belfast, BT1 1LD
Tel: 028 9032 6688

### National Association of Schoolmasters / Union of Women Teachers (NASUWT )
Ben Madigan House, Edgewater Road
Belfast, BT3 9JQ
Tel: 028 9078 4480
Fax: 028 9078 4489
Web: www.teachersunion.org.uk
Regional Officer: Else Margrain

### National Association of Teachers in Further & Higher Education (NATFHE)
475 Lisburn Road, Belfast, BT9 7EZ
Tel: 028 9066 5501
Fax: 028 9066 9225
Web: www.natfhe.org.uk
Regional Officer: Jim McKeown

### National Union of Journalists (NUJ)
Headland House
308–312 Gray's Inn Road
London, WC1X 8DT
Tel: 0207 278 7916

### National Union of Rail, Maritime & Transport Workers (RMT)
180 Hope St, Glasgow, G2 2UE
Tel: 0141 332 1117
Fax: 0141 333 9583
Regional Organiser: Steve Todd

### NI Public Service Alliance (NIPSA)
Harkin House, 54 Wellington Park
Belfast, BT9 6DP
Tel: 028 9066 1831
Fax: 028 9066 5847
Web: www.nipsa.org.uk
General Secretary: John Corey

### National Union of Students (NUS-USI)
NUS-USI, 29 Bedford Street
Belfast, BT2 7EJ
Tel: 028 9024 4641
Fax: 028 9043 9659
Email: info@nistudents.com
Web: www.nistudents.com
Convenor 2004–2005:
Damien Kavanagh

### Belfast Institute of Further and Higher Education Students Union
Room A24, College Square East
Belfast, BT1 6DJ
Union Tel: 028 9026 5059
Union Fax: 028 9026 5101
College Tel: 028 9026 5000

### Queen's University of Belfast Students Union
University Road, Belfast, BT7 1PE
Union Tel: 028 9097 3106
Union Fax: 028 9023 6900
Email: info@qubsu.org
College Tel: 028 9024 5133
Web: www.qubsu.org

### University of Ulster Students Union
Cromore Road, Coleraine, BT52 1SA
Union Tel: 028 7032 4319
Union Fax: 028 7032 4915
College Tel: 08700 400 700
Email: su.president@uusu.org
Web: www.uusu.org

*Jordanstown Site*
Shore Road, Co Antrim, BT37 0QB
Union Tel: 028 9036 6050
Union Fax: 028 9036 6817
Email: su.edwel@uusu.org
Email: vp.jordanstown@uusu.org
College Tel: 08700 400 700

*Derry Site*
Magee College, Northlands Road
Derry, BT48 7JL
Union Tel: 028 7137 5226
Union Fax: 028 7137 5415
College Tel: 08700 400 700
Email: vp.magee@uusu.org

*Belfast Site*
York Street, Belfast, BT15 1ED
Union Tel: 028 9026 7302
Union Fax: 028 9026 7351
College Tel: 08700 400 700
Email: vp.belfast@uusu.org
Email: su.enquiries@uusu.org

### Public Commerce Services Union (PCS)
10 Mounthill Court, Cloughmills
Co Antrim, BT44 9QU
Tel: 028 2563 3096
Contact: Alastair Donaghy

### Royal College of Nursing
17 Windsor Avenue, Belfast, BT9 6EE
Tel: 028 9066 8236
Fax: 028 9038 2188
Board Secretary: Martin Bradley

### Services Industrial Professional Technical Union (SIPTU)
3 Antrim Road, Belfast, BT15 2BE
Tel: 028 9074 7010
Regional Secretary: Jack Nash

### Ulster Farmers' Union
475 Antrim Road, Belfast, BT15 3DA
Tel: 028 9037 0222
Fax: 028 9037 1231
Web: info@ufunq.com
Chief Executive: Clarke Black

### Ulster Teachers' Union (UTU)
94 Malone Road, Belfast, BT9 5HP
Tel: 028 9066 2216
Fax: 028 9066 3055
Web: www.utu.edu/home.html
Secretary: Avril Hall-Callaghan

### Union of Construction, Allied Trades & Technicians (UCATT)
Rooms 108 / 110, Midland Building,
Whitla Street, Belfast, BT15 1JP
Tel: 028 9075 1866
Fax: 028 9075 1867
Email: admin@ucatt.org.uk
Regional Secretary: Terry Lally

### Union of Shop, Distributive & Allied Workers (USDAW)
40 Wellington Park, Belfast, BT9 6DN
Tel: 028 9066 3773
Fax: 028 9066 2133
Area Organiser: Bob Gourley

### UNISON
Unit 4, Fortwilliam Business Park
Dargan Road, Belfast, BT3 9LZ
Tel: 028 9077 0813
Fax: 028 9077 9772
Regional Secretary: Patricia McKeown

### Affiliated Councils of Trade Unions
Belfast & District
c/o Transport House
102 High Street, Belfast, BT1
Contact: Pearse McKenna

*Belfast & District*
c/o BURC, 45/47 Donegall Street
Belfast BT1 2FH
Contact: Mr K Doherty

*Craigavon & District*
13 The Brambles, Craigavon, BT66 6LP
Contact: Mr D Harte

*Derry*
c/o Disability Action, 58 Strand Road
Derry, BT48 7AJ
Contact: Mr K McAdams

*Fermanagh*
c/o ATGWU, 3 Queen Street
Enniskillen, BT74 7JR
Contact: Ms M Steward

*Newry*
24 Cherrywood Grove, Newry, BT34 1JJ
Contact: Mr J Murphy

*North Down*
c/o NIPSA, Dept of Education
Rathgael House, Balloo Road,
Bangor, BT19 7PG
Contact: Ms J McNulty

*Strabane*
139 Belldoo, Strabane, BT82 9QL
Contact: Mr B Forbes

*Omagh*
7 Sunningdale, Omagh, BT78 1JX
Contact: Mr A McCabe

## Charitable, Support and Voluntary Organisations

Northern Ireland has an extensive and very active voluntary sector, which includes a wide range of charitable and support organisations. Many of these organisations are affiliated to an umbrella body, the Northern Ireland Council for Voluntary Action (NICVA); an organisation that has been appointed on occasions by the European Commission as an intermediary body to distribute substantial EU funding in Northern Ireland.

It is worth noting that as a region of the UK, Northern Ireland records very high comparative levels of deprivation and it is not surprising therefore that so much voluntary endeavour is required. For example, Northern Ireland has considerably higher levels of homelessness and disability than UK averages and the charities and support groups operating in these areas are necessarily significant players.

### Action Cancer
Action Cancer House
1 Marlborough Park, Belfast BT9 6XS
Tel: 028 9080 3344
Fax: 028 9080 3356
Web: www.actioncancer.org
Chief Executive: Robin McRoberts

### Action for Dysphasic Adults NI
Graham House
Knockbracken Healthcare Park
Saintfield Road, Belfast BT8 8BH
Tel: 028 9040 1389
Fax: 028 9050 8025
Web: www.speechmatters.org
Chief Executive: Jackie White

### Action Multiple Sclerosis
Knockbracken Healthcare Park
Saintfield Road, Belfast, BT8 8BH
Tel: 028 9079 0707
Fax: 028 9040 2010
Email: info@actionms.co.uk
Web: www.actionms.co.uk
Director: Anne Walker

### ADAPT Fund for Ireland
109 Royal Avenue, Belfast BT1 1FF
Tel: 028 9023 1211
Fax: 028 9024 0878
Email: info@adaptni.org
Development Manager:
Caroline Shiels

### Age Concern NI
3 Lower Crescent, Belfast, BT7 1NR
Tel: 028 9024 5729
Fax: 028 9023 5497
Chief Executive: Chris Common

### Aids Helpline NI
7 James Street South
Belfast, BT2 8DN
Tel: 028 9024 9268
Free Helpline: 0800 137437
Fax: 028 9032 9845
Web: www.aidshelpline.org.uk
Director: Geraldine Campbell

### Alcoholics Anonymous
7 Donegall Street Place
Central Service Office
Belfast, BT1 2FN
Tel: 028 9043 4848
Fax: 028 9043 4848
Web: www.alcoholicsanonymous.ie

### Alzheimers Disease Society
86 Eglantine Avenue, Belfast, BT9 6EU
Tel: 028 9066 4100
Fax: 028 9066 4440
Regional Manager: Mike McIlwrath

### Amnesty International NI Region
397 Ormeau Road, Belfast, BT7 3GP
Tel: 028 9064 3000
Fax: 028 9069 0989
Web: www.amnesty.org
NI Programme Director: Patrick Corrigan

### Anti-Poverty Network
Room 3, 58 Howard Street
Belfast, BT1 6PJ
Tel: 0845 120 3771
Development Co-ordinator:
Frances Dowds

### Ards Society for Mentally Handicapped Children
203 South Street
Newtownards, BT23 4JY
Tel: 028 9181 5363

### Armagh Confederation of Voluntary Groups
1 College Street, Armagh, BT61 9BT
Tel: 028 3752 2282
Fax: 028 3752 2286
Web: www.acvg.com
Co-ordinator: Andrea Clark

### Arthritis Care NI
Enkalon Business Park
25 Randalstown Road
Antrim, BT41 4LJ
Tel: 028 9448 1380
Fax: 028 9446 9761
Web: www.arthritiscare.org.uk
Acting Director: Marcus Cooper

### Arthritis Research Campaign
10 Alberta Parade, Belfast, BT5 5EH
Tel: 028 9046 1529
Fax: 028 9046 1529
Area Appeals Manager:
Charlotte Trinder

### Arts and Disability Forum
Ground Floor, 109 - 113 Royal Avenue
Belfast, BT1 1FF
Tel: 028 9023 9450
Fax: 028 9024 7770
Web: www.adf.ie
Director: Avril Crawford

### ASH
c/o Ulster Cancer Foundation
40–42 Eglantine Avenue
Belfast, BT9 6DJ
Tel: 028 9049 2007
Fax: 028 9066 0081
Web: www.ulstercancer.org
Head of Education and Training:
Gerry McElwee

### Advice NI
1 Rushfield Avenue, Belfast, BT7 3FP
Tel: 028 9064 5919
Fax: 028 9049 2313
Web: www.aiac.net
Director: Bob Stronge

### Association of Mental Health
80 University Street, Belfast, BT7 1HE
Tel: 028 9032 8474
Fax: 028 9023 4940
Chief Executive: Alan Ferguson

### Association for Spina Bifida & Hydrocephalus
Graham House
Knockbracken Healthcare Park
Saintfield Road, Belfast, BT8 8BH
Tel: 028 9079 8878
Fax: 028 9079 7071
Regional Manager: Brendan Heaney

Barnardo's
NI Regional Office
542–544 Upper Newtownards Road
Belfast, BT4 3HE
Tel: 028 9067 2366
Fax: 028 9067 2399
Web: www.barnardos.org.uk
Senior Director: Linda Wilson

BBC Children in Need
Broadcasting House, Ormeau Ave
Belfast, BT2 8HQ
Tel: 028 9033 8221
Fax: 028 9033 8922
National Co-ordinator:
Sheila Jane Malley

Belfast Central Mission
5 Glengall Street, Belfast, BT12 5AD
Tel: 028 9024 1917
Fax: 028 9024 0577
Superintendent: Donald Kerr

Belfast and Co Down Railway Trust
9 Abbey Gardens, Millisle, Newtownards
Tel: 0800 980 1242
Contact: Bob Pue

Belfast Common Purpose
Beacon House, 27 Clarendon Road
Belfast, BT1 3BG
Tel: 028 9089 2273

Blind Centre for Northern Ireland
70 North Road, Belfast, BT5 5NJ
Tel: 028 9050 0999
Fax: 028 9065 0001
Web: www.bcni.co.uk
Chief Executive: Dean Huston

Board for Social Responsibility
Church of Ireland House
61–67 Donegall Street
Belfast, BT1 2QH
Tel: 028 9023 3885
Fax: 028 9032 1756
Web: www.cofiadopt.org.uk
Chief Executive: Ian Slane

Brainwaves NI
68 Cable Road, Whitehead
Co Antrim, BT38 9PZ
Tel: 028 9337 2505
Fax: 028 9335 3995
Honorary Secretary: Kate Ferguson

British Deaf Association
3rd Floor, Wilton House
5–6 College Street North
Belfast, BT1 6AR
Tel: 028 9038 7700
Tel: 028 9072 7407
Web: www.britishdeafassociation.org.uk
NI Director: Majella McAteer

British Heart Foundation
PO Box 221, Lisburn, BT28 3WF
Tel: 028 9262 7637

British Red Cross
87 University Street, Belfast, BT7 1HP
Tel: 028 9024 6400
Fax: 028 9032 6102
Regional Director: Norman McKinley

British Red Cross Therapeutic Care Service
71 High Street, Bangor, BT20 5BD
Tel: 028 9146 6915
Fax: 028 9146 6915
Regional Service Co-ordinator: Norma Groves

Bryson House
28 Bedford Street, Belfast, BT2 7FE
Tel: 028 9032 5835
Fax: 028 9043 9156
Co-Directors: Jo Marley and
John McMullan

Bryson House is a Northern Ireland Charity committed to identifying and developing sustainable responses to existing and emerging social needs. The charity provides a range of services including environmental, family and caring, training and voluntary services.

Bryson House Charity
7a Main Street, Ballynahinch, BT24 8DN
Tel: 028 9756 4366
Web: www.brysonhouse.org
Project Manager: Margaret Coffey

C A C D P
5 College Square North, Belfast, BT1 6AR
Tel: 028 9043 8161
Fax: 028 9043 8161
Minicom: 028 9043 8161
National Development Officer Northern Ireland: Cilla Mullan

Carers Northern Ireland
58 Howard Street, Belfast, BT1 6PJ
Tel: 028 9043 9843
Fax: 028 9032 9299
Email: info@carersni.demon.co.uk
Director: Helen Ferguson

Cancer Research Campaign Northern Ireland
Unit 1, Pavilions, 22A Kinnegar Drive
Holywood Road, Belfast, BT18 9JQ
Tel: 028 9042 7766
Fax: 028 9042 1822
Email: northernireland@crc.org.uk
Web: www.crc.org.uk
Fundraising Manager: Barbara Blundell

Charles Sheils Charity
Circular Road, Dungannon, BT71 6BJ
Tel: 028 8772 2138
Superintendent: Averill Griffith

Chernobyl Children Appeal
44A Church Street
Ballymena, BT43 6DF
Tel: 028 2563 2767
Fax: 028 2563 2240

Chest Heart & Stroke Association
Chamber Commerce House
22 Great Victoria Street
Belfast, BT2 7LX
Tel: 028 9032 0184
Fax: 028 9033 3487
Web: www.nicha.com
Chief Executive: Andrew Dougal

Children in NI
216 Belmont Road, Belfast, BT4 2AT
Tel: 028 9065 2713
Fax: 028 9065 0285
Web: www.childcareni.org.uk
Director: Pauline Leeson

Childline
3rd Floor Offices
The War Memorial Building
9–13 Waring Street, Belfast, BT1 2EU
Tel: 028 9032 7773
Web: www.childline.org.uk
Director: Patrick Shannon

Children in Crossfire
2 St Joseph's Avenue, Derry, BT48 6TH
Tel: 028 7126 9898
Fax: 028 7126 6630
Email:
ciara.donnelly@childreincrossfire.org
Director: Richard Moore

Children's Law Centre
3rd Floor, Philip House
123–137 York Street
Belfast, BT15 1AB
Tel: 028 9024 5704
Fax: 028 9024 5679
Email: info@childrenslawcentre.org
Director: Paddy Kelly

Christian Aid Ireland
30 Wellington Park, Belfast, BT9 6DL
Tel: 028 9038 1204
Fax: 028 9038 1737

Cleft Lip & Palate Association
43 Ashley Avenue, Belfast, BT9 7BT
Tel: 028 9066 5115
Web: www.clapa.com

### Community Arts Forum
15 Church St, Belfast, BT1 1PG
Tel: 028 9024 2910
Fax: 028 9031 2264
Web: www.community-arts-forum.org
Director: Heather Floyd

### Community Evaluation NI
295 Ormeau Road, Belfast, BT7 3GG
Tel: 028 9064 6355
Fax: 028 9064 1118
Web: www.ceni.org
Email: info@ceni.org
Director: Mr Brendan McDonnell

### Community Relations Council

**Community Relations Council**

6 Murray Street, Belfast, BT1 6DN
Tel: 028 9022 7500
Fax: 028 9022 7551
Email: info@community-relations.org.uk
Web: www.community-relations.org.uk
Chief Executive: Dr Duncan Morrow

The Community Relations Council (CRC) was established in 1990 as a registered charity. It aims to help organisations and individuals to create a society free from sectarianism.

CRC is a development agency for peace in Northern Ireland and provides advice and support to community relations initiatives and projects in the voluntary and community sector. Almost 500 grants are awarded each year. CRC also offers advice and guidance to public sector organisations in meeting the section 75 (2) statutory duty under the NI Act (1998) to promote 'Good Relations'.

### Community Relations Resource Centre
21 College Square East
Belfast, BT1 6DE
Tel: 028 9022 7555
Email: info@community-relations.org.uk
Manager: Ellana Tomassa

### Community Work Education and Training Network
Philip House, 123–137 York Street
Belfast, BT15 1AB
Tel: 028 9023 2618
Fax: 028 9031 2216
Email: cwetn@compuserve.com
Co-ordinator: Peggy Flanagan

### Conservation Volunteers NI
159 Ravenhill Road, Belfast, BT6 0BP
Tel: 028 9064 5169
Fax: 028 9064 4409
Web: www.cvni.org.uk
Email: info@cvni.org.uk
Operations Manager: Ian Humphreys

### Community Technical Aid NI Ltd
445 Ormeau Road, Belfast
Tel: 028 9064 2227
Fax: 028 9064 2467
Email: info@communitytechnicalaid.org
Director: Colm Bradley

### Community Transport Association
Graham House
Knockbracken Health Care Park
Saintfield Road, Belfast, BT8 8BH
Tel/Fax: 028 9040 3535
Regional Co-ordinator: Bryan Myles

### Concern Worldwide NI
47 Frederick Street, Belfast, BT1 LW
Tel: 028 9033 1100
Fax: 028 9033 1111
Email: infobelfast@concern.org.uk
Head of NI Operations: David Gough

### Co-operation Ireland
Glendinning House, 6 Murray Street
Belfast, BT1 6DN
Tel: 028 9032 1462
Fax: 028 9089 1000
Web: www.cooperationireland.org
Email: info@cooperationireland.org
Chief Executive: Tony Kennedy
Operations Director:
Anne Anderson Porter

Co-operation Ireland is a charitable organisation unique to Northern Ireland. Its central mission is to develop practical cooperation between people North and South of the border. It is increasingly expanding its role in reconciling different traditions North and South, to include reconciliation of the different traditions within the North. Co-operation Ireland operates numerous social, economic, youth and community programmes.

### Corrymeela Community Belfast
8 Upper Crescent, Belfast, BT7 1NT
Tel: 028 9050 8080
Fax: 028 9050 8070
Email: enquiries@corrymeela.org.uk
Leader of the Community:
Dr David Stevens

### Council for the Homeless NI
72 North Street, Belfast, BT1 1LD
Tel: 028 9024 6440
Fax: 028 9024 1266
Email: info@chni.org.uk
Director: Ms Ricky Rowledge

### Crossroads Caring for Carers
Head Office, 7 Regent Street
Newtownards, BT23 4AB
Tel: 028 9181 4455
Fax: 028 9181 2112
Email: mail@crossroadscare.co.uk
Chief Executive: Christine Best

### CRUSE Bereavement Care NI
Knockbracken Heathcare Park
Saintfield Road, Belfast, BT8 8BH
Tel: 028 9079 2419
Fax: 028 9079 2474
Regional Manager: Ann Townsend
Cruse is the leading bereavement charity in the UK. The organisation currently has 178 branches and over 6,300 volunteers throughout the UK.

### Cystic Fibrosis Trust
12 Selshion Manor
Portadown, BT62 1AF
Tel: 028 3833 4491
Regional Manager: Tom Mallon

### Diabetics UK
Bridgewood House, Newforge Lane
Belfast, BT9 5NW
Tel: 028 9066 6646
Fax: 028 9066 6333
Email: n.ireland@diabetes.org.uk
Web: www.diabetes.org.uk
National Director: Kate Fleck

### Disability Action
Portside Business Park
189 Airport Road West
Belfast, BT3 9ED
Tel: 028 9029 7880
Fax: 028 9029 7881
Textphone: 028 9029 7882
Web: www.disabilityaction.org
Chief Executive: Monica Wilson

### Downs Syndrome Association NI
Graham House
Knockbracken Healthcare Park
Saintfield Road, Belfast, BT7 8BH
Tel: 028 9070 4606
Fax: 028 9070 4075
Web: www.downs-syndrome.org.uk
Email: downs-sysdrome@cinni.org
Regional Director: Alan Hanna

### Downtown Women's Centre
109–113 Royal Avenue
Belfast, BT1 1FF
Tel: 028 9024 3363
Fax: 028 9023 7884
Director: May Desilva

### East Belfast Independent Advice Centre
85 Castlereagh Street
Belfast, BT5 4NS
Tel: 028 9096 3003
Fax: 028 9096 3004
Manager: Karen McNamee

### Family Planning Association NI
113 University Street, Belfast, BT7 1HP
Tel: 028 9032 5488
Fax: 028 9031 2212
Director: Dr Audrey Simpson

### Federation of Women's Institutes
209–211 Upper Lisburn Road
Belfast, BT10 0LL
Tel: 028 9030 1506
Fax: 028 9043 1127
Email: wini@btconnect.com
General Secretary: Irene Sproule

### Friends in the West
Rathmourne House
143 Central Promenade
Newcastle, BT33 0EU
Tel: 028 4372 3300
Fax: 028 4372 6210
Contact: Julian Armstrong

### Friends of the Earth
7 Donegall Street Place, Belfast, BT1 2FN
Tel: 028 9023 3488
Fax: 028 9024 7556
Web: www.foe.co.uk/ni
Director (NI): John Woods

### Gamblers Anonymous
18 Donegall Street, Belfast, BT1 2GP
Tel: 028 9024 9185
Web: www.gambersanonymous.org

### Gay Lesbian Youth Northern Ireland
Email: admin@glyni.org.uk
Web: www.glyni.org.uk

### Gingerbread
169 University Street, Belfast, BT7 1HR
Tel: 028 9023 1417
Fax: 028 9024 0740
Email: enquiries@gingerbreadni.org
Director: Marie Cavanagh

### Guide Dogs for the Blind
15 Sandown Park South
Belfast, BT5 6HE
Tel: 028 9047 1453
Fax: 028 9065 5097
Email: belfast@gdba.org.uk
District Team Manager: Peter Swan

### Habitat for Humanity NI
Unit 29, Forset Enterprise Park
Springfield Road, Belfast, BT12 7DY
Tel: 028 9024 3686
Fax: 028 9033 1878
Email: belfast@habitat.co.uk
Executive Director: Peter Farquharson

### Help the Aged
Ascot House, Shaftesbury Square
Belfast, BT2 7DB
Tel: 028 9023 0666
Fax: 028 9024 8183
Advice: 0800 808 7575
Web: www.helptheaged.org.uk
Email: helptheagedni@hta.org.uk
NI Executive: Grace Henry

### Home Start
533 Antrim Road, Belfast, BT15 3BS
Tel: 028 9077 8999
Fax: 028 9078 1656
Web: www.home-start.org.uk
Scheme Organiser: Patricia Friel

### International Fund for Ireland
PO Box 2000, Belfast, BT4 1WD
Tel: 028 9076 8832
Fax: 028 9076 3313
Joint Director General:
Mr Sandy Smith

### International Voluntary Service
34 Shaftsbury Square
Belfast, BT2 7DB
Tel: 028 9023 8147
Fax: 028 9024 4356
Co-ordinator: Colin McKinty

### Lifestart Family Centre
13 Dunluce Court, Derry, BT48 0PA
Tel: 028 7126 9833
Fax: 028 7126 0233
Contact: Margaret McCann

### Macmillan Cancer Relief
82 Eglantine Avenue, Belfast, BT9 6EU
Tel: 028 9066 1166
Fax: 028 9066 3661
Fundraising Manager: Paul Sweeney

### Make a Wish Foundation UK
Bryson House, 28 Bedford Street
Belfast, BT2 7FE
Tel: 028 9080 5580
Regional Manager: Stephen Wilkie

### Marie Curie Cancer Care
60 Knock Road, Belfast, BT5 6LQ
Tel: 028 9088 2060
Fundraising Manager: Lynne Davidson

### Meningitis Research Foundation
71 Botanic Avenue, Belfast, BT7 1JL
Tel: 028 9032 1283
Fax: 028 9032 1284
Freephone: 0800 800 3344
Email: info@meningitis-ni.org
NI Manager: Diane McConnell

### Mencap
416 Ormeau Road, Belfast, BT7 3HY
Tel: 028 9049 2666
Fax: 028 9049 3373
Web: www.mencap.org
Regional Director: Maureen Piggott

Mencap offers a range of services, information and support for children and adults with learning difficulties.

### Multiple Sclerosis Society – Northern Ireland
The Resource Centre
34 Annadale Avenue, Belfast, BT7 3JJ
Tel: 028 9080 2802
Web: www.mssocietyni.co.uk
Director: Kieran Harris

### National Deaf Children's Society
Wilton House, 5–6 College Square North
Belfast, BT1 6AR
Tel: 028 9031 3170
Fax: 028 9027 8205
Email: nioffice@ndcsni.co.uk
Director: Pauline Walker

### The National Trust
Rowallane House, Saintfield, BT24 7LH
Tel: 028 9751 0721
Fax: 028 9751 1242
Web: www.nationaltrust.org.uk
Director: Ruth Laird

The National Trust is a registered charity, which owns and manages a range of historic properties and estates on behalf of the public and for their future preservation. The Trust now cares for over 248,000 hectares of countryside, almost 600 miles of coastline and more than 200 buildings and gardens.

### Nexus Institute Belfast
119 University Street, Belfast, BT7 1HP
Tel: 028 9032 6803
Fax: 028 9023 7392
Email: dominica@nexusinstitute.org
Director: Dominica McGowan

### Nexus Institute Derry
38 Clarendon Street, Derry, BT48 7ET
Tel: 028 7126 0566
Fax: 028 7130 8399
Web: www.nexusinstitute.org
Project Manager: Helena Bracken

### Northern Ireland Children's Holiday Scheme
547 Antrim Road, Belfast, BT15 3BU
Tel: 028 9037 0373
Fax: 028 9078 1161
Email: niches@utvinternet.com
Director: Jackie Chalk

### Northern Ireland Foster Care Association
216 Belmont Road, Belfast, BT4 2AT
Tel: 028 9067 3441
Fax: 028 9067 3241
Email: info.nifca@dnet.co.uk
Director: Kate Lewis

### Northern Ireland Gay Rights Association
c/o 46 Malone Avenue, Belfast, BT9 6ER
Tel: 028 9066 5257
Fax: 028 9066 4111
Email: nigra@hotmail.com

### Northern Ireland Leukaemia Research Fund
University Floor, Tower Block
Belfast City Hospital, Lisburn Road
Belfast, BT9 7AB
Tel: 028 9032 2603
Fax: 028 9026 3927
Secretary: Frances Parker

### NI Council for Ethnic Minorities (NICEM)
Ascot House, 24-31 Shaftesbury Square
Belfast, BT2 7DB
Tel: 028 9023 8645
Fax: 028 9031 9485
Secretary: Frances Parker

### NIPPA Childhood Fund
6c Wildflower Way
Apollo Road, Belfast, BT12 6TA
Tel: 028 9066 2825
Fax: 028 9038 1270
Web: www.nippa.org

1a Pottinger Street, Culleybackey
Ballymena, BT42 1BP
Tel: 028 2588 2345
Fax: 028 2588 2338
Chief Executive: Siobhan Fitzpatrick

### Northern Ireland Agoraphobia & Anxiety Society
29–31 Lisburn Road, Belfast, BT9 7AA
Tel: 028 9023 5170
Fax: 028 9024 5535
Contact: Fiona McFarland

### Northern Ireland Association of Citizens Advice Bureaux
11 Upper Crescent, Belfast, BT7 1NT
Tel: 028 9023 1120
Fax: 028 9023 6522
Email: info@citizensadvice.co.uk
Chief Executive: Derek Alcorn

The Citizens Advice Bureau originated as an emergency service and now addresses debt and consumer issues, benefits, housing, legal matters, employment and immigration.
Each bureau is affiliated to the National Association of Citizens Advice Bureau (NACAB).

### Northern Ireland Cancer Fund For Children
Curlew Pavillion, Portside Business Park
Airport Road West, Belfast, BT3 9ED
Tel: 028 9080 5599
Fax: 028 9073 8747
Web: www.nicsc.com
Contact: Gillian Creevy

### Northern Ireland Council For Voluntary Action (NICVA)
61 Duncairn Gardens, Belfast, BT15 2GB
Tel: 028 9087 7777
Fax: 028 9087 7799
Email: info@nicva.org
Director: Seamus McAleavey

The Northern Ireland Council for Voluntary Action is an umbrella group for Northern Ireland charities, community and voluntary groups.

### Northern Ireland Hospice
74 Somerton Road, Belfast, BT15 3LH
Tel: 028 9078 1836
Fax: 028 9037 0585
Web: www.nihospice.com
Email: information@nihospice.com
Acting Chief Executive: Liz Duffin

### Northern Ireland Hospice Children's Service
18 O'Neill Road
Newtownabbey, BT36 6WB
Tel: 028 9077 7635
Fax: 028 9077 7144
Web: www.nihospice.com
Email: children@nihospice.com
Head of Home: Patricia O'Callaghan

### Northern Ireland ME Association
Bryson House
28 Bedford Street, Belfast
Tel: 028 9043 9831
Fax: 028 9043 9831

### Northern Ireland Mixed Marriage Association
28 Bedford Street, Belfast, BT2 7FE
Tel: 028 9023 5444
Fax: 028 9043 4544
Web: www.nimma.org.uk
Email: nimma@nireland.com
Contact: Nigel Speirs

### Northern Ireland Preschool Playgroup Association
1A Pottinger Street, Cullybackey
Ballymena, BT42 1BP
Tel: 028 2588 2345
Fax: 028 2588 2338
Training Co-ordinator:
Jennifer Montgomery

### Northern Ireland Transplant Association
51 Circular Road, Belfast, BT4 2GA
Tel: 028 9076 1394
Web: www.nita.org.uk
Email: nitransplant@email.com
Chairman: David Robinson

### Northern Ireland Women's Aid Federation
129 University Street, Belfast, BT7 1HP
Tel: 028 9024 9041
Fax: 028 9023 9296
Web: www.niwaf.org
Email: niwaf@dnet.co.uk
Director: Hilary Sidwell

### NSPCC NI
Jennymount Business Park
North Derby Street, Belfast, BT15 3HN
Tel: 028 9035 1135
Fax: 028 9035 1100
Web: www.nspcc.org.uk
Divisional Director NI: Ian Elliott

### Organisation of the Unemployed NI
14 May Street, Belfast, BT1 4NL
Tel: 028 9031 0862
Fax: 028 9031 4975

### Oxygen Therapy Centre
100 Shore Road, Magheramorne, Larne
Tel: 028 2827 4670
Fax: 028 2827 4670
Email:
info@oxygentherapycentre.co.uk
Centre co-ordinator: Joanne McAuley

### Oxfam Northern Ireland
52–54 Dublin Road, Belfast, BT2 7HN
Tel: 028 9023 0220
Fax: 028 9023 7771
Web: www.oxfamireland.org
Email: oxfam@oxfamni.org.uk
Corporate Services Manager:
Julie McSorley

### PAPA (Parents and Professionals and Autism) NI
Knockbracken Health Park
Saintfield Road, Belfast, BT8 8BH
Tel: 028 9040 1729
Fax: 028 9040 3467
Web: www.autismni.org
Director: Arlene Cassidy

### Parents Advice Centre
Franklin House, 12 Brunswick Street
Belfast, BT2 7GE
Tel: 028 9031 0891
Fax: 028 9031 2475
Web: www.pachelp.org
Email: belfast@pachelp.org
Chief Executive: Pip Jaffa

### Parkinson's Disease Society
Parkinson's Disease Society

Northern Ireland Regional Office
Dunsilly Lodge, Dunsilly
Antrim, Northern Ireland, BT41 2JH
Tel / Fax: (028) 9442 8928

Bill Canning
Regional Manager

The Aims of the PDS

To help people with Parkinson's and their relatives with the problems arising from Parkinson's

To collect and disseminate information on Parkinson's

To encourage and provide funds for research into Parkinson's

Providing a community support worker service to people with Parkinson's and their families

Promoting the development of Parkinson's Disease Nurse Specialists, nurses specially trained in Parkinson's management

There are branches throughout Northern Ireland which meet regularly
Antrim (HQ): 028 9442 8929
Development Worker: 028 4277 2999
Belfast: 028 9026 3796
Enniskillen: 028 6863 3133
Armagh: 028 3752 3758
Omagh: 028 8289 8339
Portstewart: 028 7083 3747

National Helpline: 0808 800 0303

### PHAB
Jennymount Business Park
North Derby Street, Belfast, BT15 3HN
Tel: 028 9050 4800
Fax: 028 9075 4321
Web: www.phabni.org
Email: info@phabni.org
Chief Executive: Trevor Boyle

### Praxis Care Group
29–31 Lisburn Road, Belfast, BT9 7AA
Tel: 028 9023 4555
Fax: 028 9024 5535
Chief Executive: Nevin Ringland

Praxis Care is a new charity formed out of the amalgamation of four established charities in the mental health area – Praxis Mental Healthcare, Respond, Northern Ireland Agoraphobia and Challenge.

### The Princes Trust
Block 5, 5 Jennymount Court
North Derby Street, Belfast, BT15 3HN
Tel: 028 9074 5454
Fax: 028 9074 8416
Web: www.princes-trust.org.uk
Email: ptnire@princes-trust.org.uk
Director: Siobhan Craig

### Prisoners Enterprise Project (South Belfast)
127–145 Sandy Row, Belfast, BT12 5ET
Tel: 028 9024 4449
Fax: 028 9024 4471
Co-ordinator: Bill Newman

### The Rainbow Project
2-6 Union Street, Belfast, BT1 2JF
Tel: 028 9031 9030
Fax: 028 9031 9031
Web: www.rainbow-project.com
Email: info@rainbow-project.com
Chairman: Frank Toner

### Rape Crisis and Sexual Abuse Centre
29 Donegall Street, Belfast, BT1 2FG
Tel: 028 9024 9696
Fax: 028 9032 1830

### Reach Across
21 The Diamonds, Derry, BT48 6HP
Tel: 028 7128 0048
Fax: 028 7128 0058
Web: www.reach-across.co.uk
Email: reach-across@hotmail.com
Youth co-ordinator:
Barney McGuigan

### Relate NI
3 Glengall Street, Belfast, BT12 5AB
Tel: 0870 2426091
Web: www.relateni.org
Email: office@relateni.org
Chief Executive: Gerald Clark

### Respond
25–31 Lisburn Road, Belfast, BT9 7AA
Tel: 028 9031 0883
Fax: 028 9024 5535
Director: Irene Sloan

### RETHINK
Windhurst
Knockbracken Healthcare Park
Saintfield Road, Belfast, BT8 8BH
Tel: 028 9040 2323
Fax: 028 9040 1616
Email: info.nireland@rethink.org
Director: Liz Cuddy

### Royal National Institute for the Blind
40 Linenhall Street, Belfast, BT2 8BA
Tel: 028 9032 9373
Fax: 028 9027 8119
Web: www.info@rnib.org.uk
Contact: Mike Thornicroft

### Royal National Institute for the Deaf (RNID)
Wilson House, 5 College Square North
Belfast, BT1 6AR
Tel: 028 9023 9619
Fax: 028 9031 2032
Director: Brian Symington

### Royal National Lifeboat Institution
Unit 1, Lifeboat House
Lesley Office Park, 393 Holywood Road
Belfast, BT4 2LS
Tel: 028 9047 3665
Fax: 028 9047 3668
Regional Manager: Patricia Mathison

### Royal Society for the Prevention of Accidents (RoSPA)
Nella House, Dargan Crescent
Belfast, BT3 9JP
Tel: 028 9050 1160
Fax: 028 9050 1164
Home Safety Manager: Janice Bisp

### Royal Society for the Protection of Birds (RSPB)
Belvoir Park Forest, Belvoir Drive
Belfast, BT8 4QT
Tel: 028 9049 1547
Fax: 028 9049 1669
Web: www.rspb.org.uk
Assistant Director: Clive Mellon

### Save the Children Fund
15 Richmond Park, Belfast, BT10 0HB
Tel: 028 9062 0000
Fax: 028 9043 1314
Web: www.scfuk.org.uk
Area Manager: Arlene Patterson

### Shelter (Northern Ireland)
1–5 Coyles Place, Belfast, BT9 1EL
Tel: 028 9024 7752
Fax: 028 9024 7710
Campaign Officer: Laurence Moffat

### Simon Community Northern Ireland
57 Fitzroy Avenue, Belfast, BT7 1HT
Tel: 028 9023 2882
Fax: 028 9032 6839
Chief Executive: Carol O'Bryan

Simon Community is one of Northern Ireland's largest charities, with over 200 staff with an annual budget in excess of £4m. Simon Community provides a wide range of services to homeless people including the provision of over 1,000 short-stay accommodation places all across Northern Ireland. In addition to lobbying for more appropriate accommodation for homeless people and better access to public services Simon Community is also focusing on the causes of homelessness and policy changes that could lead to greater prevention of this growing social problem.

### Spina Bifida and Hydrocephalus Association (NI) (ASBAH)
Graham House
Knockbracken Healthcare Park
Saintfield Road, Belfast, BT8 8BH
Tel: 028 9079 8878
Fax: 028 9079 7071
Web: www.asbah.org
Email: margarety@asbah.org
Regional Manager: Margaret Young

### St John's Ambulance
35 Knockbracken Healthcare Park
Belfast, BT8 8RA
Tel: 028 9079 9393
Fax: 028 9079 3303
Chief Executive: John Hugh

### Tara Counselling & Personal Development Centre
11 Holmview Terrace, Omagh
Co Tyrone, BT79 0AH
Tel: 028 8225 0024
Fax: 028 8225 0023
Administration Officer: Nuala Quinn

### Trocaire
50 King Street, Belfast, BT1 6AD
Tel: 028 9080 8030
Fax: 028 9080 8031
Web: www.trocaire.org
Regional Manager: Roisin Shannon

### Twins & Multiple Birth Association
PO Box 42, Belfast, BT5 5PQ
Tel: 028 9065 4609
Fax: 028 9065 4609
Web: www.tambni.org

### Ulster Society for the Prevention of Cruelty to Animals (USPCA)
PO Box 103, Belfast, BT6 8US
Tel: 028 9081 4242
Fax: 028 9081 5151
Web: www.planetpets-uspca.co.uk
Manager: Paddy Duffy

### Ulster Cancer Foundation
40–42 Eglantine Avenue
Belfast, BT9 6DX
Tel: 028 9049 2007
Fax: 028 9066 0081
Web: www.ulstercancer.org
Email: info@ulstercancer.org
Chief Executive: Arlene Spiers

### Ulster Wildlife Trust
Ulster Wildlife Centre
3 New Line, Crossgar
Downpatrick, BT30 9EP
Tel: 028 4483 0282
Fax: 028 4483 0888
Email: ulsterwt@clx.co.uk
Chief Executive: Heather Thompson

### Victim Support NI
Annsgate House, 70–74 Ann Street
Belfast, BT1 4EH
Tel: 028 9024 4039
Fax: 028 9031 3838
Email: info@victimsupportni.org.uk

### Voluntary Service Belfast
34 Shaftsbury Square
Belfast, BT2 7DB
Tel: 028 9020 0850
Fax: 028 9020 0860
Email: info@vsb.org.uk
Director: Bill Osborne

### War on Want
1 Rugby Avenue, Belfast, BT7 1RD
Tel: 028 9023 2064
Fax: 028 9032 8019
Director: Linda McClelland
Web: www.waronwant.org

### The Woodland Trust
1 Dufferin Court, Dufferin Avenue
Bangor, BT20 3BX
Tel: 028 9127 5787
Fax: 028 9127 5942
Email: wtni@woodland-trust.org.uk
Operations Director: Patrick Cregg

### Women's Aid Belfast
Womens Aid, 49 Malone Road
Belfast, BT9 6RY
Tel: 028 9066 6049
Fax: 028 9068 2874
Web: www.belfastwomensaid.co.uk
Email: admin@belfastwomensaid.org.uk
Management co-ordinator:
Margot Hesketh

### Women's Aid Coleraine
23 Abbey Street, Coleraine, BT52 1DU
Tel: 028 7032 1263
Administrator: Evelyn Morrow

### Women's Aid Craigavon
198 Union Street, Lurgan
Craigavon, BT66 8EQ
Tel: 028 3834 3256
Fax: 028 3832 2277
Email:
info@craigavon
banbridgewomensaid.org.uk

### Women's Aid Fermanagh
14A High Street, Enniskillen, BT74 7EH
Tel: 028 6632 8898
Fax: 028 6632 8859
Team Leader: Mary McCann

### Women's Aid Newry
7 Downshire Place
Newry, Co Down, BT34 1DZ
Tel: 028 3025 0765
Fax: 028 3026 9606
Co-ordinator: Arlene Havern

### Women's Forum NI
PO Box 135, Belfast, BT5 5WA
Tel: 028 9446 0251
Fax: 028 9446 0251
Email: anneking@lineone.net
Vice Chairman: Ms Rosemary Rainey

### Women's Support Network
2nd Floor, 109-113 Royal Avenue,
Belfast, BT1 1FF
Tel: 028 9023 6923
Email: info@womensupportnetwork.org

## Youth and Community Organisations

An Crann / The Tree
10 Arthur St, Belfast, BT1 4GD
Tel: 028 9024 0209
Fax: 028 9024 0219
Email: ancrann1@compuserve.com
Honorary Secretary: Dennis Greig

Ardglass Development Association
19 High Street, Ardglass, BT30 7TU
Tel: 028 4484 2404
Chairperson: Mary McCargoe

Ballymena Community Forum
Glendun Drive, Ballymena, BT43 6SR
Tel: 028 2565 1032
Fax: 028 2565 1035
Web:
www.ballymenacommunityforum.org
Contact: Corinna Peterson

Ballynafeigh Community Development Association
283 Ormeau Road, Belfast, BT7 3GG
Tel: 028 9049 1161
Fax: 028 9049 2393
Web: www.bcda.net
Contact: Katie Hanlon

Ballysillan Community Forum
925–927 Crumlin Road
Belfast, BT14 8AB
Tel: 028 9039 1272
Fax: 028 9039 1259
Manager: Dale Harrison

Belfast Community Theatre Workshop
Crescent Arts Centre
2–4 University Road, Belfast, BT7 1AH
Tel: 028 9031 0900
Fax: 028 9024 6748
Email: bct.comm.arts@ntlworld.com
Contact: Fintan Brady

Belfast Interface Project
Glendinning House, 6 Murray Street
Belfast, BT1 6DN
Tel: 028 9024 2828
Fax: 028 9024 2828
Email: bip@cinni.org
Support Worker: Marnie Kennedy

Belfast Travellers Education & Development Group
Blackstaff Complex, 77 Springfield Road Belfast, BT12 7AE
Tel: 028 9020 3337
Fax: 028 9080 9191
Email: info@ b-t-e-d-g@niireland.com
Director: Derek Hanway

Belfast Unemployed Resource Centre
45–47 Donegall Street
Belfast BT1 2FG
Tel: 028 9096 1111
Fax: 028 9096 1110
Manager: Joyce Green

Belfast Youth and Community Group
1–5 Donegall Lane, Belfast, BT1 2LZ
Tel: 028 9024 4640
Fax: 028 9031 5629
Email: bycg@dial.pipex.com

Belfast Economic Resource Centre
1–5 Coyles Place, Belfast, BT7 1EL
Tel: 028 9024 1924
Fax: 028 9024 6985
Email: office@boysandgirlsclub-ni.org.uk
Director of Programmes:
Terry Watson

Business in the Community
Albertbridge Road, Belfast BT5 4HD
Tel: 028 9046 0606
Email: gillian.mckee@bitcni.org.uk
PR Director: Gillian McKee

Boys Brigade Northern Ireland Headquarters
National Training Centre
Rathmore House, 126 Glenarm Road
Larne, BT40 1DZ
Tel: 028 2827 2794
Fax: 028 2827 5150
Director: Rev George McClelland

Catholic Guides of Ireland, Northern Region
285 Antrim Road, Belfast, BT15 2GZ
Tel: 028 9074 0835
Fax: 028 9074 1311
Email: guides@northern.freeserve.co.uk
Chairperson: Eilish Smyth

Central Community Relations Unit
Block A, Level 5, Room A5.18
Castle Buildings, Stormont
Belfast, BT4 3SG
Tel: 028 9052 8258
Fax: 028 9052 8426
Principal Officer: Denis Ritchie

Challenge for Youth
40–46 Edward Street, Belfast, BT1 2LP
Tel: 028 9023 6893
Fax: 028 9024 0718
Chief Executive: David Gardiner

Children's Law Centre
Philip House, York Street
Belfast, BT15 1AB
Tel: 028 9024 5704
Fax: 028 9024 5679
Email: info@childrenslawcentre.org
Director: Paddy Kelly

Children's Project NI
290 Antrim Road, Belfast, BT15 5AN
Tel: 028 9074 1536
Fax: 028 9080 5578
Email: cpnibfast@yahoo.co.uk
Director: Gary Rocks

Chinese Welfare Association (NI)
133–135 University Street
Belfast, BT7 1HP
Tel: 028 9028 8277
Fax: 028 9028 8278
Email: cwa.anna@cinni.org
Chief Executive: Anna Lo

Clogher Valley Rural Centre
Creebought House, 47 Main Street
Clogher, Co Tyrone, BT76 0AA
Tel: 028 8554 8872
Fax: 028 8554 8203
Manager: Sean Kelly

Colin Glen Trust
163 Stewartstown Road
Belfast, BT17 0HW
Tel: 028 9061 4115
Fax: 028 9060 1694
Email: info@colinglentrust.org
Chief Executive: Tim Duffy

Community Arts Forum
15 Church Street, Belfast, BT1 1PG
Tel: 028 9024 2910
Fax: 028 9031 2264
Web: www.cast.ie
Email: admin@cast.ie
Contact: Lizzie Devlin

Community Bridges Programme
16 Donegall Square South
Belfast, BT1 5JF
Tel: 028 9031 3220
Fax: 028 9031 3180
Email: community.bridge@dnet.co.uk
Programme Coordinator: Joe Hinds

Community Change
Philip House, 123-127 York Street
Belfast, BT15 1AB
Tel: 028 9023 2587
Fax: 028 9031 2216
Email: info@communitychange-ni.org
Head of Agency: Alison Wightman

Community Development & Health Network
30A Mill Street, Newry, BT34 1EY
Tel: 028 3026 4606
Fax: 028 3026 4626
Email: cdhn@btconnect.com
Director: Ruth Sutherland

### Community Dialogue
373 Springfield Road, Belfast, BT12 7DG
Tel: 028 9032 9995
Fax: 028 9033 0482
Email: admin@commdial.org
Web: www.commdial.org
Directors: Brian Lennon, David Halloway

### Community Empowerment Larne
Stylux Business Park
Lower Waterloo Road, Larne, BT40 1NT
Tel: 028 2826 7552
205a Linn Road, Larne
Tel: 028 2827 3953
Development Officer: Eric Cahoon

### Community Evaluation (NI)
297 Ormeau Road, Belfast, BT7 3GG
Tel: 028 9064 6355
Fax: 028 9064 1118
Email: info@ceni.org
Director: Brendan McDonnell

### Community Relations Council
6 Murray Street, Belfast, BT1 6DN
Tel: 028 9022 7500
Fax: 028 9022 7551
Email: info@community-relations.org.uk
Web: www.community-relations.org.uk
Chief Executive: Dr Duncan Morrow

### Community Technical Aid NI
445–449 Ormeau Road
Belfast, BT7 3GQ
Tel: 028 9064 2227
Fax: 028 9064 2467
Email: info@communitytechnicalaid.org
Director: Colm Bradley

### Contact Youth Counselling
139 Ravenhill Road, Belfast, BT6 8DR
Tel: 0808 8088 000

### Community Transport Association UK
Graham House, Saintfield Road
Belfast, BT7 8BH
Tel/Fax: 028 9040 3535
Email: bryan@communitytransport.com
Regional Development Officer:
Bryan Myles

### Community Work Education and Training Network
Philip House, York Street
Belfast, BT15 1AB
Tel: 028 9023 2618
Fax: 028 9031 2216
Co-ordinator: Peggy Flanagan

### Counteract
Philip House, 123–137 York Street
Belfast, BT15 1AB
Tel: 028 9023 7023
Fax: 028 9031 3585
Email: counteract@btconnect.com
Director: William Robinson

### Devenish Partnership Forum
26 Yoan Road, Kilmacormick
Enniskillen, BT74 6EI
Tel: 028 6632 7808
Fax: 028 6632 7808
Email: devenish.partnership@cinni.org
Manager: John Guthrie

### Duke of Edinburgh Award NI
28 Wellington Park, Belfast, BT9 6DL
Tel: 028 9050 9550
Fax: 028 9050 9555
Email: nireland@theaward.org
Secretary: Eric Rainey MBE

### Dunlewey Substance Advice Centre NI Ltd
226 Stewartstown Road
Belfast, BT17 0LB
Tel: 028 9061 1162
Fax: 028 9060 3751
Email: dsac@btconnect.com
Director: Annette Goodall

### East Belfast Community Development Agency
269 Albertbridge Road
Belfast, BT5 4PY
Tel: 028 9045 1512
Fax: 028 9073 8039
Email: info@ebcda.com
Director: Michael Briggs

### Enkalon Foundation
25 Randalstown Road
Antrim, BT41 4LJ
Tel: 028 9446 3535
Fax: 028 9446 5733
Email: enkfoundation@lineone.net
Secretary: John Wallace

### Falls Community Council
275–277 Falls Road, Belfast, BT12 6FD
Tel: 028 9020 2030
Fax:028 9020 2031
Email: info@fallscommunitycouncil.org
Contact: Marie Maguire

### Fermanagh Access and Mobility Group
36 Eastbridge Street
Enniskillen, BT74 7BT
Tel: 028 6634 0275
Email: fermanaghaccess@swiftsoft.net
Chairperson: Gerry Maguire

### Fermanagh Rural Community Initiative
Unit 3, 56A Temo Road
Enniskillen, BT74 6HR
Tel: 028 6632 6478
Fax: 028 6632 5984
Email: info@frci.org.uk
Manager: Ciaran Rooney

### Fermanagh Volunteer Bureau
12 Belmore Street
Enniskillen, BT74 6AA
Tel: 028 6632 8438
Fax: 028 6632 2061
Email: info@fermanaghvb.org
Chairperson: Martin Lawson

### Girls Brigade Northern Ireland
16 May Street, Belfast, BT1 4NL
Tel: 028 9023 1157
Fax: 028 9032 3633
Email: info@girlsbrigadeni.com
Director: Doreen Tennis

### Greater Shankill Community Council
177 Shankill Road, Belfast, BT13 1FP
Tel: 028 9032 5536
Fax: 028 9024 4469
Manager: Bill Patterson

### Greater Shankill Partnership Early Years Project
Alessie Centre, 60 Shankill Road
Belfast, BT13 2BB
Tel: 028 9087 4000
Fax: 028 9087 4009
Email: irene@earlyyears.org.uk
Project Manager: Irene Cooke

### Greater Twinbrook and Poleglass Community Forum
Unit W2, Dairyfarm Centre
Stewartstown Road, Belfast, BT17 0AW
Tel: 028 9060 4004
Fax: 028 9060 4104
Director: Sean Gibson

### Greater West Belfast Community Association
76–78 Hamill Street, Belfast, BT12 4AA
Tel: 028 9032 8295
Fax: 028 9032 8295
Email: gwbcarc@aol.com
Office Admin: Angela Forde

### Groundwork NI
63-75 Duncairn Gardens
Belfast, BT15 2GB
Tel: 028 9074 9494
Fax: 028 9075 2373
Email: info@groundworkni.co.uk
Director: Mary McKee

### Guide Association
Lorne House, Station Road, Craigavad
Holywood, BT18 0BP
Tel: 028 9042 5212
Fax: 028 9042 6025
Email: ulsterhq@guides.org.uk
Ulster Administrator: Claire Bradley

### Holywell Trust
10-12 Bishop Street, Derry, BT48 6PW
Tel: 028 7126 1941
Fax: 028 7126 9332
Web: www.holywelltrust.com
Director: Eamonn Deane

### Housing Rights Service
Middleton Building, 10-12 High Street
Belfast, BT1 2BA
Tel: 028 9024 5640
Fax: 028 9031 2200
Email: hrs@housing-rights.org.uk
Director: Janet Hunter

### Horizon Project
234 Upper Lisburn Road
Belfast, BT10 0TA
Tel: 028 9060 5424
Fax: 028 9060 5423
Email:
horizonbel@admins.freeserve.co.uk
Co-ordinator: George Simms

### Initiative on Conflict Resolution and Ethnicity (INCORE)
Aberfoyle House, Northland Road
Derry, BT48 7JA
Tel: 028 7137 5500
Fax: 028 7137 5510
Email: incore@incore.ulst.ac.uk
Director: Professor Gillian Robinson

### Larne Community Development Project
Unit 25, Ledcom Industrial Estate
Larne, BT40 3AW
Tel: 028 2826 7976
Email: info@larnecdp.org.uk
Chairperson: Geoffrey Kerr

### Law Centre NI Belfast
124 Donegall Street, Belfast, BT1 2GY
Tel: 028 9024 4401
Fax: 028 9023 9938
Email: admin.belfast@lawcenteni.org
Director: Les Allamby

### Leonard Cheshire NI Regional Office
5 Boucher Plaza, 4–6 Boucher Road
Belfast, BT12 6HR
Tel: 028 9024 6247
Fax: 028 9024 6395
Email: info@ni.leonard-cheshire.org.uk
Regional Director: Roisin Foster

### Lifestart Foundation NI
11A Bishops Street, Derry BT48 6PL
Tel: 028 7136 5363
Fax: 028 7136 5334
Director: Dolores McGuinness

### Ligoniel Improvement Association
148 Ligoniel Road, Belfast
BT14 8DT
Tel: 028 9039 1225
Fax: 028 9039 1723
Email: wolfehill@freeuk.com
Director: Tony Morgan

### LINC Resource Centre
218 York Street, Belfast, BT15 1GY
Tel: 028 9074 5983
Fax: 028 9075 4302
Email: billy.linc@cinni.lorg
Programme Manager: Billy Mitchell
Chairperson: Theresa Cullen

### Link Community Association
7 Avoca Park, Belfast, BT11 9BH
Tel: 028 9020 0774
Fax: 028 9020 0774
Chairperson: Barbara Lynn

### Lower North Belfast Community Council
The Castleton Centre
30–42 York Road, Belfast, BT15 3HE
Tel: 028 9020 8100
Fax: 028 9020 1103
Programmes Manager: Ian Crozier

### Lurgan Council for Voluntary Action
Mount Zion House, Edward Street
Lurgan, BT66 6DB
Tel: 028 3832 2066
Fax: 028 3834 8612
Email: info@lcva.co.uk
Director: Edwin Graham

### Magnet Young Adult Centre
81a Hill Street, Newry, BT34 1DG
Tel: 028 3026 9070
Fax: 028 3026 9070
Senior Youth Worker: Eugene Donnelly

### Mediation Northern Ireland
10 Upper Crescent, Belfast, BT7 1NT
Tel: 028 9043 8614
Fax: 028 9031 4430
Web: www.mediationni.org
Email: info@mediationnorthernireland.org
Director: Brendan McAllister

### Mornington Community Project NI
117 Ormeau Road, Belfast, BT7 1SH
Tel: 028 9033 0911
Fax: 028 9023 4730
Director: Ken Humphrey

### Multicultural Resource Centre
9 Lower Crescent, Belfast, BT7 1NR
Tel: 028 9024 4639
Fax: 028 9032 9581
Web: www.mcrc-ni.org
Contact: Caroline Coleman

### National Energy Action
64–66 Upper Church Lane
Belfast, BT1 4QL
Tel: 028 9023 9909
Fax: 028 9043 9191
Email: northern.ireland@nea.org.uk
Director: Majella McCloskey

### Newtownabbey Community Development Agency
Ferbro Buildings, 333 Antrim Road
Newtownabbey, BT36 5DZ
Tel: 028 9083 8088
Fax: 028 9083 0108
Director: Victor Robinson

### NIACRO Belfast
169 Ormeau Road, Belfast, BT7 1SQ
Tel: 028 9032 0157
Fax: 028 9023 4084
Chief Executive: Alwyn Lyner

### NIACRO Community Relations Project
16 Russell Street, Armagh, BT61 9AA
Tel: 028 3751 5910
Fax: 028 3751 5919

### Northern Ireland Council for Ethnic Minorities (NICEM)
3rd Floor, Ascot House
24–31 Shaftesbury Square
Belfast, BT2 7DB
Tel: 028 9023 8645
Fax: 028 9031 9485
Email: nicem@nireland.freeserve.co.uk
Web: www.nicem.org.uk
Executive Director: Patrick Yu

### Peace People
Fredheim, 224 Lisburn Road
Belfast, BT9 6GE
Tel: 028 9066 3465
Fax: 028 9068 3947
Email: info@peacepeople.com
Chairperson: Gerry Grehan

### The Phoenix Centre
Mount Zion House, Edward Street
Lurgan, BT66 6DB
Tel: 028 3832 7614
Fax: 028 3832 7614
Manager: Pearl Snowdon

### Poleglass Residents Association
Sallygarden Lane, Bell Steel Road
Poleglass, Belfast, BT17 0PB
Tel: 028 9062 7250
Fax: 028 9062 7250
Chairperson: Sue Ramsay

### Prison Link
80-90 North Street, Belfast, BT1 1LD
Tel: 028 9026 2489
Fax: 028 9026 2450

### Quaker House Belfast Joint Project
7 University Avenue, Belfast, BT7 1GX
Tel: 028 9024 9293
Email: quaker.house@ntlworld.com
Representative: Mark Chapman

### Rural Community Network
38a Oldtown Street
Cookstown, BT80 8EF
Tel: 028 8676 6670
Fax: 028 8676 6006
Email: info@ruralcommunitynetwork.org
Chairperson: Roy Hanna

### Sandy Row Community Forum
c/o Sandy Row Community Centre
63–75 Sandy Row, Belfast, BT12 5ER
Tel: 028 9023 8446
Fax: 028 9023 8446
Chairperson: Ernie Corbett

### Scout Association
Old Milltown Road, Belfast, BT8 7SP
Tel: 028 9049 2829
Fax: 028 9049 2830
Email: info@scoutsni.com
Executive Commissioner:
Ken Gillespie

### Scouting Foundation Northern Ireland
12A Lisburn Enterprise Centre
Ballinderry Road, Lisburn, BT28 2BP
Tel: 028 9266 7696
Contact: Declan Cooper

### Shankill Lurgan Community Projects
53 Edward Street BT66 6DB
Tel: 028 3832 4680
Fax: 028 3834 3466
Manager: Hugh Casey

### Share Holiday Village
Smiths Strand, Lisnaskea, BT92 0EQ
Tel: 028 6772 2122
Fax: 028 6772 1893
Email: info@sharevillage.org
Director: Oliver Wilkinson

### Speedwell Project
Parkanaur Forest Park
Dungannon, BT70 3AA
Tel: 028 8776 7392
Fax: 028 8776 1794
Email: speedwell.trust@btinternet.com
Director: Jean Kelly

### Strabane Community Unemployment Resource Centre
13a Newton Street
Strabane, BT82 8DN
Tel: 028 7138 3927
Fax: 028 7138 3927
Manager: Betty Bradley

### South Tyrone Empowerment Programme
2 Coalisland Road, Dungannon
BT71 6LA
Tel: 028 8772 9002
Fax: 028 8772 9008

### Training for Women Network Ltd
Unit 10B Weavers Court, Linfield Road
Belfast, BT12 5GL
Tel: 028 9031 9888
Fax: 028 9031 1116
Chairperson: Alice Higgins

### Traveller Movement NI
30 University Street, Belfast, BT7 1FZ
Tel: 028 9020 2727
Fax: 028 9020 2005
Email: info@tmni.org

### Ulster Community Investment Trust
13–19 Linenhall Street
Belfast, BT2 8AA
Tel: 028 9031 5003
Fax: 028 9031 5008
Email: info@ucitld.com
Chief Executive: Brian Howe

### University for Industry Learndirect
400 Springfield Road, Belfast
Tel: 028 9090 0070
Email: info@ufi.com
Head of UFI in Northern Ireland:
Mark Langhammer

### WAVE Trauma Centre
5 Chichester Park South
Belfast, BT15 5DW
Tel: 028 9077 9922
Fax: 028 9078 1165
Email: personnel@wavebelfast.co.uk
Chief Executive: Sandra Peake

### West Belfast Economic Forum
148–158 Springfield Road
Belfast, BT12 7DR
Tel: 028 9087 4545
Fax: 028 9087 5050
Email: info@wbef.org
Contact: Una Gillespie

### West Belfast Parent Youth Group
141–143 Falls Road, Belfast, BT12 6AF
Tel: 028 9023 6669
Fax: 028 9023 5564
Email: marieosbourne@btconnect.co.uk
Centre Manager: Marie Osborne

### Women into Politics
109–113 Royal Avenue, Belfast, BT1 1FF
Tel: 028 9024 3363
Fax: 028 9023 7884
Director: May DeSilvia

### Women's Resource & Development Agency
6 Mount Charles, Belfast, BT7 1NZ
Tel: 028 9023 0212
Fax: 028 9024 4363
Email: info@wrda.net
Director: Anne O'Reilly

### Young Persons Project
2 Old Lurgan Road
Portadown, BT63 5SG
Tel: 028 3839 1155
Fax: 028 3839 3718
Manager: Peadar White

### YMCA National Council
Memorial House, 9–13 Waring Street
Belfast, BT1 2EU
Tel: 028 9032 7757
Fax: 028 9043 8809
Email: admin@ymca-ireland.org
National Secretary: Stephen Turner

### Youth Initiatives
Cloona House, 31 Colin Road
Poleglass, BT17 0LG
Tel: 028 9030 1174

### Youth Link NI
143a University St, Belfast, BT7 1HP
Tel: 028 9032 3217
Fax: 028 9032 3247
Email: info@youthlink.org.uk
Director: Rev Patrick White

### YouthAction Northern Ireland
Hampton, Glenmachan Park
Belfast, BT4 2PJ
Tel: 028 9076 0067
Fax: 028 9076 8799
Director: June Trimble

### YouthNet
7 James Steet South, Belfast, BT2 8DN
Tel: 028 9033 1880
Fax: 028 9033 1977
Email: info@youthnet.co.uk
Director: Denis Palmer

### Youth Council For Northern Ireland
Forestview, Purdy's Lane
Belfast, BT8 7AR
Tel: 028 9064 3882
Fax: 028 9064 3874

## Religious, Political and Cultural Organisations

Despite the fact that Northern Ireland has endured many years of conflict it is a deeply religious place by Western European standards.

Church attendances remain the highest of any region in the UK and there is a high ratio of churches to population. The Community is overwhelmingly Christian with the main four churches being Roman Catholic, Presbyterian, Church of Ireland and Methodist, with a strong evangelical tradition within Northern Ireland Protestantism. Most of the other major world religions are represented in Northern Ireland in relatively small numbers. The section below lists the various Churches found in Northern Ireland, with additional contact details for the larger institutions.

Irish Council of Churches
Inter-Church Centre
48 Elmwood Avenue, Belfast, BT9 6AZ
Tel: 028 9066 3145
Fax: 028 9066 4160
Email: irish.church@btconnect.com
Web: www.irishchurches.org

Bahá'Í Faith
64 Old Dundonald Road
Dundonald, BT16 1XS
Tel: 028 9048 0500
Fax: 028 9041 0100

Baptist Union of Ireland
19 Hillsborough Road
Moira, BT67 0HQ
Tel: 028 9261 9267

Belfast Islamic Centre
38 Wellington Park, Belfast, BT9 6DN
Tel: 028 9066 4465
Fax: 028 9091 3148
Web: www.belfastislamiccentre.org.uk
Contact: Jamal Iweida

Belfast Synagogue
49 Somerton Road, Belfast, BT15 3LH
Tel: 028 9077 7974

Bethel Temple
95 Main St, Portglenone
Ballymena, BT44 8HR
Tel: 028 2582 1167
Contact: David Lamont

Buddhist Centre
40d Donegall Pass, Belfast, BT7 1BS
Tel: 028 9023 8090
Web: www.potalacentre.org.uk

Roman Catholic Church

The Roman Catholic Church administers Ireland as a single unit, divided into 4 ecclesiastical Provinces. The Province of Armagh comprises of 6 dioceses, which together cover the whole of Northern Ireland and a proportion of the Republic of Ireland.

### Catholic Bishops in the Province of Armagh

*Most Rev Séan Brady, Archbishop of Armagh*
Ara Coeli, Cathedral Road
Armagh, BT61 7QY
Tel: 028 3752 2045
Fax: 028 3752 6182

*Most Rev Seamus Hegarty, Bishop of Derry*
Bishop's House,
St Eugene's Cathedral
Derry, BT48 9AP
Tel: 028 7126 2302
Fax: 028 7137 1960

*Most Rev Francis Lagan, Auxiliary Bishop of Derry*
9 Glen Road, Strabane
Co Tyrone, BT82 8BX
Tel: 028 7188 4533
Fax: 028 7188 4551

*Most Rev Patrick Walsh, Bishop of Down and Connor*
Lisbreen, 73 Somerton Road
Belfast, BT15 4DE
Tel: 028 9077 6185
Fax: 028 9077 9377

*Most Rev Anthony Farquhar, Auxiliary Bishop of Down and Connor*
Lisbreen, 73 Somerton Road
Belfast, BT15 4DE
Tel: 028 9077 6185
Fax: 028 9077 9377

*Most Rev John McAreavey, Bishop of Dromore*
Bishop's House, 44 Armagh Road
Newry BT35 6PN
Tel: 028 3026 2444
Fax: 028 3026 0496

Christian Brothers
The Abbey Monastery, Courtney Hill
Newry, BT34 2EA
Tel: 028 3026 4475

Church of Ireland
Church of Ireland House
61–67 Donegall Street
Belfast, BT1 2QH
Tel: 028 9032 2268
Fax: 028 9032 1635

The Church of Ireland divides the island of Ireland into two Provinces, Armagh and Dublin. The majority of its members are in Northern Ireland; this congregation is administered under the province of Armagh.

The General Synod of the Church of Ireland, consisting of the archbishops and bishops, with 216 representatives of the clergy and 432 representatives of the laity, has chief legislative power in the Church.

### Church of Ireland Bishops in the Province of Armagh

*The Most Rev and Right Honourable the Lord Eames of Armagh*
The See House, Cathedral Close
Armagh, BT61 7EE
Tel: 028 3752 7144
Fax: 028 3752 7823

*The Right Rev Michael Jackson Lord Bishop of Clogher*
The See House, Fivemiletown
Co Tyrone, BT75 0QP
Tel/Fax: 028 8952 2475

*The Right Rev Ken Good, Lord Bishop of Derry and Raphoe*
The See House, 112 Culmore Road
Derry, BT48 8JF
Tel: 028 7135 1206
Fax: 028 7135 2554

*The Right Rev H C Miller, Lord Bishop of Down and Dromore*
The See House
32 Knockdere Park South
Belfast, BT5 7AB
Tel: 028 9023 7602
Fax: 028 9065 0584

*The Right Rev Alan Harper, Lord Bishop of Connor*
Bishop's House
113 Upper Road, Greenisland
Carrickfergus, BT38 8RR
Tel: 028 9086 3165
Fax: 028 9036 4266

### Church of Jesus Christ of the Latter Day Saints
403 Holywood Road, Belfast, BT4 2GU
Tel: 028 9076 8250
President: Eric Noble

### Child Evangelism Fellowship of Ireland
199 Templmore Avenue
Belfast, BT5 4FN
Tel: 028 9073 2263
Directors: Mr and Mrs Henry Berry

### Christian Renewal Centre
44 Shore Road, Rostrevor
Newry, BT34 3ET
Tel: 028 4173 8492
Fax: 028 4173 8996

### Elim Pentecostal Church
120a Alexandra Park Avenue
Belfast, BT15 3GJ
Tel: 028 9074 4404
Fax: 028 9074 8422
Senior Minister: Brian Madden

### Free Presbyterian Church
Martyrs Memorial
356 Ravenhill Road, Belfast
Moderator: Rev Ian Paisley

### International Society for Krishna Consciousness
Inis Rath Island, Geaglum
Derrylin, Enniskillen, Co Fermanagh
Tel: 028 6772 1512

### Jehovah's Witnesses
9 Belmont Park, Belfast BT4 3DU

### Methodist Church in Ireland
Mission House, 13 University Road
Belfast, BT7 1NA
Tel: 028 9032 0078
Fax: 028 9043 8700

The Methodist Church divides Ireland into eight district synods, each containing a number of circuits. Each synod is headed by a District Superintendent. The Methodist Conference meets around the island every year, and elects a President as overall head of the Church.
President: Rev Fletcher
35 Thomas Street
Portadown, BT62 3NU
Tel: 028 3833 3030

Secretary: Rev W Graham
1 Fountainville Avenue
Belfast, BT9 6AN
Tel: 028 9032 4554
Fax: 028 9023 9467

**District Superintendents**

Belfast District: Rev R McElhinney
8 Richill Crescent
Belfast, BT5 6HF
Tel0: 028 9065 3470

Down District: Rev Kenneth Todd
9 Maxwell Park
Bangor, BT20 3SH
Tel: 028 9146 5324

Lakelands District: Rev Ken Robinson
'Aldersgate'
47 Chanterhill Road
Enniskillen, BT74 6DE
Tel: 028 6632 2244

North East District: Rev Aian Ferguson
32 Harwood Gardens
Carrickfergus, BT38 7US
Tel: 028 9336 2202

North West District: Rev Harold Agnew
9 Dergmoney Place
Omagh, BT78 1HS
Tel: 028 8224 2372

Portadown District: Rev Maurice Laverty
5 The Hollows
Gilford Road
Lurgan, BT66 7FF
Tel: 028 3832 3367

**Methodist Administration**

Trustees of the Methodist Church in Ireland
1 Fountainville Avenue
Belfast, BT9 6AN
Tel: 028 9032 4554
Fax: 028 9023 9467

### Presbyterian Church in Ireland
Church House, Fisherwick Place
Belfast, BT1 6DW
Tel: 028 9032 2284
Fax: 028 9024 8366
Web: www.presbyterianireland.org
General Assembly Moderator:
Rev Ken Newell

Clerk of the Assembly:
Rev Dr Donal Watts

The Presbyterian Church in Ireland is divided into congregations or parishes, collectively containing over 280,000 members. The congregations are grouped into 21 district presbyteries. Eighteen of these are in the North, with the majority of Presbyterians in the South of Ireland in Dublin and the border counties. The Church is governed by an annual General Assembly, which is composed of representatives from every congregation. The General Assembly elects a Moderator each June, to act as the chief public representative of Presbyterians in Ireland.

### Quakers Religious Society of Friends
5 Glenside Avenue, Drumbo
Lisburn, BT27 5LQ
Tel: 028 9082 6708
Contact: Rosemary Calvert

### Salvation Army
12 Station Mews, Sydenham
Belfast, BT4 1TL
Tel: 028 9067 5000
Fax: 028 9067 5011
Web: www.salvationarmy.org.uk
Divisional Communications Manager:
Linda Campbell

### Seventh Day Adventist Church
9 Newry Road
Banbridge, BT32 3HF
Tel: 028 4062 4592
Email: banbridge@adventist.ie

### Sikh Cultural Centre
Simpsons Brae, Derry, BT47 6DL
Tel: 028 7134 3523

### Ulster Humanist Association
25 Riverside Drive, Lisburn, BT27 4HE
Tel: 028 9267 7264

## Cultural Organisations

Grand Orange Lodge of Ireland

Schomberg House, 368 Cregagh Road
Belfast, BT6 9EY
Tel: 028 9070 1122
Fax: 028 9040 3700

Grand Master: Robert S Saulters
Deputy Grand Master: Roy Kells MBE
Deputy Assistant Grand Masters: Rev Stephen Dickinson, William Ross
Grand Secretary: Denis J Watson

The Orange Order is possibly Northern Ireland's best-known 'cultural' organisation, with an active membership of over 100,000 men and women. It is a Protestant organisation steeped in the heritage of Protestant struggle for religious freedoms in the seventeenth century. The Order has formal links all over the world with similar institutions and is best known for its colourful militaristic marches during the summer.

Latin American Community and Cultural Association

Tel: 028 9031 9963
Email: launida@mcrc.co.uk
Chairperson: Cony Ortiz

Ulster Scots Heritage Council

218 York Street, Belfast BT15 1GY
Tel: 028 9074 6939
Fax: 028 9074 6980
Acting Director: William Humprey

Ulster Scots Historical & Cultural Society

40 Teenaght Road, Claudy, Londonderry
Tel: 07714 989 345
Contact: William Houston

## Political Organisations

Committee on the Administration of Justice

45–47 Donegall St, Belfast, BT1 2BR
Tel: 028 9096 1122
Web: www.caj.org.uk
Director: Maggie Beirne

New Ireland Group

c/o 85 Charlotte Street
Ballymoney, BT53 6AZ
Tel: 028 2766 2235
Contact: John Robb

### Political Parties

*(Details of Northern Ireland's main political parties are set out in Chapter 2).*

## Sporting, Leisure and Arts Organisations

Badminton Union of Ireland

House of Sport, Upper Malone Road
Belfast, BT9 5LA
Tel: 028 9038 3810
Contact: Leslie Dewart

Belfast Giants Ice Hockey Club

Unit 3, Ormeau Business Park
8 Cromac Avenue, Belfast BT7 2JA
Tel: 028 9059 1111
Contact: Richard Gowdy

British Association for Shooting and Conservation

The Courtyard Cottage
Galgorm Castle, Ballymena
Tel: 028 9260 5050

British Horse Society (NI Region)

60 Windmill Road
Hillsborough, BT26 6LX
Tel: 028 9268 3801
Fax: 028 9268 3801
Web: www.bhsireland.co.uk
Contact: Susan Irwin

Canoeing Association of Northern Ireland (CANI)

Unit 2, Riversedge
13-15 Ravenhill Road, Belfast, BT6 8DN
Tel: 028 9073 8884
Contact: David Bell

Disability Sports NI

Unit 10 Ormeau Business Park
8 Cromac Avenue, Belfast, BT7 2JA
Tel: 028 9050 8255
Fax: 028 9050 8256
Web: www.dsni.co.uk
Email: email@dsdni.co.uk
Contact: Kevin O'Neill

Eventing Ireland

98 Shore Street, Killyleagh, BT30 9QJ
Tel: 028 4482 8734
Fax: 028 4482 1166
Secretary: Margaret Spiers

Fitness Northern Ireland

The Robinson Centre, Montgomery Road, Belfast, BT6 9HS
Tel: 028 9070 4080
Contact: Ms I Rea

Gaelic Athletic Association

House of Sport, Upper Malone Road
Belfast, BT9 5LA
Tel: 028 9038 3815
Fax: 028 9068 2757
Contact: Seamus McGrattan

The Gaelic Athletic Association is Northern Ireland's leading participant sports organisation. It presides over Gaelic football, hurling, camogie and handball, as well as a range of other cultural activities.

Golfing Unions of Ireland, Ulster Branch

58a High Street, Holywood, BT18 9AE
Tel: 028 9042 3708
Fax: 028 9042 6766
Branch Secretary: Brendan Edwards

International Swimming Teachers Association

4 Firfields, Lough Road
Antrim, BT41 4DJ
Tel: 028 9448 7050
Email: natiinfo@aol.com
Regional Organiser NI: Des Cossum

Irish Amateur Swimming Association

House of Sport, Upper Malone Road,
Belfast, BT9 5LA
Tel: 028 9038 3807
Fax: 028 9068 2757
Contact: Claire Hamilton

Irish Bowling Association

78 North Road, Belfast, BT5 5NL
Tel: 028 9065 5076
Fax: 028 9065 5076
Honorary Secretary: Mr J Humphreys

Irish Football Association (IFA)

20 Windsor Avenue, Belfast, BT9 6EE
Tel: 028 9066 9458
General Secretary: David Bowen
The IFA presides over soccer in Northern Ireland.

Ulster Branch, Irish Hockey Association

House of Sport, Upper Malone Road
Belfast, BT9 5LA
Tel: 028 9038 3819
Fax: 028 9068 2757
Email: alan@ulsterhockey.com
Development Officer: Alan McMurray

Irish Indoor Bowling Association

204 Kings Road, Belfast, BT5 7HX
Tel: 028 9048 3536
Secretary: Mr D Hunter

**Irish Ladies Golf Union, Northern District**
7 Hillcrest Avenue
Newtownabbey, BT23 7AW
Tel: 028 4461 2286
Contact: Maureen Mawhinney

**Irish Rugby Football Union (Ulster Branch)**
85 Ravenhill Park, Belfast, BT6 0DG
Tel: 028 9049 3111
Fax: 028 9049 1522
Web: www.ulsterrugby.com
Email: lyn@ulsterrugby.com
Honorary Secretary: Mr J Eagleson

**Irish Table Tennis Association**
House of Sport, Upper Malone Road
Belfast, BT9 5LA
Tel: 028 9038 3811
Contact: Jing Yi Gao

**Irish Water Polo Association, Ulster Branch**
78 Wateresk Road
Castlewellan, BT31 9EZ
Contact: Ms J Lightbody

**Irish Water Skiing Federation, Northern Ireland Sub-Committee**
2 Shelling Hill, Lisburn, BT27 5NZ
Contact: Mr P Gray

**Irish Women's Bowling Association**
30 Cromlyn Fold
Hillsborough, BT26 6SD
Tel: 028 9268 8254
Fax: 028 9268 8808
Honorary Secretary: Ms J Fleming

**Irish Women's Indoor Bowling Association**
101 Skyline Drive, Lambeg
Lisburn, BT27 4HW
Secretary: Mrs D Miskelly

**Karate Association (NIKW)**
Oliver Brunton Schools of Karate NI
35 College Street, Belfast, BT1 6BU
Tel: 028 9061 6453
Chairman: Oliver Brunton

**Motorcycle and Car Club Ltd**
Beaghmore, Cranagill
Portadown, BT62 1SE
Tel: 028 3885 1407
Contact: Ronnie Tronton

**Motor Cycle Union of Ireland**
23 Kinnegar Rocks
Donaghadee, BT21 0EZ
Contact: Mr T Reid

**Mountaineering Council of Ireland**
c/o Tullymore Mountain Centre
Bryansford, Co. Down, BT33 0PT
Tel: 028 4372 5354
Development Officer: Stewart Magill

**Northern Ireland Amateur Fencing Union**
58 St Anne's Crescent
Newtownabbey, BT36 5JZ
Contact: Mr J Courtney

**Northern Ireland Amateur Gymnastics Association**
House of Sport, Upper Malone Road
Belfast, BT9 5LA
Tel: 028 9038 3813
Contact: Lynda Phillips

**Northern Ireland Weightlifters' Association**
130 Brooke Drive, Belfast, BT11 9NR
Tel: 028 9080 3876
Secretary: Sean Dougan

**Northern Ireland Area of British Model Flying Association**
'Strawberry Hill', 28 Carlston Avenue
Cultra, Holywood BT18 0NF
Tel: 028 9042 4113
Email: mauricedoyle@freenet.co.uk
Secretary: Maurice Doyle

**Northern Ireland Athletics Federation**
Athletics House, Old Coach Road
Belfast, BT9 5PR
Tel: 028 9060 2707
Fax: 028 9030 9939
Web: www.niathletics.org
Email: info@niathletics.org
Secretary: John Allen

**Northern Ireland Boys Football Association**
15 Beechgrove Rise, Belfast, BT6 0NH
Tel: 028 9079 4677
Contact: Mr J Weir

**Northern Ireland Cricket Association**
House of Sport, Upper Malone Road
Belfast, BT9 5LA
Tel: 028 9038 3805
Fax: 028 9068 2757
Email: brian@nica.freeserve.co.uk
Cricket Development Officer:
Brian Walsh

**Northern Ireland Federation of Sub Aqua Clubs**
56 Ballykeel Road
Moneyreagh, BT23 6BW
Contact: Mr R Armstrong

**Northern Ireland Ice Hockey Association**
25 Channing Street, Belfast, BT5 5GP
Contact: Mrs B Carter

**Northern Ireland Ice Skating Association**
15 Bromcote Street, Bloomfield Road
Belfast, BT5 5JL
Tel: 028 9096 6876
Contact: Mr J Passmore

**Northern Ireland Ju Jitsu Association**
281 Coalisland Road
Dungannon, BT71 6ET
Tel: 028 8774 6940
Secretary: Joe Canning

**Northern Ireland Olympic Wrestling Association**
312 Stranmillis Road, Belfast, BT9 5EB
Contact: Mr P Mooney

**Northern Ireland Orienteering Association**
62 Wheatfield Crescent
Belfast, BT14 7HT
Contact: Ms V Cordner

**Netball Northern Ireland**
House of Sport, Upper Malone Road
Belfast, BT9 5LA
Tel: 028 9038 3806
Fax: 028 9068 2757
Netball Development Officer:
Kate Harrup

**Northern Ireland Schools Football Association**
20 Moira Drive, Bangor, BT20 4RN
Contact: Mr B Gilliland

**Northern Ireland Ski Council**
43 Ballymaconnell Road
Bangor, BT20 5PS
Tel: 028 9145 0275
Web: www.niweb.com/niid/sport/skiing

**Northern Ireland Sports Association for People with Learning Disabilities**
1 Clare Hill Road, Moira, BT67 0PB
Contact: Mr N Logan

Northern Ireland Ten Pin Bowling Federation
13 Wanstead Road
Dundonald, BT16 2EJ
Contact: Ms K Payne

Northern Ireland Trampoline Association
Fir Tree Grove, 40 Monlough Road
Ballygowan, BT23 6NH
Contact: Mr T Clifford

Northern Ireland Tug of War Association
22 Annahugh Road
Loughall, BT61 8RQ
Contact: Mr C McKeever

Northern Ireland Volleyball Association
21 Broughton Park, Belfast, BT6 0BD
Contact: Mr D Orr

Northern Ireland Women's Football Association
11 Ravenhill Gardens, Belfast, BT6 8GP
Contact: Ms M Muldoon

Northern Cricket Union of Ireland
33 Dalboyne Park, Lisburn, BT28 3BU
Contact: Mr W Carroll

Northern Ireland Aikido Association
57 Glenview Avenue, Belfast, BT5 7LZ
Contact: Mr P Bradley

Northern Ireland American Football Association
108 Victoria Rise
Carrickfergus, BT38 7UR
Contact: Ms L Sleator

Northern Ireland Archery Society
10 Llewellyn Drive, Lisburn, BT27 4AQ
Contact: Mr K Blair

Northern Ireland Billiards and Snooker Association
2 Rockgrove Valley
Ballymena, BT43 5HF

Northern Ireland Blind Sports
12 Sandford, Belfast, BT5 5NW
Secretary: Ms L Royle

Northern Ireland Cricket Association
20 Pine Street, Waterside
Derry, BT47 3QW
Contact: Mr B Dougherty

Northern Ireland Judo Federation
c/o Judo Office, House of Sport
Upper Malone Road, Belfast, BT9 5LA
Tel: 028 9038 3814
Contact: Miss L Bradley

Northern Ireland Karting Association
44 Mill Cottage Park
Mallusk, BT22 2FF
Tel: 028 9181 4987
Fax: 028 9182 2190
Contact: Mr K Wilkinson

Northern Ireland Martial Arts Commission
c/o House of Sport
Upper Malone Road, Belfast, BT9 5LA
Tel: 028 9267 4758
Web: www.sportsni.org
Contact: Tom Lamont

Northern Ireland Pool Association
8 Birch Drive, Bangor, BT19 1RY
Contact: Mr J Humphrey

Northern Ireland Ski Council
43 Ballymaconnell Road
Bangor, BT20 5PS
Contact: Mr P White

Northern Ireland Sports Council
House of Sport, Upper Malone Road
Belfast, BT9 5LA
Tel: 028 9038 1222
Fax: 028 9068 2757
Chief Executive: Eamonn McCartan

The Sports Council is the leading government agency charged with the development of all sport across Northern Ireland.

Northern Ireland Sports Forum
c/o House of Sport
Upper Malone Road, Belfast, BT9 5LA
Tel: 028 9038 3825
Contact: Lynn Greenwood

Northern Women's Cricket Union of Ireland
18 Belvedere Park, Belfast, BT9 5GS
Contact: Miss S Owens

Royal Life Saving Society, Ulster Branch
4 Albert Drive, Belfast, BT6 9JH
Tel: 028 9070 5644
Web: www.rlssdirect.co.uk
Contact: Karen McCurry

Royal Scottish Country Dance Society
Tel: 028 9266 5834
Contact: Brian Patterson

Royal Ulster Yacht Club
101 Clifton Road, Bangor, BT20 5HY
Tel: 028 9146 5002

Royal Yachting Association (Northern Ireland Council)
House of Sport, Upper Malone Road
Belfast, BT9 5LA
Tel: 028 9038 1222
Contact: Lisa Waugh

Taekwondo Association of Northern Ireland
20 Lester Avenue, Lisburn, BT28 3QD
Contact: Mr S Nicholson

Ulster Angling Federation
4 Mill Road, Annalong, BT34 4RH
Tel: 028 4376 8531
Contact: Mr A Kilgore

Ulster Aviation Society
16 Ravelston Avenue
Newtownabbey, BT36 6PF
Tel: 028 9084 4100

Ulster Basketball Association
2 Ravensdene Crescent
Belfast, BT6 0DB
Tel: 028 9064 8000
Contact: Ms M Matthews

Ulster Branch, Badminton Union of Ireland
House of Sport, Upper Malone Road
Belfast, BT9 5LA
Contact: Mr T Clarke

Ulster Branch, Irish Amateur Rowing Union
47 Colenso Parade, Belfast' BT9 5AN
Contact: Ms C Harrison

Ulster Branch, Irish Hockey Association
Hockey Office, House of Sport
Upper Malone Road, Belfast, BT9 5LA
Tel: 028 9038 3826
Contact: Mr W Clarke

Ulster Branch, Irish Table Tennis Association
38 Ballynahinch Road
Carryduff, Belfast, BT8 8DL
Tel: 028 9081 3378
Contact: Mr M Guy

Ulster Branch, Irish Triathlon Association
c/o R G Connell and Son
13 Main Street, Limavady
Derry, BT49 0EP
Tel: 028 7772 2617
President: Peter Jack

*Community Arts, Lisburn*

Ulster Branch, Tennis Ireland
17 Tennyson Avenue
Bangor, BT20 3SS
Tel: 028 9146 5155
Contact: Mr G Stevenson

Ulster Camogie Council
10 Stang Road, Cabra
Hilltown, BT34 5TG
Contact: Ms H McAleavey

Ulster Coarse Fishing Federation
29 Georgian Villas, Hospital Road,
Omagh, BT79 0AT
Contact: Mr R Refausse

Ulster Council, Irish Federation of Sea Anglers
17 Coolshinney Close
Magherafelt, BT45 5DR
Tel: 028 7963 3198
Fax: 028 7963 3198
Secretary: Mr P Divito

Ulster Cycling Federation
c/o Mrs Rose Reilly, 18 Belturbet Road
Cornahoule, BT92 9AZ
Contact: Mr P N Clarke

Ulster Deaf Sports Council
Wilton House, 5 College Square North
Belfast, BT1 6AR
Tel: 028 9031 2255

Ulster Federation of Rambling Clubs
40 Clontara Park, Lisburn, BT27 4LB
Tel: 028 9260 1030
Honorary Secretary: Mr H Goodman

Ulster Flying Club
Newtownards Airport, Portaferry Road
Newtownards, BT23 8SG
Tel: 028 9131 3327
Fax: 028 9131 4575
Chief Flying Instructor:
David Hodgkinson

Ulster Gliding Club
Ballyscullion, Seacoast Road
Bellarena
Tel: 028 7775 0301

Ulster Handball Council
13 Dunmurry Lodge
Belfast, BT10 0GR
Contact: Mr R Maguire

Ulster Hang Gliding and Paragliding Club
35 Chester Park, Bangor
Tel: 07801 883524
Secretary: Ian Haslett

Ulster Provincial Council, Irish Amateur Boxing Association
10 Tonagh Heights
Draperstown, BT45 7DD
Tel: 028 7962 8450
Fax: 028 7962 8450
Secretary: Mr J Noonan

Ulster Region Swim Ireland
House of Sport, Upper Malone Road
Belfast, BT9 5LA
Tel: 028 9038 3807
Fax: 028 9068 2757
Web: www.swim-ulster.com
Email: ann@swim-ulster.com
Development Officer: Ruth McQuillan

Ulster Squash
18 Dundela Avenue, Belfast, BT4 3BQ
Contact: Mrs R Irvine

Ulster Society of Amateur Dancing
47 Upper Lisburn Road, Finaghy
Belfast, BT10 0GX

Ulster Vintage Car Club
11 Ballynahinch Road, Saintfield
Ballynahinch, BT24 7AE

Ulster Women's Hockey Union
168 Upper Newtownards Road
Belfast, BT4 3ES
Contact: Mrs J Patterson

Yoga Fellowship of Northern Ireland
19 Elsmere Park, Belfast, BT5 7QZ
Tel: 028 9079 1213
Contact: Mrs M Harper

Wild Geese Skydiving Club
116 Carrowreagh Road
Garvagh, BT51 5LQ
Tel: 028 2955 8609
Fax: 028 2955 7050
Web: www.wildgeese.demon.co.uk
Chief Instructor: Maggie Penny

World Ju-Jitsu Federation Northern Ireland
PO Box 1263
Belfast East Delivery, Belfast
Tel: 028 9079 7041

World Kickboxing Network NI
Dundela Social Club
Wilgar Street, Belfast, BT4 3BL
Tel: 028 9065 6414
Contact: Billy Murray

## Arts

Belfast Festival at Queen's
25 College Gardens, Belfast, BT9 6BS
Tel: 028 9097 2600
Fax: 028 9097 2630
Web: www.belfastfestival.com
Contact: Anthony McGrath

Cathedral Quarter Arts Festival
35 Donegall Street, Belfast, BT1 2FG
Tel: 028 9023 2403
Fax: 028 9031 9884
Web: www.cqaf.com
Contact: Sean Kelly

Cinemagic
1st Floor, 49 Botanic Avenue
Belfast, BT7 1JL
Tel: 028 9031 1900
Fax: 028 9031 9709
Email: Ingrid@cinemagic.org.uk
Web: www.cinemagic.org.uk
Contact: Joan Birney

Classical Music Society
Room MC210
University of Ulster, Magee
Northland Road, Derry, BT48 7JL
Tel: 028 7137 5550
Fax: 028 7137 5549

Community Arts Forum
15 Church Street, Belfast, BT1 1PG
Tel: 028 9024 2910
Fax: 028 9031 2264
Web: www.caf.ie
Email: admin@caf.ie
Director: Heather Floyd

Crescent Arts Centre
2–4 University Road, Belfast, BT7 1NH
Tel: 028 9024 2338
Fax: 028 9024 6748
Email: info@crescentarts.org
Manager: Liz Donnan

Feile an Phobail
Tel: 028 9031 3440
Email: 028 9031 3440

Northern Ireland Film Commission
21 Ormeau Avenue, Belfast, BT2 8HD
Tel: 028 9023 2444
Fax: 028 9023 9918
Email: info@nifc.co.uk
Chief Executive: Richard Williams

Northern Ireland Media Education Association (NIMEA)
c/o Brooklands Primary School
Brooklands Avenue
Dundonald, BT16 2PA
Tel: 028 9048 7589
Contact: David McCartney

Government Buildings, Dublin

# Republic of Ireland

# Chapter 11

# Republic Of Ireland - Fast Facts

## GDP 1995-2002 (€m)

| Year | GDP at current market prices | GDP at constant market prices | % change in GDP at constant prices |
|---|---|---|---|
| 1995 | 52,641 | 52,641 | n/a |
| 1996 | 58,080 | 56,891 | 8.1 |
| 1997 | 67,123 | 63,201 | 11.1 |
| 1998 | 77,543 | 68,663 | 8.6 |
| 1999 | 89,614 | 76,410 | 11.3 |
| 2000 | 102,895 | 84,113 | 10.1 |
| 2001 | 114,743 | 89,320 | 6.2 |
| 2002 | 129,344 | 95,499 | 6.9 |

Source: CSO, Dept of Finance

## GDP per capita & per person at work*

| Year | per head | per person at work | persons at work (000) |
|---|---|---|---|
| 1970 | 6,591 | 18,465 | 1,053 |
| 1975 | 7,396 | 21,897 | 1,073 |
| 1980 | 8,208 | 24,149 | 1,156 |
| 1985 | 8,324 | 27,308 | 1,079 |
| 1990 | 10,689 | 33,045 | 1,160 |
| 1995 | 12,967 | 37,426 | 1,248 |
| 2000 | 18,963 | 43,219 | 1,588 |
| 2001 | 19,559 | 45,586 | 1,647 |

Source: CSO, Dept of Finance

## Unemployment 1988-2002

| Year | Seeking full-time (000) | Total unemployed | Standardised unemployment rate (%) |
|---|---|---|---|
| 1988 | 195 | 217 | 16.3 |
| 1990 | 150 | 172 | 12.9 |
| 1992 | 185 | 207 | 15.1 |
| 1994 | 186 | 211 | 14.7 |
| 1996 | 151 | 179 | 11.9 |
| 1998 | 105 | 127 | 7.8 |
| 2000 | 61 | 75 | 4.3 |
| 2002 | 66 | 77 | 4.2 |

Source: CSO, Dept of Finance

## Population by Province 2002

| Province | Male | Female | Total |
|---|---|---|---|
| Leinster | 1,038,015 | 1,067,564 | 2,105,579 |
| Munster | 550,118 | 550,496 | 1,100,614 |
| Connacht | 233,194 | 231,102 | 464,296 |
| Ulster (part of) | 124,837 | 121,877 | 246,714 |
| State | 1,946,164 | 1,971,039 | 3,917,203 |

Source: CSO

## Population 1901-2002

| Year | Male | Female | Total |
|---|---|---|---|
| 1901 | 1,610,085 | 1,611,738 | 3,221,823 |
| 1951 | 1,506,597 | 1,453,996 | 2,960,593 |
| 1971 | 1,495,760 | 1,482,488 | 2,978,248 |
| 1981 | 1,729,354 | 1,714,051 | 3,443,405 |
| 1991 | 1,753,418 | 1,772,301 | 3,525,719 |
| 2002 | 1,946,164 | 1,971,039 | 3,917,203 |

Source: CSO

## Rates of Births, Marriages and Deaths 1950-2003

| | | Rate | |
|---|---|---|---|
| Year | Birth | Marriage | Death |
| 1950 | 21.4 | 5.4 | 12.7 |
| 1960 | 21.5 | 5.5 | 11.5 |
| 1970 | 21.9 | 7.1 | 11.4 |
| 1980 | 21.8 | 6.4 | 9.8 |
| 1990 | 15.1 | 5.1 | 8.9 |
| 2000 | 14.3 | 5.1 | 8.2 |
| 2001 | 15.0 | 5.0 | 7.7 |
| 2002 | 15.5 | 5.1 | 7.5 |
| 2003 | 15.5 | 5.1 | 7.2 |

Source: CSO

## Life Expectancy (Years) 1926-2002

| From Birth | Males | Females |
|---|---|---|
| 1926 | 57.4 | 57.9 |
| 2002 | 75.1 | 80.3 |

Source: CSO

## Overview

Since 1920, the island of Ireland has been divided into two parts – Northern Ireland, which remains part of the United Kingdom and the Republic of Ireland, an independent sovereign state (originally known as the Irish Free State until 1949) which consists of the provinces of Leinster, Munster and Connaught and the three Ulster counties of Cavan, Donegal and Monaghan.

The current population is around 4 million, the highest it has been since 1871. (The 1841 census recorded the population of the area which is now the Republic of Ireland at 6.5 million, but this had halved by 1901 following a devastating famine in which millions either died or emigrated). Over 40% of the population of Ireland live within approximately 100km of the capital Dublin. The population is currently growing at a rate of 1.16% per annum (high by European standards). In terms of religion, the vast majority of the population are of the Roman Catholic faith (88%), with around 3% belonging to the Church of Ireland.

The Irish economy has been performing very well over the past decades, which has led it to being given the name the 'Celtic tiger'. Growth averaged 8% annually in the period 1995-2002. The global slowdown, especially in the information technology sector, pressed growth down to 2.1% in 2003, although it has since bounced back to over 5%. Agriculture, once the most important sector, has now been overtaken by industry and services. Industry accounts for 46% of GDP and about 80% of exports and employs 28% of the labour force. As the numbers employed in both industry and the services sector increase, agriculture, once the biggest employer, now only accounts for 6.5% of the labour force. Per capita GDP in Ireland is 10% above that of the average for the four big European economies. Unemployment at 4.4% of the total labour force has fallen significantly by 2003 from the 13.5% recorded in 1983.

The Republic of Ireland joined in launching the euro currency system in January 1999 along with 10 other EU nations. On 1 January 2002 the euro became the sole currency, replacing the Irish pound or 'punt'.

**Republic of Ireland Key facts:**

**Area**: 70,182 sq km (27,097 sq miles)

**Population**: 3,917,203

**Life Expectancy** at birth (2001-03): Male 75.3 Female 80.3

**Currency**: Euro (€1 = 100 cent)

**Climate**: temperate maritime with mild winters and cool summers

**Terrain**: mostly level, interior plans surrounded by hills and low mountains; sea cliffs on west coast. Highest point: Carrauntoohil, Co Kerry 1,041m

**Language**: Official language is technically Irish, but English is predominantly written and spoken

International dialling code: +353

Internet domain: .ie

National holiday: St Patrick's Day 17th March

## The System of Government in the Republic of Ireland

An increasing number of Northern Ireland organisations are finding themselves interacting with government bodies and organisations in the Republic. What follows below is an overview of the system of government and politics, together with contact details for the main central and local government organisations.

### The Oireachtas

The Oireachtas (National Parliament) of the Republic of Ireland, under the terms of the 1937 constitution consists of a President and two houses: Dáil Éireann and Seanad Éireann.

### The President

The President of Ireland is elected directly by the people – every citizen with a right to vote in Dáil elections may vote in presidential elections. Candidates for the presidency must be over 35 years of age and must be nominated either by:

- Not less than 20 members of Dáil or Seanad Éireann or
- Not less than 4 administrative counties (including county boroughs).

Former or retiring presidents may become candidates on their own nomination. The term of office is 7 years and a president may not serve more than 2 terms. Mary McAleese is the eighth President of Ireland; she is about to enter her second term of office without re-election as no opponent was successful in receiving a nomination to contest the election.

**Former Presidents of Ireland**

| Year of Election | President |
|---|---|
| 1938 | Douglas Hyde |
| 1945 | Seán T Ó Ceallaigh |
| 1959 | Eamon deValera |
| 1973 | Erskine Childers |
| 1974 | Cearbhall Ó Dálaigh |
| 1975 | Patrick J Hillery |
| 1990 | Mary Robinson |
| 1997 | Mary McAleese |

#### Powers and Functions

The formal powers and functions of the President are prescribed in the Constitution. The President, who does not have an executive or policy role, exercises these powers on the advice of the government. The Taoiseach is appointed by the President on the nomination of the Dáil. The President also appoints members of the government, on the nomination of the Taoiseach and with the prior approval of the Dáil. Other office holders appointed by the President, on the advice of the government, include judges, the Attorney General, the Comptroller and Auditor General, and commissioned officers of the Defence Forces, of which the President is the Supreme Commander.

The President's signature is required on all bills before they can become law. The President has an absolute discretion to refer a Bill to the Supreme Court to get a judgement on its constitutionality (but not a Money Bill or a Bill to amend the Constitution). Before making a referral the President must first consult the Council of State. The constitutionality of any Bill signed following a referral may not be subsequently challenged in the courts.

The President of Ireland represents the Irish people when making state visits abroad, and when receiving foreign heads of state on visits to Ireland.

If the President dies during the term of office, or is incapacitated, abroad or removed from office, the Constitution provides for a Commission to act in his or her place. This Commission consists of the Chief Justice, the Ceann Comhairle (Chairperson) of Dáil Éireann and the Cathaoirleach (Chairperson) of Seanad Éireann.

## The Houses of the Oireachtas

**President of Ireland**
Áras an Uachtaráin
Phoenix Park, Dublin 8
Tel: 01 617 1000 / Fax: 01 617 1001
Web: www.gov.ie/aras
President: Mary McAleese

**Houses of the Oireachtas**
Leinster House
Kildare Street, Dublin 2
Tel: 01 618 3000
Web: www.irlgov.ie/oireachtas
Email: info@oireachtas.irlgov.ie

The two Houses of the Oireachtas are Dáil Éireann (the 'lower' house, elected by the people) and Seanad Éireann (the 'upper' house, whose members are nominated).

Elections to the Dáil must, by law, take place at least once every five years. For these general elections, the country is currently divided into 42 constituencies, each of which elects three, four or five members. The Constitution stipulates that there must be one member elected for every 20,000 to 30,000 people, and that the constituencies must be revised at least once every 12 years.

Every citizen who has reached the age of 21 years is eligible for membership of the Dáil or Seanad, except the President of Ireland, the Comptroller and Auditor General, a judge, a member of the defence or policy forces on full pay, a civil servant or a member of the board of a state-sponsored body. It is not permitted to be a member of both the Dáil and the Seanad.

The present (29th) Dáil Éireann has 166 members, known as Teachtaí Dála (TDs), who were elected in 2002. Every citizen who has reached the age of eighteen years (and who has not been disqualified by law) has the right to vote in Dáil elections. The voting system used for these elections is proportional representation by means of the single transferable vote.
Seanad Éireann has 60 members; 11 are nominated directly to the house by the Taoiseach; 43 are elected from five panels of candidates – the Cultural and Educational Panel, the Agricultural Panel, the Labour Panel, the Industrial and Commercial Panel and the Administrative Panel. The remaining six are elected by certain universities.

The maximum term of the Dáil is five years. A Presidential Proclamation sets out the date of dissolution of the outgoing Dáil and the date on which the new Dáil will meet. A general election for membership of the Dáil must take place not later than 30 days after the dissolution, and the newly elected Dáil must meet within 30 days from the polling date. An election for the Seanad takes place not later than 90 days after a dissolution of Dáil Éireann.

Sitting days for the Oireachtas are usually in the period January to July and September to December. Both the Dáil and Seanad normally sit every Tuesday, Wednesday and Thursday.

The Oireachtas has the sole power of legislating for the state. Government policy and administration may be examined and criticised in both houses, but the government is responsible to the Dáil only. The Dáil may assert its overriding authority over the Seanad on all bills.

## The Government

The government exercises the legislative power of the state. The government consists of between seven and fifteen members. The Taoiseach heads the government and is appointed by the President on nomination from the Dáil. The Taoiseach then nominates the other members of the government for the approval of the Dáil. One member of the government is nominated as Tánaiste (Deputy) by the Taoiseach. The Taoiseach also nominates the Attorney General for appointment by the President. The Taoiseach, the Tánaiste and the Minister for Finance must all be members of the Dáil. The rest of the government must be members of either the Dáil or the Seanad, but no more than two may come from the Seanad.

The government is responsible to the Dáil alone. Each member of the government usually heads one of the departments of state – they are assigned to these positions by the Taoisceach. Ministers of state assist government ministers in their parliamentary and departmental work. They are appointed by the government on the nomination of the Taoiseach.

The Attorney General, who cannot be a member of the government, advises the government in all legal matters. The Attorney General is not always a member of the Houses of the Oireachtas.

The government is collectively responsible to the Dáil for its conduct of the state's affairs. If the Taoiseach resigns, all members of the government are deemed to have resigned.

**Current members of the government (October 2004)**

| Department | Minister | Ministers of State |
|---|---|---|
| Taoiseach | Bertie Ahern | Tom Kitt/Noel Treacy |
| Tánaiste and Health & Children | Mary Harney | Brian Lenihan/Tim O'Malley/Sean Power |
| Finance | Brian Cowen | Tom Parlon |
| Communications, Marine & Natural Resources | Noel Dempsey | Pat the Cope Gallagher |
| Foreign Affairs | Dermot Ahern | Noel Treacy/Conor Lenihan |
| Arts, Sport & Tourism | John O'Donoghue | |
| Enterprise, Trade & Employment | Michéal Martin | Michael Ahern/Tony Killeen |
| Social & Family Affairs | Seamus Brennan | |
| Justice, Equality & Law Reform | Michael McDowell | Frank Fahey/Brian Lenihan |
| Transport | Martin Cullen | Ivor Callely |
| Community, Rural & Gaeltacht Affairs | Éamon Ó Cuív | |
| Agriculture & Food | Mary Coughlan | John Browne/Brendan Smith |
| Education & Science | Mary Hanafin | Síle de Valera/Brian Lenihan |
| Defence | Willie O'Dea | Tom Kitt |
| Environment, Heritage & Local Government | Dick Roche | Noel Ahern/Batt O'Keefe |

## Main Political Parties

**Fianna Fail**
65-66 Lower Mount Street, Dublin 2
Tel: 01 676 1551
Web: www.fiannafail.ie / Email: info@fiannafail.ie
President: Bertie Ahern, TD

**Fine Gael**
National Headquarters
51 Upper Mount Street, Dublin 2
Tel: 01 619 8444
Web: www.finegael.ie / Email: finegael@finegael.ie
Leader: Enda Kenny, TD

**Progressive Democrats**
25 South Frederick Street, Dublin 2
Tel: 01 679 4399
Web: www.progressivedemocrats.ie
Leader: Mary Harney, TD

**Irish Labour Party**
17 Ely Place, Dublin 2
Tel: 01 678 4700
Web: www.labour.ie
Leader: Pat Rabbite, TD

**Sinn Féin**
44 Parnell Square, Dublin 1
Tel: 01 872 6100
Web: www.sinnfein.ie / Email: sfadmin@eircom.net
President: Gerry Adams

**The Green Party**
5A Fownes Street, Dublin 2
Tel: 01 679 0012
Web: www.greenparty.ie
Email: info@greenparty.ie
Leader: Trevor Sargent, TD

**2002 General Election: % 1st preference votes & no of seats by party**

| Party | % | no of seats |
|---|---|---|
| Fianna Fail | 41.5 | 81 |
| Fine Gael | 22.5 | 31 |
| Labour | 10.8 | 21 |
| Progressive Democrats | 4 | 8 |
| Sinn Fein | 6.5 | 5 |
| Green Party | 3.9 | 6 |
| Others | 10.9 | 14 |
| Turnout | 62.7 | |

## Members of the 29th Dáil

Listed below are the members of the Dáil. Members can be contacted by telephone on 01 618 3000 or via their email addresses, which are given below. Written correspondence can be directed to members at the address below.

Dáil Eireann
Leinster House
Kildare Street, Dublin 2

Abbreviations used for the political parties are as follows:

| | |
|---|---|
| FF | Fianna Fáil |
| FG | Fine Gael |
| Lab | The Labour Party |
| PD | Progressive Democrats |
| SF | Sinn Féin |
| Ind | Independent |
| Gr | The Green Party |
| Soc | Socialist Party |

## A-Z of Dail Deputies

**Ahern, Bertie**
FF, Dublin Central
Email: taoiseach@taoiseach.irlgov.ie

**Ahern, Dermot**
FF, Louth
Email: dahern@iol.ie

**Ahern, Michael**
FF, Cork East
Email: michael_ahern@entemp.ie

**Ahern, Noel**
FF, Dublin North-West
Email: noel_ahern@oireachtas.irlgov.ie

**Allen, Bernard**
FG, Cork North-Central
Email: Bernard.allen@oireachtas.irlgov.ie

**Andrews, Barry**
FF, Dún Laoghaire
Email: bandrews@oireachtas.ie

**Ardagh, Seán**
FF, Dublin South-Central
Email: sean@ardagh.org

**Aylward, Liam**
FF, Carlow-Kilkenny
Email: liam.aylward@agriculture.gov.ie

**Blaney, Niall**
Ind, Donegal North-East
Email: nblaney@oireachtas.ie

**Boyle, Dan**
Gr, Cork South-Central
Email: dboyle@oireachtas.ie

**Brady, John**
FF, Meath

**Brady, Martin**
FF, Dublin North-East
Email: martin_brady@oireachtas.irlgov.ie

**Breen, James**
Ind, Clare
Email: jamesbreentd@eircom.net

**Breen, Pat**
FG, Clare
Email: pat.breen@oireachtas.irlgov.ie

**Brennan, Séamus**
FF, Dublin South
Email: seamusbrennantd@transport.ie

**Broughan, Thomas P**
Lab, Dublin North-East
Email:
Thomas_P_Broughan@oireachtas.irlgov.ie

**Browne, John**
FF, Wexford
Email:
john.browne_ff@oireachtas.irlgov.ie

**Bruton, John**
FG, Meath
Email: john_bruton@oireachtas.irlgov.ie

**Bruton, Richard**
FG, Dublin North-Central
Email:
richard_bruton@oireachtas.irlgov.ie

**Burton, Joan**
Lab, Dublin West
Email: joan.burton@oireachtas.irlgov.ie

**Callanan, Joe**
FF, Galway East
Emai: jcallanan@iolfree.ie

**Callely, Ivor**
FF, Dublin Norh-Central
Email: ivor_callely@health.irlgov.ie

**Carey, Pat**
FF, Dublin North-West
Email: pat_carey@oireachtas.ie

**Carty, John**
FF, Mayo

**Cassidy, Donie**
FF, Westmeath

**Collins, Michael**
FF, Limerick West
Email:
michael.collins@oireachtas.irlgov.ie

**Connaughton, Paul**
FG, Galway East
Email:
paul.connaughton@oireachtas.irlgov.ie

**Connolly, Paudge**
Ind, Cavan-Monaghan

**Costello, Joe**
Lab, Dublin Central
Email: joe.Costello@oireachtas.ie

**Coughlan, Mary**
FF, Donegal South-West
Email: minister@welfare.ie

**Coveney, Simon**
FG, Cork South-Central
Email:
simon.coveney@oireachtas.irlgov.ie

**Cowen, Brian**
FF, Laois-Offaly
Email: tullamoredfa@eircom.net

**Cowley, Jerry**
Ind, Mayo
Email: jcowley@oireachtas.ie

**Crawford, Seymour**
FG, Cavan-Monaghan
Email: seymourc@eircom.net

**Cregan, John**
FF, Limerick West

**Crowe, Seán**
SF, Dublin South-West
Email: sean.crowe@oireachtas.ie

**Cuffe, Ciarán**
Gr, Dún Laoghaire
Email: ciaran@ciarancuffe.com

**Cullen, Martin**
FF, Waterford

**Curran, John**
FF, Dublin Mid-West

**Davern, Noel**
FF, Tipperary South
Email: ndavern@oireachtas.ie

**de Valera, Síle**
FF, Clare
Email: desclare@hotmail.com

**Deasy, John**
FG, Waterford,
Email: deasyjohn@eircom.net

**Deenihan, Jimmy**
FG, Kerry North
Email: jdeenihan@eircom.net

**Dempsey, Noel**
FF, Meath

**Dempsey, Tony**
FF, Wexford

**Dennehy, John**
Email: john.dennehy@oireachtas.ie

**Devins, Jimmy**
FF, Sligo-Leitrim

**Durkan, Bernard J**
FG, Kildare North

**Ellis, John**
FF, Sligo-Leitrim

**English, Damien**
FG, Meath
Email: denglish@oireachtas.ie

**Enright, Olwyn**
FG, Laois-Offaly
Email: olwyn.enright@oireachtas.ie

**Fahey, Frank**
FF, Galway West
Email: frank_fahey@entemp.ie

**Ferris, Martin,**
SF, Kerry North
Email: mferris@oireachtas.ie

**Finneran, Michael**
FF, Longford-Roscommon
Email:
michael.finneran@oireachtas.irlgov.ie

**Fitzpatrick, Dermot**
FF, Dublin Central
Email:
dermot_Fitzpatrick@oireachtas.irlgov.ie

**Fleming, Seán**
FF, Laois-Offaly

**Flynn, Beverley**
FF, Mayo
Email: bflynn@oireachtas.ie

**Fox, Mildred**
Ind, Wicklow
Email: mildred_fox@oireachtas.irlgov.ie

**Gallagher, Pat the Cope**
FF, Donegal South-West
Email: contactme@patthecope.com

**Gilmore, Eamon**
Lab, Dún Laoghaire
Email: eamon_gilmore@oireachtas.ie

**Glennon, Jim**
FF, Dublin North
Email: jglennon@oireachtas.ie

**Gogarty, Paul**
Gr, Dublin Mid-West
Email: paultd@id.ie

**Gormley, John**
Gr, Dublin South-East
Email: johngormley@eircom.net

**Grealish, Noel**
PD, Galway West
Email: noel.grealish@oireachtas.ie

**Gregory, Tony**
Ind, Dublin Central
Email: tony.gregory@oireachtas..ie

**Hanafin, Mary**
FF, Dún Laoghaire
Email:

**Harkin, Marian**
Ind, Sligo-Leitrim
Email: marianharkin1@eircom.net

**Harney, Mary**
PD, Dublin Mid-West

**Haughey, Seán**
FF, Dublin North-Central
Email:
sean_haughey@oireachtas.irlgov.ie

**Hayes, Tom**
FG, Tipperary South

**Healy, Seamus**
Ind, Tipperary South

**Healy-Rae, Jackie**
Ind, Kerry South

**Higgins, Joe**
Soc, Dublin West

**Higgins, Michael D**
Lab, Galway West
Email:
michael.d.higgins@oireachtas.irlgov.ie

**Hoctor, Máire F**
FF, Tipperary North
Email: maire_hoctor@oireachtas.irlgov.ie

**Hogan, Phil**
FG, Carlow-Kilkenny
Email: philip.hogan@oireachtas.irlgov.ie

**Howlin, Brendan**
Lab, Wexford
Email:
brendan.howlin@oireachtas.irlgov.ie

**Jacob, Joe**
FF, Wicklow

**Keaveney, Cecilia**
FF, Donegal North-East
Email:
cecilia.keaveney@oireachtas.irlgov.ie

**Kehoe, Paul**
FG, Wexford
Email: paul.kehoe@oireachtas.irlgov.ie

**Kelleher, Billy**
FF, Cork North-Central
Email: billykelleher@eircom.net

**Kelly, Peter**
FF, Longford-Roscommon
Email: cllrpeterkelly@eircom.net

**Kenny, Enda**
FG, Mayo
Email: enda.Kenny@oireachtas.irlgov.ie

**Killeen, Tony**
FF, Clare
Email: t.killeen@oireachtas.irlgov.ie

**Kirk, Seámus**
FF, Louth

**Kitt, Tom**
FF, Dublin South
Email: tomkitt@tomkitttd.ie

**Lenihan, Brian**
FF, Dublin West

**Lenihan, Conor**
FF, Dublin South-West
Email: conor.lenihan@oireachtas.ie

**Lowry, Michael**
Ind, Tipperary North
Email: michael.lowry@oireachtas.irlgov.ie

**Lynch, Kathleen**
Lab, Cork North-Central
Email:
kathleen.lynch@oireachtas.irlgov.ie

**Martin, Micheál**
FF, Cork South-Central

**McCormack, Pádraic**
FG, Galway West
Email:
padraic.mccormack@oireachtas.irlgov.ie

**McCreevy, Charlie**
FF, Kildare North

**McDaid, James**
FF, Donegal North-East
Email: james_mcdaid@transport.ie

**McDowell, Michael**
PD, Dublin South-East
Email: minister@justice.ie

**McEllistrim, Thomas**
FF, Kerry North
Email: cllrmcellistrim@eircom.net

**McGinley, Dinny**
FG, Donegal South-West
Email:
dinny_mcginley@oireachtas.irlgov.ie

**McGrath, Finian**
Ind, Dublin North-Central
Email: finian.mcgrath@oireachtas.ie

**McGrath, Paul**
FG, Westmeath
Email: paul.mcgrath@oireachtas.irlgov.ie

**McGuinness, John**
FF, Carlow-Kilkenny
Email: johnmcg@eircom.net

**McHugh, Paddy**
Ind, Galway East

**McManus, Liz**
Lab, Wicklow
Email: liz_mcmanus@oireachtas.irlgov.ie

**Mitchell, Gay**
FG, Dublin South-Central

**Mitchell, Olivia**
FG, Dublin South
Email: olivia.mitchell@oireachtas.irlgov.ie

**Moloney, John**
FF, Laois-Offaly
Email: moloneyjo@eircom.net

**Morgan, Arthur**
SF, Louth
Email: amorgan@oireachtas.ie

**Moynihan, Donal**
FF, Cork North-West

**Moynihan, Michael**
FF, Cork North-West

**Moynihan-Cronin, Breeda**
Lab, Kerry South
Email: bmoynihancronin@eircom.net

**Mulcahy, Michael**
FF, Dublin South-Central
Email: michael.mulcahy@oireachtas.ie

**Murphy, Gerard**
FG, Cork North-West
Email: gerard.murphy@oireachtas,ie

**Naughten, Denis**
FG, Longford-Roscommon
Email: denis.naughten@oireachtas.ie

**Neville, Dan**
FG, Limerick West
Email: daniel.neville@oireachtas.ie

**Nolan, M.J.**
FF, Carlow-Kilkenny
Email: mj.nolan@oireachtas.ie

**Noonan, Michael**
FG, Limerick East
Email:
Michael.noonan@oireachtas.irlgov.ie

**Ó Caoláin, Caoimhgín**
SF, Cavan-Monaghan
Email: ocaolain@oireachtas.ie

**O'Connor, Charlie**
FF, Dublin South-West
Email: coconnor@oireachtas.ie

**Ó Cuiv, Éamon**
FF, Galway West

**O'Dea, Willie**
FF, Limerick East
Email: willie.odea@oceanfree.net

**O'Donnell, Liz**
PD, Dublin South
Email: liz.odonnell@oireachtas.ie

**O'Donoghue, John**
FF, Kerry South

**O'Donovan, Denis**
FF, Cork South-West
Email: denis.odonovan@oireachtas.ie

**O'Dowd, Fergus**
FG, Louth
Email: fergus.odowd@oireachtas.irlgov.ie

**Ó Fearghail, Seán**
FF, South Kildare
Email: sofearghail@oireachtas.ie

**O'Flynn, Noel**
FF, Cork North-Central
Email: noflynn@eircom.net

**O'Hanlon, Rory**
FF, Cavan-Monaghan
Email: rory.ohanlon@oireachtas.ie

**O'Keeffe, Batt**
FF, Cork South-Central
Email: batt.okeeffe@oireachtas.irlgov.ie

**O'Keeffe, Jim**
FG, Cork South-West
Email: jimokeeffe@eircom.net

**O'Keeffe, Ned**
FF, Cork East

**O'Malley, Fiona**
PD, Dún Laoghaire
Email: fiona.omalley@oireachtas.ie

**O'Malley, Tim**
PD, Limerick East
Email:

**O'Shea, Brian**
Lab, Waterford
Email: brian.oshea@oireachtas.irlgov.ie

**Ó Snodaigh, Aengus**
SF, Dublin South-Central
Email: sinnfeindsc@iolfree.ie

**O'Sullivan, Jan**
Lab, Limerick East
Email: jan.osullivan@oireachtas.ie

**Parlon, Tom**
PD, Laois-Offaly
Email: info@tomparlon.ie

**Pattison, Séamus**
Lab, Carlow-Kilkenny
Email: seamus.pattison@oireachtas.ie

**Penrose, William**
Lab, Westmeath

**Perry, John**
FG, Sligo-Leitrim
Email: john_perry@oireachtas.irlgov.ie

**Power, Peter**
FF, Limerick East
Email: ppower@oireachtas.ie

**Power, Séan**
FF, Kildare, South
Email: sean.power@oireachtas.irlgov.ie

**Quinn, Ruaírí**
Lab, Dublin South-West
Email: ruairi.quinn@oireachtas.irlgov.ie

**Rabbite, Pat**
Lab, Dublin South-West
Email: pat.rabbitte@oireachtas.irlgov.ie

**Ring, Michael**
FG, mayo
Email: michael_ring@oireachtas.irlgov.ie

**Roche, Dick**
FF, Wicklow
Email: dick.roche@oireachtas.irlgov.ie

**Ryan, Eamon**
GR, Dublin South
Email: eamon.ryan@oireachtas.ie

**Ryan, Séan**
Lab, Dublin North
Email: sean-ryan@oireachtas.irlgov.ie

**Sargent, Trevor**
Gr, Dublin North
Email: trevor.sergeant@oireachtas.ie

**Sexton, Mae**
PD, Longford-Roscommon
Email: maesexton@eircom.net

**Sherlock, Joe**
Lab, Cork East
Email: jsherlock@oireachtas.ie

**Shortall, Roisin**
Lab, Dublin North-West
Email: roisin.shortall@oireachtas.ie

**Smith, Brendan**
FF, Cavan-Monaghan
Email:
brendan.smith@oireachtas.irlgov.ie

**Smith, Michael**
FF, Tipperary North
Email:

**Stagg, Emmet**
Lab, Kildare North
Email: emmet.stag@oireachtas.irlgov.ie

**Stanton, David**
FG, Cork East
Email: dstanton@eircom.net

**Timmins, William**
FG, Wicklow
Email; billy.timmins@oireachtas.irlgov.ie

**Treacy, Noel**
FF, Galway East
Email:

**Twomey, Dr Liam**
Ind, Wexford

**Upton, Mary**
Lab, Dublin South-Central
Email: mary.upton@oireachtas.ie

**Wall, Jack**
Lab, Kildare South
Email: jack.wall@oireachtas.ie

**Wallace, Dan**
FF, Cork North-Central

**Wallace, Mary**
FF, Meath,
Email: mwtd@iol.ie

**Walsh, Joe**
FF, Cork South-West
Email: minjoe@indigo.ie

**Wilkinson, Ollie**
FF, Waterford
Email; ollie.wilkinson@oireachtas.ie

**Woods, Michael**
FF, Dublin North-East
Email: compass@indigo.ie

**Wright, G.V**
FF, Dublin North
Email: gv.wright@oireachtas.irlgov.ie

## TDs by Constituency (Dáil Eireann)

**Carlow-Kilkenny**
Liam Aylward, FF
John McGuinness, FF
M.J.Nolan, FF
Philip Hogan, FG
Séamus Pattison, Lab

**Cavan-Monaghan**
Brendan Smith, FF
Seymour Crawford, FG
Caoimhgín Ó Caoláin, SF
Paudge Connolly, Ind
Dr Rory O'Hanlon, Ind

**Clare**
Síle de Valera, FF
Tony Killeen, FF
Pat Breen, FG
James Breen, Ind

**Cork East**
Michael Ahern, FF
Ned O'Keeffe, FF
David Stanton, FG
Joe Sherlock, Lab

**Cork North-Central**
Billy Kelleher, FF
Noel O'Flynn, FF
Dan Wallace, FF
Bernard Allen, FG
Kathleen Lynch, Lab

**Cork North-West**
Michael Moynihan, FF
Donal Moynihan, FF
Gerard Murphy, FG

**Cork South-Central**
John Dennehy, FF
Micheál Martin, FF
Batt O'Keeffe, FF
Simon Coveney, FG
Dan Boyle, Gr

**Cork South-West**
Joe Walsh, FF
Denis O'Donovan, FF
Jim O'Keeffe, FG

**Donegal North-East**
Cecilia Keaveney, FF
James McDaid, FF
Niall Blaney, Ind

**Donegal South-West**
Mary Coughlan, FF
Pat the Cope Gallagher, FF
Dinny McGinley, FG

**Dublin Central**
Bertie Ahern, FF
Dermot Fitzpatrick, FF
Joe Costello, Lab
Tony Gregory, Ind

**Dublin Mid-West**
John Curran, FF
Mary Harney, PD
Paul Nicholas Gogarty, Gr

**Dublin North**
Jim Glennon, FF
G.V. Wright, FF
Séan Ryan, Lab
Trevor Sargent, Gr

**Dublin North-Central**
Ivor Callely, FF
Seán Haughey, FF
Richard Bruton, FG
Finian McGrath, Ind

**Dublin North-East**
Martin Brady, FF
Michael Woods, FF
Tommy Broughan, Lab

**Dublin North-West**
Noel Ahern, FF
Pat Carey, FF
Róisín Shortall, Lab

**Dublin South**
Séamus Brennan, FF
Tom Kitt, FF
Olivia Mitchell, FG
Liz O'Donnell, PD
Eamon Ryan, Gr

**Dublin South-Central**
Seán Ardagh, FF
Michael Mulchay, FF
Gay Mitchell, FG
Mary Upton, Lab
Aengus Ó Snodaigh, SF

**Dublin South-East**
Eoin Ryan, FF
Ruairí Quinn, Lab
Michael McDowell, PD
John Gormley, Gr

**Dublin South-West**
Conor Lenihan, FF
Charlie O'Donnor, FF
Pat Rabbitte, Lab
Seán Crowe, SF

**Dublin West**
Brian Lenihan, FF
Joan Burton, Lab
Joe Higgins, Soc

**Dún Laoghaire**
Barry Andrews, FF
Mary Hanafin, FF
Eamon Gilmore, Lab
Fiona O'Malley, PD
Ciaran Cuffe, G

**Galway East**
Joe Callanan, FF
Noel Treacy, FF
Paul Connaughton, FG
Paddy McHugh, Ind

**Galway West**
Frank Fahey, FF
Éamon Ó Cuív, FF
Pádraic McCormack, FG
Michael D Higgins, Lab
Noel Grealish, PD

**Kerry North**
Tom McEllistrim, FF
Jimmy Deenihan, FG
Martin Ferris, SF

**Kerry South**
John O'Donoghue, FF
Breeda Moynihan-Cronin, Lab
Jackie Healy-Rae, Ind

**Kildare North**
Charlie McCreevy, FF
Bernard J Durkan, FG
Emmet Stagg, Lab

**Kildare South**
Seán Ó Fearghaíll, FF
Seán Power, FF
Jack Wall, Lab

**Laois-Offaly**
Brian Cowen, FF
Seán Fleming, FF
John moloney, FF
Olwyn Enright, FG
Tom Parlon, PD

**Limerick East**
Willie O'Dea, FF
Peter Power, FF
Michael Noonan, FG
Jan O'Sullivan, Lab
Tim O'Malley, PD

**Limerick West**
John Cregan, FF
Dan Neville, FG
Michael Collins, Ind

**Longford-Roscommon**
Michael Finneran, FF
Peter Kelly, FF
Denis Naughten, FG
Mae Sexton, PD

**Louth**
Dermot Ahern, FF
Seámus Kirk, FF
Fergus O'Dowd, FG
Arthur Morgan, SF

**Mayo**
John Carty, FF
Beverley Cooper-Flynn, FF
Enda Kenny, FG
Michael Ring, FG
Jerry Cowley, Ind

**Meath**
Johnny Brady, FF
Noel Dempsey, FF
Mary Wallace, FF
John Bruton, FG
Damien English, FG

**Sligo-Leitrim**
Jimmy Devins, FF
John Ellis, FF
John Perry, FG
Marian Harkin, Ind

**Tipperary North**
Márie Hoctor, FF
Michael Smith, FF
Michael Lowry, Ind

**Tipperary South**
Noel Davern, FF
Tom Hayes, FG
Seamus Healy, Ind

**Waterford**
Martin Cullen, FF
Ollie Wilkinson, FF
John Deasy, FG
Brian O'Shea, Lab

**Westmeath**
Donie Cassidy, FF
Paul McGrath, FG
Willie Penrose, Lab

**Wexford**
John Browne, FF
Tony Dempsey, FF
Paul Kehoe, FG
Liam Twomey, FG
Brendan Howlin, Lab

**Wicklow**
Joe Jacob, FF
Dick Roche, FF
Billy Godfrey-Timmins, FG
Liz McManus, Lab
Mildred Fox, Ind

## Members of Seanad Eireann (Senators)

**Bannon, James, FG**
Email: james.bannon@oireachtas.irlgov.ie

**Bohan, Eddie, FF**
Email: eddie@e.j.bohan.com

**Bradford, Paul, FG**
Email: pbradford@eircom.net

**Brady, Cyprian, FF**

**Brennan, Michael, FF**

**Browne, Fergal, FG**
Email: fergal.browne@oireachtas.ie

**Burke, Paddy, FG**
Email: paddy.burke@oireachtas.irlgov.ie

**Burke, Ulick, FG**
Email: ulick.burke@oireachtas.irlgov.ie

**Callanan, Peter, FF**
Email: peter.callanan@oirechtas.ie

**Coghlan, Paul, FG**
Email: paul.coghlan@oireachtas.irlgov.ie

**Coonan, Noel J, FG**
Email: noelcoonan@eircom.net

**Cox, Margaret, FF**
Email: Margaret.cox@oireachtas.irlgov.ie

**Cummins, Maurice, FG**
Email: maurice.cummins@indigo.ie

**Daly, Brendan, FF**
Email: Brendan.daly@oireachtas.ie

**Dardis, John, PD**
Email: john.dardis@oireachtas.ie

**Dooley, Timmy, FF**
Email: timmy.dooley@oireachtas.ie

**Feeney, Geraldine, FF**
Email:
geraldine.feeney@oireachtas.irlgov.ie

**Feighan, Frank, FG**
Email: feighanf@eircom.net

**Finucane, Michael, FG**
Email:
michael.finucane@oireachtas.irlgov.ie

**Fitzgerald, Liam, FF**

**Glynn, Camillus, FF**
Email: camillus.glynn@oireachtas.irlgov.ie

**Hanafin, John, FF**
Email: hanafinj@eircom.net

**Hayes, Brian, FG**
Email: brian_hayes@oireachtas.ie

**Henry, Mary, Ind**
Email: mary.henry@oireachtas.ie

**Higgins, Jim, FG**
Email: jim.Higgins@oireachtas.ie

**Kenneally, Brendan, FF**
Email:
Brendan.kenneally@oireachtas.irlgov.ie

**Kett, Tony, FF**
Email tkett@crc.ie

**Kiely, Rory, FF**
Email: rory.kiely@oireachtas.ie

**Kitt, Michael P, FF**
Email: michael.kitt@:oireachtas.ie

**Leyden, Terry, FF**
Email: leydenterry@eircom.net

**Lydon, Don, FF**
Email: don.lydon@oireachtas.irlgov.ie

**MacSharry, Marc, FF**
Email: mmacsharry@oireachtas.ie

**McCarthy, Michael, Lab**
Email:
michael.mccarthy@oireachtas.irlgov.ie

**McDowell, Derek, Lab**
Email:
derek.mcdowell@oireachtas.irlgov.ie

**McHugh, Joe, FG**
Email: joe.mchugh@oireachtas.ie

**Mansergh, Martin**
Email: mmansergh@oireachtas.ie

**Minihan, Joh, PD**
Email: jminihan@oireachtas.ie

**Mooney, Paschal, FF**
Email:
paschal.mooney@oireachtas.irlgov.ie

**Morrissey, Tom, PD**
Email: tmorrissey@oireachtas.ie

**Moylan, Patrick, FF**
Email: pat.moylan@oireachtas.ie

**Norris, David, Ind**

**O'Brien, Francis, FF**
Email: francis.obrien@oireachtas.ie

**O'Meara, Kathleen, Lab**
Email:
kathleen_omeara@oireachtas.irlgov.ie

**Ó Murchú, Labhrás, FF**
Email: labhras.omurchu@oireachtas.ie

**O'Rourke, Mary, FF**

**O'Toole, Joe, Ind**
Email: jotoole@oireachtas.ie

**Ormonde, Ann, FF**
Email: ann.ormonde@oireachtas.ie

**Phelan, Kieran, FF**
Email: kieran.phelan@oireachtas.ie

**Quinn, Feargal, Ind**
Email: himself@feargalquinn.ie

**Ross, Shane, Ind**
Email: shane.ross@oireachtas.ie

**Ryan, Brendan, Lab**
Email: brendan.ryan@oireachtas.ie

**Scanlon, Eamon, FF**
Email: escanlonmcc@eircom.net

**Terry, Sheila, FG**
Email: sheila.terry@fingalcoco.ie

**Tuffy, Joanna, Lab**
Email: jtuffy@oireachtas.ie

**Walsh, Jim, FF**
Email: jim.walsh@oireachtas.ie

**Walsh, Kate P, PD**
Email: katewalsh@eircom.net

**White, Mary M, FF**
Email: lirchocolates@eircom.net

**Wilson, Diarmuid, FF**
Email: diarmuid.wilson@oireachtas.ie

## Government Departments: Contact Details

**Department of Agriculture and Food**
Kildare Street, Dublin 2
Tel: 01 607 2000 / Fax: 01 661 6263
Web: www.irlgov.ie/daff
Minister: Mary Coughlan
Ministers of State: John Browne, Brendan Smith
Secretary General: John Malone

**Department of Arts, Sport and Tourism**
Kildare Street, Dublin 2
Tel: 01 631 3800 / Fax: 01 661 1201
Web: www.gov.ie/arts-sport-tourism
Minister: John O'Donoghue
Secretary General: Philip Furlong

**Department of Communications, Marine & Natural Resources**
29-31 Adelaide Road, Dublin 2
Tel: 01 678 2000 / Fax: 01 661 8214
Web: www.dcmnr.gov.ie
Minister: Noel Dempsey
Minister of State: Pat the Cope Gallagher
Secretary General: Brendan Tuohy

**Department of Community, Rural and Gaeltacht Affairs**
'Dún Aimhirgin', 43-49 Mespil Road, Dublin 4
Tel: 01 647 3000 / Fax: 01 647 3051
Web: www.pobail.ie
Minister: Éamon Ó Cuív
Secretary General: Gerry Kearney

**Department of Defence**
Parkgate Infirmary Road, Dublin 7
Tel: 01 804 2000 / Fax: 01 670 3399
Web: www.defence.ie
Minister: Willie O'Dea
Minister of State: Tom Kitt
Secretary General: David J. O'Callaghan

**Department of Education and Science**
Marlborough Street, Dublin 1
Tel: 01 873 4700 / Fax: 01 878 7932
Web: www.irlgov.ie/educ
Minister: Mary Hanafin
Ministers of State: Síle de Valera, Brian Lenihan
Secretary General: John Dennehy

**Department of Enterprise, Trade and Employment**
Kildare Street, Dublin 2
Tel: 01 631 2121 / Fax: 01 631 2827
Web: www.entemp.ie
Minister: Michéal Martin
Ministers of State: Michael Ahern, Tony Killeen
Secretary General: Paul Haran

**Department of Environment, Heritage and Local Government**
Custom House, Dublin 1
Tel: 01 888 2000 / Fax: 01 888 2888
Web: www.environ.ie
Minister: Dick Roche
Ministers of State: Noel Ahern, Batt O'Keefe
Secretary General: Niall Callan

**Department of Finance**
Government Buildings, Upper Merrion Street, Dublin 2
Tel: 01 676 7571 / Fax: 01 678 9936
Web: www.finance.gov.ie
Minister: Brian Cowen
Minister of State: Tom Parlon
Secretary General: Tom Considine

**Department of Foreign Affairs**
80 St Stephen's Green, Dublin 2
Tel: 01 478 0822 / Fax: 01 478 1484
Web: www.irlgov.ie/iveagh
Minister: Dermot Ahern
Minister of State: Noel Treacy, Conor Lenihan
Secretary General: Dermot Gallagher

**Department of Health and Children**
Hawkins House, Dublin 2
Tel: 01 635 4000 / Fax: 01 635 4001
Web: www.doh.ie
Minister: Mary Harney
Ministers of State: Brian Lenihan, Tim O'Malley, Sean Power
Secretary General: Michael Kelly

**Department of Justice, Equality and Law Reform**
72-76 St Stephen's Green, Dublin 2
Tel: 01 602 8202 / Fax: 01 661 5461
Web: www.justice.ie
Minister: Michael McDowell
Ministers of State: Frank Fahey, Brian Lenihan
Secretary General: Tim Dalton

**Department of Social and Family Affairs**
Áras Mhic Dhiarmada
Store Street, Dublin 1
Tel: 01 874 8444 / Fax: 01 704 3868
Web: www.welfare.ie
Minister: Seamus Brennan
Secretary General: John Hynes

**Department of the Taoiseach**
Government Buildings
Upper Merrion Street Dublin 2
Tel: 01 662 4888 / Fax: 01 678 9791
Web: www.taoiseach.gov.ie
Taoiseach: Bertie Ahern
Ministers of State: Tom Kitt, Noel Treacy
Secretary General: Dermot McCarthy

**Department of Transport**
44 Kildare Street Dublin 2
Tel: 01 670 7444 / Fax: 01 677 3169
Web: www.transport.ie
Minister: Martin Cullen
Minister of State: Ivor Callely
Secretary General: Julie O'Neill

## System of Local Government in the Republic of Ireland

The elected local authorities in the Republic of Ireland are the 29 county councils, 5 city councils and 80 borough and town councils. County councils have a membership of between 20 and 48 and city councils have between 15 and 52 members. All borough and 3 town councils have 12 members with the remaining town councils each having 9 members.

Members of these authorities are elected every 5 years, using a system of proportional representation. The last council elections took place in June 2004.

### Responsibilities

The main areas in which local authorities have responsibilities are as follows:

- Housing and building;
- Road transportation and safety;
- Water supply and sewerage;
- Development incentives and control (planning);
- Environmental protection;
- Recreation and amenities;
- Agriculture, education, health and welfare

The functions of local government are divided into reserved functions, which are performed directly by the elected members of the authority and executive functions, performed by the city or county manager. Reserved functions comprise mainly decisions on major matters of policy and principle and include issues such as budgeting, borrowing money and development plans. Executive functions include the employment of staff, collection of rates and day-to-day administration.

### Local Authorities

**Carlow County Council**
County Offices
Athy Road, Carlow
Tel: 029 917 0300
Fax: 059 914 1503
Web: www.carlow.ie
County Manager: Joseph Crockett

*Town Councils*
Carlow
Tel: 059 913 1759
Town Clerk: Joe Watters

**Cavan County Council**
Courthouse, Cavan
Tel: 049 433 1799
Fax: 049 436 1565
Web: www.cavancoco.ie
County Manager (Acting):
Seamus Neely

*Town Councils*
Belturbet
Town Clerk (Acting):
Mary Fitzpatrick

Cavan
Town Hall, Cavan
Tel: 049 433 1397
Town Clerk (Acting):
Mary Fitzpatrick

Cootehill
Town Clerk: Jim Smith

**Clare County Council**
New Road, Ennis
Tel: 065 682 1616
Fax: 065 682 8233
Web: www.clare.ie
County Manager: Alec Fleming

*Town Councils*
Ennis
Tel: 065 682 8040
Town Clerk: Simon Moroney

Kilkee
Tel: 065 905 6040
Town Clerk: Liam O'Connor

Kilrush
Tel: 065 905 1047
Town Clerk:
Imy Whelan-Breen

Shannon
Tel: 061 362319
Town Clerk:
Tomás MacCormaic

Cork City Council
City Hall, Cork
Tel: 021 492 4000
Web: www.corkcity.ie
City Manager: Joe Gavin

**Cork County Council**
County Hall
Carrigrohane Road, Cork
Web: www.corkcoco.com
County Manager:
Maurice Moloney

*Town Councils*
Bandon
Town Clerk: Gerald Long

Bantry
Town Clerk: Maria O'Donoghue

Cobh
Tel: 021 481 1307
Town Clerk: Paraig Lynch

Fermoy
Tel: 025 31201
Town Clerk: Rose Carroll

Kinsale
Tel: 021 477 2154
Town Clerk: Ray Owens

Macroom
Tel: 026 41545
Town Clerk: Kevin Curran

Mallow
Tel: 022 21542
Town Clerk: Pat O'Connor

Midleton
Tel: 021 463 1580
Town Clerk: Joe McCarthy

Passage West
Town Clerk: Niall O'Keeffe

Skibbereen
Tel: 028 21721
Town Clerk: Noreen Murphy

Youghal
Tel: 024 92926

**Donegal County Council**
County House, Lifford
Tel: 074 917 2222
Web: www.Donegal.ie
County Manager: Michael McLoone

*Town Councils*
Ballyshannon
Tel: 071 985 1179
Town Clerk (Acting): Marie Little

Buncrana
Tel: 074 936 1198
Town Clerk: Paul Doyle

Bundoran
Tel: 071 984 1230
Town Clerk: Joe McNulty

Letterkenny
Tel: 074 912 5399
Town Clerk: Paddy Doherty

**Dublin City Council**
Civic Offices
Wood Quay, Dublin 8
Tel: 01 672 2222
Web: www.dublincity.ie
City Manager: John Fitzgerald

**Dún Laoghaire-Rathdown County Council**
County Hall
Marine Road
Dún Laoghaire
Tel: 01 205 4700
Fax: 01 280 6969
Web: www.dlrcoco.ie
County Manager: Derek Brady

**Fingal County Council**
County Hall, PO Box 174
Swords, Fingal, Co Dublin
Tel: 01 890 5000
Fax: 01 890 5809
Web: www.fingalcoco.ie
County Manager:
William Soffe

*Town Councils*
Balbriggan
Tel: 01 841 2178
Town Clerk: David Storey

**Galway City Council**
City Hall, College Road, Galway
Tel: 091 536400
Fax: 091 567493
Web: www.galwaycity.ie
City Manager: John Tierney

**Galway County Council**
Áras an Chontae
Prospect Hill, Galway
Tel: 091 509000
Fax: 091 509010
Web: www.galway.ie
County Manager:
Donal O'Donoghue

*Town Councils*
Ballinasloe
Tel: 090 964 2263

Loughrea
Town Clerk: Imelda Deely

Tuam
Town Clerk: Angela Holian

**Kerry County Council**
Áras an Chontae, Tralee
Tel: 066 712 1111
Fax: 066 712 2466
Web: www.kerrycoco.ie
County Manager:
Martin D Nolan

*Town Councils*
Killarney
Town Hall, Killarney
Tel: 064 31023

Listowel
Áras an Phiarsaigh, Charles Street, Listowel
Tel: 0687 21004

Tralee
Town Hall, Princes Quay, Tralee
Tel: 066 712 1633

**Kildare County Council**
St Mary's, Naas
Tel: 045 873800
Fax: 045 876875
Web: www.Kildare.ie
County Manager: niall Bradley

*Town Councils*
Athy
Municipal Offices, Rathstewart, Athy
Tel: 059 863 1444
Town Clerk: Helen Dowling

Droichead Nua
Town Hall, Droichead Nua
Tel: 045 431785
Town Clerk: Paul Kelly

Leixlip
Newtown House
Leixlip
Tel: 01 624 5777

Naas
Town Hall, Naas
Tel: 045 897232

**Kilkenny County Council**
County Hall
John Street, Kilkenny
Tel: 056 779 4000
Fax: 056 779 4004
Web: www.kilkennycoco.ie
County Manager:
Michael Malone

*Borough Council*
Kilkenny
Tel: 056 779 4500
Fax: 056 779 4509
Town Clerk: Donal O'Brien

**Laois County Council**
Áras an Chontae
Portlaoise
Tel: 0502 64000
Fax: 0502 22313
Web: www.laois.ie
County Manager:
Martin Riordan

*Town Councils*
Mountmellick
Town Manager: Declan Byrne

Portlaoise
Town Manager: Peter Scully

**Leitrim County Council**
Áras an Chontae
Carrick-on-Shannon
Tel: 071 962 0005
Fax: 071 962 1982
Web: www.leitrimcoco.ie
County Manager:
Daniel McLoughlin

**Limerick City Council**
City Hall, Limerick
Tel: 061 415799
Fax: 061 415266
Web: www.limerickcity.ie
City Manager: Tom Mackey

**Limerick County Council**
County Hall
Dooradoyle, Limeric
Tel: 061 496000
Fax: 061 496001
Web: www.lcc.ie
County Manager:
Edmond Gleeson

**Longford County Council**
Áras an Chontae
Great Water Street
Longford
Tel: 043 46231
Fax: 043 4123
Web: www.longfordcoco.ie
County Manager:
Michael Killeen

*Town Council*
Granard
Town Clerk: Michael Clancy

Longford
Market Square, Longford
Tel: 043 46474

**Louth County Council**
County Hall
Millennium Centre, Dundalk
Tel: 042 933 5457
042 933 4549
Web: www.louthcoco.ie
County Manager:
Martina Maloney

*Borough Council*
Drogheda
Fair Street, Drogheda
Tel: 041 987 6100
Town Clerk: Des Foley

*Town Councils*
Ardee
Market Square House, Ardee
Tel: 041 685 6083
Town Clerk: Ann Duff

Dundalk Town Hall
Crowe Street, Dundalk
Tel: 042 933 2276
Town Clerk: Frank Pentony

**Mayo County Council**
Áras an Chontae, Castlebar
Tel: 094 902 4444
Fax: 094 902 3937
Web: www.mayococo.ie
County Manager: Des Mahon

*Town Councils*
Ballina
Tel: 096 76100
Town Clerk: Carmel Murphy

Castlebar
Tel: 094 902 3350
Town Clerk: Marie Crowley

Westport
Tel: 098 50400
Town Clerk: Ann Moore

**Meath County Council**
County Hall, Navan
Tel: 046 902 1581
Fax: 046 902 1463
Web: www.meath.ie
County Manager:
Tom Dowling

*Town Councils*
Kells
Town Hall, Kells
Tel: 046 924 0064
Town Clerk: Bill Sweeney

Navan
Town Hall, Watergate Street, Navan
Tel: 046 902 9078
Town Clerk: Fergus Muldoon

Trim
Mill Street, Trim
Tel: 046 943 1238
Town Clerk: Larry McEntee

**Monaghan County Council**
County Offices, Monaghan
Tel: 047 30500
Fax: 047 82739
Web: www.monaghan.ie
County Manager:
Declan Nelson

*Town Councils*
Ballybay
The Square, Ballybay
Tel: 047 38113
Town Clerk: Susan Deery

Carrickmacross
The Old Fever Hospital
Shercock Road
Carrickmacross
Tel: 042 966 1618
Town Clerk: Frances Matthews

Castleblaney
Main Street, Castleblaney
Tel: 042 974 0058
Town Clerk: Marie Deighan

Clones
Courthouse, Clones
Tel: 047 5101
Town Clerk: Geraldine Killen

Monaghan
Town Hall
Dublin Street, Monaghan
Tel: 047 82079
Town Clerk: Tony McDonagh

**North Tipperary County Council**
Courthouse, Nenagh
Tel: 067 31771
Fax: 067 33134
Web: www.tipperarynorth.ie
County Manager:
Terry O'Niadh

*Town Councils*
Nenagh
Town Hall, Nenagh
Tel: 067 31214
Town Clerk: Jacqueline Ryan

Templemore
Town Hall, Templemore
Tel: 0504 31496
Town Clerk: Jacqueline Ryan

Thurles
Slievenamon Road, Thurle
Tel: 0504 21433
Town Clerk: Michael Ryan

**Offaly County Council**
Áras an Chontae, Charleville Road, Tullamore
Tel: 0506 46800
Fax: 0506 46868
Web: www.offaly.ie
County Manager:
Niall Sweeney

*Town Councils*
Birr
Town Hall, Birr
Tel: 0509 20187
Town Clerk: Edel O'Brien

Edenderry
Town Hall, Edenderry
Tel: 046 973 1256
Town Clerk: Deirdre Hunt

Tullamore
Town Hall, Cormac Street
Tullamore
Tel: 0506 52470

**Roscommon County Council**
Courthouse, Roscommo
Tel: 090 663 7100
Fax: 090 663 7108
Web:www.roscommoncoco.ie
County Manager: John Tiernan

*Town Council*
Boyle
Town Clerk: Eileen Callaghan

**Sligo County Council**
County Hall
Riverside, Sligo
Tel: 071 915 6666
Fax: 071 914 111
Web: www.sligococo.ie
County Manager:
Hubert Kearns

*Borough Council*
Sligo
City Hall, Sligo
Tel: 071 914 2141
Fax: 071 914 1056
Web: www.sligoborough.ie
Town Clerk: John McNabola

**South Dublin County Council**
County Hall
Tallaght, Dublin 24
Tel: 01 414 9000
Fax: 01 414 9111
Web: www.southdublin.ie
County Manager: Joe Horan

**South Tipperary County Council**
Áras an Chontae
Emmet Street, Clonmel
Tel: 052 34455
Fax: 052 24355
Web: www.southtippcoco.ie
County Manager:
Edmond O'Connor

*Borough Council*
Clonmel
Town Hall, Clonmel
Tel: 052 83800
Town Clerk: Billy Doyle

*Town Councils*
Carrick-on-Suir
Town Hall, Carrick-on-Suir
Tel: 051 640032
Town Clerk: Ger Walsh

Cashel
Friar Street, Cashel
Tel: 062 64700
Town Clerk: Seamus Maher

Tipperary
Dan Breen House, Tipperary
Tel: 062 51179
Town Clerk: David Coleman

**Waterford City Council**
City Hall, Waterford
Tel: 051 309900
Fax: 051 879124
Web: www.waterfordcity.ie
City Manager: Conn Murray

**Waterford County Council**
Waterford County Civic Office
Davitt's Quay, Dungarvan
Tel: 058 22000
Fax: 058 42911
Web: www.waterfordcoco.ie
County Manager:
Donal Connolly

*Town Councils*
Dungarvan
Civic Office
Davitt's Quay, Dungarvan
Tel: 058 41111
Town Clerk: Brian White

Lismore
Waterford County Council
Area Office, Lismore
Tel: 058 53580
Town Clerk (Acting):
Eric Flynn

Tramore
Waterford County Council Offices
Tank Field, Tramore
Tel: 051 386303
Town Clerk (Acting):
John O'Sullivan

**Westmeath County Council**
Mullingar
Tel: 044 32000
Fax: 044 42330
Web: www.westmeathcoco.ie
County Manager:
Ann McGuinness

*Town Councils*
Athlone
The Crescent
Station Road, Athlone
Tel: 090 644 210
Town Clerk: John Walsh

Mullingar
County Buildings, Mullingar
Tel: 044 32000
Town Clerk: Caroline Byrne

**Wexford County Council**
County Hall
Spawell Road, Wexford
Tel: 053 65000
Fax: 053 43406
Web: www.wexford.ie
County Manager: Eddie Breen

*Borough Council*
Wexford
Municipal Buildings, Wexford
Tel: 053 4261
Town Clerk: Patrick Collins

*Town Councils*
Enniscorthy
Market Square, Enniscorthy
Tel: 054 3354
Town Clerk: Donal Minnock

Gorey
Market House, Gorey
Tel: 055 21205
Town Clerk: Martin Whelan

New Ross
The Tholsel, New Ross
Tel: 051 42128
Town Clerk (Acting):
Gerald Mackey

**Wicklow County Council**
County Buildings, Wicklow
Tel: 0404 20100
Fax: 0404 67792
Web: www.wicklow.ie
County Manager:
Edward J Sheehy

*Town Councils*
Arklow
Town Hall, Arklow
Town Clerk: Rosemarie Dennison

Bray
Civic Office
Main Street, Bray
Tel: 01 274 4900
Town Clerk: Catherine Halligan

Greystones
Mill Road, Greystones
Tel: 01 287 669
Town Clerk: Myra Porter

Wicklow
Town Hall, Wicklow
Tel: 0404 6732
Town Clerk: Frank O'Toole

## Regional Authorities

In addition to local authorities, local government in the Republic of Ireland has an additional 'layer' in the form of eight regional authorities. These regional authorities are statutory bodies comprising local elected representatives selected by constituent local authorities. Their main tasks are to promote the co-ordination of public services in their region and to review and advise on the implementation of EU Structural and Cohesion Funds Programmes.

The eight regional authorities are:

**Border –** comprises counties Cavan, Donegal, Leitrim, Louth, Monaghan and Sligo

**Dublin –** comprises Dublin City Council, Dun Laoghaire-Rathdown County Council, Fingal County Council and South Dublin County Council

**Mid-East –** comprises counties Meath, Kildare and Wicklow

**Midland –** Laois, Longford, Offaly, Westmeath

**Mid-West –** comprises Clare, North Tipperary and Limerick County Councils, as well as Limerick City

**South-East –** comprises counties of Carlow, Kilkenny, South Tipperary, Waterford and Wexford as well as Waterford City

**South-West –** comprises Cork city, along with counties Cork and Kerry

**West –** comprises counties Galway and Mayo, Roscommon, Sligo and Galway city.

## The Republic of Ireland and the EU

**European Commission Representation in Ireland**
European Union House
18 Dawson Street Dublin 2
Tel: 01 634 1111 / Fax: 01 634 1112
Web: www.euireland.ie
Director: Peter Doyle

The European Commission Representation in Ireland informs the Irish public of developments at EU level and keeps the Commission abreast of developments in Ireland of interest to the rest of the EU.

**European Parliament**
Office in Ireland: EU House
43 Molesworth Street Dublin 2
Tel: 01 605 7900 / Fax: 01 605 7999
Web: www.europarl.ie

Elections to the European Parliament took place during June 2004, at which time Ireland elected MEPs to fill 13 seats – Ireland had previously had a representation of 15 but this was reduced as a result of enlargement of the EU on 1 May 2004.

For European Parliament elections, the Republic is divided into four constituencies, as follows:

**Dublin –** comprises Dublin city and county – 4 seats

**East –** comprises Leinster counties except Dublin – 3 seats

**North West –** comprises Connaught counties plus Clare, Donegal, Monaghan and Leitrim – 3 seats

**South –** comprises Munster counties excluding Clare – 3 seats

## Members of the European Parliament

**Dublin**
Fine Gael: Gay Mitchell
Fianna Fail: Eoin Ryan
Labour Party: Proinsias de Rossa
Sinn Féin: Mary Lou McDonald

**East**
Fine Gael: Avril Doyle, Mairead McGuinness
Fianna Fail: Liam Aylward
Independent: Marian Harkin

**North West**
Fine Gael: Jim Higgins
Fianna Fail: Sean O'Neachtain

**South**
Fine Gael: Simon Coveney
Fianna Fail: Brian Crowley
Independent: Kathy Sinnott

**European Parliament Election 2004**

| | Dublin | East | North West | South |
|---|---|---|---|---|
| Electorate | 821,723 | 806,598 | 688,804 | 802,359 |
| Total Poll | 435,136 | 471,895 | 435,910 | 498,394 |
| % Turnout | 52.95 | 58.50 | 63.29 | 62.12 |
| Spoiled Votes | 13,239 | 18,717 | 14,487 | 14,124 |
| Valid Poll | 421,987 | 453,178 | 421,423 | 484,270 |
| Seats | 4 | 3 | 3 | 3 |
| Quota | 84,380 | 113,295 | 105,356 | 121,068 |
| Candidates | 12 | 13 | 9 | 10 |

**European Parliament Election 2004**
**1st preference votes %**

| | Dublin | East | North West | South |
|---|---|---|---|---|
| Fianna Fail | 23.22 | 25.08 | 27.10 | 41.02 |
| Fine Gael | 21.51 | 40.55 | 23.96 | 24.56 |
| Labour Party | 22.53 | 13.05 | 3.31 | 4.12 |
| Green Party | 9.59 | 5.64 | n/a | 2.25 |
| Sinn Fein | 14.32 | 8.68 | 15.5 | 6.74 |
| Others | 8.84 | 6.99 | 30.13 | 21.30 |

Source: www.europarl.ie

FLORES-MARTIN
ABASCAL

# Chapter 12

# Northern Ireland and the European Union

## Introduction

The European Union was established following World War Two, with the process of European integration launched on 9 May 1950 when France officially proposed to create 'the first concrete foundation of a European federation'. Six countries Belgium, Germany, France, Italy, Luxembourg and the Netherlands joined. Since then there have been five waves of accessions:

- 1973: Denmark, Ireland and the United Kingdom;
- 1981: Greece;
- 1986: Spain and Portugal;
- 1995: Austria, Finland and Sweden;
- 2004: Czech Republic, Hungary, Estonia, Malta, Cyprus, Poland, Latvia, Slovenia, Lithuania, Slovakia

The EU currently has 25 member states. The European Union is built on a unique institutional system and is based on the rule of law and democracy; its member states delegate sovereignty to common institutions representing the interests of the Union as a whole.

All decisions and procedures are derived from the basic treaties ratified by the member states. Whilst the role of the Commission is traditionally perceived to be to uphold the interests of the Union as a whole, each national government is represented by the Council of Ministers and individual citizens by the European parliament, which is a directly elected legislature.

Two other institutions, the Court of Justice and the Court of Auditors support the 'institutional triangle' of Commission, Council and parliament and are supported by a further five bodies:

- European Central Bank;
- Economic and Social Committee;
- Committee of the Regions;
- European Investment Bank;
- European Ombudsman.

The principal objectives of the Union are to:

- Establish European Citizenship (Fundamental Rights; Freedom of Movement; Civil and Political Rights);
- Ensure freedom, security and justice (Cooperation in the field of Justice and Home Affairs);
- Promote economic and social progress (single market; euro, the common currency; job creation; regional development; environmental protection);
- Assert Europe's role in the world (common foreign and security policy; the European Union in the world).

## The Institutions of the European Union

### The European Council of Ministers

Rue de la Loi 175, B–1048 Brussels
Tel: +32 2 285 61 11 / Fax: +32 2 285 7397
Web: www.ue.eu.int
Email: public.info@consilium.eu.int

The Council of the European Union consists of relevant ministers from all of the member states, and is the European Union's main decision-making body. Its representatives come together regularly at ministerial level. According to the matters on the agenda, the Council meets in different compositions: foreign affairs, finance, education, telecommunications, etc. It co-ordinates the broad economic, foreign and security policies of member states and shares legislative and budgetary authority with the European parliament. The Council generally co-ordinates the activities of member states and adopts measures in the fields of policing and judicial co-operation in criminal matters.

The Council of Ministers is supported by the Committee of the Permanent Representatives (COREPER), which prepares the positions for the ministers prior to their Council meetings. Each country has its own permanent representation team.

### European Commission

200 rue de la Loi, B–1049, Brussels
Tel: +32 2 299 11 11
Web: www.europa.eu.int
Email: sg-info@cec.eu.int
President: José Manuel Barroso

NI Representation
Windsor House, 9–15 Bedford Street
Belfast, BT2 7EG
Tel: 028 9024 0708 / Fax: 028 9024 8241
Head of Representation: Eddie McVeigh

The European Commission's members are nominated by the member states. It initiates draft legislation, presents legislative proposals to parliament and the Council and is the executive body of the European Union, implementing legislation, budget and programmes adopted by the European parliament and the Council of the European Union. In addition, the Commission represents the EU internationally, negotiates international agreements (chiefly trade and co-operation) and acts as guardian of the Treaties with the Court of Justice, ensuring that Community law is properly applied.

The Commission consists of 20 Commissioners. A President, assisted by two Vice-Presidents, heads the Commission. Each member state has at least one of its nationals serving on the Commission at any one time, and the larger member states – France, Germany, Italy, Spain and the United Kingdom – have, at present, two. The members of the Commission are appointed 'by common accord' of the governments of the member states for a renewable term of five years. The seat of the European Commission is in Brussels.

The Commission enjoys wide legislative powers delegated from the Council and certain autonomous legislative powers under the Treaties: but its principal role is setting the general policy agenda for the European Union. Although the Council adopts European legislation, in most cases these institutions may only act on legislative proposals from the Commission itself. In the past, the right of legislative initiative has enabled the Commission to act as the engine of European integration.

The Commission also has important investigative, enforcement and quasi-judicial functions, including the power to act against member states believed to be in breach of Community law. It also has powers in relation to the supervision and enforcement of the Community's rules on competition and state aids. The latter can extend to the imposition of extremely heavy fines (subject to rights of appeal) on individuals, undertakings or groups of undertakings found to be breach of the law.
The European Commission is not simply an executive body; in particular, it has a key role to play in the management of the European Union's annual budget of over 80 billion euro. Most of this sum represents, running the Community's Common Agricultural Policy.

**The European Commission***

| | |
|---|---|
| **President:** | **José Manuel Barroso** |
| **Vice Presidents:** | |
| Institutional Relations and Communication Strategy | Margot Wallström |
| Enterprise and Industry | Günter Verheugen |
| Transport | Jacques Barrot |
| Administrative Affairs, Audit and Anti-Fraud | Siim Kallas |
| Justice, Freedom and Security | Franco Frattini |
| **Members of the Commission:** | |
| Information Society and Media | Viviane Reding |
| Environment | Stavros Dimas |
| Economic and Monetary Affairs | Joaquin Almunia |
| Regional Policy | Danuta Hübner |
| Fisheries and Maritime Affairs | Joe Borg |
| Financial Programming and Budget | Dalia Grybauskaite |
| Science and Research | Janez Potocnik |
| Education, Training, Culture and Multi-linguism | Jan Figel |
| Health and Consumer Protection | Markos Kyprianou |
| Enlargement | Olli Rehn |
| Development and Humanitarian Aid | Louis Michel |
| Energy | Laszlo Kovacs |
| Competition | Neelie Kroes |
| Agriculture and Rural Development | Mariann Fischer Boel |
| External Relations and European Neighbourhood Policy | Benita Ferrero Waldner |
| Internal Market and Services | Charlie McCreevy |
| Employment, Social Affairs and Equal Opportunities | Vladimir Spidla |
| Trade | Peter Mandelson |
| Taxation and Customs Union | Ingrida Udre |
| **Secretariat General of the Commission:** | |
| Secretary-General | David O'Sullivan |
| Deputy Secretary-Generals | Eckart Guth<br>Enzo Moavero Milanesi |
| Assistant | Cesare Onestini |

*As proposed for approval by the European Parliament

**Directorates-General**

Each Directorate-General is headed by a Director-General reporting to the Commissioner who takes overall political and operational responsibility for the work of the Directorate-General. An individual Commissioner's portfolio may well cover the work of more than one Directorate-General. The allocation of portfolios to individual Commissioners is decided collectively, although the President makes initial proposals. The Commissioners meet collectively as the College of Commissioners once a week, act by majority and operate under the political guidance of the President.

**European Commission Directorates-General**

| | |
|---|---|
| Legal Services | Michel Petite |
| Press & Communication Service | Jorge de Oliveira e Sousa |
| Policy Advisory Group | Ricardo Levi |
| Economic & Financial Affairs | Klaus Regling |
| Enterprise | Horst Reichenbach |
| Competition | Philip Lowe |
| Employment & Social Affairs | Odile Quintin |
| Agriculture | José Manuel Silva Rodriguez |
| Transport & Energy | François Lamoureux |
| Environment | Catherine Day |
| Research | Achilleas Mitsos |
| Joint Research Centre | Barry McSweeney |
| Information Society | Fabio Colasanti |
| Fisheries | Jörgen Holmquist |
| Internal Market | Alexander Schaub |
| Regional Policy | Graham Meadows |
| Taxation & Custom Unit | Robert Verrue |
| Education & Culture | Nikolaus Van Der Pas |
| Health & Consumer Protection | Robert Madelin |
| Justice & Home Affairs | Jonathan Faull |
| External Relations | Eneko Landaburu |
| Trade | Mogens Peter Carl |
| Development | Athanassios Theodorakis |
| Enlargement | Fabrizio Barbaso |
| Europe Aid Co-operation Office | Koos Richelle |
| Humanitarian Aid Office – ECHO | Costanza Adinolfi |
| Eurostat | Michel Vanden Abeele |
| Personnel & Administration | Claude Chêne |
| Internal Audit Service | Walter Deffaa |
| Budget | Luis Romero Requena |
| European Anti-Fraud Office | Franz-Hermann Brüner |
| Joint Interpreting & Conference Service | Marco Benedetti |
| Translation Service | Juhani Lönnroth |
| Office for Official Publications | Thomas L Cranfield |
| Office for Administration & Payment of Individual Entitlements | Edith Kitzmantel |
| Office for Infrastructure & Logistics | Piet Verleysen<br>Martine Reicharts |
| European Personnel Selection Office | Erik Halskov |

## The European Parliament

Strasbourg
Allée du Printemps
B.P. 1024/F
F–67070 Strasbourg Cede
Tel: +33 03 08 17 40 01
Fax: +33 03 88 25 65 01
Email: civis@europarl.eu.int
Web: www.europarl.eu.int

Brussels
Rue Wiertz
B-1047 Brussels
Tel: +322 284 2111
Fax: +322 284 6974

Luxembourg
Plateau du Kirchberg
BP 1601, L-2929 Luxembourg
Tel: +352 43001
Fax: +352 43 00 294 94

Elected every five years by individual citizens in each of the member states, the European parliament represents the democratic voice of the 374 million citizens that live within the European Union.

The European parliament is composed of members from each of the 25 member states in broad proportion to their population. The parliament shares legislative and budgetary authority with the European Council and exercises democratic and political supervision over the other institutions.

The European parliament has three essential functions:

- Shares with the Council the power to legislate, i.e. to adopt European laws (directives, regulations, decisions), assisting in maintaining the democratic legitimacy of the texts adopted;
- Shares budgetary authority with the Council and can therefore influence spending. At the end of the procedure it adopts the budget in its entirety;
- The parliament exercises democratic supervision over the Commission approving the nomination of Commissioners. It has the right to censure the Commission, and also exercises political supervision over all the institutions.

The UK has an entitlement of 78 European parliament seats out of a total of 732. Of this, Northern Ireland returns 3 MEPs by an election held every 5 years. In this case Northern Ireland is a single constituency, and the three European MPs are elected by proportional representation, the Single Transferable Vote (STV).

The most recent elections to the European Parliament were held in June 2004. Full details of the results from the 2004 Northern Ireland European election are set out in Chapter 2 on pages 118-119.

## Northern Ireland MEPs

**Jim Allister**
DUP

European Political Group: Non-attached
Constituency contact:
139 Holywood Road, Belfast
Tel: 028 9065 5011

Brussels contact:
European Parliament
Rue Wierz
ASP 08F154
B-1047, Brussels, Belgium
Tel: + 322 228 45275
Fax: + 322 284 9275

**Bairbre de Brún**
Sinn Féin

European Political Group: Confederal Group of the European United Left - Nordic Green Left
Constituency contact:
Connolly House
147 Andersonstown Road
Belfast, BT11 9BW
Tel: 028 9080 8404

Brussels contact:
European Parliament
Bât. Altiero Spinelli, 07F247
Rue Wierz 60
B-1047, Brussels, Belgium
Tel: + 322 284 5222
Fax: +322 284 9222
Assistant: Mark McGregor

**Jim Nicholson**
Ulster Unionist Party

European Political Group: European People's Party and European Democrats
Constituency contact: Cunningham House
429 Holywood Road, Belfast, BT4 2LN
Tel: 028 9076 5500
Fax: 028 9024 6738

Brussels contact:
European Parliament
Rue Wiertz
B-1047, Belgium
Tel: + 322 284 5933
Fax: + 322 284 9933

## The European Court of Justice

Luxembourg L-2925
Tel: +352 43031 / Fax: +352 4303 2600
Web: www.curia.eu.int

The European Court of Justice ensures that Community law is uniformly interpreted and effectively applied. It has jurisdiction in disputes involving member states, EU institutions, businesses and individuals.

The Court of Justice currently consists of 25 Judges and eight Advocates General who are appointed for a renewable term of six years. The task of the Judges and Advocates General is to make reasoned submissions on the cases brought before the European Court of Justice in advance of the Court handing down its final decision.

The European Court of Justice is the highest and sole judicial authority in matters of Community law. Its responsibilities encompass three main areas:

- Monitoring the application of Community law;
- Interpretation of Community law;
- Further shaping of Community law.

The Court of Justice acts as a constitutional court when disputes between Community institutions are before it or legislative instruments are up for review; as an administrative court when reviewing the administrative acts of the Commission or of national authorities applying Community legislation; as a labour court or industrial tribunal when dealing with freedom of movement, social security and equal opportunities; as a fiscal court when dealing with matters concerning the validity and interpretation of directives in the fields of taxation and customs law; as a criminal court when reviewing Commission decisions imposing fines; and as a civil court when hearing claims for damages or interpreting the Brussels convention on the enforcement of judgements in civil and commercial matters.

## The European Court of Auditors

12 Rue Alcide De Gasperi
L-1615 Luxembourg
Tel: +352 43981 / Fax: +352 439342
Web: www.eca.eu.int

The Court of Auditors checks that all the Union's revenue has been received and all its expenditure incurred in a lawful and regular manner and that financial management of the EU budget has been sound. The Court of Auditors consists of one member from each member state, currently 25.

The duties of the Court of Auditors include:

- Examining the accounts of all revenue and expenditure of the Community;
- Examining the accounts of all revenue and expenditure of all bodies set up by the Community;
- Ascertaining whether all revenue has been received and all expenditure incurred in a 'lawful and regular manner' and whether financial management has been sound;
- Assisting the European parliament and the Council in exercising their powers of control over the implementation of the budget;
- Submitting annual reports at the close of each financial year;
- Submitting observations, opinions or special reports on specific questions.

## European Central Bank

Kaiserstrasse 29, D-60311 Frankfurt, Germany
Tel: +49 691 3440 / Fax: +49 691 344 6000
Web: www.ecb.int

The European Central Bank frames and implements European monetary policy; it conducts foreign exchange operations and ensures the smooth operation of payment systems. Its chief tasks are to maintain the stability of the European currency, the Euro, and control the amount of currency in circulation.

In order to carry out its tasks the European Central Bank's independence is guaranteed by numerous legal provisions. The European Central Bank consists of a Governing Council and an Executive Board. The Governing Council comprises the governors of the national central banks and the members of the Executive Board of the European Central Bank. The Executive Board, which is made up of the President, Vice President and four other members, is effectively in charge of running the European Central Bank.

### The European Single Currency

Following agreement by EU leaders in 1998 on European and Monetary Union, 1st January 1999 saw the adoption of the single currency by France, Spain, Portugal, Germany, The Netherlands, Austria, Belgium, Finland, Italy, Luxembourg and Ireland. From 1st January 2002 notes and coins became available and the European Single Currency became a reality.

The Euro zone is comparable in size with the United States economy, already including 320 million consumers and accounting for one fifth of the world's GDP. Northern Ireland is the only region of the UK to have a land border with a country operating in the Euro zone and the impact has been substantial.

## European Investment Bank

100 Boulevard Konrad Adenauer
L-2950 Luxembourg
Tel: +352 43791 / Fax: +352 437704
Web: www.eib.eu.int

The European Investment Bank exists to assist the Community in its role as financing agency for a 'balanced and steady development' of the common market. It provides loans and guarantees in all economic sectors, especially to promote the development of less-developed regions, to modernise or convert undertakings or create new jobs and to assist projects of common interest to several member states. The 14 member states are members of the Bank.

## European Economic and Social Committee

Rue Ravenstein 2, 1000 Brussels, Belgium
Tel: +32 2 546 9011 / Fax: +32 2 513 4893
Email: info@esc.eu.int / Web: www.esc.eu.int

The Economic and Social Committee is a consultative body made up of representatives of Europe's main interest groups: employers' organisations, trade unions, farmers, consumer groups, professional associations, etc. From the 25 member states 317 members of the committee are selected. It is non-political, and exists to advise the European Parliament, European Commission and the European Council. It supports the role of civil society organisations in non-EC countries to foster better relations with similar bodies, termed 'institution building'. The Committee is divided into three groups: employers, workers and various interests. They draw up opinions on draft EU legislation and issues affecting European society.

Northern Ireland has two representatives attached to the European Economic and Social Committee:

*Claire Whitten*
Contact Details: Pi$^2$, 33 Clarendon Dock, Belfast, BT1 3BW
Tel: 028 9051 1231 / Fax: 028 9051 1201
Email: claire@pi2online.com
Group III: Various Interests
Committee Membership: Economic and Monetary Union and Social Cohesion; Agriculture, Rural Development and the Environment

*John Simpson*
Contact Details: 3 Glenmachan Drive, Belfast, BT4 2RE
Tel: 028 9076 9399 / Fax: 028 9076 0558
Email: johnvsimpson@aol.com
Group III: Various Interests
Committee Membership: Economic and Monetary Union and Social Cohesion; Single Market, Production and Consumption

## The European Committee of the Regions

Bertha Von Suttner Building
Rue Montoyer, 92–102
B–1040 Brussels, Belgium
Tel: +32 2 282 2211 / Fax: +32 2 282 2325
Web: www.cor.eu.int

The European Committee of the Regions was established under the Maastricht Treaty, to represent local and regional authorities in the European Union. Its aim is to strengthen social and economic cohesion of member states, towards European integration. The Committee meets in plenary session 5 times a year to measure opinions on relevant issues. The Committee of the Regions consists of 344 representatives of regional and local authorities in the member states. The UK currently has 24 representatives on the Committee.

There are a number of areas in which the Council or the Commission are required to seek the views of the Committee, namely:

- Education
- Culture;
- Public Health;
- Trans-European networks;
- Transport
- Telecommunications and energy infrastructure;
- Economic and Social Cohesion;
- Employment policy;
- Social legislation.

The Council also consults the Committee regularly, but without any legal obligation.

**Northern Ireland Members of the Committee of the Regions**

*Dermot Nesbitt MLA*
Political Party: UUP
Contact: 21 Downpatrick Road, Crossgar, BT30 9EQ
Tel: 028 4483 1561 / Fax: 028 4483 1722
Email: dermotnesbitt@hotmail.com
Type of Membership: Full Member
Political Group: European People's Party

*Alban Maginness MLA*
Political Party: SDLP
Contact: 228 Antrim Road, Belfast, BT15 2AN
Tel: 028 9022 0520 / Fax: 028 9022 0522
Email: a.maginness@sdlp.ie
Type of Membership: Full Member
Political Group: Party of European Socialists

*George Savage*
Political Party: UUP
Contact: 'Watties Hill'
147 Dromore Road, Donacloney, Craigavon, BT66 7NR
Tel: 028 3882 0401 / Fax: 028 3882 0401
Type of Membership: Alternate Member
Political Group: European People's Party

*Margaret Ritchie MLA*
Political Party: SDLP
Contact: 19 Annacloy Road, Downpatrick, BT30 9AE
Tel: 028 4461 2882 / Fax: 028 4461 9574
Type of Membership: Alternate Member
Political Group: Party of European Socialists

# Northern Ireland in Europe

Northern Ireland has a recognised presence in Europe and is no longer seen as a region on the periphery but as a keen participant within the structures of the European Union.

Improvements in infrastructure, the peace dividend (to which the Special Support Programme for Peace and Reconciliation has contributed over £370 million) and further resources from the EU Structural Funds aimed at promoting economic development have heightened awareness of the important role of the EU within the region.

Northern Ireland has faced great social and economic disadvantage and in the recent past the region has focused upon gaining economic parity with other member states of the European Union. The categorisation of Northern Ireland as 'lagging behind' in the early 1990s saw the region being eligible for Objective 1 status under the EU's Structural Funds. Nonetheless, even with the economic progress that has been made Northern Ireland as a region has a GDP per capita that is still only 80% of the EU average.

The European Commission has worked to develop relationships with Northern Ireland and the establishment of the Northern Ireland Executive Brussels office operated by the Office of the First Minister and Deputy First Minister reinforces a growing profile for the interests of Northern Ireland government within the Community. This, coupled with the work of the Commission's representation in Belfast ensures that Brussels is au fait with Northern Ireland developments and vice versa.

Local authorities are an increasingly important level of government in European terms, with much of the European funding in Northern Ireland administered by Local Strategy Partnerships. Councils account for a major proportion of the membership of LSPs and are influential in the distribution of European support.

## Northern Ireland in a European Context

Northern Ireland has three MEPs with a range of knowledge and experience of working for Northern Ireland; two Northern Ireland representatives on the Committee of the Regions and two representatives on the Economic and Social Committee.

At the UK level, EU policy is a non-transferred matter and the majority of decisions on EU policy are taken at national level. Under devolution, the local role is formalised in the Memorandum of Understanding and the Concordats on Co-ordination of European Union Policy and the Joint Ministerial Council (JMC). Policy is still made through London; the difference under devolution was the ability for the Northern Ireland departments to influence policy on those specific issues which have a clear regional perspective. The Concordats make specific reference to the involvement of the North/South Ministerial Council.

EU policies and legislation impact on a wide range of matters in Northern Ireland including 80 per cent of policies in the Programme for Government of the first Assembly and up to 60 per cent of all legislation. The degree to which Northern Ireland can influence EU policy depends primarily on its input through London.

Since EU policy decisions are taken at national level it is argued that Northern Ireland should focus on defining areas where there are distinctions in the Northern Ireland position and where returns can be maximised. Due to resource constraints only a limited number of areas may be chosen as priority areas. The experience of other regional parliaments suggests that if there is insufficient planning or co-ordination, the outcome will be volumes of effort with little realisable benefit for Northern Ireland.

During devolution there was some disquiet that Assembly Committees had little opportunity to exert influence on the development and implementation of policy; their first view of European Directive and Commission decisions often occured when the department brought sub-ordinate legislation forward. One plan to address this concern would be for OFMDFM to take a more proactive approach to build capacity within all departments to become engaged with European issues, particularly beyond the remit of implementing legislation. This will be supported by plans to form a Standing Committee on EU Affairs within the next Assembly, should devolution return. Other possibilities under consideration include: the establishment of an Assembly Information Desk in Brussels, possibly in the Office of the Northern Ireland Executive in Brussels, or operating as a shared resource with other regions; appointment of a Junior Minister with responsibility for European Affairs, to manage relationships with the European Parliament and Commission and to support and co-ordinate European matters within any future Assembly.

## OFMDFM: European Policy and Co-ordination Unit (EPCU)

The European Policy and Co-ordination Unit comes under OFMDFM's Strategy and European Affairs Division. The Unit has the lead responsibility among Northern Ireland departments in seeking to make a positive contribution to, and get the most benefit for Northern Ireland from involvement with the European Union. In doing so, it works closely with the Office of the Northern Ireland Executive in Brussels (see below). The Unit seeks to do this through activities in three broad areas:

- Development of a clear strategy on the Northern Ireland Executive's EU Policy priorities;
- Creation of effective mechanisms to ensure Northern Ireland interests are properly championed both in London and Brussels;
- Ensuring that policy-makers in Northern Ireland are up-to-date with all relevant EU policy developments and that Northern Ireland departments comply with EC directives.

### European Policy Issues

Contact: Alison Coey
Tel: 028 9052 3105
Fax: 028 9052 2552
Email: alison.coey@ofmdfmni.gov.uk

Contact: Paul Geddis
Tel: 028 9052 8445
Fax: 028 9052 2552
Email: paul.geddis@ofmdfmni.gov.uk

Following a consultation period during 2004, work is currently underway on a new Northern Ireland European Strategy. Further details may be obtained from:

European Strategy Consultation Team
European Policy & Co-ordination Unit
Block E, Castle Buildings, Stormont, Belfast, BT4 3SR
Tel: 028 9052 3125
Email: info.europe@ofmdfmni.gov.uk

### Office of the Northern Ireland Executive in Brussels

Rue Wiertz, 50 Wiertzstraat, B-1050 Brussels
Contact: Tony Canavan
Tel: + 322 290 1330
Fax: + 322 2990 1332
Email: tony.canavan@ofmdfmni.gov.uk

The Brussels office, which opened in 2001, provides the focal point for developing and progressing the Northern Ireland Executive's policy approach to Europe. Its main functions are:

- Monitoring the development of EU policies relevant to NI and providing up-to-date information to Ministers and departments;
- Ensuring that Northern Ireland interests are taken fully into account in the work of the EU institutions and the development of UK policy on EU matters;
- Raising the positive profile of Northern Ireland among European policy-makers and opinion-formers;
- Pursuing co-operation of practical benefit to Northern Ireland with other European regions;
- Facilitating improved contacts with the EU by the NI non-governmental and local government sectors.

## European Funding and Northern Ireland

European funding falls broadly into the following categories:

- Structural Funds Packages, which are drawn up between the European Commission and regional authorities, to identify the needs and priorities of the particular region. Packages are managed at regional level and projects are based in the region in question.
- Community initiatives which are special forms of assistance, which aim to address problems identified by the European Commission as being common throughout the EU. They are financed by the Structural Funds and managed at regional level.
- EU funding programmes which are thematic and correspond with EU policy areas. They are managed by the Directorates-General and all projects must be transactional in nature.
- Ad hoc calls for proposals issued by various Directorates-Generals of the European Commission.
- Aid to applicant countries and to other non-member states of the EU in order to support economic restructuring and democratic reforms.

### EU Structural Funds

Four main inter related funds known as the Structural Funds are used to finance EU activities for social and economic development throughout the regions. These are:

**The European Regional Development Fund (ERDF)**
Provides financial support to regional development programmes in order to reduce socio-economic imbalances.

**The European Social Fund (ESF)**
The main instrument of community social policy and provides financial assistance for vocational training, retraining and job creation schemes.

**The European Agricultural Guidance and Guarantee Fund (EAGGF)**
Financial instrument for agriculture and rural development policy and finances development in rural areas throughout the European Union.

**The Financial Instrument for Fisheries Guide (FIFG)**
Enhances the competitiveness of the fisheries sector and strives to maintain the balance between fishing capacity and resources.

Within the 2000–2006 period the total budget for the Structural Funds Europe wide amounts to 195 billion euro, including 10.44 billion euro for the Community Initiatives representing over one third of the European Union's total budget.

### Reform of the Structural Funds

Agenda 2000 was the action programme concluded in 1999 at the Berlin European Council to strengthen Community policies and to give the European Union a new financial framework in consideration of the potential full membership of the EU of 12 countries from Central and Eastern Europe by 2010.

The European Commission has accordingly refined its priority objectives for the classification of the regions. The Structural Funds are then used in different combinations in order to address the three priority objectives.

**Objective One**
Aims to promote development and structural adjustment of regions whose development are lagging behind. Regions with a GDP per capita of less than 75% of the Community average are eligible for Objective 1 funding.

**Objective Two**
Aims to support the economic and social conversion of areas experiencing structural problems. For the 2000–2006 period, areas with structural difficulties have been divided into four distinctive categories: industrial, rural, urban and fisheries dependent zones.

**Objective Three**
Aims to support the adaptation and modernisation of education, training and employment policies and systems. It replaces the former Objectives 3 and 4 and reflects the new Title on Employment in the Treaty of Amsterdam.

**Transitional Support**
Under the terms of the Agenda 2000 reforms those regions which were eligible for Objective 1 funding during the 1994–1999 period but who have lost this entitlement for 2000–2006 will be given transitional assistance. This system of phasing out support is designed to avoid a sudden cessation of European funding and to consolidate the achievements of structural assistance in the previous period.

Northern Ireland has been classified as an Objective 1 in Transition region for the funding period 2000–2006 as the level of GDP per capita had attained 82 per cent of the EU average; seven per cent above the threshold for Objective 1 status.

## The Cohesion Fund

A Cohesion Fund was set up in 1993 to run alongside the Structural Funds. The role of the fund is to finance transport and environment infrastructure in those member states where GDP is less than 90 per cent of the EU average (Greece, Ireland, Spain, Portugal). Eighteen billion euro has been allocated to the Cohesion fund for 2000–2006.

## The EU Structural Funds

### The Community Support Framework in Northern Ireland (CSF)

The details of the Structural Funds assistance to Northern Ireland are laid down in the Northern Ireland Community Support Framework (CSF) 2000–2006. The CSF for the region was agreed following the submission of the Northern Ireland Structural Funds Plan and the subsequent negotiations between the European Commission and the Northern Ireland authorities.
A total of 1.3 billion euro has been allocated to the Northern Ireland Community Support Framework for the period 2000–2006 (The breakdown is 57% ERDF, 33% ESF, 8% EAGGF and 2% FIFG).

The Northern Ireland Community Support Framework 2000–2006 aims to achieve a transition to a more peaceful, stable, prosperous, fair and outward looking society, sustained by a better physical environment. This aim is carried over into five priorities and nine Horizontal Principles, while the CSF itself is divided into two operational programmes.

- Northern Ireland Programme for Building Sustainable Prosperity 2000–2006; 890 million euro (£590 m);
- EU Programme for Peace and Reconciliation in Northern Ireland and the Border Region of Ireland 2000–2004; 425 million euro (£280 m).

## Northern Ireland Programme for Building Sustainable Prosperity 2000–2006

This Transitional Objective 1 operational programme is the largest component of the Community Support Framework, accounting for 68 per cent of the Structural Funds allocated. This programme will therefore be the main instrument for the realisation of the economic and social development identified in the Community Support Framework. The designated priorities under the programme are set out in the table below, along with the relevant points of contact in government.

## Programme for Building Sustainable Prosperity

**Priority 1 Economic Growth and Competitiveness**

1.1a Business Support - Enterprise
1.1b Business Support - Competitiveness
Arora Upritchard, Invest NI Tel: 028 9054 5218
arora.upritchard@investni.com
1.1c Business Support - Small Business Network
Maeve Hamilton, Invest NI
maeve.hamilton@detini.gov.uk
1.2 Research and Technology Development
Boyd McDowell, Invest NI
boyd.mcdowell@investni.com
1.3a Tourism - Strategic Marketing
1.3b Tourism - Enhancing the Business of Tourism
Sandra Adair, NITB
Tel: 028 9023 1221 s.adair@nitb.com
1.4 Local Economic Development
Ian Kidd, DETI Tel: 028 9052 9237
ian.kidd@detini.gov.uk
1.5 Information Society
Lorna Martin, DETI lorna.martin@detini.gov.uk
1.6a Roads and Transport - Roads
Leslie White, DRD leslie.white@drdni.gov.uk
1.6b Roads and Transport - Transport
Michael Pollock, DRD michael.pollock@drdni.gov.uk
1.7 Telecommunications, Trevor Forsythe, IRTU
Tel: 028 9262 3138
trevor.forsythe@irtu.detni.gov.uk
1.8a Energy Infrastructure
1.8b Energy Efficiency, David Stanley, DETI
david.stanley@detini.gov.uk

**Priority 2 Employment**

2.1 Education and Skills Development
2.2 Tackling the Flows into Long Term Unemployment
2.3 Promoting a Labour Market Open to All
European Unit, DEL
2.4 Improving Opportunities for Lifelong Learning
2.5 Education and Training ICT and Infrastructure Support
David Bradley, Department of Education
david.bradley@deni.gov.uk
2.6 Developing Entrepreneurship
2.7 Human Resource Development in Companies
2.8 The Advancement of Women
European Unit, DEL bsp@delni.gov.uk

**Priority 3 Urban and Social Revitalisation**

3.1 Urban Revitalisation
Don Harley, European Unit, DSD
Tel: 028 9056 9307 eugrants@dsdni.gov.uk
3.2 Advice and Information Services
3.3 Community Sustainability
James Hare Voluntary & Community Unit, DSD
Tel: 028 9056 9784
3.4 Investing in Early Learning
David Bradley, Department of Education
Tel: 028 9127 9292 david.bradley@deni.gov.uk

**Priority 4 Agriculture, Rural Development, Forestry and Fisheries**

4.1 Training
Ian Titterington, DARD Agri-Food Development Service
bsp.afds@dardni.gov.uk
4.2a Improving Processing and Marketing of Agricultural Products
Gillian Heal, DARD Food Policy Division
gillian.heal@dardni.gov.uk
4.2b Food Processing Development
Ian Titterington, DARD Agri-Food Service
bsp.afds@dardni.gov.uk
4.3 Forestry
Stuart Morwood, DARD Forest Service
grants.forestservice@dardni.gov.uk
4.4 Setting up of Farm Relief and Farm Management Services
Carol Allen, DARD Rural Development Division
cu.rdd@dardni.gov.uk
4.5 Marketing of Quality Agricultural Products
Cathy Moore, DARD Food Policy Division
cathy.moore@dardni.gov.uk
4.6 Basic Services for the Rural Economy
Rural Development Council bsp@rdc.org.uk
4.7 Renovation and Development of Villages and Protection and Conservation of the Rural Heritage
4.8 Diversification of Agricultural Activities and Activities Close to Agriculture to Provide Multiple Activities or Alternative Incomes
4.9 Development and Improvement of Infrastructure Connected with the Development of Agriculture
4.10 Encouragement for Tourist and Craft Activities
Carol Allen, DARD Rural Development Division
cu.rdd@dardni.gov.uk
4.11 Protection of the Environment in Connection with Agriculture, Forestry and Landscape Conservation and the Improvement of Animal Welfare
Rural Development Council bsp@rdc.org.uk
4.12 Financial Engineering
Carol Allen, DARD Rural Development Division
cu.rdd@dardni.gov.uk
4.13 Fisheries, David Crawford,
DARD Fisheries Division Tel: 028 9052 0042
david.crawford@dardni.gov.uk

**Priority 5 The Environment**

5.1 Sustainable Management of the Environment and Promotion of the Natural and Built Heritage
Brian Finlay, DRD Water Service
brian.finlay@waterni.gov.uk
Raymond Anderson, DOE Environment & Heritage Service bsp5.1@doeni.gov.uk

**Priority 6 Technical Assistance**

6.1a Management and Implementation of Programme
6.1b Programme Information and Publicity
Ashley Williams, DFP European Division
ashley.williams@dfpni.gov.uk

## EU Programme for Peace and Reconciliation in Northern Ireland and the Border Region of Ireland 2000–2004 (PEACE II)

Peace II accounts for 38 per cent of the Structural Funds allocated and complements the Programme for Building Sustainable Prosperity. It also aims to build upon the creative cross-community approaches to funding adopted under the Special Support Programme for Peace and Reconciliation 1994 –1999 (Peace I). 425m euro has been made available to Northern Ireland and the border regions under Peace II during the period 2000-04

### Special EU Programmes Body

EU House
6 Cromac Place
Belfast BT7 2JB
Tel: 028 9026 6660
Email: info@seupb.org
Chief Executive: Pat Colgan

The full text of the PEACE II Operational Programme can be found at: www.europe-dfpni.gov.uk

Application details can be found at: www.eugrants.org/
Information on Peace I can be found at: www.eu-peace.org/
It should be noted that not all measures are currently open for funding applications. Applicants are advised to check with the relevant implementing body to determine which are open

The Special EU Programmes Body is the key player in managing the overall allocation process relating to Peace II and is the best source of information on the initiative.

The Peace II Programme is designed to address the legacy of 'The Troubles' and aims to reinforce progress towards a peaceful and stable society and to promote reconciliation. It also aims to take the opportunities arising from the peace process and contribute to reconciliation by promoting appropriate cross community contacts. Two specific objectives can be identified in relation to the overall aim of the Programme:

- Objective 1 Addressing the legacy of conflict
- Objective 2 Taking opportunities arising from Peace

The Priorities for the PEACE II Programme along with funding allocations are set out in the tables to the right.
The five priorities have been sub divided into an extensive list of measures aimed at achieving the key objectives of the programme. Details of the measures, the bodies appointed to implement them, and contact information are set out in the tables on the next two pages.

The intermediary funding bodies associated with the various measures and relevant abbreviations are set out according to the key (shown right).

| | |
|---|---|
| Priority 1 | **Economic Renewal**<br>This has an allocation of 153.67 million euro in Northern Ireland |
| Priority 2 | **Social Integration, Inclusion and Reconciliation**<br>This has an allocation of 107.04 million euro in Northern Ireland |
| Priority 3 | **Locally Based Regeneration and Development Strategies**<br>This has an allocation of 86.05 million euro in Northern Ireland |
| Priority 4 | **Outward and Forward Looking Region**<br>This has an allocation of 86.05 million euro in Northern Ireland. |
| Priority 5 | **Cross Border Co-operation**<br>This has an allocation of 39.72 million euro in Northern Ireland. |

**Table Explaining Abbreviations**

| | |
|---|---|
| DETI | Department of Enterprise, Trade and Investment |
| DRD | Department for Regional Development |
| EGSA | Educational Guidance Service for Adults |
| ADM/CPA | Area Development Management/Combat Poverty Agency |
| TWN | Training for Women Network |
| DARD | Department of Agriculture and Rural Development |
| RDC | Rural Development Council |
| CRC | Community Relations Council |
| SELB | Southern Education and Library Board |
| NIPPA | Northern Ireland Pre Schools Playgroup Association |
| DSD | Department for Social Development |
| OFMDFM | Office of the First Minister and Deputy First Minister |
| LSP | Local Strategy Partnership |
| SEUPB | Special EU Programmes Body |
| DCAL | Department of Culture, Arts and Leisure |
| DEL | Department for Employment and Learning |
| CFNI | Community Foundation for Northern Ireland |
| RCN | Rural Community Network |
| DCMNR | Department for Communications, Marine and Natural Resources (ROI) |
| NITB | Northern Ireland Tourist Board |

### Peace II Measures and Contacts

| Measure | | Implementing Body | Contact | Telephone |
|---|---|---|---|---|
| **1.** | **Economic Renewal** | | | |
| 1.1 | Business Competitiveness and Development | | | |
| 1.1a | Economic Revitalisation | Invest NI | Elaine Brown | 028 9023 9090 |
| 1.1b | Trade Development | Invest NI | Arora Upritchard | 028 9054 5218 |
| 1.1c | Financial Engineering | DETI | Maeve Hamilton | 028 9025 7330 |
| 1.1d | Business Competitiveness | DRD | Michael Pollock | 028 9025 7330 |
| 1.1e | Business Competitiveness in the Border Region | ADM/CPA | Ailish Quinn | 00353 477 1340 |
| 1.2 | Sustainable Tourism Development | | | |
| 1.2a | Water Based Tourism | DCAL | Barry Davidson | 028 9025 8870 |
| | | DCAL | Kathleen Conlon | |
| 1.2b | Natural Resource Rural Tourism Initiative | S. Armagh Tourism Initiative | Michelle Boyle | 028 3086 8900 |
| | | Mourne Heritage Trust | Camilla Fitzpatrick | 028 4372 4059 |
| | | Causeway Heritage Trust | Peter Harper | 028 2075 2100 |
| | | Fermanagh LSP | Helen Maguire | 028 6632 5050 |
| | | Sperrins Tourism Ltd | Kathleen McBride | 028 8674 7700 |
| 1.3 | New Skills and New Opportunities | ADM/CPA | Ailish Quinn | 00353 477 1340 |
| | | DEL | John Neill | 028 9025 7777 |
| | | PROTEUS | Pat Donnelly | 028 9037 1023 |
| | | EGSA | Kevin Donaghy | 028 9024 4274 |
| 1.4 | Promoting Entrepreneurship | Invest NI | Kerry Thompson | |
| | | ADM/CPA | Ailish Quinn | 00353 477 1340 |
| 1.5 | Positive Action for Women | ADM/CPA | Ailish Quinn | 00353 477 1340 |
| | | TWN | Karen Sweeney | 028 9077 7199 |
| | | Playboard | Caroline Mills | 028 9080 3380 |
| | | DEL European Unit | Seamus Camplisson | 028 9025 7777 |
| 1.6 | Training for Farmers (NI) | DARD | | 028 9054 7111 |
| 1.7 | Diversification of Agricultural Activities (NI) | | | |
| 1.7a | Obtaining Alternative Employment | DARD | | 028 9054 7111 |
| 1.7b | Part-time Employment | RDC | | 028 8676 6980 |
| 1.8 | Technology Support for the Knowledge Based Economy (NI) | | | |
| 1.8a | Innovation Technology and Networking | Invest NI | Nigel Carr | 028 9262 3029 |
| 1.8b | Information Age | DETI Information Age Unit | | 028 9052 9900 |
| 1.9 | Investment in Agricultural Holdings (NI) | DARD | | 028 9054 7111 |
| 1.10 | Basic Services for the Rural Economy and Population | | | |
| 1.10a | Retail Services | RDC | | 028 8676 6980 |
| 1.10b | ICT | RDC | | 028 8676 6980 |
| **2** | **Social Integration, Inclusion and Reconciliation** | | | |
| 2.1 | Reconcilitation for Sustainable Peace | ADM/CPA | Ailish Quinn | 00353 477 1340 |
| | | CRC | Jim Dennison | 028 9022 7500 |
| | | OFMDFM | Pauline Morgan | 028 9052 8400 |
| | | Dept of Education | Linda Scott | 028 9127 9302 |
| 2.2 | Developing Children | ADM/CPA | Ailish Quinn | 00353 477 1340 |
| | | YESIP | Kieran Shields | 028 3741 5381 |
| 2.3 | Skilling and Building | CFNI | Felicity McCartney | 028 9024 5927 |
| 2.4 | Reconciliation of Victims | | | |
| 2.4a | Pathways to Inclusion | CFNI | Felicity McCartney | 028 9024 5927 |
| 2.4b | Integration and Reconciliation | CFNI | Felicity McCartney | 028 9024 5927 |
| 2.4c | Inclusion of Target Groups in Border Region | ADM/CPA | Ailish Quinn | 00353 477 1340 |
| 2.5 | Investing in Childcare | NIPPA | Siobhan Fitzpatrick | 028 9066 5220 |
| 2.6 | Promoting Active Citizenship | ADM/CPA | Ailish Quinn | 00353 477 1340 |
| 2.7 | Developing Weak Community Infrastructure | ADM/CPA | Ailish Quinn | 00353 477 1340 |
| | | CFNI | Felicity McCartney | 028 9024 5927 |

Continued on next page

| Measure | | Implementing Body | Contact | Telephone |
|---|---|---|---|---|
| 2.8 | Accompanying Infrastructure and Equipment Support | SELB | Gregory Butler | 028 3751 2200 |
| | | ADM/CPA | Ailish Quinn | 00353 477 1340 |
| | | CFNI | Felicity McCartney | 028 9024 5927 |
| | | NIPPA | Siobhan Fitzpatrick | 028 9066 5220 |
| 2.9 | Renovation and Development of Villages and Protection and Conservation of Rural Heritage (NI) | | | |
| 2.9a | Conservation of the Rural Heritage | RCN | Michael Hughes | 028 8676 6670 |
| 2.9b | Renovation | RDC | | 028 8676 6980 |
| 2.10 | Encouragement for Tourism & Craft Activities | RDC | | 028 8676 6980 |
| 2.11 | Area Based Regeneration | DSD | Don Harley | 028 9056 9307 |
| | | Contact Local LSP | | |
| **3** | **Locally Based Regeneration and Development Strategies** | | | |
| 3.1 | Local Economic Initiatives for Developing the Social Economy | Contact Local LSP | | |
| 3.2 | Locally Based Human Resource Training and Development Strategies | Contact Local LSP | | |
| 3.3 | Building Better Communities Border Region | Contact Local Task Force | | |
| 3.4 | Improving Our Rural Communities | Contact Local Task Force | | |
| **4** | **Outward and Forward Looking Region** | | | |
| 4.1 | Networking | OFMDFM | Kenny Knox | 028 9052 2563 |
| 4.2a | Marketing the Region as a Tourism Destination | NITB | Sandra Adair | 028 9023 1221 |
| | | Cavan Co Council Task Force | Vincent Reynolds | 00353 49 433 2427 |
| | | Donegal Co Council Task Force | Gary Martin | 00353 74 72433 |
| | | Leitrim Co Council Task Force | Sean Kielty | 00353 78 50498 |
| | | Louth Co Council Task Force | Mary Mulholland | 00353 42 935 3150 |
| | | Monaghan Co Council Task Force | Adge King | 00353 47 38140 |
| | | Sligo Co Council Task Force | Padraig Flanaghan | 00353 71 56697 |
| 4.2b | Enhancing the Region as a Tourism Destination | NITB | Sandra Adair | 028 9023 1221 |
| | | Cavan Co Council Task Force | Vincent Reynolds | 00353 49 433 2427 |
| | | Donegal Co Council Task Force | Francis Coyle | 00353 74 72433 |
| | | Leitrim Co Council Task Force | Sean Kielty | 00353 78 50498 |
| | | Louth Co Council Task Force | Therese McArdle | 00353 42 935 3116 |
| | | Monaghan Co Council Task Force | Adge King | 00353 47 38140 |
| | | Sligo Co Council Task Force | Padraig Flanaghan | 00353 71 56697 |
| **5** | **Cross Border Co-operation** | | | |
| 5.1 | Increasing Cross Border Development Opportunities | Co-operation Ireland | Des Fegan | 028 9032 1462 |
| 5.2 | Improving Cross Border Public Sector Co-operation | SEUPB | Brenda Hegarty | 028 8225 5750 |
| 5.3 | Developing Cross Border Reconciliation and Understanding | ADM/CPA | Ailish Quinn | 00353 477 1340 |
| 5.4 | Promotion of Joint Approaches to Social, Education, Training and Human Resource Devt | ADM/CPA | Ailish Quinn | 00353 477 1340 |
| 5.5 | Education, Cross Border School and Youth Co-operation | Dept of Education (NI) | Linda Scott | 028 9127 9302 |
| | | Dept of Education (RoI) | Mary O'Driscoll | |
| 5.6 | Agriculture and Rural Development Co-operation | | | |
| 5.6a | Cross Border Community Development | North South Rural Voice | Gwen Lanigan | 00 353 42 969 0806 |
| 5.6b | Cross Border Diversification | DARD | | |
| 5.7 | Cross Border Fishing and Aquaculture | DARD | David Crawford | 028 9052 0042 |
| | | DCMNR | Sean Murray | |
| **6** | **Technical Assistance** | | | |
| 6.1 | Programme Information and Publicity | SEUPB | | 028 9026 6660 |
| 6.2a | Management, Monitoring and Evaluation | DSD | Don Harley | 028 9056 9307 |
| 6.2b | Internal Co-ordination | SEUPB | Marion Barriskell | 028 8225 5750 |

## Other European Union Initiatives

### The Community Initiatives

Community Initiatives are special forms of assistance proposed by the Commission to Member states. Implemented throughout the European Union they are financed by Structural Funds aimed at solving specific problems and are additional in financial terms to a region's Community Support Framework. The Community Initiatives have three defining features:

- Encouraging transactional, cross border and interregional co-operation;
- Increased involvement of people on the ground 'bottom up approach';
- Support through a real partnership of those involved in Community initiatives.

**Reform of Community Initiatives**

The number of Community Initiatives has been reduced with the reform of the Structural Funds under Agenda 2000. There are now 4 Community Initiatives for the period 2000–06 each financed by a Structural Fund; 118 million euro has been allocated to Northern Ireland for this purpose. These are:

- Interreg III
- Leader +
- EQUAL
- Urban II

Details of these initiatives are set out below.

### INTERREG III

The main objective is to strengthen economic and social cohesion in the Community through the promotion of cross border, transnational and international co-operation and balanced development of the community territory. This is to be achieved through the promotion of integrated regional development within neighbouring regions.

INTERREG III has 3 strands:

- Strand A: cross-border co-operation
- Strand B: transnational co-operation
- Strand C: interregional co-operation

81 million euro has been allocated to Northern Ireland for INTERREG.

For general information on the Interreg IIIA Initiative, contact:

**The Interreg IIIA Secretariat**
Special EU Programmes Body
European Union House
Castle Meadow Court
Dublin Road
Monaghan
Tel: 0808 127 5005 (Freephone from Northern Ireland)
1800 80 5005 (Freephone from Republic of Ireland)
Fax: + 353 477 1258
Email: interreg@seupb.ie

The Implementing Bodies for Interreg IIIA are:

**Northwest Region Cross Border**
Interreg IIIA Partnership
16A The Diamond
Derry, BT48 6HW
Tel: 028 7137 0808
Email: interreg@derrycity.gov.uk
Contact: Eamon Molloy

**Irish Central Border Area**
Interreg IIIA Partnership
The INTEC Centre
36 East Bridge Street
Enniskillen
BT74 7BT
Tel: 028 6632 2556
Email: info@icban.com
Contact: Kate Burns

**East Border Region**
Interreg IIIA Partnership
Town Hall
Bank Parade
Newry, BT35 6HR
Tel: 028 3025 2684
Email: interreg@eastborderregion.com
Contact: Pamela Arthurs

### Business: European Information Centres

Aimed at providing the business community (with emphasis on the SME sector) with information on European developments. The centre has access to EU databases including Tenders Electronic Daily (TED) carrying daily listings for requests for tenders for EU public contracts.

**Euro Info Centre**
Invest NI, Upper Galwally, Belfast BT8 6TB
Tel: 028 9023 9090
Fax: 028 9049 0490

### Northern Ireland Innovation Relay Centre (IRC)

The IRC funded by the EU aims to promote the transfer of innovative technology to and from Northern Ireland.

**Innovation Relay Centre**
Invest NI, 17 Antrim Road, Lisburn BT28 3AL
Tel: 028 9023 9090
Fax: 028 9049 0490

## Leader +

Leader + encourages the design and implementation of innovative development strategies for rural areas. Leader + achieves this by establishing partnerships at a local level. Leader + comprises three strands:

- Strand 1: support for integrated and innovative development strategies for rural areas
- Strand 2: support for interregional and transnational co-operation
- Strand 3: networking for all EU rural areas

15 million euro has been allocated to Northern Ireland.

Contact:
Rural Development Division, DARD, Dundonald House, Belfast BT4 3SB
Tel: 028 9052 5435/ Fax: 028 9052 4776
Email: leader+.rdd@dardni.gov.uk / Web: www.dardni.gov.uk

The Northern Ireland LEADER+ Programme is being implemented by 12 LEADER+ Groups, each covering a specific geographic area:

**Coleraine Local Action Group for Enterprise Ltd**
Area covered: Coleraine Borough Council area excluding towns of Coleraine, Portrush and Portstewart
Tel: 028 2955 8066
Email: info@collage.ltd.com

**Craigavon & Armagh Rural Development (CARD)**
Area covered: Armagh City and District Council Area and Craigavon Borough Council area, excluding the urban localities of Armagh City, Lurgan, Brownlow and Portadown.
Tel: 028 3831 2588
Email: maria.mcguinness@craigavon.gov.uk

**East Tyrone Rural**
Area covered: Cookstown District Council Area and Dungannon & South Tyrone Borough Council excluding the urban areas of Cookstown and Dungannon
Tel: 028 8676 4714
Email: drew.robinson@cookstown.gov.uk

**Fermanagh Local Action Group**
Area covered: Co Fermanagh excluding Enniskillen town
Tel: 028 6862 1600
Email: info@fermanaghleader.co.uk

**Newry & Mourne Local Action Group**
Area covered: Newry & Mourne District Council area excluding the City of Newry and town of Warrenpoint
Tel: 028 3026 3177
Email: michaelmccoy@btconnect.com

**Magherafelt Area Partnership Ltd**
Area covered: Magherafelt District Council area excluding the town of Magherafelt
Tel: 028 7939 7979 / Email: info@magherafelt.eu.com

**North Antrim Leader**
Area covered: Moyle District Council area and the Borough Council areas of Ballymena, Ballymoney and Larne, excluding the towns of Ballycastle, Ballymena, Ballymoney and Larne
Tel: 028 2177 2138
Email: north-antrim-leader@antrim.net

**REAP South Antrim (Rural Economic Action Partnership)**
Area covered: District Council areas of Antrim, Carrickfergus and Newtownabbey excluding the towns of Carrickfergus and Antrim and the urban areas of Newtownabbey
Tel: 028 9446 3113 ext 343
Web: www.reapsouthantrim.com
Email: admin@reapsouthantrim.com

**Roe Valley Rural Development Ltd**
Area covered: rural wards of Limavady Borough Council area
Tel: 028 7776 0306
Email: karen.quigley@limavady.gov.uk

**Rural Area Partnership in Derry**
Area covered: Derry City Council area excluding the urban area of Derry City
Tel: 028 7133 7149
Email: leaderplus@globalnet.co.uk

**The Rural Down Partnership**
Area covered: Rural areas of Ards, Banbridge and Down Council areas, excluding the towns of Newtownards, Comber, Downpatrick, Ballynahinch and Banbridge
Tel: 028 4066 0609
Email: therese.rafferty@banbridgedc.gov.uk

**West Tyrone Rural Ltd**
Area covered: Strabane District Council area and Omagh District Council area excluding the urban areas of Strabane and Omagh towns
Tel: 028 8225 2647
Email: info@westtyronerural.com

## EQUAL

Equal aims to promote new means to tackle all forms of exclusion, discrimination and inequality in relation to the labour market and leads on from two earlier initiatives: ADAPT and EMPLOYMENT.

The Northern Ireland EQUAL Programme will target two priorities:

- Employability
- Equal opportunities for men and women

12 million euro has been allocated to Northern Ireland for this project.
Contact: Pat Donnelly,
PROTEUS, 8 Edgewater Road, Belfast, BT3 9JQ
Tel: 028 9037 1023 / Fax: 028 9077 3543
Email: equal@proteus-ni.org
Web: www.proteus-ni.org

## Urban II

The initiative aims to promote the design and implementation of innovative development models for the economic and social regeneration of urban areas in crisis and aims to strengthen exchanges of information and experience on sustainable urban development in the EU.
Approximately 50 towns with a population of 10,000+ may be eligible for the Urban initiative. The urban areas included may be inside or outside Objective 1 and 2 areas and must fulfil at least three of the following conditions:

- High long term unemployment;
- Low rate of economic activity;
- High level of poverty and exclusion;
- The need for structuring adjustment due to economic and social difficulties;
- High proportion of immigrants, ethnic minorities or refugees;
- Low level of education, major gaps in terms of qualifications and a high rate of pupil failure;
- Unstable demographic environment;
- Particularly poor environmental conditions.

10 million euro has been allocated to Northern Ireland.

Each Urban programme must include measures for strengthening information exchanges and sharing experience on the regeneration of urban areas in crisis.

Contact:
Department for Social Development
Tel: 028 9056 9263

## Other Centrally Managed Programmes
## SME Development Initiatives

Entrepreneurs or Businesses seeking European business and commercial information and assistance with Community funding should contact:

Euro Info Centre Invest NI
Upper Galwally, Belfast, BT8 6TB
Tel: 028 9023 9090 / Fax: 028 9049 0490

**Joint European Venture Programme**
The programme aims to stimulate the establishment of joint ventures between European SMEs. JEV has an indicative budget of 85 million euro.

Contact:
Greater London Enterprise Ltd
28 Park Street
London SE1 9EQ
Tel: 0207 403 0300 / Fax: 0207 403 1742

**Business Angels Networks**
Under the Business Angels programme the Commission finances up to 50% of the costs of feasibility studies for the creation of business networks, as well as a maximum of 50% of the costs of pilot actions aimed at establishing a regional or national network.

**European Business Angels Network**
Avenue des Arts 12, Bte 7
B–1210 Brussels
Belgium
Tel: 00 32 22 18 43 13 / Fax: 00 32 22 18 45 83
Email: info@eban.org
Web: www.eban.org

**Mutual Guarantee Scheme**
Mutual Guarantee Schemes involve private groupings of companies, often linked to sector specific interest groups, to provide loan insurance to banks.

Enterprise Directorate General, Access to Finance,
Rue de la Loi 200 (SC-27 04/04), B–1049 Brussels
Tel: 00 322 295 91 86 / Fax: 00 322 295 21 54

**I-TEC**
I-TEC is part of the Innovation Programme of the European Commission and aims to encourage early stage investments in technologically innovative SMEs.

Enterprise Directorate General
Innovation Programme
Rue Alcide de Gasperi
L–2920 Luxembourg
Tel: 00 352 4301 39194 / Fax: 00 352 4301 34544

**PROTEUS**
Proteus is the contact point for the EQUAL initiative and some measures under PEACE II, as well as its role administering training and employment programmes on behalf of the Department for Employment and Learning.

8 Edgewater Office Park, Edgewater Road, Belfast, BT3 9JQ
Tel: 028 9037 1023 / Fax: 028 9077 3543
Email: administrator@proteus-ni.org

**The European Employment Service (EURES)**
Eures links to a network of over 400 centres throughout Europe providing information on vacancies, recruitment and living and working conditions throughout Europe.

EURES Section, Gloucester House, Chichester Street
Belfast, BT1 4RA
Tel: 028 9025 2270 / Fax: 028 9025 2288
Email: siobhan.burns@delni.gov.uk
Web: www.europa.eu.int/eures

**Rural Carrefours**
Carrefours are part of a regional network providing information to all sectors of the agricultural and rural community. They provide regional information and will assist in the search for European partners and help place students seeking work placements in other EU member states.

Carrefour Ulster
Clogher Valley Rural Centre
47 Main Street, Clogher, BT76 0AA
Tel:028 8554 9438 / Fax:028 8554 8203
Email: carrefours_Ulster@dnet.co.uk
Web: www.carrefour.org.uk/carrefour_ulster.htm

**The European Resource Centre for Schools and Colleges**
Norwich Union House, 7 Fountain Street
Belfast, BT1 5EG
Tel: 028 9024 8220 / Fax: 028 9023 7592
Email: jonathan.stewart@britishcouncil.org

**The British Council**
Education and Training Group
Norwich Union House
7 Fountain Street, Belfast BT1 5EG
Tel: 028 9024 8220 /Fax: 028 9023 7592

**European Bureau**
Youth Council for Northern Ireland
Forestview, Purdy's Lane, Belfast BT8 7AR
Tel: 028 9064 3882 /Fax: 028 9064 3874
Email: bsweeney@youthcouncil-ni.org.uk
Web: www.youthcouncil-ni.org.uk

## Local Strategy Partnerships

The Local Strategy Partnership Boards established to oversee the implementation of Priority 3 Locally Based Regeneration and Development Initiatives will have responsibility for measures relating to the social economy and human resource and development initiatives under Peace II.

Priority 3 accounts for approximately 20 per cent of the EU's Structural Funds allocation to the EU Programme for Peace and Reconciliation in Northern Ireland. The EU allocations will be supplemented by national public and private funds to produce a total of 114.73 million euros.

It is envisaged that the role of LSPs will develop into a long-term strategy and that they will establish a remit extending beyond the distribution of EU Structural funds. In furtherance of these aims the central decision making role of the Northern Ireland Partnership Board has not been repeated for Peace II. Responsibility for decision making will rest at local level and the Special EU Programmes Body and the Monitoring Committee will focus upon:

- Ensuring compliance with the Structural Funds Regulations, the Peace II Programme document and the Programme Complement and
- Playing a supportive role for LSPs in association with the new Regional Partnership Board.

The overall strategic aim of Peace II is to 'reinforce progress toward a peaceful and stable society and to promote reconciliation'. Applications under the programme must contain at least one of two of the specific objectives i.e. they must address the legacy of conflict and/or take the opportunities arising from peace. Peace II Partnerships focus on specific needs in the partnership areas and involve a more structured contribution from the statutory sector which it is hoped will ensure greater sustainability and avoid the criticisms levelled of a lack of sustainability following Peace I.

Local Strategy Partnerships (LSPs) consist of two strands:

- Government (local government and statutory sector);
- The 'four pillars' of the: Voluntary sector; Business; Agriculture; Trade Unions.

The aim is to achieve a balance of local interests and the development of a structured involvement of the statutory sector in the Partnerships. Partnerships are required to be inclusive and provide equity of standing between the various strands and seek to be open and accountable to their local communities, demonstrate fairness in the allocation of funding in their control and produce structures and mechanisms to enable auditing of all aspects of their work.

Whilst there is no definitive membership quota set for membership of the LSPs it is recommended that a maximum of twenty-eight should not be exceeded. Nominations for members of the LSP occur at a local level and the procedure for processing nominations is determinable at individual local level. However, the process utilised must be documented and submitted to the SEUPB for approval as part of the Global Grant Allocation Agreement.

A listing of Local Strategy Partnerships including contact details is set out on the following page (A–Z).

## A-Z Listing of Local Strategy Partnerships

**Antrim LSP**
The Steeple, Antrim, BT41 1BJ
Tel: 028 9446 3113
Fax: 028 9446 4469
Partnership Manager: Claire Higgins

**Ards LSP**
Council Offices
Crepe Weavers Industrial Estate
20 Comber Road, BT23 4RX
Tel: 028 9182 6913
Fax: 028 9182 8040
Partnership Manager: Tom Rowley

**Armagh LSP**
The Palace Demesne
Armagh, BT60 4EL
Tel: 028 3752 9642
Fax: 028 3752 9631
Partnership Manager: Denise O'Hare

**Ballymena LSP**
Ardeevin, 80 Galgorm Road
Ballymena, BT42 1AB
Tel: 028 2566 0444
Fax: 028 2563 9785
Director of the LSP: Majella McAlister

**Ballymoney LSP**
Borough Offices
Riada House, 14 Charles Street
Ballymoney, BT53 6DZ
Tel: 028 2766 0200
Fax: 028 2766 5150
Partnership Manager: Margaret Drain

The Bridge Partnership
Civic Building, Downshire Road
Banbridge, BT32 3JY
Tel: 028 4066 0609
Fax: 028 4066 0601
Partnership Manager: Joanne Morgan

**Belfast LSP**
5th Floor, Premier Business Centre
20 Adelaide Street, BT2 8GB
Tel: 028 9032 8532
Fax: 028 9032 7306
Chief Executive: Dr Eddie Jackson

**Carrickfergus LSP**
Carrickfergus Museum and Civic Centre,
Antrim Street
Carrickfergus, BT38 7DG
Tel: 028 9335 8046
Fax: 028 9336 0868
Partnership Co-ordinator: Alan McCay

**Castlereagh LSP**
Civic and Administrative Offices
Bradford Court, Upper Galwally
Belfast, BT8 6RB
Tel: 028 9079 2501
Partnership Coordinator: Mike Wilson

**Coleraine LSP**
Cloonavin, 66 Portstewart Road
Coleraine, BT52 1RR
Tel: 028 7034 7050
Partnership Manager: Patricia McCallion

**Cookstown LSP**
Gortalowry House, 94 Church Street
Cookstown, BT80 8HX
Tel: 028 8676 4714
Partnership Manager: Maggie Bryson

**Craigavon LSP**
Civic Centre, Lakeview Road
Craigavon, BT64 1AL
Tel: 028 3831 2577
Partnership Manager: Jillian McAreavey

**Derry LSP**
Exchange House, Queen's Quay
Derry, BT48 7AS
Tel: 028 7130 8466
Partnership Manager: Oonagh McGillion

**Down LSP**
Magh-inis House, 8-10 Irish Street
Downpatrick, BT30 6BP
Tel: 028 4461 7667
Partnership Manager: David Patterson

**Dungannon and South Tyrone LSP**
Bank Buildings, Market Square
Dungannon, BT70 1AB
Tel: 028 8772 0315
Programme Manager: Ursula Quinn

**Fermanagh LSP**
Unit 31 Enniskillen Business Centre
Lackaghboy Industrial Estate
Tempo Road, Enniskillen BT74 4RL
Tel: 028 6632 9225
Partnership Manager: Helen Maguire

**Larne LSP**
C/O LEDCOM
LEDCOM Industrial Estate
Bank Road, Larne, BT40 3AW
Tel: 028 2827 0742
Project Officer: Patricia Brennan

**Limavady Area Partnership Ltd**
7 Connell Street,
Limavady, BT49 0HA
Tel: 028 7776 0306
Project Officer: Paul Beattie

**Lisburn Partnership**
Unit 2a, The Sidings Office Park
Antrim Road, Lisburn, BT28 3AJ
Tel: 028 9260 5406
Partnership Manager: Alice O'Kane

**Magherafelt Area Partnership**
Council Offices
50 Ballyronan Road
Magherafelt, BT45 6EN
Tel: 028 7939 7979
Strategy Manager: Chris McCarney

**Moyle LSP**
Sheskburn House
7 Mary Street, Ballycastle, BT54 6QH
Tel: 028 2076 2225
Project Officer: Caitriona McNeill

**Newry and Mourne LSP**
European House
16a Canal Quay, Newry, BT34 6BP
Tel: 028 3026 6933
Programme Manager: Deirdre Convery

**Newtownabbey LSP**
Mossley Mill
Newtownabbey, BT36 5QA
Tel: 028 9034 0194
Fax: 028 9034 0196
Partnership Coordinator: David Hunter

**North Down LSP**
Town Hall
The Castle, Bangor, BT20 4BT
Tel: 028 9127 8028
Project Officer: Jan Nixey

**Omagh LSP**
2nd Floor Tourist Information Centre
1 Market Street, Omagh, BT78 1EE
Tel: 028 8225 0202
Partnership Manager: Harry Parkinson

**Strabane LSP**
47 Derry Road
Strabane, BT82 8DY
Tel: 028 7138 1309
Fax: 028 7138 1346
Project Officer: Patrick O'Doherty

## Future of EU Funding under Peace II

There has been considerable speculation as to whether or not Northern Ireland will continue to receive such sizeable financial support from the European Union beyond the expiry date of existing programmes. Combined with the loss of Objective 1 status, there is a potential shortfall in the years ahead. The current Peace II programme has a monetary value of €707 million, representing a major injection into the Northern Ireland economy.

The Special EU Programmes Body (SEUPB), the managing authority for the EU Programme for Peace and Reconciliation (Peace II) has recently launched a public consultation on the possible extension of the EU funding programme and urged all concerned to take part and help make a case for further European funding.

SEUPB has been asked by the Department of Finance and Personnel to advise on the nature of any possible extension. This follows a decision from the European Council inviting the EU Commission to examine the possibility of extending the Peace II programme up to 2006.

As part of the overall review, SEUPB has opened up a short and focused consultation with all interested parties beginning with programme Implementing Bodies. The full context for the possible extension and details of how organisations and individuals can take part in the consultation are available from SEUPB at the addresses below:

**Belfast**
EU House, 6 Cromac Place
Belfast, BT7 2JB
Tel: 028 9026 6660
Fax: 028 9026 6661
Email: info@seupb.org

**Monaghan**
EU House, Castle Meadow Court
Monaghan
Tel: +353 477 7003
Fax: +353 477 1258
Email: interreg@seupb.ie

**Omagh**
EU House, 13 Kelvin Road
Omagh, BT78 1LB
Tel: 028 8225 5750
Fax: 028 8224 8427
Email: omagh@seupb.org

CHEQUES CASHED
ON THE SPOT
&
LOANS 4 U
TO LET
Retail Unit
c.75.45 sq.m. (813 sq.ft.)
Brown
McConnell
Clark
(028) 9032 0634
TO LET

# Chapter 13

## Lifestyle and Leisure in Northern Ireland

## Where to Eat and Drink in Northern Ireland

Northern Ireland has made great progress in recent years in terms of the overall quality and range of offerings to diners. There are an increasing number of genuinely international-class restaurants serving local and international cuisine of the highest standard. In addition, many of Northern Ireland's cafes and bars have upgraded their fare with many bars serving good quality local dishes at reasonable prices.

The advent of relative 'peace' in Northern Ireland has encouraged hoteliers and restaurateurs to invest in their industry and many good quality restaurants, bars and brasseries have opened up.

The same applies to pubs, clubs and nightlife generally. The Dublin Road/Great Victoria Street stretch of South Belfast is possibly Northern Ireland's liveliest district in terms of bars, clubs and nightlife and is unrecognisable from the quiet area that existed 15 or 20 years ago. Also there is an increasing revitalisation of town centres across Northern Ireland in terms of the growing numbers of bars and restaurants on offer.

## Restaurants

The following is a list of some well known Northern Ireland restaurants and eateries in A-Z format. The list is by no means exhaustive and there is no negative inference in relation to any premises that may have been omitted.

### Belfast

**Aldens Restaurant**
229 Upper Newtownards Road Belfast, BT4 3JH
Tel: 028 9065 0079
A modern restaurant, Aldens has given east Belfast a taste of the gourmet experience.

**ba soba Noodle Bar**
38 Hill Street,
Cathedral Quarter
Belfast, BT1 2LB
Tel: 028 9058 6868
ba soba is Belfast's first noodle bar specialising in noodle dishes and curries.

**Bar Seven Restaurant & Bar**
Odyssey Pavillion
Queen's Quay
Belfast, BT3 9QQ
Tel: 028 9046 7073

**Beatrice Kennedy**
44 University Road, BT7
Tel: 028 9020 2290
A gourmet restaurant.

**Bokhara Indian Restaurant**
143-149 High Street
Holywood
Tel: 028 9042 6767
Quality Indian restaurant.

**Bourbon**
60 Great Victoria Street
Belfast, BT2 7BB
Tel: 028 9033 2121
The taste and style of New Orleans in Belfast.

**Café Aero**
44 Bedford Street
Belfast, BT2 7FF.
Tel: 028 9024 4844
Café Aero is a contemporary fine dining restaurant.

**Cafe Paul Rankin**
27-29 Fountain Street
Belfast
Tel: 028 9031 5090
Café Paul Rankin offers casual dining.

**Cafe Milano**
92-94 Lisburn Road
Belfast, BT9 6AG.
Tel: 028 9068 9777
A bustling new Italian restaurant.

**Café Vincents**
78-80 Botanic Avenue
Belfast
Tel: 028 9024 2020
Eclectic cuisine with a French influence.

**Cayenne**
7 Lesley House
Shaftesbury Square
Belfast, BT2 7DB
Tel: 028 9033 1532
Cayenne belongs to Paul and Jeanne Rankin of television's 'Gourmet Ireland'.

**Chokdee**
44 Bedford Street
Belfast, BT2 7FF
Tel: 028 9024 8800
Pan Asian Cuisine in modern surroundings.

**Connor**
11A Stranmillis Road
Belfast
Tel: 028 9066 3266
Bright, modern airy restaurant offering a wide range of dining options from coffee to evening meals.

**Copperfields Bar & Restaurant**
9-21 Fountain Street
Belfast, BT1 5EA
Tel: 028 9024 7367
Centrally located in the heart of Belfast, this is a traditional bar and restaurant.

**Cutters River Grill**
Lockview Road, Stranmillis
Tel: 028 9066 3388
Situated on the banks of the river Lagan, in what was originally an Old Boat House.

**Deanes Restaurant & Brasserie**
36-40 Howard Street
Belfast, BT1 6PF
Tel: 028 9056 0000
One of Belfast's smartest eateries and home to award-winning chef Michael Deane. One of Northern Ireland's three Michelin Star award - winning restaurants.

**Giraffe**
54-56 Stranmillis Road,
Belfast
Tel: 028 9050 9820
Giraffe situated in the heart of the university area is a well-established eatery with a 'bring your own' policy offering casual dining and an extensive menu.

**Harry Ramsden's**
Yorkgate Complex,
150A York Street, Belfast
Tel: 028 9074 9222
Offering world famous fish and chips in a traditional environment with a fine selection of dishes to choose from.

**Indian Ocean**
Odyssey Pavillion
Queen's Quay
Belfast, BT3 9QQ
Tel: 028 9046 6888

**Indie**
159 Stranmillis Road
Belfast, BT9 5AJ
Tel: 028 9066 8100
Web: www.indiespice.com

**Ink Restaurant**
Four Winds, Newton Park
Belfast
Tel: 028 9070 7970
Contemporary European cooking with global influences.

**The John Hewitt Bar & Restaurant**
51 Donegall Street
Tel: 028 9023 3768
The John Hewitt is very much traditional in style with the emphasis on conversation, traditional music, art displays and 'craic'.

**La Salsa**
Odyssey Complex
2 Queen's Quay
Belfast, BT3 9QQ
Tel: 028 9046 0066

**L'etoile**
407 Ormeau Road
Belfast, BT7
Tel: 028 9020 1300
French Cuisine in intimate surroundings.

**Madison's**
59-63 Botanic Avenue
Belfast BT7 1JL
Tel: 028 9050 9800
70 seater 'Award Winning' restaurant.

**Malone House Restaurant**
Barnett Demesne
Malone Road
Belfast, BT9 5PB
Tel: 028 9068 1246
Period house located in verdant surroundings in Upper Malone, offering highly regarded Irish food.

**Malone Lodge Hotel**
60 Eglantine Avenue
Belfast, BT9 6DY
Tel: 028 9038 8000
Fax: 028 9038 8088
Located in the leafy Victorian suburbs of the University area of South Belfast contemporary dishes incorporate the best of fresh local produce, organic when available.

**McHugh's Bar & Restaurant**
29-31 Queen's Square
Belfast, BT1 3FG
Tel: 028 9050 9990
Famous for being the oldest building in Belfast McHugh's offers everything from Oriental cuisine, to traditional pub grub.

**The Morning Star**
17-19 Pottinger's Entry
Belfast, BT1 4DT
Tel: 028 9023 5986
Halfway down Pottinger's Entry, in the heart of Belfast, the Morning Star is one of the city's most historic pubs. Food is available in both the public bar and upstairs restaurant/lounge, with its discreet booths.

**Nick's Warehouse**
35-39 Hill Street
Belfast, BT1 2LB
Tel: 028 9043 9690
Fax: 028 9023 0514
Nick's Warehouse is located in the city near to St Anne's Cathedral.

**The Northern Whig**
2 Bridge Street
Belfast BT1 1LU
Tel: 028 9050 9888
Formerly home to the old Northern Whig printing press, this unique building has been restored with a contemporary eastern European influence.

**Olio Restaurant**
17 Brunswick Street
Belfast, BT2 7GE
Tel: 028 9024 0239
Fax: 028 9024 2290
Conveniently situated close to Belfast's Grand Opera House. Pasta and main course specialities blend with a selection of traditional favourites. Fresh baked fish is a speciality.

**The Oxford Exchange**
Grill Bar Restaurant, 1st Floor
St George's Market, Belfast
Tel: 028 9024 0014
Situated on the first floor of St George's Market in the developing Market Quarter of Belfast, Oxford Exchange offers quality dining in stylish surroundings.

**Rain City**
33-35 Malone Road, Belfast
Tel: 028 9068 2929
Café/Grill owned by Paul and Jeanne Rankin.

**The Red Panda Chinese Restaurant**
60 Great Victoria Street
Tel: 028 9080 8700
Odyssey Pavillion
Tel: 028 9046 6644
Located opposite the Europa Hotel and recently opened in the Odyssey Pavillion, this is the largest of the Chinese restaurants in the city.

**Restaurant Porcelain at TEN sq**
10 Donegall Square, Belfast
Tel: 028 9024 1001
A fusion of Japanese and European.

*Restaurant Porcelain at TEN sq*

**Roscoff**
7-11 Linenhall Street
Belfast, BT2 8AA
Tel: 028 9031 1150
International cuisine and seafood.

**Ryan's Bar & Grill**
116-118 Lisburn Road
Belfast
Tel: 028 9050 9851
Offers a varied menu adding a touch of European culture with carafes of draught wine.

**Shenanagan Rooms**
21 Howard Street
Belfast, BT1 6NB
Tel: 028 9023 0603
Downstairs the emphasis is on bar snacks. Upstairs a full Bistro menu operates.

**Shu**
253 Lisburn Road, Belfast
Tel: 028 9038 1655
AA Sea Food Restaurant of the year.

**Sonoma Restaurant**
Hilton Belfast
4 Lanyon Place
Belfast, BT1 3LP
Tel: 028 9027 7000
Fax: 028 9027 7277

The Sonoma restaurant offers a contemporary menu featuring the best of local produce with pre theatre available before performances at the Waterfront Hall and The Odyssey Arena.

**Speranza**
16-19 Shaftesbury Square
Belfast
Tel: 028 9023 0213

**The Square**
89 Dublin Road, Belfast
Tel: 028 9023 9933
Always busy. Menus change regularly. Booking required.

**Suwanna Thai Restaurant**
117 Great Victoria Street
Belfast
Tel: 028 9043 9007

**Ta Tu Bar & Grill**
701 Lisburn Road
Belfast, BT9 7GU
Tel: 028 9038 0818
Winner of the Glen Dimplex Award for Best Bar Interior in Ireland, the restaurant offers gourmet dining.

**Tedford's Restaurant**
5 Donegal Quay
Belfast, BT1 3EF
Tel: 028 9043 4000
Located in an historic Belfast building, formerly a ship's chandlers dating from 1851, this atmospheric restaurant overlooks the River Lagan.

**The Wok**
126 Great Victoria Street
Belfast
Tel: 028 9023 3828

**The Water Margin**
159-161 Donegall Pass
Belfast
Tel: 028 9032 6888

**Wrap Works Mexican Cantina**
199 Lisburn Road, Belfast
Tel: 028 9022 1141

*Bushmills Inn, Co. Antrim*

## Co Antrim

**Bureau Bar Bistro**
637 Shore Road
Whiteabbey, BT37 0ST
Tel: 028 9086 6111

**Bushmills Inn Hotel**
25 Main Street
Bushmills, BT57 8QG
Tel: 028 2073 2339
Fax: 028 2073 2048

**Clenaghans**
48 Soldierstown Road
Aghalee, BT28 0ES
Tel: 028 9265 2952
Fax: 028 9265 2251

**Galgorm Manor**
136 Fenaghy Road
Ballymena, BT42 1EA
Tel: 028 2588 1001
Fax: 028 2588 0080

**The Ginger Tree (Japanese)**
29 Ballyrobert Road
Glengormley
Tel: 028 9084 8176

**The Harbour Bar**
Harbour Road, Portrush
Tel: 028 7082 2430

**Londonderry Arms Hotel**
20-28 Harbour Road
Carnlough, BT44 0EU
Tel: 028 2888 5255
Fax: 028 2885 5263

**Lynden Heights**
97 Drumnagreagh Road
Ballygally, BT40 2RP
Tel: 028 2858 3560

**Marine Hotel**
1-3 North Street
Ballycastle, BT54 6BN
Tel: 028 2076 2222
Fax: 028 2076 9507

**Rosspark Hotel**
20 Doagh Road
Kells, Ballymena, BT42 3LZ
Tel: 028 2589 1663
Fax: 028 2589 1477
'Restaurant at Rosspark' offers locally caught fresh salmon and Northern Irish beef.

**The Smuggler's Inn**
306 Whitepark Road,
Bushmills
Tel: 028 2073 1577

**Snappers Restaurant**
21 Ballyreagh Road, Portrush
Tel: 028 7082 4945

**Tidy Doffer**
133 Ravernet Road
Lisburn, BT27 5NF
Tel: 028 9268 9188
Fax: 028 9262 8949

**Treffners**
Hilton Templepatrick
Castle Upton Estate
Templepatrick, BT39 0DD
Tel: 028 9044 5542
Fax: 028 9044 5511
Treffners restaurant offers an international menu, complemented by an extensive selection of wines and great views over the golf course.

## Co Armagh

**Ashburn Hotel**
81 William Street
Lurgan, BT66 6JB
Tel: 028 3832 5711

**De Averell House**
No 3 Seven Houses
47 Upper English Street
Armagh City, BT61 7LA
Tel: 028 3751 1213

**Moneypenny's Restaurant**
The Montagu Arms
9-19 Church Street
Tandragee
Tel: 028 3884 0219

**The Old Barn Restaurant**
7 Mowhan Road, Armagh
Tel: 028 3755 2742

**The Oriel**
2 Bridge Street Gilford
Tel: 028 3883 1543

**The Planters Tavern**
4 Banbridge Road
Waringstown, BT66 7QA
Tel: 028 3888 1510

**The Seagoe Hotel**
22 Upper Church Lane
Portadown, BT63 5JE
Tel: 028 3833 3076

**The Stonebridge Restaurant**
Stonebridge Roundabout
74 Legacorry Road
Richill, BT61 9LF
Tel: 028 3887 0024

**The Town House**
21 Church Street
Portadown, BT62 3LN
Tel: 028 3833 2555

## Co Down

**The Brass Monkey**
16 Trevor Hill
Newry, BT34 1DN
Tel: 028 3026 3176

**The Buck's Head**
77 Main Street
Dundrum, BT33 0LU
Tel: 028 4375 1868

**The Burrendale Hotel and Country Club**
51 Castlewellan Road
Newcastle, BT33 0JY
Tel: 028 4372 2599

**The Cuan**
The Square
Stangford, BT30 7ND
Tel: 028 4488 1222

**Dufferin Arms Coaching Inn**
35 High Street
Killyleagh, BT30 9QF
Tel: 028 4482 8229

**Four Trees Bar & Bistro**
61-63 Main Street
Moira, BT67 0LQ
Tel: 028 9261 1437

**Harry's Bar**
7 Dromore Street
Banbridge, BT32 4BS
Tel: 028 4066 2794

**The Coach Inn Brasserie**
Church Square
Banbridge, BT32 4AS
Tel: 028 4062 9774

**The Hillside**
21 Main Street
Hillsborough, BT26 6AE
Tel: 028 9268 2765
Fax: 028 9268 9888

**The Lobster Pot**
9-11 The Square
Strangford, BT30 7ND
Tel: 028 4488 1288
Fax: 028 4488 1288

**Normans Inn**
86 Main Street
Moira, BT67 0LH
Tel: 028 9261 1318
Fax: 028 9261 1318

The Old Inn
11-15 Main Street
Crawfordsburn, BT19 1JH
Tel: 028 9185 3255
Fax: 028 9185 2775

The Old Schoolhouse Inn
100 Ballydrain Road
Comber, BT23 6EA
Tel: 028 9754 1182
Fax: 028 9754 2583

Papa Joes New Orleans Restaurant
7 Hamilton Road, Bangor
Tel: 028 9146 1529

The Portaferry Hotel
10 The Strand
Portaferry, BT22 1PE
Tel: 028 4272 8231

The Pot Belly Restaurant
59A Banbridge Road
Gilford, BT63 6DL
Tel: 028 3883 1404

Shanks Restaurant
The Blackwood Golf Centre
150 Crawfordsburn Road
Bangor, BT19 1GB
Tel: 028 9185 3313

The Slieve Croob Inn
119 Clanvaraghan Road
Castlewellan, BT31 9LA
Tel: 028 4377 1412

Wine & Co.
57 High Street, Holywood
Tel: 028 9042 6083

### Co Fermanagh

Encore Steak House
66 Main Street, Ballinamallard
Tel: 028 6638 8606

Franco's
Queen Elizabeth Road
Enniskillen
Tel: 028 6632 4424

Oscar's Restaurant
29 Belmore Street, Enniskillen
Tel: 028 6632 7037

Picasso's Restaurant
52A Belmore Street
Enniskillen
Tel: 028 6632 2226

### Co Derry

Ardtara Country House
8 Gorteade Road
Upperlands
Maghera, BT46 5SA
Tel: 028 7964 4490

Beech Hill Country House Hotel
32 Ardmore Road
Derry, BT47 3QP
Tel: 028 7134 9279

Bohill Hotel & Country Club
69 Cloyfin Road
Coleraine, BT52 2NY
Tel: 028 7034 4406

Brown Trout Golf & Country Inn
209 Agivey Road
Aghadowey (near Coleraine)
BT51 4AD
Tel: 028 7086 8209

Decks Bar & Restaurant
1 Campsie Business Park
McLean Road
Eglinton, BT47 3XX
Tel: 028 7186 0912
Fax: 028 7186 0053

### Co Tyrone

Ardbeg Lodge
32 Dungannon Road
Ballygawley
Tel: 028 8556 8517

Corick House
20 Corick Road
Clogher, BT76 0BZ
Tel: 028 8554 8216
A licensed Gourmet

The Indigo
10 Gortmerron Link Road
Dungannon
Tel: 028 8772 7121

The Mellon Country Inn
134 Beltany Road
Omagh, BT78 5RA
Tel: 028 8166 1224

Salley's Restaurant
90 Moore Street
Aughnacloy
Tel: 028 8555 7979

Viscounts Restaurant
10 Northland Row
Dungannon, BT71 6AW
Tel: 028 8775 3800

*Deane's Brasserie, Belfast*

## Bars, Pubs and Clubs

Public Houses, known as 'pubs' or 'bars', are at the heart of many people's social lives throughout Northern Ireland, whether as drinking places or just meeting spots. They are also good places to hear live music – folk, traditional, jazz, blues and rock. Several of the pubs listed stay open until 1am or later.

### Belfast

Apartment
Donegall Square West
Belfast
Tel: 028 9050 9777

Bambu Beach Club
Odyssey Pavilion
Queen's Quay, Belfast
Tel: 028 9046 0011
Hawaiian-themed nightclub

Bar RED TENsq
10 Donegall Square, Belfast
Tel: 028 9024 1001

Bittles Bar
103 Victoria Street, Belfast
Tel: 028 9031 1088

Benedicts of Belfast
7-21 Bradbury Place, Belfast
Tel: 028 9059 1999

The Bodega Bar
4 Callender Street, Belfast
Tel: 028 9024 3177

Coyote Odyssey
Odyssey Pavilion
Queen's Quay, Belfast
Tel: 028 9046 7080

Culpa
1 Bankmore Square
Dublin Road, Belfast
Tel: 028 9023 3555

Bar 12
13 Lower Crescent, Belfast.
Tel: 028 9032 3349.
An oak panelled, imaginative Gothic style bar.

Bar Bacca
42 Franklin Street, Belfast
Tel: 028 9023 0200
Winner of the Theme Magazine Bar and Restaurant Award for Best Bar in All Ireland in May 2002.

The Botanic Inn
23-27 Malone Road
Belfast BT9 6RU
Tel: 028 9050 9740
Popular haunt for Belfast's students and watching major sporting events.

Chelsea Wine Bar
346 Lisburn Road, Belfast
Tel: 028 9068 7177

The Crown Liquor Saloon
46 Great Victoria Street
Belfast
Tel: 028 9027 9901
Traditional Irish bar opposite the Grand Opera House.

Duke of York
7-11 Commercial Court
Belfast
Tel: 028 9024 1062

The Empire
40-42 Botanic Avenue
Belfast
Tel: 028 9032 8110
Music hall and comedy club.

The Fly Bar
5-6 Lower Crescent, Belfast
Tel: 028 9050 9750
This is one of the more popular venues in Belfast, consisting of three floors.

The Globe
36 University Road, Belfast
Tel: 028 9050 9840
Karaoke, Tuesday to Friday

Irene and Nans
12 Brunswick Street, Belfast
Tel: 028 9023 9123
Fax: 028 9023 0201
Irene and Nans is a haven for cocktail connoisseurs and foodies with kitsch surroundings.

Kremlin
96 Donegall Street, Belfast
Tel: 028 9080 9700
Northern Ireland's premier gay and lesbian venue.

La Lea
43 Franklin Street, Belfast
Tel: 028 9023 0200
Fax: 0285 9023 0201
This trendy nightclub has a sumptuous decorative style.

Lavery's Bar and Gin Palace
12-16 Bradbury Place, Belfast
Tel: 028 9087 1106
One of Belfast's busiest and most famous pubs with probably the widest diversity of clientele of any bar in Belfast.

M-Club
23-31 Bradbury Place, Belfast
Tel: 028 9023 3131
M-Club has established itself as a student haunt on Thursdays, a 70's party on Fridays and the ultimate Club night on Saturdays.

McHugh's
29-31 Queen's Square
Belfast
Tel: 028 9050 9990

Madison's
59-63 Botonic Avenue
Belfast
Tel: 028 9050 9800

Magennis's
83 May Street, Belfast
Tel: 028 9023 0295
Traditional bar close to St George's Market and the Waterfront Hall offering live music and food.

Mezza(nine)
38-42 Great Victoria Street
Belfast
Tel: 028 9024 7447
Part of the Robinson's Bar Complex

Mercury Bar & Grill
451 Ormeau Road, Belfast
Tel: 028 9064 9017

Milk Bar/Club
10-14 Tomb Street, Belfast
Tel: 028 9027 8876
Trendy nightclub.

The Edge Bar & Restaurant
Mays Meadow
Laganbank Road, Belfast
Tel: 028 9032 2000
Waterfront facility, enjoying spectacular views from balconies.

The Morning Star
17-19 Pottinger's Entry
Belfast
Tel: 028 9032 3976

Morrisons Lounge Bars
21 Bedford Street, Belfast
Tel: 028 9032 0030

The Northern Whig
2 Bridge Street, Belfast
Tel: 028 9050 9880
Fax: 028 9050 9888

The Parlour
2-4 Elmwood Avenue, Belfast
Tel: 028 9068 6970

Pat's Bar
Prince's Dock Street, Belfast
Tel: 028 9074 4524

Robinson's Bars
Great Victoria Street, Belfast
Tel: 028 9024 4774
Several bars in one. One of Belfast's best know public houses.

Rotterdam Bar
Pilot Street, off Corporation Street, Belfast, BT3 5HZ
Tel: 028 9074 6021
Fax: 028 9075 3275

Shu
253 Lisburn Road, Belfast
Tel: 028 9038 1655

TaTu
Lisburn Road, Belfast
Tel: 028 9038 0818
Trendy bar and restaurant.

Wetherspoons
35 Bedford Street, Belfast
Tel: 028 9072 7890

## Co Antrim

Kellys Complex
Bushmills Road, Portrush
Tel: 028 7082 3539
Includes Lush! Nightclub

Traks Nightclub
Station Square, Portrush
Tel: 028 7082 2112

## Co Armagh

Bennetts Bar
4 Mandeville Street
Portadown
Tel: 028 3835 0778

Courthouse Bar
William Street, Lurgan
Tel: 028 3832 9161

Lynesses'
1 The Square, Richhill
Tel: 028 3887 1874

McConville Bros
1 Mandeville Street
Portadown
Tel: 028 3833 2070

McKeever and Sons
28-29 Woodhouse Street
Portadown
Tel: 028 3833 2054

The Cellar Bar
50 Church Place, Lurgan
Tel: 028 3832 7994

The Met
109 Drumcairn Road, Armagh
Tel: 028 3751 1360

## Co Down

Bar 15
13-15 High Street, Bangor
Tel: 028 9127 1060

Newcastle Arms
Railway Street, Newcastle
Tel: 028 4372 2853

Norman's Inn
86 Main Street, Moira
Tel: 028 9261 1318

The Four Trees
61-63 Main Street, Moira
Tel: 028 9261 1437

The Plough Inn
3 The Square, Hillsborough
Tel: 028 9268 2985

Primrose Bar & Restaurant
30 Main Street, Ballynahinch
Tel: 028 9756 3177

Wee Minnies
1 Wall Road, Gilford
Tel: 028 3883 2361

## Co Fermanagh

Bar M
33 Darling Street, Enniskillen
Tel: 028 6632 2059

Blake's of the Hollow
6 Church Street, Enniskillen
Tel: 028 6632 2143

Charlie's
1 Church Street, Enniskillen
Tel: 028 6632 5303

Pat's Bar
1-5 Townhall Street
Enniskillen
Tel: 028 6632 2040

The Necarne Arms
2 Church Street, Irvinestown
Tel: 028 6862 1572

The Mayfly Inn
Main Street, Kesh
Tel: 028 6863 1281

## Co Londonderry

Anchor Inn
38 Ferryquay Street
Londonderry
Tel: 028 7136 8601

Castle Bar
Waterloo Street, Derry
Tel: 028 7126 3118

Clarendon Bar
46-48 Strand Road, Derry
Tel: 028 7126 3705

Cosmopolitan Bar
29 Strand Road, Derry
Tel: 028 7126 6400

Mullen's
13 Little James Street, Derry
Tel: 028 7126 5300

Peadar O'Donnell's
Waterloo Street, Derry
Tel: 028 7137 2318

River Inn Bar & Cellars
36-38 Shipquay Street, Derry
Tel: 028 7136 7463

Shenanigans
78 The Promenade
Portstewart
Tel: 028 7083 6000

The Metro
3 Bank Place, Londonderry
Tel: 028 7126 7401

The Strand
35 Strand Road, Derry
Tel: 028 7136 6910

## Co Tyrone

The Fort
30 Scotch Street, Dungannon
Tel: 028 8772 2620

Halliday's Bar
9-13 Perry Street, Dungannon
Tel: 028 8772 2198

Sally O'Brien's
35 John Street, Omagh
Tel: 028 8224 2521

Utopia Nightclub & Bar
55-57 Market Street, Omagh
Tel: 028 8225 1192

*Irene and Nans, Belfast*

## Cinema, Theatre and the Arts

### Cinema

After many years of decline in cinema attendances, Northern Ireland has seen a substantial increase in investment, with new multi-screen cinema complexes in many of the main population centres. Many big screen stars hail from Northern Ireland, such as Kenneth Branagh and Liam Neeson, and the region has produced award winning films and shorts.

### Main Cinemas in Northern Ireland

Antrim Cineplex
1 Fountain Hill
Antrim, BT41 1LZ
Tel: 028 9446 1111 (info)
Tel: 028 9446 9500 (booking)

Armagh City Filmhouse
Market Street
Armagh, BT61 7BU
Tel: 028 3751 1033

Bangor Multiplex
1 Valentines Road
Castle Park
Bangor, BT20 4JH
Tel: 028 9146 5007

Carrickfergus Omniplex Cinema Ltd
Unit 4 Rodger's Quay
Carrickfergus
Tel: 028 9335 1111

Cinema Studio
Gillygooly Road, Omagh
Tel: 028 8224 2034

Enniskillen Omniplex
Factory Road, Enniskillen
Tel: 028 6632 4777

Global Cinema
Oaks Road, Dungannon
Tel: 028 8772 7733

IMC Multiplex Cinema
Larne Road Link
Ballymena, BT42
Tel: 028 2563 1111

Lisburn Omniplex
Lisburn Leisure Park
Governor's Road
Lisburn, BT28 1PR
Tel: 028 9266 3664

Movie House Cinemas Ltd
51 St Lurach's Road
Maghera, BT46 5JE
Tel: 028 7964 2936

Movie House Cinemas Ltd
13 Glenwell Road
Glengormley, BT36 7RF
Tel: 028 9083 3424

Movie House Cinemas Ltd
14 Dublin Road
Belfast, BT2 7HN
Tel: 028 9024 5700

Movie House Cinemas Ltd
100-150 York Street, Belfast
Tel: 028 9075 5000

Movieland
Ards Shopping Centre
Circular Road
Newtownards, BT23 4EU
Tel: 028 9182 0000

Newry Omniplex Cinema
Quays Shopping Centre
Albert Basin, Newry
Tel: 028 3025 2233

Playhouse Cinema
Main Street, Portrush
Tel: 028 7082 3917

Queen's Film Theatre
Ashby Building
Stranmillis Road, Belfast
Tel: 0800 328 2811
The best of cinema from around the world, contemporary and classic.

Ritz Multiplex Cinemas
1-2 Burn Road
Cookstown, BT80 8DN
Tel: 028 8676 5182

Sheridan IMAX® Cinema
The Odyssey Pavilion
Queen's Quay
Belfast, BT3 9QQ
Tel: 028 9046 7000
Web: www.belfastimax.com
The 380 seat Sheridan IMAX® cinema features a host of 2D and 3D movies.

The Strand Cinema
152-154 Holywood Road
Belfast, BT4 1NY
Tel: 028 9067 3500

Strand Multiplex
Quayside Centre, Strand Road
Derry, BT48
Tel: 028 7137 3900

Warner Village Cinemas
Odyssey Pavilion
2 Queen's Quay
Belfast, BT3 9QQ
Tel: 0871 224 0240

West Belfast Cineplex Ltd
Kennedy Centre
Falls Road, Belfast
Tel: 028 9060 0988

### Theatres and Arts Venues

Northern Ireland has a relatively small number of purpose-built theatres and professional theatre companies, but this should not disguise the fact that there is great enthusiasm for the dramatic arts throughout the region. There is a particularly vibrant amateur theatre sector within Northern Ireland. The main theatrical venues are set out below.

Ardhowen Theatre
97 Dublin Road
Enniskillen, BT74 6BR
Tel: 028 6632 3233 (Admin)
Tel: 028 6632 5440 (Box Office)
Fax: 028 6632 7012

Ards Arts Centre
Town Hall, Conway Square
Newtownards, BT23 4DB
Tel: 028 9181 0803

Ballyearl Arts and Leisure Centre
The Courtyard Theatre
585 Doagh Road
Newtownabbey, BT36 5RZ
Tel: 028 9084 8287

Bangor Drama Club Studio Theatre
38A Central Avenue
Bangor, BT20 3AW
Tel: 028 9145 4706 (Box Office)

Burnavon Arts & Cultural Centre
Burn Road
Cookstown, BT80 8DN
Tel: 028 8676 7994 (Admin)
Tel: 028 8676 9949 (Box Office)

Belfast Waterfront Hall & Conference Centre
2 Lanyon Place
Belfast, BT1 3WH
Tel: 028 9033 4455 (Box Office)
Tel: 028 9033 4400 (General Enquiries)
Fax: 028 9024 9862
Web: www.waterfront.co.uk

Clotworthy Arts Centre
Castle Gardens
Randalstown Road
Antrim, BT41 4LH
Tel: 028 9442 8000

Craigavon Civic Centre
Craigavon
Tel: 028 3831 2423

Crescent Arts Centre
24 University Road
Belfast, BT7 1NH
Tel: 028 9024 2338
Converted Victorian school, presenting workshops in all kinds of dance, circus and other skills. Occasional studio performances.

Down Arts Centre
2-6 Irish Street
Downpatrick, BT30 6BN
Tel: 028 4461 5283

Flax International Arts Centre
Brookfield Mill
333 Crumlin Road
Belfast, BT14 7EA
Tel: 028 9035 2333

Golden Thread Theatre
333 Crumlin Road
Belfast, BT14 7EA
Tel: 028 9074 5241

*Grand Opera House, Belfast*

Grand Opera House
Great Victoria Street, Belfast
Tel: 028 9024 1919
(Box Office)
Tel: 028 9024 0411 (Admin)
Web: www.goh.co.uk

Island Hall and Studio Theatre
Lagan Valley Island, Lisburn
Tel: 028 9250 9254
(Box Office)

Lyric Theatre
55 Ridgeway Street
Belfast, BT9 5FB
Tel: 028 9038 1081
(Box Office)
Tel: 028 9038 5685
(Admin)
Web: www.lyrictheatre.co.uk

Market Place Theatre
Market Street
Armagh, BT61 6AT
Tel: 028 3752 1821
(Box Office)

Millennium Forum
Newmarket Street, Derry
Tel: 028 7126 4426 (Admin)
Tel: 028 7126 4455
(Box Office)

Newry Arts Centre
1A Bank Parade
Newry, BT34 2NT
Tel: 028 3031 3180

Old Museum Arts Centre
7 College Square North
Belfast, BT1 6AR
Tel: 028 9023 5053

The Playhouse
5-7 Artillery Street
Londonderry, BT48 6RG
Tel: 028 7126 8027

Portadown Town Hall
15-17 Edward Street
Portadown, BT62 3LX
Tel: 028 3833 5264

Riverside Theatre
University of Ulster
Cromore Road
Coleraine, BT52 1SA
Tel: 028 7032 3232
(Box Office)
Tel: 028 7034 4141 (Admin)
Fax: 028 7032 4924

St Columb's Theatre & Arts Centre
Orchard Street
Derry, BT48 6EG
Tel: 028 7126 2880

Ulster Hall
Bedford Street Belfast
Tel: 028 9032 3900 (admin)
Fax: 028 9024 7199

King's Hall Exhibition & Conference Centre
Lisburn Road, Belfast
Tel: 028 9066 5225

Ulster Orchestra
Elmwood Hall
University Road
Ticket Hotline:
028 9066 8798

The Ulster Orchestra has established itself as one of the major symphony orchestras in the United Kingdom.

Much loved in Belfast and beyond, successful tours of Europe, Asia and America, and over fifty commercial recordings, broadcasts for BBC television, Radio 3 and Radio Ulster plus regular appearances at the Henry Wood Promenade concerts, have added to the orchestra's growing international reputation.

Waterside Theatre
The Ebrington Centre
Glendermott Road
Derry, BT47 6BG
Tel: 028 7131 4000

## Art Galleries

Ulster Museum
Botanic Gardens, Belfast
Tel: 028 9038 3000
Fax: 028 9038 3003
Irish artists include Sir John Lavery, Andrew Nicholl and William Conor.

Ormeau Baths Gallery
18A Ormeau Avenue, Belfast
Tel: 028 9032 1402
Bookshop, contemporary art.

Arches Gallery
2 Holywood Road
Belfast, BT4 1NT
Tel: 028 9045 9031
Irish artists.

Bell Gallery
13 Adelaide Park, Belfast
Tel: 028 9066 2998
Irish artistic, graphics.

Catalyst Arts Gallery
2nd Floor, 5 College Court
Belfast, BT1 6BS
Tel: 028 9031 3303

Craigavon Arts
Pinebank Art Centre,
Tullygally Road, Craigavon
Tel: 029 3834 1618

Tom Caldwell Gallery
49 Lisburn Road
Belfast, BT9 7EX
Tel: 028 9066 1890
Living Irish artists.

Cavehill Gallery
18 Old Cavehill Road, Belfast
Tel: 028 9077 6784
Irish Artists.

Eakin Gallery
237 Lisburn Road, Belfast
Tel: 028 9066 8522
Irish Artists.

Fenderesky Gallery
2 University Road, Belfast
Tel: 028 9023 5245
Contemporary Art.

Arttank
58 Lisburn Road
Belfast, BT9 6AF
Tel: 028 9023 0500
Irish and international art

McGilloway Gallery
6 Shipquay Street, Derry
Tel: 028 7136 6011
Open 10am-5.30pm Mon-Sat.
Modern Irish paintings.

Old Museum Arts Centre
7 College Square North
Belfast
Tel: 028 9023 3332

Prentice Gallery
20 Armagh Road
Portadown, BT62 3DP
Tel: 028 3835 3377

Waring Gallery
87 Main Street Moira
Tel: 028 9261 9100

## Major Events 2005

### Arctic Traditions
18 May 2004
28 February 2005
Ulster Museum, Belfast

Kayaks, dog sleds, harpoons, seal oil lamps and clothing are common to all. Many changes have taken place in Inuit life since they were first visited in the 18th century.
Tel: 028 9038 3000

### 'All Change – The Social Impact of The Railways.'
25 September 2004-
25 January 2005
Armagh County Museum,

An exhibition on an atmospheric and nostalgic journey into a bygone era when railway transport reigned supreme.
Tel: 028 3752 3070
Web: www.magni.org.uk

### Ulster's Railways Exhibition
30 November 2004-
28 February 2005
North Down Heritage Centre, Bangor, Co Down

A major touring exhibition on Ulster's Railways.
Tel: 028 9127 1200
Web: www.northdown.gov.uk

### Apassionata
January
Odyssey Arena, Belfast

An equestrian extravaganza, featuring all the royal breeds.
Contact: Odyssey Box Office
Tel: 028 9073 9074
Web: www.odysseyarena.com

### Johann Strauss Gala
22 January
Waterfront Hall, Belfast

Magical show recreating the beauty and Romance of the grand ballrooms of 19th century Vienna.
Contact: Waterfront Hall Box Office
Tel: 028 9033 4455
Web: www.waterfront.co.uk

### Moscow State Circus
26-30 January
Waterfront Hall, Belfast

The World famous Moscow State Circus returns to the UK, bringing a brand new show featuring a 35 strong cast performing in Northern Ireland for the very first time.
Contact: Waterfront Hall Box Office
Tel: 028 9033 4455
Web: www.waterfront.co.uk

### Ulster Orchestra Out of the Blue!
February

A series of master classes and concerts. The orchestra's main concert season takes place in Belfast between the months of September and May, in both the Ulster Hall and Waterfront Hall.
Tel: 028 9066 8798

### The Nutcracker
1- 5 February
Grand Opera House, Belfast

Scottish Ballet production of the classic 'The Nutcracker'- with the music of Tchaikovsky.
Tel: 028 9024 0411
Web: www.goh.co.uk

### Between the Lines
March–April (tbc)
Crescent Arts Centre, Belfast

Belfast's annual literary festival. Features readings and workshops from local, national and international authors.
Contact: Belfast City Council
Tel: 028 9032 0202
Web: www.belfastcity.gov.uk

### Classical Spectacular
5 March
Odyssey Arena, Belfast

Contact: Odyssey Box Office
Tel: 028 9073 9074
Web: www.odysseyarena.com

### Titanic made in Belfast
5 March-2 April
Belfast

Celebration of the energy, skill and creativity that helped make Belfast the biggest shipbuilding port in the world.
Tel: 028 9032 0202

### Soccermagic
Sunday 13 March (tbc)
Odyssey Arena, Belfast

Northern Ireland's largest celebrity football match. Over 100 celebrities from the world of film, television and music compete.
Contact: Odyssey Box Office
Tel: 028 9073 9074
Web: www.odysseyarena.com

### Barry Manilow's Copacabana – The Musical
15-19 March
New Lyric Operatic Company
Grand Opera House, Belfast

Tel: 028 9024 0411
Web: www.goh.co.uk

### Saint Patrick's Day
17 March
Celebrations all over Ireland

Includes carnival parades and cross-community festivals.
Contact: Belfast and Northern Ireland Welcome Centre
Tel: 028 9024 6609
Web: www.gotobelfast.com

### Ballycastle and District Horse Ploughing Match & Heavy Horse Show.
17 March
Ballycastle, Co Antrim

Contact: Ballycastle Tourist Information Centre
Tel: 028 2076 2024
Web: www.moyle-council.org

### Easter Extravaganza & Craft Fair.
28 March
The Argory, Moy
Co Armagh

Craft Fair and children's entertainment.
Tel: 028 8778 4753
Fax: 028 8778 9598
Web: www.ntni.org.uk

### Belfast Film Festival
7-16 April
Belfast

Mix of international and local films screened at venues across the city, with music, seminars and discussions.
Tel: 028 9032 5913

### Madama Butterfly
15 April
Waterfront Hall, Belfast

With exquisite Japanese water garden, waterfalls and stunning aquariums filled with golden fish.
Tel: 028 9033 4455
Web: www.waterfront.co.uk

### 6th Cathedral Quarter Arts Festival
28 April-8 May
North Belfast

Vibrant arts festival in Belfast's historic North city centre.
Tel: 028 9023 2403
Web: www.cqaf.com

### Northern Ireland Game Fair
30 April-1 May
Ballywalter Estate
Co Down

Game and country sports fair, with displays, demonstrations and competitions.
Tel: 028 9260 5050
Email: nire@basc.org.uk
Web: www.basc.org.uk

### Vintage and Classic Vehicle Rally
30 April
The Argory, Moy
Co Armagh

Exhibits of cars, tractors, motorcycles and stationary engines.
Tel: 028 8778 4753

The Lord Mayor's Show
May (tbc)
Belfast City Centre

A civic festivity of colour makes its way round the city centre in this annual parade.
Contact: Belfast City Council
Tel: 028 9032 0202
Web: www.belfastcity.gov.uk

Belfast City Marathon
2 May
Starts at City Hall
Contact: Belfast City Council
Tel: 028 9027 0345
Web: www.belfastcity.gov.uk

P&O Kingdoms of Down Open Championship
4-6 May
Co Down

International tournament, played over the courses of Scrabo Golf Club, Clandeboye Golf Club and the Royal County Down Golf Club in Newcastle on the final day. The competition is open to all golfers who are members of an affiliated club.
Tel: 028 4482 8686

Rod Stewart in Concert
24 May
Odyssey Arena, Belfast

Contact: Odyssey Box Office
Tel: 028 9073 9074
Web: www.odysseyarena.com

Blues on the Bay Festival
26 -30 May (tbc)
Warrenpoint

Blues and Jazz Festival
Contact: Peter Thompson
Tel: 028 4175 2256

Castle Ward Opera Season
31 May-end June
Strangford, Co Down

Opera in an enchanted setting. Mozart's 'The Magic Flute' and Bizet's 'Carmen'.
Tel: 028 9066 1090

Feis na nGleann
June
Co Antrim

Over two weekends in June, celebrations include traditional music, singing and dancing, hurling, language and choir competitions.
Contact: Marie McAllister
Tel: 028 2888 5507

North Antrim Agricultural Show
3-4 June
Ballymoney, Co Antrim

Annual show held at Ballymoney showgrounds.
Contact: Ann V Morrison
Tel: 028 2075 2327
Web: www.naaa.co.uk

Midsummer Concerts at Mussenden Temple
10-11 June
Downhill Estate, Castlerock
Co Londonderry

Contact: Concert Booking & Information Line
Tel: 07790 103590
Web: www.ntni.org.uk

Omagh Agricultural Show
2 July
Omagh, Co Tyrone

Tel: 028 8224 2500

Twelfth of July Parades
12 July
Venues throughout Northern Ireland

Parades to celebrate the culture and heritage of the Loyal Orange Institution.
Tel: 028 9024 6609

Strangford Lough Race Week
13-16 July
Strangford, Co Down

Championship racing on Strangford Lough.
Tel: 028 4461 2233

Belfast Rose Week
18-24 July
Sir Thomas and Lady Dixon Park, Belfast

Tel: 028 9027 0467
Web: www.gotobelfast.com

Northern Ireland Milk Cup
31 July-5 August
Co Londonderry

One of Europe's premier youth soccer tournaments. Attracts teams from all over the world.
Contact: Jim Sandford
Tel: 07860 841193
Web: www.nimilkcup.org

Danny Boy Festival
August
Limavady

Limavady family arts festival with an international flavour, taking place across the borough of Limavady.
Contact: Limavady Borough Council
Tel: 028 7776 0304

Féile an Phobail
5-14 August
West Belfast

Concerts, debates, tours, exhibitions, drama and street theatre at various venues in West Belfast.
Tel: 028 9031 3440
Fax: 028 9031 9150
Email: info@feilebelfast.com
Web: www.feilebelfast.com

Oul' Lammas Fair
29-30 August
Ballycastle, Co Antrim

Ireland's oldest, traditional market fair. Horse trading, street entertainment and market stalls.
Contact: Ballycastle Tourist Information Centre
Tel: 028 2076 2024

Belfast Festival at Queen's
21 October-6 November (tbc)
Belfast

The largest festival of its kind in Ireland, combining the best of Irish, UK and international culture each year.
Contact: Festival Box Office
Tel: 028 9097 2626
Web: www.belfastfestival.com

BT Ghostly Halloween
22 October
Ardress House,
Portadown, Co Armagh

Ghostly storytelling, children's entertainment, fancy dress competition, scary face painting.
Normal admission for house tours.
Tel & Fax: 028 3885 1236
Web: www.ntni.org.uk

Banks of the Foyle Halloween Festival
October
Derry City

A week long programme of events featuring the annual River Foyle fireworks display on Monday 31 October with revellers taking to the streets in a mix of music, costume and fun.
Tel: 028 7137 6545

Christmas Concert at Castle Coole
December (tbc)
Enniskillen, Co Fermanagh

An evening of festive songs and music in the Grand Hall at 8pm.
Tel: 028 6632 2690
Web: www.ntni.org.uk

Santa's Grotto
3, 10 & 17 December
Mount Stewart House,
Newtownards, Co Down

Includes visit to Santa and special woodland trail with prizes.
Tel: 028 4278 8387/8487
Web: www.ntni.org.uk

## Exhibitions/Shows

**Holiday World Belfast**
21–23 January 2005
King's Hall, Belfast
Tel: 028 9066 5225
Web: www.kingshall.co.uk
Email: info@kingshall.co.uk

**Northern Ireland Motorcycle Show**
18–20 February 2005
Odyssey Arena, Belfast
Visitors can see all 2005 models on display, as well as a wide range of other goods catering to every biker's needs.
Contact: Nutt Promotions
Tel: 028 7035 1199

**Wedding Journal Show**
25–27 February 2005
King's Hall, Belfast
Belfast King's Hall gets romantic for the annual brides fair.
Tel: 028 9066 5225
Web: www.kingshall.co.uk
Email: info@kingshall.co.uk

**Balmoral Show**
May 2005
King's Hall, Belfast
Northern Ireland's largest agricultural show, featuring showing classes and entertainment for all the family.
Tel: 028 9066 5225
Web: www.kingshall.co.uk
Email: info@kingshall.co.uk

**Wedding Extravaganza 2005**
16–18 September 2005
Odyssey Arena, Belfast
An array of everything needed to plan a wedding, pre-nuptial events, honeymoon and future lives together.
Contact: 028 9080 1898

**Belfast Craft Fair**
2–4 December 2005
King's Hall, Belfast
Tel: 028 9066 5225
Web: www.kingshall.co.uk
Email: info@kingshall.co.uk

**Ideal Home Exhibition**
7–11 September 2005
King's Hall, Belfast
Tel: 028 9066 5225
Web: www.kingshall.co.uk
Email: info@kingshall.co.uk

## Museums

**Armagh County Museum**
The Mall East, Armagh
Tel: 028 3752 3070

**Ballymena Museum**
3 Wellington Court, Ballymena
Tel: 028 2564 2166

**Down County Museum**
The Mall, Downpatrick
Tel: 028 4461 5218

**Fermanagh County Museum**
Enniskillen Castle
Castle Barracks, Enniskillen
Tel: 028 6632 5000

**Flame – The Gasworks Museum of Ireland**
44 Irish Quarter West, Carrickfergus
Tel: 028 9336 9575

**Foyle Valley Railway Museum**
Foyle Road, Londonderry
Tel: 028 7126 5234

**Harbour Museum**
Harbour Square, Londonderry
Tel: 028 7137 2411

**Irish Linen Centre and Lisburn Museum**
Market Square, Lisburn
Tel: 028 9266 3377

**North Down Heritage Centre**
Town Hall
Castle Park Avenue, Bangor
Tel: 028 9127 1200

**Regimental Museum of the Royal Irish Regiment**
St Patrick's Barracks
Meenagh Drive, Ballymena
Tel: 028 2566 1383

**Museums & Galleries of NI (MAGNI)**
Ulster Folk & Transport Museum
Tel: 028 9042 8428
Ulster Museum
Tel: 028 9038 3000
Ulster American Folk Park
Tel: 028 8224 3292
Armagh County Museum
Tel: 028 3752 3070

**Royal Inniskilling Fusiliers Museum**
The Castle, Enniskillen
Tel: 028 6632 3142

**Royal Irish Fusiliers Museum**
Sovereigns House
The Mall, Armagh
Tel: 028 3752 2911

**Ulster American Folk Park**
Mellon Road, Castletown
Omagh
Tel: 028 8224 3292

**Ulster Folk & Transport Museum**
Cultra, Holywood
Tel: 028 9042 8428

**Ulster Museum**
Botanic Gardens, Belfast
Tel: 028 9038 3000

*Ulster Museum, Belfast*

*Tower Museum, Derry*

## Sports and Leisure

### Sports

Northern Ireland's main sports are football (soccer, Gaelic and rugby) golf, hockey and cricket. There is also a high level of interest in motorcycling and car rallying. Most other sports are to an extent minority pursuits, but Northern Ireland boasts a strong record in amateur boxing and bowls. The recently formed ice hockey team, the 'Belfast Giants', has established a regular following of 5,000 enthusiasts.

### Soccer

As a small, albeit enthusiastic, footballing country, Northern Ireland has limited expectations in terms of international football success, but the team has performed with credit in the World Cups of 1958 and 1982.

Home of the legendary forward George Best, Northern Ireland has produced many top-class players (although seldom enough at one time to support a good international side). Home internationals are played at Windsor Park in Belfast, the home of Irish League club, Linfield.

The International team tends to be made up of professional footballers playing in the upper divisions of the English football league, although occasionally a locally based player breaks through to the International side. Much hope has been pinned on the latest Northern Ireland manager Lawrie Sanchez who is currently taking the team through the qualifying stages for the 2006 World Cup finals.

At local level the 'Irish League' constitutes the main attraction. It is primarily part-time football (with a handful of full-time professionals) and comprises a number of teams from Belfast, and a team from most of each of Northern Ireland's largest provincial towns.

The local game suffers from a number of fundamental difficulties. As a spectacle it suffers when compared with the televised glamour of the English 'premiership', and the cream of top young local players tend to leave the local game to play 'across the water'.

Attendance at Irish League games are poor (except for the exciting 'Big-Two' derby clashes between Belfast clubs Linfield and Glentoran) and crowd trouble and sectarianism on the terraces have on occasions made it very difficult for the games' promoters to push up attendances.

Like most activities in Northern Ireland soccer does not escape the impact of political divisions. A sizeable minority of soccer supporters give their first loyalty to the international team from the Irish Republic. Indeed the top team from Northern Ireland's second city 'Derry City' plays in the Republic of Ireland League rather than the Irish League. This conflict of affiliation also has a negative impact on local attendances at games.

Nonetheless, despite its difficulties most of the different interests in the game came together under the auspices of former Culture Minister Michael McGimpsey to devise a strategy to improve the image and attractiveness of the game and to put Irish League football on a more sustainable financial footing. The Irish Football Association administers the game at all levels and is hopeful that government will provide a new multipurpose stadium for soccer, to be shared with other sports.

### Gaelic Sports

There are a number of Gaelic Sports including football, hurling and camogie all administered by the Gaelic Athletic Association (GAA). Gaelic Football has now become the largest participation sport in Northern Ireland.

Again Northern Ireland's political divisions are reflected in this sport which tends to be pursued predominantly, although not exclusively by the Catholic, Nationalist community. The GAA has recently reversed a rule which excluded participation in Gaelic games by members of the security forces, and is currently under pressure to rescind a policy, which prohibits the use of GAA facilities (sports arenas) for other 'foreign games'.

Gaelic Sport is organised on an all-island basis both at club and County level, and its highest prize is the All-Island County Championship (the 'Sam Maguire'). Clubs are organised at a 'parish' level and most own their own pitches and clubhouses.

Northern Ireland counties have been successful in this prestigious All-Ireland competition in the 1990s notably Armagh, Down, Derry and most recently Tyrone. Most of the 6 counties of Northern Ireland have extensive football leagues at club level.

Despite its high-level of participation and level of spectator attendances as well as TV coverage, Gaelic football remains a completely amateur sport. However pressure is building within the GAA, as it has done in recent years in athletics and rugby, to allow the top players to share in some of the commercial value created.

#### Hurling

Hurling is played less widely than football, although areas in county Antrim and Down and Derry have a renowned passion for the sport. It is a uniquely Irish game which pre-dates Gaelic football although the Northern counties have traditionally been weak in an all-Ireland context.

#### Handball

Although in comparison to football and hurling it is something of a minority sport, handball is a popular gaelic sport pursuit. Unlike Olympic handball played between teams this is a sport for individuals or pairs played in an 'alley' similar to a squash court, except there are no racquets!

### Rugby Union

Rugby Union has a strong following in Northern Ireland. It tends to be a predominantly, but by no means exclusively, Protestant and middle-class game. Although its organisation is all-island, the sport is based on club and provincial rather than county structures.

Northern Ireland rugby is synonymous with the 'Ulster' team, which showcases Northern Ireland's best players in both the inter-provincial series against the three other Irish provinces and in international competition such as the Celtic Cup and the Heineken Cup.

In recent times Ulster has won the increasingly important European Cup, a competition featuring the best club and provincial sides from the British Isles, France and Italy. The Ulster team was crowned European Champions in 1999 after a Lansdowne Road final at the end of an exciting campaign which re-ignited

Ulster Rugby at Ravenhill

wider interest in the local game. More recently in 2003 Ulster registered another major success in winning the Celtic Cup.

Northern Ireland players have also contributed prominently to the Irish National Team and to the British Lions with Ballymena's Willie John McBride and North's Mike Gibson ranking among the all-time greats of the game. In more recent times players like David Humphreys, Willie Anderson and Paddy Johns have served the national game with distinction.

Rugby Union is undergoing continuous change. Several years ago the game adopted professional status, and many top-level players departed to play outside Northern Ireland. However, with Ulster's success many of the best local players have largely been retained within Northern Ireland in a thoroughly professional set-up. As well as at the Ireland and Ulster level there is an enthusiastic following for rugby at town and club level.

## Cricket

As in Britain, cricket is a popular summer sport in Northern Ireland although it tends to draw very small numbers of spectators.

Much of the cricket activity outside Greater Belfast is based around village sides and villages such as Sion Mills (near Strabane) who once famously humiliated the mighty West Indies and Waringstown (near Lurgan) have become synonymous with the game. Although a very 'British' game, cricket is organised on an all-island basis and there is a National side covering all of Ireland. This team competes with other minor cricketing countries and some of the English County sides but is not competitive at the top international level.

## Hockey

Hockey (both men and ladies) is a popular sport right across Northern Ireland although more a participant than a spectator sport.

It is organised in local leagues for clubs – often closely associated with neighbouring rugby and cricket clubs although the international games are organised on an all-island basis. In the men's game Lisnagarvey (near Lisburn) have been the best team in Ireland for long stretches. In the ladies game Pegasus and Portadown have been regularly at the top.

Northern Ireland players can opt to play for Ireland or for Great Britain and many have played with distinction in major international championships including the Olympic Games.

## Boxing

Although it can be seen as affirming certain stereotypical images of the 'fighting Irish', Northern Ireland has regularly produced top quality international boxers both as amateurs and professionals. There is a long history of heroic medal winning performances in Olympic and Commonwealth Championships for amateurs and, for such a small place, a number of local boxers have made it to World Champion in the professional ring. Names such as Barry McGuigan, Dave McAuley and Wayne McCullough have all held world championship belts.

## Motorsport

Northern Ireland has a large and very enthusiastic following for motor sports, in particular motorcycle road racing and car rallying. Although becoming increasingly expensive and specialist in nature motorsports have major spectator appeal.

A motorcycle race, the North West 200, which takes place every year at Portrush is by far the largest spectator event in Northern Ireland's sporting calendar drawing huge crowds and a top quality international field for the racing.

Northern Ireland has always produced motorcyclists of the highest quality, including Isle of Man TT legend and 'King of the Road' Joey Dunlop and circuit racer Jeremy McWilliams. Car rallying is also hugely popular in Northern Ireland with the highlights being the Circuit of Ireland Rally and the Ulster Rally.

## Athletics

Since the era of Mary Peters and Mike Bull in the 1970s, Northern Ireland has rarely made the headlines in international athletics. However there is a strong record over the years of track and field participation in top competition.

Highlights of the local scene are the Belfast Marathon and the major cross-country events at Mallusk and Stormont which usually attract world-class fields. Locally there are 47 clubs in Northern Ireland – affiliated to the IAAF.

North West 200 Road Race

## Golf in Northern Ireland

Northern Ireland is perfect golfing country with plenty of fine parkland and coastal links courses. There are nearly a hundred 18- and 9-hole golf courses including world-famous championship courses such as Royal Portrush and Royal County Down. Northern Ireland continues to produce world-class golfers; in recent years Ronan Rafferty, David Feherty and Darren Clarke have all reached the top international level of the game.

The following listing includes all of Northern Ireland's 18-hole golf courses, along with details of their location, best days to visit and contact information.

### Belfast Area

**Balmoral Golf Club**
518 Lisburn Road
Belfast, BT9 6GX
Tel: 028 9038 1514
Fax: 028 9066 6759

18 Holes, 6,034 yds, par 69
Parkland course, 3 miles south-west of city centre. Best days for visitors: Monday and Thursday

**Belvoir Park Golf Club**
73 Church Road
Newtownbreda
Belfast, BT8 7AN
Tel: 028 9049 1693
Fax: 028 9064 6113

18 Holes, 6,516 yds, par 71
Parkland course, 3 miles south of city centre. Best days for visitors: Monday, Tuesday and Thursday

**Dunmurry Golf Club**
91 Dunmurry Lane
Dunmurry, Belfast, BT17 9JS
Tel: 028 9061 0834

18 Holes, 5,832 yds, par 68
Parkland course, 4 miles south-west of city centre. Best days for visitors: Tuesday and Thursday

**Fortwilliam Golf Club**
Downview Avenue
Belfast, BT15 4EZ
Tel: 028 9037 0770
Fax: 028 9078 1891

18 Holes, 5,973 yds, par 69
Parkland course, 3 miles north of city centre. Best days for visitors: weekday mornings

**Knock Golf Club**
Summerfield
Upper Newtownards Road
Belfast, BT16 2QX
Tel: 028 9048 3251
Fax: 028 9048 3251

18 Holes, 6,435 yds, par 71
Parkland course, 4 miles east of city centre. Best days for visitors: Monday, Wednesday and Thursday mornings; Tuesday and Friday afternoons

**Malone Golf Club**
240 Upper Malone Road
Dunmurry, Belfast, BT17 9LB
Tel: 028 9061 2758

18 Holes, 6,600 yds, par 71
Parkland course, 4 miles south of city centre. Best days for visitors: any day except Tuesday and Saturday

**Mount Ober Golf & Country Club**
20-24 Ballymaconaghy Road
Knockbracken
Belfast, BT8 6SB
Tel: 028 9079 5666

18 Holes, 5,182 yds, par 68
Parkland course, 4 miles south-east of city centre. Best days for visitors: any day except Saturday

**Rockmount Golf Club**
28 Drumalig Road
Carryduff, Belfast, BT8 8EQ
Tel: 028 9081 2279
18 Holes, 6,373 yds, par 72
Parkland course, 2 miles south of Carryduff. Best days for visitors: any day except Wednesday and Saturday

**Shandon Park Golf Club**
73 Shandon Park
Belfast, BT5 6NY
Tel: 028 9080 5030
Fax: 028 9040 2773

18 Holes, 6,282 yds, par 70
Parkland course, 4 miles east of city centre. Best days for visitors: any day except Tuesday and Saturday

### Co Antrim

**Aberdelaghy Golf Course**
Bell's Lane, Lambeg
Lisburn, BT27 4QH
Tel: 028 9266 2738
Fax: 028 9260 3432

18 Holes, 4,526 yds, par 62
Parkland course, 1 mile north of Lisburn. Best days for visitors: any day except Saturday morning

**Allen Park Golf Centre**
45 Castle Road
Antrim, BT41 4NA
Tel: 028 9442 9001
Fax: 028 9442 9001

18 Holes, 6,683 yds, par 72
Parkland course, 2 miles west of Antrim. Best days for visitors: any day

**Ballycastle Golf Club**
2 Cushendall Road
Ballycastle, BT54 6QP
Tel: 028 2076 2536

18 Holes, 5,940 yds, par 70
Links/Parkland course, just south-east of Ballycastle. Best days for visitors: weekdays

**Ballyclare Golf Club**
25 Springvale Road
Ballyclare, BT39 9JW
Tel: 028 9332 2696
Fax: 028 9332 2696

18 Holes, 5,699 yds, par 71
Parkland course, 2 miles north of town . Best days for visitors: Monday, Tuesday and Wednesday

**Ballymena Golf Club**
128 Raceview Road
Ballymena, BT42 4HY
Tel: 028 2586 1487
Fax: 028 2586 1487

18 Holes, 5,795 yds, par 67
Parkland course, 2 miles east of Ballymena on A42. Best days for visitors: any day except Tuesday and Saturday

**Cairndhu Golf Club**
192 Coast Road
Ballygally, Larne, BT40 2QG
Tel: 028 2858 3324
Fax: 028 2858 3324

18 Holes, 6,112 yds, par 69
Parkland course, 4 miles north of Larne Best days for visitors: weekdays

**Carrickfergus Golf Club**
35 North Road
Carrickfergus, BT38 8LP
Tel: 028 9336 3713
Fax: 028 9336 3023

18 Holes, 5,759 yds, par 68
Parkland course, west of Carrickfergus. Best days for visitors: any day except Tuesday, Saturday and Sunday afternoon

**Galgorm Castle Golf & Country Club**
200 Galgorm Road
Ballymena, BT42 1HL
Tel: 028 2564 6161
Fax: 028 2565 1151

18 Holes, 6,736 yds, par 72
Parkland course, 1 mile south-west of Ballymena. Best days for visitors: any day

**Gracehill Golf Club**
141 Ballinlea Road
Stranocum
Ballymoney, BT53 8PX
Tel: 028 2075 1209
Fax: 028 2075 1074

18 Holes, 6,600 yds, par 72
Parkland course, 7 miles north-east of Ballymoney . Best days for visitors: weekdays

### Greenacres Golf Centre
153 Ballyrobert Road
Ballyclare, BT39 9RT
Tel: 028 9335 4111

18 Holes, 6,020 yds, par 71 Parkland course, 3 miles from Corr's Corner. Best days for visitors: any day except Saturday morning

### Hilton Templepatrick ****

Hilton
Templepatrick
Hotel & Country Club

Hilton Templepatrick
Castle Upton Estate
Templepatrick, BT39 0DD
Tel: 028 9443 5500
Fax: 028 9443 5511
Email: hilton.templepatrick@hilton.com
Web: www.hilton.co.uk/templepatrick

18 Holes, 7,100 yds, par 71 Parkland course, 5 miles from Belfast International Airport. Best days for visitors: any day.

### Lisburn Golf Club
68 Eglantine Road
Lisburn, BT27 5RQ
Tel: 028 9267 7216

18 Holes, 6,672 yds, par 72 Parkland course, 2 miles south of Lisburn
Best days for visitors: weekdays

### Massereene Golf Club
51 Lough Road
Antrim, BT41 4DQ
Tel: 028 9442 8096

18 Holes, 6,375 yds, par 71 Parkland/sandy course, 1 mile south of Antrim. Best days for visitors: any day except Friday and Saturday

### Royal Portrush Golf Club
Bushmills Road
Portrush, BT56 8JQ
Tel: 028 7082 2311

(1) 18 Holes, 6,818 yds, par 73 (2) 18 Holes, 6,273 yds, par 70. Two links courses: (1) Dunluce (2) Valley, 1 mile east or Portrush. Best days for visitors: weekdays except Wednesday and Friday afternoon (Green fees are expensive).

### Whitehead Golf Club
McCrea's Brae
Whitehead, BT38 9NZ
Tel: 028 9337 0820
Fax: 028 9337 0825

18 Holes, 6,050 yds, par 68 Parkland course, just north of Whitehead. Best days for visitors: any day except Saturday; members only on Sunday.

## Co Armagh

### Ashfield Golf Club
Freeduff Cullyhanna
Newry, BT35 0JJ
Tel: 028 3086 8180
Fax: 028 3086 8611

18 Holes, 5,645 yds, par 67 Parkland course, 4 miles north of Crossmaglen off B30. Best days for visitors: any day

### County Armagh Golf Club
7 Newry Road
Armagh, BT60 1EN
Tel: 028 3752 5861
Fax: 028 3752 5861

18 Holes, 6,212 yds, par 70 Parkland course, in palace demesne. Best days for visitors: weekdays and Sunday

### Craigavon Silverwood Golf Centre
Turmoyra Lane
Lurgan, BT66 6NG
Tel: 028 3832 6606
Fax: 028 3834 7272

18 Holes, 6,188 yds, par 72 Parkland course, 2 miles north of Lurgan. Best days for visitors: any day

### Loughgall Country Park
11-14 Main Street
Loughgall, BT61 8HZ
Tel: 028 3889 2900
Fax: 028 3889 2902

18 Holes, 5,937 yds, par 69 Parkland course, 100 yards from Loughgall village. Best days for visitors: any day

### Lurgan Golf Club
The Demesne
Windsor Avenue
Lurgan, BT67 9BN
Tel: 028 3832 2087
Fax: 028 3831 6166

18 Holes, 5,995 yds, par 70 Parkland course, in Lurgan
Best days for visitors: Monday, Thursday and Friday morning

### Portadown Golf Club
192 Gilford Road
Portadown, BT63 5LF
Tel: 028 3835 5356

18 Holes, 6,147 yds, par 70 Parkland course, in Portadown. Best days for visitors: any day except Tuesday and Saturday

### Tandragee Golf Club
11 Markethill Road
Tandragee, BT62 2ER
Tel: 028 3884 1272
Fax: 028 3884 0664

18 Holes, 6,285 yds, par 70 Parkland course, just south of Tandragee
Best days for visitors: any day except Saturday and Thursday

## Co Down

### Ardglass Golf Club
Castle Place
Ardglass, BT30 7TP
Tel: 028 4484 1219
Fax: 028 4484 1841

18 Holes, 5,776 yds, par 68 Seaside course, in Ardglass
Best days for visitors: weekdays

### Banbridge Golf Club
116 Huntly Road
Banbridge, BT32 3UR
Tel: 028 4066 2211
Fax: 028 4066 9400

18 Holes, 5,468 yds, par 67 Parkland course, north-west of Banbridge. Best days for visitors: any day except Tuesday and Saturday

### Bangor Golf Club
Broadway
Bangor, BT20 4RH
Tel: 028 9127 0922

18 Holes, 6,410 yds, par 71 Parkland course, in Bangor. Best days for visitors: Monday, Wednesday and Friday

### Blackwood Golf Centre
150 Crawfordsburn Road
Bangor, BT19 1GB
Tel: 028 9185 2706
Fax: 028 9185 3785

18 Holes, 6,500 yds, par 70 Parkland course, 2 miles west of Bangor. Best days for visitors: any day

### Bright Castle Golf Club
14 Coniamstown Road
Bright
Downpatrick, BT30 8LU
Tel: 028 4484 1319

18 Holes, 7,143 yds, par 73 Parkland course, 4 miles south of Downpatrick. Best days for visitors: any day

### Carnalea Golf Club
Station Road
Bangor, BT19 1EZ
Tel: 028 9127 0368
Fax: 028 9127 3989

18 Holes, 5,548 yds, par 67 Seaside meadowland course, 1 mile west of Bangor. Best days for visitors: any day except Sunday

Clandeboye Golf Club
Tower Road, Conlig
Newtownards, BT23 3PN
Tel: 028 9127 1767
Fax: 028 9147 3711

(1) 18 Holes, 6,559 yds, par 71 (2) 18 Holes, 5,755 yds, par 68. Two parkland /heathland courses (1) Dufferin course (2) Ava Course, 2 miles south of Bangor. Best days for visitors: weekdays, weekend after 2.30pm

Cloverhill Golf Club
Lough Road
Mullaghbawn, Newry
Tel: 028 3088 9374

18 Holes, 6,090 yds, par 70 Parkland course, 7 miles North West of Newry

Donaghadee Golf Club
Warren Road
Donaghadee, BT21 0PQ
Tel: 028 9188 3624
Fax: 028 9188 8891

18 Holes, 6,091 yds, par 69 Seaside course, north side of Donaghadee. Best days for visitors: Monday, Wednesday and Friday

Downpatrick Golf Club
43 Saul Road
Downpatrick, BT30 6PA
Tel: 028 4461 5947

18 Holes, 6,120 yds, par 69 Parkland course, 1 mile from Downpatrick. Best days for visitors: any day, booking is advisable

Down Royal Park Golf Club
Dunygarton Road
Maze, BT27 5RT
Tel: 028 9262 1339

18 Holes, 6,824 yds, par 72 Heathland course, within Down Royal racecourse. Best days for visitors: any day

Edenmore Golf Club
70 Drumnabreeze Road
Magheralin, Craigavon
BT67 0RH
Tel: 028 9261 1310

18 Holes, 6,244 yds, par 71 Parkland course, 1.5 miles south-east of Magheralin. Best days for visitors: any day except Saturday morning

Holywood Golf Club
Nun's Walk, Demesne Road
Holywood, BT18 9LE
Tel: 028 9042 3135

18 Holes, 5,885 yds, par 67 Parkland course, 1 mile south of Holywood. Best days for visitors: any day except Thursday and Saturday

Kilkeel Golf Club
Mourne Park, Ballyardle
Newry, BT34 4LB
Tel: 028 4176 5095
Fax: 028 4176 5579

18 Holes, 6,625 yds, par 72 Parkland course, 3 miles west of town. Best days for visitors: Monday, Wednesday-Friday

Kirkistown Castle Golf Club
142 Main Road, Cloughey
Newtownards, BT22 1JA
Tel: 028 4277 1233

18 Holes, 6,142 yds, par 70 Links course, 15 miles south-east of Newtownards – A20 and B173. Best days for visitors: any day except Saturday

Ringdufferin Golf Course
36 Ringdufferin Road
Toye, Killyleagh, BT30 9PH
Tel: 028 4482 8812

18 Holes, 5,136 yds, par 66 Drumlin course, 2 miles north of Killyleagh. Best days for visitors: any day

Royal Belfast Golf Club
Station Road, Craigavad
Holywood, BT18 0BT
Tel: 028 9042 8165

18 Holes, 5,961 yds, par 69 Parkland course, 7 miles north-east of Belfast. Best days for visitors: by arrangement with Club, visitors require letter of introduction (Green fees are expensive)

Royal County Down Golf Club
36 Golf Links Road
Newcastle, BT33 0AN
Tel: 028 4372 3314

(1) 18 Holes, 7,037 yds, par 74 (2) 18 Holes, 4.681 yds, par 63. Two links courses, (1) Championship (2) Annesley 30 miles south of Belfast Best days for visitors: (1) Monday, Tuesday, Thursday and Friday (2) any day except Saturday morning

Scrabo Golf Club
233 Scrabo Road
Newtownards, BT23 4SL
Tel: 028 9181 2355
Fax: 028 9182 2919

18 Holes, 6,257 yds, par 71 Undulating course, 1? miles south-west of Newtownards follow Scrabo Country Park signs. Best days for visitors: Monday Tuesday and Thursday, Sunday after 11.30am

Spa Golf Club
20 Grove Road
Ballynahinch, BT24 8PN
Tel: 028 9756 2365
Fax: 028 9756 4158

18 Holes, 6,494 yds, par 72 Parkland course, 1 mile south of town. Best days for visitors: Monday-Thursday

Warrenpoint Golf Club
Lower Dromore Road
Warrenpoint, BT34 3LN
Tel: 028 4175 3695
Fax: 028 4175 2918

18 Holes, 6,200 yds, par 70 Parkland course, 1 mile west of town.. Best days for visitors: Monday, Thursday and Friday

**Co Fermanagh**

Castle Hume Golf Club
Castle Hume
Enniskillen, BT74 6HZ
Tel: 028 6632 7077

18 Holes, 6,900 yds, par 71 Parkland course, 3.5 miles north of Enniskillen. Best days for visitors: any day

Enniskillen Golf Club
Castle Coole
Enniskillen, BT74 6HZ
Tel: 028 6632 5250

18 Holes, 6,189 yds, par 69 Parkland course, in Castle Coole estate half a mile east of town. Best days for visitors: any day

**Co Derry**

Castlerock Golf Club
65 Circular Road
Castlerock, BT51 4TJ
Tel: 028 7084 8314
Fax: 028 7084 9440

18 Holes, 6,687 yds, par 72 Two links courses, 6 miles west of Coleraine. Best days for visitors: Monday-Thursday

City of Derry Golf Club
49 Victoria Road
Prehen, Derry, BT47 2PU
Tel: 028 7134 6369

18 Holes, 6,487 yds, par 71 Parkland course, 2 miles south of city.
Best days for visitors: weekdays until 4.30pm

Foyle International Golf Centre
12 Alder Road
Derry, BT48 8DB
Tel: 028 7135 2222

18 Holes, 6,678 yds, par 71 Parkland course, just north of Derry. Best days for visitors: any day

Moyola Park Golf Club
15 Curran Road,
Castledawson, BT45 8DG
Tel: 028 7946 8468

18 Holes, 6,517 yds, par 71 Parkland course, in Castledawson
Best days for visitors: weekdays except Wednesday

Portstewart Golf Club
117 Strand Road
Portstewart, BT55 7PG
Tel: 028 7083 2015

(1) 18 Holes, 6,779 yds, par 73 (2) 18 Holes, 4,730 yds, par 64. Links course, (1) Strand (2) Old - 1 mile from town centre. Best days for visitors: (1) Monday, Tuesday, Thursday and Friday (2) any day

Radisson Roe Hotel & Golf Resort
Roe Park
Limavady, BT49 9LB
Tel: 028 7776 0105

18 Holes, 6,001 yds, par 70 Parkland course, 1 mile west of Limavady. Best days for visitors: any day

**Co Tyrone**

Dungannon Golf Club
34 Springfield Lane
Dungannon, BT70 1QX
Tel: 028 8772 2098

18 Holes, 5,861 yds, par 69 Parkland course, 1 mile west of Dungannon. Best days for visitors: Monday, Thursday and Friday morning

Killymoon Golf Club
200 Killymoon Road
Cookstown, BT80 8TW
Tel: 028 8676 3762

18 Holes, 6,149 yds, par 69 Parkland course, south side of Cookstown. Best days for visitors: Monday-Wednesday and Friday, ladies Thursday

Newtownstewart Golf Club
38 Golf Course Road
Newtownstewart, BT78 4HU
Tel: 028 8166 1466

18 Holes, 5,341 yds, par 69 Parkland course, 2 miles south-west of town. Best days for visitors: any day

Omagh Golf Club
83A Dublin Road
Omagh, BT78 1HQ
Tel: 028 8224 3160

18 Holes, 5,885 yds, par 68 Parkland course, just south of town. Best days for visitors: any day except Tuesday and Saturday

Strabane Golf Club
33 Ballycolman Road
Strabane, BT82 9PH
Tel: 028 7138 2271

18 Holes, 6,055 yds, par 69 Parkland course, 1 mile south of town Best days for visitors: weekdays except Tuesday

## Motorsport/Karting

Below is a list of venues in Northern Ireland where groups or individuals can avail of organised karting and motorsport activities.

Alltrak Rallysport
61 Mullantine Road
Portadown
Tel: 028 3833 1919

Bishopscourt Racing Circuit
29 Lismore Road
Downpatrick, BT30 7EY
Tel: 028 4484 2202

Fast Track Karting Club
3 Edergoole Avenue, Omagh
Tel: 028 8225 0170

Gosford Karting
49 Dinnahorra Road
Markethill, Armagh
Tel: 028 3755 1248

Landrover Experience
Clandeboye Courtyard
Bangor, BT19 1RN
Tel: 0870 2644457

Raceview Indoor Karting
Woodside Industrial Estate
1 Woodside Road East
Ballymena, BT42 4HX
Tel: 028 2565 1000

Rally School Ireland
Unit 8
Graham Industrial Estate
Dargan Crescent
Belfast, BT36 9JP
Tel: 028 9077 3777

Superdrive Motorsports Centre
7 Derryneskan Road
Portadown, BT62 1UH
Tel: 028 3885 2545

Ultimate Karting
11 Kilbride Road, Doagh
Ballyclare, BT39 0Q4
Tel: 028 9334 2777

## Riding Schools/ Equestrian Centres

Ballyknock Riding School
38 Ballyknock Road
Hillsborough, BT26 6EF
Tel: 028 9269 2144

Birr House Riding Centre
81 Whinney Hill
Dundonald, BT16 0UA.
Tel: 028 9042 5858

The Burn Equestrian Centre
Knockbracken Healthcare Park, Saintfield Road
Belfast, BT8 8BH
Tel: 028 9040 2384

Danescroft
21 Waterloo Road
Lisburn, BT27 5NW
Tel: 028 9260 2621

Drumgooland House and Equestrian Centre
29 Dunnanew Road
Seaforde, BT30 8PJ
Tel: 028 4481 1956

Ecclesville Equestrian Centre
11 Ecclesville Road
Fintona, BT78 2EF
Tel: 028 8284 0591

The Forest Stables
100 Cooneen Road
Fivemiletown, BT75 0NQ
Tel: 028 8952 1991

Galgorm Parks Riding School
112 Sand Road
Ballymena, BT42 1DN
Tel: 028 2588 0269

Heathview Equestrian
60 Upper Gransha Road
Donaghadee, BT21 0LZ
Tel: 028 9181 3388

Hill Farm Riding Centre
47 Altikeeragh Road
Castlerock, BT51 4SR
Tel: 028 7084 8629

Island Equestrian Centre
49 Ballyrashane Road
Coleraine, BT52 2NL
Tel: 028 7034 2599

Islandmagee Riding Centre
103 Browns Bay Road
Islandmagee, BT40 3TL
Tel: 028 9338 2108

Lagan Valley Equestrian Centre
170 Upper Malone Road
Dunmurry, Belfast, BT17 9JZ
Tel: 028 9061 4853

Lessans Riding Stables
126 Monlough Road
Saintfield
Tel: 028 9751 0141

Maddybenny Stud
Maddybenny Farm
Coleraine, BT52 2PT
Tel: 028 7082 3603

Mossvale Equestrian Centre
18 Church Road, Dromara
Dromore, BT25 2NS
Tel: 028 9753 2279

Mount Pleasant Trekking Centre
15 Bannonstown Road
Castlewellan, BT31 9BG
Tel: 028 4377 8651

Moy Riding School
131 Derrycaw Road
Moy, BT71 6NA
Tel: 028 8778 4440

Newcastle Riding Centre
35 Carnacaville Road
Castlewellan, BT31 9HD
Tel: 028 4372 2694

The Rainbow Equestrian Centre
24 Hollow Road, Islandmagee
Larne, BT40 3RL
Tel: 028 9338 2929

Tullynewbank Stables
25 Tullynewbank Road
Glenavy, BT29 4PQ
Tel: 028 9445 4657

## Leisure

Northern Ireland has a proportionately large variety of leisure facilities for an area of its size. The climate and landscape facilitate outdoor pursuits such as hiking, mountain climbing and camping, and many of the lakes and rivers host watersports facilities. There are also many swimming pools, leisure and activity centres equipped with the latest fitness suites, some of which are listed below.

### Leisure and Recreation Centres

Andersonstown Leisure Centre
Andersonstown Road
Belfast, BT11 9BY
Tel: 028 9062 5211

Antrim Forum
Lough Road
Antrim, BT41 4DQ
Tel: 028 9446 4131

Ards Leisure Centre
William Street
Newtownards, BT23 4EJ
Tel: 028 9181 2837
Fax: 028 9182 0807

Avoniel Leisure Centre
Avoniel Road
Belfast, BT5 4SF
Tel: 028 9045 1564

Ballynahinch Community Centre
55 Windmill Street
Ballynahinch, BT24 8HB
Tel: 028 9756 1950
Fax: 028 9756 5606

Ballysillan Leisure Centre
Ballysillan Road
Belfast, BT14 7QQ
Tel: 028 9039 1040

Banbridge Leisure Centre
14 Downshire Road
Banbridge, BT32 3JY
Tel: 028 4062 8800

Bangor Castle Leisure Centre
Castle Park Avenue
Bangor, BT20 4BN
Tel: 028 9127 0271

Bawnacre Centre
Castle Street
Irvinestown, BT94 1EE
Tel: 028 6862 1177

Beechmount Leisure Centre
Falls Road
Belfast, BT12 6FD
Tel: 028 9032 8631

Belfast Indoor Tennis Arena
Ormeau Embankment
Belfast, BT6 8LT
Tel: 028 9045 8024

Brandywell Sports Centre
Lone Moor Road
Derry, BT48
Tel: 028 7126 3902

Brooke Park Leisure Centre
Rosemount Avenue
Derry, BT48 0HH
Tel: 028 7126 2637

Carrickfergus Leisure Centre
Prince William Way
Carrickfergus, BT38 7HP
Tel: 028 9335 1711

Cascades Leisure Centre
51 Thomas Street
Portadown, BT62 3AF
Tel: 028 3833 2802

Castlepark Centre
11 Water Road
Lisnaskea, BT92 0LZ
Tel: 028 6772 1299

Comber Leisure Centre
Castle Street
Comber, BT23 5DY
Tel: 028 9187 4350
Fax: 028 9187 0099

Coleraine Leisure Centre
Railway Road
Coleraine, BT52 1PE
Tel: 028 7035 6432

Cookstown Leisure Centre
Fountain Road
Cookstown, BT80 8QF
Tel: 028 8676 3853

Craigavon Leisure Centre
Brownlow Road, Craigavon
Tel: 028 3834 1333

Derg Valley Leisure Centre
6 Strabane Road
Castlederg, BT81 7HZ
Tel: 028 8167 0727

Down Leisure Centre
114 Market Street
Downpatrick, BT30 6LZ
Tel: 028 4461 3426
Fax: 028 4461 6905

Dundonald International Ice Bowl
111 Old Dundonald Road
Dundonald
Belfast, BT16 1XT
Tel: 028 9080 9100

Dungannon Leisure Centre
Circular Road
Dungannon, BT71 6BH
Tel: 028 8772 0370

Dungiven Sports Pavilion
3 Chapel Road
Dungiven, BT47 2AN
Tel: 028 7774 2074

Ecclesville Centre
11 Ecclesville Road
Fintona, BT78 2EF
Tel: 028 8284 0591

Glenmore Activity Centre
43 Glenmore Park, Hilden
Lisburn, BT27 4RT
Tel: 028 9266 2830

Greenvale Leisure Centre
Greenvale Park
Magherafelt, BT45 6DR
Tel: 028 7963 2796

Grove Activity Centre
15 Ballinderry Park
Knockmore
Lisburn, BT28 1ST
Tel: 028 9267 1131

Grove Leisure Centre
York Road Belfast, BT15 3HF
Tel: 028 9035 1599

Joey Dunlop Leisure Centre
33 Garryduff Road
Ballymoney, BT53 7DB
Tel: 028 2766 5792

Kilkeel Leisure Centre
Mourne Esplanade
Kilkeel, BT34 4DB
Tel: 028 4176 4666

Kilmakee Activity Centre
52A Rowan Drive
Seymour Hill, Dunmurry
Belfast, BT17 9QA
Tel: 028 9030 1545

Kiltonga Leisure Centre
Belfast Road
Newtownards, BT23 4TJ
Tel: 028 9181 8511
Fax: 028 9182 3400

Lagan Valley LeisurePlex
12 Lisburn Leisure Park
Governors Road
Lisburn, BT28 1LP
Tel: 028 9267 2121
Fax: 028 9267 4322

Lakeland Forum
Broadmeadow, Enniskillen
Tel: 028 6632 4121

Larne Leisure Centre
Tower Road
Larne, BT40 1AB
Tel: 028 2826 0478

Lisnagelvin Leisure Centre
Richill Park, Waterside
Derry, BT47 5QZ
Tel: 028 7134 7695

Lough Moss Centre
Hillsborough Road
Carryduff
Tel: 028 9081 4884

Loughside Leisure Centre
Shore Road
Belfast, BT15 4HP
Tel: 028 9078 1524

Maghera Leisure Centre
Coleraine Road
Maghera
Tel: 028 7954 7400

Meadowbank Recreation Ground
Ballyronan Road
Magherafelt
Tel: 028 7963 1680

Millburn Community Centre
Linden Avenue
Coleraine, BT52 2AN
Tel: 028 7034 2625

Newcastle Centre
10-14 Central Promenade
Newcastle, BT33
Tel: 028 4372 5034
Fax: 028 4372 2400

Newry Sports Centre
Patrick Street
Newry, BT35 8TR
Tel: 028 3031 3130

Olympia Leisure Centre
Boucher Road
Belfast, BT12 6HR
Tel: 028 9023 3369

Omagh Leisure Complex
Old Mountfield Road
Omagh, BT79
Tel: 028 8224 6711

Orchard Leisure Centre
37-39 Folly Lane
Armagh, BT60 1AT
Tel: 028 3751 5920

Queen's Leisure Complex
Sullivan Place
Holywood, BT18 9JF
Tel: 028 9042 1234

Queen's University (Malone Sports Facilities)
Dub Lane
Belfast, BT9 5NB
Tel: 028 9062 3946

Riversdale Leisure Centre
Lisnafin Park, Strabane
Tel: 028 7138 2672

The Robinson Centre
Montgomery Road
Belfast, BT6 9HS
Tel: 028 9070 3948

St Columb's Park Leisure Centre
Limavady Road
Derry, BT47 6JY
Tel: 028 7134 3941

Seapark Sports Ground
Seapark Recreation Park
Holywood, BT18 0LP
Tel: 028 9042 2894

Sentry Hill Sports Complex
Old Ballymoney Road
Ballymena, BT43 6NE
Tel: 028 2565 6101

Seven Towers Leisure Centre
Trostan Avenue
Ballymena, BT43 7BL
Tel: 028 2564 1427

Shankill Leisure Centre
Shankill Road
Belfast, BT13 2BD
Tel: 028 9024 1434

Sheskburn Recreation Centre
7 Mary Street
Ballycastle, BT54 6QH
Tel: 028 2076 3300

Sixmile Leisure Centre
Ballynure Road
Ballyclare, BT39 9YU
Tel: 028 9334 1818
Fax: 028 9335 4357

Templemore Swimming Centre
Templemore Avenue
Belfast, BT5 4FW
Tel: 028 9045 7540

Templemore Sports Complex
Buncrana Road
Derry, BT48 8LQ
Tel: 028 7128 9200

Trillick Enterprise Leisure Centre
Gargadis Road
Trillick, BT78 3
Tel: 028 8956 1333

The Valley Leisure Centre
40 Church Road, Whiteabbey
Newtownabbey, BT36 7LN
Tel: 028 9086 1211
Fax: 028 9085 3211

Waves Leisure Complex
22 Robert Street
Lurgan, BT66 8BE
Tel: 028 3832 2906

Whiterock Leisure Centre
Whiterock Road
Belfast, BT12 7RG
Tel: 028 9023 3239

## Private Fitness Clubs

Arena Health and Fitness - Yorkgate
100-150 York Street
Belfast, BT15 1WA
Tel: 028 9074 1235
Fax: 028 9074 1239

Arena Health and Fitness - Finaghy
37-39 Finaghy Road North
Belfast, BT10 0JB
Tel: 028 9062 9789

David Lloyd Racquet and Fitness Club
Old Dundonald Road
Belfast, BT16 1DL
Tel: 028 9041 3300
Fax: 028 9041 3339

Elysium Health and Leisure Club
Culloden Hotel, Bangor Road
Craigavad
Tel: 028 9042 5315

Esporta Health Club
Mertoun Hall
106 Belfast Road
Holywood, BT18 9QY
Tel: 028 9076 5000

Fitness First
1 Circular Road
Toscana Retail Park, Bangor
Tel: 028 9147 0000

*Ballymena*
Unit 3 Pennybridge Industrial Estate, Larne Road, Ballymena
Tel: 028 2563 1333

*Belfast*
Unit 2 Lesley Retail Centre
Boucher Road, Belfast
Tel: 028 9038 1868

*Connswater*
Arches Retail Park
Bridge End, Belfast
Tel: 028 9045 0505

*Londonderry*
Unit 1 Lesley Retail Park
Londonderry
Tel: 028 7127 5500

*Newtownabbey*
Unit 1 Shore Road Retail Park
Newtownabbey
Tel: 028 9086 9888

LA Fitness
Ramada Hotel, Shaws Bridge
Belfast, BT8 7XT
Tel: 028 9064 1800
Fax: 028 9064 1611

*Belfast*
Adelaide Street, Belfast
Tel: 028 9032 8816

*Armagh*
Armagh City Hotel
Friary Road, Armagh
Tel: 028 3752 5705

Living Well Health Clubs
Hilton Belfast
Lanyon Place, Belfast
Tel: 028 9027 7490

Hilton Templepatrick
Castle Upton Estate,
Templepatrick
Tel: 028 9443 5566

Newforge Leisure & Fitness Club
18B Newforge Lane, Belfast
Tel: 028 9068 5117

Peak Physique
721A Lisburn Road, Belfast
Tel: 028 9066 7887

*Queen's Arcade, Belfast*

## Shopping in Northern Ireland

It would be impossible to take a comprehensive look at lifestyle and leisure in Northern Ireland without taking into consideration one particular leisure activity – shopping!

In recent years, Northern Ireland has begun to attract the large national retail chains, which had, to a large extent previously been absent from Northern Ireland's high streets. Leading this influx has been the large supermarket chains of Sainsbury's and Tesco, both of which now have a significant presence in towns and cities across Northern Ireland. Many of the larger of these supermarkets offer extended opening times, some even opening 24 hours.

British department store Debenham's, which has been the flagship store in Castle Court for many years has also opened additional outlets in Northern Ireland, at Craigavon and Newry. Despite the presence of many of the large national and international chains, there are some not yet present in Northern Ireland, such as Scandinavian furniture giant, IKEA, which, despite rumours has yet to find a suitable location in the province. Similarly Dublin department store Brown Thomas has not yet established a presence in the north. There are plans for the location of Northern Ireland's first John Lewis store, at a site near the existing Sprucefield development.

A recent survey has shown Belfast to be in the top 20 retail centres in the UK – coming in at number 17. Belfast's attraction lies in its compact retail centre based, to a large extent, around the Royal Avenue and Donegall Place areas. In the survey the city ranked positively in terms of accessibility and also car-parking, but less well in terms of public transport provision and shopper facilities.

One trend in shopping in Northern Ireland has seen the development of many large 'out-of-town' retail centres which often have the appeal of being less congested than town centres and easily accessible by car. An added benefit is that these retail areas often offer free parking, unlike town centres where parking can cost anything up to £1.60 per hour.

There is concern in some quarters that the development of these large retail parks, with the incoming national chains, will have a detrimental effect on Northern Ireland's family-run businesses, which have in many cases operated in town centres for long numbers of years. Some also fear that by taking shoppers away from town centres, traditional shopping areas will become deserted and run-down and that this will lead to a deterioration in the overall appearance of our towns.

Another trend which is starting to emerge in Northern Ireland is that of 'factory outlet villages' such as The Linen Green in Moygashel, which has been operating for a number of years on the site of a former linen mill near Dungannon. These outlet villages see top, often designer, names (such as Paul Costello or Ramsay) set up outlet or discount stores selling their goods at greatly reduced prices. In 2004, Northern Ireland's first and only international outlet shopping centre opened with over 50 stores at Junction One near Antrim.

Some of Northern Ireland's most exclusive retail outlets are to be found, not in the largest cities and towns but in provincial villages and small towns such as Holywood, Hillsborough or Moira.

*Castlecourt, Belfast*

*Royal Avenue, Belfast*

*Castlecourt*

It is becoming increasingly common for people to visit these towns to spend time browsing amongst the unique shops selling unusual, often hand-crafted goods or services (such as Scandinavian wood products, luxury food items, upmarket interior design services). Shopping is then combined with a visit to a local coffee bar or delicatessen for refreshment!

The trend for shopping and the 'café lifestyle' is most apparent in Belfast's trendy Lisburn Road area, which offers a host of designer shops along with a wide variety of eateries, perfect for whiling away an idle Saturday afternoon!

Below is a list of Northern Ireland's main shopping centres, arranged in a convenient A-Z format.

## Shopping Centres

Abbey Centre
Longwood Road
Newtownabbey
Tel: 028 9086 8018

Ards Shopping Centre
22C Circular Road
Newtownards
Tel: 028 9181 5444

Bloomfield Centre
South Circular Road, Bangor
Tel: 028 9127 0797

Bow Street Mall
Bow Street, Lisburn
Tel: 028 9267 5438

Buttercrane Shopping Centre
Buttercrane Quay, Newry
Tel: 028 3026 4627

Carryduff Shopping Centre
Church Road, Carryduff
Tel: 028 9081 3001

Castle Centre
Market Square, Antrim
Tel: 028 9442 8269

Castle Court
Royal Avenue, Belfast
Tel: 028 9023 4591

Connswater Shopping Centre
Bloomfield Avenue, Belfast
Tel: 028 9045 0111

Diamond Centre
Bridge Street, Coleraine
Tel: 028 7032 1123

Donegall Arcade
5-7 Castle Place, Belfast
Tel: 028 9043 9562

Erneside Shopping Centre
The Point, Enniskillen
Tel: 028 6632 5705

Fairhill Shopping Centre
Fairhill Lane, Ballymena
Tel: 028 2565 1199

The Flagship Centre
Main Street, Bangor
Tel: 028 9145 6700

Flax Centre
Ardoyne Avenue, Belfast
Tel: 028 9059 3366

Forestside Shopping Centre
Upper Galwally, Belfast
Tel: 028 9049 4990

Foyleside Shopping Centre
Orchard Street, Londonderry
Tel: 028 7137 7575

High Street Mall
High Street, Portadown
Tel: 028 3836 2251

InShops Centres Ltd
Hi Park Centre
High Street, Belfast
Tel: 028 9032 9719

Junction One
Ballymena Road, Antrim
Tel: 028 9442 9111

Kennedy Centre
Falls Road, Belfast
Tel: 028 9020 3303

Lisburn Square
3 Lisburn Square, Lisburn
Tel: 028 9264 1384

**Lisnagelvin Shopping Centre**
Lisnagelvin Road, Londonderry
Tel: 028 7132 9336

**The Mall Shopping Centre**
The Mall West, Armagh
Tel: 028 3751 8336

**Meadow Lane Shopping Centre**
Moneymore Road, Magherafelt
Tel: 028 7963 4081

**Meadows Shopping Centre**
Meadow Lane, Portadown
Tel: 028 3836 3000

**Millennium Court**
William Street, Portadown
Tel: 028 3835 1710

**Northcott Shopping Centre**
Ballyclare Road, Glengormley
Tel: 028 9034 2977

**Oaks Centre**
Oaks Road, Dungannon
Tel: 028 8772 9694

**Park Centre**
Donegall Road, Belfast
Tel: 028 9032 3451

**The Quays**
The Quays, Newry
Tel: 028 3025 6000

**Richmond Shopping Centre**
Richmond Street, Londonderry
Tel: 028 7126 0525

**Rushmere Shopping**
Central Way, Craigavon
Tel: 028 3834 3350

**Springhill Shopping Centre**
Killeen Avenue, Bangor
Tel: 028 9127 0185

**Tower Centre**
Wellington Street, Ballymena
Tel: 028 2564 8921

**Westwood Centre**
Kennedy Way, Belfast
Tel: 028 9061 1255

**Yorkgate Centre**
100-150 York Street, Belfast
Tel: 028 9074 0990

*Donegall Arcade, Belfast*

*Junction One, Antrim*

*Shoppers in Belfast*

Carrick-a-Rede Rope Bridge, Co Antrim

Visitors Guide to Northern Ireland

# Chapter 14

## Introduction

This chapter of the Northern Ireland Yearbook 2005 aims to provide useful information for anyone visiting Northern Ireland. It includes details of how to get here, the public transport system as well as a comprehensive list of where to stay and things to see and do. Further information in relation to places to eat, culture and the arts and other leisure activities is included in Chapter 13. We hope that the practical information, timetables, reservations contacts and general information will be of interest and practical use to those visiting Northern Ireland and also those arranging trips for family, friends and colleagues.

## Travelling to and From Northern Ireland

### By Air

Northern Ireland has three airports: Belfast International, Belfast City and City of Derry which between them serve a variety of destinations in the UK and beyond. In addition to the regular year-round services, there are also a large number of flights from Northern Ireland airports to popular holiday destinations during the summer months. It should be noted that lists are subject to change, and new routes may be added. Passengers are advised to check with airlines for confirmation of flight operating schedules.

### Belfast International Airport

Belfast, BT29 4AB
Tel: 028 9448 4848
Web: www.bial.co.uk
Email: info.desk@bial.co.uk

Belfast International Airport is also known as Aldergrove, and is the largest of the three airports in Northern Ireland. Situated near Templepatrick, 20 miles outside Belfast, it is one of the busiest airports in the United Kingdom, carrying over 4 million passengers annually. The airport operates 24 hours a day, 365 days per year as it is not subject to any noise restrictions. During 2003 Concorde paid a visit to Belfast International Airport during its final tour of the UK prior to being withdrawn from service. During his visit to Northern Ireland President Bush, with his Airforce One entourage, also landed at Belfast International Airport.

**Flight Information**

Airlines currently operating from Belfast International Airport and the destinations to which they fly are as follows:

**Flights from Belfast International Airport**

| Destination | Carrier | Booking Line |
|---|---|---|
| Alicante | easyjet | 0870 6000 000 |
| Amsterdam | easyJet | 0870 6000 000 |
| Bristol | easyJet | 0870 6000 000 |
| Edinburgh | easyJet | 0870 6000 000 |
| Glasgow | easyJet | 0870 6000 000 |
| Liverpool | easyJet | 0870 6000 000 |
| London Luton | easyJet | 0870 6000 000 |
| London Stansted | easyJet | 0870 6000 000 |
| London Gatwick | easyJet | 0870 6000 000 |
| Malaga | easyjet | 0870 6000 000 |
| Newcastle | easyJet | 0870 6000 000 |
| Nice | easyjet | 0870 6000 000 |
| Paris CDG | easyjet | 0870 6000 000 |
| Barcelona | Jet2.com | 0870 737 8282 |
| Leeds Bradford | Jet2.com | 0870 737 8282 |
| Prague | Jet2.com | 0870 737 8282 |
| Aberdeen | Eastern Airways | 01652 680600 |
| Manchester | bmibaby | 08702 642229 |
| Cardiff | bmibaby | 08702 642229 |
| Teesside | bmibaby | 08702 642229 |
| East Midlands | bmibaby | 08702 642229 |

**Flights from Belfast City Airport**

| | | |
|---|---|---|
| Birmingham | flybe | 08705 676676 |
| Bristol | flybe | 08705 676676 |
| Edinburgh | flybe | 08705 676676 |
| Exeter | flybe | 08705 676676 |
| Glasgow | flybe | 08705 676676 |
| Isle of Man | flybe | 08705 676676 |
| Jersey | flybe | 08705 676676 |
| Leeds Bradford | flybe | 08705 676676 |
| London City | flybe | 08705 676676 |
| London Gatwick | flybe | 08705 676676 |
| Newcastle | flybe | 08705 676676 |
| Southampton | flybe | 08705 676676 |
| Blackpool | Flykeen | 0800 083 7783 |
| Isle of Man | Flykeen | 0800 083 7783 |
| Manchester | British Airways | 0870 850 9850 |
| London Heathrow | bmi | 01332 854000 |
| Cork | Aer Arann | 0800 587 2324 |

**Flights from Derry City Airport**

| | | |
|---|---|---|
| Birmingham | Aer Arann | 0800 587 2324 |
| London Stansted | ryanair | 0871 246 0000 |
| Dublin | British Airways | 0870 850 9850 |
| Glasgow | British Airways | 0870 850 9850 |
| Manchester | Aer Arann | 0800 587 2324 |

*EasyJet*
Amsterdam, Bristol, Liverpool, London Luton, London Gatwick, Newcastle, Glasgow, Edinburgh, London Stansted, Alicante, Malaga, Nice and Paris CDG.
To book: Online at www.easyJet.com
Booking line: 0870 6000 000

Note that check-in for all easyJet flights closes 40 minutes prior to departure.

*Jet2.com*
Barcelona, Leeds Bradford, Prague
To book: Online at www.jet2.com
Booking line: 0870 737 8282

*Eastern Airways*
Aberdeen
To book: Online at www.easternairways.com
Booking line: 01652 680600

*bmibaby*
Manchester, Cardiff, Teeside, East Midlands
To book: Online at www.bmibaby.com
Booking line: 0870 264 2229

**Other passenger information**

*Access*

Belfast International Airport is located around 20 miles outside Belfast, near the village of Templepatrick. It is served by the Airbus, which leaves every 30 minutes from Belfast's Great Victoria Street bus centre. Single ticket from Belfast to the Airport is £6.00, with a return costing £9.00. For more information on the Airbus service go to www.translink.co.uk or telephone the information line on 028 9066 6630.

*Parking*

All Belfast International Airport car parks operate a 'pay-on-foot' system and payment machines are located in the exit hall of the terminal and in each of the car parks. Payment is accepted by cash or alternatively ticketless car parking is available through use of a credit card on entry to and exit from the car park.

The short term car park is located close to the terminal building and is ideal for short stays or pick-up. Additional days will be charged at £17 per day or part thereof.

The main car park offers the best value parking for up to 3 days so is suitable for short business trips or weekends.

Additional days will be charged at £6.00 per day or part thereof. The long stay car park is located within easy walking distance of the terminal building, and is regularly patrolled. Pre-booked car parking is available in the long stay car park for passengers parking for 7 days or more. To pre-book contact the booking centre on 0870 013 4747. Additional days will be charged at £3.00 per day or part thereof.

**Belfast International Airport Car Parking Rates**

| | |
|---|---|
| **Short Term Tariffs** | |
| 15 mins | £0.60 |
| up to 30 mins | £2.00 |
| 30mins – 1hr | £3.50 |
| 1-1.5hrs | £4.50 |
| 1.5hrs – 2hrs | £5.50 |
| 2 – 4hrs | £7.00 |
| 4 – 6hrs | £9.00 |
| 6 – 8hrs | £11.00 |
| 8 – 12hrs | £16.00 |
| 12 – 24hrs | £18.00 |
| 24 – 48hrs | £29.00 |
| **Main Stay Tariffs** | |
| Up to 1hr | £3.00 |
| Up to 2hrs | £3.50 |
| Up to 1 day | £7.00 |
| Up to 2 days | £14.00 |
| Up to 3 days | £20.00 |
| Up to 4 days | £26.00 |
| **Long Stay Tariffs** | |
| Up to 2hrs | £10.00 |
| Up to 7 days | £26.00 |
| Up to 8 days | £29.00 |
| Up to 9 days | £32.00 |
| Up to 10 days | £35.00 |
| Up to 11 days | £38.00 |
| Up to 12 days | £41.00 |
| Up to 13 days | £44.00 |
| Up to 14 days | £47.00 |

**Car parking at Belfast International Airport is also provided by:**

*Boal Car Park*
Tel: 028 9445 3812

*McCausland Car Park*
Tel: 028 9442 2022

*Cosmo Car Park*
Tel: 028 9445 2565

**Car Hire**

Car hire from Belfast International Airport is available through:

*Avis Rent A Car*
Tel: 028 9442 2333

*Hertz*
Tel: 028 9442 2533

*Budget*
Tel: 028 9442 3332

*National Car Rental*
Tel: 0870 191 0605

*Europcar*
Tel: 028 9442 3444

*Thrifty Car Rental*
Tel: 028 9442 2777

In addition to passenger services, Belfast International Airport is the fifth largest regional air cargo centre in the UK. Aircraft handling agents at the airport include:

*Aer Lingus*
Tel: 028 9442 2735
Fax: 028 9442 2493

*BA World Cargo*
Tel: 028 9442 2995
Fax: 028 9445 2570

*Servisair*
Tel: 028 9442 2574
Fax: 028 9442 2070

*Reed Aviation*
Tel: 028 9448 4929

## Belfast City Airport

Belfast, BT3 9JH, Tel: 028 9093 9093
Web: www.belfastcityairport.com
Email: info@belfastcityairport.com

Belfast City Airport is located just three miles outside Belfast on the southern shore of Belfast Lough. The Airport is on the site of a former airfield used by Shorts Manufacturing Company. The Airport has recently undergone a major refurbishment and passenger traffic has grown rapidly as the airport serves more and more destinations. There are plans to further develop facilities at the airport to enable the accommodation of larger planes and more frequent flights, however, there is some local opposition to this, especially in relation to late-night flights.

**Flight information**

Airlines currently operating from Belfast City Airport and the destinations to which they fly are as follows:

*flybe*
Birmingham, Bristol, London Gatwick, Leeds Bradford, London City, Newcastle, Southampton, Glasgow, Edinburgh, Exeter, Isle of Man, Jersey
To book: Online at www.flybe.com
Tel: 08705 676 676

*Flykeen:* Blackpool, Isle of Man
To book: Online at www.flykeen.com
Tel: 0800 083 7783

*British Airways:* Manchester
To book: Tel: 0870 850 9850

*bmi:*
London Heathrow
To book: Online at www.flybmi.com
Tel: 01332 854000

**Other passenger information**

*Access*

Belfast City Airport is located just a couple of miles outside the city. It can be accessed by rail services to Sydenham from both Great Victoria Street and Central Stations. A shuttle bus service operates to bring passengers from the railway station to the terminal building.

It is also served by Belfast City Airlink, a bus service which leaves the airport terminal for Great Victoria Street Bus Station every 40 minutes, at a cost of £2.50 for a single journey. Number 21 Citybus operates every 20 minutes from Sydenham railway station (a 5 minute walk from the terminal building) to the City Hall in the city centre.

The Airporter service operates 6 coaches daily to Londonderry. For booking information contact 028 7136 9996.

**Belfast City Airport Car Parking Rates**

| | |
|---|---|
| **Short Stay Tariffs** | |
| First 15 mins | £0.50 |
| Up to 30 mins | £1.70 |
| 30 mins – 1hr | £2.70 |
| 1 – 1.5hrs | £4.00 |
| 1.5 – 2hrs | £5.00 |
| 2 – 4hrs | £7.00 |
| 4 – 8hrs | £11.00 |
| 8 – 12hrs | £14.00 |
| 12 – 24hrs | £16.00 |
| **Main Stay Tariffs** | |
| First 15 mins | £0.50 |
| Up to 2hrs | £3.00 |
| 2 – 24hrs | £7.00 |
| 1 – 2 days | £14.00 |
| 2 – 3 days | £20.00 |
| 3 – 4 days | £26.00 |
| 4 – 5 days | £30.00 |
| 5 – 6 days | £32.00 |
| 6 – 7 days | £32.00 |
| £2.50 per day thereafter | |

**Car Hire**

Car hire from Belfast City Airport is available through:

*Avis Rent A Car*
Tel: 028 9045 2017

*Europcar*
Tel: 028 9045 0904

*Hertz*
Tel: 028 9073 2451

*Budget*
Tel: 028 9045 1111

*National Car Rental*
Tel: 028 9073 9400

## City of Derry Airport

Airport Road, Eglinton, BT47 3GY
Tel: 028 7181 0784
Web: www.cityofderryairport.com
Email: info@cityofderryairport.com

City of Derry Airport (formerly Eglinton Airport) has undergone significant development in recent years with passenger numbers increasing from 61,461 in 1997 to 204,390 in 2002.

**Flight Information**

Destinations served from City of Derry Airport are: London Stansted, Manchester, Glasgow, Dublin, Birmingham, Majorca, Lanzarote and Reus (Salou). Detailed timetable information can be accessed at www.cityofderryairport.com.
To book contact airlines directly as follows:

*Ryanair*
Flights to London Stansted and connecting flights to UK and Europe via Stansted and Dublin.
To book: Online at www.ryanair.com
Booking line: 0871 246 0000

*British Airways*
Direct flights to Glasgow and Dublin with connecting flights via these airports.
To book: Online at www.britishairways.com
Booking line: 0870 850 9850

*Aer Arran*
Direct flights to Birmingham and Manchester
To book: Online at www.aerarran.ie
Booking line: 0800 587 2324

**Other passenger information**

*Access*

The airport is located 7 miles north-east of Derry City on the main A2 Derry to Coleraine road. A typical taxi fare to Derry City Centre from the airport is around £8.00. The airport is served by bus from Derry's Foyle Street bus station.

**Derry City Airport Car Parking Rates**

| | |
|---|---|
| **Short Stay Tariffs** | |
| First 15 mins | Free |
| Up to 30 mins | £2.00 |
| 30 mins – 1hr | £2.70 |
| 1hr – 2hrs | £3.50 |
| Over 2hrs | £7.00 |
| **Long Stay Tariffs** | |
| Up to 1 day | £7.00 |
| Up to 2 days | £13.00 |
| Up to 3 days | £19.00 |
| Up to 7 days | £24.00 |
| Up to 8 days | £27.00 |
| Up to 9 days | £29.00 |
| Up to 10 days | £32.00 |
| Up to 11 days | £34.00 |
| Up to 12 days | £36.00 |
| Up to 13 days | £38.00 |
| Up to 14 days | £40.00 |
| Subsequent days | £3.00 |

**Car Hire**

*Abe King:* 028 9335 2557

*Ford:* 028 7136 7137

*Avis:* 028 7181 1708

*Hertz:* 028 7181 1994

*Europcar:* 028 7181 2773

## Travelling by Sea

### Seacat

Seacat Terminal
Donegall Quay
Belfast, BT1 3AL
Operations Manager: John Burrows

From Belfast, Seacat operates services to both Troon and the Isle of Man. Both are fast craft services carrying cars and passengers but not freight.

For 2005 the Troon service is in operation from 18th March, with 2 services per day in the off-peak season (March-June and September-October) and three services per day in the peak summer season (July and August).

Belfast to the Isle of Man operates twice per week from March until September with a crossing time of 2 hours 45 minutes.

For detailed passenger information or reservations: Tel: 08705 523 523
www.seacat.co.uk

### Stenaline

Stenaline operates services on the Belfast to Stranraer route using both the Stena HSS, which makes the crossing in 1 hour 45 minutes and their Superferry on which the sailing takes 3 hours 15 minutes. Latest check in times for all services is 30 minutes before sailing.

Stenaline also operates the Larne to Fleetwood service, which takes 8-9 hours. Both routes operate all year round.

**For reservations:** Tel: 028 9074 7747
**Ferry check:** Tel: 08705 755 755
www7.stenaline.co.uk

### P&O Irish Sea

P&O operates services from Larne to Troon and Cairnryan. The Larne to Troon service is seasonal – exact details of dates are not yet available for 2005. The Larne to Cairnryan route operates all year round and is serviced by both fast craft vessels and the traditional ferry.

For detailed passenger information or reservations: Tel: 0870 2424 777
Web: www.poirishsea.com

### Norse Merchant Ferries

In addition to their freight services, Norse Merchant Ferries operates a passenger service between Belfast and Liverpool. There are 12 sailings weekly with the night cruiser service operating from Monday to Sunday and the day breaker service in operation Tuesday to Saturday. The crossing takes 8 hours and latest check in time for all sailings is 1 hour before sailing.

For detailed passenger information or reservations:
Tel: 0870 600 4321
www.norsemerchant.com

## By Rail

### To and from Dublin

The Enterprise is a direct rail service which runs from Belfast to Dublin 8 times daily in each direction (5 times on Sunday). The service departs from Central Station and stops at Portadown and Newry en route to Dublin. The journey takes around 2 hours. For further details on the Enterprise service and for other rail services see information on Translink and NI Railways included later in the chapter on page 474.

*Lisburn Station*

### To and from Great Britain

NIR Travel operates a 'Rail and Sail' service to Great Britain using Stena Line to sail to Stranraer and Seacat to sail to Troon. Passengers make their own way to the port in Belfast, where they travel as a foot passenger on the boat, they then board a train in Scotland for onward travel to destinations throughout Great Britain or onwards to Europe if required. Full details of this service can be obtained from NIR Travel on 028 9024 2420.

## By Bus

### To and from Dublin

Ulsterbus Service 200 runs from Belfast's Europa Bus Centre to Busaras in Dublin serving Dublin Airport en route. The service runs 8 times daily Monday – Saturday and 5 times on Sundays and the journey takes approximately 3 hours. For further details on bus services see information on Ulsterbus included later in the chapter.

### To and from Great Britain

Ulsterbus Tours operate a service to Great Britain where passengers board their bus at Belfast's Europa Bus Centre, which takes them to the ferry port, where they board the ferry as a foot passenger. On disembarking, they then board a bus for onward travel to destinations throughout Great Britain or onwards to Europe if required. Full details of this service can be obtained from Ulsterbus Tours on 028 9033 7002/3.

# Getting Around Northern Ireland

## The Public Transport System

The provision of public transport services in Northern Ireland is overseen by the Northern Ireland Transport Holding Company (NITHCo). NITHCo is responsible to the Department for Regional Development for the operation of its subsidiary companies Citybus, Northern Ireland Railways and Ulsterbus. These companies are responsible for the delivery of public transport services. The role of NITHCo is to approve the strategic direction of the operating companies, which each retain their legal status but are marketed under the generic brand-name of Translink. The operations of Citybus, NI Railways and Ulsterbus are managed by a single integrated Executive Team.

## Translink

Translink currently employs approximately 3,500 employees and over 75 million passenger journeys are made on its services each year.

The company is split into 6 divisions:

**Operations, Marketing and Human Resources**
Central Station
East Bridge Street, Belfast, BT1 3PB
Tel: 028 9089 9400

**Finance, Infrastructure and Property**
Milewater Road, Belfast, BT3 9BG
Tel: 028 9035 1201

**Mechanical Engineering**
York Road, Belfast

Chief Executive: Keith Moffatt

Detailed passenger information for all Translink services can be obtained from the General Enquiries Line on 028 9066 6630. This is also available as a Textphone service on 028 9038 7505. Alternatively updated information is available online at www.translink.co.uk.

## Citybus Services

Bus services within the Greater Belfast area are operated by Citybus. This includes approximately 60 routes in Belfast, serviced by a fleet of over 250 buses. Traditionally Citybuses have been red, but newer buses are being introduced which are green and red in colour. Citybus services depart and terminate in the city centre, but always display the route name and number of their outward journey (even on inward journeys to the city centre).

**Bus Lanes**

Citybus are gradually introducing a system of Quality Bus Corridors (QBCs) on main arterial routes into the city. With specially designated bus lanes and low floor buses these lead to faster journey times. Currently operating are QBCs from Newtownabbey (City Express) and from the Ormeau Road and Four Winds in the south of the city. These are the first of 15 routes to be introduced in Belfast.

**Park and Ride**

Park and ride facilities are currently available in East Belfast at Station Street, Bridge Street and Middlepath Street. The park and ride facility serving North Belfast is located at York Street.

**Easibus**

The Easibus network has been designed to meet local community needs by providing a service to health centres and clinics, local shops, housing for the elderly and a main shopping centre in the area. Easibus services do not follow normal Citybus practice of starting and finishing in the city centre, but instead serve local communities.
The Easibus service in Belfast currently serves the areas around the Connswater, Forestside and Abbey Centre retail areas. There are also Easibus services operating in Bangor and Derry.

For more information on the Easibus service contact a local Translink depot or the general Translink enquiry line on 028 9066 6630 or:

Belfast: Tel: 028 9073 1117
Bangor: Tel: 028 9127 1143 or
028 9147 0111
Derry: Tel: 028 7126 8688

**Nightlink**

8 Nightlink services provide a late night service from Belfast City Centre to various local towns. All services depart from Donegall Square West on Saturdays only at 0100 and 0200. The fare is £3.50 per person.

Nightlink serves the following destinations:

- Antrim
- Ballynahinch (0100) and Ballynahinch/Downpatrick (0200)
- Bangor
- Carrickfergus
- Comber/Ballygowan
- Lisburn
- Newtownabbey
- Newtownards

**Centrelink**

Belfast's main bus and rail stations, as well as principal shopping areas and the Waterfront Hall are linked by the Centrelink service (100), which is supported by the Department for Regional Development and Marks and Spencer. Rail and bus users with valid tickets can use the service for free, otherwise a Day Ticket can be purchased which allows passengers to get on and off the bus as often as required over the course of a single day. The service operates every 12 minutes at peak periods.

**Citybus Ticketing**

*Smartlink*

In 2003 Translink introduced a new system of ticketing using the Smartlink card. Smartlink is a plastic card which can be loaded with either a certain number of journeys in advance (the Smartlink Multi-Journey Card) or a week or month's worth of unlimited travel (the Smartlink Travel Card).

*Smartlink Multi-Journey Card*

This card can be loaded with a number of journeys from a minimum of 5 to 40 at any one time. The card holds a maximum of 50 journeys in total, which are valid for 3 months from date of purchase. The card offers a saving of 22% on standard single journey fares.

*Smartlink Travel Cards*
These cards allow unlimited travel across the Citybus network for either 1 week or 1 month (discounted rates are available for children's travel cards). Weekly cards are valid for 7 consecutive days from date of first use (not purchase) and monthly cards are valid for a calendar month from date of first use. Smartlink Multi-Journey and Travel Cards can be bought or topped up at ticket agents in the Greater Belfast area and at the Citybus kiosk in Donegall Square West.

*Day Tickets*
Day Tickets offer unlimited travel on all Citybus services including the extended zone. These are available from the driver onboard.

**Citybus Contacts**
Director of Operations: Philip O'Neill
Tel: 028 9089 9408

Central Area Operations Manager:
Billy Gilpin
Tel: 028 9035 4061

*Citybus Depots and District Managers*
Falls: Damien Bannon
Tel: 028 9030 1732

Newtownabbey: Gerry Mullan
Tel: 028 9036 5355

Short Strand: Roy Sloan
Tel: 028 9045 8345

**Citybus Ticket and Information Kiosk:**
Donegall Square West
Opening hours:
Monday – Saturday
0800 – 1800
Closed Sunday

**Translink Information Line**
General Travel Enquiries:
Tel: 028 9066 6630
Textphone: 028 9038 7505
Open 0700–2200,
364 days per year

Private Hire Enquiries/Tours Enquiries/Credit Card Bookings:
Tel: 028 9045 8484

Lost Property Enquiries:
Tel: 028 9045 8345
Open 0900 – 1330
Monday – Friday

## Ulsterbus Services

Ulsterbus is responsible for virtually all bus services in Northern Ireland except those in the Greater Belfast area which are operated by Citybus. Ulsterbus currently has 21 main passenger facilities across Northern Ireland, employing 1,250 drivers and operating approximately 1,100 buses.

From Belfast, North and East bound Ulsterbus services depart from the Laganside Buscentre while those going to the South and West depart from the Europa Buscentre in Great Victoria Street.

The Goldline service is a high frequency express service to all main towns Northern Ireland wide. Goldline service 200 runs between Belfast (Europa Buscentre) and Dublin 8 times daily from Monday to Saturday and 5 times on Sundays with a journey time of approximately 3 hours.

**Flexibus**
Flexibus offers minibus and mini-coach hire (for up to 25 people) in the greater Belfast area and throughout Northern Ireland, and also carries out contract work for schools, churches and industry. Flexibus has a fleet of over 40 vehicles including a replica of a 1930s Charabanc.

For further information or a quotation contact Flexibus:
Tel: 028 9023 3933
Fax: 028 9031 5991

**Ulsterbus Ticketing**
*Return tickets*
Offer a saving over the cost of two single tickets.

*Ten Journey Tickets*
Valid for 10 journeys in either direction between specific points for one month from date of purchase.

*40 Journey Commuter Tickets*
Valid for 40 single journeys within 3 months from date of purchase. Two or more people can travel together on the same ticket providing the ticket holder travels the further distance. These tickets are transferable so can be passed on to someone else to make the same journey on Ulsterbus.

*Monthly Tickets*
Valid for unlimited travel between designated points one month from date of purchase.

*Sunday Rambler Tickets*
Unlimited travel on all scheduled Ulsterbus services within Northern Ireland on Sundays.

**Ulsterbus Contacts**
General Travel Enquiries:
Open 0700–2200, 364 days per year
Tel: 028 9066 6630 /
Textphone: 028 9038 7505

Ulsterbus Coach Hire: Contact local bus depot or Tel: 028 9033 7006

*Ulsterbus Tours Travel Centre*
Europa Bus Centre, Glengall Street
Belfast, BT12 5AH
Tel: 028 9033 7004

Lost Property Enquiries:
Tel: 028 9033 7000

**Main Ulsterbus Stations**

| | |
|---|---|
| Belfast Europa: | 028 9033 7001 |
| Belfast Laganside: | 028 9033 7015 |
| Antrim: | 028 9442 8729 |
| Armagh: | 028 3752 2266 |
| Ballyclare: | 028 9335 2311 |
| Ballymena: | 028 2565 2214 |
| Banbridge: | 028 4062 3633 |
| Bangor: | 028 9127 1143 |
| Coleraine: | 028 7032 5400 |
| Cookstown: | 028 8676 6440 |
| Craigavon: | 028 3834 2511 |
| Derry City: | 028 7126 2261 |
| Downpatrick: | 028 4461 2384 |
| Dungannon: | 028 8772 2251 |
| Enniskillen: | 028 6632 2633 |
| Larne: | 028 2827 2345 |
| Limavady: | 028 7776 2101 |
| Lisburn: | 028 9266 2091 |
| Londonderry County: | 028 7126 2261 |
| Magherafelt: | 028 7963 2218 |
| Newcastle: | 028 4372 2296 |
| Newry: | 028 3026 3531 |
| Newtownabbey: | 028 9036 5355 |
| Newtownards: | 028 9181 2391 |
| Omagh: | 028 8224 2711 |
| Strabane: | 028 7138 2393 |

## Northern Ireland Railways Services

The present railway system in Northern Ireland comprises approximately 210 route miles, including the Belfast/Dublin main line, a line to Coleraine and Londonderry, with a branch line from Coleraine to Portrush, and suburban routes from Belfast to Portadown, Bangor and Larne. The Antrim/Bleach Green line was re-opened in 2001 as part of a £16.2 million project which is planned to include new stations at Mossley West and Templepatrick. NI Railways currently employs around 700 staff.

NI Railways trains are a mixture of two types of diesel train dating from the 1970s and 1980s but procurement is currently underway to replace 23 train sets to replace the oldest existing trains. This project is expected to be completed with the new trains in service by 2005/06.

In addition to its passenger services, NI Railways also operates both a parcel and freight service.

### Stations

NI Railways has in recent years undertaken a major building and refurbishment programme to upgrade and replace many of its main stations. Belfast's new Central Station was officially opened by the Minister for Regional Development in March 2003 and includes an extended park and ride scheme as well as a new traffic management system. Major projects have also been completed at Bangor, Coleraine and Carrickfergus.

### Enterprise Service

The Enterprise is the flagship Belfast to Dublin service which is jointly operated by Iarnród Eireann and NI Railways. 8 services operate in each direction Monday to Saturday and 5 services run in each direction on Sundays. Passengers in possession of a valid Enterprise ticket are entitled to free onward travel on the Centrelink service in Belfast and via the Dart between Connolly Station and Tara Street in Dublin.

The executive 1st Plus service on the Enterprise allows passengers to reserve a seat in advance. 1st Plus passengers can also avail of half price secure parking at Belfast Central Station on presentation of a 1st Plus ticket.

*Ticket and Seat Reservations:*
Belfast Tel: 028 9089 9409
Dublin Tel: 01 703 4070

### NIR Travel

NIR Travel provides short break holidays by rail with hotel breaks available in both Dublin and Scotland.

For more information contact:
028 9024 2420

### NI Railways Ticketing

*Single*
Valid on day of issue only, between two stations.

*Day Return*
Valid on day of issue only, with return journey on the same day.

*Monthly Return*
Outward journey is valid on day of issue only, return journey is valid up to one month from the date shown on the ticket.

*7 Day Weekly Ticket*
Seven days' unlimited travel between any two designated stations, valid from Monday to Sunday.

*Monthly Moneysavers*
Unlimited travel between any two designated stations for a full calendar month plus unrestricted travel over the entire NI Railways network at weekends.

*Contract Tickets*
Books of 40 single tickets may be purchased for some journeys in Northern Ireland. For further details contact Translink's general enquiries line on 028 9066 6630.

*Sunday Day Tracker*
Unlimited travel on all scheduled train services within Northern Ireland.

*Group Travel*
Discount of up to 15% for parties of 10 or more passengers on all services. Further details are available from NIR Travel on 028 9024 2420.

### Cross Border Rail Tickets

*Single*
Available for Enterprise Class and 1st Plus travel.

*Day Return*
Available Monday to Thursday and on Saturday for Enterprise Class only. (This is a promotional ticket and may be withdrawn at any time).

*Family Day Return*
Available for Enterprise Class only and valid for two adults and up to four children.

*One Month Return*
Available for 1st Plus and Enterprise Class travel. Return journey is valid for up to one month from date shown on ticket.

*Family One Month Return*
Available for Enterprise Class travel only and valid for two adults and up to four children.

*Cross Border Contract Tickets*
Books of 20 single journey tickets are available between Belfast/Dublin and Portadown/Dublin. Contact NIR Travel on 028 9024 2420 for further information.

*7 Day Weekly Ticket*
7 days' unlimited travel between Portadown or Newry to selected cross border stations (valid Monday – Sunday).

### NI Railways Contacts

General Travel Enquiries:
Tel: 028 9066 6630
Textphone: 028 9038 7505
Open 0700 – 2200,
364 days per year
Lost Property Enquiries:
Tel: 028 9074 1700

Credit/debit card sales
and reservations:
Tel: 028 9089 9409

### NI Railways Managers

Rail Services Manager: Seamus Scallon
Conductors Standards Manager:
Hilton Parr
Enterprise Manager: Ken McKnight

Each of the above managers can be contacted at Central Station, Belfast on 028 9089 9400.

**Main Northern Ireland Railway Stations**

| | |
|---|---|
| Botanic | 028 9089 9400 |
| Central | 028 9089 9400 |
| Great Victoria Street | 028 9043 4424 |
| Yorkgate | 028 9074 1700 |
| Antrim | 028 9446 9051 |
| Ballymena | 028 2565 2277 |
| Ballymoney | 028 2766 3241 |
| Bangor | 028 9127 1143 |
| Carrickfergus | 028 9335 1286 |
| Coleraine | 028 7032 5400 |
| Larne | 028 2826 0604 |
| Lisburn | 028 9266 2294 |
| Londonderry | 028 7134 2228 |
| Lurgan | 028 3832 2052 |
| Newry | 028 3026 9271 |
| Portadown | 028 3835 1422 |
| Portrush | 028 7082 2395 |

## Other fare information – bus and rail

### Concession Fares

*Senior Citizens*

Senior citizens (65 years and over) can avail of free travel on bus and rail services throughout Northern Ireland provided they are in possession of a valid Smart Pass.

*Blind Persons*

Blind Persons are entitled to free travel on all scheduled local and cross-border bus and train services on presentation of a Blind Persons Concession Pass.

*Students*

Concessions are available on certain tickets to students on presentation of a valid Translink Student Discount Card.

*Young People/Children*

A 50% reduction is available on all local, cross border and cross channel fares to young persons aged 5-16. Between the ages of 16 and 21 concession fares are available on rail season tickets only.

*Jobseekers/Gateway*

Reduced bus and rail fares are available to any person who is unemployed and seeking active employment, or any person on the Gateway period of a New Deal Initiative on presentation of an authenticated permit and JS40.

### Integrated Bus & Rail Tickets

*Freedom of Northern Ireland Tickets*

1 day, 3 out of 8 day and 7 day Freedom of Northern Ireland Tickets can be purchased from all main bus and rail stations, offering unlimited travel on all bus and rail services throughout Northern Ireland.

*Pupil Tickets*

Pupil tickets are available for return travel from home to school. Application forms are available at main bus and rail stations or from:

Pupil Ticket Office, Translink
Milewater Road, Belfast, BT3 9BG Tel: 028 9035 4074

*Translink Commuter Travelcards*

Commuter Travelcards are valid for 1 year and offer at least 15% discount compared with the purchase of monthly tickets. They provide unlimited travel between two chosen points (by one mode or a combination of modes of travel) and also provide freedom of the Northern Ireland network at weekends.

*Bangor Bus and Rail Station*

*Bangor Ticketline Tickets*

A pilot integrated ticketing scheme operates in the Bangor area. Tickets allow travel on either train or bus between any central zone station and Bangor and outer surrounding areas.

## Airport Connections

For detailed passenger information on all airport services call Translink's General Enquiries line on 028 9066 6630 or access online at www.translink.co.uk

### Belfast International Airport

The Airbus service No 300 operates between Europa Buscentre and Belfast International Airport. The service operates every 30 minutes from 0545 to 2230 Monday to Saturday and approximately every hour from 0615 to 2130 on Sundays.

*Antrim Airlink*

The Antrim Airlink service No 309 operates between Antrim bus and rail stations and Belfast International Airport.

### Belfast City Airport

Belfast City Airlink service No 600 departs from Europa Buscentre to Belfast City Airport serving Sydenham station. Trains operate to Sydenham station from both Great Victoria Street and Central Stations, and these services connect with the Airlink at Sydenham station.

### City of Derry Airport

Ulsterbus Service No 143 from Derry's Foyle Street Bus Station and Service No 234 from Coleraine operate to the City of Derry Airport.

### Dublin Airport

Ulsterbus Goldline Service No 200 operates between Europa Buscentre and Dublin Airport. Enterprise train services to Dublin Connolly leave from Central Station.

## Car Hire and Taxi Services

Car hire is a popular way of exploring Northern Ireland, especially the more remote rural areas which may be less well served by public transport. Cars can be hired from various locations throughout Northern Ireland. Details of car hire firms operating from the 3 airports are detailed earlier in this chapter. *(Other companies across Northern Ireland offering car hire are listed on page 476).*

### Driving Information

General rules of the road are the same as in Great Britain, ie drive on the left; overtake on the right. Speed limits are 30 miles per hour in built up areas, 60mph on single carriageways and 70 mph on motorways and dual carriageways. Seatbelts are compulsory for drivers and all passengers; motorcyclists must wear crash helmets. Parking is available on-street or in car parks.

### Taxis

Taxis are relatively inexpensive in Northern Ireland. Public taxis, often black 'London' Hackney cabs, can pick up in the street or from taxi ranks. Alternatively, there are many private taxi firms, many of which have waiting rooms. In some buildings (such as airports, shopping centres) there will be a freephone available which automatically connects to a local taxi firm.

## Car Hire Companies

A2B Autos
187 Corkey Road, Ballymena, BT44 9JB
Tel: 028 2764 1064

Annagh Motors Car Hire
51 Church Street, Banbridge, BT32 4AA
Tel: 028 4066 2495

Avis Rent a Car
69-71 Great Victoria Street
Belfast, BT2 7AF
Tel: 028 9024 0404

Ballyclare Car Hire
Site 31, Dennison Industrial Estate
Ballyclare, BT39 9EB
Tel: 028 9335 2557

Ballykelly Car & Van Hire
22 Ballykelly Road
Banbridge, BT32 4PS
Tel: 028 4062 4966

Ballymena Car Hire
59 Shankbridge Road
Ballymena, BT42 3DL
Tel: 028 2589 2525

Beatties Car Hire
Quarter Road, Camlough
Bessbrook, BT35 7EY
Tel: 028 3083 9535

Brown & Day
Hilltop Garage, 4 Main Street
Claudy, BT47 4HR
Tel: 028 7133 8102

Budget Rent a Car
Unit 1, 96-102 Great Victoria Street
Belfast, BT2 7BE
Tel: 028 9023 0700

Burnside Vehicle Rentals
Unit 3 Ivan Wilson Complex
277 Dunhill Road
Coleraine, BT51 3QJ
Tel: 0870 444 1451

Carrick Self Drive
77B Irish Quarter West
Carrickfergus, BT38 8BW
Tel: 028 9335 1113

Charles Hurst Ltd
62 Boucher Road
Belfast BT12 6LR
Tel: 028 9038 3539

Comber Commercial Centre
3C Killinchy Street
Comber, BT23 5AP
Tel: 028 9187 3245

Corrigans Car Hire
72 Old Caulfield Road
Dungannon, BT70 3NG
Tel: 028 8776 1482

Dan Dooley Rent a Car
175B Airport Road, Aldergrove
Crumlin, BT29 4D
Tel: 028 9445 2522

Desmond Motors Ltd
City of Derry Airport
Airport Road, Eglinton, BT48 7PN
Tel: 028 7181 2222

Direct Self Drive
57A Kilkeel Road,
Annalong, BT34 4TJ
Tel: 028 4376 8190

Enterprise Rent a Car
Unit 3 Building 10, Central Park Mallusk
Newtownabbey, BT36 4FS
Tel: 028 9084 3749

Europcar
105 Great Victoria Street
Belfast, BT2 7AG
Tel: 028 9031 3500

Gallen Vehicle Hire
96 Drumlegagh Road South
Omagh, BT78 4TW
Tel: 028 8224 6966

Garryduff Car, Van & Minibus Hire
97C Garryduff Road
Ballymoney, BT53 7DH
Tel: 028 2766 7170

Holmes Motors
2-20 Beersbridge Road
Belfast, BT5 4RU
Tel: 028 9045 1850

Kingdom Car Hire
14 Coolmillish Road
Markethill, BT60 1QA
Tel: 028 3755 1169

Kings Self Drive
96 Oldstone Road
Muckamore, Antrim, BT41 4SP
Tel: 028 9446 6645

Lakeside Self Drive Car Hire Ltd
Ballybrack Road, Sixmilecross
Carrickmore, BT79 9LU
Tel: 028 8076 1060

Lindsay Ford Rental
397 Upper Newtownards Road
Belfast, BT4 3LG
Tel: 028 9065 4687

Lochside Garages Ltd
Tempo Road
Enniskillen, BT74 6HR
Tel: 028 6632 4366

Low Cost Car & Van Hire
12 Church Street
Bangor, BT20 3HT
Tel: 028 9127 1535

McCausland Car Park
21-31 Grosvenor Road
Belfast, BT12 4GN
Tel: 028 9033 3777

MPC Vehicle Rentals
2 Monaghan Road
Armagh, BT60 4DA
Tel: 028 3752 3775

National Car Rental
90-92 Grosvenor Road
Belfast, BT12 5AX
Tel: 028 9032 5520

National-Alamo
277 Dunhill Road
Coleraine, BT51 3QJ
Tel: 0870 191 0613

Nova Rent a Car Reservations Ltd
1 Castle Street
Portaferry, BT22 1PD
Tel: 028 4272 8189

SJS Vehicle Hire
1-6 Loves Hill, Castledawson Road
Magherafelt, BT45 8DP
Tel: 028 7946 9889

Saville's Vauxhall Rental
70 Belfast Road
Lisburn, BT27 4AU
Tel: 028 9263 3622

## Tourism Information for Visitors

**Northern Ireland Tourist Board (NITB)**
St Anne's Court, 59 North Street, Belfast, BT1 1NB
Tel: 028 9023 1221/Fax: 028 9024 0960
Corporate Website: www.nitb.com
Visitor Information: www.discovernorthernireland.com
16 Nassau Street, Dublin 2
Tel: +353 (0) 1 679 1977 / Fax: +353 (0) 1 679 1863

*Mussenden Temple*

The Northern Ireland Tourist Board is responsible for implementing strategy for the development, promotion and marketing of Northern Ireland as a tourist destination. Detailed visitor information, including places to stay and things to see and do can be accessed on their visitor website www.discovernorthernireland.com.

**Tourism Ireland Limited (TIL)**
Beresford House, 2 Beresford Road, Coleraine, BT52 1GE
Tel: 028 7035 9200 / Fax: 028 7032 6932
Web: www.tourismireland.com

TIL was established as one of the six 'areas of co-operation' under the Belfast Agreement. With offices in Coleraine and Dublin, it is responsible for marketing the entire island of Ireland overseas as a tourist destination.

**Sperrins Tourism Limited**
30 High Street
Moneymore, BT45 7PB
Tel: 028 8674 7700
Fax: 028 8674 7754
Web: www.sperrinstourism.com
Email: info@sperrinstourism.com

## Regional Tourism Organisations (RTOs)

Northern Ireland's RTOs are responsible primarily for co-ordinating and implementing marketing activity on behalf of and with private sector and local authority members, as well as advising local businesses on tourism opportunities. Together they represent over 1700 private sector businesses and 11 local authorities across Northern Ireland. They are public/private membership companies limited by guarantee.

**Belfast Visitor and Convention Bureau**
Belfast Welcome Centre
47 Donegall Place
Belfast, BT1 5AD
Tel: 028 9023 9026
Web: www.gotobelfast.com
Email: info@belfastvisitor.com

**Causeway Coast & Glens**
11 Lodge Road
Coleraine BT52 1LU
Tel: 028 7032 7720
Web: www.causewaycoastandglens.com
Email: mail@causewaycoastandglens.com

**Kingdoms of Down**
40 West Street
Newtownards, BT23 4EN
Tel: 028 9182 2881
Web: www.kingdomsofdown.com
Email: info@kingdomsofdown.com

**Derry Visitor & Convention Bureau**
44 Foyle Street
Londonderry, BT48 6AT
Tel: 028 7126 7284
Web: www.derryvisitor.com
Email: info@derryvisitor.com

**Fermanagh Lakeland Tourism**
Wellington Road
Enniskillen, BT74 7EF
Tel: 028 6634 6736
Web: www.fermanaghlakelands.com
Email: info@fermanaghlakelands.com

*Fermanagh Tourist Information Centre*

## Tourist Information Centres (TICs)

In addition to the Regional Tourism Organisations, there is a network of Tourist Information Centres located in villages, towns and cities, across Northern Ireland, as well as at important tourist attractions. Staff at Tourist Information Centres can provide information about local visitor attractions as well as providing an accommodation booking service. Details of Northern Ireland's Tourist Information Centres are set out on the following page (it should be noted that opening hours do vary, with some Tourist Information Centres operating on a seasonal basis).

## Tourist Information Centres

**Antrim**
16 High Street, Antrim, BT41 4AN
Tel: 028 9442 8331
Fax: 028 9448 7844

**Armagh**
Old Bank Building, 40 English Street
Armagh, BT61 7BA
Tel: 028 3752 1800
Fax: 028 3752 8329

**Ballycastle**
Sheskburn House
7 Mary Street, BT54 6QH
Tel: 028 2076 2024
Fax: 028 2076 2515

**Ballymena**
76 Church Street, Ballymena, BT43 6DF
Tel: 028 2563 8494
Fax: 028 2563 8495

**Banbridge**
200 Newry Road, Banbridge, BT32 3NB
Tel: 028 4062 3322
Fax: 028 4062 3114

**Bangor**
34 Quay Street
Bangor, BT20 5ED
Tel: 028 9127 0069
Fax: 028 9127 4466

**Belfast Welcome Centre**
47 Donegall Place
Belfast, BT1 5AD
Tel: 028 9024 6609
Fax: 028 9031 2424

**Carrickfergus**
Museum and Civic Centre
11 Antrim Street
Carrickfergus, BT38 7DG
Tel: 028 9335 8049
Fax: 028 9335 0350

**Coleraine**
Railway Road
Coleraine, BT52 1PE
Tel: 028 7034 4723
Fax: 028 7035 1756

**Cookstown**
The Burnavon
Burn Road, Cookstown, BT80 8DN
Tel: 028 8676 6727
Fax: 028 8676 5853

**Downpatrick**
St Patrick 's Centre, 53A Market Street
Downpatrick, BT30 6LZ
Tel: 028 4461 2233
Fax: 028 4461 2350

**Fermanagh**
Wellington Road
Enniskillen, BT74 7EF
Tel: 028 6632 3110
Fax: 028 6632 5511

**Giant's Causeway**
44 Causeway Road
Bushmills, BT57 8SU
Tel: 028 2073 1855
Fax: 028 2073 2537

**Hillsborough**
The Courthouse, The Square
Hillsborough, BT26 6AG
Tel: 028 9268 9717
Fax: 028 9268 9773

**Kilkeel**
28 Bridge Street
Kilkeel, BT34 4AD
Tel: 028 4176 2525
Fax: 028 4176 9947

**Killymaddy**
190 Ballygawley Road
Dungannon, BT70 1TF
Tel: 028 8776 7259
Fax: 028 8776 7911

**Larne**
Narrow Gauge Road
Larne, BT40 1XB
Tel: 028 2826 0088
Fax: 028 2826 0088

**Limavady**
Council Offices
7 Connell Street, BT49 0HA
Tel: 028 7776 0307
Fax: 028 7772 2010

**Lisburn**
15 Lisburn Square
Lisburn, BT28 1AN
Tel: 028 9266 0038
Fax: 028 9260 7889

**Londonderry**
44 Foyle Street
Londonderry, BT48 6AP
Tel: 028 7126 7284
Fax: 028 7137 7992

**Magherafelt**
Bridewell Centre
6 Church Street
Magherafelt, BT45 6AN
Tel: 028 7963 1510

**Newcastle**
Newcastle Centre
10-14 Central Promenade
Newcastle, BT33 0AA
Tel: 028 4372 2222
Fax: 028 4372 2400

**Newry**
Town Hall
Newry, BT35 6HR
Tel: 028 3026 8877
Fax: 028 3026 8833

**Newtownards**
31 Regent Street
Newtownards, BT23 4AD
Tel: 028 9182 6846
Fax: 028 9182 6681

**Omagh**
1 Market Street
Omagh, BT78 1EE
Tel: 028 8224 7831
Fax: 028 8224 0774

**Portaferry (seasonal)**
The Stables
Castle Street
Portaferry, BT22 1NZ
Tel: 028 4272 9882
Fax: 028 4272 9822

**Portrush (seasonal)**
Dunluce Centre
Sandhill Drive
Portrush, BT56 8BF
Tel: 028 7082 3333
Fax: 028 7082 2256

**Strabane (seasonal)**
Abercorn Square
Strabane, BT82 8AN
Tel: 028 7188 3735
Fax: 028 7138 1348

# Where to Stay in Northern Ireland

## Hotels

Until relatively recently Northern Ireland has been undersupplied with quality hotel accommodation. In fact, on some occasions when there has been a major international event in the region, hotel accommodation has been insufficient to meet demand. However, over the last few years hoteliers, supported by government tourism policy and the Northern Ireland Tourist Board, have invested heavily in new and improved accommodation. Most of the leading hotels now have well-equipped leisure centres. A number of the big international hotel chains have recently established a presence, including Hilton, Radisson, Ramada and Holiday Inn.

The following is a list of hotels arranged first by county (beginning with those in Belfast), and then in alphabetical order. Where a rating is available, the hotels have been rated according to the Northern Ireland Tourist Board's 'star' system. A description of each category in the system follows below.

*(See Chapter 13 for details of places to eat and drink in Northern Ireland).*

### NITB Star System

**Five Star** *****
Hotels of an international standard with luxurious and spacious guest accommodation including suites. High quality restaurants with table d'hôte and à la carte and dinner menus.

**Four Star** ****
Large hotels with a high standard of comfort and service in well appointed premises. All bedrooms ensuite. Cuisine meets exacting standards. Comprehensive room service.

**Three Star** ***
Good facilities with a wide range of services. All bedrooms ensuite. Food available all day.

**Two Star** **
Good facilities with a reasonable standard of accommodation, food and services. Most bedrooms are ensuite.

**One Star** *
Hotels with acceptable standards of accommodation and food. Some bedrooms have ensuite facilities.

### Belfast

Balmoral Hotel **
Black's Road, Dunmurry
Belfast, BT10 0NF
Tel: 028 9030 1234
Fax: 028 9060 1455
Web: www.balmoralhotelbelfast.co.uk
43 Rooms

Beechlawn House Hotel ***
4 Dunmurry Lane, Belfast, BT17 9RR
Tel: 028 9060 2010
Fax: 028 9060 2080
Web: www.beechlawnhotel.co.uk
42 Rooms

Belfast City Travelodge**
15 Brunswick Street, Belfast BT2 7GE
Tel: 028 9033 3555
Fax: 028 9023 2999
Web: www.travelodge.co.uk
Rooms: 90

Benedicts of Belfast ***
7-21 Bradbury Place, Belfast, BT7 1RQ
Tel: 028 9059 1999
Fax: 028 9059 1990
Web: www.benedictshotel.co.uk
32 Rooms

The Crescent Townhouse**
13 Lower Crescent, Belfast, BT7 1NR
Tel: 028 9032 3349
Fax: 028 9032 0646
Email: info@crescenttownhouse.com
Web: www.crescenttownhouse.com
17 Rooms

Culloden Hotel *****
Bangor Road, Holywood, BT18 0EX
Tel: 028 9042 1066
Fax: 028 9042 6777
Web: www.hastingshotels.com
79 Rooms

Days Hotel ***
40 Hope Street, Belfast, BT12 5EE
Tel: 028 9024 2494
Fax: 028 9024 2495
Web: www.dayshotelbelfast.com
244 Rooms

Dukes Hotel ***
65-67 University Street
Belfast, BT7 1HL
Tel: 028 9023 6666
Fax: 028 9023 7177
Web: www.welcome-group.co.uk
20 Rooms

Europa Hotel ****
Great Victoria Street, Belfast, BT2 7AP
Tel: 028 9027 1066
Fax: 028 9032 7800
Web: www.hastingshotels.com
240 Rooms

Express Holiday Inn ***
106 University Street, Belfast, BT7 1HP
Tel: 028 9031 1909
Fax: 028 9031 1910
Web: www.holidayinn-ireland.com
114 Rooms

Hilton Belfast *****

Hilton

4 Lanyon Place
Belfast, BT1 3LP
Tel: 028 9027 7000
Fax: 028 9027 7277
Email: hilton.belfast@hilton.com
Web: www.hilton.co.uk/belfast

Hilton Belfast is Belfast City centre's only five star hotel and is located in the stylish Laganside riverfront area adjacent to the Waterfront Hall and close to the Odyssey Arena. 195 guest rooms, including an outstanding selection of suites and corner studios, 3 Executive floors, Executive Club Lounge and LivingWell Health Club with pool on-site. Hilton Belfast is only a short walk from a selection of chic bars, restaurants and the city centre's shopping.

Holiday Inn Belfast ****
22-26 Ormeau Avenue
Belfast, BT2 8HS
Tel: 028 9027 1706
Fax: 028 9062 6546
Web: www.belfast.holiday-inn.com
170 Rooms

Ivanhoe Inn and Hotel
556 Saintfield Road, Belfast, BT8 8EU
Tel: 028 9081 2240
Fax: 028 9081 5516
Web: www.ivanhoeinn.co.uk
21 Rooms

Jurys Inn Belfast***

Fisherwick Place
Great Victoria Street
Belfast, BT2 7AP
Tel: +44 (0) 28 9053 3500
Fax: +44 (0) 28 9053 3511
Email: jurysinnbelfast@jurysdoyle.com
Web: www.jurysdoyle.com

In the heart of Belfast, within walking distance of the best restaurants and bars; 190 rooms accommodating 3 adults or 2 adults and 2 children; Innfusion Restaurant serves breakfast and dinner; The Inn Pub serves snacks; Six meeting rooms are available for seminars, training or meetings.

Lansdowne Hotel ***
857 Antrim Road, Belfast, BT15 4EF
Tel: 028 9077 3317
Fax: 028 9078 1588
Web: www.welcome-group.co.uk
25 Rooms

Malmaison Belfast ****
34-38 Victoria Street, Belfast, BT1 3GH
Tel: 028 9022 0200
Web: www.malmaison.com

Malone Lodge Hotel ****
60 Eglantine Avenue, Belfast, BT9 6DY
Tel: 028 9038 8000
Fax: 028 9038 8088
Email: info@malonelodgehotel.com
Web: www.malonelodgehotel.com
50 Rooms

Park Avenue Hotel ***
158 Holywood Road, Belfast, BT4 1PB
Tel: 028 9065 6520
Fax: 028 9047 1417
Web: www.parkavenuehotel.co.uk
56 Rooms

Radisson SAS Hotel****
The Gasworks, 3 Cromac Place
Belfast, BT7 2JB
Tel: 028 9043 4065
Fax: 028 9043 4066
Email: info.belfast@radissonsas.com
120 Rooms

Ramada Hotel ****
177 Milltown Road
Shaws Bridge, Belfast, BT8 7XP
Tel: 028 9092 3500
Fax: 028 9092 3600
Web: www.ramadabelfast.com
120 Rooms

Stormont Hotel ****
587 Upper Newtownards Road
Belfast, BT4 3LP
Tel: 028 9065 1066
Fax: 028 9048 0240
Web: www.hastingshotels.com
109 Rooms

TENsq Boutique Hotel ****
10 Donegall Square South,
Belfast, BT1 5JD
Tel: 028 9024 1001
Fax: 028 9024 3210
Web: www.tensquare.co.uk
Rooms: 23

Wellington Park Hotel ****
21 Malone Road
Belfast, BT9 6RU
Tel: 028 9038 5050
Fax: 028 9038 5055
Web: www.mooneyhotelgroup.com
75 Rooms

## Co Antrim

Adair Arms Hotel ***
1-7 Ballymoney Road
Ballymena, BT43 5BS
Tel: 028 2565 3674
Fax: 028 2564 0436
44 Rooms

Ballygally Castle Hotel ***
274 Coast Road, Ballygally, BT40 2QR
Tel: 028 2858 1066
Fax: 028 2858 3681
Web: www.hastingshotels.com
44 Rooms

Bushmills Inn ***
9 Dunluce Road, Bushmills, BT57 8QG
Tel: 028 2073 2339
Fax: 028 2073 2048
Web: www.bushmillsinn.com
32 Rooms

Chimney Corner Hotel **
630 Antrim Road
Newtownabbey, BT36 4RH
Tel: 028 9084 4925
Fax: 028 9084 4352
Web: www.chimneycorner.co.uk
63 Rooms

Comfort Hotel ***
73 Main Street, Portrush, BT56 8BN
Tel: 028 7082 6100
Fax: 028 7082 6160
Web: www.comforthotelportrush.com
50 Rooms

Corr's Corner **
315 Ballyclare Road
Newtownabbey, BT36 4TQ
Tel: 028 9084 9221
Fax: 028 9083 2118
Web: www.corrscorner.co.uk
Email: info@corrscorner.co.uk
30 Rooms

Dobbins Inn Hotel **
6-8 High Street
Carrickfergus, BT38 7AF
Tel: 028 9335 1905
Web: www.dobbinsinnhotel.co.uk
Email: info@dobbinsinnhotel.co.uk
15 Rooms

Dunadry Hotel & Country Club ****
2 Islandreagh Drive, Dunadry, BT41 2HA
Tel: 028 9443 4343
Fax: 028 9443 3389
Email: reservations@mooneyhotelgroup.com
Web: www.mooneyhotelgroup.com
83 Rooms

Fitzwilliam International ****
Belfast International Airport, BT29 4ZY
Tel: 028 9445 7000
Fax: 028 9442 3500
Web: www.fitzwilliaminternational.com
106 Rooms

Galgorm Manor ****
136 Fenaghy Road, Cullybackey
Ballymena, BT42 1EA
Tel: 028 2588 1001
Fax: 028 2588 0080
Web: www.galgorm.com
25Rooms

Glenavna House Hotel ***
588 Shore Road
Newtownabbey, BT37 0SN
Tel: 028 9086 4461
Fax: 028 9086 2531
Web: www.glenavna.com
32 Rooms

The Golf Links Hotel (Kelly's)
Bushmills Road, Portrush, BT56 8JQ
Tel: 028 7082 3539
Fax: 028 7082 5140
Web: www.kellysportrush.co.uk

Hilton Templepatrick ****

Hilton
Templepatrick
Hotel & Country Club

Hilton Templepatrick
Castle Upton Estate
Templepatrick, BT39 0DD
Tel: 028 9443 5500
Fax: 028 9443 5511
Email: hilton.templepatrick@hilton.com
Web: www.hilton.co.uk/templepatrick

Hilton Templepatrick Hotel and Country Club four star hotel is located in the magnificent Castle Upton Estate. Situated only five minutes from Belfast International Airport and twenty minutes from the city centre. With 129 bedrooms featuring wonderful views, the best of local international cuisine and a host of leisure and conference facilities, Hilton Templepatrick Hotel and Country club is one of the most prestigious hotels in Northern Ireland.

Leighinmohr House Hotel ***
Leighinmohr Avenue
Ballymena, BT42 2AN
Tel: 028 2565 2313
Fax: 028 2565 6669
Web: www.leighinmohrhotel.com
20 Rooms

Londonderry Arms Hotel ***
20 Harbour Road
Carnlough, BT44 0EU
Tel: 028 2888 5255
Fax: 028 2885 5263
Web: www.glensofantrim.com
35 Rooms

Magherabuoy House Hotel ***
41 Magheraboy Road
Portrush, BT56 8NX
Tel: 028 7082 3507
Fax: 028 7082 4687
Web: www.magherabuoy.co.uk
38 Rooms

Marine Hotel ***
1-3 North Street
Ballycastle, BT54 6BN
Tel: 028 2076 2222
Fax: 028 2076 9507
Web: www.marinehotel.net
32 Rooms

Peninsula Hotel **
15 Eglinton Street
Portrush, BT56 8DX
Tel: 028 7082 2293
Fax: 028 7082 4315
Web: www.peninsulahotel.co.uk
24 Rooms

The Port Hotel
53-57 Main Street
Portrush, BT56 8BN
Tel: 028 7082 5353

Quality Hotel ***
75 Belfast Road
Carrickfergus, BT38 8PH
Tel: 028 9336 4556
Fax: 028 9335 1620
Web: www.choicehotelseurope.com
68 Rooms

Rosspark Hotel ***
20 Doagh Road, Kells
Ballymena, BT42 3LZ
Tel: 028 2589 1663
Fax: 028 2589 1477
Web: www.rossparkhotel.com
39 Rooms

Royal Court Hotel ***
233 Ballybogey Road
Portrush, BT56 9NF
Tel: 028 7082 2236
Fax: 028 7082 3176
Web: www.royalcourthotel.co.uk
18 Rooms

The Smugglers Inn
306 Whitepark Road
Bushmills, BT57 8SN
Tel: 028 2073 1577
Fax: 028 2073 1072
Web: www.smugglers-inn.co.uk
12 Rooms

Templeton Hotel ***
882 Antrim Road
Templepatrick, BT39 0AH
Tel: 028 9443 2984
Fax: 028 9443 3406
Web: www.templetonhotel.com
24 Rooms

Tullyglass Hotel ***
Galgorm Road
Ballymena, BT42 1HJ
Tel: 028 2565 2639
Fax: 028 2564 6938
Web: www.tullyglass.com
35 Rooms

## Co Armagh

Ashburn Hotel **
81 William Street
Lurgan, BT66 6JB
Tel: 028 3832 5711
Fax: 028 3834 7194
Web: www.theashburnhotel.com
12 Rooms

Armagh City Hotel ***
2 Friary Road
Armagh, BT60 4FR
Tel: 028 3751 8888
Fax: 028 3751 2777
Web: www.mooneyhotelgroup.com
102 Rooms

Carngrove Hotel **
2 Charlestown Road
Portadown, BT63 5PW
Tel: 028 3833 9222
Fax: 028 3833 2899
35 Rooms

Charlemont Arms Hotel **
57-65 English Street
Armagh, BT61 7LB
Tel: 028 3752 2028
Fax: 028 3752 6979
Web: www.charlemontarmshotel.com
30 Rooms

Seagoe Hotel ***
Upper Church Lane
Portadown, BT63 5JE
Tel: 028 3833 3076
Fax: 028 3835 0210
Web: www.seagoe.com
36 Rooms

## Co Down

Bannville House Hotel
174 Lurgan Road, Banbridge, BT32 4NR
Tel: 028 4062 8884
Fax: 028 4062 7077
Web: www.bannvillehouse.co.uk
20 Rooms

Burrendale Hotel & Country Club ***
51 Castlewellan Road
Newcastle, BT33 0JY
Tel: 028 4372 2599
Fax: 028 4372 2328
Web: www.burrendale.com
69 Rooms

Canal Court Hotel ***
Merchant's Quay, Newry, BT35 3FC
Tel: 028 3025 1234
Fax: 028 3025 1177
Web: www.canalcourthotel.com
51 Rooms

Clandeboye Lodge Hotel ***
10 Estate Road, Bangor, BT19 1NR
Tel: 028 9185 2500
Fax: 028 9185 2772
Email: info@clandeboyelodge.com
Website: www.clandeboyelodge.com
43 Rooms

Downshire Arms Hotel
95 Newry Street
Banbridge, BT32 3EF
Tel: 028 4066 2638
Fax: 028 4062 6811
Web: www.downshirearmshotel.com

Kilmorey Arms Hotel **
41-43 Greencastle Street
Kilkeel, BT34 4BH
Tel: 028 4176 2220
Fax: 028 4176 5399
Web: www.kilmoreyarmshotel.co.uk
25 Rooms

La Mon Country House Hotel ***
The Mills, 41 Gransha Road
Castlereagh, BT23 5RF
Tel: 028 9044 8631
Fax: 028 9044 8026
Web: www.lamon.co.uk
71 Rooms

Marine Court Hotel ***
18-20 Quay Street, Bangor, BT20 5ED
Tel: 028 9145 1100
Fax: 028 9145 1200
Web: www.marinecourthotel.net
52 Rooms

Millbrook Lodge Hotel **
5 Drumaness Road
Ballynahinch, BT24 8LS
Tel: 028 9756 2828
Fax: 028 9756 5405
Web: www.millbrooklodge.co.uk
16 Rooms

Mourne Country Hotel **
52 Belfast Road, Newry, BT34 1TR
Tel: 028 3026 7922
Fax: 028 3026 9922
43 Rooms

The Old Inn ***
15 Main Street, Crawfordsburn, BT19 1JH
Tel: 028 9185 3255
Fax: 028 9185 2775
Web: www.theoldinn.com
32 Rooms

The Portaferry Hotel ***
10 The Strand, Portaferry, BT22 1PE
Tel: 028 4272 8231
Fax: 028 4272 8999
Web: www.portaferryhotel.com
14 Rooms

Royal Hotel **
26-28 Quay Street, Bangor, BT20 5ED
Tel: 028 9127 1866
Fax: 028 9146 7810
Web: www.the-royal-hotel.com
50 Rooms

Slieve Donard Hotel ****
Downs Road, Newcastle, BT33 0AH
Tel: 028 4372 1066
Fax: 028 4372 1166
Web: www.hastingshotels.com
124 Rooms

Strangford Arms Hotel ***
92 Church Street
Newtownards, BT23 4AL
Tel: 028 9181 4141
Fax: 028 9181 1010
Web: www.strangfordhotel.co.uk
37 Rooms

White Gables Hotel ***
14 Dromore Road
Hillsborough, BT26 6HS
Tel: 028 9268 2755
Fax: 028 9268 9532
31 Rooms

## Co Fermanagh

Fort Lodge Hotel **
72 Forthill Street, Enniskillen, BT74 6AJ
Tel: 028 6632 3275
Fax: 028 6632 0275
36 Rooms

Hotel Carlton **
2 Main Street, Belleek, BT93 3FX
Tel: 028 6865 8282
Fax: 028 6865 9005
Web: www.hotelcarlton.co.uk
19 Rooms

Killyhevlin Hotel ****
Dublin Road, Enniskillen, BT74 6RW
Tel: 028 6632 3481
Fax: 028 6632 4726
Web: www.killyhevlin.com
43 Rooms

Lough Erne Hotel **
Main Street, Kesh, BT93 1TF
Tel: 028 6863 1275
Fax: 028 6863 1423
Web: www.loughernehotel.com
16 Rooms

Mahon's Hotel **
Mill Street, Irvinestown, BT94 1GS
Tel: 028 6862 1656
Fax: 028 6862 8344
Web: www.mahonshotel.co.uk
18 Rooms

Manor House Resort Hotel ****
Killadeas, Enniskillen, BT94 1NY
Tel: 028 6862 2200
Fax: 028 6862 1545
Web: www.manor-house-hotel.com
81 Rooms

Railway Hotel *
34 Forthill Street, Enniskillen, BT74 6AJ
Tel: 028 6632 2084
Fax: 028 6632 7480
Web: www.railwayhotelenniskillen.com
19 Rooms

## Co Londonderry

Beech Hill Country House Hotel ****
32 Ardmore Road, Derry, BT47 3QP
Tel: 028 7134 9279
Fax: 028 7134 5366
Web: www.beech-hill.com
27 Rooms

Brown Trout Golf & Country Inn ***
209 Agivey Road
Aghadowey, BT51 4AD
Tel: 028 7086 8209
Fax: 028 7086 8878
Web: www.browntroutinn.com
15 Rooms

Broomhill Hotel ***
Limavady Road, Derry, BT47 6LT
Tel: 028 7134 7995
Fax: 028 7134 9304
42 Rooms

Bushtown House Hotel and Country Club ***
283 Drumcroone Road
Coleraine, BT51 3QT
Tel: 028 7035 8367
Fax: 028 7032 0909
Web: www.bushtownhotel.com
40 Rooms

City Hotel
14-18 Queen's Quay
Derry, BT48 7AS
Tel: 028 7136 5800
Fax: 028 7136 5801
Web: www.greatsouthernhotels.com
145 Rooms

Da Vinci's Hotel Complex***
15 Culmore Road, Derry, BT48 8TB
Tel: 028 7127 9111
Fax: 028 7127 9222
Web: www.davincishotel.co.uk
70 Rooms

Everglades Hotel ****
41-53 Prehen Road, Derry, BT47 2NH
Tel: 028 7132 1066
Fax: 028 7134 9200
Web: www.hastingshotels.com
64 Rooms

Inn at the Cross
171 Glenshane Road
Londonderry, BT47 3EN
Tel: 028 7130 1480
Fax: 028 7130 1394
19 Rooms

Lodge Hotel and Travelstop***
Lodge Road, Coleraine, BT52 1NF
Tel: 028 7034 4848
Fax: 028 7035 4555
Web: www.thelodgehotel.com
56 Rooms

Radisson SAS Roe Park Resort ****
Roe Park, Limavady, BT49 9LB
Tel: 028 7772 2222
Fax: 028 7772 2313
Web: www.radissonroepark.com
118 Rooms

Tower Hotel ****
Tower Hotel Derry ****
Butcher Street
Londonderry, BT48 6HL
Tel: 028 7137 1000
Fax: 028 7137 7123
Web: www.towerhotelgroup.com
Email: reservations@thd.ie
General Manager: Ian Hyland

Travel Lodge **
22-24 Strand Road, Derry, BT48 7AB
Tel: 028 7127 1271
Fax: 028 7127 1277
Web: www.travelodge.co.uk
39 Rooms

Waterfoot Hotel & Country Club ***
14 Clooney Road, Derry, BT47 6TB
Tel: 028 7134 5500
Fax: 028 7131 1006
Web: www.thewaterfoothotel.co.uk
48 Rooms

White Horse Hotel ***
68 Clooney Road, Derry, BT47 3JP
Tel: 028 7186 0606
Fax: 028 7186 0371
Web: www.whitehorsehotel.biz
57 Rooms

## Co Tyrone

Fir Trees Hotel **
Dublin Road, Strabane, BT82 9EA
Tel: 028 7138 2382
Fax: 028 7138 3116
24 Rooms

Four Ways Hotel *
41-45 Main Street, Fivemiletown, BT75 0PG
Tel: 028 8952 1260
Fax: 028 8952 2061
10 Rooms

Glenavon House Hotel ***
52 Drum Road, Cookstown, BT80 8JQ
Tel: 028 8676 4949
Fax: 028 8676 4396
Web: www.glenavonhotel.co.uk
53 Rooms

Greenvale Hotel **
57 Drum Road, Cookstown, BT80 8QS
Tel: 028 8676 2243
Fax: 028 8676 5539
74 Rooms

Silverbirch Hotel ***
5 Gortin Road, Omagh, BT79 7DH
Tel: 028 8224 2520
Fax: 028 8224 9061
Web: www.silverbirchhotel.com
46 Rooms

Tullylagan Country House Hotel **
40B Tullylagan Road
Cookstown, BT80 8UP
Tel: 028 8676 5100
Fax: 028 8676 1715
Web: www.tullylagan.freeserve.co.uk
15 Rooms

Valley Hotel **
60 Main Street
Fivemiletown, BT75 0PW
Tel: 028 8952 1505
Fax: 028 8952 1688
22 Rooms

## Camping and Caravanning

### Co Antrim

Ballymacrea Caravan and Camping Park
Portrush
Tel: 028 7082 4507

Ballyness Caravan Park
Bushmills
Tel: 028 2073 2393

Bush Caravan Park
Bushmills
Tel: 028 2073 1678

Carnfunnock Country Park and Caravan Park
Larne
Tel: 028 2827 3797 (out of season)
Tel: 028 2827 0541 (in season)

Carrick Dhu Caravan Park
Portrush
Tel: 028 7082 3712

Curran Court Caravan Park
Larne
Tel: 028 2827 3797

Cushendall Caravan Park
Cushendall
Tel: 028 2177 1699

Cushendun Caravan Park
Cushendun
Tel: 028 2176 1254

Drumaheglis Marina and Caravan Park
Ballymoney
Tel: 028 2766 6466

Glenariff Forest and Caravan Park
Glenariff
Tel: 028 2175 8232

Jordanstown Lough Shore Park
Newtownabbey
Tel: 028 9034 0000

Portballintrae Caravan Park
Portballintrae
Tel: 028 2073 1478

Silvercliffs Holiday Village
Ballycastle
Tel: 028 2076 2550

Sixmilewater Marina and Caravan Park
Antrim
Tel: 028 9446 4131

Watertop Farm
Cushendall
Tel: 028 2076 2576

### Co Armagh

Gosford Forest Park and Caravan Park
Markethill
Tel: 028 3755 1277

Kinnego Marina Caravan Park
Lurgan
Tel: 028 3832 7573

### Co Down

Annalong Caravan Park
Annalong, Newcastle
Tel: 028 4376 8248

The Camping and Caravanning Club Site
Killyleagh
Tel: 028 4482 1883

Castleward Caravan Park
Strangford
Tel: 028 4488 1680

Castlewellan Forest Park and Caravan Park
Castlewellan
Tel: 028 4377 8664

Chestnutt Caravan Park
Kilkeel
Tel: 028 4176 2653

Cranfield Caravan Park
Kilkeel
Tel: 028 4176 2572

Dundonald Touring Caravan Park
Belfast
Tel: 028 9080 9100

Kilbroney Caravan Park
Rostrevor
Tel: 028 4173 8134

Lakeside View Caravan Park
Hillsborough
Tel: 028 9268 2098

Rathlin Caravan Park
Millisle
Tel: 028 9186 1386

Sandycove Holiday Park
Ballywalter
Tel: 028 4275 8062

Sandilands Caravan Park
Kilkeel
Tel: 028 4176 3634

Tollymore Forest Park Caravan Park
Newcastle
Tel: 028 4372 2428

Windsor Caravan Park
Newcastle
Tel: 028 4372 3367

### Co Fermanagh

Blaney Caravan Park
Blaney
Tel: 028 6864 1634

Castle Archdale Caravan Park and Camping Site
Irvinestown
Tel: 028 6862 1333

Lakeland Caravan Park
Kesh
Tel: 028 6863 1578

Share Holiday Village
Lisnaskea
Tel: 028 6772 2122

### Co Londonderry

Castlerock Holiday Park
Castlerock
Tel: 028 7084 8381

Golden Sands Forest Park
Limavady
Tel: 028 7775 0324

Juniper Hill Caravan Park
Portstewart
Tel: 028 7083 2023

Tullans Farm Caravan Park
Coleraine
Tel: 028 7034 2309

### Co Tyrone

Ballyronan Marina and Caravan Park
Ballyronan, Cookstown
Tel: 028 7941 8399

Clogher Valley Country Caravan Park
Clogher
Tel: 028 8554 8932

Drum Manor Forest Park and Caravan Park
Cookstown
Tel: 028 8676 2774

Dungannon Park and Caravan Park
Dungannon
Tel: 028 8772 7327

Killymaddy Tourist Amenity Centre
Dungannon
Tel: 028 8776 7259

Round Lake Caravan Park
Fivemiletown, Co Tyrone
Tel: 028 8952 1949

## Hostels

### Belfast

The Ark
18 University Street
Belfast, BT7 1FZ
Tel: 028 9032 9626
Web: www.arkhostel.com
Email: info@arkhostel.com

Arnie's Backpackers
63 Fitzwilliam Street
Belfast, BT9 6AX
Tel: 028 9024 2867
Web: www.arniesbackpackers.co.uk

Belfast International Youth Hostel
22 Donegall Road
Belfast, BT12 5JN
Tel: 028 9032 4733
Email: info@hini.org.uk

The Linen House Hostel
18 Kent Street
Belfast, BT1 2JA
Tel: 028 9058 6444
Web: www.belfasthostel.com
Email: bookings@belfasthostel.com

### Co Antrim

Ballycastle Backpackers
4 North Street, Ballycastle, BT54 6BN
Tel: 028 2076 3612
Email: am@bcbackpackers.fsnet.co.uk

Castle Hostel
62 Quay Road, Ballycastle, BT54 6BH
Tel: 028 2076 2337
Email: info@castlehostel.com

Colliers Barn
50 Cushendall Road
Ballycastle, BT54 6QR
Tel: 028 2076 2531

Glendun Court
PO Box 14, Glenville Road
Whiteabbey, BT37 0UN
Tel: 028 9085 3005
Web: www.csni.com

Metropole House
70 Eglinton Street, Portrush, BT56 8DY
Tel: 028 7082 3511

Mill Rest
49 Main Street, Bushmills, BT57 8QA
Tel: 028 2073 1222
Email: info@hini.org.uk

Portrush Independent Youth Hostel (Macool's)
35 Causeway Street,
Portrush, BT56 8AB
Tel: 028 7082 4845
Email: scilley@portrush.hostel.fsnet.co.uk

Sheep Island View
42A Main Street, Ballintoy, BT54 6LX
Tel: 028 2076 9391
Email: sheepisland@hotmail.com

Soerneog View Hostel
Ouig, Rathlin Island
Ballycastle, BT54 6RT
Tel: 028 2076 3954

Whitepark Bay Hostel
157 Whitepark Road
Ballintoy, BT54 6NH
Tel: 028 2073 1745
Email: info@hini.org.uk

### Co Armagh

Armagh City International Youth Hostel
39 Abbey Street, Armagh, BT61 7EB
Tel: 028 3751 1800
Email: info@hini.org.uk

Waterside Hostel & Activity Centre
Oxford Island, Lurgan, BT66 6NJ
Tel: 028 3832 7573
Email: kinnego.marina@craigavon.gov.uk

### Co Down

Ballinran Mourne Centre
42 Ballinran Road, Kilkeel, BT34 4JA
Tel: 028 4176 5727
Email: kenmuir@clara.co.uk

Barholm
11 The Strand, Portaferry, BT22 1PE
Tel: 028 4272 9598
Email: barholm.portaferry@virgin.net

Cnocnafeola Cultural & Activity Centre
Bog Road, Atticall, Kilkeel, BT34 4RZ
Tel: 028 4176 5859
Email: info@cnocnafeolacentre.com

Glenada Holiday & Conference Centre
29 South Promenade
Newcastle, BT33 0EX
Tel: 028 4372 2402
Email: info@glenada-conferences.freeserve.co.uk

Greenhill YMCA – Outdoor Centre
Donard Park, Newcastle, BT33 0GR
Tel: 028 4372 3172
Email: greenhill@ymca-ireland.org

Newcastle Hostel
30 Downs Road, Newcastle, BT33 0AG
Tel: 028 4372 2133
Web: www.hini.org.uk
Email: info@hini.org.uk

### Co Fermanagh

The Bridges Youth Hostel
Belmore Street, Enniskillen, BT74 6AA
Tel: 028 6634 0110
Email: info@hini.org.uk

Lough Melvin Holiday Centre
Main Street, Garrison, BT93 4ET
Tel: 028 6865 8142
Email:
enquiry@loughmelvinholidaycentre.com

Share Holiday Village
Smith's Strand, Lisnaskea, BT92 0EQ
Tel: 028 6772 2122
Web: www.sharevillage.org
Email: info@sharevillage.org

Field Studies Council Derrygonnelly Centre
Tir Navar, Creamery Street
Derrygonnelly, BT93 6HW
Tel: 028 6864 1673
Email: fsc.derrygonnelly@ukonline.co.uk

### Co Londonderry

Derry City Hostel
4-6 Magazine Street
Londonderry, BT48 6HJ
Tel: 028 7128 0280
Web: www.derrycityyouthhostel.com
Email: derrycitytours@aol.com

Derry City Independent Hostel
44 Great James Street,
Londonderry, BT48 7DB
Tel: 028 7137 7989
Web: www.derry-hostel.co.uk
Email: derryhostel@hotmail.com

Downhill Hostel
12 Mussenden Road, Downhill
Coleraine, BT51 4RP
Tel: 028 7084 9077
Web: www.downhillhostel.com
Email: downhillhostel@hotmail.com

Dungiven Castle
Upper Main Street, Dungiven, BT47 4LF
Tel: 028 7774 2428
Email: enquiries@dungivencastle.com

The Flax Mill
Mill Lane, Gortnaghey Road
Dungiven, BT47 4PY
Tel: 028 7774 2655

Hostel 56
56 Rainey Street
Magherafelt, BT45 5AH
Tel: 028 7963 2096
Web: www.hostel56.club24.co.uk

Kilcronaghan Activity & Conference Centre
10 Rectory Road, Tobermore
Magherafelt, BT45 5QP
Tel: 028 7962 7826
Email: manager@kilcronaghan.co.uk

Rick's Causeway Independent Hostel
4 Victoria Terrace, Atlantic Circle
Portstewart, BT55 7BA
Tel: 028 7083 3789

Wild Geese Parachute Club
116 Carrowreagh Road
Garvagh, BT51 5LQ
Tel: 028 2955 8609
Email:
parachute@wildgeese.demon.co.uk

## Co Tyrone

Gortin Accommodation Suite and Activity Centre
62 Main Street, Gortin
Omagh, BT79 8NH
Tel: 028 8164 8346
Web: www.gortin.net
Email: visit.gortin@virgin.net

Gortin Hostel and Outdoor Centre
198 Glenpark Road, Gortin
Omagh, BT79 8PJ
Tel: 028 8164 8083

Omagh Hostel
9A Waterworks Road
Omagh, BT79 7JS
Tel: 028 8224 1973
Web: www.omaghhostel.co.uk
Email: marella@omaghhostel.co.uk

# Things to See and Do

## Guided Tours

Belfast City Black Taxi Tours
Tel: 028 9030 1832
Mob: 07712 673178
Web: www.allirelandtours.com
Email: martin@allirelandtours.com

Tour includes famous sites of Belfast and includes the political murals from both traditions. Tours can be arranged to suit.

Belfast City Hall
Tel: 028 9027 0456

Built in 1906 from Portland Stone, Belfast City Hall is a fine example of Classical Renaissance style. Home of Belfast City Council, the tour includes the oak-furnished Council Chamber.

Belfast City Sightseeing
Tel: 028 9062 6888
Web: www.city-sightseeing.com

Tours of the city from open-top bus or luxury coach. Tours depart from Castle Place.

Black Taxi Tours
Tel: 028 9064 2264
Web: www.belfasttours.com
Email: michael@belfasttours.com

Visits some of the well-known sites of Belfast with commentary provided – includes the political wall murals.

Citybus Tours
Tel: 028 9066 6630

Operated by Translink during the months of May - September inclusive. Includes tours of Belfast City, the Belfast Living History Tour and the Titanic Tour.

Due North
Tel: 028 3083 3149
Mob: 07929 823660
Web: www.duenorth-ni.com
Email: info@duenorth-ni.com

Specialists in providing individualised and personalised tours of Northern Ireland.

Historical Pub Walking Tour of Belfast
Tel: 028 9268 3665
Web: www.belfastpubtours.com
Email: judy@belfastpubtours.com

Tour around Belfast's famous and historic pubs. Leaves from Crown Dining Room on Thursdays at 7pm and Saturdays at 4pm from May until the end of October.
Lasts approximately 2 hours.

Intercomm Tourism
Tel: 028 9035 2165
Web: www.irishhistoricaltours.com

Political, educational and cultural tour package.

KM Tour Guiding Services
Tel: 028 3884 0054
Mob: 07801 541600
Web: www.kmtgs.co.uk
Email: info@kmtgs.co.uk

Complete Blue Badge Guiding Service for Northern Ireland offering tours and visits to Northern Ireland's top tourist attractions.

Lagan Boat Company (NI) Ltd
Tel: 028 9024 6609 for details of scheduled tour bookings
Tel: 028 9033 0844 for private hire and information

Guided Titanic and River Lagan boat tours departing from Donegall Quay.

Mini Coach Tours
Tel: 028 9031 5333
Web: www.minicoachni.co.uk
Email: info@minicoachni.co.uk

Daily tours of Belfast and The Giant's Causeway also overnight tours including Belfast, The Giant's Causeway and Londonderry. Also provide airport and ferry transfers.

NI Tour Guide Association
Tel: 028 9028 0925

Blue Badge Tour Guides are available to provide tours in all areas of Northern Ireland.

Ulsterbus Tours
Tel: 028 9066 6630

Operated by Translink, Ulsterbus tours visit main attractions in Northern and Southern Ireland. Depart daily from the Europa Bus Centre.

## Places to Visit

The following list highlights places of interest to visit across Northern Ireland. It is worth noting that opening hours at many of the attractions are limited, especially during winter months so it is worth phoning to check before making a trip to any of the following places. Admission charges may also be payable at some attractions.

### In and Around Belfast

Belfast Castle
Antrim Road, Belfast, BT15 5GR
Tel: 028 9077 6925
www.belfastcastle.co.uk

Impressive sandstone building 400ft above sea level on the slopes of Cave Hill.

Belfast Telegraph Newspapers
124 Royal Avenue, Belfast
Tel: 028 9026 4226
www.belfasttelegraph.co.uk

View the printing works and see the next edition being made up for the camera. Admission free.

Belfast Zoo
Antrim Road, Belfast, BT36 7PN
Tel: 028 9077 6277
www.belfastzoo.co.uk

Zoo set in landscaped parkland housing over 160 species of rare/endangered animals.

Botanic Gardens
Stranmillis Road, Belfast
Tel: 028 9032 4902

City park hosting the Ulster Museum and the Victorian Palm House, full of exotic plants. Admission free.

City Hall
Donegall Square, Belfast, BT1 5GS
Tel: 028 9027 0456
www.belfastcity.gov.uk

A magnificent building in Portland stone, the centrally-located City Hall is seat of Belfast City Council. Tours last 1 hour. Admission free.

Colin Glen Forest Park
163 Stewartstown Road
Belfast, BT17 0HW
Tel: 028 9061 4115
www.colinglentrust.org

Wooded river glen consisting of 200 acres of scenic woodland, grassland, waterfalls and ponds.

Crown Liqueur Saloon
46 Great Victoria Street, Belfast
Tel: 028 9027 9901
www.belfasttelegraph.co.uk/crown

Gas-lit Victorian pub with fine tiles, woodwork and glass – now National Trust owned.

Fernhill House: The People's Museum
Glencairn Road, Belfast, BT13 3PT
Tel: 028 9071 5599

Recreated 1930s terraced 'kitchen house' telling history of Shankill district, Home Rule crisis and both World Wars.

Giant's Ring
Shaw's Bridge, Belfast
www.ntni.org.uk

Prehistoric enclosure over 200m in diameter, with a dolmen in the centre. Admission free.

Grovelands
Stockman's Lane, Belfast
Tel: 028 9032 0202
www.belfastcity.gov.uk

Sunken garden and small ornamental gardens with art deco entrance gates. Admission free.

Lagan Lookout Centre
Donegall Quay
Belfast
Tel: 028 9031 5444
www.laganlookout.com

Background to the River Lagan's weir explained, industrial and folk history of the city. Platform views of river activities.

Lagan Valley Regional Park
Tel: 028 9049 1922

1700 hectares of countryside and 21km of river stretching from Governor's Bridge in Belfast to the former Union Locks in Lisburn. Admission free.

Linen Hall Library
17 Donegall Square North
Belfast, BT1 5GB
Tel: 028 9032 1707
Web: www.linenhall.com

Belfast's oldest library dating from 1788, internationally recognised as a unique and vital resource for Irish and local studies. Admission free.

Malone House
Barnett Demesne, Upper Malone Road
Belfast, BT9 5PB
Tel: 028 9068 1246
Web: www.malonehouse.co.uk

Early 19th century house in parkland. Also has restaurant and art gallery. Admission free.

Minnowburn Beeches
Shaw's Bridge, Belfast
Web: www.ntni.org.uk

Woodlands and walks in Lagan Valley.

Odyssey
Queen's Quay, Belfast, BT3 9QQ.
Tel: 028 9045 1055

Main features are an indoor arena, home of Belfast Giants Ice Hockey team, W5 interactive discovery centre, Sheridan IMAX and the Warner Village 12-screen multiplex cinema.

Police Museum
Brooklyn, 65 Knock Road, Belfast
Tel: 028 9065 0222 extn 22499
Web: www.psni.police.uk/museum

Uniforms, photographs and equipment relating to the Irish Constabulary since its formation in 1822 and the Royal Ulster Constabulary since 1922. Admission free.

Public Record Office of Northern Ireland (PRONI)
66 Balmoral Avenue, Belfast, BT9 6NY
Tel: 028 9025 5905
Web: www.proni.gov.uk

PRONI is the official place of deposit for public and private records in Northern Ireland with records dating from 1219.

Queen's University Visitors' Centre

Lanyon Building, Queen's University
University Road, Belfast, BT7 1NN
Tel: 028 9033 5252
Web: www.qub.ac.uk/vcentre
Exhibition, information, memorabilia.
Admission free.

Royal Ulster Rifles Museum

War Memorial Building
5 Waring Street, Belfast
Tel: 028 9023 2086
Preserves relics of the Royal Ulster Rifles and its predecessor foot regiments.

Sir Thomas and Lady Dixon Park

Upper Malone Road, Belfast
Tel: 028 9032 0202
Web: www.belfastcity.gov.uk

One of the world's best rose gardens which hosts the Belfast International Rose Trials each year. Admission free.

St Anne's Cathedral

Donegall Street, Belfast
Tel: 028 9032 8332
Web: www.belfastcathedral.org

St Anne's Cathedral is built on the site of Belfast's first Church of Ireland parish. Cathedral has excellent glass mosaics and Irish marble and the largest Celtic cross in Ireland. Admission free.

St George's Market

Tel: 028 9043 5704

The last surviving Victorian covered market in Belfast. Market days on Friday and Saturday.

Streamvale Open Dairy Farm

38 Ballyhanwood Road, Belfast
Tel: 028 9048 3244

Chance to see farming at work – pets' corner, milking parlour, animal feeding and rides and nature trail.

Ulster Museum

Stranmillis Road (in Botanic Gardens)
Belfast, BT9 5AB
Tel: 028 9038 3000
Web: www.ulstermuseum.org.uk

Northern Ireland's largest museum, housing major permanent and visiting collections, as well as a permanent exhibition of Irish art. Admission free.

whowhatwherewhenwhy-W5

whowhatwherewhenwhy W5

At Odyssey, 2 Queen's Quay
Belfast, BT3 9QQ
Tel: 028 9046 7700
Web: www.w5online.co.uk

An amazing place to visit for adults and children alike.

W5 is the award winning interactive discovery centre located at the Odyssey complex in Belfast. As one of Northern Ireland's premier visitor attractions the centre has 140 amazing interactive exhibits, which offer fantastic fun for visitors of all ages.

Opening Hours:
Mon-Saturday 10.00am-6.pm.
Sunday 12.00pm-6.00pm.
Last Admission 5.00pm

Please note, during school term time W5 will close one hour earlier on Monday to Thursday with last admission at 4pm.

In addition to the exhibits W5 also offer live science shows and run a special programme of changing events.

World War II Exhibition

9 Waring Street, Belfast
Tel: 028 9032 0392

## Co Antrim

Andrew Jackson Centre

Boneybefore, Carrickfergus
Tel: 028 9336 6455
Web: www.carrickfergus.org

Close to site of ancestral home of Andrew Jackson, 7th US President 1829-37, whose parents emigrated in 1765 from Carrickfergus.

Antrim Castle Gardens

Randalstown Road, Antrim
Tel: 028 9442 8000

Restored 17th century Anglo-Dutch water gardens with parterre, ponds, and woodland and riverside walks.

Arthur Ancestral Home

Dreen, Cullybackey
Tel: 028 2563 8494

Restored 18th century farmhouse with open flax-straw thatched roof. Ancestral home of Chester Alan Arthur, 21st US President 1881-85.

Ballance House

118A Lisburn Road, Glenavy
Tel: 028 9264 8492

Birthplace in 1839 of John Ballance, New Zealand Prime Minister 1891-93. Historic house and museum.

Ballycastle Museum

59 Castle Street, Ballycastle
Tel: 028 2076 2024

Folk/social history of the Glens in the town's 18th century courthouse. Admission free.(only open July & August)

Ballycastle – Rathlin Island Ferry

14 Bayview Road, Ballycastle
Tel: 028 2076 9299

Ballymena Museum

3 Wellington Court
Ballymena BT43 6EG
Tel: 028 2564 2166

Diverse programme of exhibitions, talks, tours and other events exploring the rich heritage of Ballymena borough. Admission free.

Ballymoney Museum
Tel: 028 2766 0245

Local history exhibits. Admission free. (only open during summer months)

Benvarden Gardens
Dervock, Ballymoney
Tel: 028 2074 1331

18th century walled garden with herbaceous borders, kitchen garden and Victorian woodland pond. Stable yard with coach and cart houses and mini museum.

Brookhall Historical Farm
2 Horse Park, Ballinderry Road, Lisburn
Tel: 028 9262 1712

Farming museum with duck pond, rare breed animals, gardens, farming implements from a bygone era.

Carnfunnock Country Park
Coast Road, Larne
Tel: 028 2827 0541 or 028 2826 0088

Maze in the shape of Northern Ireland. Walled garden, barbecue/picnic sites, children's activity centre with outdoor adventure playground, forest walks, orienteering, golf activities, miniature railway and modern visitor centre.

Carrick-a-Rede Rope Bridge
Larrybane, Ballintoy, Ballycastle
Tel: 028 2073 1582
Web: www.ntni.org.uk

Swinging rope bridge spans a 60 ft wide chasm, giving access to the salmon fishery. Also 1 mile walk along the cliff path.

Carrickfergus Castle
Marine Highway, Carrickfergus
Tel: 028 9335 1273

Castle started in 1180 by John de Courcy and garrisoned until 1928. Exhibition on the castle's history.

Dunluce Castle
3 miles east of Portrush
Tel: 028 2073 1938

Dramatic ruins on a rocky headland – most of the fortifications date from the 16th and 17th centuries.

Dunluce Family Entertainment Centre
Sandhill Drive, Portrush
Tel: 028 7082 4444

Has soft-play adventure playground, a computerised treasure hunt, motion simulator, restaurant and shops.

East Strand Beach
Causeway Street, Portrush

Beach stretches from Portrush to the White Rocks with views over the Skerries to the Scottish Islands. Backed by an extensive dune system and the famous Royal Portrush golf course.

ECOS Environmental Centre
Kernohans Lane, Broughshane Road
Ballymena
Tel: 028 2566 4400
Web: www.ecoscentre.com

Environmental centre with interactive exhibits highlighting environmental issues; focus on biodiversity, sustainability and alternative energy production from sustainable sources on site in the 150 acre park.

Flame – The Gasworks Museum of Ireland
Irish Quarter West, Carrickfergus
Tel: 028 9336 9575

The only Victorian coal-fired gasworks in Ireland built in 1855 to light street lamps, it produced gas until 1964. Site has recently been completely restored.

Ford Farm Park and Museum
8 Low Road, Islandmagee
Tel: 028 9335 3264
Web: www.ford-farm.co.uk

Museum, animals, shoreline walks, birdwatching, demonstrations by arrangement – butter-making and spinning.

Giant's Causeway
Bushmills
Tel: 028 2073 1855
Web: www.ntni.org.uk

Ireland's first World Heritage site – over 40,000 stone columns. Various walks and coastal paths.

Glenariff Forest Park
Ballymena/Waterfoot Road
Tel: 028 2955 6000

Spectacular glen walk with three waterfalls. Scenic path and trails to mountain viewpoints.

Hilden Brewery
Hilden House, Hilden, Lisburn
Tel: 028 9266 3863

Guided tour of Ireland's oldest independent brewery in the 19th century courtyard of Hilden House.

Irish Linen Centre and Lisburn Museum
Market Square, Lisburn
Tel: 028 9266 3377

Weaving workshop with hand looms, audio visuals. Exhibitions on local history. Linen/craft shop. Admission free.

Lagan Valley LeisurePlex
12 Lisburn Leisure Park,
Lisburn, BT28 1LP
Tel: 028 9267 2121

Water attractions including a free-form leisure pool, competition and diving pools.

Larne Interpretive Centre
Narrow Gauge Road, Larne
Tel: 028 2826 0088

Story of the building of the Antrim coast road. Admission free.

Larne – Islandmagee Ferry
Tel: 028 2827 4085

Leslie Hill Open Farm
Macfin Road, Ballymoney
Tel: 028 2766 6803

Horse-trap and and pony rides through an 18th century estate. Deer, ornamental fowl, pets, farm animals, walled garden, lakes and trails. Carriages, horse-drawn machines and threshing barn.

Old Bushmills Distillery
Distillery Road, Bushmills
Tel: 028 2073 1521
Web: www.whiskeytours.ie

Oldest licensed whiskey distillery in the world, established in 1608. One hour guided tour and whiskey tasting.

Patterson's Spade Mill
751 Antrim Road, Templepatrick
Tel: 028 9443 3619
Web: www.ntni.org.uk

Last water-powered spade mill in Ireland. All original equipment in working order. Spade-making demonstrations.

Portrush Countryside Centre
Lansdowne Crescent
Bath Road, Portrush
Tel: 028 7082 3600

Countryside centre with seashore exhibition, touch tank and live sea creatures. Opportunities for rock pool rambles, fossil hunts and bird watching. Admission free.

Rathlin Island Boathouse Visitors' Centre
Rathlin Island Harbour
Tel: 028 2076 3951

History, photographs and artefacts.

Royal Irish Regiment Museum
Depot Royal Irish
St Patrick's Barracks, Ballymena
Tel: 028 2566 1383

Regimental history from 1689.

TACT Wildlife Centre
2 Crumlin Road, Crumlin
Tel: 028 9442 2900

200 year old walled garden with bird sanctuary.

Waterworld
Portrush
Tel: 028 7082 2001

Indoor water centre – giant water flumes, fun pools, water cannon, pirate ships and Jacuzzis.

Whitepark Bay Nature Trail
Ballintoy
Web: www.ntni.org.uk

1 mile trail shows vegetation types developed on sand and chalk. Geological features displayed. Free access always.

## Co Armagh

Ardress House
64 Ardress Road
Tel: 028 3885 1236

17th century famhouse with Adam-style drawing room, fine furniture and paintings. Farmyard with rare breeds. Woodland and riverside walks.

Argory
144 Derrycaw Road, Moy, BT71 6NA
Tel: 028 8778 4753

House dating from 1820 overlooking the Blackwater river and set in wooded countryside. Stable yard and sundial garden.

Armagh Ancestry
38A English Street, Armagh
Tel: 028 3752 1802

Provides a pathway for tracing Armagh ancestors using comprehensive genealogical database.

Armagh County Museum
The Mall East, Armagh
Tel: 028 3752 3070

History of Co Armagh – military, archaeology, railway, costume and local history collections.

Armagh Observatory
College Hill, Armagh
Tel: 028 3752 2928

Modern astronomical research institute with a rich heritage. Grounds include Robinson dome with a 10 inch telescope, Lindsay sundial and the Armagh Astropark. Admission free.

Armagh Planetarium
College Hill, Armagh
Tel: 028 3752 4725

Public telescope, daily audio-visual presentation, exhibition areas.

Armagh Public Library
Abbey Street, Armagh
Tel: 028 3752 3142

Library was established in 1771 and was the first public library outside Dublin. Repository of a fine collection of antiques and ancient manuscripts.

Ballydougan Pottery Visitors' Centre
Bloomvale House
171 Plantation Road, Craigavon
Tel: 028 3834 2201
Web: www.ballydouganpottery.co.uk

Bloomvale House has been home to generations of craftspeople since 1785 and is currently where Ballydougan Pottery is crafted.

Dan Winter's House (Ancestral Home)
The Diamond, Loughgall
Tel: 028 3885 1344

Traditionally thatched, mud-walled farmyard cottage, where decision to form the Orange Order was made by Dan Winter and others following the Battle of the Diamond.

Derrymore House
Newry
Tel: 028 3083 8361

Thatched 18th century mansion was home to Isaac Corry, General-in-Chief of the Irish Volunteers and later Chancellor of the Irish Parliament.

Gosford Forest Park
Markethill
Tel: 028 3755 1277

Estate has associations with Dean Jonathan Swift. Heritage poultry, rare breeds of cattle and sheep in open paddocks, deer-park, walled garden, nature trails and treks.

Keady and District Community Initiative
Unit 3, The Old Mill, Main Street, Keady
Tel: 028 3753 9928

The story of local linen production from 1840s including model of a working mill, weaving loon, local history exhibits, photographs, music recordings.

Loughgall Country Park
11-14 Main Street, Loughgall
Tel: 028 3889 2900

188 hectare estate of open farmlands and orchards, with 18 hole golf course, 37 acre coarse fishery, bridle path, walks, children's play area and football pitch.

Millworker's House
6 College Square East, Bessbrook
Tel: 028 3083 7143

Restored terrace house built in 1881 depicting the home of a linen millwoker in Bessbrook in the late 19th century.

Moneypenny's Lock
Castle Street, Portadown
Tel: 028 3832 2205

Restored lock-keeper's house, stables and bothy on the Newry canal. Also 2 mile walk along the towpath.

Oxford Island/Lough Neagh Discovery Centre
Oxford Island, Craigavon
Tel: 028 3832 2205
Web: www.oxfordisland.com

4 miles of footpaths, 5 birdwatching hides, woodland, ponds, wildflower meadows, picnic and play areas. Centre houses exhibition about history, culture and wildlife in and around Lough Neagh. Also has craft shop and café with views of the lough.

Palace Stables Heritage Centre
Friary Road, Armagh
Tel: 028 3752 9629
Web: www.visit-armagh.com

Restored Georgian stable block featuring the life of the palace in 1786. Costumed interpreters recreate the grandeur and squalor of the Georgian period.

Peatlands Park
Off Junction 13 M1
Tel: 028 3885 1102

Woods, open bogs, nature reserves and bog garden with 1 mile trip on narrow-gauge railway.

Royal Irish Fusiliers Museum
Sovereign's House
The Mall East, Armagh
Tel: 028 3752 2911

Story of the regiment from 1793-1968 with large model of the capture of the Imperial French Eagle at the Battle of Barossa 1813. Also contains militaria from the Armagh, Cavan and Monaghan militias.

Slieve Gullion Forest Park
Newry
Tel: 028 3086 8900

8 mile drive up and round this thickly wooded park. Mountain-top trail at 1,880 ft to megalithic cairns and lake with views of Ring of Gullion, Mourne Mountains and Cooley Mountains. Admission free.

St Patrick's Cathedral (Church of Ireland)
Cathedral Close, Armagh
Tel: 028 3752 3142
Web: www.stpatricks-cathedral.org

Present Cathedral dates from the 13th century, built on site where St Patrick established his chief church in 445 AD. Admission free.

St Patrick's Cathedral (Roman Catholic)
Cathedral Road, Armagh
Tel: 028 3752 2802

Building begun in 1840 but suspended during Famine years. Dedicated for worship in 1873 but interior decoration not completed until 20th century. Admission free.

St Patrick's Trian Visitor Complex
40 English Street, Armagh
Tel: 028 3752 1801
Web: www.visit-armagh.com

3 different exhibitions trace Armagh's history, its association with St Patrick and also the adventures of Gulliver, in the 'Land of Lilliput'.

Tayto Factory
Tandragee Castle, Tandragee
Tel: 028 3884 0249
Web: www.tayto.com

Factory inside the grounds of a castle formerly owned by Duke of Manchester. Factory tour demonstrates potato storage techniques and the process of crisp-making.

## Co Down

Annalong Corn Mill
Marine Park, Annalong
Tel: 028 4376 8736

Built in around 1830 and powered by a waterwheel, the mill overlooks the harbour in Annalong.

Ark Open Farm
296 Bangor Road, Newtownards
Tel: 028 9182 0445

Over 80 rare species of cattle, pigs, sheep, goats, ponies, ducks, poultry and llamas in 40 acres of countryside.

Ballycopeland Windmill
Millisle
Tel: 028 9054 3037

Late 18th century tower mill in use until 1915 and still in working order. Visitor centre at the miller's house with an electrically operated model of the mill.

Brontë Homeland Interpretive Centre
Drumballyroney, Rathfriland
Tel: 028 4063 1152

Drumballyroney school and church where Patrick Brontë, father of the novelist sisters, taught and preached.

Butterfly House
Seaforde Nursery, Seaforde
Tel: 028 4481 1225

Set in Seaforde Gardens, with large flight area with hundreds of free-flying exotic butterflies. Reptiles and insects behind glass. Parrots, maze, viewing tower, rare plants, nursery garden, play area.

Castle Espie
78 Ballydrain Road, Comber
Tel: 028 9187 4146

Ireland's largest collection of ducks, geese and swans with viewing from hides, waterfowl gardens, woodland walks.

Castle Ward
Strangford
Tel: 028 4488 1204

18th century mansion with facades in different styles – Classical and Gothic. Victorian laundry, restored 1830s cornmill, disused leadmine and sawmill. Exhibition in Strangford Lough Wildlife Centre and guided tours and boat trips.

Castlewellan Forest Park
Main Street, Castlewellan
Tel: 028 4377 8664

Queen Anne style courtyards, tropical birds, hedge maze. Features a national arboretum, initiated in 1740 and also 3 mile trail around the lake with sculptures created from the park's natural materials.

Cranfield Beach
Rostrevor to Kilkeel Road
Tel: 028 4176 2525

South-facing beach at the mouth of Carlingford Lough with Mourne Mountains as its backdrop.

Crawfordsburn Country Park
Helen's Bay
Tel: 028 9185 3621

Beaches, woodland and meadows, coastal and riverside walks. Restored gun site at Grey Pint Fort.
Admission free.

Delamont Country Park
Downpatrick to Comber Road
Tel: 028 4482 8333

Strangford stone and Ireland's longest miniature railway. Allows access to, and views over, Strangford Lough.

Down Cathedral and St Patrick's Grave
English Street, Downpatrick
Tel: 028 4461 4922

Church of Ireland Cathedral built in 1183 as a Benedictine Monastery. St Patrick's grave is reputedly within the graveyard. Church contains magnificent stain glass windows and box pews.
Admission free.

Down County Museum
The Mall, Downpatrick
Tel: 028 4461 5218
Web: www.downcountymuseum.com

Restored 18th century gaol containing exhibitions and the history of county Down. Includes restored cell block with life-size figures of prisoners and their jailers.

Downpatrick Railway Museum
Railway Station, Market Street
Downpatrick
Tel: 028 4461 5779

Working engines and steam locomotive on display along with photographic display and model railway.

Exploris Aquarium
The Ropewalk, Castle Street, Portaferry
Tel: 028 4272 8062

Presents marine life on a journey from Strangford Lough to the Irish Sea, with thousands of species on view. New seal sanctuary.

Grey Abbey
Greyabbey
Tel: 028 9054 3037

Ruined Cistercian abbey founded in 1193 by Affreca, wife of John de Courcy. Parkland setting with medieval 'physick' garden.

Hillsborough Castle and Gardens
Main Street, Hillsborough
Tel: 028 9268 1300

18th century mansion, built in 1770s by the first Marquis of Downshire. Formerly the home of the Governor of Northern Ireland the Castle is now the official residence of the Secretary of State. Gardens feature extensive rose garden and lakeside walks.

Hillsborough Courthouse
The Square, Hillsborough
Tel: 028 92 68 9717

Exhibition in Georgian courthouse on working of courts through stories, pictures and games. Admission free.

Inch Abbey
Downpatrick

Ruins of Cistercian monastery founded in 1180s by John de Courcy. Situated on island in the Quoile, reached by a causeway.

Mount Stewart House and Gardens
Portaferry Road, Newtownards
Tel: 028 4278 8387

Childhood home of Lord Castlereagh with fine gardens and vistas. Temple of the Winds overlooks Strangford Lough.

Murlough National Nature Reserve
Dundrum
Tel: 028 4375 1467

Sand dune system with heath and woodland surrounded by estuary and sea. Guided walks and nature trail.

Newry Museum
Arts Centre, Bank Parade, Newry
Tel: 028 3026 6232

Demonstrates history of the Gap of the North. Also contains robes of the Order of St Patrick and period furniture in a restored 18th century room, including Nelson's table from HMS Victory.
Admission free.

North Down Heritage Centre
Castle Park Avenue, Bangor
Tel: 028 9127 1200

Contains the Ballycroghan Swords dating from 500 BC and a 9th century handbell found near Bangor. Also features toy and railway displays and vintage films. Observation beehive in summer.

Pickie Family Fun Park
The Marina, Bangor
Tel: 028 9127 4430

Swan pedal boats, paddling pools, mini railway, playground, go-karts and superslide.

Portaferry Visitor Centre
Castle Street, Portaferry
Tel: 028 4272 9882

Restored stable featuring exhibitions on the heritage and environment of Portaferry and Strangford Lough.

Quoile Countryside Centre
Downpatrick
Tel: 028 4461 5520

Displays on the wildlife of the Quoile pondage where a barrage has changed the saltwater estuary to fresh water. Includes birdwatching hide.

Rowallane Garden
Saintfield
Tel: 028 9751 0131

Rare trees, shrubs and plants including magnificent rhododendrons and azaleas.

Scarva Visitor Centre
Main Street, Scarva
Tel: 028 3883 2163

History of canals in Ireland, the building of the Newry canal and the history of Scarva. Admission free.

Scrabo Country Park
Newtownards
Tel: 028 9181 1491

Contains Scrabo Tower (with 122 steps to the top), which was built in 1857 as a memorial to the 3rd Marquis of Londonderry.

Silent Valley
Head Road, Kilkeel
Tel: 028 9074 1166

Silent Valley and Ben Crom reservoirs supply 30 million gallons of water per day to Belfast and County Down. Beautiful parkland before the dams.

Somme Heritage Centre
233 Bangor Road, Newtownards
Tel: 028 9182 3202

Highlights Ireland's contribution to the First World War, including reconstructed trenches of the Battle of the Somme.

St Patrick Centre
53A Lower Market Street
Downpatrick, BT30 6LZ
Tel: 028 4461 9000

Exhibition explores the legacy of St Patrick and recalls the story of the saint.

Strangford – Portaferry Ferry
Tel: 028 4488 1637

Tollymore Forest Park
Bryansford Road, Newcastle
Tel: 028 4372 2428

Park has numerous stone follies and bridges and a magnificent Cork Oak in the arboretum. Wildlife and forestry exhibits in barn.

Tyrella Beach
Tel: 028 4482 8333

Miles of flat sandy beach with dune conservation area – car free zone with waymarked walks.

Ulster Folk and Transport Museum
Cultra, Holywood
Tel: 028 9042 8428

Illustrates past Ulster traditions including typical Ulster town of the early 1900s. Transport Museum presents Ireland's most comprehensive transport collection including 'Titanic' and 'Flight Experience' exhibitions.

Ulster Wildlife Centre
3 New Line, Crossgar
Tel: 028 4483 0282

Victorian walled garden providing a sample of the natural heritage of Ulster. Habitats recreated include wild bogland, meadows, woodland and wildlife pond. Admission free.

## Co Fermanagh

Belleek China
Belleek, BT93 3FY
Tel: 028 6865 8501

Home of the world-famous porcelain. Tours allow visitors to watch craftsmen at work.

Castle Archdale Country Park
Castle Archdale
Tel: 028 6862 1588

Woodland and loughshore walks, marina, pony trekking, nature trail. Allows access to White Island. Castle Archdale at War exhibition on the Battle of the Atlantic.

Castle Balfour
Main Street, Lisnaskea
Tel: 028 6632 3110

Built around 1618 by Sir James Balfour, a Scottish planter, the castle was in continuous occupation until the early 19th century.

Castle Caldwell Forest Park
Belleek
Tel: 028 6634 3032

RSPB reserve, wildfowl hides, shore walks.

Castle Coole
Dublin Road, Enniskillen
Tel: 028 6632 2690

Designed by James Wyatt for the Earls of Belmore and completed in 1798. Grounds feature mature oak woodland and lake.

Crom Estate
Newtownbutler
Tel: 028 6773 8118

Over 2,000 acres of woodland, farmland and loughs support rare plants and wildlife. Walks around the estate take in the ruins of Crom old castle.

Devenish Island
Tel: 028 6862 1588

Famous for its perfect 12th century round tower and ruined Augustinian abbey. Graveyard holds intricately carved 15th century high cross.

Enniskillen Castle and Museum
Castle Barracks, Enniskillen
Tel: 028 6632 5000
Web: www.enniskillencastle.co.uk

Famous castle, once the stronghold of Gaelic Maguire chieftains. History, wildlife and landscape of the area presented in Fermanagh County Museum. Museum of the Royal Inniskilling Fusiliers in the castle keep.

ExploreErne Exhibition
Gateway Centre, Corry, Belleek
Tel: 028 6865 8833

The story of the formation of the lough and its effect on the people who live round its shores.

Fermanagh Crystal
Main Street, Belleek
Tel: 028 6865 8631

Design, marking and cutting of hand-cut lead glass.

Florence Court
Florencecourt
Tel: 028 6634 8249

Built by Earls of Enniskillen in 18th century. Features 1780s walled garden.

Florencecourt Forest Park
Florencecourt
Tel: 028 6634 3032

Walks and walled garden. Grounds boast 200 year old Irish oaks and the original Irish yew tree.

Forthill Park and Cole's Monument
Enniskillen
Tel: 028 6632 5050

Town park on steep hill. Monument built in 1857 commemorating Sir Galbraith Lowry-Cole who was one of Wellington's generals. 108 steps to the top of the monument.

Lough Navar Forest
Derrygonnelly
Tel: 028 6634 3032

7 mile drive through the forest to magnificent panorama over Lower Lough Erne with viewpoints and picnic areas.

Marble Arch Caves and Cuilcagh
Mountain Park, Florencecourt
Tel: 028 6634 8855

Guided tour included walk through ancient ash woodland and boat journey along subterranean river, continuing on foot past a variety of cave formations.

Monea Castle
Monea
Tel: 028 6632 3110

Imposing plantation castle build around 1618 by Malcolm Hamilton. Abandoned in 1750 following a fire.

Roslea Heritage Centre
Monaghan Road, Roslea
Tel: 028 6775 1750

An 1874 schoolhouse with old school desks. Among traditional farming implements on display is a McMahon space, once manufactured locally.

Sheelin Lace Museum
Bellanaleck
Tel: 028 6634 8052

Items of Irish lace dating form 1850 to 1900, including wedding dresses and veils, baby dresses, bonnets and parsols.

Tully Castle
Churchhill

Fortified house and bawn built in 1613 and burned by the Maguires in 1641. Formal garden and visitor centre.

Vintage Cycle Museum
64 Main Street, Brookeborough
Tel: 028 8953 1206

Over 100 bicycles including folding army bike, ice-cream tricycle, tandems, 1950s children's cycles and bicycle with levers. Also toys and household memorabilia.

White Island
Kesh
Tel: 028 6862 1333

Main feature of the ruined 12th century church is its Romanesque doorway. The archaic stone figures set into the wall predate the church.

## Co Londonderry

Bellaghy Bawn
Castle Street, Bellaghy
Tel: 028 7938 6812

Exhibits inside this restored fortified house of 1618 include local history, the Ulster Plantation and the writings of Bellaghy-born Seamus Heaney and other poets.

Benone Strand
Benone
Tel: 028 7775 0555

White beach backed by sand dunes and dramatic cliffs.

Castledawson Open Farm
Leitrim Road, Castledawson
Tel: 028 7946 8207

Rare fowl breeds, goats, rabbits, Jacob and Soya sheep, Dexter cattle, guinea pigs, miniature Shetland ponies, emus.

Derry's Walls
Derry City
Tel: 028 7126 7284

Derry is the only completely walled city in Ireland, its walls have withstood several sieges, the most celebrated 105 days. Fine views from the top of the walls which encircle the old city.

Downhill Castle and Mussenden Temple
Mussenden Road, Castlerock
Tel: 028 7084 8728

Ruins of 18th century palace of the eccentric Earl – Bishop of Derry. Mussenden Temple on the cliff top was built by the Bishop in 1783 as a summer library.

Earhart Centre and Wildlife Sanctuary
Ballyarnet, Londonderry
Tel: 028 7135 4040

Cottage exhibition on Amelia Earhart, the first woman to fly the Atlantic solo who landed in the field here in 1932.

Fifth Province
Calgach Centre, Butcher Street
Tel: 028 7137 3177

Presentation using a variety of dramatic effects and audio-visual techniques which depicts the unique history of the Celtic nation.

Foyle Valley Railway Centre
Foyle Road, Derry
Tel: 028 7126 5234

Built on the site of the Great Northern Railway terminus. Features narrow-gauge networks that carried the Donegal Railway and the Londonderry and Lough Swilly Railway. Diesel railcars of 1932 and 1940 on 6 mile track.

Garvagh Museum and Heritage Centre
Main Street, Garvagh
Tel: 028 2955 7924

Stone Age artefacts from the Bann Valley. Boat from nearby Eel fishery and farming implements.

Guildhall
Guildhall Square, Derry
Tel: 028 7137 7335

The original building, named in honour of the London Guilds, was officially opened in 1890 as the administrative centre of the Londonderry Corporation. The neo-gothic building stands on land reclaimed from the River Foyle; its clock tower is the largest of its kind in Ireland.

Harbour Museum
Harbour Square, Derry
Tel: 028 7137 7331

The maritime history of Derry including a replica of 30 ft Curragh in which St Columba sailed to Iona in 563 AD. Admission free.

Hezlett House
107 Sea Road, Castlerock
Tel: 028 7084 8567

Thatched 17th century former rectory with cruck/truss roof and 19th century furnishings.

Magilligan – Greencastle Ferry
Tel: + (353) 778 1901
Ferry from Co Londonderry to Donegal

Plantation of Ulster Visitor Centre
50 High Street, Draperstown
Tel: 028 7962 7800

The story of the Ulster Plantation, Hugh O'Neil and the 'Flight of the Earls'.

Portstewart Strand
Portstewart
Tel: 028 7083 6396

Two miles of strand and sand dunes with waymarked nature trail.

Roe Valley Country Park
Limavady
Tel: 028 7772 2074

Home to Ulster's first domestic hydro-electric power station opened in 1896 – much of the original equipment is still preserved.

Springhill House
20 Springhill Road, Moneymore
Tel: 028 8674 8210

17th century manor house with family belongings and costume museum.

St Columb's Cathedral
London Street, Derry
Tel: 028 7126 7313

Built in 1633 with stained glass depicting heroic scenes from the Great Siege of 1688-89. The keys of the gates which were closed against the Jacobites are displayed in the chapterhouse.

Tower Museum
Union Hall Place, Derry
Tel: 028 7137 2411

History of the city from prehistoric times.

William Clark & Sons Ltd
Upperlands, Maghera
Tel: 028 7954 7200

Linen fabrics for the clothing industry are made here. Beetling machines in operation. Tour passes the dams which used to power the old linen mill and still supply the water for manufacturing processes. Booking essential.

Workhouse Museum
23 Glendermott Road, Derry
Tel: 028 7131 8328
History of the workhouse, Irish famine and city's role during World War II.

## Co Tyrone

An Creagán Visitor Centre
Creggan, Omagh
Tel: 028 8076 1112

Archaeological history and stories of the area with interpretive displays and bog walks.

Castle Caulfield
Castlecaulfied

Ruins of mansion built by Sir Toby Caulfield in 1619. Gatehouse with murder holes and Caulfield arms.

Castlederg Visitor Centre
26 Lower Strabane Road, Castlederg
Tel: 028 8167 0795

Local exhibits and displays highlight the area's heritage.

Coach and Carriage Museum
Blessingbourne, Fivemiletown
Tel: 028 8952 1221

Coaches on display including an 1825 London-to-Oxford stagecoach and a 1910 country doctor's buggy.

Drum Manor Forest Park
Cookstown
Tel: 028 8676 2774

Demonstration shrub garden, walled butterfly garden, arboretum. Lakes, heronry, nature trail.

Gortin Glen Forest Park
Gortin, Omagh
Tel: 028 8167 0666

5 mile forest drive with pull-in places for fine views. Trails also lead to viewpoints.

Grant Ancestral Home
Dergina, Ballygawley
Tel: 028 8555 7133

1738 birthplace of John Simpson, great grandfather of Ulysses Simpson Grant, 18th US President 1869-77.

Gray's Printers' Museum
49 Main Street, Strabane
Tel: 028 7188 0055

Associated with famous Ulster-Americans, including John Dunlap, printer of the American Declaration of Independence.

Kinturk Cultural Centre
7 Kinturk Road, Cookstown
Tel: 028 8673 6512

History of the Lough Neagh fishing and eel industry including displays of old traditional boats and equipment.

Sperrin Heritage Centre
274 Glenelly Road
Cranagh, Gortin
Tel: 028 8164 8142

'Treasure of the Sperrins' exhibition unearths the regions rich geological composition and the story of gold.

The Linen Green
Moygashel
Tel: 028 8775 3761

Designer outlet village including visitors' centre depicting the history behind Moygashel linen.

Tyrone Crystal
Killybrackey, Dungannon
Tel: 028 8772 5335

Guided tour of the blowing, marking, cutting and finishing stages of Tyrone Crystal.

Ulster-American Folk Park
Castletown, Omagh
Tel: 028 8224 3292

Outdoor museum of emigration to North America tells the story of people who left Ireland during the 18th and 19th centuries.

Wellbrook Beetling Mill
Cookstown
Tel: 028 8674 8210

Water-powered 18th century linen hammer mill. Linen making demonstrations.

Wilson Ancestral Home
Strabane
Tel: 028 7138 2204

Ancestral home of James Wilson, 28th President of the USA.

## Northern Ireland's Forests

Northern Ireland's forests are expanding and the Forest Service encourages this growth and manages its forests in a responsible and environmentally friendly manner. Its forests are open throughout the year, providing facilities and areas for recreational activities such as walking. Forests are listed below by county.

The Forest Service Headquarters
Customer Service Manager
Dundonald House
Upper Newtownards Road
Belfast, BT4 3SB
Tel: 028 9052 4480
Fax: 028 9052 4570

Co Antrim
Ballycastle Forest, Glenarm Forest, Glenariff Forest Park, Tardree Forest, Ballyboley Forest, Ballypatrick Forest, Portglenone Forest, Randalstown Forest, Rea's Wood

Co Armagh
Gosford Forest Park, Slieve Gullion Forest Park

Co Down
Tollymore Forest Park, Castlewellan Forest Park, Donard Forest, Rostrevor Forest, Drumkeeragh Forest, Belvoir Park Forest, Cairn Wood

Co Fermanagh
Florence Court Forest Park, Ely Lodge Forest, Lough Navar Forest, Castle Caldwell Forest, Castle Archdale Forest, Marble Arch Wood, Spring Grove.

Co Londonderry
Coleraine Woods – Sommerset, Mountsandel, Castleroe, Springwell Forest, Binevenagh

Co Tyrone
Gortin Glen Forest Park, Drum Manor Forest Park, Parkanaur Forest Park, Pomeroy Forest, Seskinore Forest, Knockmany Forest, Fardross Forest

## Other Visitor Information

### Weather

Average daytime/night time temperatures, degree C (degrees F)

| | DAY °C (°F) | NIGHT °C (°F) |
|---|---|---|
| January/ February | 7 (44) | 1 (34) |
| March/ April | 10 (51) | 3 (38) |
| May/June | 16 (61) | 8 (46) |
| July/ August | 18 (65) | 10 (51) |
| September/ October | 15 (59) | 8 (46) |
| November/ December | 8 (47) | 3 (37) |

**Average Annual Rainfall:** 43 inches

### Currency

Northern Ireland uses the Pound Sterling, as in Great Britain. However, the main banks each issue their own banknotes, as well as the more familiar Bank of England and Bank of Scotland. Mastercard/Access and Visa are generally accepted; Diner's Club and American Express less so. Cheques with a bankers' card are also widely accepted.

In towns, most banks have opening hours of 9.30am - 4.30pm, sometimes closing for lunch, or closing early on Friday. A few may open on Saturday mornings, but most do not, and in smaller towns and villages the bank may not be open every day.

Cash dispensers are numerous, and accept most UK bank cards, as well as all types of credit card. Banks such as TSB and Lloyd's do not have branches in Northern Ireland, although cash may be withdrawn via cash dispensers.

For travel to the Republic of Ireland, money must be changed into Euros, the common currency for most of the European Union. The Euro is commonly accepted in border areas and in larger stores in Belfast and some of the bigger towns.

### Shopping

Northern Ireland has most of the high street stores seen in both Great Britain and the Republic of Ireland. Shopping hours are generally 9.00am to 5.30 pm, although in smaller towns shops close for lunch and may close early (or not even open) on one day of the week. In larger towns shops are often open late on Thursday nights, and many open on Sunday from 1pm to 5pm. Some of the larger supermarkets are open 24 hours a day, except Sunday. Most towns also have a market day once a week.
*(For a list of shopping centres and more detail on shopping see Chapter 13, page 443).*

**Northern Ireland Towns 'Closed' Days**

| | |
|---|---|
| Antrim | Wednesday |
| Armagh | Wednesday |
| Ballycastle | Wednesday |
| Ballyclare | Thursday |
| Ballymena | Wednesday |
| Ballymoney | Monday |
| Ballymoney | Monday |
| Banbridge | Thursday |
| Bangor | Thursday |
| Bushmills | Thursday |
| Carrickfergus | Wednesday |
| Coleraine | Thursday |
| Comber | Wednesday |
| Cookstown | Wednesday |
| Downpatrick | Wednesday |
| Dungannon | Wednesday |
| Enniskillen | Wednesday |
| Holywood | Wednesday |
| Larne | Tuesday |
| Limavady | Thursday |
| Randalstown | Tuesday & Saturday |
| Warrenpoint | Wednesday |
| Lisburn | Wednesday |
| Londonderry | Thursday |
| Lurgan | Wednesday |
| Magherafelt | Tuesday |
| Newcastle | Thursday |
| Newry | Wednesday |
| Newtownards | Thursday |
| Omagh | Wednesday |
| Portadown | Thursday |
| Portstewart | Thursday (except July and August) |
| Strabane | Thursday |

**Travelling Distances**

| Road Distances from Belfast | Miles |
|---|---|
| Armagh | 40 |
| Cork | 262 |
| Dublin | 103 |
| Enniskillen | 83 |
| Larne | 23 |
| Derry | 73 |
| Newcastle | 31 |
| Newry | 38 |
| Omagh | 68 |
| Portrush | 61 |
| Rosslaire | 202 |
| Shannon | 211 |
| Sligo | 125 |

### Emergency Services

To contact the police, fire brigade, ambulance or coastguard in an emergency, dial 999 or 112.

### Medical & Dental Services

Certain hospitals have 24 hour A&E departments which will treat serious injuries and sudden illness. *(See Chapter 5 page 240 for list of hospitals)*

### Police Service of Northern Ireland

In non-emergency situations (such as to report lost or stolen property) the police can be contacted at the following local stations.

**Main Police Stations**

| | |
|---|---|
| Armagh | Tel: 028 3752 3311 |
| Ballymena | Tel: 028 2565 3355 |
| Belfast | Tel: 028 9065 0222 |
| Coleraine | Tel: 028 7034 4122 |
| Cookstown | Tel: 028 8676 6000 |
| Downpatrick | Tel: 028 4461 5011 |
| Dungannon | Tel: 028 8775 2525 |
| Enniskillen | Tel: 028 6632 2823 |
| Larne | Tel: 028 2827 2266 |
| Londonderry | Tel: 028 7136 7337 |
| Magherafelt | Tel: 028 7963 3701 |
| Newry | Tel: 028 3026 5500 |
| Newtownards | Tel: 028 9181 8080 |
| Omagh | Tel: 028 8224 6177 |
| Portadown | Tel: 028 3833 2424 |

## Consulates

American Consulate General
Queen's House, 14 Queen Street, Belfast
Tel: 028 9032 8239

Canadian Consulate
35 The Hill, Groomsport, Bangor
Tel: 028 9127 2060

Consul for the Netherlands
14-16 West Bank Road, Belfast, BT3 9JL
Tel: 028 9037 0223

Denmark, Sweden and Iceland
MWS Maclaran, c/o G Heyn & Sons Ltd
1 Corry Place, Belfast
Tel: 028 9035 0035

French Honorary Consul
University of Ulster
Shore Road
Newtownabbey
BT37 0QB
Tel: 028 9036 6546

German Consul
Frank Hewitt
Chamber of Commerce
22 Great Victoria Street
Belfast, BT2 7BJ
Tel: 028 9024 4113

Italy
O D'Agostino,
7 Richmond Park, Belfast
Tel: 028 9066 8854

New Zealand Consulate
118A Lisburn Road, Glenavy
Tel: 028 9264 8098

Norway, Portugal, Greece
c/o M F Ewings (Shipping) Ltd
15 Corporation Square, Belfast
Tel: 028 9024 2242

## Phone Numbers

The Northern Ireland Dialling Code (028) or (28) is used as a prefix when dialling from outside the region, or when making internal calls using a mobile phone. All Belfast numbers are composed of (028) followed by 90 and six digits.

## Pharmacies

General hours for pharmacies are 9.00am – 5.30pm Monday to Saturday although some may open late and on Sundays on a rota basis – details can usually be obtained in local press or from pharmacies.

## Postal Services

Post Offices and red post boxes are all over the city; Main Post Office is at Castle Junction and late mailings are accepted at Tomb Street Sorting Office. Small books of UK stamps are available in most convenience stores and petrol stations.

## Cars - Breakdown

Automobile Association Emergency
Tel: 0800 88 77 66

RAC
Tel: 0800 82 82 82

Green Flag
Tel: 051 0636

Ulster Automobile Club
Tel: 028 9042 6262

## DOE Traffic Watch

Tel: 08457 123321

## Car Parking

Multi-storey and off-street car parks have hourly tariffs dependent on location. On-street pay and display zones are clearly marked. Pay heed to restriction notices drawing attention to morning and evening rush hour clearways and bus lanes when in operation.

## Places of Worship

Main Sunday services of major Christian denominations are advertised in the Saturday edition of the Belfast Telegraph. Places of worship for most faith communities are listed in Yellow Pages. The two cathedrals in central Belfast are St. Anne's Cathedral (Anglican/Church of Ireland) on Donegall Street and St. Peter's Cathedral (Roman Catholic) on Derby Street.

## Pub Hours

Generally Mon-Sat, 11.30am-11pm, Sundays, 12.30-10pm. Many bars in Belfast have later opening hours on Thursday, Friday and Saturday nights. Children are not permitted on licensed premises. No alcohol may be served to under 18s

## Smoking

No smoking applies on public transport and in most public buildings. Increasingly restaurants are adopting a no-smoking policy; most have a smoke free area. Unlike the Republic of Ireland where a smoking ban has been introduced, smoking is still permitted in most bars and hotels in Northern Ireland.

## Tipping

It is now a generally accepted practice in restaurants to leave a gratuity of 10-15 per cent for good service. Some restaurants may add on an obligatory 10 or 12.5 per cent service charge on large group bookings.

# Reference Section

# Index

ORDNANCE SURVEY®
OF NORTHERN IRELAND

MALIN HEAD

FANAD HEAD

BALLYLIFFIN

CARNDONAGH

TORY ISLAND

HORN HEAD

BLOODY FORELAND

DUNFANAGHY

CARRICKART

BUNCRANA

City of D
Airpor

FALCARRAGH

CREESLOUGH

RATHMULLAN

DERRYBEG

MILLFORD

A2

Donegal International
Airport

GWEEDORE

GLENVEAGH NATIONAL
PARK

RATHMELTON

N13

LONDON

ARAN ISLAND

ANNAGARY

BURTONPORT

DUNGLOW

LETTERKENNY

N14

RIVER FOYLE

CO LONDON

FINTOWN

CO DONEGAL

GLENTIES

BALLYBOFEY

STRABANE

N15

A5

NEWTOWNSTEWART

ARDARA

GORTIN

GLENCOLUMBKILLE

CASTLEDERG

RIVER STRULE

CARRICK

KILLYBEGS

DONEGAL

OMAGH

PETTIGOE

FINTONA

BALLYSHANNON

KESH

IRVINESTOWN

A47

LOWER L ERNE

A32

AUGHER

BUNDORAN

BELLEEK

A26

DERRYGONNELLY

CLOGHER

TEMPO

A4

FIVEMILETOWN

N15

ENNISKILLEN

N16

BELCOO

A4

CO FERMANAGH

SLIGO

LISNASKEA

A34

MC

N4

UPPER
LOUGH
ERNE

A509

N17

LOUGH
ALLEN

N54

## NORTHERN IRELAND

- 🛈 Tourist Information
- A24 Main Route
- M1 Motorway
- Secondary Route
- Railway
- ✈ Airport
- ⛴ Car Ferry

RATHLIN ISLAND

GIANTS CAUSEWAY
BALLINTOY  BALLYCASTLE
PORTRUSH
PORTSTEWART
BUSHMILLS
A29
COLERAINE
A44
A2
CUSHENDUN
A37
LIMAVADY
BALLYMONEY
A26
CUSHENDALL
A54
GARVAGH
BUSH RIVER
GLENS OF ANTRIM
CO ANTRIM
DUNGIVEN
PORTGLENONE
A43
CARNLOUGH
GLENARM
A6
MAGHERA
A42
RIVER BANN
12
11
M2
BALLYMENA
10
RIVER MAIN
A36
A26
A8
PERRINS
CASTLEDAWSON
A31
MAGHERAFELT
RANDALSTOWN
BALLYCLARE
A57
LARNE
ISLAND MAGEE
WHITEHEAD
A29
MONEYMORE
2 M22
6
ANTRIM
5
M2
CARRICKFERGUS
COOKSTOWN
BALLINDERRY RIVER
Belfast International Airport
A52
4
Belfast City Airport
BANGOR
DONAGHADEE
MILLISLE
CRUMLIN
BELFAST
HOLYWOOD
A48
NEWTOWNARDS
LOUGH NEAGH
A501
A30
A26
LISBURN
A3
A20
COMBER
GREYABBEY
BALLYWALTER
ONE
COALISLAND
M1
9
KIRCUBBIN
UNGANNON
14
13
12
M12
10
7
6
SAINTFIELD
A21
A22
A20
PORTAVOGIE
GHNACLOY
PORTADOWN
CRAIGAVON
LURGAN
HILLSBOROUGH
DROMORE
A49
A7
KILLYLEAGH
PORTAFERRY
STRANGFORD
A50
A26
RIVER LAGAN
A1
BALLYNAHINCH
A25
ARMAGH
TANDRAGEE
A24
DOWNPATRICK
A28
RIVER BANN
BANBRIDGE
CO DOWN
A50
CLOUGH
CO ARMAGH
A25
CASTLEWELLAN
KILLOUGH
ARDGLASS
ETOWN
A3
RATHFRILAND
DUNDRUM
KEADY
A25
NEWCASTLE
A29
NEWRY
MOURNES
N2
WARRENPOINT
ANNALONG
ROSTREVOR
A2
CROSSMAGLEN
N1
KILKEEL

To Cairnryan, Fleetwood & Troon
To Stranraer & Troon
To Liverpool & Heysham

Miles
0   10   20
0   10   20   30
Kilometres

©Crown Copyright 2004

## Belfast City Centre

The capital city of Northern Ireland, Belfast is also its administrative, industrial and commercial centre. It has a population of around 350,000 and enjoys an enviable setting, facing out to sea and cradled on all sides by ranges of hills and mountains. The name Belfast itself is derived from the Irish béal feirste. This literally means 'mouth of the river' and came from Belfast's position at the head of the River Lagan, which becomes Belfast Lough as it joins the Irish Sea. Originally a small town, Belfast saw its population increase significantly with the Industrial Revolution.

In 1888, Belfast became a city by royal charter and by the end of the 19th century had overtaken Dublin in terms of population. By the beginning of the Second World War, during which Belfast experienced bombing at the hands of German planes targeting its shipyards and engineering works, its population had exceeded 400,000.

The city also suffered heavily in economic and social terms during the 'Troubles', when it became a frequent target of paramilitary bombs. In recent years however it has enjoyed a major revival of cultural activities and a more positive atmosphere, with new hotels, restaurants and entertainment venues springing up all over the city.

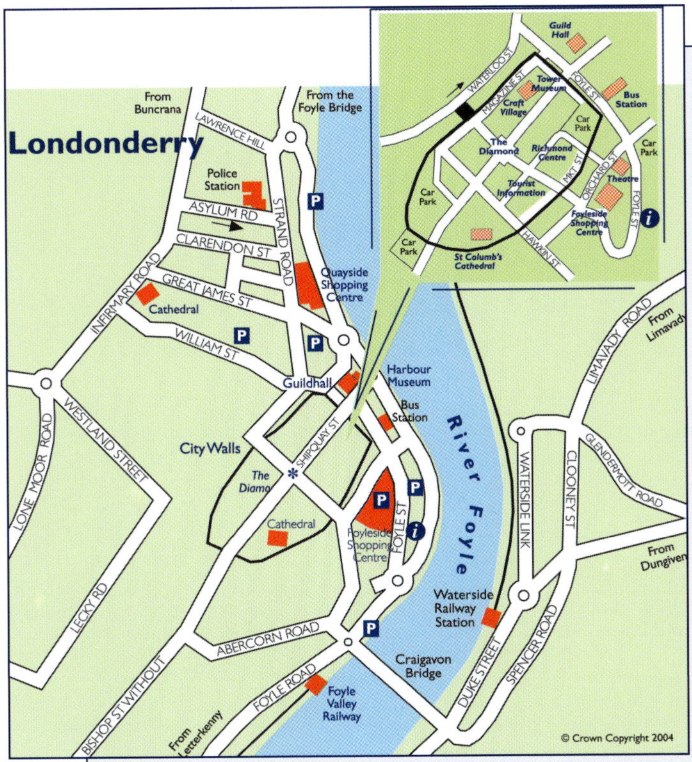


## Derry/Londonderry

Derry, the 'Maiden City', is located on the river Foyle in the north west of Northern Ireland, and has a population of around 100,000. It is one of the oldest settlements on the island of Ireland. The name Derry comes from the Irish word Doire or Daire, meaning oak grove, in particular one surrounded by water or a peat bog. This was the case in Derry, the grove being on an island in the River Foyle. The water beside the island gradually dried out, leaving a boggy area that became known as the 'Bogside'. In the early seventeenth century, King James I gave the City of London responsibility for settling this area of Ireland. Derry was fortified in 1613 and renamed Londonderry by royal charter as part of the Plantation of Ulster. The debate over what the city should be called is a long-standing one with some people adopting the phrase 'Stroke City' as a humourous and inoffensive option.

Although much smaller than Belfast and no bigger than a typical English town, the inhabitants of Derry are very proud of their City status and their rich heritage.

Despite its image as a divided city Derry is developing a vibrant cultural life and a new economic self-confidence. Architecturally the city boasts the famous City Walls and the Guildhall, which are both must-see sights for any visitor. With the emergence of new hotels, bars and restaurants Derry city has become more appealing as a place for people to visit as well as to live and work.

## Armagh City

Armagh is similarly an historical city, first founded on the hill fort of Ard Mhacha in the 4th century AD. It has a population of less than 20,000 and barely merits inclusion in the top 10 of Northern Ireland's towns (by population). Important in terms of Ulster and Ireland as a whole, it is the ancient city of St Patrick. Both Church of Ireland and Catholic cathedrals in the city are named after the patron saint of Ireland and both churches' archbishops are based in the ecclesiastical city.

Armagh city also boasts an observatory (founded in 1765) and planetarium. Of particular note also is the fine Regency and Georgian architecture that is prominent around the City Centre in the area of the Mall. This combined with its unique history makes Armagh a most interesting and distinctive city to visit. The county of Armagh is known as the Orchard County; famous for fruit growing, in particular apples.

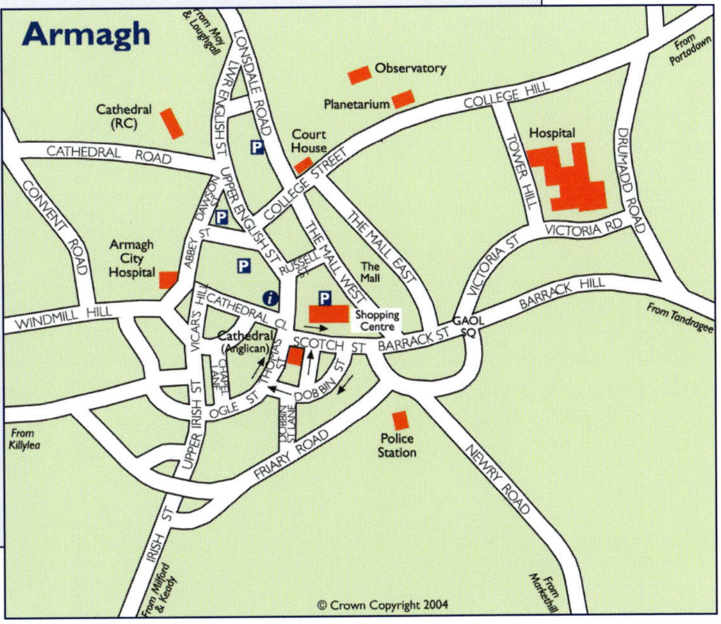

# Lisburn

Lisburn, some 8 miles southwest of Belfast and increasingly merging with the south western outskirts of the city, was a small village until plantation. The English government invited French Huguenots to settle there, who nurtured the growing linen industry by the introduction of new Dutch looms. Lisburn quickly became a major linen producer, although today this industry has declined. The River Lagan runs through the centre of Lisburn and although the linen industry based around the river has declined, Lisburn remains an important centre for commerce and industry in Northern Ireland and is also a popular residential location, acting as a 'commuter town' for Belfast.

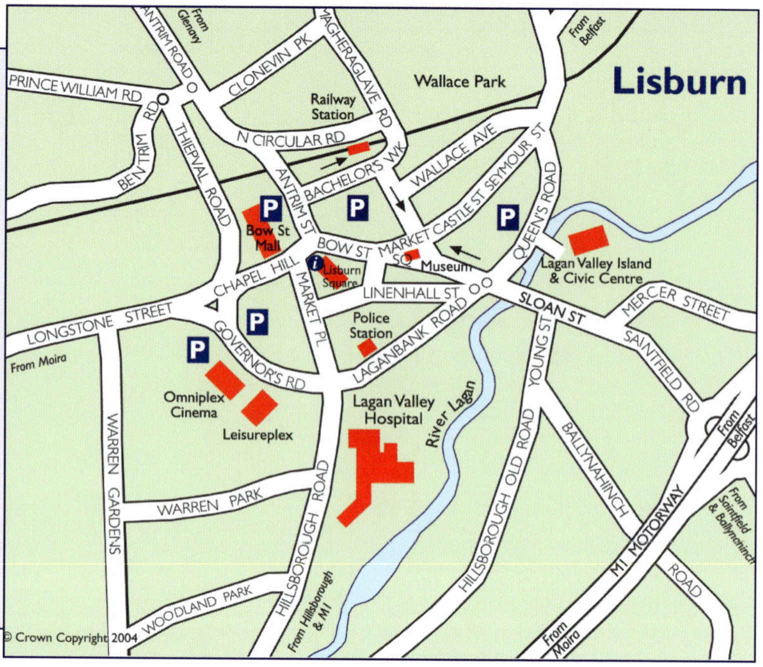


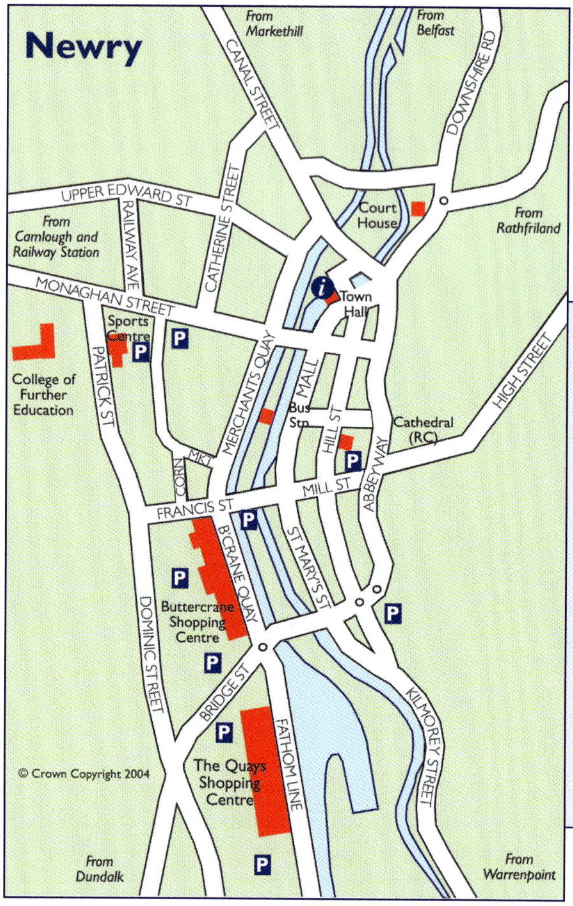


# Newry

Newry is notable for having the first inland waterway in the British Isles, which contributed greatly to the town's prosperity in the nineteenth century. The canal had 14 locks and provided a means to export mainly linen and stone. By 1840 its importance had declined, however. The name Newry is derived from the Gaelic for a yew tree, which was according to legend planted by St Patrick in the area. Newry has experienced rapid growth in population and economic activity in recent years and today is a busy city benefiting from its close proximity to the border with the Republic of Ireland. The city itself is strategically located some forty miles south of Belfast and only sixty miles north of Dublin.

# Northern Ireland Mileage Chart

| | | | | | | | | | | | | | | | | | | | | | | | | | | | | | | |
|---|---|---|---|---|---|---|---|---|---|---|---|---|---|---|---|---|---|---|---|---|---|---|---|---|---|---|---|---|---|---|
| **Antrim** | | | | | | | | | | | | | | | | | | | | | | | | | | | | | | |
| 42 | **Armagh** | | | | | | | | | | | | | | | | | | | | | | | | | | | | | |
| 41 | 84 | **Ballycastle** | | | | | | | | | | | | | | | | | | | | | | | | | | | | |
| 11 | 54 | 28 | **Ballymena** | | | | | | | | | | | | | | | | | | | | | | | | | | | |
| 32 | 54 | 72 | 42 | **Bangor** | | | | | | | | | | | | | | | | | | | | | | | | | | |
| **19** | **41** | **58** | **28** | **14** | **Belfast** | | | | | | | | | | | | | | | | | | | | | | | | | |
| 6 | 40 | 46 | 17 | 33 | **19** | **Belfast International Airport** | | | | | | | | | | | | | | | | | | | | | | | | |
| 91 | 75 | 114 | 92 | 122 | **109** | 97 | **Belleek** | | | | | | | | | | | | | | | | | | | | | | | |
| 27 | 70 | 26 | 16 | 53 | **39** | 33 | 108 | **Carnlough** | | | | | | | | | | | | | | | | | | | | | | |
| 40 | 61 | 19 | 28 | 71 | **58** | 46 | 95 | 42 | **Coleraine** | | | | | | | | | | | | | | | | | | | | | |
| 28 | 24 | 57 | 28 | 60 | **46** | 33 | 63 | 45 | 37 | **Cookstown** | | | | | | | | | | | | | | | | | | | | |
| 25 | 49 | 63 | 36 | 5 | **8** | 26 | 108 | 44 | 63 | 53 | **Craigavad** | | | | | | | | | | | | | | | | | | | |
| 30 | 73 | 16 | 19 | 61 | **48** | 35 | 110 | 10 | 35 | 47 | 35 | **Cushendall** | | | | | | | | | | | | | | | | | | |
| 47 | 68 | 26 | 35 | 78 | **65** | 53 | 92 | 49 | 7 | 43 | 71 | 41 | **Downhill** | | | | | | | | | | | | | | | | | |
| 38 | 52 | 85 | 55 | 27 | **22** | 35 | 119 | 64 | 85 | 60 | 30 | 74 | 91 | **Downpatrick** | | | | | | | | | | | | | | | | |
| 45 | 13 | 67 | 39 | 56 | **42** | 42 | 68 | 55 | 47 | 11 | 51 | 58 | 54 | 53 | **Dungannon** | | | | | | | | | | | | | | | |
| 86 | 50 | 110 | 82 | 97 | **84** | 83 | 25 | 98 | 91 | 54 | 101 | 101 | 88 | 95 | 43 | **Enniskillen** | | | | | | | | | | | | | | |
| 45 | 76 | 13 | 32 | 76 | **63** | 50 | 110 | 40 | 15 | 52 | 69 | 29 | 22 | 82 | 62 | 106 | **Giant's Causeway** | | | | | | | | | | | | | |
| 22 | 31 | 59 | 32 | 24 | **12** | 19 | 106 | 49 | 61 | 45 | 20 | 53 | 67 | 18 | 36 | 82 | 85 | **Hillsborough** | | | | | | | | | | | | |
| 21 | 65 | 41 | 21 | 38 | **25** | 22 | 111 | 14 | 49 | 48 | 29 | 25 | 56 | 52 | 66 | 108 | 54 | 35 | **Larne** | | | | | | | | | | | |
| 45 | 62 | 33 | 42 | 77 | **63** | 50 | 82 | 56 | 14 | 38 | 71 | 48 | 11 | 82 | 48 | 78 | 29 | 65 | 63 | **Limavady** | | | | | | | | | | |
| 84 | 42 | 125 | 95 | 96 | **82** | 82 | 37 | 111 | 103 | 59 | 91 | 114 | 101 | 93 | 49 | 12 | 118 | 77 | 104 | 90 | **Lisnaskea** | | | | | | | | | |
| 55 | 71 | 51 | 52 | 87 | **73** | 61 | 62 | 68 | 32 | 48 | 81 | 67 | 29 | 93 | 63 | 61 | 47 | 79 | 76 | 18 | 73 | **Londonderry** | | | | | | | | |
| 26 | 16 | 66 | 36 | 37 | **23** | 23 | 89 | 52 | 66 | 30 | 34 | 55 | 72 | 34 | 22 | 64 | 70 | 13 | 46 | 70 | 58 | 81 | **Lurgan** | | | | | | | |
| 23 | 40 | 40 | 18 | 55 | **41** | 29 | 79 | 34 | 21 | 16 | 47 | 37 | 28 | 61 | 27 | 69 | 36 | 45 | 44 | 23 | 75 | 34 | 48 | **Maghera** | | | | | | |
| 43 | 40 | 91 | 61 | 38 | **33** | 41 | 115 | 70 | 90 | 55 | 44 | 80 | 97 | 13 | 48 | 90 | 95 | 24 | 56 | 88 | 82 | 99 | 30 | 66 | **Newcastle** | | | | | |
| 47 | 19 | 88 | 58 | 52 | **38** | 45 | 93 | 75 | 88 | 44 | 46 | 77 | 94 | 30 | 32 | 69 | 92 | 27 | 60 | 81 | 60 | 89 | 23 | 60 | 21 | **Newry** | | | | |
| 54 | 36 | 83 | 55 | 82 | **69** | 60 | 37 | 71 | 64 | 27 | 85 | 74 | 61 | 80 | 28 | 27 | 79 | 66 | 75 | 51 | 39 | 34 | 49 | 42 | 75 | 55 | **Omagh** | | | |
| 48 | 60 | 87 | 57 | 24 | **29** | 44 | 128 | 66 | 87 | 69 | 30 | 76 | 93 | 9 | 62 | 103 | 91 | 24 | 52 | 92 | 102 | 102 | 43 | 70 | 21 | 39 | 88 | **Portaferry** | | |
| 46 | 67 | 19 | 34 | 78 | **64** | 52 | 102 | 49 | 6 | 43 | 68 | 34 | 13 | 84 | 54 | 98 | 9 | 65 | 55 | 20 | 92 | 38 | 72 | 27 | 90 | 94 | 71 | 93 | **Portrush** | |
| 62 | 56 | 64 | 58 | 93 | **80** | 67 | 51 | 74 | 45 | 46 | 89 | 77 | 42 | 99 | 48 | 47 | 60 | 86 | 82 | 31 | 59 | 15 | 69 | 40 | 94 | 75 | 20 | 108 | 51 | **Strabane** |

*Courtesy of Northern Ireland Tourist Board*

# 2004

| | January | February | March | April | May | June |
|---|---|---|---|---|---|---|
| Mon | 5 12 19 26 | 2 9 16 23 | 1 8 15 22 29 | 5 12 19 26 | 3 10 17 24 31 | 7 14 21 28 |
| Tue | 6 13 20 27 | 3 10 17 24 | 2 9 16 23 30 | 6 13 20 27 | 4 11 18 25 | 1 8 15 22 29 |
| Wed | 7 14 21 28 | 4 11 18 25 | 3 10 17 24 31 | 7 14 21 28 | 5 12 19 26 | 2 9 16 23 30 |
| Thu | 1 8 15 22 29 | 5 12 19 26 | 4 11 18 25 | 1 8 15 22 29 | 6 13 20 27 | 3 10 17 24 |
| Fri | 2 9 16 23 30 | 6 13 20 27 | 5 12 19 26 | 2 9 16 23 30 | 7 14 21 28 | 4 11 18 25 |
| Sat | 3 10 17 24 31 | 7 14 21 28 | 6 13 20 27 | 3 10 17 24 | 1 8 15 22 29 | 5 12 19 26 |
| Sun | 4 11 18 25 | 1 8 15 22 29 | 7 14 21 28 | 4 11 18 25 | 2 9 16 23 30 | 6 13 20 27 |

| | July | August | September | October | November | December |
|---|---|---|---|---|---|---|
| Mon | 5 12 19 26 | 2 9 16 23 30 | 6 13 20 27 | 4 11 18 25 | 1 8 15 22 29 | 6 13 20 27 |
| Tue | 6 13 20 27 | 3 10 17 24 31 | 7 14 21 28 | 5 12 19 26 | 2 9 16 23 30 | 7 14 21 28 |
| Wed | 7 14 21 28 | 4 11 18 25 | 1 8 15 22 29 | 6 13 20 27 | 3 10 17 24 | 1 8 15 22 29 |
| Thu | 1 8 15 22 29 | 5 12 19 26 | 2 9 16 23 30 | 7 14 21 28 | 4 11 18 25 | 2 9 16 23 30 |
| Fri | 2 9 16 23 30 | 6 13 20 27 | 3 10 17 24 | 1 8 15 22 29 | 5 12 19 26 | 3 10 17 24 31 |
| Sat | 3 10 17 24 31 | 7 14 21 28 | 4 11 18 25 | 2 9 16 23 30 | 6 13 20 27 | 4 11 18 25 |
| Sun | 4 11 18 25 | 1 8 15 22 29 | 5 12 19 26 | 3 10 17 24 31 | 7 14 21 28 | 5 12 19 26 |

# 2005

| | January | February | March | April | May | June |
|---|---|---|---|---|---|---|
| Mon | 3 10 17 24 31 | 7 14 21 28 | 7 14 21 28 | 4 11 18 25 | 2 9 16 23 30 | 6 13 20 27 |
| Tue | 4 11 18 25 | 1 8 15 22 | 1 8 15 22 29 | 5 12 19 26 | 3 10 17 24 31 | 7 14 21 28 |
| Wed | 5 12 19 26 | 2 9 16 23 | 2 9 16 23 30 | 6 13 20 27 | 4 11 18 25 | 1 8 15 22 29 |
| Thu | 6 13 20 27 | 3 10 17 24 | 3 10 17 24 31 | 7 14 21 28 | 5 12 19 26 | 2 9 16 23 30 |
| Fri | 7 14 21 28 | 4 11 18 25 | 4 11 18 25 | 1 8 15 22 29 | 6 13 20 27 | 3 10 17 24 |
| Sat | 1 8 15 22 29 | 5 12 19 26 | 5 12 19 26 | 2 9 16 23 30 | 7 14 21 28 | 4 11 18 25 |
| Sun | 2 9 16 23 30 | 6 13 20 27 | 6 13 20 27 | 3 10 17 24 | 1 8 15 22 29 | 5 12 19 26 |

| | July | August | September | October | November | December |
|---|---|---|---|---|---|---|
| Mon | 4 11 18 25 | 1 8 15 22 29 | 5 12 19 26 | 3 10 17 24 31 | 7 14 21 28 | 5 12 19 26 |
| Tue | 5 12 19 26 | 2 9 16 23 30 | 6 13 20 27 | 4 11 18 25 | 1 8 15 22 29 | 6 13 20 27 |
| Wed | 6 13 20 27 | 3 10 17 24 31 | 7 14 21 28 | 5 12 19 26 | 2 9 16 23 30 | 7 14 21 28 |
| Thu | 7 14 21 28 | 4 11 18 25 | 1 8 15 22 29 | 6 13 20 27 | 3 10 17 24 | 1 8 15 22 29 |
| Fri | 1 8 15 22 29 | 5 12 19 26 | 2 9 16 23 30 | 7 14 21 28 | 4 11 18 25 | 2 9 16 23 30 |
| Sat | 2 9 16 23 30 | 6 13 20 27 | 3 10 17 24 | 1 8 15 22 29 | 5 12 19 26 | 3 10 17 24 31 |
| Sun | 3 10 17 24 31 | 7 14 21 28 | 4 11 18 25 | 2 9 16 23 30 | 6 13 20 27 | 4 11 18 25 |

# 2006

| | January | February | March | April | May | June |
|---|---|---|---|---|---|---|
| Mon | 2 9 16 23 30 | 6 13 20 27 | 6 13 20 27 | 3 10 17 24 | 1 8 15 22 29 | 5 12 19 26 |
| Tue | 3 10 17 24 31 | 7 14 21 28 | 7 14 21 28 | 4 11 18 25 | 2 9 16 23 30 | 6 13 20 27 |
| Wed | 4 11 18 25 | 1 8 15 22 | 1 8 15 22 29 | 5 12 19 26 | 3 10 17 24 31 | 7 14 21 28 |
| Thu | 5 12 19 26 | 2 9 16 23 | 2 9 16 23 30 | 6 13 20 27 | 4 11 18 25 | 1 8 15 22 29 |
| Fri | 6 13 20 27 | 3 10 17 24 | 3 10 17 24 31 | 7 14 21 28 | 5 12 19 26 | 2 9 16 23 30 |
| Sat | 7 14 21 28 | 4 11 18 25 | 4 11 18 25 | 1 8 15 22 29 | 6 13 20 27 | 3 10 17 24 |
| Sun | 1 8 15 22 29 | 5 12 19 26 | 5 12 19 26 | 2 9 16 23 30 | 7 14 21 28 | 4 11 18 25 |

| | July | August | September | October | November | December |
|---|---|---|---|---|---|---|
| Mon | 3 10 17 24 31 | 7 14 21 28 | 4 11 18 25 | 2 9 16 23 30 | 6 13 20 27 | 4 11 18 25 |
| Tue | 4 11 18 25 | 1 8 15 22 29 | 5 12 19 26 | 3 10 17 24 31 | 7 14 21 28 | 5 12 19 26 |
| Wed | 5 12 19 26 | 2 9 16 23 30 | 6 13 20 27 | 4 11 18 25 | 1 8 15 22 29 | 6 13 20 27 |
| Thu | 6 13 20 27 | 3 10 17 24 31 | 7 14 21 28 | 5 12 19 26 | 2 9 16 23 30 | 7 14 21 28 |
| Fri | 7 14 21 28 | 4 11 18 25 | 1 8 15 22 29 | 6 13 20 27 | 3 10 17 24 | 1 8 15 22 29 |
| Sat | 1 8 15 22 29 | 5 12 19 26 | 2 9 16 23 30 | 7 14 21 28 | 4 11 18 25 | 2 9 16 23 30 |
| Sun | 2 9 16 23 30 | 6 13 20 27 | 3 10 17 24 | 1 8 15 22 29 | 5 12 19 26 | 3 10 17 24 31 |

# **Northern Ireland** Year Planner 2005

| | January | February | March | April | May | June |
|---|---|---|---|---|---|---|
| Tue | | 1 | 1 | | | |
| Wed | | 2 | 2 | | | 1 |
| Thu | | 3 | 3 | | | 2 |
| Fri | | 4 | 4 | 1 | | 3 |
| Sat | 1 New Year's Day | 5 | 5 | 2 | | 4 |
| Sun | 2 | 6 | 6 | 3 | 1 | 5 |
| Mon | 3 | 7 | 7 | 4 | 2 | 6 |
| Tue | 4 | 8 | 8 | 5 | 3 | 7 |
| Wed | 5 | 9 | 9 | 6 | 4 | 8 |
| Thu | 6 | 10 | 10 | 7 | 5 | 9 |
| Fri | 7 | 11 | 11 | 8 | 6 | 10 |
| Sat | 8 | 12 | 12 | 9 | 7 | 11 |
| Sun | 9 | 13 | 13 | 10 | 8 | 12 |
| Mon | 10 | 14 | 14 | 11 | 9 | 13 |
| Tue | 11 | 15 | 15 | 12 | 10 | 14 |
| Wed | 12 | 16 | 16 | 13 | 11 | 15 |
| Thu | 13 | 17 | 17 St. Patrick's Day | 14 | 12 | 16 |
| Fri | 14 | 18 | 18 | 15 | 13 | 17 |
| Sat | 15 | 19 | 19 | 16 | 14 | 18 |
| Sun | 16 | 20 | 20 | 17 | 15 | 19 |
| Mon | 17 | 21 | 21 | 18 | 16 | 20 |
| Tue | 18 | 22 | 22 | 19 | 17 | 21 |
| Wed | 19 | 23 | 23 | 20 | 18 | 22 |
| Thu | 20 | 24 | 24 | 21 | 19 | 23 |
| Fri | 21 | 25 | 25 | 22 | 20 | 24 |
| Sat | 22 | 26 | 26 | 23 | 21 | 25 |
| Sun | 23 | 27 | 27 | 24 | 22 | 26 |
| Mon | 24 | 28 | 28 | 25 | 23 | 27 |
| Tue | 25 | | 29 | 26 | 24 | 28 |
| Wed | 26 | | 30 | 27 | 25 | 29 |
| Thu | 27 | | 31 | 28 | 26 | 30 |
| Fri | 28 | | | 29 | 27 | |
| Sat | 29 | | | 30 | 28 | |
| Sun | 30 | | | | 29 | |
| Mon | 31 | | | | 30 | |
| Tue | | | | | 31 | |
| Wed | | | | | | |